E. Jerome McCarthy received his Ph.D. from the University of Minnesota in 1958. Since then he has taught at the Universities of Oregon, Notre Dame, and Michigan State. He has been deeply involved in teaching and developing new teaching materials. Besides writing various articles and monographs, he is the author of textbooks on data processing and social issues in marketing.

Now 61 years old, Dr. McCarthy is active in making presentations to academic conferences and business meetings. He has worked with groups of teachers throughout the country and has addressed international conferences in South America, Africa, and India.

Dr. McCarthy received the American Marketing Association's Trailblazer Award in 1987. And he was voted one of the "top five" leaders in Marketing Thought in 1975 by marketing educators. He was also a Ford Foundation Fellow in 1963–64, studying the role of marketing in economic development. In 1959–60 he was a Ford Foundation Fellow at the Harvard Business School working on mathematical methods in marketing.

Besides his academic interests, Dr. McCarthy is involved in consulting for, and guiding the growth of, several businesses. He has worked with top managers from Steelcase, Dow Chemical, Dow-Corning, 3M, Bemis, Grupo Industrial Alfa, and many smaller companies. He is director of several organizations. His primary interests, however, are in (1) "converting" students to marketing and marketing strategy planning and (2) preparing teaching materials to help others do the same. This is why he has continued to spend a large part of his time revising and improving marketing texts. This is a continuing process, and this edition incorporates the latest thinking in the field.

William D. Perreault, Jr., received his Ph.D. from the University of North Carolina at Chapel Hill in 1973. He has taught at the University of Georgia and Stanford University. He is currently Kenan Professor and Associate Dean at the University of North Carolina School of Business. At UNC, he has twice received awards for teaching excellence. In 1987, the Decision Sciences Institute recognized him for innovations in marketing education, and *Ad Week* magazine recently profiled him as one of the "10 best young marketing professors in America."

Dr. Perreault is a well-known author, and his ideas about marketing management, marketing research, and marketing education have been published in many journals. He is a past editor of the *Journal of Marketing Research* and has served on the review board of the *Journal of Marketing* and other publications. In 1985, the American Marketing Association recognized his long-run contributions to marketing research with the prestigious William O'Dell Award.

Dr. Perreault has served as Vice President and on the Board of Directors of the AMA, and as chairman of an advisory committee to the U.S. Bureau of the Census, and he is now a trustee of the Marketing Science Institute. He has worked as a marketing consultant to many organizations, including IBM, Libby-Owens-Ford, Whirlpool, Owens/Corning Fiberglas, the Federal Trade Commission, and a variety of wholesale and retail firms. He has served as an advisor evaluating educational programs for the U.S. Department of Education, Venezuelan Ministry of Education, Andenberg Foundation, and American Assembly of Collegiate Schools of Business.

The Irwin Series in Marketing

Consulting Editor
Gilbert A. Churchill, Jr.
University of Wisconsin, Madison

Basic Marketing
A Managerial Approach

E. Jerome McCarthy, Ph.D.
Michigan State University

William D. Perreault, Jr., Ph.D.
University of North Carolina

Tenth Edition

Homewood, IL 60430
Boston, MA 02116

©Richard D. Irwin, Inc., 1960, 1964, 1968, 1971,
1975, 1978, 1981, 1984, 1987, and 1990

Sponsoring editor: Elizabeth S. MacDonell
Developmental editor: Nancy J. Barbour
Coordinating editor: Linda G. Davis
Project editor: Ethel Shiell
Production manager: Carma W. Fazio
Photo researcher: Michael J. Hruby
Designer: Lucy Lesiak Design
Compositor: Carlisle Communications, Ltd.
Typeface: 9/12 Helvetica
Printer: Von Hoffmann Press, Inc.

Library of Congress Cataloging-in-Publication Data

McCarthy, E. Jerome (Edmund Jerome)
    Basic marketing: a managerial approach/E. Jerome McCarthy,
William D. Perreault.—10th ed.
        p.   cm.
    ISBN 0-256-06865-8.—ISBN 0-256-08398-3 (International ed.)
    1. Marketing—Management.   I. Perreault, William D.   II. Title.
HF5415.13.M369   1990
    658.8—dc20   89–35299
                                                                      CIP

Printed in the United States of America

2 3 4 5 6 7 8 9 0 VH 7 6 5 4 3 2 1 0

Preface

The first edition of *Basic Marketing* pioneered an innovative structure—using the "four Ps" with a managerial approach—for the introductory marketing course. In the 30 years since publication of that first edition, there have been constant changes in marketing management. Some of the changes have been dramatic, and others have been subtle. Throughout all of these changes, *Basic Marketing*—and the supporting materials to accompany it—have been more widely used than any other teaching materials for introductory marketing. It is gratifying that the "four Ps" has proved to be an organizing structure that has worked well for millions of students and teachers.

Of course, this position of leadership is not the result of a single strength—or one long-lasting innovation. On the contrary, with each new edition of *Basic Marketing* we have seized the opportunity to introduce innovations—and to set new standards of excellence. And our belief that attention to quality in every aspect of the text and support materials does make a difference is consistently reaffirmed by the enthusiastic response of students and teachers alike.

We believe that the tenth edition of *Basic Marketing* is the highest quality teaching and learning resource ever available for the introductory course. The whole text and all of the supporting materials have been critically revised, updated, and rewritten. As in past editions, clear and interesting communication has been a priority. Careful explanations provide a crisp focus on the important "basics." At the same time, we have researched and carefully integrated hundreds of new examples that bring the concepts alive to heighten your interest and motivate learning.

The tenth edition focuses special attention on changes taking place in today's dynamic markets. For example, throughout the tenth edition you'll see how computers and other advances in information technology are shaping new marketing opportunities and strategies. You'll learn about the changing relationships between producers and middlemen—including the increasing importance of big retail chains. You'll see how increasingly intense competition—both in the United States and around the world—is affecting marketing strategy planning. You'll even see why Russia and other centrally planned economies are making efforts to become more market oriented. Some other marketing texts have attempted to describe such changes. But what sets *Basic Marketing* apart is that the explanations and examples not only highlight the changes that are taking place today, but also equip students to see *why* these changes are taking place—and what changes to expect in the future. That is an important distinction—because marketing is dynamic.

The text has been redesigned, too. A more open format has allowed us to be even more effective in incorporating illustrations—full-color graphs, figures, photographs—to reinforce key points and facilitate learning. We have done extensive research to refine and improve these learning elements as part of an overall redesign that makes important concepts and points even clearer to students.

The aim of all this revising, refining, editing, and illustrating was to make sure that each student really does get a good feel for a market-directed system and how he or she can help it—and some company—run better. We believe marketing

v

is important and interesting—and we want every student who reads *Basic Marketing* to share our enthusiasm.

The emphasis of *Basic Marketing* is on marketing strategy planning. Twenty-three chapters introduce the important concepts in marketing management and help the student see marketing through the eyes of the marketing manager. The organization of the chapters and topics was carefully planned. But we took special care in writing so that it is possible to rearrange and use the chapters in many ways to fit various needs.

The first two chapters deal with the nature of marketing—focusing both on its macro role in society and its micro role in businesses and other organizations. The first chapter stresses that the effectiveness of our macro-marketing system depends on the decisions of many producers and consumers. That sets the stage for the second chapter—and the rest of the book—which focuses on how business-people and, in particular, marketing managers develop marketing strategies to satisfy specific target markets.

Chapter 3 introduces a strategic planning view of how managers can find new market opportunities. The emphasis is on identifying target markets with market segmentation and positioning approaches. This strategic view alerts students to the importance of evaluating opportunities in the external environments affecting marketing—and these are discussed in Chapter 4. Chapter 5 is a contemporary view of getting information—from marketing information systems and marketing research—for marketing management planning.

The next three chapters take a closer look at customers so students will better understand how to segment markets and satisfy target market needs. Chapter 6 introduces the demographic dimensions of the consumer market, and Chapters 7 and 8 study the behavioral features of the consumer market and how intermediate customers—like manufacturers, channel members, and government purchasers—are similar to and different from final consumers.

The next group of chapters—Chapters 9 to 19—is concerned with developing a marketing mix out of the four Ps: Product, Place (involving channels of distribution and customer service levels), Promotion, and Price. These chapters are concerned with developing the "right" Product and making it available at the "right" Place with the "right" Promotion and the "right" Price—to satisfy target customers and still meet the objectives of the business. These chapters are presented in an integrated, analytical way, so students' thinking about planning marketing strategies develops logically.

Chapter 20 ties the four Ps into planning and implementing whole marketing plans and programs. Chapter 21 discusses controlling marketing plans and programs, using examples to emphasize important points. Chapter 22 applies the principles of the text to international marketing. While there is an international emphasis throughout the text, this separate chapter is provided for those wishing special emphasis on international marketing.

The final chapter considers how efficient the marketing process is. Here we evaluate the effectiveness of both micro- and macro-marketing—and we consider the challenges facing marketing managers now and in the future. After this chapter, the student might want to look at Appendix C—which is about career opportunities in marketing.

Some textbooks treat "special" topics—like services marketing, marketing for nonprofit organizations, industrial marketing, and marketing ethics—in separate chapters. We have not done this because we are convinced that treating such topics separately leads to an unfortunate compartmentalization of ideas. We think they are too important to be isolated in that way. Instead, they are interwoven and illustrated throughout the text to emphasize that marketing thinking is crucial in all aspects of our society and economy.

Really understanding marketing and how to plan marketing strategies can build self-confidence—and it can help prepare a student to take an active part in the business world. To move students in this direction, we deliberately include a variety of frameworks, models, classification systems, and "how-to-do-it" techniques, which should speed the development of "marketing sense"—and enable the student to analyze marketing situations in a confident and meaningful way. Taken seriously, they are practical and they work. In addition, because they are interesting and understandable, they equip students to see marketing as the challenging and rewarding area it is.

Basic Marketing can be studied and used in many ways—the *Basic Marketing* text material is only the central component of a *Professional Learning Units Systems* (our *P.L.U.S.*) for students and teachers. Instructors can select from our units to develop their own personalized systems. Many combinations of units are possible—depending on course objectives.

So students will see what is coming in each *Basic Marketing* chapter, behavioral objectives are included on the first page of each chapter. And to speed student understanding, important new terms are shown in red and defined immediately. Further, a glossary of these terms is presented at the end of the book. Within chapters, major section headings and second-level headings (placed in the margin for clarity) immediately show how the material is organized *and* summarize key points in the text. Further, we have placed photos in the margin right beside the paragraph they illustrate to provide a visual reminder of the ideas. All of these aids help the student understand important concepts—and speed review before exams.

Understanding of the text material can be deepened by analysis and discussion of specific cases. *Basic Marketing* features two different types of cases. New with this edition, a special case report appears as an offset in each chapter. Each case illustrates how a particular company has developed its marketing strategy—with emphasis on a topic covered in that chapter. These cases have been specially developed to provide an excellent basis for critical evaluation and discussion of a specific concept. In addition, there are several suggested cases at the end of each chapter. The focus of these cases is on problem solving. They encourage students to apply—and really get involved with—the concepts developed in the text.

End-of-chapter questions and problems offer additional opportunities. They can be used to encourage students to investigate the marketing process and develop their own ways of thinking about it. These can be used for independent study or as a basis for written assignments or class discussion.

Some professors and students want to follow up on text readings. Each chapter is supplemented with detailed references—to both "classic" articles and current readings in business publications. These can guide more detailed study of the topics covered in a chapter.

In addition, with this edition of *Basic Marketing* we introduce a totally new teaching/learning unit: *Applications in Basic Marketing.* This collection of marketing "clippings"—from publications such as *The Wall Street Journal, Fortune,* and *Business Week*—provides convenient access to short, interesting, and current discussions of marketing issues. There are a variety of short clippings related to each chapter in *Basic Marketing.* In addition, we will revise this collection *each year* so that it can include timely material that is available in no other text. It is a sign of the commitment of our publisher to the introductory marketing course that this innovative new supplement will be provided free of charge; the most recent edition of *Applications in Basic Marketing* will come shrink-wrapped with each new copy of the tenth edition of *Basic Marketing*!

At the end of each chapter there is also a suggested computer-aided problem. These exercises stimulate a problem-solving approach to marketing strategy planning and give students "hands-on" experience that shows how logical analysis of alternative strategies can lead to improved decision making. The problems and related software are explained in the new edition of *Computer-Aided Problems to Accompany Basic Marketing*. The computer program that accompanies the booklet was specifically developed for use by students who study *Basic Marketing*. The new version of the software includes a graphics capability. The revised computer-aided problem booklets and software are provided free to instructors on request.

There are more components to *P.L.U.S.* A separate *Learning Aid* provides several more units and offers further opportunities to obtain a deeper understanding of the material. The *Learning Aid* can be used by the student alone or with teacher direction. Portions of the *Learning Aid* help students to review what they have studied. For example, there is a brief introduction to each chapter, a list of the important new terms (with page numbers for easy reference), true-false questions (with answers and page numbers) that cover *all* the important terms and concepts, and multiple-choice questions (with answers) that illustrate the kinds of questions that may appear in examinations. In addition, the *Learning Aid* has cases, exercises, and problems—with clear instructions and worksheets for the student to complete. As with the text, computer-aided problems have been developed to accompany the *Learning Aid*. The *Learning Aid* exercises can be used as classwork or homework—to drill on certain topics and to deepen understanding of others by motivating application and then discussion. In fact, reading *Basic Marketing* and working with the *Learning Aid* can be the basic activity of the course.

Another element to accompany *Basic Marketing* is *The Marketing Game! The Marketing Game!* is a microcomputer-based competitive simulation. It was developed specifically to reinforce the target marketing and marketing strategy planning ideas discussed in *Basic Marketing*. Students make marketing management decisions—blending the four Ps to compete for the business of different possible target markets. The innovative design of *The Marketing Game!* allows the instructor to increase the number of decision areas involved as students learn more about marketing. In fact, some instructors may want to use the advanced level of the game—perhaps as the basis for a second course.

Basic Marketing—and all of our accompanying materials—have been developed to promote student learning and get students involved in the excitement and challenges of marketing management. Additional elements of *P.L.U.S.* have been specifically developed to help an instructor offer a truly professional course that meets the objectives he or she sets for students. Complete Instructor's Manuals accompany all of the *P.L.U.S.* components. A separate *Lecture Guide to Accompany Basic Marketing*—newly revised and updated for this edition—offers a rich selection of lecture material and ideas. A high-quality selection of Color Transparencies—and the newly revised *Basic Marketing Videotapes*—are also available. In addition, thousands of objective test questions—written by the authors to really work with the text—give instructors a high-quality resource. The newly revised COMPUTEST III program for microcomputers allows the instructor to select from any of these questions, change them as desired, or add new questions—and quickly print out a finished test customized to the instructor's course.

In closing, we return to a point raised at the beginning of this preface: *Basic Marketing* has been the leading textbook in marketing for three decades. We take the responsibilities of that leadership seriously. We know that you want and deserve the very best teaching and learning materials possible. It is our commitment to bring you those materials—today with this edition and in the future with subsequent editions. *Basic Marketing* is not just a passing fad. We believe that the substance it offers today—and will offer tomorrow—must reach beyond some short-term view. Improvements, changes, and development of new elements must be ongoing—because needs change. You are an important part of this evolution, of this leadership. We encourage your feedback. Thoughtful criticisms and suggestions from students and teachers alike have helped to make *Basic Marketing* what it is. We hope that you will help make it what it will be in the future.

E. Jerome McCarthy
William D. Perreault, Jr.

Acknowledgments

Planning and preparing this revision of *Basic Marketing* has been a three-year effort. The resulting text—and all of the teaching and learning materials that accompany it—represents a blending of our career-long experiences, influenced and improved by the inputs of more people than it is possible to list.

Faculty and students at our current and past academic institutions—Michigan State University, University of North Carolina, Notre Dame, University of Georgia, Northwestern University, University of Oregon, University of Minnesota, and Stanford University—have significantly shaped the book. Faculty at Notre Dame had a profound effect when the first editions of the book were developed. Professor Yusaku Furuhashi had a continuing impact on the multinational emphasis. Similarly, Professor Andrew A. Brogowicz of Western Michigan University has contributed many fine ideas. Thought-provoking reviews provided by William R. George, Gilbert A. Churchill, and Barbara A. McCuen were especially significant in shaping the previous edition. Charlotte Mason and Nicholas Didow have provided a constant flow of helpful suggestions.

We are especially grateful to our many students who have criticized and made comments about materials in *Basic Marketing*. Indeed, in many ways, our students have been our best teachers.

Many improvements in the current edition were stimulated by feedback from a number of colleagues around the country. Feedback took many forms. We received valuable insights—and hundreds of detailed suggestions—from professors who kept class-by-class diaries while teaching from *Basic Marketing*. Participants in focus group interviews shared their in-depth ideas about ways to improve teaching and materials used in the first marketing course. Professors who provided comprehensive comparative reviews helped us see ways to build on our strengths and identify where improvements would be most helpful to students and faculty. And responses to detailed surveys gave us ideas and insights for ways to update and improve not only the text but also the whole set of teaching and learning materials that accompany it. For all of these suggestions and criticisms we are most appreciative. In particular, we would like to recognize the helpful contributions of:

Linda Anglin	Kathy Daruty	Ron Hoverstad
Barry Ashman	Roger Davis	Dan Howard
Kenneth Baker	Vincent Deni	Harry Howren
James Baylor	Theresa DiNovo	Bernard Johnson
Kip Becker	John Dunseth	Gary Karns
James Bedtke	Pat Farmer	M. L. King
Jim Boespflug	John Flood	Ronald King
Joseph Bonnice	Bill Franklin	Eugene Klippel
Gail Bracken	George Glisan	Bob Kosmedek
Stephan Calcich	James Gould	John Krane
Wayne Cioffari	Roy Grundy	Kathleen Krentler
Gerald Crawford	Debra Haley	Donald Lindgren
Ken Crocker	Ronald Halsac	Ernest Manshel
Lawrence Dandurand	Hendrick Helmers	Susan Marine

Joesph McAloon	Robert Pettengill	Joseph Sirgy
Howard McCoy	Joseph Plummer	Rosann Spiro
Barbara McCuen	Raymond Polchow	Vernon Stauble
Robert McInnis	Arthur Prell	Jerry Stiles
Mark Miller	Donald Rahtz	David Stringer
Malcolm Morris	Richard Reid	Glori Sundberg
Linda Morris	Mike Reilly	Ruth Taylor
David Morris	Elizabeth Rogol	Stephan Thomas
William Moser	Stan Scott	David Tonks
Japhet Nkonge	Vern Seguin	Ron Tremmel
Wayne Norvell	Irwin Shapiro	Gerald Waddle
Glenn Olsen	Edwin Simpson	Karen Zwissler
Daniel Outland	Susan Sipkoff	

The designers, artists, editors, and production people at Richard D. Irwin, Inc., who worked with us on this edition warrant special recognition. All of them have shared our commitment to excellence and brought their own individual creativity to the project.

We owe a special debt of gratitude to Linda G. Davis. She provided valuable help in researching photos and case histories, and she typed thousands of manuscript pages through countless revisions of the text and all the accompanying materials. Her hard work and dedication to quality throughout the whole process was exemplary. We could not have asked for better support.

Our families have been patient and consistent supporters through all phases of developing *Basic Marketing*. The support has been direct and substantive. Joanne McCarthy and Pam Perreault provided invaluable editorial assistance—and many fresh ideas through each draft and revision. The quality of their inputs is matched only by their energy and enthusiasm about the book. Carol McCarthy helped research and reorient the "Career Planning in Marketing" appendix—reflecting her needs and experiences as a college student looking for a career in advertising. Similarly, Mary McCarthy Zang provided creative inputs on visual aspects of the project.

We are indebted to all the firms that allowed us to reproduce their proprietary materials here. Similarly, we are grateful to associates from our business experiences who have shared their perspectives and feedback, and enhanced our sensitivity to the key challenges of marketing management.

A textbook must capsulize existing knowledge while bringing new perspectives and organization to enhance it. Our thinking has been shaped by the writings of literally thousands of marketing scholars and practitioners. In some cases it is impossible to give unique credit for a particular idea or concept because so many people have played important roles in anticipating, suggesting, shaping, and developing it. We gratefully acknowledge these contributors—from the early thought-leaders to contemporary authors—who have shared their creative ideas. We respect their impact on the development of marketing and more specifically this book.

To all of these persons—and to the many publishers who graciously granted permission to use their materials—we are deeply grateful. Responsibility for any errors or omissions is certainly ours, but the book would not have been possible without the assistance of many others. Our sincere appreciation goes to everyone who helped in their own special way.

E. Jerome McCarthy
William D. Perreault, Jr.

Contents

Computer-Aided Problems
(See separate booklet)

Basic Marketing
A Managerial Approach

Chapter 1

Marketing's Role in Society

When You Finish This Chapter, You Should

1. Know what marketing is and why you should learn about it.

2. Understand the difference between micro-marketing and macro-marketing.

3. Know why and how macro-marketing systems develop.

4. Know why marketing specialists—including middlemen and facilitators—develop.

5. Know the marketing functions and who performs them.

6. Understand the important new terms (shown in red).

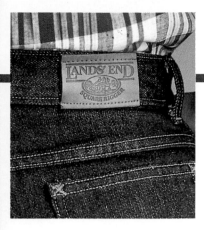

Marketing affects almost every aspect of your daily life.

When it's time to roll out of bed in the morning, does your General Electric alarm wake you with a buzzer—or by playing your favorite radio station? Is the station playing rock, classical, or country music? Will you slip into your Lands' End jeans, your shirt from L. L. Bean, and your Nikes, or does the day call for your Brooks Brothers suit? Will breakfast be Kellogg's Mueslix cereal—made with grain from America's heartland—or some extra large eggs and Hormel bacon cooked in a Panasonic microwave imported from Japan? Will it be decaffeinated Maxwell House coffee—grown in Colombia—or some calcium-enriched Citrus Hill orange juice? Maybe you're late and plan to get an Egg McMuffin at the McDonald's drive-thru. When you leave home, will it be in a Acura, on a Huffy bike, or on the bus that the city bought from General Motors?

When you think about it, you can't get very far into a day without bumping into marketing—and what the whole marketing system does for you. It affects every aspect of our lives—often in ways we don't even consider.

In this chapter, you'll see what marketing is all about and why it's important to you. We'll also explore how marketing fits into our whole economic system.

MARKETING—WHAT'S IT ALL ABOUT?

Marketing is more than selling or advertising

If forced to define marketing, most people, including some business managers, say that marketing means "selling" or "advertising." It's true that these are parts of marketing. But *marketing is much more than selling and advertising.*

All tennis rackets can hit the ball over the net—but there are many variations to meet the needs of different people.

How did all those tennis rackets get here?

To illustrate some of the other important things that are included in marketing, think about all the tennis rackets being swung with varying degrees of accuracy by tennis players around the world. Most of us weren't born with a tennis racket in our hand. Nor do we make our own tennis rackets. Instead, they are made by firms like Wilson, Spalding, Kennex, Head, and Prince.

Most tennis rackets are intended to do the same thing—hit the ball over the net. But a tennis player can choose from a wide assortment of rackets. There are different shapes, materials, weights, handle sizes, and types of strings. You can buy a prestrung racket for less than $15. Or you can spend more than $250 just for a frame!

This variety in sizes and materials complicates the production and sale of tennis rackets. The following list shows some of the many things a firm should do before and after it decides to produce tennis rackets.

1. Analyze the needs of people who play tennis and decide if consumers want more or different tennis rackets.
2. Predict what types of rackets—handle sizes, shapes, weights, and materials—different players will want and decide which of these people the firm will try to satisfy.
3. Estimate how many of these people will be playing tennis over the next several years and how many rackets they'll buy.
4. Predict exactly when these players will want to buy tennis rackets.
5. Determine where these tennis players will be—and how to get the firm's rackets to them.
6. Estimate what price they are willing to pay for their rackets—and if the firm can make a profit selling at that price.
7. Decide which kinds of promotion should be used to tell potential customers about the firm's tennis rackets.

8. Estimate how many competing companies will be making tennis rackets, how many rackets they'll produce, what kind, and at what prices.

The above activities are not part of **production**—actually making goods or performing services. Rather, they are part of a larger process—called *marketing*—that provides needed direction for production and helps make sure that the right products are produced and find their way to consumers.

Our tennis racket example shows that marketing includes much more than selling or advertising. We'll describe marketing activities in the next chapter. And you'll learn much more about them before you finish this book. For now, it's enough to see that marketing plays an essential role in providing consumers with need-satisfying goods and services.

HOW MARKETING RELATES TO PRODUCTION

Production is a very important economic activity. Whether for lack of skill and resources or just lack of time, most people don't make most of the products they use. Picture yourself, for example, building a 10-speed bicycle, a compact disc player, or a digital watch—starting from scratch! We also turn to others to produce services—like health care, air transportation, and entertainment. Clearly, the high standard of living that most Americans enjoy is made possible by specialized production.

Tennis rackets, like mousetraps, don't sell themselves

Although production is a necessary economic activity, some people overrate its importance in relation to marketing. Their attitude is reflected in the old saying: "Make a better mousetrap and the world will beat a path to your door." In other words, they think that if you just have a good product, your business will be a success.

The "better mousetrap" idea probably wasn't true in Grandpa's time, and it certainly isn't true today. In modern economies, the grass grows high on the path to the Better Mousetrap Factory—if the new mousetrap is not properly marketed. We have already seen, for example, that there's a lot more to marketing tennis rackets than just making them. This is true for most goods and services.

The point is that production and marketing are both important parts of a total business system aimed at providing consumers with need-satisfying goods and services. Together, production and marketing provide the four basic economic utilities—form, time, place, and possession utilities—that are needed to provide consumer satisfaction. Here, **utility** means the power to satisfy human needs. See Exhibit 1–1.

Tennis rackets do not automatically provide utility

Form utility is provided when someone produces something tangible—for instance, a tennis racket. But just producing tennis rackets doesn't result in consumer satisfaction. The product must be something that consumers want—or there is no need to be satisfied—and no utility.

This is how marketing thinking guides the production side of business. Marketing decisions focus on the customer and include decisions about what goods and services to produce. It doesn't make sense to provide goods and services consumers don't want when there are so many things they do want or need. Let's take our "mousetrap" example a step further. Some customers don't want *any kind* of

Exhibit 1–1 Types of Utility and How They Are Provided

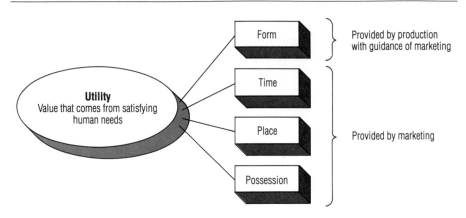

mousetrap. They may want someone else to exterminate the mice for them. Marketing is concerned with what customers want—and it should guide what is produced and offered. This is an important idea that we will develop more completely later.

Even when marketing and production combine to provide form utility, consumers won't be satisfied until possession, time, and place utility are also provided. **Possession utility** means obtaining a product and having the right to use or consume it. Customers usually exchange money or something else of value for possession utility.

Time utility means having the product available *when* the customer wants it. And **place utility** means having the product available *where* the customer wants it. Tennis rackets that stay at a factory don't do anyone any good. Time and place utility are important for services, too. For example, neighborhood emergency-care health clinics have recently become very popular. People just walk in as soon as they feel sick, not a day later when their doctor can schedule an appointment.

Stated simply, marketing provides time, place, and possession utility. It should also guide decisions about what goods and services should be produced to provide form utility. We'll look at how marketing does this later in this chapter. First, we want to discuss why you should study marketing, and then we'll define marketing.

MARKETING IS IMPORTANT TO YOU

Why you should study marketing

One reason for studying marketing is that you—as a consumer—pay for the cost of marketing activities. Marketing costs about 50 cents of your consumer dollar. For some goods and services, the percentage is much higher.

Another important reason for learning about marketing is that marketing affects almost every aspect of your daily life. All the goods and services you buy, the stores where you shop, and the radio and TV programs paid for by advertising are there because of marketing. Even your job résumé is part of a marketing campaign to sell yourself to some employer! Some courses are interesting when you take them but never relevant again once they're over. Not so with marketing—you'll be a consumer dealing with marketing for the rest of your life.

Still another reason for studying marketing is that there are many exciting and rewarding career opportunities in marketing. Marketing is often the route to the top. Throughout this book you will find information about opportunities in different areas of marketing—in sales, advertising, product management, marketing research, physical distribution, and other areas. And, Appendix C is all about career planning in marketing.

Even if you're aiming for a nonmarketing job, you'll be working with marketing people. Knowing something about marketing will help you understand them better. It will also help you do your own job better. Marketing is important to the success of every organization. Remember, a company that can't successfully sell its products doesn't need accountants, financial managers, production managers, personnel managers, computer programmers, or credit managers.

Even if you're not planning a business career, marketing concepts and techniques apply to nonprofit organizations, too. Many nonprofit organizations have a marketing manager. And the same basic principles used to sell soap are also used to "sell" ideas, politicians, mass transportation, health-care services, conservation, museums, and even colleges. Think about the school where you take this course. If you didn't know about its offerings—or if they didn't interest you—you would simply pick some other school.[1]

An even more basic reason for studying marketing is that marketing plays a big part in economic growth and development. Marketing stimulates research and new ideas—resulting in new goods and services. Marketing gives customers a choice among products. If these products satisfy customers, fuller employment, higher incomes, and a higher standard of living can result. An effective marketing system is important to the future of our nation—and all nations.[2]

Marketing stimulates product improvement and gives customers a choice.

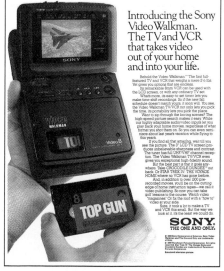

HOW SHOULD WE DEFINE MARKETING?

As we said earlier, some people define marketing too narrowly as "selling and advertising." On the other hand, one authority defined marketing as "the creation and delivery of a standard of living."[3] That definition is too broad.

An important difference between the two definitions may be less obvious. The first definition is a *micro*-level definition. It focuses on activities performed by an individual organization. The second is a *macro*-level definition. It focuses on the economic welfare of a whole society.

Micro- or macro-marketing?

Which view is correct? Is marketing a set of activities done by individual firms or organizations? Or is it a social process?

To answer this question, let's go back to our tennis racket example. We saw that a producer of tennis rackets has to perform many customer-related activities besides just making rackets. The same is true for an insurance company, an art museum, or a family-service agency. This supports the idea of marketing as a set of activities done by individual organizations.

On the other hand, people can't live on tennis rackets and art museums alone! In an advanced economy like ours, it takes thousands of goods and services to satisfy the many needs of society. A typical K mart stocks 25,000 different items. A society needs some sort of marketing system to organize the efforts of all the producers and middlemen needed to satisfy the varied needs of all its citizens. So marketing is also an important social process.

The answer to our question is that *marketing is both a set of activities performed by organizations and a social process.* In other words, marketing exists at both the micro and macro levels. Therefore, we will use two definitions of marketing—one for micro-marketing and another for macro-marketing. The first looks at customers and the organizations that serve them. The second takes a broad view of our whole production-distribution system.

MICRO–MARKETING DEFINED

Micro-marketing is the performance of activities that seek to accomplish an organization's objectives by anticipating customer or client needs and directing a flow of need-satisfying goods and services from producer to customer or client. Let's look at this definition.[4]

Applies to profit and non-profit organizations

To begin with, this definition applies to both profit and nonprofit organizations. Profit is the objective for most business firms. But other types of organizations may seek more members—or acceptance of an idea. Customers or clients may be individual consumers, business firms, nonprofit organizations, government agencies, or even foreign nations. While most customers and clients pay for the goods and services they receive, others may receive them free of charge or at a reduced cost through private or government support.

More than just persuading customers

You already know that micro-marketing isn't just selling and advertising. Unfortunately, many executives still think it is. They feel that the job of marketing is to "get rid of" whatever the company happens to produce. In fact, the aim of marketing is to identify customers' needs—and meet those needs so well that the product

The aim of marketing is to identify customers' needs—and to meet these needs so well that the product almost "sells itself."

(goods and/or services) almost "sells itself." If the whole marketing job has been done well, the customer doesn't need much persuading. He should be ready to buy.

Begins with customer needs

Marketing should begin with potential customer needs—not with the production process. Marketing should try to anticipate needs. And then marketing, rather than production, should determine what goods and services are to be developed— including decisions about product design and packaging; prices or fees; credit and collection policies; use of middlemen; transporting and storing policies; advertising and sales policies; and, after the sale, installation, warranty, and perhaps even disposal policies.

Marketing does not do it alone

This does not mean that marketing should try to take over production, accounting, and financial activities. Rather, it means that marketing—by interpreting customers' needs—should provide direction for these activities and try to coordinate them. After all, the purpose of a business or nonprofit organization is to satisfy customer or client needs. It is not to supply goods and services that are convenient to produce and *might* sell or be accepted free.

THE FOCUS OF THIS TEXT—MANAGEMENT— ORIENTED MICRO–MARKETING

Since most of you are preparing for a career in business, the main focus of this text will be on micro-marketing. We will see marketing through the eyes of the marketing manager. But most of this material will also be useful for those who plan to work for nonprofit organizations.

Marketing managers must remember that their organizations are just small parts of a larger macro-marketing system, however. Therefore, the rest of this chapter will look at the macro-view of marketing. Let's begin by defining macro-marketing and reviewing some basic ideas. Then, in Chapter 2, we'll explain the marketing management decision areas we will be discussing in the rest of the book.

MACRO—MARKETING DEFINED

Macro-marketing is a social process that directs an economy's flow of goods and services from producers to consumers in a way that effectively matches supply and demand and accomplishes the objectives of society.

Emphasis is on whole system

Like micro-marketing, macro-marketing is concerned with the flow of need-satisfying goods and services from producer to consumer. However, the emphasis with macro-marketing is not on the activities of individual organizations. Instead, the emphasis is on *how the whole marketing system works*. This includes looking at how marketing affects society and vice versa.

Every society needs a macro-marketing system to help match supply and demand. Different producers in a society have different objectives, resources, and skills. Likewise, not all consumers share the same needs, preferences, and wealth. In other words, within any society there are both heterogeneous supply capabilities and heterogeneous demands for goods and services. The role of a macro-marketing system is to effectively match this heterogeneous supply and demand *and* at the same time accomplish society's objectives.

Is it effective and fair?

The effectiveness and fairness of a particular macro-marketing system must be evaluated in terms of that society's objectives. Obviously, all nations don't share the same objectives. For example, Swedish citizens receive many "free" services—like health care and retirement benefits. Goods and services are fairly evenly distributed among the Swedish population. By contrast, until recently, Russia placed much less emphasis on producing goods and services for individual consumers—and more on military spending. In Venezuela, the distribution of goods and services is very uneven—with a big gap between the "have-nots" and the elite "haves." Whether each of these systems is judged "fair" or "effective" depends on the objectives of the society.

Let's look more closely at macro-marketing.[5] And to make this more meaningful to you, consider (1) what kind of a macro-marketing system we have and (2) how effective and fair it is.

EVERY SOCIETY NEEDS AN ECONOMIC SYSTEM

All societies must provide for the needs of their members. Therefore, every society needs some sort of **economic system**—the way an economy organizes to use scarce resources to produce goods and services and distribute them for consumption by various people and groups in the society.

How an economic system operates depends on a society's objectives and the nature of its political institutions.[6] But, regardless of what form these take, all economic systems must develop some method—along with appropriate economic institutions—to decide what and how much is to be produced and distributed by whom, when, and to whom. How these decisions are made may vary from nation to nation. But the macro-level objectives are basically similar: to create goods and services and make them available when and where they are needed—to maintain or improve each nation's standard of living.

HOW ECONOMIC DECISIONS ARE MADE

There are two basic kinds of economic systems: planned systems and market-directed systems. Actually, no economy is entirely planned or market-directed. Most are a mixture of the two extremes.

Government planners may make the decisions

In a **planned economic system** government planners decide what and how much is to be produced and distributed by whom, when, and to whom. Producers generally have little choice about what goods and services to produce. Their main task is to meet their assigned production quotas. Prices are set by government planners and tend to be very rigid—not changing according to supply and demand. Consumers usually have some freedom of choice—it's impossible to control every single detail! But the assortment of goods and services may be quite limited. Activities such as market research, branding, and advertising usually are neglected. Sometimes they aren't done at all.

Government planning may work fairly well as long as an economy is simple and the variety of goods and services is small. It may even be necessary under certain conditions—during wartime, for example. However, as economies become more complex, government planning becomes more difficult. It may even break down. Planners may be overwhelmed by too many complex decisions. And consumers may lose patience if the planners don't respond to their needs. Labor strikes in Poland illustrate this. The Polish workers want the government to change the plan—so that needed consumer products will be available. To try to reduce such con-

In 1989 over a million Chinese consumers came together to protest the economic decisions made by government planners.

sumer dissatisfaction, planners in the Soviet Union, China, and other socialist countries have put more emphasis on marketing (branding, advertising, and market research) in recent years.[7]

A market-directed economy adjusts itself

In a **market-directed economic system,** the individual decisions of the many producers and consumers make the macro-level decisions for the whole economy. In a pure market-directed economy, consumers make a society's production decisions when they make their choices in the marketplace. They decide what is to be produced and by whom—through their dollar "votes."

Price is a measure of value

Prices in the marketplace are a rough measure of how society values particular goods and services. If consumers are willing to pay the market prices, then apparently they feel they are getting at least their money's worth. Similarly, the cost of labor and materials is a rough measure of the value of the resources used in the production of goods and services to meet these needs. New consumer needs that can be served profitably—not just the needs of the majority—will probably be met by some profit-minded businesses.

In summary, in a market-directed economic system the prices in both the production sector (for resources) and the consumption sector (for goods and services) vary to allocate resources and distribute income according to consumer preferences. The result is a balance of supply and demand and the coordination of the economic activity of many individuals and institutions.

Greatest freedom of choice

Consumers in a market-directed economy enjoy maximum freedom of choice. They are not forced to buy any goods or services, except those that must be provided for the good of society—things such as national defense, schools, police and fire protection, highway systems, and public-health services. These are provided by the community—and the citizens are taxed to pay for them.

Similarly, producers are free to do whatever they wish—provided that they stay within the rules of the game set by government *and* receive enough dollar "votes" from consumers. If they do their job well, they earn a profit and stay in business. But profit, survival, and growth are not guaranteed.

Conflicts can result

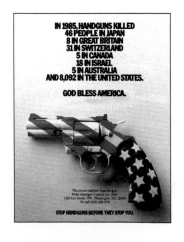

Conflicts and difficulties can come from producers and consumers making free choices. This is called the **micro-macro dilemma:** what is "good" for some producers and consumers may not be good for society as a whole.

Gun control is an example. Each year thousands of people are killed with handguns. There are producers who make and sell handguns at a profit. And there are many consumers who feel strongly about their right to own guns. But others argue that handguns are a threat to society. They want handgun sales banned and sales of all weapons limited. Should gun producers be allowed to sell guns to consumers who want them?

Sometimes such decisions don't involve a matter of life and death but are still important. Many Americans want the convenience of soft drinks in cheap, disposable aluminum cans. But often these same cans end up sprinkled along the roads and must be picked up at taxpayer expense. Should only can buyers (through special charges)—or all of us—have to pay for this littering?

The role of government

The American economy is mainly market-directed—but not completely. Society assigns supervision of the system to the government. For example, besides setting and enforcing the "rules of the game," the federal government controls interest rates and the supply of money. It also sets import and export rules that affect international competition, regulates radio and TV broadcasting, sometimes controls wages, and prices, and so on. Government also tries to be sure that property is protected, contracts are enforced, individuals are not exploited, no group unfairly monopolizes markets, and producers deliver the kinds and quality of goods and services they claim to be offering.

You can see that some of these government activities are needed to make sure the economy runs smoothly. However, some people worry that too much government "guidance" is a threat to the survival of our market-directed system—and the economic and political freedom that goes with it. In the past decade, there has been much less "interference" by federal government—especially in markets for services such as banking, transportation, and communications. The vigorous competition among airlines is a good example of what follows. A few years ago a government agency controlled airline prices and routes. Now that agency doesn't exist, and these decisions are made by marketing managers—and consumers.[8]

ALL ECONOMIES NEED MACRO–MARKETING SYSTEMS

At this point, you may be saying to yourself: all this sounds like economics—where does marketing fit in? Studying a macro-marketing system is a lot like studying an economic system except we give more detailed attention to the "marketing" components of the system—including consumers and other customers, middlemen, and marketing specialists. The focus is on the activities they perform—and how the interaction of the components affects the effectiveness and fairness of a particular system.

In general, we can say that no economic system—whether centrally planned or market-directed—can achieve its objectives without an effective macro-marketing system. To see why this is true, we will look at the role of marketing in primitive economies. Then we will see how macro-marketing tends to become more and more complex in advanced economic systems.

Marketing involves exchange

In a **pure subsistence economy**, each family unit produces everything it consumes. There is no need to exchange goods and services. Each producer-consumer unit is totally self-sufficient. No marketing takes place because *marketing doesn't occur unless two or more parties are willing to exchange something for something else.*

What is a market?

The term *marketing* comes from the word **market**—which is a group of sellers and buyers who are willing to exchange goods and/or services for something of value. Of course, some negotiation may be needed. This can be done face-to-face at some physical location (for example, a farmers' market). Or it can be done indirectly—through a complex network of middlemen who link buyers and sellers who are far apart.

In primitive economies, exchanges tend to occur in central markets. **Central markets** are convenient places where buyers and sellers can meet face-to-face to exchange goods and services. We can understand macro-marketing better by seeing how and why central markets develop.

Central markets help exchange

Imagine a small village of five families—each with a special skill for producing some need-satisfying product. After meeting basic needs, each family decides to specialize. It's easier for one family to make two pots and another to make two baskets than for each one to make one pot and one basket. Specialization makes labor more efficient and more productive. It can increase the total amount of form utility created.

If these five families each specialize in one product, they will have to trade with each other. As Exhibit 1–2A shows, it will take the five families 10 separate exchanges to obtain some of each of the products. If the families live near each other, the exchange process is relatively simple. But if they are far apart, travel back and forth will take time. Who will do the traveling—and when?

Faced with this problem, the families may agree to come to a central market and trade on a certain day. Then each family makes only one trip to the market to trade with all the others. This reduces the total number of trips to five, which makes exchange easier, leaves more time for producing and consuming, and also provides for social gatherings. In total, much more time, place, possession, and even form utility is enjoyed by each of the five families.

Money system speeds trading

While a central meeting place simplifies exchange, the individual bartering transactions still take a lot of time. Bartering only works when someone else wants what you have, and vice versa. Each trader must find others who have products of about equal value. After trading with one group, a family may find itself with extra baskets, knives, and pots. Then it has to find others willing to trade for these products.

Exhibit 1–2

A. Ten exchanges required when a central market is not used

B. Only five exchanges are required when a middleman in a central market is used

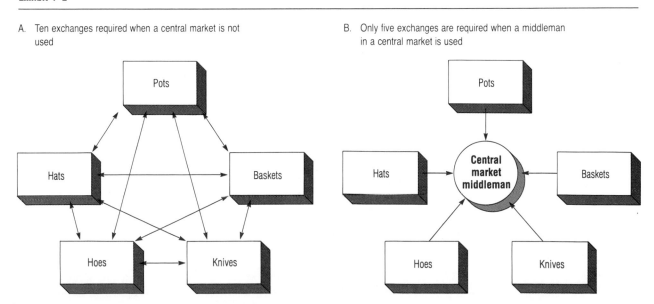

A money system changes all this. A seller only has to find a buyer who wants his products and agrees on the price. Then the seller is free to spend this income to buy whatever he wants.

Middlemen help exchange even more

The development of a central market and a money system simplifies the exchange process among the five families in our imaginary village. But a total of 10 separate transactions is still required. Thus, it still takes a lot of time and effort to carry out exchange among the five families.

This clumsy exchange process is made much simpler by the appearance of a **middleman**—someone who specializes in trade rather than production. A middleman is willing to buy each family's goods and then sell each family whatever it needs. He charges for his services, of course. But this charge may be more than offset by savings in time and effort.

In our simple example, using a middleman at a central market reduces the necessary number of exchanges for all five families from 10 to 5. See Exhibit 1–2B. Each family has more time for production, consumption, and leisure. Also, each family can specialize in production—creating more form utility. Meanwhile, by specializing in trade, the middleman provides additional time, place, and possession utility. In total, all the villagers may enjoy greater economic utility—and greater consumer satisfaction—by using a middleman in the central market.

Note that the reduction in transactions that results from using a middleman in a central market becomes more important as the number of families increases. For example, if the population of our imaginary village increases from 5 to 10 families, 45 transactions are needed without a middleman. Using a middleman requires only one transaction for each family.

Today such middlemen—offering permanent trading facilities—are known as *wholesalers* and *retailers.* The advantages of working with middlemen increase as the number of producers and consumers, their distance from each other, and the number and variety of competing products increase. That is why there are so many wholesalers and retailers in modern economies.

THE ROLE OF MARKETING IN ECONOMIC DEVELOPMENT

Modern economies have advanced well beyond the five-family village, but the same ideas still apply. The main purpose of markets and middlemen is to make exchange easier and allow greater time for production, consumption, and other activities—including recreation.

Effective marketing system is necessary

Although it is tempting to conclude that more effective macro-marketing systems are the result of greater economic development, just the opposite is true. *An effective macro-marketing system is necessary for economic development.* Improved marketing may be the key to growth in less-developed nations.

Breaking the vicious circle of poverty

Without an effective macro-marketing system, the less-developed nations may not be able to escape the "vicious circle of poverty." Many people in these nations can't leave their subsistence way of life to produce for the market because there

Pepsi Barters with Cashless Buyers

Every country has a money system. However, government planners in developing nations often won't let local customers spend cash on foreign-made products. They want the money—and the opportunities for jobs and economic growth—to stay in the local economy. To facilitate exchange in these markets, American firms have turned to *counter-trade*—a special type of bartering. The U.S. company takes its payment in products, not money. For example, soft-drink bottlers in Mexico trade locally grown broccoli for Pepsi concentrate. Then PepsiCo finds a market for the broccoli in the United States. Consumers in Nicaragua sip Pepsi because the company takes sesame seeds and molasses in trade. Distribution systems and middlemen have not yet developed in these countries to handle this sort of exchange. In pursuing its own opportunities, Pepsi is also stimulating economic development. Pepsi is not alone in using countertrade. About 6 percent of all U.S. exports rely on countertrade. [9]

are no buyers for what they produce. And there are no buyers because everyone else is producing for their own needs. As a result, distribution systems and middlemen do not develop.

Breaking this vicious circle of poverty may require major changes in the inefficient micro- and macro-marketing systems that are typical in less-developed nations. At the least, more market-oriented middlemen are needed to move surplus output to markets where there is more demand. Peace Corps workers often help organize local production-distribution efforts—to show the possibilities. For example, local fresh vegetables have been assembled by producers cooperatives in East Africa and shipped to nearby cities where prices were much higher.[10]

Without an effective macro-marketing system, people can't leave their subsistence way of life.

Mexican farmers do not have a local market for their broccoli, but PepsiCo has helped them find customers in the United States.

CAN MASS PRODUCTION SATISFY A SOCIETY'S CONSUMPTION NEEDS?

Urbanization brings together large numbers of people. They must depend on others to produce most of the goods and services they need to satisfy their basic needs. Also, in advanced economies, many consumers have higher discretionary incomes. They can afford to satisfy higher-level needs as well. A modern economy faces a real challenge to satisfy all these needs.

Economies of scale mean lower cost

Fortunately, advanced economies can often take advantage of mass production with its **economies of scale**—which means that as a company produces larger numbers of a particular product, the cost for each of these products goes down. You can see that a one-of-a-kind, custom-built car would cost much more than a mass-produced standard model.

Of course, even in our advanced society, not all goods and services can be produced by mass production—or with economies of scale. Consider medical care. It's difficult to get productivity gains in labor-intensive medical services—like brain surgery. Nevertheless, from a macro-marketing perspective, it is clear that we are able to devote resources to meeting these "quality of life" needs because we are achieving efficiency in other areas.

Thus, modern production skills can help provide great quantities of goods and services to satisfy large numbers of consumers. But mass production alone does not solve the problem of satisfying consumers' needs. Effective marketing is also needed.

Effective marketing is needed to link producers and consumers

Effective marketing means delivering the goods and services that consumers want and need. It means getting products to them at the right time, in the right place, and at a price they're willing to pay. That's not an easy job—especially if you think about the variety of goods and services a highly developed economy can produce—and the many kinds of goods and services consumers want.

Effective marketing in an advanced economy is more difficult because producers and consumers are separated in several ways. As Exhibit 1–3 shows, exchange between producers and consumers is hampered by spatial separation, separation in time, separation in information and values, and separation of ownership. Exchange is further complicated by "discrepancies of quantity" and "discrepancies of assortment" between producers and consumers. That is, each producer specializes in producing and selling large amounts of a narrow assortment of goods and services, but each consumer wants only small quantities of a wide assortment of goods and services.[11]

Marketing functions help narrow the gap

The purpose of a macro-marketing system is to overcome these separations and discrepancies. The "universal functions of marketing" help do this.

The **universal functions of marketing** are: buying, selling, transporting, storing, standardization and grading, financing, risk taking, and market information. They must be performed in all macro-marketing systems. *How* these functions are

Exhibit 1–3   Marketing Facilitates Production and Consumption

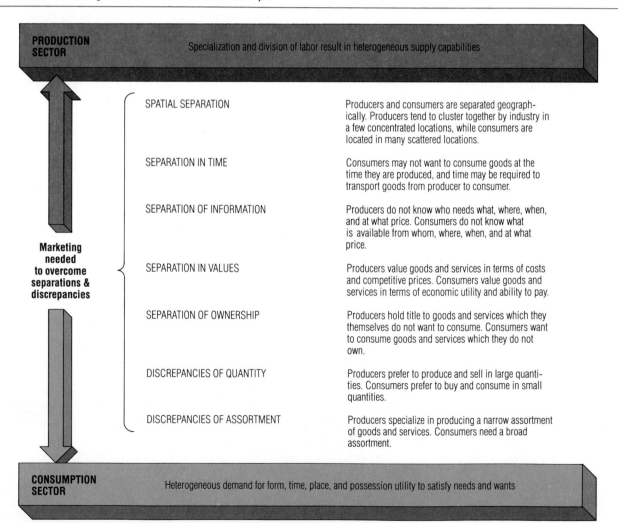

PRODUCTION SECTOR — Specialization and division of labor result in heterogeneous supply capabilities

Marketing needed to overcome separations & discrepancies

SPATIAL SEPARATION — Producers and consumers are separated geographically. Producers tend to cluster together by industry in a few concentrated locations, while consumers are located in many scattered locations.

SEPARATION IN TIME — Consumers may not want to consume goods at the time they are produced, and time may be required to transport goods from producer to consumer.

SEPARATION OF INFORMATION — Producers do not know who needs what, where, when, and at what price. Consumers do not know what is available from whom, where, when, and at what price.

SEPARATION IN VALUES — Producers value goods and services in terms of costs and competitive prices. Consumers value goods and services in terms of economic utility and ability to pay.

SEPARATION OF OWNERSHIP — Producers hold title to goods and services which they themselves do not want to consume. Consumers want to consume goods and services which they do not own.

DISCREPANCIES OF QUANTITY — Producers prefer to produce and sell in large quantities. Consumers prefer to buy and consume in small quantities.

DISCREPANCIES OF ASSORTMENT — Producers specialize in producing a narrow assortment of goods and services. Consumers need a broad assortment.

CONSUMPTION SECTOR — Heterogeneous demand for form, time, place, and possession utility to satisfy needs and wants

performed—and *by whom*—may differ among nations and economic systems. But they are needed in any macro-marketing system. Let's take a closer look at them now.

Exchange usually involves buying and selling. The **buying function** means looking for and evaluating goods and services. The **selling function** involves promoting the product. It includes the use of personal selling, advertising, and other mass selling methods. This is probably the most visible function of marketing.

The **transporting function** means the movement of goods from one place to another. The **storing function** involves holding goods until customers need them.

Standardization and grading involve sorting products according to size and quality. This makes buying and selling easier because it reduces the need for inspection and sampling. **Financing** provides the necessary cash and credit to produce, transport, store, promote, sell, and buy products. **Risk taking** involves bearing the uncertainties that are part of the marketing process. A firm can never be sure that customers will want to buy its products. Products can also be damaged, stolen, or outdated. The **market information function** involves the collection, analysis, and distribution of all the information needed to plan, carry out, and control marketing activities.

WHO PERFORMS MARKETING FUNCTIONS?

Producers, consumers, and marketing specialists

From a macro-level viewpoint, these marketing functions are all part of the marketing process—and must be done by someone. None of them can be eliminated. In a planned economy, some of the functions may be performed by government agencies. Others may be left to individual producers and consumers. In a market-directed economy, marketing functions are performed by producers, consumers, and a variety of marketing specialists. See Exhibit 1–4.

Facilitators—including transportation firms and advertising specialists—may help a marketing manager with one or more of the marketing functions.

Exhibit 1–4 Model of U.S. Macro-Marketing System*

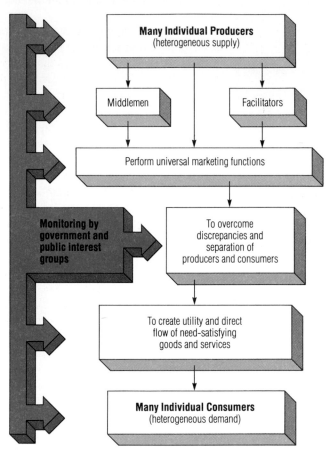

*Our nation's macro-marketing system must interact with the
macro-marketing systems of many other nations.

**Specialists perform some
functions**

Earlier in this chapter, you saw how producers and consumers benefited when
marketing specialists (middlemen) took over some buying and selling. Producers
and consumers also benefit when marketing specialists perform the other marketing functions. So we find marketing functions being performed not only by marketing middlemen but also by a variety of other **facilitators**—firms that provide one or
more of the marketing functions other than buying or selling. These include advertising agencies, marketing research firms, independent product-testing laboratories,
public warehouses, transporting firms, and financial institutions (including banks).
Through specialization or economies of scale, marketing middlemen and facilitators
are often able to perform the marketing functions better—and at a lower cost—
than producers or consumers can. This allows producers and consumers to spend
more time on production and consumption.

**Functions can be shifted
and shared**

From a macro viewpoint, all of the marketing functions must be performed by
someone. But, *from a micro viewpoint, not every firm must perform all of the functions. Further, not all goods and services require all the functions at every level of*

their production. "Pure services"—like a plane ride—don't need storing, for example. But storing is required in the production of the plane and while the plane is not in service.

Some marketing specialists perform all the functions. Others specialize in only one or two. Marketing research firms, for example, specialize only in the market information function. The important point to remember is this: *responsibility for performing the marketing functions can be shifted and shared in a variety of ways, but no function can be completely eliminated.*

HOW WELL DOES OUR MACRO–MARKETING SYSTEM WORK?

It connects remote producers and consumers

A macro-marketing system does more than just deliver goods and services to consumers—it allows mass production with its economies of scale. Also, mass communication and mass transportation allow products to be shipped where they're needed. Oranges from California are found in Minnesota stores—even in December—and electronic parts made in New York State are used in making products all over the country.[12]

It encourages growth and new ideas

In addition to making mass production possible, our market-directed, macro-marketing system encourages **innovation**—the development and spread of new ideas and products. Competition for consumers' doilars forces firms to think of new and better ways of satisfying consumer needs.

It has its critics

In explaining marketing's role in society, we described some of the benefits of our macro-marketing system. This approach is reasonable because our macro-marketing system has provided us—at least in material terms—with one of the highest standards of living in the world. It seems to be "effective" and "fair" in many ways.

We must admit, however, that marketing—as we know it in the United States—has many critics! Marketing activity is especially open to criticism because it is the part of business most visible to the public. There is nothing like a pocketbook issue for getting consumers excited!

Typical complaints about marketing include:

Advertising is too often annoying, misleading, and wasteful.

Products are not safe—or the quality is poor.

Marketing makes people too materialistic—it motivates them toward "things" instead of social needs.

Easy consumer credit makes people buy things they don't need and really can't afford.

Packaging and labeling are often confusing and deceptive.

Middlemen add to the cost of distribution—and raise prices without providing anything in return.

Marketing creates interest in products that pollute the environment.

Too many unnecessary products are offered.

Marketing serves the rich and exploits the poor.

Note that some of these complaints deal with the whole macro-marketing system. Others apply to practices of specific firms and are micro-marketing oriented.

Consumer complaints should be taken seriously

Such complaints cannot and should not be taken lightly.[13] They show that many Americans aren't happy with some parts of our marketing system. Certainly, the strong public support for consumer protection laws proves that not all consumers feel they are being treated like kings and queens. But some of the complaints occur because people don't understand what marketing is. As you go through this book, we'll discuss some of these criticisms—to help you understand marketing better. Then, we will return to a more complete appraisal of marketing in our final chapter.

CONCLUSION

In this chapter, we defined two levels of marketing: micro-marketing and macro-marketing. Macro-marketing is concerned with the way the whole economy works. Micro-marketing focuses on the activities of individual firms. We discussed the role of marketing in economic development—and the functions of marketing and who performs them. We ended by raising some of the criticisms of marketing—both of the whole macro system and of the way individual firms work.

We emphasized macro-marketing in this chapter, but the major thrust of this book is on micro-marketing. By learning more about market-oriented decision making, you will be able to make more efficient and socially responsible decisions. This will help improve the performance of individual firms and organizations (your employers). And, eventually, it will help our macro-marketing system work better.

We'll see marketing through the eyes of the marketing manager—maybe *you* in the near future. And we will show how you can contribute to the marketing process. Along the way, we'll discuss the impact of micro-level decisions on society. Then, in Chapter 23—after you have had time to understand how and why producers and consumers think and behave the way they do—we will evaluate how well both micro-marketing and macro-marketing perform in our market-directed economic system.

Questions and Problems _____

1. List your activities for the first two hours after you woke up this morning. Briefly indicate how marketing affected your activities.

2. It is fairly easy to see why people do not beat a path to a mousetrap manufacturer's door, but would they be similarly indifferent if some food processor developed a revolutionary new food product that would provide all necessary nutrients in small pills for about $100 per year per person?

3. Distinguish between macro- and micro-marketing. Then explain how they are interrelated, if they are.

4. Distinguish between how economic decisions are made in a planned economic system and how they are made in a market-directed economy.

5. A committee of the American Marketing Association defined marketing as "the process of planning and executing the conception, pricing, promotion, and distribution of ideas, goods, and services to create exchanges that satisfy individual and organizational objectives." Does this definition consider macro-marketing? Explain your answer.

6. Identify a "central market" in your city and explain how it facilitates exchange.

7. Discuss the nature of marketing in a socialist economy. Would the functions that must be provided and the development of wholesaling and retailing systems be any different than in a market-directed economy?

8. Discuss how the micro-macro dilemma relates to each of the following products: seat belts in cars, nuclear power, high–performance automobiles, and bank credit cards.

9.   Describe a recent purchase you made and indicate why that particular product was available at a store and, in particular, at the store where you bought it.

10.   Refer to Exhibit 1–3, and give an example of a purchase you recently made that involved separation of information and separation in time between you and the producer. Briefly explain how these separations were overcome.

11.   Define the functions of marketing in your own words. Using an example, explain how they can be shifted and shared.

12.   Explain, in your own words, why the emphasis in this text is on micro-marketing.

13.   Explain why a small producer might want an advertising agency to be a facilitator to take over some of its advertising activities.

14.   Explain why a market-directed macro-marketing system encourages innovation. Give an example.

Suggested Cases

1.   McDonald's "Fast-Food" Restaurant

4.   Bill's Cleaning, Inc.

Suggested Computer-Aided Problem

1.   Revenue, Cost, and Profit Relationships

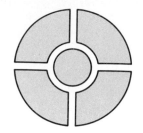

Chapter *2*

Marketing's Role within the Firm

When You Finish This Chapter, You Should

1. Know what the marketing concept is—and how it should affect a firm's strategy planning.

2. Understand what a marketing manager does.

3. Know what marketing strategy planning is—and why it will be the focus of this book.

4. Understand target marketing.

5. Be familiar with the four Ps in a marketing mix.

6. Know the difference between a marketing strategy, a marketing plan, and a marketing program.

7. Understand the important new terms (shown in red).

"A master plan to hit the target" is not a Rambo story line—but the goal of a good marketing manager.

Marketing and marketing management are important in our society—and in business firms. As you saw in Chapter 1, marketing is concerned with anticipating needs and directing the flow of goods and services from producers to consumers. This is done to satisfy the needs of consumers and achieve the objectives of the firm (the micro view) and of society as a whole (the macro view).

To get a better understanding of marketing, we are going to look at things from the point of view of the marketing manager—the one who makes a company's important marketing decisions. To get you thinking about the ideas we will be developing in this chapter and the rest of the book, let's consider a few decisions recently made by marketing managers.

In the 1980s, consumer interest in health and fitness increased demand for athletic shoes. Firms like Nike, Reebok, and Converse—as well as competing producers from Taiwan and Korea—battled to win a profitable share of the $9 billion market. To come out on top in these "sneakers wars," Nike's managers had to make many decisions.

Nike's marketing research showed that consumer needs were changing. Consumers wanted fashionable, high-performance shoes for activities like aerobics, walking, and racquetball. Nike's marketing managers had to decide what new products to develop to meet these needs. They had to decide whether to rely on the familiar Nike name and label or to design a whole new look. Marketing managers also had to decide who would be the main target—and the best way to reach them. This included picking a theme for the advertising campaign and determining how much to spend on advertising—and where to spend it. Managers also had to decide how to promote the shoes to their wholesalers and retailers—the middlemen who actually distribute the products to places where the customers can buy them.

They had other decisions to make. In such large quantities a pair of shoes costs only $25 to produce. Should the price stay at about $70 a pair, or would a different price be more profitable? Should Nike offer introductory price rebates to help attract customers away from other brands? Should Nike start in some introductory regions of the country or distribute the new products in as many places as possible all at once? Should they try to expand the number of middlemen who carried Nike products, or should they focus on the ones who had sold their products in the past? Nike's managers did a good job with these decisions. Within a few years Nike dramatically increased its share of the market and its profits—in an increasingly competitive market.[1]

We've mentioned only a few of many decisions Nike's marketing managers had to make, but you can see that each of these decisions affects the others. Making marketing decisions is never easy. But knowing what basic decision areas have to be considered helps you to plan a better, more successful strategy. This chapter will get you started by giving you a framework for thinking about all the marketing management decision areas—which is what the rest of this book is all about.

MARKETING'S ROLE HAS CHANGED A LOT OVER THE YEARS

From our Nike example, it's clear that marketing decisions are very important to a firm's success. But marketing hasn't always been so complicated. In fact, it's only in the last 30 years or so that an increasing number of producers, wholesalers, and retailers have adopted modern marketing thinking. Instead of just focusing on producing or selling *products*, these firms focus on *customers*—and try to integrate the company's total effort to satisfy them.

We will discuss five stages in marketing evolution: (1) the simple trade era, (2) the production era, (3) the sales era, (4) the marketing department era, and (5) the marketing company era. We'll talk about these eras as if they applied generally to all firms—but keep in mind that *some managers still have not made it to the final stages.* They are stuck in the past.

Specialization permitted trade—and middlemen met the need

When societies first moved toward some specialization of production and away from a subsistence economy where each family raised and consumed everything it produced, traders played an important role. Early "producers for the market" made products that were needed by themselves and their neighbors. (Recall the five-family example in Chapter 1.) As bartering became more difficult, societies moved into the **simple trade era**—a time when families traded or sold their "surplus" output to local middlemen. These specialists resold the goods to other consumers or distant middlemen. This was the early role of marketing—and it didn't change much until the Industrial Revolution brought larger factories a little over a hundred years ago.

From the production to the sales era

From the Industrial Revolution until the 1920s, most companies were in the production era. The **production era** is a time when a company focuses on production of a few specific products—perhaps because few of these products are available in the market. "If we can make it, it will sell" is management thinking characteristic of the production era.

In 1891. a firm could easily sell the safety razors it could produce—because there were few available in the market.

By about 1930, companies had more production capability than ever before. Now the problem wasn't just to produce—but to beat the competition and win customers. This led many firms to enter the sales era. The **sales era** is a time when a company emphasizes selling because of increased competition.

To the marketing department era

For most firms, the sales era continued until at least 1950. By then, sales were growing rapidly in most areas of the economy. The problem was deciding where to put the company's effort. Someone was needed to tie together the efforts of research, purchasing, production, shipping, and sales. As this situation became more common, the sales era was replaced by the marketing department era. The **marketing department era** is a time when all marketing activities are brought under the control of one department to improve short-run policy planning and to try to integrate the firm's activities.

To the marketing company era

Since 1960, most firms have developed at least some staff with a marketing management outlook. Many of these firms have even graduated from the marketing department era into the marketing company era. The **marketing company era** is a time when, in addition to short-run marketing planning, marketing people develop long-range plans—sometimes 10 or more years ahead—and the whole company effort is guided by the marketing concept.

WHAT DOES THE MARKETING CONCEPT MEAN?

The **marketing concept** means that an organization aims *all* its efforts at satisfying its *customers*—at a *profit*. See Exhibit 2–1. The marketing concept is a simple but very important idea.

It is not really a new idea in business—it's been around for a long time. But some managers act as if they are stuck at the beginning of the production era—when there were shortages of most products. They show little interest in customers' needs. These managers still have a **production orientation**—making whatever products are easy to produce and *then* trying to sell them. They think of customers existing to buy the firm's output rather than of firms existing to serve customers and—more broadly—the needs of society.

Well-managed firms have replaced this production orientation with a marketing orientation. A **marketing orientation** means trying to carry out the marketing con-

Exhibit 2–1   Firms with a Marketing Orientation Carry Out the Marketing Concept

Customer satisfaction

Total company effort

The marketing concept

Profit as an objective

cept. Instead of just trying to get customers to buy what the firm has produced, a marketing-oriented firm tries to produce what customers need.

Three basic ideas are included in the definition of the marketing concept: (1) a customer orientation, (2) a total company effort, and (3) profit—not just sales—as an objective. These ideas deserve more discussion.

A customer orientation guides the whole system

"Give the customers what they need" seems so obvious that it may be hard for you to see why the marketing concept requires special attention. However, people don't always do the logical and obvious—especially when it means changing what they have done in the past. In a typical company 30 years ago, production managers thought mainly about getting out the product. Accountants were interested only in balancing the books. Financial people looked after the company's cash position. And salespeople were mainly concerned with getting orders. Each department thought of its own activity as the center of the business—with others working around "the edges." No one was concerned with the whole system. As long as the company made a profit, each department went merrily on—"doing its own thing." Unfortunately, this is still true in many companies today.

Work together . . . do a better job

Ideally, all managers should work together because the output from one department may be the input to another. But some managers tend to build "fences" around their own departments as seen in Exhibit 2–2A. There may be meetings to try to get them to work together—but they come and go from the meetings worried only about protecting their own "turf."

We use the term *production orientation* as a shorthand way to refer to this kind of narrow thinking—and lack of a central focus—in a business firm. But keep in mind that this problem may be seen in sales-oriented sales representatives, advertising-oriented agency people, finance-oriented finance people, directors of nonprofit organizations, and so on. It is not just a criticism of people who manage production. They aren't necessarily any more guilty of narrow thinking than anyone else in a firm.

Exhibit 2–2

A. A business as a box
(most departments have high fences)

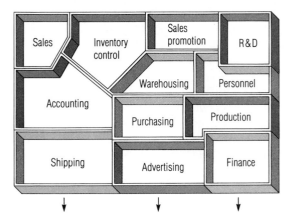

Each department sees its activities as what is most important.

B. Total system view of a
business (implementing marketing concept;
still have departments but all guided by
what customers want)

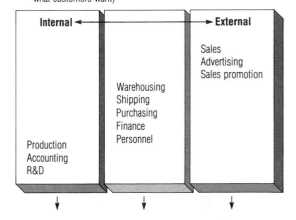

All departments work together to provide customer satisfaction.

The "fences" come down in an organization that has accepted the marketing concept. There are still departments, of course, because specialization makes sense. But the total system's effort is guided by what customers want—instead of what each department would like to do.

In such a firm, it is more realistic to view the business as a box with both internal and external activities as shown in Exhibit 2–2B. Some internal departments—production, accounting, and research and development (R&D)—are mainly concerned with affairs inside the firm. The external departments are concerned with

*Marketing is being more widely
accepted by nonprofit organizations.*

outsiders—sales, advertising, and sales promotion. Finally, some departments—warehousing, shipping, purchasing, finance, and personnel—work with both insiders and outsiders.

The important point is to have a guiding focus that *all* departments adopt. It helps the organization work as a total "system" rather than a lot of separate parts. The marketing concept, however, is more complete than many systems-oriented ideas. It actually specifies a high-level objective—customer satisfaction—that is logical for each and every part of the system. It also specifies a profit objective, which is necessary for the system's survival.

A nonprofit organization does not measure "profit" in the same way as a for-profit firm. But, as with any business firm, a nonprofit organization needs support to survive and achieve its objectives. This support may not come from those who receive the benefits the organization produces—animals protected by the World Wildlife Fund, for example. But if supporters don't think the benefits are worth what it costs to provide them, they will—and should—put their time and money elsewhere. So the marketing concept makes sense for nonprofit organizations, too.

It's easy to slip into a production orientation

The marketing concept may seem obvious, but it's very easy to slip into a production-oriented way of thinking. For example, a retailer might prefer only weekday hours—avoiding nights, Saturdays, and Sundays when many customers would prefer to shop. Or a company might rush to produce a clever new product developed in its lab—rather than first finding if it will fill an unsatisfied need. A community theater group might decide to do a play that the actors and the director like—never stopping to consider what the audience might want to see.

Take a look at Exhibit 2–3. It shows some differences in outlook between adopters of the marketing concept and typical production-oriented managers. As the exhibit suggests, the marketing concept—if taken seriously—is really very powerful. It forces the company to think through what it is doing—and why. And it motivates the company to develop plans for accomplishing its objectives.

ADOPTION OF THE MARKETING CONCEPT HAS NOT BEEN EASY OR UNIVERSAL

The marketing concept seems so logical that you would think it would have been quickly adopted by most firms. But this isn't the case. Many firms are still production oriented. In fact, the majority are either production oriented—or regularly slip back that way—and must consciously refocus on customers' interests in their planning.

The marketing concept was first accepted by consumer products companies such as General Electric and Procter & Gamble. Competition was intense in some of their markets—and trying to satisfy customers' needs more fully was a way to win in this competition. Widespread publicity about the success of the marketing concept at companies like General Electric and Procter & Gamble helped spread the message to other firms.[2]

Producers of industrial commodities—steel, coal, paper, glass, chemicals—have accepted the marketing concept slowly if at all. Similarly, many retailers have been slow to accept the marketing concept—in part because they are so close to final consumers that they "feel" they really know their customers.

Exhibit 2–3   Some Differences in Outlook between Adopters of the Marketing Concept and the Typical Production-Oriented Managers

Topic	Marketing orientation	Production orientation
Attitudes toward customers	Customer needs determine company plans	They should be glad we exist, trying to cut costs and bringing out better products
Product offering	Company makes what it can sell	Company sells what it can make
Role of marketing research	To determine customer needs and how well company is satisfying them	To determine customer reaction, if used at all
Interest in innovation	Focus on locating new opportunities	Focus is on technology and cost cutting
Importance of profit	A critical objective	A residual, what's left after all costs are covered
Role of customer credit	Seen as a customer service	Seen as a necessary evil
Role of packaging	Designed for customer convenience and as a selling tool	Seen merely as protection for the product
Inventory levels	Set with customer requirements and costs in mind	Set to make production more convenient
Transportation arrangements	Seen as a customer service	Seen as an extension of production and storage activities, with emphasis on cost minimization
Focus of advertising	Need-satisfying benefits of products and services	Product features and how products are made
Role of sales force	Help the customer to buy if the product fits his needs, while coordinating with rest of firm	Sell the customer, don't worry about coordination with other promotion efforts or rest of firm

Service industries are catching up

Marketing concept applies directly to nonprofit organizations

"Service" industries—including airlines, banks, investment firms, lawyers, physicians, accountants, and insurance companies—were slow to adopt the marketing concept, too. But this has changed dramatically in the last decade, partly due to government regulation changes that enabled many of these businesses to be more competitive.[3]

Banks used to be open for limited hours that were convenient for bankers—not customers. Many closed during lunch hour! But now financial services are less regulated, and banks compete with companies like Merrill Lynch or American Express for checking accounts and retirement investments. The banks stay open longer, often during evenings and on Saturdays. They also offer more services for their customers—automatic banking machines that take credit cards or a "personal banker" to give financial advice. Most banks now aggressively advertise their special services and even interest rates so customers can compare bank offerings.

The same ideas apply to nonprofit organizations. Only the objectives against which possible plans are measured are different. The YMCA, the Girl Scouts, colleges, symphony orchestras, and the Post Office, for example, are all seeking to satisfy some consumer groups and at least survive—even though they aren't seeking profits.[4]

A simple example shows how marketing concept thinking helped one nonprofit service organization do a better job achieving its objectives. A police chief in a small town was trying to fight increased robberies in residential areas. He asked the town manager for a larger budget—for more officers and cars to patrol neigh-

Many service industries have begun to apply the marketing concept.

borhoods. The town manager wasn't convinced a bigger police budget would solve the problem. Instead she tried a different approach. One police officer was taken "off the beat" and put in charge of a "community watch" program. This officer helped neighbors organize to look after each others' property and notify the police of any suspicious situations. He also set up a program to engrave ID numbers on belongings and installed signs warning thieves that a "community watch" was in effect. Break-ins all but stopped—without increasing the police budget. What the town *really* needed was more effective crime prevention—not just more police officers.

Throughout this book, we'll be discussing the marketing concept and related ideas as they apply in many different settings. Often we'll simply say "in a firm" or "in a business"—but remember that most of the ideas can be applied in *any* type of organization.

How far should the marketing concept go?

The marketing concept is so logical that it's hard to argue with it. Yet, it does raise some important questions—for which there are no easy answers.

Should all consumer needs be satisfied?

When a firm focuses its efforts on satisfying some consumers—to achieve its objectives—the effect on society may be completely ignored. (Remember that we discussed this micro-macro dilemma in Chapter 1.)

Further, some consumers want products that may not be safe or good for them in the long run. Some critics argue that businesses should not offer cigarettes, high-heeled shoes, alcoholic beverages, sugar-coated cereals, softdrinks, and many processed foods—because they aren't "good" for consumers in the long run. These critics raise the basic question: Is the marketing concept really desirable?[5]

Many marketing managers and socially conscious marketing companies are trying to resolve this problem. Their definition of customer satisfaction includes long-range effects—as well as immediate customer satisfaction. They try to balance consumer, company, *and* social interests.

What if it cuts into profits?

Being more socially conscious often seems to lead to positive customer response. For example, Gerber had great success when it improved the nutritional quality of its baby food.

But what about products consumers want but that may be risky to use? Bicycles, for example, are one of the most dangerous products identified by the Consumer Product Safety Commission. Should Schwinn stop production? What about skis, mopeds, and scuba equipment? Who should decide if these products will be offered to consumers? Is this a micro-marketing issue or a macro-marketing issue?

Being socially conscious and trying to carry out the marketing concept can be difficult. But business managers have to face this problem. We will discuss some of the social and ethical issues faced by marketing management throughout the text.

Does it go far enough?

Some critics say that the marketing concept doesn't go far enough in today's highly competitive markets. They think of marketing as "warfare" for customers—and argue that a marketing manager should focus on competitors, not customers. That viewpoint, however, misses the point. The marketing concept idea isn't just to satisfy customers—but to do it at a profit through an integrated, whole-company effort. All three must be considered simultaneously. Profit opportunities depend not only on outdoing some other firm—but also on doing the right thing. In fact, often the best way to beat the competition is to be first to find and satisfy a need that others have not even considered. The competition between Pepsi and Coke illustrates this.

Coke and Pepsi were spending millions of dollars on promotion—fighting head-to-head for the same cola customers. They put so much emphasis on the competitor that they missed opportunities. Then, Pepsi recognized consumer interest in a potential new product idea: a soft drink based on fruit juice. Pepsi's Slice brand soft drink was first on the market, and that helped Slice win loyal customers and space on middlemen's shelves.

THE MANAGEMENT JOB IN MARKETING

Now that you know about the marketing concept—a philosophy to guide the whole firm—let's look more closely at how a marketing manager helps a firm to achieve its objectives. The marketing manager is a manager, so let's look at the marketing management process.

The **marketing management process** is the process of (1) *planning* marketing activities, (2) directing the *implementation* of the plans, and (3) *controlling* these plans. Planning, implementation, and control are basic jobs of all managers—but here we will emphasize what they mean to marketing managers.

Exhibit 2–4 shows the relationships among the three jobs in the marketing management process. The jobs are all connected to show that the marketing management process is continuous. In the planning job, managers set guidelines for the implementing job—and specify expected results. They use these expected results in the control job—to determine if everything has worked out as planned. The link from the control job to the planning job is especially important. This feedback often leads to changes in the plans—or to new plans.

Exhibit 2–4   The Marketing Management Process

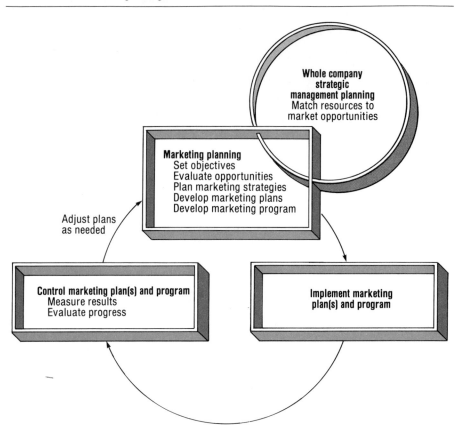

Whole company
strategic
management planning
Match resources to
market opportunities

Marketing planning
Set objectives
Evaluate opportunities
Plan marketing strategies
Develop marketing plans
Develop marketing program

Adjust plans
as needed

Control marketing plan(s) and program
Measure results
Evaluate progress

**Implement marketing
plan(s) and program**

**Marketing managers
should seek new
opportunities**

Exhibit 2–4 shows that marketing managers must seek attractive new opportunities—as customers' needs change or as the organization's ability to meet customers' needs changes. In the next two chapters, we will discuss how marketing managers seek and evaluate opportunities. For now, however, note that marketing managers cannot be satisfied just planning present activities. Markets are dynamic. Consumers' needs, competitors, and the environment keep changing.

Consider Parker Brothers, a company that seemed to have a "Monopoly" in family games. While it continued selling board games, firms like Atari and Nintendo zoomed in with "video game" competition. Of course, not every opportunity is "good" for every company. Really attractive opportunities are those that fit with what the whole company wants—and is able to do.

**Strategic management
planning concerns the
whole firm**

The job of planning strategies to guide a whole company is called **strategic (management) planning**—the managerial process of developing and maintaining a match between an organization's resources and its market opportunities. This is a top management job that includes planning not only for marketing activities but also for production, research and development, and other functional areas. We won't discuss whole-company planning in this text, but you need to understand that marketing department plans are not whole company plans.

On the other hand, company plans should be market-oriented. And the marketing manager's plans can set the tone and direction for the whole company. So we will use *strategy planning* and *marketing strategy planning* to mean the same thing.[6]

WHAT IS MARKETING STRATEGY PLANNING?

Marketing strategy planning means finding attractive opportunities and developing profitable marketing strategies. But what is a "marketing strategy?" We have used these words rather casually so far. Now let's see what they really mean.

What is a marketing strategy?

A **marketing strategy** specifies a target market and a related marketing mix. It is a "big picture" of what a firm will do in some market. Two interrelated parts are needed:

1. A **target market**—a fairly homogeneous (similar) group of customers to whom a company wishes to appeal.
2. A **marketing mix**—the controllable variables the company puts together to satisfy this target group.

Exhibit 2–5   A Marketing Strategy

The importance of target customers in this process can be seen in Exhibit 2–5, where the customer—the "C"—is at the center of the diagram. The customer is surrounded by the controllable variables that we call the "marketing mix." A typical marketing mix includes some product, offered at a price, with some promotion to tell potential customers about the product, and a way to reach the customer's place.

Compaq Computer's strategy aims at business-oriented users of microcomputers in urban areas. Compaq's strategy calls for a reliable, high-performance product that is compatible with popular business-oriented software produced by other firms. The strategy calls for the product to be readily available through full-service computer stores in major cities. To avoid the types of conflicts that IBM and Apple have had with their middlemen, Compaq does not sell directly to the final customers with its own sales force. However, the company supports the whole effort with much promotion—including personal selling to managers of computer stores, advertising to computer buyers, and sales promotion to both customers and computer stores. Compaq's pricing is more or less competitive with other well-known brands.[7]

SELECTING A MARKET—ORIENTED STRATEGY IS TARGET MARKETING

Target marketing is not mass marketing

Note that a marketing strategy specifies some *particular* target customers. This approach is called "target marketing" to distinguish it from "mass marketing." **Target marketing** says that a marketing mix is tailored to fit some specific target customers. In contrast, **mass marketing**—the typical production-oriented approach—vaguely aims at "everyone" with the same marketing mix. Mass marketing assumes that everyone is the same—and considers everyone a potential customer. It may help to think of target marketing as the "rifle approach" and mass marketing as the "shotgun approach."

"Mass marketers" may do target marketing

Commonly used terms can be confusing here. The terms *mass marketing* and *mass marketers* do not mean the same thing. Far from it! *Mass marketing* means trying to sell to "everyone," as we explained above. *Mass marketers* like General

A marketing-oriented manager sees everyone as different and practices target marketing.

Foods and Sears are aiming at clearly defined target markets. The confusion with mass marketing occurs because their target markets usually are large and spread out.

Target marketing—can mean big markets and profits

Target marketing is not limited to small market segments—only to fairly homogeneous ones. A very large market—even what is sometimes called the "mass market"—may be fairly homogeneous, and a target marketer will deliberately aim at it. For example, there is a very large group of young urban professionals (sometimes called yuppies) who are homogeneous on many dimensions—including a high income level. This group accounts for about 70 percent of all stereo equipment purchases—so it should be no surprise that it is a major target market for companies like Sony and Pioneer.

The basic reason for a marketing manager to focus on some specific target customers is to gain a competitive advantage—by developing a more satisfying marketing mix that should also be more profitable for the firm.

DEVELOPING MARKETING MIXES FOR TARGET MARKETS

There are many marketing mix variables

There are many possible ways to satisfy the needs of target customers. A product can have many different features and quality levels. Service levels can be adjusted. The package can be of various sizes, colors, or materials. The brand name and warranty can be changed. Various advertising media—newspapers, magazines, radio, television, billboards—may be used. A company's own sales force or other sales specialists can be used. Different prices can be charged. Price discounts may be given, and so on. With so many possible variables, the question is: is there any way to help organize all these decisions and simplify the selection of marketing mixes? And the answer is: yes.

The four "Ps" make up a marketing mix

It is useful to reduce all the variables in the marketing mix to four basic ones:

> Product.   Promotion.
> Place.   Price.

It helps to think of the four major parts of a marketing mix as the "four Ps."

**Exhibit 2–6
A Marketing Strategy—Showing the
Four Ps of a Marketing Mix**

Exhibit 2–6 emphasizes their relationship and their common focus on the customer—"C."

Customer is not part of the marketing mix

The customer is shown surrounded by the four Ps in Exhibit 2–6. Some students assume that the customer is part of the marketing mix—but this is not so. The customer should be the *target* of all marketing efforts. The customer is placed in the center of the diagram to show this. The C stands for some specific customers—the target market.

Exhibit 2–7 shows some of the variables in the four Ps—which will be discussed in later chapters. For now, let's just describe each P briefly.

Product—the right one for the target

The Product area is concerned with developing the right "product" for the target market. This offering may involve a physical good, a service, or a blend of both. Keep in mind that Product is not limited to "physical goods." For example, the Product of H & R Block is a completed tax form. The important thing to remember is that your good—and/or service—should satisfy some customers' needs.

Along with other Product decisions, we will talk about developing and managing new products and whole product lines. We'll also discuss the characteristics of various kinds of products so that you will be able to make generalizations about product classes. This will help you to develop whole marketing mixes more quickly.

Place—reaching the target

Place is concerned with getting the "right" product to the target market's Place. A product isn't much good to a customer if it isn't available when and where it's wanted.

Exhibit 2–7 Strategy Decision Areas Organized by the Four Ps

Product	Place	Promotion	Price
Physical good	Objectives	Objectives	Objectives
Service	Channel type	Promotion blend	Flexibility
Features	Market exposure	Salespeople	Level over
Quality level	Kinds of	Kind	product life
Accessories	middlemen	Number	cycle
Installation	Kinds and	Selection	Geographic terms
Instructions	locations of	Training	Discounts
Warranty	stores	Motivation	Allowances
Product lines	How to handle	Advertising	
Packaging	transporting	Targets	
Branding	and storing	Kinds of ads	
	Service levels	Media type	
	Recruiting	Copy thrust	
	middlemen	Prepared by	
	Managing	whom	
	channels	Sales promotion	
		Publicity	

Marketing managers for Minute Maid know that different target markets may require different marketing mixes.

A product reaches customers through a channel of distribution. A **channel of distribution** is any series of firms (or individuals) from producer to final user or consumer.

Sometimes a channel system is quite short. It may run directly from a producer to a final user or consumer. Often it is more complex—involving many different kinds of middlemen and specialists. See Exhibit 2–8. And if a marketing manager has several different target markets, several channels of distribution might be needed.

We will also see how physical distribution—transporting and storing—relates to the other Place decisions and the rest of the marketing mix.

Promotion—telling and selling the customer

The third P—Promotion—is concerned with telling the target market about the "right" product. Promotion includes personal selling, mass selling, and sales promotion. It is the marketing manager's job to blend these methods.

Personal selling involves direct communication between sellers and potential customers. Personal selling is usually face-to-face, but sometimes the communication is over the telephone. Personal selling lets the salesperson adapt the firm's marketing mix to each potential customer. But this individual attention comes at a price. Personal selling can be very expensive. Often this personal effort has to be blended with mass selling and sales promotion.

Mass selling is communicating with large numbers of customers at the same time. The main form of mass selling is **Advertising**—any *paid* form of nonpersonal presentation of ideas, goods, or services by an identified sponsor. **Publicity**—any *unpaid* form of nonpersonal presentation of ideas, goods, or services—is another important form of mass selling.

Sales promotion refers to those promotion activities—other than advertising, publicity, and personal selling—that stimulate interest, trial, or purchase by final customers or others in the channel. This can involve use of coupons, point-of-

Exhibit 2–8   Four Examples of Basic Channels of Distribution for Consumer Products

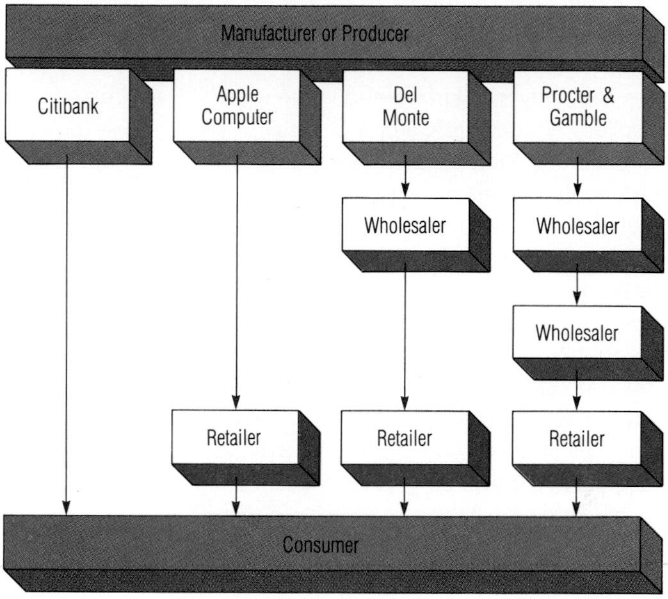

of-purchase materials, samples, signs, catalogs, novelties, and circulars. Sales promotion specialists try to help the personal selling and mass selling people.

Price—making it right

In addition to developing the right Product, Place, and Promotion, marketing managers must also decide the right Price. In setting a price, they must consider the kind of competition in the target market—and the cost of the whole marketing mix. They must also try to estimate customer reaction to possible prices. Besides this, they also must know current practices as to markups, discounts, and other terms of sale. Further, they must be aware of legal restrictions on pricing.

If customers won't accept the Price, all of the planning effort will be wasted. So you can see that Price is an important area for a marketing manager.

Each of the four Ps contributes to the whole

All four Ps are needed in a marketing mix. In fact, they should all be tied together. But is any one more important than the others? Generally speaking, the answer is no—all contribute to one whole. When a marketing mix is being developed, all (final) decisions about the Ps should be made at the same time. That's why the four Ps are arranged around the customer (C) in a circle—to show that they all are equally important.

Let's sum up our discussion of marketing mix planning thus far. We develop a *Product* to satisfy the target customers. We find a way to reach our target customers' *Place.* We use *Promotion* to tell the target customers (and middlemen) about the product that has been designed for them. And we set a *Price* after estimating expected customer reaction to the total offering and the costs of getting it to them.

Both jobs must be done together

It is important to stress—it cannot be overemphasized—that selecting a target market *and* developing a marketing mix are interrelated. Both parts must be de-

---

Kid's Shoe Producer Builds Success on a Shoestring

It has only been a few years since 24 year-old Jeffrey Silverman started Toddler University (TU), Inc., but the company's children's shoes are already hot sellers. Stride Rite Corp. and Wohl Shoe Co. (makers of the Buster Brown brand) were already targeting the same market, but Silverman saw a way to get a toe up on the competition by serving customers better. First, he improved the product. Unlike most rigid high-topped infant shoes, he makes softer shoes with more comfortable rubber soles. The shoes last longer because they are stitched rather than glued. He also patented a special insert so parents can adjust the width. Since there are 11 sizes of children's shoes—and five widths—retailers usually

need to stock 55 pairs of each model. The adjustable width helps relieve this stocking problem—and that attracts retailers to sell the line. It also makes it possible for TU to resupply sold-out inventory faster than competitors—within a week. These advantages helped TU win the business of the big Kids 'R' Us apparel chain away from Buster Brown shoes. To help Kids 'R' Us promote its footwear, TU provides the stores with "shoe rides"—electric-powered rocking replicas of its shoes. The rides not only attract kids to the shoe department, but since they are coin-operated they pay for themselves in a year. TU prices its shoes at $35–$40 a pair. This is a premium price, but with today's smaller families parents are willing to spend more on each child.[8]

---

cided together. It is *strategies* that must be evaluated against the company's objectives—not alternative target markets or alternative marketing mixes.

Understanding target markets leads to good strategies

The needs of a target market virtually determine the nature of an appropriate marketing mix. So it is necessary for marketers to analyze their potential target markets with great care. This book will explore ways of identifying attractive market opportunities and developing appropriate strategies.

These ideas can be seen more clearly with an example in the home decorating market.

The needs of a target market virtually determine the nature of an appropriate marketing mix.

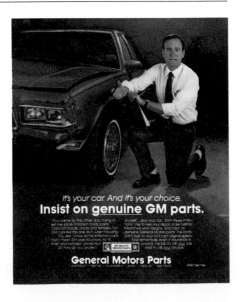

Strategy planning in the British home decorating market

The experience of a paint producer in England illustrates the strategy planning process—and how strategy decisions help decide how the plan is carried out.

First, the paint producer's marketing manager interviewed many potential customers and studied the needs for the products he could offer. By combining several kinds of customer needs and some available demographic data, he came up with the view of the market shown in Exhibit 2–9. In the following description of these markets, note that useful marketing mixes come to mind immediately.

There turned out to be a large (but hard to describe) market for "general-purpose paint"—about 60 percent of the potential for all kinds of paint products. The producer did not consider this market because he did not want to compete "head-on" with the many companies already in this market. The other four markets are placed in the four corners of a market diagram to show that they are different markets. He called these markets Helpless Homemaker, Handy Helper, Crafty Craftsman, and Cost-Conscious Couple.

The producer found that the *Helpless Homemaker* really didn't know much about home painting or specific products. This customer needed a helpful paint retailer who could supply not only paint and other supplies—but also much advice. And the retailer who sold the paint would want it to be of fairly high quality so that the Homemaker would be satisfied with the results.

The *Handy Helper* was a jack-of-all-trades who knew a great deal about painting. He wanted a good-quality product and was satisfied to buy from an old-fashioned paint store or lumber yard—which usually sells to customers who know just what they want. The *Crafty Craftsman* knew more than most paint sales reps, so he didn't want much help from a retailer either. These older men didn't really want to buy standard paint at all. They wanted color tints, oils, and other things to mix their own custom colors.

Finally, the *Cost-Conscious Couple* was young, had low income, and lived in an apartment. In England, an apartment dweller must paint the apartment during the course of the lease. This is an important factor for some tenants as they choose their paint. If you were a young apartment dweller with limited income, what sort of paint would you want? Some couples in England, the producer discovered, did not want very good paint! In fact, something not much better than whitewash would do fine.

Exhibit 2–9   The Home Decorating Market (Paint Area) in England

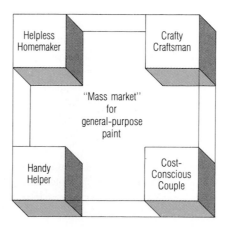

The paint producer decided to cater to Cost-Conscious Couples with a marketing mix flowing from the description of that market. That is, knowing what he did about them, he offered a low-quality paint (Product), made it available in lower-income apartment neighborhoods (Place), aimed his price-oriented ads at these areas (Promotion), and, of course, offered an attractive low price (Price). The producer has been extremely successful with this strategy—giving *his* customers what they really want—even though other paint buyers might say that the product quality was too low.

THE MARKETING PLAN IS A GUIDE TO IMPLEMENTATION AND CONTROL

Now that the key ideas of marketing strategy planning have been introduced, we can return to our overview of the marketing management process. You will see how a marketing strategy leads to a marketing plan and ultimately to implementation and control (see Exhibit 2–4).

Marketing plan fills out marketing strategy

A marketing strategy sets a target market and a marketing mix. It is a "big picture" of what a firm will do in some market. A marketing plan goes farther. A **marketing plan** is a written statement of a marketing strategy *and* the time-related details for carrying out the strategy. It should spell out the following in detail: (1) what marketing mix will be offered, to whom (that is, the target market), and for how long; (2) what company resources (shown as costs) will be needed at what rate (month by month perhaps); and (3) what results are expected (sales and profits perhaps monthly or quarterly). The plan should also include some control procedures—so that whoever is to carry out the plan will know if things are going wrong. This might be something as simple as comparing actual sales against expected sales—with a "warning flag" to be raised whenever total sales fall below a certain level.

Implementation puts plans into operation

After a marketing plan is developed, a marketing manager knows *what* needs to be done. Then he is concerned with **implementation**—putting marketing plans into operation.

Strategies work out as planned only when they are effectively implemented. Many **operational decisions**—short-run decisions to help implement strategies—may be needed.

Managers should make operational decisions within the guidelines set down during strategy planning. They develop product policies, place policies, and so on as part of strategy planning. Then, operational decisions within these policies probably will be necessary—while carrying out the basic strategy. Note, however, that as long as these operational decisions stay within the policy guidelines, managers are making no change in the basic strategy. If the controls show that operational decisions are not producing the desired results, however, the managers may have to reevaluate the whole strategy—rather than just "working harder" at implementing it.

It's easier to see the difference between strategy decisions and operational decisions if we illustrate these ideas using our paint producer example. Possible four-P or basic strategy policies are shown in the left-hand column in Exhibit 2–10, and likely operational decisions are shown in the right-hand column.

Exhibit 2–10   Relation of Strategy Policies to Operational Decisions for Paint Manufacturer

Marketing mix variable	Strategy policies	Likely operational decisions
Product	Carry as limited a line of colors and sizes as will satisfy the target market.	Add, change, or drop colors and/or can sizes as customer tastes and preferences dictate.
Place	Try to obtain distribution in every conceivable retail outlet that will handle this type of paint in the areas where the target customers live or buy.	If a new retailer opens for business in these market areas, immediately solicit his order.
Promotion	Promote the "low price" and "satisfactory quality" to meet the needs of the market.	Regularly change the point-of-purchase and advertising copy to produce a "fresh" image. Media changes may be necessary also. Salespeople have to be trained, motivated, etc.
Price	Maintain a low "one-price" policy without "specials" or other promotional deals	If paint companies in other markets cut prices, do not follow.

It should be clear that some operational decisions are made regularly—even daily—and such decisions should not be confused with planning strategy. Certainly, a great deal of effort can be involved in these operational decisions. They might take a good part of the sales or advertising manager's time. But they are not the strategy decisions that will be our primary concern.

Our focus has been—and will continue to be—on developing marketing strategies. But it is also important to see that eventually marketing managers must develop and implement marketing plans. We discuss this more fully in Chapter 20.[9]

Several plans make a whole marketing program

Most companies implement more than one marketing strategy—and related marketing plan—at the same time. They may have several products—some of them quite different—that are aimed at different target markets. The other elements of the marketing mix may vary, too. Gillette's Right Guard deodorant, Atra Plus razor blades, and Liquid Paper typewriter correction fluid all have different marketing mixes. Yet the strategies for each must be implemented at the same time.[10]

A **marketing program** blends all of the firm's marketing plans into one "big" plan. See Exhibit 2–11. This program, then, is the responsibility of the whole company. Typically, the whole *marketing program* is an integrated part of the whole-company strategic plan we discussed earlier.

Ultimately, marketing managers plan and implement a whole marketing program. In this text, however, we will emphasize planning one marketing strategy at a time, rather than planning—or implementing—a whole marketing program. This is practical, because it is important to plan each strategy carefully. Too many marketing managers fall into "sloppy thinking." They try to develop too many strategies all at once—and don't develop any very carefully. Good plans are the building blocks of marketing management. We'll talk about merging plans into a marketing program in Chapter 20.

Exhibit 2–11   Elements of a Firm's Marketing Program

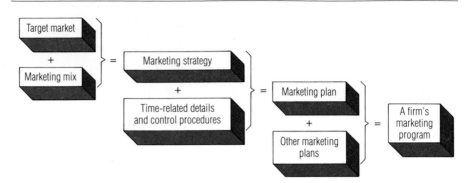

Control is analyzing and correcting what you've done

The control job provides the feedback that leads managers to modify their marketing strategies. To maintain control, a marketing manager uses a number of tools—like computer sales analysis, marketing research surveys, and accounting analysis of expenses and profits. All of Chapter 21 is devoted to the important topic of controlling marketing plans and programs.

In addition, as we talk about each of the marketing decision areas, we will discuss some of the control problems. This will help you understand how control keeps the firm on course—or shows the need to plan a new course.

All marketing jobs require planning and control

At first, it might appear that planning and control are of concern only to high-level management—or in really large companies. This is not true. Every organization needs planning—and without control it's impossible to know if the plans are working.

This means that marketing strategy planning may be very important to you soon—maybe in your present job or college activities. In Appendix C, on marketing careers, we present some strategy planning ideas for getting a marketing job.

THE IMPORTANCE OF MARKETING STRATEGY PLANNING

We emphasize the planning part of the marketing manager's job for a good reason. The "one-time" strategy decisions—the decisions that decide what business the company is in and the strategies it will follow—usually determine success—or failure. An extremely good plan might be carried out badly and still be profitable, while a poor but well-implemented plan can lose money. The case histories that follow show the importance of planning—and why we emphasize marketing strategy planning throughout this text.

Henry Ford's strategy worked—until General Motors caught up

Henry Ford is famous for developing techniques to mass produce cars. His own view of his approach, however, was that mass production developed *because* of his basic decision to build an affordable car for the masses. Earlier cars were almost custom-built for wealthy buyers. Ford decided on a different strategy. He wanted to produce a car that could appeal to most potential buyers.

Certainly, new production ideas were needed to carry out Ford's strategy. But the really important decision was the initial market-oriented one that there was a market for millions of cars in the $500 price range. Much of what followed was just implementing his decision. Ford's strategy to offer a low-priced car was an outstanding success—and millions of Model Ts were sold during the 1910s and 1920s. But there was a defect in his strategy. To keep the price down, Ford offered a very basic car in "any color you want as long as it's black."

In the 1920s, General Motors felt there was room for a new strategy. It hit on the idea of looking at the market as having several segments (based on price and quality)—and offered a full line of cars with different styles and colors in each price range. The GM strategy was not an immediate success. But GM stuck with it and slowly caught up with Ford. In 1927, Ford finally closed down his assembly line for 18 months, switched his strategy, and introduced the more market-oriented Model A. By then GM was already well on its way to the strong market position it still holds.

General Motors didn't see all the opportunities

While GM was successfully capturing a giant share of the car market, it was neglecting another very important market—for car replacement parts. GM saw supplying parts as more of a "necessary evil" than an important business in itself. As a result, this profitable market was left to many smaller suppliers. Even today, GM does not have the dominance in the repair parts and service market that it has in the car market. In other words, GM's successful strategy was concerned with making and selling *cars*—not with the broader business of meeting customers' needs for personal transportation and keeping the cars moving.

GM also failed to learn the lesson that it had, years earlier, hammered home to Ford. GM concentrated on producing and trying to sell what it wanted—high-priced big cars—even after rising gas prices changed some consumers' preferences to smaller, more economical cars. Foreign producers—Toyota, Honda, Nissan—had aimed at that target market in their own countries much earlier, and they successfully seized the opportunity when U.S. firms were slow to respond. They also upgraded quality and features to respond to preferences of U.S. buyers.

This tough competition hit Chrysler first. The company came close to bankruptcy. Lee Iacocca brought in new marketing managers to help lead Chrysler to a marketing orientation. They went after specific target markets with fuel-efficient Voyager minivans, front-wheel-drive family sedans, and sporty LeBaron convertibles. GM also responded—with a view to world markets—with products like the Saturn. Ford put a new emphasis on "quality first" and targeted specific markets with successful offerings like the Sable and Escort.

Although U.S. producers were achieving successes and fending off competition for some target markets, they were slow to see opportunities posed by the growing number of wealthy, middle-aged professionals. They wanted high performance luxury cars, not the sluggish Cadillacs and Lincolns Detroit had been selling for 20 years. Mercedes, Volvo, BMW, and other European firms were quicker in developing marketing mixes that appealed to this target market. Here too, U.S. producers have improved their marketing mixes and responded to the changing market. Even so, it probably will be a long, hard battle for Detroit automakers to recapture customers lost to foreign competition.[11]

Time for new strategies in the watch industry

The conventional watch makers—both domestic and foreign—had always aimed at customers who thought of watches as high-priced, high-quality symbols to mark special events—like graduations or retirement. Advertising was concentrated around Christmas and graduation time and stressed a watch's symbolic appeal. Expensive jewelry stores were the main retail outlets.

This commonly accepted strategy of the major watch companies ignored people in the target market that just wanted to tell the time—and were interested in a reliable, low-priced watch. So the U.S. Time Company developed a successful strategy around its "Timex" watches—and became the world's largest watch company. Timex completely upset the watch industry—both foreign and domestic— not only by offering a good product (with a one-year repair or replace guarantee) at a lower price, but also by using new, lower-cost channels of distribution. Its watches were widely available in drugstores, discount houses, and nearly any other retail stores that would carry them.

Marketing managers at Timex soon faced a new challenge. Texas Instruments, a new competitor in the watch market, took the industry by storm with its low-cost but very accurate electronic watches—using the same channels Timex had originally developed. But other firms quickly developed a watch that used a more stylish liquid crystal display for the digital readout. Texas Instruments could not change quickly enough to keep up—and the other companies took away its customers. The competition became so intense that Texas Instruments stopped marketing watches altogether.

While Timex and others were focusing on lower priced watches, Seiko captured a commanding share of the high-priced "gift" market for its stylish and accurate quartz watches by obtaining strong distribution. All of this forced many traditional watch makers—like some of the once-famous Swiss brands—to close their factories.

In 1983 Swatch launched its colorful, affordable plastic watches—and it changed what consumers see when they look at their watches. Swatch promoted its watches as fashion accessories and set them apart from those of other firms, whose ads squabbled about whose watches were most accurate and dependable. Swatch was also able to attract new middlemen by focusing its distribution on upscale fashion and department stores. The marketing mix Swatch developed around its "fashion watch" idea was so successful it didn't just increase Swatch's share of the market. The total size of the watch market increased because many consumers bought several watches to match different fashions.

Swatch's success prompted Timex, Seiko, and others to pay more attention to consumer fashion preferences. For example, Timex developed its fashionable "Watercolors" line targeted at teens. Timex has also emphasized better styling to compete in the higher-priced market—and broadened its offering to defend its position in the low- to mid-priced segment.

Changes continue in this market. For example, Seiko is working on a watch powered by a tiny generator that translates the movement of the wearer's wrist into energy so consumers won't need to worry about changing a battery.[12]

Creative strategy planning needed for survival

Dramatic shifts in strategy—like those described above—may surprise conventional, production-oriented managers. But such changes are becoming much more common—and should be expected. Industries or firms that have accepted the marketing concept realize that they cannot define their line of business in terms of the products they currently produce or sell. Rather, they have to think about the basic consumer needs they serve—and how those needs may change in the future. If they are too nearsighted, they may fail to see what's coming until too late.

Creative strategy planning is becoming even more important because firms can no longer win profits just by spending more money on plant and equipment. Moreover, domestic and foreign competition threatens those who can't create more satisfying goods and services. New markets, new customers, and new ways of doing

Timex is constantly developing new marketing strategies to meet consumers' needs—and stay ahead of competitors.

We have watches that go with clothes you don't even know you have.
TIMEX WATERCOLORS

Suitable for dinner. The Timex Carriage Collection.

things must be found if companies are to operate profitably in the future—and contribute to our macro-marketing system.

STRATEGY PLANNING DOESN'T TAKE PLACE IN A VACUUM

Strategy planning takes place within a framework

Our examples show that a marketing manager's strategy planning cannot take place in a vacuum. Instead, the manager works with controllable variables within a framework involving many uncontrollable variables (which must be considered even though the manager can't control them). Exhibit 2–12 illustrates this framework and shows that the typical marketing manager must be concerned about the competitive environment, economic and technological environment, political and legal environment, cultural and social environment, and the resources and objectives of the firm. We discuss these uncontrollable variables in more detail in the next two chapters. But clearly, the framework in which the marketing manager operates affects strategy planning.

MARKET–ORIENTED STRATEGY PLANNING HELPS NONMARKETING PEOPLE, TOO

While market-oriented strategy planning is helpful to marketers, it is also needed by accountants, production and personnel people, and all other specialists. A market-oriented plan lets everybody in the firm know what "ballpark" they are playing in—and what they are trying to accomplish. In other words, it gives direction to the whole business effort. An accountant can't set budgets if there is no plan, except perhaps by mechanically projecting last year's budget. Similarly, a financial manager can't project cash needs without some idea of expected sales to target customers—and the costs of satisfying them.

Exhibit 2–12   Marketing Manager's Framework

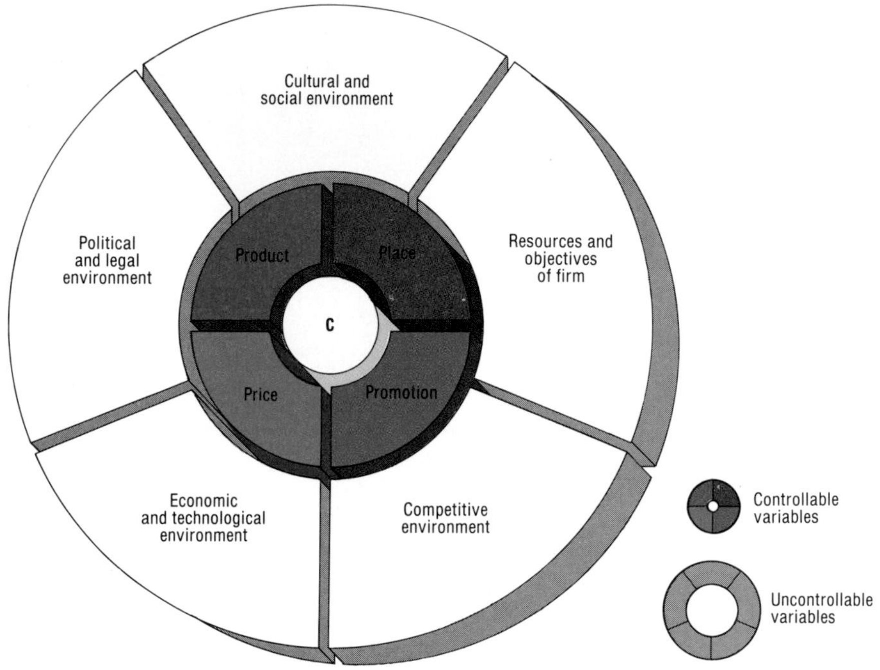

We will use the term *marketing manager* for editorial convenience, but really, when we talk about marketing strategy planning, we are talking about the planning that a market-oriented manager should do when developing a firm's strategic plans. This kind of thinking should be done—or at least understood—by everyone in the organization who is responsible for planning. And this means even the lowest-level salesperson, production supervisor, retail buyer, or personnel counselor.

CONCLUSION

Marketing's role within a marketing-oriented firm is to provide direction for a firm. The marketing concept stresses that the company's efforts should focus on satisfying some target customers—at a profit. Production-oriented firms tend to forget this. Often the various departments within a production-oriented firm let their natural conflicts of interest lead them to building fences.

The job of marketing management is one of continuous planning, implementing, and control. The marketing manager must constantly study the environment— seeking attractive opportunities and planning new strategies. Possible target markets must be matched with marketing mixes the firm can offer. Then, attrac-

tive strategies—really, whole marketing plans—are chosen for implementation. Controls are needed to be sure that the plans are carried out successfully. If anything goes wrong along the way, this continual feedback should cause the process to be started over again—with the marketing manager planning more attractive marketing strategies.

A marketing mix has four variables: the four Ps— Product, Place, Promotion, and Price. Most of this text is concerned with developing profitable marketing mixes for clearly defined target markets. So, after several chapters on analyzing target markets, we will discuss each of the four Ps in greater detail.

Questions and Problems

1. Define the marketing concept in your own words and then explain why the notion of profit is usually included in this definition.

2. Define the marketing concept in your own words and then suggest how acceptance of this concept might affect the organization and operation of your college.

3. Distinguish between "production orientation" and "marketing orientation," illustrating with local examples.

4. Explain why a firm should view its internal activities as part of a "total system." Illustrate your answer for (a) a large grocery products producer, (b) a plumbing wholesaler, and (c) a department store chain.

5. Does the acceptance of the marketing concept almost require that a firm view itself as a "total system?"

6. Distinguish clearly between a marketing strategy and a marketing mix. Use an example.

7. Distinguish clearly between mass marketing and target markcting. Use an example.

8. Why is the customer placed in the center of the four Ps in the text diagram of a marketing strategy (Exhibit 2–6)? Explain, using a specific example from your own experience.

9. Explain, in your own words, what each of the four Ps involves.

10. Evaluate the text's statement, "A marketing strategy sets the details of implementation."

11. Distinguish between strategic and operational decisions, illustrating for a local retailer.

12. Distinguish between a strategy, a marketing plan, and a marketing program, illustrating for a local retailer.

13. Outline a marketing strategy for each of the following new products: (a) a radically new design for a toothbrush, (b) a new fishing reel, (c) a new "wonder drug," (d) a new industrial stapling machine.

14. Provide a specific illustration of why marketing strategy planning is important for all businesspeople, not just for those in the marketing department.

Suggested Cases

2. Alta Foods, Inc.

5. Dow Chemical Company

32. Castco, Inc.

Suggested Computer-Aided Problem

2. Target Marketing

Appendix A

Economics Fundamentals

When You Finish This Appendix, You Should

1. Understand the "law of diminishing demand."

2. Know what a market is.

3. Understand demand and supply curves—and how they set the size of a market and its price level.

4. Know about elasticity of demand and supply.

5. Know why demand elasticity can be affected by availability of substitutes.

6. Recognize the important new terms (shown in red).

A good marketing manager should be an expert on markets—and the nature of competition in markets. The economist's traditional demand and supply analysis are useful tools for analyzing markets. In particular, you should master the concepts of a demand curve and demand elasticity. A firm's demand curve shows how the target customers view the firm's Product—really its whole marketing mix. And the interaction of demand and supply curves helps set the size of a market—and the market price. These ideas are discussed more fully in the following sections.

PRODUCTS AND MARKETS AS SEEN BY CUSTOMERS AND POTENTIAL CUSTOMERS

Economists provide useful insights

How potential customers (not the firm) see a firm's product (marketing mix) affects how much they are willing to pay for it, where it should be made available, and how eager they are for it—if they want it at all. In other words, their view has a very direct bearing on marketing strategy planning.

Economists have been concerned with market behavior for years. Their analytical tools can be quite helpful in summarizing how customers view products and how markets behave.

Economists see individual customers choosing among alternatives

Economics is sometimes called the "dismal" science—because it says that most customers have a limited income and simply cannot buy everything they want. They must balance their needs and the prices of various products.

Economists usually assume that customers have a fairly definite set of preferences—and that they evaluate alternatives in terms of whether the alternatives will make them feel better (or worse) or in some way improve (or change) their situation.

But what exactly is the nature of a customer's desire for a particular product?

Usually economists answer this question in terms of the extra utility the customer can obtain by buying more of a particular product—or how much utility would be lost if the customer had less of the product. (Students who wish further discussion of this approach should refer to indifference curve analysis in any standard economics text.)

It is easier to understand the idea of utility if we look at what happens when the price of one of the customer's usual purchases changes.

The law of diminishing demand

Suppose that a consumer buys potatoes in 10-pound bags at the same time he buys other foods such as bread and rice. If the consumer is mainly interested in buying a certain amount of food and the price of the potatoes drops, it seems reasonable to expect that he will switch some of his food money to potatoes and away from some other foods. But if the price of potatoes rises, you expect our consumer to buy fewer potatoes and more of other foods.

The general relationship between price and quantity demanded illustrated by this food example is called the **law of diminishing demand**—which says that if the price of a product is raised, a smaller quantity will be demanded and if the price of a product is lowered, a greater quantity will be demanded.

A group of customers makes a market

When our hypothetical consumers are considered as a group, we have a "market." It's reasonable to assume that many consumers in a market will behave in a similar way. That is, if price declines, the total quantity demanded will increase—and if price rises, the quantity demanded will decrease. Experience supports this reasoning, especially for broad product categories or commodities such as potatoes.

The relationship between price and quantity demanded in a market is what economists call a "demand schedule." An example is shown in Exhibit A–1. The third column shows that the total revenue (sales) in the potato market—at possible prices—is equal to the quantity demanded times the price at those possible prices. Note that as prices go lower, the total *unit* quantity increases, yet the total *revenue* decreases. Fill in the blank lines in the third column and observe the behavior of total revenue—an important number for the marketing manager. We will explain what you should have noticed—and why—a little later.

The demand curve— usually down-sloping

If your only interest is seeing at which price customers will be willing to pay the greatest total revenue, the demand schedule may be adequate. But a demand curve "shows" more. A **demand curve** is a graph of the relationship between price

Exhibit A–1   Demand Schedule for Potatoes (10-pound bags)

Point	(1) Price of potatoes per bag (P)	(2) Quality demanded (bags per month) (Q)	(3) Total revenue per month (P × Q = TR)
A	$1.60	8,000,000	$12,800,000
B	1.30	9,000,000	_____
C	1.00	11,000,000	11,000,000
D	0.70	14,000,000	_____
E	0.40	19,000,000	_____

and quantity demanded in a market—assuming that all other things stay the same. Exhibit A–2 shows the demand curve for potatoes—really just a plotting of the demand schedule. Demand curves show the price on the vertical axis and the quantity demanded on the horizontal axis. It shows how many potatoes potential customers will demand at various possible prices. This is a "down-sloping demand curve."

Most demand curves are down-sloping. This just means that if prices are decreased, the quantity customers demand will increase.

Note that the demand curve only shows how customers will react to various prices. In a market, we see only one price at a time—not all of these prices. The curve, however, shows what quantities will be demanded—depending on what price is set.

You probably think that most businesspeople would like to set a price that would result in a large sales revenue. Before discussing this, however, we should consider the demand schedule and curve for another product to get a more complete picture of demand-curve analysis.

Exhibit A–2   Demand Curve for Potatoes (10-pound bags)

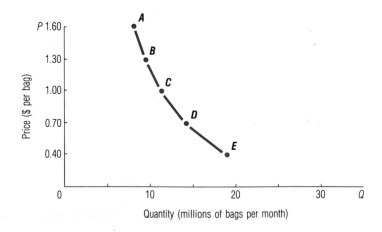

Exhibit A–3   Demand Schedule for 10-Cubic-Foot Refrigerators

Point	(1) Price per refrigerator (P)	(2) Quantity demanded per year (Q)	(3) Total revenue per year (P × Q = TR)
A	$300	20,000	$ 6,000,000
B	250	70,000	17,500,000
C	200	130,000	26,000,000
D	150	210,000	31,500,000
E	100	310,000	31,000,000

Refrigerator demand curve looks different

A different demand schedule is the one for standard 10-cubic-foot refrigerators shown in Exhibit A–3. Column (3) shows the total revenue that will be obtained at various possible prices and quantities. Again, as the price goes down, the quantity demanded goes up. But here, unlike the potato example, total revenue increases as prices go down—at least until the price drops to $150.

Every market has a demand curve—for some time period

These general demand relationships are typical for all products. But each product has its own demand schedule and curve in each potential market—no matter how small the market. In other words, a particular demand curve has meaning only for a particular market. We can think of demand curves for individuals, groups of individuals who form a target market, regions, and even countries. And the time period covered really should be specified—although this is often neglected because we usually think of monthly or yearly periods.

The difference between elastic and inelastic

The demand curve for refrigerators (see Exhibit A–4) is down-sloping—but note that it is flatter than the curve for potatoes. It is important that we understand what this flatness means.

Exhibit A–4   Demand Curve for 10-Cubic-Foot Refrigerators

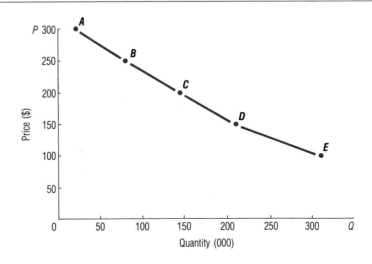

We will consider the flatness in terms of total revenue—since this is what interests business managers.*

When you filled in the total revenue column for potatoes, you should have noticed that total revenue drops continually if the price is reduced. This looks undesirable for sellers—and illustrates inelastic demand. **Inelastic demand** means that although the quantity demanded increases if the price is decreased, the quantity demanded will not "stretch" enough—that is, it is not elastic enough—to avoid a decrease in total revenue.

In contrast, **elastic demand** means that if prices are dropped, the quantity demanded will stretch (increase) enough to increase total revenue. The upper part of the refrigerator demand curve is an example of elastic demand.

But note that if the refrigerator price is dropped from $150 to $100, total revenue will decrease. We can say, therefore, that between $150 and $100, demand is inelastic—that is, total revenue will decrease if price is lowered from $150 to $100.

Thus, elasticity can be defined in terms of changes in total revenue. *If total revenue will increase if price is lowered, then demand is elastic. If total revenue will decrease if price is lowered, then demand is inelastic.* (Note: A special case known as "unitary elasticity of demand" occurs if total revenue stays the same when prices change.)

Total revenue may increase if price is raised

A point that is often missed in discussions of demand is what happens when prices are raised instead of lowered. With elastic demand, total revenue will *decrease* if the price is *raised*. With inelastic demand, however, total revenue will *increase* if the price is *raised*.

The possibility of raising price and increasing dollar sales (total revenue) at the same time is attractive to managers. This only occurs if the demand curve is inelastic. Here, total revenue will increase if price is raised, but total costs probably will not increase—and may actually go down—with smaller quantities. Keep in mind that profit is equal to total revenue minus total costs. So—when demand is inelastic—profit will increase as price is increased!

The ways total revenue changes as prices are raised are shown in Exhibit A–5. Here, total revenue is the rectangular area formed by a price and its related quantity. The larger the rectangular area, the greater the total revenue.

P_1 is the original price here, and the total potential revenue with this original price is shown by the area with blue shading. The area with red shading shows the total revenue with the new price, P_2. There is some overlap in the total revenue areas, so the important areas are those with only one color. Note that in the left-hand figure—where demand is elastic—the revenue added (the red-only area) when the price is increased is less than the revenue lost (the blue-only area). Now, let's contrast this to the right-hand figure, when demand is inelastic. Only a small blue revenue area is given up for a much larger (red) one when price is raised.

An entire curve is not elastic or inelastic

It is important to see that it is *wrong to refer to a whole demand curve as elastic or inelastic.* Rather, elasticity for a particular demand curve refers to the change in total revenue between two points on the curve—not along the whole curve. You saw the change from elastic to inelastic in the refrigerator example. Generally, however, nearby points are either elastic or inelastic—so it is common to refer to a

---

* Strictly speaking, two curves should not be compared for flatness if the graph scales are different, but for our purposes now, we will do so to illustrate the idea of "elasticity of demand." Actually, it would be more correct to compare two curves for one product—on the same graph. Then both the shape of the demand curve and its position on the graph would be important.

Exhibit A–5   Changes in Total Revenue as Prices Increase

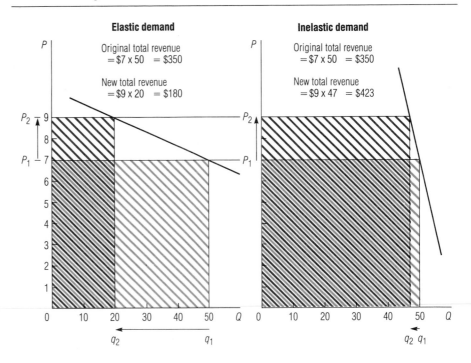

whole curve by the degree of elasticity in the price range that normally is of interest—the *relevant range.*

Demand elasticities affected by availability of substitutes and urgency of need

At first, it may be difficult to see why one product has an elastic demand and another an inelastic demand. Many factors affect elasticity—such as the availability of substitutes, the importance of the item in the customer's budget, and the urgency of the customer's need and its relation to other needs. By looking more closely at one of these factors—the availability of substitutes—you will better understand why demand elasticities vary.

Substitutes are products that offer the buyer a choice. For example, many consumers see grapefruit as a substitute for oranges and hot dogs as a substitute for hamburgers. The greater the number of "good" substitutes available, the greater will be the elasticity of demand. From the consumer's perspective, products are "good" substitutes if they are very similar (homogeneous). If consumers see products as extremely different—or heterogeneous—then a particular need cannot easily be satisfied by substitutes. And the demand for the most satisfactory product may be quite inelastic.

As an example, if the price of hamburger is lowered (and other prices stay the same), the quantity demanded will increase a lot—as will total revenue. The reason is that not only will regular hamburger users buy more hamburger, but some consumers who formerly bought hot dogs or steaks probably will buy hamburger, too. But if the price of hamburger is raised, the quantity demanded will decrease—perhaps sharply. Still, consumers will buy some hamburger—depending on how much the price has risen, their individual tastes, and what their guests expect (see Exhibit A–6).

In contrast to a product with many "substitutes"—such as hamburger—consider a product with few or no substitutes. Its demand curve will tend to be inelastic. Salt

Exhibit A–6   Demand Curve for Hamburger (a product with many substitutes)

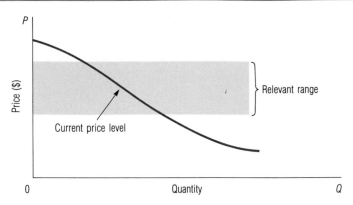

is a good example. Salt is needed to flavor food. Yet no one person or family uses great quantities of salt. So it is not likely that the quantity of salt purchased will change much as long as price changes are *within a reasonable range.* Of course, if the price is dropped to an extremely low level, manufacturers may buy more—say, for low-cost filler instead of clay or sand (Exhibit A–7). Or, if the price is raised to a staggering figure, many people will have to do without. But these extremes are outside the relevant range.

Demand curves are introduced here because the degree of elasticity of demand shows how potential customers feel about a product—and especially whether they see substitutes for the product. But to get a better understanding of markets, we must extend this economic analysis.

MARKETS AS SEEN BY SUPPLIERS

Customers may want some product—but if suppliers are not willing to supply it, then there is no market. So we'll study the economist's analysis of supply. And then we'll bring supply and demand together for a more complete understanding of markets.

Exhibit A–7   Demand Curve for Salt (a product with few substitutes)

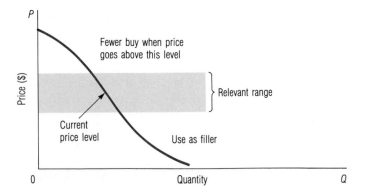

Economists often use the kind of analysis we are discussing here to explain pricing in the marketplace. This is not our intention. Here we are interested in how and why markets work—and the interaction of customers and potential suppliers. The discussion in this appendix does not explain how individual firms set prices—or should set prices. That will come in Chapters 18 and 19.

Supply curves reflect supplier thinking

Generally speaking, suppliers' costs affect the quantity of products they are willing to offer in a market during any period. In other words, their costs affect their supply schedules and supply curves. While a demand curve shows the quantity of products customers will be willing to buy at various prices, a **supply curve** shows the quantity of products that will be supplied at various possible prices. Eventually, only one quantity will be offered and purchased. So a supply curve is really a hypothetical (what-if) description of what will be offered at various prices. It is, however, a very important curve. Together with a demand curve, it summarizes the attitudes and probable behavior of buyers and sellers about a particular product in a particular market—that is, in a product-market.

Some supply curves are vertical

We usually assume that supply curves tend to slope upward—that is, suppliers will be willing to offer greater quantities at higher prices. If a product's market price is very high, it seems only reasonable that producers will be anxious to produce more of the product—and even put workers on overtime or perhaps hire more workers to increase the quantity they can offer. Going further, it seems likely that producers of other products will switch their resources (farms, factories, labor, or retail facilities) to the product that is in great demand.

On the other hand, if a very low price is being offered for a particular product, it's reasonable to expect that producers will switch to other products—thus reducing supply. A supply schedule (Exhibit A–8) and a supply curve (Exhibit A–9) for potatoes illustrate these ideas. This supply curve shows how many potatoes would be produced and offered for sale at each possible market price in a given month.

In the very short run (say, over a few hours, a day, or a week), a supplier may not be able to increase the supply at all. In this situation, we would see a vertical supply curve. This situation is often relevant in the market for fresh produce. Fresh strawberries, for example, continue to ripen, and a supplier wants to sell them quickly—preferably at a higher price—but in any case, he wants to sell them.

If the product is a service, it may not be easy to expand the supply in the short run. Additional barbers or medical doctors are not quickly trained and licensed, and they only have so much time to give each day. Further, the prospect of much

Exhibit A–8   Supply Schedule for Potatoes (10-pound bags)

Point	Possible market price per 10-lb. bag	Number of bags sellers will supply per month at each possible market price
A	$1.60	17,000,000
B	1.30	14,000,000
C	1.00	11,000,000
D	0.70	8,000,000
E	0.40	3,000,000

Note: This supply curve is for a month to emphasize that farmers might have some control over when they deliver their potatoes. There would be a different curve for each month.

Exhibit A–9   Supply Curve for Potatoes (10-pound bags)

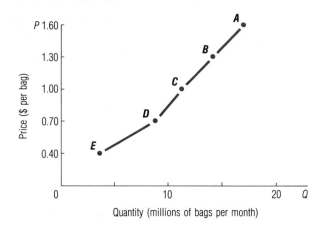

higher prices in the near future cannot easily expand the supply of many services. For example, a "hit" play or an "in" restaurant or nightclub is limited in the amount of "product" it can offer at a particular time.

Elasticity of supply

The term *elasticity* also is used to describe supply curves. An extremely steep or almost vertical supply curve—often found in the short run—is called **inelastic supply** because the quantity supplied does not stretch much (if at all) if the price is raised. A flatter curve is called **elastic supply** because the quantity supplied does stretch more if the price is raised. A slightly up-sloping supply curve is typical in longer-run market situations. Given more time, suppliers have a chance to adjust their offerings. And competitors may enter or leave the market.

DEMAND AND SUPPLY INTERACT TO DETERMINE THE SIZE OF THE MARKET AND PRICE LEVEL

We have treated market demand and supply forces separately. Now we must bring them together to show their interaction. The *intersection* of these two forces determines the size of the market and the market price—at which point (price and quantity) the market is said to be in *equilibrium*.

The intersection of demand and supply is shown for the potato data discussed above. The demand curve for potatoes is now graphed against the supply curve in Exhibit A–9. See Exhibit A–10.

In this potato market, demand is inelastic—the total revenue of all the potato producers would be greater at higher prices. But the market price is at the **equilibrium point**—where the quantity and the price sellers are willing to offer are equal to the quantity and price that buyers are willing to accept. The $1.00 equilibrium price for potatoes yields a smaller *total revenue* to potato producers than a higher price would. This lower equilibrium price comes about because the many producers are willing to supply enough potatoes at the lower price. *Demand is not the only determiner of price level. Cost also must be considered—via the supply curve.*

Exhibit A–10   Equilibrium of Supply and Demand for Potatoes (10-pound bags)

Some consumers get a surplus

It is important to note that not everyone gets *only* his money's worth in a sales transaction. Presumably, a sale takes place only if both buyer and seller feel they will be better off after the sale. But sometimes the price is better than "right."

The price we are talking about is the market price set by demand and supply forces. Typically, demand curves are down-sloping, and some of the demand curve is above the equilibrium price. This is simply a graphic way of showing that some customers are willing to pay more than the equilibrium price if they have to. In effect, some of them are getting a "bargain" by being able to buy at the equilibrium price. Economists have traditionally called these bargains the **consumer surplus**—that is, the difference to consumers between the value of a purchase and the price they pay.

It is important to see that there is such a surplus because some business critics assume that consumers do badly in any business transaction. In fact, a sale takes place only if the consumer feels he is at least "getting his money's worth." As we can see here, some are willing to pay much more than the market price.

DEMAND AND SUPPLY HELP US UNDERSTAND THE NATURE OF COMPETITION

The elasticity of demand and supply curves—and their interaction—help predict the nature of competition a marketing manager is likely to face. For example, an extremely inelastic demand curve means that the manager will have much choice in strategy planning—and especially price setting. Apparently customers like the product and see few substitutes. They are willing to pay higher prices before cutting back much on their purchases.

Clearly, the elasticity of a firm's demand curves makes a big difference in strategy planning, but there are other factors that affect the nature of competition. Among these are the number and size of competitors and the uniqueness of each firm's marketing mix. These ideas are discussed more fully in Chapters 3 and 4. Those discussions presume a real understanding of the contents of this appendix—so now you should be ready to handle them and later material involving demand and supply analysis (especially Chapters 18 and 19).

CONCLUSION

The economist's traditional demand and supply analysis provides useful tools for analyzing the nature of demand and competition. It is especially important that you master the concepts of a demand curve and demand elasticity. How demand and supply interact helps determine the size of a market—and its price level. It also helps explain the nature of competition in different market situations. These ideas are discussed in Chapters 3 and 4 and then built on throughout the text. So careful study of this appendix will build a good foundation for later work.

Questions and Problems

1.   Explain in your own words how economists look at markets and arrive at the "law of diminishing demand."

2.   Explain what a demand curve is and why it is usually down-sloping.

3.   What is the length of life of the typical demand curve? Illustrate your answer.

4.   If the general market demand for men's shoes is fairly elastic, how does the demand for men's dress shoes compare to it? How does the demand curve for women's shoes compare to the demand curve for men's shoes?

5.   If the demand for razor blades is inelastic above and below the present price, should the price be raised? Why or why not?

6.   If the demand for steak is highly elastic below the present price, should the price be lowered?

7.   Discuss what factors lead to inelastic demand and supply curves. Are they likely to be found together in the same situation?

8.   Why would a marketing manager prefer to sell a product that has no close substitutes? Are "high profits" almost guaranteed?

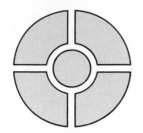

Chapter *3*

Finding Target Market Opportunities with Market Segmentation

When You Finish This Chapter, You Should

1. Understand how to find marketing opportunities.

2. Know about the different kinds of marketing opportunities.

3. Know about defining generic markets and product-markets.

4. Know what market segmentation is.

5. Know three approaches to market-oriented strategy planning.

6. Know how to segment product-markets into submarkets.

7. Know dimensions that may be useful for segmenting markets.

8. Know a seven-step approach to market segmentation that you can do yourself.

9. Know what positioning is—and why it is useful.

10. Understand the important new terms (shown in red).

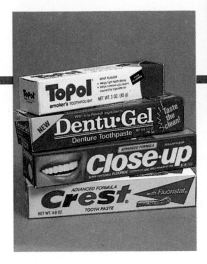

Finding attractive target markets is part of marketing strategy planning.

Motel 6 saw an opportunity. Most motels were pretty much alike—but some travelers were not satisfied with what they offered. These customers didn't want to pay extra for room service, a fancy restaurant, or someone to turn down their sheets at night. They just wanted a clean room, a good location, and a budget price for a one-night stay. Marketing managers for Motel 6 identified several groups of customers—vacation travelers in the 55-plus age bracket, salespeople who pay their own travel expenses, and young families—with similar "budget-oriented" interests. Then they developed a marketing mix specifically targeted at these segments. They built less costly motels without showy lobbies, swimming pools, and restaurants. They located near highways and inexpensive eateries like McDonald's that appealed to their target customers. They used radio ads—rather than costly TV and print ads—to convey their message. They set the price low—about half what most motels charged. This budget-oriented strategy was very profitable—and other motels began to copy it. To stay ahead, Motel 6 has made some changes—like adding free color TVs and free local calls—while sticking with its basic strategy.[1]

Other motels and hotels are also targeting segments of the market with special needs. For example, Marriott's Residence Inns target guests who want a nice place to stay for a week or more. Residence Inns feature fully equipped kitchens and grocery shopping services, fireplaces, and convenient recreation areas. The Ritz-Carlton in Atlanta caters to its Japanese guests by offering room information in their language, traditional slippers, green tea, and sake. The staff is even tutored in Japanese culture. The Hyatt Regency in Los Angeles attracts upscale business travelers with fancy conference rooms and a full library of general interest, business, and research books.[2]

WHAT ARE ATTRACTIVE OPPORTUNITIES?

The main focus of this book is on marketing strategy planning—an important part of which is finding attractive target markets. But how do you identify a target market and decide if it offers good opportunities? Why would a company like Marriott that in the past had focused on motels seek to serve travelers in a new way—by offering food preparation services to airlines?

In this chapter and the next chapter you will learn how to find possible market opportunities and choose the ones to be turned into strategies and plans. We will look first at how to identify attractive target markets. See Exhibit 3–1.

Possible opportunities are evaluated against screening criteria. We will be covering screening criteria in more detail in the next chapter. For now, however, you should see in Exhibit 3–1 that these criteria grow out of analysis of the company's resources, the long-run trends in the uncontrollable environments facing the firm, as well as the objectives of top management.

Attractive opportunities for a particular firm are those that the firm has some chance of doing something about—given its resources and objectives. Marketing strategy planning tries to match opportunities to the firm's resources—what it can do—and its objectives—what it wants to do.

Breakthrough opportunities are best

How many opportunities a firm "sees" depends on the thinking of top management—and the objectives of the firm. Some want to be innovators and eagerly search out new opportunities. Others are willing to be creative imitators of the leaders. And others are risk-avoiding "me-too" marketers.

Exhibit 3–1   Finding and Evaluating Marketing Opportunities

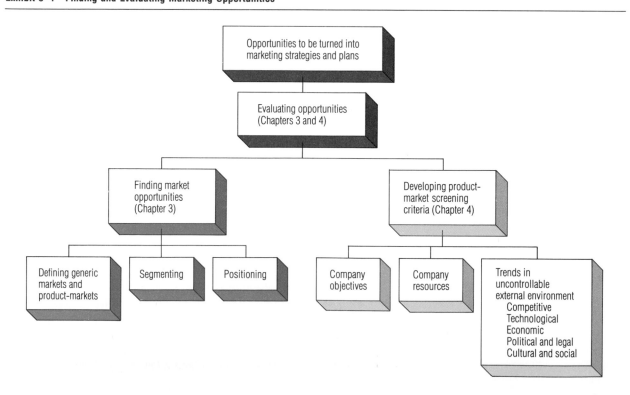

Throughout this book, we will emphasize finding **breakthrough opportunities**—opportunities that help innovators develop hard-to-copy marketing strategies that will be very profitable for a long time. Finding breakthrough opportunities is important because imitators are always waiting to try to "share" the profits—if they can.

Competitive advantage is needed—at least

Even if a breakthrough opportunity isn't possible, a firm should try to obtain a competitive advantage to increase its chances for profit or survival. **Competitive advantage** means that a firm has a marketing mix that the target market sees as better than a competitor's mix.

The search for breakthrough opportunities and competitive advantage sometimes involves only "fine-tuning" a firm's marketing mix(es). Sometimes it may require new facilities, new people, and totally new ways of solving problems. But it is vital to have some competitive advantage—so the promotion people have something unique to sell and success doesn't hinge on offering lower and lower prices.[3]

TYPES OF OPPORTUNITIES TO PURSUE

Most people have unsatisfied needs—and alert marketers can find opportunities all around them. Starting with the firm's present product-markets is useful. By carefully defining its markets, the firm may see new opportunities. Or it may see opportunities beyond its present activities.

It helps to see the kinds of opportunities firms may find. Exhibit 3–2 shows the four broad possibilities: market penetration, market development, product development, and diversification. We will look at these separately, but some firms may pursue more than one type of opportunity at the same time.

Attractive opportunities are often fairly close to markets the firm already knows.

Exhibit 3-2   Four Basic Types of Opportunities

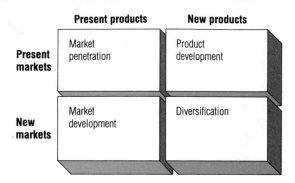

Market penetration

Market penetration is trying to increase sales of a firm's present products in its present markets—probably through a more aggressive marketing mix. The firm may try to increase the customers' rate of use or attract competitors' customers or current nonusers. For example, Coca Cola has increased advertising to encourage people to take a morning Coke break instead of a coffee break and to switch from Pepsi to Diet Coke.

New promotion appeals alone may not be effective. A firm may need to add more stores in present areas for greater convenience. Short-term price cuts or coupon offers may help. AT&T has increased advertising and offered special discounts to encourage customers to choose AT&T over other long-distance telephone services.

Obviously, effective planning is aided by a real understanding of why some people are buying now and what will motivate them to shift brands, buy more, or begin or resume buying.

Market development

Market development is trying to increase sales by selling present products in new markets. This may only involve advertising in different media to reach new target customers. Or it may mean adding channels of distribution or new stores in new areas. For example, McDonald's is reaching new customers by opening outlets in airports, office buildings, zoos, casinos, hospitals, and military bases. And it's rapidly expanding into international markets with outlets in places like Brazil, Hong Kong, and Australia.

Market development may also involve a search for new uses for a product, as when Lipton provides recipes showing how to use its dry soup mixes to make party dip for potato chips.

Product development

Product development is offering new or improved products for present markets. Here, the firm should know the market's needs; it may see ways of adding or modifying product features, creating several quality levels, or adding more types or sizes to better satisfy them. Computer software firms like Microsoft boost sales by introducing new versions of popular programs. Microsoft has also developed other types of new products for its customers. It now sells computer books and even computer hardware.

Diversification

Diversification is moving into totally different lines of business—which may include entirely unfamiliar products, markets, or even levels in the production-marketing system. Until recently, Sony was strictly a producer of electronic equipment. With its purchase of CBS records, it has expanded into producing music—and it is considering other moves that will take it further yet from its traditional business.

Which opportunities come first?

Usually, attractive opportunities are fairly close to markets the firm already knows. It makes sense to build on a firm's strengths and avoid its weaknesses. This may allow the firm to capitalize on changes in its present markets—or more basic changes in the uncontrollable environments.

Most firms think first of greater market penetration. They want to increase profits where they already have experience and strengths. But if they already have as big a share as they can get in their present markets, they may think of market development—finding new markets for their present products—including expanding regionally, nationally, or even internationally.

Marketers who have a good understanding of their present markets may see opportunities in product development—especially because they already have a way of reaching their present customers.

The most challenging opportunities involve diversification. Here, both new products *and* new markets are involved. The further the opportunity is from what the firm is already doing, the more attractive it may look to the optimists—and the harder it will be to evaluate. Opportunities that are far from a firm's current experiences involve higher risks. The landscape is littered with failed efforts at diversification. For example, Holiday Corporation learned fast that making mattresses (like the ones used in its Holiday Inn motels) was *not* one of its strengths.[4]

SEARCH FOR OPPORTUNITIES CAN BEGIN BY UNDERSTANDING MARKETS

Breakthrough opportunities from understanding target markets

When marketing managers really understand their target markets, they may see breakthrough opportunities, as this Eastman Kodak example shows. Eastman Kodak—maker of cameras and photographic supplies—also produces an industrial product, X-ray film. At first, Kodak felt all this market wanted was faster X-ray pictures at cheaper prices. But closer study showed that the real need in hospitals and health-care units was saving the radiologist's time. Time was precious—but just giving the radiologist a faster picture wasn't enough. Something more was needed to help do the whole job faster—and better.

Kodak came to see that its business was not just supplying X-ray pictures, but also helping to improve the health care supplied to patients. As a result, Kodak came up with new time-savers for radiologists: a handy cassette film pack and a special identification camera that records all vital patient data directly on X ray at the time the X ray is made. Before, such tagging had to be done during developing, which took more time and created the risk of error. This new marketing mix aimed at satisfying a different need. And it worked very well.

What is a company's market?

What is a company's market is an important but sticky question. A **market** is a group of potential customers with similar needs and sellers offering various products—that is, ways of satisfying those needs.

Market-oriented managers develop marketing mixes for *specific* target markets. This is very different from production-oriented managers—who just see a mass market of customers who are pretty much the same. Target marketers aim at specific "somebodies."

Getting the firm to focus on specific target markets is vital. Target marketing requires a "narrowing down" process—to get beyond mass market thinking. But this narrowing down process is often misunderstood. Exhibit 3–3 shows the narrowing down process we will be talking about.

Don't just focus on the product

Some production-oriented managers ignore the tough part of defining markets. To make the narrowing down process easier, they just describe their markets in terms of *products* they sell. For example, producers and retailers of greeting cards might define their market as the "greeting-card" market. But this production-oriented approach ignores customers—and customers make a market! This also leads to missed opportunities. Hallmark isn't missing these opportunities. Instead, Hallmark aims at the "personal-expression" market. It offers all kinds of products that can be sent as "memory makers"—to express one person's feelings towards another. Hallmark has expanded far beyond Christmas and birthday cards—the major greeting card days—to jewelry, gift wrap, plaques, candles, and puzzles as well as to all-occasion and humorous cards.[5]

From generic markets to product-markets.

It's useful to think of two basic types of market. A **generic market** is a market with *broadly* similar needs—and sellers offering various—*often diverse*—ways of satisfying those needs. In contrast, a **product-market** is a market with *very* similar needs and sellers offering various *close substitute* ways of satisfying those needs.[6]

A generic market description looks at markets broadly and from a customer's viewpoint. Status-seekers, for example, have several very different ways to satisfy

Exhibit 3–3   Narrowing Down to Target Markets

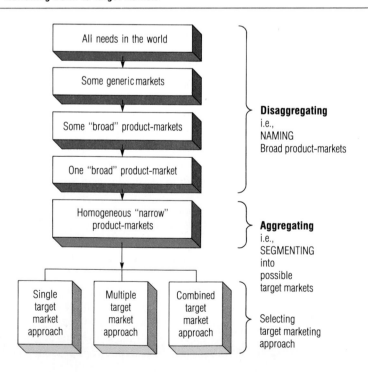

Chewing gum and toothpaste may compete in the same generic market.

status needs. A status-seeker might buy a new Mercedes, a Lindblad tour, or designer fashions from Neiman-Marcus. Any one of these *very different* products may satisfy this status need. Sellers in this generic status-seeker market have to focus on the need(s) the customers want satisfied—not on how one seller's product (car, vacation, or designer label) is better than that of another producer.

It is sometimes hard to understand and define generic markets because *quite different product types may compete with each other.* But if customers see all these products as substitutes—as competitors in the same generic market—then marketers must deal with this complication.

Suppose, however, that one of our status-seekers decides to satisfy this status need with a new, expensive car. Then—in this product-market—Mercedes, Cadillac, and BMW may compete with each other for the status-seeker's dollars. In this *product*-market concerned with cars *and* status (not just transportation!), consumers compare similar products to satisfy their status need.

Most companies quickly narrow their focus to product-markets because of the firm's past experience, resources, or management preferences. And we will usually be thinking of product-markets when we refer to markets. But, when looking for opportunities, the broader generic market view should be considered.

Broaden market definitions to find opportunities

Broader market definitions—including generic market definitions and broader product-market definitions—can help firms find opportunities. But deciding *how* broad to go isn't easy. Too narrow a definition will limit a firm's opportunities—but too broad a definition will make the company's efforts and resources seem insignificant.

Our strategy planning process helps in defining relevant markets. Here we are trying to match opportunities to a firm's resources and objectives, so the *relevant market for finding opportunities* should be bigger than the firm's present product-market—but not so big that the firm couldn't expand and be an important competitor. A small manufacturer of screwdrivers, for example, shouldn't define its market as broadly as "the worldwide tool users market" or as narrowly as "our present screwdriver customers." But it may have the production and/or marketing potential to consider "the U.S. handyman's hand-tool market." Careful naming of your product-market can help you see possible opportunities.

NAMING PRODUCT–MARKETS AND GENERIC MARKETS

Product-related terms are not—by themselves—an adequate description of a market. A complete product-market definition includes a four-part description.

What:	1. Product Type
To Meet What:	2. Customer (User) Needs
For Whom:	3. Customer Types
Where:	4. Geographic Area

In other words, a product-market description must include customer-related terms—not just product-related terms. We will refer to these four-part descriptions as product-market "names" because most managers label their markets when they think, write, or talk about them. Such a four-part definition can be clumsy, however, so it's often practical to use a "nickname"—as long as everyone understands the underlying four-part terms. And it's desirable to have the nickname refer to people—not products—because, as we've emphasized, people make markets!

Product type should meet customer needs

Product type describes the goods and/or services the customers want. (Note: a particular product type may include no physical good. Many products are pure services.)

Customer (user) needs refer to the needs the product type will satisfy for the customer. At a very basic level, product types usually provide functional benefits such as nourishing, protecting, warming, cooling, transporting, cleaning, holding, drilling, assembling, and so forth. We should identify such "basic" needs first. But usually it's necessary to go beyond these "basic" needs to emotional needs—such as needs for fun, excitement, pleasing appearance, or status. Correctly defining the need(s) relevant to a market is crucial and requires a good understanding of customers. These topics are discussed more fully in Chapters 7 and 8.

Both product type and customer need(s) should be defined together. Sometimes naming the product type reveals the needs at the same time. For example, floor-wax products are for waxing. In other cases, naming the needs requires much thought because the same product type may satisfy several needs—or even several sets of needs. Cars, for example, can be for transporting *and* socializing *and* status *and* fun. When a single product may satisfy different needs, marketers have a basis for identifying two or more different product-markets.

Customer type refers to the final consumer or user of a product type. Here, we want to choose a name that describes all present (possible) types of customers.

The emphasis in defining customer type should be on identifying the final consumer or user of the product type, rather than the buyer—if they are different. If the product type flows through middlemen on the way to final customers, marketers should avoid treating middlemen as a customer type—unless these middlemen actually use the product in their own business.

Exhibit 3–4   Relationship between Generic and Product-Market Definitions

A generic market definition consists of:
Product type + Customer (user) needs + Customer types + Geographic area, which together form the Product-market definition.

The *geographic area* is where a firm is competing—or thinking of competing—for customers. While naming the geographic area may seem trivial, it should be taken seriously. Just understanding geographic boundaries of a market can suggest new opportunities. A supermarket in Los Angeles is not catering to all consumers in the Los Angeles area—so there may be opportunities for expansion to unsatisfied customers in that market. Similarly, if a firm is only aiming at the U.S. market, this may suggest world market opportunities.

No product type in generic market names

A generic market description *doesn't include any product-type terms.* It consists of the last three parts of a product-market definition—omitting the product type. This emphasizes that any product type that satisfies the needs of the customer can be a competitor in this generic market. Recall that in our "status-seeker" market example, very different product types were competitors. Exhibit 3–4 shows the relationship between generic market and product-market definitions.

Creativity is needed in naming markets

Creative analysis of the needs and attitudes of present and potential target markets—in relation to the benefits being offered by the firm and competitors—will help you see new opportunities. Later, we'll study the many possible dimensions of markets. But for now you should see that defining markets only in terms of current products is not the best way to find new opportunities—or plan marketing strategies.

MARKET SEGMENTATION DEFINES POSSIBLE TARGET MARKETS

Market segmentation is a two-step process

Market segmentation is a two-step process of: (1) *naming* broad product-markets and (2) *segmenting* these broad product-markets in order to select target markets and develop suitable marketing mixes.

This two-step process isn't well understood. First-time market segmentation efforts often fail because beginners start with the whole "mass market" and try to find one or two demographic characteristics to segment this market. Customer behavior is usually too complex to be explained in terms of just one or two demographic characteristics. For example, not all old men—or all young women—buy the same products or brands. Other dimensions usually must be considered—starting with customer needs.

Naming broad product-markets is disaggregating

The first step in effective market segmentation is naming a broad product-market of interest to the firm. This involves "breaking apart"—disaggregating—all possible needs into some generic markets and broad product-markets in which the firm may be able to operate profitably. See Exhibit 3–3. No one firm can satisfy everyone's needs. So, the naming—disaggregating—step involves "brainstorming" about very different solutions to various generic needs and selecting some broad areas—broad product-markets—where the firm has some resources and experience. This means that a car manufacturer would probably ignore all the possible opportunities in food and clothing markets and focus on the generic market, "transporting people in the world," and probably on the broad product-market, "cars and trucks for transporting people in the world."

Disaggregating is a practical, "rough-and-ready" approach that tries to "narrow down" the marketing focus to product-market areas where the firm is more likely to have a competitive advantage—or even to find breakthrough opportunities. It looks easy, but it actually requires a lot of thought and judgment about what the firm may be able to do for some consumers—and do better than some or all competitors—so it will have a competitive advantage.

Market grid is a visual aid to market segmentation

Assuming that any market may consist of submarkets, it helps to picture a market as a rectangle with boxes representing smaller, more homogeneous product-markets. See Exhibit 3–5.

Think of the whole rectangle as representing a generic market—or broad product-market. Now, think of the boxes as submarkets—product-markets. In the generic "transporting market" discussed above, for example, we might see submarkets for bicycles, mopeds, motorcycles, airplanes, ships, buses, and "others."

Segmenting is an aggregating process

Marketing-oriented managers think of **segmenting** as an aggregating process—clustering together people with similar needs into a "market segment." A **market segment** is a (relatively) homogeneous group of customers who will respond to a marketing mix in a similar way.

This part of the market segmentation process (see Exhibit 3–3) takes a different approach than the naming part. Here, we are looking for similarities rather than basic differences in needs. Segmenters start with the idea that each person is "one of a kind" but that it may be possible to aggregate some more or less homogeneous people into a product-market.

Segmenters see each of these one-of-a-kind people as having a unique set of dimensions. This is shown in Exhibit 3–6A. Here the many dots show each per-

Exhibit 3–5 Market Grid Diagram with Submarkets (numbered)

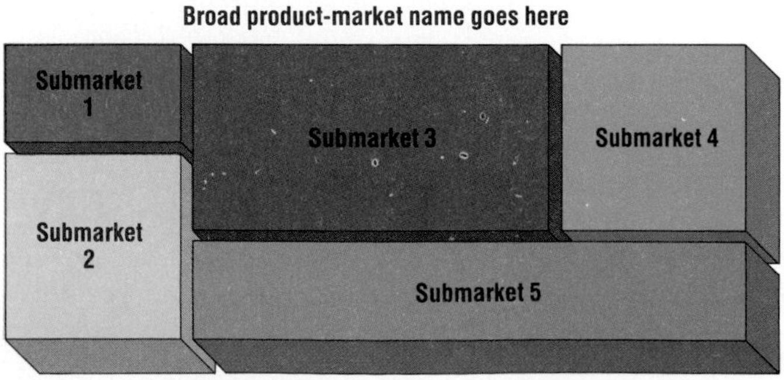

Broad product-market name goes here

- Submarket 1
- Submarket 2
- Submarket 3
- Submarket 4
- Submarket 5

Exhibit 3–6   Every Individual Has His or Her Own Unique Position in a Market—Those with Similar Positions Can Be Aggregated into Potential Target Markets

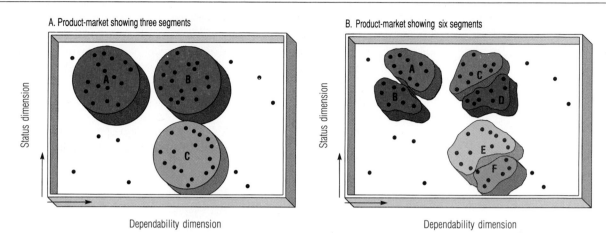

A. Product-market showing three segments

B. Product-market showing six segments

son's position in a product-market with two dimensions—need for status and need for dependability. While each person's position is unique, you can see that many of them are similar in terms of how much status and dependability they want. So a segmenter may aggregate these people into three (an arbitrary number) relatively homogeneous submarkets—A, B, and C. Group A might be called "Status Oriented" and Group C "Dependability Oriented." Members of Group B want both and might be called the "Demanders."

How far should the aggregating go?

The segmenter wants to aggregate individual customers into some workable number of relatively homogeneous target markets—and then treat each target market differently.

Look again at Exhibit 3–6A. Remember we talked about three segments. But this was an arbitrary number. As Exhibit 3–6B shows, there may really be six segments. What do you think—does this broad product-market consist of three segments or six segments?

Another difficulty with segmenting is that some potential customers just don't "fit" neatly into market segments. For example, not everyone in Exhibit 3–6B was put into one of the groups. Forcing them into one of the groups would have made these segments more heterogeneous—and harder to please. Further, forming additional segments for them probably wouldn't be profitable. They are too few and not very similar in terms of the two dimensions. These people are simply too "unique" to be catered to and may have to be ignored—unless they are willing to pay a high price for special treatment.

The number of segments that should be formed depends more on judgment than on some scientific rule. But the following guidelines can help.

Criteria for segmenting a broad product-market

Ideally, "good" market segments meet the following criteria (see Exhibit 3–7):

1. *Homogeneous (similar) within*—the customers in a market segment should be as similar as possible with respect to their likely responses to marketing mix variables *and* their segmenting dimensions.

Exhibit 3-7   Criteria for Segmenting

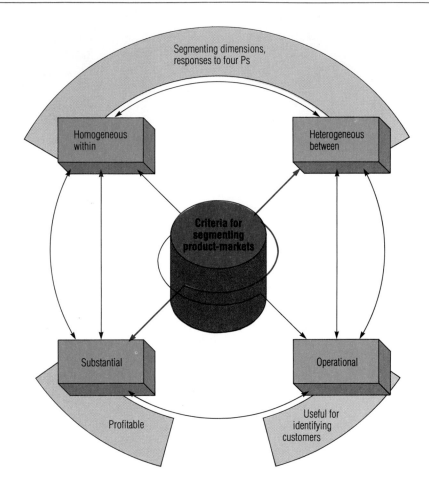

2. *Heterogeneous (different) between*—the customers in different segments should be as different as possible with respect to their likely responses to marketing mix variables *and* their segmenting dimensions.
3. *Substantial*—the segment should be big enough to be profitable.
4. *Operational*—the segmenting dimensions should be useful for identifying customers and deciding on marketing mix variables.

It is especially important that segments be *operational*. This means you should avoid dimensions that have no practical use. A personality trait such as moodiness, for example, might be found among the traits of heavy buyers of a product, but how could you use this fact? Personal salespeople would have to give a personality test to each buyer—an impossible task. Similarly, advertising media buyers or copywriters couldn't make much use of this information. So although moodiness might be related in some way to previous purchases, it would not be a useful dimension for segmenting.

The need for segments to be operational may lead marketers to include demographic dimensions such as age, income, location, and family size to help in planning marketing mixes. Information on these dimensions is readily available, and this can be very useful—at least for Place and Promotion planning. In fact, it is difficult to make some Place and Promotion decisions without such information.

Segmenting dimensions should be useful for identifying customers and deciding on marketing mix variables.

Target marketers aim at specific targets

Once you accept the idea that broad product-markets may have submarkets, you can see that target marketers usually have a choice among many possible target markets.

There are three basic ways of developing market-oriented strategies in a broad product-market.

1. The **single target market approach**—segmenting the market and picking one of the homogeneous segments as the firm's target market.
2. The **multiple target market approach**—segmenting the market and choosing two or more segments, each of which will be treated as a separate target market needing a different marketing mix.
3. The **combined target market approach**—combining two or more submarkets into one larger target market as a basis for one strategy.

Note that all three approaches involve target marketing—they all aim at specific—and clearly defined—target markets. See Exhibit 3–8. For convenience, we'll call people who follow the first two approaches the "segmenters" and the people who use the third approach "combiners."

Combiners try to satisfy pretty well

Combiners try to increase the size of their target markets by combining two or more segments—perhaps to gain some economies of scale, to reduce risk, or just because they don't have enough resources to develop more than one marketing mix.

Combiners look at various submarkets for similarities rather than differences. Then they try to extend or modify their basic offering to appeal to these "combined" customers with just one marketing mix. See Exhibit 3–8. For example, combiners may try a new package, more service, a new brand, or new flavors. But even if they make product or other marketing mix changes, they are not trying to uniquely satisfy smaller submarkets. Instead, combiners try to improve the general appeal of their marketing mix to appeal to a bigger "combined" target market.

Exhibit 3–8   Target Marketers Have Specific Aims

In a product-market area

A segmenter	A combiner

Using single
target market
approach—
can aim at one
submarket with
one marketing mix

Using multiple
target market
approach—
can aim at two
or more submarkets
with different
marketing mixes

Using combined
target market
approach—
aims at two
or more submarkets
with the same
marketing mix

The strategy

Strategy one

Strategy three

Strategy two

The strategy

Segmenters try to satisfy "very well"

Segmenters, on the other hand, aim at one or more homogeneous segments and try to develop a different marketing mix for each segment. They want to satisfy each one very well.

Segmenters may make more basic changes in marketing mixes—perhaps in the product itself—because they are aiming at smaller target markets.

Heinz uses a multiple target market approach that treats consumers and hotels as separate segments that need different marketing mixes.

Instead of assuming that the whole market consists of a fairly similar set of customers (like the mass marketer does) or merging various submarkets together (like the combiner), a segmenter sees submarkets with their own demand curves—as shown in Exhibit 3–9. Segmenters believe that aiming at one—or some—of these smaller markets will provide greater satisfaction to the target customers and greater profit potential for the firm.

Segmenting may produce bigger sales

Note that a segmenter is not settling for a smaller sales potential. Instead, by aiming at only a part of a larger product-market, the segmenter hopes to get a much larger share of his target market(s). In the process, total sales may be larger. The segmenter may even get a monopoly in "his" market(s).

Should you segment or combine?

Which approach should be used? This depends on the firm's resources, the nature of competition, and—most important—the similarity of customer needs, attitudes, and buying behavior.

It is tempting to aim at larger combined markets instead of smaller segmented markets. If successful, such a strategy can result in economies of scale. Also, offering one marketing mix to two or more submarkets usually requires less investment—and may seem less risky—than offering different marketing mixes to different submarkets.

Too much aggregating is risky

Combiners must be careful not to aggregate too far. As they enlarge the target market, it becomes less homogeneous—and individual differences within each submarket may begin to outweigh the similarities. This makes it harder to develop marketing mixes that can do an effective job of reaching and satisfying potential customers within each of the submarkets.

A combiner faces the continual risk of innovative segmenters "chipping away" at the various segments of the combined target market—by offering more attractive marketing mixes to more homogeneous submarkets.[7]

In the extreme, a combiner may create a fairly attractive marketing mix but then watch segmenters capture one after another of its submarkets with more targeted marketing mixes—until finally the combiner is left with no customers at all!

In general, it's usually safer to be a segmenter—that is, to try to satisfy some customers *very* well instead of many just *fairly* well. That's why many firms use the

Exhibit 3–9   There May Be Different Demand Curves in Different Market Segments

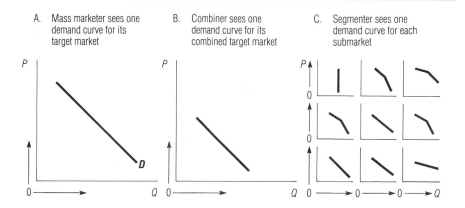

A. Mass marketer sees one demand curve for its target market

B. Combiner sees one demand curve for its combined target market

C. Segmenter sees one demand curve for each submarket

AFG Finds a Window of Opportunity with Segmenting

In the 1970s, AFG Industries of California, manufactured sheets of plain old window glass used in construction. AFG was competing head-on against larger producers who had stronger distribution channels and lower costs. Recurring downturns in construction further shattered AFG's thin profit margins. In searching for new opportunities, marketing managers at AFG looked beyond the construction product-market and focused on the needs of companies that used tempered and colored glass in their production. There were many possibilities—so they focused their efforts where AFG could develop a competitive advantage. They used a multiple target market approach and planned marketing mixes for "niche" segments that bigger producers didn't target. Because of careful segmenting, AFG now sells 70 percent of the glass for microwave oven doors and 75 percent of the glass for shower enclosures and patio tabletops. Segments that buy specialty glass now account for more than half of AFG's fast-growing $400 million in sales. And instead of competing to sell commodity glass, AFG earns the best profit margins in its industry.[8]

single or multiple target market approach instead of the combined target market approach. Procter & Gamble, for example, offers many products that seem to compete directly with each other (e.g., Tide versus Cheer or Crest versus Gleem). However, P&G offers "tailor-made" marketing mixes to each submarket that is large enough—and profitable enough—to deserve a separate marketing mix. This approach can be extremely effective but may not be possible for a smaller firm with more limited resources. A smaller firm may have to use the single target market approach—aiming at the one submarket niche where it sees the best opportunity.

Profit is the balancing point

Target marketers develop and implement whole strategies—they don't just segment markets. In practice, this means that cost considerations probably encourage

Sony's new filmless camera will probably compete in the same broad product-market as Pentax's 35mm autofocus camera—but it may appeal to a different submarket with different needs.

more aggregating—to obtain economies of scale—while demand considerations suggest less aggregating—to satisfy needs more exactly.

Profit is the balancing point. It determines how unique a marketing mix the firm can afford to offer to a particular group.

WHAT DIMENSIONS ARE USED TO SEGMENT MARKETS?

Market segmentation forces a marketing manager to decide which product-market dimensions might be useful for planning marketing mixes. The dimensions should help guide marketing mix planning. Exhibit 3–10 shows the kinds of dimensions we'll be talking about in Chapters 6 through 8—and their probable effect on the four Ps. Ideally, we would like to describe any potential product-market in terms of all three types of customer-related dimensions—plus a product type description—because these dimensions will help us develop better marketing mixes.

Consumers have many dimensions. And several may be useful for segmenting a broad product-market. Exhibit 3–11 shows some possible consumer market segmenting dimensions and their typical breakdowns. As Exhibit 3–11 shows, there are customer-related dimensions and situation-related dimensions—either of which may be more important in some cases.[9]

Exhibit 3–12 shows some possible dimensions for segmenting industrial markets and typical breakdowns.

With so many possible segmenting dimensions—and knowing that several dimensions may be needed to show what is really important in specific product-markets—how should we proceed?

What are the qualifying and determining dimensions?

To select the important segmenting dimensions, it is useful to think about two different types of dimensions. **Qualifying dimensions** are the dimensions that are relevant to including a customer type in a product-market. **Determining dimensions** are the dimensions that actually affect the customer's purchase of a specific product or brand in a product-market. These are the segmenting dimensions we are seeking.

Exhibit 3–10 Relation of Potential Target Market Dimensions to Marketing Mix Decision Areas

Potential target market dimensions	Effects on decision areas
1. Geographic location and other demographic characteristics of potential customers	Affects size of *Target Markets* (economic potential) and *Place* (where products should be made available) and *Promotion* (where and to whom to advertise)
2. Behavioral needs, attitudes, and how present and potential goods or services fit into customers' consumption patterns	Affects *Product* (design, packaging, length or width of product line) and *Promotion* (what potential customers need and want to know about the product offering, and what appeals should be used)
3. Urgency to get need satisfied and desire and willingness to compare and shop	Affects *Place* (how directly products are distributed from producer to consumer, how extensively they are made available, and the level of service needed) and *Price* (how much potential customers are willing to pay)

Exhibit 3–11   Possible Segmenting Dimensions and Typical Breakdowns for Consumer Markets

Dimensions	Typical breakdowns
Customer related	
Geographic	
Region	Pacific, Mountain, West North Central, West South Central, East North Central, East South Central, South Atlantic, Middle Atlantic, New England
City, county, MSA size	Under 5,000; 5,000–19,999; 20,000–49,999; 50,000–99,999; 100,000–249,999; 250,000–499,999; 500,000–999,999; 1,000,000–3,999,999; 4,000,000 or over
Demographic	
Age	Infant, under 6; 6–11; 12–17; 18–24; 25–34; 35–49; 50–64; 65 and over
Sex	Male, female
Family size	1, 2, 3–4, 5 or more
Family life cycle	Young, single; young, married, no children; young, married, youngest child under 6; young, married, youngest child 6 or over; older, married, with children; older, married, no children under 18; older, single; other
Income	Under $5,000; $5,000–$9,999; $10,000–$14,999; $15,000–$19,999; $20,000–$29,999, $30,000–$39,999, $40,000 and over
Occupation	Professional and technical; managers, officials, and proprietors; clerical sales; craftsmen, foremen; operatives; farmers; retired; students; housewives; unemployed
Education	Grade school or less, some high school, high school graduate, some college, college graduate
Race	White, Black, Oriental, other
Nationality.	American, British, French, German, etc.
Social class	Lower-lower, upper-lower, lower-middle, upper-middle, lower-upper, upper-upper
Situation related	
Benefits offered	
Need satisfiers	PSSP, economic, and more detailed needs
Product features.	Situation specific, but to satisfy specific or general needs
Consumption or use patterns	
Rate of use.	Heavy, medium, light, nonusers
Use with other products . . .	Situation specific, e.g., gas with a traveling vacation
Brand familiarity.	Insistence, preference, recognition, nonrecognition, rejection
Buying situation	
Kind of store	Convenience, shopping, specialty
Kind of shopping	Serious versus browsing, rushed versus leisurely
Depth of assortment	Out of stock, shallow, deep
Type of product	Convenience, shopping, specialty, unsought

Note: Terms used in this table are explained in detail later in the text.

A prospective car buyer, for example, has to have enough money—or credit—to buy a car. He also must have—or be able to get—a driver's license. This still doesn't guarantee that he'll buy a car. He may just rent one, or continue borrowing his parents' or friends' cars, or hitchhike. He may not get around to actually buying a car until his status with his buddies is falling because he doesn't have "wheels." This need may lead him to buy *some* car. But this dimension is not determining with respect to a specific brand or a specific model.

Exhibit 3–12   Possible Segmenting Dimensions for Industrial Markets

Type of organization	Manufacturing, institutional, government, public utility, military, farm, etc.

Demographics	Size
	   Number of employees
	   Sales volume
	SIC code
	Number of facilities
	Geographic location:
	   East, Southeast, South, Midwest, Mountains, Southwest, West
	   Large city⟶rural

Type of product	Installations, accessories, components, raw materials, supplies, services
Type of buying situation	Decentralized⟶centralized Buyer⟶multiple buying influence Straight rebuy⟶modified rebuy⟶new buy
Source loyalty	Weak⟶strong loyalty Last resort⟶second source⟶first source
Kinds of commitments	Contracts, agreements, financial aids
Reciprocity	None⟶complete

Note: Terms used in this table are explained in detail later in the text.

Determining dimensions may be very specific

How specific the determining dimensions are depends on whether you are concerned with a general product type or a specific brand. See Exhibit 3–13. The more specific you want to be, the more particular the determining dimensions may be. In a particular case, the determining dimensions may seem minor. But they are important because they *are* the determining dimensions. In the car status-seekers market, for example, paint colors or the brand name may determine which cars people buy.

Qualifying dimensions are important, too

The qualifying dimensions help identify the "core features" that must be offered to everyone in a product-market. Qualifying and determining dimensions work together in marketing strategy planning.

Exhibit 3–13   Finding the Relevant Segmenting Dimensions

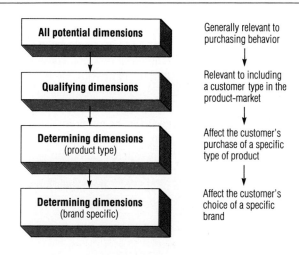

**Different dimensions
needed for different
submarkets**

Note that each different submarket within a broad product-market may be motivated by a different set of dimensions. In the snack food market, for example, health food enthusiasts are interested in nutrition, dieters may care only about calories, and economical shoppers with lots of kids may want volume to "fill them up." The related submarkets might be called: health-conscious snack food market, dieters' snack food market, and kids' snack food market. They would be in different boxes in a market grid diagram for the snack food market.

A SEVEN–STEP APPROACH TO SEGMENTING CONSUMER PRODUCT–MARKETS

Now let's go on to a logical, seven-step approach to market segmentation. Marketing research could help fine-tune some of the decisions made with this approach. But even without additional research *this approach works*—and has led to successful strategies. It is especially useful for finding the determining dimensions for product types. When you want to get down to dimensions for specific brands—especially when there are several competing brands—more sophisticated techniques may be needed.

To be sure you understand the approach, we will review each step separately, explain its importance, and use an ongoing example to show how each step works. The example is rental housing—in particular, the apartment market in a big urban area.

1: Name the broad product-market.

First, decide what broad product-market the firm wants to be in. This may be stated in the firm's objectives. Or if the firm is already in some product-market, its current position might be a good starting point. If it is just starting out, however, then many more choices are open—although the available resources, both human and financial, will limit the possibilities. It is better to build on the firm's strengths while avoiding its weaknesses—and competitors' strengths.

Example: A firm is building and renting small utility apartments for low-income families. A narrow view—considering only the products now being produced—might lead the firm to think only of more low-income housing. A bigger view might see such apartments as only a small part of the total apartment market or total rental housing market—or even the total housing market in the firm's geographic area. Taking an even bigger view, the firm could consider expanding to other geographic areas—or moving into other kinds of products (like office buildings or shopping centers).

There has to be some balance between naming the product-market too narrowly (same old product, same old market) and naming it too broadly (the whole world and all its needs). Here, the firm decided on the whole apartment renter's market in one city—because this is where the firm had some experience.

2: List potential customers' needs.

Write down as many relevant needs as you can—considering all of the potential customers in the broad product-market. This is a "brainstorming" step. The list doesn't have to be complete yet, but should provide enough input to really stimulate thinking in the next steps. Possible needs can be seen by thinking about *why* some people buy the present offerings in this broad product-market.

Example: In the apartment renter's market, it is fairly easy to list some possible needs: basic shelter, parking, play space, safety and security, distinctiveness, economy, privacy, convenience (to something), enough living area, attractive interiors, and good supervision and maintenance to assure trouble-free and comfortable living.

3: Form "homogeneous" submarkets—i.e., "narrow" product-markets.

Assuming that some people will have different needs than others, form one submarket around yourself (or some "typical" customer) and then aggregate similar people into this segment as long as they could be satisfied by the same marketing mix. Write the important need dimensions of these people in a column to help decide whether each new person should be included in the first segment. Also, note the people-related characteristics (including demographics) of the product-markets you are forming—so you can name them later.

For example, if the people in one market (column) are college students looking for a "party environment," this will help you understand what they want and why—and will help you name the market (perhaps as "the partyers").

People who are not "homogeneous"—who don't fit in the first segment—should be used to form a new submarket. List their different need dimensions in another column. Continue this classifying until three or more submarkets emerge.

Obviously, some judgment is needed here. But you should have some ideas about how you behave—and you can see that others have different needs and attitudes. We all have different preferences, but experienced observers do tend to agree, at least roughly, on how and why people behave.

Example: A college student living off campus probably wants an apartment to provide basic shelter, parking, economy, convenience to school and work, and enough room somewhere to have parties. An older married couple, on the other hand, has quite different needs—perhaps for basic shelter and parking, but *also* for privacy and good supervision so that they don't have to put up with the music that might appeal to the partyers.

4: Identify the determining dimensions.

Review the list of need dimensions for each possible segment (column) and identify the determining dimensions (perhaps putting parentheses around them). Although the qualifying dimensions are important—perhaps reflecting "core needs" that should be satisfied—they are not the *determining* dimensions we are seeking now.

Careful thinking about the needs and attitudes of the people in each possible segment will help identify which are the determining dimensions. They may not seem very different from market to market, but if they are determining to those people then they *are* determining!

Example: With our apartment renters, the need for basic shelter, parking, and safety and security are probably not determining. Everyone has these qualifying needs. Ignoring these common needs helps you see the determining dimensions— such as the needs for privacy, club facilities, strong management, and so on. See Exhibit 3–14.

5: Name (nickname) the possible product-markets.

Review the determining dimensions—market by market—and name (nickname) each one based on the relative importance of the determining dimensions (and aided by your description of the customer types). A market grid is a good way to help visualize this broad product-market and its narrow product-markets.

Draw the market grid as a rectangle with boxes inside representing smaller,

Exhibit 3–14   Segmenting the Broad Apartment Renters Market in a Metropolitan Area

	Need dimensions (benefits sought)	Customer-related characteristics	Nickname of product-market
1	Shelter Parking Security (Common facilities) (Close-in location) (Economy) Friendly management	Young, unmarried, active, fun-loving, party-going	**Swingers**
2	Shelter Parking Security (Distinctive design) (Privacy) (Interior variety) (Strong management) Club facilities	Older and more mature than swingers. Also, more income and education. More desire for comfort and individuality	**Sophisticates**
3	Shelter Parking Security (Room size) (Play space) (Economy)	Young families with children and not enough income to afford own home	**Family**
4	Shelter Parking Security (Close-in location) (Strong management) (Economy)	Single adults, widows, or divorcees. Not much discretionary income and want to be near job	**Job-centered**
5	Shelter Parking Security (Distinctive design) (Close-in location) (Strong management)	Former suburban home owners who now want to be close to city attractions	**Urban-centered**
6	Shelter Parking Security (Privacy) (Strong management) Club facilities	Younger, but no longer swingers. Want a home but don't have enough money yet. Both work so economy not necessary	**Newly married**

Apartment Renters in a Metro Area

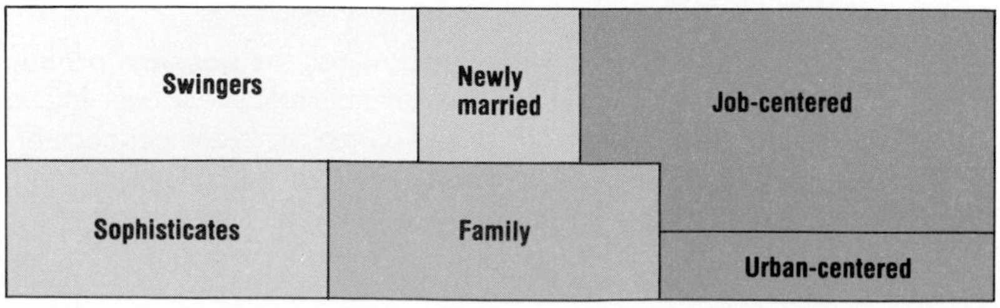

more homogeneous segments. See Exhibit 3–14. Think of the whole rectangle as representing the broad product-market with its name on top. Now think of each of the boxes as narrow product-markets. Since the markets within a broad product-market usually require very different dimensions, don't try to use the same two dimensions to name the markets—or to label the sides of the market grid boxes. Rather, just think of the grid as showing the relative sizes of product-market segments. Then, label each segment with its nickname.

Example: We can identify the following apartment renter submarkets: swingers, sophisticates, family-oriented, job-centered, and urban-centered. See Exhibit 3–14. Note that each segment has a different set of determining dimensions (benefits sought) that follows directly from customer type and needs.

6: Evaluate why product-market segments behave as they do.

After naming the markets as we did in Step 5, think about what else is known about each segment to help you understand how and why these markets behave the way they do. Different segments may have similar—but slightly different—needs. This may explain why some competitive offerings are more successful than others. It also can lead to splitting and renaming some segments.

Example: Newly married couples might have been treated as "swingers" in Step 5 because the "married" characteristic did not seem important. But with more thought, we see that while some newly married couples are still swingers at heart, others have begun to shift their focus to buying a home. For these newly marrieds, the apartment is a temporary place. Further, they are not like the sophisticates and probably should be treated as a separate market. The point here is that these market differences might only be discovered in Step 6. It is at this step that the "newly married" market would be named—and a related column created to describe the new segment.

7: Make a rough estimate of the size of each product-market segment.

Remember, we are looking for *profitable* opportunities. So now we must try to tie our product-markets to demographic data—or other customer related characteristics—to make it easier to estimate the size of these markets. We aren't trying to estimate our likely sales yet. Now we only want to provide a basis for later forecasting and marketing mix planning. The more we know about possible target markets, the easier those jobs will be.

Fortunately, much demographic data is available. And bringing in demographics adds a note of economic reality. Some possible product-markets may have almost no market potential. Without some hard facts, the risks of aiming at such markets are great.

To refine the market grid, redraw the inside boxes so that they give a better idea of the size of the various segments. This will help highlight the larger—and perhaps more attractive—opportunities.

Example: It's possible to tie the swingers to demographic data. Most of them are between 21 and 35. The U.S. Census Bureau publishes detailed age data by city. Given age data and an estimate of what percentage are swingers, it's easy to estimate the number of swingers in a metropolitan area.

Market dimensions suggest a good mix

Once we have followed all seven steps, we should at least be able to see the outlines of the kinds of marketing mixes that would appeal to the various markets. Let's take a look.

We know that swingers are active, young, unmarried, fun-loving, and party-going. The determining dimensions (benefits sought) in Exhibit 3–14 show what the swingers want in an apartment. (It's interesting to note what they do *not* want—strong management. Most college students will probably understand why!)

A Dallas-area apartment complex made a very successful appeal to local swingers by offering a swimming pool, a putting green, a nightclub with bands and other entertainment, poolside parties, receptions for new tenants, and so on. And to maintain the image, management insists that tenants who get married move out shortly—so that new swingers can move in.

As a result, apartment occupancy rates have been extremely high. At the same time, other builders often have difficulty filling their apartments—mostly because their units are just "little boxes" with few unique and appealing features.

SEVEN–STEP APPROACH APPLIES IN INDUSTRIAL MARKETS, TOO

A similar seven-step approach can be used for industrial markets, too. The major change is in the first step—selecting the broad product-market. The needs are different.

Industrial customers usually have basic functional needs. Their demands are derived from final consumer demands—so the industrial market is concerned with purchases that help produce finished products. The functions industrial buyers are concerned about include, but are not limited to: forming, bending, grading, digging, cutting, heating, cooling, conducting, transmitting, containing, filling, cleaning, analyzing, sorting, training, and insuring.

Defining the relevant broad product-market using both geographic dimensions and basic functional needs usually ensures that the focus is broad enough—that is, not exclusively on the product now being supplied to present customers. But it also keeps the focus from vaguely expanding to "all the industrial needs in the world."

It is better to focus on needs satisfied by products, *not* product characteristics themselves. New ways of satisfying the need may be found—and completely surprise and upset current producers—if the product-market is defined too narrowly. For example, desktop computers and printers now compete in what some producers thought was the "typewriter market." And telephone calls and fax machines are replacing letters—further reducing the need for typing. Perhaps this broad product-market is concerned with "thought processing and transmitting." Certainly, the "typewriter" view is too narrow. Market-oriented strategy planners try to avoid surprises that result from such tunnel vision.

After the first step in the seven-step approach, the other steps are similar to segmenting consumer markets. The main difference is that segmenting dimensions like those shown in Exhibit 3–12 and discussed in Chapter 8 are used.[10]

MORE SOPHISTICATED TECHNIQUES MAY HELP IN SEGMENTING

The seven-step approach is inexpensive, logical, practical—*and it works*. But computer-aided methods can help, too. A detailed review of the possibilities is beyond the scope of this book. But a brief discussion of some approaches will give you a flavor of how computer-aided methods work.

Different toothpastes may be targeted at different segments with different needs.

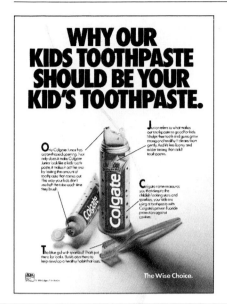

Clustering usually requires a computer

Clustering techniques try to find similar patterns within sets of data. "Clustering" groups customers who are similar on their segmenting dimensions into homogeneous segments. Clustering approaches use computers to do what previously was done with much intuition and judgment.

The data to be clustered might include such dimensions as demographic characteristics, the importance of different needs, attitudes toward the product, and past buying behavior. The computer searches all the data for homogeneous groups of people. When it finds them, marketers study the dimensions of the people in the groups to see why the computer clustered them together. If the results make some sense, they may suggest new, or at least better, marketing strategies.[11]

A cluster analysis of the toothpaste market, for example, might show that some people buy toothpaste because it tastes good (the sensory segment), while others are concerned with the effect of clean teeth on their social image (the sociables). Others are worried about decay (the worriers), and some are just interested in the best value for their money (the economic men). See Exhibit 3–15. Each of these market segments calls for a different marketing mix—although some of the four Ps may be similar.

Finally, a marketing manager has to decide which one (or more) of these segments will be the firm's target market(s).

You can see that these techniques only *aid* the manager. Judgment is still needed to develop an original list of possible dimensions—and then to name the resulting clusters.

Positioning segments by product features

Another approach to segmenting—**positioning**—shows where customers locate proposed and/or present brands in a market. It requires some formal marketing research but may be helpful when competitive offerings are quite similar. The results are usually plotted on graphs to help show where the products are

Exhibit 3–15   Toothpaste Market Segment Description

	Segment name			
	The sensory segment	**The sociables segment**	**The worriers segment**	**The independent segment**
Principal benefit sought	Flavor, product appearance	Brightness of teeth	Decay prevention	Price
Demographic strengths	Children	Teens, young people	Large families	Men
Special behavioral characteristics	Users of spearmint flavored toothpaste	Smokers	Heavy users	Heavy users
Brands disproportionately favored	Colgate, Stripe	Macleans, Plus White Ultra Brite	Crest	Brands on sale
Personality characteristics	High self-involvement	High sociability	High hypochondriasis	High autonomy
Life-style characteristics	Hedonistic	Active	Conservative	Value-oriented

"positioned" in relation to competitors. Usually, the products' positions are related to two product features that are important to the target customers.

Assuming the picture is reasonably accurate, managers then decide whether they want to leave their product (and marketing mix) alone or reposition it. This may mean *physical changes* in the product or simply *image changes based on promotion.* For example, most beer drinkers can't pick out their "favorite" brand in a blind test—so physical changes might not be necessary (and might not even work) to reposition a beer brand.

The graphs for positioning decisions are obtained by asking product users to make judgments about different brands—including their "ideal" brand—and then using computer programs to summarize the ratings and plot the results. The details of positioning techniques—sometimes called "perceptual mapping"—are beyond the scope of this text. But Exhibit 3–16 shows the possibilities.[12]

Exhibit 3–16 shows the "product space" for different brands of bar soap using two dimensions—the extent to which consumers think the soaps moisturize and deodorize their skin. For example, consumers see Dial as quite low on moisturizing but high on deodorizing. Lifebuoy and Dial are close together—implying that consumers think of them as similar on these characteristics. Dove is viewed as different and is further away on the graph. Remember that positioning maps are based on *customers' perceptions*—the actual characteristics of the products (as determined by a chemical test) might be different!

The circles on Exhibit 3–16 show sets of consumers clustered near their "ideal" soap preferences. Groups of respondents with a similar ideal product are circled to show apparent customer concentrations. In this graph, the size of the circles suggests the size of the segments for the different ideals.

Ideal clusters 1 and 2 are the largest and are close to two popular brands—Dial and Safeguard. It appears that customers in cluster 1 want more moisturizing than they see in Dial and Lifebuoy. However, exactly what these brands should do about this isn't clear. Perhaps both of these brands should leave their physical products alone—but emphasize moisturizing more in their promotion to make a stronger appeal to those who want moisturizers.

Exhibit 3–16 "Product Space" Representing Consumers' Perceptions for Different Brands of Bar Soap

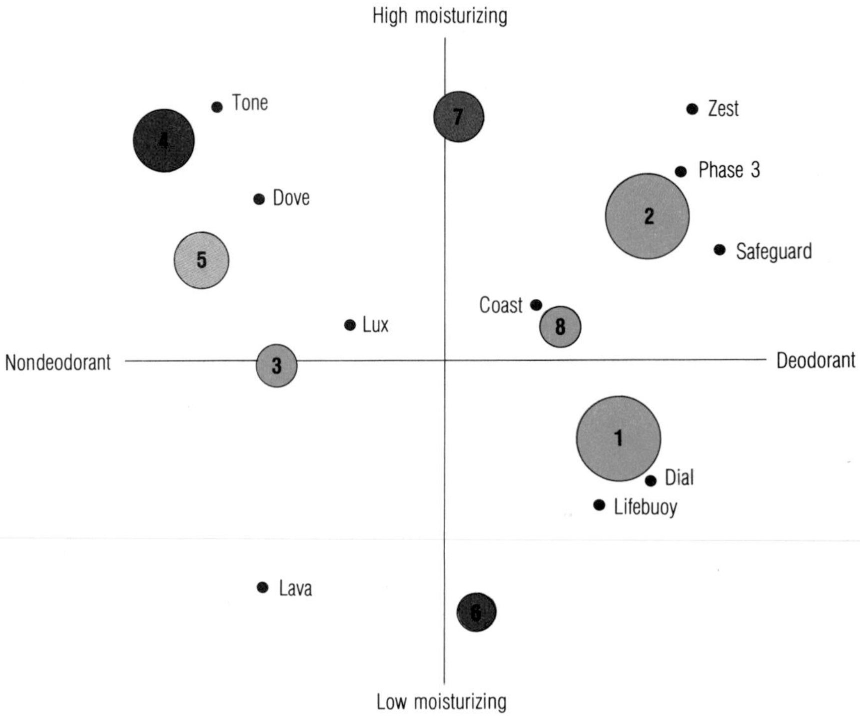

Lava doesn't seem to satisfy any of the ideal clusters very well. Therefore, some attempt probably should be made to reposition Lava—either through physical or image changes.

Note that ideal cluster 7 is not near any of the present brands. This may suggest an opportunity for introducing a new product—a strong moisturizer with some deodorizers. If some firm chooses to follow this approach, we would think of it as a segmenting effort.

Combining versus segmenting

Positioning analysis may lead a firm to combining—rather than segmenting—if managers think they can make several general appeals to different parts of a "combined" market. For example, by varying its promotion, Coast might try to appeal to clusters 8, 1, and 2 with one product. On the other hand, there may be clearly defined submarkets—and some parts of the market may be "owned" by one product or brand. In this case, segmenting efforts may be practical—moving the firm's own product into another segment of the general market area where competition is weaker.

Positioning as part of broader analysis

The major value of positioning is to help managers understand how customers see their market. It is a visual aid to understanding a product-market. But positioning usually focuses on specific product features—that is, it is product-oriented. There is the risk that important *customer*-related dimensions—including needs and attitudes—may be overlooked. But as part of a broader analysis of target markets, positioning can be very useful. The first time such an analysis is done, managers may be shocked to see how much customers' perceptions of a market differ from their own. For this reason alone, positioning is useful.

Premature emphasis on product features is dangerous, however. And it's easy to do if you start with a product-oriented definition of a market—as in the bar soap example. This leads to positioning bar soaps against bar soaps. But this can make a firm miss more basic shifts in markets. For example, bars might be losing popularity to liquid soaps. Or other products, like bath oils or bubble baths, may be part of the relevant competition. Such shifts would not be seen by only looking at alternative bar soap brands—the focus is just too narrow.

As we emphasize throughout the text, you must understand potential needs and attitudes when planning marketing strategies. If customers are treating quite different products as substitutes, then a firm has to position itself against those products, too. It must avoid focusing on physical product characteristics that are not the determining dimensions of the target market.

CONCLUSION

Creative strategy planning is needed for survival in our increasingly competitive markets. In this chapter, we discussed how to find attractive target market opportunities. We saw that carefully defining generic markets and product-markets can help find new opportunities. The shortcomings of a too narrow product-oriented view of markets were emphasized.

We also discussed market segmentation—the process of naming and then segmenting broad product-markets to find potentially attractive target markets. Some people try to segment markets by starting with the "mass market" and then dividing it into smaller submarkets based on a few dimensions. But this can lead to poor results. Instead, market segmentation should first focus on a broad product-market, and then group similar customers into homogeneous submarkets. The more similar the potential customers are, the larger the submarkets can be. Four criteria for evaluating possible product-market segments were presented.

Once a broad product-market has been segmented,

marketing managers can use one of three approaches to market-oriented strategy planning: (1) the single target market approach, (2) the multiple target market approach, and (3) the combined target market approach. In general, we encourage marketers to be segmenters rather than combiners.

We discussed a practical—"rough-and-ready"—seven-step approach to market segmentation that works for both consumer and industrial markets. We also discussed some computer-aided segmenting approaches—clustering techniques and positioning.

In summary, good marketers should be experts on markets and likely segmenting dimensions. By creatively segmenting markets, they may spot opportunities—even breakthrough opportunities—and help their firms to succeed against aggressive competitors offering similar products. Segmenting is basic to target marketing. And the more you practice segmenting, the more meaningful market segments you will see.

Questions and Problems

1. Distinguish between an attractive opportunity and a breakthrough opportunity. Give an example.

2. Explain how new opportunities may be seen by defining a firm's markets more precisely. Illustrate for a situation where you feel there is an opportunity—namely, an unsatisfied market segment—even if it is not very large.

3. Distinguish between a generic market and a product-market. Illustrate your answer.

4. Explain the major differences among the four basic types of opportunities discussed in the text and cite examples for two of these types of opportunities.

5. Explain why a firm may want to pursue a market penetration opportunity before pursuing one involving product development or diversification.

6. Explain what market segmentation is.

7. List the types of potential segmenting dimensions and explain which you would try to apply first, second, and third in a particular situation. If the nature of the situation would affect your answer, explain how.

8. Explain why segmentation efforts based on attempts to divide the mass market using a few demographic dimensions may be very disappointing.

9. Illustrate the concept that segmenting is an aggregating process by referring to the admissions policies of your own college and a nearby college or university.

10. (a) Evaluate how "good" the seven submarkets identified in the market for apartments are (Exhibit 3–14) with respect to the four criteria for selecting good market segments. (b) Same as (a) but evaluate the four corner markets in the British home decorating market (Exhibit 2–9).

11. Review the types of segmenting dimensions listed in Exhibits 3–11 and 3–12, and select the ones you think should be combined to fully explain the market segment you personally would be in if you were planning to buy a new car today. List several dimensions and try to develop a shorthand name, like "swinger," to describe your own personal market segment. Then try to estimate what proportion of the total car market would be accounted for by your market segment. Next, explain if there are any offerings that come close to meeting the needs of your market. If not, what sort of a marketing mix is needed? Would it be economically attractive for anyone to try to satisfy your market segment? Why or why not?

12. Identify the determining dimension or dimensions that explain why you bought the specific brand you did in your most recent purchase of a (a) soft drink, (b) shampoo, (c) shirt or blouse, and (d) larger, more expensive item, such as a bicycle, camera, boat, and so on. Try to express the determining dimension(s) in terms of your own personal characteristics rather than the product's characteristics. Estimate what share of the market would probably be motivated by the same determining dimension(s).

13. Apply the seven-step approach to segmenting consumer markets to the college-age market for off-campus recreation, which can include eating and drinking. Then evaluate how well the needs in these market segments are being met in your geographic area. Is there an obvious breakthrough opportunity waiting for someone?

14. Explain how the first step in the seven-step approach to segmenting markets would have to be changed to apply it in industrial markets. Illustrate your answer.

15. Explain how positioning can help a marketing manager identify target market opportunities.

Suggested Cases

3. Gerber Products Company

7. Pillsbury's Häagen-Dazs

15. McMiller's Ski Shop

32. Castco, Inc.

Suggested Computer-Aided Problem

3. Segmenting Customers

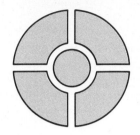

Chapter 4

Evaluating Opportunities in Uncontrollable Environments

When You Finish This Chapter, You Should

1. Know the uncontrollable variables the marketing manager must work with.

2. Understand why company objectives are important in guiding marketing strategy planning.

3. See how the resources of the firm may limit its search for opportunities.

4. Know the effect of the different kinds of competitive situations on strategy planning.

5. Understand how the economic and technological environment can affect strategy planning.

6. Know why you can go to prison by ignoring the political and legal environment.

7. Understand how to screen and evaluate marketing strategy opportunities.

8. Understand the important new terms (shown in red).

Marketing managers do not plan strategies in a vacuum. They have to work with several uncontrollable variables when choosing target markets and developing the four Ps. Marketing planning at Rubbermaid shows why this is important.

Top executives at Rubbermaid had set ambitious objectives for the firm. They wanted to achieve sales of $2 billion by 1992—about double what sales had been in 1988. Their profit objectives were equally ambitious.

Marketing managers for Rubbermaid had built a respected brand name in plastic kitchenware—but after evaluating the firm's uncontrollable environments they knew that just working harder at their current strategy would not be enough to achieve the firm's objectives. Sales growth was slipping because the target market was not growing as fast as in the past. Competition was also becoming more intense. For example, Tupperware had introduced new products and for the first time it was supplementing its Tupperware parties and other promotion efforts with aggressive advertising. Rubbermaid's profit margins were also being squeezed by uncontrollable increases in the cost of raw materials.

The marketing managers realized that new strategies would be required to achieve the company's objectives. Research showed that there were good opportunities for the firm to develop a new marketing mix targeted at consumers who wanted high-quality plastic toys. Rubbermaid had the money to move quickly. It acquired Little Tikes Co.—a small firm that was already producing sturdy plastic toys—and immediately expanded its product assortment. This helped to speed Rubbermaid's entry in the market. Marketing managers also took advantage of Rubbermaid's strong relationships with retailers to get scarce shelf space for the new toys—and they developed new ads to stimulate consumer interest. However, unlike many toy companies, Rubbermaid was sensitive to parents' concerns about TV ads targeted at children. It aimed its cost-effective print ads at parents.

Rubbermaid marketing managers also realized that there were opportunities for growth in European markets. Rubbermaid was less well-known there, and it had not developed strong distribution. Developing new strategies to expand sales in Europe involved a number of new challenges. The political, legal, and cultural environments there were very different than on Rubbermaid's home turf. However, by adapting its strategies to these uncontrollable environments, Rubbermaid is rapidly increasing its profits. Already the company is earning 10 percent of its total profits from European sales—and it expects that before long one fourth of its profits will come from that market.[1]

THE UNCONTROLLABLE ENVIRONMENTS

The Rubbermaid case shows why marketing managers need to understand the uncontrollable environments. You saw in the last chapter that finding target market opportunities takes a real understanding of what makes customers tick. Now you need to see that uncontrollable environments affect the attractiveness of possible opportunities—and marketing strategy planning.

As we saw in Chapter 2 (see Exhibit 2–12), the uncontrollable environments fall into five basic areas:

1. Objectives and resources of the firm.
2. Competitive environment.
3. Economic and technological environment.
4. Political and legal environment.
5. Cultural and social environment.

To achieve its objectives in a changing environment, Rubbermaid is developing new marketing strategies.

Exhibit 3–1 shows how Chapters 3 and 4 fit together. In Chapter 3 we talked about finding attractive opportunities. Now we'll see how to evaluate them—given the uncontrollable variables a marketing manager faces.

OBJECTIVES SHOULD SET FIRM'S COURSE

A company must decide where it's going, or it may fall into the trap expressed so well by the quotation: "Having lost sight of our objective, we redoubled our efforts." Company objectives should shape the direction and operation of the whole business. So we will treat this matter in some depth—discussing its effect both on finding attractive opportunities and developing marketing strategies.

Setting objectives that really guide the present and future development of the company is difficult. This process forces top management to look at the whole business, relate its present objectives and resources to the external environment, and then decide what the firm wants to accomplish in the future.

It would be convenient if a company could set one objective—such as making a profit—and let that serve as the guide. Actually, however, setting objectives is much more complicated, which helps explain why it's often done poorly—or not done at all.

Three basic objectives provide guidelines

The following three objectives provide a useful starting point for setting objectives for a firm. They should be sought *together* because—in the long run—a failure in even one of the three areas can lead to total failure of the business. A business should:

1. Engage in specific activities that will perform a socially and economically useful function.
2. Develop an organization to carry on the business and implement its strategies.
3. Earn enough profit to survive.[2]

Should be socially useful

The first objective says that the company should do something useful for society. This isn't just a "do-gooder" objective. Businesses exist on the approval of consumers. If the activities of a business appear to be against the consumer "good," that firm can be wiped out almost overnight by political or legal action—or consumers' own negative responses.

The first objective also implies that a firm should try to satisfy customer needs. This is why the marketing manager should be heard when the company is setting objectives. But setting whole-company objectives—within resource limits—is ultimately the responsibility of top management. In this sense, whole-company objectives are "uncontrollable" by the marketing manager.

A firm should define its objectives broadly—setting need-satisfying objectives rather than production-oriented objectives. Because customer needs change, too narrow a view may lead the company into a product-market in which the product itself will soon be obsolete.[3]

Should organize to innovate

In a macro-marketing sense, consumers have granted businesses the right to operate—and to make a profit if they can. With this right comes the responsibility for businesses to be dynamic agents of change, adjusting their offerings to meet new needs. Our competitive system is supposed to encourage innovation and efficiency. A business firm should develop an organization that will ensure that these consumer-assigned tasks are carried out effectively—and that the firm itself continues to prosper.

Should earn some profit

Certainly it's true that in the long run a firm must make a profit to survive. But just saying that a firm should try to make a profit isn't enough. The time period involved must also be specified since long-run profit maximization may require losing money during the first few years of a plan. On the other hand, seeking only short-term profits may steer the firm from opportunities that would offer larger long-run profits.

Further, trying to maximize profit won't necessarily lead to big profits. Competition in a particular industry may be so fierce that failure may be almost guaranteed. For example, Greyhound Corp. struggled to maximize profits selling long distance bus travel, but low airfares attracted much of the business. Even the maximum possible profit was disappointing. In a situation like this, it might be better to set a *target* rate of profit return that will lead the firm into areas with more promising possibilities.

Setting profit objectives is further complicated by the need to specify the degree of risk that management is willing to assume for larger returns. Very large profits are possible in the oil exploration business, for example, but the probability of success on each hole is quite low.

Objectives should be explicit

These three general objectives provide guidelines, but a firm has to develop its own *specific* objectives. In spite of their importance, objectives are seldom stated explicitly. And too often they are stated after the fact! If company objectives aren't clear and specific from the start, different managers may hold unspoken and conflicting objectives. This is a common problem—especially in large companies.

The whole firm must work toward the same objectives

As objectives are made more specific, care is necessary. Objectives chosen by top management should be compatible with each other—or frustrations and even failure may result. For example, top management may set a 25 percent return on investment each year as one objective, while at the same time specifying that the current plant and equipment be used as fully as possible.

On the surface this may seem reasonable, but competition may make it impossible to use the resources fully *and* achieve the target return. For example, efficient U.S. papermakers like Weyerhaeuser set the objective of operating at nearly full capacity so that they can keep their costs low—and keep foreign competitors out of the market. This does not mean, however, that top executives should expect marketing managers to find a way to pile up profits by the ream and earn a 25 percent return on investment. To earn that high a profit in the short term would require Weyerhaeuser marketing managers to set prices at too high a level—a level that would attract competitors into the market. That would soon prevent Weyerhaeuser from running its plant and equipment at full capacity. In a situation like this, conflicting objectives can lead to disaster. Managers may try to achieve the return on investment objective during the year and then, at the end of the year, find that it is impossible to keep running at full capacity. The two objectives are impossible to achieve together![4]

Top-management myopia may straitjacket marketing

We are assuming that it is the marketing manager's job to work within the framework of objectives provided by top management. But some of these objectives may limit marketing strategies—perhaps damaging the whole business. This is another reason why it is desirable for the marketing manager to help shape the company's objectives.

Some top managements want a large sales volume or a large market share because they feel this assures greater profitability. But recently, many large firms with big market shares have gone bankrupt. W. T. Grant was the largest retail bankruptcy in history. Braniff Airlines went under, and so did International Harvester. These firms sought large market shares—but earned little profit. Increasingly, companies are shifting their objectives toward *profitable* sales growth rather than just larger market share—as they realize that the two don't necessarily go together.[5]

Objectives should lead to marketing objectives

You can see why the marketing manager should be involved in setting company objectives. These objectives should guide the search for and evaluation of opportunities—as well as later planning of marketing strategies. Particular marketing objectives should be set within the framework of these larger, company objectives. As shown in Exhibit 4–1, there should be a hierarchy of objectives—moving from company objectives to marketing department objectives. For each marketing strategy, there should also be objectives for each of the four Ps—as well as more detailed objectives. For example, in the Promotion area, we need objectives for advertising, sales promotion, *and* personal selling.

Both company objectives and marketing objectives should be realistic and achievable. Overly ambitious objectives are useless if the firm lacks the resources to achieve them.

Exhibit 4–1   A Hierarchy of Objectives

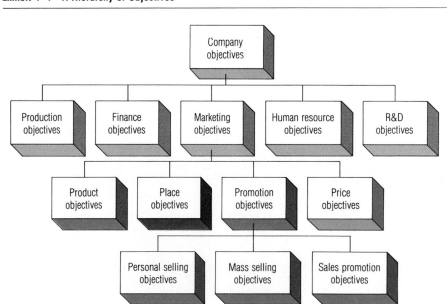

COMPANY RESOURCES MAY LIMIT SEARCH FOR OPPORTUNITIES

Every firm has some resources—hopefully some unique ones—that set it apart from other firms. Breakthrough opportunities—or at least some competitive advantage—come from making use of these strengths while avoiding direct competition with firms having similar strengths.

To find its strengths, the firm must evaluate functional areas (production, research and engineering, marketing, general management, and finance) as well as present products and markets. By analyzing successes or failures in relation to the firm's resources, management can discover why the firm was successful—or why it failed—in the past.

Harley-Davidson's motorcycle business was on the ropes and it was losing customers to Japanese competitors. The competitors' prices were so low that Harley initially thought the Japanese were "dumping" motorcycles in the United States at prices below cost. However, careful analysis revealed that Japanese manufacturing approaches were yielding operating costs fully 30 percent lower than Harley's. Studying the Japanese firms helped Harley identify ways to use its resources more efficiently and improve the quality of its products. With these resource-use problems resolved, new opportunities opened up—and Harley was again on the road to achieving its objectives.[6]

The pressure of competition focused Harley's attention on manufacturing resources. Other resources that should be considered—as part of an evaluation of strengths and weaknesses—are discussed in the following sections.

Financial strength

Some opportunities require large amounts of capital just to get started. Money may be required for R&D, production facilities, marketing research, or advertising—before the first sale is made. And even a really good opportunity may not be profitable for years. So lack of financial strength is often a barrier to entry into an otherwise attractive market.

A familiar brand name—and other marketing strengths—can be an advantage in seeking new opportunities.

Producing capability and flexibility

In many businesses, the cost of production per unit decreases as the quantity produced increases. Therefore, smaller producers can be at a great cost disadvantage if they try to win business from larger competitors.

On the other hand, new—or smaller—firms sometimes have the advantage of flexibility. They are not handicapped with large, special-purpose facilities that are obsolete or poorly located. U.S. Steel (USX), Bethlehem, and other large steel producers once enjoyed economies of scale. But today, they have trouble competing with producers using smaller, more flexible plants. Similarly, poorly located or obsolete retail or wholesale facilities can severely limit marketing strategy planning.

Firms that own or have assured sources of supply have an important advantage—especially in times of short supply. Big firms often control their own sources of supply. Companies that don't have guaranteed supply sources may have difficulty meeting demand—or even staying in business.

Marketing managers at Cummins Engine, a diesel engine producer, recently had to deal with this problem. At first they were pleased when customers greeted the introduction of a new engine with brisker than expected sales. When demand exceeded Cummins's normal output of 200 engines a day, the company switched to overtime and made other changes. But Cummins's suppliers couldn't keep pace. Unfinished engines piled up waiting for missing parts. It took several months to resolve the problem—and customers were lost as orders went unfilled. To maintain control, Cummins is now making some of the needed parts in-house.[7]

Marketing strengths

Our marketing strategy framework helps in analyzing current marketing resources. In the product area, for example, a familiar brand can be a big strength or a new idea or process may be protected by a *patent*. A patent owner has a 17-year monopoly to develop and use its new product, process, or material as he chooses. If one firm has a strong patent, competitors may be limited to second-rate offerings—and their efforts may be doomed to failure.

Good relations with established middlemen—or control of good locations—can be important resources in reaching some target markets. When Bic decided to compete with Gillette by selling disposable razors, Bic's other products had already proved profitable to drugstores, grocery stores, and other retailers who could reach the target market. So these retailers were willing to give Bic scarce shelf space.

Promotion and price resources must be considered, too. Westinghouse already has a skilled sales force. Marketing managers know these sales reps can handle new products and customers. And low-cost facilities may enable a firm to undercut competitors.

Finally, thorough understanding of a target market can give a company an edge. Many companies fail in new product-markets because they don't really understand the needs of the new customers—or the new competitive environment.

THE COMPETITIVE ENVIRONMENT

A manager may be able to avoid head-on competition

The **competitive environment** affects the number and types of competitors the marketing manager must face—and how they may behave. Although a marketing manager can't control these factors, he may be able to choose strategies that will avoid head-on competition. Or, where competition is inevitable, he can plan for it.

A marketing manager operates in one of four kinds of market situations. We'll discuss three kinds: pure competition, oligopoly, and monopolistic competition. The fourth kind, monopoly, isn't found very often and is like monopolistic competition. (Note: the following materials assume some familiarity with economic analysis—and especially the nature of demand curves and demand elasticity. For those needing a review of these materials, see Appendix A, which follows Chapter 2.)

Understanding these market situations is important because the freedom of a marketing manager—especially his control over price—is greatly reduced in some situations. The important dimensions of these situations are shown in Exhibit 4–2.

When competition is pure

Many competitors offer about the same thing

Pure competition is a market situation that develops when a market has:

1. Homogeneous (similar) products.
2. Many buyers and sellers, who have full knowledge of the market.
3. Ease of entry for buyers and sellers; that is, new firms have little difficulty starting in business—and new customers can easily come into the market.

More or less pure competition is found in many agricultural markets. In the potato industry, for example, there are thousands of producers—and they are in pure competition. Let's look more closely at these producers.

In pure competition, each of these many small producers sees a flat demand curve. Although the industry as a whole has a down-sloping demand curve, each individual producer has a demand curve that is flat at the **equilibrium price**—the going market price.

To explain this more clearly, let's look at the relation between the industry demand curve and the demand curve facing the individual potato farmer—shown in Exhibit 4–3. Assume that the equilibrium price for the industry is $1. This means

Exhibit 4–2   Some Important Dimensions Regarding Market Situations

Important dimensions / Types of situations	Pure competition	Oligopoly	Monopolistic competition	Monopoly
Uniqueness of each firm's product	None	None	Some	Unique
Number of competitors	Many	Few	Few to many	None
Size of competitors (compared to size of market)	Small	Large	Large to small	None
Elasticity of demand facing firm	Completely elastic	Kinked demand curve (elastic and inelastic)	Either	Either
Elasticity of industry demand	Either	Inelastic	Either	Either
Control of price by firm	None	Some (with care)	Some	Complete

Exhibit 4–3   Interaction of Demand and Supply in the Potato Industry and the Resulting Demand Curve Facing Individual Potato Producers

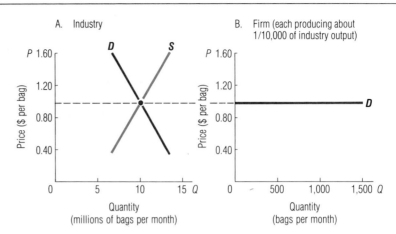

the producer can sell as many bags of potatoes as he chooses at $1. The quantity that all producers choose to sell makes up the supply curve.

A small producer has little effect on overall supply. If this individual farmer raises 1/10,000th of the quantity offered in the market, for example, you can see that there will be little effect if he goes out of business—or doubles his production.

The reason an individual producer's demand curve is flat is that the farmer probably couldn't sell any potatoes above the market price. And there is no point in selling below the market price! So, in effect, the individual producer has no control over price.

Markets tend to become more competitive

Not many markets are *purely* competitive. But many are close enough so we can talk about "almost" pure competition situations—those in which the marketing manager has to accept the going price.

Such highly competitive situations aren't limited to agriculture. Wherever *many* competitors sell *homogeneous* products—such as textiles, lumber, coal, printing, and laundry services—the demand curve seen by *each producer* tends to be flat.

Markets tend to become more competitive, moving toward pure competition (except in oligopolies—see below). On the way to pure competition, prices and profits are pushed down until some competitors are forced out of business. Eventually, in long-run equilibrium, the price level is only high enough to keep the survivors in business. No one makes any profit—they just cover costs. It's tough to be a marketing manager in this situation!

When competition is oligopolistic

A few competitors offer similar things

Not all markets move toward pure competition. Some become oligopolies.

Oligopoly situations are special market situations that develop when a market has:

1. Essentially homogeneous products—such as basic industrial chemicals or gasoline.

Hammermill would like to avoid head-on competition from other paper producers, but that is difficult if potential customers view the products as essentially similar.

2. Relatively few sellers—or a few large firms and many smaller ones who follow the lead of the larger ones.
3. Fairly inelastic industry demand curves.

It's important to keep in mind that oligopoly situations don't just apply to whole industries and national markets. Competitors who are focusing on the same local target market often face oligopoly situations. A suburban community might have several gas stations—all of whom provide essentially the same product. In this case, the "industry" consists of the gas stations competing with each other in the local product-market.

The demand curve facing each firm is unusual in an oligopoly situation. Although the industry demand curve is inelastic throughout the relevant range, the demand curve facing each competitor looks "kinked." See Exhibit 4–4. The current market price is at the kink.

There is a market price because the competing firms watch each other carefully—and know it's wise to be at the kink. Each marketing manager must expect that raising his own price above the market price will cause a big loss in sales. Few, if any, competitors will follow his price increase. So his demand curve is relatively flat above the market price. If he lowers his price, he must expect competitors to follow. Given inelastic industry demand, his own demand curve is inelastic at lower prices—assuming he keeps "his share" of this market at lower prices. Since lowering prices along such a curve will drop total revenue, he should leave his price at the kink—the market price.

Actually, however, there are price fluctuations in oligopolistic markets. Sometimes this is caused by firms that don't understand the market situation and cut their prices to get business. In other cases, big increases in demand or supply change the basic nature of the situation and lead to price cutting. Price cuts can

Exhibit 4–4   Oligopoly—Kinked Demand Curve—Situation

A. Industry situation

B. Each firm's view
of its demand curve

(smaller than industry quantity)

be drastic—such as Du Pont's price cut of 25 percent for Dacron. This happened when Du Pont decided that industry production capacity already exceeded demand, and more plants were due to start production.

As in pure competition, oligopolists face a long-run trend toward an equilibrium level—with profits driven toward zero. This may not happen immediately—and a marketing manager may try to delay price competition by relying more on other elements in the marketing mix. For example, Clorox Bleach uses the same basic chemicals as other bleaches. But marketing managers for Clorox may help to set it apart from other bleaches by offering an improved pouring spout, with ads that demonstrate its stain-killing power, or by getting it better shelf positions in supermarkets. This approach is extremely difficult, however. In oligopoly situations there is little to prevent competitors from imitating the leader. If potential customers view the products as essentially similar, a firm must rely on lower costs to obtain a competitive advantage.

**When competition is
monopolistic**

A price must be set

You can see why marketing managers want to avoid pure competition or oligopoly situations. They prefer a market in which they have more control. **Monopolistic competition** is a market situation that develops when a market has:

1. Different (heterogeneous) products—in the eyes of some customers.
2. Sellers who feel they do have some competition in this market.

The word *monopolistic* means that each firm is trying to get control in its own little market. But the word *competition* means that there are still substitutes. The vigorous competition of a purely competitive market is reduced. Each firm has its own down-sloping demand curve. But the shape of the curve depends on the similarity of competitors' products and marketing mixes. Each monopolistic competitor has freedom—but not complete freedom—in its own market.

Judging elasticity will help set the price

Since a firm in monopolistic competition has its own down-sloping demand curve, it must make a decision about price level as part of its marketing strategy planning. Here, estimating the elasticity of the firm's own demand curve is helpful. If it is highly inelastic, the firm may decide to raise prices to increase total revenue. But if demand is highly elastic, this may mean many competitors with acceptable substitutes. Then the price may have to be set near that of the competition. And the marketing manager probably should try to develop a better marketing mix.

Why compete in pure competition?

Why would anyone compete in profitless pure competition? One reason is that the firm is already in the industry. Or the firm enters without knowing what's happening—and must stick it out until it runs out of money. Production-oriented firms are more likely to make such a mistake.

Another reason that marketing managers find themselves in perfect competition is that they have not stopped to anticipate how current or potential competitors will react to a new strategy. If no other firm has identified a potential opportunity, it may appear attractive on the surface. It's easy to make the mistake of assuming that there won't be competition in the future—or of discounting how aggressive competition may become. The problem is that a successful strategy will attract the interest of others who are eager to jump in for a share of the profit—even if profits only hold up for a short time. That is why it is important to find opportunities where you can sustain a competitive advantage over the longer run.

Avoiding pure competition is sensible—and certainly fits with our emphasis on target marketing. In fact, the reasons for avoiding pure competition help explain why learning about effective target marketing is fundamentally different than learning about effective decision making in other areas of business. Accounting, production, and financial managers for competing firms can learn about and use the same, standardized approaches—and they will work well in each case. By contrast, marketing managers for competing firms can't just learn about and adopt the same "good" marketing strategy. That would just lead to head-on competition.

Pure competition cannot always be avoided

Despite their desire to avoid pure competition, some firms find that they can't. In some industries, new firms keep entering—replacing the casualties—possibly because they don't have more attractive alternatives and can at least earn a living. Examples include small retailers and wholesalers—especially in less-developed economies. Also, farmers continually try to shift their production to more profitable crops, but since there are many thousands of other farmers making similar choices, almost pure competition is typical.

ECONOMIC ENVIRONMENT

The **economic and technological environment** affects the way firms—and the whole economy—use resources. We will treat the economic and technological environments separately to emphasize that the technological environment provides a *base* for the economic environment. Technical skills and equipment affect the way an economy's resources are converted into output. The economic environment, on the other hand, is affected by the way all of the parts of our macro-economic system interact. This, then, affects such things as national income, economic growth, and inflation.

Economic conditions change rapidly

The economic environment can—and does—change quite rapidly. The effects can be far reaching—and require changes in marketing strategy.

Even a well-planned marketing strategy may fail if the country goes through a rapid business decline. As consumers' incomes drop, they must shift their spending patterns. They may simply have to do without some products. Many companies aren't strong enough to survive such bad times.

Inflation and interest rates affect buying

Inflation is a fact of life in many economies. Some Latin American countries have had from 25 to 100 percent inflation per year for many years. In contrast, the 6 to 20 percent levels reached in recent years in the United States sound "low." Still, inflation must be considered in strategy planning. It can lead to government policies that reduce income, employment, *and* consumer spending.

The government-encouraged recession of 1980–83 was the most severe since the Great Depression of the 1930s. But it was generally agreed that some pulling back was necessary to stop spiraling prices. Exhibit 4–5 shows how rapidly the cost of living rose in the 1970s—and why the government chose such drastic action in 1980. After that, inflation subsided. Many experts expect the inflation rate to increase again in the near future.

The interest rate—the charge for borrowing money—affects the total price borrowers must pay for products. So the interest rate affects when—and if—they will buy. This is an especially important factor in some industrial markets. But it also affects consumer purchases, especially for homes, cars, and other "high-ticket" items usually bought on credit.

The global economy is connected

In the past, marketing managers often focused their attention on the economy of their home country. It's no longer that simple. The economies of the world are connected—and at an increasing pace changes in one economy affect others. One reason for this is that the amount of international trade is increasing—and it is affected by changes in and between economies.

Changes in the *exchange rate*—how much our dollar is worth in another country's money—have an important effect on international trade. When the "dollar is

Exhibit 4–5   Rising Cost of Living in the United States, 1950–1986 (using consumer price index, 1967 = 100)

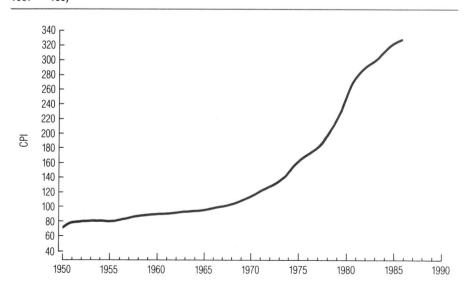

strong," it's worth more in foreign countries. This sounds good—but it makes U.S. products more expensive overseas and foreign products cheaper in the United States. Companies like Caterpillar (tractors) lose foreign customers to producers from other countries. A marketing manager isn't safe from these forces just because his firm is not involved in foreign trade. Here at home, new competition arises as foreign products gain a competitive edge due to their lower prices. Many companies find themselves helpless during such economic change. In fact, a country's whole economic system can change as the balance of imports and exports shifts—affecting jobs, consumer income, and national productivity.

You can see that the marketing manager must watch the economic environment carefully. In contrast to the cultural and social environment, economic conditions change continuously. And they can move rapidly—up or down—requiring strategic responses.

TECHNOLOGICAL ENVIRONMENT

The technological base affects opportunities

Underlying any economic environment is the **technological base**—the technical skills and equipment that affect the way an economy's resources are converted to output. Technological developments certainly affect marketing. Many argue, for example, that we are moving from an industrial society to an information society. Telecommunications make possible mass promotion via radio, TV, and telephone—reducing the relative importance of other media. Computers allow more sophisticated planning and control of business. And we are in the middle of an explosion of "hi-tech" products—from robots in factories to home refrigerators that "talk."

As we move through the text, you should see that some of the big advances in business have come from early recognition of new ways to do things. Marketers

Rapid changes in information technology are creating many new market opportunities.

should help their firms see such opportunities by trying to understand the "why" of present markets—and what is keeping their firms from being more successful. Then, as new technological developments come along, they will be alert to possible uses of those technologies—and see how opportunities can be turned into profits.

The rapid pace of technological change opens up new opportunities, but it also poses challenges for marketers. For many firms, success hinges on how quickly new ideas can be brought to market. It's easy for a firm to slip into a production orientation in the flush of excitement that follows a new discovery in a research and development lab. That makes it more important than ever for marketing thinking to guide the production process—starting at the beginning with decisions about where basic R&D effort will be focused.

Marketers must also help their firms decide what technical developments will be acceptable to society. With the growing concern about environmental pollution and the quality of life, some attractive technological developments may be rejected because of their long-run effects on the environment. Perhaps what's good for the firm and the economy's economic growth may not be good for the cultural and social environment—or be acceptable in the political and legal environment. A marketer's closeness to the market should give him a better feel for current trends—and help his firm avoid serious mistakes.[8]

POLITICAL ENVIRONMENT

The attitudes and reactions of people, social critics, and governments all affect the political environment.

Consumerism is here—and basic

Consumerism is a social movement that seeks to increase the rights and powers of consumers. In the last 30 years, consumerism has emerged as a major political force. The basic goals of modern consumerism haven't changed much since 1962 when President Kennedy's "Consumer Bill of Rights" affirmed consumers' rights to safety, to be informed, to choose, and to be heard.

Twenty years ago, consumerism was much more visible. There were frequent consumer boycotts, protest marches, and much media attention. Today, consumer groups provide information and work on special projects, like product safety standards. Publications like *Consumer Reports* provide product comparisons and information on other consumer concerns.

Business is responding to public expectations

Many companies have responded to the spirit of consumerism. For example, Chrysler has adopted a consumer bill of rights and Ford has set up a "consumer board" to help resolve consumer complaints. Many firms have established a consumer affairs position to directly represent consumer interests within the company.

Clearly, top management—and marketing managers—must continue to pay attention to consumer concerns. The old, production-oriented ways of doing things are no longer acceptable.[9]

Nationalism can be limiting in international markets

Strong sentiments of **nationalism**—an emphasis on a country's interests before everything else—may also affect the work of some marketing managers. These feelings can reduce sales—or even block all marketing activity—in some international markets. For many years, Japan has made it difficult for U.S. firms to do

Wal-Mart, a mass-merchandiser chain, promotes its "Buy American" policy.

business there—in spite of the fact that the Japanese producers of cars, color TVs, VCRs, and other products have established profitable markets in the United States.

The "Buy American" policy in many government contracts and business purchases reflects this same attitude in the United States. And there is support for protecting U.S. producers from foreign competition—especially producers of footwear, textiles, production machinery, and cars.

Nationalistic feelings can determine whether a firm can enter markets because businesses often must get permission to operate. In some political environments, this is only a routine formality. In others, a lot of red tape and personal influence are involved, and bribes are sometimes expected. This raises ethical issues for marketing managers—and legal issues too—since it's illegal for U.S. firms to offer such bribes. Clearly, that can make it difficult for a U.S. firm to compete with a company from a country that doesn't have similar laws.

Political environment may offer new opportunities

The political environment is not always antibusiness. Some governments (like the People's Republic of China) decide that encouraging business is good for their people. These countries encourage foreign investors.

Within the United States, special programs and financial incentives have been established to encourage urban redevelopment and minority business. Government loan guarantees made it possible for troubled firms—Lockheed and Chrysler—to develop profitable new marketing strategies. State and local governments also try to attract and hold businesses—sometimes with tax incentives.

Some business managers have become very successful by studying the political environment and developing strategies that use these political opportunities.

LEGAL ENVIRONMENT

Changes in the political environment often lead to changes in the legal environment—and in the way existing laws are enforced.

Trying to encourage competition

American economic and legislative thinking is based on the idea that competition among many small firms helps the economy. Therefore, attempts by business to limit competition are thought to be against the public interest.

As industries grew larger after the Civil War, some became monopolies controlled by wealthy businessmen—the "robber barons." This made it hard for smaller producers to survive. A movement grew—especially among Midwestern farmers—to control monopolists.

Beginning in 1890, a series of laws were passed that were basically antimonopoly or procompetition. The names and dates of these laws are shown in Exhibit 4–6.

Antimonopoly law and marketing mix planning

Specific application of antimonopoly law to the four Ps will be presented in later chapters. For our discussion here, you should know what kind of proof the government must have to get a conviction under each of the major laws. You should also know which of the four Ps are most affected by each law. Exhibit 4–7 provides such a summary—with a phrase following each law to show what the government must prove to get a conviction. Note how the wording of the laws is moving toward protecting consumers.

Prosecution is serious— you can go to jail

Businesses and *business managers* are subject to both criminal and civil laws. Penalties for breaking civil laws are limited to blocking or forcing certain actions— along with fines. Where criminal law applies, jail sentences can be imposed. For example, several managers at Beech-Nut Nutrition Company were recently fined $100,000 each and sentenced to a year in jail. In spite of unfair ads claiming that Beech-Nut's apple juice was 100 percent natural, they tried to bolster profits by secretly using low cost artificial juices. The people responsible paid a price for bad judgment, and so did the firm. The bad publicity from the incident resulted in a big drop in Beech-Nut sales.[10]

Exhibit 4–6   Outline of Federal Legislation Now Affecting Competition in Marketing

Year	Antimonopoly (procompetition)	Anticompetition	Antispecific practices
1890	Sherman Act		
1914	Clayton Act Federal Trade Commission Act		Clayton Act
1936	Robinson-Patman Act	Robinson-Patman Act	Robinson-Patman Act
1938			Wheeler-Lea Amendment
1950	Antimerger Act		Antimerger Act
1975	Magnuson-Moss Act		Magnuson-Moss Act

Exhibit 4–7   Focus (mostly prohibitions) of Federal Antimonopoly Laws on the Four Ps

Law	Product	Place	Promotion	Price
Sherman Act (1890) Monopoly or conspiracy in restraint of trade	Monopoly or conspiracy to control a product	Monopoly or conspiracy to control distribution channels		Monopoly or conspiracy to fix or control prices
Clayton Act (1914) Substantially lessens competition	Forcing sale of some products with others—tying contracts	Exclusive dealing contracts (limiting buyers' sources of supply)		Price discrimination by manufacturers
Federal Trade Commission Act (1914) Unfair methods of competition		Unfair policies	Deceptive ads or selling practices	Deceptive pricing
Robinson-Patman Act (1936) Tends to injure competition		Prohibits paying allowances to "direct" buyers in lieu of middlemen costs (brokerage charges)	Prohibits "fake" advertising allowances or discrimination in help offered	Prohibits price discrimination on goods of "like grade and quality" without cost justification, and limits quantity discounts
Wheeler-Lea Amendment (1938) Unfair or deceptive practices	Deceptive packaging or branding		Deceptive ads or selling claims	Deceptive pricing
Antimerger Act (1950) Lessens competition	Buying competitors	Buying producers or distributors		
Magnuson-Moss Act (1975) Unreasonable practices	Product warranties			

Consumer protection laws are not new

There is more to the legal environment than just the antimonopoly laws. Some consumer protections are built into the English and U.S. common law system. A seller has to tell the truth (if asked a direct question), meet contracts, and stand behind the firm's product (to some reasonable extent). Beyond this, it is expected that vigorous competition in the marketplace will protect consumers—*so long as they are careful.*

Focusing only on competition didn't protect consumers very well in some areas, however. So the government found it necessary to pass other laws—usually involving specific types of products.

Foods and drugs are controlled

Consumer protection laws go back at least to 1906, when the Pure Food and Drug Act was passed. Unsanitary meat-packing practices in the Chicago stockyards stirred consumer support for this act. After much debate, Congress decided to pass a general law to control the quality and labeling of food and drugs in inter-state commerce. This was a major victory for consumer protection. Before the law, it was assumed that common law and the old warning "let the buyer beware" would take care of consumers.

Later acts corrected some loopholes in the law. The law now bans the shipment of unsanitary and poisonous products and requires much testing of drugs. The Food and Drug Administration (FDA) attempts to control manufacturers of these products. It can seize products that violate its rules—including regulations on branding and labeling.

In general, the FDA has done a good job. But complaints over a proposal to ban the use of saccharin—commonly used to sweeten diet soft drinks—forced the government to rethink how much protection consumers really want. In this case, many users felt that the government should first ban the use of other products whose bad effects had been more thoroughly proven—such as alcohol and cigarettes.

Product safety is controlled

The Consumer Product Safety Act (of 1972) is another important consumer protection law—it set up the Consumer Product Safety Commission. This group has broad power to set safety standards and can impose penalties for failure to meet these standards. Again, there is some question as to how much safety consumers really want—the Commission found the bicycle the most hazardous product under its control!

But given that the Commission has the power to *force* a product off the market—or require expensive recalls to correct problems—it is obvious that safety

---

The government regulates the marketing of many goods and services.

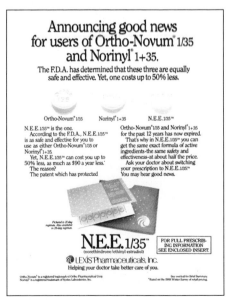

must be considered in product design. This uncontrollable variable must be treated seriously by marketing managers.[11]

State and local laws vary

Besides federal legislation—which affects interstate commerce—marketers must be aware of state and local laws. There are state and city laws regulating minimum prices and the setting of prices, regulations for starting up a business (licenses, examinations, and even tax payments), and in some communities, regulations prohibiting certain activities—such as door-to-door selling or selling on Sundays or during evenings.

Consumerists and the law say, "Let the seller beware"

The old rule about buyer-seller relations—*let the buyer beware*—has shifted to *let the seller beware*. The shift to proconsumer laws and court decisions suggests that there is more interest now in protecting consumers rather than competition. This may upset production-oriented managers. But times have changed—and managers will just have to adapt to this new political and legal environment.[12]

Know the laws—follow the courts and federal agencies

Often, laws are vaguely phrased by legislators—to convey intent but not specific detail. It's then up to the courts and government agencies to spell out the details. As a result, the way a law is interpreted and enforced sometimes changes over time. For example, during the last 10 years government agencies have been less interested in regulating business firms and instead have focused more attention on encouraging competition.

Because legislation must be interpreted by federal agencies and the courts, you should carefully study both legislative developments and the thinking of the courts and agencies. See Exhibit 4–8 for a description of some important federal regulatory agencies that should be considered in marketing strategy planning.

If marketing managers have a better understanding of the intent of the lawmakers and interpreters, there will be less conflict between business and government—and fewer costly mistakes. Managers should accept the political and

Exhibit 4–8   Some Important Federal Regulatory Agencies

Agencies	Responsibilities
Federal Trade Commission (FTC)	Enforces laws and develops guidelines regarding unfair business practices
Food and Drug Administration (FDA)	Enforces laws and develops regulations to prevent distribution and sale of adulterated or misbranded foods, drugs, cosmetics, and hazardous consumer products
Consumer Product Safety Commission (CPSC)	Enforces the Consumer Product Safety Act—which covers any consumer product not assigned to other regulatory agencies
Interstate Commerce Commission (ICC)	Regulates interstate rail, bus, truck, and water carriers
Federal Communications Commission (FCC)	Regulates interstate wire, radio, and television
Environmental Protection Agency (EPA)	Develops and enforces environmental protection standards
Office of Consumer Affairs (OCA)	Handles consumers' complaints

legal environment as simply another framework in which business must function. After all, it is the consumers—through their government representatives—who determine the kind of economic system they want.

CULTURAL AND SOCIAL ENVIRONMENT

The **cultural and social environment** affects how and why people live and behave as they do—which affects customer buying behavior and eventually the economic, political, and legal environment. Since we will discuss how the cultural and social environment relates to buying behavior in Chapters 6 through 8, we will present only a few examples here to emphasize the possible impact of this variable on marketing strategy planning.

A trend toward health and fitness

In the last decade, the American culture has put much more emphasis on health and fitness. There is concern, for example, about the amount of salt, calories, and fiber in diets—so many firms now offer "salt-free" or "low-cal" or "high-fiber" food products. Responding to such consumer interests can be profitable. A California egg producer who bred a flock of chickens to lay low-cholesterol eggs has a hard-boiled success with eggs that sell at about three times the normal price.

The fitness emphasis also sparked interest in a wide range of exercise-related products—and the growth of companies such as Nike (athletic shoes), Nautilus (exercise equipment), and Schwinn (bicycles, exercise cycles).

Identifying how best to work with cultural changes sometimes requires creativity. Some people might not see a link between paper towels and health—but marketing managers for Bounty paper towels did. Wrapping meats and vegetables in a wet paper towel to steam cook them in a microwave oven eliminates the need to add butter or margarine. Bounty developed new ads and packaging to remind con-

Increased interest in health and fitness has created new opportunities for Schwinn.

Where's the Beef?

Health-conscious U.S. consumers have been switching from beef to chicken and fish. From 1976 to 1988, per capita beef consumption fell 23 percent—and poultry consumption rose 60 percent. To fight this trend, beef producers banded together and spent $23 million on an ad campaign. Celebrities like James Garner and Cybill Shepherd confessed their craving for beef and touted it as "real food for real people." In a culture where consumers want less fat and cholesterol in their food, the ads didn't have much effect. It also didn't help that Mr. Garner made the news with heart trouble. Most beef products are still being outflanked by market-oriented poultry firms—like

Holly Farms and Perdue Chickens. They are giving consumers what they want—healthy food *and* convenience at a reasonable price—with new products like precooked chicken nuggets and chicken fingers that are ready for microwave heating. A few beef producers, however, are waking up to the marketing concept. Rather than just expecting advertising to sell what they are producing, they're responding to trends in the external environment. For example, they are developing new feeds so that the cattle will have less fat. They are cutting the meat into smaller, healthier servings—trimming fat and bones before packaging it. Prepackaging also reduces butcher expenses at supermarkets—and helps to make beef prices more competitive.[13]

sumers of this idea—and to inform them that Bounty towels were specifically designed to work well for that purpose.[14]

Changes come slowly

Changes in basic cultural values and social attitudes come slowly. An individual firm can't hope to encourage big changes in the short run. Instead, it should identify current attitudes and work within these constraints—as it seeks new and better opportunities.

HOW TO EVALUATE OPPORTUNITIES

A progressive firm is constantly looking for new opportunities. Once some opportunities have been identified, they must be screened and evaluated. Usually, it isn't possible for a firm to pursue all of its opportunities, so it must try to match its opportunities to its resources and objectives. The first step is to quickly screen out the obvious mismatches. Then, the others can be analyzed more carefully. Let's look at some approaches for screening and evaluating opportunities.

Developing and applying screening criteria

After you analyze the firm's resources (for strengths and weaknesses), the environmental trends the firm faces, and the objectives of top management, you merge them all into a set of product-market screening criteria. These criteria should include both quantitative and qualitative components. The quantitative components summarize the firm's objectives: sales, profit, and return on investment (ROI) targets. (Note: ROI analysis is discussed briefly in Appendix B, which follows Chapter 18.) The qualitative components summarize what kinds of businesses the firm wants to be in, what businesses it wants to exclude, what weaknesses it should avoid, and what resources (strengths) and trends it should build on.[15]

Developing screening criteria is difficult—but worth the effort. They summarize in one place what the firm wants to accomplish—in quantitative terms—as well as roughly how and where it wants to accomplish it. The criteria should be realistic—that is, they should be achievable. Opportunities that pass the screen should be able to be turned into strategies that the firm can implement with the resources it has.

Exhibit 4–9 illustrates the product-market screening criteria for a small sales company (retailer and wholesaler). These criteria help the firm's managers eliminate unsuitable opportunities—and find attractive ones to turn into strategies and plans.

Whole plans should be evaluated

You need to forecast the probable results of implementing whole product-market strategic plans to apply the quantitative part of the screening criteria because it is implemented plans that generate sales, profits, and return on investment (ROI). For a rough screening, you only need to estimate the likely results of implementing each opportunity over a logical planning period. If a product's life is likely to be three years, for example, then a good strategy may not produce profitable results during the first six months to a year. But evaluated over the projected three-year life, the product may look like a winner. When evaluating the potential of possible opportunities (product-market strategic plans) it is important to evaluate similar things—that is, *whole* plans.

Exhibit 4–9   An Example of Product-Market Screening Criteria for a Sales Company (retail and wholesale—$5 million annual sales)

1. **Quantitative criteria**
   a. Increase sales by $750,000 per year for the next five years.
   b. Earn ROI of at least 25 percent before taxes on new ventures.
   c. Break even within one year on new ventures.
   d. Opportunity must be large enough to justify interest (to help meet objectives) but small enough so company can handle with the resources available.
   e. Several opportunities should be needed to reach the objectives—to spread the risks.

2. **Qualitative criteria**
   a. Nature of business preferred.
      (1) Goods and services sold to present customers.
      (2) "Quality" products that can be sold at "high prices" with full margins.
      (3) Competition should be weak and opportunity should be hard to copy for several years.
      (4) Should build on our strong sales skills.
      (5) There should be strongly felt (even unsatisfied) needs—to reduce promotion costs and permit "high" prices.
   b. Constraints.
      (1) Nature of businesses to exclude.
         (a) Manufacturing.
         (b) Any requiring large fixed capital investments.
         (c) Any requiring many people who must be "good" all the time and would require much supervision (e.g., "quality" restaurant).
      (2) Geographic.
         (a) United States and Canada only.
      (3) General.
         (a) Make use of current strengths
         (b) Attractiveness of market should be reinforced by more than one of the following basic trends: technological, demographic, social, economic, political.
         (c) Market should not be bucking any basic trends.

Opportunities that pass the screen—or all opportunities, if screening criteria are not used—should be evaluated in more detail before being accepted as *the* product-market strategic plans for implementation. Usually, there are more opportunities than resources, and you have to choose among them—to match the firm's opportunities to its resources and objectives. The following approaches can be useful in selecting among possible strategic plans.

Total profit approach can help evaluate possible plans

The total profit approach to evaluating plans requires forecasts of potential sales and costs during the life of the plan to estimate likely profitability.

The prospects for each plan may be evaluated over a five-year planning period, with monthly and/or annual estimates of sales and costs. This is shown graphically in Exhibit 4–10.

Note that quite different marketing plans can be evaluated at the same time. In this case, a much improved product and product concept (Product A) is being compared with a "me-too" product for the same target market. In the short run, the "me-too" product will make a profit sooner and might look like the better choice—if only one year's results are considered. The improved product, on the other hand, will take a good deal of pioneering—but over its five-year life will be much more profitable.

Return-on-investment (ROI) approach can help evaluate possible plans, too

Besides evaluating the profit potential of possible plans, you may also want to calculate the return on investment (ROI) of resources needed to implement plans. One plan may require a heavy investment in advertising and channel development, for example, while another relies primarily on lower price.

ROI analyses can be useful for selecting among possible plans because equally profitable plans may require vastly different resources and offer different rates of return on investment. Some firms are very concerned with ROI. Such firms may borrow money for working capital, and there is little point in borrowing to implement strategies that won't even return enough to meet the cost of borrowing.

PLANNING GRIDS HELP EVALUATE A PORTFOLIO OF OPPORTUNITIES

When a firm has many possibilities to evaluate, it usually has to compare quite different ones. This problem is easier to handle with graphical approaches—such

Exhibit 4–10   Expected Sales and Cost Curves of Two Strategies over Five-Year Planning Periods

as the nine-box strategic planning grid developed by General Electric and used by many other companies. Such grids can help evaluate a firm's whole portfolio of strategic plans or businesses.

General Electric looks for green positions

General Electric's strategic planning grid—see Exhibit 4–11—forces company managers to make three-part judgments (high, medium, and low) about the business strengths and industry attractiveness of all proposed or existing product-market plans. As you can see from Exhibit 4–11, this approach helps a manager organize information about the company's uncontrollable environments (discussed earlier in this chapter) along with information about its strategy.

The industry attractiveness dimension helps managers answer the question: "Does this product-market plan look like a good idea?" The answer is influenced by judgments about factors such as the size of the market and its growth rate, the nature of competition, the potential environmental or social impact of the plan, and how laws might affect it. Note that an opportunity may be attractive for *some* company—but not well suited to the strengths (and weaknesses) of a particular firm. That is why the GE grid also considers the business strengths dimension.

The business strengths dimension focuses on the ability of the company to pursue a product-market plan effectively. To make judgments along this dimension, a manager evaluates whether the firm has people with the right talents and skills to implement the plan, if the plan is consistent with the firm's image and profit objectives, and if the firm could establish a profitable market share given its technical capability, costs, and size.

GE feels that opportunities that fall into the green boxes in the upper left-hand corner of the grid are its growth opportunities. Managers give these opportunities high marks on both industry attractiveness and business strengths. The red boxes in the lower right-hand corner of the grid, on the other hand, suggest a no-growth policy. Existing red businesses may continue to generate earnings, but GE figures they no longer deserve much investment. The yellow businesses are the borderline cases—they can go either way. An existing yellow business may be continued and supported, but a proposal for a new yellow business has a greater chance of being rejected by top management.

Exhibit 4–11   General Electric's Strategic Planning Grid

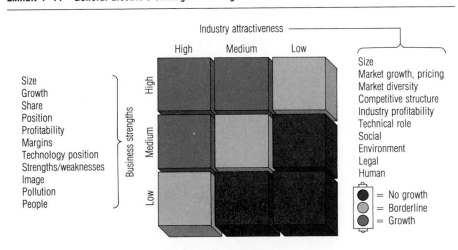

GE's "stop light" evaluation method is a very subjective, multiple-factor approach. GE has concluded that there are too many traps and possible errors if it tries to use oversimplified, single-number criteria—like ROI and market share—for judging "attractiveness" or "strength." Instead, top managers review written summaries of about a dozen factors that help them make summary judgments. Then they make a collective judgment. The approach generally leads to agreement and, further, a good understanding about why some businesses or new opportunities are supported while others are not. Further, it appears that high-high green businesses are uniformly good on almost any quantitative or qualitative measure used. This interaction among the relevant variables makes it practical to blend them all into a "stop light" framework.[16]

Factors can change to reflect objectives

The various factors General Electric considers reflect its objectives. The various "business strength" factors are related to the size of business GE wants to be in—and the business' growth potential and profitability. The "industry attractiveness" variables also reflect GE's objectives to be involved in industries where the firm has a good chance of growth and profitability—while still contributing to the economy. Of course, another firm might modify the evaluation to put more emphasis on other factors—depending on its objectives and the type of product-market plans it is considering. While attention to specific factors may change depending on the firm, the use of many factors helps ensure that all the company's concerns are considered when its managers are evaluating alternative opportunities.

MULTIPRODUCT FIRMS HAVE A DIFFICULT STRATEGY PLANNING JOB

Multiproduct firms—like General Electric—obviously have a more difficult strategic planning job than a firm with only a few products or product lines aimed at the same or similar target markets. They have to develop strategic plans for very different businesses. And they must try to balance the plans and needed resources in such a way that the whole company reaches its objectives. This requires analyses of the various alternatives, using approaches similar to the General Electric strategic planning grid, and approval of strategic plans that make sense for the whole company—even if it means getting needed resources by "milking" some businesses and eliminating others.

Details on how to manage such a complicated firm are beyond our scope. But you should be aware (1) that there are such firms and (2) that the principles in this text are applicable—they just have to be extended. For example, some firms use strategic business units (SBUs), and some use portfolio management.

Strategic business units may help

Some multiproduct firms have tried to improve their operations by forming strategic business units. A **strategic business unit (SBU)** is an organizational unit (within a larger company) that focuses its efforts on some product-markets and is treated as a separate profit center. Forming SBUs formally recognizes that a company is composed of quite different activities. Sara Lee, for example, has an SBU that produces baked goods that sell to consumers and restaurants—and another SBU that produces and markets Hanes brand T-shirts and underwear.

Some SBUs may be growing rapidly and require a great deal of attention and resources. Others may only be in the middle in terms of profitability and should be "milked"—that is, they should be allowed to generate cash for the businesses with more potential. There also may be product lines with poor market position, low profits, and poor growth prospects. These should be dropped or sold.

Companies that set up strategic business units usually do change their attitudes and methods of operation. Managers are rated in terms of achieving their strategic plans—rather than short-term profits or sales increases. With SBUs, the emphasis is on developing plans, which, when accepted, are implemented aggressively. Under this concept, some managers are rewarded for successfully phasing out product lines, while other managers are moving ahead aggressively—expanding sales in other markets.

The point here is that each manager is carrying out a market-oriented strategic plan approved by top management. The manager's job is to help develop effective plans and then implement them to ensure that the company's resources are used effectively—and that the firm accomplishes its objectives.

Some firms use portfolio management

Some top managements handle strategic planning for a multiproduct firm with an approach called **portfolio management**—which treats alternative products, divisions, or strategic business units (SBUs) as though they were stock investments, to be bought and sold using financial criteria. Such managers make trade-offs among very different opportunities. They treat the various alternatives as investments that should be supported, "milked," or sold off—depending on profitability and return on investment (ROI). In effect, they evaluate each alternative just like a stock market trader evaluates a stock.[17]

This approach makes some sense if the alternatives are really quite different. Top managers feel they can't become very familiar with the prospects for all of their alternatives. So they fall back on the easy-to-compare quantitative criteria. And because the short run is much clearer than the long run, they place heavy emphasis on *current* profitability and return on investment. This puts great pressure on the operating managers to "deliver" *in the short run*—perhaps even neglecting the long run.

Neglecting the long run is risky—and this is the main weakness of the portfolio approach. This weakness can be overcome by enhancing the portfolio management approach with market-oriented strategic plans. They make it possible for managers to more accurately evaluate the alternatives' short-run and long-run prospects.

CONCLUSION

Innovative strategy planning is needed for survival in our increasingly competitive markets. In this chapter, we discussed the uncontrollable environments and how they affect marketing strategy planning. We saw how the firm's own resources and objectives may help guide or limit the search for opportunities. Then, we went on to look at the rest of the uncontrollable variables. They are important because changes in these environments present new opportunities—as well as problems—that a marketing manager must deal with in marketing strategy planning.

A manager must study the competitive environment. How well established are competitors? What action might they take? What is the nature of competition: pure, oligopolistic, or monopolistic?

The economic environment—including chances of recessions or inflation—also affects the choice of strategies. And the marketer must try to anticipate, understand, and deal with these changes—as well as changes in the technological base underlying the economic environment.

The marketing manager must also be aware of legal restrictions—and be sensitive to changing political climates. The acceptance of consumerism has already forced many changes.

The social and cultural environment affects how people behave—and what marketing strategies will be successful.

Developing good marketing strategies within all these uncontrollable environments isn't easy. You can see that marketing management is a challenging job that requires much integration of information from many disciplines.

Eventually, procedures are needed for screening and evaluating opportunities. We explained an

approach for developing screening criteria—from an analysis of the strengths and weaknesses of the company's resources, the environmental trends it faces, and top management's objectives. We also considered some quantitative techniques for evaluating opportunities. And we discussed ways for evaluating and managing quite different opportunities—using the GE strategic planning grid, SBUs, and portfolio management.

Now we can go on—in the rest of the book—to discussing how to turn opportunities into profitable marketing plans and programs.

Questions and Problems

1. Explain how a firm's objectives may affect its search for opportunities.

2. Specifically, how would various company objectives affect the development of a marketing mix for a new type of baby shoe? If this company were just being formed by a former shoemaker with limited financial resources, list the objectives he might have. Then discuss how they would affect the development of his marketing strategy.

3. Explain how a firm's resources may limit its search for opportunities. Cite a specific example for a specific resource.

4. Discuss how a company's financial strength may have a bearing on the kinds of products it produces. Will it have an impact on the other three Ps as well? If so, how? Use an example in your answer.

5. If a manufacturer's well-known product is sold at the same price by many retailers in the same community, is this an example of pure competition? When a community has many small grocery stores, are they in pure competition? What characteristics are needed to have a purely competitive market?

6. List three products that are sold in purely competitive markets and three that are sold in monopolistically competitive markets. Do any of these products have anything in common? Can any generalizations be made about competitive situations and marketing mix planning?

7. Cite a local example of an oligopoly—explaining why it is an oligopoly.

8. Discuss the probable impact on your hometown of a major technological breakthrough in air transportation that would permit foreign producers to ship into any U.S. market for about the same transportation cost that domestic producers incur.

9. Which way does the U.S. political and legal environment seem to be moving (with respect to business-related affairs)?

10. Why is it necessary to have so many laws regulating business? Why hasn't Congress just passed one set of laws to take care of business problems?

11. What and who is the government attempting to protect in its effort to preserve and regulate competition?

12. For each of the *major* laws discussed in the text, indicate whether in the long run this law will promote or restrict competition (see Exhibit 4–7). As a consumer without any financial interest in business, what is your reaction to each of these laws?

13. Are consumer protection laws really new? Discuss the evolution of consumer protection. Is more such legislation likely?

14. Explain the components of product-market screening criteria—which can be used to evaluate opportunities.

15. Explain the differences between the total profit approach and the return-on-investment approach to evaluating alternative plans.

16. Explain General Electric's strategic planning grid approach to evaluating opportunities.

17. Distinguish between the operation of a strategic business unit and a firm that only pays lip service to adopting the marketing concept.

Suggested Cases _____

2. Alta Foods, Inc.

6. Inland Steel Company

Suggested Computer-Aided Problem _____

4. Company Resources

Chapter **5**

Getting Information for Marketing Decisions

When You Finish This Chapter, You Should

1. Know about marketing information systems.

2. Understand a scientific approach to marketing research.

3. Know how to define and solve marketing problems.

4. Know about getting secondary and primary data.

5. Understand the role of observing, questioning, and using experimental methods in marketing research.

6. Understand the important new terms (shown in red).

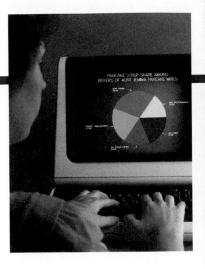

Marketing research isn't just to prove that you're right. It helps you find out.

Marketing managers at Kraft, Inc., faced a problem. Like many food producers, Kraft's marketing mix relies heavily on promotion. But managers were never certain what level of promotion spending was right. And the "right" level seemed to vary not only for different products, but also in different markets—depending on how Kraft stacked up against its competition.

To help its marketing managers plan better strategies, Kraft responded with a computerized information system. A manager can now use a special computer program to help him pick two markets that are very similar for a specific product—in terms of market share, sales volume, competition, promotion spending, and other factors. The manager can then vary the promotion level in one of the two matched markets. After data is collected for a month or two, the system can produce graphs that compare the sales and share in the two markets before and after the test. The system is effective and easy to use. Now, over 200 people from brand managers to sales reps—and even Kraft's ad agency people—are using the system. And Kraft is making better decisions faster.[1]

The Jacksonville Symphony Orchestra wanted to broaden its base of support and increase ticket sales. This required a marketing strategy to attract new audiences. To get better information about the opportunities, it hired a marketing research firm to conduct informal interviews with small groups of current subscribers, former subscribers, and qualified prospects. These interviews helped the marketing managers refine their ideas about what these target "customers" liked and did not like about the orchestra—and what kinds of music future audiences might want. These ideas were then tested with a larger, more representative sample. Interviewers telephoned 500 people and asked them how interested they would be in various orchestra programs, event locations, and guest artists.

The information from the research was carefully analyzed to plan the orchestra's program for the year—and to develop promotion to reach the new target audience. The result? Subscription ticket sales nearly doubled from the previous year.[2]

MARKETING MANAGERS NEED INFORMATION

These examples show that successful planning of marketing strategies requires information—information about potential target markets and their likely responses to marketing mixes as well as about competition and other uncontrollable variables. Information is also needed for implementation and control. Without good marketing information, managers have to use intuition or guesses—and in our fast-changing and competitive economy, this invites failure.

On the other hand, managers seldom have all the information they need to make the best decision. Both customers and competitors can be unpredictable. Getting more information may cost too much or take too long. So managers often must decide if they need more information and—if so—how to get it. In this chapter, we'll talk about how marketing managers can get the information they need to plan successful strategies.

MARKETING INFORMATION SYSTEMS CAN HELP

Marketing managers for some companies make decisions based almost totally on their own judgment—with very little hard data. When it's time to make a deci-

Claritas has developed decision support systems that make it easier for a marketing manager to work with a marketing information system.

sion, they may wish they had more information. But by then it's too late to do anything about it, so they do without.

MIS makes available data accessible

There is a difference between information that is *available* and information that is readily *accessible*. Some information is just not available—for example, details of competitors' plans. In other cases, information is available, but not without time-consuming collection. Such information is not really accessible. For example, a company may have records of customer purchases, what was sold by sales reps last month, or what is in the warehouse. But, if a manager can't get this information when he needs it, it isn't useful.

Some firms like Kraft have realized that it doesn't pay to wait until they have important questions they can't answer. They are working to develop a *continual flow of information*—and to make it more accessible to managers whenever they need it.

A **marketing information system (MIS)** is an organized way of continually gathering and analyzing data to provide marketing managers with information they need to make decisions. In some companies, an MIS is set up by marketing specialists. In other companies, it is set up by a group that provides *all* departments in the firm with information.

The technical details of setting up and running an MIS are beyond the scope of this course. But, you should understand what an MIS is so you know some of the possibilities. Exhibit 5-1 shows the elements of a complete MIS.

Marketing managers must help develop an MIS

Marketing managers often don't know in advance exactly what questions they will have—or when. But they do know what data they have routinely used or needed in the past. They can also foresee what types of data might be useful. They should communicate these needs to the MIS manager so the information will be there when they want it.

Exhibit 5–1   Elements of a Complete Marketing Information System

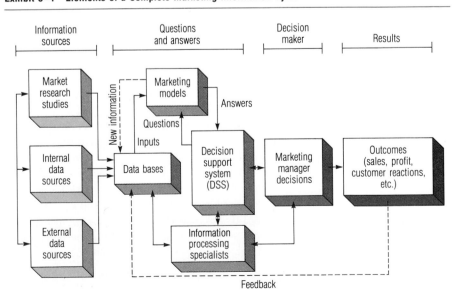

Decision support systems put managers "on-line"

An MIS system organizes incoming data in a data base so that it is available when it's needed. Most firms with an MIS have information processing specialists who help managers get standard reports and output from the data base.

To get better decisions, some MIS systems provide marketing managers with a decision support system. A **decision support system (DSS)** is a computer program that makes it easy for a marketing manager to get and use information *as he is making decisions*. Typically the DSS helps change raw data—like product sales for the previous day—into more *useful information*. For example, it may draw graphs to show relationships in data—perhaps comparing yesterday's sales to the sales on the same day in the last four weeks.

Some decision support systems go even further. They allow the manager to see how answers to questions might change in various situations. For example, a manager may want to estimate how much sales will increase if the firm expands into a new market area. The DSS will ask the manager for *his* judgment about how much business could be won from each competitor in that market. Then, using this input and drawing on data in the data base, the system will make an estimate using a marketing model. A **marketing model** is a statement of relationships among marketing variables. (Note: for more discussion on marketing models, see the discussion of "response functions" in Chapter 20.)

In short, the decision support system puts the individual manager "on-line" so he can study available data and make better marketing decisions—faster.[3]

Information makes managers greedy for more

Once marketing managers see how a functioning MIS—and perhaps a DSS—can help their decision making, they are eager for more information. They realize that they can improve all aspects of their planning—blending individual Ps, combining the four Ps into mixes, and developing and selecting plans. Further, they can monitor the implementation of current plans, comparing results against plans and making necessary changes more quickly. (Note: the sales and cost analysis techniques discussed in Chapter 21 are often used in an MIS.) Marketing information systems will become more widespread as managers become more sensitive to the possibilities and computer costs continue to drop.

Many firms are not there yet

Of course, not every firm has a complete MIS system. And in some firms that do, managers don't know how to use the system properly. A major problem is that many managers are used to doing it the "old way"—and they don't think through what information they need.

One sales manager thought he was progressive when he asked his assistant for an MIS report listing each sales rep's sales for the previous month and the current month. The assistant provided the report—but later was surprised to see the sales manager working on the list with a calculator. He was figuring the percentage change in sales for the month and ranking the reps from largest increase in sales to smallest. The computer could have done all of that—quickly—but the sales manager got what he *asked for*, not what he really needed. An MIS can provide information—but it is the marketing manager who knows what problem is to be solved. It's the job of the manager—not the computer or the MIS specialist—to ask for the right information in the right form.

MIS use is growing rapidly. Low-cost microcomputers make a powerful MIS affordable—even in small firms. And marketing information systems will become even more widespread as marketing becomes more sensitive to the possibilities.

There is a lot of opportunity for students who are able and willing to apply quantitative techniques to solve real marketing problems.[4]

New questions require new answers

Routinely analyzing incoming data can be valuable to marketing managers. But incoming data shouldn't be their only source of information for decision making. MIS systems tend to focus on recurring information needs. But marketing managers must try to satisfy ever-changing needs in dynamic markets. So marketing research must be used—to supplement the data already available in the MIS system.

WHAT IS MARKETING RESEARCH?

Research provides a bridge to customers

The marketing concept says that marketing managers should meet the needs of customers. Yet today, many marketing managers are isolated in company offices—far from potential customers. It is just not possible for managers to keep up with all of the changes taking place in their markets.

This means marketing managers have to rely on help from **marketing research**—procedures to develop and analyze new information to help marketing managers make decisions. One of the important jobs of a marketing researcher is to get the "facts" that are not currently available in the MIS.

Continued improvements in research methods are making marketing research information more dependable. This has encouraged firms to put more money and trust in research. Managers in some consumer product companies don't make any major decisions without the support—and sometimes even the official approval—of the marketing research department. As a result, some marketing research directors rise to high levels in the organization.

Who does the work?

Most large companies have a separate marketing research department to plan and carry out research projects. These departments often use outside specialists—including interviewing and tabulating services—to handle technical assignments. Further, specialized marketing consultants and marketing research organizations may be called in to take charge of a research project.

Small companies (those with less than $4 or $5 million in sales) usually don't have separate marketing research departments. They depend on salespeople or top managers to conduct what research they do.[5]

Effective research usually requires cooperation

Good marketing research requires much more than just technical tools. It requires cooperation between researchers and marketing managers. Good marketing researchers must keep both marketing research *and* marketing management in mind to be sure their research focuses on real problems.

Marketing managers must be involved in marketing research, too. Many marketing research details can be handled by company or outside experts. But marketing managers must be able to explain what their problems are—and what kinds of information they need. They should be able to communicate with specialists in the specialists' language. Marketing managers may only be "consumers" of research. But they should be informed consumers—able to explain exactly what they want from the research. They should also know about some of the basic decisions made during the research process so they know the limitations of the findings.

For this reason, our discussion of marketing research won't emphasize mechanics—but rather how to plan and evaluate the work of marketing researchers.[6]

THE SCIENTIFIC METHOD AND MARKETING RESEARCH

The scientific method—combined with the strategy planning framework we discussed in Chapter 2—can help marketing managers make better decisions.

The **scientific method** is a decision-making approach that focuses on being objective and orderly in *testing* ideas before accepting them. With the scientific method, managers don't just *assume* that their intuition is correct. Instead, they use their intuition and observations to develop **hypotheses**—educated guesses about the relationships between things or about what will happen in the future. Then, they test their hypotheses before making final decisions.

A manager who relies only on intuition might introduce a new product without testing consumer response. But a manager who uses the scientific method might say, "I think (hypothesize) that consumers currently using the most popular brand will prefer our new product. Let's run some consumer tests. If at least 60 percent of the consumers prefer our product, we can introduce it in a regional test market. If it doesn't pass the consumer test there, we can make some changes and try again."

The scientific method forces an orderly research process. Some managers don't carefully specify what information they need. They blindly move ahead—hoping that research will provide "the answer." Other managers may have a clearly defined problem or question but lose their way after that. These "hit-or-miss" approaches waste both time and money.

Carefully planned marketing research can help managers avoid costly errors.

FIVE–STEP APPROACH TO MARKETING RESEARCH

The **marketing research process** is a five-step application of the scientific method that includes:

1. Defining the problem.
2. Analyzing the situation.
3. Getting problem-specific data.
4. Interpreting the data.
5. Solving the problem.

Exhibit 5–2 shows the five steps in the process. Note that the process may lead to a solution before all of the steps are completed. Or, as the feedback arrows show, researchers may return to an earlier step if needed. For example, the interpreting step may point to a new question—or reveal the need for additional information—before a final decision can be made.

DEFINING THE PROBLEM—STEP 1

Defining the problem is the most important—and often the most difficult—step in the marketing research process. Sometimes it takes up over half the total time spent on a research project. But it's time well spent if the objectives of the research are clearly defined. The best research job on the wrong problem is wasted effort.

Finding the right problem level almost solves the problem

The strategy planning framework introduced in Chapter 2 can be useful here. It can help the researcher identify the real problem area—and what information is needed. Do we really know enough about our target markets to work out all of the four Ps? Do we know enough to decide what celebrity to use in an ad—or how to handle a price war in New York City or Tokyo? If not, we may want to do research rather than rely on intuition.

The importance of understanding the nature of the problem—and then trying to solve it—can be seen by looking at a Dr Pepper ad campaign that missed the target. Competition between Coke and Pepsi had heated up, and sales of Dr Pepper

Exhibit 5–2   Five-Step Scientific Approach to Marketing Research Process

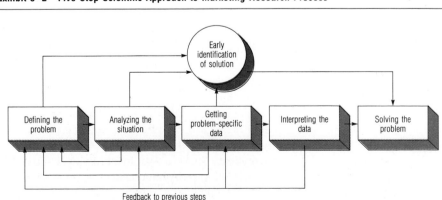

began to slide. Dr Pepper's managers defined the problem as weak promotion so they developed a new promotion effort to go after the "big cola" market. Dr Pepper commercials invited everyone to join the parade and "be a Pepper too." These snappy ads seemed to be a hit. Consumer surveys rated them among the most remembered on TV.

When sales were still disappointing, Dr Pepper put more personal selling emphasis on food stores—because research showed that the "big cola" customers relied on that channel. But this strategy didn't help either.

With two strikes against them, the marketing managers went back for a more careful look at the problem. This time they realized that they needed to know more about their target market before they could plan their marketing mix. To solve this problem, they conducted another survey that revealed some surprising information. Dr Pepper's prospects were very different than the target market the company had selected. An ad agency executive explained, "the Dr Pepper prospect believes he should live life in accordance with his own personal values and not try to meet other people's expectations." In contrast, the cola drinker "tends to follow the latest trends and seek peer approval." The "be a pepper" slogan turned off customers who might tend to choose Dr Pepper—that is, people like the present Dr Pepper customers.

Having finally identified its most likely consumers, Dr Pepper switched its emphasis to channels these buyers used—like vending machines and fast-food restaurants. And its ads showed individualists who would stop at nothing to get a Dr Pepper. With these changes, sales began to rise.[7]

The moral of this story is that our strategy planning framework can be useful for guiding the problem definition step—as well as the whole marketing research process. First, marketing managers should understand their target markets—and know that they have needs their firm can satisfy. Then, managers can focus on lower-level problems—namely, how sensitive the target market is to a change in one or more of the marketing mix ingredients. Without such a framework, marketing researchers can waste time—and money—working on the wrong problem.

Don't confuse problems with symptoms

The problem definition step sounds simple—and that's the danger. As the Dr Pepper case shows, it is easy to confuse symptoms with the problem. Suppose a firm's MIS shows that the company's sales are decreasing in certain territories while expenses are remaining the same—resulting in a decline in profits. Will it help to define the problem by asking: How can we stop the sales decline? Probably not. This would be like fitting a hearing-impaired patient with a hearing aid without first trying to find out *why* he is having trouble hearing.

It's easy to fall into the trap of mistaking symptoms for the problem. Then, research objectives are confused. Relevant questions may be ignored—while unimportant questions are analyzed in expensive detail.

Setting research objectives may require more understanding

Sometimes the research objectives are very clear. A manager wants to know if the targeted households have tried a new product and what percent of them bought it a second time. But often research objectives aren't so simple. The manager might also want to know *why* some didn't buy—or whether they had even heard of the product. Companies rarely have enough time and money to study everything. The manager must narrow his research objectives. One good way is to develop a "research question" list that includes all the possible problem areas.

Then, the items on the list can be considered more completely—in the situation analysis step—before final research objectives are set.

ANALYZING THE SITUATION—STEP 2

What information do we already have?

When the marketing manager thinks the real problem has begun to surface, a situation analysis is useful. A **situation analysis** is an informal study of what information is already available in the problem area. It can help define the problem and specify what additional information—if any—is needed.

Pick the brains around you

The situation analysis usually involves informal talks with informed people. Informed people can be others in the firm, a few good middlemen who have close contact with customers, or others knowledgeable about the industry. In industrial markets—where relationships with customers are close—researchers may even call the customers themselves. Informed customers may have already worked on the same problem—or know about a source of helpful information. Their inputs can help to sharpen the problem definition, too.

Situation analysis helps educate a researcher

The situation analysis is especially important if the researcher is a research specialist who doesn't know much about the management decisions to be made—or if the marketing manager is dealing with unfamiliar areas. They both must be sure they understand the problem area—including the nature of the target market, the marketing mix, competition, and other external factors. Otherwise, the researcher may rush ahead and make costly mistakes—or simply discover "facts" that management already knows. The following case illustrates this danger.

A marketing manager at the home office of a large retail chain hired a research firm to do in-store interviews to learn what customers liked most—and least—about some of its stores in other cities. Interviewers diligently filled their questionnaires. When the results came in, it was apparent that neither the marketing manager nor the researcher had done his homework. No one had even talked with the local store managers! Several of the stores were in the middle of some messy remodeling—so all the customers' responses concerned the noise and dust from the construction. The "research" was a waste of money. You can imagine why this retailer—one of the largest in the country—doesn't want to be named! But the point is: even big companies make marketing research mistakes if they don't take the situation analysis seriously.

Secondary data may provide the answers—or some background

The situation analysis should also find relevant **secondary data**—information that has been collected or published already. Later, in Step 3, we will cover **primary data**—information specifically collected to solve a current problem . Too often researchers rush to gather primary data when much relevant secondary information is already available—at little or no cost! See Exhibit 5–3.

Much secondary data is available

Ideally, much secondary data is already available from the firm's MIS. Data that has not been organized in an MIS may be available from the company's files and reports. Secondary data also is available from libraries, trade associations, and government agencies.

Exhibit 5–3   Sources of Secondary and Primary Data

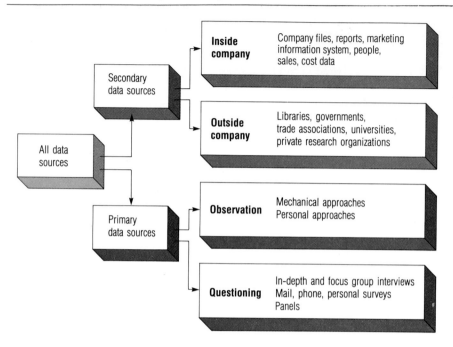

One of the first places a researcher should look for secondary data—after looking within the firm—is a good library. The *Index of Business Periodicals* helps identify all published references to a topic. And some computerized index services are available through libraries and private firms. Lockheed's DIALOGUE system, for example, allows a distant researcher to access a computer and get summaries of articles written on a specific subject. This can be a big time saver and help the researcher "cover all the bases."

Government data is inexpensive

Federal and state governments publish data on almost every subject. Government data is often useful in estimating the size of markets. In the next chapter—and throughout the book—you will get a feel for what types of data are available. Almost all government data is available in inexpensive publications—much of it in computer form ready for further analysis.

Sometimes it's more practical to use summary publications for leads to more detailed documents. The most useful of these summaries—the *Statistical Abstract of the United States*—is like an almanac. It is issued each year and gives more than 1,500 summary tables from published sources. Detailed footnotes are a guide to more specific information on a topic.

The U.S. Department of Commerce distributes statistics compiled by all other federal departments. Commerce Department branch and field offices in many major cities provide assistance in locating specific data. Some city and state governments have similar agencies for local data. For example, if a swimming pool company wants leads on new prospects and knows that a building permit is needed to build a new home, the company could check the building permit list and call the owners—before the homes were finished.

Private sources are useful, too

Many private research organizations—as well as advertising agencies, newspapers, and magazines—regularly compile and publish data. A good business library

National Decision Systems helps marketing managers find the secondary data they need to make better marketing decisions.

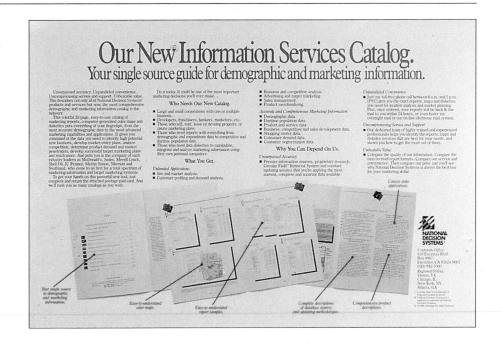

is valuable for sources such as *Sales & Marketing Management, Industrial Marketing, Advertising Age,* and the publications of the National Industrial Conference Board. Some information is available inexpensively as a customer service to clients of advertising agencies or buyers of advertising space or time. Often a company's suppliers can provide useful information.

The *Encyclopedia of Associations* lists trade and professional associations that can be a good source of information. For example, the American Marketing Association has an information center with many marketing publications. Most trade associations compile data from and for their members. Some also publish magazines that focus on important topics in the industry. *Chain Store Age,* for example, has much information on retailing.

Standard & Poor's Industry Surveys is another source of information on whole industries. And the local telephone company or your library usually has copies of the Yellow Pages for many cities. These may be a big help in estimating how much competition there is in certain lines of business—and where it is located.[8]

Situation analysis yields a lot—for very little

The virtue of a good situation analysis is that it can be very informative but takes little time. It is inexpensive compared with more formal research efforts—like a large-scale survey. It can help focus further research—or even eliminate the need for it entirely. The situation analyst is really trying to determine the exact nature of the situation—and the problem. Too-hasty researchers may try to skip this step in their rush to get out questionnaires. Often these researchers find the real problem only when the questionnaires are returned—and then they must start over. One marketing expert put it this way: "Some people never have time to do research right the first time, but they seem to have time to do it over again."

Determine what else is needed

At the end of the situation analysis, you can see which research questions—from the list developed during the problem definition step—remain unanswered.

Then you have to decide exactly what information is needed to answer those questions—and how to get it.

This often requires discussion between technical experts and the marketing manager. Often a written **research proposal**—a plan that specifies what information will be obtained and how—is used to be sure that no misunderstandings occur later. The research plan may include information about costs, what data will be collected, how it will be collected, who will analyze it and how, and how long the process will take. Then the marketing manager must decide if it makes sense to go ahead—if the time and costs involved seem worthwhile. It's foolish to pay $100,000 for information to solve a $50,000 problem! When the decision is not clear-cut, marketing managers should know more about the next steps in the marketing research process.

GETTING PROBLEM–SPECIFIC DATA—STEP 3

Gathering primary data

The next step is to plan a formal research project to gather primary data. There are different methods for collecting primary data. Which approach to use depends on the nature of the problem and how much time and money are available.

In most primary data collection, the researcher tries to learn what customers think about some topic—or how they behave under some conditions. There are two basic methods for obtaining information about customers: *questioning* and *observing*. Questioning can range from qualitative to quantitative research. And many kinds of observing are possible.

Qualitative questioning—open-ended with a hidden purpose

Qualitative research seeks in-depth, open-ended responses, not "yes" or "no" answers. The researcher tries to get people to share their thoughts on a topic—without giving them many directions or guidelines about what to say.

A researcher might ask different consumers "What do you think about when you decide where to shop for food?" One person may talk about convenient location, another about service, and others about the quality of the fresh produce. The real advantage of this approach is *depth*. Each person can be asked follow-up questions so the researcher really understands what *that* respondent is thinking. The depth of the qualitative approach gets at the details—even if a lot of judgment is involved in summarizing it all.

Some types of qualitative research don't use specific questions. For example, a cartoon may show a situation—such as a woman and a man buying coffee in a supermarket. The respondent may be asked to explain what the woman is saying to the man. Or the consumer might simply be shown a product or an ad and asked to comment.

Focus groups focus the discussion

The most widely used form of qualitative questioning in marketing research is the **focus group interview**, which involves interviewing 6 to 10 people in an informal group setting. The focus group also uses open-ended questions, but here the interviewer wants to get group interaction—to stimulate thinking and get immediate reactions.

A skilled focus group leader can learn a lot from this approach. A typical session may last an hour so participants can cover a lot of ground. Sessions are often videotaped so different managers can form their own impressions of what happened.[9] However, conclusions reached from watching a focus group session vary depending on who watches it! A typical problem—and serious limitation—with qualitative research is that it's hard to measure the results objectively. The results seem to depend so much on the point of view of the researcher.

Some researchers use qualitative research to prepare for quantitative research. Qualitative research can provide good ideas—hypotheses. But other approaches—perhaps based on more representative samples and objective measures—are needed to *test* the hypotheses.

Structured questioning gives more objective results

When researchers use identical questions and response alternatives, they can summarize the information quantitatively. Samples can be larger and more representative, and various statistics can be used to draw conclusions. For these reasons, most survey research is **quantitative research**—which seeks structured responses that can be summarized in numbers, like percentages, averages, or other statistics. For example, a marketing researcher might calculate what percentage of respondents had tried a new product—and then figure an average "score" for how satisfied they were with the experience.

Fixed responses speed answering and analysis

Survey questionnaires usually provide fixed responses to questions to simplify analysis of the replies. This multiple-choice approach also makes it easier and faster for respondents to reply. Simple fill-in-a-number questions are also widely used in quantitative research. A questionnaire might ask an industrial buyer "From approximately how many suppliers do you currently purchase electronic parts?" Fixed responses are also more convenient for computer analysis, which is how most surveys are analyzed.

Quantitative measures of attitudes, too

One common approach to measuring consumers' attitudes and opinions is to have respondents indicate how much they agree or disagree with a questionnaire statement. A researcher interested in what target consumers think about frozen pizzas, for example, might include statements like those at the top of Exhibit 5–4.

Another approach is to have respondents *rate* a product, feature, or store. Figure 5–4 shows commonly used rating "scales." Sometimes rating scales are labeled with adjectives like *excellent, good, fair,* and *poor.*

Surveys by mail, phone, or in person

Decisions about what specific questions to ask—and how to ask them—are usually related to how respondents will be contacted—by mail, on the phone, or in person.

Mail surveys are the most common and convenient

The mail questionnaire is useful when extensive questioning is necessary. With a mail questionnaire, respondents can complete the questions at their convenience. They may be more willing to fill in personal or family characteristics—since a mail questionnaire can be returned anonymously. But the questions must be simple and easy to follow, since no interviewer is there to help.

A big problem with mail questionnaires is that many people don't complete or return them. The **response rate**—the percent of people contacted who complete the questionnaire—is usually around 25 percent in consumer surveys. And it can be even lower. Also, respondents may not be representative. People who are most interested in the questionnaire topic may respond—but answers from this group may be very different from the answers of the typical "don't care" group.[10]

Mail surveys are economical if a large number of people respond. But they may be quite expensive if the response rate is low. Further, it can take a month or more

Exhibit 5–4   Sample Questioning Methods to Measure Attitudes and Opinions

---

A. Please check your level of agreement with each of the following statements.

	Strongly agree	Agree	Uncertain	Disagree	Strongly disagree
1. I add extra toppings when I prepare a frozen pizza.	____	____	____	____	____
2. A frozen pizza dinner is more expensive than eating at a fast food restaurant.	____	____	____	____	____

B. Please rate how important each of the following is to you in selecting a brand of frozen pizza:

	Not at all important				Very important
1. Price per serving	____	____	____	____	____
2. Toppings available	____	____	____	____	____
3. Amount of cheese	____	____	____	____	____
4. Cooking time	____	____	____	____	____

C. Please check the rating which best describes your feelings about the last frozen pizza which you prepared.

	Poor	Fair	Good	Excellent
1. Price per serving	____	____	____	____
2. Toppings available	____	____	____	____
3. Amount of cheese	____	____	____	____
4. Cooking time	____	____	____	____

to get the data—and this is too slow for some decisions. Moreover, it is difficult to get respondents to expand on particular points. In spite of these limitations, the convenience and economy of mail surveys makes them popular for collecting primary data.

Telephone surveys—fast and effective

Telephone interviews are growing in popularity. They are effective for getting quick answers to simple questions. Telephone interviews allow the interviewer to probe and really learn what the respondent is thinking. On the other hand, the telephone is usually not a very good contact method if the interviewer is trying to get confidential personal information—such as details of family income. Respondents are not certain who is calling or how such personal information might be used.

Research firms—with up to 50 interviewers calling at the same time on long distance lines—can complete 1,000 or more "nationwide" interviews in one evening. In addition, with computer-aided telephone interviewing, answers are immediately recorded on a computer, resulting in fast data analysis. The popularity of telephone surveys is partly due to their speed and high response rates.[11]

Personal interview surveys—can be in-depth

A personal interview survey is usually much more expensive per interview than a mail or telephone survey. But it's easier to get and keep the respondent's atten-

The U.S. Bureau of the Census used public service advertising to encourage people to respond to the census questionnaire.

Out of sight...   Out of mind.

What benefits do you get for not filling out the Census? Zero. If the Census doesn't know who you are or where you live or what you do, they can't see you. And the less you participate in the Census, the less chance your community has for growth. That's because the Census is one way our government determines how much funding your neighborhood needs. For better clinics, schools and jobs. Yes, they do ask some personal questions, but none of your answers become public. The Census is not connected with taxes, police or welfare agencies. So spread the word. Census time is time for everyone to speak up. Let America know you're here— and start counting yourself in.

Stand right up for who you are.
Answer the census.

tion when the interviewer is right there. The interviewer can also help explain complicated directions—and perhaps get better responses. For these reasons, personal interviews are commonly used for industrial customers. To reduce the cost of locating consumer respondents, interviews are sometimes done at a store or shopping mall. This is called a mall intercept interview because the interviewer stops a shopper and asks for responses to the survey.

Researchers have to be careful that having an interviewer involved doesn't affect the respondent's answers. Sometimes people won't give an answer they consider embarrassing. Or they may try to impress or please the interviewer. For example, when asked what magazines they read, respondents may report a "respectable" magazine like *National Geographic*—even if they never read it—but fail to report magazines like *Playboy* or *Playgirl*.

Sometimes questioning has limitations. Then, observing may be more accurate or economical.

Observing—what you see is what you get

Observing—as a method of collecting data—focuses on a well-defined problem. Here we are not talking about the casual observations that may stimulate ideas in the early steps of a research project.

With the observation method, researchers try to see or record what the subject does naturally. They don't want the observing to *influence* the subject's behavior.

A museum director wanted to know which of the many exhibits was most popu-

Information Resources Rolls Out a Research Innovation

Information Resources, Inc. (IRI), a marketing research firm, built its initial success by helping marketers harness the power of scanner data collected at supermarket checkout counters. Now it's on a roll testing its new VideOcart—a shopping cart with a computer screen that displays ads and gathers marketing research data. The cart collects data about the path the shopper takes through the store, time spent in various parts of the store, and shopper opinions. The data are "dumped" from VideOcart at the checkout stand through a radio transmitter hooked to a personal computer. Grocers use the information to analyze shopping patterns and plan better product placement on shelves. VideOcart also displays point-of-purchase ads, with the computer instantly sequencing ads for products as the consumer approaches them on the shelf.[12]

lar. A survey didn't help. Visitors seemed to want to please the interviewer—and usually said that all of the exhibits were interesting. Putting observers near exhibits—to record how long visitors spent at each one—didn't help either. The curious visitors stood around to see what was being recorded—and that messed up the measures. Finally, the museum floors were waxed to a glossy shine. Several weeks later, the floors around the exhibits were inspected. It was easy to tell which exhibits were most popular—based on how much wax had worn off the floor!

In some situations, consumers are recorded on videotape. Later, researchers can study the tape by running the film at very slow speed or actually analyzing each frame. This technique is used to study the routes consumers follow through a grocery store—or how they select products in a department store.

Observation data can be plotted on graphs or maps. Taubman Company, a shopping center developer in San Francisco, wondered if one of its shopping centers was attracting customers from all the surrounding areas. Taubman hired a firm to record the license plate numbers of cars in the parking lot. Using registration information, the addresses of all license holders were then obtained and plotted on a map. Very few customers were coming from one large area. The developer aimed direct mail advertising at that area and generated a lot of new business.

Observing is common in advertising research

Observation methods are common in advertising research. For example, A. C. Nielsen Company has developed a device called the "people meter" that adapts the observation method to television audience research. This machine is attached to the TV set in the homes of selected families. It records when the set is on and what station is tuned in. The results are widely used to rate the popularity of TV shows. Some claim that once families get used to the meter, it no longer influences their behavior. Note, however, that the meter only records what channel is on—not whether anyone is watching it.

Checkout scanners see a lot

Computerized scanners at retail checkout counters, a major breakthrough in observing, help researchers collect very specific—and useful—information. Often this type of data feeds directly into a firm's MIS. Managers of a big department store can see exactly what products have sold each day—and how much money each department earned. But the scanner also has wider applications for marketing research.

Data from electronic scanning at the supermarket helps retailers to decide what brand they will sell.

Information Resources, Inc., uses a **consumer panel**—a group of consumers who provide information on a continuing basis. Whenever a panel member shops for groceries, he gives an ID number to the clerk, who keys in the number. Then the scanner records every purchase—including brands, sizes, prices, and any coupons used. For a fee, clients can evaluate actual customer purchase patterns—and answer questions about the effectiveness of their discount coupons. Did the coupons draw new customers, or did current customers simply use them to stock up? If consumers switched from another brand, did they go back to their old brand the next time? The answers to such questions are important in planning marketing strategies—and scanners can help marketing managers get the answers.

Some members of the consumer panel are also tied into a special TV cable system. With this system, a company can direct advertisements to some houses and not others. Then, researchers can evaluate the effect of the ads by comparing the purchases of consumers who saw the ads with those who didn't.

The use of scanners to "observe" what customers actually do is changing consumer research methods. Companies can turn to firms like Information Resources, Inc., as a single source of complete information about customers' attitudes, shopping behavior, and media habits. The information available is so detailed that the possibilities are limited more by imagination—and money—than by technology.[13]

Experimental method controls conditions

A marketing manager can get a different kind of information—with either questioning or observing—using the experimental method. With the **experimental method**, researchers compare the responses of groups that are similar except on the characteristic being tested. Researchers want to learn if the specific characteristic—which varies among groups—*causes* differences in some response among the groups. The "response" might be an observed behavior—like the purchase of a product—or the answer to a specific question—like "How much do you like the taste of our new product?"

Marketing managers for Mars—the company that makes Snickers candy bars—used the experimental method to help solve a problem. Other candy and snack foods were taking customers. But why? Surveys showed that many consumers thought the shrinking candy bar was too small. But they also didn't want to pay more for a larger bar. Mars' managers wanted to know if making their candy bar bigger would increase sales enough to offset the higher cost. To decide, they needed more information.

The company carefully varied the size of candy bars sold in *different* markets. Otherwise, the marketing mix stayed the same. Then researchers tracked sales in each market area to see the effect of the different sizes. They saw a difference—a big difference—immediately. It was clear that the added sales would more than offset the cost of a bigger candy bar. So marketing managers at Mars made a decision that took them in the opposite direction from other candy companies. And, yes, it proved to be a sweet success.

The experimental method isn't used as often as surveys and focus groups because it's hard to set up controlled situations where only one marketing variable is different. But there are probably other reasons, too. Many managers don't understand the valuable information they can get from this method. Further, they don't like the idea of some researcher "experimenting" with their business.[14]

INTERPRETING THE DATA—STEP 4

What does it really mean?

When data has been collected it has to be analyzed to decide what it all means. In quantitative research, this step usually involves statistics. **Statistical packages**—easy-to-use computer programs that analyze data—have made this step easier. As we noted earlier, some firms provide *decision support systems* so a manager can use a statistical package to interpret data himself. More often, however, technical specialists are involved at the interpretation step.

SPSS is a microcomputer statistical software program that makes it easy to summarize marketing research data.

The details of statistical analysis are beyond the scope of this book. But a good manager should know enough to understand what a research project can—and can't—do.[15]

Is your sample really representative?

It's usually impossible for marketing managers to collect all the information they want about everyone in a **population**—the total group they are interested in. Marketing researchers typically study only a **sample**, a part of the relevant population. How well a sample *represents* the total population affects the results. Results from a sample that is not representative may not give a true picture.

The manager of a retail store might want a phone survey to learn what consumers think about the store's hours. If interviewers make all of the calls during the day, the sample will not be representative. Consumers who work outside the home during the day won't have an equal chance of being included. Those interviewed might say the limited store hours are "satisfactory." Yet it would be a mistake to assume that *all* consumers are satisfied. Marketing managers must be aware of how representative a sample really is.

Random samples tend to be representative

You can see that getting a representative sample is very important. One method of doing so is **random sampling**, where each member of the population has the same chance of being included in the sample. Great care must be used to ensure that sampling is really random—not just haphazard.

If a random sample is chosen from a population, it will tend to have the same characteristics and be representative of the population. "Tend to" is important because it is only a tendency—the sample is not exactly the same as the population.

Much marketing research is based on nonrandom sampling because of the high cost and difficulty of obtaining a truly random sample. Sometimes nonrandom samples give very good results—especially in industrial markets where the number of customers may be relatively small and fairly similar. But results from nonrandom samples must be interpreted—and used—with care.

Research results are not exact

An estimate from a sample—even a representative one—usually varies somewhat from the true value for a total population. Managers sometimes forget this. They assume that survey results are exact. Instead, when interpreting sample estimates, managers should think of them as *suggesting* the approximate value.

If random selection is used to develop the sample, then methods are available for stating the likely accuracy of the sample value. This is done in terms of **confidence intervals**—the range on either side of an estimate that is likely to contain the true value for the whole population. Some managers are surprised to learn how wide that range can be.

Consider a wholesaler who has 1,000 retail customers. He wants to learn how many of these retailers carry a product from a competing supplier. If he randomly samples 100 retailers and 20 say yes, then the sample estimate is 20 percent. But with that information he can only be 95 percent confident that the percentage of all retailers is in the confidence interval between 12 and 28 percent.[16]

The larger the sample size, the greater the accuracy of estimates from a random sample. With a larger sample, a few unusual responses are less likely to make a big difference.

You can see that the nature of the sample—and how it is selected—makes a big difference in how the results of a study can be interpreted. Managers must consider this factor when planning data collection—to make sure that the final results can be interpreted with enough confidence to be useful in marketing strategy planning.

Validity problems can destroy research

Even if the sampling is carefully planned, it is also important to evaluate the quality of the research data itself.

Managers and researchers should be sure that research data really measures what it is supposed to measure. Many of the variables that are of interest to marketing managers are difficult to measure accurately. Questionnaires may let us assign numbers to consumer responses, but that still doesn't mean that the result is precise. An interviewer might ask "How much did you spend on soft drinks last week?" A respondent may be perfectly willing to cooperate—and be part of the representative sample—but just not be able to remember.

Validity concerns the extent to which data measures what it is intended to measure. Validity problems are important in marketing research because most people want to help and will try to answer—even when they don't know what they're talking about. Further, a poorly worded question can mean different things to different people—and invalidate the results. A manager must be sure that he only pays for research results that are representative—and valid.

Poor interpretation can destroy research

Besides sampling and validity problems, a marketing manager must consider whether the analysis of the data supports the *conclusions* drawn in the interpretation step. Sometimes technical specialists pick the right statistical procedure—their calculations are exact—but they misinterpret the data because they don't understand the management problem. In one survey, car buyers were asked to rank five cars in order from "most preferred" to "least preferred." One car was ranked first by slightly more respondents than any other car so the researcher reported it as the "most liked car." That interpretation, however, ignored the fact that 70 percent of the respondents ranked the car *last*!

Interpretation problems like this can be subtle but crucial. Some people draw misleading conclusions—on purpose—to get the results they want. A marketing manager must decide whether *all* of the results support the interpretation—and are relevant to his problem.

Marketing manager and researcher should work together

Marketing research involves some technical details. But you can see that the marketing researcher and the marketing manager must work together to be sure that they really do solve the problems facing the firm. If the whole research process has been a joint effort, then the interpretation step can move quickly to decision making—and solving the problem.

SOLVING THE PROBLEM—STEP 5

The last step is solving the problem

In the problem solution step, managers use the research results to make marketing decisions.

Some researchers—and some managers—are fascinated by the interesting tidbits of information that come from the research process. They are excited if the research reveals something they didn't know before. But if research doesn't have action implications, it has little value—and suggests poor planning by the researcher and the manager.

When the research process is finished, the marketing manager should be able to apply the findings in marketing strategy planning—the choice of a target market or the mix of the four Ps. If the research doesn't provide information to help guide these decisions, the company has wasted research time and money.

We emphasize this step because it is the reason for and logical conclusion to the whole research process. This final step must be anticipated at each of the earlier steps.

HOW MUCH INFORMATION DO YOU NEED?

Information is costly—but reduces risk

We have been talking about the benefits of good marketing information, but dependable information can be expensive. A big company may spend millions developing an information system. A large-scale survey can cost from $20,000 to $100,000—or even more. The continuing research available from companies such as Information Resources, Inc., can cost a company well over $100,000 a year. And a market test for 6 to 12 months may cost $200,000 to $500,000 per test market!

Companies that are willing and able to pay the cost often find that marketing information pays for itself. They are more likely to select the right target market and marketing mix—or see a potential problem before it becomes a costly crisis.

What is the value of information?

The high cost of good information must be balanced against its probable value to management. Managers never get all the information they would like to have. Very detailed surveys or experiments may be "too good" or "too expensive" or "too late" if all the company needs is a rough sampling of retailer attitudes toward a new pricing plan—by tomorrow. Money is wasted if research shows that a manager's guesses are wrong—and the manager ignores the facts. For example, GM faced an expensive disaster with its 1986 Riviera, which was released even after extensive research predicted a flop.[17]

Marketing managers must take risks because of incomplete information. That's part of their job and always will be. But they must weigh the cost of getting more data against its likely value. If the risk is not too great, the cost of getting more information may be greater than the potential loss from a poor decision. A decision to expand into a new territory with the present marketing mix, for example, might be made with more confidence after a $25,000 survey. But just sending a sales rep into the territory for a few weeks to try to sell the potential customers would be a lot cheaper. And, if successful, the answer is in and so are some sales.

Faced with many risky decisions, the marketing manager should only seek help from research for problems where the risk can be reduced at a reasonable cost.[18]

CONCLUSION

Marketing managers face difficult decisions in selecting target markets and managing marketing mixes. And, managers rarely have all the information they would like to have. But they don't have to rely only on intuition. Good information usually can be obtained to improve the quality of their decisions.

Computers are helping marketing managers become full-fledged members of the information age.

Both large and small firms are setting up marketing information systems (MIS)—to be certain that routinely needed data is available and accessible quickly.

Marketing managers deal with rapidly changing environments. Available data is not always adequate to answer the detailed questions that arise. Then, a marketing research project may be required to gather new information.

Marketing research should be guided by the scientific method. The scientific approach to solving marketing problems involves five steps: defining the problem, analyzing the situation, obtaining data, interpreting

data, and solving the problem. This objective and organized approach helps to keep research on target—reducing the risk of doing costly research that isn't necessary or doesn't solve the problem.

Our strategy planning framework can be helpful in finding the real problem. By finding and focusing on the real problem, the researcher and marketing manager may be able to move quickly to a useful solution—without the cost and risks of gathering primary data in a formal research project. With imagination, they may even be able to find the "answers" in their MIS or in other readily available secondary data.

Questions and Problems

1. Discuss the concept of a marketing information system and why it is important for marketing managers to be involved in planning the system.

2. In your own words, explain why a decision support system (DSS) can add to the value of a marketing information system. Give an example of how a decision support system might help.

3. Discuss how output from a MIS might differ from the output of a typical marketing research department.

4. Discuss some of the likely problems facing the marketer in a small firm that has just purchased an inexpensive personal computer to help develop a marketing information system.

5. Explain the key characteristics of the scientific method and show why these are important to managers concerned with research.

6. How is the situation analysis different from the data collection step. Can both these steps be done at the same time to obtain answers sooner? Is this wise?

7. Distinguish between primary data and secondary data and illustrate your answer.

8. If a firm were interested in estimating the distribution of income in the state of Florida, how could it proceed? Be specific.

9. If a firm were interested in estimating sand and clay production in Georgia, how could it proceed? Be specific.

10. Go to the library and find (in some government publication) three marketing-oriented "facts" that you

did not know existed or were available. Record on one page and show sources.

11. Explain why a company might want to do focus group interviews rather than doing individual interviews with the same people.

12. Distinguish between qualitative and quantitative approaches to research—and give some of the key advantages and limitations of each approach.

13. Define what is meant by response rate and discuss why a marketing manager might be concerned about the response rate achieved in a particular survey. Give an example.

14. Explain how you might use different types of research (focus groups, observation, survey, and experiment) to forecast market reaction to a new kind of margarine, which is to receive no promotion other than what the retailer will give it. Further, assume that the new margarine's name will not be associated with other known products. The product will be offered at competitive prices.

15. Marketing research involves expense—sometimes considerable expense. Why does the text recommend the use of marketing research even though a highly experienced marketing executive is available?

16. Discuss the concept that some information may be too expensive to obtain in relation to its value. Illustrate.

Suggested Cases

8. Mario's

9. Holiday Inn versus Days Inn

Suggested Computer-Aided Problem

5. Marketing Research

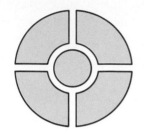

Chapter **6**

Demographic Dimensions of the U.S. Consumer Market

When You Finish This Chapter, You Should

1. Know about population and income trends—and how they affect marketers.

2. Understand how population is growing—but at different rates for different age groups.

3. Know about the distribution of income.

4. Know how final consumer spending is related to population, income, family life cycle, and other variables.

5. Know how to estimate likely consumer purchases for broad classes of products.

6. Understand the important new terms (shown in red).

Markets are people with money to spend to satisfy needs.

AT&T is wooing senior citizens with daytime long-distance discounts, phone amplifiers, and automatic emergency dialing attachments. United, American, and other airlines are offering discounts to older travelers. General Motors is doing research to see if older consumers will react favorably to bigger buttons, simpler operating instructions, and larger doors. Sales of Post Natural Bran Flakes went up 10 percent after older celebrities like Lena Horne and Steve Allen were featured in its ads. American Express Company is offering special financial-planning services as part of a strategy targeted at retirees. Across the country, marketing managers are trying to reach older consumers.

Why all this attention to consumers 50 and older? This group now makes up about 25 percent of the population—but has about half of the disposable income! Senior citizens buy $800 billion worth of goods and services each year. And, they are the fastest-growing age group. In the next 10 years, the number of adults will grow by about 14 percent, but the number of people over 50 will increase by nearly 25 percent. By the year 2000, 76 million Americans will be 50 or older. We are moving away from a youth oriented culture—and the "graying of America" is creating new marketing opportunities.[1]

Target marketers focus on the customer

Target marketers believe that the *customer* should be the focus of all business and marketing activity. These marketers hope to develop unique marketing strategies by finding unsatisfied customers and offering them more attractive marketing mixes. They want to work in less-competitive markets with more inelastic demand curves. Finding these attractive opportunities takes real knowledge of what potential customers want. This means finding those market dimensions that make a difference—in terms of population, income, needs, attitudes, and buying behavior.

147

Three important questions should be answered about any potential market:

1. What are its relevant segmenting dimensions?
2. How big is it?
3. Where is it?

The first question is basic. Management judgment—perhaps aided by analysis of existing data and new findings from marketing research—is needed to pick the right dimensions.

To help build your judgment regarding buying behavior, this and the following two chapters will discuss what we know about various kinds of customers and their buying behavior. Keep in mind that we aren't trying to make generalizations about average customers or how the mass market behaves—but rather how *some* people in *some* markets behave. You should expect to find differences.

Get the facts straight—for good marketing decisions

Everybody "knows" that there are lots of retired people in Florida, many Californians speak Spanish, and the population in the Sun Belt states is growing fast. Generalities like these may be partly true—but "partly true" isn't good enough when it comes to making marketing strategy decisions. Marketing managers need to know the facts about the size, location, and characteristics of their target markets.

Fortunately, much useful information is available on the demographic dimensions of the U.S. consumer market. Most of it is free because it has been collected by government agencies like the Bureau of the Census. When valid data is available, managers have no excuse for basing their decisions on guesses. Look at the data in the next few chapters in terms of selecting relevant market dimensions—and estimating the potential in different market segments. Also, check your own assumptions against this data. Now is a good time to get your facts straight!

POPULATION—PEOPLE WITH MONEY MAKE MARKETS

Where does your state stand?

Exhibit 6–1 is a map of the United States showing the relative population for each state. The "high areas" on this map emphasize the concentration of population in different geographic regions. Note that California is the most populated state with New York a distant second. Third place Texas has almost as large a population as New York, but it is more spread out. More generally, the heavy concentration of population in the Northeast makes this market more than one and a half times bigger than the whole West Coast.

The most populated U.S. areas developed near inexpensive water transportation—on ocean harbors (East and West Coasts), along major rivers (like the Mississippi), or in the Great Lakes region. Obviously, these markets are attractive to many marketers. But this can also mean tough competition—as in the big urban East and West Coast markets.

Marketers anxious to avoid the extremely competitive East and West Coast markets often view the midwestern and southern states as unique target markets. Note, too, the few people in the plains and mountain states, which explains why some national marketers pay less attention to these areas. Yet these states can provide an opportunity for an alert marketer looking for less competitive markets.

Exhibit 6–1   Map of United States Showing Population by State (all figures in thousands)

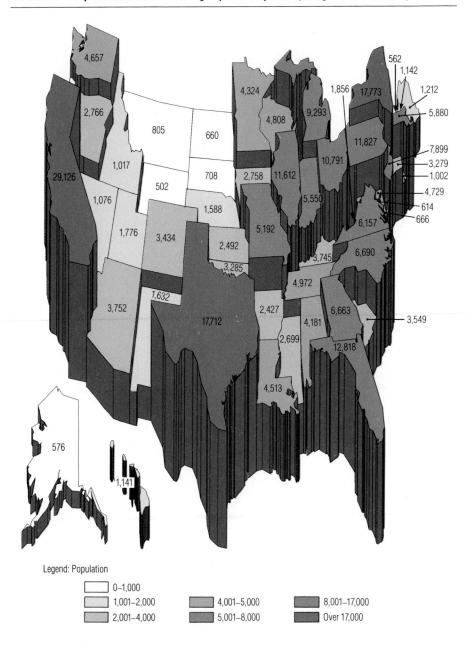

Legend: Population

- ☐ 0–1,000
- ☐ 1,001–2,000
- ☐ 2,001–4,000
- ☐ 4,001–5,000
- ☐ 5,001–8,000
- ☐ 8,001–17,000
- ☐ Over 17,000

Where are the people today and tomorrow?

Population figures for a single year don't show the dynamic aspects of markets. The U.S. population has been growing continuously since the founding of the country—more than doubling from 1930 to 1990—until it reached about 250 million. But—and this is important to marketers—the population did *not* double everywhere. Marketers are always looking for fast-growing markets. They want to know where recent growth has occurred—and where growth is likely to occur in the future.

Exhibit 6–2 shows the percentage change in population—growth or decline—in different regions of the country. The states with the darkest shading are growing the fastest, and the lightest ones are actually losing population. Arizona, Nevada, New Mexico, Florida, Georgia, and Alaska are growing the fastest—with expected increases of about 20 percent during the 1990s—while others will grow only a little. And Iowa, West Virginia, North Dakota, and 10 other states are declining.

Notice that some of the most populated areas in Exhibit 6–1 are not growing the fastest. For example, people are moving out of the Northeast and the north central states to the Sun Belt of the South and West. California, Texas, and Florida are expected to account for over half of the total U.S. population growth from now until the turn of the century!

These different rates of growth are especially important to marketers. Sudden growth in one area may create a demand for many new shopping centers—while retailers in declining areas face tougher competition for a smaller number of customers. In growing areas, demand may increase so rapidly that profits may be good even in poorly planned facilities.[2]

These maps summarize state-level data to give the big picture. Keep in mind, however, that much more detailed population data is available. Detailed census data—or updated estimates—are available for very small geographic areas. Just as we have mapped population changes at the state level, a local marketer can divide a big metropolitan area into many smaller areas to see "where the action is." By the end of the decade, census data may be getting out of date—but by then local and state government planning groups may be able to provide updates.

Population will keep growing but . . .

The world's population is growing fast and is expected to nearly double in the next 20 years—but this is not true of the United States. Our own population growth has slowed dramatically. It was less than 1 percent a year during the last decade.

Exhibit 6–2   Percent Change in Population by State, 1990–2000

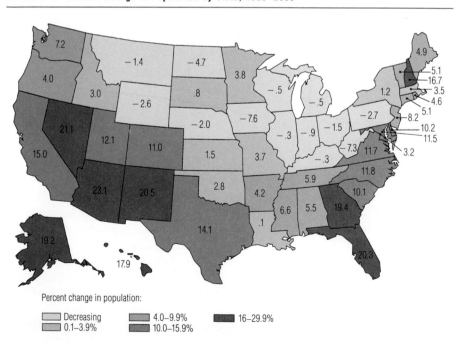

Percent change in population:

☐ Decreasing
☐ 0.1–3.9%
☐ 4.0–9.9%
☐ 10.0–15.9%
■ 16–29.9%

In fact, many U.S. marketers who enjoyed rapid and profitable growth know that the domestic "picnic" is over. They are now turning to international markets where population—and sales revenues—are likely to continue to grow.

This doesn't mean, however, that our population growth has stopped. The U.S. population will continue to grow—at least for another 60 years or so. The big questions are: How much and how fast? The Census Bureau predicts that the population will hit an all-time high of 300 million by 2050 and then begin to decline. Most of our future growth is expected to come from immigration. In fact, even now the total U.S. population would start to decline if immigration were cut off. Let's look at some of these trends—and what they mean to marketing managers.[3]

Birthrate—boom or bust?

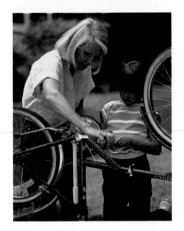

The U.S. **birthrate**—the number of babies per 1,000 people—has fluctuated greatly in the last 50 years. The pattern is clear from Exhibit 6–3. A post-World War II "baby boom" began as returning soldiers started families, and it lasted about 15 years into the early 1960s. Then the situation changed. There was a "baby bust" in the 70s as more women stayed in the work force and couples waited longer to have children. When you see the dip in the birthrate—and think about the declining market for baby products—you can understand why Johnson & Johnson started to promote its baby shampoo to adults who wanted a gentle product.

The birthrate hit a low in 1976 and then went up again—but only slightly. It is starting to drop now and this trend is expected to continue. These shifts are easy to explain. As the baby boom generation entered its child-bearing years there were simply more women to have babies. Now this baby "boomlet" is passing. In addition, the number of children per family is low. There may be less need for big family homes and large, family-size food packages—and more demand for small apartments, out-of-home entertainment, travel, and smaller food packages.

Exhibit 6–3   Changes in the U.S. Birthrate, 1935–1986

With fewer children in a family, parents tend to spend more money on each child.

With fewer children, parents can spend more money on each child. For example, expensive bikes, home video games, and designer clothes for children have all done well in recent years because parents can indulge one or two children more easily than a house full.[4]

Age distribution is changing

Because population is growing slowly, the average age is rising. In 1970, the average age of the population was 28—but by the year 2000 the average age will jump to about 37.

Stated another way, the percentage of the population in different age groups is changing. Exhibit 6–4 shows the number of people in different age groups in 1980 and 1990—and how the size of these groups will look in 2000. Note the big increases in the 25–44 age group from 1980 to 1990—and how that growth will carry over to the 45–64 age groups from 1990 until 2000.

The major reason for the changing age distribution is that the post-World War II baby boom produced about one fourth of our present population. This large group crowded into the schools in the 1950s and 60s—and then into the job market in the 1970s. In the 1980s, they were swelling the middle-aged group. And early in the 21st century, they will reach retirement—still a dominant group in the total population. According to one population expert, "It's like a goat passing through a boa constrictor."

Some of the effects of this big market are very apparent. For example, recording industry sales exploded—to the beat of rock and roll music and the Beatles—as the baby boom group moved into their record-buying teens. Soon after, colleges added facilities and faculty to handle the surge—then had to cope with excess capacity and loss of revenue when the student-age population dwindled. To relieve financial strain many colleges are now adding special courses and programs for adults to attract the now-aging baby boom students. On the other hand, the fitness industry and food producers who offer low-calorie foods are reaping the benefit of a middle-aged "bulge" in the population.

Medical advances help people live longer and are also adding to the proportion of the population in the senior citizen group. Note from Exhibit 6–4 that the over-65 age group grew by 23 percent in the last decade—and will grow another 10 percent before the turn of the century. These dramatic changes are creating new opportunities for such industries as tourism, health care, and financial services.[5]

Household composition is changing

We often think of the "typical" American household as a married couple with two children—living in the suburbs. This never was true and is even less true now. Although almost all Americans marry, they are marrying later, delaying child bearing, and having fewer children. Couples with no children under 18 now account for half of all families.

And couples don't stay together as long as they used to. The United States has the highest divorce rate in the world—about 38 percent of marriages end in divorce. But divorce does not seem to deter people from marrying again. Almost 80 percent of divorced people remarry "in what is described as the triumph of hope over experience." Still, even with all this shifting around, about two thirds of all adults are married.

Exhibit 6–4   Population Distribution by Age Groups for the Years 1980, 1990, and 2000

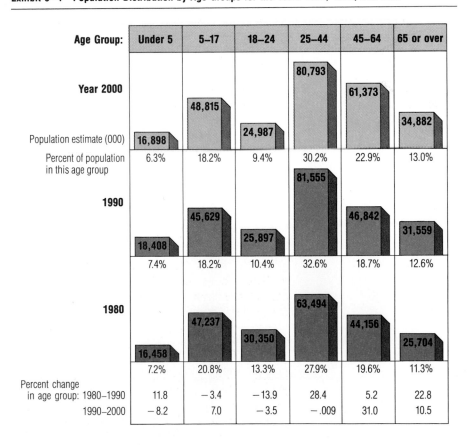

Age Group:	Under 5	5–17	18–24	25–44	45–64	65 or over
Year 2000				80,793	61,373	
		48,815				34,882
Population estimate (000)	16,898		24,987			
Percent of population in this age group	6.3%	18.2%	9.4%	30.2%	22.9%	13.0%
1990				81,555		
		45,629			46,842	
	18,408		25,897			31,559
	7.4%	18.2%	10.4%	32.6%	18.7%	12.6%
1980				63,494		
		47,237	30,350		44,156	
	16,458					25,704
	7.2%	20.8%	13.3%	27.9%	19.6%	11.3%
Percent change in age group: 1980–1990	11.8	−3.4	−13.9	28.4	5.2	22.8
1990–2000	−8.2	7.0	−3.5	−.009	31.0	10.5

Sony Tunes in to Kids

Sony isn't just playing around with its new strategy that targets toy-buying adults. This is a growing market because of the number of baby-boomers with young children. As Sony's $3 million introductory ad campaign announced, "after years of giving people smaller electronics, Sony now makes electronics for smaller people."

Sony's research showed that no competitor was targeting children in the 4 to 11 age range. They are too old for products from toy companies like Fisher-Price, but are not yet ready for products that appeal to young teens. Sony's new line of products, called "My First Sony," includes cassette players, Walkman stereos, radios, and walkie-talkies. They were designed to be durable—which appealed to parents—and kids liked the colorful plastic cases. Sony's familiar brand name helped recruit new middlemen—toy store chains, mass-merchandisers, and major department stores. Sony's price, from $35 to $60, is higher than for most toys, but Sony marketing managers think that upscale parents are willing to pay extra for Sony's "added durability and play value."

Sony's ad campaign appeared on prime-time TV and in magazines like *People* rather than on children's shows—because it was targeted at the parents rather than the kids. In the ads, several children hold up Sonys and sing, "I'd like a bike, I'd like a pony, but what I'd love is my first Sony!"[6]

Nonfamily households are increasing

Many households are not families in the usual sense. *Single-adult households* account for 24 percent of all households—more than 21 million people! These households include young adults who leave home when they finish school, as well as divorced or widowed people who live alone.

In some big cities, the percentage of single-person households is even higher—around 30 percent in New York and Washington, D.C. These people need smaller apartments, smaller cars, smaller food packages, and, in some cases, less-expensive household furnishings because many singles don't have much money. Other singles have ample discretionary income and are attractive markets for top-of-the-line stereos and clothing, "status" cars, travel, nice restaurants, and "trendy" bars.

There are also several million unmarried people living together—some in groups but most as couples. Some of these arrangements are temporary—as in college towns or in large cities where recent graduates go for their first "real" job. But the majority are older couples who choose not to get married.

The number of these nontraditional households is still relatively small. But marketers should pay special attention to them because they are growing at a much higher rate than the traditional family households. In fact, since 1970 their number has quadrupled. And they have different needs and attitudes than the stereotypical American family. To reach this market, some banks have changed their policies about loans to unmarried couples for homes, cars, and other major purchases. And some insurance companies have designed coverage for unmarried couples.[7]

The shift to urban and suburban areas

Migration from rural to urban areas has been continuous in the United States since 1800. In 1920, about half the population lived in rural areas. By 1950, the number living on farms dropped to 15 percent—and by 1987, it was only 2 percent. We have become an urban and suburban society.[8]

From city to suburbs—and then a trickle back

Since World War II, there has been a continuous flight to the suburbs by middle-income consumers. By 1970, more people were living in the suburbs than in the central cities. Retailers moved too—following their customers. Lower-income consumers—often with varied ethnic backgrounds—have moved in, changing the nature of markets in the center of the city.

Industries too have been fleeing the cities, moving many jobs closer to the suburbs. Today's urban economic system is not as dependent on central cities. A growing population must go somewhere—and the suburbs can combine pleasant neighborhoods with easy transportation to higher-paying jobs nearby or in the city.

Purchase patterns are different in the suburbs. For example, a big city resident may not need or own a car. But with no mass transportation, living carless in the suburbs is difficult. And in some areas, it almost seems that a minivan—to carpool kids and haul lawn supplies or pets—is a necessity.

Some families, however, have become disenchanted with the suburban dream. They found it to be a nightmare of commuting, yard and house work, rising local taxes, and gossiping neighbors. Many of these people have moved back to the city—creating a market for luxury condominiums, home repair products, and interesting restaurants. Ten years ago, many people thought that this flow back to the city would increase—reversing the trend to suburbia. But instead, for each person who has moved back to the city during the last decade, two others have moved out!

Local political boundaries don't define market areas

These continuing shifts—to and from urban and suburban areas—mean that the usual practice of reporting population by city and county boundaries can result in misleading descriptions of markets. Marketers are more interested in the size of homogeneous *marketing* areas than in the number of people within political boundaries. To meet this need, the U.S. Census Bureau has developed a separate population classification based on metropolitan statistical areas. Much data is reported on the characteristics of people in these areas. The technical definition of these areas has changed over time. But, basically, a **Metropolitan Statistical Area (MSA)** is an integrated economic and social unit with a large population nucleus. Generally, an MSA centers on one city or urbanized area of 50,000 or more inhabitants and includes bordering urban areas.

The largest MSAs—basically those with a population of more than a million—are called Consolidated Metropolitan Statistical areas. More detailed data is available for areas within these sprawling, giant urban areas.

Big targets are attractive—but very competitive

Some national marketers sell only in these metro areas because of the large, concentrated population. They know that having so many customers packed into a small area can simplify the marketing effort. They can use fewer middlemen and still offer products conveniently. One or two local advertising media—a city newspaper or TV station—can reach most residents. If a sales force is needed, it will incur less travel time and expense because people are closer together.

Metro areas are also attractive markets because they offer greater sales potential than their large population alone suggests. Consumers in these areas have more money to spend because wages tend to be higher. In addition, professionals—with higher salaries—are concentrated there. But, it is wise to remember that competition for consumer dollars is usually stiff in an MSA.[9]

The mobile ones are an attractive market

Of course, none of these population shifts is necessarily permanent. People move, stay awhile, and then move again. In fact, about 18 percent of Americans

move each year—about half of them to a new city. Both the long-distance and local mobiles are important market segments.

Often people who move in the same city are trading up to a bigger or better house or neighborhood. They tend to be younger and better educated people "on the way up" in their careers. Their income is rising—and they have money to spend. Buying a new house may spark many other purchases, too. The old sofa may look shabby in the new house. And the bigger yard may require a new lawnmower—or even a yard service.

Many market-oriented decisions have to be made fairly quickly after moves. People must find new sources of food, clothing, medical and dental care, and household products. Once they make these basic buying decisions, they may not change for a long time. An alert marketer tries to locate these potential customers early to inform them of his offering.[10] Note that retail chains, "national" brands, and franchised services that are available in different areas have a competitive advantage with mobiles. The customer who moves to a new town may find the familiar Kroger grocery store sign down the street and never even try the local competitors.

INCOME—PEOPLE WITH MONEY MAKE MARKETS

So far, we have been concerned mainly with the *number* of different types of people—and *where* they live. But people without money are not potential customers. And the amount of money people can spend affects the products they are likely to buy. So most marketers study income levels, too.

Growth may continue

Income comes from producing and selling goods and services in the marketplace. A widely available measure of the output of the whole economy is the **gross national product (GNP)**—the total market value of goods and services produced in a year. U.S. GNP has increased at the rate of approximately 3 percent a year since 1880. This means that GNP doubled—on the average—every 20 years. Total U.S. GNP is now over $4.2 trillion dollars, or about $17,500 per capita.

Recently, this growth slowed—and even declined for a while. This decline in GNP may not just be due to temporarily bad economic conditions. GNP is related to the output of employees. When the population growth rate slows, there are fewer young workers and more retired people. This may become a serious political problem—everyone expects the economy to deliver more, while fewer young people are available to support the older ones.

More people are in middle and upper income levels

Total GNP figures are more meaningful to marketing managers when converted to family or household income—and its distribution. Family incomes in the United States have generally increased with GNP. But, even more important to marketers, the *distribution* of income has changed drastically over time.

Fifty years ago, the U.S. income distribution looked something like a pyramid. Most families were bunched together at the low end of the income scale—just over a subsistence level—to form the base of the income pyramid. There were many fewer families in the middle range, and a relative handful formed an elite market at the top.

By the 1970s, real income (buying power) had risen so much that most families —even those near the bottom of the income distribution—could afford a comfortable standard of living. And the proportion of people with middle incomes was much larger. Such middle-income people enjoyed real choices in the marketplace.

This was a revolution that broadened markets and drastically changed our marketing system. Products viewed as luxuries in most parts of the world are sold to "mass" markets in the United States. And these large markets lead to economies of scale, which boost our standard of living even more. Such a situation is found in the United States, Canada, many Western European countries, Australia, New Zealand, and Japan.

Real income growth has dropped—but for how long?

The shifting in the income distribution—and the increased number of families with more money to spend—is reflected by the trend in median family income from 1960 to 1986. See Exhibit 6–5. Note, though, that (real) median income stopped its continuous rise during the inflation-ridden 1970s—and then actually dropped some. Since 1982, it has been increasing again. But there is concern that there will be another downturn in the 1990s.

There is heated debate about what will happen to consumer incomes—and income distribution—in the future. Some business analysts feel that the lack of income growth is a sign of worse things to come. They think that America's middle-class standard of living is threatened by a decline in the manufacturing sector of the economy. These analysts argue that industries that traditionally paid high wages are now replacing workers with machines—to be able to compete with low-cost foreign producers. At the same time, the new jobs are coming from growth of the lower-paying service industries. But other analysts are not so pessimistic. They agree that the percentage of the work force earning middle-income wages has declined recently—but they think this is a temporary shift, not a long-term trend.

What happens to income levels will be critical to you—and to American consumers in general. It is easy for both consumers and marketing managers to be lulled by the promise of a constantly increasing standard of living. Adjustments in consumer thinking—and in marketing strategy—will be required if growth does not resume.

The higher-income groups receive a big share

Higher-income groups receive a very large share of the total income. This can be seen in Exhibit 6–6, which divides all families into five equal size groups—from

Exhibit 6–5   Median Family Income, 1960–1986 (in 1986 dollars)

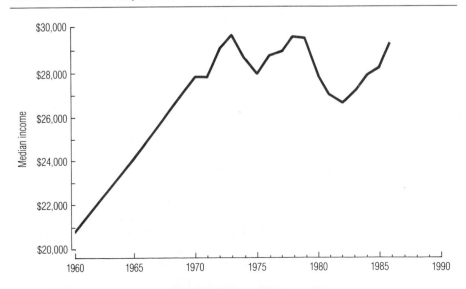

Exhibit 6–6   Percent of Total Income Going to Different Income Groups in 1986

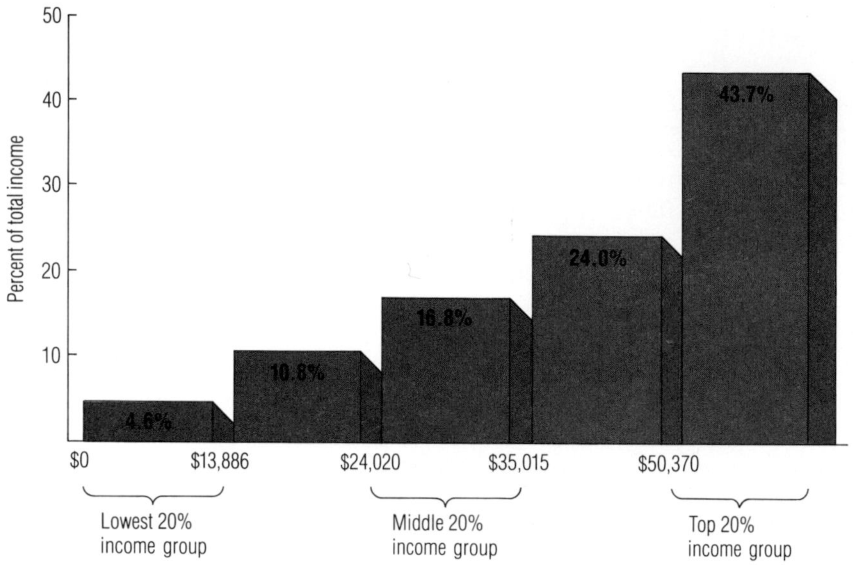

lowest income to highest. Note that although the median income of U.S. families in 1986 was about $29,450, the top 20 percent of the families—those with incomes over $50,370—received almost 44 percent of the total income. This gave them extra buying power, especially for luxury items. Well-to-do families with incomes over $82,270—the top 5 percent nationally—got more than 17 percent of the total income.

At the lower end of the scale, almost 13 million families had less than $13,886 income. They account for 20 percent of all families but receive less than 5 percent of the total income. Even this low-income group—over half of whom are below the poverty level of $11,000 for a family of four—is an attractive market for some basic commodities, especially food and clothing. These consumers may receive food stamps, medicare, and public housing, which increases their buying power. Some marketers target this group, usually with a lower-price marketing mix.

How much income is "enough"?

The importance of income distribution cannot be stressed too much. Companies have made serious marketing strategy errors by overestimating the amount of income in various target markets. It is easy for marketers to make such errors because of people's natural tendency to associate with others like themselves—and to assume that almost everyone lives like they do.

The 1986 median family income of about $29,450 is a useful reference point because some college graduates start near this level. And a young working couple together can easily go way over this figure. This may seem like a lot of money at first—but it is surprising how soon needs and expenses rise and adjust to available income.

Income is not equally distributed geographically

Earlier, we said that population is concentrated in some areas of the country—and that consumers in urban areas tend to have higher incomes than their country cousins. The map in Exhibit 6–7 compares median income by state. The high spots on the map are areas with high median incomes. Companies often map the income of different areas when picking markets. A market area—a city, county,

Exhibit 6–7   Median per Capita Income by State (1986)

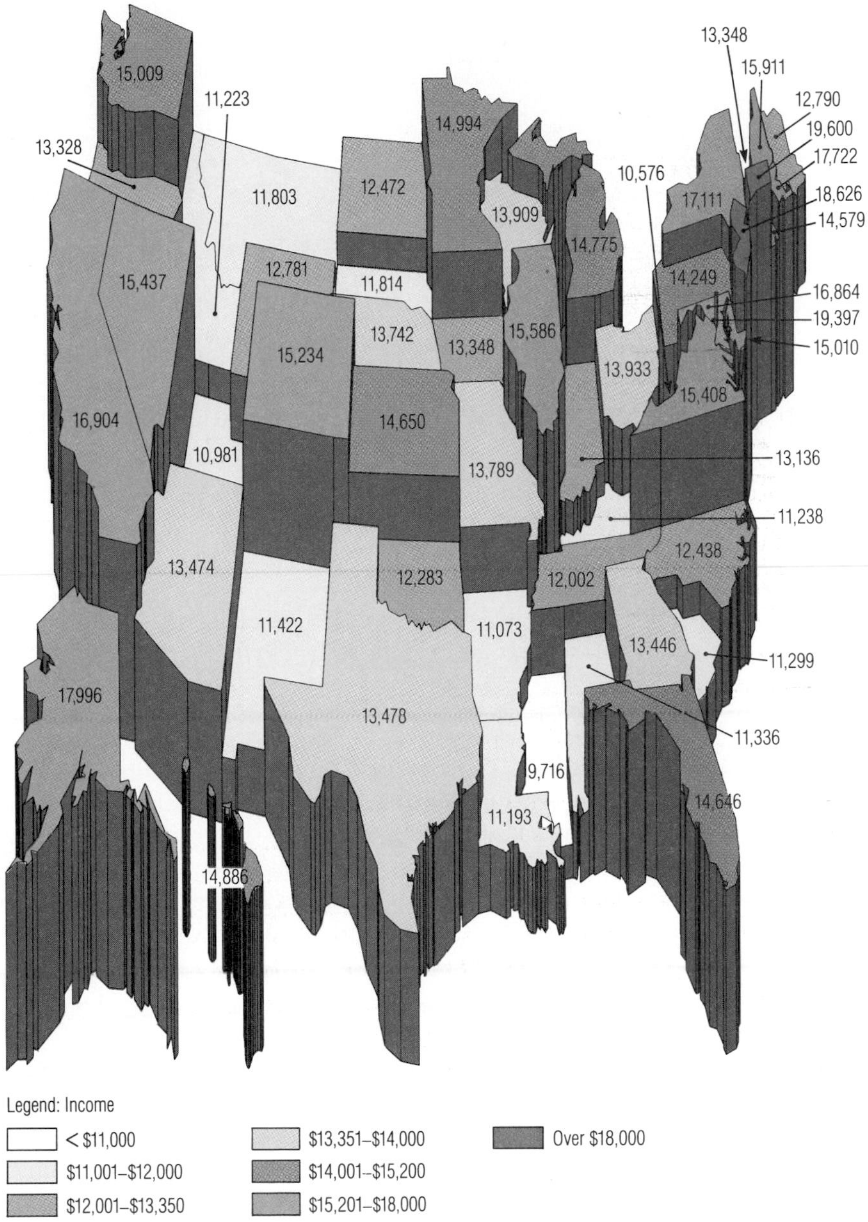

Legend: Income

< $11,000	$13,351–$14,000	Over $18,000
$11,001–$12,000	$14,001–$15,200	
$12,001–$13,350	$15,201–$18,000	

MSA, or state—that has more income will often be more attractive. A chain of retail children's wear stores moved into the Washington, D.C. suburbs because there are a lot of young families with high incomes there.[11]

CONSUMER SPENDING PATTERNS ARE RELATED TO POPULATION AND INCOME

We have been using the term *family income* because consumer budget studies show that most consumers spend their incomes as part of family or household

*Purchases of luxury items come
from discretionary income.*

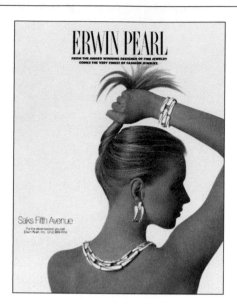

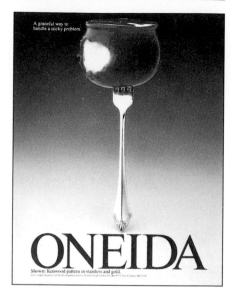

units. They usually pool their incomes when planning major expenditures. Thus, most of our discussion will concern how families or households spend their income.

**Disposable income is what
you get to spend**

Families don't get to spend all of their income. **Disposable income** is what is left after taxes. Out of this disposable income—together with gifts, pensions, cash savings, or other assets—the family makes its expenditures. Some families don't spend all their disposable income—they save part of it. Therefore, when trying to estimate potential sales in target markets, we should distinguish among income, disposable income, and what consumers actually spend.

**Discretionary income is
elusive**

Most families spend a good portion of their income on such "necessities" as food, rent or house payments, car and home furnishings payments, and insurance. A family's purchase of "luxuries" comes from **discretionary income**—what is left of disposable income after paying for necessities.

Discretionary income is an elusive concept because the definition of necessities varies from family to family and over time. It depends on what they think is necessary for their lifestyle. A color TV might be purchased out of discretionary income by a lower-income family but be considered a necessity by a higher-income family. But if many people in a lower-income neighborhood buy color TVs, then they might become a "necessity" for the others—and severely reduce the discretionary income available for other purchases.

The majority of U.S. families do not have enough discretionary income to afford the lifestyles seen on TV and in other mass media. On the other hand, some young adults and older people without family responsibilities have a lot of discretionary income. They may be especially attractive markets for stereos, cameras, new cars, foreign travel, and various kinds of recreation—tennis, skiing, boating, concerts, and fine restaurants.

Expenditure data tells how target markets spend

Obviously, wealthy families spend more money than poor ones—and on different things.[12] But, how it is spent—and how spending varies for different target markets—is important to marketers.

Currently the Bureau of Labor Statistics (BLS) and the U.S. Census Bureau publish the most comprehensive and easily available data on family spending.

Exhibit 6–8 shows the annual spending by urban families for several family income levels and for major categories of expenditures. This data can serve as reference points—and should keep you from making wild guesses based only on your own experience. The amount spent on major categories—such as food, housing, clothing, transportation, and so on—does vary by income level. And the relationships are logical when you realize that many of the purchases in these categories are "necessities."

Data such as that in Exhibit 6–8 can help you understand how potential target customers spend their money. Let's make this more concrete. Suppose you are a marketing manager for a swimming pool producer. You're considering a mail advertisement directed to consumers in an urban neighborhood of families with an average annual income of $25,000 a year. Looking at the center column of Exhibit 6–8, you can see how families at this income level spend their money. For example, the exhibit shows that—after paying for housing, transportation, and other basic items—families at this income level have about $3,000 a year left for entertainment, education, personal care, and other expenditures. If a swimming pool costs at least $2,000 a year—including maintenance and depreciation—the average family in this income category would have to make a big change in lifestyle to buy a pool.

Data like this won't tell you whether a specific family will buy a pool. But it does supply useful input to help make a sound decision. If more information is needed—perhaps about the strength of the target market's attitudes toward recreation products—then some marketing research may be needed. For example, you might want to see a budget study on consumers who already have a pool to see how they adjusted their spending patterns—and how they felt before and after the purchase.

Exhibit 6–8 Family Spending (in dollars and percent of spending) for Several Family Income Levels (in 1986 dollars)

Spending category	$15,000–$19,999		$20,000–$29,999		$30,000–$39,999	
	$	%	$	%	$	%
Food	$ 2,881	15.8%	$ 3,321	14.4%	$ 3,954	14.1%
Housing	5,685	31.1	6,750	29.3	8,025	28.6
Clothing	876	4.8	1,121	4.9	1,392	5.0
Transportation	3,763	20.6	5,151	22.4	6,226	22.2
Health care	1,194	6.5	1,103	4.8	1,101	3.9
Personal care	178	1.0	204	.9	255	.9
Education	171	.9	178	.8	229	.8
Reading	114	.6	146	.6	173	.6
Entertainment	834	4.6	1,052	4.6	1,513	5.4
Alcohol	223	1.2	303	1.3	327	1.2
Tobacco	228	1.2	257	1.1	270	1.0
Insurance and pensions	1,292	7.1	2,254	9.8	3,379	12.0
Contributions	564	3.1	853	3.7	748	2.7
Miscellaneous	264	1.5	313	1.4	453	1.6
Total spending	$18,266	100.0%	$23,008	100.0%	$28,043	100.0%

EXPENDITURE PATTERNS VARY WITH OTHER MEASURABLE FACTORS

Income has a direct bearing on spending patterns, but other important factors are involved.

Spending affected by urban-rural location

Consumer spending data show that the location of a consumer's family affects the family's spending habits. (We won't present detailed data here but will summarize a few important differences. Detailed BLS data can help you answer specific questions.)

Expenditures on transportation, housing, and food vary by geographic location. Consumers in central cities spend a lower percentage of their income on transportation and more on housing than those in rural areas outside MSAs—probably because of higher land and construction costs, and greater population density. A rural family spends a larger *percentage* on food, but the absolute amount is not very different.

Also, by region of the country

Geographic boundaries are also related to spending. Total expenditures in the South are lower than in other regions—but this isn't surprising. You can't spend what you don't have, and incomes in the South are lower (see Exhibit 6–7). But the important differences involve the relative shares going for food and housing. Consumers in the northeastern part of the United States tend to spend more on these categories (especially for food, utilities, and housing costs).

Stage of family life cycle affects spending

Marital status, age, and the age of any children in a family are other demographic dimensions that affect spending patterns. Put together, these dimensions tell us about the life cycle stage of a family.[13] See Exhibit 6–9 for a summary of stages in the life cycle and buying behavior.

Young people and families accept new ideas

Singles and young couples seem to be more willing to try new products and brands—and they are careful, price-conscious shoppers. Younger people often earn less than older consumers, but they spend a greater proportion of their income on discretionary items because they don't have the major expenses of home ownership, education, and family rearing. Although many young people are waiting longer to marry, most do "tie the knot" eventually. These younger families—especially those with no children—are still accumulating durable goods, such as automobiles and home furnishings. They spend less on food. It is only as children arrive and grow that family spending shifts to soft goods and services, such as education, medical, and personal care. This usually happens when the family head reaches the 35–44 age group. To meet expenses, people in this age group often make more purchases on credit, and they save less of their income.

Divorce—increasingly a fact of American life—disrupts the family life cycle pattern. Divorced parents don't spend like other "singles." The mother usually has custody of the children, and the father may pay child support. The mother and children typically have much less income than two-parent families. Such families spend a larger percent of their income on housing, child care, and other necessities—with little left for discretionary purchases. If a single parent remarries, the family life cycle may start over again.

Exhibit 6–9   Stages in the Family Life Cycle

Stage	Characteristics and buying behavior
1. Singles: unmarried people living away from parents	Feel "affluent" and "free." Buy basic household goods. More interested in recreation, cars, vacations, clothes, cosmetics and personal care items.
2. Divorced or separated	May be financially squeezed to pay for alimony or maintaining two households. Buying may be limited to "necessities"—especially for women who have no job skills.
3. Newly married couples: no children	Both may work and so they feel financially well-off. Buy durables: cars, refrigerators, stoves, basic furniture—and recreation equipment and vacations.
4. Full nest I: youngest child under six	Feel squeezed financially because they are buying homes and household durables—furniture, washers, dryers, and TV. Also buying child-related products—food, medicines, clothes, and toys. Really interested in new products.
5. Full nest II: youngest child over five	Financially are better off as husband earns more and/or wife goes to work as last child goes to school. More spent on food, clothing, education, and recreation for growing children.
6. Full nest III: older couples with dependent children	Financially even better off as husband earns more and more wives work. May replace durables and furniture, and buy cars, boats, dental services, and more expensive recreation and travel. May buy bigger houses.
7. Empty nest: older couples, no children living with them, head still working	Feel financially "well-off." Home ownership at peak, and house may be paid for. May make home improvements or move into apartments. And may travel, entertain, go to school, and make gifts and contributions. Not interested in new products.
8. Sole survivor, still working	Income still good. Likely to sell home and continue with previous lifestyle.
9. Senior citizen I: older married couple, no children living with them, head retired	Big drop in income. May keep home but cut back on most buying as purchases of medical care, drugs, and other health-related items go up.
10. Senior citizen II: sole survivor, not working	Same as senior citizen I, except likely to sell home, and has special need for attention, affection, and security.

Reallocation for teenagers

Once children become teenagers, further shifts in spending occur. Teenagers eat more, want to wear expensive clothes, and develop recreation and education needs that are hard on the family budget. The parents may be forced to reallocate their expenditures to cover these expenses—spending less on durable goods, such as appliances, automobiles, household goods, and houses. A family can easily spend $10,000 a year to send a son or daughter to college.

Many teenagers do earn much or all of their own spending money—and this has made them an attractive market. The amount of money involved may surprise you: America's 24 million teens spend $53 billion a year—an average of about $185 a month! But marketers who have catered to teenagers are feeling the decline in birthrate and probably will face harder times in the future. Motorcycle manufacturers, for example, have already been hurt because teenagers are their heaviest buyers.[14]

Selling to the empty nesters

An important category is the **empty nesters**—people whose children are grown and who are now able to spend their money in other ways. Usually these people are in the 50–64 age group. But this is an elusive group because some people marry later and are still raising a family at this age.

Empty nesters are an attractive market for many items. They have paid for their homes, and the big expenses of raising a family are behind them. They are more interested in travel, small sports cars, and other things they couldn't afford before. Much depends on their income, of course. But this is a high-income period for many workers—especially white-collar workers.

Senior citizens are a big new market

Finally, the **senior citizens**—people over 65—should not be neglected. The number of people over 65 is increasing rapidly because of modern medicine, improved sanitary conditions, and better nutrition. This group now makes up about 13 percent of the population—and is growing.

Our senior citizens are more prosperous than ever before. Their income is lower than in their peak earning years, but most do have money to spend. They don't just squeak by on social security. Such prosperity is a dramatic change. In 1960, about a third of all senior citizens had incomes below the poverty level. Now, only about 13 percent are considered "poor"—barely higher than the average for all adults.

Older people also have very different needs. Many firms are already catering to senior citizens—and more will be serving this market. For example. some companies have developed housing and "life-care" centers designed to appeal to older people. Casio makes a calculator with large, easy-to-read numbers. Publix Super Markets, a big Florida chain, trains employees to cater to older customers. Check-out clerks, for example, give older customers two light bags instead of one heavier one. Some travel agents are finding that senior citizens are an eager market for expensive tours and cruises. Other companies offer diet supplements and drug products—often in special easy-to-open packages. And senior citizen discounts at

Many firms are catering to the increasing number of senior citizens.

drugstores are more than just a courtesy—the elderly are the biggest market for medicines.

Keep in mind, however, that older people are not all the same. With a group this large, generalities can be dangerous. Different senior citizen target markets have different needs—and require different marketing strategies.

Do ethnic groups buy differently?

America may be called the "melting pot," but ethnic groups deserve special attention when analyzing markets. For example, more than 1 out of 10 families speaks a language other than English at home. Some areas have a much higher rate. In Miami and San Antonio, for example, about one out of three families speaks Spanish. This obviously affects promotion planning. Similarly, brand preferences vary for some ethnic groups.

Ethnic dimensions must be studied and watched carefully because they can be subtle and fast-changing. This is also an area where stereotyped thinking is the most common—and misleading. Some marketing managers have treated all 31 million black consumers as "the black market," ignoring other relevant segmenting dimensions. For example, young, middle-income, black working couples are a distinctive, almost ignored market—but they account for a large share of the $220 billion spent by black consumers each year. These working couples have accepted the values of middle America—but they have their own needs and ways of thinking. And they live in different areas and respond to different media.[15]

The demographics for ethnic groups may vary, too. The median age of U.S. blacks and Spanish-speaking people is much lower than that of whites—and the birthrate is higher. This means that many more are in earlier stages of the life cycle and, therefore, are a better market for certain products—especially durable goods.

Separate strategies may be needed for these ethnically or racially defined markets. Some of these strategies may require only changes in Place and Promotion—but they will be separate strategies. More marketers are paying attention to ethnic groups now because the size of these markets is increasing. For example, the market of Hispanic consumers more than doubled from about 9 million consumers in 1970 to about 22 million now. To put this in perspective, there are as many Hispanics in the United States as there are Canadians in Canada—and they spend $140 billion a year. Moreover, by 2015 the U.S. Hispanic population is expected to reach 40 million.[16]

When the wife earns, the family spends

Another group that deserves attention is the growing number of women—especially married women—with paying jobs. In 1950, only 24 percent of wives worked outside the home. But this figure rose to more than 55 percent in the 80s, and by 1995 it will probably be 60 percent. Among women in the 35–44 age group, the percentage is already over 70.

The flood of women into the job market has boosted economic growth and is changing the U.S. economy. Women's wages average only about 65 percent of men's wages, although this gap is narrowing. Even so, working women are generating income and creating new opportunities for marketers. Working women spend more on clothes and food and purchase more personal services—child care and cleaning help, for example.

In families where the wife works, about 40 percent of all the family spending power comes from her income. This is one reason why the median family income is as high as it is. Families with working wives also spend more on clothing, child care, alcohol and tobacco, home furnishings and equipment, and cars. In short, when a wife works outside the home, it affects the family's spending habits. This fact must be considered when analyzing markets and planning marketing strategies.[17]

CONCLUSION

We studied population data to get the facts straight on how nearly 250 million people are spread over the United States. We learned that the potential of a given market cannot be determined by population figures alone. Income, stage in life cycle, geographic location of people, and other factors are important, too. We talked about some of the ways that these dimensions—and changes in them—affect marketing strategy planning.

We also noted the growth of metropolitan areas. The high concentration of population and spending power in these markets has already made them attractive target markets. Competition in these markets is often tough, however.

One of the outstanding characteristics of Americans is their mobility. Managers must pay attention to changes in markets. High mobility makes even relatively new data suspect. Data can only aid a manager's judgment—not replace it.

American consumers are among the most affluent in the world. They have more discretionary income and can afford a wide variety of "luxuries."

The kind of data discussed in this chapter can be very useful for estimating the market potential within possible target markets. But, unfortunately, it is not very helpful in explaining specific customer behavior— why people buy *specific* products and *specific* brands. Yet such detailed forecasts are important to marketing managers. Better forecasts can come from a better understanding of consumer behavior—the subject of the next chapter.

Questions and Problems

1. Discuss how slower population growth— especially the smaller number of young people—will affect businesses in your local community.

2. Discuss the impact of our "aging culture" on marketing strategy planning.

3. Name three specific examples of firms that have developed a marketing mix to appeal to the baby boom group of consumers.

4. Some demographic characteristics are likely to be more important than others in determining market potential. For each of the following characteristics, identify two products for which this characteristic is *most* important: (*a*) size of geographic area, (*b*) population, (*c*) income, (*d*) stage of life cycle.

5. Name three specific examples (specific products or brands—not just product categories) and explain how demand will differ by geographic location *and* urban-rural location.

6. Explain how the continuing mobility of consumers—as well as the development of big metropolitan areas—should affect marketing strategy planning in the future. Be sure to consider the impact on the four Ps.

7. Explain how the redistribution of income has affected marketing planning thus far—and its likely impact in the future.

8. Explain why the concept of the Metropolitan Statistical Area was developed. Is it the most useful breakdown for retailers?

9. Explain why mobile consumers can be an attractive market.

10. Briefly discuss how the increasing number of women who work outside the home is likely to affect the demand for each of the following products: (*a*) food freezers, (*b*) VCRs, (*c*) Girl Scout uniforms.

Suggested Cases _____

8. Mario's   10.   Polar Ice Rink

Suggested Computer-Aided Problem _____

6.   Demographic Analysis

Chapter 7

Behavioral Dimensions of the Consumer Market

When You Finish This Chapter, You Should

1. Know about the various "black box" models of buyer behavior.

2. Understand how psychological variables affect an individual's buying behavior.

3. Understand how social influences affect an individual's and household's buying behavior.

4. See why the purchase situation has an effect on consumer behavior.

5. Know how consumers use problem-solving processes.

6. Have some "feel" for how a consumer handles all the behavioral variables and incoming stimuli.

7. Understand the important new terms (shown in red).

Which car will the customer buy—a BMW or a Cadillac Seville?

For years, Cadillac's marketing mix was targeted toward older consumers who wanted a big luxury car with a "living-room" quiet drive. Cadillac consistently promoted its image and built a strong customer following.

By 1987, marketing managers at Cadillac had shifted their aim to the growing number of high-paid professionals in their early 40s who were buying BMWs, Mercedes, Turbo Saabs, or Volvos. To appeal to this market, Cadillac introduced the Allante convertible and sporty Seville and Eldorado models with sleek new designs, snappy performance, and better handling. Promotion focused on these changes and "the new spirit of Cadillac." Ads showed middle-aged people driving Cadillacs and enjoying fast-paced lifestyles.

Cadillac's efforts didn't have much effect at first. The new target market didn't pay much attention to Cadillac's advertising—even in "their" magazines. They wanted a car that had status with their "group." They still thought of Cadillac as a car for their parents. Older Cadillac buyers were not impressed either. They complained about the smaller size—and many switched to big Lincolns.

Cadillac made more changes to appeal to its target—and the market changed too. Yuppie status symbols were no longer "in." Higher prices and a number of new luxury cars in the market—like the Acura, Lexus, and Infiniti—motivated buyers to study the choices more carefully. Many younger buyers decided that Cadillac did have something for them. And Cadillac increased the size of some models to satisfy older customers. It seems that Cadillac is now doing a better job of meeting customers' needs—and things are looking up.[1]

CONSUMER BEHAVIOR—WHY DO THEY BUY WHAT THEY BUY?

How can marketing managers predict which specific products consumers will buy—and in what quantities? Why does a consumer choose a particular product?

In the last chapter, we discussed basic data on population, income, and consumer spending patterns in U.S. markets. With this information, we can predict basic *trends* in consumer spending patterns.

Unfortunately, when many firms sell similar products, demographic analysis isn't much help in predicting which products and brands consumers will purchase. Yet whether his products and brands will be chosen—and to what extent—is extremely important to a marketing manager.

To find better answers, we need to understand more about people—and their consumer behavior. For this reason, many marketers have turned to the behavioral sciences for help. In this chapter, we will explore some of the thinking from economics, psychology, sociology, and the other behavioral disciplines. Our Cadillac example illustrates some of the ideas we'll be discussing. Note that consumers' attitudes toward Cadillac had been learned over a long period of time. Advertising didn't have much effect at first because it was selectively ignored. Customers' beliefs—right or wrong—and friends' opinions did have an effect. A car purchase is motivated by certain needs, but it was not until the new target market did more extended problem solving that they decided that Cadillac was meeting these needs.

THE BEHAVIORAL SCIENCES HELP UNDERSTAND BUYING PROCESS

Buying in a black box

Exhibit 7–1 shows a simplified—"black box"—view of customer buying behavior. Potential customers are exposed to various stimuli, including competitors' marketing mixes. Somehow, a person takes in some or all of these stimuli and then, for some reason, responds.

Exhibit 7–1   Simplified Buyer Behavior Model

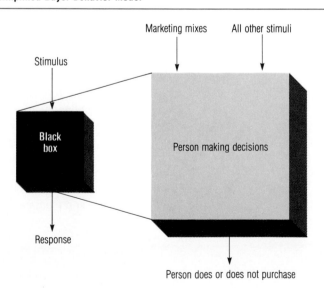

This is a simple version of the classic **stimulus-response model**, which says that people respond in some predictable way to a stimulus. However, the model doesn't explain *why* people behave the way they do.

Although we can't directly observe a consumer's decision-making process, there is much research—and many different opinions—about how it works. These different theories lead to different forecasts about how consumers will behave.

Most economists assume that consumers are **economic men**—people who know all the facts and logically compare choices in terms of cost and value received to get the greatest satisfaction from spending their time and money. It was a logical extension of the economic-man theory that led us to look at consumer spending patterns in Chapter 6. There is value in this approach. Consumers must at least have income to be in a market. But most marketing managers think that buyer behavior is not as simple as the economic-man model suggests.

How we will view consumer behavior

Consumers have many dimensions. Let's try to combine these dimensions into a better model of how consumers make decisions. Exhibit 7–2 presents a more detailed view "inside" the black box. We see that psychological variables, social influences, and the purchase situation all affect a person.

These topics will be discussed in the next few pages. Then we'll look at the consumer's problem-solving process.

PSYCHOLOGICAL INFLUENCES WITHIN AN INDIVIDUAL

Here we will discuss some variables of special interest to marketers—including motivation, perception, learning, attitudes, and lifestyle. Much of what we know about these *psychological (intrapersonal) variables* draws from ideas originally developed in the field of psychology.

Exhibit 7–2 More Complete Buyer Behavior Model

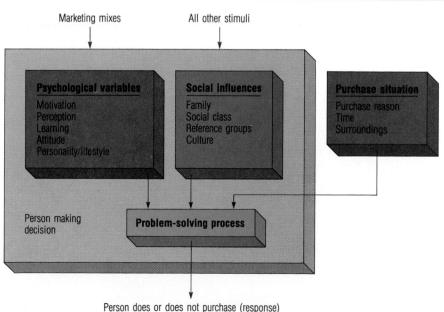

Needs motivate consumers

Everybody is motivated by needs and wants. **Needs** are the basic forces that motivate a person to do something. Some needs are concerned with a person's physical well-being. Other needs are concerned with the individual's self-view and relationship with others. Needs are more basic than wants. **Wants** are "needs" that are learned during a person's life. For example, everyone needs water or some kind of liquid, but some people also have learned to want "Perrier with a twist."

When a need is not satisfied, it may lead to a drive. The need for liquid, for example, leads to a thirst drive. A **drive** is a strong stimulus that encourages action to reduce a need. Drives are internal—they are the reasons behind certain behavior patterns. In marketing, a product purchase is the result of a drive to satisfy some need.

Some critics imply that marketers can somehow manipulate consumers to buy products against their will. But marketing managers can't create internal drives in consumers. Most marketing managers realize that trying to get consumers to act against their will is a waste of time. Instead, a good marketing manager studies what consumer drives and needs already exist and how they can be satisfied better.

Consumers seek benefits to meet needs

We all are a bundle of needs and wants. Exhibit 7–3 lists some important needs that might motivate a person to some action. This list, of course, is not complete. But thinking about such needs can help you see what *benefits* consumers might seek from a marketing mix.

When a marketing manager defines a product-market, the needs may be quite specific. For example, the food need might be as specific as wanting a thick-crust pepperoni pizza.

Exhibit 7–3   Possible Needs Motivating a Person to Some Action

Physiological needs			
Hunger	Thirst	Activity	Sleep
Sex	Body elimination	Self-preservation	Warmth/coolness
Rest			

Psychological needs			
Aggression	Curiosity	Being responsible	Dominance
Family preservation	Imitation	Independence	Love
Nurturing	Order	Personal fulfillment	Playing—competitive
Playing—relaxing	Power	Pride	Self-expression
Self-identification	Tenderness		

Desire for			
Acceptance	Achievement	Acquisition	Affection
Affiliation	Appreciation	Beauty	Companionship
Comfort	Fun	Distance—"space"	Distinctiveness
Esteem	Fame	Happiness	Identification
Knowledge	Prestige	Pleasure	Recognition
Respect	Retaliation	Self-satisfaction	Sociability
Status	Sympathy	Variety	

Freedom from			
Anxiety	Depression	Discomfort	Fear
Harm	Imitation	Loss	Pain
Pressure	Ridicule	Sadness	Illness

Several needs at the same time

Some psychologists argue that a person may have several reasons for buying—at the same time. Maslow is well known for his five-level hierarchy of needs. We will discuss a similar four-level hierarchy that is easier to apply to consumer behavior.[2] The four levels are illustrated in Exhibit 7–4, along with an advertising slogan that illustrates how a company has tried to appeal to each need. The lowest-level needs are physiological. Then come safety, social, and personal needs. As a study aid, think of the "PSSP needs."

The **physiological needs** are concerned with biological needs—food, drink, rest, and sex. The **safety needs** are concerned with protection and physical well-being (perhaps involving health food, medicine, and exercise). The **social needs** are concerned with love, friendship, status, and esteem—things that involve a person's interaction with others. The **personal needs**, on the other hand, are concerned with an individual's need for personal satisfaction—unrelated to what others think or do. Examples include self-esteem, accomplishment, fun, freedom, and relaxation.

Motivation theory suggests that we never reach a state of complete satisfaction. As soon as lower-level needs are reasonably satisfied, those at higher levels become more dominant. It is important to see, however, that a particular product may satisfy more than one need at the same time. A hamburger in a friendly environment, for example, might satisfy not only the physiological need to satisfy hunger but also some social need. In fact, marketing managers should realize that most consumers try to fill a *set* of needs rather than just one need or another in sequence. Also, exactly which set of needs is to be satisfied can vary from one group to another.

Economic needs affect how we satisfy basic needs

The need hierarchy idea can help explain *why* consumers will buy, but the economic needs help explain *what* specific product features they will select.

Exhibit 7–4   The PSSP Hierachy of Needs

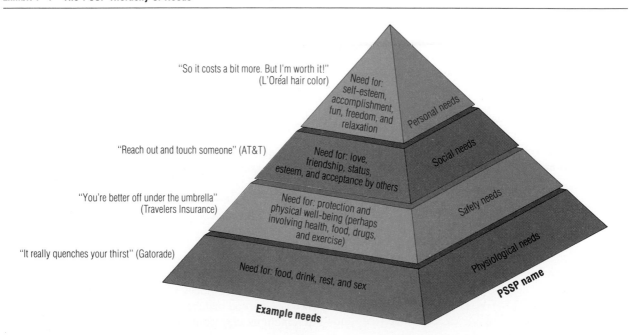

The Purina Dog Chow ad focuses on the need for love while the Benedryl ad focuses on physical well-being.

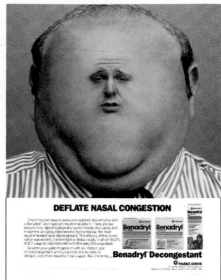

Economic needs are concerned with making the best use of a consumer's time and money—as the consumer judges it. Some consumers look for the lowest price. Others will pay extra for convenience. And others may weigh price and quality for the best value. Some economic needs are:

1. Economy of purchase or use.
2. Convenience.
3. Efficiency in operation or use.
4. Dependability in use.
5. Improvement of earnings.

Marketing managers should be alert to new ways to appeal to economic needs. This does not just mean offering lower and lower prices. Many consumers face a "poverty of time." Carefully planned place decisions can make it easier and faster for customers to make a purchase. Products can be designed to require less service—or to last longer. Promotion can explain product benefits in terms of measurable factors like specific dollar savings, the length of the guarantee, and the time or money saved by using the product.

Perception determines what is seen and felt

Consumers select varying ways to meet their needs. Some of this is because of differences in **perception**—how we gather and interpret information from the world around us.

We are constantly bombarded by stimuli—ads, products, stores—yet we may not hear or see anything. This is because we apply the following selective processes:

1. **Selective exposure**—our eyes and minds seek out and notice only information that interests us.
2. **Selective perception**—we screen out or modify ideas, messages, and information that conflict with previously learned attitudes and beliefs.
3. **Selective retention**—we remember only what we want to remember.

These selective processes help explain why some people are not affected by some advertising—even offensive advertising. They just don't see or remember it!

Our needs affect these selective processes. And current needs receive more attention. For example, Goodyear tire retailers advertise some "sale" in the newspaper almost weekly. Most of the time we don't even notice these ads—until we need new tires. Only then do we tune in to Goodyear's ads.

Marketers are interested in these selective processes because they affect how target consumers get and retain information. This is also why marketers are interested in how consumers *learn.*

Learning determines what response is likely

Learning is a change in a person's thought processes caused by prior experience. A little girl tastes her first Häagen-Dazs ice cream cone, and learning occurs! In fact, almost all consumer behavior is learned.[3]

Experts describe a number of steps in the learning process. We have already discussed the idea of a drive as a strong stimulus that encourages action. Depending on the **cues**—products, signs, ads, and other stimuli in the environment—an individual chooses some specific response. A **response** is an effort to satisfy a drive. The specific response chosen depends on the cues and the person's past experience.

Reinforcement of the learning process occurs when the response is followed by satisfaction—that is, reducing the drive. Reinforcement strengthens the relationship between the cue and the response. And it may lead to a similar response the next time the drive occurs. Repeated reinforcement leads to the development of a habit—making the individual's decision process routine. The relationships of the important variables in the learning process are shown in Exhibit 7–5.

Exhibit 7–5   The Learning Process

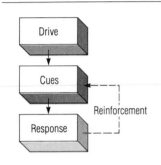

The learning process can be illustrated by a thirsty person. The thirst *drive* could be satisfied in a variety of ways. But if the person happened to walk past a vending machine and saw a 7UP sign—a *cue*—then he might satisfy the drive with a *response*—buying a 7UP. If the experience is satisfactory, positive *reinforcement* will occur, and our friend may be quicker to satisfy this drive in the same way in the future. This emphasizes the importance of developing good products that live up to the promises of the firm's advertising. People can learn to like or dislike 7UP—reinforcement and learning work both ways.

Good experiences can lead to positive attitudes about a firm's product. Bad experiences can lead to negative attitudes that even good promotion won't be able to change. In fact, the subject of attitudes, an extremely important one to marketers, is discussed more fully in a later section.

Positive cues help a marketing mix

Sometimes marketers try to identify cues or images that have positive associations from some other situation and relate them to their marketing mix. Many people associate the smell of lemons with a fresh, natural cleanliness. Lemon scent is often added to household cleaning products—Joy dishwashing detergent and Pledge furniture polish, for example—because it has these associations.

Some firms copy favorable cues associated with a competitor's popular product—hoping that the same consumer response will carry over to their product. They may use a similar package or brand name. Campbell's soup—long a consumer favorite—has a label with distinctive colors and lettering. Some lesser-known brands of soup use look-alike colors and type styles on their labels. They hope that consumers' positive feelings toward Campbell will encourage purchase of *their* soup. Ideally, they hope the buyer will simply respond to the cue with the same learned response and not discriminate between Campbell's and their brand.

Sometimes marketers try to identify cues that have positive associations from other situations and relate them to their marketing mix.

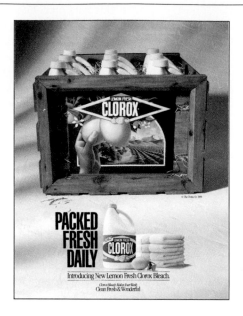

Some needs may be learned

Many needs are culturally (or socially) learned. The need for food, for instance, may lead to many specific food wants. Many Japanese enjoy raw fish, and their children learn to like it. Few Americans, however, have learned to like raw fish.

Some critics argue that marketing efforts encourage people to spend money on learned wants totally unrelated to any "basic need." For example, Europeans are less concerned about body odor, and few buy or use a deodorant. Yet Americans spend millions of dollars on such products. Advertising says that using Ban deodorant "takes the worry out of being close." But is marketing activity the cause of the difference in the two cultures? Most research says that advertising can't convince buyers of something contrary to their basic attitudes.

Attitudes relate to buying

An **attitude** is a person's point of view toward something. The "something" may be a product, an advertisement, a salesperson, a firm, or an idea. Attitudes are an important topic for marketers because attitudes affect the selective processes, learning, and eventually the buying decisions people make.

Because attitudes are usually thought of as involving liking or disliking, they have some action implications. Beliefs are not so action-oriented. A **belief** is a person's opinion about something. Beliefs may help shape a consumer's attitudes but don't necessarily involve any liking or disliking. It is possible to have a belief—say, that Listerine has a medicinal taste—without really caring what it tastes like. On the other hand, beliefs about a product may have a positive or negative effect in shaping consumers' attitudes. For example, a person with a headache is unlikely to switch to a new pain medicine unless he believes it will be more effective than what he has used in the past.

In an attempt to relate attitude more closely to purchase behavior, some marketers have stretched the attitude concept to include consumer "preferences" or "intention to buy." The intention to buy is of most interest to managers who must

Some products are purchased because of culturally learned needs.

forecast how much of their brand customers will buy. Forecasts would be easier if attitudes were good predictors of intentions to buy. Unfortunately, the relationships usually are not that simple. A person may have positive attitudes toward a Jacuzzi hot tub but no intention of buying one.

Research on consumer attitudes can sometimes help a marketing manager get a better picture of markets. For example, consumers who have very positive attitudes toward a new product idea might indicate a good opportunity—especially if they have negative attitudes about competitors' offerings. Or they may have beliefs that would discourage them from liking the product category or wanting to buy it.

Marketers generally try to understand the attitudes of their potential customers and work with them. We'll discuss this idea again when we review the way consumers evaluate product alternatives. For now, we want to emphasize that it is more economical to work with consumer attitudes than to try to change them. Attitudes tend to be enduring. Changing present attitudes—especially negative ones—is probably the most difficult job that marketers face.[4]

Personality affects how people see things

Much research has been done on how personality affects people's behavior, but the results have generally been disappointing to marketers. A trait like neatness can be associated with users of certain types of products—like cleaning materials. But personality traits haven't been much help in predicting which specific products or brands people will choose.[5]

Further, we haven't found a way to use personality to help in strategy planning. Part of the problem is that most personality measures were originally developed to identify people whose behavior was abnormal. Most consumer behavior, on the other hand, is quite normal. As a result, marketers have stopped focusing on personality measures borrowed from psychologists and instead developed life-style analysis.

Marketing Managers for Nuprin Give Competitors a Headache

Ask pharmacists about pain relievers and they're likely to talk about the ingredients—using tongue-twister words like analgesics, acetaminophen, and ibuprofen. In contrast, most consumers just think about a brand of pain pill—like Tylenol, Nuprin, Advil, or Bayer Aspirin. Consumer attitudes about these different brands affect each brand's share of the $2 billion people spend on pain killers each year.

Marketing managers at Bristol-Myers Company faced a challenge. Research showed that their Nuprin brand gave more pain relief than Tylenol, the most popular brand. But, Nuprin ads had failed to get across that message. Consumers didn't want to listen—they seemed to believe that one pain killer was about as good as another. This prompted Nuprin to try a different approach. Nuprin developed ads that focused on a super-

ficial product difference, its yellow color, and pitched Nuprin as "little, yellow, different, better." Black-and-white TV ads showed people giving testimonials that their worst pains—toothaches, back pain, headaches—were relieved with Nuprin. Only the yellow Nuprin tablets were shown in color. The ads resulted in more favorable attitudes toward Nuprin, and by the end of the year Nuprin's sales were growing faster than sales of any other brand. One advertising specialist explained the success this way: "you have to convince consumers that the product is different before they will believe the product is better. That Nuprin is yellow is superficial to the product superiority, yet it opens people's minds that this product is different." Consumer beliefs—right or wrong—can have a significant impact on whether a strategy succeeds.[6]

Psychographics or life-style analysis focuses on activities, interests, and opinions

Psychographics or **life-style analysis** is the analysis of a person's day-to-day pattern of living as expressed in his Activities, Interests, and Opinions—sometimes referred to as "AIOs." A number of variables for each of the AIO dimensions are shown in Exhibit 7–6—along with some demographics that are used to add detail to the life-style profile of a target market.

Life-style analysis assumes that a marketer can plan more effective strategies to reach his target market if he knows more about them. Understanding the life-style of target customers has been especially helpful in providing ideas for advertising themes. Let's see how it adds to a typical demographic description. It may not help Mercury marketing managers much to know that an average member of the target market for a Sable station wagon is 34.8 years old, married, lives in a

Exhibit 7–6   Life-Style Dimensions

Activities	Interests	Opinions	Demographics
Work	Family	Themselves	Age
Hobbies	Home	Social issues	Education
Social events	Job	Politics	Income
Vacation	Community	Business	Occupation
Entertainment	Recreation	Economics	Family size
Club membership	Fashion	Education	Dwelling
Community	Food	Products	Geography
Shopping	Media	Future	City size
Sports	Achievements	Culture	Stage in life cycle

General Mills has changed "Betty Crocker's" appearance as consumer attitudes and lifestyles have changed.

The original Betty, 1936   1955   1965   1972   1980   1986

three-bedroom home, and has 2.3 children. Lifestyles help marketers paint a more human portrait of the target market. For example, life-style analysis might show that the 34.8-year-old is also a community-oriented consumer with traditional values who especially enjoys spectator sports and spends much time in other activities with the whole family. An ad might show the Sable being used by a happy family at a ball game so the target market could really identify with the ad. And the ad might be placed in a magazine like *Sports Illustrated* whose readers match the target life-style profile.[7]

SOCIAL INFLUENCES AFFECT CONSUMER BEHAVIOR

We have been discussing some of the ways that needs, attitudes, and other psychological variables influence the buying process. Now, we'll see that these variables—and the buying process—are usually affected by relations with other people, too. We will look at how the individual interacts with family, social class, and other groups who may have influence. Keep in mind that many ideas about social (interpersonal) influence on buyer behavior were originally developed in sociology, anthropology, and social psychology.

Who is the real decision maker in family purchases?

Although one person in a household usually makes the purchase, in planning strategy it's important to identify the real decision maker.

Not long ago, the wife was the family purchasing agent. She had the time to shop and run errands. So most promotion for food and household items was aimed at women. But now as more women work—and as night and weekend shopping become more popular—men and older children are doing more shopping and decision making.

Although one member of the family may go to the store and make a specific purchase, it is important in planning marketing strategy to know who else may be involved. Other family members may have influenced the decision or really decided what to buy. Still others may use the product.

You don't have to watch much Saturday morning TV to see that Kellogg's and General Mills know this. Cartoon characters like "Cap'n Crunch" and "Tony the Tiger" tell kids about the goodies found in certain cereal packages—and urge them

Buying responsibilities and influence vary greatly, depending on the product and the family.

to remind Dad or Mom to pick up that brand on their next trip to the store. Older sons and daughters may even influence big purchases like cars and television sets.

Family considerations may overwhelm personal ones

A husband or wife may have strong personal preferences for various products and services. However, such individual preferences may be changed if the other spouse has different priorities. One might want to take a family vacation to Disneyland—when the other wants a new RCA video recorder and Sony large-screen TV. The actual outcome in such a situation is unpredictable. The preferences of one spouse might change because of affection for the other—or because of the other's power and influence.

Buying responsibility and influence vary greatly depending on the product and the family. A marketer trying to plan a strategy will find it helpful to research his target market. Remember, many buying decisions are made jointly, and thinking only about who actually buys the product can misdirect the marketing strategy.[8]

Social class affects attitudes, values, and buying

Up to now, we have been concerned with the individual and his relation to his family. Now let's consider how society looks at an individual and perhaps the family—in terms of social class. A **social class** is a group of people who have approximately equal social position as viewed by others in the society.

Almost every society has some social class structure. The U.S. class system is far less rigid than in most countries. Children start out in the same social class as their parents—but they can move to a different social class depending on their educational levels or the jobs they hold.

Marketers want to know what buyers in various social classes are like. Simple approaches for measuring social class groupings are based on a person's *occupation*, *education*, and *type and location of housing*. By using marketing research surveys or available census data, marketers can get a feel for the social class of a target market.

Note that income level is not included in this list. There is *some* general relationship between income level and social class. But the income level of people within the same social class can vary greatly, and people with the same income level may be in different social classes.

To develop better marketing strategies, marketing managers need to understand the differences among social classes. Exhibit 7–7 illustrates a multilevel social class structure. (Note the relative sizes of the groupings.) Although we use traditional technical terms like *upper, middle,* and *lower,* a word of warning is in order. The terms may seem to imply "superior" and "inferior." But, in sociological and marketing usage, no value judgment is intended. We cannot say that any one class is "better" or "happier" than another.

Characteristics of social classes in the United States

The **upper class** (2 percent of the population) consists of people from old, wealthy families (upper-upper) as well as the socially prominent new rich (lower-upper). Such people often live in large homes with luxury features. They are a good market for antiques, art, rare jewelry, luxury travel, and unique designer products. They may avoid mass-merchandisers in favor of exclusive shops where they receive special services.

The **upper-middle class** (11 percent of the population) consists of successful professionals, owners of small businesses, or managers of large corporations. These people are concerned about their quality of life. They view their purchases as symbols of success, so they want quality products. They want to be seen as socially acceptable. They support the arts and are community-minded. They are ambitious for their children and, in general, are more "future-oriented" than the lower-class groups.

The **lower-middle class** (36 percent of the population) consists of small business people, office workers, teachers, and technicians—the white-collar workers.

Exhibit 7–7   Relative Sizes of Different Social Class Groups

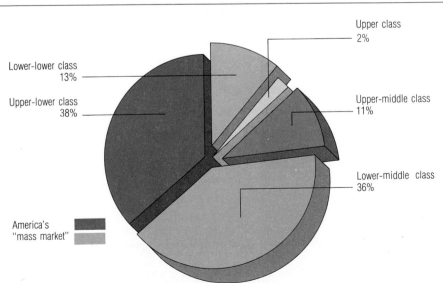

The American moral code and the emphasis on hard work have come from this class. This has been the most "conforming" segment of society. They are home- and family-oriented. We speak of America as a middle-class society, but the middle-class value system stops here. More than half of our society is *not* middle class.

The **upper-lower class** (38 percent of the population) consists of factory production line workers, skilled workers, and service people—the blue-collar workers. Most earn good incomes but are still very concerned about security. They are less confident in their own judgments about products and may rely more on salespeople and advertising.

The **lower-lower class** (13 percent of the population) consists of unskilled laborers and people in very low status occupations. These people usually don't have much income but are good markets for "necessities" and products that help them enjoy the present.[9]

What do these classes mean?

Social class studies suggest that an old saying—"A rich man is simply a poor man with more money"—is not true. Given the same income as a middle class person, a person belonging to the lower classes handles himself and his money very differently. The various classes shop at different stores. They prefer different treatment from salespeople. They buy different brands of products—even though prices are about the same. And they have different spending-saving attitudes. Some of these differences are shown in Exhibit 7–8.

Reference groups are relevant, too

A **reference group** is the people to whom an individual looks when forming attitudes about a particular topic. People normally have several reference groups for different topics. Some they meet face-to-face. Others they may just wish to imitate. In either case, they may take values from these reference groups and make buying decisions based on what the group might accept.

We are always making comparisons between ourselves and others. So reference groups are more important when others will be able to "see" which product or which brand is being used. Influence is stronger for products that relate to status in the group. For one group, owning an expensive fur coat may be a sign of "having arrived." A group of animal lovers might view it as a sign of bad judgment. In either case, owning a coat would affect the consumer's status with the group.[10]

Reaching the opinion leaders who are buyers

An **opinion leader** is a person who influences others. Opinion leaders aren't necessarily wealthier or better educated. And opinion leaders on one subject are

Exhibit 7–8   Characteristics and Attitudes of Middle and Lower Classes

Middle classes	Lower classes
Plan and save for the future	Live for the present
Analyze alternatives	"Feel" what is "best"
Understand how the world works	Have simplistic ideas about how things work
Feel they have opportunities	Feel controlled by the world
Willing to take risks	"Play it safe"
Confident about decision making	Want help with decision making
Want long-run quality or value	Want short-run satisfaction

not necessarily opinion leaders on another subject. Capable homemakers with large families may be consulted for advice on family budgeting. Young women may be opinion leaders for new clothing styles and cosmetics. Each social class tends to have its own opinion leaders. Some marketing mixes are aimed especially at these people since their opinions affect others and research shows that they are involved in many product-related discussions with "followers."[11]

Culture surrounds the other influences

Culture is the whole set of beliefs, attitudes, and ways of doing things of a reasonably homogeneous set of people. We can think of the American culture, the French culture, or the Latin American culture. People within these cultural groupings are more similar in outlook and behavior. And sometimes it is useful to think of subcultures within such groupings. For example, within the American culture, there are various religious and ethnic subcultures.

From a target marketing point of view, a marketing manager will probably want to aim at people within one culture or subculture. If a firm is developing strategies for two cultures, it often needs two different marketing plans.[12]

The attitudes and beliefs that we usually associate with culture tend to change slowly. So once a marketer develops a good understanding of the culture he is planning for, he should concentrate on the more dynamic variables discussed above.

INDIVIDUALS ARE AFFECTED BY THE PURCHASE SITUATION

Purchase reason can vary

Why a consumer is making a purchase can affect buying behavior. For example, a student buying a pen for his own use might pick up an inexpensive Bic. But if the same student wanted to buy a pen as a gift for a friend, he might choose a Cross.

Time affects what happens

Time is also a purchase situation influence. When a purchase is made—and the time available for shopping—also influence behavior. A leisurely dinner induces different behavior than grabbing a quick cup of 7-Eleven coffee on the way to work.

Surroundings affect buying, too

Surroundings can affect buying behavior. The excitement of an auction may stimulate impulse buying. Surroundings may discourage buying, too. For example, some people don't like to stand in a checkout line and have others look at what they are buying—even if the other shoppers are complete strangers.

Needs, benefits sought, attitudes, motivation, and even how a consumer selects certain products all vary depending on the purchase situation. So different purchase situations may require different marketing mixes—even when the same target market is involved.[13]

CONSUMERS USE PROBLEM–SOLVING PROCESSES

The variables we have been discussing affect *what* products a consumer finally decides to purchase. It is also important for marketing managers to understand *how* buyers use a problem-solving process to select particular products.

Most consumers seem to use the following five-step problem-solving process:

1. Becoming aware of—or interested in—the problem.
2. Recalling and gathering information about possible solutions.
3. Evaluating alternative solutions—perhaps trying some out.
4. Deciding on the appropriate solution.
5. Evaluating the decision.[14]

Exhibit 7–9 presents an expanded version of this basic process. Note that this exhibit integrates the problem-solving process with the whole set of variables we've been reviewing.

Exhibit 7–9   Consumer's Problem-Solving Process

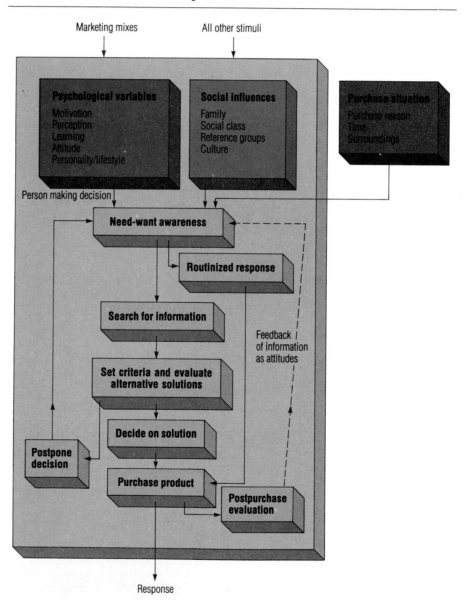

When a consumer evaluates information about purchase alternatives, he may weigh not only a product type in relation to other types of products, but also differences in brands within a product type *and* the stores where the products may be available. This can be a very complicated evaluation procedure, and, depending on their choice criteria, consumers may make seemingly "irrational" decisions. If convenient service is crucial, for example, a buyer might pay list price for an "unexciting" car from a very convenient dealer. Marketers need a way to analyze these decisions.

Grid of evaluative criteria helps

Based on studies of how consumers seek out and evaluate information about products, researchers suggest that marketing managers use an evaluative grid showing features common to different products (or marketing mixes). For example, Exhibit 7–10 shows some of the features common to three different cars a consumer might consider.

The grid encourages marketing managers to view each product as a "bundle" of features or "attributes." The pluses and minuses in Exhibit 7–10 indicate one consumer's attitude toward each feature of each car. If members of the target market don't rate a feature of the marketing manager's brand with "pluses," it may indicate a problem. The manager might want to change the product to improve that feature—or perhaps use more promotion to emphasize an already acceptable feature. The consumer in Exhibit 7–10 has a minus under gas mileage for the Nissan. If the Nissan really gets better gas mileage than the other cars, promotion might focus on mileage to improve consumer attitudes toward this feature and toward the whole product.

Some consumers will reject a product if *one* feature is below standard—regardless of how favorably they might regard the product's other features. The consumer represented in Exhibit 7–10 might avoid the Saab, which he saw as less than satisfactory on ease of service, even if it were superior in all other aspects. In other instances, a consumer's overall attitude toward the product might be such that a few good features could make up for some shortcomings. The comfortable interior of the Toyota (Exhibit 7–10) might make up for less exciting styling—especially if the consumer viewed comfort as really important.

Exhibit 7–10   Grid of Evaluative Criteria for Three Car Brands

Brands	Gas mileage	Ease of service	Comfortable interior	Styling
Nissan	–	+	+	–
Saab	+	–	+	+
Toyota	+	+	+	–

Note: Pluses and minuses indicate a consumer's evaluation of a feature for a brand.

Of course, consumers don't use a grid like this. However, constructing such a grid helps managers think about what evaluative criteria are really important to their target consumers, what consumers' attitudes are toward their product (or marketing mix) on each criteria, and how consumers combine the criteria to reach a final decision. Having a better understanding of the process should help a manager develop a better marketing mix.[15]

Three levels of problem solving are useful

The basic problem-solving process shows the steps a consumer may go through while trying to find a way to satisfy his needs—but it doesn't show how long this process will take or how much thought he will give to each step. Individuals who have had a lot of experience solving certain problems can move quickly through some of the steps or almost directly to a decision.

It is helpful, therefore, to recognize three levels of problem solving: extensive problem solving, limited problem solving, and routinized response behavior. See Exhibit 7–11. These problem-solving approaches are used for any kind of product.

Extensive problem solving is involved when a need is completely new or important to a consumer—and much effort is taken to decide how to satisfy the need. For example, a music lover who wants higher quality sound might decide to buy a compact audiodisc player—but not have any idea what to buy. After talking with friends to find out about good places to buy a player, she might visit several of the stores to find out about different brands and their features. After thinking about her needs some more, she might buy a portable Sony unit—so she could use it in her apartment and in her car.

Limited problem solving is involved when a consumer is willing to put *some* effort into deciding the best way to satisfy a need. Limited problem solving is typical when a consumer has some previous experience in solving a problem, but is not certain which choice is best at the current time. If our music lover wanted some new disks for her player, she would already know what type of music she enjoys. She might go to a familiar store and check out what disks they had in stock for her favorite types of music.

Routinized response behavior involves regularly selecting a particular way of satisfying a need when it occurs. Routinized response behavior is typical when a consumer has considerable experience in how to meet a need. There is no need for additional information. For example, our music lover might routinely buy the latest recording by her favorite band as soon as it is available. Most marketing managers would like their target consumers to buy their products in this routinized way.

Routinized response behavior is also typical for **low involvement purchases**—purchases that do not have high personal importance or relevance for the

Exhibit 7–11   Problem-Solving Continuum

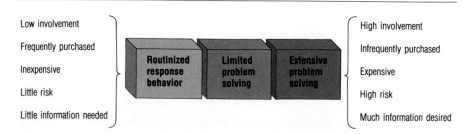

customer. Let's face it, buying a box of salt is probably not one of the burning issues in your life.[16]

Problem solving is a learning process

The reason problem solving becomes simpler with time is that people learn from experience—both positive and negative things. As a person approaches the problem-solving process, he brings attitudes formed by previous experiences and social training. Each new problem-solving process may then contribute to or modify this attitude set.

New concepts require an adoption process

When consumers face a really new concept, their previous experience may not be relevant to problem-solving. These situations involve the **adoption process**—the steps individuals go through on the way to accepting or rejecting a new idea. It is similar to the problem-solving process, but, in the adoption process, the role of learning is clearer—and so is promotion's potential contribution to a marketing mix.

In the adoption process, an individual moves through some fairly definite steps:

1. Awareness—the potential customer comes to know about the product but lacks details. He may not even know how it works or what it will do.
2. Interest—*if* he becomes interested, he gathers general information and facts about the product.
3. Evaluation—he begins to give the product a mental trial, applying it to his personal situation.
4. Trial—he may buy the product so that he can experiment with it in use. A product that is either too expensive to try or isn't available for trial may never be adopted.
5. Decision—he decides on either adoption or rejection. A satisfactory evaluation and trial may lead to adoption of the product and regular use. According to psychological learning theory, reinforcement leads to adoption.
6. Confirmation—the adopter continues to rethink the decision and searches for support for the decision—that is, further reinforcement.[17]

Marketing managers for 3M, the company that makes Scotch tape, worked with the adoption process when they introduced Post-It note pads. Test market ads increased awareness—they explained how Post-It notes could be applied to a surface and then easily removed. But test market sales were slow because most con-

Marketing managers offer trial sizes of products free—to speed the adoption process.

sumers were not interested. They didn't see the benefit. To encourage trial, 3M distributed free samples. Using the samples confirmed the benefit—and when the samples were used up consumers started buying Post-Its. As Post-It distribution expanded to other market areas, 3M used samples to speed consumers through the trial stage and the rest of the adoption process.[18]

Dissonance may set in after the decision

After a buyer makes a decision, he may have second thoughts. He may have chosen from among several attractive alternatives—weighing the pros and cons and finally making a decision. Later doubts, however, may lead to **dissonance**— tension caused by uncertainty about the rightness of a decision. Dissonance may lead a buyer to search for additional information to confirm the wisdom of his decision and so reduce tension. Without this confirmation, the adopter might buy something else next time—or not comment positively about the product to others.[19]

SEVERAL PROCESSES ARE RELATED AND RELEVANT TO STRATEGY PLANNING

Exhibit 7–12 shows the interrelation of the problem-solving process, the adoption process, and learning. It is important to see this interrelation—and to understand that promotion can modify or accelerate it. Also note that the potential buyers' problem-solving behavior should affect how firms design their physical distribution systems. If customers aren't willing to travel far to shop, a firm may need more outlets to get their business. Similarly, customers' attitudes help determine what price to charge. Clearly, knowing how a target market handles these processes will aid marketing strategy planning.

Exhibit 7–12   Relation of Problem-Solving Process, Adoption Process, and Learning (given a problem)

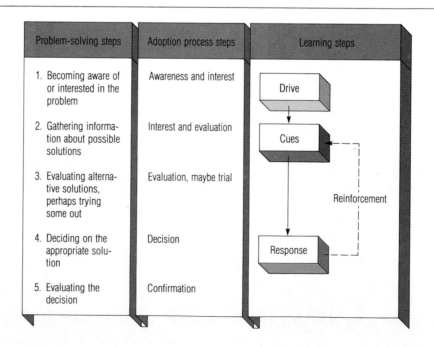

CONCLUSION

In this chapter, we analyzed the individual consumer as a problem solver who is influenced by psychological variables, social influences, and the purchase situation. All of these variables are related, and our model of buyer behavior helps integrate them into one process. Marketing strategy planning requires a good grasp of this material. Assuming that everyone behaves the way you do—or even like your family or friends do—can lead to expensive marketing errors.

Consumer buying behavior results from the consumer's efforts to satisfy needs and wants. We discussed some reasons why consumers buy and saw that consumer behavior can't be fully explained by only a list of needs.

We also saw that our society is divided into social classes, a fact that helps explain some consumer behavior. And we discussed the impact of reference groups and opinion leaders.

We presented a buyer behavior model to help you interpret and integrate the present findings—as well as any new data you might get from marketing research.

As of now, the behavioral sciences can only offer insights and theories, which the marketing manager must blend with intuition and judgment in developing marketing strategies.

Marketing research may have to be used to answer specific questions. But if a firm has neither the money nor the time for research, then marketing managers have to rely on available descriptions of present behavior and "guesstimates" about future behavior. Popular magazines and leading newspapers often reflect the public's shifting attitudes. And many studies of the changing consumer are published regularly in the business and trade press. This material—coupled with the information in these last two chapters—will help your marketing strategy planning.

Remember that consumers—with all their needs and attitudes—may be elusive, but they aren't invisible. Research has provided more data and understanding of consumer behavior than business managers generally use. Applying this information may help you find your breakthrough opportunity.

Questions and Problems

1. What is the behavioral science concept that underlies the "black box" model of consumer behavior? Does this concept have operational relevance to marketing managers; that is, if it is a valid concept, can they make use of it?

2. Explain what is meant by a hierarchy of needs and provide examples of one or more products that enable you to satisfy each of the four levels of need.

3. Cut out two recent advertisements: one full-page color ad from a magazine and one large display from a newspaper. Indicate which needs are being appealed to in each case.

4. Explain how an understanding of consumers' learning processes might affect marketing strategy planning. Give an example.

5. Briefly describe your own *beliefs* about the potential value of wearing seat belts when driving a car, your *attitude* toward seat belts, and your *intention* about wearing seat belts the next time you drive.

6. Explain psychographics and life-style analysis. Explain how it might be useful for planning marketing strategies to reach college students as compared to the "average" consumer.

7. A supermarket chain is planning to open a number of new stores to appeal to the Hispanics in southern California. Give some examples that indicate how the four Ps might be adjusted to appeal to the Hispanic subculture.

8. How should the social class structure affect the planning of a new restaurant in a large city? How might the four Ps be adjusted?

9. What social class would you associate with each of the following phrases or items?

   a. Sport cars.
   b. The *National Inquirer.*
   c. *New Yorker* magazine.
   d. *Playboy* magazine.
   e. People watching soap operas.

f. TV bowling shows.

g. Men who drink beer after dinner.

h. Families who dress formally for dinner regularly.

i. Families who are distrustful of banks (keep money in socks or mattresses).

j. Owners of French poodles.

In each case, choose one class if you can. If you can't choose one class, but rather feel that several classes are equally likely, then so indicate. In those cases where you feel that all classes are equally interested or characterized by a particular item, choose all five classes.

10. Illustrate how the reference group concept may apply in practice by explaining how you personally are influenced by some reference group for some product. What are the implications of such behavior for marketing managers?

11. Give two examples of recent purchases where your purchase decision was influenced by the specific purchase situation. Briefly explain how your decision was affected.

12. Give an example of a recent purchase in which you used extended problem solving. What sources of information did you use in making the decision?

13. On the basis of the data and analysis presented in Chapters 6 and 7, what kind of buying behavior would you expect to find for the following products: *(a)* a haircut, *(b)* shampoo, *(c)* ballpoint pens, *(d)* baseball gloves, *(e)* sport coats, *(f)* a cordless telephone, *(g)* life insurance, *(h)* personal computers, and *(i)* a new checking account? Set up a chart for your answer with products along the left-hand margin as the row headings and the following factors as headings for the columns: *(a)* how consumers would shop for these products, *(b)* how far they would go, *(c)* whether they would buy by brand, *(d)* whether they would wish to compare with other products, and *(e)* any other factors they should consider. Insert short answers—words or phrases are satisfactory—in the various boxes. Be prepared to discuss how the answers you put in the chart would affect each product's marketing mix.

Suggested Cases

1. McDonald's "Fast-Food" Restaurant

9. Holiday Inn versus Days Inn

11. Nike and Walking Shoes

Suggested Computer-Aided Problem

7. Selective Processes

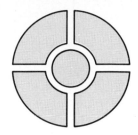

Chapter 8

Industrial and Intermediate Customers and Their Buying Behavior

When You Finish This Chapter, You Should

1. Know who the intermediate customers are.

2. Know about the number and distribution of manufacturers.

3. Understand the problem-solving behavior of industrial buyers.

4. See why multiple influence is common in purchase decisions of intermediate customers.

5. Know the basic methods used in industrial buying.

6. Know how buying by service firms, retailers, wholesalers, and governments is similar to—and different from—industrial buying.

7. Understand the important new terms (shown in red).

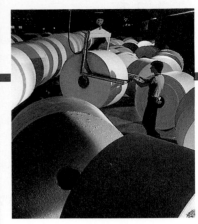

Intermediate customers buy more than final consumers!

Duall/Wind, a plastics producer, was a major supplier of small parts for Polaroid instant cameras. But, when Duall/Wind decided to raise its prices, Polaroid balked. Polaroid's purchasing manager demanded that Duall/Wind show a breakdown of all its costs, from materials to labor to profit. As Duall/Wind's president said, "I had a tough time getting through my head that Polaroid wanted to come right in here and have us divulge all that." But Polaroid is a big account—and it got the information it wanted.

You can see that Polaroid takes buying seriously. It works at limiting supplier price increases by knowing suppliers' businesses as well as—or better than—suppliers do themselves. Instead of just accepting price hikes, a Polaroid buyer does an analysis and suggests ways the supplier can operate at lower cost. Then Polaroid refuses to pay a higher price until the supplier streamlines its operation.[1]

Most industrial buyers look at more than price. Many are downright picky about quality control and on-time delivery. For example, when Toshiba ordered a three-ton industrial burner from tiny Pyronics, Inc., of Cleveland, a buyer from Toshiba negotiated "visitation rights" during the 16-week building process. To make certain that everything would be as promised, he demanded a quality control graph showing just where Pyronics would be at each stage of production. The technique was new to Pyronics—so the buyer taught the company how to use it.[2]

INTERMEDIATE CUSTOMERS—A BIG OPPORTUNITY

Most of us think the term *customer* means only the individual final consumer. But many marketing managers aim at customers who are not final consumers. In fact, more purchases are made by businesses and other intermediate customers than by final consumers. **Intermediate customers** are any buyers who buy for resale or to produce other goods and services. Exhibit 8–1 shows the different types of intermediate customers. There are more than 6 million intermediate customers in the United States. These customers do many different jobs—and many different market dimensions are needed to describe all the different intermediate customer markets.

This chapter will discuss these intermediate consumers: who they are, where they are, and how they buy. We will emphasize the buying behavior of manufacturers. But other intermediate customers seem to buy in much the same way. In fact, buyers for all kinds of organizations are often loosely referred to as "industrial buyers." To keep the discussion specific, we will focus on the United States, but most of the ideas apply to international markets as well.

Exhibit 8–1   Examples of Different Types of Intermediate Customers

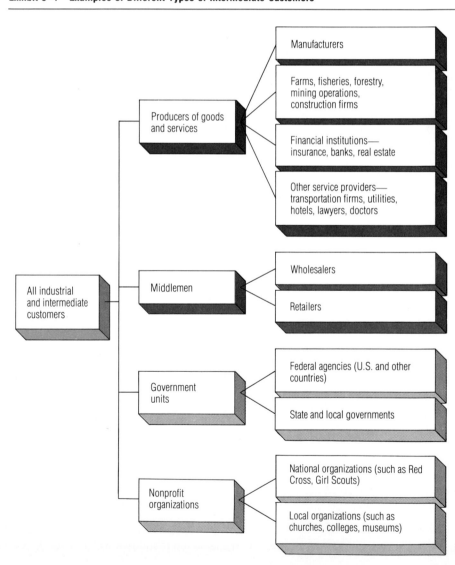

There are great marketing opportunities in serving intermediate customers, and a student heading toward a business career has a good chance of working in this area.

INTERMEDIATE CUSTOMERS ARE DIFFERENT

Intermediate customers buy for a purpose

Intermediate buyers purchase goods and services to meet needs—just as final consumers do. But here the needs are usually easier to define because the buyers are trying to satisfy their customers. A business firm wants to make a profit by producing or reselling products. A town government wants to meet its legal and social obligations to citizens. A country club wants to help its members enjoy their leisure time. Such organizations buy goods and services that will help them meet the demand for the goods and services that they in turn supply to their markets.

Even small differences are important

Understanding how and why intermediate customers buy is important because competition is often rugged in intermediate markets. Even "trivial" differences may affect the success of a marketing mix.

Since sellers usually approach each intermediate customer directly—through a sales representative—they have more chance to adjust the marketing mix for each individual customer. Sellers may even have a special marketing strategy for each individual customer. This is carrying target marketing to its extreme. But when the customer's size and sales volume make this possible, it may be not only desirable but necessary in order to compete.

In such situations, the individual sales rep has to carry more responsibility for strategy planning. This fact is relevant to your career planning since these jobs are very challenging—and they pay well, too.

MANUFACTURERS ARE IMPORTANT CUSTOMERS

There are not many big ones

One of the most striking facts about manufacturers is how few there are compared to final consumers. In the industrial market, there are over 355,000 factories. Exhibit 8–2 shows that the majority of these are quite small—half have less than 10 workers. But these small firms account for only about 3 percent of manufacturing activity. In small plants, the owners often do the buying. And they buy less formally than buyers in the relatively few large manufacturing plants—which employ most of the workers and produce a large share of the value added by manufacturing. For example, plants with 250 or more employees make up only about 4 percent of the total—yet they employ nearly 55 percent of the production employees and produce over 60 percent of the value added by manufacturers. Because these large plants are so important, it may be desirable to segment industrial markets on the basis of size.

Customers cluster in geographic areas

In addition to concentration by size, industrial markets are concentrated in big metropolitan areas—especially in New York, Pennsylvania, Ohio, Illinois, Texas, and California.[3]

The buyers for some of these larger manufacturers are even further concentrated in home offices—often in large metropolitan areas. U.S. Gypsum, one of the

Exhibit 8–2   Size Distribution of Manufacturing Establishments, 1986

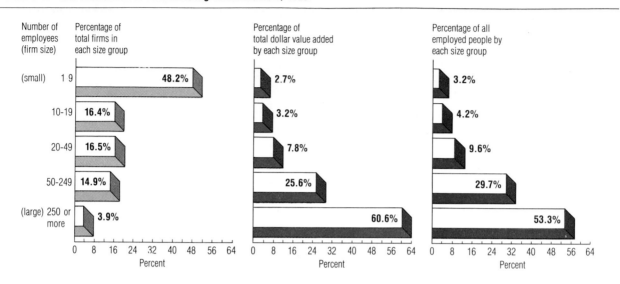

largest building materials manufacturers, does most of the buying for over 50 plants from its Chicago offices. In such a case, a sales rep may be able to sell to plants all over the country without leaving a base city. This makes selling easier for competitors, too, so the market may be extremely competitive. The importance of such big buyers has led some companies to set up "national account" sales forces specially trained to cater to these needs. A geographically bound salesperson can be at a real disadvantage against such competitors.

Concentration by industry

In addition to concentration by size of firm and geographic location, there is also concentration by industry. Manufacturers of advanced electronics systems are concentrated in California's famous Silicon Valley near San Francisco and along Boston's Route 128. The steel industry is heavily concentrated in the Pittsburgh, Birmingham (Alabama), and Chicago areas.

Much data is available on industrial markets by SIC codes

The products an industrial customer needs to buy depend on the business it is in. Because of this, sales of a product are often concentrated among customers in similar businesses. For example, apparel manufacturers are the main customers for buttons. Marketing managers who can relate their own sales to their customers' type of business can focus their efforts—and detailed information is available to help. The federal government regularly collects and publishes data by **Standard Industrial Classification (SIC) codes**—groups of firms in similar lines of business. The number of establishments, sales volumes, and number of employees—broken down by geographic areas—are given for each SIC code.

SIC code breakdowns start with such broad industry categories as food and related products (code 20), tobacco products (code 21), textile mill products (code 22), apparel (code 23), and so on. Within each two-digit industry breakdown, much more detailed data may be available for three-digit and four-digit industries (that is, subindustries of the two- or three-digit industries). Exhibit 8–3 gives an example of more detailed breakdowns within the apparel industry. Four-digit detail isn't available for all industries in every geographic area because the government does not provide data when only one or two plants are located in an area.

Exhibit 8–3   Illustrative SIC Breakdown for Apparel Industries

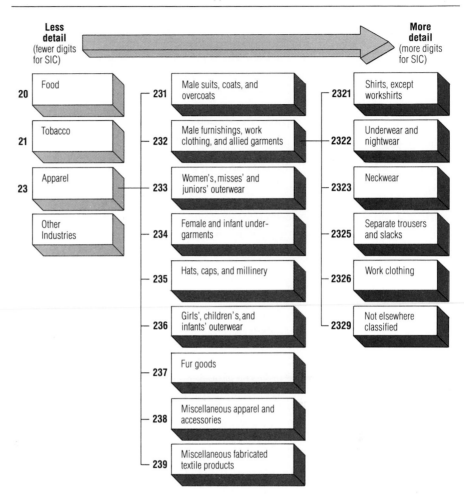

Many firms find their *current* customers' SIC codes and then look at SIC-coded lists for similar companies that may need the same goods and services. Other companies look at which SIC categories are growing or declining to discover new opportunities. If companies aiming at industrial target markets know exactly who they are aiming at, readily available data organized by SIC codes can be valuable. Most trade associations and private organizations that gather industrial market data also use SIC codes.

SIC codes are not perfect. Some companies have sales in several categories but are listed in only one—the code with the largest sales. In addition, some newer businesses don't fit any of the categories very well. So, although a lot of good information is available, the codes must be used carefully.[4]

BUYERS ARE PROBLEM SOLVERS

Some people think of industrial buying as entirely different from consumer buying—but there are many similarities. In fact, the problem-solving framework introduced in Chapter 7 can be applied here.

Three kinds of buying processes are useful

In Chapter 7, we discussed problem solving by consumers and how it might vary from extended problem solving to routine buying. In industrial markets, we can adapt these concepts slightly and work with three similar buying processes: a new-task buying process, a modified rebuy process, or a straight rebuy.[5] See Exhibit 8–4.

New-task buying occurs when a firm has a new need and the buyer wants a great deal of information. New-task buying can involve setting product specifications, sources of supply, and an order routine that can be followed in the future if results are satisfactory.

A **straight rebuy** is a routine repurchase that may have been made many times before. Buyers probably don't bother looking for new information or new sources of supply. Most of a company's small or recurring purchases are of this type—but they take only a small part of an organized buyer's time.

The **modified rebuy** is the in-between process where some review of the buying situation is done—though not as much as in new-task buying. Sometimes a competitor will get lazy enjoying a straight rebuy situation. An alert marketer can turn these situations into opportunities by providing more information.

Note that a particular product may be bought in any of the three ways. Careful market analysis is needed to determine how the firm's products are bought—and by whom. A new-task buy takes much longer than a straight rebuy—and the seller's promotion has much more chance to have an impact. This can be seen in Exhibit 8–5, which shows the time and many influences involved in the purchase of a special drill.[6]

Purchasing agents are buying specialists

Some producers are so large that they need buying specialists. **Purchasing agents** are buying specialists for their employers. Most industrial buyers are serious and well educated. In large companies, they usually specialize by product area and are real experts. Salespeople usually have to see the purchasing agent first—before they contact any other employee. These buyers hold important positions and take a dim view of sales reps who try to go around them.

Rather than being "sold," buyers want salespeople to provide accurate information that will help them buy wisely. They like information on new goods and ser-

Exhibit 8–4   Industrial Buying Processes

Type of process / Characteristics	New-task buying	Modified rebuy	Straight rebuy
Time required	Much	Medium	Little
Multiple influence	Much	Some	Little
Review of suppliers	Much	Some	None
Information needed	Much	Some	Little

Exhibit 8–5   Decision Network Diagram of the Buying Situations: Special Drill

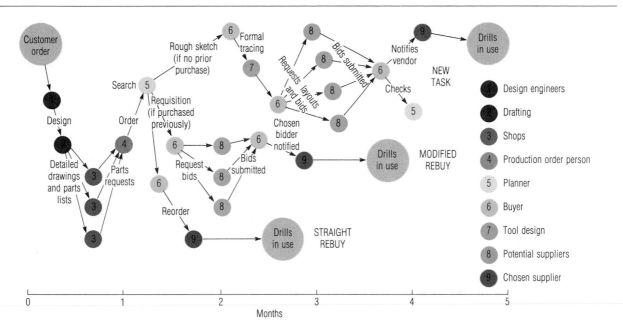

vices, and tips on potential price changes, strikes, and other changes in business conditions.

Of course, industrial buyers don't just rely on salespeople for information. They get information from a variety of sources to make certain that they have all the facts. See Exhibit 8-6. How much information a buyer will collect depends on the importance of the purchase and the level of uncertainty about what choice might be best. The time and expense of searching for and analyzing a lot of information may not be justified for a minor purchase. But a major purchase often requires real detective work.

Basic purchasing needs are economic

Industrial buyers are usually less emotional in their buying than final consumers. Buyers look for certain product characteristics—including economy both in original

Exhibit 8–6   Major Sources of Information Used by Industrial Buyers

	Marketing sources	Nonmarketing sources
Personal sources	• Salespeople • Others from supplier firms • Trade shows	• Buying center members • Outside business associates • Consultants and outside experts
Impersonal sources	• Advertising in trade publications • Sales literature • Sales catalogs	• Rating services • Trade associations • News publications • Product directories

Industrial buyers usually focus on economic needs when they make purchase decisions.

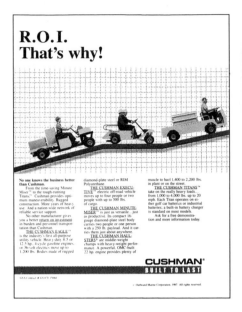

cost and in use, productivity, uniformity, purity, and ability to make the buyer's final product better.

In addition to product characteristics, buyers consider the seller's reliability and general cooperativeness; the ability to provide speedy maintenance and repair, steady supply under all conditions, and reliable and fast delivery; and any past and present relationships (including previous favors).

The matter of dependability deserves further emphasis. There is nothing worse to a purchasing agent and a production manager than shutting down a production line because sellers haven't delivered the goods. Product quality is important, too. The cost of a small item may have little to do with its importance. If it causes a larger unit to break down, it may result in a large loss completely out of proportion to its own cost.

Many buyers use **vendor analysis**—formal rating of suppliers on all relevant areas of performance. Evaluating suppliers and how they are working out results in better buying decisions.[7]

Emotional needs are relevant, too

Vendor analysis tries to focus on economic factors, but industrial purchasing does have emotional overtones. Modern buyers are human—and they want friendly relationships with suppliers. Some buyers seem eager to imitate progressive competitors—or even to be the first to try new products. Such "innovators" might deserve special attention when new products are being introduced.

Buyers are also human with respect to protecting their own interests—and their own position in the company. "Looking good" is a serious matter for some purchasing agents. They have to buy a wide variety of products from many sources and make decisions involving many factors beyond their control. If a new source delivers low-quality materials, you can guess who will be blamed. Poor service or late delivery also reflect on the buyer's ability. Therefore, anyone or anything that helps the buyer look good has a definite appeal. In fact, this one factor may make the difference between a successful and unsuccessful marketing mix.

Although industrial buyers are influenced by their own needs, most are careful to avoid a conflict between their own self-interests and company outcomes. Marketers must be careful here. A salesperson who offers one of his company pens to a buyer may view the "giveaway" as part of the promotion effort—but the customer's firm may have a policy against a buyer accepting *any* gift.

A seller's marketing mix should satisfy *both* the needs of the buyer's company as well as the buyer's individual needs. Therefore, sellers need to find an overlapping area where both can be satisfied. See Exhibit 8–7 for a summary of this idea.

Multiple buying influences in a buying center

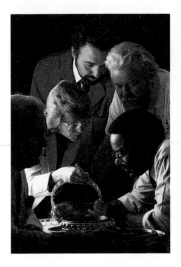

Much of the work of the typical purchasing agent consists of straight rebuys. When a purchase requisition comes in, the purchasing agent places an order without consulting anyone else. But, in many cases—especially new-task buying—multiple buying influence is important. **Multiple buying influence** means the buyer shares the purchasing decision with several people—perhaps even top management. Possible buying influences include:

1. *Users*—perhaps production line workers or their supervisors.
2. *Influencers*—perhaps engineering or R&D people who help write specifications or supply information for evaluating alternatives.
3. *Buyers*—the purchasing agents who have the responsibility for working with suppliers and arranging the terms of the sale.
4. *Deciders*—the people in the organization who have the power to select or approve the supplier—usually the purchasing agent for small items, but perhaps top management for larger purchases.
5. *Gatekeepers*—people who control the flow of information within the organization—perhaps purchasing agents who shield users or other deciders. Gatekeepers can also include receptionists, secretaries, research assistants, and others who influence the flow of information about potential purchases.

An example shows how the different buying influences work.

Exhibit 8–7 A Model of Individual Industrial Buyer Behavior—Showing Overlapping Needs

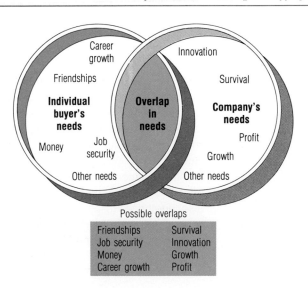

GE knows that there is multiple buying influence when a new facility is built, so promotion targeted at people who influence lighting specifications is part of GE's marketing mix.

Suppose Adidas wants to buy a machine to attach running shoe soles to the tops. Different vendors are eager for the business. Several people (influencers) help to evaluate the choices. A finance manager worries about the high cost and suggests leasing the machine. The quality control people want a machine that will do a more accurate job—although it's more expensive. The production manager is interested in speed of operation. The production line workers and their supervisors want the machine that is easiest to use so workers can continue to rotate jobs.

The company president asks the purchasing department to assemble all the information but retains the power to select and approve the supplier (to be the decider). The purchasing manager's administrative assistant (a gatekeeper) has been deciding what information to pass on to higher-ups as well as scheduling visits for salespeople. After all these buying influences are considered, one of the purchasing agents for the firm will be the buyer. He will be responsible for making recommendations and arranging the terms of the sale.

It is helpful to think of a **buying center** as all the people who participate in or influence a purchase. Different people may make up a buying center from one decision to the next. This makes the marketing job difficult.

The salesperson must study each case carefully. Just learning who to talk with may be hard, but thinking about the various roles in the buying center can help. See Exhibit 8–8.

The salesperson may have to talk to every member of the buying center—stressing different topics for each. This not only complicates the promotion job but also lengthens it. Approval of a routine order may take anywhere from a week to several months. On very important purchases—a new computer system, a new plant, or major equipment—the selling period may stretch out to a year or more.[8]

Exhibit 8-8   Multiple Influence and Roles in the Buying Center

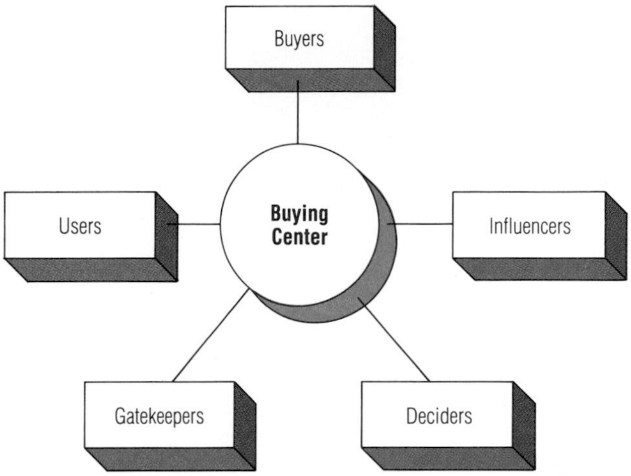

BASIC METHODS AND PRACTICES IN INDUSTRIAL BUYING

Should you inspect, sample, describe, or negotiate?

Industrial buyers (really, buyers of all types, including final consumers) use four basic approaches to evaluating and buying products: (1) inspection, (2) sampling, (3) description, and (4) negotiated contracts. Understanding the differences in these buying methods is important in strategy planning, so let's look at each approach.

Inspection looks at everything

Inspection buying means looking at every item. It's used for products that are not standardized and require examination. Here each product is different—as in the case of livestock or used equipment. Such products are often sold in open markets—or at auction if there are several potential buyers. Buyers inspect the goods and either "haggle" with the seller or bid against competing buyers.

Sampling looks at some

Sampling buying means looking at only part of a potential purchase. As products become more standardized—perhaps because of careful grading or quality control—buying by sample becomes possible. For example, a power company might buy miles of heavy electric cable. A sample section might be heated to the melting point to be certain the cable is safe.

Prices may be based on a sample. Although demand and supply forces may set the general price level, the actual price may vary depending on the quality of a specific sample. For example, this kind of buying is used in grain markets where the actual price is based on a sample that has been withdrawn from a carload of grain and analyzed.

People in less-developed economies do a lot of buying by inspection or sampling—regardless of the product. The reason is skepticism about quality—or lack of faith in the seller.

Industrial buyers may only inspect a portion of a potential purchase, but the quality of the sample may affect the price or acceptability of the whole order.

Specifications describe the need

Description (specification) buying means buying from a written (or verbal) description of the product. Most manufactured items and many agricultural commodities are bought this way—often without inspection. When quality can almost be guaranteed, buying by description—grade, brand, or specification—may be satisfactory, especially when there is mutual trust between buyers and sellers. This method, of course, reduces the cost of buying and is used by buyers whenever practical.

Services are usually purchased by description. Since a service is usually not performed until it is purchased, buyers have nothing to inspect ahead of time.

Once the purchase needs are specified, it's the buyer's job to get the best deal possible. If there are several suppliers interested in the business, the buyer will often request competitive bids. **Competitive bids** are the terms of sale offered by different suppliers in response to the buyer's purchase specifications. If different suppliers' quality, dependability, and delivery schedules all meet the specs, the buyer will select the low-price bid. But a creative marketer needs to look carefully at the purchaser's specs—and the need—to see if there are other elements of his marketing mix that could provide a competitive advantage.

Negotiated contracts handle relationships

Negotiated contract buying means agreeing to a contract that allows for changes in the purchase arrangements.

Sometimes, the buyer knows roughly what the company needs but can't fix all the details in advance. The specifications or total requirements may change as the job progresses. This situation is common, for example, in research and development work and in the building of special-purpose machinery or buildings. In such cases, the general project is described, and a basic price may be agreed on—perhaps even based on competitive bids—but with provision for changes and price adjustments up or down. Or a supplier may be willing to accept a contract that provides some type of incentive—such as full coverage of costs plus a fixed fee or full costs plus a profit percentage tied to costs. The whole contract may even be subject to renegotiation as the work proceeds.

Buyers and suppliers form partnerships

To be sure of dependable quality, a buyer may develop loyalty to certain suppliers. This is especially important when buying nonstandardized products. When a supplier and buyer develop a "working partnership" over the years, the supplier practically becomes a part of the buyer's organization. (Sometimes the buyer will design a product—and simply ask the supplier to build and deliver it at a fair price.)

When a seller proposes a new idea that saves the buyer's company money, the buyer usually rewards the seller with orders, and this encourages future suggestions. In contrast, buyers who use a bid system exclusively—either by choice or necessity, as in some government and institutional purchasing—may not be offered much beyond basic goods and services. They are interested primarily in price.

Until recently, Ford, Chrysler, and GM relied heavily on bids—convinced this approach would result in lower prices from competing suppliers. But Japanese competition made them rethink this approach. Japanese producers and their suppliers often work together very closely. They view the effort as a partnership. Suppliers are consulted before design changes are made, to make certain that a planned change won't create problems. Now the Detroit automakers are also using

Industrial and intermediate buyers prefer dependable suppliers whose products are available when they are needed.

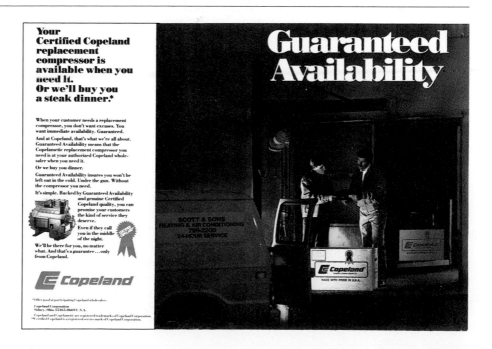

this approach, often giving a single supplier a long-term contract to supply a needed part. In return, they are expecting—and getting—more help from the supplier. In fact, Ford credits suggestions from its suppliers for the improved quality of its new cars.[9]

But most buyers seek several sources to spread their risk

Even if a firm has developed the best marketing mix possible, it probably won't get all of its industrial customers' business. Buyers often look for several dependable sources of supply to protect themselves from unpredictable events, such as strikes, fires, or floods in one of their suppliers' plants. Still, a good marketing mix is likely to win a larger share of the total business.[10]

Most buyers try to routinize buying

Most firms use a buying procedure that tries to routinize the process. When some person or unit wants to buy something, a **requisition**—a request to buy something—is filled out. After approval by some operating supervisor, the requisition is forwarded to the buyer for placement with the "best" seller.

Approved requisitions are converted to purchase orders as quickly as possible. Straight rebuys are usually made the day the requisition is received, while new-task and modified rebuys take longer. If time is important, the buyer may place the order by telephone—and then a confirming purchase order is typed and sent out.

It pays to know the buyer

Notice the importance of being one of the regular sources of supply. For straight rebuys, the buyer may place an order without even calling other potential sources. Sellers' sales reps regularly call on these buyers—but *not* to sell a particular item. Rather, they want to maintain relations, become a source, and/or point out new developments that might cause the buyer to reevaluate his present straight rebuy procedure and give some business to the sales rep's company.

Having a favorable image can be profitable for a seller. Unless a buyer has to allocate a definite share of the business to each of several sources, a favored source will probably get a larger share. Moving from a 20 percent to a 30 percent share may not seem like much from a buyer's point of view, but for the seller it's a 50 percent increase in sales!

Some buy by computer

Some buyers delegate a large part of their routine order placing to computers. They program decision rules that tell the computer how to order and leave the details of following through to the machine. When economic conditions change, buyers modify the computer instructions. When nothing unusual happens, however, the computer system continues to routinely rebuy as needs develop—printing out new purchase orders to the regular suppliers.

Obviously, it's a big "sale" to be selected as a major supplier and routinely called up in the buyer's computer program. It's also obvious that such a buyer will be more impressed by an attractive marketing mix for a whole *line* of products than just a lower price for a particular order. It may be too expensive and too much trouble to change the whole buying system just because somebody is offering a low price on a particular day.[11]

Ingersol Lands an $8 Million Sale to Boeing Co.

A recent purchase by Boeing Company, the giant airplane manufacturer, illustrates a trend toward closer working partnerships between industrial customers and their suppliers. Boeing is a big customer for machine tools—the equipment it uses to make airplane parts. Like other manufacturers, Boeing's usual process had been to design parts for its planes first and then get bids from machine suppliers. The supplier whose machines met Boeing's specs at the lowest price would get the order. Japanese machine tool suppliers, like Toshiba, had been beating American suppliers in this price-oriented competition.

Recently Boeing needed to buy machines to produce landing-gear parts, and it tried a different approach. Boeing invited potential suppliers to study its operations and recommend how the landing-gear parts could be designed so that the machines to produce them would be more efficient. Ingersol, an American machine-tool company, seized the opportunity. It helped Boeing design the landing-gear parts so that the total cost of both the machines and the parts they produced would be lower. Ingersol's proposals also helped Boeing speed up the production process. Instead of just trying to sell machines at the lowest price, Ingersol helped Boeing develop a better way to make its airplane. Ingersol's Japanese competitors could not provide this kind of help—and Ingersol won the $8 million contract![12]

Inventory policy may determine purchases

Industrial firms generally try to maintain an adequate inventory—certainly enough to keep production lines moving. There is no greater disaster in a factory than to have a production line close down.

No buyer wants to run out of needed products, but keeping too much inventory is expensive. Firms are now paying more attention to inventory costs—and looking to their suppliers for help in controlling them. This often means that a supplier must be able to provide **"just-in-time" delivery**—reliably getting products there *just* before the customer needs them.

Just-in-time relationships between buyers and sellers require a lot of coordination. For example, an automobile producer may ask a supplier of automobile seats to load the delivery truck so that the color and style of seats is in the planned order of cars on the assembly line. This reduces the buyer's costs because the seats will only need to be handled one time. However, it may increase the supplier's costs. Most buyers realize they can't just push costs back onto their suppliers without giving them something in return. Often what they give is a longer-term contract that shares both the costs and benefits of the working partnership.

Anticipating the future may lead to buying fluctuations

Demand at the manufacturer level may fluctuate much more than demand at the final consumer level. Manufacturers try to *predict* the behavior of middlemen and other producers. If manufacturers believe prices are going to drop further, they may postpone all purchases. If they think prices are at their lowest point, they may buy in large quantities in anticipation of future needs.

Producers also try to predict changes in demand by final consumers. For example, if Black and Decker sees that consumer purchases of small appliances are slowing down—perhaps because of a bad economy—it may stop buying electric motors. It doesn't want a big inventory of motors *or* finished appliances. During such a cutback, a seller probably couldn't stimulate sales—even by reducing price or offering more favorable credit terms. The buyer is just not in the market at that time.

Reciprocity helps sales, but . . .

Reciprocity means trading sales for sales—that is, "if you buy from me, I'll buy from you." If a company's customers also can supply products that the firm buys, then the sales departments of both buyer and seller may try to "trade" sales for sales. Purchasing agents generally resist reciprocity but often face pressure from their sales departments.

When prices and quality are otherwise competitive, an outside supplier seldom can break a reciprocity relationship. The supplier can only hope to become an alternate source of supply—and wait for the competitor to let its quality slip or prices rise.

In the past, the U.S. Justice Department tried to block reciprocal buying on the grounds that it is an attempt to monopolize—that is, to restrict the normal operation of the free market. However, in recent years the government has been more lenient in this area.[13]

PRODUCERS OF SERVICES—SMALLER AND MORE SPREAD OUT

Marketing managers need to keep in mind that the service side of our economy is large and has been growing fast. There may be good opportunities in providing these companies with the products they need to support their operations. But there are also challenges.

There are about 2 million services firms—about 6 times as many as there are manufacturers. Some of these—like a large hotel chain or a telephone company—are big companies. But, as you might guess given the large number of firms, most of them are small. They are also more spread out around the country than manufacturing concerns. Factories often locate where transportation facilities are good, where raw materials are available, and where it is less costly to produce goods in quantity. Service operations, in contrast, usually have to be close to their customers.

SIC data is coming

The basic SIC system was set up when America was primarily a manufacturing economy—with less emphasis on services. In 1987 the SIC codes were updated. The new SIC system will provide better information on service firms, but it may be some time before detailed data is available.

Buying is usually not as formal

Purchases by small service firms are often handled by whoever is in charge. This may be a doctor, lawyer, owner of a local insurance agency, or manager of a hotel. Suppliers who usually deal with manufacturers may have trouble adjusting to this market. Personal selling is still an important part of Promotion, but reaching these customers in the first place often requires more advertising. And service firms may need much more help in buying than a large manufacturer.

One company, Canon, capitalized on such needs. Canon knew that Xerox, a familiar name in office copiers, was very successful selling to larger accounts. But Xerox's sales force was not serving the needs of smaller service firms like law offices. Canon seized this opportunity. It developed promotion materials to help first-time buyers understand differences in copiers. It emphasized that its machines were easy to use and maintain. And Canon also used retail channels to make the

Canon developed a marketing mix to serve the needs of service firms and other small businesses.

copiers available in smaller areas where there wasn't enough business to justify using a sales rep. As a result, Canon has been very successful in this market.[14]

RETAILERS AND WHOLESALERS BUY FOR THEIR CUSTOMERS

Most retail and wholesale buyers see themselves as purchasing agents for their target customers—remembering the old saying that "Goods well bought are half sold." Typically, retailers do *not* see themselves as sales agents for particular manufacturers. They buy what they think they can sell. And wholesalers buy what they think their retailers can sell. They don't try to make value judgments about the desirability or "worth" of what they are selling. Rather, they focus on the needs and attitudes of *their* target customers. For example, Super Valu—an $8 billion a year food wholesaler—calls itself "the retail support company." As a top manager at Super Valu put it, "Our mandate is to try to satisfy our retailer customers with *whatever it takes.*"[15]

They must buy too many items

Most retailers carry a large number of items—drugstores up to 12,000 items, hardware stores from 3,000 to 25,000, and grocery stores up to 20,000 items—and they just don't have the time to pay close attention to every one. Often retail buyers are annoyed by the number of wholesalers' and manufacturers' representatives who call on them. Retailers think that their sales of each item are so small that they can't afford to spend much time on each product.

Wholesalers, too, handle so many items that they can't give a lot of attention to each one. Drug wholesalers may stock up to 125,000 items, and wholesalers of textiles and sewing supplies may stock up to 250,000 items.[16]

Retailers and wholesalers usually buy most of their products on a routine, automatic reorder basis—straight rebuys—once they make the initial decision to stock specific products. Sellers to these markets must understand the size of the buyer's job and have something useful to say and do when they call. For example, they might try to save the middleman time by taking inventory, setting up displays, or arranging shelves—while trying to get a chance to talk about specific products and maintain the relationship.

In larger firms, on the other hand, buyers spend more time on individual items. Buyers may specialize in certain lines. Some large chains like Sears buy in such large lots that they assign buyers to find additional and lower-cost sources of supply.[17]

They must watch inventories and computer output

Because retailers and wholesalers buy and stock such a large number of items, they have to watch their inventories carefully. Smart retailers and wholesalers try to carry adequate but not excessive inventories. Instead, they want to maintain a selling stock and some reserve stock—and then depend on a continual flow through the channel.

Most larger firms now use sophisticated computer-controlled inventory control systems. Scanners at retail check-out counters keep track of what goes out the door—and computers use this data to update the records. Even small firms are using automated control systems that can print daily unit control reports showing sales of every product on the manager's shelves. This fact is important to marketing managers selling to such firms, because buyers with this kind of information know their needs and become more demanding about dependable delivery. They also know more about how goods move—and where promotion assistance might be desirable.

Automatic computer ordering is a natural outgrowth of such systems. McKesson Corporation—a large wholesaler of drug products—gave computers to drugstores so the stores could keep track of inventory and place orders directly into McKesson's computer. Once a retailer started using the service, McKesson's share of that store's business usually doubled or tripled. Many competing wholesalers went out of business—and the survivors installed their own computerized systems.[18]

Some are not "open to buy"

Just as manufacturers sometimes try to reduce their inventory and are "not in the market," retailers and wholesalers stop buying for similar reasons. No amount of special promotion or price cutting will induce them to buy in these situations.

In retailing, another dimension may become important. Buyers may be controlled by a miniature profit and loss statement for each department or merchandise line. In an effort to make a profit, the buyer tries to forecast sales, merchandise costs, and expenses. The figure for "cost of merchandise" is the amount the buyer has budgeted to spend over the budget period. If the money has not yet been spent, the buyer is **open to buy**—that is, the buyer has budgeted funds that he can spend during the current period.[19]

Owners or professional buyers may buy

The buyers in small stores and for many wholesalers are the owners or managers since there is a very close relationship between buying and selling. In larger operations, buyers may specialize in certain lines—and they may also supervise the salespeople who sell what they buy. These buyers are in close contact with their customers *and* with their salespeople, who are sensitive to the effectiveness of the buyer's efforts—especially when they are on commission. A buyer may even

Buyers for the Toys "R" Us chain are real experts who specialize by specific product lines.

buy some items to satisfy the preferences of salespeople. Therefore, the salespeople should not be neglected in the promotion effort. The multiple buying influence may be important.

As sales volumes rise, a buyer may specialize in buying only—and have no responsibility for sales. Sears is an extreme case, but it has a buying department of more than 3,000—supported by a staff department exceeding 1,400. These professional buyers frequently know more than their suppliers about prices, quality, and trends in the market. Obviously, they are big potential customers and must be approached differently than the typical small retailer.

Resident buyers may help a firm's buyers

Resident buyers are independent buying agents who work in central markets (New York, Chicago, Los Angeles, etc.) for several retailer or wholesaler customers in outlying areas. They buy new styles and fashions and fill-in items as their customers run out of stock during the year. Some resident buyers have hundreds of employees—and buy more than $1 billion worth of goods a year.

Resident buying organizations fill a need. They help small channel members (producers and middlemen) reach each other inexpensively. Resident buyers usually are paid an annual fee based on their purchases.

Committee buying is impersonal

In some large companies—especially chains selling foods and drugs—the major decisions to add or drop lines or change buying policies may be handled by a *buying committee.* The seller still calls on and gives a "pitch" to a buyer—but the buyer does not have final responsibility. In such companies, the buyer prepares forms summarizing proposals for new products. The forms are passed on to the committee for evaluation. The seller may not get to present his story to the buying committee in person.

This rational, almost cold-blooded approach reduces the impact of a persuasive salesperson. It has also become a necessity due to the flood of new products. Consider the problem facing grocery chains. In an average week, 150 to 250 new items are offered to the buying offices of a large chain like Safeway. If the chain accepted all of them, it would add 10,000 new items during a single year! Obviously, buyers must be hard-headed and impersonal. In fact, food stores reject about 90 percent of all new items.

Wholesalers' and manufacturers' marketing managers must develop good marketing mixes when buying becomes this sophisticated and competitive. Such situations are likely to become more common as computers improve sales analysis and inventory control. Obviously, how possible target markets buy should affect marketing strategy planning.

THE GOVERNMENT MARKET

Size and diversity

Some marketers ignore the government market because they think that government "red tape" is "more trouble than it's worth." They probably don't realize how big the government market really is. Government is the largest customer group in the United States—and in many other countries. About 21 percent of the U.S. gross national product is spent by various government units—and the figure is much higher in more planned economies. Different government units in this country spend about $870 *billion* a year to buy almost every kind of product. They run not only schools, police departments, and military organizations, but also supermarkets, public utilities, research laboratories, offices, hospitals, and even liquor stores. These huge government expenditures cannot be ignored by an aggressive marketing manager.

Government agencies are important customers for a wide variety of products.

Bid buying is common

Government buyers are expected to spend money wisely—in the public interest—so their purchases are usually subject to much public review. To avoid charges of favoritism, most government customers buy by specification using a mandatory bidding procedure. Often the government buyer is required to accept the lowest bid that meets the specifications. You can see how important it is for the buyer to write precise and complete specifications. Otherwise, sellers may submit a bid that fits the "specs" but doesn't really match what is needed. By law, a government unit might have to accept the lowest bid—even for an unwanted product.

Writing specifications is not easy—and buyers usually appreciate the help of well-informed salespeople. Salespeople *want* to have input on the specifications so their product can be considered or even have an advantage. One company may get the business—even with a bid that is not the lowest—because the lower bids don't meet minimum specifications. At the extreme, some buyers who want a specific brand or supplier may try to write the description so that no other supplier will be able to meet all the specs. This kind of loyalty, though it sounds great, might be viewed as illegal "bid rigging."

Specification and bidding difficulties aren't problems in all government orders. Some items that are bought frequently—or for which there are widely accepted standards—are purchased routinely. The government unit simply places an order at a previously approved price. To share in this business, a supplier must be on the list of "approved suppliers." The list is updated occasionally, sometimes by a bid procedure. School supplies, construction materials, and gasoline are bought this way. Buyers and sellers agree on a price that will stay the same for a specific period—perhaps a year.

However, this kind of arrangement can be risky when prices are changing rapidly. Usually the risk is with the seller since prices typically go up. But sometimes it works the other way. For example, the state of North Carolina had contracts with "approved" sellers of microcomputers. The prices were set in the contract. But, after the contracts were signed, Korean computer manufacturers offered lower-price computers. IBM, Zenith, and other major producers quickly lowered their prices. But, by law, state agencies that ordered microcomputers had to buy from the approved vendors—and at a "special" price that was 20 percent higher than current retail prices!

Negotiated contracts are common, too

Contracts may be negotiated for items that are not branded or easily described, for products that require research and development, or in cases where there is no effective competition. Depending on the government involved, the contract may be subject to audit and renegotiation, especially if the contractor makes a larger profit than expected.

Negotiation is often necessary when there are many intangible factors. Unfortunately, this is exactly where favoritism and "influence" can slip in. Such influence is not unknown—especially in city and state government. Nevertheless, negotiation is an important buying method in government sales—so a marketing mix should emphasize more than just low price.[20]

Learning what government wants

There are more than 83,000 local government units (school districts, cities, counties, and states) as well as many federal agencies that make purchases. Keeping on top of all of them is nearly impossible. Potential suppliers should focus on the government units they want to cater to and learn the bidding methods of those units. Then it is easier to stay informed since most government contracts are advertised. Target marketing can make a big contribution here—making sure the marketing mixes are well matched with the different bidding procedures.

A marketer can learn a lot about potential government target markets from various government publications. The federal government's *Commerce Business Daily* lists most current purchase bid requests. The Small Business Administration's *U.S. Purchasing, Specifications, and Sales Directory* explains government procedures to encourage competition for such business. Various state and local governments also offer guidance. And trade magazines and trade associations provide information on how to reach schools, hospitals, highway departments, park departments, and so on. These are unique target markets and must be treated as such when developing marketing strategies.

CONCLUSION

In this chapter, we considered the number, size, location, and buying habits of various intermediate customers to try to identify logical dimensions for segmenting markets. We saw that the nature of the buyer and the buying situation are relevant. We also saw that the problem-solving models of buyer behavior introduced in Chapter 7 apply here—with modifications.

The chapter focused mainly on buying by manufacturers, but buying by other intermediate customers is similar. Some differences in buying by wholesalers and retailers were considered. We described the government market as an extremely large, complex set of markets that require much market analysis—but also offer opportunities for target marketers.

A clear understanding of intermediate customer buying habits, needs, and attitudes can aid marketing strategy planning. And since there are fewer intermediate customers than final consumers, it may even be possible for some marketing managers (and their salespeople) to develop a unique strategy for each potential customer.

This chapter offered some general principles that are useful in strategy planning—but the nature of the products being offered may require adjustments in the plans. The nature of specific industrial products is discussed in Chapter 9. These variations by product may provide additional segmenting dimensions to help a marketing manager fine-tune marketing strategies.

Questions and Problems

1. Discuss the importance of thinking "target marketing" when analyzing intermediate customer markets. How easy is it to isolate homogeneous market segments in these markets?

2. Explain how SIC codes might be helpful in evaluating and understanding industrial markets. Give an example.

3. Compare and contrast the problem-solving approaches used by final consumers and by industrial buyers.

4. Describe the situations that would lead to the use of the three different buying processes for a particular product—such as computer tapes.

5. Compare and contrast the buying processes of final consumers and industrial buyers.

6. Briefly discuss why a marketing manager should think about who is likely to be involved in the "buying center" for a particular industrial purchase. Is the buying center idea useful in consumer buying? Explain your answer.

7. Why would an industrial buyer want to get competitive bids? What are some of the situations when competitive bidding can't be used?

8. Discuss the advantages and disadvantages of "just-in-time" supply relationships from the industrial buyer's point of view. Are the advantages and disad-

vantages merely reversed from the seller's point of view?

9. IBM has a long-term negotiated contract with Microsoft, a supplier that provides the software operating system for IBM computers. Discuss several of the issues that IBM might want the contract to cover.

10. Discuss how much latitude an industrial buyer has in selecting the specific brand and the specific source of supply for a product once it has been requisitioned by some production department. Consider this question with specific reference to pencils, paint for the offices, plastic materials for the production line, a new factory, and a large printing press. How should the buyer's attitudes affect the seller's marketing mix?

11. How does the kind of industrial product affect manufacturers' buying habits and practices? Consider fabric for furniture, a lathe, glue for a box factory, and lubricants for production machinery.

12. Considering the nature of retail buying, outline the basic ingredients of promotion to retail buyers. Does it make any difference what kinds of products are involved? Are any other factors relevant?

13. The government market is obviously an extremely large one, yet it is often slighted or even ignored by many firms. "Red tape" is certainly one reason, but there are others. Discuss the situation and be sure to include the possibility of segmenting in your analysis.

14. Based on your understanding of buying by manufacturers and governments, outline the basic ingredients of promotion to each type of customer. Use two products as examples for each type. Is the promotion job the same for each pair?

Suggested Cases

5. Dow Chemical Company

6. Inland Steel Company

Suggested Computer-Aided Problem

8. Vendor Analysis

Chapter 9

Elements of Product Planning

When You Finish This Chapter, You Should

1. Understand what "Product" really means.

2. Know the key differences between goods and services.

3. Know the differences among the various consumer and industrial product classes.

4. Understand how the product classes can help a marketing manager plan marketing strategies.

5. Understand what branding is and how to use it in strategy planning.

6. Understand the importance of packaging in strategy planning.

7. Understand the important new terms (shown in red).

The product must satisfy customers—what they want is what they'll get.

Marketing managers for Campbell's V-8 Juice wondered why sales to health conscious consumers—an important target market—were weak. Research revealed that these consumers didn't specifically shop for the V-8 brand. In fact, they didn't even spend any time on the canned goods aisle of the grocery store. Instead, they usually chose one of the well-known brands of juice that was conveniently available in the refrigerated section. Armed with a better understanding of how the target customers shopped for the product, Campbell's packaged V-8 in refrigerator cartons—and sales jumped 15 percent.

Volvo marketing managers decided that offering their upscale customers a reliable car wasn't enough. Owning the car had to be hassle-free, too. So Volvo offered a three-year unlimited mileage warranty that covered not only parts and labor but also provided a 24-hour roadside service program. Volvo is not alone in looking at the role of services and warranties in product planning. For example, AT&T guarantees customers of its long-distance phone services immediate credit for any misdialed calls—even if the mistake is the customer's fault.[1]

These examples highlight some important topics we'll discuss in this chapter. First, we'll look at how customers see a firm's product. Then, we'll talk about product classes to help you understand marketing strategy planning better.

We will also talk about branding and packaging. Most goods need some packaging. And both goods and services should be branded. A successful marketer wants to be sure that satisfied customers know what to ask for the next time.

In summary, we will talk about the strategy planning of producers—and middlemen—who make these Product decisions. These strategy decisions are shown in Exhibit 9–1.

Exhibit 9–1   Strategy Planning for Product

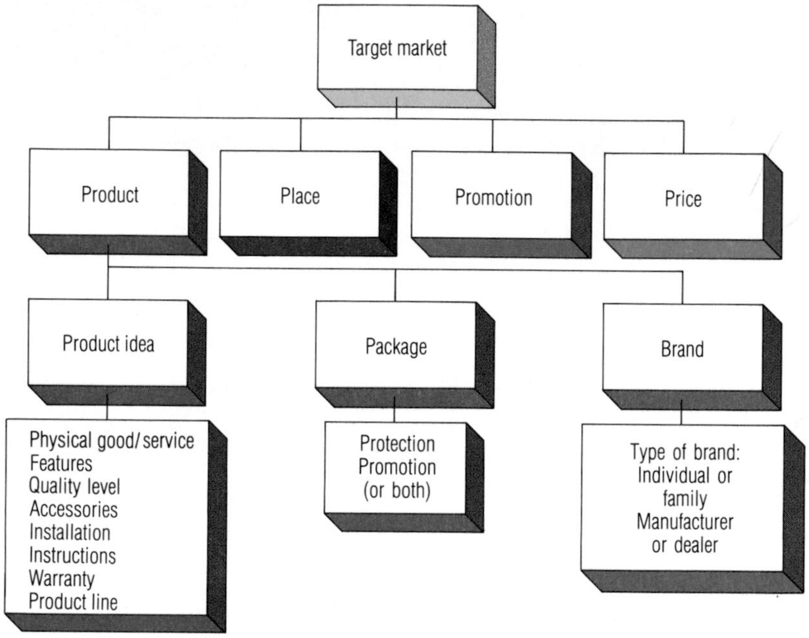

WHAT IS A PRODUCT?

Customers buy satisfaction, not parts

First, we have to define what we mean by a "product."

When Chrysler sells a Voyager minivan, is it just selling a certain number of nuts and bolts, some sheet metal, an engine, and four wheels?

When Procter & Gamble sells a box of laundry detergent, is it just selling a box of chemicals?

When Federal Express sells an overnight delivery service, is it just selling so much wear and tear on an airplane and so much pilot fatigue?

The answer to all these questions is *no.* Instead, what they are really selling is the satisfaction, use, or benefit that the customer wants.

All customers care about is that their minivans look good and keep running. They want to clean with their detergent—not analyze it. And when they send a package by Federal Express, they really don't care how it gets there. They just want their package to arrive on time.

In the same way, when producers and middlemen buy products, they are interested in the profit they can make from their purchase—through its use or resale—not how the products were made.

Product means the need-satisfying offering of a firm. The idea of "Product" as potential customer satisfaction or benefits is very important. Many business managers—trained in the production side of business—get wrapped up in the technical details. They think of Product in terms of physical components, like transistors and screws. These are important to *them,* but components have little effect on the way most customers view the product. Most customers just want a product that satisfies their needs.

Product quality and customer needs

Because consumers buy satisfaction, not just parts, marketing managers must be constantly concerned with product quality. This may seem obvious, but what is obvious is sometimes easy to overlook. In the 1980s, many U.S. firms learned this lesson the hard way when Japanese and European competitors stole market share by offering customers higher quality products. It's important to see, however, what "high quality" means. Much attention has been focused on better quality control in production—so that products work as they should and so that consumers really get what they think they're buying. But quality means more than that.

From a marketing perspective, **quality** means the ability of a product to satisfy a customer's needs or requirements. This definition focuses on a customer's view of a product's fitness for some purpose. For example, the "best" quality clothing for casual wear on campus may be a pair of jeans—not a pair of dress slacks made of a higher grade fabric.

Among different types of jeans, the one with the strongest stitching and the most comfortable or durable fabric might be thought of as having the highest grade or *relative quality* for its product type. Marketing managers often focus on relative quality when comparing their products to competitors' offerings. However, a product with more features—or even better features—is not a high-quality product if the features are not what the target market wants or needs.

Quality and satisfaction depend on the total product offering. If potato chips get stale on the shelf because of poor packaging, the consumer will be dissatisfied. A broken button on a shirt will disappoint the customer—even if the laundry did a nice job cleaning and pressing the collar. A powerful computer is a poor-quality product if it won't work with the software the customer wants to use. [2]

Goods and/or services are the product

You already know that a product may be a physical *good* or a *service* or a *blend* of both. But this view of Product must be understood completely. It's too easy to slip into a limited, physical product point of view. We want to think of a

Because consumers buy satisfaction, not just parts, marketing managers must be constantly concerned with product quality.

product in terms of the needs it satisfies. If the objective of a firm is to satisfy customer needs, it must see that service can be part of its product—or service alone may *be* the product—and must be provided as part of a total marketing mix.

Exhibit 9–2 shows this bigger view of Product. It shows that a product can range from a 100 percent emphasis on physical goods—for commodities like common nails—to a 100 percent emphasis on service, like advice from a lawyer. Regardless of the emphasis involved, the marketing manager must consider most of the same elements in planning products and marketing mixes. Given this, we usually won't make a distinction between goods and services but will call all of them *Products.* Sometimes, however, understanding the differences in goods and services can help fine-tune marketing strategy planning. So let's look at some of these differences next.

DIFFERENCES IN GOODS AND SERVICES

How tangible is the Product?

Because a good is a physical thing, it can be seen and touched. You can try on a Gant shirt, thumb through the latest *People* magazine, smell PopsRite popcorn as it pops. A good is a *tangible* item. When you buy it, you own it. And it's usually pretty easy to see exactly what you'll get.

On the other hand, a **service** is a deed performed by one party for another. When you provide a customer with a service, the customer can't "keep" it. Rather, a service is experienced, used, or consumed. You go see a Touchstone Studios movie, but afterwards all you have is a memory. You ride in a Checker taxi, but you don't own the taxi. Services are not physical—they are *intangible.* You can't "hold" a service. And it may be hard to know exactly what you'll get when you buy it.

Most products are a combination of tangible and intangible elements. Texaco gas and the credit card to buy it are tangible—the credit the card grants is not. A McDonald's hamburger is tangible—but the fast service is not.

Is the product produced before it is sold?

Goods are usually produced in a factory and then sold. A Sony TV may be stored in a warehouse or store—waiting for a buyer. By contrast, services are often

Exhibit 9–2   Examples of Possible Blends of Physical Goods and Services in a Product

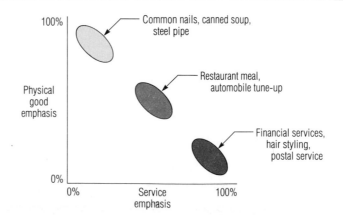

A good is a physical thing; a service is a deed performed by one party for another.

sold first, then produced. And they are produced and consumed in the same time frame. You can't perform a deed and then "put it on the shelf." Thus, goods producers may be far away from the customer, but service providers often work in the customer's presence.

A worker in a Sony TV factory can be in a bad mood—and customers will never know. And a faulty TV can be caught by a quality control inspector. But a rude bank teller can drive customers away. The growing use of computers and machines in service businesses is part of an attempt to avoid this problem. An "automatic teller machine" can't do everything, but it's never rude.

Services can't be stored or transported

Services can't be stored, and this makes it harder to balance supply and demand. An example explains the problem.

MCI is a major supplier of long-distance telephone services. Even when demand is high—during peak business hours or on Mother's Day—customers expect the service to be available. They don't want to hear "Sorry, all lines are busy." So MCI must have enough equipment and employees to deal with peak demand times. But when customers aren't making many calls, MCI's facilities are idle. MCI might be able to save money with less capacity (equipment and people), but then it will sometimes have to face dissatisfied customers.

It is often difficult to have economies of scale when the product emphasis is on service. Services can't be produced in large, economical quantities and then transported to customers. In addition, *services often have to be produced in the presence of the customer*. Thus, services often require a duplication of equipment and people at places where the service is actually provided. Merrill Lynch sells investment advice along with financial "products." That advice could, perhaps, be "produced" more economically in a single building in New York. But Merrill Lynch uses small facilities all over the country—to be conveniently available. Customers want the "personal touch" from the stock broker who is telling them how to invest their money.[3]

Think about the whole Product

Providing the right product—when and where and how the customer wants it—is a challenge. This is true whether the product is primarily a service, primarily a good, or, as is usually the case, a blend of both. Marketing managers must think about the "whole" Product they provide, and then make sure that all of the elements fit together—and work with the rest of the marketing strategy. Sometimes a single product isn't enough to meet the needs of target customers. Then, assortments of different products may be required.

WHOLE PRODUCT LINES MUST BE DEVELOPED, TOO

A **product assortment** is the set of all product lines and individual products that a firm sells. A **product line** is a set of individual products that are closely related. The seller may see them as related because they are produced and/or operate in a similar way, are sold to the same target market, are sold through the same types of outlets, or are priced at about the same level. Procter & Gamble, for example, has many product lines in its product assortment—including coffee, detergents, toothpastes, shampoo, toilet tissue, and disposable diapers. But Hertz has one product line—different types of cars to rent. An **individual product** is a particular product within a product line. It usually is differentiated by brand, level of service offered, price, or some other characteristic. For example, each size of a brand of soap is an individual product.

Each individual product may require a separate strategy. So we will focus mainly on developing one marketing strategy at a time. But remember that a marketing manager may have to plan *several* strategies to develop an effective marketing program for a whole company.

PRODUCT CLASSES HELP PLAN MARKETING STRATEGIES

When planning strategies, it isn't necessary to treat *every* product as unique. Some classes of products require similar marketing mixes. These product classes are a useful starting point for developing marketing mixes for new products—and evaluating present mixes. Exhibit 9–3 summarizes the product classes.

Exhibit 9–3   Product Classes

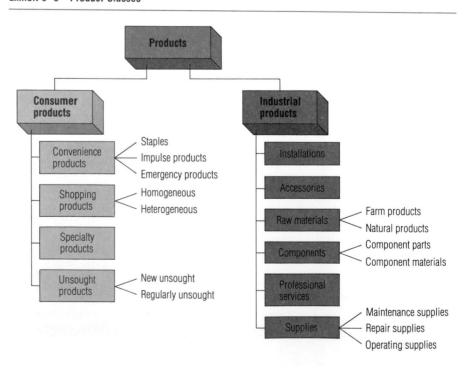

Gatorade is sold as a consumer product and also as an industrial product.

Product classes start with type of customer

All products fit into one of two broad groups—based on the type of customer that will use them. **Consumer products** are those products meant for the final consumer. **Industrial products** are products meant for use in producing other products. Note, however, that the same product might be in both groups. 3M's Post-it™ note pads are sold to both final consumers and industrial customers—and require (at least) two different strategies.

There are product classes within each of these two groups. The basis for the classes is different in each group because final consumers and industrial customers usually view purchases differently. Consumer product classes are based on *how consumers think about and shop for products.* Industrial customers typically do little shopping—especially compared to final consumers. Usually the seller comes to the industrial buyer. So industrial product classes are based on *how buyers think about products and how the products will be used.*

We'll talk about consumer product classes first.

CONSUMER PRODUCT CLASSES

Consumer product classes are based on how consumers think about and shop for products. Consumer products are divided into four groups: (1) convenience, (2) shopping, (3) specialty, and (4) unsought. See Exhibit 9–4 for a summary of how these product classes are related to marketing mixes.[4]

CONVENIENCE PRODUCTS—PURCHASED QUICKLY WITH LITTLE EFFORT

Convenience products are products a consumer needs but isn't willing to spend much time or effort shopping for. These products are bought often, require little selling, don't cost much, and may even be bought by habit.

Exhibit 9–4   Consumer Product Classes and Marketing Mix Planning

1. **Convenience products.**
   a. *Staples*—need maximum exposure—need widespread distribution at low cost.
   b. *Impulse products*—need maximum exposure—need widespread distribution but with assurance of preferred display or counter position.
   c. *Emergency products*—need widespread distribution near probable point of use.
2. **Shopping products.**
   a. *Homogeneous*—need enough exposure to facilitate price comparison.
   b. *Heterogeneous*—need adequate representation in major shopping districts or large shopping centers near other, similar shopping products.
3. **Specialty products**—can have limited availability, but in general should be treated as a convenience or shopping product (in whichever category product would normally be included), to reach persons not yet sold on its specialty products status.
4. **Unsought products**—need attention directed to product and aggressive promotion in outlets, or must be available in place where similar products would be sought.

Convenience products are of three types—staples, impulse products, and emergency products—again based on *how customers think about products,* not the features of the products themselves.

Staples—purchased regularly, by habit

Staples are products that are bought often and routinely—without much thought. Examples include most packaged foods used frequently in every household.

Because staples are purchased often, they are sold in convenient places like food stores, discount stores, vending machines, or directly at your home. Branding is important with staples. It helps customers cut shopping effort and encourages repeat buying of satisfying brands.

Impulse products—bought immediately on sight

Impulse products are products that are bought quickly—as *unplanned* purchases—because of a strongly felt need. True impulse products are items that the customer had not planned to buy, decides to buy on sight, may have bought the same way many times before, and wants "right now." An ice cream seller at a beach sells impulse products. If sun bathers don't buy an ice cream bar, the need goes away, and the purchase won't be made later.

Typical buyer behavior affects Place—and the whole marketing mix—for impulse products. If the buyer doesn't see an impulse product at the "right" time, the sale may be lost. As a result, impulse products are put where they will be seen and bought—near checkout counters or in other heavy traffic areas of a store. Gum, candy bars, and magazines are often sold this way in grocery stores. And life insurance is sold at convenient booths or vending machines in airports.[5]

Emergency products—purchased only when urgently needed

Emergency products are products that are purchased immediately when the need is great. The customer doesn't have time to shop around. Price isn't important. Examples are ambulance services, umbrellas or raincoats during a rainstorm, tire chains during a snowstorm, or a bag of ice just before a party.

Meeting customers' emergency needs may require a different marketing mix—especially regarding Place. Some small neighborhood stores carry "emergency" products to meet these needs—staying open "7 till 11" and stocking "fill-in" items like milk or bread. A wrecker service for cars is available 24 hours a day. Higher prices are usually charged for these products. But customers don't mind because they think of these purchases as "emergencies."

SHOPPING PRODUCTS—ARE COMPARED

Shopping products are products that a customer feels are worth the time and effort to compare with competing products.

Shopping products can be divided into two types depending on what customers are comparing: (1) homogeneous and (2) heterogeneous shopping products.

Homogeneous shopping products—the price must be right

Homogeneous shopping products are shopping products that the customer sees as basically the same and wants at the lowest price. Some consumers feel that certain sizes and types of refrigerators, television sets, washing machines, and even cars are very similar. They are shopping for the best price.

To avoid head-on price competition, firms may try to change the product and use promotion to emphasize their product differences. For example, Wachovia bank in the Southeast offers a "personal banker" to provide customers with information and advice. However, if the customers don't think the differences are real or important, they'll just look at price.

Low-price items are seen this way, too

Even some inexpensive products like butter or coffee may be thought of as homogeneous shopping products. Some customers carefully read food store ads for the lowest prices and then go from store to store getting the bargains. They don't do this for staples.

Heterogeneous shopping products—the product must be right

Heterogeneous shopping products are shopping products that the customer sees as different and wants to inspect for quality and suitability. Examples are furniture, clothing, dishes, and some cameras. Quality and style are more important than price.

Often the buyer of heterogeneous shopping products wants and expects some kind of help in buying. And if the product is expensive, the buyer may want *personalized* services, such as alteration of clothing or installation of appliances.

For nonstandardized products, it's harder to compare prices. Once the customer has found the right product, price may not matter as long as it's "reasonable." This is also true when service is a major part of the product: for example, a visit to a doctor or a car repair service.

Branding may be less important for heterogeneous shopping products. The more consumers want to make their own comparisons of price and quality, the less they rely on brand names or labels. Some retailers carry competing brands so consumers don't have to go to a competitor to compare items.

SPECIALTY PRODUCTS—NO SUBSTITUTES PLEASE!

Specialty products are consumer products that the customer really wants and is willing to make a special effort to find. Shopping for a specialty product doesn't mean comparing—the buyer wants that special product and is willing to search for it. It's the customer's *willingness to search*—not the extent of searching—that makes it a specialty product.

The brand a consumer wants

Specialty products don't have to be expensive, once-in-a-lifetime purchases. Most of us will wait for a specific barber or hairdresser who is able to provide a "just right" haircut. *Any* branded product that consumers insist on by name is a specialty product. Consumers have been observed asking for a drug product by its brand name and—when offered a chemically identical substitute—actually leaving the store in anger.

UNSOUGHT PRODUCTS—NEED PROMOTION

Unsought products are products that potential customers don't yet want or know they can buy. Therefore, they don't search for them at all. In fact, consumers probably won't buy these products if they see them—unless Promotion can show their value.

There are two types of unsought products. **New unsought products** are products offering really new ideas that potential customers don't know about yet. Informative promotion can help convince customers to accept or even seek out the product—ending their unsought status. Products like Dannon's Yogurt, Litton's microwave ovens, Sony's videotape recorders, and California Wine Coolers are all popular items now, but initially they were new, unsought products because they were innovations and consumers didn't know what benefits they offered.

Regularly unsought products are products—like gravestones, life insurance, and encyclopedias—that stay unsought but not unbought forever. There may be a need, but potential customers aren't motivated to satisfy it. And there probably is little hope that such products will move out of the unsought class for most consumers. For this kind of product, personal selling is *very* important.

Many nonprofit organizations try to "sell" their unsought products. For example, the Red Cross supplies blood to disaster victims. Few of us see donating blood as a big need. So the Red Cross regularly holds blood drives to remind prospective donors of how important it is to give blood.

ONE PRODUCT MAY BE SEEN AS SEVERAL CONSUMER PRODUCTS

We've been looking at product classes one at a time. But the same product might be seen in different ways by different target markets—at the same time. Each of these markets might need a different marketing mix.

A tale of four motels

Motels are a good example of a service that can be seen as four different kinds of consumer products. Some tired motorists are satisfied with the first motel they come to—a convenience product. Others shop for basic facilities at the lowest price—a homogeneous shopping product. Some shop for the kind of place they want at a fair price—a heterogeneous shopping product. And others study tourist guides, talk with traveling friends, and phone ahead to reserve a place in a recommended motel—a specialty product.

How an individual views a motel may vary, too. During a cross-country move, one type of motel may be needed. Another may be needed for a family vacation.

Perhaps one motel could satisfy *all* potential customers. But it would be hard to produce a marketing mix attractive to everyone—easy access for convenience, good facilities at the right price for shopping product buyers, and qualities special enough to attract the specialty product travelers. As a result, very different kinds of motels may at first seem to be competing with each other. But they are really aiming at different markets.

Of course, marketing strategy planners would like to know more about potential customers than how they buy specific products. But these product classes are a good place to start strategy planning.

INDUSTRIAL PRODUCTS ARE DIFFERENT

Industrial product classes are useful for developing marketing mixes, too, since industrial firms use a system of buying related to these product classes.

Before looking at industrial product differences, however, we will note some important similarities that have a direct impact on marketing strategy planning.

One demand derived from another

The outstanding characteristic of the industrial products market is **derived demand**—the demand for industrial products is derived from the demand for final consumer products. For example, about one fifth of all steel products are sold to auto manufacturers. Even a steel company with a good marketing mix will lose sales to the auto manufacturers if demand for cars is down.[6]

Price increases might not reduce quantity purchased

The fact that demand for most industrial products is derived means that total *industry* demand for such products is fairly inelastic. To satisfy their customers' needs, industrial firms buy what they need to produce their own products—almost regardless of price. This is because each input to the production process usually costs only a small fraction of the total cost of the product. Even if the cost of buttons doubles, for example, the shirt producer needs them. And the increased cost of the buttons won't have much effect on the price of the shirt—or on the number of shirts final consumers demand.

But suppliers may face almost pure competition

Although the total industry demand for industrial products may be inelastic, the demand facing *individual sellers* may be extremely elastic. This is true if competitive products are similar and there are many sellers—that is, if the market approaches pure competition. Further, industrial buyers make the market as competitive as they can. Their job is to buy as economically as possible—so they are quick to tell suppliers that competitors are offering lower prices.

Tax treatment affects buying, too

How a firm's accountants—and the tax laws—treat a purchase is also important to industrial customers. A **capital item** is a long-lasting product that can be used and depreciated for many years. Often it is very expensive. The customer pays for the capital item when he buys it, but for tax purposes the cost is spread over a number of years. This may increase current profits—and taxes—as well as reducing the cash available for other purchases.

An **expense item** is a product whose total cost is treated as a business expense in the year when it is purchased. This reduces current profits and taxes. It doesn't affect long-run profits. Business managers think about a decision's impact on taxes and profits, so this affects the way they look at the products they buy.

INDUSTRIAL PRODUCT CLASSES—HOW THEY ARE DEFINED

Industrial product classes are based on how buyers think about products—and how the products will be used. Expensive and/or long-lasting products are treated differently than inexpensive items. Products that become a part of a firm's own product are seen differently from those that only aid production. Finally, the relative size of a particular purchase can make a difference. A band-saw might be a very important purchase for a small cabinet shop—but not for a large furniture manufacturer like Drexel.

The classes of industrial products are: (1) installations, (2) accessories, (3) raw materials, (4) components, (5) supplies, and (6) professional services. See Exhibit 9–5 for a summary of how these product classes are related to marketing mix planning.

INSTALLATIONS—MAJOR CAPITAL ITEMS

Installations are important capital items—buildings, land rights, and major equipment. One-of-a-kind installations—like office buildings and custom-made equipment—generally require special negotiations for each sale. Standard major equipment is more homogeneous and is treated more routinely. Even so, negotiations for installations can stretch over months or even years.

Specialized services are needed as part of the product

The customer's expected return on an installation is based on efficient operation. The supplier may have to provide special services to assure this efficiency. The more homogeneous the physical product, the more likely that the seller will try to differentiate the product by offering special services—such as installing the ma-

Exhibit 9–5   Industrial Products and Marketing Mix Planning

1. **Installations.**
   a. *Buildings (used) and land rights*—need widespread and/or knowledgeable contacts, depending on specialized nature of product.
   b. *Buildings (new)*—need technical and experienced personal contact, probably at top-management level (multiple buying influence).
   c. *Major equipment.*
      (1) Custom-made—need technical (design) contacts by person able to visualize design applications and present them to high-level and technical management.
      (2) Standard—need experienced (not necessarily highly technical) contacts by person able to visualize applications and present to high-level and technical management.
2. **Accessory equipment**—need fairly widespread and numerous contacts by experienced and sometimes technically trained personnel.
3. **Raw materials.**
   a. *Farm products*—need contacts with many small farmer producers and fairly widespread contact with users.
   b. *Natural products*—need fairly widespread contacts with users.
4. **Component parts and materials**—need technical contacts to determine specifications required—widespread contacts usually not necessary.
5. **Supplies.**
   a. *Maintenance*—need very widespread distribution for prompt delivery.
   b. *Repairs*—need widespread distribution for some, and prompt service from factory for others (depends on customers' preferences).
   c. *Operating supplies*—need fair to widespread distribution for prompt delivery.
6. **Professional services**—most need very widespread availability.

chine in the buyer's plant, training employees in its use, supplying repair service, and taking trade-ins.

Firms selling equipment to dentists, for example, may assign a service representative to stay with the dentist until he can use the equipment easily. They will even provide plans for a building to hold the dental equipment. The cost is included in the price.

Small number of customers at any one time

Installations are long-lasting products so they aren't bought very often. The number of potential buyers *at any particular time* usually is small. For custom-made machines, there may be only a half-dozen potential customers—compared to a thousand or more potential buyers for similar standard machines.

Potential customers are generally in the same industry. Their plants are likely to be near each other—which makes personal selling easier. The textile industry, for example, is concentrated in and around North Carolina. And the aircraft industry—from a world view—is located in the United States.

Installations—a "boom-or-bust" business

Installations are a "boom-or-bust" business. During the upswing of a business cycle, businesses want to expand capacity rapidly. And, because the potential return on a new investment may be very attractive, firms may accept any reasonable price. In this situation, the demand for installations may be quite inelastic up to a certain price. And supplier capacity may be less than quantity demanded, which reduces competition. But during a downswing, buyers have little or no need for new installations, and sales fall off sharply.

Even during good times when the buyers' demand can be very inelastic, the situation for sellers may be different. If there are many possible suppliers—such as building contractors—buyers of installations may be able to request bids and buy in a very competitive market.

May have to be leased or rented

If a customer wants to actually *own* an installation, he purchases it outright—and treats it as a capital item. But, since installations are relatively expensive, some target markets prefer to lease or rent. That way, the payment is not made all at once and capital can be invested in other opportunities. The customer treats lease payments as an expense item.

Leasing also makes it easier for a firm to make changes if its needs change. For example, many firms lease computers so they can expand to bigger systems as the firm grows. And short-term needs may conflict with the desire for long-term flexibility. So multiple buying influence is common—and top managers are often involved. This multiple buying influence makes promotion more difficult.[7]

ACCESSORIES—IMPORTANT BUT SHORT–LIVED CAPITAL ITEMS

Accessories are short-lived capital items—tools and equipment used in production or office activities. Examples include Canon's small copy machines, Sharp's fax machines, Rockwell's portable drills, Clark's electric lift trucks, IBM's electronic typewriters, and Steelcase's filing cabinets.

Since these products cost less and last a shorter time than installations, multiple buying influence is less important. Operating people and purchasing agents—rather than top managers—may make the purchase decision. As with installations, some customers may wish to lease or rent.

**More target markets re-
quiring different market-
ing mixes**

Accessories are more standardized than installations. And they are usually needed by more customers. IBM's robotics systems, for example, can cost over $1 million and are sold as custom installations to large manufacturers. But IBM's PS/2 desktop computers are accessory equipment for just about every type of business. And these different types of customers are spread out geographically.

Because the market for less expensive and more standardized accessories is larger, more competitors are likely. So, although individual buyers may have inelastic demands, they still may be able to buy in fairly competitive markets.

The larger number of different kinds of customers—and increased competition—mean that different marketing mixes are needed for accessory equipment.

**Special services may
be attractive**

Ordinarily, engineering services or special advice is less important for accessory equipment because of its simpler operation. Yet some companies manage to add attractive services to their accessories. Office furniture suppliers, for example, usually offer decorating services and advice on office layout.

RAW MATERIALS—FARM AND NATURAL PRODUCTS ARE EXPENSE ITEMS

**They become part of a
physical good**

Raw materials are unprocessed expense items—such as logs, iron ore, wheat, and cotton—that are handled as little as needed to move them to the next production process. Unlike installations and accessories, *raw materials become part of a physical good—and are expense items.*

We can break raw materials into two types: (1) farm products and (2) natural products. **Farm products** are grown by farmers—examples are oranges, wheat, sugar cane, cattle, poultry, eggs, and milk. **Natural products** are products that occur in nature—such as fish and game, timber and maple syrup, and copper, zinc, iron ore, oil, and coal.

**They involve grading, stor-
ing, and transporting**

The need for grading is one of the important differences between raw materials and other industrial products. Nature produces what it will—and someone must sort and grade raw materials to satisfy various market segments. Some of the top grades of fruits and vegetables find their way into the consumer products market.

Procter & Gamble's Flint River plant processes 5,000 tons of wood a day. It is an important raw material for making disposable diapers.

The lower grades are treated as industrial products and used in juices, sauces, and soup.

Raw materials are usually produced in specific geographic areas. Much wheat is grown in the Midwest. Timber is important in the Northwest. West Virginia is a center for coal mining. In addition, many raw materials are produced seasonally. Oranges and shrimp can only be harvested at certain times of the year. Yet the demand for raw materials is geographically spread out and fairly constant all year. As a result, storing and transporting are important.

Large buyers may want long-term contracts

Most buyers of raw materials have specific uses in mind and generally want ample supplies in the right grades. Birds Eye needs fresh vegetables for its production lines. International Paper needs logs to make paper. Such buyers can't afford to run out of materials.

Thus, raw materials customers often sign long-term contracts—sometimes at guaranteed prices—for a supplier's output. The supplier then becomes a part of the buyer's operation—thus removing one more producer from the "open" market. Such a situation may be desirable from the supplier's point of view—if it isolates him from pure competition. Another way for a customer to assure supply is to buy producers of raw materials. This makes it difficult or impossible for independent producers—like family farmers or small coal mines—to compete.

Farm products markets are more competitive

Most raw materials have an inelastic *industry* (product-market) demand—in the short run anyway. But remember that industry demand becomes more elastic when good substitutes are available. For example, buyers for a restaurant chain might switch to chicken if beef gets too expensive.

Individual producers of farm products usually face tougher competition than suppliers of natural products. There are a large number of farmers—and nearly pure competition may exist. They have to take the market price.

Natural products are usually produced by fewer and larger companies. As in other oligopoly situations, they can adjust supply to maintain stable prices. For example, the amount of iron ore mined in any one year can be adjusted up or down—at least within limits. And most natural products are less perishable than farm products—so they are more easily stored to wait for better market conditions.

COMPONENTS—IMPORTANT EXPENSE ITEMS

The whole is no better than . . .

Components are processed expense items that become part of a finished product. They need more processing than raw materials and require different marketing mixes than raw materials—even though they both become part of a finished product.

Component *parts* include those items that are (1) finished and ready for assembly or (2) nearly finished—requiring only minor processing (such as grinding or polishing) before being assembled into the final product. Disk drives included in personal computers, batteries in cars, and motors for appliances are examples. They all go directly into a finished product. Some simpler component parts, like rivets and electronic transistors and resistors, may be inexpensive as individual items but are used in very large quantities.

Component *materials* are items such as wire, paper, textiles, or cement. They have already been processed, but they must be processed further before becoming part of the final product.

Major component parts are often custom made to the buyer's specifications. Small operating supplies are usually more standardized and are often purchased with straight rebuys.

Since components become part of the firm's own product, quality is extremely important. The buyer's own name and whole marketing mix are at stake.

Components must meet specifications

Some components are custom-made. Much negotiation may be necessary between the engineering staffs of both buyer and seller to arrive at the right specifications. Multiple buying influence is typical here. Top management becomes involved if the component is very expensive or if it is extremely important to the final product. New task buying—to set the specifications and select sources—is seen here.

Other components are produced in quantity to accepted standards or specifications. Production people in the buying firm may specify quality—but the purchasing agent does the buying. And he often wants several dependable sources of supply. Modified rebuys and straight rebuys are seen here.

Industrial buyers want assurances of availability and prompt delivery. A purchasing agent does everything possible to avoid a plant shutdown caused by lack of components. Moreover, "just-in-time delivery" means that the buyer can save the expense of a large inventory.

Market may be very competitive

Although the industry demand for components may be fairly inelastic, there are usually many willing suppliers and an extremely competitive market. In fact, components often compete in international markets. Producing components can require a lot of expensive labor. Often components are bought from suppliers in countries like Korea or Mexico where labor costs are very low. This "out-sourcing" has made competition among components sellers in the United States even more intense.

Profitable replacement markets may develop

Since component parts go into finished products, a replacement market often develops. This market can be both large and very profitable—as in the case of car tires and batteries.

The replacement market (*after market*) may involve new target markets. The part originally may be a component part when it is sold in the *OEM* (*original equipment market*). But as a replacement, the same product might become a consumer product. The target markets are different—and different marketing mixes are usually necessary.[8]

SUPPLIES—SUPPORT MAINTENANCE, REPAIR, AND OPERATIONS

Supplies are expense items that do not become part of a finished product. Buyers may treat these items less seriously. Although supplies are necessary, most are not as vital to continued operations as the products in the first four classes. When a firm cuts its budget, orders for supplies may be the first to go.

They're called MRO supplies

Supplies can be divided into three types: (1) maintenance, (2) repair, and (3) operating supplies—giving them their common name: "MRO supplies."

Maintenance supplies include products such as paint, light bulbs, and sweeping compounds. *Repair supplies* are products like filters, bearings, and gears that are needed to fix worn or broken equipment or facilities. *Operating supplies* include products such as lubricating oils and greases, grinding compounds, typing paper, paper clips, coal or electricity, and insurance needed for day-to-day operations.[9]

Important operating supplies

Operating supplies that are needed regularly and at large expense receive special treatment from buyers. Many companies buy coal and fuel oil in railroad-car quantities. Usually there are several sources for such homogeneous products, and large volumes may be purchased in highly competitive markets. Or contracts may be negotiated—perhaps by top-level executives. Such contracts have several advantages. Later purchase orders can be drawn routinely against them as straight rebuys. They sometimes assure lower prices. And they eliminate the buyer's concern about a dependable source for these important operating supplies.

Maintenance and small operating supplies

These products are similar to consumers' convenience products—and they are so numerous that a purchasing agent can't possibly be an expert in buying all of them. Branding may become important for such products. It makes product identification and buying easier for such "nuisance" purchases.

Each requisition for maintenance and small operating supplies may be for relatively few items. A purchase order may amount to only $1 or $2. Although the cost of handling a purchase order may be from $5 to $10, the item will be ordered because it is needed—but buyers won't spend much time on it. As this suggests, such items are usually purchased as a straight rebuy.

Industry demand for supplies is fairly inelastic—and sellers may see quite inelastic demand curves, too. Since relatively small amounts of money are involved—and shopping around for bargains is hardly worth the time—a purchasing agent may find a few dependable suppliers with good assortments and buy from them. A new company offering only one supply item may have trouble entering such a market.

Repair supplies

The original supplier of installations or accessory equipment may be the only source for repair needs. The cost of repairs relative to the cost of disrupted production may be so small that buyers are willing to pay the price charged—whatever it is.

Demand for repairs is quite inelastic. But if the demand is large and steady—say, for truck mufflers or power transmission belts—there may be many suppliers. The market then may become quite competitive even though each buyer's demand is inelastic.

PROFESSIONAL SERVICES—PAY TO GET IT DONE

Professional services are specialized services that support the operations of a firm. They are usually an expense item. Engineering or management consulting services can improve the plant layout or the efficiency of a company. Design services can supply designs for a physical plant, products, and promotion materials. Advertising agencies help promote the firm's products. Accounting, data processing, and legal services help in their special areas. Water treatment services rid the firm's water system of pollutants. Food services help improve morale.

Here, the emphasis is completely on the *service* part of the product. Goods may be supplied, as with food service, but the customer is primarily interested in the service. Professional services are often purchased because the buyer either can't afford to have the necessary "pros" on the permanent payroll or chooses not to.

The cost of buying professional services outside the firm is compared with the cost of having company people do them. For special skills needed only occasionally, an outsider can be the best source. And the number of service specialists is growing in our complex economy.

The demand for professional services is often inelastic—if the supplier has a unique product. And the supply may be fairly inelastic, too. Some suppliers—engineers, architects, and lawyers—follow commonly accepted fee schedules. The competition among them is usually based on quality and type of service, not on price.

PRODUCT CLASSES AND MARKETING MIXES ARE RELATED

This focus on product classes may not seem exciting but it is vital because how customers see products affects how they buy them. This obviously has a direct effect on planning marketing mixes.

We will be referring to product classes as we talk about other elements of the marketing mix. In the rest of this chapter, however, we will focus on other strategy decisions related to Product—including branding, packaging, and warranty policies.

BRANDING NEEDS A STRATEGY DECISION, TOO

There are so many brands—and we're so used to seeing them—that we take them for granted. In the grocery products area alone, there are more than 70,000 brands. Brands are of great importance to their owners. They help identify the company's marketing mix—and they help consumers recognize the firm's products and advertising. Branding is an important decision area that many businesspeople ignore. So we will treat it in some detail.

What are branding, brand name, and trademark?

Branding means the use of a name, term, symbol, or design—or a combination of these—to identify a product. It includes the use of brand names, trademarks, and practically all other means of product identification.

Brand name has a narrower meaning. A **brand name** is a word, letter, or a group of words or letters.

Trademark is a legal term. A **trademark** includes only those words, symbols, or marks that are legally registered for use by a single company.

The word *Buick* can be used to explain these differences. The Buick car is branded under the brand name "Buick" (whether it is spoken or printed in any manner). When "Buick" is printed in a certain kind of script, however, it becomes a trademark. A trademark need not be attached to the product. It need not even be a word. A symbol can be used. Exhibit 9–6 shows some common trademarks.

These differences may seem technical. But they are very important to business firms that spend a lot of money to protect and promote their brands.

BRANDING—WHY IT DEVELOPED

Brands provide identification

Branding started during the Middle Ages—when craft guilds (similar to labor unions) and merchant guilds formed to control the quantity and quality of production. Each producer had to mark his goods so output could be cut back when necessary. This also meant that poor quality—which might reflect unfavorably on other guild products and discourage future trade—could be traced back to the guilty producer. Early trademarks were also a protection to the buyer, who could then know the source of the product.

More recently, brands have been used mainly for identification. The earliest and most aggressive brand promoters in America were the patent medicine companies. They were joined by the food manufacturers, who grew in size after the Civil War. Some of the brands started in the 1860s and 1870s (and still going strong) are Borden's Condensed Milk, Quaker Oats, Pillsbury's Best Flour, and Ivory Soap. Today, familiar brands exist for most product categories, ranging from crayons ("Crayola") to real estate services ("Century 21").

Exhibit 9–6   Recognized Trademarks and Symbols Help in Promotion

**Brands make consumers'
shopping easier**

Well-recognized brands make shopping easier. Think of trying to buy groceries, for example, if you had to evaluate the advantages and disadvantages of each of 17,000 items every time you went to a supermarket.

Many customers are willing to buy new things—but having gambled and won, they like to buy a "sure thing" the next time. Even on infrequent purchases, consumers often rely on well-known brands as an indication of quality.

**Branding helps
branders, too**

Brand promotion has advantages for branders as well as customers. A good brand speeds up shopping for the customer—and thus reduces the marketer's selling time and effort. And, when customers repeatedly purchase by brand, the brander is protected against competition from other firms. This can increase sales volume and reduce promotion costs.

Good brands can improve the company's image—speeding acceptance of new products marketed under the same name. For example, many consumers quickly tried Diet Coke when it was introduced because they liked other Coke products.

CONDITIONS FAVORABLE TO BRANDING

Most marketing managers accept branding and are concerned with seeing that their brands succeed.

The following conditions are favorable to successful branding:

1. The product is easy to identify by brand or trademark.
2. The product quality is the best "value" for the price. And the quality is easy to maintain.
3. Dependable and widespread availability is possible. When customers start using a brand, they want to be able to continue using it.
4. The demand for the general product class is large.
5. The demand is strong enough so that the market price can be high enough to make the branding effort profitable.
6. There are economies of scale. If the branding is really successful, costs should drop and profits should increase.
7. Favorable shelf locations or display space in stores will help. This is something retailers can control when they brand their own products. Producers must use aggressive salespeople to get favorable positions.

ACHIEVING BRAND FAMILIARITY IS NOT EASY

Brand acceptance must be earned with a good product and regular promotion. **Brand familiarity** means how well customers recognize and accept a company's brand. The degree of brand familiarity affects the planning for the rest of the marketing mix—especially where the product should be offered and what promotion is needed.

**Five levels of brand
familiarity**

Five levels of brand familiarity are useful for strategy planning: (1) rejection, (2) nonrecognition, (3) recognition, (4) preference, and (5) insistence.

Some brands have been tried and found wanting. **Brand rejection** means that potential customers won't buy a brand unless its image is changed. Rejection may

Hershey's marketing mix—including a familiar brand name—has helped develop brand insistence by some customers.

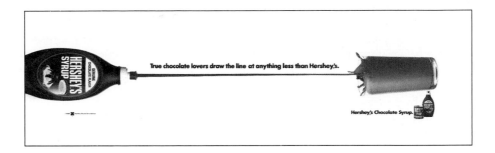

suggest a change in the product—or perhaps only a shift to target customers who have a better image of the brand. Overcoming a negative image is difficult—and it can be very expensive.

Brand rejection is a big concern for service-oriented businesses because it's hard to control the quality of service. A business traveler who gets a dirty room in a Hilton Hotel might not return. Yet it's difficult for Hilton to ensure that every maid does a good job every time.

Some products are seen as basically the same. **Brand nonrecognition** means a brand is not recognized by final customers at all—even though middlemen may use the brand name for identification and inventory control. Examples here are school supplies, pencils, and inexpensive dinnerware.

Brand recognition means that customers remember the brand. This can be a big advantage if there are many "nothing" brands on the market. Even if consumers can't recall the brand without help, they may be reminded when they see it in a store among other less familiar brands.

Most branders would like to win **brand preference**—which means that target customers usually choose the brand over other brands, perhaps because of habit or past experience.

Brand insistence means customers insist on a firm's branded product and are willing to search for it. This is an objective of many target marketers. Here, the firm may enjoy a very inelastic demand curve.

The right brand name can help

A good brand name can help build brand familiarity. It can help tell something important about the company or its product. Exhibit 9–7 lists some characteristics of a good brand name. Some successful brand names seem to break all these rules, but many of them got started when there was less competition.

Exhibit 9–7   Characteristics of a Good Brand Name

● Short and simple	● Suggestive of product benefits
● Easy to spell and read	● Adaptable to packaging/labeling needs
● Easy to recognize and remember	● Not offensive, obscene, or negative
● Easy to pronounce	● Always timely (does not get out of date)
● Can be pronounced in only one way	● Adaptable to any advertising medium
● Can be pronounced in all languages (for international markets)	● Legally available for use (not in use by another firm)

Sunkist Brand Name Is a Sweet Deal

After 75 years of promotion, the Sunkist brand name is familiar to almost every consumer. It's associated with the fresh, sweet oranges that usually bear the trademark. The trademark itself is owned by Sunkist Growers, a farmer's cooperative. But the Sunkist name isn't limited to the fruit grown by members of the cooperative. It has been licensed for use on more than 400 products in 30 countries. For example, Ceiba Consumer Pharmaceuticals licenses the brand for its Sunkist Vitamin C tablets. Cadbury Schweppes, a soft-drink company, has a license for its Sunkist Orange Soda. Lipton, originally famous for its tea, licenses the brand name for use with its line of Sunkist fruit juices, frozen juice bars, and Sunkist Fun Fruits, a line of fruit snacks.

How much is a brand name worth? Licensees are often willing to pay royalties ranging from 4 to 8.5 percent of the wholesale sales. Sunkist earns about $13 million a year in license fees. That's a sweet return—especially since it requires no new investment from the Sunkist growers.[10]

PROTECTING BRAND NAMES AND TRADEMARKS

Common law protects the rights of the owners of trademarks and brand names. And the Lanham Act of 1946 spells out what kinds of marks (including brand names) can be protected and the exact method of protecting them. The law applies to goods shipped in interstate or foreign commerce.

The Lanham Act does not force registration. But a good reason to register under the Lanham Act is to protect a trademark to be used in international markets. Before a trademark can be protected in a foreign country, some nations require that it be registered in its home country.

You must protect your own   A brand can be a real asset to a company. Each firm should try to see that its brand doesn't become a common descriptive term for its kind of product. When this happens, the brand name or trademark becomes public property—and the owner loses all rights to it. This happened with the names cellophane, aspirin, shredded wheat, and kerosene. There was concern that "Teflon" and "Scotch Tape" might become public property. And Miller Brewing Company tried—unsuccessfully—to protect its "Lite" beer by suing other brewers who wanted to use the word "light."[11]

WHAT KIND OF BRAND TO USE?

Keep it in the family   Branders of more than one product must decide whether they are going to use a **family brand**—the same brand name for several products—or individual brands for each product. Examples of family brands are the Kraft food products and Sears' Craftsman tools and Kenmore appliances.

The use of the same brand for many products makes sense if all are similar in type and quality. The main benefit is that the goodwill attached to one or two products may help the others. Money spent to promote the brand name benefits more than one product—which cuts promotion costs for each product. Using a family brand makes it easier, faster, and less expensive to introduce new products. This can be an important competitive advantage, and it explains why many firms are

Sunkist licenses its brand and trademark for use by other firms.

expanding the number of products sold under family brand names that have been developed over a long period of time. For example, Clorox, a leading brand name in bleach, has introduced a new detergent under the Clorox name.

A special kind of family brand is a **licensed brand**—a well-known brand that sellers pay a fee to use. For example, the creators of "Sesame Street" allow different sellers to brand their products with the Sesame Street name and trademark—for a fee. In this case, many different companies are in the "family."[12]

Individual brands for outside and inside competition

A company uses **individual brands**—separate brand names for each product—when its products are of varying quality or type. If the products are really different, such as Elmer's glue and Borden's ice cream, individual brands can avoid confusion.

Sometimes firms use individual brands to encourage competition within the company. Each brand is managed by a different group within the firm. Some managers think that internal competition keeps everyone alert. The theory is that if anyone is going to take business away from their firm, it ought to be their own brand. This kind of competition is found among General Motors' brands. Chevrolet, Pontiac, Oldsmobile, Buick, and even Cadillac compete with each other in some markets.

Many firms that once used this approach have reorganized. Faced with slower market growth, they found they had plenty of competitive pressure from other firms. The internal competition just made it more difficult to coordinate different marketing strategies. For example, Procter & Gamble has a number of different brands of bar soap. A few years ago the managers for the individual brands were fighting it out—often going after the same target market with similar marketing mixes. Now, one manager has responsibility for developing a coordinated marketing plan for all products in the bar soap category. The result is a better-integrated effort.

Generic "brands"

Products that some consumers see as "commodities" may be difficult or expensive to brand. Some manufacturers and middlemen have responded to this problem with **generic products**—products that have no brand at all other than identification of their contents and the manufacturer or middleman. Generic products are usually offered in plain packages at lower prices.

A decade ago, some target markets were interested in buying generic products. But price cuts by branded competitors narrowed the price gap—and won back many customers. Now, generics account for only about 1.5 percent of grocery store sales—and in many product categories they have disappeared altogether. However, generics still capture significant market share in a few product categories—especially prescription drugs.[13]

WHO SHOULD DO THE BRANDING?

Manufacturer brands versus dealer brands

Manufacturer brands are brands created by manufacturers. These are sometimes called "national brands" because the brand is promoted all across the country or in large regions. Such brands include Kellogg's, Stokely, Whirlpool, Ford, and IBM. Many creators of service-oriented firms—like McDonald's, Orkin Pest Control, and Midas Muffler—spend a lot of money promoting their brands in the same way that other producers do.

Dealer brands are brands created by middlemen. These are sometimes called "private brands." Examples of dealer brands include the brands of Kroger, Ace Hardware, and Sears. Some of these are advertised and distributed more widely than many national brands.

Manufacturer brands— more prestige, less control

The major advantage of selling a popular manufacturer's brand is that the product is already presold to some target customers. Such products may bring in new customers and can encourage higher turnover with reduced selling cost. If quality slips, the manufacturer receives the blame, not the middleman. The customer can be shifted to another brand. The middleman doesn't lose *his* customer.

The major disadvantage of manufacturers' brands is that manufacturers normally offer lower gross margins than the middleman might be able to earn with his own brands. In addition, the manufacturer maintains control of the brand and may withdraw it from a middleman at any time. Customers may go elsewhere if the brand is not available. Here, loyalty is tied to the brand rather than to the retailer or wholesaler.

Dealer brands—more control, more responsibility

The advantages of dealer brands are—roughly—the reverse of the disadvantages of manufacturers' brands. The middleman may be able to buy products at lower prices and obtain higher gross margins, even with lower retail prices. The middleman can also control the point of sale and give the dealer brand special shelf position or promotion.

With dealer brands, the middlemen can even change suppliers. For example, if the company that manufactures Lady Kenmore sewing machines for Sears can't supply the quality or price Sears wants, that supplier can be dropped. Customers may not even know that the manufacturer is different.

Dealer branders take on more responsibility. They must promote their own product. This may be costly, especially if turnover is slow. They must also take the blame for poor quality. And getting consistently good quality at low prices may be difficult—especially during times of short supply. Dealer branders usually have to buy in fairly large quantities from suppliers—thus assuming the risk and cost of carrying inventory.

Dealer brands can succeed when . . .

Dealers who do their own branding must assume much responsibility for marketing strategy planning—and it can be costly. Therefore, the decision to go into dealer branding should not be made lightly. A middleman has a greater chance of success if the following conditions exist:

1. The market is large enough and well established. Dealers may find it expensive to pioneer the introduction of new products.
2. No manufacturers' brands are strongly entrenched in the market.
3. The product is available in a dependable quality and quantity and at a reasonable cost, assuring a good margin if the brand is accepted.
4. Product quality can be easily and economically determined by inspection or use. Customers are more willing to experiment if a dealer brand is not much of a risk.
5. Manufacturers' brands are overpriced. Then the dealer brand can be priced under them, yet with a sufficient gross margin to cover higher promotion costs.
6. The right promotion is not so expensive as to use up the extra gross margin.
7. Business conditions are depressed. Customers are more price conscious then, which helps the sale of a lower-priced dealer brand.

Who's winning the battle of the brands?

The **battle of the brands** is the competition between dealer brands and manufacturer brands. The "battle" is just a question of whose brands will be more popular—and who will be in control.

At one time, manufacturer brands were much more popular than dealer brands. But manufacturer brands may be losing the battle. Now sales of both kinds of brands are about equal—but sales of dealer brands are expected to continue growing. Middlemen have some advantages in this battle. They can control shelf space—and they often price their own brands lower. Customers benefit from the "battle." Price differences between manufacturer brands and well-known dealer brands have already narrowed due to the competition.[14]

THE STRATEGIC IMPORTANCE OF PACKAGING

Packaging involves promoting and protecting the product. Packaging can be important to both sellers and customers. Packaging can make a product more convenient to use or store. It can prevent spoiling or damage. Good packaging makes products easier to identify and promotes the brand at the point of purchase and even in use.

Packaging can make the difference

A new package can make *the* important difference in a new marketing strategy—by meeting customers' needs better. A better box, wrapper, can, or bottle may help create a "new" product—or a new market. For example, Campbell's soup is now available in single-serving bowls that can be heated in a microwave, Quaker State Oil is packaged with a twist-off top and pouring spout to make it more convenient for customers of self-service gas stations, and Pringles come in a resealable can that keeps them fresh.

Sometimes a new package improves a product by making it easier or safer to use. Kodak increased sales of its light-sensitive X-ray film by packing each sheet in a separate foil pack—making the film easier to handle. Many drug and food products now have special seals to prevent product tampering.

Packaging can make the important difference in a marketing strategy—by meeting customer needs better.

Packaging sends a message—even for services

Packaging can tie the product to the rest of the marketing strategy. Expensive perfume may come in a crystal bottle, adding to the prestige image. L'eggs panty-hose comes in plastic eggs to make the product stand out in store displays and remind customers of the name.

In a way, the appearance of service providers or the area where a service is provided is a form of packaging. Disney sends the message that its parks are a good place for family vacations by keeping them spotless. Lawyers put their awards and diplomas on the wall so that clients know they provide a high-quality product.

Packaging may lower distribution and promotion costs

Better protective packaging is very important to manufacturers and wholesalers. They often have to pay the cost of goods damaged in shipment, and goods damaged in shipment also may delay production—or cause lost sales.

Retailers need good packaging, too. Packaging that provides better protection can reduce storing costs by cutting breakage, preventing discoloration, and stopping theft. Packages that are easier to handle can cut costs by speeding price marking, improving handling and display, and saving space.

A good package sometimes gives a firm more promotion effect than it could possibly afford with advertising. The package is seen in stores—when customers are actually doing the buying. The package may be seen by many more potential customers than the company's advertising. An attractive package may speed turnover so much that total costs will drop as a percentage of sales.

Or . . . it may raise total costs

In other cases, costs (and prices) may rise because of packaging. But customers may be more satisfied because the packaging improves the product by offering much greater convenience or reducing waste.

Packaging costs as a percentage of a manufacturer's selling price vary widely—ranging from 1 to 70 percent. When sugar producers like Domino sell sugar in 100-pound bags, the cost of packaging is only 1 percent of the selling price. In two- and five-pound cartons, it's 25 to 30 percent. And for individual serving packages, it's 50 percent. But consumers don't want to haul a 100-pound bag home. They are quite willing to pay more for convenient sizes. Restaurants use one-serving envelopes of sugar to eliminate the cost of filling and washing sugar bowls—and because customers prefer the sanitary little packages.[15]

WHAT IS SOCIALLY RESPONSIBLE PACKAGING?

Some consumers say that some package designs are misleading—perhaps on purpose. Who hasn't been surprised by a candy bar half the size of the package? Others feel that the great variety of packages makes it hard to compare values. And some are concerned about whether the packages are biodegradable or can be recycled.

Laws reduce confusion—and clutter

Consumer criticism finally led to the passage of the **Federal Fair Packaging and Labeling Act** (of 1966)—which requires that consumer goods be clearly labeled in easy-to-understand terms—to give consumers more information. The law also calls on government agencies and industry to try to reduce the number of package sizes and make labels more useful.[16]

Food products must now show nutrition information as well as weight or volume. But there is some question whether many consumers understand this information or what to do with it—or even if this is the information they want. At the same time, it is difficult or impossible to provide the kind of information they *do* want—for example, regarding taste and texture.

Some consumers like the convenience of disposable packages. But they can also be a problem. Empty packages litter our streets. Some plastic packages will not decompose even if they lie in a city dump for decades. Empty aerosol cans may explode, and empty bottles often become broken glass.

Marketing managers must be aware of these problems because some tough decisions may be involved. And some states have laws that force the issue. For example, in some states a consumer pays a deposit on bottles and cans—until they are returned. This can cause problems. Channels of distribution are usually set up to distribute products, not return empty packages. Some supermarkets have installed efficient handling systems. And Reynolds Aluminum works with communities to set up centers to buy and recycle cans. But can and bottle returns add new marketing costs.

Unit-pricing is a possible help

Some retailers—especially large supermarket chains—make it easier for consumers to compare packages with different weights or volumes. They use **unit-pricing**—which involves placing the price per ounce (or some other standard measure) on or near the product. This makes price comparison easier.

Research has shown that many consumers don't bother to use unit price information. Because of this, some critics say that unit-pricing is unnecessary. But some consumers do appreciate unit-pricing, and even consumers who don't use it benefit from the price competition it encourages. Big differences in unit prices often disappear when unit-pricing is used.[17]

Universal product codes allow more information

To speed handling and fast-selling products, government and industry representatives have developed a **universal product code (UPC)** that identifies each prod-

uct with marks that can be "read" by electronic scanners. A computer then matches each code to the product and its price. Supermarkets and other high-volume retailers have been eager to use these codes. They reduce the need to mark the price on every item. They also reduce errors by cashiers—and make it easy to control inventory and track sales of specific products. Exhibit 9–8 shows a universal product code mark.

The codes can help consumers, too. They speed the checkout process. Also, most systems now include a printed receipt showing the name, size, and price of each product bought. These codes will become even more widely used in the future because they do lower operating costs.[18]

WARRANTIES ARE IMPORTANT, TOO

**Warranty should mean
something**

Common law says that producers must stand behind their products. And the federal **Magnuson-Moss Act** (of 1975) says that producers must provide a clearly written warranty if they choose to offer any warranty. A **warranty** explains what the seller promises about its product. The warranty does not have to be strong. In fact, the written warranty can *reduce* the responsibility a producer would have under common law.

Federal Trade Commission (FTC) guidelines try to ensure that warranties are clear and definite—and not "deceptive" or "unfair." Some firms used to say their products were "fully warranted" or "absolutely guaranteed." However, they didn't state the time period or spell out the meaning of the warranty. Now a company has to make clear whether it's offering a "full" or "limited" warranty—and the law de-

AT&T and Volvo use promotion to highlight their special service warranties.

fines what "full" means. Also, the warranty must be available for inspection before the purchase. Most firms offer a limited warranty—if they offer one at all.

Some firms use warranties to help create different strategies. They design more quality into their products and offer stronger warranties or replacement—not just repair—if there is a problem. In other cases, the basic price for a product may include a warranty that covers a short time period or that covers parts but not labor. Consumers who want more or better protection pay extra for an extended warranty or a service contract.

Customers might like a strong warranty, but it can be very expensive—even economically impossible—for small firms. Backing up warranties can be a problem, too. Some customers abuse products—and then demand a lot of service on warranties. Although manufacturers may be responsible, they may have to depend on reluctant or poorly trained middlemen to do the job. For example, when energy prices began to rise, many consumers bought chain saws to cut their own firewood. To reach this target market, Homelite began to distribute its chain saws through chains like K mart to reach homeowners in the suburbs. But Homelite had to set up its own service centers because the retail chains had no repair facilities. In situations like this, it's hard for a small firm to compete with larger firms with many service centers.

Deciding on the warranty is a matter for strategy planning. Specific decisions should be made about what the warranty will cover—and then the warranty should be communicated clearly to the target customers. A warranty can make the difference between success and failure for a whole marketing strategy.[19]

CONCLUSION

In this chapter, we looked at Product very broadly. A product may not be a physical good at all. It may be a service. Or it may be some combination of goods and services—like a meal at a restaurant. Most importantly, we saw that a firm's Product is *what satisfies the needs of its target market.*

Consumer product and industrial product classes were introduced to simplify your study of marketing and help in planning marketing mixes. The consumer product classes are based on consumers' buying behavior. Industrial product classes are based on how buyers see the products and how they are used. Knowing these product classes—and learning how marketers handle specific products within these classes—will speed the development of your "marketing sense."

The fact that different people may see the same product in different product classes helps explain why seeming competitors may succeed with very different marketing mixes.

Branding and packaging can create new and more satisfying products. Variations in packaging can make a product attractive to different target markets. A specific package may have to be developed for each strategy. Packaging offers special opportunities to promote the product and inform customers.

The main value of brands to customers is as a guarantee of quality. This leads to repeat purchasing. For marketers, such "routine" buying means lower promotion costs and higher sales.

Should brands be stressed? The decision depends on whether the costs of brand promotion and honoring the brand guarantee can be more than covered by a higher price or more rapid turnover—or both. The cost of branding may reduce other costs by reducing pressure on the other three Ps.

Branding gives marketing managers a choice. They can add brands and use individual or family brands. In the end, however, customers express their approval or disapproval of the whole Product (including the brand).

The degree of brand familiarity is a measure of the marketing manager's ability to carve out a separate market. And brand familiarity affects Place, Price, and Promotion decisions.

Warranties are also important in strategy planning. A warranty need not be strong—it just has to be clearly stated. But some customers find strong warranties attractive.

So it should be clear that Product is concerned with much more than physical goods and service. To succeed in our increasingly competitive markets, the marketing manager must also be concerned about packaging, branding, and warranties.

Questions and Problems

1. Define, in your own words, what a Product is.

2. Discuss several ways in which physical goods are different from pure services. Give an example of a good and then an example of a service that illustrates each of the differences.

3. What "products" are being offered by a shop that specializes in bicycles? By a travel agent? By a supermarket? By a new car dealer?

4. What kinds of consumer products are the following: (a) watches, (b) automobiles, (c) toothpastes? Explain your reasoning. Draw a picture of the market in each case to help illustrate your thinking.

5. Consumer services tend to be intangible, and goods tend to be tangible. Use an example to explain how the lack of a physical good in a "pure service" might affect efforts to promote the service.

6. How would the marketing mix for a staple convenience product differ from the one for a homogeneous shopping product? How would the mix for a specialty product differ from the mix for a heterogeneous shopping product? Use examples.

7. Give an example of a product that is a *new* unsought product for most people. Briefly explain why it is an unsought product.

8. In what types of stores would you expect to find: (a) convenience products, (b) shopping products, (c) specialty products, and (d) unsought products?

9. Cite two examples of industrial products that require a substantial amount of service in order to be useful "products."

10. Explain why a new architectural firm might want to lease a blueprint machine rather than buy it.

11. Would you expect to find any wholesalers selling the various types of industrial products? Are retail stores required (or something like retail stores)?

12. What kinds of industrial products are the following: (a) lubricating oil, (b) electric motors, (c) a firm that provides landscaping and grass mowing for an apartment complex? Explain your reasoning?

13. How do raw materials differ from other industrial products? Do the differences have any impact on their marketing mixes? If so, what specifically?

14. For the kinds of industrial products described in this chapter, complete the following table (use one or a few well-chosen words).

Products	1	2	3
Installations			
Buildings and land rights			
Major equipment			
Standard			
Custom-made			
Accessories			
Raw materials			
Farm products			
Natural products			
Components			
Supplies			
Maintenance and small operating supplies			
Operating supplies			
Professional services			

1. Kind of distribution facility(ies) needed and functions they will provide.
2. Caliber of salespeople required.
3. Kind of advertising required.

15. Is there any difference between a brand name and a trademark? If so, why is this difference important?

16. Is a well-known brand valuable only to the owner of the brand?

17. Suggest an example of a product and a competitive situation where it would *not* be profitable for a firm to spend large sums of money to establish a brand.

18. List five brand names and indicate what product is associated with the brand name. Evaluate the strengths and weaknesses of the brand name.

19. Explain family brands. Sears and A&P use family brands, but they have several different family brands. If the idea is a good one, why don't they have just one brand?

20. In the past Sears emphasized its own dealer brands. Now it is carrying more well-known manufacturers' brands. What are the benefits to Sears of carrying more manufacturers' brands?

21. What does the degree of brand familiarity imply about previous and future promotion efforts? How does the degree of brand familiarity affect the Place and Price variables?

22. You operate a small hardware store with emphasis on manufacturers' brands and have barely been breaking even. Evaluate the proposal of a large wholesaler who offers a full line of dealer-branded hardware items at substantially lower prices? Specify any assumptions necessary to obtain a definite answer.

23. Give an example where packaging costs probably: (*a*) lower total distribution costs and (*b*) raise total distribution costs.

Suggested Cases

1. McDonald's "Fast-Food" Restaurant

13. Office Systems, Inc.

14. Kodak's Ektar

Suggested Computer-Aided Problem

9. Branding Decision

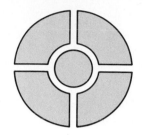

Chapter **10**

Product Management and New-Product Development

When You Finish This Chapter, You Should

1. Understand how product life cycles affect strategy planning.

2. Know what is involved in designing new products and what "new products" really are.

3. Understand the new-product development process.

4. See why product liability must be considered in screening new products.

5. Understand the need for product or brand managers.

6. Understand the important new terms (shown in red).

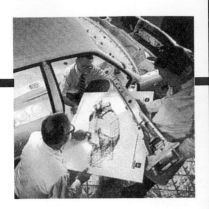

Product management is a dynamic, full-time job for product managers.

Fax machines that can copy a letter, illustration, or photograph and transmit it anywhere in the world over standard phone lines—in just minutes—are becoming standard equipment in business offices. Fax machines are not only changing how companies communicate, but they are also taking business and profits away from overnight delivery services like Federal Express and Express Mail.

When Litton first introduced microwave ovens, most consumers saw them as an expensive and unnecessary novelty. Now they have altered the way of life of millions of American households—and prompted almost every firm that competes in the broad food preparation product-market to alter its market strategy.

Sony, a pioneer in developing videocassette recorders, was one of the first firms to put VCRs on the market. Other firms quickly followed—and the competition drove down prices and increased demand. As sales of VCRs continued to grow, Sony doggedly stuck to its Beta format VCRs in spite of the fact most consumers were buying VHS-format machines offered by competitors. It was not until a decade later that Sony finally "surrendered" and offered a VHS-format machine. However, by then the booming growth in VCR sales had ebbed, and competitors controlled 90 percent of the market. Although Sony was slow to see its mistake, its lost opportunities were minor compared to those of American producers who sat on the sidelines and watched as the whole VCR market was captured by foreign producers.[1]

These innovations show that products, markets, and competition change over time. This makes marketing management an exciting challenge. Developing new products and managing existing products to meet changing conditions is important to the success of every firm. In this chapter, we will look at some important ideas in these areas.

MANAGEMENT OF PRODUCTS OVER THEIR LIFE CYCLES

Products—like consumers—go through life cycles. So product planning and marketing mix planning are important. Competitors are always developing and copying new ideas and products—making existing products out-of-date more quickly than ever.

Product life cycle has four major stages

The **product life cycle** describes the stages a new product idea goes through from beginning to end. The product life cycle is divided into four major stages: (1) market introduction, (2) market growth, (3) market maturity, and (4) sales decline.

A particular firm's marketing mix for a product usually must change during the product's life cycle. There are several reasons. Customers' attitudes and needs may change over the product's life cycle. The product may be aimed at entirely different target markets at different stages. And the nature of competition moves toward pure competition or oligopoly.

Further, total sales of the product—by all competitors in the industry—vary in each of its four stages. They move from very low in the market introduction stage—to high at market maturity—and then back to low in the sales decline stage. More importantly, the profit picture changes, too. These general relationships can be seen in Exhibit 10–1. Note that sales and profits do not move together over time. *Industry profits decline while industry sales are still rising.*[2]

Market introduction— investing in the future

In the **market introduction** stage, sales are low as a new idea is first introduced to a market. Customers aren't looking for the product. They don't even know about it. Informative promotion is needed to tell potential customers about the advantages and uses of the new product.

Even though a firm promotes its new product, it takes time for customers to learn that the product is available. The introduction stage usually is marked by losses—with much money spent for Promotion, Product, and Place development. Money is being invested in the hope of future profits.

Exhibit 10–1 Life Cycle of a Typical Product

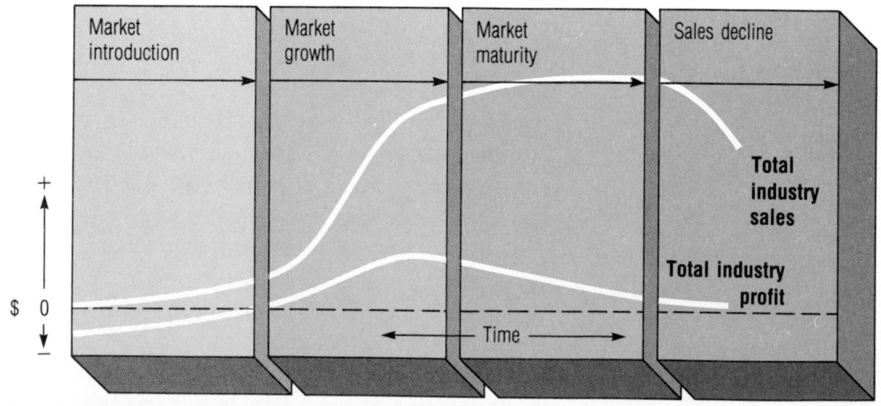

During the market introduction stage of the product life cycle, informative promotion is needed to tell potential customers about the advantages and uses of the new product.

Market growth—profits go up and down

In the **market growth** stage, industry sales are growing fast—but industry profits rise and then start falling. The innovator begins to make big profits as more and more customers buy. But competitors see the opportunity and enter the market. Some try to improve the product to compete better. This results in much product variety. Others just copy the most successful product. Monopolistic competition—with down-sloping demand curves—is typical of the market growth stage.

This is the time of biggest profits *for the industry. But it is also when industry profits begin to decline* as competition increases. See Exhibit 10–1.

Some firms make big strategy planning mistakes at this stage by not understanding the product life cycle. They see the big sales and profit opportunities of the early market growth stage but ignore the competition that will soon follow. When they realize their mistake, it may be too late.

Market maturity— sales level off, profits continue down

The **market maturity** stage occurs when industry sales level off—and competition gets tougher. Many aggressive competitors have entered the race for profits—except in oligopoly situations. Industry profits go down throughout the market maturity stage because promotion costs rise and some competitors cut prices to attract business. Less efficient firms can't compete with this pressure—and they drop out of the market. Even in oligopoly situations, there is a long-run downward pressure on prices.

New firms may still enter the market at this stage—increasing competition even more. Note that late entries skip the early life-cycle stages, including the profitable market growth stage. And they must try to take a share of the market from established firms, which is difficult and expensive.

Cellular telephones are still in the growth stage of the product life cycle.

Persuasive promotion becomes more important during the market maturity stage. Products may differ only slightly if at all. Most competitors have discovered the most effective appeals—or copied the leaders. Although each firm may still have its own demand curve, the curves become increasingly elastic as the various products become almost the same in the minds of potential consumers.

In the United States, the markets for most cars, boats, television sets, and many household appliances are in market maturity.[3] This stage may continue for many years—until a basically new product idea comes along. This is true even though individual brands or models may come and go.

Sales decline—a time of replacement

During the **sales decline** stage, new products replace the old. Price competition from dying products becomes more vigorous—but firms with strong brands may make profits until the end. These firms have down-sloping demand curves because they have successfully differentiated their products.

As the new products go through their introduction stage, the old ones may keep some sales by appealing to the most loyal customers or those who are slow to try new ideas. These conservative buyers might switch later—smoothing the sales decline.

PRODUCT LIFE CYCLES VARY IN LENGTH

How long a whole product life cycle will take—and the length of each stage—varies a lot across products. The cycle may vary from 90 days—in the case of a toy like Rubik's Cube—to possibly 100 years for gas-powered cars.

The product life cycle concept does not tell a manager precisely *how long* the cycle will last. But often a good "guess" is possible based on the life cycle for similar products. Sometimes marketing research can help, too. However, it is more important to expect and plan for the different stages than to know the precise length of each cycle.

Some products move fast

A new product will move through the early stages of the life cycle more quickly when it has certain characteristics. For example, the greater the *comparative advantage* of a new product over those already on the market, the more rapidly its sales will grow. Sales growth is also faster when the product is *easy to use* and if its advantages are *easy to communicate.* If the product *can be tried* on a limited basis—without a lot of risk to the customer—it can usually be introduced more quickly. Finally, if the product is *compatible* with the values and experiences of target customers, they are likely to buy it more quickly.

NutraSweet low-calorie sweetener is a good example. NutraSweet offered real benefits—fewer calories compared to sugar without the bitter aftertaste of existing diet sweeteners. Free samples of NutraSweet chewing gum made it easy for consumers to try the product. And NutraSweet worked well in many products—like diet soft drinks—that were already a part of consumers' lifestyles.[4]

Product life cycles are getting shorter

Although the life of different products varies, in general product life cycles are getting shorter. This is partly due to rapidly changing technology. One new invention may make possible many new products that replace old ones. Plastics changed many products—and created new ones. Tiny electronic "microchips" led to hundreds of new products—from Texas Instruments' calculators and Pulsar digital watches to electronic fuel control on GM cars and Apple's desktop computers.

Some markets move quickly to market maturity—if there are fast "copiers." In the highly competitive grocery products industry, cycles are down to 12 to 18 months for really new ideas. Simple variations of a new idea may have even shorter life cycles. Competitors sometimes copy flavor or packaging changes in a matter of weeks or months.

Patents for a new product may not be much protection in slowing down competitors. Competitors can often find ways to copy the product idea without violating a specific patent. Worse, some firms find out that an unethical competitor has simply disregarded the patent protection. A product's life may be over before a patent case can get through the courts. By then, the copycat competitor may even be out of business.[5]

The early bird usually makes the profits

The increasing speed of the product life cycle means that firms must be developing new products all the time. Further, they must try to have marketing mixes that will make the most of the market growth stage—when profits are highest.

During the growth stage, competitors are likely to be introducing product improvements. Fast changes in marketing strategy may be required here because profits don't necessarily go to the innovator. Sometimes fast copiers of the basic idea will share in the market growth stage. Duncan Hines' new soft chocolate chip cookies were an instant success. Nabisco, Keebler, Frito-Lay, and other cookie makers followed fast—with product improvements, lower prices, and even more varieties. Within a year, Nabisco's "Almost Home" brand led the market. At that time, it was estimated that the Duncan Hines brand had lost $100 million. You can see that copiers can be even faster than the innovator in adapting to the market's needs. Marketers must be flexible *but also* they must fully understand the needs and attitudes of their target markets.[6]

The short happy life of fashions and fads

The sales of some products are influenced by **fashion**—the currently accepted or popular style. Fashion-related products tend to have short life cycles. What is "currently" popular can shift rapidly. A certain color or style of clothing—harem pants, miniskirts, or four-inch-wide ties—may be in fashion one season and outdated the next. Marketing managers who work with fashions often have to make really fast product changes.

How fast is fast enough? The Limited, a retail chain that specializes in women's fashions, tracks consumer preferences every day through point-of-sale computers. Based on what's selling, new product designs are sent by satellite to suppliers around the U.S.—and in Hong Kong, South Korea, and Singapore. Within days clothing from those distant points begins to collect in Hong Kong. About four times a week a chartered jet brings it to the Limited's distribution center in Ohio, where items are priced and then shipped to stores within 48 hours. In spite of the speed of this system, a top manager at the Limited has commented that it's "not fast enough" for the 1990s.[7]

It's not really clear why a particular fashion becomes popular. Most present fashions are adaptations or revivals of previously popular styles. Designers are always looking for styles that will satisfy consumers who crave distinctiveness. The speed of fashion changes increases the cost of producing and marketing products. There are losses due to trial and error in finding acceptable styles, then producing them on a limited basis because of uncertainty about the length of the cycle. These increased costs are not always charged directly to the consumer since some firms lose their investment and go out of business. But in total, fashion changes cost consumers money.

A **fad** is an idea that is fashionable only to certain groups who are enthusiastic about it—but these groups are so fickle that a fad is even more short-lived than a

A certain color or style may be in fashion one season and outdated the next.

© 1988 Gable Estates & Co. Represented by The Roger Richman Agency, Inc., Beverly Hills, CA

regular fashion. Many toys—like Hasbro's Transformers and Kenner's Care Bears—do well during a short-lived cycle. Some teenagers' music tastes are fads. Exhibit 10–2 summarizes the shape of typical life cycles for fashions, fads, and styles. Note that the pattern for a style may go up and down as it comes back into fashion over time.[8]

PRODUCT LIFE CYCLES SHOULD BE RELATED TO SPECIFIC MARKETS

Each market should be carefully defined

The way we define a market makes a difference in the way we see product life cycles—and who the competitors are. If a market is defined too broadly, there may be many competitors—and the market may appear to be in market maturity. On the other hand, if we focus on a narrow area—and a particular way of satisfying specific needs—then we may see much shorter product life cycles, as improved product ideas come along to replace the old.

The market for word processing software appeared to be approaching market maturity—where only minor product changes were expected. However, innovators with a broader view of needs in the market saw new growth opportunities. Desktop publishing software that processes words *and* pictures *and* provides a typeset look is becoming very popular—and appears to be in the growth stage of the product life cycle. Software firms that defined their market too narrowly missed this opportunity.

Exhibit 10–2   Patterns of Fashion, Fad, and Style Cycles for Fashion Products

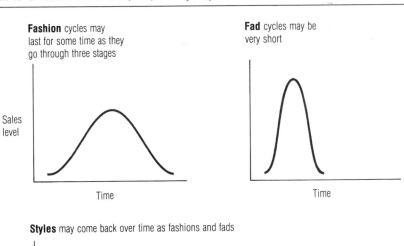

Fashion cycles may last for some time as they go through three stages

Sales level

Time

Fad cycles may be very short

Time

Styles may come back over time as fashions and fads

Sales level

Time

Each market segment has its own product life cycle

Individual products don't have product life cycles

Sometimes existing products can become "new" products in a new market. Sales of Dow Chemical's Saran Wrap fell sharply in the early 1970s when small plastic food storage bags became popular. But sales picked up again by the end of the decade. The product didn't change, but customers' needs did. Saran Wrap filled a new need—for a wrap that would work well in microwave cooking.

Remember that product life cycles describe industry sales and profits for a product idea within a particular product-market—not the sales and profits of an individual product or brand. Individual products or brands may be introduced or withdrawn during any stage of the product life cycle. Further, their sales and profits may vary up and down throughout the life cycle—sometimes moving in the opposite direction of industry sales and profits.

A "me-too" product introduced during the market growth stage, for example, may reach its peak and start to decline even before the market maturity stage begins. Or it may never get any sales at all and suffer a quick death. Market leaders may enjoy high profits during the market maturity stage—even though industry profits are declining. Weaker products, on the other hand, may not earn a profit during any stage of the product life cycle. Sometimes the innovator brand loses so much in the introduction stage that it has to drop out just as others are reaping big profits in the growth stage.

This means that sales of *individual* products often do not follow the general product life cycle pattern—and expecting such patterns can be dangerous for strategy planners. It's the life cycle for the product idea—in the whole product-market—that marketing managers must consider when planning their strategies. In fact, it might be more sensible to think in terms of "market life cycles" or "product-market life cycles" rather than product life cycles—but we will use the term *product life cycle* because it is commonly accepted and widely used.

PLANNING FOR DIFFERENT STAGES OF THE PRODUCT LIFE CYCLE

Length of cycle affects strategy planning

The probable length of the cycle affects strategy planning—realistic plans must be made for the later stages. In fact, where a product is in its life cycle—and how fast it's moving to the next stage—should affect strategy planning. Exhibit 10–3 shows the relationship of the product life cycle to the marketing mix variables. The technical terms in this figure are discussed later in the book.

Introducing new products

Exhibit 10–3 shows that a marketing manager has to do a lot of work to introduce a really new product—and this should be reflected in the strategy planning. Money must be spent designing and developing the new product. Even if the product is unique, this doesn't mean that everyone will immediately come running to the producer's door. The firm will have to build channels of distribution—perhaps offering special incentives to win cooperation. Promotion is needed to build demand *for the whole idea*—not just to sell a specific brand. Because all this is expensive, it may lead the marketing manager to try to "skim" the market—charging a relatively high price to help pay for the introductory costs.

The correct strategy, however, depends on how fast the product life cycle is likely to move—that is, how quickly the new idea will be accepted by customers—and how quickly competitors will follow with their own versions of the product. When the early stages of the cycle will be fast, a low initial (penetration) price may make sense to help develop loyal customers early and keep competitors out.

Exhibit 10–3 Typical Changes in Marketing Variables over the Product Life Cycle

	Market introduction	Market growth	Market maturity	Sales decline
Competitive situation	Monopoly or monopolistic competition	Monopolistic competition or oligopoly	Monopolistic competition or oligopoly heading toward pure competition	
Product	One or few	Variety—try to find best product Build brand familiarity	All "same" Battle of brands	Some drop out
Place	Build channels Maybe selective distribution		Move toward more intensive distribution	
Promotion	Pioneering informing Build primary demand	Informing and persuading ⟶ Persuading and Build selective demand ⟶ reminding Frantically competitive		
Price	Skimming or penetration	Meet competition (especially in oligopoly) ⟶ or Price dealing and price cutting ⟶		

(Chart shows Industry sales and Industry profit curves over Time, with $ and + / 0 / − axis.)

Also relevant is how quickly the firm can change its strategy as the life cycle moves on. Some firms are very flexible. They are able to compete effectively with larger, less adaptable competitors by adjusting their strategies more frequently.

Managing maturing products

Having some competitive advantage is important as you move into market maturity. Even a small advantage can make a big difference—and some firms do very well by careful management of maturing products. They are able to capitalize on a slightly better product—or perhaps lower production and/or marketing costs. Or they are simply more successful at promotion—allowing them to differentiate their more or less homogeneous product from competitors. For example, graham crackers were competing in a mature market and sales were flat. Nabisco used the same ingredients to create three flavors of "bite-sized" Teddy Grahams and then promoted them heavily. These changes captured new sales and profits for Nabisco.[9]

An important point to remember here, however, is that industry profits are declining in market maturity. Top management must see this, or it will continue to expect the attractive profits of the market growth stage—profits that are no longer possible. If top managers don't understand the situation, they may place impossible burdens on the marketing department—causing marketing managers to think about collusion with competitors, deceptive advertising, or some other desperate attempt to reach impossible objectives.

Product life cycles keep moving. But even though a company has no competitive advantage, it doesn't have to sit by and watch its products go through a complete product life cycle. It has choices. It can improve the product—for the same or a different market—and let it start on a different cycle. Or it can withdraw the product before it completes the cycle. These two choices are shown in Exhibit 10–4.

Product life cycles can be extended

When a firm's product wins the position of "the product that meets my needs," its life will last as long as it continues to meet these needs. If the needs change, the product may have to change—but the target consumers will continue to buy it if it still meets their needs. An outstanding example is Procter & Gamble's Tide. Introduced in 1947, this powdered detergent gave consumers a much cleaner wash than they were able to get before because it did away with soap film. Tide led to a whole new generation of powdered laundry products that cleaned better with fewer suds. The demands on Tide continued to change because of new washing machines and fabrics—so the powdered Tide sold today is much different than the one sold in 1947. In fact, powdered Tide has had at least 55 (sometimes subtle) modifications.

Do product modifications—like those made with powdered Tide—create a wholly new product that should have its own product life cycle? Or are they technical adjustments of the original product idea? We will take the latter position—focusing on the product idea rather than changes in features. This means that some of these Tide changes were made in the market maturity stage. It also means that—for strategy planning purposes—"new" brands that are similar to present competitors must immediately enter the product life cycle stage of the already competing brands.

New and different product concepts do result in new product life cycles. For example, by 1985 industry sales of powdered detergents were declining as liquid detergents like Wisk were attracting away some customers. To share in the growth stage profits for liquid detergents, Procter & Gamble introduced Liquid Tide. Al-

Exhibit 10–4   Significantly Improved Product Starts a New Cycle, but Maybe with Short Introductory Stage

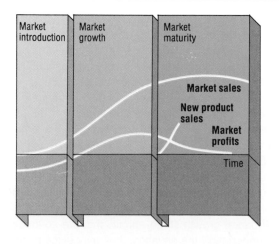
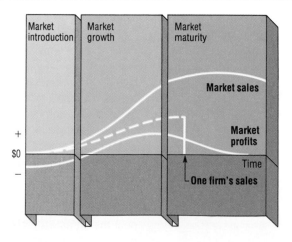

though the familiar Tide brand name was used, Liquid Tide appears to be a different product concept that competes in a different product-market.

Liquid Tide has been very successful. At the same time, powdered Tide continues to sell well. Although powdered detergents in general appear to be in the decline stage, powdered Tide still meets some customers' needs for a dependable powdered detergent that "does the job."[10]

Phasing out dying products

Not all strategies have to be "exciting" growth strategies. If prospects are poor in some product-market, a phase-out strategy may be needed. The need for phasing out becomes more obvious as the sales decline stage arrives. But even in market maturity, it may be clear that a particular product is not going to be profitable enough to reach the company's objectives using the current strategy. Then, the wisest move may be to develop a strategy that helps the firm phase out of the product-market—perhaps over several years.

Marketing plans are implemented as ongoing strategies. Salespeople are making calls, inventory is moving in the channel, advertising is scheduled for several months into the future, and so on. So usually it isn't possible to avoid losses if management ends a plan abruptly. Because of this, it's sometimes better to phase out the product gradually. Managers order materials more selectively so production can end with a minimum of unused inventory. Salespeople are shifted to other jobs, and advertising and other promotion efforts are canceled or phased out quickly since there is no point in promoting for the long run anymore. These various actions obviously affect morale within the company—and they may cause middlemen to pull back, too. So the company may have to offer price inducements in the channels. Employees should be told that a phase-out strategy is being implemented—and reassured that they will be shifted to other jobs as the plan is completed.

Obviously, there are some difficult implementation problems here. But phase-out is also a *strategy*—and it must be market-oriented to cut losses. In fact, it is possible to "milk" a dying product for some time if competitors move out more quickly. This situation occurs when there is still ongoing demand—although it is declining—and some customers are willing to pay attractive prices to get their "old favorite."

Clearly, whole product life cycles should be planned for each strategy. This has a direct bearing on evaluating the prospects for different kinds of opportunities as discussed in Chapter 4. Now you can see that opportunities have different product life cycles—and that product life cycles should be considered when estimating the attractiveness of alternative opportunities.

NEW–PRODUCT PLANNING

Competition is strong and dynamic in most markets. So it is essential for a firm to keep developing new products—as well as modifying its current products—to meet changing customer needs and competitors' actions. Not having an active new-product development process means that consciously—or subconsciously—the firm has decided to "milk" its current products and go out of business. New-product planning is not an optional matter. It has to be done just to survive in today's dynamic markets.

What is a new product?

A **new product** is one that is new *in any way* for the company concerned. A product can become "new" in many ways. A fresh idea can be turned into a new product—and start a new product life cycle. For example, Alza Corporation developed time-release "skin patches" that are replacing pills and injections for some medications. Variations on an existing product idea can also make a product "new." 3M—producer of Scotch Tape—recently introduced "Magic Plus" tape, which sticks to paper but can be easily removed without damaging the surface. Even small changes in an existing product can make it "new."

FTC says product is "new" only six months

A product can be called "new" for only a limited time. Six months is the limit according to the **Federal Trade Commission (FTC)**—the federal government agency that polices antimonopoly laws. To be called new—says the FTC—a product must be entirely new or changed in a "functionally significant or substantial respect." While six months may seem a very short time for production-oriented managers, it may be reasonable, given the short life cycles of many products.

New markets can lead to "new" products

Sometimes existing products can become "new" products in a new market. Du Pont's TEFLON® fluorocarbon resin is a good example. It was developed more than 50 years ago and has enjoyed sales growth as a nonstick coating for cookware, as an insulation for aircraft wiring, and as a lining for chemically resistant equipment. But marketing managers for Teflon are not waiting to be stuck with declining profits in those mature markets. They are constantly developing strategies for new markets where Teflon will meet needs. For example, Teflon is now selling well as a special coating for the wires used in high speed communications between computers.[11]

Videodisc players were a flop during their introduction in the home-entertainment market. Consumers didn't see any advantage over cheaper video-tape players. But now a new market is developing. Interactive video systems—

Du Pont has developed new opportunities by finding new markets for Teflon.

To Handle Tomorrow's High Data Speeds, Use Plenum Cable Insulated With Teflon® Today.

Soon, your system is going to run at higher data rates. But if your twisted pair cable isn't built for speed, you'll get bogged down with "jitter"—fluctuations in timing of network signals. That can lead to increased bit error rate, system slowdown, and cable obsolescence. Unless you install plenum cable made with TEFLON® fluorocarbon resin.

In tests, cables insulated with TEFLON demonstrated superior performance compared to PVC and other materials, because TEFLON dramatically reduces a cable's contribution to jitter. And that means reliable data transmission, whether you're running at 10 megabits today or 20 megabits or more with your next generation system.

TEFLON also allows for longer cable runs, thanks to a dielectric constant of 2.1 — the lowest of any insulation. Cable made with TEFLON also cuts installation costs by 50% because it meets building codes without conduit.

The bottom line is simple: Use cable insulation of TEFLON now, and you'll be ready to run at higher transmission speeds later. To learn more, write for our free brochure on twisted pair cable for high-speed networks: Du Pont Company, 595 Colonial Park Drive, Roswell, GA 30075.

DU PONT

which tie videodisc players to computers—are being used by business firms as a selling aid. Customers can "shop" for products by viewing pictures on a video screen.[12]

AN ORGANIZED NEW–PRODUCT DEVELOPMENT PROCESS IS CRITICAL

Identifying and developing new product ideas—and effective strategies to go with them—is often the key to a firm's success and survival. But this isn't easy. New-product development demands effort, time, and talent—and still the risks and costs of failure are high. Experts estimate that consumer-product companies spend at least $20 million to introduce a new brand—and 70 to 80 percent of these new brands are flops.[13]

A new product may fail for many reasons. Not offering a unique benefit or underestimating the competition are common mistakes. Sometimes the idea is good, but there are design problems—or the product costs much more to produce than was expected. Some companies rush to get a product on the market—perhaps without developing a complete marketing plan.[14]

Not moving fast enough can be a problem, too. The fast pace of change for many products means that speedy entry into the market may be a key to competitive advantage. A few years ago, marketing managers at Xerox were alarmed that Japanese competitors were taking market share with innovative new models of copiers. It turned out that the competitors were developing new models twice as fast as Xerox, and at half the cost. For Xerox to compete, it had to slash its five-year product development cycle.[15]

To be able to move quickly and also avoid expensive new-product failures, it is useful to follow an organized new-product development process. The following pages describe such a process, which moves logically through five steps: (1) idea generation, (2) screening, (3) idea evaluation, (4) development (of product and marketing mix), and (5) commercialization.[16] See Exhibit 10–5.

The general process is similar for both consumer and industrial markets. There are some significant differences, but we will emphasize the similarities in the following discussion.

Exhibit 10–5   New-Product Development Process

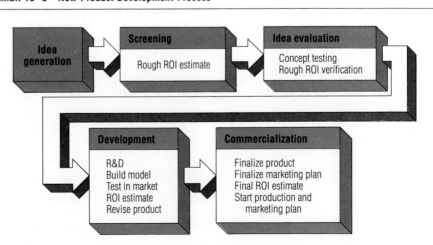

Process tries to kill new ideas—economically

An important element in this new-product development process is continued evaluation of new ideas' likely profitability and return on investment. In fact, it is desirable to apply the hypothesis-testing approach discussed in Chapter 5 to new-product development. The hypothesis tested is that the new idea will *not* be profitable. This puts the burden on the new idea—to prove itself or be rejected. Such a process may seem harsh, but experience shows that most new ideas have some flaw that can lead to problems—and even substantial losses. Marketers try to discover those flaws early, and either find a remedy or reject the idea completely. Applying this process requires much analysis of the idea—both within and outside the firm—*before* research and development (R&D) or engineering spend any money to develop a physical item. This is a major departure from the usual production-oriented approach—which develops a product first and then asks sales to "get rid of it."

Booz, Allen & Hamilton—a consulting firm—has been studying new product introductions for some time. Its research shows the importance of an organized new-product development process. In a 1968 study, it found that about 58 ideas were evaluated for each successful new product. Of course, as shown in Exhibit 10–6, some ideas were rejected at each stage of the process. When the study was repeated in 1981, only about seven ideas were required for each successful new product.[17] The researchers say that this dramatic change is because many companies are doing a better job of generating good new-product ideas. As a result, firms can concentrate more resources in the later stages of the new-product development process on ideas with the highest potential.

Of course, the actual new product success rate varies among industries and companies. But many companies *are* improving the way they develop new products. It's important to see that if a firm doesn't use an organized process like this, it may bring many bad or weak ideas to market—at a big loss.

Step 1: Idea generation

New ideas can come from a company's own sales or production staff, middlemen, competitors, consumer surveys, or other sources such as trade associations, advertising agencies, or government agencies. Analyzing new and different views

Exhibit 10–6   Surviving New-Product Ideas during an Organized New-Product Development Process

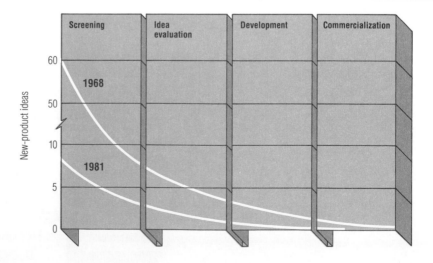

Marketing research often plays an important role in avoiding expensive new-product failures.

of the company's markets helps a marketing manager spot opportunities that have not yet occurred to competitors—or even to potential customers. Basic studies of present consumer behavior point up opportunities, too.

When looking for ideas, the consumer's viewpoint is all-important. It may be helpful to consider the image that potential customers have of the firm and its product. The Maryland Cup Corporation—the world's largest manufacturer of paper drinking straws and a leading manufacturer of paper drinking cups—was able to move into producing plastic food containers of all types because customers identified the company with the "disposable container" business—rather than just the straw and cup business.

No one firm can always be first with the best new ideas. So the search for ideas should include attention to what current or potential competitors are doing. For example, Ford Motor Company has new-product specialists who buy cars made by other firms as soon as they are available. Then they take the cars apart to search for new ideas or improvements made by the other firms. Many other companies use similar approaches.[18]

Research shows that many new ideas in industrial markets come from customers who identify a need they have. Then they approach a supplier with the idea—and perhaps even with a particular design or specification.

But finding new-product ideas should not be left to chance. Companies need a formal procedure for seeking new ideas. The checkpoints discussed below—as well as the hierarchy of needs and other behavioral elements discussed earlier—should be reviewed regularly to assure a continual flow of new—but sound—ideas. The importance of a continual flow is obvious. It makes it possible to spot an opportunity early—while there is still time to do something about it. Although later steps will eliminate many ideas, a company must have some that succeed.

Step 2: Screening

Screening involves evaluating the new ideas with the product-market screening criteria described in Chapter 4. Recall that these criteria include the combined output of a resource (strengths and weaknesses) analysis, a long-run trends analysis, and the objectives of the company. See Exhibit 3–1. The criteria include the nature of the product-markets the company would like to be in—as well as those it wants to avoid. Further, the qualitative criteria include statements that help the company select ideas that will allow it to lead from its strengths and avoid its weaknesses. Ideally, a company matches its resources to the size of its opportunities. A "good" new idea should eventually lead to a product (and marketing mix) that will give the firm a competitive advantage—hopefully one that will last.

Some companies screen based on consumer welfare

The firm's final choice in product design should fit with the company's overall objectives—and make good use of the firm's resources. But it is also desirable to create a need-satisfying product that will appeal to consumers—in the long run as well as the short run. Ideally, the product will increase consumer welfare, too—not just satisfy a whim. Different kinds of new-product opportunities are shown in Exhibit 10–7. Obviously, a socially responsible firm tries to find "desirable" opportunities rather than "deficient" ones. This may not be as easy as it sounds, however. Some consumers want "pleasing products" instead of "desirable products." They emphasize immediate satisfaction and give little thought to their own long-term welfare. And some competitors are quite willing to offer what consumers want in the short run. Generating "socially responsible" new-product ideas is a challenge for new-product planners. Consumer groups are helping to force this awareness on more firms.

Exhibit 10–7
Types of New-Product Opportunities

Safety must be considered

Real acceptance of the marketing concept certainly leads to the design of safe products. But some risky products are purchased because they provide thrills and excitement—for example, bicycles, skis, and hang gliders. Even so, safety features usually can be added—and are desired by some potential customers.

The **Consumer Product Safety Act** (of 1972) set up the Consumer Product Safety Commission to encourage more awareness of safety in product design—and better quality control. The commission has a great deal of power. It can set safety standards for products. It can order costly repairs or return of "unsafe products." And it can back up its orders with fines and jail sentences. The Food and Drug Administration has similar powers for food and drugs.

Product safety complicates strategy planning because not all customers—even those who want better safety features—are willing to pay more for safer products. Some features cost a lot to add and increase prices considerably. These safety concerns must be considered at the screening step because a firm can later be held liable for unsafe products.

Products can turn to liabilities

Product liability means the legal obligation of sellers to pay damages to individuals who are injured by defective or unsafe products. Product liability is a serious matter. Liability settlements may exceed not only the company's insurance coverage, but also its total assets!

The courts have been enforcing a very strict product liability standard. Producers may be held responsible for injuries related to their products, no matter how

Adopting the marketing concept should lead to the development of safe products.

the items are used or how well they are designed. Riddell—whose football helmets protect the pros—recently was hit with a $12 million judgment for a high school football player who broke his neck. The jury concluded that Riddell should have put a sticker on the helmet to warn players of the danger of butting into opponents! Cases and settlements like this are common.

The question of liability is a serious concern—and changes in state and federal laws are underway. But, until product liability questions are resolved, marketing managers must be even more sensitive when screening new product ideas.[19]

ROI is a crucial screening criterion

Getting by the initial screening criteria doesn't guarantee success for the new idea. But it does show that at least the new idea is "in the right ballpark" *for this firm*. If many ideas pass the screening criteria, then a firm must set priorities for which ones go on to the next step in the process. This can be done by comparing the ROI (return on investment) for each idea—assuming the firm is ROI-oriented. The most attractive alternatives are pursued first.

Step 3: Idea evaluation

When an idea moves past the screening step, it is evaluated more carefully. Note that no tangible product has yet been developed—and this can handicap the firm in getting feedback from customers. For help in idea evaluation, firms use **concept testing**—getting reactions from customers about how well a new product idea fits their needs. Concept testing uses market research—ranging from informal focus groups to formal surveys of potential customers.

It is often possible to make a rough ROI estimate after some market research. Even informal focus groups are useful—especially if they show that potential users aren't excited about the new idea. If results are discouraging, it may be best to kill the idea at this stage. Remember, in this hypothesis-testing process, we are looking for any evidence that an idea is *not* a good opportunity for this firm—and should be rejected.

Product planners must think about intermediate customers as well as final consumers. Middlemen may have special concerns about handling a proposed product. A Utah ice cream maker was considering a new line of ice cream novelty products—and he had visions of a hot market in California. But, he had to drop his idea when he learned that grocery store chains wanted payments of $20,000 each just to put his frozen novelties in their freezers. Without the payment, they didn't want to risk using profitable freezer space on an unproven product. This is not an unusual case. It often becomes clear at the idea evaluation stage that other members of the channel of distribution will not cooperate.[20]

Idea evaluation is more precise in industrial markets. Here, potential customers are more informed about their needs—and their buying is more economical and less emotional. Further, given the derived nature of demand in industrial markets, most needs are already being satisfied in some way. So new products are substitutes for existing ways of doing things. This means that fewer interviews with well-informed people can help determine the range of product requirements—and whether there is an opportunity.

A large manufacturer of food machinery and equipment did not use this process. It completed the design of a large citrus juicer without adequately studying the juice industry. Management went ahead with engineering development—confident that the machine would find a market. After spending nearly $1 million on design and engineering work, the company learned that the machine was built for the top of the market rather than for the bulk of potential users—the smaller processors. The machine was too big and expensive—and only a few firms could afford it. If the company had spent a few thousand dollars to determine how many citrus processors there were by size, types of machines used and wanted, and related facts, it might have avoided a costly mistake.

Whatever research methods are used, the idea evaluation step should gather enough information to help decide whether there is an opportunity, whether it fits with the firm's resources, *and* whether there is a basis for developing a competitive advantage. With such information, the firm can estimate likely ROI in the various market segments and decide whether to continue the new-product development process.[21]

Step 4: Development

Product ideas that survive the screening and idea evaluation steps must now be analyzed further. Usually, this involves some research and development (R&D) and engineering to design and develop the physical part of the product. Input from the earlier efforts helps guide this technical work.

But it is still desirable to test models and early versions of the product in the market. This process may have several cycles—building a model or producing limited quantities of a product, testing it, revising product specifications based on the tests, and so on—*before* pilot plant production.

With actual products, potential customers can see how the idea has been converted into a tangible product. Using small focus groups, panels, and larger surveys, marketers can get reactions to specific features and to the whole product idea. Sometimes that reaction kills the idea. For example, Coca-Cola Foods believed it had a great idea with Minute Maid Squeeze-Fresh, frozen orange juice

Computer-aided design is helping to speed up the new-product development process.

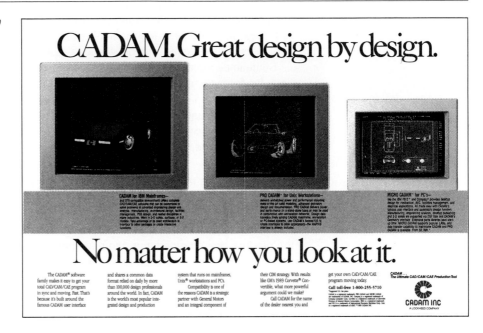

concentrate in a squeeze bottle. The idea was that consumers would prefer to mix one glass at a time rather than find space for another half-gallon jug in the refrigerator. When the product was actually tested it was a bomb. Consumers had loved the idea, but hated the product. It was messy to use, and no one knew how much concentrate to squeeze in the glass.[22]

In other cases, testing can lead to revision of product specifications for different markets. Sometimes months or even years of research are necessary to focus on precisely what different market segments will find acceptable. It took Procter & Gamble over 10 years and $800 million to develop Pringles Potato Chips!

Full-scale market testing is often used to get reactions in real market conditions or to test product variations and variations in the marketing mix. For example, a firm may test alternative brands, prices, or advertising copy in different test cities. Note that the firm is testing the whole marketing mix, not just the product.

Test marketing can be risky. It not only tests ideas for the company, but also may give information to the competition. In fact, a company in Chicago—Marketing Intelligence Services—monitors products in test markets and then sells the information to competing firms.

But *not* testing is dangerous, too. In 1986, Frito-Lay was so sure it understood consumers' snack preferences that it introduced a three-item cracker line called MaxSnax without market testing. Even with network TV ad support, the line met with overwhelming consumer indifference. By the time Frito-Lay pulled the product from store shelves it had lost $52 million. Market tests can be very expensive. Yet they can discover problems that otherwise might go undetected—and destroy the whole strategy.[23]

If the new-product development process is used carefully, the market test will provide a lot more information to the firm than to its competitors. Of course, the company must test specific variables—rather than just vaguely testing whether a new idea will "sell." After the market test, an estimate of likely ROI for various strategies will determine whether the idea moves on to commercialization.

Sometimes a market test is not run because it isn't practical. In fashion markets, for example, speed is extremely important, and products are usually just tried in the market. And durable products—which have high fixed production costs and long production lead times—may have to go directly to the market. In these cases, it is especially important that the early steps be done carefully to reduce the chances for failure.[24]

Step 5: Commercialization

A product idea that survives this far can finally be placed on the market. First, the new-product people decide exactly which product form or line to sell. Then, they complete the marketing mix—really a whole strategic plan. And top management has to approve an ROI estimate for the plan before it is implemented. Finally, the product idea emerges from the new-product development process—but success requires the cooperation of the whole company.

Putting a product on the market is expensive. Manufacturing facilities have to be set up and enough product has to be produced to fill the channels of distribution. Further, introductory promotion is costly—especially if the company has to develop new channels of distribution.

Because of the size of the job, some firms introduce their products city by city or region by region—in a gradual "roll out"—until they have complete market coverage. Roll outs also permit more market testing—although that is not their purpose. All implementation efforts should be controlled—to be sure the marketing plan is still on target.

NEW–PRODUCT DEVELOPMENT: A TOTAL COMPANY EFFORT

Top-level support is vital

Some companies seem to be particularly successful at developing new products. There are many differences in how these companies are organized. A key element that they all have in common is enthusiastic top-management support that new product development is important. New products tend to upset old routines that managers of established products often try in subtle but effective ways to maintain. So someone with top-level support needs to be responsible for new-product development.[25]

Put someone in charge

In addition, rather than just leaving new-product development to anyone who happens to be interested—perhaps in engineering, R&D, or sales—it is better to put someone in charge. This can be a person, a department, or a committee.

A new-product development department or committee helps ensure that new ideas are carefully evaluated—and good ones profitably marketed. Who is involved in this evaluation is important. Overly conservative managers may kill too many—or even all—new ideas. Or they may create delays. Delays lead to late introduction—and give competitors a head start. A delay of even a few months can make the difference between a product's success or failure.

3M's Smooth–Running Innovation Machine

Minnesota Mining & Manufacturing (3M) spins out new products faster and better than just about any other company. The company knows that finding new-product opportunities is critical to success. In fact, more than a quarter of 3M's sales (over $10 billion!) come from products that did not exist five years ago. That is no accident—it's a company guideline that applies to every division. Another guideline—the "15 percent rule"—allows virtually every employee to spend up to 15 percent of the workweek on anything related to new-product opportunities. Post-It Notes, Scotch Tape, and hundreds of other profitable new products were developed with this "free time."

3M also motivates innovation by rewarding new-product champions, sharing ideas among divisions, and recognizing that many new ideas may need to be considered before you find a good opportunity. Perhaps most important, 3M works at getting close to customers and their needs. This simple idea has been part of 3M's market orientation for decades. For example, back in the 1920s, a 3M inventor joined a sales rep at an automobile assembly line to get ideas for ways to improve 3M sandpaper. He noticed that workers had trouble keeping paint borders straight on the two-tone cars popular at the time. Rather than dismissing that problem as irrelevant to producing sandpaper, he went back to the lab and invented masking tape. Breakthrough opportunities don't just happen at 3M—the company continually works at finding them.[26]

Market needs guide R&D effort

Many new-product ideas come from scientific discoveries and new technologies. That is why firms often assign specialists to study the technological environment in search of new ways to meet customers' needs. Many firms have their own R&D group that works on developing new products and new-product ideas. We've touched on this earlier, but the relationship between marketing and R&D warrants special emphasis.

The R&D effort is usually handled by scientists and engineers who have special technical training and skills. Their work can make an important contribution to a firm's competitive advantage—especially if it competes in "high-tech" markets. However, it is important to see that technical creativity by itself is not enough. The R&D effort must be guided by the type of new-product development process we have been discussing.

From the idea generation stage to the commercialization stage, the R&D specialists and the marketing people must work together to evaluate the feasibility of new ideas. It isn't sensible for a marketing manager to develop elaborate marketing plans for a product that the firm simply can't produce—or produce profitably. It also doesn't make sense for the R&D people to "do their own thing" trying to develop a technology or product that does not have potential for the firm and its markets. Clearly, a balancing act is involved here. But the critical point is the basic one we have been emphasizing throughout the whole book: marketing-oriented firms seek to satisfy customer needs at a profit with an integrated, whole-company effort.

A complicated, integrated effort is needed

Developing new products should be a total company effort. The whole process—involving people in management, research, production, promotion, packaging, and branding—must move in steps from early exploration of ideas to development of the product and marketing mix. Even with a careful development process, many new products do fail. This usually happens, however, when some steps in the process have been skipped. Because speed can be important, it's always tempting to skip needed steps when some part of the process seems to indicate that the company has a "really good idea." But the process moves in steps—gathering different kinds of information along the way. Skipping some of the steps may lead to missing an important aspect that will make a whole strategy less profitable—or actually cause it to fail.

Eventually, the "new" product is no longer "new"—and it becomes just another product. About this time, the "new-product people" turn the product over to the regular operating people—and go on to developing other new ideas.

NEED FOR PRODUCT MANAGERS

Product variety leads to product managers

When a firm has only one or a few related products, everyone is interested in them. But when many new products are being developed, someone should be put in charge of new-product planning to be sure it is not neglected. Similarly, when a firm has several different kinds of products, management may decide to put someone in charge of each kind—or even each brand—to be sure they are not lost in the rush of everyday business. **Product managers** or **brand managers** manage specific products—often taking over the jobs formerly handled by an advertising manager. That gives a clue to what is often their major responsibility—Promotion—since the products have already been developed by the "new-product" people.

Product managers are especially common in large companies that produce many kinds of products. Several product managers may serve under a marketing manager. Sometimes these product managers are responsible for the profitable operation of a particular product's whole marketing effort. Then, they have to coordinate their efforts with others—including the sales manager, advertising agencies, and production and research people, and even channel members. This is likely to lead to difficulties if the product manager has no control over the marketing strategy for other related brands—or authority over other functional areas whose efforts he is expected to direct and coordinate!

To avoid these problems, in some companies the product manager serves mainly as a "product champion"—concerned with planning and getting the promotion effort implemented. A higher-level marketing manager with more authority coordinates the efforts and integrates the marketing strategies for different products into an overall plan.

The activities of product managers vary a lot depending on their experience and aggressiveness—and the company's organizational philosophy. Today, companies are emphasizing marketing *experience*—because this important job takes more than academic training and enthusiasm. But it is clear that someone must be responsible for developing and implementing product-related plans—especially when a company has many products.[27]

CONCLUSION

New-product planning is an increasingly important activity in a modern economy because it is no longer very profitable to just sell "me-too" products in highly competitive markets. Markets, competition, and product life cycles are changing at a fast pace.

The product life cycle concept is especially important to marketing strategy planning. It shows that different marketing mixes—and even strategies—are needed as a product moves through its cycle. This is an important point because profits change during the life cycle—with most of the profits going to the innovators or fast copiers.

We pointed out that a new product is not limited to physical newness. We call a product "new" if it is new in any way—to any target market. But the FTC takes a narrower view of what you can call "new."

New products are so important to business survival that firms need some organized process for developing them. Such a process was discussed—and it is obvious that new-product development must be a total company effort to be successful.

The failure rate of new products is high—but it is lower for better-managed firms that recognize product development and management as vital processes. Some firms appoint product managers to manage individual products and new-product committees to ensure that the process is carried out successfully.

Questions and Problems

1. Explain how industry sales and industry profits behave over the product life cycle.

2. Cite two examples of products that you feel are currently in each of the product life cycle stages.

3. Explain how different conclusions might be reached with respect to the correct product life cycle stage(s) in the automobile market—especially if different views of the market are held.

4. Explain why the product life cycle concept does not apply to individual brands. Give an example of a new brand that is not entering the life cycle at the market introduction stage.

5. Discuss the life cycle of a product in terms of its probable impact on a manufacturer's marketing mix. Illustrate using personal computers.

6. What are some of the characteristics of a new product that will help it to move through the early stages of the product life cycle more quickly? Briefly discuss each characteristic—illustrating with a product of your choice.

7. What is a new product? Illustrate your answer.

8. Explain the importance of an organized new-product development process and illustrate how it might be used for (*a*) a new frozen-food item, (*b*) a new children's toy, (*c*) a new large-screen TV for home use.

9. Explain the role of product or brand managers. Are they usually put in charge of new-product development?

10. Discuss the social value of new-product development activities that seem to encourage people to discard products that are not "all worn out." Is this an economic waste? How worn out is "all worn out?" Must a shirt have holes in it? How big?

Suggested Cases

7. Pillsbury's Häagen-Dazs

12. Union Carbide

14. Kodak's Ektar

18. Tandy versus IBM

22. Outdoor Sports, Inc.

Suggested Computer-Aided Problem

10. Growth Stage Competition

Chapter **11**

Place and Development of Channel Systems

When You Finish This Chapter, You Should

1. Understand how and why marketing specialists adjust discrepancies of quantity and assortment.

2. Understand what product classes suggest about Place objectives.

3. Know about the different kinds of channel systems.

4. Understand how much market exposure is "ideal."

5. Understand how to obtain cooperation and avoid conflict in channel systems.

6. Know how channel systems can shift and share functions.

7. Understand the important new terms (shown in red).

You may build a "better mousetrap," but if it's not in the right place at the right time, it won't do anyone any good.

During the 1980s, Compaq Computer's sales grew faster than any other new company in history. It took advantage of market growth by quickly introducing new models of personal computers for market segments neglected by IBM and other producers.

Good relationships with strong middlemen contributed to Compaq's success. Initially, Compaq didn't have the resources to try to sell direct to big corporate accounts. Instead, it recruited computer dealers to help reach the business market. Most dealers handled several brands of computer. But many of them focused on selling Compaq's line. Compaq was a cooperative supplier who helped the dealer get whatever sales it could. Other major suppliers—like IBM and Apple—reserved some of the biggest accounts for their own salespeople.

By 1989, the market had changed. Sales growth was slowing and competition was becoming more intense. IBM and other producers were pushing for a larger share of the sales made by local dealers. IBM was particularly interested in getting more attention from Businessland, one of the largest chains. Along with other changes in its marketing mix—like more help in training Businessland salespeople—IBM offered the chain a 44 percent discount off list price. That was a larger discount than IBM offered other dealers—and it was more than Compaq's discount. The change meant that Businessland would make more profit by emphasizing the IBM line—even after boosting its sales commissions and advertising on IBM equipment.

Compaq had been working with Businessland for seven years, and Businessland generated 7 percent of Compaq's sales. However, Compaq and Businessland now had conflicting objectives—so marketing managers at Compaq decided to drop Businessland as a distributor. They thought that other dealers who had not been offered IBM's "special favors" would be motivated to work harder at selling Compaqs—so that is where they put their emphasis.[1]

As this example shows, offering customers a good product at a reasonable price is important to a successful marketing strategy. But it's not the whole story. Managers must also think about **Place**—making products available in the right quantities and locations—when customers want them.

Place often requires the selection and use of marketing specialists—middlemen and facilitators—to provide target customers with time, place, and possession utilities. But many variations are possible. Cross pens are sold by a selected group of stores—while Bic pens are sold by many more retailers. Many industrial products are sold by the producer direct to the customer. But most consumer products are sold to middlemen, who later sell to final consumers.

The many Place variations raise important questions. Why are some products sold by the producer direct to final customers, while others are sold with the help of middlemen? Why are some products carried by many retailers—and others by only a few? In the next four chapters, we'll deal with these important questions. See Exhibit 11–1 for a "picture" of the Place decision areas we're going to discuss.

In this chapter, we will first consider Place objectives—and how they relate to product classes. Then we'll take a look at some of the activities needed to provide Place. We will show why specialists are often involved and how they come together to form a **channel of distribution**—any series of firms or individuals who participate in the flow of goods and services from producer to final user or consumer. We will also consider how much market exposure is "ideal." Finally, we'll

Exhibit 11–1   Strategy Decision Areas in Place

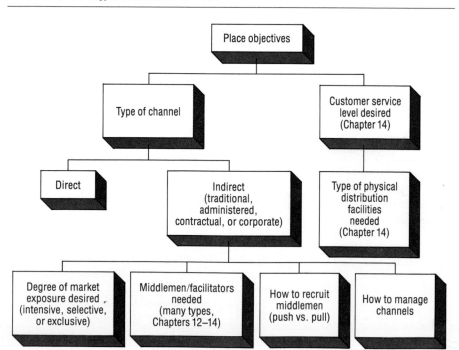

discuss how relations among channel members can be managed to reduce conflict and improve cooperation.

"IDEAL" PLACE OBJECTIVES SUGGESTED BY PRODUCT CLASSES

Obviously, the needs and attitudes of potential target markets should be considered when developing Place. We expect that people in a particular target market have similar attitudes and, therefore, can be satisfied with the same Place system. In our discussion of the product classes we covered their attitudes about urgency to have needs satisfied and willingness to shop. Now you should be able to use the product classes to suggest how Place should be handled.

The relationship between product classes and ideal Place objectives was shown in Exhibit 9–4 for consumer products and Exhibit 9–5 for industrial products. Study these figures carefully—they provide the framework for dealing with Place as part of a marketing strategy. In particular, the product classes help us to decide how much market exposure we will need in each geographic area.

The marketing manager must also consider Place objectives in relation to the product life cycle; see Exhibit 10–3. *Place decisions have long-run effects.* They are harder to change than Product, Price, and Promotion decisions. Effective working arrangements with others in the channel may take several years—and a good deal of money—to develop. Legal contracts with channel partners may also limit changes. And it's hard to move retail stores and wholesale facilities once leases are signed and customer movement patterns are settled.

Place system is not automatic

Just as there are no automatic classifications of products, we can't automatically decide the one "best" Place arrangement. If two or three market segments hold different views of a product, then different Place arrangements may be required.

DISCREPANCIES REQUIRE CHANNEL SPECIALISTS

All producers want to be sure that their products reach the target customers. But the assortment and quantity of products customers want may be different than the assortment and quantity of products normally produced. Specialists develop to adjust these discrepancies. Remember that we discussed this briefly in Chapter 1. Now we will go into more detail so you will be able to plan different kinds of channels of distribution.[2]

Discrepancies of quantity and assortment

Discrepancy of quantity means the difference between the quantity of products it is economical for a producer to make and the quantity final users or consumers normally want. For example, most manufacturers of golf balls produce large quantities—perhaps 200,000 to 500,000 in a given time period. The average golfer, however, wants only a few balls at a time. Adjusting for this discrepancy usually requires middlemen—wholesalers and retailers.

Producers typically specialize by product—and therefore another discrepancy develops. **Discrepancy of assortment** means the difference between the lines a typical producer makes and the assortment final consumers or users want. Most golfers, for example, need more than golf balls. They want golf shoes, gloves,

Specialists help adjust discrepancies between the quantity it is economical to produce and the quantity a consumer wants to buy.

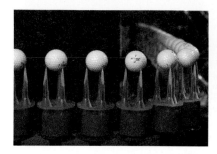  

clubs, a bag, and so forth. And they usually prefer not to shop around for each item. So, again, there is a need for middlemen to adjust these discrepancies.

In actual practice, bringing products to customers isn't as simple as in the golf example. Specializing only in golfing products may not achieve all the economies possible in a channel of distribution. Retailers who specialize in sports products usually carry even wider assortments. And they buy from a variety of wholesalers who specialize by product line. Some of these wholesalers are supplied by other wholesalers. These complications will be discussed later. The important thing to remember is that discrepancies in quantity and assortment cause distribution problems for producers—and explain why specialists develop.

Channel specialists adjust discrepancies with re-grouping activities

Regrouping activities adjust the quantities and/or assortments of products handled at each level in a channel of distribution.

There are four regrouping activities: accumulating, bulk-breaking, sorting, and assorting. When one or more of these activities is needed, a marketing specialist may develop to fill this need.

Adjusting quantity discrepancies by accumulating and bulk-breaking

Accumulating involves collecting products from many small producers. This is common for agricultural products. It is a way of getting the lowest transporting rate—by combining small quantities that then can be shipped in truckload or carload quantities.

Wholesalers often accumulate products from many producers and then break bulk to provide the smaller quantities needed by retailers.

Bulk-breaking involves dividing larger quantities into smaller quantities as products get closer to the final market. Sometimes this even starts at the producer's level. A golf ball producer may need 25 wholesalers to help sell its output. And the bulk-breaking may involve several levels of middlemen. Wholesalers may sell smaller quantities to other wholesalers—or directly to retailers. Retailers continue breaking bulk as they sell individual items to their customers.

Adjusting assortment discrepancies by sorting and assorting

Different types of specialists are needed to adjust assortment discrepancies. Two types of regrouping activities may be needed: sorting and assorting.

Sorting means separating products into grades and qualities desired by different target markets. This is a common process for farm products and raw materials. Nature produces what it will—and then these products must be sorted to meet the needs of different target markets.

Sorting may separate out low-quality products that the producer's regular middlemen don't want. Minor defects in the stitching on an Arrow shirt, for example, wouldn't be acceptable to buyers for Lord & Taylor department stores—or their target market. This forces Arrow's marketing manager to offer these shirts—perhaps at little profit—as "seconds" in special "outlet stores."

Assorting means putting together a variety of products to give a target market what it wants. This usually is done by those close to the final consumer or user—retailers or wholesalers who try to supply a wide assortment of products for the convenience of their customers. A grocery store is a good example. But some assortments involve very different products. A wholesaler selling Yazoo tractors and mowers to golf courses might also carry Pennington grass seed, Scott fertilizer, and even golf ball washers or irrigation systems—for its customers' convenience.

Watch for changes

Sometimes these discrepancies are adjusted badly—especially when consumer wants and attitudes shift rapidly. When videotapes became popular, an opportunity developed for a new specialist. Large numbers of consumers were suddenly interested in having an assortment of movies and other tapes available—in one place. Electronics stores had focused only on selling the tape players and blank tapes. Videotape rental stores emerged to meet the new need.

Rapid shifts in buying habits or preferences can result in discrepancies of assortment—and new marketing opportunities.

Specialists should develop to adjust discrepancies *if they must be adjusted.* But there is no point in having middlemen just because "that's the way it's always been done." Sometimes a breakthrough opportunity can come from finding a better way to reduce discrepancies—perhaps eliminating some middlemen specialists. For example, Dell Computer in Austin, Texas, found that it could sell computers direct to customers—at very low prices—by advertising in computer magazines and taking orders by mail or phone. With this approach, Dell not only bypassed retail stores and the wholesalers who served them, but also avoided the expense of setting up a large field sales organization. This gave Dell a cost advantage and resulted in a low price and a marketing mix that appealed to some target segments.

Middlemen supply needed information

Economists often assume that customers have "perfect information" about all producers—and that producers know which customers need what product, where, when, and at what price. But this assumption is rarely true. Specialists often develop to help provide information to bring buyers and sellers together.

For example, most consumers don't know much about the wide variety of home and auto insurance policies available from many different insurance companies. A local independent insurance agent may help them decide which policy—and which insurance company—best fits their needs.

Marketing manager must choose type of channel

Middlemen specialists can help make a channel more efficient. But there may be problems getting the different firms in a channel to work together well. How well they work together depends on the type of relationship they have. This should be carefully considered since marketing managers usually have choices about what type of channel system to join—or develop.

Marketing managers must choose among direct and indirect channel systems. See Exhibit 11–1. We'll talk about direct channels first and then the various indirect channels. (Exhibit 11–2 summarizes some characteristics of indirect channel systems.)

Exhibit 11–2   Types of Indirect Channel Systems

Type of channel / Characteristic	Traditional	Vertical marketing systems		
		Administered	Contractual	Corporate
Amount of cooperation	Little or none	Some to good	Fairly good to good	Complete
Control maintained by	None	Economic power and leadership	Contracts	Ownership by one company
Examples	Typical channel of "independents"	General Electric, Miller's Beer, O.M. Scott & Sons (lawn products)	McDonald's, Holiday Inn, IGA, Ace Hardware, Super Valu, Coca-Cola, Chevrolet	Florsheim Shoes, Firestone Tire

DIRECT CHANNEL SYSTEMS MAY BE BEST, SOMETIMES

Some producers prefer to handle the whole distribution job themselves. They don't want to rely on independent middlemen—who have different objectives. Or they think they can adjust the discrepancies as well as available middlemen. And some just want to control a large organization. In any case, there often *are* great advantages in selling direct to the final user or consumer.

If a firm is in direct contact with its customers, it is more aware of changes in customer attitudes. It is in a better position to adjust its marketing mix quickly—

The Franklin Mint uses a direct-to-customer channel; Travelers Insurance is sold through independent middlemen.

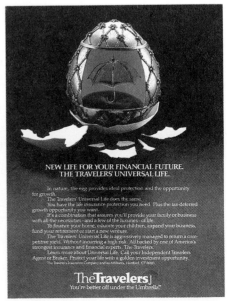

there is no need to convince other channel members to help. If aggressive selling effort or special technical service is needed, the marketing manager can be sure that the sales force receives the necessary training and motivation. In contrast, middlemen often carry products of several competing producers. So they aren't willing to give any one item the special emphasis its producer wants.

Direct-to-user channels are not uncommon. Many industrial products are sold direct. This is understandable since there are fewer transactions and orders are larger. In some cases, producers and customers have to talk directly about product specifications or leasing details. Of course, some consumer products are sold direct, too. Tupperware, Avon cosmetics, Electrolux vacuum cleaners, Amway cleaning products, and Fuller Brush products are examples.

Service firms often use direct channels. If the service must be produced in the presence of the customers, there may be little need for middlemen.

INDIRECT CHANNELS MAY BE BEST, SOMETIMES

Although a producer might prefer to handle the whole distribution job, this is just not economically possible for many kinds of products. When Apple Computer introduced its Macintosh personal computer, the firm hoped to use its own sales force to sell to corporate customers. But a year after the Macintosh came out, profits from this market were poor—only about 30 percent of Apple's sales came from its own sales force. Apple concluded that it had to develop better channel relationships with computer middlemen if the company was to compete profitably.[3]

Typically, producers have to use middlemen—like it or not. This means that they must either join or develop one of the indirect channel systems described below and summarized in Exhibit 11–2.

Traditional channel systems are common

In **traditional channel systems** the various channel members make little or no effort to cooperate with each other. They buy and sell from each other—and that's all. Each channel member does only what it considers to be in its own best interest. It doesn't worry much about the effect of its policies on other members of the channel. This is shortsighted, but it's easy to see how it can happen. The objectives of the various channel members may be different. For example, General Electric wants a wholesaler of electrical building supplies to sell *GE* products. But if the wholesaler carries an assortment of products from different producers, he may not care whose products are sold—as long as his customers are happy and he earns a good profit margin.

Specialization has the potential to make a channel more efficient—but not if the specialists are so independent that the channel doesn't work smoothly. For example, in some very "independent" traditional channels, buyers may wait until sellers desperately need to sell—hoping to force the price down. This leads to erratic production, inventory, and employment patterns that can only increase total costs.

Traditional channel members have their independence—but they may pay for it, too. As we will see, such channels are declining in importance—with good reason. But they are still typical—and very important—in some industries.

Vertical marketing systems focus on final customers

In contrast to traditional channel systems are **vertical marketing systems**—channel systems in which the whole channel focuses on the same target market at the end of the channel. Such systems make sense—and are growing—because if the final customer doesn't buy the product, the whole channel suffers. There are three types of vertical marketing systems—corporate, administered, and contractual.

Corporate channel systems shorten channels

Some corporations develop their own vertical marketing systems by internal expansion and/or by buying other firms. With **corporate channel systems**—corporate ownership all along the channel—we might say the firm is going "direct." But actually the firm may be handling manufacturing, wholesaling, *and* retailing—so it's more accurate to think of the firm as a vertical marketing system.

Vertical integration is at different levels

Corporate channel systems are often developed by **vertical integration**—acquiring firms at different levels of channel activity. Firestone, for example, has rubber plantations in Liberia, tire plants in Ohio, and Firestone wholesale and retail outlets all over the United States. Sherwin Williams produces paint, but it also operates 2,000 retail outlets.

Corporate channel systems are not always started by producers. A retailer might integrate into wholesaling—and perhaps even manufacturing. A&P has fish canning plants. Genesco and Florsheim make their own shoes. J. C. Penney controls textile plants.

There are many possible advantages to vertical integration—stability of operations, assurance of materials and supplies, better control of distribution, better quality control, larger research facilities, greater buying power, and lower executive overhead. The economies of vertical integration benefit the consumer, too, through lower prices and better products.

Provided that the discrepancies of quantity and assortment are not too great at each level in a channel—that is, that the firms fit together well—vertical integration can be extremely efficient and profitable.

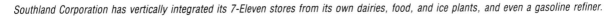

Southland Corporation has vertically integrated its 7-Eleven stores from its own dairies, food, and ice plants, and even a gasoline refiner.

Administered and contractual systems may work well

Firms can often gain the advantages of vertical integration without building an expensive corporate channel. A firm can develop administered or contractual channel systems instead. In **administered channel systems**, the channel members informally agree to cooperate with each other. They can agree to routinize ordering, standardize accounting, and coordinate promotion efforts. In **contractual channel systems**, the channel members agree by contract to cooperate with each other. With both of these systems, the members achieve some of the advantages of corporate integration while retaining some of the flexibility of a traditional channel system.

An appliance producer, for example, developed an informal arrangement with the independent wholesalers in its administered channel system. It agreed to keep production and inventory levels in the system balanced—using sales data from the wholesalers. Every week, its managers make a thorough analysis of up to 130,000 major appliances located in the many warehouses operated by its 87 wholesalers throughout the country. This helps the producer plan production and shipments to maintain adequate inventory levels and helps the wholesalers manage their inventories. The wholesalers can be sure that they have enough inventory, but not the expense of too much or the need to worry about it. And the producer has better information to plan its manufacturing and marketing efforts.

Middlemen in the grocery, hardware, and drug industries develop and coordinate similar systems. Electronic cash registers keep track of what is sold. The information is sent to the wholesaler's computer, and orders are automatically entered when needed. This reduces buying and selling costs, inventory investment, and customer frustration with "out-of-stock" items throughout the channel.

Vertical marketing systems—new wave in the marketplace

Smoothly operating channel systems are more efficient and successful.

In the consumer products field, corporate chains that are at least partially vertically integrated account for about 25 percent of total retail sales. Other vertical systems account for an additional 37.5 percent. Thus, vertical systems in the consumer products area have a healthy majority of retail sales. Such systems should continue to increase their share of total retail sales in the future. Vertical marketing systems are becoming the major competitive units in the U.S. distribution system.[4]

THE BEST CHANNEL SYSTEM SHOULD ACHIEVE IDEAL MARKET EXPOSURE

You may think that all marketing managers should want their products to have maximum exposure to potential customers. This isn't true. Some product classes require much less market exposure than others. **Ideal market exposure** makes a product available widely enough to satisfy target customers' needs but not exceed them. Too much exposure only increases the total cost of marketing.

Ideal exposure may be intensive, selective, or exclusive

Intensive distribution is selling a product through all responsible and suitable wholesalers or retailers who will stock and/or sell the product. **Selective distribution** is selling through only those middlemen who will give the product special attention. **Exclusive distribution** is selling through only one middleman in a particular geographic area. As we move from intensive to exclusive distribution, we give up exposure in return for some other advantage—including, but not limited to, lower cost.

Wrigley's uses intensive distribution, while Godiva uses exclusive distribution for its high-quality chocolates.

In practice, this means that Wrigley's chewing gum is handled—through intensive distribution—by about a million U.S. outlets. Rolls Royces are handled—through exclusive distribution—by only a limited number of middlemen across the country.

Intensive distribution—sell it where they buy it

Intensive distribution is commonly needed for convenience products and industrial supplies—such as pencils, paper clips, and typing paper—used by all plants and offices. Customers want such products nearby.

The seller's intent is important here. Intensive distribution refers to the *desire* to sell through *all* responsible and suitable outlets. What this means depends on customer habits and preferences. If target customers normally buy a certain product at a certain type of outlet, ideally, you would specify this type of outlet in your Place policies. If customers prefer to buy Sharp portable TVs only at TV stores, you would try to sell at all TV stores to achieve intensive distribution. Today, however, many customers buy small portable TVs at a variety of convenient outlets—including Eckerd drugstores, a local K mart, or over the phone from the Sharper Image catalog. This means that an intensive distribution policy requires use of these outlets—and more than one channel—to reach one target market.

Selective distribution—sell it where it sells best

Selective distribution covers the broad area of market exposure between intensive and exclusive distribution. It may be suitable for all categories of products. Only the better middlemen are used here. The usual reason for going to selective distribution is to gain some of the advantages of exclusive distribution—while still achieving fairly widespread market coverage.

A selective policy might be used to avoid selling to wholesalers or retailers who (1) have a poor credit rating, (2) have a reputation for making too many returns or requesting too much service, (3) place orders that are too small to justify making calls or providing service, or (4) are not in a position to do a satisfactory job.

Selective distribution is becoming more popular than intensive distribution as firms see that they don't need 100 percent coverage of a market to justify or support national advertising. Often, the majority of sales come from relatively few customers—and the others buy too little compared to the cost of working with them. That is, they are unprofitable to serve. This is called the "80/20 rule"—80 percent of a company's sales often come from only 20 percent of its customers *until it becomes more selective in choosing customers.*

Esprit—a producer of colorful, trendy clothing—was selling through about 4,000 department stores and specialty shops nationwide. But Esprit found that about half of the stores generated most of the sales. Sales analysis also showed that sales in Esprit's own stores were about 400 percent better than sales in other sales outlets. As a result, Esprit cut back to about 2,000 outlets and moved to open more of its own stores—and profits increased.[5]

Selective distribution can produce greater profits not only for the producer, but for all channel members because of the closer cooperation among them. Transactions become more routine, requiring less negotiation in the buying and selling process. Wholesalers and retailers are more willing to promote products aggressively if they know they are going to obtain the majority of sales produced through their own efforts. They may carry more stock and wider lines, do more promotion, and provide more service—all of which lead to more sales.

Selective distribution makes sense for shopping and specialty products and for those industrial products that need special efforts from channel members. It reduces competition between different channels and gives each middleman a greater opportunity for profit.

When selective distribution is used by producers, fewer sales contacts have to be made—and fewer wholesalers are needed. A producer may be able to contact selected retailers directly. Hanes sells men's underwear this way.

In the early part of the life cycle of a new unsought good, a producer's marketing manager may have to use selective distribution to encourage enough middlemen to handle the product. The manager wants to get the product out of the unsought category as soon as possible—but he can't if it lacks distribution. Well-known middlemen may have the power to get such a product introduced but sometimes on their own terms—which often include limiting the number of competing wholesalers and retailers. The producer may be happy with such an arrangement at first but dislike it later when more retailers want to carry the product.

Exclusive distribution sometimes makes sense

Exclusive distribution is just an extreme case of selective distribution—the firm selects only one middleman in each geographic area. Besides the various advantages of selective distribution, producers may want to use exclusive distribution to help control prices and the service offered in a channel.

Unlike selective distribution, exclusive distribution usually involves a verbal or written agreement stating that channel members will buy all or most of a given product from the seller. In return, these middlemen are granted the exclusive rights to that product in their territories. Many middlemen are so anxious to get a producer's exclusive franchise that they will do practically anything to satisfy the producer's demands. Retailers of shopping products and specialty products often try to

Acura's Drive for Exclusive Distribution

Marketing managers for Acura, the luxury car division of Honda Motor Co., decided to set up new channels of distribution to introduce the car to U.S. consumers. In return for the right to sell the car, each new dealer agreed to focus his effort exclusively on Acura and its target market. Acura also required its dealers to build expensive new showrooms. At first, the strategy seemed to be a big success. Acura lured buyers away from competitors like BMW, Mercedes, and Cadillac. Surveys also showed that Acura owners were more satisfied than buyers of other cars. However, after three years, nearly half of Acura's dealers were still losing money or making only a small profit. Although sales were steady, they often didn't offset the big investment in new facilities. Most other car dealers were earning profits from more than one line of cars. Further, the new and reliable Acuras simply didn't keep the service department busy—and service usually produces a large share of a car dealer's profit.

Acura realized that long-run success would depend on having strong channel partners. To help its troubled dealers pull in more customers, Acura increased its advertising. Development of a new sports model also expanded dealer sales opportunities. And Acura worked with dealers to identify ways to earn more profit from service and used cars. Even so, many Acura dealers worried that the drive for improved profits might be a long and lonely one.[6]

get exclusive distribution rights in their territories. And owners of fast-food franchises—like McDonald's—willingly pay a share of sales and follow McDonald's strategy to keep the exclusive right to a market.

But is limiting market exposure legal?

Exclusive distribution is a vague area in the antimonopoly laws. Courts currently focus on whether an exclusive distribution arrangement hurts competition.

Horizontal arrangements among competitors are illegal

Horizontal arrangements—among *competing* retailers, wholesalers, or producers—to limit sales by customer or territory have consistently been ruled illegal by the Supreme Court. Such arrangements are considered as obvious collusion—reducing competition and harming customers.

Vertical arrangements may or may not be legal

The legality of vertical arrangements—between producers and middlemen—is not as clear-cut. A 1977 Supreme Court decision (involving Sylvania and distribution of TV sets) reversed a 1967 ruling that vertical relationships limiting territories or customers are always illegal. Now, possible good effects can be weighed against possible restrictions on competition by channel planners.

This view looks at competition between whole channels—rather than just focusing on competition at one level of distribution. Sylvania had a very small share of the overall market for television sets. It couldn't compete on price with bigger producers who sold through self-service stores. Sylvania decided to target customers who saw TVs as a heterogeneous shopping product. These people preferred stores that specialized in TVs, had a good selection on hand, and provided advice before the purchase—and repair service afterwards. Such retailers faced added costs to provide these services. They didn't want customers to inspect TV sets, get information at their store, and then be able to buy a set somewhere else—at a lower price. In other words, they didn't want other retailers to get a "free ride" on their investment in inventory and higher-paid sales help. Sylvania argued that it needed exclusive sales territories to attract these middlemen. This reduced competition at the retail level somewhat, and made it possible for Sylvania to compete with other producers. The Supreme Court basically agreed with Sylvania in the 1977 decision.

The Sylvania decision does *not* mean that all vertical arrangements are legal. Rather, it says that a firm has to be able to legally justify any exclusive arrangements.

Vertical relationships will probably change in the future to ensure that channels work better. There may be less price competition and more service competition—because producers may be able to control their channels and will choose to control their prices. Under the 1967 ruling, the price-cutting "maverick" who came in after the introductory work had been done could not be stopped. Now that may be changed, as long as a firm can show some good reason for limiting distribution—such as building stronger retailers who can and will offer advertising and sales support as well as better repair services. Major changes may come in the distribution of products as diverse as appliances, TVs, oil, tires, bicycles, hearing aids, beer, and auto accessories. And the federal government has already given approval for soft drink companies—like Coca Cola—to grant bottlers exclusive territories.[7]

Caution is suggested

In spite of the 1977 Supreme Court ruling, firms should be extremely cautious about entering into *any* exclusive distribution arrangements. The antimonopoly rules still apply. The courts can force a change in expensively developed relationships. And—even worse—the courts can award triple damages if they rule that competition has been hurt.

The same cautions apply to selective distribution. Here, however, less formal arrangements are typical—and the possible impact on competition is more remote. It is now more acceptable to carefully select channel members when building a channel system. Refusing to sell to some middlemen, however, should be part of a logical plan which has long-term benefits to consumers.

CHANNEL SYSTEMS CAN BE COMPLEX

Trying to achieve the desired degree of market exposure can lead to complex channels of distribution. Different channels may be required to reach different segments of a broad product-market—or to be sure that each segment is reached. Sometimes this results in competition between different channels.

Exhibit 11–3 shows the many channels used by companies that produce roofing shingles. It also shows (roughly) what percent of the sales go to different channel members. Shingles are both consumer products (sold to do-it-yourselfers) and industrial products (sold to building contractors and roofing contractors). This helps explain why some channels develop. But note that the shingles go through different wholesalers and retailers—independent and chain lumberyards, hardware stores, and mass-merchandisers. This can cause problems because different wholesalers and retailers want different markups. It also increases competition—

Exhibit 11–3   Sales of Roofing Shingles Are Made through Many Kinds of Wholesalers and Retailers

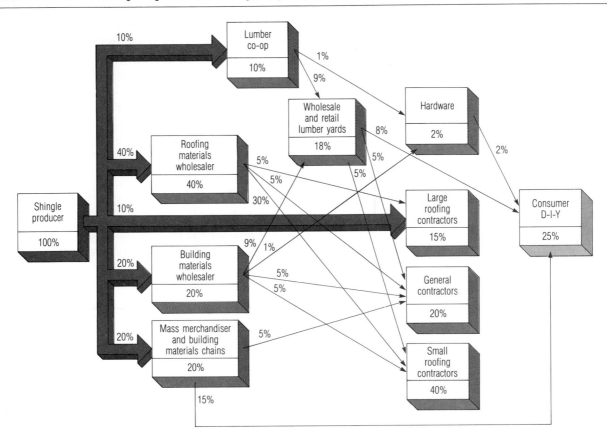

including price competition. And the competition among different middlemen may result in conflicts between the middlemen and the producer.

Dual distribution systems may be needed

Dual distribution occurs when a producer uses several competing channels to reach the same target market—perhaps using several middlemen in addition to selling directly. Dual distribution is becoming more common. Big retail chains want to deal directly with producers. They want large quantities—and low prices. The producer sells directly to retail chains, and relies on wholesalers to sell to smaller accounts. Some established middlemen resent this because they don't appreciate *any* competition—but especially price competition set up by their own suppliers. Other times, producers are forced to use dual distribution because their present channels are doing a poor job or aren't reaching some potential customers.

Sometimes there's not much choice of middlemen

The shingles example suggests that there are plenty of middlemen around to form almost any kind of channel system. But this isn't true. Sometimes there is only one middleman serving a market. To reach this market, producers may have no choice but to use this one middleman—if he is willing.

In other cases, there is no middleman at all! Then a producer has to go directly to target customers. If this isn't economically possible, the product may die. Some products aren't wanted in big enough volume and/or at high enough prices to support the regrouping activities needed to reach potential customers.

HOW TO RECRUIT MIDDLEMEN

A producer has a special challenge ensuring that the product reaches the end of the channel. To reach its target market, a producer may have to recruit middlemen.

The two basic methods of recruiting middlemen are pushing and pulling.[8]

Pushing policy—get a hand from the firms in the channel

Pushing (a product through a channel) means using normal promotion effort—personal selling, advertising, and sales promotion—to help sell the whole marketing mix to possible channel members. This approach emphasizes the importance of building a channel and securing the wholehearted cooperation of channel members. The producer in effect tries to develop a team that will work well to "push" the product down the channel to the final user.

Pulling policy—makes them reach for it out there

By contrast, **pulling** means getting consumers to ask middlemen for the product. This usually involves highly aggressive and expensive promotion to final consumers or users—perhaps using coupons or samples—and temporary bypassing of middlemen. Such an approach is risky. But if the promotion works, the middlemen are forced to carry the product to satisfy customer requests.

Pulling may be necessary if many products are already competing in all desired outlets, and channel members are reluctant to handle a new product. But channel members should be told about the planned pulling effort—so they can be ready if the promotion is successful.

CHANNELS MUST BE MANAGED

Some conflict is natural

Our discussion of vertical marketing systems makes it clear there are many good reasons for cooperation within a channel system. But there are also reasons

---

Toshiba uses promotion to sell possible channel members on the marketing mix for its fax machines. Canon's fax machine ad is targeted to final consumers—to help pull the product through the channel.

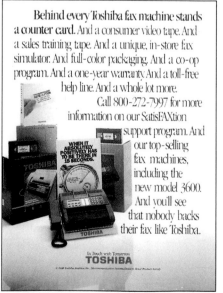

Sherwood, a producer of industrial gas control products, arranged this promotion in a trade magazine to help its middlemen reach the target market at the end of the channel.

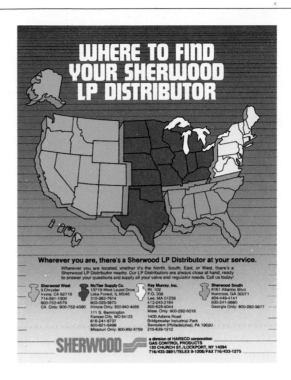

why conflicts arise—and these should be anticipated and managed, if possible. For example, horizontal conflicts occur when middlemen's territories overlap and they argue over taking each other's business.

Vertical conflicts also occur. Policies that may be "good" for the producer—perhaps expanding *its* sales by lowering suggested retail prices (by reducing the middlemen's margins)—may not be quite as "good" for the middlemen. And dual distribution conflicts can easily happen unless channel systems are carefully planned. This leads us to the channel captain concept.

Channel captain can guide channel planning

Each channel system should act as a unit, perhaps directed by a **channel captain**—a manager who helps direct the activities of a whole channel and tries to avoid—or solve—channel conflicts.

The concept of a single channel captain is logical. But some channels—including most traditional ones—don't have a recognized captain. The various firms don't act as a system. The reason may be lack of leadership or the fact that members of the system don't understand their interrelationship. Many managers— concerned with individual firms immediately above and below them—seem unaware that they are part of a channel.[9]

But, like it or not, firms are interrelated—even if poorly—by their policies. And there is potential for conflict in the buyer-seller relationship. So it makes sense to try to avoid channel conflicts by planning for channel relations.

Producer or middleman?

In the United States, producers frequently take the lead in channel relations. Middlemen often wait to see what the producer intends to do and what he wants done. After the producer sets Price, Promotion, and Place policies, middlemen decide whether their roles will be profitable—and whether they want to join in the producer's plans.

Some middlemen dominate their channels

Some large or well-located middlemen do take the lead. These middlemen analyze the types of products their customers want and then seek out producers— perhaps small ones—who can provide these products at reasonable prices. This is becoming more common in the United States—and it is already typical in many foreign markets. In Japan, for example, very large wholesalers ("trading companies") are often the channel captains.

Channel captains who are middlemen often develop their own dealer brands. Strong retailers like Sears or K mart—and wholesalers like Ace Hardware—in effect act like producers. They specify the whole marketing mix for a product and merely delegate production to a factory.

Some strong middlemen use their power to control channel relationships. Wal-Mart, the third largest retail chain, is constantly looking for ways to cut its own costs—and sometimes that means cutting costs in the channel. Buyers for Wal-Mart look at the "value added" by a wholesaler. If they think Wal-Mart can be more efficient without the wholesaler, then they tell the producer that the chain will only buy "direct"—usually at a lower price than was paid to the wholesaler.[10]

Middlemen are closer to the final user or consumer and are in an ideal position to assume the channel captain role. It is even possible that middlemen—especially retailers—will dominate the marketing system of the future.

The whole channel competes with other channels

It is extremely important for a whole channel system to view itself in competition with other systems. Without this view, one firm might adopt policies clearly unfavorable to another member of the same system. In the short run, a stronger firm might succeed in forcing its policies by sheer weight of market power. Yet, in the long run, this might lead to failure—not only of a weaker channel member but of the whole team.[11]

Product-market commitment can guide strategy

It helps to think of all the members of a vertical marketing system having a *product-market commitment*—with all members focusing on the same target market at the end of the channel and sharing the various marketing functions in appropriate ways.

The job of the channel captain is to arrange for the performance of the necessary functions in the most effective way. This might be done as shown in Exhibit 11–4 in a producer-dominated channel system. Here, the producer has selected the target market and developed the Product, set the Price structure, done some consumer and channel Promotion, and developed the Place setup. Middlemen are then expected to finish the Promotion job in their respective places.

In a middleman-dominated channel system, we would see quite a different diagram. Let's use Sears as an extreme example. In a Sears-dominated channel, the middleman part of the job would be larger while producers would be almost solely concerned with manufacturing the product to meet Sears's specifications.

A coordinated channel system can help everyone

A channel system in which the members have accepted a common product-market commitment can work very well—even though not everyone in the channel system is strongly market oriented. As long as someone—say, the channel captain—is market oriented, it may be possible to win the confidence and support of production-oriented firms and make the whole channel work effectively.

Computerland is working with small producers in Korea to develop a Computer-land brand of personal computer and accessories. The producers don't know much

Exhibit 11–4   How Channel Strategy Might Be Handled in a Producer-Dominated System

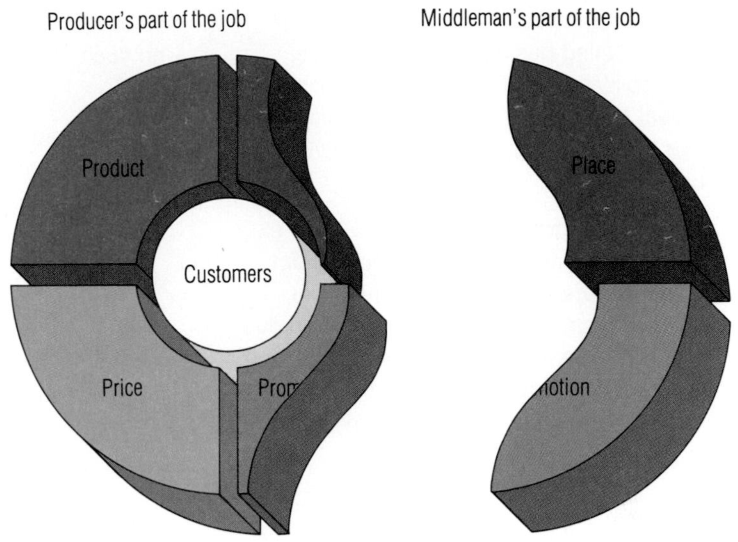

Producer's part of the job   Middleman's part of the job

Product

Customers

Price   Promotion   Place   Promotion

about the U.S. market. But, if Computerland correctly analyzes market needs and relays them clearly to the producers, the relationship will be profitable for both the producers and Computerland—and the whole channel will compete effectively.

The choice of who will lead a marketing channel—and who will perform specific marketing functions in a channel—are important strategy decisions. They must be based not only on costs but also on how Place fits in with the rest of the marketing strategy.

CONCLUSION

In this chapter we discussed the role of Place and noted that Place decisions are especially important because they may be difficult and expensive to change.

Marketing specialists—and channel systems—develop to adjust discrepancies of quantity and assortment. Their regrouping activities are basic in any economic system. And adjusting discrepancies provides opportunities for creative marketers.

Channel planning requires deciding on the degree of market exposure desired. The ideal level of exposure may be intensive, selective, or exclusive. The legality of limiting market exposure should also be considered to avoid having to undo an expensively developed channel system or face steep fines.

The importance of planning channel systems was discussed—along with the role of a channel captain. We stressed that channel systems compete with each other—and that vertical marketing systems seem to be winning.

In this broader context, the "battle of the brands" is only a skirmish in the battle between various channel systems. And, we emphasized that producers are not necessarily channel captains. Often, middlemen control or even dominate channels of distribution. Producers have to consider the degree of this control when they are deciding whether to push or pull their product though a channel system—or to simply join some channel captain's system.

Questions and Problems

1. Explain "discrepancies of quantity and assortment" using the clothing business as an example. How does the application of these concepts change when selling coal to the steel industry? What impact does this have on the number and kinds of marketing specialists required?

2. Explain the four regrouping activities with an example from the building supply industry (nails, paint, flooring, plumbing fixtures, etc.). Do you think that many specialists develop in this industry, or do producers handle the job themselves? What kinds of marketing channels would you expect to find in this industry, and what functions would various channel members provide?

3. Travel agents are middleman who help other members of the channel by providing information. Would it make sense for a travel agent to specialize in providing information about one airline? Why or why not? Would it make sense for a travel agent to specialize in certain types of travel—like tours of overseas vacation spots? Why or why not?

4. Discuss the Place objectives and distribution arrangements that are appropriate for the following products (indicate any special assumptions you have to make to obtain an answer):
   a. A postal scale for products weighing up to two pounds.
   b. Children's toys: (1) radio-controlled model airplanes costing $80 or more, (2) small rubber balls.
   c. Heavy-duty, rechargeable, battery-powered nut tighteners for factory production lines.
   d. A chemical used in making roofing shingles.

5. Give an example of a producer that uses two or more different channels of distribution. Briefly discuss what problems this might cause.

6. Find an example of vertical integration within your city. Are there any particular advantages to this vertical integration? If so, what are they? If there are no such advantages, how do you explain the integration?

7. Explain how a "channel captain" can help traditional independent firms compete with a corporate (integrated) channel system.

8. What would happen if retailer-organized integrated channels (either formally integrated or administered) dominated consumer product marketing?

9. How does the nature of the product relate to the degree of market exposure desired?

10. Why would middlemen want to be exclusive distributors for a product? Why would producers want exclusive distribution? Would middlemen be equally anxious to get exclusive distribution for any type of product? Why or why not? Explain with reference to the following products: chewing gum, razor blades, golf clubs, golf balls, steak knives, stereo equipment, and industrial woodworking machinery.

11. Explain the present legal status of exclusive distribution. Describe a situation where exclusive distribution is almost sure to be legal. Describe the nature and size of competitors and the industry, as well as the nature of the exclusive arrangement. Would this exclusive arrangement be of any value to the producer or middleman?

12. Discuss the promotion a new grocery products producer would need in order to develop appropriate channels and move products through those channels. Would the nature of this job change for a new dress producer? How about for a new small producer of installations?

13. Discuss the advantages and disadvantages of either a pushing or pulling policy for a very small producer just entering the candy business with a line of inexpensive candy bars. Which policy would probably be most appropriate?

Suggested Cases

13. Office Systems, Inc.

17. National Sales Company

18. Tandy versus IBM

19. Nelson Company

34. Kenny Chrysler, Inc.

38. ALCO Manufacturing Co.

Suggested Computer-Aided Problem

11. Intensive versus Selective Distribution

Chapter 12

Retailing

When You Finish This Chapter, You Should

1. Understand about retailers planning their own marketing strategies.

2. Know about the many kinds of retailers that work with producers and wholesalers as members of channel systems.

3. Understand the differences among the conventional and non-conventional retailers—including those who accept the mass-merchandising concept.

4. Understand scrambled merchandising and the "wheel of retailing."

5. See why size or belonging to a chain can be important to a retailer.

6. Understand the important new terms (shown in red).

If products aren't sold, nobody makes any money.

Consumer needs are changing—and some retailers have gone out of business because they didn't adapt to the changes. Other retailers are growing fast because they have identified good ways to meet the needs of their target markets. For example, Wal-Mart, with ambitions to be the number one retailer in the country, opened about 150 stores last year. McDonald's lit up the golden arches on 600 new burger stations. Benetton found over 200 intersections that seemed just right for new sweater shops. And Woolworth Co. opened 1,100 new stores. That's right, Woolworth. Could we be talking about the old Woolworth five-and-ten-cent stores that sell sewing notions, trinkets, and doodads?

Not exactly. Woolworth is changing. The company now operates more than 40 different types of retail stores that sell varied product lines. Its newer specialty stores—located mostly in shopping malls—include Footlocker (running shoes and sporting togs), Champs (sporting goods), Kids Mart (children's clothing), Afterthoughts (fashion accessories), and Herald Square (party supplies). In fact, Woolworth now operates more specialty stores than anyone in the world.

With all this change, Woolworth is not giving up its variety store roots. It is closing some of the older stores. But it is improving profits in others by trimming product assortments on slow-moving items, concentrating attention on more profitable items, and reducing operating costs. It is also experimenting with a new type of variety store called Woolworth Express. These stores are about one fifth the size of a traditional Woolworth. Only brisk selling products— like health and beauty aids, greetings cards, and videotapes—get shelf space. The product assortment is like what you find in a drugstore—but without the pharmacy. As one Woolworth marketing manager puts it, today's drugstores have really become "variety stores with overblown health and beauty departments." In the 1980s these stores took customers away from Woolworth. Now Woolworth is returning the favor.

Woolworth is not alone in changing its strategy. After a hundred years in business, Sears now offers consumers "low everyday prices" and more manufacturers' brand products. And Sears plans to drop its big "wish book" and instead is using smaller catalogs that focus on specific product lines.[1]

As these cases show, retailing is very competitive—and constantly changing. Retailers must select their own target markets and marketing mixes very carefully.

Retailing covers all of the activities involved in the sale of products to final consumers. Retailing is important to all of us. As consumers, we spend $1.6 *trillion* (that's $1,600,000,000,000!) a year buying goods and services from retailers. If the retailing effort isn't effective, everyone in the channel suffers—and some products aren't sold at all. So retailing is important to marketing managers of consumer products at *all* channel levels.

What are the different kinds of retailers, and why did they develop? How do their strategies vary? How is retailing changing now? What trends are likely in the future? In this chapter, we'll try to answer these questions. We'll talk about the major decision areas shown in Exhibit 12–1. We won't cover the promotion and pricing decisions of retailers in detail here. These are similar for all firms, and they are discussed in later chapters.

PLANNING A RETAILER'S STRATEGY

Retailers are directly involved with final consumers—so their strategy planning is critical to survival. If a retailer loses a customer to a competitor, the retailer is the one who suffers. Producers and wholesalers still make *their* sale regardless of which retailer sells the product. Retailers must be guided by the old maxim: "Goods well bought are half sold."

A retailer usually sells more than just one kind of product. We can think of the retailer's *whole offering*—assortment of goods and services, advice from salesclerks, convenience in parking, and the like—as its "Product." In the case of service retailing—dry cleaning, lawn care, fast food, or one-hour photo processing, for

Exhibit 12–1 Strategy Decision Areas for a Retailer

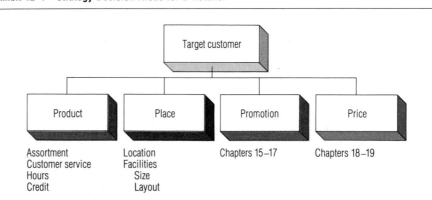

Product	Place	Promotion	Price
Assortment	Location	Chapters 15–17	Chapters 18–19
Customer service	Facilities		
Hours	Size		
Credit	Layout		

Target customer

example—the *retailer is also the producer*. So most of what we said in the Product area applies here. Now, let's look at why customers choose particular retailers.

Consumers have reasons for buying from particular retailers

Different consumers prefer different kinds of retailers—but why they do is often ignored by retailers. Just renting a store and assuming that customers will come running is all too common among beginning small retailers—and the failure rate is high. More than three fourths of new retailing ventures fail during the first year. To avoid this fate, a new retailer—or one trying to adjust to changing conditions—should carefully identify possible target markets and try to understand why these people buy where they do.[2]

Economic needs—which store has the best value?

Consumers consider many factors in choosing a particular retailer. Some of the most important ones relate to their economic needs. The price the retailer charges is obviously relevant here. Other economic factors include:

1. Convenience.
2. Variety of selection.
3. Quality of products.
4. Help from salespeople.
5. Reputation for integrity and fairness in dealings.
6. Special services offered—delivery, credit, returned-goods privileges.
7. Value offered.

Emotional needs—the importance of social class

Consumers may also have important emotional reasons for preferring particular retailers. Some people get an ego boost from shopping in a "prestige" store. Others just want to shop in a store where they won't feel "out of place."

Different stores do seem to attract customers from different social classes. People like to shop where salespeople and other customers are similar to themselves.

The emotional needs a store fills are related to its target market(s). Dollar General—a chain of 1,300 general merchandise stores—has been very successful with a "budget" image that appeals to lower-class customers. Saks Fifth Avenue works at its upper-class image. But not all stores have—or want—a particular class image. Some try to avoid creating one—because they want to appeal to a wide market. Macy's, for example, has departments that carry very expensive merchandise—and others that handle products for the masses.

There is no one "right" answer as to whom a store should appeal. But ignorance about emotional dimensions—including social class appeal—could lead to serious errors in marketing strategy planning.[3]

Product classes help understand store types

Retail strategy planning can be simplified by extending our earlier discussion of consumer product classes—convenience products, shopping products, and specialty products—to define three types of stores.

A **convenience store** is a convenient place to shop—either because it is centrally located near other shopping or because it is "in the neighborhood." Such stores attract many customers because they are so handy. Easy parking, fast check-out, and easy-to-find merchandise add to the convenience. **Shopping stores** attract customers from greater distances because of the width and depth of their assortments. They may also appeal to customers with displays, demonstrations, information, and knowledgeable salesclerks. **Specialty stores** are those for which customers have developed a strong attraction. For whatever reasons—service, selection, or reputation—some customers consistently buy at these stores. They insist on the store—just as some customers insist on a certain brand of a product.

Store types based on how customers see store

It is important to see that these store types refer to *the way customers think about the store*—not just the kind of products the store carries. Different market segments might see or use a particular store differently. Remember that this was true with the product classes, too. So a retailer's strategy planning must consider potential customers' attitudes toward *both* the product and the store. Classifying market segments by how they see both the store type and the product class—as shown in Exhibit 12–2—helps to make this clear.

When planning strategy, a retailer will get a better understanding of a market by estimating the relative size of each of the boxes shown in Exhibit 12–2. By identifying which competitors are satisfying which market segments, the retailer may see that some boxes are already "filled." He may find that he and his competitors are all charging head-on after the same customers and completely ignoring others.

For example, houseplants used to be sold only by florists or greenhouses. This was fine for customers who wanted a "shopping store" variety. But for others, going to such outlets was too much trouble, so they just didn't buy plants. Then, some retailers went after the "convenience store" segment—with small house plant departments or stores in neighborhood shopping centers. They found a big market willing to buy plants—at convenience stores.

Whole channel system is involved

Store-product classes are also important to manufacturers and wholesalers. If, for example, the majority of a manufacturer's target customers patronize convenience stores, then intensive distribution may be necessary. Similarly, if a large group of customers treat particular stores—or a chain—as specialty stores, manufacturers will have to be in those stores if they want to reach such customers. Unfortunately, if the stores use dealer brands the manufacturers may be blocked from reaching the desired customers.

Exhibit 12–2   How Customers View Store-Product Combinations

Product class \ Store type	Convenience	Shopping	Specialty
Convenience	Will buy any brand at most accessible store	Shop around to find better service and/or lower prices	Prefer store. Brand may be important
Shopping	Want some selection but will settle for assortment at most accessible store	Want to compare both products and store mixes	Prefer store but insist on adequate assortment
Specialty	Prefer particular product but like place convenience too	Prefer particular product but still seeking best total product and mix	Prefer both store and product

TYPES OF RETAILERS AND THE NATURE OF THEIR OFFERINGS

There are about 1.5 million retailers in the United States—and they are constantly evolving. Retailers differ in terms of the product assortments they sell. A paint store and a fabric store, for example, both have depth in their separate lines. By contrast, a department store might have less depth in any one line—but more different lines and more variety in each line. Some retailers expect customers to serve themselves. Others provide helpful salesclerks as well as credit, delivery, trade-ins, gift wrap, special orders, and returns. Some retailers charge the full price suggested by a manufacturer—and others offer discount prices. Some retailers have prestige locations—downtown or at a mall with other stores. Some sell from vending machines or in a customer's home—without any store at all.

Each retailer's offering represents some *mix* of all of these different characteristics. So any classification of retailers based on a single characteristic is incomplete. But it is helpful to describe basic types of retailers—and some differences in their strategies.

Let's look first at the conventional retailers—and then see how others modify the conventional offering and succeed because they meet the needs of *some* consumers.

CONVENTIONAL RETAILERS—TRY TO AVOID PRICE COMPETITION

Single-line, limited-line retailers specialize by product

A hundred and fifty years ago, **general stores**—which carried anything they could sell in reasonable volume—were the main retailers. But after the Civil War, the growing number and variety of consumer products made it hard for a general store to offer depth and width in all its traditional lines. So some stores specialized in dry goods, apparel, furniture, or groceries. Now, most conventional retailers are **single-line** or **limited-line stores** that specialize in certain lines of related products rather than a wide assortment. Many stores specialize not only in a single line—such as clothing—but also in a *limited line* within the broader line. For example, within the clothing line, a store might carry *only* shoes, formal wear, men's casual wear, or even neckties—but offer depth in that limited line. This specialization will probably continue as long as customer demands are varied and large enough to support such stores.

Single-line, limited-line stores are being squeezed

The main advantage of these stores is that they can satisfy some target markets better. Some even achieve specialty-store status by adjusting their marketing mixes—including store hours, credit, and product assortment—to suit certain customers. But these stores face the costly problem of having to stock some slow-moving items in order to satisfy the store's target market. Further, many of these stores have the disadvantage of being small—with high expenses relative to sales. Stores of this type have traditionally applied the retailing philosophy of "buy low and sell high." If they face much competition, they may expand assortment—to specialize further. By avoiding competition on identical products, they try to keep prices up.

Conventional retailers like this have been around for a long time and are still found in every community. They are a durable lot and clearly satisfy some people's needs. But they will continue to be squeezed by retailers who have modified their mixes in the various ways suggested in Exhibit 12–3. Let's look closer at some of these other types of retailers.

Exhibit 12–3   Types of Retailers and the Nature of Their Offerings

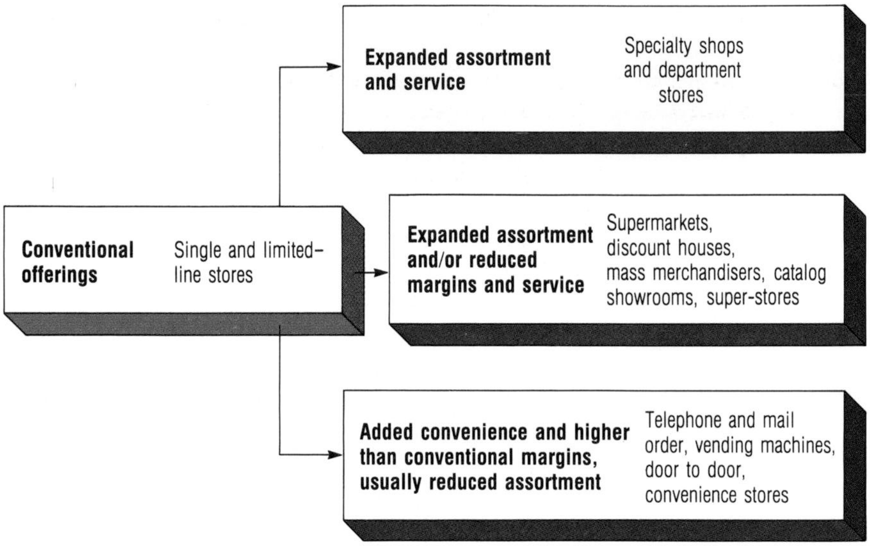

Expanded assortment and service	Specialty shops and department stores	
Conventional offerings Single and limited-line stores	**Expanded assortment and/or reduced margins and service**	Supermarkets, discount houses, mass merchandisers, catalog showrooms, super-stores
	Added convenience and higher than conventional margins, usually reduced assortment	Telephone and mail order, vending machines, door to door, convenience stores

EXPAND ASSORTMENT AND SERVICE—TO COMPETE AT A HIGH PRICE

Specialty shops usually sell shopping products

A **specialty shop**—a type of conventional limited-line store—is usually small and has a distinct "personality." Specialty shops often sell special types of shopping products—such as high-quality sporting goods, exclusive clothing, cameras, or even microwave ovens.[4] They aim at a carefully defined target market by offering a unique product assortment, knowledgeable salesclerks, and better service. For example, specialty shops have developed to satisfy people who want help in selecting computer software. The clerks are themselves experts. They know the many different software packages that are available. They are eager to explain or demonstrate the advantages of the different offerings to their customers. These stores also carry computer books and magazines as well as diskettes and other computer accessories.

Don't confuse specialty *shops,* specialty *stores,* and specialty *products.* A specialty store is a store that has become *the* store for some customers. A successful specialty shop might achieve a specialty-store status among a small group of target customers. But the owner probably would rather be well known among a larger group as a "good" shopping store because of the distinctiveness of his line and the special services he offers. A specialty shop might carry specialty products—but only if such products fit into its narrow line and will benefit by the additional service and display the specialty shop offers. For example, "The Kitchen Korner"—a specialty *shop*—is a specialty *store* for some gourmet-cook customers. And the owner of "The Kitchen Korner" is willing—because it fits into "The Kitchen Korner's" line—to carry Calphalon cookware, which is considered a specialty *product* by its gourmet-cook customers.

The specialty shop's major advantage is that it caters to certain types of customers who the management and salespeople come to know well. This simplifies buying, speeds turnover, and cuts costs due to obsolescence and style changes. Specialty shops probably will continue to be a part of the retailing scene as long as customers have varied tastes—and the money to satisfy them.

Department stores combine many limited-line stores and specialty shops

Department stores are larger stores that are organized into many separate departments and offer many product lines. Each department is like a separate limited-line store or specialty shop. Department stores usually handle a wide variety of products—such as women's ready-to-wear and accessories, men's and children's wear, textiles, housewares, and home furnishings. Some well-known department stores are Bloomingdale's in New York, Filene's in Boston, Bullock's in Los Angeles, Marshall Field's in Chicago, Rich's in Atlanta, Dayton's in Minneapolis, and Dillard's in Little Rock.

Department stores are often considered the retailing leaders in a community. They usually do lead in customer services—including credit, merchandise return, delivery, fashion shows, and Christmas displays. They are also leaders because of their size. In a recent study, U.S. department stores averaged about $15.4 million in annual sales—compared to about $1.2 million for the average retail store. The biggest—Macy's, May Company, and Dayton-Hudson—each top $500 million in sales annually. Although department stores account for less than 1 percent of the total number of retail stores, they make almost 10 percent of total retail sales.[5]

Department stores generally try to cater to customers seeking shopping products. But some special departments—a beauty salon or optical department, for example—may help attract customers. If these departments require people with special skills, the store may lease out space for the department. Decisions about the department's operation are then left to the proprietor—who usually pays some share of sales as rent.

At first, most department stores were located downtown—close to other, similar stores. Many downtown stores began to suffer after World War II, however, as middle- and upper-income groups moved to the suburbs.

Following their customers, most department stores also opened suburban branches—usually in shopping centers. This helped offset some of the problems of downtown stores. But traditional department stores still face many challenges. Their share of retail business has been declining since the 1970s. Well-run limited-line stores are competing with good service—and they often carry the same brands. An even bigger threat has come with price competition from mass-merchandising retailers who operate with lower costs and sell larger volumes.[6] We'll discuss them next.

EVOLUTION OF MASS–MERCHANDISING RETAILERS

Mass-merchandising is different than conventional retailing

So far we've been describing retailers primarily in terms of their product *assortment.* This reflects traditional thinking about retailing. We could talk about supermarkets and discount houses in these terms, too. But then we would miss some important differences—just as some conventional retailers did when these stores first appeared.

Conventional retailers believe the demand in their area is fixed—and they have a "buy low and sell high" philosophy. Some modern retailers reject these ideas. They accept the **mass-merchandising concept**—which says that retailers should offer low prices to get faster turnover and greater sales volumes—by appealing to larger markets. To understand mass-merchandising better, let's look at its evolution from the development of supermarkets and discounters to the modern mass-merchandisers like K mart and Wal-Mart.

Supermarkets started the move to mass-merchandising

A **supermarket** is a large store specializing in groceries—with self-service and wide assortments. As late as 1930, most food stores were relatively small single- or limited-line operations. In the early Depression years, some innovators felt that they could increase sales by charging lower prices. They introduced self-service, provided a very broad product assortment in large stores, and offered low prices. Their early experiments in vacant warehouses were an immediate success. Profits came from large volume sales—not from "high" traditional markups. Many conventional retailers—both independents and chains—quickly copied the innovators.[7]

Supermarkets sell convenience products—but in quantity. Their target customers don't want to shop for groceries every day like grandma did. To make volume shopping easier, supermarkets typically carry 30,000 product items. Stores are large—averaging around 31,000 square feet. According to the Food Marketing Institute, $2 million is considered the minimum annual sales volume for a store to be called a supermarket. In 1988, there were about 30,500 supermarkets—and they handled more than half of all food store sales. Today, supermarkets are beginning to reach the saturation level, yet new ones still do well when they are wisely located.[8]

Present-day supermarkets are planned for maximum efficiency. Scanners at check-out counters make it possible to carefully analyze the sales and profit of each item—and allocate more shelf space to faster-moving and higher-profit items. This helps sell more products—faster. It also reduces the investment in inventory, makes stocking easier, and minimizes the cost of handling products. *Survival* depends on such efficiency. Grocery competition is keen, and net profits after taxes in grocery supermarkets usually run a thin 1 percent of sales—*or less!*

This thin profit margin puts pressure on supermarket managers to increase sales volume—which is hard to do in such a competitive market. One food industry consultant put it this way: "The supermarket is sort of like an old DC-3 airplane. It's been great fun to fly, but . . . it doesn't go fast enough anymore."

To make sales "go faster," some supermarket operators are opening "super warehouse" stores. These stores are big—50,000 to 100,000 square feet. They carry more nonperishable items than supermarkets— package goods and canned items with fast turnover. They don't stock perishable items like produce or meat. Prices are lower than in supermarkets. These super warehouse stores have been very successful. For example, Cub—a super warehouse innovator—sells about four times as much as the typical supermarket—and its labor cost as a percent of sales is about half that of the typical supermarket.[9]

Catalog showroom retailers preceded discount houses

Catalog showroom retailers sell several lines out of a catalog and display showroom—with backup inventories. Before 1940, catalog sellers were usually wholesalers who also sold at discounted prices to friends and members of groups—such as labor unions or church groups. In the 1970s, however, these operations expanded rapidly by aiming at final consumers and offering attractive catalogs and improved facilities. Catalog showroom retailers—like Service Merchandise, Consumers Distributing, and Best—grew because they offer big price savings and deliver almost all the items in the catalogs from backroom warehouses. They emphasize well-known manufacturers' brands of jewelry, gifts, luggage, and small appliances. They offer few services.[10]

This Service Merchandise catalog showroom is offering new customer services, including a drive-in window.

Early catalog retailers didn't bother conventional retailers because they were not well publicized and accounted for only a small portion of total retail sales. If the early catalog retailers had moved ahead aggressively—as the current catalog retailers have—the retailing scene might be different. But instead, discount houses developed.

Discount houses upset some conventional retailers

Right after World War II, some retailers moved beyond offering discounts to selected customers. These **discount houses** offered "hard goods" (cameras, TVs, appliances)—at substantial price cuts—to customers who would go to the discounter's low-rent store, pay cash, and take care of any service or repair problems themselves. These retailers sold at 20 to 30 percent off the list price being charged by conventional retailers for similar or the same nationally advertised brands. They focused on fast turnover—at lower prices.

In the early 1950s—with war shortages finally over—manufacturers' brands became more available. The discount houses were able to get any brands they wanted—and to offer fuller assortments. At this stage, many discounters "turned respectable"—moving to better locations and offering more services and guarantees. They began to act more like regular retailers. But they kept their prices lower than conventional retailers to keep turnover high.

Conventional retailers fight back by cutting prices

The discount house strategy was a new approach to "hard goods" retailing. Faced with discount house competition, some conventional hard goods retailers resorted to price cutting on highly competitive items. But these purely defensive moves were just that—price cutting—while discounters made a standard practice of selling everything with lower-than-usual markups at "everyday" low prices.

Mass-merchandisers are more than discounters

Mass-merchandisers are large, self-service stores with many departments that emphasize "soft goods" (housewares, clothing, and fabrics) but still follow the discount house's emphasis on lower margins to get faster turnover. Mass-merchandisers—like K mart and Wal-Mart—have check-out counters in the front of the store and little or no sales help on the floor. More conventional retailers—like the

department stores—still offer some service and have sales stations and cash registers in most departments. The conventional retailer may try to reorder sizes and maintain complete stocks in the lines it carries. Mass-merchandisers do less of this. They want to move merchandise—fast—and are less concerned with continuity of lines and assortment.

The average mass-merchandiser has nearly 60,000 square feet of floor space. This is twice the size of the average supermarket. K mart—the largest mass-merchandiser and the second largest retailer—has about 2,300 general merchandise stores nationally. And the average K mart store has annual sales of over $9 million.[11]

Mass-merchandisers have grown rapidly. In fact, they expanded so rapidly in some areas that they were no longer taking customers from conventional retailers—but from each other. Profits have been declining. And many stores have gone bankrupt. Seeing the declining potential in major metropolitan areas, some mass-merchandisers—especially Wal-Mart—have concentrated on opening stores in smaller towns. This has really upset some small-town merchants—who felt they were safe from this competitive "rat-race."[12]

Consumers appreciate mass-merchandisers

The success of mass-merchandisers shows that some customers weren't fully satisfied with the conventional retailers' strategies. Obviously, there is a demand for this type of retailing.

Since 1980 other retailers—focusing on single product lines—have adopted the mass-merchandisers' approach with great success. Perhaps one of the best examples is Toys "R" Us, which stocks many brands of toys and other products for children. Similarly, hardware mass-merchandisers like Hechingers and Builders Square offer depth of assortment in home-improvement products. Payless Drugstores, B. Dalton Books, and Circuit City (electronics) are also attracting large numbers of customers with their convenient assortment and low prices in a specific product category. These stores are sometimes called "category killers" because it's so hard for other, less specialized, retailers to compete. But the idea here isn't just to have the best selection; the key is these retailers' emphasis on earning profits through faster turnover and higher sales volume.[13]

Super-stores meet all routine needs

Some supermarkets and mass-merchandisers have moved toward becoming **super-stores**—very large stores that try to carry not only foods, but all goods and services that the consumer purchases *routinely*. Such a store may look like a mass-merchandiser, but it's different in concept. A super-store is trying to meet *all* the customer's routine needs—at a low price. These stores combine the concepts of both supermarkets and mass-merchandisers—so they are sometimes called *combination* super-stores.

Super-stores carry about 50,000 items. In addition to foods, a super-store carries personal care products, medicine, some apparel, toys, some lawn and garden products, gasoline—and services such as dry cleaning, travel reservations, bill paying, and banking. They attract more customers—and each customer tends to spend more because of the convenience of "one-stop" shopping. A super-store may have weekly sales that are six or seven times larger than a supermarket. Some super-stores are very large—over 200,000 square feet is no longer unusual. To help put that size in perspective, consider the Bigg's super-store in Cincinnati; it has 57 check-out registers!

Some mass-merchandisers and supermarket chains are moving in this direction. Many experts believe super-stores will continue to spread. If so, existing supermarkets may suffer. Their present buildings and parking lots are not large enough to convert to super-stores.[14]

New mass-merchandising formats keep coming

Retailers are constantly trying and refining new mass-merchandising store formats. For example, some retailers have opened stores that are basically "malls without walls"—220,000 square-foot stores that take the convenience of one-stop shopping even further than the super-stores.

The warehouse club is another retailing format that is gaining popularity. Price Club and Sam's Warehouse are two examples. Consumers usually pay an annual membership fee to shop in these large, bare-bones facilities. They are like the super warehouse stores for food, but they also carry appliances, yard tools, and other items that many consumers see as homogeneous shopping items—and want at the lowest possible price.[15]

SOME RETAILERS FOCUS ON ADDED CONVENIENCE

Supermarkets, discounters, and mass-merchandisers provide many different products "under one roof." Yet they are inconvenient in other ways. There may be few customer services. Or check-out lines may be longer. It may be hard to find the right product in the store. Or stores may be in less convenient locations. The savings may justify these inconveniences when a consumer has a lot to buy. But there are times when convenience is much more important—even if the price is a little higher. Let's look at some retailers who have met a need by focusing on convenience.

Convenience (food) stores must have the right assortment

Convenience (food) stores are a convenience-oriented variation of the conventional limited-line food stores. Instead of expanding their assortment, however, convenience stores limit their stock to "pick-up" or "fill-in" items like bread, milk, ice cream, and beer. Stores such as 7-Eleven, Majik Market, Stop-N-Go, and Circle K fill needs between major shopping trips to a supermarket. They are offering convenience—not assortment—and often charge prices 10 to 20 percent higher than those charged at nearby supermarkets. They earn approximately 4 percent on sales—rather than the 1 percent earned by supermarkets. This helps explain why the number of such stores increased from 2,500 in 1960 to 33,000 in 1980. The number of convenience stores continued to grow in the 1980s, but at a slower pace.

Because of the trend toward self-service gas, many of these stores now sell gas as well as food. And many are making the food even more convenient by selling sandwiches, soup, and other eat-on-the-run snacks. Thus, many of these stores are competing not only with grocery stores and gas stations but also with fast-food outlets. All of this competition is beginning to put pressure on convenience store profits—but they continue to be successful because they meet the needs of some target markets.[16]

Vending machines are convenient

Automatic vending is selling and delivering products through vending machines. Although the growth in vending machine sales has been impressive, such sales account for only about 1.5 percent of total U.S. retail sales. But 16 percent of all cigarettes sold in the United States, 20 percent of candy bars, and 25 percent of canned and bottled soft drinks are sold through machines. For some target markets, this retailing method cannot be ignored. And it may require other marketing mix changes. For example, granola bars started out as "health food," but now they compete with traditional candy bars. To make granola bars available where other candy is sold, Quaker and other producers are making smaller bars that fit in standard vending machines.

The major disadvantage to automatic vending is high cost. The machines are expensive to buy, stock, and repair relative to the volume they sell. Marketers of similar nonvended products can operate profitably on a margin of about 20 percent. The vending industry requires about 41 percent to break even. So they must charge higher prices. If costs come down—and consumers' desire for convenience rises—we may see more growth in this method of retailing. Automatic bank teller machines—which give a customer cash, using a "money card"—provide a hint of how technology is changing automatic vending. For example, "token cards" have already become popular with consumers in Japan. They buy the card in advance and then use it to pay for vending machine products—including telephone calls.[17]

Shop at home—with telephone, TV, and direct-mail retailing

Telephone and direct-mail retailing allow consumers to shop at home—usually placing orders by mail or a toll-free long-distance telephone call—and charging the purchase to a credit card. Typically, catalogs and ads on TV let customers "see" the offerings, and purchases are delivered by mail or United Parcel Service (UPS). Some consumers really like the convenience of this type of retailing—especially for products not available in local stores.

Mail-order sales now account for about 4 percent of all retail sales. During the 1980s, many new firms entered this market as sales were growing at the rapid rate of about 15 percent per year. In 1988, over 12 billion catalogs were distributed—an average of 135 per household! With computer mailing lists to help target customers, companies like Sharper Image, Renovator's Supply, and Horchow Collection were extremely successful with catalogs for narrow lines—electronic gadgets, antique hardware, and expensive gift items.[18]

The early mail-order houses—Sears, Roebuck and Montgomery Ward—were pioneers in catalog selling. But now department stores like Bloomingdale's and limited-line stores like Western Auto are seeing the profit possibilities and are selling this way. Not only can they get additional business, but costs may also be lower because they can use warehouse-type buildings and limited sales help. And shoplifting—a big expense for most retailers—isn't a problem. After-tax profits for mail-order retailers average 7 percent of sales—more than twice the profit margins for most other types of retailers. However, the increasing competition and slower growth in sales—about 10 percent per year—are beginning to reduce these margins.

Put the "catalog" on cable TV

Some companies have tried to offer "electronic shopping," which allows consumers to connect their personal computers or a push-button phone to central computer systems. This has proved too complicated for most consumers. However, Home Shopping Network and others have been more successful by devoting cable TV channels to home shopping. These channels don't sell the records and gadgets that have been sold on late-night TV for years. Instead, they display furni-

The Home Shopping Network has been successful by appealing to some consumers who want the convenience of in-home shopping.

ture, clothing, and appliances, which the consumer can order by phone. This approach yielded sales of about $1.4 billion in 1989, a big increase from $200 million in 1986. Some experts think that sales will mushroom to $20 billion a year as shopping channels become more popular in the next decade.[19]

Door-to-door retailers—
give personal attention

Door-to-door selling means going directly to the consumer's home. It accounts for less than 1 percent of retail sales—but it meets some consumers' needs for convenience and personal attention. Door-to-door selling can also be useful with unsought products—like encyclopedias.

Hard times have hit door-to-door retailers. Finding customers at home—especially during the day—is becoming difficult because more adults are working outside the home. Many of the firms in this line of business are now trying to get a foothold in other channels of distribution.

RETAILING TYPES ARE EXPLAINED BY CONSUMER NEEDS FILLED

We've talked about many different types of retailers and how they evolved. Earlier, we noted that no single characteristic provided a good basis for classifying all retailers. Now it helps to see the three-dimensional view of retailing presented in Exhibit 12–4. It positions different types of retailers in terms of three consumer-oriented dimensions: (1) width of assortment desired; (2) depth of assortment desired, and (3) a price/service combination. Price and service are combined because they are often indirectly related. Services are costly to provide. So, a retailer that wants to emphasize low prices usually has to cut some services—and stores with a lot of service must charge prices that cover the added costs.

Exhibit 12–4   A Three-Dimensional View of the Market for Retail Facilities and the Probable Position of Some Present Offerings

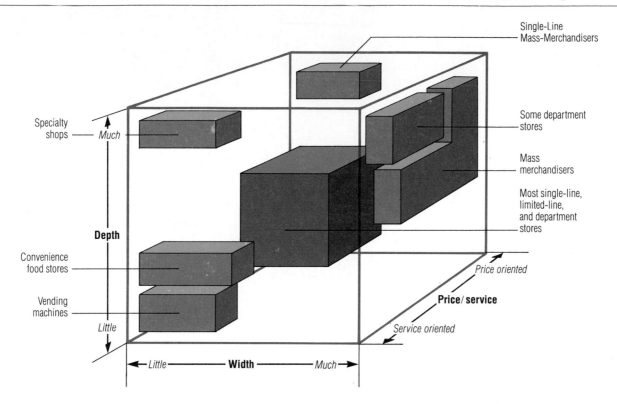

We can position most existing retailers within this three-dimensional market diagram. Exhibit 12–4, for example, suggests the *why* of vending machines. Some people—in the front lower left-hand corner—have a strong need for a specific item and are not interested in width of assortment, depth of assortment, or price.

WHY RETAILERS EVOLVE AND CHANGE

Exhibit 12–4 compares different types of *existing* stores. Now, we'll look at some ways that retailing is changing.

Scrambled merchandising— mixing product lines for higher profits

Conventional retailers tend to specialize by product line. But most modern retailers have moved toward **scrambled merchandising**—carrying any product lines they think they can sell profitably. Supermarkets and "drugstores" are selling anything they can move in volume—pantyhose, magazines, antifreeze and motor oil, potted plants, and videotapes. Mass-merchandisers aren't just selling everyday items, but also cameras, jewelry, and even home computers. Why has scrambled merchandising become so common?

To survive, a retailer must consistently show at least some profit. But typical retailers' net profit margins on sales are very slim—from 0 to 5 percent. And new types of retailers are continually evolving and putting even more pressure on profits. So a firm looking for better profits wants to sell more fast-moving, high-profit

Microwave popcorn is promoted to video store managers and pantyhose are promoted to grocery chain buyers—because many retailers scramble their merchandise lines to earn higher profits.

items. And it is exactly these items that are scrambling across traditional lines and appearing in unexpected places.

Exhibit 12–5 shows the ranges of gross margins conventional retailers have found necessary to stay in business and make *some* profit. *Some* is emphasized because usually the net profit—the difference between a seemingly big gross margin and apparently necessary expenses—is only 1 or a few percent.

Mass-merchandisers and discounters like to operate on gross margins and markups of 15 to 30 percent. But—as shown in Exhibit 12–5—conventional retailers usually need much higher percentages. This exhibit should give you a better idea of the *why* of scrambled merchandising—and suggest possible directions it will take. Exhibit 12–5 shows, for example, why scramblers want to sell bakery goods, jewelry, appliances, refreshments, and gifts. Try to analyze why some of the conventional retailers have such high gross margins and why other types of retailers can operate more economically.[20]

The wheel of retailing keeps rolling

The **wheel of retailing theory** says that new types of retailers enter the market as low-status, low-margin, low-price operators and then—if they are successful—evolve into more conventional retailers offering more services with higher operating costs and higher prices. Then they are threatened by new low-status, low-margin, low-price retailers—and the wheel turns again.

Early department stores began this way. Then they became higher priced—and they added "bargain basements" to serve the more price-conscious customers. The supermarket was started with low prices and little service. Mass-merchandisers have gone through the same cycle.

Some innovators start with high margins

The wheel of retailing theory, however, doesn't explain all major retailing developments. Vending machines entered as high-cost, high-margin operations. Convenience food stores are high-priced. Suburban shopping centers have not had a low-price emphasis.

Exhibit 12–5   Illustrative Gross Margins in Selected Retail Trades for Recent Years

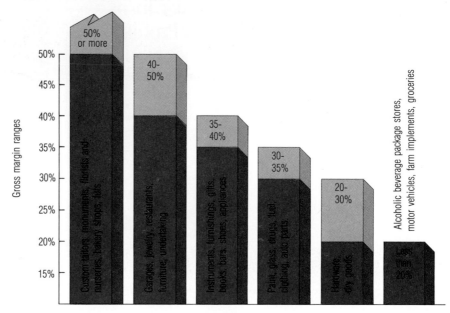

Product life-cycle
concept applies to
retailer types, too

We've seen that people's needs help explain why different kinds of retailers developed. But we have to apply the product life-cycle concept to understand this process better. A retailer with a new idea may have big profits—for a while. But if it's a really good idea, he can count on speedy imitation—and a squeeze on his profits. Other retailers will "scramble" their product mix to sell products that offer them higher margins or faster turnover.

The cycle is illustrated by what has happened with video movies. As the popularity of VCRs grew, video stores cropped up across the country. The first ones charged from $5 to $10 a night for a tape. As more competitors entered, however, prices (and profits) were driven down. Competition heated up even more as supermarkets, convenience stores, and drugstores started to carry the most popular tapes—sometimes renting them for as little as 99 cents a night. Many of the original video stores couldn't cover their costs trying to compete at that price—and they have gone out of business.

The cycle on video stores has moved very quickly. Sometimes the cycle is much slower. But these cycles do exist—and some conventional retailers are far along in their life cycles and may be declining. Recent innovators are still in the market growth stage. See Exhibit 12–6.

Some retailers are confused by the scrambling going on around them. They don't see this evolutionary process. And they don't understand that some of their more successful competitors are aiming at different target markets—instead of just "selling products."

It's not surprising to find that some modern success stories in retailing are firms that moved into a new market and started another "product life cycle"—by aiming at needs along the edges of the market shown in Exhibit 12–4. The convenience food stores, for example, don't just sell food. They deliberately sell a particular

Exhibit 12–6   Retailer Life Cycles—Timing and Years to Market Maturity

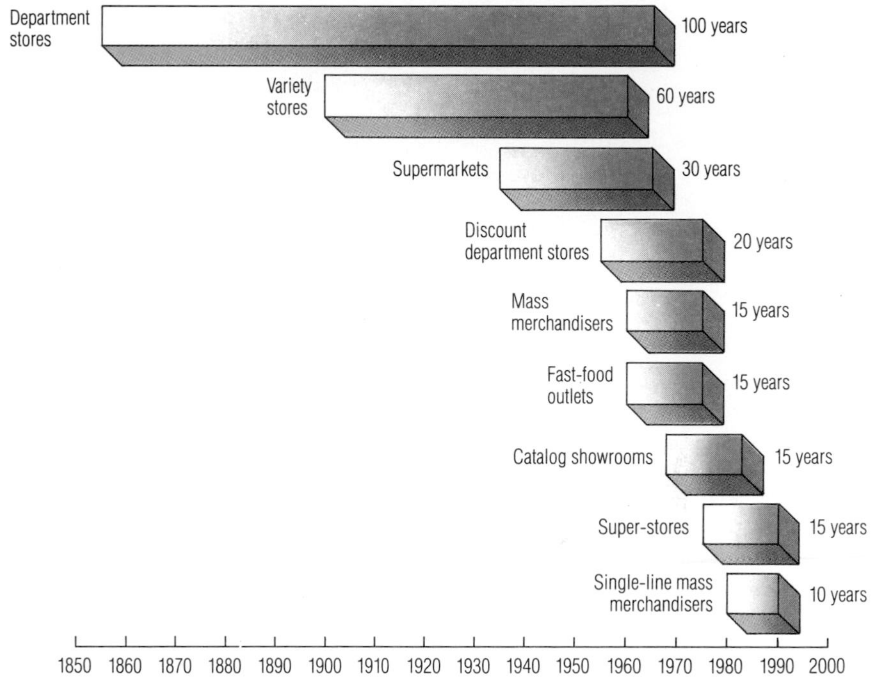

Department stores — 100 years
Variety stores — 60 years
Supermarkets — 30 years
Discount department stores — 20 years
Mass merchandisers — 15 years
Fast-food outlets — 15 years
Catalog showrooms — 15 years
Super-stores — 15 years
Single-line mass merchandisers — 10 years

1850 1860 1870 1880 1890 1900 1910 1920 1930 1940 1950 1960 1970 1980 1990 2000

assortment-service combination to meet a different need. This is also true of specialty shops and some of the mass-merchandisers and department store chains.[21]

Competition leads to price pressure

In discussing the retail life cycle, we focused on how retail innovators change over time—moving toward more service and higher prices. But it is also important to see that the evolving retail scene also forces many existing stores to adopt new methods and to respond to price competition.

In the 1990s we see the effect of this price competition everywhere. Department stores that once had two or three "price-off" sales a year now have them much more often—perhaps several times a month. The gap between department store prices and mass-merchandiser prices has narrowed. Even catalog showrooms are feeling the pinch. Supermarkets try to retain services their customers want—but they are cutting their prices even more to compete with superwarehouse stores. Mass-merchandisers fight with each other for customers—advertising weekly "specials" featuring even lower prices.[22]

RETAILER SIZE AND PROFITS

We've talked about different types of retailers and how they evolved. Now let's look at the size of stores and how they are owned—because this too is related to retailer strategy planning. It is another area that has seen much change—and it helps to explain why some retailers are becoming more powerful members of the channel of distribution.

The number of retailers is very large

There are lots of retailers—partly because it's so easy to enter retailing. Kids can open and close a lemonade stand in one day. A more serious retailer—with relatively little capital—can rent an empty store and be in business in a few weeks. There are about 1.5 million retailers compared to about 416,000 wholesalers and 355,000 manufacturers.

But a few big ones do most of the business

The large number of retailers might suggest that retailing is a field of small businesses. To some extent this is true. As shown in Exhibit 12–7, about 60 percent of all the retail stores had annual sales of less than $250,000 during the 1982 census. But that's only part of the story. Those same retailers accounted for only about eight cents of every $1 in retail sales!

The larger retail stores—such as larger supermarkets and other stores selling more than $2.5 million annually—do most of the business. Only about 4 percent of the retail stores are this big, yet they account for over 50 percent of all retail sales.

The government will not publish updated statistics on retailer size and sales until sometime in 1992. However, the general pattern that you see in Exhibit 12–7 is expected to stay the same. The largest retailers account for the vast majority of all retail sales—and that means that a manufacturer or wholesaler often needs to work with them to reach the target market at the end of the channel.

On the other hand, the many small retailers can't be ignored. They do reach many consumers—and often are valuable channel members. But they frequently cause difficult problems for producers and wholesalers. Their large number—and

Exhibit 12–7   Distribution of Stores by Size and Share of Total Retail Sales (United States, 1982)

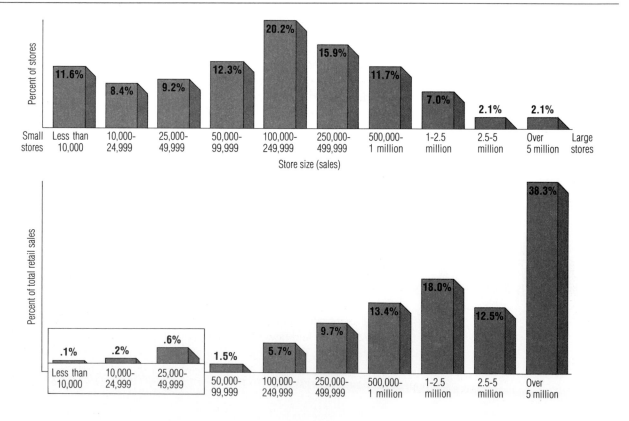

relatively small sales volume—make working with them expensive. They often require separate marketing mixes.

Small size may be hard to overcome

Small retailers often have trouble making enough money to cover expenses. But even the average retail store is too small to gain economies of scale—and that is sometimes what is required to be competitive.

Well-managed larger stores can usually get some economies of scale. They can buy in quantity at lower prices, take advantage of mass advertising, and hire specialists. But larger size alone doesn't guarantee more efficient operation. For example, individual departments in a department store might not be any larger than independent limited-line stores—and so there may be little possibility for volume buying.[23]

Being in a chain may help

One way for a retailer to achieve economies of scale is with a corporate chain. A **(corporate) chain store** is one of several stores owned and managed by the same firm. Most chains have at least some central buying for different stores, which allows them to take advantage of quantity discounts or opportunities for vertical integration. They may also have advantages over independent stores in promotion and management because they can spread the costs to many stores. Often, retail chains have their own dealer brands, too. Chains grew slowly until after World War I—then spurted ahead during the 1920s. Chains have continued to grow. They now account for about 53 percent of retail sales—and about 22 percent of all retailers.

Chains have done even better in certain lines. They have 99 percent of the department store business. Sears and May Company are in this category. Safeway, Kroger, A&P, and other supermarket chains have about 70 percent of grocery sales. Mass-merchandisers like K mart are usually operated as chains. That gives them more buying power—and makes it easier to fight price competition.

Chain stores—like J. C. Penney—win a very large share of all retail business.

Toys "R" Us Is a Winner at Marketing Toys

Toys "R" Us is serious about retailing. Although the toy market has only been growing at about 2 percent a year, sales for the Toys "R" Us chain have increased at about 25 percent a year. In 1988, consumers spent about $13 billion on toys—and nearly a fourth of that was at Toys "R" Us. What explains this success? Each store—and there are more than 300 of them—is in a convenient location and offers low prices on 18,000 toys. The chain's buying clout means that it can get good prices from toy producers. In addition, it uses computers to spot fast selling toys before they are hits—so it can buy early and avoid problems with running out of stock that trouble other toy retailers. In fact, stores like K mart and Service Merchandise often reduce the size of their toy departments when a Toys "R" Us opens nearby. Their smaller, seasonal selections and occasional sales just are not competitive. Customers will drive right by them for the service, prices, and selection at a Toys "R" Us.

Several other large chains, like Child World and Lionel, use similar strategies. Toys "R" Us continues to be the market leader, but in some of its markets these competitors have put pressure on profits. In an effort to find profitable new opportunities, Toys "R" Us is opening new stores in overseas markets where small shops and department stores still dominate toy distribution. For example, 70 percent of the toys in Europe are sold at Christmas. As a result, Toys "R" Us expects that its new stores will quickly be able to capture most of the off-season market.[24]

Independents form chains, too

The growth of corporate chains has encouraged the development of both cooperative chains and voluntary chains.

Cooperative chains are retailer-sponsored groups—formed by independent retailers—to run their own buying organizations and conduct joint promotion efforts. Sales of cooperative chains have been rising as they learn how to meet the corporate chain competition. Examples include Associated Grocers, Certified Grocers, and True Value Hardware.

Voluntary chains are wholesaler-sponsored groups that work with "independent" retailers. Some are linked by contracts stating common operating procedures—and requiring the use of common store front designs, store name, and joint promotion efforts. The wholesaler-sponsor often provides training programs, computer and accounting assistance, and dealer brands. Examples include IGA and Super Valu in groceries, Ace in hardware, and Western Auto in auto supplies.

Franchisers form chains, too

In a **franchise operation**, the franchiser develops a good marketing strategy, and the retail franchise holders carry out the strategy in their own units. The franchiser acts iike a voluntary chain operator—or a producer! Each franchise holder benefits from the experience, buying power, and image of the larger company. In return, the franchise holder usually signs a contract to pay fees and commissions—and to strictly follow franchise rules designed to continue the successful strategy. Examples of well-known franchise operations are shown in Exhibit 12–8.

Voluntary chains tend to work with existing retailers, while some franchisers like to work with—and train—newcomers. For newcomers, a franchise often reduces the risk of starting a new business. Government studies show that only about 5

Exhibit 12–8   Examples of Some Well-Known Franchise Operations

percent of new franchise operations fail in the first few years—compared to about 70 percent for other new retailers. One reason for this is better training. For example, a six-week course at "Dunkin Donuts University" trains a franchise holder to run a donut shop. Some franchise holders also get help in locating or building a store and with initial promotion.

Franchise holders' sales are growing fast. And you see the evidence all around you. If you need your car's muffler fixed, you stop at a Midas Muffler. If you get a late-night craving for pizza, you call Domino's. If you want to lose a few pounds, perhaps you join a Jazzercise class. The Commerce Department estimates that by the year 2000 franchise holders will account for half of all retail sales. One important reason for this growth is that franchising is especially popular with service firms, one of the fastest-growing sectors of the economy.[25]

LOCATION OF RETAIL FACILITIES

Location can spell success or failure for a retail facility. But, what's a "good location" depends on target markets, competitors, and costs. Let's review some of the ideas a retailer should consider in selecting a location.

Downtown and shopping strips—evolve without a plan

Most cities have a "central business district" where many retail stores are found. At first, it may seem that such a district was developed according to some plan. Actually, the location of individual stores is more an accident of time—and what spaces were available.

As cities grow, "shopping strips" of convenience stores develop along major roads. Generally, they emphasize convenience products. But a variety of single-line and limited-line stores may enter too, adding shopping products to the mix. Some retailers have been "dressing up" the stores in these unplanned strips. The expense of remodeling these locations is small compared to the higher rents at big shopping centers. But, even so, these strips aren't the planned shopping centers that have developed in the last 30 years.

Planned shopping centers—not just a group of stores

A **planned shopping center** is a set of stores planned as a unit to satisfy some market needs. The stores sometimes act together for promotion purposes. Many centers are enclosed to make shopping more pleasant. Free parking is usually provided. There are now about 30,000 shopping centers in the United States—but different types of shopping centers serve different needs.

Neighborhood shopping centers consist of several convenience stores. These centers usually include a supermarket, drugstore, hardware store, beauty shop, laundry, dry cleaner, gas station, and perhaps others—such as a bakery or appliance shop. They normally must serve 7,500 to 40,000 people living within a 6- to 10-minute driving distance.

Community shopping centers are larger and offer some shopping stores as well as the convenience stores found in neighborhood shopping centers. They usually include a small department store that carries shopping products (clothing and home furnishings). But most sales in these centers are convenience products. These centers must serve 40,000 to 150,000 people within a radius of five to six miles.

Regional shopping centers are the largest centers and emphasize shopping stores and shopping products. Most of these are enclosed malls, which make shopping easier in bad weather. They usually include one or more large department stores and as many as 200 smaller stores. Stores that feature convenience products are often placed at the edge of the center—so they won't get in the way of customers primarily interested in shopping. Some regional shopping centers feature entertainment—movie theaters, restaurants, and even art displays—to help attract customers.

Regional centers usually serve 150,000 or more people. They are like downtown shopping districts of larger cities. Regional centers usually are found near populated suburban areas. They draw customers from a radius of 7 to 10 miles—or even farther from rural areas where shopping facilities are poor. Regional shopping centers being built now often cover 2 million square feet—as large as 40 football fields!

During the 1980s, many "discount malls" developed. These shopping centers are often as large as regional shopping centers, and all the stores claim to sell at

The mix of stores in a shopping center is planned—to make it convenient for consumers to shop.

discounted prices. Many of these malls feature "factory outlet" stores that sell "seconds" or discontinued lines. Such malls target budget shoppers who are willing to drive long distances for a big assortment of "deals."[26]

WHAT DOES THE FUTURE LOOK LIKE?

The changes in retailing in the last 30 years have been rapid—and they seem to be continuing. Scrambled merchandising may become even more scrambled. Some people are forecasting larger stores, while others are predicting smaller ones.

More customer-oriented retailing may be coming

Any effort to forecast trends in such a situation is risky, but our three-dimensional picture of the retailing market (Exhibit 12–4) can help. Those who suggest bigger and bigger stores may be primarily concerned with the center of the diagram. Those who look for more small stores and specialty shops may be anticipating more small—but increasingly wealthy—target markets able to afford higher prices for special products.

To serve small—but wealthy—markets, convenience stores continue to spread. And sales by "electronic" retailing are expected to grow. For example, Compusave Corporation now has an "electronic catalog" order system. A videodisc player hooked to a TV-like screen allows the consumer to see pictures and descriptions of thousands of products. The product assortment is similar to that at a catalog store—and the prices are even lower. When a selection is made, the consumer

Machines like this one make it convenient for a consumer to give gifts without the hassle of shopping, wrapping, and delivering.

inserts a credit card, and the computer places the order and routes it to the consumer's home. These machines are being installed in shopping centers around the country. They are popular among hurried, cost-conscious consumers.[27]

American consumers simply don't have as much time to shop as they once did—and a growing number are willing to pay for convenience. Stores will probably continue to make shopping more convenient by staying open later, carrying assortments that make "one-stop" shopping possible, and being sure the stocks don't run out. This interest in convenience and saving time should also lead to growth of "in-home" shopping.

In-home shopping will become more popular

More consumers will "let their fingers do the walking"—and telephone shopping will become more popular, too. Mail-order houses and department stores already find phone business attractive. Telephone supermarkets—now a reality—sell only by phone and deliver all orders. Linking the phone to closed-circuit TV lets customers see the products—at home—while hearing prepared sales presentations. Selling to consumers at home through a home computer has not been very successful so far—but it may become more popular in the future.

We now have far greater electronic capabilities than we are using. There is no reason why customers can't shop in the home—saving time and gasoline. Such automated retailing might take over a large share of the convenience products and homogeneous shopping products business.

Some retailers are becoming more powerful

We will continue to see growth in retail chains, franchises, and other cooperative arrangements. These arrangements can help retailers serve their customers better—and also give the retailer more power in the channel. A "battle of the titans" is emerging as powerful retail chains put pressure on big manufacturers for better purchasing arrangements and more promotion support.

We may also see more vertical arrangements in channel systems. This will affect present manufacturers—who already see retailers developing their own brands and using manufacturers mainly as production arms.

Large manufacturers may go into retailing themselves—for self-protection. Rexall Corporation, Sherwin-Williams, Benetton, Van Heusen, and others already control or own retail outlets.

Retailing will continue to be needed, but the role of individual retailers may have to change. Customers will always have needs. But retail *stores* aren't necessarily the only way to satisfy them.

Retailers must face the challenge

One thing is certain—change in retailing is inevitable. For years, conventional retailers' profits have declined. Even some of the newer discounters and shopping centers have not done well. Department stores and food and drug chains have seen profits decline. Old style variety stores have done even worse. Some shifted into mass-merchandising operations, which are also becoming less attractive as limited-line stores try to "meet competition" with lower margins.

A few firms—especially Wal-Mart—have avoided this general profit squeeze. But the future doesn't look too bright for retailers who can't—or won't—change. New technical developments—like automatic check-out counters—require capital to save labor costs. But the same developments are available to all competitors. In our competitive markets, the benefits are passed on to the consumers—but the firms are stuck with higher fixed costs.

No easy way for more profit

In fact, it appears that the "fat" has been squeezed out of retailing—and there isn't an easy route to big profits anymore. To be successful in the future, retailers will need careful strategy planning and implementation. This means more careful market segmenting to find unsatisfied needs that (1) have a long life expectancy and (2) can be satisfied with low levels of investment. This is a big order. But imaginative marketers will find more profitable opportunities than the conventional retailer, who doesn't know that the product life cycle is moving along—and is just "hoping for the best."[28]

CONCLUSION

Modern retailing is scrambled—and we will probably see more changes in the future. In such a dynamic environment, a producer's marketing manager must choose very carefully among the available kinds of retailers. And retailers must plan their marketing mixes with their target customers' needs in mind—while at the same time becoming part of an effective channel system.

We described many types of retailers—and we saw that each has its advantages and disadvantages. We also saw that modern retailers have discarded conventional practices. The old "buy low and sell high" philosophy is no longer a safe guide. Lower margins with faster turnover is the modern philosophy as more retailers move into mass-merchandising. But even this is no guarantee of success as retailers' product life cycles move on.

Scrambled merchandising will continue as retailing evolves to meet changing consumer demands. But important breakthroughs are still possible because consumers probably will continue to move away from conventional retailers. Convenience products, for example, may be made more easily available by some combination of electronic ordering and home delivery or vending. The big, all-purpose department store may not be able to satisfy anyone's needs exactly. Some combination of mail-order and electronic ordering might make a larger assortment of products available to more people—to better meet their particular needs.

Our society needs a retailing function—but all the present retailers may not be needed. It is safe to say that the future retail scene will offer the marketing manager new challenges and opportunities.

Questions and Problems

1. Identify a specialty store selling convenience products in your city. Explain why you think it is that kind of store and why an awareness of this status would be important to a manufacturer. Does it give the retailer any particular advantage? If so, with whom?

2. What sort of a "product" are specialty shops offering? What are the prospects for organizing a chain of specialty shops?

3. Many department stores have a bargain basement. Does the basement represent just another department, like the lingerie department or the luggage department? Or is some whole new concept involved?

4. Distinguish among discount houses, price cutting by conventional retailers, and mass-merchandising. Forecast the future of low-price selling in food, clothing, and appliances.

5. In view of the wide range of gross margins (and expenses) in various lines of trade, what will the supermarket or scrambled merchandising outlet of the future be like? Use care here. Are products with high gross margins necessarily highly profitable?

6. Discuss a few changes in the uncontrollable environment that you think help to explain why telephone and mail-order retailing has been growing so rapidly.

7. Apply the "wheel of retailing" theory to your local community. What changes seem likely? Will established retailers see the need for change, or will entirely new firms have to develop?

8. What advantages does a retail chain have over a retailer who operates with a single store? Does a small retailer have any advantages in competing against a chain? Explain your answer.

9. Discuss the kinds of markets served by the three types of shopping centers. Are they directly competitive? Do they contain the same kinds of stores? Is the long-run outlook for all of them similar?

10. Explain the growth and decline of various retailers and shopping centers in your own community. Use the text's three-dimensional drawing (Exhibit 12–4) and the product life-cycle concept. Also, treat each retailer's whole offering as a "product."

Suggested Cases

11. Nike and Walking Shoes

16. Visual Tools, Inc.

20. Hudson's, Inc.

Suggested Computer-Aided Problem

12. Mass-Merchandising

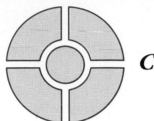

Chapter **13**

Wholesaling

When You Finish This Chapter, You Should

1. Understand what wholesalers are and the wholesaling functions they *may* provide for others in channel systems.

2. Know the various kinds of merchant wholesalers and agent middlemen.

3. Understand when and where the various kinds of merchant wholesalers and agent middlemen are most useful to channel planners.

4. Know what progressive wholesalers are doing to modernize their operations and marketing strategies.

5. Understand why wholesalers have lasted.

6. Understand the important new terms (shown in red).

"I can get it for you wholesale," the man said. But could he? Would it be a good deal?

Frieda Caplan and her two daughters, Jackie and Karen, run Produce Specialties, a wholesale firm that each year supplies supermarkets with $15 million worth of exotic fruits and vegetables. It is a sign of the firm's success that kiwifruit, artichokes, pearl onions, and mushrooms no longer seem very exotic. All of these crops were once viewed as unusual. Few U.S. farmers produced them. Consumers didn't know about them. Traditional produce wholesalers didn't want to handle them because they had a limited market. Produce Specialties helped to change all of that.

Caplan realized that some supermarkets were putting more emphasis on their produce departments—and wanted to offer consumers more choice. She looked for products that would help them meet this need. For example, the funny looking, egg-shaped kiwifruit with its fuzzy brown skin was popular in New Zealand, but it was virtually unknown to American consumers. Caplan worked with a number of small farmer-producers to insure that she could provide the retailers with an adequate supply. She packaged kiwi with interesting recipes and promoted kiwi *and* her brand name to consumers. Because of her efforts, many supermarkets now carry kiwi—which has become a $40 million crop for California farmers. Because demand for kiwi has grown, other wholesalers now handle them. Even so, Caplan has a competitive advantage with many supermarkets because she offers a high-quality assortment of kiwi and other specialty produce.[1]

American Hospital Supply (AHS) provides hospitals with about 70 percent of all the items they need—and does it within 24 hours. This is no small feat. To meet its customers' varied needs, AHS carries about 120,000 products—from hundreds of producers.

To stay the leader in its field, AHS is constantly looking for ways to help hospitals reduce costs. For example, AHS assigned a sales rep to work *full-time* for Nashville's Hospital Corp. of America—which controls purchasing for many hospitals. The AHS rep helped control inventory and handling costs, which can eat up a large part of a hospital's budget. Further, AHS offered a "cash refund" to encourage hospitals to buy in larger quantities. In return, over 350 hospitals agreed not to seek competitive bids on products carried by AHS. AHS's success prompted other suppliers to offer similar plans. So AHS is seeking new opportunities by shifting more of its personal selling effort to nursing homes, doctors' offices, and clinics.[2]

These examples show that wholesalers are a vital link in a channel system—and in the whole marketing process—helping both their suppliers and their customers. It also shows that wholesalers—like other businesses—must select their target markets and marketing mixes carefully. But you can understand wholesalers better if you look at them as members of channels. Wholesalers are middlemen.

In this chapter, you will learn more about wholesalers. You'll see how they have evolved, how they fit into various channels, why they are used, and what functions they perform.

WHAT IS A WHOLESALER?

It's hard to define what a wholesaler is because there are so many different wholesalers doing different jobs. Some of their activities may even seem like manufacturing. As a result, some wholesalers call themselves "manufacturer and dealer." Some like to identify themselves with such general terms as merchant, jobber, dealer, or distributor. And others just use the name that is commonly used in their trade—without really thinking about what it means.

To avoid a long technical discussion on the nature of wholesaling, we will use the U.S. Bureau of the Census definition:

Wholesaling is concerned with the *activities* of those persons or establishments which sell to retailers and other merchants, and/or to industrial, institutional, and commercial users, but who do not sell in large amounts to final consumers.

So, **wholesalers** are firms whose main function is providing *wholesaling activities*.

Note that producers who take over wholesaling activities are not considered wholesalers. However, if branch warehouses are set up at *separate locations,* these establishments are counted as wholesalers by the U.S. Census Bureau.

POSSIBLE WHOLESALING FUNCTIONS

Wholesalers may perform certain functions for both their suppliers and the wholesalers' own customers—in short, for those above and below them in the channel. These *wholesaling functions* really are variations of the basic marketing functions—buying, selling, grading, storing, transporting, financing, risk taking, and gathering market information. These wholesaling functions are basic to the following discussion and should be studied carefully now. But keep in mind that these functions are provided by some—*but not necessarily all*—wholesalers.

What a wholesaler might do for customers

1. Regroup goods—to provide the quantity and assortment wanted by customers, at the lowest possible cost.
2. Anticipate needs—forecast customers' demands and buy accordingly.
3. Carry stocks—carry inventory so customers don't have to store a large inventory.
4. Deliver goods—provide prompt delivery at low cost.
5. Grant credit—give credit to customers, perhaps supplying their working capital. Note: this financing function may be very important to small customers, and it is sometimes the main reason why they use wholesalers rather than buying directly from producers.
6. Provide information and advisory service—supply price and technical information as well as suggestions on how to install and sell products. Note: the wholesaler's sales reps may be experts in the products they sell.
7. Provide part of the buying function—offer products to potential customers so they don't have to hunt for supply sources.
8. Own and transfer title to products—help by completing a sale without the need for other middlemen, speeding the whole buying and selling process.

What a wholesaler might do for producer-suppliers

1. Provide part of a producer's selling function—going to producer-suppliers instead of waiting for their sales reps to call.
2. Store inventory—reduce a producer's need to carry large stocks and so cut his warehousing expenses.
3. Supply capital—reduce a producer's need for working capital by buying his output and carrying it in inventory until it's sold.

A wholesaler often helps its customers by carrying needed products and providing prompt delivery at low cost.

If your store's sales are moving faster than your distributor, make a quick call to us.

For convenience stores, nothing is more inconvenient than running out when customers are running in.

That's why Southland maintains a 99.7% in-stock rate. Why placing an electronic order takes only seconds. Why we deliver on the day we promise, in less than 30 minutes.

Stores with brisk sales need a system that knows how to move.

Call Southland. We're ready to roll.

To find out more, call the Southland Distribution Center near you.
Northeast—Falmouth, VA (703) 371-5000, Midwest—Champaign, IL (217) 398-1800, West—San Bernardino, CA (714) 887-7921.

4. Reduce credit risk—selling to customers the wholesaler knows and taking the loss if these customers don't pay.

5. Provide market information—as an informed buyer and seller closer to the market, the wholesaler reduces the producer's need for market research.[3]

Functions are crucial in many channels

The importance of these wholesaling functions can be seen more clearly by looking at a specific case. George Mims is a heating contractor. His company sells heating systems—and his crew installs them in new buildings. Mr. Mims gets a lot of help from Air Control Company, the wholesaler who supplies this equipment. When Mims isn't certain what type of furnace to install, Air Control's experts give him good technical advice. Air Control also stocks an inventory of products from different producers. This means that Mr. Mims can order a piece of equipment when he's ready to install it. He doesn't have to tie up capital in a big inventory—or wait for a part to be shipped cross country from a producer. Air Control even helps finance his business. Mims doesn't have to pay for his purchases until 30 days after he takes delivery. By then, he has finished his work and been paid by his customers. Mr. Mims' whole way of doing business would be different without this wholesaler providing wholesaling functions.

KINDS AND COSTS OF AVAILABLE WHOLESALERS

Exhibit 13–1 compares the number, sales volume, and operating expenses of some major types of wholesalers. The differences in operating expenses suggest that each of these types performs—or does not perform—certain wholesaling functions. But which ones and why?

Exhibit 13–1 shows that the 338,000 merchant wholesalers account for 58 percent of wholesale dollar sales. But why do manufacturers use merchant wholesalers—costing 13 percent of sales—when manufacturers' sales branches cost only 6.8 percent?

Why use either when agent middlemen cost only 4.5 percent? Is the use of wholesalers with higher operating expenses the reason why marketing costs so much—if, in fact, it does?

Exhibit 13–1   Wholesale Trade by Type of Wholesale Operation

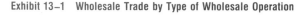

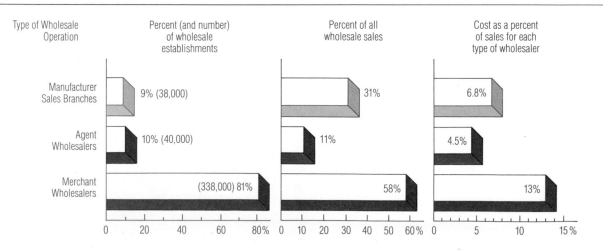

To answer these questions, we must understand what these wholesalers do—and don't do. Exhibit 13–2 gives a big-picture view of the wholesalers described in more detail below. Note that a major difference is whether they *own* the products they sell.

Wholesaler provides access to a target market

One of the main assets of a wholesaler is its customers. A particular wholesaler may be the only one who reaches certain customers. The producer who wants to reach these customers *may have no choice but to use that wholesaler.* "What customers does this wholesaler serve?" should be one of the first questions you ask when planning a channel of distribution.[4]

Learn the pure to understand the real

The next important question should be "What functions does this particular wholesaler provide?" Wholesalers typically specialize by product line. But they do provide different functions. And they probably will keep doing what they are doing—no matter what others might like them to do!

To help you understand wholesaling better, we'll discuss "pure types" of wholesalers. In practice, it may be hard to find examples of these pure types because many wholesalers are mixtures. Further, the names commonly used in a particular industry may be misleading. Some so-called brokers actually behave as limited-function merchant wholesalers. And some "manufacturers' agents" operate as full-service wholesalers. This casual use of terms makes it all the more important for you to thoroughly understand the pure types before trying to understand the blends—and the names given to them in the business world.

Exhibit 13–2   Types of Wholesalers

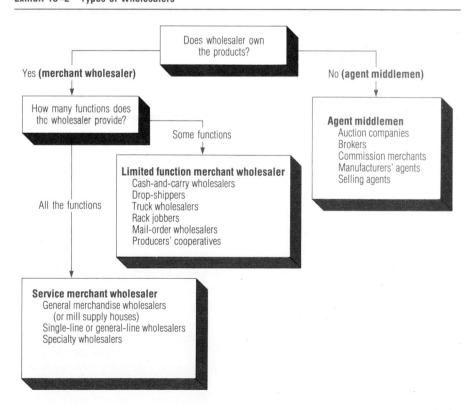

In the following pages, we'll discuss the major types of wholesalers identified by the U.S. Census Bureau. Remember, detailed data are available by kind of business, by product line, and by geographic territory. Such detailed data can be valuable in strategy planning—especially to learn whether potential channel members are serving a target market. You can also learn what sales volume current middlemen are achieving.

MERCHANT WHOLESALERS ARE THE MOST NUMEROUS

Merchant wholesalers own (take title to) the products they sell. For example, a wholesale lumber yard that buys plywood from the producer is a merchant wholesaler. It actually owns—"takes title to"—the plywood for some period of time before selling to its customers. In Exhibit 13–1, we can see that about four out of five wholesaling establishments are merchant wholesalers—and they handle about 58 percent of wholesale sales.

As you might guess based on the large number of merchant wholesalers, they often specialize by certain types of products or customers. They also tend to service relatively small geographic areas. And several wholesalers may be competing for the same customers. For example, restaurants, hotels, and cafeterias purchase about $80 billion worth of food a year—mostly from merchant wholesalers who specialize in food distribution. But, over 3,500 wholesalers share this business. Even the very largest—Sysco Corp, Staley Continental, and Sara Lee's PYA/Monarch—have only about a 3 percent share each.[5]

Merchant wholesalers also differ in how many of the wholesaling functions they provide. There are two basic kinds of merchant wholesalers: (1) service (sometimes called full-service wholesalers) and (2) limited-function or limited-service wholesalers. Their names explain their difference.

Service wholesalers provide all the functions

Service wholesalers provide all the wholesaling functions. Within this basic group are three types: (1) general merchandise, (2) single-line, and (3) specialty.

General merchandise wholesalers are service wholesalers who carry a wide variety of nonperishable items such as hardware, electrical supplies, plumbing supplies, furniture, drugs, cosmetics, and automobile equipment. These wholesalers originally developed to serve the early retailers—the general stores. Now, with their broad line of convenience and shopping products, they serve hardware stores, drugstores, electric appliance shops, and small department stores. In the industrial products field, the *mill supply house* operates in a similar way. A mill supply house carries a broad variety of accessories and supplies for industrial customers.

Single-line (or general-line) wholesalers are service wholesalers who carry a narrower line of merchandise than general merchandise wholesalers. For example, they might carry only food, or wearing apparel, or certain types of industrial tools or supplies. In consumer products, they serve the single- and limited-line stores. In industrial products, they cover a wider geographic area and offer more specialized service.

Specialty wholesalers are service wholesalers who carry a very narrow range of products—and offer more information and service than other service wholesalers. A consumer products specialty wholesaler might carry only health foods or oriental foods instead of a full line of groceries. Or a specialty wholesaler might carry only automotive items and sell exclusively to mass-merchandisers.

Specialty wholesalers often know a great deal about the final target markets in their channel. For example, a mass-merchandiser chain might have automotive items in all of its stores. But the number and types of cars in different geographic areas vary and thus affect what items a particular store will need. There are more Toyotas in Los Angeles—and more Ford pickup trucks in the Midwest. Specialty wholesalers have such information—and they advise the busy store manager about what to stock. Some wholesalers even arrange the stock on the mass-merchandisers' shelves . . . to match the needs of local customers.

An industrial products specialty wholesaler might limit himself to fields requiring special technical knowledge or service—perhaps electronics or plastics. The Cadillac Plastic and Chemical Company in Detroit became a specialty wholesaler serving the needs of both plastics makers and users. Neither the large plastics producers nor the merchant wholesalers with wide lines was able to give technical advice to each of the many customers (who often have little knowledge of which product would be best for them). Cadillac carries 10,000 items and sells to 25,000 customers, ranging in size from very small firms to General Motors.

Limited-function wholesalers provide some functions

Limited-function wholesalers provide only *some* wholesaling functions. Exhibit 13–3 shows the functions typically provided—and not provided. In the following paragraphs, we will discuss the main features of these wholesalers. Some are not very numerous. In fact, they are not counted separately by the U.S. Census Bureau. Nevertheless, these wholesalers are very important for some products.

Exhibit 13–3   Functions Provided by Different Types of Limited-Function Merchant Wholesalers

Functions	Cash-and-Carry	Drop-shipper	Truck	Mail-order	Coopera-tives	Rack jobbers
For customers						
Anticipates needs	X		X	X	X	X
"Regroups" products (one or more of four steps)	X		X	X	X	X
Carries stocks	X		X	X	X	X
Delivers products			X		X	X
Grants credit		X	Maybe	Maybe	Maybe	Consignment (in some cases)
Provides information and advisory services		X	Some	Some	X	
Provides buying function		X	X	X	Some	X
Owns and transfers title to products	X	X	X	X	X	X
For producers						
Provides producers' selling function	X	X	X	X	X	X
Stores inventory	X		X	X	X	X
Helps finance by owning stocks	X		X	X	X	X
Reduces credit risk	X	X	X	X	X	X
Provides market information	X	X	Some	X	X	Some

Cash-and-carry wholesalers want cash

Cash-and-carry wholesalers operate like service wholesalers—except that the customer must pay cash.

Some retailers, such as small auto repair shops, are too small to be served profitably by a service wholesaler. So service wholesalers set a minimum charge—or just refuse to grant credit to a small business that may have trouble paying its bills. Or the wholesaler may set up a cash-and-carry department to supply the small retailer for cash on the counter. The wholesaler can operate at lower cost because the retailers take over many wholesaling functions. And using cash-and-carry outlets may enable the small retailer to stay in business.

Drop-shipper does not handle the products

Drop-shippers own the products they sell—but they do not actually handle, stock, or deliver them. These wholesalers are mainly involved in selling. They get orders—from wholesalers, retailers, or industrial users—and pass these orders on to producers. Then the producer ships the order directly to the customers. Because drop-shippers do not have to handle the products, their operating costs are lower.

Drop-shippers commonly sell products so bulky that additional handling would be expensive and possibly damaging. Also, the quantities they usually sell are so large that there is little need for regrouping—for example, rail-carload shipments of coal, lumber, oil, or chemical products.

Truck wholesalers deliver—at a cost

Truck wholesalers specialize in delivering products that they stock in their own trucks. By handling perishable products in general demand—tobacco, candy, potato chips, and salad dressings—truck wholesalers may provide almost the same functions as full-service wholesalers. Their big advantage is that they deliver perishable products that regular wholesalers prefer not to carry. Some truck wholesalers operate 24 hours a day, every day—and deliver an order within hours. A 7-Eleven store that runs out of potato chips on a busy Friday night doesn't want to be out of stock all weekend!

Truck wholesalers call on many small service stations and "back-alley" garages—providing local delivery of the many small items these customers often forget to pick up from a service wholesaler. Truck wholesalers' operating costs are relatively high because they provide a lot of service.

Mail-order wholesalers reach outlying areas

Mail-order wholesalers sell out of catalogs that may be distributed widely to smaller industrial customers or retailers. These wholesalers operate in the hardware, jewelry, sporting goods, and general merchandise lines. Their markets are often small industrial or retailer customers who might not be called on by other middlemen.[6]

For example, Mountain West—located in Phoenix—uses a catalog to sell a complete line of burglar alarms and other specialized security products to installers and small electronics stores all over the country. Many of these customers—especially those in smaller towns—don't have a local wholesaler.

Producers' cooperatives do sorting

Producers' cooperatives operate almost as full-service wholesalers—with the "profits" going to the cooperative's customer-members. Cooperatives develop in agricultural markets where there are many small producers. Examples of such organizations are Sunkist (citrus fruits), Sunmaid Raisin Growers Association, and Land O'Lakes Creameries, Inc.

Mail-order wholesalers sell out of catalogs—usually to widely spread customers.

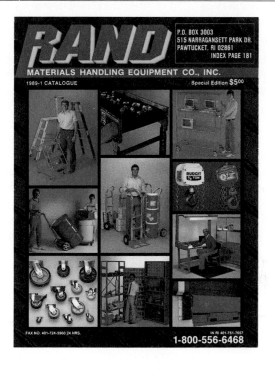

Successful producers' cooperatives emphasize sorting—to improve the quality of farm products offered to the market. Some also brand these improved products—and then promote the brands. For example, the California Almond Growers Exchange has captured most of the retail market with its Blue Diamond brand.

Farmers' cooperatives sometimes succeed in restricting output and increasing price by taking advantage of the normally inelastic demand for agricultural commodities. In most businesses, it is not legal for a wholesaler to arrange for producers to band together to "fix" prices and output in this way. However, for more than 50 years agricultural cooperatives have been specifically excluded from these regulations.[7]

Rack jobbers sell hard-to-handle assortments

Rack jobbers specialize in nonfood products that are sold through grocery stores and supermarkets—and they often display them on their own wire racks. Most grocers don't want to bother with reordering and maintaining displays of nonfood items (housewares, hardware items, and books and magazines) because they sell small quantities of so many different kinds of products. Rack jobbers are almost service wholesalers—except that they usually are paid cash for what is sold or delivered.

This is a relatively expensive operation—with operating costs of about 18 percent of sales. The large volume of sales from these racks has encouraged some large chains to experiment with handling such items themselves. But chains often find that rack jobbers can provide this service as well as—or better than—they can themselves. For example, a rack jobber that wholesales paperback books studies which titles are selling in the local area—and applies that knowledge in many stores. A chain has many stores—but often in different areas where preferences vary. It may not be worth the extra effort for the chain to study the market in each area.

RCA TV Wholesalers Get a Bad Signal

For years, RCA relied on help from merchant wholesalers to distribute TVs to retailers in different regions of the country. With that help RCA had become the best selling TV in the United States. Recently, however, RCA dropped 10 of its 26 independent wholesalers. As a marketing manager for RCA put it, "the cost of maintaining two-step distribution can't be justified anymore." A key reason for the change is that TV retailing is increasingly dominated by big specialty chains such as Circuit City Stores. In addition, mass-merchandisers like Sears and Montgomery Ward are expanding their TV departments. These chains are taking over many of the functions previously performed by the wholesalers—and they want to buy large quantities at low prices direct from the producer.

Without the RCA TVs, many of the wholesalers will go out of business. And without the help of the wholesalers many small retailers will find it even harder to compete with the big chains. In the past, the local wholesaler's truck would deliver an order within a few days. The wholesaler also helped with financing—even on small orders. Now, direct shipments from RCA's distant warehouses may take a month. Thus, the small retailers will need to place larger orders longer in advance—and cope with the cost of carrying more inventory.[8]

AGENT MIDDLEMEN ARE STRONG ON SELLING

They don't own the products

Agent middlemen are wholesalers who do not own the products they sell. Their main purpose is to help in buying and selling. They usually provide even fewer functions than the limited-function wholesalers. In certain trades, however, they are extremely valuable. They may operate at relatively low cost, too—sometimes 2 to 6 percent of their selling price.

Agent middlemen—like merchant wholesalers—normally specialize by customer type and by product or product line. So it's important to determine exactly what each one does.

In the following paragraphs, we will mention only the most important points about each type. Study Exhibit 13–4 for details on the functions provided by each. It is obvious from the number of empty spaces in Exhibit 13–4 that agent middlemen provide fewer functions than merchant wholesalers.

Manufacturers' agents— free-wheeling sales reps

A **manufacturers' agent** sells similar products for several noncompeting producers—for a commission on what is actually sold. Such agents work almost as members of each company's sales force—but they are really independent middlemen. More than half of all agent middlemen are manufacturers' agents.

Their big "plus" is that they already call on some customers and can add another product line at relatively low cost—and at no cost to the producer until something is sold! If an area's sales potential is low, a company may use a manufacturers' agent instead of its own sales rep because the agent can do the job at lower cost. A small producer often has to use agents everywhere because its sales volume is too small or too spread out to justify paying its own sales force.

Manufacturers' agents are very useful in fields where there are many small manufacturers who need to contact customers. These agents are often used in the sale of machinery and equipment, electronic items, automobile products, clothing and apparel accessories, and some food products. They may cover one city or several states.

Exhibit 13–4   Functions Provided by Different Types of Agent Middlemen

Functions	Manufac- turers' agents	Brokers	Com- mission merchants	Selling agents	Auction companies
For customers					
Anticipates needs	Sometimes	Some			
"Regroups" products (one or more of four steps)	Some		X		X
Carries stocks	Sometimes		X		Sometimes
Delivers products	Sometimes		X		
Grants credit			Sometimes	X	Some
Provides information and advisory services	X	X	X	X	
Provides buying function	X	Some	X	X	X
Owns and transfers title to products		Transfers only	Transfers only		
For producer					
Provides selling function	X	Some	X	X	X
Stores inventory	Sometimes		X		X
Helps finance by owning stocks					
Reduces credit risk				X	Some
Provides market information	X	X	X	X	

This agent's main job is selling. The agent—or the agent's customer—sends the orders to the producer. The agent, of course, gets credit for the sale. Agents seldom have any part in setting prices or deciding on the producer's other policies. Basically, they are independent, aggressive salespeople.

Agents can be especially useful in introducing new products. For this service, they may earn 10 to 15 percent commission. (In contrast, their commission on large-volume established products may be quite low—perhaps only 2 percent.) The higher rates for new products often become the agent's major disadvantage for the producer. A 10 to 15 percent commission rate may seem small when a product is new and sales volume is low. Once the product is selling well, the rate seems high. About this time, the producer often begins using its own sales reps—and the manufacturers' agents must look for other new products to sell. Agents are well aware of this possibility. Most try to work for many producers so they aren't dependent on only one or a few lines.

Brokers provide information

Brokers bring buyers and sellers together. Brokers usually have a *temporary* relationship with the buyer and seller while a particular deal is negotiated. Their "product" is information about what buyers need—and what supplies are available. They aid in buyer-seller negotiation. If the transaction is completed, they earn a commission from whichever party hired them.

Usually, some kind of broker will develop whenever and wherever market information is inadequate. Brokers are especially useful for selling seasonal products. For example, brokers may represent a small food canner during the canning season—then go on to other activities.

Some kind of broker will develop whenever and wherever market information is inadequate.

Brokers are also active in sales of used machinery, real estate, and even ships. These products are not similar, but the needed marketing functions are. In each case, buyers don't come into the market often. Someone with knowledge of available products is needed to help both buyers and sellers complete the transaction quickly and inexpensively.

Commission merchants handle and sell products in distant markets

Commission merchants handle products shipped to them by sellers, complete the sale, and send the money—minus their commission—to each seller.

Commission merchants are common in agricultural markets where farmers must ship to big-city central markets. They need someone to handle the products there—as well as to sell them—since the farmer can't go with each shipment. Although commission merchants don't own the products, they generally are allowed to sell them at the market price—or the best price above some stated minimum. Newspapers usually print the prices in these markets, so the producer-seller has a check on the commission merchant. Costs are usually low because commission merchants handle large volumes of products—and buyers usually come to them.

Commission merchants are sometimes used in other trades—such as textiles. Here, many small producers want to reach buyers in a central market without having to maintain their own sales force.

Selling agents—almost marketing managers

Selling agents take over the whole marketing job of producers—not just the selling function. A selling agent may handle the entire output of one or more producers—even competing producers—with almost complete control of pricing, selling, and advertising. In effect, the agent becomes each producer's marketing manager.

Financial trouble is one of the main reasons a producer calls in a selling agent. The selling agent may provide working capital, but may also take over the affairs of the business.

Selling agents are especially common in highly competitive fields—like textiles and coal. They are also used for marketing lumber, certain food products, clothing items, and some metal products. In all these industries, marketing is much more important than production for the survival of firms. The selling agent provides the necessary financial assistance and marketing know-how.

Auction companies—speed up the sale

Auction companies provide a place where buyers and sellers can come together and complete a transaction. Auction companies are not numerous, but they are important in certain lines—such as livestock, fur, tobacco, and used cars. For these products, demand and supply conditions change rapidly—and the product must be seen to be evaluated. Buyers and sellers, therefore, are brought together by the auction company. Then demand and supply interact to determine the price while the products are being inspected.

Facilities can be plain to keep overhead costs low. Frequently, auction sheds are close to transportation sources so that the commodities can be reshipped quickly. The auction company charges a set fee or commission for the use of its facilities and services.

International marketing is not so different

We find agent middlemen in international trade, too. Most operate like those just described. **Export or import agents** are basically manufacturers' agents. **Export or import commission houses** and **export or import brokers** are really brokers. A **combination export manager** is a blend of manufacturers' agent and selling agent—handling the entire export function for several producers of similar but non-competing lines.

Agent middlemen are more common in international trade because financing is often critical. Many markets have only a few well-financed merchant wholesalers. The best many producers can do is get local representation through agents—and then arrange financing through banks that specialize in international trade.

Agent middlemen in overseas markets are usually experts on local business customs and rules concerning imported products. Sometimes it's not even possible for a marketing manager from a U.S. firm to work through a country's government "red tape" without the help of a local agent. Because of the work that this may require, commissions are sometimes quite high compared with those of similar agents in the United States.

Agent middlemen can also help international firms adjust to unfamiliar market conditions in foreign markets. A decade ago Brazilian shoe producers had only a small share of the U.S. footwear market. This was true even though their low labor costs—about 70 cents an hour compared to $6 an hour for American workers—gave them a big cost advantage. And they could produce a quality product. But the Brazilian producers had trouble anticipating rapidly changing American styles. So a number of export agents developed. These specialists traveled in the United States, keeping Brazilian producers informed about style changes. They also helped identify retailers looking for lower prices for fashionable shoes. With this information, Brazilian firms were able to export $850 million worth of shoes to the United States.[9]

MANUFACTURERS' SALES BRANCHES PROVIDE WHOLESALING FUNCTIONS, TOO

Manufacturers' sales branches are separate businesses that producers set up away from their factories. For example, computer producers such as IBM set up local branches to provide service, display equipment, and handle sales. About 9 percent of wholesalers are owned by manufacturers—but they handle 31 percent of total wholesale sales. One reason the sales per branch are so high is that the branches are usually placed in the best market areas. This also helps explain why their operating costs are often lower. But cost comparisons between various channels can be misleading, since sometimes the cost of selling is not charged to the branch. If all the expenses of the manufacturers' sales branches were charged to them, they probably would be more costly than they seem now.

The U.S. Census Bureau collects much data showing the number, kind, location, and operating expenses of manufacturers' sales branches. Such data can help marketers analyze competitors' distribution systems and probable costs. If competitors are using branches, it may mean that no good specialists are available—or at least none who can provide the functions needed.[10]

OTHER SPECIALIZED MIDDLEMEN—FACILITATORS— FILL UNIQUE ROLES

Factors—like a credit department

In competitive markets, producers are often short of cash—working capital—and aren't able to borrow at a bank. So some producers are willing to sell their accounts receivable—for less than the amount due—to get cash quicker and be able to pay their bills on time. To sell its accounts receivable, such a producer might turn to a factor.

Factors are wholesalers of credit. In buying accounts receivable, factors provide their clients with working capital—the financing function. A factor may provide advice on customer selection and collection, too. In effect, the factor may assume the function of a credit department—relieving its clients of this expense.

Field warehousing—cash for products on hand

If a firm has accounts receivable, it can use a factor or even borrow at a bank. But if it has financial problems and its products are not yet sold, then borrowing may be more difficult. Then the company may wish to use a **field warehouser**—a firm that segregates some of a company's finished products on the company's own property and issues warehouse receipts that can be used to borrow money.

In field warehousing, the producer's own warehouse is used to save the expense of moving the goods to another location. But an area is formally segregated by the field warehouser. The producer retains title to the goods, but control of them passes to the field warehouser. A receipt, which can be used as collateral in borrowing, is issued. These field warehousing organizations usually know capital sources—and they may be able to arrange loans at lower cost than is possible locally.

Sales finance companies— do floor planning

Some **sales finance companies** finance inventories. **Floor planning** is the financing of display stocks for auto, appliance, and electronics retailers. Many auto dealers don't own any of the cars on their display floors. They may have only a 10 percent interest in each of them—the other 90 percent belongs to a sales finance company. When they sell a car, the sales finance company gets its share, and the dealer keeps the rest.

In effect, these companies are providing part of the retailer's financing function. But because the products are usually well branded—and therefore easily resold—there is relatively little risk.

WHOLESALERS TEND TO CONCENTRATE TOGETHER

Different wholesalers are found in different places

Some wholesalers—such as grain elevator operators—are located close to producers. But most wholesaling is done in or near large cities. About 40 percent of all wholesale sales are made in the 15 largest Metropolitan Statistical Areas.

This heavy concentration of wholesale sales in large cities is caused, in part, by the concentration of manufacturers' sales offices and branches in these attractive markets. It also is caused by the tendency of agent middlemen to locate in these large cities—near the many large wholesalers and industrial buyers. Some large producers buy for many plants through one purchasing department located in the general offices in these cities. And large general merchandise wholesalers often are located in these transportation and commerce centers. This is true not only in the United States but also in world markets. Wholesalers tend to concentrate together—near transporting, storing, and financing facilities as well as near large populations.

When a number of competing wholesalers are located together, competition can be tough. And channel relations are usually dynamic as producers and middlemen seek lower costs and higher profits.

In 1968, when Sanyo began exporting consumer products to the United States, the company had little brand recognition and no established channels of distribution. Small electronics wholesalers—like Pinros and Gar Corp. in New York City—worked to develop retail customers for Sanyo. By 1984, 90 U.S. wholesalers had helped develop a large market share for Sanyo's audio and video equipment lines. But Sanyo was finding it costly to work with so many wholesalers. So Sanyo selected 20 of its largest wholesalers—in different geographic areas—to handle the job. This move made sense for Sanyo, but the smaller wholesalers—like Pinros and Gar—lost product lines that had generated millions of dollars in sales each

Some progressive wholesalers are using computer-controlled warehouses and automated conveyor systems to reduce costs and improve service to customers.

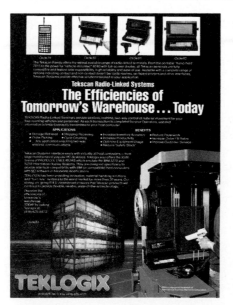

year. Many wholesalers try to protect themselves from such losses by handling competing lines—or by demanding long-term arrangements and exclusive territories.[11]

COMEBACK AND FUTURE OF WHOLESALERS

In the late 1800s, wholesalers held a dominant position in U.S. marketing. The many small producers and small retailers needed their services. As producers became larger, some bypassed the wholesalers. When retail chains also began to spread rapidly, many people predicted a gloomy future for wholesalers. Because chain stores normally assume the wholesaling functions, it was thought that the days of independent wholesalers were numbered.

Not fat and lazy, but enduring

Some analysts and critics felt that the decline of wholesalers might be desirable from a macro point of view because many wholesalers had apparently grown "fat and lazy"—contributing little more than bulk-breaking. Their salespeople were often just order takers. The selling function was neglected. High-caliber management was not attracted to wholesaling.

Our review here, however, shows that wholesaling functions *are* necessary—and wholesalers have not been eliminated. True, their sales volume declined from 1929 to 1939, but wholesalers have since made a comeback. By 1954, they regained the same relative importance they had in 1929—and they continue to hold their own.

Producing profits, not chasing orders

Wholesalers held their own, in part, because of new management and new techniques. To be sure, many still operate in the old ways—and changes in wholesaling have not been as rapid as those in retailing. Yet progressive wholesalers have become more concerned with their customers—and with channel systems. Some are offering more services. Others are developing voluntary chains that bind them more closely to their customers. Their customers' ordering can now be done routinely by telephone—or directly by computer-to-computer hookups.

Some modern wholesalers no longer require all customers to pay for all the services offered simply because certain customers use them. This traditional practice encouraged limited-function wholesalers and direct channels. Now some wholesalers are making a basic service available at a minimum cost—then charging additional fees for any special services required. In the grocery field, for instance, basic servicing might cost the store 3 to 4 percent of wholesale sales. Then promotion assistance and other aids are offered at extra cost.

Most modern wholesalers have streamlined their operations to cut unnecessary costs and improve profits. They use computers to keep track of inventory—and to order new stock only when it is really needed. Computerized sales analysis helps them identify and drop unprofitable products. Wholesalers are also becoming more selective in picking customers. They are using a selective distribution policy—when cost analysis shows that many of their smaller customers are unprofitable. With these less desirable customers gone, wholesalers give more attention to more profitable customers. In this way, they help to promote healthy retailers who are able to compete in any market.

Some wholesalers renamed their salespeople "store advisers" or "supervisors" to reflect their new roles. These representatives provide many management advisory services—including location analysis, store design and modernization, legal assistance on new leases or adjustments in old leases, store-opening services, sales training and merchandising assistance, and advertising help. Such salespeople—who really act as management consultants—must be more competent than the "good ol' boy" order takers of the past.

Progress—or fail

Training a modern wholesaler's sales force isn't easy. It's sometimes beyond the management skills of small wholesale firms. In some fields—such as the plumbing industry—wholesaler trade associations or large suppliers have taken over the job. They organize training programs designed to show the wholesaler's salespeople how they, in turn, can help their customers manage their businesses and promote sales. These programs give instruction in bookkeeping, figuring markups, collecting accounts receivable, advertising, and selling—all in an effort to train the wholesalers' salespeople to improve the effectiveness of other channel members.

Many wholesalers are now modernizing their warehouses and physical handling facilities. Products are marked with bar codes that can be read with hand-held scanners—so inventory, shipping, and sales records can be easily and instantly updated. Computerized order-picking systems speed the job of assembling orders. New storing facilities are carefully located to minimize the costs of both incoming freight and deliveries. Delivery vehicles travel to customers in a computer-selected sequence that reduces the number of miles traveled.

Realizing that their own survival is linked to their customers' survival, some wholesalers offer central bookkeeping facilities for their retailers. Such wholesalers are becoming more channel system minded—they no longer try to overload retail-

Many modern wholesalers now use "bar code" labels that can be quickly read by a computer scanner to constantly update inventory information.

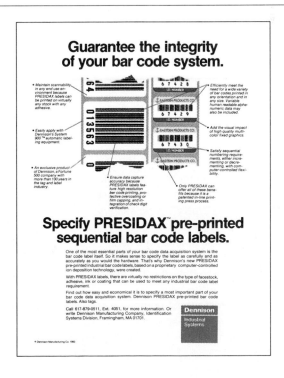

ers' shelves. Now they are trying to clear the merchandise *off* retailers' shelves. They follow the old adage, "Nothing is really sold until it is sold at retail."

Wholesalers are helping retailers reduce costs, too. Retailers can wait until they really need a product to order it—and the order can be instantly placed with a fax machine, toll-free telephone line, or computer hookup.

Perhaps good-bye to some

Not all wholesalers are progressive, however. Some of the smaller, less efficient ones may fail. While the average operating expense ratio is 13 percent for merchant wholesalers, some small wholesalers have expense ratios of 20 to 30 percent or higher.

Low cost, however, is not all that's needed for success. Some wholesalers will disappear as the functions they have provided in the past are shifted and shared in different ways in the channel. Cost-conscious buyers for Wal-Mart, Lowes, and other chains are refusing to deal with some of the middlemen who represent small producers. They want to negotiate directly with the producer—not just accept whatever price has traditionally been available from a wholesaler. Efficient delivery services like UPS and Federal Express are making it easy and inexpensive for many producers to ship directly to their customers. The customer knows that having a wholesaler "down the street" is not the only way to be sure of getting needed orders by 10 o'clock the next morning.

The wholesalers who do survive will need to be efficient, but that does not mean they will all have low costs. The higher operating expenses of some wholesalers are a result of the special services they offer to *some* customers. Truck wholesalers are usually small—and have high operating costs. Yet some customers are willing to pay the higher cost of this service. Although full-service wholesalers may seem expensive, some will continue operating because they offer the wholesaling functions and sales contacts some small producers need.

To survive, each wholesaler must develop a good marketing strategy. Profit margins are not large in wholesaling—typically ranging from less than 1 percent to 2 percent. And they have been declining in recent years as the competitive squeeze has tightened.

Wholesaling will last—but weaker, less progressive wholesalers may not.[12]

CONCLUSION

Wholesalers can provide functions for those both above and below them in a channel of distribution. These services are closely related to the basic marketing functions. There are many types of wholesalers. Some provide all the wholesaling functions—while others specialize in only a few. Eliminating wholesalers would not eliminate the need for the functions they provide. And we cannot assume that direct channels will be more efficient.

Merchant wholesalers are the most numerous and account for just over half of wholesale sales. Their distinguishing characteristic is that they take title to (own) products. Agent middlemen, on the other hand, act more like sales representatives for sellers or buyers—and they do not take title.

Despite various predictions of the end of wholesalers, they continue to exist. And the more progressive ones have adapted to a changing environment. Wholesaling hasn't experienced the revolutions we saw in retailing, and none seem likely. But some smaller—and less progressive—wholesalers will probably fail, while larger and more market-oriented wholesalers will continue to provide these necessary functions.

Questions and Problems

1. Discuss the evolution of wholesaling in relation to the evolution of retailing.

2. Does a wholesaler need to worry about new-product planning, just as a producer needs to have an organized new-product development process? Explain your answer.

3. What risks do merchant wholesalers assume by taking title to goods? Is the size of this risk about constant for all merchant wholesalers?

4. Why would a manufacturer set up its own sales branches if established wholesalers were already available?

5. What is an agent middleman's marketing mix? Why do you think that many merchant middlemen handle competing products from different producers, while manufacturers' agents usually handle only noncompeting products from different producers?

6. Discuss the future growth and nature of wholesaling if low-margin retailing and scrambled merchandising become more important. How will wholesalers have to adjust their mixes if retail establishments become larger and the retail managers more professional? Will wholesalers be eliminated? If not, what wholesaling functions will be most important? Are there any particular lines of trade where wholesalers may have increasing difficulty?

7. Which types of wholesalers would be most appropriate for the following products? If more than one type of wholesaler could be used, describe each situation carefully. For example, if size or financial strength of a company has a bearing, then so indicate. If several wholesalers could be used in this same channel, explain this, too.
   a. Women's shoes.
   b. Fresh peaches.
   c. Machines to glue packing boxes.
   d. Auto mechanics' tools.
   e. An industrial accessory machine.
   f. Used construction equipment.
   g. Shoelaces.

8. Would a drop-shipper be desirable for the following products: coal, lumber, iron ore, sand and gravel, steel, furniture, or tractors? Why or why not? What channels might be used for each of these products if drop-shippers were not used?

9. Explain how field warehousing could help a marketing manager.

10. Discuss some of the ways in which use of computer systems affect wholesalers' operations.

11. Which types of wholesalers are likely to become more important in the next 25 years? Why?

Suggested Cases

17. National Sales Company

19. Nelson Company

Suggested Computer-Aided Problem

13. Merchant versus Agent Wholesaler

Chapter 14

Physical Distribution

When You Finish This Chapter, You Should

1. Understand why physical distribution (PD) is such an important part of Place *and* marketing.

2. Understand why the PD customer service level is a marketing strategy variable.

3. Know about the advantages and disadvantages of the various transporting methods.

4. Know what storing possibilities a marketing manager can use.

5. Understand the distribution center concept.

6. Understand the physical distribution concept and why it requires coordination of storing and transporting.

7. See how computers are being used to improve transporting and storing decisions.

8. Understand the important new terms (shown in red).

Customers don't want excuses—they want products available when and where they need them.

About 30 years ago, Ralph Ketner opened a typical small town grocery store in Salisbury, North Carolina. He had a dream of lower food prices for all consumers. Ketner's dream grew into Food Lion—one of the fastest growing supermarket chains in the United States—because he did cut costs and prices.

Ketner realized that the high costs of storing and transporting affected what his customers had to pay for groceries. As he added stores, Ketner set up a large, centrally located and computer-controlled warehouse—a distribution center. With this approach, he was able to get price breaks from suppliers by ordering in large quantities. And he saved on transporting costs by using economical railroad deliveries direct to his distribution center. Since Ketner was a big customer, he could demand "on schedule" deliveries from suppliers. Then he used his own trucks to speed the flow of food to his stores. "Hidden costs"—like the cost of holding inventory and the cost of spoiled produce—were reduced. Computer scanners at checkout counters tracked sales so that fast-moving items could be reordered just in time—before they ran out. And less popular sizes and brands that sat on store shelves were eliminated, so turnover and profits would grow. Ketner passed some of the savings on to his customers as lower prices. And the customers responded—speeding his growth and expansion.

Where he opened stores, small competitors went out of business. And bigger competitors—like A&P and Kroger—saw that they had a simple choice: losing customers—and profits—or copying Ketner's methods and offering their own customers lower prices.[1]

This case shows how important *physical distribution* is to individual firms—and to the whole macro-marketing system. The many challenges and opportunities in this area are the focus of this chapter.

PHYSICAL DISTRIBUTION GETS IT TO CUSTOMERS

Choosing the right channel of distribution is crucial in getting products to the target market's Place. But that alone is usually not enough to assure that products are available at the right time and in the right quantities. Whenever the product includes a physical good, Place requires physical distribution decisions. **Physical distribution (PD)** is the transporting and storing of goods to match target customers' needs with a firm's marketing mix—both within individual firms and along a channel of distribution.

Nearly half of the cost of marketing is spent on PD activities. They are very important to the firm—and to the macro-marketing system. Possession utility is not possible until time and place utility have been provided.

From the beginning, we've emphasized that marketing strategy planning is based on meeting customers' needs. Planning for physical distribution is no exception. So let's start by looking at PD through a customer's eyes.

Customers want products— not excuses

Customers don't care how a product was moved or stored—or what some channel member had to do to provide it. Rather, customers think in terms of the PD **customer service level**—how rapidly and dependably a firm can deliver what they—the customers—want. Marketing managers need to understand the customer's point of view.

Fast and reliable delivery is important to many customers.

Here's something that will help everyone sleep better. Except our competition.

At UPS, we have something that will help assure you a restful night's sleep when it comes to overnight delivery.

It's guaranteed UPS Next Day Air.®

For some time UPS has been the only company fast and reliable enough to deliver overnight to every single address coast to coast. And we guarantee it, or you don't pay for it.

What's more, we'll even guarantee delivery in the morning to the vast majority of people across the country.

And because of our efficiency, we're still able to do all of this for up to half what other companies charge.

All of which is guaranteed to give our competition a restless night's sleep.

And you a comfortable one.

We run the tightest ship in the shipping business.

What does this really mean? It means that Toyota wants to have enough wind-shields delivered to make cars *that* day—not late so production stops *or* early so there are a lot of extras to move around or store. It means that a business executive who rents a car from Avis wants it to be ready when he gets off the plane. It means you want your Lay's potato chips to be whole when you buy a bag at the snack bar—not crushed into crumbs from rough handling in a warehouse.

Physical distribution should be invisible

PD is—and should be—a part of marketing that is "invisible" to most customers. PD only gets the customer's attention when something goes wrong. At that point, it may be too late to do anything that will keep a customer happy.

Usually we don't think much about physical distribution. This probably means that our market-directed macro-marketing system works pretty well—that a lot of individual marketing managers have made good decisions in this area. But it doesn't mean that the decisions are always clear-cut or simple. In fact, many "trade-offs" may be required.

Trade-offs of costs, service, and sales

Most physical distribution decisions involve trade-offs between costs, customer service level, and sales. If the customer service level is wrong—if product availability is not dependable or timely—customers will buy elsewhere and profits will be lost. If you want the current top-selling CD and the store where you usually go doesn't have it, you're likely to buy it elsewhere. Perhaps the first store could keep your business by guaranteeing one-day delivery of your CD—using special delivery from the supplier. In this case, the manager is trading the cost of storing a large inventory for the extra cost of speedy delivery.

Either way, providing a higher service level will increase PD costs. The higher cost of PD may result in a higher price to the customer. Or the store may hope that the better service will greatly increase the quantity sold at the usual price. But, either approach will reduce profits if the service level is higher than customers want or are willing to pay for. Exhibit 14–1 illustrates these relationships.

Exhibit 14–1   Trade-Offs among Physical Distribution Costs, Customer Service Level, and Sales

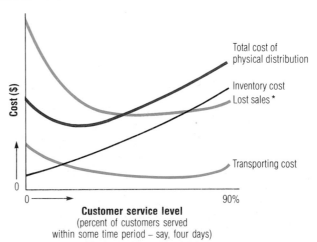

*Note: Sales may be lost because of poor customer service or because of the high price charged to pay for too high a customer service level.

The important point is that trade-offs must be made in the PD area. The lowest-cost approach may not be best—if customers aren't satisfied. A higher service level may make a better strategy. Further, if different channel members or target markets want different customer service levels, several different strategies may be needed.[2]

Now that you see why PD and the customer service level are an important part of Place—and whole marketing strategies—let's look more closely at some of these PD decisions.

DECIDING WHO WILL HAUL AND STORE IS STRATEGIC

Functions can be shifted and shared

As a marketing manager develops the Place part of a strategy, it is important to decide how transporting and storing functions can and should be divided within the channel. Who will store and transport the goods—and who will pay for these services? Who will coordinate all of the PD activities?

Just deciding to use certain types of wholesalers or retailers doesn't automatically—or completely—answer these questions. A wholesaler may use its own trucks to haul goods from a producer to its warehouse and from there to retailers—but only because the manufacturer gives a transportation allowance. Another wholesaler may want the goods delivered.

PD decisions affect the rest of a strategy

When developing a marketing strategy, the marketing manager must decide how these functions are to be shared since this will affect the other three Ps—especially Price. There is no "right" sharing arrangement. Physical distribution can be varied endlessly in a marketing mix and in a channel system. And note that competitors may share these functions in different ways—with different costs.

PD decisions are important because they can make (or break) a strategy. Channel Master—a firm making inexpensive "rabbit ear" TV antennas—illustrates these ideas. The growth of cable TV was hurting sales. So the firm developed a new product—a large dish-like antenna used by motels to receive HBO and other TV signals from satellites. The product looked like it could be a big success, but the small company didn't have the money to invest in a large inventory. So Channel Master decided to work only with wholesalers who were willing to buy (and pay for) several units—to be used for demonstrations and to ensure that buyers got immediate delivery.

In the first few months, the firm had a hefty $2 million in sales. Channel Master recovered its development cost just providing inventory for the channel. And the wholesalers paid the interest cost of carrying inventory—over $300,000 the first year. Here, the wholesalers helped share the risk of the new venture—but it was a good decision for them, too. They won many sales from a competing channel whose customers had to wait several months for delivery. And, because Channel Master was the first to sell these middlemen, it became a market leader.

THE TRANSPORTING FUNCTION—ADDS VALUE

Transporting aids economic development and exchange

Transporting is the marketing function of moving goods. It provides time and place utilities. However, the value added to products by moving them must be greater than the cost of the transporting—or there is little reason to ship in the first place.

Many firms have their own truck fleets.

Transporting can help achieve economies of scale in production. If production costs can be reduced by producing larger quantities in one location, these savings may more than offset the added cost of transporting the finished products to customers.

The value added by transporting is clearly illustrated by what happened after the introduction of the first practical steam locomotive in 1829. In the United States, the railroads made it possible to ship midwest farm products to eastern industrial areas—dramatically lowering food prices. Even after adding the cost of transporting, it was cheaper to grow food in the fertile plains and transport it to the East than to try to grow the same products locally. Today, without transporting, there could be no mass distribution with its regrouping activities—or any urban life as we know it.[3]

Transporting can be costly

Transporting costs may limit the target markets that a marketing manager can consider. Shipping costs increase delivered cost—and that's what really interests customers. Transport costs add little to the cost of products that are already valuable relative to their size and weight. But transporting costs can be a large part of the total cost for heavy products of low value—like many minerals and raw materials. This is illustrated in Exhibit 14–2, which shows transporting costs as a percent of total sales dollars for several products.[4]

There used to be many regulations

Until the 1980s, the government had a lot of control over transporting. Routes had to be approved by the government—as did rates and services. Because of these rates, carriers typically did not compete on Price. And some carriers were approved to carry some products but not others.

All of this caused higher prices and much waste. For example, the rules required a carrier that took Cummins diesel engines from the Midwest to California to

Exhibit 14–2   Transporting Costs as a Percent of Selling Price for Different Products

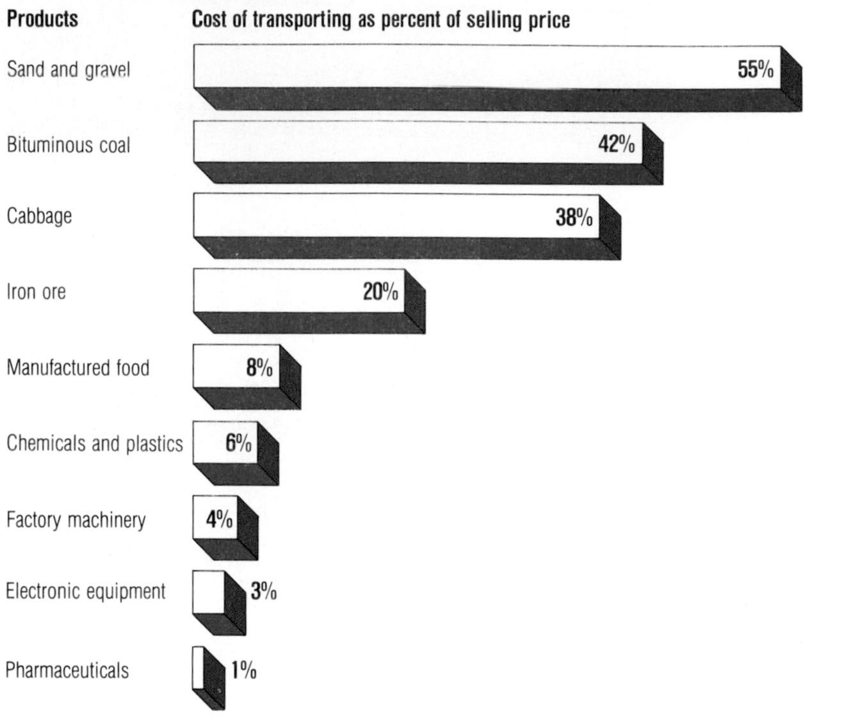

Products	Cost of transporting as percent of selling price
Sand and gravel	55%
Bituminous coal	42%
Cabbage	38%
Iron ore	20%
Manufactured food	8%
Chemicals and plastics	6%
Factory machinery	4%
Electronic equipment	3%
Pharmaceuticals	1%

use an extra long route going out—and to make the return trip empty. Other carriers took California vegetables to the Midwest—and they too went home empty.

Now you have more transporting choices

Today, most of the rules have been relaxed. A marketing manager generally has many carriers in one or more modes competing for the firm's transporting business. Or a firm can do its own transporting. So knowing about the different modes is important.[5]

FIVE MODES OF TRANSPORTATION CARRY THE LOAD

There are five basic modes of freight movement: railroads, trucks, waterways, pipelines, and airplanes.

Railroads—workhorse of the nation

A common measure of the importance of various transportation methods is ton-miles carried. A **ton-mile** means the movement of 2,000 pounds (one ton) of goods one mile. If, for example, 10 tons of sand were carried 10 miles, the total movement would be 100 ton-miles. Exhibit 14–3 shows the annual ton-miles of intercity freight moved in the United States by each mode. It also shows that freight volume carried by each mode has grown dramatically since 1960.

Exhibit 14–3 shows that railways are the workhorse of the U.S. transportation system. Following in importance are trucks, pipelines, and barges. Relatively speaking, airplanes don't move much freight. While the railroads still account for the largest share (36 percent) of ton-miles, the exhibit shows that *growth* in the other modes—especially trucks and airplanes—has been rapid since 1960.

Exhibit 14–3   Intercity Freight Movement in the United States, 1960 and 1986

Total intercity
ton miles
(billions)

■	1960
■	1986

(36%)
896

(44%)
579

(25%)
627

(22%)
285

(16%)
393

(23%)
579

(17%)
220

(17%)
229

(.07%)
.9

(.24%)
7

Rail   Truck   Inland waterways   Pipelines   Airways

But goods keep on truckin'—part of the way

Looking only at ton-miles, however, does not tell the whole story. At least 75 percent of all freight moves by trucks—at least part of the way from producer to user. Trucks haul the bulk of short-haul cargo. The trucking industry slogan: "If you have it, it came by truck," is certainly true for consumer products—although many industrial products are still delivered by railroads or other transporting modes.

WHICH TRANSPORTING ALTERNATIVE IS BEST?

Transporting function must fit the whole strategy

The transporting function should fit into the whole marketing strategy. But picking the best transporting alternative can be difficult. What is "best" depends on the product, other physical distribution decisions, and what service level the company wants to offer. The best alternative should not only be as low-cost as possible, but also provide the level of service (for example, speed and dependability) required. See Exhibit 14–4. The exhibit makes it clear that different modes have different strengths and weaknesses.[6] It is important to see that low transporting cost is *not* the only criterion for selecting the best mode.

Railroads—large loads moved at low cost

The railroads are important mainly for carrying heavy and bulky goods—such as raw materials, steel, chemicals, cars, canned goods, and machines—over long distances. By handling large quantities, the railroads are able to transport at relatively low cost. For example, the average cost to ship by rail runs about 3 to 4 cents per ton-mile.

Railroad freight moves more slowly than truck shipments. Thus it is not as well suited for perishable items or those in urgent demand. Railroads are most efficient at handling full carloads of goods. Less-than-carload (LCL) shipments take a lot of handling and rehandling, which means they usually move more slowly and at a higher price per pound than carload shipments.

Exhibit 14–4   Relative Benefits of Different Transport Modes

Mode \ Transporting features	Cost per ton mile	Door-to-door delivery speed	Number of locations served	Ability to handle variety of goods	Frequency of scheduled shipments	Dependability in meeting schedules
Rail	light	light	best	best	medium	light
Water	best	medium	medium	best	worst	light
Truck	light	good	best	light	good	good
Pipeline	good	worst	worst	worst	best	good
Air	worst	best	light	medium	medium	worst

Scale: Worst (○ white) → Best (● dark)

Competition has forced railroads to innovate

Railroads had low profits for many years—in part because trucks took a large share of the most profitable business. Now railroads are cutting costs to improve profits. Relaxed government regulations have helped. Many railroads have merged to reduce overlap in equipment—and routes. And they have increased prices where competition from truck and water transport is weak.

Railroads are also catering to the needs of new target customers with a variety of specially designed railcars.[7]

To offset the shortcomings of low speed and high cost—and still encourage the business of small shippers—some railroads encourage **pool car service**, which allows groups of shippers to pool their shipments of like goods into a full car. Sometimes local retailers buying from a single area such as Los Angeles combine their shipments in single cars. Local truckers then deliver the goods when they arrive. When different commodities are shipped in the same car, it is called a *mixed car* rather than a pool car—and the highest rate for any of the commodities applies to the whole shipment.

Another example of a special railroad service is **diversion in transit**, which allows redirection of carloads already in transit. A Florida grower can ship a carload of oranges toward the Northeast as soon as they are ripe. While they head north, the grower can find a buyer or identify the market with the best price. Then—for a small fee—the railroad reroutes the car to this destination.

Trucks are more expensive, but flexible and essential

The flexibility of trucks makes them better at moving small quantities of goods for shorter distances. They can travel on almost any road. They go where the rails can't. And, by using the interstate highway system, trucks can give extremely fast service. Truckers also compete with railroads for the high-value items in somewhat the same way retailers compete in "scrambled merchandising." This is reflected in their rates, which average about 13 cents per ton-mile.

Critics complain that trucks congest traffic and damage highways. But trucks are essential to our present macro-marketing system.[8]

Railroads and their suppliers have introduced many specialized new services to better serve transporting needs.

Ship it overseas— but slowly

Water transportation is the slowest shipping mode—but it is usually the lowest-cost way of shipping heavy freight. Water transportation is very important for international shipments. Often it is the only practical approach. This explains why port cities like Boston, New York, New Orleans, and Los Angeles are important centers for international trade.

Inland waterways are important, too

In the United States, the inland waterways (like the Great Lakes and Mississippi River) are used mostly for bulky, nonperishable products—such as iron ore, grain, steel, petroleum products, cement, gravel, sand, and coal. When winter ice closes freshwater harbors, alternate transportation must be used. Some shippers—such as those moving iron ore—ship their total annual supply during the summer months and store it near their production facilities for winter use. Here, low-cost transporting combined with storing reduces *total* cost.

Pipelines move oil and gas

In the United States, pipelines are used primarily by the petroleum industry to move oil and natural gas. Only a few cities in the United States are more than 200 miles from a major pipeline system. Of course, the majority of the pipelines are in the Southwest—connecting the oil fields and refineries. From there, the more flexible railroads, trucks, and ships usually take over—bringing refined and graded products to customers.

Airfreight is expensive but fast

The most expensive cargo transporting mode is airplane—but it is fast! Airfreight rates normally are at least twice as high as trucking rates—but the greater

Water transportation is slow—but it's very important for international shipments.

speed may offset the added cost. Trucks took the cream of the railroads' traffic. Now airplanes are taking the cream of the cream.

High-value, low-weight goods—like high-fashion clothing and industrial parts for the electronics and metal-working industries—are often shipped by air. Airfreight is also creating new transporting business. Perishable products that previously could not be shipped are now being flown across continents and oceans. Tropical flowers from Hawaii, for example, now are jet-flown to points all over the United States. And airfreight is also becoming very important for small emergency deliveries—like repair parts, special orders, and business documents that "absolutely" need to be there the next day.

But airplanes may cut the total cost of distribution

An important advantage of using planes is that the cost of packing, unpacking, and preparing the goods for sale may be reduced or eliminated. Planes may help a firm reduce inventory costs by eliminating outlying warehouses. Valuable by-products of airfreight's speed are less spoilage, theft, and damage. Although the *transporting* cost of air shipments may be higher, the *total* cost of distribution may be lower. As more firms realize this, airfreight firms—like Federal Express, Airborne, and Emery Air Freight—are enjoying rapid growth.[9]

Put it in a container— and move between modes easily

We've described the modes separately. But products are often moved by several different modes and carriers during their journey. This is especially common for international shipments. Japanese firms—like Panasonic—ship stereos to the United States and Canada by boat. When they arrive on the West Coast, they are loaded on trains and sent across the country. Then, the units are delivered to a wholesaler by truck or rail. Loading and unloading the goods several times used to be a real problem. Parts of a shipment would become separated, damaged, or even stolen. And handling the goods—perhaps many times—raised costs and slowed delivery.

CSX uses satellite communications to keep tabs on every container as it moves between different transportation modes.

Many of the these problems are reduced with **containerization**—grouping individual items into an economical shipping quantity and sealing them in protective containers for transit to the final destination. This protects the products and simplifies handling during shipping. Some containers are as large as truck bodies.

Piggyback—a ride on two modes

This idea is also carried further. **Piggyback service** loads truck trailers—or flatbed trailers carrying containers—on railcars to provide both speed and flexibility. Railroads now pick up truck trailers at the producer's location, load them onto specially designed rail flatcars, and haul them as close to the customer as rail lines run. The trailers are then hooked up to a truck tractor and delivered to the buyer's door. Similar services are offered on ocean-going ships—allowing door-to-door service between the United States and foreign cities.

ECONOMIES OF SCALE IN TRANSPORTING

Most transporting rates—the prices charged for transporting—are based on the idea that large quantities of a good can be shipped at a lower transport cost per pound than small quantities. Whether a furniture producer sends a truck to deliver one sofa or a full carload, the company still has to pay for the driver, the truck, the gas, and other expenses like insurance.

Transporters often give much lower rates for quantities that make efficient use of their transport facilities. Thus, transport costs per pound for less-than-full carloads or truckloads are often twice as high as for full loads. These quantity rate differences are another reason for the development of wholesalers. They buy in large quantities to get the advantage of economies of scale in transporting. Then they sell in the smaller quantities their customers need.

Freight forwarders accumulate economical shipping quantities

Freight forwarders combine the small shipments of many shippers into more economical shipping quantities. Freight forwarders do not own their own transporting facilities—except perhaps for delivery trucks. Rather, they wholesale air, ship, rail, and truck space. They accumulate small shipments from many shippers and reship in larger quantities to obtain lower transporting rates.

Many marketing managers regularly use freight forwarders to make the best use of available transporting facilities. Freight forwarders can be especially helpful to a marketing manager who ships many small shipments to foreign markets. They handle an estimated 75 percent of the general cargo shipped from U.S. ports to foreign countries.[10]

Should you do it yourself?

To cut transporting costs, some marketing managers do their own transporting rather than buy from specialists. Large producers, like Levi Strauss, often buy or lease their own truck fleets. Shell Oil and other large petroleum, iron ore, and gypsum rock producers have their own ships. Some firms now buy their own planes for airfreight.

Deregulation is enabling more firms to "do it themselves." Before deregulation, it was often more costly for a firm to use its own trucks. The company could truck its products to customers in distant markets, but the government rules often required that the trucks come back empty. Now a company with its own trucks can contract with noncompeting firms to bring their products back on the return trip. The extra revenue reduces the firm's own transporting costs.[11]

THE STORING FUNCTION

Store it and smooth out sales, increase profits and consumer satisfaction

Storing is the marketing function of holding goods. It provides time utility. **Inventory** is the amount of goods being stored.

Storing is necessary when production of goods doesn't match consumption. This is common with mass production. U. S. Steel, for example, might produce thousands of steel bars of one size before changing the machines to produce another size. Changing the production line can be costly and time-consuming. It is often cheaper to produce large quantities of one size—and store the unsold quantity—than to have shorter production runs. Thus, storing goods allows the producer to achieve economies of scale in production.

Storing helps keep prices steady

Some products—such as agricultural commodities—can only be produced seasonally although they are in demand year-round. If crops could not be stored when they mature, all of the crop would be thrown onto the market—and prices might drop sharply. Consumers might benefit temporarily from this "surplus." But later in the year—when supplies were scarce and prices high—they would suffer. Storing thus helps stabilize prices during the consumption period—although prices usually do rise slightly over time to cover storing costs.

Some buyers purchase in large quantities to get quantity discounts from the producer or transporter. Then, the extra goods must be stored until there is demand. And goods are sometimes stored as a hedge against future price rises, strikes, shipping interruptions, and other disruptions.

Holly Farms Gets Egg on Its Face

Holly Farms's marketing managers thought that a new, preroasted chicken product was just the ticket for today's busy consumers. It was a big success in a year of test marketing in Atlanta. But Holly Farms had to revise its strategy when it tried national distribution. As with other perishable food products, the Holly Farm label indicated a date by which the chicken should be sold. Many grocers refused to buy the roast chicken because they worried that they had only a few days after it was delivered to sell it. Shelf life had not been a problem with Holly Farms's raw chicken. It sold in higher volume and moved off shelves more quickly.

The source of the problem was that it took nine days to ship the roast chicken from the plant in North Carolina to stores around the country. Coupled with slow turnover, that didn't leave grocers enough selling time. To address the problem, Holly Farms developed new packaging that allowed grocers to store the chicken longer. Holly Farms also shifted its promotion budget to put more emphasis on in-store promotions to speed up sales once the chicken arrived. To give grocers even more flexibility, Holly Farms is considering separate transportation arrangements for its roast chicken and raw chicken.[12]

Storing varies the channel system

Storing allows producers and middlemen to keep stocks at convenient locations—ready to meet customers' needs. In fact, storing is one of the major activities of some middlemen.

Most channel members provide the storing function for some length of time. Even final consumers store some things for their future needs. Since storing can be provided anywhere along the channel, the storing function offers several ways to vary a firm's marketing mix—and its channel system—by (1) adjusting the time goods are held, (2) sharing the storing costs, and (3) delegating the job to a specialized storing facility. This latter variation would mean adding another member to the distribution channel.

Which channel members store the product—and for how long—affects the behavior of all channel members. For example, the producer of Snapper Lawnmowers tries to get wholesalers to inventory a wide selection of its machines. That way, retailers can carry smaller inventories since they can be sure of dependable local supplies. And they might decide to sell Snapper—rather than Toro or some other brand that they would have to store at their own expense.

If final customers "store" the product, more of it may be used or consumed. Soft-drink producers like Pepsi know this so they offer six packs and two-liter bottles. They want customers to have an "inventory" in the refrigerator when thirst hits.

Goods are stored at a cost

Storing can increase the value of goods—and make them more available when customers want them. But a manager must remember that *storing always involves costs,* too. Car dealers, for example, must store cars on their lots—waiting for the right customer. If a new car on the lot is dented or scratched, there is a repair cost. If a car isn't sold before the new models come out, its value drops. There is also a risk of fire or theft—so the retailer must carry insurance. And, of course, there is the cost of leasing or owning the display lot where the cars are stored. All of these costs add to the expense of maintaining inventory—to provide the kind of service customers expect.[13]

SPECIALIZED STORING FACILITIES CAN BE VERY HELPFUL

New cars can be stored outside on the dealer's lot. Fuel oil can be stored in a specially designed tank. Coal and other raw materials can be stored in open pits. But most products must be stored inside protective buildings. Often, there are choices among different types of specialized storing facilities. The right choice may reduce costs—and serve customers better.

Private warehouses are common

Private warehouses are storing facilities owned or leased by companies for their own use. Most manufacturers, wholesalers, and retailers have some storing facilities either in their main buildings or in a warehouse district. A sales manager often is responsible for managing a manufacturer's finished-goods warehouse—especially if sales branches are located away from the factory. In retailing, storing is so closely tied to selling that the buyers may control this function.

Private warehouses are used when a large volume of goods must be stored regularly. Private warehouses can be expensive, however. If the need changes, the extra space may be hard—or impossible—to rent to others.

Public warehouses fill special needs

Public warehouses are independent storing facilities. They can provide all the services that a company's own warehouse can provide. A company might choose a public warehouse if it doesn't have a regular need for space. For example, Tonka Toys uses public warehouses because its business is seasonal. Tonka pays for the space only when it is used. Public warehouses are also useful for manufacturers who must maintain stocks in many locations—including foreign countries.

Public warehouses are located in all major metropolitan areas and many smaller cities. Many rural towns also have public warehouses for locally produced agricultural commodities. See Exhibit 14–5 for a comparison of private and public warehouses.[14]

Exhibit 14–5   A Comparison of Private Warehouses and Public Warehouses

Characteristics / Type of Warehouse	Private	Public
Fixed investment	Very high	No fixed investment
Unit cost	High if volume is low. Very low if volume is very high	Low: charges are made only for space needed
Control	High	Low managerial control
Adequacy for product line	Highly adequate	May not be convenient
Flexibility	Low: fixed costs have already been committed	High: easy to end arrangement

**Warehousing facilities
have modernized**

The cost of physical handling is a major storing cost. Goods must be handled once when put into storage—and again when removed to be sold. Further, especially in the typical old "downtown" warehouse districts, traffic congestion, crowded storage areas, and slow elevators delay the process—and increase the costs.

Today, modern one-story buildings are replacing the old multistory warehouses. They are located away from downtown traffic. They eliminate the need for elevators—and permit the use of power-operated lift trucks, battery-operated motor scooters, roller-skating order pickers, electric hoists for heavy items, and hydraulic ramps to speed loading and unloading. Most of these new warehouses use lift trucks and pallets (wooden "trays" that carry many cases) for vertical storage and better use of space. Computers monitor inventory, order needed stock, and track storing and shipping costs. Some warehouses even have computer-controlled order picking systems that speed the process of locating and assembling the assortment required to fill a particular order.[15]

THE DISTRIBUTION CENTER—A DIFFERENT KIND OF WAREHOUSE

Is storing really needed?

Discrepancies of assortment or quantity between one channel level and another are often adjusted at the place where goods are stored. It reduces handling costs to regroup and store at the same place—*if both functions are required.* But sometimes regrouping is required when storing isn't.

Don't store it, distribute it

A **distribution center** is a special kind of warehouse designed to speed the flow of goods and avoid unnecessary storing costs. Anchor Hocking moves over a million pounds of its housewares products through its distribution center each day. Faster inventory turnover and easier bulk-breaking reduce the cost of carrying inventory. This is important. These costs may run as high as 35 percent a year of

The Best Buy retail chain built a new 400,000-square-foot distribution center to speed the flow of products from different producers to its 40 stores in an eight-state market area.

the value of the average inventory. The lower costs and faster turnover lead to bigger profits.

Today, the distribution center concept is widely used by firms at all channel levels. But the basic benefits of this approach are still the same as they were over 20 years ago when the idea was pioneered. In fact, a good way to see how the distribution center works is to consider an early application.

Pillsbury's distribution system was overwhelmed by expanding product lines and sales

Pillsbury—the manufacturer of baking products—used to ship in carload quantities directly from its factories to large middlemen. Initially, plants were as close to customers as possible, and each plant produced the whole Pillsbury line. As lines expanded, however, no single plant could produce all the various products. When customers began to ask for mixed carload shipments and faster delivery, Pillsbury added warehouse space—and started hauling goods from plant to plant. Over time, Pillsbury set up 100 branch warehouses—controlled by 33 sales offices. Accounting, credit, and other processing operations were duplicated in each sales office. PD costs were high, but the customer service level was still a problem. It took Pillsbury a week just to process an order. And the company had no effective control over its inventories. Pillsbury needed a change to distribution centers.

The distribution center brings it all together

Pillsbury first specialized production at each plant to a few product lines. Then Pillsbury sent carload shipments directly to the distribution centers—almost eliminating storing at the factories. The distribution centers were controlled by four regional data processing centers, which quickly determined where and when goods were to be shipped. Centralized accounting got invoices to customers faster—resulting in quicker payment. Because each distribution center always had adequate inventory, it could ship orders the most economical way. And because the field sales organization no longer handled physical distribution or inventory, it could focus on sales. Pillsbury could guarantee customers delivery within three days.

There are many variations of the distribution center. The Pillsbury example shows it within an integrated operation. But public warehouses offer similar services.

PHYSICAL DISTRIBUTION CONCEPT FOCUSES ON THE WHOLE DISTRIBUTION SYSTEM

Partly to simplify discussion we've talked about the transporting and storing functions as if they were separate activities. In our examples, however, it's obvious that they are related. In fact, the transporting and storing functions often affect other areas of the firm, too—as we saw in the Pillsbury case. Recognizing how these areas relate leads us to think about the *whole* physical distribution function.

Physical distribution concept—an idea for now

The **physical distribution (PD) concept** says that all transporting and storing activities of a business and a channel system should be coordinated as one system—which should seek to minimize the cost of distribution for a given customer service level. It may be hard to see this as a startling development. But until just a few years ago, even the most progressive companies treated PD functions as separate and unrelated activities.

Firms spread the responsibility for different distribution activities among various departments—production, shipping, sales, warehousing, and others. No one person was responsible for coordinating storing and shipping decisions—or for seeing how they related to customer service levels. Sometimes the costs for these activities were not even calculated. And the *total* cost of physical distribution was not obvious. This is still the case in many firms.[16]

Focusing on individual functional activities may actually increase total distribution costs for the firm—and even for the whole channel. It may also lead to the wrong customer service level.

Decide what service level to offer

With the physical distribution concept, a firm decides what aspects of service are most important to its customers—and what specific service level to provide. Increasing service levels may be very profitable in highly competitive situations where the firm has little else to differentiate its marketing mix. Dow Chemical sells homogeneous basic chemicals that are also sold by many other suppliers. Increasing the service level—perhaps through faster delivery or wider stocks—might allow Dow to make headway in a market without changing Product, Price, or Promotion. Competitors might not realize what has happened—or that Dow's improved customer service level makes its marketing mix better.

What aspects of customer service are most important depend on target market needs. Xerox might focus on how long it takes to deliver copy machine repair parts once it receives an order. When a copier breaks down, customers want the repair "yesterday." The service level might be stated as "we will deliver emergency repair parts within 24 hours." Such a service level might require that almost all such parts be kept in inventory, that order processing be very fast, and that the parts be sent by airfreight. Obviously, supplying this service level will affect the total cost of the PD system. But it may also beat competitors who don't provide this service level.[17]

Finding the lowest total cost for the right service level

In selecting a PD system, the **total cost approach** involves evaluating each possible PD system—and identifying *all* of the costs of each alternative. This approach uses the tools of cost accounting and economics. Costs that otherwise might be ignored—like carrying costs—are considered. The possible costs of lost sales due to a lower customer service level may also be considered. Sometimes, total cost analyses show that unconventional physical distribution methods will provide service as good as or better than conventional means—and at a lower cost. See the following example.

Evaluating rail/warehouse versus airfreight

The Good Earth Vegetable Company was shipping produce to distant markets by train. The cost of shipping a ton of vegetables by train averaged less than half the cost of airfreight. So the company thought rail was the best method. But then Good Earth managers did a more complete analysis. To their surprise, they found the airfreight system was faster and cheaper. See Exhibit 14–6.

Exhibit 14–6 compares the costs for the two distribution systems—airplane and railroad. Because shipping by train was slow, Good Earth had to keep a large inventory in a warehouse to fill orders on time. And the company was surprised at the extra cost of carrying the inventory "in transit." Good Earth's managers also found that the cost of spoiled vegetables during shipment and storage in the warehouse was much higher when they used rail shipping.

Identifying all the alternatives is sometimes difficult

In a total cost analysis of this kind, managers should evaluate all practical alternatives. Sometimes, however, there are so many possible combinations that it is difficult to study each one completely. For example, there may be hundreds of pos-

Exhibit 14–6   Comparative Costs of Airplane versus Rail and Warehouse

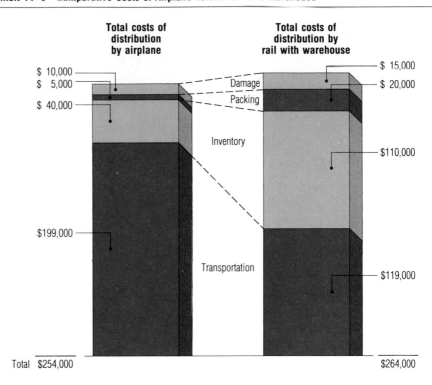

sible locations for a warehouse. And each location might require different combinations of transporting and storing costs.

Some companies use computer simulation to compare the many possible alternatives.[18] But typically, the straightforward total cost analysis discussed above is practical—and it will show whether there is need for a more sophisticated analytical approach.

FUTURE PHYSICAL DISTRIBUTION PROBLEMS AND OPPORTUNITIES

Coordinating PD activities among firms

Coordinating all of the elements of PD has always been a challenge—even in a single firm. Trying to coordinate PD in the whole channel usually wasn't done at all. Firms had trouble keeping track of inventory levels, when to order, and where goods were when they moved. Today, marketing managers for some firms are finding solutions to these challenges—with help from computers.

Many firms now continuously update their marketing information systems—so they can immediately find out what products have sold, the level of the current inventory, and when goods being transported will arrive. And coordination of physical distribution decisions throughout channels of distribution will continue to improve as more firms are able to have their computers "talk to each other" directly.

Improved information flow and coordination affects other PD activities, too. Instantaneous computer-to-computer order processing, for example, can have the same effect on the customer service level as faster, more expensive transportation. And knowing what a customer has in stock can improve a supplier's own inventory planning.

Subaru of America uses a sophisticated computer system to help coordinate the distribution of more than 180,000 imported vehicles each year.

Better coordination of PD activities is a key reason why the marketing strategy for Pepperidge Farm's new line of premium cookies has been a success. A few years ago, the company was spending a lot of money making the wrong products and delivering them—too slowly—to the wrong market. Poor information was the problem. Delivery truck drivers took orders from retailers, which were assembled manually at regional offices and then mailed to Pepperidge's bakeries. Now, the company has an almost instantaneous computerized information link between sales, delivery, inventory, and production. Hundreds of the company's 2,200 drivers use hand-held computers to record the inventory at each stop along their routes. They phone the information into a computer at the bakeries—so that cookies in short supply will be produced. The right assortment of fresh cookies is quickly shipped to local markets, and delivery trucks are loaded with what retailers need that day. Pepperidge Farm now moves cookies from its bakeries to store shelves in about 3 days; most cookie producers take about 10 days. That means fresher cookies for consumers—and helps to support Pepperidge Farm's high-quality strategy and premium price.[19]

In summary, using computers to coordinate information is helping some firms and channels compete successfully for customers—and increase their own profits.

Transporting industry is changing

There have already been drastic changes in transporting since deregulation. Many transporting firms—including some big ones—have gone out of business. But deregulation has given market-oriented managers new opportunities. Some firms are meeting the challenge of change and earning bigger profits while serving their customers better.

The changes since deregulation also show how valuable the "rules of the game" can be. And the "rules" may change again. Some shippers and transporters want the government to put some of the regulations back in place. This is an uncontrollable part of the marketing environment that marketing managers need to watch carefully.[20]

Energy costs are a problem   In the last two decades, the cost of fuel has fluctuated drastically. Fuel costs directly affect transporting costs. Lower fuel costs might lead to new market opportunities. And if fuel costs increase, truck and air transport will be less attractive, and the rails will be more appealing. Lower speed limits on trucks may make the railroads look even better. Another energy crisis might force even more radical changes—such as limiting the use of private cars and stimulating mass transportation. Such shifts could affect where people live and work, what they produce and consume, and where and how they buy. In other words, these changes could affect our future macro-marketing system. An alert marketing manager should try to anticipate and plan for this future.[21]

CONCLUSION

This chapter dealt with physical distribution activities—and how they provide *time* and *place* utility. We looked at the PD customer service level and why it is important. We discussed various modes of transporting and their advantages and disadvantages. We also discussed the types of warehousing available. Examples were given of distribution centers, which can cut storing and handling costs.

We emphasized that customer service level, transporting, and storing are all related. The physical distribution concept is concerned with coordinating all the storing and transporting activities into a smoothly working system—to deliver the desired service level at the lowest cost. Computerized information links—within firms and among firms in the channel—are increasingly important in blending all of the activities into a smooth-running system.

A marketing manager often wants to improve service and may select a higher-cost alternative to improve his marketing mix. Or the total cost approach might reveal that it is possible *both* to reduce costs and to improve service—perhaps by eliminating warehouses and using airplanes to speed delivery.

Effective marketing managers make important strategic decisions about physical distribution. But acceptance of the physical distribution concept continues to be slow. Many so-called "marketing managers" do not see physical distribution as part of their job—even though it accounts for half the cost of marketing. This may enable creative marketing managers to cut their PD costs while maintaining or improving their customer service levels. And production-oriented competitors may not even understand what is happening.

Questions and Problems

1. Explain how adjusting the customer service level could improve a marketing mix. Illustrate.

2. Briefly explain which aspects of customer service you think would be most important for a producer that sells fabric to a firm that manufactures furniture.

3. Briefly describe a purchase you have made where the customer service level had an effect on the product you selected or where you purchased it.

4. Discuss the relative advantages and disadvantages of railroads, trucks, and airlines as transporting methods.

5. Discuss why economies of scale in transportation might encourage a producer to include a regional merchant wholesaler in the channel of distribution for its consumer product.

6. Discuss some of the ways that air transportation can change other aspects of a Place system.

7. Explain which transportation mode would probably be most suitable for shipping the following goods to a large Chicago department store:

   a. 300 pounds of Alaskan crab.

   b. 15 pounds of screwdrivers from New York.

c. Three dining room tables from High Point, North Carolina.

d. 500 high-fashion dresses from the garment district in New York City.

e. A 10,000-pound shipment of machines from England.

f. 600,000 pounds of various appliances from Evansville, Indiana.

How would your answers change if this department store were the only one in a large factory town in Ohio?

8. Indicate the nearest location where you would expect to find large storage facilities. What kinds of products would be stored there? Why are they stored there instead of some other place?

9. Indicate when a producer or middleman would find it desirable to use a public warehouse rather than a private warehouse. Illustrate, using a specific product or situation.

10. Discuss the distribution center concept. Is this likely to eliminate the storing function of conventional wholesalers? Is it applicable to all products? If not, cite several examples.

11. Clearly differentiate between a warehouse and a distribution center. Explain how a specific product would be handled differently by each.

12. Explain the total cost approach and why it may be controversial in some firms. Give examples of where conflicts might occur between different departments.

13. Discuss some of the ways that computers are being used to improve PD decisions.

Suggested Cases

19. Nelson Company

29. Fruitco, Inc.

Suggested Computer-Aided Problem

14. Total Distribution Cost

Chapter 15

Promotion—Introduction

When You Finish This Chapter, You Should

1. Know the advantages and disadvantages of the promotion methods that a marketing manager can use in strategy planning.

2. Understand the importance of promotion objectives.

3. Know how the communication process should affect promotion planning.

4. Know how the adoption processes can guide promotion planning.

5. Know how promotion blends have to change because of the size of the budget, the product life cycle, the nature of competition, the target of the promotion, and the nature of the product.

6. Know how typical promotion budgets are blended.

7. Know who plans and manages promotion blends.

8. Understand the importance and nature of sales promotion.

9. Understand the important new terms (shown in red).

People won't buy your product if they've never heard of it.

Procter & Gamble was one of the first firms to use radio and TV advertising when those media were new. For the past 30 years, P&G has continued to be one of the heaviest advertisers on these media. But P&G's marketing managers don't just rely on network advertising to promote their products. They are constantly testing new ways to communicate with target customers. For example, to better reach the increasing number of Hispanic households, they are placing ads in a new Spanish-language magazine that is distributed free—along with samples of P&G products—to dentists' and doctors' offices in Hispanic neighborhoods. They are also testing ads on POP Radio, a new radio service that plays music in supermarkets and drugstores and provides information about products to consumers while they are shopping—at the point of purchase. They have also been getting publicity by sponsoring golf tournaments and other sporting events.

To generate more interest in P&G products, they are supplementing their advertising on TV shows like Dallas with special tie-in sales promotions—including sweepstakes contests and coupons distributed in newspaper inserts. To reach teenagers and other target groups, P&G representatives give away free product samples at Six Flags amusement parks. Sales promotions targeted at retailers are also used to help get retailers' support—and the best shelf space.

And, of course, P&G salespeople are also an important part of the promotion blend. They work closely with middlemen—not only to get orders but also to explain P&G's marketing mix, get cooperation on point-of-purchase displays, and help coordinate marketing effort among the members of the channel.[1]

Promotion is communicating information between seller and potential buyer to influence attitudes and behavior. The marketing manager's promotion job is to tell target customers that the right Product is available at the right Place at the right Price.

What the marketing manager communicates is determined when the target customers' needs and attitudes are known. *How* the messages are delivered depends on what blend of the various promotion methods the marketing manager chooses.

SEVERAL PROMOTION METHODS ARE AVAILABLE

As the P&G examples show, a marketing manager can choose from several promotion methods—personal selling, mass selling, and sales promotion (see Exhibit 15–1).

Personal selling—flexibility is its strength

Personal selling involves direct face-to-face communication between sellers and potential customers. Face-to-face selling also provides immediate feedback—which helps salespeople to adapt. Salespeople are included in most marketing mixes. But personal selling can be very expensive. So it's often desirable to combine personal selling with mass selling and sales promotion.

Mass selling—reaching millions at a price or even free

Mass selling is communicating with large numbers of potential customers at the same time. It's less flexible than personal selling. But when the target market is large and scattered, mass selling can be less expensive.

Advertising is the main form of mass selling. **Advertising** is any *paid* form of nonpersonal presentation of ideas, goods, or services by an identified sponsor. It includes the use of such media as magazines, newspapers, radio and TV, signs, and direct mail. While advertising must be paid for, another form of mass selling—publicity—is "free."

Exhibit 15–1   Basic Promotion Methods and Strategy Planning

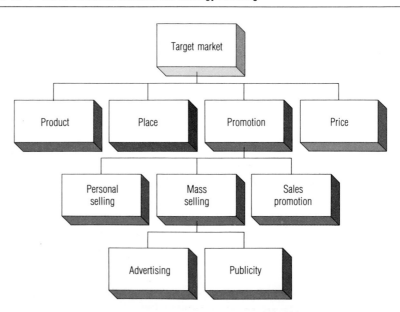

Promotion planning must consider the whole channel.

Publicity is "free"

Publicity is any *unpaid* form of nonpersonal presentation of ideas, goods, or services. Of course, publicity people are paid. But they try to attract attention to the firm and its offerings *without having to pay media costs.* For example, book publishers try to get authors on TV "talk shows" because this generates a lot of interest—and book sales—at no cost to the publisher.

When Coleco introduced its Cabbage Patch dolls, it held press parties for reporters and their children. A number of reporters wrote "human interest" stories about their kids "adopting" the cute dolls. Those stories prompted more media attention—and a very successful product introduction without Coleco doing any introductory advertising.[2]

If a firm has a really new message, publicity may be more effective than advertising. Trade magazines, for example, may carry articles featuring the newsworthy products of regular advertisers—in part because they *are* regular advertisers. The firm's publicity people write the basic "copy" and then try to convince magazine editors to print it. Each year, magazines print photos and stories about new cars—and often the source of the information is the auto producers. This publicity may even raise more interest than the company's paid advertising. A consumer might not pay any attention to an ad—but might carefully read a long magazine story with the same information.

Some companies prepare videotapes that are designed to get free publicity for their products on TV news shows. For example, one video—distributed to TV stations at Halloween—discussed a government recommendation that parents use makeup rather than masks for young children. The story was effectively tied to a new makeup product for children made by PAAS Products.[3]

Large firms have specialists to handle publicity. Usually though, publicity is treated as just another kind of advertising— and it often isn't used as effectively as it could be. In most firms, publicity deserves much more attention than it gets now.[4]

Sales promotion tries to spark immediate interest

Sales promotion refers to promotion activities—other than advertising, publicity, and personal selling—that stimulate interest, trial, or purchase by final customers or others in the channel. Sales promotion may be aimed at consumers, at middlemen, or even at a firm's own employees. Examples include coupons, samples of consumer products, special sweepstakes and contests, point-of-purchase materials, and displays at trade shows. Other examples are listed in Exhibit 15–2.

It's hard to generalize about sales promotion because it includes such a wide variety of activities. But usually its objective is to complement mass selling and personal selling.

We'll talk more about sales promotion later in this chapter. First, however, you need to understand the role of the whole promotion blend—personal selling, mass selling, and sales promotion combined—so you can see how promotion fits into the rest of the marketing mix.

WHICH METHODS TO USE DEPENDS ON PROMOTION OBJECTIVES

Overall objective is to affect behavior

The different promotion methods can all be viewed as different forms of communication. But good marketers aren't interested in just "communicating." They want to communicate information that will encourage customers to choose *their* product. They know that if they have a better offering, informed customers are more likely to buy. Therefore, they are interested in (1) reinforcing present attitudes that might lead to favorable behavior or (2) actually changing the attitudes and behavior of the firm's target market. In terms of demand curves, promotion may help the firm make its present demand curve more inelastic, or shift the demand curve to the right, or both. These possibilities are shown in Exhibit 15–3.

The buyer behavior model introduced in Chapter 7 showed the many influences on buying behavior. You saw there that affecting behavior is a tough job—but it is the overall objective of Promotion.

Exhibit 15–2   Examples of Sales Promotion Activities

Aimed at final consumers or users	Aimed at middlemen	Aimed at company's own sales force
Contests	Price deals	Contests
Coupons	Promotion allowances	Bonuses
Aisle displays	Sales contests	Meetings
Samples	Calendars	Portfolios
Trade shows	Gifts	Displays
Point-of-purchase materials	Trade shows	Sales aids
Banners and streamers	Meetings	Training materials
Trading stamps	Catalogs	
Sponsored events	Merchandising aids	

Exhibit 15–3   Promotion Seeks to Shift the Demand Curve

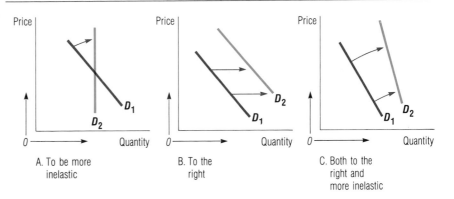

A. To be more
inelastic

B. To the
right

C. Both to the
right and
more inelastic

Informing, persuading, and reminding are basic promotion objectives

For a firm's promotion to be effective, its promotion objectives must be clearly defined—because the right promotion blend depends on what the firm wants to accomplish. It's helpful to think of three basic promotion objectives: *informing, persuading,* and *reminding* target customers about the company and its marketing mix. All are concerned with affecting behavior by providing more information.

Even more useful is a more specific set of promotion objectives that states *exactly who* you want to inform, persuade, or remind, and *why.* But this is unique to each company's strategy—and too detailed to discuss here. Instead, we will limit ourselves to the three basic promotion objectives—and how you can reach them.

Informing is educating

Potential customers must know something about a product if they are to buy at all. Therefore, *informing* may be the most important objective. For example, a cable TV company found that whenever it offered service to a new neighborhood, most of the families subscribed. The cable company's main job was informing prospects that cable was available.

A firm with a really new product may not have to do anything but inform consumers about it—and show that it meets consumer needs better than other products. When Mazda introduced its stylish and affordable Miata roadster, the uniqueness of the car simplified the promotion job. Excitement about the product also generated a lot of free publicity in automobile magazines.

Persuading usually becomes necessary

When competitors are offering similar products, the firm must not only inform customers that its product is available, but also persuade them to buy it. A *persuading* objective means the firm will try to develop or reinforce a favorable set of attitudes in the hope of affecting buying behavior. Promotion with a persuading objective often focuses on reasons why one brand is better than competing brands. Ads for Johnson & Johnson's Tylenol tout it as the pain relief medicine most often used in hospitals to help convince consumers to buy Tylenol rather than some other firm's brand.

Reminding may be enough, sometimes

If target customers already have positive attitudes about the firm's product, then a *reminding* objective might be suitable. This objective can be extremely important in some cases. Even though customers have been attracted and sold once, they are still targets for competitors' appeals. Reminding them of their past satisfaction may keep them from shifting to a competitor. Campbell's realizes that most people know about its soup—so much of its advertising is intended to remind.

PROMOTION REQUIRES EFFECTIVE COMMUNICATION

Promotion must get the attention of the target audience—and communicate effectively—or it's wasted effort. However, this isn't always easy to do. Much promotion doesn't really communicate. You might listen to the radio for hours without really being aware of the ads. Promotional communication can break down in many ways.

The same message may be interpreted differently

Different audiences may see the same message in different ways—or interpret the same words differently. Such differences are often found in international marketing when translation is a problem. General Motors, for example, had trouble in Puerto Rico with its Nova car. It discovered that, while *Nova* means "star" in Spanish, when spoken it sounds like "no va", meaning "it doesn't go." The company changed the car's name to "Caribe"—and it sold well.[5]

Semantic problems in the same language may not be so obvious—and yet the negative effects can still be serious. For example, a new children's cough syrup was advertised as "extra strength." The advertising people thought that would assure parents that the product worked well. But cautious mothers avoided the product because they feared that it might be too strong for their children.

Communication can break down

There are many reasons why a message can be misunderstood—or not heard at all. To understand this, it's useful to think about a whole **communication process**—which means a source trying to reach a receiver with a message. Exhibit 15–4 shows the elements of this communication process. Here we see that a **source**—the sender of a message—is trying to deliver a message to a **receiver**— a potential customer. Research shows that customers evaluate not only the mes-

---

Effective promotion planning must take into consideration the whole communication process.

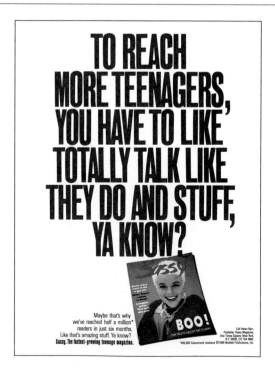

TO REACH MORE TEENAGERS, YOU HAVE TO LIKE TOTALLY TALK LIKE THEY DO AND STUFF, YA KNOW?

Maybe that's why we've reached half a million* readers in just six months. Like that's amazing stuff. Ya know?
Sassy. The fastest-growing teenage magazine.

BOO!
THE TRUTH ABOUT FAT CAMPS

Exhibit 15—4   The Communication Process

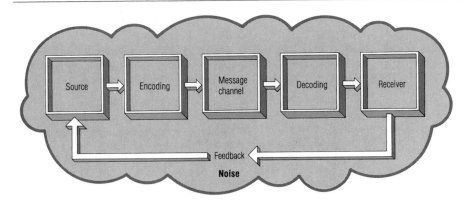

sage but also the source of the message, in terms of trustworthiness and credibility. For example, American Dental Association (ADA) studies show that Listerine mouthwash helps reduce plaque buildup on teeth. Listerine mentions the ADA endorsement in its promotion to help make the promotion message credible. Similarly, information coming from Chrysler Chairman Lee Iacocca is more impressive than the same message from an unidentified spokesperson or a junior sales rep at a car dealership.

A source can use many message channels to deliver a message. The salesperson does it in person with voice and action. Advertising must do it with magazines, newspapers, radio, TV, and other media.

A major advantage of personal selling is that the source—the seller—can get immediate feedback from the receiver. It's easier to judge how the message is being received—and change it if necessary. Mass sellers must depend on marketing research or total sales figures for feedback—and that can take too long.

The **noise**—shown in Exhibit 15—4—is any distraction that reduces the effectiveness of the communication process. Conversations during TV ads are "noise." Advertisers planning messages must recognize that many possible distractions—noise—can interfere with communications.

Encoding and decoding depend on common frame of reference

The basic difficulty in the communication process occurs during encoding and decoding. **Encoding** is the source deciding what it wants to say and translating it into words or symbols that will have the same meaning to the receiver. **Decoding** is the receiver translating the message. This process can be very tricky. The meanings of various words and symbols may differ, depending on the attitudes and experiences of the two groups. People need a common frame of reference to communicate effectively. See Exhibit 15—5.

Exhibit 15—5

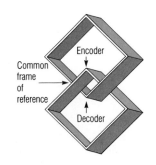

Maidenform encountered this problem with its promotion aimed at working women. The company ran a series of ads depicting women stockbrokers and doctors wearing Maidenform lingerie. The men in the ads were fully dressed. Maidenform was trying to show women in positions of authority, but some women felt the ad presented them as sex objects. In this case, the promotion people who encoded the message didn't understand the attitudes of the target market—and how they would decode the message.[6]

Message channel is important, too

The communication process is complicated even more because the receiver is aware that the message is not only coming from a source but also coming through some **message channel**—the carrier of the message. The receiver may attach more value to a product if the message comes in a well-respected newspaper or magazine, rather than over the radio. Some consumers buy products that are advertised in *Good Housekeeping* magazine, for example, because they have faith in its "seal of approval."

ADOPTION PROCESSES CAN GUIDE PROMOTION PLANNING

The adoption process discussed in Chapter 7 is related to effective communication and promotion planning. You learned the six steps in that adoption process: awareness, interest, evaluation, trial, decision, and confirmation. We saw consumer buying as a problem-solving process in which buyers go through these six steps on the way to adopting (or rejecting) an idea or product.

Now we see that the three basic promotion objectives are related to these six steps. See Exhibit 15–6. *Informing* and *persuading* may be needed to affect the potential customer's knowledge and attitudes about a product—and then bring about its adoption. Later, promotion can simply *remind* the customer about that favorable experience—and confirm the adoption decision.

The AIDA model is a practical approach

The basic adoption process fits very neatly with another action-oriented model—called AIDA—which we will use in this and the next two chapters to guide some of our discussion.

The **AIDA model** consists of four promotion jobs—(1) to get *Attention,* (2) to hold *Interest,* (3) to arouse *Desire,* and (4) to obtain *Action.* (As a memory aid, note that the first letters of the four key words spell AIDA—the well-known opera.)

The relationship of the adoption process to the AIDA jobs can be seen in Exhibit 15–6. Getting attention is necessary to make consumers aware of the company's offering. Holding interest gives the communication a chance to build the con-

Advertisers are using 3-D pop-up ads and musical microchips to grab attention.

Exhibit 15–6   Relation of Promotion Objectives, Adoption Process, and AIDA Model

Promotion objectives	Adoption process (Chapter 7)	AIDA model
Informing	Awareness Interest	Attention Interest
Persuading	Evaluation Trial	Desire
Reminding	Decision Confirmation	Action

sumer's interest in the product. Arousing desire affects the evaluation process—perhaps building preference. And obtaining action includes gaining trial, which then may lead to a purchase decision. Continuing promotion is needed to confirm the decision—and encourage additional purchases.

GOOD COMMUNICATION VARIES PROMOTION BLENDS ALONG ADOPTION CURVE

The AIDA and adoption processes look at individuals. This emphasis on individuals helps us understand how people behave. But it's also useful to look at markets as a whole. Different customers within a market may behave differently—with some taking the lead in trying new products and, in turn, influencing others.

Adoption curve focuses on market segments, not individuals

Research on how markets accept new ideas has led to the adoption curve model. The **adoption curve** shows when different groups accept ideas. It shows the need to change the promotion effort as time passes. It also emphasizes the

Getting attention does not always lead to interest, desire, or action.

The Garolini Pump.
Now Available In Kitchens.

relations among groups—and shows that some groups act as leaders in accepting a new idea.

Promotion must vary for different adopter groups

The adoption curve for a typical successful product is shown in Exhibit 15–7. Some of the important characteristics of each of these customer groups are discussed below. Which one are you?

Innovators don't mind taking some risk

The **innovators** are the first to adopt. They are eager to try a new idea—and willing to take risks. Innovators tend to be young and well educated. They are likely to be mobile and to have many contacts outside their local social group and community. Business firms in the innovator group usually are large and rather specialized. They are seeking new ways to be more effective.

An important characteristic of innovators is that they rely on impersonal and scientific information sources—or other innovators—rather than personal salespeople. They often read articles in technical publications or informative ads in special-interest magazines or newspapers.

Early adopters are often opinion leaders

Early adopters are well respected by their peers—and often are opinion leaders. They tend to be younger, more mobile, and more creative than later adopters. But unlike innovators, they have fewer contacts outside their own social group or community. Business firms in this category also tend to be specialized.

This group tends to have the greatest contact of all the groups with salespeople. Mass media are important information sources, too. Marketers should be very concerned with attracting and selling the early adopter group. Their acceptance is really important in reaching the next group because the early majority look to the early adopters for guidance. The early adopters can help the promotion effort by spreading *word-of-mouth* information and advice among other consumers.

Exhibit 15–7   The Adoption Curve

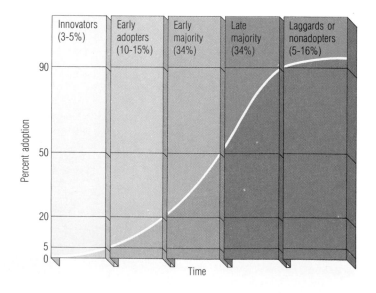

Early majority group is deliberate

The **early majority** avoid risk and wait to consider a new idea after many early adopters have tried it—and liked it. By the time members of this group start to buy, a product is probably in the market growth stage of the product life cycle and headed for success—if this group buys.

Average-sized business firms that are less specialized often fit in this category. If successful companies in their industry adopt the new idea, they will too.

The early majority have a great deal of contact with mass media, salespeople, and early adopter opinion leaders. Members usually aren't opinion leaders themselves.

Late majority is cautious

The **late majority** are cautious about new ideas. Often they are older than the early majority group—and more set in their ways. So they are less likely to follow opinion leaders and early adopters. In fact, strong social pressure from their own peer group may be needed before they adopt a new product.

Business firms in this group tend to be conservative, smaller-sized firms with little specialization.

The late majority make little use of marketing sources of information—mass media and salespeople. They tend to be oriented more to other late adopters rather than to outside sources they don't trust.

Laggards or nonadopters hang on to tradition

Laggards or **nonadopters** prefer to do things the way they have been done in the past and are very suspicious of new ideas. They tend to be older and less well educated. They may also be low in social status and income.

The smallest businesses with the least specialization are often in this category. They cling to the status quo and think it's the safe way. They don't realize that other companies are searching for better ways of doing things. The laggards stay the same—while competitors are adopting new ideas.

The main source of information for laggards is other laggards. This certainly is bad news for marketers who are trying to reach a whole market quickly—or who want to use only one promotion method. In fact, it may not pay to bother with this group.[7]

Opinion leaders help spread the word

Adoption curve research supports our earlier discussion (in Chapter 7) of the importance of *opinion leaders*—people who influence other people's attitudes and behavior. It shows the importance of early adopters. They influence the early majority—and help spread the word to many others.

Marketers know the importance of these personal conversations and recommendations by opinion leaders. If early groups reject the product, it may never get off the ground. For example, some movie goers are usually among the first to see new movies. If they think a movie is dull, they are quick to tell their friends not to waste their time and money.

But if they accept a product, then what the opinion leaders in each social group say about it can be very important. This "word-of-mouth" publicity may do the real selling job—long before the customer ever walks into the retail store. Some companies try to target promotion to encourage opinion leadership. When Canon introduced a high-quality new automatic 35 mm camera, it prepared special ads designed to help opinion leaders explain to others how the camera worked. Other firms take a simpler approach. Their ads just say "tell your friends."

We know less about the adoption process in industrial markets. It seems likely that the same general process is at work—but there is less word-of-mouth communication in these markets. This makes both personal selling and mass selling more important in communicating with industrial buyers *and* all the multiple buying influences.[8]

MAY NEED A DIFFERENT BLEND FOR EACH PRODUCT—MARKET SEGMENT

Each unique market segment may need a separate marketing mix—and a different *promotion blend*. Some mass selling specialists have missed this point. They think mainly in "mass marketing"—rather than "target marketing"—terms. Aiming at large markets may be desirable in some situations, but promotion aimed at everyone can end up hitting no one. In developing the promotion blend, you should be especially careful not to slip into a "shotgun" approach when what you really need is a "rifle" approach—with a more careful aim.

As this McGraw-Hill magazine ad suggests, it is seldom practical for personal selling to carry the whole promotion load.

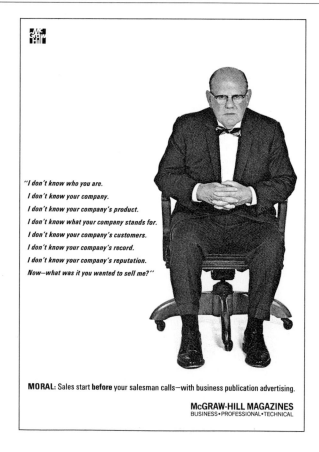

"I don't know who you are.
I don't know your company.
I don't know your company's product.
I don't know what your company stands for.
I don't know your company's customers.
I don't know your company's record.
I don't know your company's reputation.
Now—what was it you wanted to sell me?"

MORAL: Sales start **before** your salesman calls—with business publication advertising.

McGRAW-HILL MAGAZINES
BUSINESS•PROFESSIONAL•TECHNICAL

Successful promotion may be an economical blend

Once promotion objectives for a strategy are set, a marketing manager will probably use a blend of promotion methods— since some jobs can be done more economically one way than another. You can see this most clearly in industrial markets. While personal selling dominates most industrial promotion budgets, mass selling is necessary, too. Personal sales representatives nearly always have to complete the sale, but it is seldom practical for them to carry the whole promotion load. The cost of the typical industrial sales call is over $250.[9] This relatively high cost is because salespeople have only limited time and they spend much of it on nonselling activities—traveling, paperwork, sales meetings, and strictly service calls. Less than half of their time is available for actual selling.

The job of reaching all the buying influences is made more costly and difficult by the constant turnover of buyers and influencers. An industrial salesperson may be responsible for several hundred customers and prospects—with many buying influences per company. He doesn't have enough time to get the company's whole message across to every potential customer. A firm invests too much in a salesperson to use his time and skill answering questions that could be better handled through mass selling. It may cost an industrial advertiser much less than a dollar per reader to advertise in a trade magazine to a targeted group of possible buyers or influencers. After the mass selling does the ground work, the salesperson can concentrate on answering specific questions—and closing the sale.

FACTORS AFFECTING THE SELECTION OF A PROMOTION BLEND

Most business firms develop a *promotion blend* of some kind because the three promotion methods complement each other. But what blend is right in a particular situation?

Each promotion blend should be designed to achieve the firm's promotion objectives in each marketing strategy. The particular blend a firm selects also depends on other factors—including (1) the promotion budget available, (2) the stage of product in its life cycle, (3) the nature of competition, (4) the target of the promotion, and (5) the nature of the product.

Size of promotion budget affects promotion efficiency

There are some economies of scale in promotion. An ad on network TV might cost less *per person* reached than an ad on local TV. Similarly, citywide radio, TV, and newspapers may be cheaper than neighborhood newspapers or direct personal contact. But the *total cost* for some "mass media" may force small firms—or those with small promotion budgets—to use promotion alternatives that are more expensive per contact. For example, a small retailer might want to use local television but find that he has only enough money for an ad in the Yellow Pages—and an occasional newspaper ad.

When the promotion budget is limited, sales promotion and direct mail may be attractive possibilities. The cost per person reached may be high with direct mail, but direct-mail selling can be carefully targeted to the desired target market so there is little wasted expense. Some companies, like Radio Shack, try to get the name and address of every customer to build their own mailing lists. This is easy to do when most customers pay by check or credit card. Computerized mailing lists can also be purchased very inexpensively. For less than 5 cents a name,

This magazine is for marketers who use direct-mail promotion to get their message to their target market.

a company selling medical supplies can buy a list of all the doctors in certain ZIP code areas—with the names printed on mailing labels. Thousands of such specific lists are available. Most special-interest magazines sell their subscription lists.

Stage of product in its life cycle

A new product seldom becomes a spectacular success overnight. The adoption curve helps explain why. Further, the product must go through the product life cycle stages described in Chapter 10—market introduction, market growth, market maturity, and sales decline. During these stages, promotion blends may have to change to achieve different promotion objectives.

Market introduction stage—"this new idea is good"

During market introduction, the basic promotion objective is informing. If the product is a really new idea, the promotion must build **primary demand**—demand for the general product idea—for example, cellular telephones or laser printers for computers—not just the company's own brand. There may be few potential innovators during the introduction stage, and personal selling can help find them. Salespeople also are needed to find good channel members and persuade them to carry the new product. Sales promotion may be targeted at salespeople or channel members to get them interested in selling the new product. And sales promotion may also encourage customers to try it.

Market growth stage—"our brand is best"

In the market growth stage, more competitors enter the market and promotion emphasis shifts from building primary demand to stimulating **selective demand**—demand for a company's own brand. The main job is to persuade customers to buy—and keep buying—the company's product.

Now that more potential customers are trying and adopting the product, mass selling may become more economical. But personal salespeople must still work in the channels—expanding the number of outlets.

Market maturity stage—"our brand is better, really"

In the market maturity stage, more competitors have entered the market. Promotion becomes more persuasive. At this stage, mass selling and sales promotion may dominate the promotion blends of consumer products firms. Industrial products may require more aggressive personal selling—perhaps supplemented by more advertising. The total dollars allocated to promotion may rise as competition increases.

If a firm already has high sales—relative to competitors—it may have a real advantage in promotion at this stage. If, for example, Nabisco has twice the sales for a certain type of cookie as Keebler, its smaller competitor, and they both spend the same *percentage* of total sales on promotion—Nabisco will be spending twice as much and will probably communicate to more people. Nabisco may get even more than twice as much promotion because of economies of scale.

Firms that have strong brands are able to use reminder-type advertising at this stage to be sure customers remember the product name. This may be much less expensive than persuasive efforts.

Sales decline stage—"let's tell those who still want our product"

During the sales decline stage, the total amount spent on promotion usually decreases as firms try to cut costs to remain profitable. Since some people may still want the product, firms need more targeted promotion to reach these customers.

On the other hand, some firms may increase promotion to try to slow the cycle—at least temporarily. Crayola had almost all of the market for children's crayons, but sales had been slowly declining as new kinds of markers came along. Crayola slowed the cycle with more promotion spending—and a message to parents to buy their kids a "fresh box."

Nature of competition requires different promotion

Firms in monopolistic competition may favor mass selling because they have differentiated their marketing mixes and have something to talk about. As a market tends toward pure competition—or oligopoly—it is difficult to predict what will happen. Competitors in some markets try to "out-promote" each other. The only way for a competitor to stay in this kind of market is to match rivals' promotion efforts—unless the whole marketing mix can be improved in some other way. We see a lot of such competitive advertising in our daily newspapers—and in "cents-off" coupons at grocery store check-out counters.

In markets that are drifting toward pure competition, some companies resort to price cutting. Lower prices may be offered to middlemen, customers, or both. This *may* increase the number of units sold—temporarily—but it may also reduce total revenue and the amount available for promotion *per unit.* And competitive retaliation may reduce the temporary sales gains—and drag price levels down faster. The cash flowing into the business may decline—and promotion may have to be cut back.

Target of promotion helps set the blend

Promotion can be directed to five different groups: final consumers, industrial customers, retailers, wholesalers, and even a company's own employees. The right promotion blend for each group can be different.

Coupons have become a big part of promotion—because they encourage action.

Promotion to final consumers

The large number of potential customers almost forces producers of consumer products and retailers to emphasize mass selling and sales promotion. Sales promotion—such as contests or free samples—may build consumer interest and short-term sales of a product. Effective mass selling may build enough brand familiarity so that little personal selling is needed—as in self-service and discount operations.

Personal selling can be effective, too. Some retailers—specialty shops in particular—rely heavily on well-informed salespeople. But aggressive personal selling to final consumers usually is found only in relatively expensive channel systems, such as those for fashionable clothing, furniture, consumer electronics, and automobiles.

Promotion to industrial customers

Industrial customers are much less numerous than final consumers—and there is more reason to emphasize personal selling. Industrial customers may have technical questions or need adjustments in the marketing mix. Producers' or wholesalers' sales reps can be more flexible in adjusting their companies' appeals to suit each customer. They also are able to call back later and provide confirmation and additional information. Personal selling becomes more practical as the size of each purchase increases. And larger unit purchases are more typical in industrial markets.

When it is hard to identify all of the companies—or even industries—that might use a product, ads in trade publications can inform potential customers that the product is available and stimulate inquiries. Then a salesperson can follow up.

Promotion to retailers

Much promotion to retailers is concerned with informing. Mass selling in trade magazines can be valuable here—especially when the firm is promoting a new offering. But salespeople handle most of the important communication with retailers. They can answer retailers' questions about what promotion will be directed toward the final consumer, the retailers' own part in selling the product, and important details on prices, markups, and promotion assistance and allowances.

Another reason personal selling is so important in dealing with retailers is that marketing mixes may have to be adjusted from one geographic territory to another to meet competitive situations. The mixes in highly competitive urban areas, for example, may emphasize price more than those in outlying areas.

Since the producer's or wholesaler's sales reps cannot *guarantee* the retailer a profit, the promotion must also be persuasive. The sales rep must convince the retailer that demand for the product exists—and that making a profit will be easy. Retailers must be convinced that the producer or wholesaler has their interests at heart.

Retailers don't want empty promises. They want to know what they can expect in return for their cooperation and help. If a number of suppliers are offering similar products and competing for attention and shelf space, the retailer is likely to emphasize the one with the best profit potential. Special sales promotions may be very important in persuading him of that potential.

Sales promotions targeted at retailers usually focus on short-term arrangements that will improve the retailers' profits. For example, a soft-drink bottler might offer a convenience store a free case of drinks with each two cases it buys. The free case improves the store's profit margin on the whole purchase. Or a supplier might offer a price discount if the retailer is willing to use a special point-of-purchase display. Other types of sales promotions—such as contests that offer vacation trips for high-volume retailers—are also common.

Much of the promotion to retailers is done by producers' or wholesalers' salespeople.

Promotion to wholesalers

Promotion to wholesalers is very similar to promotion to retailers—except that wholesalers are less numerous and perhaps even more aware of demand and cost. They respond to economic arguments. They want to know about the promotion the producer intends to direct at final customers and retailers. They also want personal attention from producers' sales reps to be certain that any problems will be handled promptly. A good sales rep helps to cement the relationship between producer and wholesaler.

Promotion to employees

Some companies put a lot of emphasis on promotion to employees—especially salespeople. Sales promotions—like contests that give free trips to big sellers—are common in many businesses. And some large companies are trying to design ads targeted at customers that also communicate to employees—and boost the employees' image. This is especially important in service-oriented industries where the quality of the employees' efforts is a big part of the product. General Motors, for example, promotes "Mr. Goodwrench"—the well-qualified mechanic who provides friendly, expert service. The ad communicates primarily to customers—but it also reminds service people that what they do is important and appreciated.

Nature of the product makes a big difference

The target customers' view of the product is the common thread that ties together all the variables in a marketing mix. The customers' view of the product affects the promotion blend, too. The product classes we introduced in Chapter 9 have a direct bearing on the Place objectives. These product classes influence the development of promotion blends, too. The way all these factors interact will be discussed in Chapter 20. Here, however, we will consider the impact of some general product characteristics on promotion blends.

Technical nature of product

An extremely technical industrial product may require a heavy emphasis on personal selling—using technically trained salespeople. This is the only sure way to make the product understood and get feedback on how customers use it. The technical sales rep meets with engineers, plant people, purchasing agents, and top managers—and can adjust the sales message to the needs of these various influences.

Mass selling, on the other hand, is practical for many consumer products because there is no technical story to be told. If there are some technical details—for example, with cars or appliances—they can be offered to interested customers, perhaps in sales promotion materials at the retailer's showroom.

Degree of brand familiarity

If a product has already won brand preference or insistence—perhaps after years of satisfactory service—aggressive personal selling may not be needed. Reminder-type advertising may be all that's necessary. Hershey Chocolate long prided itself on not having to do any advertising! In the last 15 years, however, increased competition in the United States has forced Hershey to begin using advertising and sales promotion. In Canada—where it is not well established—Hershey always has advertised aggressively.[10]

If a producer has not differentiated its product and brand, and does not intend to build brand familiarity—perhaps because of a small budget—then much heavier emphasis on personal selling makes sense. The objective is to build good channel relations and encourage channel members to recommend the product.

HOW TYPICAL PROMOTION BUDGETS ARE BLENDED

There is no one right blend

There is no one *right* promotion blend for all situations. Each one must be developed as part of a marketing mix. But to round out our discussion of promotion blends, let's look at some typical ways promotion budgets are spread across the three promotion methods in different situations.

For most wholesalers, personal selling dominates the promotion blend. They may do some trade advertising or sponsor sales promotions aimed at retailers, but most of the promotion budget usually goes to personal selling.

Producers of industrial products usually spend most of their promotion budget on personal selling. Mass selling in trade publications or exhibits at trade shows may help in attracting new prospects. Sales promotions aimed at wholesalers or the firm's own sales force may be used to motivate special effort. Even so, the total amount spent on these areas is likely to be only a small percent of the personal selling budget.

On average, producers of consumer products spend about equally on mass selling to consumers, personal selling (to middlemen) and sales promotion to middlemen and consumers. The blend varies, however, depending on the type of product. Producers of branded convenience products are now spending a larger share on sales promotion. Producers of shopping products usually put more emphasis on personal selling and less emphasis on sales promotion and mass selling. Smaller producers and firms that offer relatively undifferentiated consumer products put more emphasis on personal selling, with the rest of the budget going mainly to sales promotion. Note that here we are referring to percentages in the promotion blend—not the level of expenditures.

United uses different types of promotion to achieve different objectives.

Many companies are sponsoring special events like this Coors Bicycle Classic to help reach their target markets.

Less is spent on advertising than personal selling or sales promotion

Many people think that most promotion money is spent on advertising—because advertising is all around them. The many ads you see in magazines and newspapers and on TV are impressive— and costly. But all the special sales promotions—coupons, sweepstakes, trade shows, sporting events sponsored by firms, and the like—add up to even more money. Similarly, most retail sales are completed by salesclerks. And behind the scenes, much personal selling goes on in the channels. In total, less money is spent on advertising than on personal selling or sales promotion.

SOMEONE MUST PLAN AND MANAGE THE PROMOTION BLEND

Selecting a promotion blend is a strategic decision that should fit with the rest of a marketing strategy. Once a firm sets the outlines of its promotion blend, it must develop and implement more detailed plans for the parts of the blend. This is the job of specialists—such as sales managers and advertising managers.

Sales managers manage salespeople

Sales managers are concerned with managing personal selling. Often the sales manager is responsible for building good distribution channels and implementing Place policies. In smaller companies, the sales manager may also act as the marketing manager—and be responsible for advertising and sales promotion, too. Since most sales managers have come up through sales, they usually know more about the power of personal contact. This can be both a strength and a weakness. They may believe in—and be able to develop and motivate—an effective sales force. But they may have less interest in—and respect for—developing a whole promotion blend.

Advertising managers work with ads and agencies

Advertising managers manage their company's mass selling effort—in television, newspapers, magazines, and other media. Their job is choosing the right media and developing the ads. Advertising departments within their own firms may help in these efforts—or they may use outside advertising agencies. The advertising manager may handle publicity, too. Or it may be handled by an outside agency or by whoever handles **public relations**—communication with noncustomers, including labor, public interest groups, stockholders, and the government.

Advertising managers usually come up through advertising—and many have an exaggerated view of its potential power. They may think that advertising can do the whole promotion job—or that advertising *is* promotion.

Sales promotion managers need many talents

Sales promotion managers manage their company's sales promotion effort. They fill the gaps between the sales and advertising managers—increasing their effectiveness. In some companies, sales promotion managers have independent status, reporting to the marketing manager. Sometimes the sales promotion effort is handled by the sales or advertising departments. But sales promotion activities are so varied that firms use both inside and outside specialists. If a firm's sales promotion expenses exceed those for advertising, it probably should have a separate sales promotion manager.

Marketing manager talks to all, blends all

Because of differences in outlook and experience, the advertising, sales, and sales promotion managers may have trouble working with each other as partners or equals. This is especially true when each feels that his own approach is the most important. There may also be conflict if a shift in the promotion blend results in one manager getting a smaller budget. The marketing manager must weigh the pros and cons of the various methods. Then he must come up with an effective promotion blend—fitting in the various departments and personalities and coordinating their efforts.

To be able to evaluate a company's promotion blend, you must first know more about the individual areas of promotion decisions. We start in that direction in the next section—with more discussion of sales promotion. Then, in the following chapters, we'll take up personal selling and advertising.

Pepsi's "tipping can" shelf display gets attention—and prompts action—at the point of purchase.

SALES PROMOTION: DO SOMETHING DIFFERENT TO STIMULATE CHANGE

Sales promotion refers to those promotion activities—other than advertising, publicity, and personal selling—that stimulate interest, trial, or purchase by final customers or others in the channel. Sales promotion generally tries to complement the other promotion methods. And, if properly done, it can be very effective. But there are problems in the sales promotion area.

Sales promotion is a weak spot in marketing

Sales promotion is often a weak spot in marketing. Exhibit 15–2 shows that sales promotion includes a wide variety of activities—each of which may be custom-designed and used only once. Thus the typical company develops little skill in sales promotion. Mistakes caused by lack of experience can be very costly, too. One promotion sponsored jointly by Polaroid and Trans World Airlines proved to be a disaster. The promotion offered a coupon worth 25 percent off the price of any TWA ticket with the purchase of a $20 Polaroid camera. The companies intended to appeal to vacationers who take pictures when they travel. Instead, travel agents bought up many of the cameras. For the price of the $20 camera, they made an extra 25 percent on every TWA ticket they sold. And big companies bought thousands of the cameras to save on overseas travel expenses.[11]

Sales promotion problems are likely to be worse when a company has no sales promotion manager. If the personal selling or advertising managers are responsible for sales promotion, they often treat it as a "stepchild." They allocate money to sales promotion if there is any "left over"—or if a crisis develops. Many companies—even some large ones—don't have a separate budget for sales promotion or even know what it costs in total.

Making sales promotion work is a learned skill—not a sideline for amateurs. In fact, specialists in sales promotion have developed—both inside larger firms and as outside consultants. Some are extremely creative and might be willing to take over the whole promotion job. But it's the marketing manager's responsibility to set promotion objectives and policies that will fit in with the rest of each marketing strategy.[12]

Sales promotion spending is big—and getting bigger

The need for sales promotion experts—and perhaps separate status for sales promotion within the marketing organization—is apparent when we consider how much money is involved. Sales promotion expenditures are now over $100 billion.[13]

Spending on sales promotion is growing—sometimes at the expense of other promotion methods—for several reasons. Sales promotion has proved effective in increasingly competitive markets. Sales promotion can usually be implemented quickly—and get results sooner than advertising. It is often designed to get *action*. Act Media—a New York firm specializing in sales promotion—sent representatives to 4,800 stores around the country, where they gave away booklets of coupons for a variety of products. About 12 percent of the coupons were quickly redeemed—nearly half for products the shopper didn't ordinarily buy![14]

Sales promotion activities also help a product manager win support from an already overworked sales force. The sales force may be especially receptive to sales promotion—including promotion in the channels—because competition is growing and middlemen respond to sales promotion. The sales reps can see that their company is willing to help them win more business.

Underalls Panty Hose Races into Sports Promotions

Marketing managers for Underalls panty hose recently entered a new type of competition: stock car racing. As fans watch an Underalls-sponsored car circle the track, the brand name painted on the car gets constant exposure. TV coverage of a race may expand the reach to broader audiences. This element of Underalls' promotion blend is not as unusual as it may seem. As costs of traditional advertising media have skyrocketed, sporting event sales promotions have gained in popularity.

And producers of spark plugs and oil are no longer the only sponsors of race cars. Tide, Crisco oil, Folgers coffee, and even Eureka vacuum cleaners sponsor cars. The cost of sponsoring a race car varies from about $250,000 to $2 million, depending on the amount of publicity the firm gets. Even so, marketing managers for Underalls think it may be a cost-effective way to reach the target market. Forty percent of the fans who attend races are female—and many races are in southern states where Underalls wants to rev up sales.[15]

Earlier, we noted that sales promotion can be aimed at final consumers or users, channel members, and company employees. Let's look at some of the sales promotion tools used for these different target receivers—and what they are expected to accomplish.

Sales promotion for final consumers or users

Sales promotion aimed at final consumers or users usually is trying to increase demand or speed up the time of purchase. Such promotion might involve developing materials to be displayed in retailers' stores—including banners, sample packages, calendars, and various point-of-purchase materials. The sales promotion people also might develop the aisle displays for supermarkets. They might be responsible for "sweepstakes" contests, as well as for coupons designed to get customers to buy a product by a certain date. Each year, about 200 billion coupons are distributed. That's over 800 coupons for every man, woman, and child in America![16]

All of these sales promotion efforts are aimed at specific objectives. For example, if customers already have a favorite brand, it may be hard to get them to try anything new. Or it may take a while for them to become accustomed to a different product. A free trial size bottle of mouthwash might be just what it takes to get cautious consumers to try—and like—the new product. Such samples might be distributed house to house, by mail, at stores, or attached to other products sold by the firm.

Sales promotion directed at industrial customers might use the same kinds of ideas. In addition, the sales promotion people might set up and staff trade show exhibits. Here, attractive models are often used to encourage buyers to look at a firm's product—especially when it is displayed near other similar products in a circus-like atmosphere.

Some industrial sellers give promotion items—pen sets, cigarette lighters, watches, or more expensive items (perhaps with the firm's brand name on them)—to "remind" industrial customers of their products. This is common practice in many industries. But it can be a sensitive area, too. Some companies do not allow buyers to take any gift—of any kind—from a supplier. They fear the buyer's judgment may be influenced by the supplier who gives the best promotion items![17]

Sales promotion for middlemen

Sales promotion aimed at middlemen—sometimes called *trade promotion*—stresses price-related matters. The objective may be to encourage middlemen to stock new items, buy in larger quantity, or buy early. The tools used here are price and/or merchandise allowances, promotion allowances, and perhaps sales contests to encourage retailers or wholesalers to sell specific items—or the company's whole line. Offering to send contest winners to Hawaii, for example, may increase sales greatly.[17]

Sales promotion for own employees

Sales promotion aimed at the company's own sales force might try to encourage getting new customers, selling a new product, or selling the company's whole line. Depending on the objectives, the tools might be contests, bonuses on sales or number of new accounts, or holding sales meetings at fancy resorts to raise everyone's spirits.

Ongoing sales promotion work might also be aimed at the sales force—to help sales management. Sales promotion might be responsible for preparing sales portfolios, videotapes on new products, displays, and other sales aids. Sales promotion people might develop the sales training material that the sales force uses in working with customers and other channel members. They might develop special racks for product displays that the sales rep sells or gives to retailers. In other words, rather than expecting each individual salesperson—or the sales manager—to develop these sales aids, sales promotion might be given this responsibility.

Service-oriented firms, such as hotels or restaurants, now use sales promotions targeted at their employees. Some, for example, give a monthly cash prize for the employee who provides the "best service." And the employee's picture is displayed to give recognition.[19]

Sales promotion in mature markets

Some experts think that marketing managers—especially those who deal with consumer package goods—put too much emphasis on sales promotions. They argue that the effect of most sales promotion is temporary and that money spent on advertising and personal selling helps the firm more over the long-term. Let's take a closer look at these concerns.

There *is* heavy use of sales promotion in mature markets where competition for customers and attention from middlemen is fierce. Moreover, if the total market is not growing, sales promotions may just encourage "deal-prone" customers (and middlemen) to switch back and forth among brands. Here, all the expense of the sales promotions and the swapping around of customers simply contributes to lower profits for everyone. However, it's important to see that once a marketing manager is in this situation there may not be any choice. At this stage of the product life cycle, frequent sales promotions may be needed just to offset the effects of competitors' promotions. The only escape from this competitive rat race is for the marketing manager to seek new opportunities—with a strategy that doesn't rely solely on short-term sales promotions for competitive advantage.[20]

CONCLUSION

Promotion is an important part of any marketing mix. Most consumers and intermediate customers can choose from among many products. To be successful, a producer must not only offer a good product at a reasonable price, but also inform potential customers about the product and where they can buy it. Further, producers must tell wholesalers and retailers in the channel about their product and their marketing mix. These middlemen, in turn, must use promotion to reach their customers.

The promotion blend should fit logically into the strategy that is being developed to satisfy a particular target market. *What* should be communicated to them—and *how*—should be stated as part of the strategy planning.

The overall promotion objective is affecting buying behavior, but the basic promotion objectives are informing, persuading, and reminding.

Three basic promotion methods can be used to reach these objectives. How the promotion methods are combined to achieve effective communication can be guided by behavioral science findings. In particular, what we know about the communication process and how individuals and groups adopt new products is important in planning promotion blends.

An action-oriented framework called AIDA can help guide planning of promotion blends. But the marketing manager has the final responsibility for combining the promotion methods into one promotion blend for each marketing mix. Special factors that may affect the promotion blend are the size of the promotion budget, the stage of product in its life cycle, the particular target customers who must be reached, the nature of competition, and the nature of the product.

In this chapter, we considered some promotion basics and went into some detail on sales promotion. Sales promotion spending is big and growing. This approach is especially important in prompting action—by customers, middlemen, or salespeople. There are many different types of sales promotion, and it is a problem area in many firms because it is difficult for a firm to develop expertise with all of the possibilities. However, it must be managed carefully as part of the overall promotion blend. Thus, in the next two chapters, we'll discuss personal selling and mass selling (advertising) in more detail.

Questions and Problems

1. Briefly explain the nature of the three basic promotion methods that are available to a marketing manager. What are the main strengths and limitations of each of the approaches?

2. Relate the three basic promotion objectives to the four jobs (AIDA) of promotion, using a specific example.

3. Discuss the communication process in relation to a producer's promotion of an accessory product, say, a new electronic security system used by businesses to limit access to areas where confidential records are stored.

4. Explain how an understanding of the way individuals adopt new ideas or products (the adoption process) would be helpful in developing a promotion blend. In particular, explain how it might be desirable to change a promotion blend during the course of the adoption process. To make this more concrete, discuss it in relation to the acceptance of digital tape recorders, a new consumer electronics product that produces high-quality recordings.

5. Explain how opinion leaders should affect a firm's promotion planning.

6. Discuss how our understanding of the adoption curve should be applied to planning the promotion blend(s) for a new, wireless portable telephone that can be used in cars while traveling.

7. Discuss the nature of the promotion job in relation to the life cycle of a product. Illustrate, using microwave ovens.

8. Promotion has been the target of considerable criticism. What specific types of promotion are probably the object of this criticism? Give a specific example that illustrates your thinking.

9. Would promotion be successful in expanding the general demand for: (a) raisins, (b) air travel, (c) tennis rackets, (d) cashmere sweaters, (e) high-octane unleaded gasoline, (f) single serving, frozen gourmet dinners, (g) cement? Explain why or why not in each case.

10. What promotion blend would be most appropriate for producers of the following established products? Assume average- to large-sized firms in each case and support your answer.

    a. Candy bars.

    b. Panty hose.

    c. Castings for car engines.

    d. Car batteries.

    e. A special computer used by manufacturers for computer-aided design of new products.

    f. Inexpensive plastic raincoats.

    g. A video camera that has achieved a specialty-products status.

11. Discuss the potential conflict among the various promotion managers. How could this be reduced?

12. Explain why sales promotion is currently a "weak spot" in marketing and suggest what might be done.

13. If sales promotion spending continues to grow—often at the expense of media advertising—how do you think this might affect the rates charged by mass media for advertising time or space? How do you think it might affect advertising agencies?

Suggested Cases

18. Tandy versus IBM

21. DeWitt State Bank

22. Outdoor Sports, Inc.

Suggested Computer-Aid Problem

15. Sales Promotion

Chapter 16

Personal Selling

When You Finish This Chapter, You Should

1. Understand the importance and nature of personal selling.

2. Know the three basic sales tasks and what the various kinds of salespeople can be expected to do.

3. Know what the sales manager must do—including selecting, training, and organizing salespeople—to carry out the personal selling job.

4. Understand how the right compensation plan can help motivate and control salespeople.

5. Understand when and where the three types of sales presentations should be used.

6. Understand the important new terms (shown in red).

Today, many salespeople are problem-solving professionals.

John Akers, the top executive at IBM, faced a big challenge. Fast-growing competitors had been eating away at IBM's market share. IBM's worldwide earnings had dropped 25 percent. These were just symptoms of a more basic problem: IBM was out of touch with its customers.

Akers and his top marketing managers decided that the best way to address the problem was to put more emphasis on personal selling—and to increase the number of salespeople. The idea was not just to "sell harder," but rather to improve communication with customers, understand their needs better, and do a better job of solving their problems.

As a first step, IBM's marketing managers identified the many sales tasks that needed to be performed—consulting with customers and prospects about their problems, getting orders from new customers, making certain that regular customers' orders were handled well, and providing technical support after the sale. Then, to fill the new jobs, IBM took a dramatic step. It shifted over 11,000 employees from overstaffed areas such as manufacturing, development, and administration into sales positions.

These new salespeople knew about IBM and computers—but most of them didn't know much about the company's marketing program, working with customers, or making effective sales presentations. So IBM set up training programs in all of these areas. Much of the training focused on professional problem-solving skills and making presentations. Further, all of the newly trained salespeople had to be assigned to specific sales territories, customers, and product lines. And new compensation arrangements were needed so that they would be motivated to work hard and rewarded for producing needed results.

It will take some time to see if the changes produce all of the desired results. But already customers are saying that IBM is being more responsive to their needs—and IBM's profits are improving.[1]

Promotion is communicating with potential customers. As the IBM case suggests, personal selling is often the best way to do it. Few companies are as large as IBM, but almost every company can benefit from personal selling. While face-to-face with prospects, salespeople can get more attention than an advertisement or a display. Further, they can ask questions to find out about a customer's specific interests. They can also stay in tune with the prospect's feedback, and adjust the presentation as they move along. If—and when—the prospect is ready to buy, the salesperson is there to close the sale and take the order.

Marketing managers must decide how much—and what kind of—personal selling effort is needed in each marketing mix. Specifically, as part of their strategy planning, they must decide: (1) how many salespeople are needed, (2) what kind of salespeople are needed, (3) what kind of sales presentation should be used, (4) how salespeople should be selected and trained, and (5) how they should be supervised and motivated. The sales manager provides inputs into these strategy decisions. And once they are made, it's the sales manager's job to implement the personal selling part of a marketing strategy.

In this chapter, we'll discuss the importance and nature of personal selling so you'll understand the strategy decisions sales managers and marketing managers face. These strategy decisions are shown in Exhibit 16–1.

THE IMPORTANCE AND ROLE OF PERSONAL SELLING

We've already seen that personal selling is important in some promotion blends—and absolutely essential in others. Some feel that personal selling is the

Exhibit 16–1 Strategy Planning for Personal Selling

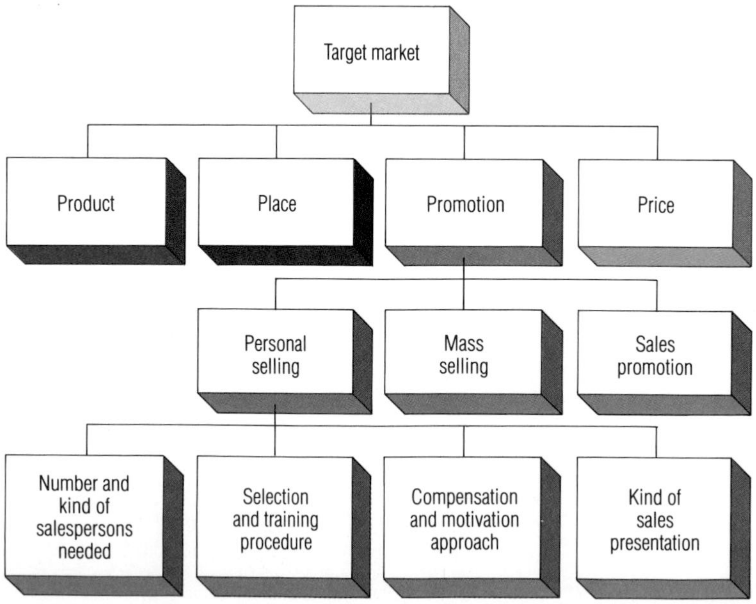

Good salespeople try to help the customer buy—by understanding the customer's needs.

dynamic element that keeps our economy going. You would better appreciate the importance of personal selling if you regularly had to meet payrolls, and somehow—almost miraculously—your salespeople kept coming in with orders just in time to keep the business from closing.

Personal selling is often a company's largest single operating expense. This is another reason why it is important to understand the decisions in this area. Bad sales management decisions can be costly not only in terms of lost sales, but also in actual out-of-pocket expenses.

Our economy needs and uses many salespeople. Census Bureau statistics show that about 1 person out of every 10 in the total labor force is in sales work. By comparison, that's about 20 times more people than are employed in advertising. Any activity that employs so many people—and is so important to the economy—deserves study.

Helping to buy is good selling

Good salespeople don't just try to *sell* the customer. Rather, they try to *help the customer buy*—by understanding the customer's needs and presenting the advantages and disadvantages of their products. Such helpfulness results in satisfied customers—and long-term relationships. Those relationships are often the basis for a firm's competitive advantage, especially when it is targeting business markets.

You may think of personal selling in terms of an old-time stereotype: a "bag of wind" with no more to offer than a funny story, a big expense account, and an engaging grin. But that isn't true any more. "Old-time" salespeople are being replaced by real professionals—problem solvers—who have something definite to contribute to their employers *and* their customers.

Salespeople represent the whole company—and customers, too

Increasingly, the salesperson is seen as a representative of the whole company—responsible for explaining its total effort to target customers rather than just "pushing" products. The sales rep is often the only link between the firm and its customers—especially if customers are far away. The salesperson may provide information about products, explain and interpret company policies, and even negotiate prices or diagnose technical problems when a product doesn't work well.

In some cases, the salesperson represents his *customers* back inside his own firm, too. Recall that feedback is an essential part of both the communication process *and* the basic management process of planning, implementing, and control. For example, the sales rep is the likely one to explain to the production manager why a customer is unhappy with product performance or quality—or to the physical distribution manager why slow shipments are causing problems.

As evidence of these changing responsibilities, some companies now give their salespeople such titles as field manager, market specialist, account representative, or sales engineer.

Sales force aids in market information function as well

The sales force can aid in the marketing information function, too. The sales rep may be the first to hear about a new competitor or a competitor's new product or strategy. And, as the following example shows, sales reps who are well attuned to customers' needs can be a key source of ideas for new products.

Ballard Medical Products is a small producer that competes with giants like Johnson & Johnson in the hospital supply business. A key factor in Ballard's success is that its salespeople have the right products to offer when they make a sales call. But that's not just luck. It's because the salespeople all have a lot of say in what products the company will produce and how they are designed. Ballard salespeople are trained as information specialists who seek and report on customer feedback. At each hospital, they work closely with the doctor and nurse specialists who use Ballard products. And when one of them says "we need a product that would solve this problem" the Ballard sales rep is right there to follow up with questions and invite suggestions. And they quickly relay the customer's needs back to Ballard's new-product group.[2]

Salespeople can be strategy planners, too

Some salespeople are expected to be marketing managers in their own geographic territories. And some become marketing managers by default because top management hasn't provided detailed strategy guidelines. Either way, salespeople may take the initiative to fill the gap. They may develop their own marketing mixes or even their own strategies. Some firms fail to give their sales reps a clear idea of who their target customers should be. Although the sales reps are assigned a territory, they may have to start from scratch with strategy planning. The salesperson may have choices about (1) what target customers to aim at, (2) which particular products to push most aggressively, (3) which middlemen to call on or to work with the hardest, (4) how to use any promotion money that may be available, and (5) how to adjust prices.

A salesperson who can put together profitable strategies—and implement them well—can rise very rapidly. The opportunity is there for those who are prepared and willing to work.

Even a starting job may offer great opportunities. Some beginning salespeople—especially those working for producers or wholesalers—are responsible for larger sales volumes than many retail stores achieve. This is a serious responsibility—and the salesperson should prepare for it.

Further, the sales job is often used as an entry-level position to evaluate a person. Success in this job can lead to rapid promotion to higher-level sales and marketing jobs—and more money and security.[3]

WHAT KINDS OF PERSONAL SELLING ARE NEEDED?

If a firm has too few salespeople—or the wrong kind—some important personal selling tasks may not be completed. And having too many salespeople—or the wrong kind—wastes money. A sales manager needs to find a good balance—the right number and the right kind of salespeople.

One of the difficulties of determining the right number and kind of salespeople is that every sales job is different. While an engineer or accountant can look forward to fairly specific duties, the salesperson's job is constantly changing. However, there are three basic types of sales tasks. This gives us a starting point for understanding what selling tasks need to be done—and how many people will be needed to do them.

Personal selling is divided into three tasks

The three **basic sales tasks** are order getting, order taking, and supporting. For convenience, we'll describe salespeople by these terms—referring to their primary task—although one person might have to do all three tasks in some situations.

As the names imply, order getters and order takers obtain orders for their company. Every marketing mix must have someone or some way to obtain orders. In contrast, supporting salespeople are not directly interested in orders. Their function is to help the order-oriented salespeople. With this variety, you can see that there is a place in personal selling for nearly everyone.

ORDER GETTERS DEVELOP NEW BUSINESS

Order getters are concerned with getting new business. **Order getting** means seeking possible buyers with a well-organized sales presentation designed to sell a product, service, or idea. The emphasis here is on getting results—orders—not on style, however. A good order getter may appear very "low-key" if he thinks it is appropriate for his target customers.

Order getters must know what they're talking about—not just be a personal contact. Order-getting salespeople work for producers, wholesalers, and retailers. They normally are well paid—many earn more than $70,000 per year.

Producers' order getters— find new opportunities

Producers of all kinds of products—especially industrial products—have a great need for order getters. They are needed to locate new prospects, open new accounts, see new opportunities, and help establish and build channel relationships.

High-caliber order getters are essential in sales of installations and accessory equipment where large sums are involved and where top-level management participates in the buying decision.

Top-level customers are more interested in ways to save or make more money than in technical details. Good order getters cater to this interest. They help the customer identify ways to solve problems, and then sell concepts and ideas—not just physical products. The products are merely the means of achieving the customer's end.

For example, Circadian, Inc., sells "high-tech" medical equipment. Changes in Medicare rules mean that doctors can no longer routinely order expensive tests in hospitals because the costs can't be recovered easily. But the doctors *can* be paid for tests done in their offices—if they have the right equipment. When a Circadian order getter calls on a doctor, he shows how the firm's testing equipment can improve patient care—and office profits. The rep can often get a $20,000 order "on the spot" because he can show that the equipment will pay for itself in the first year. The doctors don't care about technical details as long as the machines are accurate and easy to use.[4]

Order getters are also necessary in selling industrial raw materials, components, supplies, and services—but mainly for initial contacts. Since many competitors offer nearly the same product, the order getter's crucial selling job here is getting the company's name on the "approved suppliers" list.

Order getters for professional services—and other products where service is an important element of the marketing mix—face a special challenge. The customer usually can't "inspect" a service before deciding to buy. The order getter's communication and relationship with the customer may be the only basis on which to evaluate the quality of the supplier.

Industrial products order getters need the "know-how" to help solve their customers' problems. Often they need to understand both customers' general business concerns and technical details about the product and its applications. To have technically competent order getters, firms often give special training to business-trained college graduates. Such salespeople can then work intelligently with their specialist customers. In fact, they may be more technically competent in their narrow specialty than anyone they encounter—so they provide a unique service. For example, a salesperson for automated manufacturing equipment must understand

An order getter may have to deal with multiple buying influences to make a sale.

everything about a prospect's production process, as well as the technical details of converting to computer-controlled equipment.

Wholesalers' order getters—hand it to the customer, almost

Progressive merchant wholesaler sales reps are developing into counselors and store advisors rather than just order takers. Such order getters may become retailers' "partners" in the job of moving goods from the wholesale warehouse through the retail store to consumers. These order getters almost become a part of the retailer's staff—helping to check stock, write orders, conduct demonstrations—and they plan advertising, special promotions, and other retailing activities.

Agent middlemen often are order getters—particularly the more aggressive manufacturers' agents and brokers. They face the same tasks as producers' order getters. But, unfortunately for them, once the order getting is done and the customers become established and loyal, producers may try to eliminate the agents—and save money with their own order takers.

Retail order getters influence consumer behavior

Unsought products need order getters

Convincing consumers about the value of products they haven't seriously considered takes a high level of personal selling ability. Order getters must help customers see how a new product can satisfy needs now being filled by something else. Early order getters for aluminum storm windows, for example, faced a tough job. They had to convince skeptical customers that this new kind of storm window not only was as durable as wood, but also would need less maintenance in the long run. Without order getters, many of the products we now rely on—such as refrigerators and air conditioners—might have died in the market introduction stage. It is the order getter who helps bring products out of the introduction stage

Sales reps who call on retailers often serve as store advisors—to help improve the performance of the whole channel.

into the market growth stage. Without sales and profits in the early stages, the product may fail—and never be offered again.

They help sell shopping products

Order getters are helpful for selling *heterogeneous* shopping products. Consumers shop for many of these items on the basis of price and quality. They welcome useful information. Cars, furniture and furnishings, cameras, jewelry, and fashion items can be sold effectively by an aggressive, helpful order getter. Friendly advice—based on thorough knowledge of the product and its alternatives—may really help consumers and bring profits to the salesperson and retailers.

ORDER TAKERS—KEEP THE BUSINESS COMING

Order takers sell the regular or typical customers. Order takers complete most sales transactions. After a customer becomes interested in the products of a specific firm—from an order getter or a supporting salesperson or through advertising or sales promotion—an order taker is usually needed to answer any final questions and complete the sale. **Order taking** is the routine completion of sales made regularly to the target customers.

Sometimes sales managers or customers use the term *order taker* as a "put down" when referring to nonaggressive salespeople. While a particular salesperson may perform so poorly that criticism is justified, it's a mistake to downgrade the function of order taking. Order taking is extremely important. Many sales are lost just because no one ever asked for the order—and closed the sale.

Producers' order takers—train and explain

After order getters open up industrial, wholesale, or retail accounts, regular follow-up is necessary. Order takers work on improving the whole relationship with the customer, not just on completing a single transaction. Even if routine reorders

Some firms are finding new ways to handle routine order taking—so salespeople can concentrate on other selling tasks.

The Staff At Jeans International Can't Take Orders 24 Hours A Day. Their Konica Fax Can.

Whatever your business, there's a Konica Fax tailored to fit your needs. Rush orders, hot leads, or new product developments. When overnight just won't do, Konica Fax saves the day.
Sew up more business with a Konica Fax.
Call 1-800-648-7130.

© 1989 Konica Business Machines U.S.A., Inc.

Konica
COPIERS • FAX

are handled by computer, someone has to explain details, make adjustments, handle complaints, explain or negotiate new prices and terms, place sales promotion materials, and keep customers informed on new developments. It may also be necessary to train the customers' employees to use machines or products. In sales to middlemen, it may be necessary to train wholesalers' or retailers' salespeople. All these activities are part of the order taker's job.

Producers' order takers often have a regular route with many calls. To handle these calls well, they must have energy, persistence, enthusiasm, and a friendly personality that wears well over time. They sometimes have to "take the heat" when something goes wrong with some other element of the marketing mix.

Sometimes jobs that are basically order taking are used to train potential order getters and managers. Such jobs give them an opportunity to meet key customers and to better understand their needs. Frequently, they run into some order-getting opportunities.

Order takers who are alert to order-getting opportunities can make the big difference in generating new sales. Averitt Express, a trucking firm, recognized the opportunities. At most trucking firms, drivers are basically order takers and service providers. When a customer places an order, the driver picks up and delivers the shipment. In contrast, Averitt encourages its drivers to help in getting new orders. Whenever they deliver a shipment to a firm that is not a regular Averitt customer, they call on the shipping manager at the firm. They give the shipping manager sales literature about Averitt services and ask if Averitt can help handle some of that firm's shipping needs. With 700 drivers all helping out as order getters, Averitt sales have grown at a rate of 30 to 50 percent a year since 1971!

Wholesalers' order takers—not getting orders but keeping them

While producers' order takers usually handle relatively few items—and sometimes even a single item—wholesalers' order takers may sell 125,000 items or more. Most wholesale order takers just sell out of their catalog. They have so many items that they can't possibly give aggressive sales effort to many—except perhaps newer or more profitable items. There are just too many items to single any out for special attention. The order taker's strength is a wide assortment—rather than detailed knowledge of individual products.

The wholesale order taker's main job is to maintain close contact with customers—perhaps once a week—and fill any needs that develop. Sometimes such an order taker gets very close to industrial customers or retailers. Some retailers let the salesperson take inventory—and then write up the order. Obviously, this position of trust cannot be abused. After writing up the order, this order taker normally checks to be sure his company fills the order promptly and accurately. He also handles any adjustments or complaints and generally acts as a liaison between his company and customers.

Such salespeople are usually the low-pressure type—friendly and easygoing. Usually these jobs aren't as high paying as the order-getting variety—but they are attractive to many because they aren't as taxing. Relatively little traveling is required and there is little or no pressure to get new accounts. There can be a social aspect, too. The salesperson sometimes becomes good friends with customers.

Retail order takers—often they are poor salesclerks

Order taking may be almost mechanical at the retail level—for example, at the supermarket check-out counter. Even so, retail order takers play a vital role in a retailer's marketing mix. Customers expect prompt and friendly service. They will find a new place to shop rather than deal with a salesclerk who is rude or acts annoyed by having to complete a sale.

A good retail order taker helps to build satisfied customers.

Some retail clerks are poor order takers because they aren't paid much—often only the minimum wage. But they may be paid little because they do little. In any case, order taking at the retail level appears to be declining in quality. And it is likely that there will be far fewer such jobs in the future as more marketers make adjustments in their mixes and turn to self-service selling. Check-out counters are being automated with electronic scanning equipment that reads price codes directly from packages. Some supermarkets are even experimenting with systems where customers do their own scanning, and the clerk simply accepts the money.

SUPPORTING SALES FORCE—INFORMS AND PROMOTES IN THE CHANNEL

Supporting salespeople help the order-oriented salespeople—but they don't try to get orders themselves. Their activities are aimed at getting sales in the long run. For the short run, however, they are ambassadors of goodwill who may provide specialized services and information. Almost all supporting salespeople work for producers or middlemen who do this supporting work for producers. There are two types of supporting salespeople: missionary salespeople and technical specialists.

Missionary salespeople can increase sales

Missionary salespeople are supporting salespeople who work for producers—calling on their middlemen and their customers. They try to develop goodwill and stimulate demand, help the middlemen train their salespeople, and often take orders for delivery by the middlemen. Missionary salespeople are sometimes called *merchandisers* or *detailers*.

A missionary salesperson may explain promotion programs to middlemen—and even help set up special in-store displays like this one for Bartles & Jaymes.

Producers who rely on merchant wholesalers to obtain widespread distribution often use missionary salespeople. The sales rep can give a promotion boost to a product that otherwise wouldn't get much attention from the middlemen because it's just one of many they sell. A missionary salesperson for Vicks's cold remedy products, for example, might visit druggists during the "cold season" and encourage them to use a special end-of-aisle display for Vicks's cough syrup—and then help set it up. The wholesaler that supplies the drugstore would benefit from any increased sales, but might not take the time to urge use of the special display.

An imaginative missionary salesperson can double or triple sales. Naturally, this doesn't go unnoticed. Missionary sales jobs are often a route to order-oriented jobs. In fact, this position is often used as a training ground for new salespeople—and recent college grads are often recruited for these positions.

Technical specialists are experts who know product applications

Technical specialists are supporting salespeople who provide technical assistance to order-oriented salespeople. Technical specialists usually are science graduates or engineers with the know-how to explain the advantages of the company's product. They are usually more interested in showing the technical details of their product than in helping to persuade customers to buy it. Before the specialist's visit, an order getter probably has stimulated interest. The technical specialist provides the details. The order getter usually completes the sale—but only after the customer's technical people give at least tentative approval.

Today many of the decision makers who influence industrial purchases have more technical knowledge than they did in the past. As a result, firms need more technical specialists. And many companies are training their technical specialists in presentation skills to help them be not only technically accurate, but also persuasive. Technical specialists who are also good communicators often become highly paid order getters.

Three tasks may have to be blended

We have described three sales tasks—order getting, order taking, and supporting. You should understand, however, that a particular salesperson might be given two—or all three—of these tasks. Ten percent of a particular job may be order getting, 80 percent order taking, and the additional 10 percent supporting. Another company might have three different people handling the different sales tasks. This can lead to **team selling**—when different sales reps work together on a specific account. Team selling is often used by producers of "high-ticket" items. AT&T uses team selling to sell office communications systems for a whole business. Different specialists handle different parts of the job—but the efforts of the whole "team" are coordinated to achieve the desired result.

Strategy planners should specify the different types of selling tasks to be handled by the sales force. Once the tasks are specified, the sales manager needs to assign responsibility for individual sales jobs so that the tasks are completed and the personal selling objectives achieved.

THE RIGHT STRUCTURE HELPS ASSIGN RESPONSIBILITY

A sales manager must organize the sales force so that all the necessary tasks are done well. A large organization might have different salespeople specializing by different selling tasks *and* by the target markets they serve.

Different target markets need different selling tasks

Sales managers often divide sales force responsibilities based on the type of customer involved. For example, Bigelow—a company that makes quality carpet for homes and office buildings—has divided its sales force into two groups of specialists. Some Bigelow salespeople call only on architects to help them choose the best type of carpet for new office buildings. These reps know all the technical details, such as how well a certain carpet fiber will wear or its effectiveness in reducing noise from office equipment. Often no "selling" is involved because the architect only suggests specifications and doesn't actually buy the carpet.

Other Bigelow salespeople call on retail carpet stores. These reps identify stores that don't carry Bigelow carpets—and they work to establish a relationship and get that crucial first order. Once a store is sold, these reps encourage the store manager to keep a variety of Bigelow carpets in stock. They also take orders, help train the store's salespeople, and try to solve any problems that occur.

Big accounts get special treatment

Very large customers often require special selling effort—and are treated differently. Moen, a maker of plumbing fixtures, has a "regular" sales force to call on building material wholesalers and an "elite" **national accounts sales force** that sells directly to large accounts—like Lowe's or other major retail chain stores that carry plumbing fixtures.

Some salespeople specialize in telephone selling

Some firms have a group of salespeople who specialize in **telemarketing**—using the telephone to "call" on customers or prospects. A phone call has many of the benefits of a personal visit—including the ability to modify the message as feedback is received. The big advantage of telemarketing is that it saves time and money. Telemarketing is especially useful when customers are small or in hard-to-reach places. It is also important when many prospects have to be contacted to reach one who is actually interested in buying.

Telemarketing is rapidly growing in popularity. Large and small firms alike are finding that it allows them to extend the personal selling effort to new target markets. It also is a good way to increase the frequency of contact between the firm and its customers. Convenient toll-free telephone lines also make it fast and easy for the customer to place an order or get assistance.

Sales tasks are done in sales territories

Often companies organize selling tasks on the basis of **sales territory**—a geographic area that is the responsibility of one salesperson or several working together. A territory might be a region of the country, a state, or part of a city—depending on the market potential. Companies like Lockheed Aircraft Corporation often consider a whole country as *part* of a sales territory for one salesperson.

Carefully set territories can reduce travel time and the cost of sales calls. Assigning territories can also help reduce confusion about who has responsibility for a set of selling tasks. But sometimes simple geographic division of selling jobs isn't easy. A company may have different products that require very different knowledge or selling skills—even if products are being sold in the same territory or to the same customer. For example, Du Pont makes special films for hospital X-ray departments as well as chemicals used in laboratory blood tests. But a salesperson who can talk to a radiologist about what film is best for a complex X ray probably can't be expected to also know everything about blood chemistry!

Size of sales force depends on workload

Once the important selling tasks have been specified—and the responsibilities have been divided—the sales manager must decide how many salespeople are needed. The first step is estimating how much work can be done by one person in some time period. Then the sales manager can make an "educated guess" about how many people are required in total, as the following example shows.

For many years, the Parker Jewelry Company was very successful selling its silver jewelry to department and jewelry stores in the Southwest. But management wanted to expand into the big urban markets of the Northeast. They realized that most of the work for the first few years would require order getters. They felt that a salesperson would need to call on each account at least once a month to get a share of this competitive business. They estimated that a salesperson could make only four calls a day on prospective buyers and still allow time for travel, waiting, and follow-up on orders that came in. This meant that a sales rep who made calls 20 days a month could handle about 80 stores (4 a day × 20 days).

The managers looked at telephone Yellow Pages for their target cities and estimated the total number of jewelry departments and stores. Then they simply divided the total number of stores by 80 to estimate the number of salespeople needed. This helped them set up territories, too—defining areas that included about 80 stores for each salesperson. Obviously, managers might want to "fine-tune" this estimate for differences in territories—such as travel time. But the basic approach can be applied to many different situations.[5]

When a company is starting a new sales force, managers are concerned about its size. But many established firms ignore this problem. Some managers forget that over time the "right" number of salespeople may change—as selling tasks change. Then, when a problem becomes obvious, they try to change everything in a hurry—a big mistake. Finding and training effective salespeople takes time—and it is an ongoing job.

SOUND SELECTION AND TRAINING TO BUILD A SALES FORCE

Selecting good salespeople takes judgment, plus

It is important to hire *good, well-qualified* salespeople. But the selection in many companies is a hit-or-miss affair—done without serious thought about exactly what kind of person the firm needs. Managers may hire friends and relations—or who-ever is available—because they feel that the only qualifications for sales jobs are a friendly personality and nice appearance. This approach has led to poor sales—and costly sales force turnover.

Progressive companies try to be more careful. They constantly update a list of possible job candidates. They schedule candidates for multiple interviews with vari-ous executives, do thorough background checks, and even use psychological tests. Unfortunately, such techniques can't guarantee success. But using some kind of systematic approach based on several different inputs results in a better sales force than using no selection aids at all.

One problem in selecting salespeople is that two different sales jobs with identi-cal titles may involve very different selling tasks—and require different skills. One way to avoid this problem is with a carefully prepared job description.

Job descriptions should be in writing and specific

A **job description** is a written statement of what a salesperson is expected to do. It might list 10 to 20 specific tasks—as well as routine prospecting and sales report writing. Each company must write its own job specifications. But when they are written, they should provide clear guidelines about what selling tasks the job involves. This is critical to determine the kind of salespeople who should be selected—and later it provides a basis for seeing how they should be trained, how well they are performing, and how they should be paid.

To train new salespeople, IBM uses in-class lectures, role-playing exercises, and a variety of other approaches.

Good salespeople are trained, not born

The idea that good salespeople are born may have some truth—but it isn't the whole story. A *born* salesperson—if that term refers to an outgoing, aggressive kind of individual—may not do nearly as well when the going gets rough as a less extroverted co-worker who has had solid, specialized training.

A salesperson needs to be taught—about the company and its products, and about giving effective sales presentations. But this isn't always done. Many salespeople fail—or do a poor job—because they haven't had good training. New salespeople often are hired and immediately sent out on the road—or the retail selling floor—with no grounding in the basic selling steps and no information about the product or the customer. They just get a price list and a pat on the back. This isn't enough!

All salespeople need some training

It's up to sales and marketing management to be sure that the salespeople know what they're supposed to do—and how to do it. A job description is helpful in telling salespeople what they are expected to do. But showing them how to get the job done is harder—because people may be hired with different backgrounds, skills, and levels of intelligence. Some trainees are hired with no knowledge of the company or its products—and little knowledge of selling. Others may come in with a lot of industry knowledge and much selling experience—but some bad habits developed at another company. Still others may have some selling experience, but need to know more about the firm's customers and their needs. Even a firm's own sales veterans may get set in their ways and profit greatly by—and often welcome the chance for—additional training.

The kind of initial sales training should be modified based on the experience and skills of the group involved. But the company's sales training program should cover at least the following areas: (1) company policies and practices, (2) product information, and (3) professional selling skills.

Selling skills can be learned

Many companies spend the bulk of their training time on product information and company policy. They neglect training in selling techniques because they think selling is something "anyone can do." More progressive companies know that training on selling skills can pay off. For example, training can help salespeople learn how to be more effective in "cold calls" on new prospects, in listening carefully to identify a customer's real objections, and in closing the sale. Training can also help a salesperson better analyze why present customers buy from the company, why former customers now buy from competitors, and why some prospects remain only prospects. Later in this chapter, we'll talk about some key ideas in this area—especially those related to different kinds of sales presentations.

Training on selling techniques often starts in the classroom with lectures, case studies, and videotaped trial presentations and demonstrations. But a complete training program adds on-the-job observing of effective salespeople and coaching from sales supervisors.

Training is ongoing

How long the initial training period should last depends on how hard the job is— as shown in the job description. Some training programs go on for many months. For example, some new IBM sales reps don't call on an account by themselves for the first six months or more. Some form of sales training should go on indefinitely. Many companies use weekly sales meetings or work sessions, annual or semian-

---

Hewlett-Packard Salespeople Find Sales at Their Fingertips

Most salespeople try to improve sales by wearing out shoe leather—not their fingertips. But companies like Hewlett-Packard (HP) are training salespeople to work smarter, not just harder. In a carefully designed study, HP tracked how 135 of its salespeople spent their time. Then it gave each salesperson a laptop computer and training on how to use it. At first the laptops just helped with time-consuming chores like retrieving account histories and checking the status of orders on the corporate computer. Then laptop use expanded to many other sales tasks. After the six-month pilot program, HP found that the computers helped

salespeople cut time spent in meetings by 46 percent and travel time between customers and the office by 13 percent. As one HP marketing manager put it, "we changed the way people communicate."

Because of these changes, the time salespeople spent with customers shot up 27 percent—and sales increased by 10 percent. Based on that success, HP gave laptops and training to another 1,700 salespeople. HP's analysis indicated that the increase in profits from the laptops program would be $30 million— five times the cost—even if sales improvements were only half what they had been in the pilot study.[6]

---

nual conventions or conferences, and regular weekly or biweekly newsletters—as well as normal sales supervision—to keep salespeople up-to-date.[7]

COMPENSATING AND MOTIVATING SALESPEOPLE

To recruit—and keep—good salespeople, a firm has to develop an attractive compensation plan. The plan must be designed to motivate salespeople. Ideally, sales reps are paid in such a way that what they want to do—for personal interest and gain—is in the company's interest, too. Most companies focus on financial motivation—but public recognition, sales contests, and simple personal recognition for a job well done can be highly effective in encouraging greater sales effort.[8] Our main emphasis here, however, will be on financial motivation.[9]

Two basic decisions must be made in developing a compensation plan: (1) the level of compensation and (2) the method of payment.

Compensation varies with job and needed skills

To attract good salespeople, a company must pay at least the going market wage for different kinds of salespeople. Order getters are paid more than order takers, for example.

The job description explains the salesperson's role in the marketing mix. It should show whether the salesperson needs any special skills or has any special responsibilities that require higher pay levels. To be sure it can afford a specific type of salesperson, the company should estimate—when the job description is written—how valuable such a salesperson will be. A good order getter may be worth $50,000 to $100,000 to one company, but only $15,000 to $25,000 to another—just because the second firm doesn't have enough to sell! In such a case, the second company should rethink its job specifications—or completely change its promotion plans—because the "going rate" for order getters is much higher than $15,000 a year.

The sales compensation plan may need to be flexible to take into consideration differences in sales potential—and the effort required—in different territories.

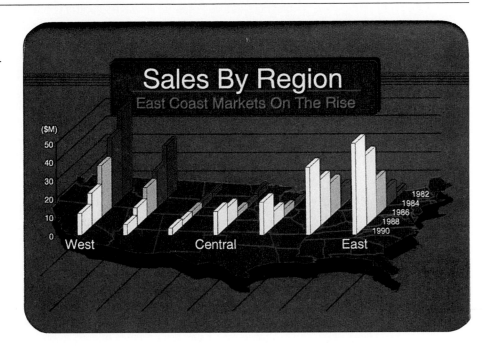

If a job requires extensive travel, aggressive pioneering, or contacts with difficult customers, the pay may have to be higher. But the salesperson's compensation level should compare—at least roughly—with the pay scale of the rest of the firm. Normally, salespeople are paid more than the office or production force, but less than top management.

Payment methods vary

Once a firm decides on the general level of compensation, it has to set the method of payment. There are three basic methods of payment: (1) *straight salary,* (2) *straight commission,* or (3) a *combination plan.* Straight salary normally supplies the most security for the salesperson—and straight commission the most incentive. These two represent extremes. Most companies want to offer their salespeople some balance between incentive and security so the most popular method of payment is a combination plan that includes some salary and some commission. Bonuses, profit sharing, pensions, insurance, and other fringe benefits may be included, too. Still, some blend of salary and commission provides the basis for most combination plans.

What determines the choice of the pay plan? Four standards should be applied: control, incentive, flexibility, and simplicity.

Salary gives control—if there is close supervision

The proportion of a salesperson's compensation that is paid as salary affects how much control the sales manager has. It also affects how much supervision is required. A salesperson on straight salary earns the same amount regardless of how he spends his time. So the salaried salesperson is expected to do what the sales manager asks—whether it is order taking, supporting sales activities, or completing sales call reports. However, control is maintained *only* if the sales manager provides close supervision. As a result, straight salary or a large salary element in the compensation plan increases the amount of sales supervision needed.

If such personal supervision would be difficult, a firm may get better control with a compensation plan that includes some commission—or even a straight commission plan with built-in direction. For example, if a company wants its salespeople to devote more time to developing new accounts, it can pay higher commission for "first orders" from a new customer. However, with a straight commission the salesperson tends to be his own boss. The sales manager is likely to get less cooperation on sales activities that will not increase the salesperson's commission earnings.

Incentives can be direct or indirect

An *incentive* plan can range anywhere from an indirect incentive (a modest sharing of company profits) to a very direct incentive—where a salesperson's income is strictly a commission on sales. The incentive should be large only if there is a direct relationship between the salesperson's effort and results. The relationship is less direct if a number of people are involved in the sale—engineers, top management, or supporting salespeople. In this case, each one's contribution is less obvious—and greater emphasis on salary may make more sense.

Strong incentives are normally offered to order-getting salespeople when a company wants to expand sales rapidly. Strong incentives may be used, too, when the company's objectives are shifting or varied. In this way, the salesperson's activities and efforts can be directed and shifted as needed. One trucking company, for example, has a sales incentive plan that pays higher commissions on business needed to balance freight movements—depending on how heavily traffic has been moving in one direction or another.

Flexibility is desirable—but difficult to achieve

Flexibility is probably the most difficult aspect to achieve. One major reason that combination plans have become more popular is that they offer a way to meet varying situations. We'll consider four major kinds of flexibility:

1. *Flexibility in selling costs.* This is important for most small companies. With limited working capital and uncertain markets, small companies like straight commission—or combination plans with a large commission element. When sales drop off, costs do too. Such flexibility is similar to using manufacturers' agents who are paid only if they deliver sales. This advantage often dominates in selecting a sales compensation method. Exhibit 16–2 shows the general relation between personal selling expense and sales volume for each of the basic compensation alternatives.
2. *Flexibility among territories.* Different sales territories have different potentials. Unless the pay plan allows for this fact, the salesperson in a growing territory might have rapidly increasing earnings for the same amount of work—while the sales rep in a poor area will have little to show for his effort. Such a situation isn't fair—and it can lead to high turnover and much dissatisfaction. Many companies set different sales objectives—or quotas—depending on the potential in each territory.
3. *Flexibility among people.* Most companies' salespeople vary in their stage of professional development. Trainees and new salespeople usually require a spe-

Exhibit 16–2   Relation between Personal Selling Expenses and Sales Volume—for Three Basic Personal Selling Compensation Alternatives

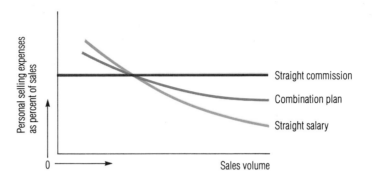

cial pay plan with emphasis on salary. This provides at least some stability of earnings.

4. *Flexibility among products.* Most companies sell several different products with different profit potentials. Unless firms recognize this fact, the salespeople may push the products that sell best—ignoring overall company profit. A flexible commission system can more easily adjust to changing profit potentials.

Simplicity

A final consideration is the need for *simplicity.* Complicated plans are hard for salespeople to understand. Salespeople become dissatisfied if they can't see a direct relationship between their effort and their income.

Simplicity is best achieved with straight salary. But in practice, it's usually better to sacrifice some simplicity to gain some incentive, flexibility, and control. The best combination of these factors depends on the job description and the company's objectives.

Sales managers must plan, implement, and control

There are no easy answers to the compensation problem. It is up to the sales manager—together with the marketing manager—to develop a good compensation plan. The sales manager's efforts must be coordinated with the whole marketing mix because personal selling objectives can be accomplished only if enough money is allocated for this job. Further, managers must regularly evaluate each salesperson's performance—and be certain that all the needed tasks are being done well. The compensation plan may have to be changed if the pay and work are out of line. And evaluating performance can also identify areas that need more attention—by the salesperson or management.[10] In Chapter 21, we'll talk more about controlling marketing activities.

PERSONAL SELLING TECHNIQUES—PROSPECTING AND PRESENTING

When we discussed the need for sales training programs, we stressed the importance of training in selling techniques. Now, let's discuss these ideas in more detail so you understand the basic steps each salesperson should follow—including prospecting, planning sales presentations, making sales presentations, and following up after the sale. Exhibit 16–3 shows the steps we'll consider. You

Exhibit 16–3   Key Steps in the Personal Selling Process

```
┌──────────────┐         ┌──────────────────┐
│ Prospecting  │────────▶│ Set effort       │         ┐
│              │         │ priorities       │         │
└──────┬───────┘         └──────────────────┘         │
       │                                              │
       ▼                                              │
┌──────────────────────────┐                          │
│ Select target customer   │                          │
└────────────┬─────────────┘                          │
             │                                        │
             ▼                                        │
┌──────────────────────────┐                          │
│ Plan sales presentation  │                          │
│ Prepared presentation    │                          │
│ Need-satisfaction approach│                         F│
│ Selling formula approach │                          E│
└────────────┬─────────────┘                          E│
             │                                        D│
             ▼                                        B│
┌──────────────────────────┐                          A│
│ Make sales presentation  │                          C│
│ Create interest          │                          K│
│ Meet objections          │                          │
│ Arouse desire            │                          │
└────────────┬─────────────┘                          │
             │                                        │
             ▼                                        │
┌──────────────────────────┐                          │
│ Close sale               │                          │
│ (get action)             │                          │
└────────────┬─────────────┘                          │
             │                                        │
      ┌──────┴───────┐                                │
      ▼              ▼                                │
┌───────────┐  ┌──────────────┐                       │
│ Follow up │─▶│ Follow up    │                       │
│ after the │  │ after the    │                       │
│ sales call│  │ purchase     │                       │
└───────────┘  └──────────────┘                       ┘
```

can see that the personal salesperson is just carrying out a planned communication process—as we discussed in Chapter 15.[11]

Prospecting—narrowing down to the right target

Although a marketing strategy should specify the segmenting dimensions for a target market, that doesn't mean that each target customer is individually identified! Narrowing the personal selling effort down to the right target requires constant, detailed analysis of markets and much prospecting. Basically, **prospecting** involves following all the "leads" in the target market to identify potential customers.

Finding prospects who are currently "live" and will help make the buying decision isn't as easy as it sounds. In industrial markets, for example, the salesperson may need to do some real detective work to find the real purchase decision makers. Multiple buying influence is common and companies regularly rearrange their organization structures and buying responsibilities.

Most salespeople use the telephone for much of their detective work. A phone call often saves the wasted expense of personal visits to prospects who are not at

Many firms now equip salespeople with portable computers—and specially developed software—to help with prospecting, communications, and other sales tasks.

We've not only changed how you work out of the office, we've changed how you work in it.

Our PCs are being seen in more and more offices.
They're also being seen out of more and more offices.
That's because not only can our machines do anything a desktop can do, they can do it just about anywhere you want.
They're small enough and rugged enough to stand up to constant traveling. And they have the power to run whatever software you're using.
What's more, our full line of PCs includes three new machines. First, our T1600, a battery powered 286. Second, our T3100e, the enhanced successor to our award winning T3100/20. And, finally, our 20MHz, 386-based T5200, a portable workstation.
All are capable of being integrated in your networked system. Or of being packed up and taken with you.
Even if you're only taking them down the hall.

In Touch with Tomorrow
TOSHIBA

all interested—or it can provide much useful information for planning a follow-up sales visit. Some "hot" prospects can even be sold on the phone.

Some companies provide "prospect lists" to make this part of the selling job easier. For example, one insurance company checks the local newspaper for marriage announcements—then a salesperson calls to see if the new couple is interested in finding out more about life insurance.

How long to spend with whom?

Once a set of possible prospects has been identified, the salesperson must decide how much time to spend on which prospects. A sales rep must "qualify" prospects—to see if they deserve more effort. He has to weigh the potential sales volume—as well as the likelihood of a sale. This requires judgment. But well-organized salespeople usually develop some system to guide prospecting because they have too many prospects. They can't "wine and dine" all of them.[12]

Some firms provide their reps with personal computers—and specially developed computer programs—to help with this process. Usually some "grading" scheme is used. A sales rep might estimate how much each prospect is likely to purchase—and the probability of getting the business, given the competition. The computer then combines this information and grades each prospect. Attractive accounts may be labeled "A"—and the salesperson may plan to call on them weekly until the sale is made or they are placed in a lower category. "B" customers might offer somewhat lower potential—and be called on monthly. "C" accounts might be called on only once a year—unless they happen to contact the salesperson. And "D" accounts might be ignored—unless the customer takes the initiative.[13]

Three kinds of sales presentations may be useful

Once a promising prospect is located, it's necessary to make a **sales presentation**—a salesperson's effort to make a sale. But someone has to plan the kind of sales presentation to be made. This is a strategy decision. The kind of presentation should be set before the sales rep is sent prospecting. And in situations where the customer comes to the salesperson—in a retail store, for instance—planners have to make sure that prospects are brought together with salespeople. Then the sales presentation must be made.

A marketing manager can choose two basically different approaches to making sales presentations: the prepared approach or the need-satisfaction approach. Another approach—the selling formula approach—is a combination of the two. Each of these has its place.

The prepared sales presentation

The **prepared sales presentation** approach uses a memorized presentation that is not adapted to each individual customer. A prepared ("canned") presentation builds on the stimulus-response model discussed in Chapter 7. This model says that a customer faced with a particular stimulus will give the desired response—in this case, a "yes" answer to the salesperson's prepared statement—which includes a request for an order.

If one "trial close" doesn't work, the sales rep tries another prepared presentation—and attempts another closing. This can go on for some time—until the salesperson runs out of material or the customer either buys or decides to leave. Exhibit 16–4 shows the relative participation of the salesperson and customer in the prepared approach. Note that the salesperson does most of the talking.

In modern selling, firms commonly use the "canned" approach when the prospective sale is low in value and only a short presentation is practical. It's also sensible when salespeople aren't very skilled. The company can control what they say—and in what order. For example, a sales rep for *Time* magazine can call a prospect—perhaps a person whose subscription is about to run out—and basically "read" the prepared presentation. The caller needs little training or ability.

But a "canned" approach has a weakness. It treats all potential customers alike. It may work for some and not for others—and the salespeople probably won't know why or learn from experience. A prepared approach may be suitable for simple order taking—but it is no longer considered good selling for complicated situations.

Need-satisfaction approach—builds on the marketing concept

The **need-satisfaction approach** involves developing a good understanding of the individual customer's needs before trying to close the sale. Here, the sales rep makes some general "benefit" statements to get the customer's attention and interest. Then he leads the customer to do most of the talking. The salesperson asks questions and *listens carefully* to understand the customer's needs. Once

Exhibit 16–4   Prepared Approach to Sales Presentation

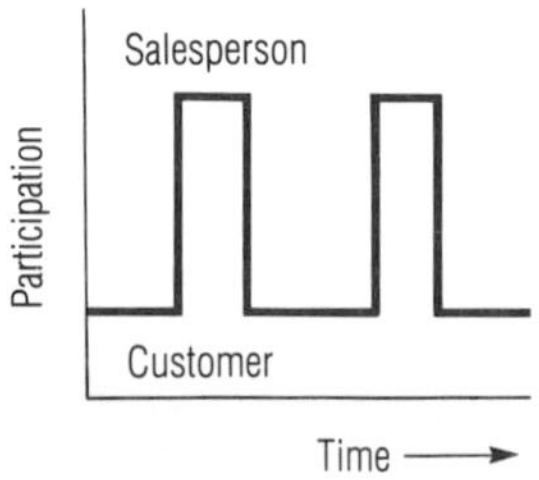

Exhibit 16–5   Need-Satisfaction Approach to Sales Presentation

Exhibit 16–6   Selling-Formula Approach to Sales Presentation

they agree on needs, the seller tries to show the customer how the product fills those needs—and to close the sale. This is a problem-solving approach—in which the customer and salesperson work together to solve the problem. Because the salesperson is almost acting as a consultant to help identify and solve the customer's problem, some people call this approach consultative selling. Exhibit 16–5 shows the participation of the customer and the salesperson during such a sales presentation.

The need-satisfaction approach is most useful if there are many subtle differences among the customers in one target market. In the extreme, each customer may be thought of as a separate target market—with the salesperson trying to adapt to each one's needs and attitudes. This kind of selling takes more skill—and time. The salesperson must be able to analyze what motivates a particular customer—and show how the company's offering would help the customer satisfy those needs.

Selling formula approach— some of both

The **selling formula approach** starts with a prepared presentation outline— much like the prepared approach—and leads the customer through some logical steps to a final close. The prepared steps are logical because we assume that we know something about the target customer's needs and attitudes.

Exhibit 16–6 shows the selling formula approach. The salesperson does most of the talking at the beginning of the presentation to be certain he communicates key points early. This part of the presentation may even have been prepared as part of the marketing strategy. As the sales presentation moves along, however, the salesperson brings the customer into the discussion to help clarify just what needs this customer has. The salesperson's job is to discover the needs of a particular customer to know how to proceed. Once it is clear what kind of customer

Which sales presentation is used depends on the situation.

this is, the salesperson comes back to show how the product satisfies this specific customer's needs—and to close the sale.

This approach can be useful for both order-getting and order-taking situations—where potential customers are similar and firms must use relatively untrained salespeople. Some office equipment and computer producers use this approach. They know the kinds of situations their salespeople meet—and roughly what they want them to say. Using this approach speeds training and makes the sales force productive sooner.

AIDA helps plan sales presentations

AIDA—Attention, Interest, Desire, Action. Each sales presentation—except for some very simple canned types—follows this AIDA sequence. The "how-to-do-it" might even be set as part of the marketing strategy. The time spent with each of the steps might vary, depending on the situation and the selling approach being used. But it is still necessary to begin a presentation by getting the prospect's *attention*, and hopefully, moving him to *action* through a close.[14]

Each sales manager—and salesperson—needs to think about this sequence in deciding what sales approach to use and in evaluating a possible presentation. Does the presentation get the prospect's attention quickly? Will the presentation be interesting? Will the benefits be clear so that the prospect is moved to buy the product? Does it consider likely objections—and anticipate problems—so the sales rep can act to close the sale when the time is right? These may seem like simple things. But too frequently they aren't done at all—and a sale is lost.

CONCLUSION

In this chapter, we discussed the importance and nature of personal selling. Selling is much more than just "getting rid of the product." In fact, a salesperson who is not provided with strategy guidelines may have to become his own strategy planner. Ideally, however, the sales manager and marketing manager work together to set some strategy guidelines: the kind and number of salespersons needed, the kind of sales presentation, and selection, training, and motivation approaches.

We discussed the three basic sales tasks: (1) order-getting, (2) order-taking, and (3) supporting. Most sales jobs are a combination of at least two of these three tasks. Once a firm specifies the important tasks, it can decide on the structure of its sales organization and the number of salespeople it needs. The nature of the job—and the level and method of compensation—also depend on the blend of these tasks. Firms should develop a job description for each sales job. This, in turn, provides guidelines for selecting, training, and compensating salespeople.

Once the sales manager's basic plan and budget have been set, he must implement the plan—including

directing and controlling the sales force. This includes assigning sales territories and controlling performance. You can see that the sales manager has more to do than jet around the country sipping martinis and entertaining customers. A sales manager is deeply involved with the basic management tasks of planning and control—as well as ongoing implementation of the personal selling effort.

We also reviewed some fundamentals of salesmanship and identified three kinds of sales presentations. Each has its place—but the need-satisfaction approach seems best for higher-level sales jobs. In these kinds of jobs, personal selling is achieving a new, professional status because of the competence and level of personal responsibility required of the salesperson. The day of the old-time "glad-hander" is passing in favor of the specialist who is creative, industrious, persuasive, knowledgeable, highly trained—and, therefore, able to help the buyer. This type of salesperson always has been—and probably always will be—in short supply. And the demand for high-level salespeople is growing.

Questions and Problems

1. What strategy decisions are needed in the personal selling area? Why should they be made by the marketing manager?

2. What kind of salesperson (or what blend of the basic sales tasks) is required to sell the following products? If there are several selling jobs in the channel for each product, then indicate the kinds of salespeople required. Specify any assumptions necessary to give definite answers.

   a. Laundry detergent.
   b. Costume jewelry.
   c. Office furniture.
   d. Men's underwear.
   e. Mattresses.
   f. Corn.
   g. Life insurance.

3. Distinguish among the jobs of producers', wholesalers', and retailers' order-getting salespeople. If one order getter is needed, must all the salespeople in a channel be order getters? Illustrate.

4. Discuss the role of the manufacturers' agent in a marketing manager's promotion plans. What kind of salesperson is a manufacturers' agent? What type of compensation plan is used for a manufacturers' agent?

5. Discuss the future of the specialty shop if producers place greater emphasis on mass selling because of the inadequacy of retail order taking.

6. Compare and contrast missionary salespeople and technical specialists.

7. How would a straight commission plan provide flexibility in the sale of a line of women's clothing products that continually vary in profitability?

8. Explain how a compensation plan could be developed to provide incentives for experienced salespeople and yet make some provision for trainees who have not yet learned their job.

9. Cite an actual local example of each of the three kinds of sales presentations discussed in the chapter. Explain for each situation whether a different type of presentation would have been better.

10. Describe a need-satisfaction sales presentation that you experienced recently. How could it have been improved by fuller use of the AIDA framework?

11. How would our economy operate if personal salespeople were outlawed? Could the economy work? If so, how? If not, what is the minimum personal selling effort necessary? Could this minimum personal selling effort be controlled by law?

Suggested Cases

23. Du Pont

24. Republic Wire, Inc.

25. Conn Furniture Company

31. American Tools, Inc.

Suggested Computer-Aided Problem

16. Sales Compensation

Chapter 17

Mass Selling

When You Finish This Chapter, You Should

1. Understand when the various kinds of advertising are needed.

2. Understand how to go about choosing the "best" medium.

3. Understand how to plan the "best" message—that is, the copy thrust.

4. Understand what advertising agencies do—and how they are paid.

5. Understand how to advertise legally.

6. Understand the important new terms (shown in red).

To reach a lot of people quickly and cheaply—use mass selling.

Marketing managers for Campbell's ready-to-serve Chunky Soup faced important decisions concerning their 1990 advertising. The previous year's ad campaign positioned Chunky soup as "taking care of the meanest appetites." It was aimed primarily at men. That campaign had helped Chunky become more popular. But for 1990 Campbell's wanted to broaden its market with a new strategy designed to appeal to families.

Along with other decisions, the Campbell's managers had to decide if they would stick with BBDO Worldwide, the ad agency that had been helping with Chunky advertising. They also needed to rethink what media to use. They knew that they wanted to spend some of the firm's $247 million ad budget on high-impact, family-oriented network TV shows—like "The Cosby Show" and "Roseanne." But they also wanted to find more cost-effective local media—perhaps radio—that would allow them to adjust better mass selling messages to regional differences. And, of course, they needed to decide on the specific objectives for the new campaign, the kind of advertising that should be developed, and how the new ads would be evaluated.[1]

Mass selling makes widespread distribution possible. Although a marketing manager might prefer to use personal selling, it can be expensive on a per-contact or per-sale basis. Mass selling is a way around this problem. It's not as flexible as personal selling, but it can reach large numbers of potential customers at the same time. Today, most promotion blends contain both personal and mass selling.

Mass selling contacts vary in cost and results. This means that marketing managers—and the advertising managers who work with them—have important strategy decisions to make. As the Campbell's case illustrates, they must decide: (1) who their target audience is, (2) what kind of advertising to use, (3) how to reach customers (via which types of media), (4) what to say to them (the copy thrust), and (5) who will do the work—the firm's own advertising department or outside agencies. See Exhibit 17–1. We'll talk about these decisions in this chapter. We'll also consider how to measure advertising effectiveness—and how to advertise legally—in an increasingly competitive environment.

THE IMPORTANCE OF ADVERTISING

$125 billion in ads in 1989

Advertising can get results in a promotion blend. But good advertising results cost money. In the United States, spending for advertising has grown continuously since World War II—and more growth is expected. In 1946, advertising spending was slightly more than $3 billion. By 1982 it was $66 billion—and by 1989 it was about $125 billion.[2]

It's all done by less than half a million people

While total advertising expenditures are large, the advertising industry itself employs relatively few people. The major expense is for media time and space. And in the United States, the largest share of this—26 percent—goes for newspaper space. Television (including cable) takes about 22 percent of the total, and direct mail about 18 percent.[3]

Many students hope for a glamorous job in advertising, but only about 500,000 people work directly in the U.S. advertising industry. This includes all people who help create or sell advertising or advertising media—advertising people in radio and television stations, newspapers, and magazines—those in advertising agen-

Exhibit 17–1   Strategy Planning for Advertising

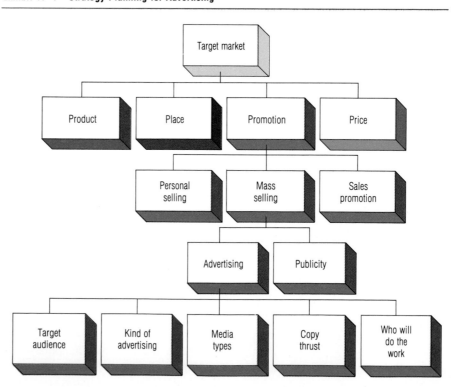

cies, and those working for retailers, wholesalers, and producers. U.S. advertising agencies employ only about half of all these people.[4]

Most advertisers aren't really spending that much

U.S. corporations spend an average of only about 1.5 percent of their sales dollar on advertising. This is relatively small compared to the total cost of marketing—perhaps 50 percent of the consumer's dollar.

Some industries—and companies—spend a much larger percentage of sales for advertising than the average of 1.5 percent. Cereal producers like General Mills and Kellogg's spend between 12 and 14 percent of sales on ads. Soft-drink companies like PepsiCo and Coca Cola spend about 6 percent of sales on advertising. K mart and J. C. Penney spend about 3 percent—although many retailers and wholesalers spend only about 1 percent. At the other extreme, some industrial products companies—those who depend on personal selling—may spend less than 1/10 of 1 percent.

Of course, percentages don't tell the whole story. General Motors only spends a little over 1 percent of sales on advertising, but it is one of the biggest advertisers. The really big spenders are very important to the advertising industry. In recent years, the top 100 advertisers accounted for about 25 percent of all advertising dollars. See Exhibit 17–2 for a list of the top 10 national advertisers in 1988.

You can see that advertising is important in certain markets—especially final consumer markets. Nevertheless, keep in mind that, in total, advertising costs much less than personal selling.

ADVERTISING OBJECTIVES ARE SET BY MARKETING STRATEGY

Every ad and every advertising campaign should have clearly defined objectives. These should grow out of the firm's overall marketing strategy—and the jobs assigned to advertising. It isn't enough for the marketing manager to say, "Promote the product." The marketing manager should decide exactly what advertising should do—although it isn't necessary to specify what each ad should accomplish.

Exhibit 17–2   Top 10 U.S. National Advertisers in 1988

Rank	Company name	Total advertising dollars—1988 ($ million)
1	Philip Morris Cos.	$2,058
2	Procter & Gamble Co.	1,507
3	General Motors Corp.	1,294
4	Sears Roebuck & Co.	1,045
5	RJR Nabisco	815
6	Grand Metropolitan PLC	774
7	Eastman Kodak Co.	736
8	McDonald's Corp.	728
9	PepsiCo Inc.	712
10	Kellogg Co.	683

Such detailed objectives should be set by the advertising manager to guide his own efforts.

Advertising should be assigned specific objectives

An advertising manager might be given one or more of the following specific objectives—along with the budget to accomplish them:

1. Aid in the introduction of new products to specific target markets.
2. Help obtain desirable outlets.
3. Prepare the way for salespeople by presenting the company's name and the merits of its products.
4. Provide ongoing contact with target customers—even when a salesperson isn't available.
5. Help "position" the brand by informing and persuading consumers about its benefits.
6. Get immediate buying action.
7. Help buyers confirm their purchasing decisions.

If you want half the market, say so!

The objectives listed above are not as specific as they could be. The advertising manager might want to sharpen them for his own purposes—or encourage the marketing manager to set more specific objectives. If a marketing manager really wants specific results, he should state what he wants. A general objective: "To help in the expansion of market share," could be rephrased more specifically: "To increase shelf space in our cooperating retail outlets by 25 percent during the next three months."

Such specific objectives obviously affect implementation. Advertising that might be right for building a good image among opinion leaders might be all wrong for getting customers into the retailers' stores.

Even more specific objectives might be needed in some cases. With new products, for example, most of the target market may have to be brought through the early stages of the adoption process. The advertising manager may use "teaser"

Producers of consumer products often rely on mass selling to inform customers about new products—and to persuade them about the benefits of established products.

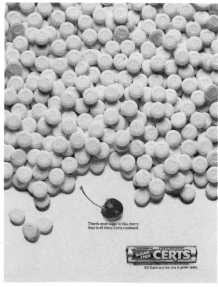

campaigns—along with informative ads. For more established products, advertising's job might be to build brand preference—as well as help purchasers confirm their decisions. This, too, leads to different kinds of advertising as shown in Exhibit 17–3.

Advertising objectives should be more specific than personal selling objectives. One of the advantages of personal selling is that the salespeople can shift their presentations to meet customers' needs. Each ad, however, is a specific communication. It must be effective not just for one customer but for thousands—or millions—of target customers. This means that advertising managers must set specific objectives for each ad—as well as a whole advertising campaign. If specific objectives aren't set, the "creative" advertising people may pursue their own objectives. They may set some general objective—like "selling the product"—and then create ads that may win artistic awards within the advertising industry but fail to achieve the expected results.

OBJECTIVES DETERMINE THE KINDS OF ADVERTISING NEEDED

The advertising objectives largely determine which of two basic types of advertising to use—product or institutional.

Product advertising tries to sell a product. It may be aimed at final users or channel members.

Institutional advertising tries to develop goodwill for a company—or even an industry—instead of a specific product. Its objective is to improve the advertiser's

Exhibit 17–3   Advertising Should Vary for Adoption Process Stages

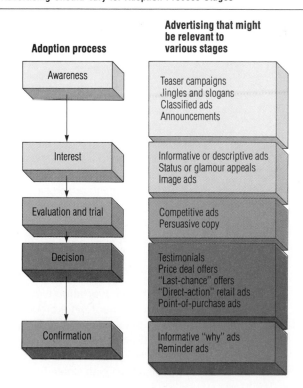

Webster's uses reminder advertising for its popular collegiate dictionary; Dow targets its institutional ads at various groups, including potential employees.

image, sales, and relations with the various groups the company deals with. This includes not only consumers but also current and prospective channel members, suppliers, shareholders, employees, and the general public. Dow, for example, appeals to college grads and other potential employees with image-oriented ads that proclaim "Dow lets you do great things."

Product advertising—know us, like us, remember us

Product advertising falls into three categories: pioneering, competitive, and reminder advertising.

Pioneering advertising—builds primary demand

Pioneering advertising tries to develop **primary demand**—demand for a product category rather than a specific brand. It's needed in the early stages of the adoption process to inform potential customers about a new product. Pioneering advertising is usually done in the early stage of the product life cycle. When Merrell Dow Pharmaceutical introduced a prescription drug to help smokers break the habit, it did pioneering advertising to inform both doctors and smokers about its breakthrough. The ad didn't even mention the name of the drug. Instead it informed smokers who wanted to quit that doctors could now help them overcome their nicotine dependence.

Competitive advertising—emphasizes selective demand

Competitive advertising tries to develop **selective demand**—demand for a specific brand rather than a product category. A firm is forced into competitive advertising as the product life cycle moves along—to hold its own against competitors. The United Fruit Company gave up a 20-year pioneering effort to promote bananas in favor of promoting its own Chiquita brand. The reason was simple. While United Fruit was single-handedly promoting bananas, it slowly lost market

The California Raisin Advisory Board's pioneering ads are intended to build primary demand for raisins. Sun Maid uses competitive advertising to develop selective demand for the Sun Maid brand.

share to competitors. It launched its competitive advertising campaign to avoid further losses.

Competitive advertising may be either direct or indirect. The **direct type** aims for immediate buying action. The **indirect type** points out product advantages to affect future buying decisions.

Most of Delta Airline's advertising is of the competitive variety. Much of it is trying for immediate sales—and the ads are the direct type with prices, timetables, and phone numbers to call for reservations. Some of its ads are the indirect type. They focus on the quality of service and number of cities served—and suggest you mention Delta's name the next time you talk to your travel agent.

Comparative advertising is even rougher. **Comparative advertising** means making specific brand comparisons—using actual product names. A recent comparative ad shows a large package of Tyco plastic toy blocks next to a smaller package of very similar Lego blocks with the headline "More or Less." The copy for the Tyco ad goes on to say "We've priced our new 600 piece Giant Storage Bucket to sell for the same as the Lego 359 piece bucket . . . so which would you choose . . . more or less?" In the same vein, a TV ad for Chevrolet trucks belittles Ford trucks—by name—as underpowered and outmoded.

A number of years ago, the Federal Trade Commission encouraged comparative ads. The FTC thought they would increase competition and provide consumers with more useful information. But this approach has led to legal as well as ethical problems—and some advertisers and their agencies now back away from it. Superiority claims are supposed to be supported by research evidence—but the guidelines aren't clear. Some firms just keep running tests until they get the results they want. Others talk about minor differences that don't reflect a product's overall benefits. Some comparative ads leave consumers confused—or even angry if the product they are using is criticized. And, in at least one case, comparative ads ap-

Tyco's comparative ad makes specific product comparisons with Lego, a competitor that sells a very similar toy.

pear to have benefited the competitive product (Tylenol) more than the advertisers' products (Datril, Anacin, and Bayer aspirin).[5]

Comparative advertising may be "a can of worms" that some advertisers wish they hadn't opened. But comparative ads seem to attract attention. So some advertisers will probably continue using this approach—as long as the government encourages it and the ad copy is not obviously false.[6]

Reminder advertising—reinforces early promotion

Reminder advertising tries to keep the product's name before the public. It may be useful when the product has achieved brand preference or insistence—perhaps in the market maturity or sales decline stages. Here, the advertiser may use "soft-sell" ads that just mention or show the name—as a reminder. For example, when Merriam-Webster came out with the new edition of its well-known Webster's Collegiate Dictionary, magazine ads showed the cover of the dictionary with the headline "America's favorite to the rescue."

Institutional advertising— remember our name in Dallas, Seattle, Boston

Institutional advertising focuses on the name and prestige of a company or industry. It may seek to inform, persuade, or remind.

A persuading kind of institutional advertising is sometimes used by large companies with several divisions to link the divisions in customers' minds. AT&T, for example, advertises the AT&T name—emphasizing the quality and research behind *all* AT&T products.

Companies sometimes rely on institutional advertising to present the company in a favorable light—perhaps to overcome image problems. Ads for a chemical company, for example, might highlight its concern about the environment.

Sometimes an advertising campaign may have both product and institutional aspects—because the federal government has taken an increasingly dim view of institutional advertising. The Internal Revenue Service has limited tax deductions for some institutional advertising—claiming it had no "business purpose."

COORDINATING ADVERTISING EFFORTS

Vertical cooperation— advertising allowances, co- operative advertising

So far, our discussion suggests that only producers do product or institutional advertising. This is not true, of course, but producers often affect the advertising done by others. Sometimes a producer knows what promotion job or advertising job should be done but finds that it can be done more effectively or more economically by someone further along in the channel. In this case, the producer may offer **advertising allowances**—price reductions to firms further along in the channel to encourage them to advertise or otherwise promote the firm's products locally.

Cooperative advertising involves middlemen and producers sharing in the cost of ads. It helps the producer get more promotion for the advertising dollar because media usually give local advertisers lower rates than national firms. In addition, a retailer is more likely to follow through when he is paying a share of the cost.

Coordination is another reason for cooperative advertising in a channel. Often one big, well-planned advertising effort is better than many different—perhaps inconsistent—local efforts. The idea of communicating with "one voice" is found in many franchise operations. Kentucky Fried Chicken uses the theme "We Do Chicken Right" in its national advertising. In the past, local franchises came up with their own ads—with themes like "Eight clucks for four bucks"—that didn't fit with the overall marketing strategy. Now, local franchises are encouraged to use a common advertising program.

Producers often get this coordination—and reduce local middlemen costs—by providing a "master" of an ad on a videotape, cassette tape, or printed sheets. The middleman's identification is added before the ad is turned over to local media.

BMW and its Atlanta dealers coordinate their advertising efforts—to get more mileage from their advertising budgets.

But cooperative advertising and advertising allowances can be abused. Some retailers ask for allowances, but then don't run the ads. Some producers have "closed their eyes" to this problem because they didn't know what to do about intense competition from other suppliers for the retailer's attention. But there are legal and ethical problems with that response. Basically, the "allowance" may have become a disguised price concession that results in price discrimination. The Federal Trade Commission has become more interested in this problem—and some manufacturers have pulled back from cooperative advertising. To avoid legal problems, smart producers insist on proof that the advertising was really done.

Horizontal cooperation— promotes different firms

Sometimes two or more firms with complementary products join together in a common advertising effort. Ads for Delta Airlines and Disney World encouraged families to travel by air and so have more time to enjoy the attractions at Disney World. Retailers in the same shopping center often share the costs of promotion efforts. They might buy full-page newspaper ads listing the individual stores or promoting "sale days." Generally, the objective is the same as in vertical cooperation—to get more for the advertising dollar.[7]

CHOOSING THE "BEST" MEDIUM—HOW TO DELIVER THE MESSAGE

For effective promotion, ads must reach specific target customers. Unfortunately, not all potential customers read all newspapers, magazines, or other printed media—or listen to all radio and TV programs. So not all media are equally effective.

What is the best advertising medium? There is no simple answer to this question. Effectiveness depends on how well the medium fits with the rest of a marketing strategy—that is, it depends on (1) your promotion objectives, (2) what target markets you want to reach, (3) the funds available for advertising, and (4) the nature of the media—including who they *reach*, with what *frequency*, with what *impact*, and at what *cost*. Exhibit 17–4 shows some of the pros and cons of major kinds of media—and some typical costs.[8]

Specialized media are small—but gaining

Exhibit 17–4 lists the *major* advertising media. These media attract the vast majority of mass selling media budgets. But advertising specialists are always looking for cost-effective new media that will help advertisers reach their target markets. For example, one company has been successful selling space for signs on bike racks that it places in front of 7-Eleven stores. Another company prints advertising on grocery bags. One company even sells hotels and auto rental companies space on advertising boards that are placed in the restrooms on airplanes!

In recent years, these specialized media have been gaining in popularity. One reason is that they are often designed to get the mass selling message to the target market close to the point of purchase. They may also offer the advantage of making an advertiser's message stand out from the usual advertising "clutter" in the mass media. There are too many specialized media to go into all of them in detail here. What is important to see is that they require the same type of strategy decisions as the more typical mass media.

Specify promotion objectives

Before you can choose the best medium, you have to decide on your promotion objectives. If the objective is to inform—telling a long story with precise detail—and if pictures are needed, then print media—including magazines and newspapers—may be better. Jockey switched its annual budget of more than $1 million to maga-

Exhibit 17–4   Relative Size and Costs, and Advantages and Disadvantages of Major Kinds of Media

Kinds of Media	Sales Volume—1988 ($ billions)	Typical costs—1988	Advantages	Disadvantages
Newspaper	$31.2	$20,640 for one-page weekday, *Milwaukee Journal*	Flexible Timely Local market Credible source	May be expensive Short life No "pass-along"
Television	$25.7	$4,000 for a 30-second spot, prime time, Milwaukee	Offers sight, sound and motion Good attention Wide reach	Expensive in total "Clutter" Short exposure Less selective audience
Direct Mail	$21.1	$65/1,000 for listing of 105,500 architects	Selected audience Flexible Can personalize	Relatively expensive per contact "Junk mail"—hard to retain attention
Radio	$7.8	$200 for one-minute drive time, Milwaukee	Wide reach Segmented audiences Inexpensive	Offers audio only Weak attention Many different rates Short exposure
Magazine	$6.1	$70,025 for one-page, 4-color in *People*	Very segmented audiences Credible source Good reproduction Long life Good "pass-along"	Inflexible Long lead times
Outdoor	$1.1	$4,200 (painted) for prime billboard, 30–60-day showings, Milwaukee	Flexible Repeat exposure Inexpensive	"Mass market" Very short exposure

zines from television when it decided to show the variety of colors, patterns, and styles of its men's briefs. Jockey felt that it was too hard to show this in a 30-second TV spot. Further, there are problems with modeling such products on television—the same problems that producers of women's undergarments face! Jockey ran its ads in men's magazines—such as *Sports Illustrated, Outdoor Life, Field and Stream, Esquire,* and *Playboy.* But aware that women buy over 80 percent of men's ordinary underwear—and 50 percent of fashion styles—Jockey also placed ads in *TV Guide, The New Yorker, People, Money, Time,* and *Newsweek.* And it ran a page of scantily clad males in *Cosmopolitan.*[9]

Match your market with the media

To guarantee good media selection, the advertiser first must *clearly* specify its target market—a necessary step for all marketing strategy planning. Then, the advertiser can chose media that are heard, read, or seen by those target customers.

Matching target customers and media is the major problem in effective media selection because it is not always certain who sees or hears what. Most of the major media use marketing research to develop profiles of the people who buy their publications—or live in their broadcasting area. But they cannot be as definite about who actually reads each page or sees or hears each show. And they seldom gather information on the market dimensions *each* advertiser may think important. Generally, media research focuses on demographic characteristics. But what if the really important dimensions are concerned with behavioral needs or attitudes that are difficult to measure—or unique to a particular product-market?

Another problem is that the audience for media that *do* reach your target market may also include people who are *not* in the target group. But *you pay for the whole audience the media delivers*—including those who aren't potential users of your product. A study of TV advertising during the Olympics illustrates the problem. Levi's Olympic ads were aimed at its target market of 18- to 24-year-old jeans buyers. Many 18- to 24-year-olds did watch the Olympics, but most of the viewers weren't in Levi's target market. A research firm concluded that Levi's—and five other top Olympic advertisers—paid about twice as much as they normally do to get their message across to those consumers who actually buy the type of product advertised.[10]

Because it is so difficult to evaluate alternative media, some media analysts focus on objective measures—such as "cost per thousand" of audience size or circulation. But advertisers who are preoccupied with keeping these costs down may ignore the relevant dimensions—and slip into "mass marketing." The media buyer may look only at the relatively low cost of "mass media" when a more specialized medium might be a much better buy. Its audience might have more interest in the product—or more money to spend—or more willingness to buy. Gillette Co. is buying advertising time on cable TV—especially MTV—to increase its penetration with teenagers and young adults, who are more willing to try new products.

Specialized media help zero in on target markets

Media are now directing more attention to reaching smaller, more defined target markets. National media may offer regional editions. *Time* magazine, for example, offers not only several regional and metropolitan editions, but also special editions for college students, educators, doctors, and business managers.

Cable TV can help the marketer zero in on a specific target market, but consumers may selectively "tune out" ads that don't interest them.

Large metro newspapers usually have several editions to cater to city and suburban areas. Where these outlying areas are not adequately covered, however, suburban newspapers are prospering—catering to the desire for local news.

Many magazines serve only special-interest groups—such as fishermen, soap opera fans, new parents, professional groups, and personal computer users. In fact, the most profitable magazines seem to be the ones aimed at clearly defined markets.

There are trade magazines in many fields—such as chemical engineering, electrical wholesaling, farming, and the defense market. *Standard Rate and Data* provides a guide to the thousands of magazines now available.

Radio—like some magazines and newspapers—has become a more specialized medium. Some stations cater to particular ethnic, racial, and religious groups—such as Hispanics, blacks, and Catholics. Others aim at specific target markets with rock, country, or classical music. Stations that play "golden oldies" have been popping up around the country—to appeal to the baby boomer crowd.

Cable TV channels—like MTV, Cable News Network, Nickelodeon, and ESPN—are also targeted at specific audiences. ESPN, for example, has an audience heavily weighted toward affluent, male viewers and MTV appeals most strongly to affluent young viewers 25–34 years old.

Perhaps the most specific medium is **direct-mail advertising**—selling directly to customers via their mailboxes. The method involves sending a specific message to a carefully selected list of names.

Some firms specialize in providing computer mailing lists—ranging from hundreds to millions of names. The diversity of these lists (See Exhibit 17–5) points out the importance of knowing your target market. Some firms are making their mailing lists more useful by merging information about other segmenting dimensions with names and addresses. For example, an auto manufacturer can get a mailing list that includes the make of car a person drives. That information is merged from vehicle registration records. Different promotion can then be targeted to people who own different types of cars.[11]

Exhibit 17–5   Examples of Available Mailing Lists

Quantity of names	Name of list
425	Small Business Advisors
40,000	Social Register of Canada
5,000	Society of American Bacteriologists
500	South Carolina Engineering Society
2,000	South Dakota State Pharmaceutical Association
250	Southern California Academy of Science
12,000	Texas Manufacturing Executives
720	Trailer Coach Association
1,200	United Community Funds of America
50,000	University of Utah Alumni
19,000	Veterinarians

Actmedia Sells Advertisers a Little Media Space

Actmedia, Inc., sells advertising space on little message boards that hang on shopping carts and shelves in grocery stores. Advertising managers for Huggies diapers, Heinz ketchup, Windex window cleaner, and other consumer products like the concept. With print and TV ads, the manager may have to rely on demographic data to select media that reach the target market. With in-store ads, the target customers are already in the store where 80 percent of the purchase decisions are made. The ads also do more than get attention; they prompt action. Actmedia promises average sales increases of at least 8 percent for the four weeks a product is advertised in-store. A marketing manager at General Foods achieved in-creases of 20 percent for impulse products like ice cream. Results like those explain why Actmedia, which started in 1972, was generating about $65 million in ad revenues by 1987.

Supermarkets like the idea, too. They get 25 percent of the revenue Actmedia receives from advertisers. Because of that incentive, about half of the nation's supermarkets are involved with Actmedia. And, to reach new target markets, Actmedia is expanding to drugstores and other types of retailers. Other advertising specialists have tried to compete with Actmedia—for example, with special in-store radio ads and ads on grocery bags—but being in the stores first gave Actmedia an advantage that has made it hard to beat.[12]

"Must buys" may use up available funds

Selecting which media to use is still pretty much an art. The media buyer may start with a budgeted amount and try to buy the best blend to reach the target audience.

Some media may be obvious "must buys"—such as *the* local newspaper for a retailer in a small or medium-sized town. Most firms that serve local markets view a Yellow Pages listing as a "must buy." Such "must buys" may even use up the available funds. If not, then the media buyer must compare the relative advantages

---

Most marketing managers who serve local markets view Yellow Pages advertising as a "must buy"— because it usually reaches customers when they are ready to buy.

and disadvantages of alternatives—and select a media *blend* that helps achieve the promotion objectives, given the available budget.

For many firms—even national advertisers—the high cost of television may eliminate it from the media blend. A 30-second commercial on a prime-time show averages about $125,000—and the price goes up rapidly for "specials" and shows that attract a large audience. In fact, many firms are moving away from television and experimenting with combinations of other media. To keep customers, the networks are offering 15-second advertising slots. That's not much time to get across an effective message!

PLANNING THE "BEST" MESSAGE—WHAT IS TO BE COMMUNICATED

Specifying the copy thrust

Once you decide *how* the messages are to reach the target audience, then you have to decide on the **copy thrust**—what the words and illustrations should communicate. This decision should flow from the promotion objectives—and the specific jobs assigned to advertising.

Carrying out the copy thrust is the job of advertising specialists. But the advertising manager and the marketing manager need to understand the process to be sure that the job is done well.

There are few tried-and-true rules in message construction. But behavioral research can help. Recall our discussion of the communication process and common frames of reference in Chapter 15. And the concepts of needs, learning, and perception discussed in Chapter 7 apply here, too. We know, for example, that consumers have a fantastic ability to selectively "tune out" messages or ideas that don't interest them. How much of the daily newspaper do you actually "see" as you page through it? We don't see everything the advertisers want us to see—or learn all they would like us to learn. How can an advertiser be more effective?

Let AIDA help guide message planning

Basically, the overall marketing strategy should determine *what* the message should say. Then management judgment—perhaps aided by marketing research—can help decide how this content can be encoded so it will be decoded as intended.

As a guide to message planning, we can make use of the AIDA concept: getting Attention, holding Interest, arousing Desire, and obtaining Action.

Billboards are good for getting attention with a simple copy thrust.

Getting attention

Getting attention is an ad's first job. If this isn't done, it doesn't matter how many people see it or hear it. Many readers leaf through magazines and newspapers without paying attention to any of the ads. Many listeners or viewers do chores—or get snacks—during commercials on radio and TV. When watching a program on videotape, they may zap past the commercial with a flick of the "fast forward" button.

Many attention-getting devices are available. A large headline, newsy or shocking statements, pictures of pretty girls, babies, "special effects"—anything that is "different" or eye-catching—may do the trick. For example, a TV ad for "the New Generation of Olds" gets attention with the playfully unexpected howls that accompany clips of astronaut training, and the "liftoff" roar as astronaut Scott Carpenter and his son drive off—tilted upward—in a new Oldsmobile. The major problem is that the attention-getting device must not detract from the next step—holding interest.

Holding interest

Holding interest is more difficult. A pretty girl may get attention—but once you've seen her, then what? A man may pause to appreciate her. Women may evaluate her. But if there is no relation between the girl and the product, observers of both sexes will move on.

More is known about holding interest than getting attention. The tone and language of the ad must fit with the experiences and the attitudes of target customers—and their reference groups. This has led many advertisers to develop ads that relate to specific emotions. They hope that the good "feeling" about the ad (and the whole marketing mix) will "stick"—even if the specific details of the copy thrust are forgotten. Many McDonald's ads, for example, don't focus on specific menu items but rather on people enjoying being with other people—at a McDonald's.

To hold interest, informative ads need to speak the target customer's language. And advertising layouts should look "right" to the customer. Print illustrations and copy should be arranged to encourage the eye to move smoothly through the ad—perhaps from the upper left-hand corner to the company or brand name at the lower right-hand corner. Ads with this natural flowing characteristic encourage *gaze motion*.[13]

Arousing desire

Arousing desire to own or use a particular product is one of an ad's most difficult jobs. The advertiser must communicate with the customer. To do this effectively, the advertiser must understand how target customers think, behave, and make decisions. Then the ad must convince the customers that the product can meet their needs. Some experts feel that an ad should focus on one "unique selling proposition" that aims at an important unsatisfied need. They discourage the typical approach of trying to tell the whole story in a single ad. Telling the whole story is the job of the whole promotion blend—not one ad.

If consumers see many different competing brands as "all the same," focusing on a unique selling proposition may be particularly important. This can help set the brand apart—and position it as especially effective in meeting the needs of the target market. For example, many Volvo ads emphasize safety. This approach makes

A unique selling proposition can help to position a brand as especially effective in meeting the needs of a target market.

sense when a brand really does have a comparative advantage on an *important* benefit.

An ad may also have the objective—especially during the market growth and market maturity stages—of supplying words that customers can use to rationalize their desire to buy. Although products may satisfy certain emotional needs, many consumers find it necessary to justify their purchases on some economic or "rational" basis. Snickers (candy bar) ads help ease the guilt of calorie-conscious snackers by assuring them that "Snickers satisfies you when you need an afternoon energy break."

Obtaining action

Getting action is the final requirement—and not an easy one. From communication research, we now know that prospective customers must be led beyond considering how the product *might* fit into their lives—to actually trying it or letting the company's sales rep come in and demonstrate it.

To communicate more effectively, the ads might emphasize strongly felt customer needs. Careful research on attitudes in the target market may help uncover such strongly felt *unsatisfied* needs.

Appealing to these needs can get more action—and also provide the kind of information buyers need to confirm their decisions. Post-purchase dissonance may set in—and obtaining confirmation may be one of the important advertising objectives. Some customers seem to read more advertising *after* the purchase than before. The ad may reassure them about the correctness of their decision—and also supply the words they use to tell others about the product.

ADVERTISING AGENCIES OFTEN DO THE WORK

An advertising manager manages a company's mass selling effort. Many advertising managers—especially those working for large retailers—have their own advertising departments that plan specific advertising campaigns and carry out the details. Others turn over much of the advertising work to specialists—the advertising agencies.

Ad agencies are specialists

Advertising agencies are specialists in planning and handling mass selling details for advertisers. Agencies play a useful role—because they are independent of the advertiser and have an outside viewpoint. They bring experience to an individual client's problems, because they work for many other clients. Further, as specialists they often can do the job more economically than a company's own department.

Some full-service agencies handle any activities related to advertising. They may even handle overall marketing strategy planning—as well as marketing research, product and package development, and sales promotion. Some agencies make good marketing partners—and almost assume the role of the firm's marketing department.

Some agencies don't offer a full line of services. *Media buying services* specialize in selecting media to fit a firm's marketing strategy. They are used when a firm wants to schedule a number of ads—perhaps in different media—and needs help finding the blend that will deliver what it needs at the lowest cost. Similarly, creative specialists create ads. These agencies handle the artistic elements of advertising, but leave media planning, research, and related services to others.

The biggest agencies handle much of the advertising

The vast majority of advertising agencies are small—with 10 or fewer employees. But the largest agencies account for most of the billings.

Recently, some big agencies merged—creating "mega-agencies" with worldwide networks. Exhibit 17–6 shows a list of 10 of these largest agencies and examples of some of the products they advertise. Part of the reason for these mergers is to combine the strengths of the individual agencies. The mega-agency can offer a marketing manager varied services wherever he may need them. This may

Exhibit 17–6   Top 10 Advertising Agency Supergroups and Examples of Products They Advertise

Rank	Supergroup	1988 gross income ($ millions)	Product
1	Young & Rubicam	$758	Johnson & Johnson Baby Powder
2	Saatchi & Saatchi Advertising Worldwide	740	Tide
3	Backer Spielvogel Bates Worldwide	690	Miller
4	McCann-Erickson Worldwide	657	Coca-Cola
5	FCB-Publicis	653	California Raisins
6	Ogilvy & Mather Worldwide	635	American Express
7	BBDO Worldwide	586	Pepsi-Cola
8	J. Walter Thompson Co.	559	Ford
9	Lintas: Worldwide	538	Chevrolet
10	D'Arcy Masius Benton & Bowles	433	Canon

be especially important for managers in large corporations—like General Motors, Procter & Gamble, and Coca-Cola—who advertise worldwide.

In spite of the growth of very large agencies, smaller agencies will probably continue to play an important role. The really big agencies are less interested in smaller accounts. Smaller agencies will continue to appeal to customers who want more "personal" attention.

It's easy to fire an ad agency

One of the advantages of using an ad agency is that the advertiser is free to cancel the arrangement at any time. This gives the advertiser extreme flexibility. Some companies even use their advertising agency as a scapegoat. Whenever anything goes wrong, they blame the agency—and shop around for a new one.

Are they paid too much?

Traditionally, most advertising agencies have been paid a commission of 15 percent on media and production costs. This arrangement evolved because media usually have two prices: one for national advertisers and a lower rate for local advertisers, such as local retailers. The advertising agency gets a 15 percent commission on national rates—but not on local rates. This makes it worthwhile for producers and national middlemen to use agencies. These national advertisers would have to pay the full media rate, anyway. So it makes sense to let the agency experts do the work—and earn their commission. Local retailers—allowed the lower media rate—seldom use agencies.

There is growing resistance to this "traditional" method of paying agencies. The chief complaint is that agencies receive the flat 15 percent commission regardless of the work performed or *the results achieved.* The commission approach also makes it hard for agencies to be completely objective about inexpensive media—or promotion campaigns that use little space or time. Much of the opposition to the traditional commission system comes from very large consumer products advertisers. They spend the most on media ads, and they think that a 15 percent fee is often too high—especially when an expensive ad campaign hasn't produced the desired results.

Advertising agencies work with marketing managers to plan ad campaigns.

Not all agencies are satisfied with the present arrangement either. Some would like to charge additional fees as their costs rise and advertisers demand more services.

The fixed commission system is most favored by accounts—such as producers of industrial products—that need a lot of service but spend relatively little on media. These are the firms the agencies would like to—and sometimes do—charge additional fees.

Fifteen percent is not required

The Federal Trade Commission worked for many years to change the method of advertising agency compensation. Finally, in 1956, the American Association of Advertising Agencies agreed it would no longer require the 15 percent commission system. This opened the way to fee increases and decreases. But, it is only in recent years that changes have become more widespread.

A number of advertisers are now "grading" the work provided by their agencies—and the agencies' pay depends on the grade. For example, General Foods has lowered its basic commission to about 13 percent. However, the company pays the agency a bonus of about 3 percent on campaigns that earn an "A" rating. If the agency only earns a "B" it loses out on the bonus. If it earns a "C" it had better improve fast—or GF will remove the account.

Variations on this approach are becoming common. For example, Carnation has directly linked its agency's compensation with how well its ads score in market research tests. Gillette and Lorillard use a sliding scale, and the percentage compensation declines with increased advertising volume. And others manage the spending of the 15 percent commission—paying for agency services on a fee basis and perhaps using some of the funds for outside suppliers or even in-house operations.

Many ad agencies dislike the idea of being so closely scrutinized by clients—or having to negotiate on what they are paid. But, if the current trends continue, they may have to get used to it.[14]

Conflicts between ad agencies and clients

The creative people in ad agencies and their more business-oriented clients often disagree. Some creative people are "production-oriented." They sometimes create an ad that they like themselves—or that will win approval within their industry—and are less concerned about how well it fits into the rest of the client's marketing mix.

You can see why this creates conflict. The advertiser's product managers or brand managers may be personally responsible for the success of particular products—and feel that they have some right to direct and even veto the work of the creative agency people. Because the advertiser is paying the bills, the agency often loses these confrontations.

MEASURING ADVERTISING EFFECTIVENESS IS NOT EASY

Success depends on the total marketing mix

It would be convenient if we could measure the results of advertising by looking at sales. Unfortunately, we can't—though the advertising literature is filled with success stories that "prove" advertising has increased sales. The total marketing mix—not just promotion generally or advertising specifically—is responsible for the sales result. And the impact of advertising that shows up in sales may be affected by what competitors do and by other changes in the uncontrollable environment.

Research can measure how well an ad captures consumer attention, but it is usually hard to tell what effect a single ad will have on sales.

TRUE CHAMPIONS.

The one exception to this is direct-mail advertising. If it doesn't produce immediate results, it's considered a failure.

Research and testing can improve the odds

Ideally, advertisers should pretest advertising before it's run—rather than relying solely on their own guesses about how "good" an ad will be. The judgment of creative people or advertising "experts" may not help much. They often judge only on the basis of originality—or cleverness—of the copy and illustrations.

Some progressive advertisers now demand laboratory or market tests to evaluate an ad's effectiveness. In addition, before ads are run generally, attitude research is sometimes used. Researchers often try to evaluate consumers' reaction to particular ads—or parts of ads. For example, American Express used focus group interviews to get reactions to a series of possible TV ads. The company wanted the ads to convey the idea that younger people could qualify for its credit cards—but it still wanted to present a prestige image. The agency prepared picture boards presenting different approaches—as well as specific copy. Four of six possible ads failed to communicate the message to the focus groups. One idea that seemed to be effective became the basis for an ad that was tested again before being launched on TV.[15]

Sometimes laboratory-type devices that measure skin moisture or eye reaction are used to gauge consumer responses. In addition, split runs on cable TV systems in test markets are now proving to be an important approach for testing ads in a normal viewing environment. Scanner sales data from retailers in those test markets can provide an estimate of how an ad is likely to affect sales. This approach is providing marketing managers with a powerful new tool—and it will become even more powerful in the future as more cable systems add new technology that allows viewers to provide immediate feedback to an ad as it appears on the TV.

**Hindsight may lead
to foresight**

After ads have been run, researchers may try to measure how much consumers recall about specific products or ads. Inquiries from customers may be used as a measure of the effectiveness of particular ads. The response to radio or television commercials—or magazine readership—can be estimated using various survey methods to check the size and composition of audiences (the Nielsen and Starch reports are examples).

While advertising research methods aren't foolproof, they are probably far better than relying on pure judgment by advertising "experts." Until more effective advertising research tools are developed, the present methods—carefully defining specific advertising objectives, choosing media and messages to accomplish these objectives, testing plans, and then evaluating the results of actual ads—seem to be most productive.[16]

HOW TO AVOID UNFAIR ADVERTISING

**FTC can control unfair
practices**

The Federal Trade Commission has the power to control unfair or deceptive business practices—including "deceptive advertising." The FTC has been policing deceptive advertising for many years. And it may be getting results now that advertising agencies as well as advertisers must share equal responsibility for false, misleading, or unfair ads.

This is a serious matter. If the FTC decides that a particular practice is unfair or deceptive, it has the power to require affirmative disclosures—such as the health warnings on cigarettes—or **corrective advertising**—ads to correct deceptive advertising. The FTC has not required corrective advertising recently, but that may be because several of its earlier actions got a lot of attention. For example, Listerine was forced to spend millions of dollars on advertising to "correct" earlier ads that claimed the mouthwash helped prevent colds. The FTC concluded that Listerine could not prove its claim. The possibility of large financial penalties and/or the need to pay for corrective ads has caused more agencies and advertisers to stay well within the law—rather than just along the edge.[17]

When the FTC found fewer outright deceptive ads in national campaigns, the agency moved more aggressively against what it felt to be other "unfair" practices. Some in the FTC felt it was unfair to target advertising at children. Others thought a case could be made against promotion that "encourages materialism"—by persuading consumers to buy things that they otherwise wouldn't. An FTC lawyer created a stir by criticizing electric hair dryers. His feeling was "that if you wait 15 minutes, your hair gets dry anyway." And there were questions about whether food and drug advertising should be controlled to protect "vulnerable" groups, such as the aged, poor, non-English-speaking, or less-educated adults. For example, there were concerns that obesity among low-income women might be caused by ads for high-calorie foods.

Not everyone agreed with this thrust, however. Congress specifically limits FTC rule making to advertising that is *deceptive* rather than *unfair*. Note, however, that while the FTC is prohibited from using "unfairness" in a rule affecting a whole industry, "unfairness" can still be used against an individual company. So advertisers *do* have to worry about being "unfair!"[18]

**What is unfair or deceptive
is changing**

What is unfair and deceptive is a difficult topic and one marketing managers will have to wrestle with for years. The social and political environment is changing. Practices considered acceptable some years ago are now questioned—or considered deceptive. Saying or even implying that your product is "best" may be viewed as deceptive.

A 1988 revision of the Lanham Act has brought new attention to this area. It prohibits advertisers from misrepresenting the qualities or characteristics of "another person's goods, services, or commercial activities." This means that companies that believe their brand names have been unfairly tarnished in another company's comparative ads are protected by federal law. By contrast, the earlier federal law only prohibited an advertiser from misrepresenting its own products.

Supporting ad claims is a fuzzy area

Supporting ad claims is a vague area—with no clear guidelines. There are many ways to "lie with statistics." And unethical and/or desperate advertisers of "me-too" products have tried many of them. Unfortunately, it only takes one such competitor in an industry to cause major shifts in market share—and affect the nature of competition in that market. As an old cliché says: one bad apple can spoil a whole barrel.

Most advertisers have good intentions and aren't trying to compete unfairly. So just clearing up what research support is needed to back up advertising claims might reduce unfair or deceptive advertising. Those in favor of self-regulation are well aware of this. This is why they have organized and work cooperatively with the government—and probably will continue to do so.[19]

Self-regulation works some of the time

Some industry groups have made efforts at self-regulation. But most of these groups fail because they lack power to enforce their guidelines. One exception is the National Advertising Division (NAD) of the Council of Better Business Bureaus. It has helped shape guidelines that are followed by many advertisers. In addition, the NAD encourages consumers, advertisers, and government agencies to complain about questionable advertising. If a complaint seems justified, the NAD asks the advertiser for proof of the claims it has made. The NAD makes its findings public—and its decisions are reviewed by a larger group representing different groups of advertisers and consumers. Most firms comply when asked to discontinue problem ads.

In the long run, the best way to avoid criticisms of being "unfair" and "deceptive" is to stop the typical production-oriented effort to differentiate "me-too" product offerings with promotion. A little "puffing" has always been acceptable—and probably always will be. But advertisers should avoid trying to pass off "me-too" products as really new or better. Some advertising agencies are already refusing such jobs.

CONCLUSION

Theoretically, it may seem simple to develop a mass selling campaign. Just pick the media and develop a message. But it's not that easy. Effectiveness depends on using the "best" medium and the "best" message, considering: (1) promotion objectives, (2) the target markets, and (3) the funds available for advertising.

Specific advertising objectives determine what kind of advertising to use—product or institutional. If product advertising is needed, then the particular type must be decided—pioneering, competitive (direct or indirect), or reminder. And advertising allowances and cooperative advertising may be helpful.

Many technical details are involved in mass selling, and specialists—advertising agencies—handle some of these jobs. But specific objectives must be set for them, or their advertising may have little direction and be almost impossible to evaluate.

Effective advertising should affect sales. But the whole marketing mix affects sales—and the results of advertising can't be measured by sales changes alone. Advertising is only a part of promotion—and promotion is only a part of the total marketing mix that the marketing manager must develop to satisfy target customers.

Questions and Problems

1.   Identify the strategy decisions a marketing manager must make in the mass selling area.

2.   Discuss the relation of advertising objectives to marketing strategy planning and the kinds of advertising actually needed. Illustrate.

3.   Give three examples where advertising to middlemen might be necessary. What are the objective(s) of such advertising?

4.   What does it mean to say that "money is invested in advertising?" Is all advertising an investment? Illustrate.

5.   Find advertisements to final consumers that illustrate the following types of advertising: (a) institutional, (b) pioneering, (c) competitive, (d) reminder. What objective(s) does each of these ads have? List the needs each ad appeals to.

6.   Describe the type of media that might be most suitable for promoting: (a) tomato soup, (b) greeting cards, (c) an industrial component material, (d) playground equipment. Specify any assumptions necessary to obtain a definite answer.

7.   Discuss the use of testimonials in advertising. Which of the four AIDA steps might testimonials accomplish? Are they suitable for all types of products? If not, for which types are they most suitable?

8.   Find a magazine ad that you think does a particularly good job of communicating to the target audience. Explain your thinking.

9.   Discuss the future of smaller advertising agencies now that many of the largest agencies are merging to form "mega-agencies."

10.   Does mass selling cost too much? How can this be measured?

11.   How would your local newspaper be affected if local supermarkets switched their weekly advertising and instead used a service that delivered weekly, free-standing ads directly to each home?

12.   Is it "unfair" to advertise to children? Is it "unfair" to advertise to less-educated or less-experienced people of any age? Is it "unfair" to advertise for "unnecessary" products? Is it "unfair" to criticize a competitor's product in an ad?

Suggested Cases

21.   DeWitt State Bank

22.   Outdoor Sports, Inc.

Suggested Computer-Aided Problem

17.   Advertising Media

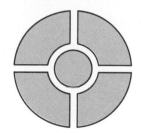

Chapter **18**

Pricing Objectives and Policies

When You Finish This Chapter, You Should

1. Understand how pricing objectives should guide pricing decisions.

2. Understand choices the marketing manager must make about price flexibility and price levels over the product life cycle.

3. Understand the legality of price level and price flexibility policies.

4. Understand the many possible variations of a price structure, including discounts, allowances, and who pays transportation costs.

5. Understand the important new terms (shown in red).

Deciding what price to charge can be agonizing.

On February 28, 1989, Sears, Roebuck and Co. closed all of its 824 stores for 42 hours. When they reopened, Sears had lowered its prices on 50,000 items. After 100 years in business, Sears had abandoned its traditional high markups and moved to "everyday low pricing."

In 1989, Sears was the largest retailer, but its share of retail sales had been declining for years. Worse, profits were far short of objectives. It was losing customers to low-price retailers like K mart, Kids "R" Us, and Circuit City. Those chains earned strong profits—in spite of low markups—because of faster turnover and lower costs. Sears had tried to attract customers with frequent, heavily promoted sales—but that had not helped profits. To make things worse, a New York consumer protection agency charged that ads for Sears sales were deceptive and gave consumers the impression that Sears sale prices were lower than they really were.

Sears marketing managers hoped that lower prices would help bring consumers back. They also made other changes. For example, they allowed consumers to pay with bank credit cards, put more emphasis on manufacturer brands, and worked to develop a more effective promotion blend.[1]

Price is one of the four major variables a marketing manager controls. Price level decisions are especially important because they affect both the number of sales a firm makes and how much money it earns.

Guided by the company's objectives, marketing managers must develop a set of pricing objectives and policies. They must spell out what price situations the firm will face and how it will handle them. These policies should explain: (1) how flexible prices will be, (2) at what level they will be set over the product life cycle, (3) to whom and when discounts and allowances will be given, and (4) how transportation costs will be handled. See Exhibit 18–1. These Price-related strategy decision areas are the focus of this chapter. In the next chapter, we will discuss how specific prices are set—consistent with the firm's pricing objectives and policies.

PRICE HAS MANY DIMENSIONS

It's not easy to define price in real-life situations because prices reflect many dimensions. Not realizing this can lead to big mistakes.

Suppose you've been saving to buy a new car and you see in an ad that the base price for the new-year model has been dropped to $9,494—5 percent lower than the previous year. At first this might seem like a real bargain. However, your view of this "deal" might change when you found out that you also had to pay a $400 transportation charge—and an extra $480 for an extended warranty. The price might look even less attractive if you discovered that options you wanted—air conditioning, power windows, and an AM-FM radio—cost $1,200 more than the previous year. Further, how would you feel if you bought the car anyway and then learned that a friend who just bought the exact same car had negotiated a much lower price?[2]

The price equation: price equals something

This example emphasizes that when a price is quoted, it is related to *some* assortment of goods and services. So **Price** is what is charged for "something." *Any business transaction in our modern economy can be thought of as an exchange of money—the money being the Price—for something.*

The something can be a physical product in various stages of completion, with or without supporting services, with or without quality guarantees, and so on. Or it could be a "pure" service—dry cleaning, a lawyer's advice, or insurance on your car.

Exhibit 18–1   Strategy Planning for Price

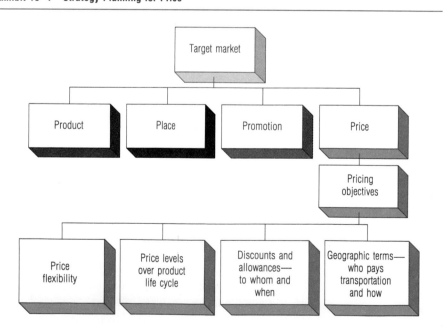

The nature and extent of this something determines the amount of money exchanged. Some customers pay list price. Others obtain large discounts or allowances because something is *not* provided. Some possible variations are summarized in Exhibit 18–2 for consumers or users and in Exhibit 18–3 for channel members. Some of these variations are discussed more fully below. But here it should be clear that Price has many dimensions.

PRICING OBJECTIVES SHOULD GUIDE PRICING

Pricing objectives should flow from—and fit in with—company-level and marketing objectives. Pricing objectives should be *explicitly stated* because they have a direct effect on pricing policies as well as the methods used to set prices.

Exhibit 18–4 shows the various types of pricing objectives we'll discuss.

PROFIT-ORIENTED OBJECTIVES

Target returns provide specific guidelines

A **target return objective** sets a specific level of profit as an objective. Often this amount is stated as a percentage of sales or of capital investment. A large

Exhibit 18–2   Price as Seen by Consumers

Price	equals	Something
List Price Less: *Discounts:* 　Quantity 　Seasonal 　Cash 　Temporary sales Less: *Allowances:* 　Trade-ins 　Damaged goods Less: *Rebate and coupon value*	equals	*Product:* 　Physical good 　Service 　Assurance of quality 　Repair facilities 　Packaging 　Credit 　Trading stamps *Place of delivery or when available*

Exhibit 18–3   Price as Seen by Channel Members

Price	equals	Something
List price Less: *Discounts:* 　Quantity 　Seasonal 　Cash 　Trade or functional 　Temporary "deals" Less: *Allowances:* 　Damaged goods 　Advertising 　Push money 　Stocking	equals	*Product:* 　Branded—well known 　Guaranteed 　Warranted 　Service—repair facilities 　Convenient packaging for handling *Place:* 　Availability—when and where *Price:* 　Price-level guarantee 　Sufficient margin to allow chance for profit *Promotion:* 　Promotion aimed at customers

Exhibit 18–4   Possible Pricing Objectives

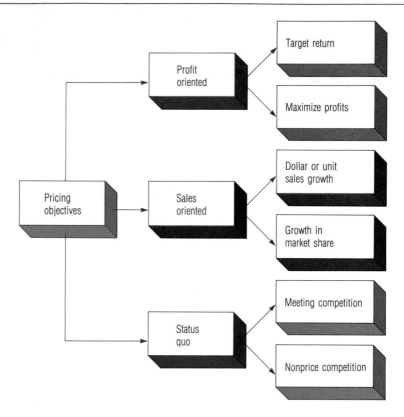

manufacturer like Motorola might aim for a 15 percent return on investment. The target for Safeway and other grocery chains might be a 1 percent return on sales.

A target return objective has administrative advantages in a large company. Performance can be compared against the target. Some companies eliminate divisions—or drop products—that aren't yielding the target rate of return. For example, General Electric sold its small appliance division to Black & Decker because it felt it could earn higher returns in other product-markets.

Some just want satisfactory profits

Some managers aim for only "satisfactory" returns. They just want returns that ensure the firm's survival and convince stockholders they are "doing a good job." Similarly, some small family-run businesses aim for a profit that will provide a "comfortable life style."[3]

Companies that are leaders in their industries—like Alcoa, Du Pont, AT&T—and those that provide critical public services—utility companies, transportation firms, defense contractors—sometimes pursue only "satisfactory" long-run targets. They are well aware that their activities are in public view. The public—and government officials—expect them to follow policies that are "in the public interest" when they play the role of price leader or wage setter. Too large a return might invite government action.[4]

But this kind of situation can lead to decisions that are not in the public interest. For example, before imported cars became popular, many GM managers were afraid of making "too much" profit—so they were not motivated to keep costs and prices low. They thought that lower costs—reflected in lower prices to consumers—might result in an even larger market share—and antitrust action by the government. Then, when low-cost foreign producers entered the U.S. market, GM was not able to quickly reduce costs—or prices.

Profit maximization can be socially responsible

A **profit maximization objective** seeks to get as much profit as possible. It might be stated as a desire to earn a rapid return on investment. Or, more bluntly, to charge "all the traffic will bear."

Some people believe that anyone seeking a profit maximization objective will charge high prices—prices that are not in the public interest. However, this point of view is not correct. Pricing to achieve profit maximization doesn't always lead to high prices. Demand and supply *may* bring extremely high prices if competition can't offer good substitutes. But this happens if and only if demand is highly inelastic. If demand is very elastic, profit maximizers may charge relatively low prices. Low prices may expand the size of the market—and result in greater sales and profits. For example, when prices of VCRs were very high, only wealthy people bought them. When Sony and its competitors lowered prices, nearly everyone bought a VCR. In other words, when demand is elastic, profit maximization may occur at a *lower* price.

Profit maximization objectives can also produce desirable results indirectly. Consumers "vote" with their purchase dollars for firms that do "the right things." The profits from this "voting" guide other firms in deciding what they should do. If a firm is earning a very large profit, other firms will try to copy or improve on what the company offers. Frequently, this leads to lower prices. IBM sold its original personal computer for about $4,500 in 1981. As Compaq, Zenith, and other competitors started to copy IBM, new features were added and prices dropped. Eight years later, customers could buy a better machine for about $600, and prices continued to drop.[5]

We saw this process at work in Chapter 10—in the rise and fall of profits during the product life cycle. Contrary to popular belief, a profit maximization objective is often socially desirable.

SALES-ORIENTED OBJECTIVES

A **sales-oriented objective** seeks some level of unit sales, dollar sales, or share of market—*without referring to profit*.

Sales growth doesn't mean big profits

Some managers are more concerned about sales growth than profits. They think sales growth leads to more profits. This kind of thinking causes problems when a firm's costs are growing faster than sales—or when managers don't keep track of their costs. Recently, many major corporations have had declining profits in spite of growth in sales. At the extreme, International Harvester kept cutting prices on its tractors—trying to reach its target sales levels in a weak economy—until it had to sell that part of its business. Generally, however, managers are now paying more attention to profits—not just sales.[6]

Market share objectives are popular

Many firms seek to gain a specified share (percent) of a market. A benefit of a market share objective is that it forces a manager to pay attention to what competi-

Price level decisions affect both the number of sales a firm makes and how much money it makes.

tors are doing in the market. In addition, it's usually easier to measure a firm's market share than to determine if profits are being maximized. Large consumer package goods firms—such as Procter & Gamble, Coca-Cola, and General Foods—often use market share objectives.

Aggressive companies often aim to increase market share—or even to control a market. Sometimes this makes sense. If a company has a large market share, it may have better economies of scale than its competitors. Therefore, if it sells at about the same price as its competitors, it gets more profit from each sale. Or lower costs may allow it to sell at a lower price—and still make a profit.

A company with a longer-run view may decide that increasing market share is a sensible objective when the overall market is growing. The hope is that larger future volume will justify sacrificing some profit in the short run.

Of course, objectives aimed at increasing market share have the same limitations as straight sales growth objectives. A larger market share—if gained at too low a price—may lead to profitless "success."

The key point regarding sales-oriented objectives is: larger sales volume, by itself, doesn't necessarily lead to higher profits.

STATUS QUO PRICING OBJECTIVES

Don't-rock-the-boat objectives

Managers who are satisfied with their current market share and profits some-time adopt **status quo objectives**—"don't-rock-the-*pricing*-boat" objectives. Managers may say that they want to "stabilize prices," or "meet competition," or even "avoid competition." This "don't-rock-the-boat" thinking is most common when the total market is not growing. Maintaining stable prices may discourage price competition and avoid the need for hard decisions.

Or stress nonprice competition instead	A status quo pricing objective may be part of an aggressive overall marketing strategy focusing on **nonprice competition**—aggressive action on one or more of the Ps other than Price.[7] Fast-food chains like McDonald's and Burger King prefer nonprice competition.

MOST FIRMS SET SPECIFIC PRICING POLICIES— TO REACH OBJECTIVES

Specific pricing policies are vital for any firm. Otherwise, the marketing manager has to rethink the marketing strategy every time a customer asks for a price.

Administered prices help achieve objectives	Price policies usually lead to **administered prices**—consciously set prices. In other words, instead of letting daily market forces decide their prices, most firms (including *all* of those in monopolistic competition) set their own prices. They may hold prices steady for long periods of time, or change them more frequently if that is what is required to meet objectives.

If a producer doesn't sell directly to final customers, it may be difficult to administer prices throughout the channel. Other channel members may also wish to administer prices to achieve their own objectives. This is what happened to Alcoa, one of the largest aluminum producers. To reduce its excess inventory, Alcoa offered its wholesalers a 30 percent discount off its normal price. Alcoa expected the wholesalers to pass most of the discount along to their customers to stimulate sales throughout the channel. Instead, wholesalers bought *their* aluminum at the lower price, but passed on only a small part of the discount to customers. As a result, the quantity Alcoa sold didn't increase much, and it still had excess inventories, while the wholesalers made more profit on the aluminum they did sell.[8]

Some firms don't even try to administer prices. They just "meet competition"— or worse, mark up their costs with little thought to demand. They act as if they have no choice in selecting a price policy.

Remember that Price has many dimensions. Managers *do* have many choices. They *should* administer their prices. And they should do it carefully because, ultimately, it is these prices that customers must be willing to pay before a whole marketing mix is a success. In the rest of this chapter, we'll talk about policies a marketing manager must set to do an effective job of administering Price.[9]

PRICE FLEXIBILITY POLICIES

One of the first decisions a marketing manager has to make is about price flexibility. Should he have a one-price or a flexible-price policy?

One-price policy—the same price for everyone	A **one-price policy** means offering the same price to all customers who purchase products under essentially the same conditions and in the same quantities. The majority of U.S. firms use a one-price policy—mainly for administrative convenience and to maintain goodwill among customers.

A one-price policy makes pricing easier. But a marketing manager must be careful to avoid a rigid one-price policy. This can amount to broadcasting a price that competitors can undercut—especially if the price is somewhat high. One reason for the growth of discount houses is that conventional retailers rigidly applied traditional margins—and stuck to them.

Flexible-price policy— different prices for different customers

A **flexible-price policy** means offering the same product and quantities to different customers at different prices. Flexible-price policies often specify a *range* in which the actual price charged must fall.

Flexible pricing is most common in the channels, in direct sales of industrial products, and at retail for expensive items and homogeneous shopping products. These situations usually call for personal selling—not mass selling. The advantage of flexible pricing is that the sales rep can make price adjustments—considering prices charged by competitors, the relationship with the customer, and the customer's bargaining ability.[10]

Most auto dealers use flexible pricing. The producer suggests a list price, but the dealers bargain for what they can get. Their salespeople negotiate prices every day. Inexperienced consumers—reluctant to "bargain"—often pay hundreds of dollars more than the dealer is willing to accept.

Flexible pricing does have disadvantages. A customer who finds that others have paid lower prices for the same marketing mix will be unhappy. For example, the Winn-Dixie supermarket chain stopped carrying products of some suppliers that refused to give it a price available to chains in other regions of the country.[11]

If buyers learn that negotiating can be in their interest, the time needed for bargaining will increase. This can affect selling costs. In addition, some sales reps let price cutting become a habit. This reduces the role of price as a competitive tool—and leads to a lower price level.

PRICE LEVEL POLICIES—OVER THE PRODUCT LIFE CYCLE

When marketing managers administer prices—as most do—they must consciously set a price level policy. As they enter the market, they have to set intro-

Exhibit 18–5 Alternative Introductory Pricing Policies

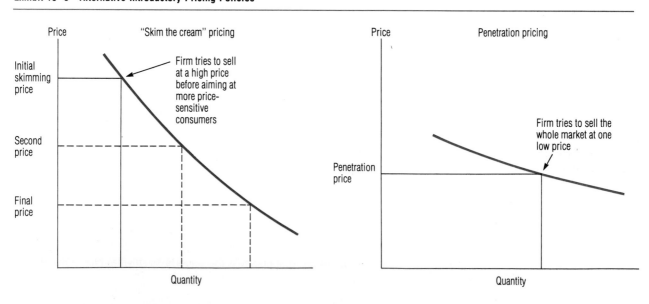

Skimming may maximize profits in the market introduction stage, but as more firms enter the market competition typically pushes prices down.

ductory prices that may have long-run effects. They must consider where the product life cycle is—and how fast it's moving. And they must decide if their prices should be above, below, or somewhere in between relative to the "market."

Let's look for a moment at a new product in the market introduction stage of its product life cycle. The price level decision should focus first on the nature of market demand. There are few (or no) direct substitute marketing mixes. And considering the demand curve for this product, a high price may lead not only to higher profit from each sale, but also to fewer units sold. A lower price might appeal to more potential customers. With this in mind, should the firm set a "high" or "low" price?

Skimming pricing—feeling out demand at a high price

A **skimming price policy** tries to sell the top ("skim the cream") of a market—the top of the demand curve—at a high price before aiming at more price-sensitive customers. Skimming may maximize profits in the market introduction stage, especially if there is little competition. A skimming policy is more attractive if demand is quite inelastic—at least at the upper price ranges.

A skimming policy usually involves a slow reduction in price over time. See Exhibit 18–5. It is important to realize that as price is reduced, new target markets are probably being sought. So, as the price level "steps-down" the demand curve, new Place and Promotion policies may be needed, too.

HEWLETT PACKARD

When Hewlett-Packard (HP) introduced its laser printer for personal computers, it initially set a high price—around $4,000. HP had a good head start on competitors—and no close substitute was available. The high-priced printer was sold mainly to computer professionals and business users with serious desktop publishing needs. Distribution was through a select group of authorized HP computer dealers whose salespeople could explain the printer. When other firms entered the market with similar printers, HP added features and lowered its price. It also did more advertising and added mail-order middlemen to reach new target markets. Then, just as competitors were entering the market to go after budget-oriented buyers, HP introduced a smaller model at a lower price. This is very typical of skimming. It involves changing prices through a series of marketing strategies over the course of the product life cycle.

Skimming is also useful when you don't know very much about the shape of the demand curve. It's safer to start with a high price that customers can refuse—and then reduce it if necessary.[12]

Penetration pricing—get volume at a low price

A **penetration pricing policy** tries to sell the whole market at one low price. Such an approach might be wise when the "elite" market—those willing to pay a high price—is small. This is the case when the whole demand curve is fairly elastic. See Exhibit 18–5.

A penetration policy is even more attractive if selling larger quantities results in lower costs because of economies of scale. Penetration pricing may be wise if the firm expects strong competition very soon after introduction.

A low penetration price may be called a "stay out" price. It discourages competitors from entering the market.

When personal computers became popular, Borland International came out with a complete programming language—including a textbook—for under $50. Business customers had paid thousands of dollars for similar systems for mainframe computers. But Borland felt that it could sell to hundreds of thousands of customers—and earn large total profits—by offering a really low price that would attract individual users as well as business firms. A low price helped Borland penetrate the market early. For several years, IBM, Microsoft, and other big companies were not able—or willing—to compete directly with Borland at that price. When they finally did match Borland's price, it already had a large base of very loyal customers who were not interested in switching to something new.

Introductory price dealing—temporary price cuts

Price cuts do attract customers. Therefore, marketers often use **introductory price dealing**—temporary price cuts—to speed new products into a market. These *temporary* price cuts should not be confused with low penetration prices, however. The plan here is to raise prices as soon as the introductory offer is over.

Established competitors often choose not to meet introductory price dealing—as long as the introductory period is not too long or too successful.

"Meeting competition" may be necessary

Regardless of their introductory pricing policy, most firms face competition sooner or later in the product life cycle. When that happens, how high or low a price is may be relative not only to the market demand curve, but also to the prices charged by competitors.

The nature of competition usually affects whether prices are set below, at, or above competition. The clearest case is pure competition. The decision is really made by the market. To offer products above or below the market price is foolish.

Meeting competitors' prices may also be the practical choice in mature markets that are moving toward pure competition. Here, there is typically downward pressure on both prices and profits. Profit margins are already thin—and for many firms they would disappear or turn into losses at a lower price. A higher price would simply prompt competitors to promote their price advantage.

Similarly, there is little choice in oligopoly situations. Pricing "at the market"—that is, meeting competition—may be the only sensible policy. To raise prices might lead to a large loss in sales—unless competitors adopt the higher price, too. And cutting prices would probably lead to similar reductions by competitors—downward along an inelastic industry demand curve. This can only lead to a decrease in total revenue for the industry and probably for each firm. Therefore, each oligopolist may choose a status quo pricing objective—and set its price at the competitive level.[13] (Note: some critics call this pricing behavior "conscious parallel action"—and imply that it is the same as intentional conspiracy among firms.)

There are alternatives in monopolistic competition

In monopolistic competition, there are more pricing options. At one extreme, some firms are clearly "above-the-market"—and they may even brag about it. Tiffany's is well known as one of the most expensive jewelry stores in the world. Other firms emphasize "below-the-market" prices in their marketing mixes. Prices offered by discounters and mass-merchandisers, such as K mart, illustrate this approach. They may even promote their pricing policy with catchy slogans like "guaranteed lowest prices" or "we'll beat any advertised price."

But, above or below what market?

These examples raise an important question. Do these various strategies contain prices that are "above" or "below" the market—or are they really different prices for different target markets? It is important in thinking about price level policies to clearly define the *relevant target market* and *competitors* when making comparisons of prices.

When making comparisons of prices, it is important for a marketing manager to clearly define the relevant target market and competitors.

Japanese Consumers Yen for Campbell Soup

In 1983, marketing managers for Campbell Soup Company mounted a new effort to enter the Japanese market. They developed "corn potage" and a line of six other soups in Japanese-style packages. In spite of a good product line, Campbell's salespeople struggled to get shelf space in Japan's small, cramped grocery stores. Progress was slow. The firm wasn't achieving its market share objective. In fact, Campbell was shipping less soup to Japan than to Albuquerque, New Mexico! In May of 1985, with a "meeting competition" retail price of 220 Japanese yen (about 91 cents) per can, Campbell was barely making a profit.

Over the next two years, there was an 89 percent rise in the exchange rate for the Japanese yen against the U.S. dollar. That meant that Campbell made more dollars for each can of soup sold in Japan—and that its profits would increase simply by holding its price level the same. However, Campbell's marketing managers seized the opportunity to be more aggressive in pursuing their market share objective. They lowered the suggested list price of Campbell soup 16 percent—to a "below market" price of 185 yen—and kept retailers' profit margins the same. With those changes, sales volume and market share doubled. Moreover, even at the lower price Campbell was making the equivalent of $1.30 a can, up nearly 50 percent from the 1985 level. Campbell used the extra money to increase promotion in the Japanese market to help recruit more retailers.[14]

Perhaps some target customers do see important differences in the product, or in the convenience of location, or in the whole marketing mix. Then what we're talking about are different marketing strategies—not just different price levels.

Consider K mart prices again from this view. K mart may have lower camera prices than conventional camera retailers, but it offers less help in the store and less selection, and it won't take old cameras in trade. K mart may be appealing to budget-oriented shoppers who are comparing prices among different mass-merchandisers. A specialty camera store—appealing to different customers—may not be a direct competitor! Thus, it may be better to think of K mart's price as part of a different marketing mix for a different target market—not as a "below-the-market" price.

Different price level policies through the channel

When a product is sold to channel members instead of final consumers, the price should be set so that the channel members can cover costs and make a profit. To achieve its objectives, a manufacturer may set different price level policies for different levels in the channel. For example, a producer of a slightly better product might set a price level that is low relative to competitors when selling to retailers, while suggesting an "above-the-market" retail price. This encourages retailers to carry the product—and to emphasize it in their marketing mix—because it yields higher profits.

MOST PRICE STRUCTURES ARE BUILT AROUND LIST PRICES

Prices start with a list price   Most price structures are built around a base price schedule or price "list." **Basic list prices** are the prices that final customers or users are normally asked to pay for products. Unless noted otherwise, "list price" refers to "basic list price" in this book.

Some channel members don't charge the suggested list price.

How these list prices are set is discussed in the next chapter. For now, however, we'll consider variations from list price—and why they are made.

DISCOUNT POLICIES—REDUCTIONS FROM LIST PRICES

Discounts are reductions from list price that are given by a seller to a buyer who either gives up some marketing function or provides the function himself. Discounts can be useful in marketing strategy planning. In the following discussion, think about what function the buyers are giving up—or providing—when they get each of these discounts.

Quantity discounts encourage volume buying

Quantity discounts are discounts offered to encourage customers to buy in larger amounts. This lets a seller get more of a buyer's business, or shifts some of the storing function to the buyer, or reduces shipping and selling costs—or all of these. Such discounts are of two kinds: cumulative and noncumulative.

Cumulative quantity discounts apply to purchases over a given period—such as a year—and the discount usually increases as the amount purchased increases. Cumulative discounts are intended to encourage *repeat* buying by a single customer by reducing the customer's cost for additional purchases. For example, a Lowes lumberyard might give a cumulative quantity discount to a building contractor who is not able to buy all of the needed materials at once. Lowes wants to reward the contractor's patronage—and discourage shopping around.

Noncumulative quantity discounts apply only to individual orders. Such discounts encourage larger orders—but do not tie a buyer to the seller after that one purchase. These discounts are often used to discourage small orders, which are expensive to handle. But they are mainly used to encourage bigger orders. Lowes lumberyard may purchase and resell insulation products made by several competing producers. Owens/Corning might try to encourage Lowes to stock larger quantities of its insulation by offering a noncumulative quantity discount. The objective would be to encourage Lowes to "push" those products to its customers.

Quantity discounts may be based on the dollar value of the entire order, or on the number of units purchased, or on the size of the package purchased. While quantity discounts are usually given as price cuts, sometimes they are given as "free" or "bonus" products. Airline frequent flier programs use this approach.

Quantity discounts can be a very useful tool for the marketing manager. Some customers are eager to get them. But marketing managers must use quantity discounts carefully. To avoid price discrimination, they must offer such discounts to all customers on equal terms.

Seasonal discounts—buy sooner and store

Seasonal discounts are discounts offered to encourage buyers to stock earlier than present demand requires. If used by producers, this discount tends to shift the storing function further along in the channel. It also tends to even out sales over the year and, therefore, permits year-round operation. If seasonal discounts are large, they may be passed along to other customers down the channel of distribution. For example, the manufacturer of Merry Tiller garden tillers offers its wholesalers a lower price if they buy in the fall—when sales are slow. The wholesalers can then offer a seasonal discount to retailers—who may try to sell the tillers during a special "fall sale."

Payment terms and cash discounts set payment dates

Most sales to businesses are made on credit. The seller sends a bill (invoice), and the buyer's accounting department processes it for payment. Some firms depend on their suppliers for temporary working capital (credit). Therefore, it is very important for both sides to clearly state the terms of payment—including the availability of cash discounts—and to understand the commonly used payment terms.

An invoice shows the terms of a sale.

SERVCO, INC.
1475 LAKE LANSING ROAD
LANSING, MI 48912

INVOICE NO.   **4238**

ORDER NO.	INVOICE DATE	
179642	1/8/90	
DATE SHIPPED	SHIPPED VIA	
1/30/90	Truck	

NO.PCS	WT.	FOB	TERMS
5	300	Lansing, MI	Net 30

SOLD TO	SHIPPED TO
Jones Supply Co.	Jones Supply Co.
220 Commercial Ave.	623 Kensington
South Gate, CA 94087	Portland, OR 90722

QUANTITY	UNIT	DESCRIPTION	UNIT PRICE	TOTAL PRICE
200	263-A	Smoke alarms	12.00	2400.00
		Thank You.		

Net means that payment for the face value of the invoice is due immediately. These terms are sometimes changed to "net 10" or "net 30"—which means payment is due within 10 or 30 days of the date on the invoice.

Cash discounts are reductions in the price to encourage buyers to pay their bills quickly. The terms for a cash discount usually modify the "net" terms.

2/10, net 30 means that a 2 percent discount off the face value of the invoice is allowed if the invoice is paid within 10 days. Otherwise, the full face value is due within 30 days. And it usually is stated or understood that an interest charge will be made after the 30-day free-credit period.

Why cash discounts are given and should be taken

Smart buyers take advantage of cash discounts. A discount of 2/10, net 30 may not look like much at first. But the 2 percent discount is earned for paying the invoice just 20 days sooner than it should be paid anyway. And if it is not taken, the company—in effect—is borrowing at an annual rate of 36 percent. That is, assuming a 360-day year and dividing by 20 days, there are 18 periods during which the company could earn 2 percent—and 18 times 2 equals 36 percent a year.

While the marketing manager can often use a cash discount as a marketing variable, this isn't always true. Purchasing agents who value cash discounts may insist that the marketing manager offer the same discount offered by competitors. In fact, some buyers automatically deduct the traditional cash discount from their invoices—regardless of the seller's invoice terms!

Some sellers find themselves in trouble when they don't state exactly when payment is due—or what the penalty will be for late payment. Customers may wait as long as possible to pay the invoice, especially if they are short of cash or if interest rates are high.

Consumers say "charge it," too

Credit sales are also important to retailers. Some stores, including most department stores, have their own credit systems. But most retailers use credit card services, such as VISA or MasterCard. The retailers pay a percent of the revenue from each credit sale for this service—from 1 to 7 percent depending on the card company and the store's sales volume. For this reason, some retailers offer discounts to consumers who pay cash.

Many consumers like the convenience of credit card buying. But some critics argue that the cards make it too easy for consumers to buy things they really can't afford. Further, because of high interest charges, credit card buying can increase the total costs to consumers.[15]

Trade discounts often are set by tradition

A **trade (functional) discount** is a list price reduction given to channel members for the job they are going to do.

A manufacturer, for example, might allow retailers a 30 percent trade discount from the suggested retail list price to cover the cost of the retailing function and their profit. Similarly, the manufacturer might allow wholesalers a *chain* discount of 30 percent and 10 percent off the suggested retail price. In this case, the wholesalers would be expected to pass the 30 percent discount on to retailers.

Trade discounts might seem to offer manufacturers or wholesalers great flexibility in varying a marketing mix. In fact, however, customary trade discounts can be so well established in the channel that the manager has to accept them as fixed when setting prices.

Special sales reduce list prices—temporarily

A **sale price** is a temporary discount from the list price. Sale price discounts encourage immediate buying. In other words, to get the sale price customers give up the convenience of buying when they want to buy—and instead buy when the seller wants to sell.

Special "sales" provide a marketing manager with a quick way to respond to changing market conditions—without changing the basic marketing strategy. For example, a retailer might use a sale to help clear extra inventory or to meet a competing store's price. Or a producer might offer a middleman a special "deal"—in addition to the normal trade discount—that makes it more profitable for the middleman to push the product. Retailers often pass some of the savings of these deal purchases along to consumers.

In recent years, sale prices and deals have become much more common. Some retailers who had an occasional sale a few years ago now have weekly sales. And for some consumer convenience products the majority of purchases by middlemen involve some sort of deal. At first it may seem that consumers benefit from all of this. But that may not be the case. Prices that change constantly may confuse customers and increase selling costs.

Sale prices should be used carefully, consistent with well thought out pricing objectives and policies. A marketing manager who constantly uses temporary sales to adjust the price level probably has not done a good job setting the normal price.[16]

ALLOWANCE POLICIES—OFF LIST PRICES

Allowances—like discounts—are given to final consumers, customers, or channel members for doing "something" or accepting less of "something."

Advertising allowances— something for something

Advertising allowances are price reductions given to firms in the channel to encourage them to advertise or otherwise promote the supplier's products locally. For example, General Electric gave an allowance (1.5 percent of sales) to its wholesalers of housewares and radios. They, in turn, were expected to spend the allowance on local advertising.

Stocking allowances—get attention and shelf space

Stocking allowances—sometimes called slotting allowances—are given to a middleman to get shelf space for a product. For example, a producer might offer a retailer cash or free merchandise to stock a new item. Stocking allowances are a recent development. So far, they have been used mainly to prompt supermarket chains to handle new products. Supermarkets don't have enough "slots" on their shelves to handle all of the available new products. They are more willing to give space to a new product if the supplier will offset their handling costs—by making space in the warehouse, adding information on computer systems, and redesigning store shelves, for example.

Some retailers are getting allowances that cover more than handling costs. The Shoprite Stores chain in New York City got an $86,000 allowance to stock $172,000 worth of Old Capital Microwave Popcorn. When the popcorn didn't sell well, Shoprite quickly took it off its shelves. With a big stocking allowance, the middleman makes extra profit—even if a new product fails and the producer loses money.

There is much controversy about stocking allowances. Critics say that retailer demands for big stocking allowances are slowing new product introductions—and making it hard for small producers to compete.[17]

PMs—push for cash

Push money (or prize money) allowances—sometimes called "PMs" or "spiffs"—are given to retailers by manufacturers or wholesalers to pass on to the retailers' salesclerks for aggressively selling certain items. PM allowances are used for new items, slower-moving items, or higher-margin items. They are often used for "pushing" furniture, clothing, consumer electronics, and cosmetics. A salesclerk, for example, might earn an additional $5 for each new model Pioneer cassette deck sold.

Bring in the old, ring up the new—with trade-ins

A **trade-in allowance** is a price reduction given for used products when similar new products are bought.

Trade-ins give the marketing manager an easy way to lower the effective price without reducing list price. Proper handling of trade-ins is important when selling durable products. Customers buying machinery, for example, buy long-term satisfaction in terms of more production capacity. If the list price less the trade-in allowance doesn't offer greater satisfaction—as the customer sees it—then no sales will be made.

Many firms replace machinery slowly—perhaps too slowly—because they value their old equipment above market value. This also applies to cars. Customers want higher trade-ins for their old cars than the current market value. This encourages the use of high, perhaps "phony," list prices for new cars so that dealers can give high trade-in allowances.

SOME CUSTOMERS GET EXTRA SOMETHINGS

Clipping coupons—more for less

Many producers and retailers offer discounts (or free items) through coupons distributed In packages, mailings, print ads, or at the store. By presenting a coupon to a retailer, the consumer is given a discount off list price ("25 cents off"). This is especially common in the grocery business—but the use of price-off coupons is growing in other lines of business too.

Retailers are willing to redeem coupons because it increases their sales—and they usually are paid for handling the coupons.

Retailers are willing to redeem producers' coupons because it increases their sales—and they usually are paid for the trouble of handling the coupon. For example, a retailer who redeems a "50 cents off" coupon might be repaid 75 cents. In effect, the coupon increases the functional discount and makes it more attractive to sell the couponed product.

"Couponing" is so common that new firms have been set up to help repay retailers for redeeming manufacturers' coupons. The total dollar amounts involved are so large that crime has become a big problem. The government recently cracked a coupon fraud that had cost producers $178 million by collecting repayment for coupons that consumers had not actually used. And some dishonest retailers have gone to jail for collecting on coupons that they "redeemed" without requiring their customers to buy the products.[18]

Cash rebates when you buy

Some producers offer **rebates**—refunds paid to consumers after a purchase has been made. Sometimes the rebate may be very large. Following Chrysler's example, some automakers offered rebates of $500 to $2,500 to promote sales of slow-moving models. Rebates are sometimes used on lower-price items—ranging from Duracell batteries to Paul Masson wines.

Rebates give the producer a way to be certain that final consumers actually get the price reduction. If the rebate amount were just taken off the price charged middlemen, they might not pass the savings along to consumers.

Some sales promotions basically lower the price a consumer pays.

LIST PRICE MAY DEPEND ON GEOGRAPHIC PRICING POLICIES

Retail list prices sometimes include free delivery. Or free delivery may be offered to some customers as an aid to closing the sale. What is included (or not included) in the retail list price may not be formally stated. That way, the retailer can adjust its marketing mix—depending on the needs or bargaining ability of a customer.

Deciding who is going to pay the freight is more important on sales to intermediate customers than to final consumers because more money is involved. Usually purchase orders specify place, time, method of delivery, freight costs, insurance, handling, and other charges. There are many possible variations for an imaginative marketing manager. Some specialized terms have developed. A few are discussed in the following paragraphs.

F.O.B. pricing is easy

A commonly used transportation term is **F.O.B.**—which means "free on board" some vehicle at some place. Typically, it is used with the place named—often the location of the seller's factory or warehouse, as in "F.O.B. Detroit" or "F.O.B. mill." This means that the seller pays the cost of loading the products onto some vehicle—usually a truck, railroad car, or ship. At the point of loading, title to the products passes to the buyer. Then the buyer pays the freight and takes responsibility for damage in transit—except as covered by the transporting company.

Variations are made easily by changing the place named in the F.O.B. description. If the marketing manager wants to pay the freight for the convenience of customers, he can use: "F.O.B. delivered" or "F.O.B. buyer's factory." In this case, title does not pass until the products are delivered. If the seller wants title to pass immediately but is willing to prepay freight (and then include it in the invoice), "F.O.B. seller's factory–freight prepaid" can be used.

F.O.B. "shipping point" pricing simplifies the seller's pricing—but it may narrow the market. Since the delivered cost varies depending on the buyer's location, a customer located farther from the seller must pay more and might buy from closer suppliers.

Zone pricing smooths delivered prices

Zone pricing means making an average freight charge to all buyers within specific geographic areas. The seller pays the actual freight charges and bills each customer for an average charge. For example, a company might divide the United

Different geographic pricing policies may be needed to expand into new territories.

States into seven zones. All customers in the same zone are billed the same amount for freight, even though the actual shipping costs might vary.

Zone pricing reduces the wide variation in delivered prices that results from an F.O.B. shipping point pricing policy. It also simplifies charging for transportation.

Uniform delivered pricing—one price to all

Uniform delivered pricing means making an average freight charge to all buyers. It is a kind of zone pricing—an entire country may be considered as one zone—that includes the average cost of delivery in the price. Uniform delivered pricing is most often used when (1) transportation costs are relatively low and (2) the seller wishes to sell in all geographic areas at one price—perhaps a nationally advertised price.

Freight-absorption pricing—competing on equal grounds in another territory

When all firms in an industry use F.O.B. shipping point pricing, a firm usually competes well near its shipping point but not farther away. As sales reps look for business farther away, delivered prices rise and the firm finds itself priced out of the market.

This problem can be reduced with **freight absorption pricing**—which means absorbing freight cost so that a firm's delivered price meets the nearest competitor's. This amounts to cutting list price to appeal to new market segments.

With freight absorption pricing, the only limit on the size of a firm's territory is the amount of freight cost it is willing to absorb. These absorbed costs cut net return on each sale—but the new business may raise total profit.

LEGALITY OF PRICING POLICIES

This chapter discusses the many pricing decisions that must be made. However, as was suggested in Chapter 4, some pricing decisions are limited by government legislation.

The first step to understanding pricing legislation is to know the thinking of legislators and the courts. Ideally, they try to help the economy operate more effectively—in the consumers' interest. In practice, this doesn't always work out. But generally their intentions are good. And if we take this view, we get a better idea of the "why" of legislation. This helps us to anticipate future rulings. We'll only look at U.S. legislation here, but many other countries have similar laws on pricing.[19]

Unfair trade practice acts control some minimum prices

Unfair trade practice acts put a lower limit on prices, especially at the wholesale and retail levels. They have been passed in more than half the states. Selling below cost in these states is illegal. Wholesalers and retailers are usually required to take a certain minimum percentage markup over their merchandise-plus-transportation costs. The most common markup figures are 6 percent at retail and 2 percent at wholesale.

If a specific wholesaler or retailer can provide "conclusive proof" that operating costs are lower than the minimum required figure, lower prices may be permitted. But it is nearly impossible to provide satisfactory proof.

Most retailers know enough about their costs to set markups larger than these minimums. The practical effect of these laws is to protect certain limited-line food retailers—such as dairy stores—from the kind of "ruinous" competition that supermarkets might offer if they sold milk as a "leader"—offering it below cost—for a long time.

Even very high prices may be OK

Generally speaking, firms can charge high prices—even "outrageously high" prices—as long as they don't conspire with their competitors to fix prices, discriminate against some of their customers, or lie.

You can't lie about prices

Phony list prices are prices that customers are shown to suggest that the price they are to pay has been discounted from "list." Some customers seem more interested in the supposed discount than in the actual price. Most businesses, Better Business Bureaus, and government agencies consider the use of phony list prices unethical. And the FTC tries to stop such pricing using the **Wheeler Lea Amendment**, which bans "unfair or deceptive acts in commerce."[20]

Price fixing is illegal—you can go to jail

Difficulties with pricing—and violations of price legislation—usually occur when competing marketing mixes are quite similar. When the success of an entire marketing strategy depends on price, there is pressure (and temptation) to make agreements with competitors (conspire). And **price fixing**—competitors getting together to raise, lower, or stabilize prices—is common and relatively easy. *But it is also completely illegal.* It is "conspiracy" under the Sherman Act and the Federal Trade Commission Act. To discourage price fixing, both companies and individual managers are held responsible. Some executives have already gone to jail!

Federal price fixing laws focus on protecting customers who purchase directly from a supplier. For example, a wholesaler could bring action against a producer-supplier for fixing prices. However, retailers or consumers who bought the producer's products from the wholesaler could not bring action. In contrast, many states have laws that allow "indirect customers" in the channel to sue the price fixer. A 1989 Supreme Court ruling cleared the way for more states to pass this type of law. The expected result will be even tougher penalties for price fixing.[21]

Antimonopoly legislation bans price discrimination unless . . .

Price level and price flexibility policies can lead to price discrimination. The **Robinson-Patman Act** (of 1936) makes illegal any **price discrimination**—selling the same products to different buyers at different prices—*if it injures competition.* This law does permit some price differences, but they must be based on (1) cost differences or (2) the need to meet competition. Both buyers and sellers are guilty if they know they are entering into discriminatory agreements. This is a serious matter—price discrimination suits are common.

What does "like grade and quality" mean?

The Robinson-Patman Act allows a marketing manager to charge different prices for similar products if they are *not* of "like grade and quality." But the problem is: How similar can products be without being considered of "like grade and quality?" The FTC position is that if the physical characteristics of a product are similar, then they are of like grade and quality. The FTC's view was upheld in a landmark U.S. Supreme Court ruling against the Borden Company. The Court held that a well-known label *alone* does not make a product different from the one with an unknown label. The issue was rather clear-cut in the Borden case. The company agreed that the physical characteristics of the canned milk it sold at different prices under different labels were basically the same.

But the FTC's "victory" in the *Borden* case was not complete. The U.S. Supreme Court agreed with the FTC in the *Borden* case with respect to like grade and quality. However, it sent the case back to the U.S. Court of Appeals to determine whether the price difference actually injured competition—which is also required by the law. The appeals court found no evidence of injury and further noted that there could be no injury unless Borden's price differential exceeded the "recognized consumer appeal of the Borden label." How to measure "consumer appeal" was not spelled out and may lead to additional suits. Eventually, what the consumer thinks about the product may be the deciding factor. For now, however, producers who want to sell several brands or dealer brands at lower prices than their main brand probably should offer physical differences—and differences that are really useful.[22]

Can cost analysis justify price differences?

The Robinson-Patman Act allows price differences if there are cost differences—say for larger quantity shipments or because middlemen take over some of the physical distribution functions. One problem is that cost arguments must be developed *before* different prices are set. The seller can't wait until a competitor, disgruntled customer, or the FTC brings a charge and then worry about justifying it. At that point, it's too late.

Justifying cost differences is a difficult job. Costs usually must be allocated to several products. But it's easy for the FTC to raise objections to whatever allocation method is used. And such objections are raised often because the FTC is especially concerned about the impact of price differences on competitors—and on small competitors in particular.[23]

Can you legally meet price cuts?

Under the Robinson-Patman Act, meeting competition is permitted as a defense in price discrimination cases. But the FTC normally takes a dim view of this argument.

A major objective of antitrust legislation is to protect competition—not competitors. And "meeting competition" in "good faith" still seems to be legal—even if it is large firms that meet the lower prices of small firms.

Are functional discounts discriminatory?

Can functional (trade) discounts be considered price discrimination? The laws are not completely clear on this issue, but court decisions appear to have settled the matter by emphasizing the functions provided. At the root of the problem is the distinction between wholesalers and retailers since wholesalers seek certain discounts from producers for providing wholesaling functions.

Generally, the courts have held that whether a firm is a wholesaler or a retailer depends not on the quantity it buys or handles, but on the nature of the functions it provides. A producer can legally refuse to give a wholesale discount to a large retail grocery chain—although the chain might handle a much larger volume than small wholesalers. The justification is that functional discounts are necessary for the small wholesaler to cover costs and still sell to retailers at prices low enough for the retailers to be competitive.

A retail chain probably would not have to pay the same price offered a small retailer, however, because a special functional discount could be set up for chain stores. As long as a functional discount seems to reflect the nature of the job required in the channel, the courts probably would consider it legal.

Special promotion allowances might not be allowed

Some firms have violated the Robinson-Patman Act by providing push money, advertising allowances, and other promotion aids to some customers and not others. The act prohibits such special allowances—*unless they are made available to all customers on "proportionately equal" terms.* No proof of injury to competition is necessary. And the FTC has been fairly successful in prosecuting such cases.

The need for such a rule is clear—once you try to control price discrimination.

Allowances for promotion aid could be granted to retailers or wholesalers without expecting that any promotion actually be done. This plainly is price discrimination in disguise.

The law does cause hardships, however. Sometimes it is difficult to provide allowances on "proportionately equal" terms to both large and small customers. And it may also be difficult to determine exactly who competing customers are. The FTC might define a list of competitors much more broadly than either the seller or the competing buyers. Supermarket operators might only be concerned about other supermarkets and the food discounters. But the FTC might think that small drugstores are also competitors for health and beauty aids.[24]

How to avoid discriminating

Because the price discrimination laws are complicated—and penalties for violations heavy—many business managers deemphasize price as a marketing variable. They think the safest course is to offer few or no quantity discounts—and to offer the same cost-based prices to *all* customers. Perhaps this is *too* conservative a reaction. But, when price differences are being considered, it may be wise for a lawyer to be involved in the discussion!

CONCLUSION

The Price variable offers an alert marketing manager many possibilities for varying marketing mixes. What pricing policies should be used depends on the pricing objectives. We looked at profit-oriented, sales-oriented, and status quo–oriented objectives.

A marketing manager must set policies about price flexibility, price levels over the product life cycle, who will pay the freight, and who will get discounts and allowances. While doing this, the manager should be aware of legislation that affects pricing policies.

In most cases, a marketing manager must set prices—that is, administer prices. Starting with a list price, a variety of discounts and allowances may be offered to adjust for the "something" being offered in the marketing mix.

Throughout this chapter, we assumed that a list price has already been set. We talked about what may be included (or excluded) in the "something"—and what objectives a firm might set to guide its pricing policies. Price setting itself was not discussed. It will be covered in the next chapter—where we show ways of carrying out the various pricing objectives and policies.

Questions and Problems

1. Identify the strategy decisions a marketing manager must make in the Price area. Illustrate your answer for a local retailer.

2. How should the acceptance of a profit-oriented, a sales-oriented, or a status quo–oriented pricing objective affect the development of a company's marketing strategy? Illustrate for each.

3. Distinguish between one-price and flexible-price policies. Which is most appropriate for a hardware store? Why?

4. Cite two examples of continuously selling above the market price. Describe the situations.

5. Explain the types of competitive situations that might lead to a "meeting competition" pricing policy.

6. What pricing objective(s) is a skimming pricing policy most likely implementing? Is the same true for a penetration pricing policy? Which policy is probably most appropriate for each of the following products: *(a)* a new type of home lawn-sprinkling system, *(b)* a new type of disposable contact lenses, *(c)* a videotape of a best selling movie, *(d)* a new children's toy?

7. Discuss unfair trade practices acts. To whom are they "unfair"?

8. How would our marketing system change if manufacturers were required to set fixed prices on *all* products sold at retail and *all* retailers were required to use these prices? Would a manufacturer's marketing mix be easier to develop? What kind of an operation would retailing be in this situation? Would consumers receive more or less service?

9. Is price discrimination involved if a large oil company sells gasoline to taxicab associations for resale to individual taxicab operators for 2½ cents a gallon less than the price charged to retail service stations? What happens if the cab associations resell gasoline not only to taxicab operators, but also to the general public as well?

10. What does the final consumer really obtain when paying the list price for the following products: *(a)* a car, *(b)* a portable CD player, *(c)* a package of frozen carrots, and *(d)* a lipstick in a jeweled case?

11. Do stocking allowances increase or reduce conflict in a channel of distribution? Explain your thinking.

12. Are seasonal discounts appropriate in agricultural businesses (which are certainly seasonal)?

13. What are the "effective" annual interest rates for the following cash discount terms: *(a)* 1/10, net 20; *(b)* 1/5, net 10; *(c)* net 25?

14. Why would a manufacturer offer a rebate instead of lowering the suggested list price?

15. How can a marketing manager change his F.O.B. terms to make his otherwise competitive marketing mix more attractive?

16. What type of geographic pricing policy is most appropriate for the following products (specify any assumptions necessary to obtain a definite answer): *(a)* a chemical by-product, *(b)* nationally advertised candy bars, *(c)* rebuilt auto parts, *(d)* tricycles?

17. How would a ban on freight absorption (that is, requiring F.O.B. factory pricing) affect a producer with substantial economies of scale in production?

Suggested Cases

13. Office Systems, Inc.

27. A-1 Photos, Inc.

28. Western Mfg., Inc.

Suggested Computer-Aided Problem

18. Cash Discounts

Appendix B

Marketing Arithmetic

When You Finish This Appendix, You Should

1. Understand the components of an operating statement (profit and loss statement).

2. Know how to compute the stockturn rate.

3. Understand how operating ratios can help you analyze a business.

4. Understand how to calculate markups and markdowns.

5. Understand how to calculate return on investment (ROI) and return on assets (ROA).

6. Understand the important new terms (shown in red).

Marketing students must become familiar with the essentials of the "language of business." Businesspeople commonly use accounting terms when talking about costs, prices, and profit. And using accounting data is a practical tool in analyzing marketing problems.

THE OPERATING STATEMENT

An **operating statement** is a simple summary of the financial results of a company's operations over a specified period of time. Some beginning students may feel that the operating statement is complex, but as we'll soon see, this really isn't true. *The main purpose of the operating statement is determining the net profit figure—and presenting data to support that figure.* This is why the operating statement is often referred to as the *profit and loss statement.*

An operating statement for a wholesale or retail business is presented in Exhibit B–1. A complete and detailed statement is shown so you will see the framework throughout the discussion, but the amount of detail on an operating statement is *not* standardized. Many companies use financial statements with much less detail than this one. They emphasize clarity and readability rather than detail. To really

Exhibit B–1 An Operating Statement (profit and loss statement)

XYZ COMPANY
Operating Statement
For the Year Ended December 31, 199X

Gross sales....................................			$540,000
Less: Returns and allowances..................			40,000
Net sales.....................................			$500,000
Cost of sales:			
Beginning inventory at cost....................		$ 80,000	
Purchases at billed cost......................	$310,000		
Less: Purchase discounts	40,000		
Purchases at net cost	270,000		
Plus freight-in..............................	20,000		
Net cost of delivered purchases		290,000	
Cost of products available for sale		370,000	
Less: Ending inventory at cost		70,000	
Cost of sales			300,000
Gross margin (gross profit).......................			200,000
Expenses:			
Selling expenses:			
Sales salaries	60,000		
Advertising expense........................	20,000		
Delivery expense	20,000		
Total selling expense		100,000	
Administrative expense			
Office salaries.............................	30,000		
Office supplies	10,000		
Miscellaneous administrative expense...........	5,000		
Total administrative expense		45,000	
General expense:			
Rent expense	10,000		
Miscellaneous general expenses	5,000		
Total general expense...................		15,000	
Total expenses			160,000
Net profit from operation........................			$ 40,000

understand an operating statement, however, you must know about its components.

**Only three basic
components**

The basic components of an operating statement are *sales*—which come from the sale of goods and services; *costs*—which come from the making and selling process; and the balance—called *profit or loss*—which is just the difference between sales and costs. So there are only three basic components in the statement: sales, costs, and profit (or loss). Other items on an operating statement are there only to provide supporting details.

**Time period covered
may vary**

There is no one time period that an operating statement covers. Rather, statements are prepared to satisfy the needs of a particular business. This may be at the end of each day or at the end of each week. Usually, however, an operating statement summarizes results for one month, three months, six months, or a full year. Since the time period does vary, this information is included in the heading of the statement as follows:

XYZ COMPANY
Operating Statement
For the (Period) Ended (Date)

Also, see Exhibit B–1.

Management uses of operating statements

Before going on to a more detailed discussion of the components of our operating statement, let's think about some of the uses for such a statement. Exhibit B–1 shows that a lot of information is presented in a clear and concise manner. With this information, a manager can easily find the relation of net sales to the cost of sales, the gross margin, expenses, and net profit. Opening and closing inventory figures are available—as is the amount spent during the period for the purchase of goods for resale. Total expenses are listed to make it easier to compare them with previous statements—and to help control these expenses.

All this information is important to a company's managers. Assume that a particular company prepares monthly operating statements. A series of these statements is a valuable tool for directing and controlling the business. By comparing results from one month to the next, managers can uncover unfavorable trends in the sales, costs, or profit areas of the business—and take any needed action.

A skeleton statement gets down to essential details

Let's refer to Exhibit B–1 and begin to analyze this seemingly detailed statement to get first-hand knowledge of the components of the operating statement.

As a first step, suppose we take all the items that have dollar amounts extended to the third, or right-hand, column. Using these items only, the operating statement looks like this:

Gross sales	$540,000
Less: Returns and allowances	40,000
Net sales	500,000
Less: Cost of sales	300,000
Gross margin	200,000
Less: Total expenses	160,000
Net profit (loss)	$ 40,000

Is this a complete operating statement? The answer is **yes**. This skeleton statement differs from Exhibit B–1 only in supporting detail. All the basic components are included. In fact, the only items we must list to have a complete operating statement are:

Net sales	$500,000
Less: Costs	460,000
Net profit (loss)	$ 40,000

These three items are the essentials of an operating statement. All other subdivisions or details are just useful additions.

Meaning of "sales"

Now let's define the meaning of the terms in the skeleton statement.

The first item is "sales." What do we mean by sales? The term **gross sales** is the total amount charged to all customers during some time period. It is certain, however, that there will be some customer dissatisfaction—or just plain errors in ordering and shipping goods. This results in returns and allowances—which reduce gross sales.

A **return** occurs when a customer sends back purchased products. The company either refunds the purchase price or allows the customer dollar credit on other purchases.

An **allowance** occurs when a customer is not satisfied with a purchase for some reason. The company gives a price reduction on the original invoice (bill), but the customer keeps the goods and services.

These refunds and price reductions must be considered when the firm computes its net sales figure for the period. Really, we're only interested in the revenue the company manages to keep. This is **net sales**—the actual sales dollars the company receives. Therefore, all reductions, refunds, cancellations, and so forth—made because of returns and allowances—are deducted from the original total (gross sales) to get net sales. This is shown below:

```
Gross sales ................................. $540,000
   Less: Returns and allowances................. 40,000
Net sales ................................... $500,000
```

Meaning of "cost of sales"

The next item in the operating statement—**cost of sales**—is the total value (at cost) of the sales during the period. We'll discuss this computation later. Meanwhile, note that after we obtain the cost of sales figure, we subtract it from the net sales figure to get the gross margin.

Meaning of "gross margin" and "expenses"

Gross margin (gross profit) is the money left to cover the expenses of selling the products and operating the business. Firms hope that a profit will be left after subtracting these expenses.

Selling expense is commonly the major expense below the gross margin. Note that in Exhibit B–1, **expenses** are all the remaining costs that are subtracted from the gross margin to get the net profit. The expenses in this case are the selling, administrative, and general expenses. (Note that the cost of purchases and cost of sales are not included in this total expense figure—they were subtracted from net sales earlier to get the gross margin. Note, also, that some accountants refer to "cost of sales" as "cost of goods sold.")

Net profit—at the bottom of the statement—is what the company earned from its operations during a particular period. It is the amount left after the cost of sales and the expenses are subtracted from net sales. *Net sales and net profit are not the same.* Many firms have large sales and no profits—they may even have losses!

DETAILED ANALYSIS OF SECTIONS OF THE OPERATING STATEMENT

Cost of sales for a wholesale or retail company

The cost of sales section includes details that are used to find the "cost of sales" ($300,000 in our example).

In Exhibit B–1, you can see that beginning and ending inventory, purchases, purchase discounts, and freight-in are all necessary in calculating costs of sales. If we pull the cost of sales section from the operating statement, it looks like this:

Cost of sales:			
Beginning inventory at cost....................			$ 80,000
Purchases at billed cost	$310,000		
Less: Purchase discounts	40,000		
Purchases at net cost	$270,000		
Plus: Freight-in	20,000		
Net cost of delivered purchases		290,000	
Cost of goods available for sale		$370,000	
Less: Ending inventory at cost		70,000	
Cost of sales			$300,000

"Cost of sales" is the cost value of what is *sold*—not the cost of goods on hand at any given time.

The inventory figures merely show the cost of goods on hand at the beginning and end of the period the statement covers. These figures may be obtained by a physical count of the goods on hand on these dates—or they may be estimated by "perpetual inventory" records that show the inventory balance at any given time. The methods used in determining the inventory should be as accurate as possible because these figures affect the cost of sales during the period and net profit.

The net cost of delivered purchases must include freight charges and purchase discounts received since these items affect the money actually spent to buy goods and bring them to the place of business. A **purchase discount** is a reduction of the original invoice amount for some business reason. For example, a cash discount may be given for prompt payment of the amount due. We subtract the total of such discounts from the original invoice cost of purchases to get the *net* cost of purchases. To this figure we add the freight charges for bringing the goods to the place of business. This gives the net cost of *delivered* purchases. When we add the net cost of delivered purchases to the beginning inventory at cost, we have the total cost of goods available for sale during the period. If we now subtract the ending inventory at cost from the cost of the goods available for sale, we finally get the cost of sales.

One important point should be noted about cost of sales. The way the value of inventory is calculated varies from one company to another—and can cause big differences in the cost of sales and the operating statement. (See any basic accounting textbook for how the various inventory valuation methods work.)

Cost of sales for a manufacturing company

Exhibit B–1 shows the way the manager of a wholesale or retail business arrives at his cost of sales. Such a business *purchases* finished products and resells them. In a manufacturing company, the "purchases" section of this operating statement is replaced by a section called "cost of production." This section includes purchases of raw materials and parts, direct and indirect labor costs, and factory overhead charges (such as heat, light, and power) that are necessary to produce finished products. The cost of production is added to the beginning finished products inventory to arrive at the cost of products available for sale. Often, a separate cost of production statement is prepared and only the total cost of production is shown in the operating statement. See Exhibit B–2 for an illustration of the cost of sales section of an operating statement for a manufacturing company.

Expenses

"Expenses" go below the gross margin. They usually include the costs of selling and the costs of administering the business. They do not include the cost of sales—either purchased or produced.

Exhibit B–2   Cost of Sales Section of an Operating Statement for a Manufacturing Firm

Cost of sales:			
Finished products inventory (beginning)		$ 20,000	
Cost of production (Schedule 1)		100,000	
Total cost of finished products available for sale		120,000	
Less: Finished products inventory (ending)		30,000	
Cost of sales			$ 90,000

Schedule 1, Schedule of cost of production

Beginning work in process inventory			15,000
Raw materials			
Beginning raw materials inventory.		10,000	
Net cost of delivered purchases		80,000	
Total cost of materials available for use		90,000	
Less: Ending raw materials inventory		15,000	
Cost of materials placed in production		75,000	
Direct labor.		20,000	
Manufacturing expenses			
Indirect labor	$4,000		
Maintenance and repairs	3,000		
Factory supplies	1,000		
Heat, light, and power.	2,000		
Total manufacturing expenses		10,000	
Total manufacturing costs			105,000
Total work in process during period			120,000
Less: Ending work in process inventory			20,000
Cost of production			$100,000

There is no "right" method for classifying the expense accounts or arranging them on the operating statement. They can just as easily be arranged alphabetically or according to amount, with the largest placed at the top and so on down the line. In a business of any size, though, it is clearer to group the expenses in some way and to use subtotals by groups for analysis and control purposes. This was done in Exhibit B–1.

Summary on operating statements

The statement presented in Exhibit B–1 contains all the major categories in an operating statement—together with a normal amount of supporting detail. Further detail can be added to the statement under any of the major categories without changing the nature of the statement. The amount of detail normally is determined by how the statement will be used. A stockholder may be given a sketchy operating statement—while the one prepared for internal company use may have a lot of detail.

COMPUTING THE STOCKTURN RATE

A detailed operating statement can provide the data needed to compute the **stockturn rate**—a measure of the number of times the average inventory is sold during a year. Note that the stockturn rate is related to the *turnover during a year*—not the length of time covered by a particular operating statement.

The stockturn rate is a very important measure because it shows how rapidly the firm's inventory is moving. Some businesses typically have slower turnover than others. But a drop in turnover in a particular business can be very alarming. It may mean that the firm's assortment of products is no longer as attractive as it was. Also, it may mean that the firm will need more working capital to handle the same volume of sales. Most businesses pay a lot of attention to the stockturn rate—trying to get faster turnover.

Three methods—all basically similar—can be used to compute the stockturn rate. Which method is used depends on the data available. These three methods—which usually give approximately the same results—are shown below.*

(1)
$$\frac{\text{Cost of sales}}{\text{Average inventory at cost}}$$

(2)
$$\frac{\text{Net sales}}{\text{Average inventory at selling price}}$$

(3)
$$\frac{\text{Sales in units}}{\text{Average inventory in units}}$$

Computing the stockturn rate will be illustrated only for Formula 1 since all are similar. The only difference is that the cost figures used in Formula 1 are changed to a selling price or numerical count basis in Formulas 2 and 3. Note: regardless of the method used, you must have both the numerator and denominator of the formula in the same terms.

If the inventory level varies a lot during the year, you may need detailed information about the inventory level at different times to compute the average inventory. If it stays at about the same level during the year, however, it's easy to get an estimate. For example, using Formula 1, the average inventory at cost is computed by adding the beginning and ending inventories at cost and dividing by 2. This average inventory figure is then divided into the cost of sales (in cost terms) to get the stockturn rate.

For example, suppose that the cost of sales for one year was $1,000,000. Beginning inventory was $250,000 and ending inventory $150,000. Adding the two inventory figures and dividing by 2, we get an average inventory of $200,000. We next divide the cost of sales by the average inventory ($1,000,000 divided by $200,000) and get a stockturn rate of 5.

The stockturn rate is covered further in Chapter 19.

OPERATING RATIOS HELP ANALYZE THE BUSINESS

Many businesspeople use the operating statement to calculate **operating ratios**—the ratio of items on the operating statement to net sales—and compare these ratios from one time period to another. They can also compare their own operating ratios with those of competitors. Such competitive data is often available

---

*Differences occur because of varied markups and nonhomogeneous product assortments. In an assortment of tires, for example, those with low markups might have sold much better than those with high markups. But with Formula 3, all tires would be treated equally.

through trade associations. Each firm may report its results to the trade association, which then distributes summary results to its members. These ratios help managers control their operations. If some expense ratios are rising, for example, those particular costs are singled out for special attention.

Operating ratios are computed by dividing net sales into the various operating statement items that appear below the net sales level in the operating statement. The net sales figure is used as the denominator in the operating ratio because it shows the sales the firm actually won.

We can see the relation of operating ratios to the operating statement if we think of there being another column to the right of the dollar figures in an operating statement. This column contains percentage figures—using net sales as 100 percent. This approach can be seen below:

Gross sales	$540,000	
Less: Returns and allowances	40,000	
Net sales	$500,000	100%
Cost of sales	300,000	60
Gross margin	$200,000	40
Expenses	160,000	32
Net profit	$ 40,000	8%

The 40 percent ratio of gross margin to net sales in the above example shows that 40 percent of the net sales dollar is available to cover sales expenses and administering the business—and to provide a profit. Note that the ratio of expenses to sales added to the ratio of profit to sales equals the 40 percent gross margin ratio. The net profit ratio of 8 percent shows that 8 percent of the net sales dollar is left for profit.

The value of percentage ratios should be obvious. The percentages are easily figured—and they are much easier to compare than large dollar figures.

Note that because these operating statement categories are interrelated, only a few pieces of information are needed to figure the others. In this case, for example, knowing the gross margin percent and net profit percent makes it possible to figure the expense and cost of sales percentages. Further, knowing just one dollar amount and the percentages lets you figure all the other dollar amounts.

MARKUPS

A **markup** is the dollar amount added to the cost of sales to get the selling price. The markup usually is similar to the firm's gross margin because the markup amount added onto the unit cost of a product by a retailer or wholesaler is expected to cover the selling and administrative expenses—and to provide a profit.

The markup approach to pricing is discussed in Chapter 19, so it will not be discussed at length here. But a simple example illustrates the idea. If a retailer buys an article that costs $1 when delivered to his store, he must sell it for more than this cost if he hopes to make a profit. So he might add 50 cents onto the cost of the article to cover his selling and other costs and, hopefully, to provide a profit. The 50 cents is the markup.

The 50 cents is also the gross margin or gross profit from that item *if* it is sold. But note that it is *not* the net profit. The selling expenses may amount to 35 cents, 45 cents, or even 55 cents. In other words, there is no guarantee that the markup will cover costs. Further, there is no guarantee that customers will buy at the marked-up price. This may require markdowns, which are discussed later in this appendix.

Markup conversions

Often it is convenient to use markups as percentages rather than focusing on the actual dollar amounts. But, markups can be figured as a percent of cost or selling price. To have some agreement, *markup (percent)* will mean percentage of selling price unless stated otherwise. So the 50-cent markup on the $1.50 selling price is a markup of 33⅓ percent. On the other hand, the 50-cent markup is a 50 percent markup on cost.

Some retailers and wholesalers use markup conversion tables. This way they can easily convert from cost to selling price—depending on the markup on selling price they want. To see the interrelation, look at the two formulas below. They can be used to convert either type of markup to the other.

$$\text{(4)}\qquad \frac{\text{Percent markup}}{\text{on selling price}} = \frac{\text{Percent markup on cost}}{100\% + \text{Percent markup on cost}}$$

$$\text{(5)}\qquad \frac{\text{Percent markup}}{\text{on cost}} = \frac{\text{Percent markup on selling price}}{100\% - \text{Percent markup on selling price}}$$

In the previous example, we had a cost of $1, a markup of 50 cents, and a selling price of $1.50. We saw that the markup on selling price was 33⅓ percent—and on cost, it was 50 percent. Let's substitute these percentage figures—in Formulas 4 and 5—to see how to convert from one basis to the other. Assume first of all that we only know the markup on selling price and want to convert to markup on cost. Using Formula 5, we get:

$$\text{Percent markup on cost} = \frac{33\tfrac13\%}{100\% - 33\tfrac13\%} = \frac{33\tfrac13}{66\tfrac23} = 50\%$$

On the other hand, if we know only the percent markup on cost, we can convert to markup on selling price as follows:

$$\text{Percent markup on selling price} = \frac{50\%}{100\% + 50\%} = \frac{50\%}{150\%} = 33\tfrac13\%$$

These results can be proved and summarized as follows:

$$\begin{array}{l}
\text{Markup } \$0.50 = \quad 50\% \text{ of cost, or } 33\tfrac13\% \text{ of selling price}\\
\underline{+ \quad\;\; \text{Cost } \$1.00 = 100\% \text{ of cost, or } 66\tfrac23\% \text{ of selling price}}\\
\text{Selling price } \$1.50 = 150\% \text{ of cost, or } 100\% \text{ of selling price}
\end{array}$$

It is important to see that only the percentage figures change while the money amounts of cost, markup, and selling price stay the same. Note, too, that when selling price is the base for the calculation (100 percent), then the cost percentage plus the markup percentage equal 100 percent. But when the cost of the product is used as the base figure (100 percent), the selling price percentage must be greater than 100 percent by the markup on cost.

MARKDOWN RATIOS HELP CONTROL RETAIL OPERATIONS

The ratios we discussed above were concerned with figures on the operating statement. Another important ratio—the **markdown ratio**—is a tool used by many retailers to measure the efficiency of various departments and their whole business. But note that it is *not directly related to the operating statement.* It requires special calculations.

A **markdown** is a retail price reduction that is required because customers won't buy some item at the originally marked-up price. This refusal to buy may be due to a variety of reasons—soiling, style changes, fading, damage caused by handling, or an original price that was too high. To get rid of these products, the retailer offers them at a lower price.

Markdowns are generally considered to be due to "business errors"—perhaps because of poor buying, original markups that are too high, and other reasons. Regardless of the cause, however, markdowns are reductions in the original price—and they are important to managers who want to measure the effectiveness of their operations.

Markdowns are similar to allowances because price reductions are made. Thus, in computing a markdown ratio, markdowns and allowances are usually added together and then divided by net sales. The markdown ratio is computed as follows:

$$\text{Markdown \%} = \frac{\$ \text{ Markdowns } + \$ \text{ Allowances}}{\$ \text{ Net sales}} \times 100$$

The 100 is multiplied by the fraction to get rid of decimal points.

Returns are *not* included when figuring the markdown ratio. Returns are treated as "consumer errors"—not business errors—and therefore are not included in this measure of business efficiency.

Retailers who use markdown ratios keep a record of the amount of markdowns and allowances in each department and then divide the total by the net sales in each department. Over a period of time, these ratios give management one measure of the efficiency of buyers and salespeople in various departments.

It should be stressed again that the markdown ratio is not calculated directly from data on the operating statement since the markdowns take place before the products are sold. In fact, some products may be marked down and still not sold. Even if the marked-down items are not sold, the markdowns—that is, the reevaluations of their value—are included in the calculations in the time period when they are taken.

The markdown ratio is calculated for a whole department (or profit center)—*not* individual items. What we are seeking is a measure of the effectiveness of a whole department—not how well the department did on individual items.

RETURN ON INVESTMENT (ROI) REFLECTS ASSET USE

Another "off the operating statement" ratio is **return on investment (ROI)**—the ratio of net profit (after taxes) to the investment used to make the net profit, multiplied by 100 to get rid of decimals. "Investment" is not shown on the operating statement. But it is on the **balance sheet** (statement of financial condition)—another accounting statement—that shows a company's assets, liabilities, and net worth. It may take some "digging" or special analysis, however, to find the right investment number.

"Investment" means the dollar resources the firm has "invested" in a project or business. For example, a new product may require $4 million in new money—for inventory, accounts receivable, promotion, and so on—and its attractiveness may be judged by its likely ROI. If the net profit (after taxes) for this new product is expected to be $1 million in the first year, then the ROI is 25 percent—that is, ($1 million ÷ $4 million) × 100.

There are two ways to figure ROI. The *direct* way is:

$$\text{ROI (in \%)} = \frac{\text{Net profit (after taxes)}}{\text{Investment}} \times 100$$

The *indirect* way is:

$$\text{ROI (in \%)} = \frac{\text{Net profit (after taxes)}}{\text{Sales}} \times \frac{\text{Sales}}{\text{Investment}} \times 100$$

This way is concerned with net profit margin and turnover—that is:

$$\text{ROI (in \%)} = \text{Net profit margin} \times \text{Turnover} \times 100$$

This indirect way makes it clearer how to *increase* ROI. There are three ways:

1. Increase profit margin (with lower costs or a higher price).
2. Increase sales.
3. Decrease investment.

Effective marketing strategy planning and implementation can increase profit margins and/or sales. And careful asset management can decrease investment.

ROI is a revealing measure of how well managers are doing. Most companies have alternative uses for their funds. If the returns in a business aren't at least as high as outside uses, then the money probably should be shifted to the more profitable uses.

Some firms borrow more than others to make "investments." In other words, they invest less of their own money to acquire assets—what we called "investments." If ROI calculations use only the firm's own "investment," this gives higher ROI figures to those who borrow a lot—which is called leveraging. To adjust for different borrowing proportions—to make comparisons among projects, departments, divisions, and companies easier—another ratio has come into use. **Return on assets (ROA)** is the ratio of net profit (after taxes) to the assets used to make the net profit—times 100.

Both ROI and ROA measures are trying to get at the same thing—how effectively the company is using resources. These measures became increasingly popular as profit rates dropped and it became more obvious that increasing sales volume doesn't necessarily lead to higher profits—or ROI, or ROA. Inflation and higher costs for borrowed funds also force more concern for ROI and ROA. Marketers must include these measures in their thinking or top managers are likely to ignore their plans—and their requests for financial resources.

Questions and Problems

1. Distinguish between the following pairs of items that appear on operating statements: *(a)* gross sales and net sales, and *(b)* purchases at billed cost and purchases at net cost.

2. How does gross margin differ from gross profit? From net profit?

3. Explain the similarity between markups and gross margin. What connection do markdowns have with the operating statement?

4. Compute the net profit for a company with the following data:

Beginning inventory (cost)	$ 150,000
Purchases at billed cost	330,000
Sales returns and allowances	250,000
Rent	60,000
Salaries	400,000
Heat and light	180,000
Ending inventory (cost)	250,000
Freight cost (inbound)	80,000
Gross sales	1,300,000

5. Construct an operating statement from the following data:

Returns and allowances	$ 150,000
Expenses	20%
Closing inventory at cost	600,000
Markdowns	2%
Inward transportation	30,000
Purchases	1,000,000
Net profit (5%)	300,000

6. Compute net sales and percent of markdowns for the data given below:

Markdowns	$ 40,000
Gross sales	400,000
Returns	32,000
Allowances	48,000

7. *(a)* What percentage markups on cost are equivalent to the following percentage markups on selling price: 20, 37½, 50, and 66⅔? *(b)* What percentage markups on selling price are equivalent to the following percentage markups on cost: 33⅓, 20, 40, and 50?

8. What net sales volume is required to obtain a stockturn rate of 20 times a year on an average inventory at cost of $100,000, with a gross margin of 25 percent?

9. Explain how the general manager of a department store might use the markdown ratios computed for his various departments. Is this a fair measure? Of what?

10. Compare and contrast return on investment (ROI) and return on assets (ROA) measures. Which would be best for a retailer with no bank borrowing or other outside sources of funds; i.e., the retailer has put up all the money that the business needs?

Chapter 19

Price Setting in the Real World

When You Finish This Chapter, You Should

1. Understand how most wholesalers and retailers set their prices—using markups.

2. Understand why turnover is so important in pricing.

3. Understand the advantages and disadvantages of average cost pricing.

4. Know how to use break-even analysis to evaluate possible prices.

5. Know how to find the most profitable price and quantity—using marginal analysis, total revenue, and total cost.

6. Know the many ways that price setters use demand estimates in their pricing.

7. Understand the important new terms (shown in red).

"How should I price this product?" is a common problem facing marketing managers.

In the last chapter, we discussed the idea that pricing objectives and policies should guide pricing decisions. We accepted the idea of a list price and went on to discuss variations from list. Now, we'll see how the basic list price is set in the first place—based on information about costs, demand, and profit margins. See Exhibit 19–1.

How should the manager of Office Depot, an office equipment store, price a new item—for example, Sharp's new model fax machine? The fax machine costs the store about $800. The store could just use the list price suggested by the producer—or it could arrive at a list price by adding the same dollar markup amount it adds to any item costing $800. The manager might even price the phone very close to cost—if the customer also buys a standard office copy machine that earns the store a good profit. Or the manager may price the phone based on estimates of demand at different price levels.[1]

There are many ways to set list prices. But—for simplicity—they can be reduced to two basic approaches: *cost-oriented* and *demand-oriented* price setting. We will discuss cost-oriented approaches first because they are most common. Also, understanding the problems of relying on a cost-oriented approach shows why demand must also be considered to make good price decisions. Let's begin by looking at how most retailers and wholesalers set cost-oriented prices.

Exhibit 19–1   Key Factors that Influence Price Setting

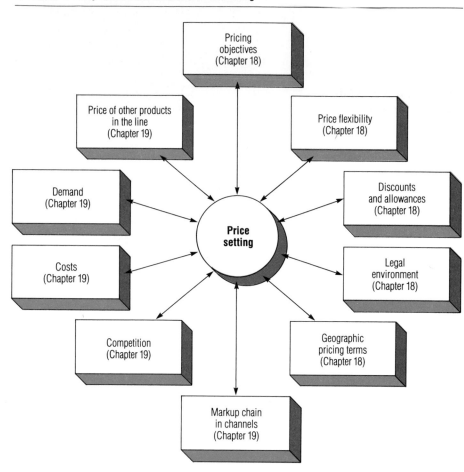

PRICING BY WHOLESALERS AND RETAILERS

Markups guide pricing by middlemen

Most retailers and wholesalers set prices by using a **markup**—a dollar amount added to the cost of products to get the selling price. For example, suppose that a Revco drugstore buys a bottle of Prell shampoo for $1. To make a profit, the drugstore obviously must sell the shampoo for more than $1. If it adds 50 cents to cover operating expenses and provide a profit, we say that the store is marking up the item 50 cents.

Markups, however, usually are stated as percentages rather than dollar amounts. And this is where confusion sometimes arises. Is a markup of 50 cents on a cost of $1 a markup of 50 percent? Or should the markup be figured as a percentage of the selling price—$1.50—and therefore be 33⅓ percent? A clear definition is necessary.

Markup percent is based on selling price—a convenient rule

Unless otherwise stated, **markup (percent)** means percentage of selling price that is added to the cost to get the selling price. So the 50-cent markup on the $1.50 selling price is a markup of 33⅓ percent. Markups are related to selling price for convenience.

There is nothing wrong with the idea of markup on cost. The important thing is to state clearly which markup percent you are using to avoid confusion.

Managers often want to change a markup on cost to one based on selling price—or vice versa. The calculations to do this are simple (see the section on markup conversion in Appendix B on marketing arithmetic).[2]

Many use a "standard" markup percent

A middleman commonly sets prices on all of his products by applying the same markup percent. This makes pricing easier! When you think of the large number of items the average retailer and wholesaler carry—and the small sales volume of any one item—this approach makes sense. Spending the time to find the "best" price to charge on every item in stock (day-to-day or week-to-week) probably wouldn't pay.

Moreover, the same markup percent is often used by different companies in the same line of business. There is a reason for this: their operating expenses are usually similar. So a standard markup is acceptable as long as it is large enough to cover the firm's operating expenses—and provide a reasonable profit.

Markups are related to gross margins

How do managers decide on a standard markup in the first place? A standard markup is usually set close to the firm's *gross margin.* Managers regularly see gross margins on their operating (profit and loss) statements. (See Appendix B on marketing arithmetic—it follows Chapter 18—if you are unfamiliar with these ideas.) Our Office Depot manager knows that there won't be any profit unless the gross margin is large enough. For this reason, he might accept a markup percent on the fax machine that is close to his usual gross margin.

Smart producers pay attention to the gross margins and standard markups of middlemen in their channel. They usually allow trade (functional) discounts that are similar to the standard markups these middlemen expect.

Markup chain may be used in channel pricing

Different firms in a channel often use different markups. A **markup chain**—the sequence of markups used by firms at different levels in a channel—determines the price structure in the whole channel. The markup is figured on the *selling price* at each level of the channel.

For example, Black & Decker's selling price for an electric drill becomes the cost paid by the Ace Hardware wholesaler. The wholesaler's selling price becomes the hardware retailer's cost. And this cost plus a retail markup becomes the retail selling price. Each markup should cover the costs of running the business—and leave a profit.

Exhibit 19–2 illustrates the markup chain for an electric drill at each level of the channel system. The production (factory) cost of the drill is $21.60. In this case, the producer is taking a 10 percent markup and sells the product for $24. The markup is 10 percent of $24 or $2.40. The producer's selling price now becomes the wholesaler's cost—$24. If the wholesaler is used to taking a 20 percent markup on selling price, the markup is $6—and the wholesaler's selling price becomes $30. $30 now becomes the cost for the hardware retailer. And if the retailer is used to a 40 percent markup, he adds $20, and the retail selling price becomes $50.

High markups don't always mean big profits

Some people—including many traditional retailers—think high markups mean high profits. But often this isn't true. A high markup may result in a price that's too high—a price at which few customers will buy. And you can't earn much if you

Exhibit 19–2   Example of a Markup Chain and Channel Pricing

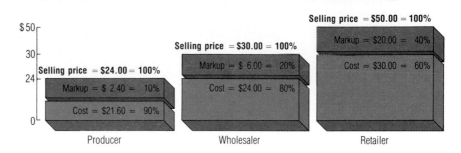

don't sell much—no matter how high your markup. But many retailers and whole-salers seem more concerned with the size of their markup on a single item than with their total profit. And their high markups may lead to low profits—or even losses.

Lower markups can speed turnover—and the stock-turn rate

Some retailers and wholesalers, however, try to speed turnover to increase profit—even if this means reducing their markups. They realize that the business is running up costs over time. If they can sell a much greater amount in the same time period, they may be able to take a lower markup—and still have a higher profit at the end of the period.

An important idea here is the **stockturn rate**—the number of times the average inventory is sold in a year. Various methods of figuring stockturn rates can be used (see the section "Computing the Stockturn Rate" in Appendix B). A low stockturn rate may be bad for profits.

At the very least, a low stockturn increases inventory carrying cost and ties up working capital. If a firm with a stockturn of 1 (once per year) sells products that cost it $100,000, it has that much tied up in inventory all the time. But a stockturn of 5 requires only $20,000 worth of inventory ($100,000 cost divided by five turn-overs a year).

Whether a stockturn rate is high or low depends on the industry and the product involved. A NAPA auto parts wholesaler may expect an annual rate of 1—while an A&P store might expect 10 to 12 stockturns for soap and detergents and 40 to 50 stockturns for fresh fruits and vegetables.

Supermarkets and mass-merchandisers run in fast company

Although some middlemen use the same "standard" markup percent on all their products, this policy ignores the importance of fast turnover. Mass-merchandisers and supermarkets know this. They put low markups on fast-selling items and higher markups on items that sell less frequently. For example, Wal-Mart may put a small markup (like 20 percent) on fast-selling health and beauty aids (like tooth-paste or shampoo) but put higher markups on appliances and clothing. Similarly, supermarket operators put low markups on fast-selling items like milk, eggs, and detergents. The markup on these items may be less than half the average markup for all grocery items, but this doesn't mean they are unprofitable. The small profit per unit is earned more often.

Items with a high stockturn rate may have a lower markup.

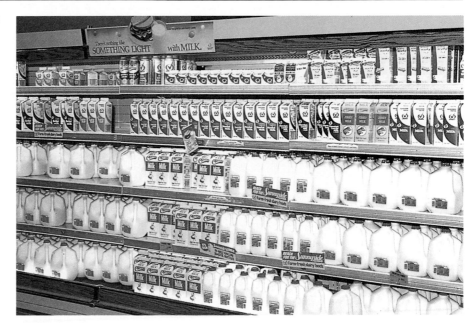

PRICING BY PRODUCERS

It's up to the producer to suggest a list price

Some markups eventually become "standard" in a trade. Most of the channel members tend to follow a similar process—adding a certain percentage to the previous price. But who sets price in the first place?

The basic list price usually is decided by the producer and/or brander of the product—a large retailer, a large wholesaler, or most often, the producer. Now we'll look at the pricing approaches of such firms. For convenience, we'll call them "producers."

Producers commonly use some cost-oriented approach. They start with a cost per unit figure and add a markup—perhaps a "standard" markup—to obtain their selling price. Or they may use some rule-of-thumb formula such as: Production cost per unit × 3 = Selling price.

Each producer usually develops rules and markups related to its own costs and objectives. Yet even the first step—selecting the appropriate cost per unit to build on—isn't easy. Let's discuss several approaches to see how cost-oriented price setting really works.

AVERAGE-COST PRICING IS COMMON AND DANGEROUS

Average-cost pricing is adding a "reasonable" markup to the average cost of a product. The average cost per unit is usually found by studying past records. The total cost for the last year may be divided by all the units produced and sold in that period to get the "expected" average cost per unit for the next year. If the total cost was $5,000 for labor and materials and $5,000 for fixed overhead expenses—such as selling expenses, rent, and manager salaries—then "expected" total cost is $10,000. If the company produced 10,000 items in that time period, the "ex-

Exhibit 19–3   Results of Average-Cost Pricing

Calculation of planned profit if 10,000 items are sold		Calculation of actual profit if only 5,000 items are sold	
Calculation of costs:		Calculation of costs:	
Fixed overhead expenses.........................	$ 5,000	Fixed overhead expenses...........................	$5,000
Labor and materials............................	5,000	Labor and materials.............................	2,500
Total costs	10,000	Total costs	$7,500
''Reasonable'' profit............................	1,000		
Total costs and planned profit	$11,000		

Calculation of ''reasonable'' price for both possibilites:

$$\frac{\text{Total costs and planned profit}}{\text{Planned number of items to be sold}} = \frac{\$11,000}{10,000} = \$1.10 = \text{''Reasonable'' price}$$

Calculation of profit or (loss):		Calculation of profit or (loss):	
Actual unit sales (10,000) times price		Actual unit sales (5,000) times price	
($1.10) = ...	$11,000	($1.10) = ...	$5,500
Minus: Total costs	10,000	Minus: Total costs	7,500
Profit (loss).............................	$ 1,000	Profit (loss)	($2,000)

Therefore: Planned (''reasonable'') profit of $1,000 is earned if 10,000 items are sold at $1.10 each.

Therefore: Planned (''reasonable'') profit of $1,000 is not earned. Instead, $2,000 loss results if 5,000 items are sold at $1.10 each.

pected'' average cost is $1 per unit. To get the price, the producer decides how much profit per unit seems ''reasonable'' and adds this to the average cost per unit. If 10 cents is considered a reasonable profit for each unit, then the new price is set at $1.10. See Exhibit 19–3.

It does not make allowances for cost variations as output changes

Average-cost pricing is simple. But it can also be dangerous. It's easy to lose money with average-cost pricing. To see why, let's follow this example further.

First, remember that the average cost of $1 per unit was based on output of 10,000 units. But if only 5,000 units are produced and sold in the next year, the firm may be in trouble. Five thousand units sold at $1.10 each ($1.00 cost plus 10 cents for ''profit'') yields a total revenue of only $5,500. The overhead is still fixed at $5,000, and the variable material and labor cost drops in half to $2,500—for a total cost of $7,500. This means a loss of $2,000, or 40 cents a unit. The method that was supposed to allow a profit of 10 cents a unit actually causes a loss of 40 cents a unit! See Exhibit 19–3.

Exhibit 19–4   Typical Shape of Average Cost Curve

The basic problem is that this method doesn't allow for cost variations at different levels of output. In a typical situation, costs are high with low output and then economies of scale set in—and the average cost per unit drops as the quantity produced increases. (See Exhibit 19–4 for the typical shape of the average cost curve.) This is why mass production and mass distribution often make sense. This behavior of costs must be considered when setting prices.

MARKETING MANAGER MUST CONSIDER VARIOUS KINDS OF COSTS

Average-cost pricing may lead to losses because there are a variety of costs—and each changes in a *different* way as output changes. Any pricing method that uses cost must consider these changes. To understand why, we need to define six types of costs.

There are three kinds of total cost

1. **Total fixed cost** is the sum of those costs that are fixed in total—no matter how much is produced. Among these fixed costs are rent, depreciation, managers' salaries, property taxes, and insurance. Such costs stay the same even if production stops temporarily.
2. **Total variable cost**, on the other hand, is the sum of those changing expenses that are closely related to output—expenses for parts, wages, packaging materials, outgoing freight, and sales commissions.

    At zero output, total variable cost is zero. As output increases, so do variable costs. If Wrangler doubles its output of jeans in a year, its total cost for denim cloth also (roughly) doubles.
3. **Total cost** is the sum of total fixed and total variable costs. Changes in total cost depend on variations in total variable cost—since total fixed cost stays the same.

There are three kinds of average cost

The pricing manager usually is more interested in cost per unit than total cost because prices are usually quoted per unit.

1. **Average cost** (per unit) is obtained by dividing total cost by the related quantity (that is, the total quantity that causes the total cost). See Exhibit 19–5.

Average fixed costs are lower when a larger quantity is produced.

Exhibit 19–5 Cost Structure of a Firm

Quantity (Q)	Total fixed costs (TFC)	Average fixed costs (AFC)	Average variable costs (AVC)	Total variable costs (TVC)	Total cost (TC)	Average cost (AC)
0	$30,000	—	—	—	$ 30,000	—
10,000	30,000	$3.00	$0.80	$ 8,000	38,000	$3.80
20,000	30,000	1.50	0.80	16,000	46,000	2.30
30,000	30,000	1.00	0.80	24,000	54,000	1.80
40,000	30,000	0.75	0.80	32,000	62,000	1.51
50,000	30,000	0.60	0.80	40,000	70,000	1.40
60,000	30,000	0.50	0.80	48,000	78,000	1.30
70,000	30,000	0.43	0.80	56,000	86,000	1.23
80,000	30,000	0.38	0.80	64,000	94,000	1.18
90,000	30,000	0.33	0.80	72,000	102,000	1.13
100,000	30,000	0.30	0.80	80,000	110,000	1.10

$$\begin{bmatrix} 110,000 \text{ (TC)} \\ -\ 80,000 \text{ (TVC)} \\ \hline 30,000 \text{ (TFC)} \end{bmatrix} \quad (Q)\ 100,000) \overline{\begin{matrix} 0.30 \text{ (AFC)} \\ 30,000 \text{ (TFC)} \\ 0.80 \text{ (AVC)} \end{matrix}} \quad \begin{bmatrix} 100,000 \text{ (Q)} \\ \times\ 0.80 \text{ (AVC)} \\ \hline 80,000 \text{ (TVC)} \end{bmatrix} \quad \begin{bmatrix} 30,000 \text{ (TFC)} \\ +\ 80,000 \text{ (TVC)} \\ \hline 110,000 \text{ (TC)} \end{bmatrix} \quad (Q)\ 100,000) \overline{\begin{matrix} 1.10 \text{ (AC)} \\ 110,000 \text{ (TC)} \end{matrix}}$$

2. **Average fixed cost** (per unit) is obtained by dividing total fixed cost by the related quantity.
3. **Average variable cost** (per unit) is obtained by dividing total variable cost by the related quantity.

An example shows cost relations

Exhibit 19–5 shows typical cost data for one firm. For simplicity, we assume that average variable cost is the same for each unit. Notice how average fixed cost goes down steadily as the quantity increases. Notice also how total variable cost increases when quantity increases, although the average variable cost remains the same. Average cost decreases continually, too. This is because while average variable cost is the same, average fixed cost is decreasing. Exhibit 19–6 shows the three "average" curves.

Exhibit 19–6 Typical Shape of Cost (per unit) Curves when AVC Is Assumed Constant per Unit

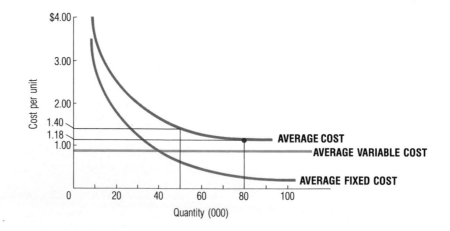

Ignoring demand is the major weakness of average-cost pricing

Average-cost pricing works well if the firm actually sells the quantity it used to set the average cost price. Losses may result, however, if actual sales are much lower than expected. On the other hand, if sales are much higher than expected, then profits may be very good. But this will only happen by luck—that is, because the firm's demand is much larger than expected.

To use average-cost pricing, a marketing manager must make *some* estimate of the quantity to be sold in the coming period. But unless this quantity is related to price—that is, unless the firm's demand curve is considered—the marketing manager may set a price that doesn't even cover a firm's total cost! This can be seen in a simple example for a firm with the cost curves shown in Exhibit 19–6. This firm's demand curve is shown in Exhibit 19–7. It is important to see that customers' demands (and their demand curve) are still important—whether management takes time to estimate the demand curve or not.

In this example, the firm will incur a loss whether management sets the price at a high $3 or a low $1.25. At $3, the firm will sell only 10,000 units for a total revenue of $30,000. But total cost will be $38,000—for a loss of $8,000. At the $1.25 price, it will sell 50,000 units—for a loss of $7,500. If management tries to estimate the demand curve—however roughly—the price probably will be set in the middle of the range—say at $2—where the firm will earn a profit of $6,000. See Exhibit 19–7.

In short, average-cost pricing is simple in theory—but often fails in practice. In stable situations, prices set by this method may yield profits—but not necessarily *maximum* profits. And note that such cost-based prices might be higher than a price that would be more profitable for the firm—as shown in Exhibit 19–7. When demand conditions are changing, average-cost pricing is even more risky.

Exhibit 19–8 summarizes the relationships discussed above. Cost-oriented pricing suggests that the total number of units to be sold determines the *average* fixed cost per unit and thus the average total cost. Then, the firm adds some amount of

Exhibit 19–7   Evaluation of Various Prices along a Firm's Demand Curve

Exhibit 19–8   Summary of Relationships among Quantity, Cost, and Price Using Cost-Oriented Pricing

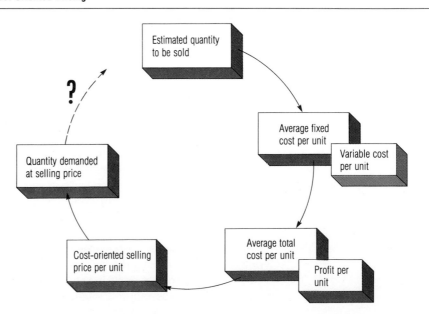

profit per unit to average total cost to get the cost-oriented selling price. But we are back where we started—when demand is considered—because the number of units sold depends on the selling price. And the quantity sold (times price) determines total revenue (and total profit or loss). A decision made in one area affects each of the others—directly or indirectly.[3] A manager who forgets this can make bad pricing decisions.

Experience curve pricing is even riskier

In recent years, some aggressive firms, including Texas Instruments, have used a variation of average-cost pricing called experience curve pricing. **Experience curve pricing** is average-cost pricing using an estimate of *future* average costs. This approach is based on the observation that over time—as an industry gains experience in certain kinds of production—managers learn new ways to reduce costs. The effect of such "learning" on costs varies in different businesses. Studies suggest that costs decrease about 15 to 20 percent each time cumulative production volume (experience) doubles—at least in some industries. So some firms set average-cost prices where they expect costs to be when products are sold in the future—not where costs actually are when the strategy is set. This approach is more common in rapidly growing markets (such as in the electronics business) because cumulative production volume (experience) grows faster.

If costs drop as expected, this approach can work fairly well. But it has the same risks as regular average-cost pricing—unless demand is included in the price setting. At the least, this means that the price setter has to estimate what quantity will be sold to be able to read the "right" price from the "experience"-based average-cost curve.[4]

SOME FIRMS ADD A TARGET RETURN TO COST

Target return pricing scores . . . sometimes

Target return pricing—adding a "target return" to the cost of a product—has become popular in recent years. With this approach, the price setter seeks to earn (1) a percentage return (say 10 percent per year) on the investment or (2) a specific total dollar return.

The method is a variation of the average-cost method since the desired target return is added into total cost. As a simple example, if a small company had $10,000 invested and wanted to make a 10 percent return on investment, it would add $1,000 to its annual total costs in setting prices.

This approach has the same weakness as other average-cost pricing methods. If the quantity actually sold is less than the quantity used in setting the price, then the target return is not earned—even though it seems to be part of the price structure. In fact, we already saw this in Exhibit 19–3. Remember that we added $1,000 as an expected "reasonable profit"—or target return. But the return was much lower when the expected quantity was not sold. (It could be higher, too—but only if the quantity sold is much larger than expected.) Target return pricing clearly does not guarantee that a firm will hit the target.

Hitting the target in the long run

Managers in some larger firms, who want to achieve a long-run target return objective, use another cost-oriented pricing approach—**long-run target return pricing**—adding a "long-run average target return" to the cost of a product. Instead of estimating the quantity they expect to produce in any one year, they assume that during several years' time their plants will produce at, say, 80 percent of capacity. They use this quantity when setting their prices.

Companies that take this longer-run view assume that there will be recession years when sales drop below 80 percent of capacity. For example, Owens/Corning Fiberglas sells insulation. In years when there is little construction, output is low, and the firm does not earn the target return. But the company also has good years when it sells more insulation and exceeds the target return. Over the long run, Owens/Corning managers expect to achieve the target return. And sometimes they're right—depending on how accurately they estimate demand!

BREAK-EVEN ANALYSIS CAN EVALUATE POSSIBLE PRICES

Some price setters use break-even analysis in their pricing. **Break-even analysis** evaluates whether the firm will be able to break even—that is, cover all its costs—with a particular price. This is important, because a firm must cover all costs in the long run or there is not much point being in business. This method focuses on the **break-even point (BEP)**—the quantity where the firm's total cost will just equal its total revenue.

Break-even charts help find the BEP

To help understand how break-even analysis works, look at Exhibit 19–9, an example of the typical break-even chart. The chart has lines that show total costs (total variable plus total fixed costs) and total revenues at different levels of production. The break-even point on the chart is at 75,000 units—where the total cost and total revenue lines intersect. At that production level, total cost and total revenue are the same—$90,000.

This chart also shows some typical assumptions that are made to simplify break-even analysis. Note that the total revenue curve is assumed to be a straight line. This means that each extra unit sold adds the same amount to total revenue. Stated differently, this assumes that *any quantity can be sold at the same price.* For this chart, we are assuming a selling price of $1.20 a unit. You can see that if

Exhibit 19–9   Break-Even Chart for a Particular Situation

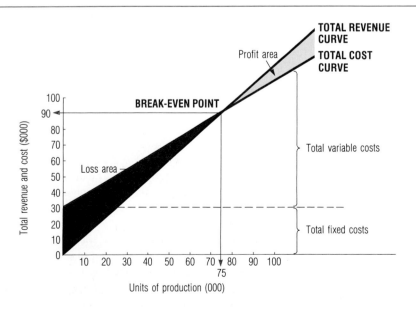

the firm sells the break-even quantity of 75,000 at $1.20 each, it will earn a total revenue of $90,000.

In addition, the total cost curve in the chart is assumed to be a straight line. This means that average variable cost (AVC) is the same at different levels of output. For Exhibit 19–9, the AVC is 80 cents per unit.

The chart shows that below the break-even point, total cost is higher than total revenue—and the firm incurs a loss. It would make a profit above the break-even point. The difference between the total revenue and total cost at a given quantity is the profit—or loss!

Break-even analysis can be very helpful—if used properly—so let's look at this approach more closely.

How to compute a break-even point

A break-even chart is an easy-to-understand "visual," but it's also useful to be able to compute the break-even point.

The BEP, in units, can be found by dividing total fixed costs (TFC) by the **fixed-cost (FC) contribution per unit**—the assumed selling price per unit minus the variable cost per unit. This can be stated as a simple formula:

$$\text{BEP (in units)} = \text{Total fixed cost} / \text{Fixed cost contribution per unit}$$

This formula makes sense when we think about it. To break even, we must cover total fixed costs. Therefore, we must figure the contribution each unit will make to covering the total fixed costs (after paying for the variable costs to produce the item). When we divide this per-unit contribution into the total fixed costs that must be covered, we have the BEP (in units).

To illustrate the formula, let's use the cost and price information in Exhibit 19–9. The price per unit is $1.20. The average variable cost per unit is 80 cents. So the FC contribution per unit is 40 cents ($1.20 − .80). The fixed cost is $30,000 (see Exhibit 19–9). Substituting in the formula:

$$\text{BEP} = \$30,000 / .40 = 75,000 \text{ units}$$

From this you can see that if this firm sells 75,000 units, it will exactly cover all its fixed and variable costs. If it sells even one more unit, then it will begin to show a profit—in this case, 40 cents per unit. Note that once the fixed costs are covered, the part of revenue formerly going to cover fixed costs is now *all profit.*

BEP can be stated in dollars, too

The BEP can also be figured in dollars. Here, the easiest method to remember is to compute the BEP in units and then multiply by the assumed per-unit price. If you multiply the selling price ($1.20) by the BEP in units (75,000) you get $90,000—the BEP in dollars.

Each possible price has its own break-even point

Often it is useful to compute the break-even point for each of several possible prices and then compare the BEP for each price to likely demand at that price. The marketing manager can quickly reject some price possibilities when the expected quantity demanded at a given price is way below the break-even point for that price.

Target profit point can be figured, too

So far in our discussion of BEP we've focused on the quantity at which total revenue equals total cost—where profit is zero. We can also vary this approach to see what quantity is required to earn a certain level of profit. The analysis is the same as described above for the break-even point in units, but the amount of target profit is added to the total fixed cost. Then, when we divide the fixed cost plus profit figure by the contribution from each unit, we get the quantity that will earn the target profit.

Break-even analysis is helpful—but not a pricing solution

Break-even analysis is helpful for evaluating alternatives. It is also popular because it's easy to use. Yet break-even analysis is too often misunderstood. Beyond the BEP, profits seem to be growing continually. And the graph—with its straight-line total revenue curve—makes it seem that any quantity can be sold at the assumed price. But this usually is not true. It is the same as assuming a perfectly horizontal demand curve at that price. In fact, most managers face down-sloping demand situations. And their total revenue curves *do not* keep going up. So, to really zero in on the most profitable price, marketers are better off estimating the demand curve itself and then using "marginal analysis," which we'll discuss next.[5]

TRADITIONAL DEMAND AND SUPPLY ANALYSIS SHOWS HOW TO MAXIMIZE PROFITS

Most demand curves are down-sloping—and most supply curves are up-sloping. The intersection of these demand and supply curves seems to determine price—and, therefore, to take care of demand-oriented pricing. Unfortunately, it's

Marketing managers know that the price which is set will affect the quantities that will be sold.

not that simple. Although such analysis is suitable for a whole industry or market, some refinements are needed for an individual firm seeking to maximize profits.

We are seeking the biggest profit

In the following pages, we'll discuss these refinements—concentrating on price setting in the many situations in which demand curves are down-sloping—that is, in monopolistic competition.[6] In these situations, the firm has carved out a market niche for itself—and it does have a pricing decision to make. By contrast, in pure or nearly pure competition, marketing managers have little difficulty with the pricing decision. They simply use the market price. (The special case of oligopoly will be treated later in the chapter.)

We'll focus on how to *maximize* profits—not just on how to seek *some* profits. This has been the traditional approach of economic analysis. And it makes sense. If you know how to make the biggest profit, you can always adjust to pursue other objectives—while knowing how much profit you are giving up!

Marginal analysis—helps find the best price

In monopolistic competition, a marketing manager faces a down-sloping demand curve. He must pick a price on that curve—and generally must offer that price to all potential buyers (to avoid price discrimination under the Robinson-Patman Act) for the life of the plan. If he chooses a lower price, additional units will be sold. But all customers—even those who might be willing to pay more—pay this lower price. Therefore, a manager should consider the effect of alternative prices on total revenue and profit.

Marginal analysis can help make the best pricing decision. **Marginal analysis** focuses on the change in total revenue and total cost from selling one more unit to find the most profitable price and quantity. This very useful—but technical—idea is treated more fully in the next few pages. Be sure to study the exhibits.

Marginal revenue helps decide—can be negative

Marginal revenue is the change in total revenue that results from the sale of one more unit of a product. Since the firm's demand curve is down-sloping, this extra unit can be sold only by reducing the price of *all* items.

Exhibit 19–10 shows the relationship between price, quantity, total revenue, and marginal revenue in a situation with a straight-line, down-sloping demand curve.

Exhibit 19–10   Marginal Revenue and Price

(1)	(2)	(3) Total revenue (1) × (2) = TR	(4) Marginal revenue MR
Quantity q	Price p		
0	$150	$ 0	
1	140	140	$ 140
2	130	260	120
3	117	351	91
4	105	420	69
5	92	460	40
6	79	474	14
7	66	462	−12
8	53	424	−38
9	42	378	−46
10	31	310	−68

If a firm can sell four units for a total revenue of $420 and five units for $460, then marginal revenue for the fifth unit is $40. Considering only revenue, it would be desirable to sell this extra unit. But will revenue continue to rise if the firm sells more units at lower prices? No! Exhibit 19–10 shows that negative marginal revenues occur at lower price levels. Obviously, this is not good for the firm! (Note: the total revenue that will be obtained if price is cut may still be positive, but the marginal revenue—the extra revenue gained—may be positive or negative.)

Marginal revenue curve and demand curve are different

The marginal revenue curve is always below a down-sloping demand curve because the price of each "last unit" must be lower to sell more. This can be seen in Exhibit 19–11 where the data in Exhibit 19–10 is plotted. The fact that the demand curve and the marginal revenue curves are different in monopolistic competition is very important. We will use both curves to find the best price and quantity.

Marginal cost—the cost of one more unit

As we've already seen, various kinds of costs behave differently. Further, there is an important kind of cost that is similar to marginal revenue: marginal cost. This cost is vital to marginal analysis.

Marginal cost is the change in total cost that results from producing one more unit. If it costs $275 to produce 9 units of a product and $280 to produce 10 units, then marginal cost is $5 for the 10th unit. In other words, marginal cost—contrasted to average cost per unit—is the additional cost of producing one more *specific unit;* average cost is the average for *all units.*

Cost structure example

Exhibit 19–12 shows how these costs can vary for a typical firm. *Fill in the missing numbers in this exhibit.* Notice that variable cost no longer is assumed constant per unit in Exhibit 19–12. Here, we use the more realistic assumption that variable costs will go down for a while and then rise.

Exhibit 19–12 illustrates three important points. *First,* total fixed costs do not change over the entire range of output—but total variable costs increase continu-

Exhibit 19–11   A Plotting of the Demand and Marginal Revenue Data in Exhibit 19–10

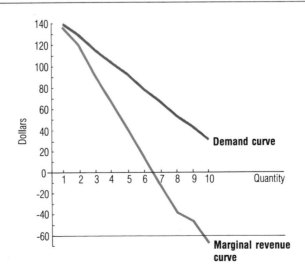

Exhibit 19–12 Cost Structure for Individual Firm (fill in the missing numbers)

(1) Quantity Q	(2) Total fixed cost TFC	(3) Average fixed cost AFC	(4) Total variable cost TVC	(5) Average variable cost AVC	(6) Total cost (TFC + TVC = TC) TC	(7) Average cost (AC = TC ÷ Q) AC	(8) Marginal cost (per unit) MC
0	$200	$ 0	$ 0	$ 0	$200	Infinity	
1	200	200	96	96	296	$296	$ 96
2	200	100	116	58	316	___	20
3	200	___	___	___	331	110.33	___
4	200	50	___	___	344	___	___
5	200	40	155	31	___	71	11
6	200	___	168	___	___	61.33	13
7	___	___	183	___	___	___	15
8	___	___	223	___	___	___	___
9	___	___	307	___	507	56.33	___
10	___	20	510	51	710	71	203

ally as more and more units are produced. Therefore, total costs—the sum of total fixed costs and total variable costs—will increase as total quantity increases.

Second, average costs will decrease—for a while—as quantity produced increases. Remember that average costs are the sum of average fixed costs and average variable costs—and here average fixed costs are going down because total fixed costs are divided by more and more units as output increases. For example, given a total fixed cost of $200, at a production level of four units, the average fixed cost is $50. At a production level of five units, the average fixed cost is $40.

Third, average costs in this table start rising for the last two units because average variable costs are increasing faster than average fixed costs are decreasing. The firm may be forced to use less efficient facilities and workers, to go into overtime work, or to pay higher prices for the materials it needs. This turn-up of the average cost curve is common after economies of scale "run out."

The marginal cost of just one more is important

The marginal cost column in Exhibit 19–12 is the most important cost column for our purposes. It shows what each extra unit costs. This suggests the *minimum* extra revenue we would like to get for that additional unit. Note that, like average cost, marginal cost drops—but it begins to rise again at a lower level of output than average cost does.

Marginal cost starts to increase at five units. This can be seen in Exhibit 19–13—which shows the behavior of the average cost, average variable cost, and marginal cost curves. Note that the marginal cost curve intersects the average variable cost and average cost curves from below *at their low points,* and then rises rapidly. This is how this curve typically behaves.

How to find the most profitable price and the quantity to produce

Since a manager must choose only *one* price level (for a time period), his pricing problem is which one to choose. This price determines the quantity that will be sold. To maximize profit, a manager should be willing to supply more units if he can obtain a marginal revenue at least equal to the marginal cost of extra units.

Exhibit 19–13   Per-Unit Cost Curves (for data in Exhibit 19–12)

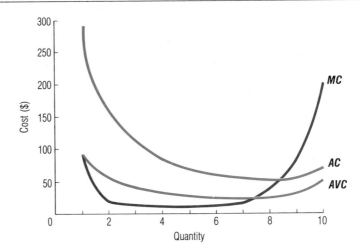

From this we get the following **rule for maximizing profit**: the firm should produce that output where marginal cost is just less than or equal to marginal revenue.*

The selling price for this optimum quantity is found by referring to the demand curve—which shows what price customers are willing to pay for the optimum quantity. Note: *the optimum price is not found on the marginal revenue curve.*

This method of finding the most profitable price and quantity is a useful tool for a marketing manager. To make sure you understand it, study the following example carefully. To make doubly sure that this approach is fully explained, we will calculate the most profitable price and quantity using total revenue and total cost curves first, and then show that the same answer is obtained with marginal curves. This will give you a check on the method—as well as help you see how the marginal revenue–marginal cost method works.

Profit maximization with total revenue and total cost curves

Exhibit 19–14 provides data on total revenue, total cost, and total profit for a firm. Exhibit 19–15 graphs the total revenue, total cost, and total profit relationships. It is clear from the graph of the total profit curve that the most profitable quantity is six—this is the quantity where we find the greatest vertical distance between the TR curve and the TC curve. Exhibit 19–14 shows that the most profitable price is $79 and a quantity of six will be sold.

You can see that, beyond a quantity of six, the total profit curve declines. A profit-maximizing marketing manager should not be interested in selling more than this number.

---

*This rule applies in the typical situations where the curves are shaped similarly to those discussed here. Technically, however, we should add the following to the rule for maximizing profit: the marginal cost must be increasing, or decreasing at a lesser rate than marginal revenue.

Exhibit 19–14   Revenue, Cost, and Profit for an Individual Firm

(1) Quantity q	(2) Price p	(3) Total revenue TR	(4) Total cost TC	(5) Profit (TR − TC)	(6) Marginal revenue MR	(7) Marginal cost MC	(8) Marginal profit (MR − MC)
0	$150	$0	$200	$ − 200			
1	140	140	296	− 156	$140	$96	$+ 44
2	130	260	316	− 56	120	20	+ 100
3	117	351	331	+ 20	91	15	+ 76
4	105	420	344	+ 76	69	13	+ 56
5	92	460	355	+ 105	40	11	+ 29
6	79	474	368	+ 106	14	13	+ 1
7	66	462	383	+ 79	− 12	15	− 27
8	53	424	423	+ 1	− 38	40	− 78
9	42	378	507	− 129	− 46	84	− 130
10	31	310	710	− 400	− 68	203	− 271

Profit maximization using marginal curves

Now we can apply the rule for maximizing profit using marginal curves. We obtain the same best quantity and price—six at $79. See Exhibit 19–16, which is based on the data for marginal revenue and marginal cost in Exhibit 19–14.

In Exhibit 19–16, the intersection of the marginal cost and marginal revenue curves occurs at a quantity of six. This is the most profitable quantity. But the best price must be obtained by going up to the demand curve and then over to the vertical axis—*not* by going from the intersection of MR and MC over to the vertical axis. Again, the best price is $79.

Exhibit 19–15   Graphic Determination of the Output Giving the Greatest Total Profit for a Firm

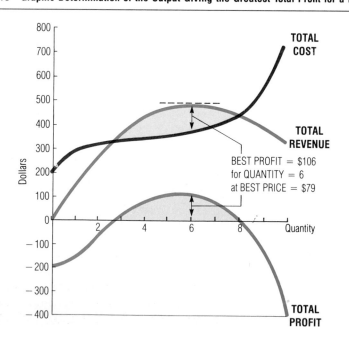

Exhibit 19–16   Alternate Determination of the Most Profitable Output and Price for a Firm

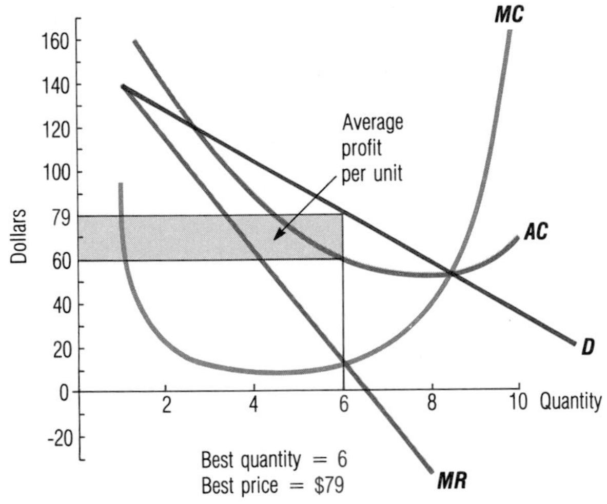

Best quantity = 6
Best price = $79

The graphic solution is supported by the data in Exhibit 19–14. At a quantity of six, marginal revenue equals $14, and marginal cost is $13. There is a profit margin of $1—suggesting that it might be profitable to offer seven rather than six units. This is not the case, however. The marginal cost of the seventh unit is $15, while its marginal revenue is actually negative. Offering to sell seven units (instead of only six) will reduce total profit by $27.

It is important to realize that *total* profit is *not* near zero when MR equals MC. **Marginal profit**—the extra profit on the last unit—is near zero. But that is exactly why the quantity obtained at the MR–MC intersection is the most profitable. Marginal analysis shows that when the firm is finding the best price to charge, it should increase the quantity it will sell as long as the last unit it considers offering will yield *extra* profits.

Again, the marketing manager must choose only *one* price. Marginal analysis is useful in helping to set the best price to charge for all that will be sold. It might help to think of the demand curve as an "iffy" curve—*if* a price is selected, *then* its related quantity will be sold. Before the marketing manager sets the actual price, all these *if-then* combinations can be evaluated for profitability. But once he sets a particular price, the results will follow—the related quantity will be sold.

A profit range is reassuring   We've been trying to find the most profitable price and quantity. But in a changing world, this is difficult. Fortunately, this "best" point is surrounded by a profitable range.

Note that in Exhibit 19–15, there are two break-even points rather than a single point, which was the case when we were discussing break-even analysis. The second break-even point falls farther to the right because total costs turn up and total revenue turns down.

These two break-even points are important. They show the range of profitable operations. Although we are seeking the point of *maximum* profit, we know that this point is an ideal rather than a realistic possibility. So it is essential that you know there is a *range of profit* around the optimum—it isn't just a single point. This means that pursuing the most profitable price is a wise policy.

How to lose less, if you must

The marginal approach to finding the most profitable output will also find the output that will be least unprofitable when market conditions are so poor that the firm must operate at a loss.

If sales are slow, the marketing manager may even have to consider stopping production. When making this decision, he should ignore fixed costs since these will continue regardless. Some fixed costs may even involve items that are so "sunk" in the business that they cannot be sold for anything near the cost shown on the company's records. An unsuccessful company's special-purpose buildings and machines may be worthless to anyone else.

Marginal costs are another matter. If the firm cannot recover the marginal cost of the last unit (or, more generally, the variable cost of the units being considered), it should stop operations temporarily or go out of business. The only exceptions involve social or humanitarian considerations—or the fact that the marginal costs of closing temporarily are high and stronger demand is expected *soon*. But if marginal costs can be covered in the short run—even though all fixed costs cannot—the firm should stay in operation.

Marginal analysis helps get the most in pure competition

Marketing managers caught in pure competition can also apply marginal methods. They don't have a price decision to make since the demand curve is flat. (Note: this means that the marginal revenue curve is flat at the same level.) But they do have output decisions. They can use the marginal revenue curve, therefore, with their own unique marginal cost curve to determine the most profitable (or least unprofitable) output level. See Exhibit 19–17. And this approach leads to a different (and more profitable) output than the lowest average-cost decision favored by some "common-sense" managers. Note in Exhibit 19–17 that the quantity associated with the lowest average cost is not the most profitable quantity.

MARGINAL ANALYSIS APPLIES IN OLIGOPOLY, TOO

Marginal analysis can be used whenever a firm can estimate its demand and cost curves. The special kinked nature of the oligopoly demand curve is no problem.

Exhibit 19–17 Finding the Most Profitable (or least unprofitable) Price and Quantity in Pure Competition (in the short run)

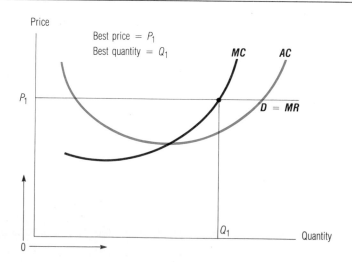

When demand kinks, marginal revenue drops fast

Exhibit 19–18 Marginal Revenue Drops Fast in an Oligopoly

As we saw in Chapter 4, each competitor in an oligopoly faces a kinked demand curve. We said then that the tendency in such situations is to avoid the use of Price—to avoid price cutting. Marginal analysis now helps us understand this situation better.

The dashed part of the marginal revenue line in Exhibit 19–18 shows that marginal revenue drops sharply at the kinked point. This is a technical but important matter. It helps explain why prices are relatively "sticky" at the kinked point. Even if costs change—and, therefore, if each firm's supply curve moves up or down—the MC curve may still cross the MR curve someplace along this drop. In this case, even though costs are changing—and there may seem to be a reason for changing the price—each firm should hold its price at the kinked price level to maximize its profits!

A price leader usually sets the price

Most of the firms in an oligopoly are aware of the economics of their situation—at least intuitively. Usually, a **price leader** sets a price for all to follow—perhaps to maximize profits or to get a certain target return on investment—and (without any collusion) other members of the industry follow. This price may be maintained for a long time—or at least as long as all members of the industry continue to make a reasonable profit.

The price leader must take this responsibility seriously. If followers are not able to make a reasonable profit at the market price, they may try secret price cuts to expand sales. If very much of this happens, the price leader will lose business, but all will lose profits. And the situation may turn into a violent price war. Or competitors may be tempted to get together and "fix prices." This sometimes happens—but *it is illegal.* Lacking an effective leader, the market may be unstable. And severe price cutting may be a continual threat.

Price leader should know costs and demand

A price leader should have a good understanding of its own and its competitors' cost structures—as well as an estimate of the industry demand curve. Setting too high a price may look attractive in the short run, but it may attract more competitors to the market and lead to trouble later—when capacity has expanded. Setting too low a price, on the other hand, can lead to action from antitrust officials who become concerned about small competitors. An optimal price may be one that is just high enough to support the marginal firm—the least efficient company whose production is needed to meet peak long-run demands.

If the price leader chooses a price that others can accept, they may follow without any need for agreement. This "conscious parallel action" is deplored by the FTC and the Justice Department, but it still hasn't been declared illegal. It's hard to see how it could be. Each firm *must* administer its prices, and meeting competition is certainly legal. In fact, the same behavior is found in pure competition. So—as long as the firms avoid conspiracy—meeting competition in any market situation probably will continue to be acceptable.

SOME PRICE SETTERS DO ESTIMATE DEMAND

Cost-oriented pricing is relatively simple and sometimes practical. But it is also clear that most cost-oriented approaches require some estimate of likely demand.

Mazda Dealers Maximize Profits, At Least in the Short-Run

During the 1980s, most American consumers just saw Mazda as a lower-priced Japanese alternative to Toyota and Honda. Mazda's marketing managers knew that they needed to build a more distinct image in the 1990s. Their plan was to offer marketing mixes that clearly established Mazda as a producer of high-performance, affordable cars. The sporty Miata convertible was their first step in that effort. Mazda designers styled the Miata for the preferences of U.S. sports car buffs. Research showed that this target market wanted a "back to basics" two-seater at a list price of about $14,000. To insure profits at that price, Mazda kept fixed development costs low. It also avoided costly features like digital controls and electronic suspension.

The marketing mix seemed to be on target. Before the Miata was even on the market, magazines praised it as the "best sports car buy in America." Spurred by the publicity, consumers poured into dealer showrooms. However, demand quickly outstripped supply. Most dealers soon had a long waiting list of buyers who were willing to pay $3,000 or more above the Miata's list price. Other consumers were angry that the dealers expected them to pay a premium—even to get on a waiting list. Mazda tried to convince its dealers to stick to the list price—that the plan to build an affordable image would be more profitable in the long-run. However, most dealers were more interested in maximizing their short-run profits, and the car maker did not have the legal right to dictate that they sell at the suggested price.[7]

And, as we've seen, estimating the demand curve may help avoid mistakes in pricing.

Actual use of demand curves is not very common in the real world. This is partly because many managers think the exact shape of the demand curve must be known to gain the benefits of this approach. They forget that the profitable "range" around the best price and quantity allows some leeway in demand estimates.

Yet we do find marketers pricing as though demand curves are there. The following sections discuss these demand-related approaches.

Value in use pricing—how much will the customer save?

Industrial buyers think about costs when making purchases. Many marketers who aim at industrial markets keep this in mind in setting prices. They use **value in use pricing**—which is setting prices that will capture some of what customers will save by substituting the firm's product for the one currently being used. For example, a producer of computer-controlled machines used to assemble cars knows that his machine doesn't just replace a standard machine. It also reduces labor costs, quality control costs, and—after the car is sold—costs of warranty repairs. He can estimate what the auto producer will save by using the machine—and then set a price that makes it less expensive for the auto producer to buy the computerized machine than to stick with his old methods.[8]

Leader pricing—make it low to attract customers

Leader pricing is setting some very low prices—real bargains—to get customers into retail stores. The idea is not to sell large quantities of the leader items, but to get customers into the store to buy other products.[9] Certain products are picked

Value in use pricing considers what a customer will save by buying a product.

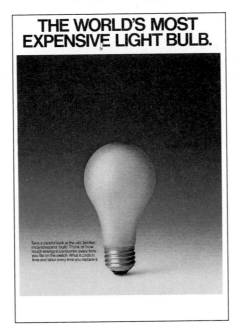

for their promotion value and priced low—but above cost. In food stores, the leader prices are the "specials" that are advertised regularly to give an image of low prices. Leader items are usually well-known, widely used items that customers don't stock heavily—milk, butter, eggs, or coffee—but on which they will recognize a real price cut.

Leader pricing may try to appeal to customers who normally shop elsewhere. But it can backfire if customers buy only the low-price leaders. To avoid hurting profits, managers often select leader items that aren't directly competitive with major lines—as when bargain-priced recording tape is the leader for a stereo equipment store.

Bait pricing—offer a "steal," but sell under protest

Bait pricing is setting some very low prices to attract customers—but trying to sell more expensive models or brands once the customer is in the store. For example, a furniture store may advertise a color TV for $199. But once bargain hunters come to the store, salesclerks point out the disadvantages of the low-price TV and try to convince them to "trade-up" to a better (and more expensive) set. Bait pricing is something like leader pricing. But here the seller *doesn't* plan to sell many at the low price. Some stores even make it very difficult to buy the "bait" item.

If bait pricing is successful, the demand for higher-quality products expands. But extremely aggressive and sometimes dishonest bait-pricing advertising has given this method a bad reputation. The Federal Trade Commission considers bait pricing a deceptive act and has banned its use in interstate commerce. Even Sears, one of the nation's most trusted retail chains, has been criticized for "bait-and-switch" pricing. But some retailers who operate only within one state continue to advertise bait prices.

Psychological pricing—some prices just seem right

Prestige pricing: make it high—but not cheap

Price lining—a few prices cover the field

Psychological pricing is setting prices that have special appeal to target customers. Some people think there are whole ranges of prices that potential customers see as the same. So price cuts in these ranges do not increase the quantity sold. But just below this range, customers may buy more. Then, at even lower prices, the quantity demanded stays the same again—and so on. Exhibit 19–19 shows the kind of demand curve that leads to psychological pricing. Vertical drops mark the price ranges that customers see as the same. Pricing research shows that there are such demand curves.[10]

Odd-even pricing is setting prices that end in certain numbers. For example, products selling below $50 often end in the number 5 or the number 9—such as 49 cents or $24.95. Prices for higher-priced products are often $1 or $2 below the next even dollar figure—such as $99 rather than $100.

Some marketers use odd-even pricing because they feel that consumers react better to these prices—perhaps seeing them as "substantially" lower than the next highest even price. Marketers using these prices seem to assume that they have a rather jagged demand curve—that slightly higher prices will substantially reduce the quantity demanded. Odd-even prices were used long ago by some retailers to force their clerks to make change. Then the clerks had to record the sale and could not pocket the money. Today, however, it's not always clear why these prices are used—or whether they really work. Perhaps it's done simply because "everyone else does it."[11]

Prestige pricing is setting a rather high price to suggest high quality or high status. Some target customers want the "best." So they will buy at a high price. But if the price seems "cheap," they worry about quality and don't buy.[12]

Prestige pricing is most common for luxury products—such as furs, jewelry, and perfume. It is also common in service industries—where the customer can't see the product in advance and relies on price to judge its quality. Target customers who respond to prestige pricing give the marketing manager an unusual demand curve. Instead of a normal down-sloping curve, the curve goes down for a while and then bends back to the left again. See Exhibit 19–20.

Price lining is setting a few price levels for a product line and then marking all items at these prices. This approach assumes that customers have a certain price in mind that they expect to pay for a product. For example, most neckties are priced between $10 and $25. In price lining, there are only a few prices within this range. Ties will not be priced at $10.00, $10.50, $11.00, and so on. They might be priced at four levels—$10, $15, $20, and $25.

Exhibit 19–19   Demand Curve when Psychological Pricing Is Appropriate

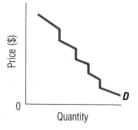

Exhibit 19–20   Demand Curve Showing a Prestige Pricing Situation

Price lining has advantages other than just matching prices to what consumers expect to pay. The main advantage is simplicity—for both clerks and customers. It is less confusing than having many prices. Some customers may consider items in only one price class. Their big decision, then, is which item(s) to choose at that price.

For retailers, price lining has several advantages. Sales may increase because (1) they can offer a bigger variety in each price class and (2) it's easier to get customers to make decisions within one price class. Stock planning is simpler because demand is larger at the relatively few prices. Price lining can also reduce costs because inventory needs are lower.

Demand-backward pricing—for gifts

Demand-backward pricing is setting an acceptable final consumer price and working backward to what a producer can charge. It is commonly used by producers of final consumer products—especially shopping products, such as women's and children's clothing and shoes. It is also used for toys or gifts for which customers will spend a specific amount—because they are seeking a $5 or a $10 gift. Here, a reverse cost-plus pricing process is used. This method has been called "market-minus" pricing.

The producer starts with the retail price for a particular item and then works backward—subtracting the typical margins that channel members expect. This gives the approximate price that the producer can charge. Then, the average or planned marketing expenses can be subtracted from this price to find how much can be spent producing the item. Candy companies do this. They alter the size of the candy bar to keep the bar at the "expected" price.

Demand estimates are needed if demand-backward pricing is to be successful. The quantity that will be demanded affects production costs—that is, where the

Demand-backward pricing starts with the retail price for a particular item and then works backward—subtracting the typical margins that channel members expect.

firm will be on its average cost curve. Also, since competitors can be expected to make the best product possible, it is important to know customer needs to set the best amount to be spent on manufacturing costs. By increasing costs a little, the product may be so improved in consumers' eyes that the firm will sell many more units. But if consumers only want novelty, additional quality may not increase the quantity demanded—and it shouldn't be offered.

PRICING A FULL LINE

Our emphasis has been—and will continue to be—on the problem of pricing an individual product, mainly because this makes our discussion clearer. But most marketing managers are responsible for more than one product. In fact, their "product" may be the whole company line! So we'll discuss this matter briefly.

Full-line pricing—market- or firm-oriented?

Full-line pricing is setting prices for a whole line of products. How to do this depends on which of two basic situations a firm is facing.

In one case, all products in the company's line are aimed at the same general target market, which makes it important for all prices to be related. For example, a producer of TV sets could offer several price and quality levels to give its target customers some choice. Then, the different prices should appear "reasonable" when the target customers are evaluating them.

In the other case, the different products in the line are aimed at entirely different target markets so there doesn't have to be any relation between the various prices. A chemical producer of a wide variety of products with several target markets, for example, probably should price each product separately.

Cost is not much help in full-line pricing

The marketing manager must try to recover all costs on the whole line—perhaps by pricing quite low on competitive items and much higher on less competitive items. Estimating costs for each product is a big problem because there is no single "right" way to assign a company's fixed costs to each of the products. Further, if any cost-oriented pricing method is carried through without considering demand, it can lead to very unrealistic prices. To avoid mistakes, the marketing manager should judge demand for the whole line as well as demand for each individual product in each target market.

As an aid to full-line pricing, the marketing manager can assemble directly variable costs on the many items in the line to calculate a price floor. To this floor he can add a "reasonable" markup based on the quality of the product, the strength of the demand for the product, and the degree of competition. But finally, the image projected by the full line must be evaluated.

Complementary product pricing

Complementary product pricing is setting prices on several products as a group. This may lead to one product being priced very low so that the profits from another product will increase—and increase the product group's total profits. A new Gillette shaver, for example, may be priced low to sell the blades, which must be replaced regularly.

Complementary product pricing differs from full-line pricing because different production facilities may be involved—so there's no cost allocation problem. Instead, the problem is really understanding the target market and the demand curves for each of the complementary products. Then, various combinations of prices can be tried to see what set will be best for reaching the company's pricing objectives.

BID PRICING AND NEGOTIATED PRICING DEPEND HEAVILY ON COSTS

A new price for every job

Bid pricing is offering a specific price for each possible job rather than setting a price that applies for all customers. Building contractors, for example, must bid on possible projects. And many companies selling services (like cleaning or data processing) must submit bids for jobs they would like to have.

The big problem in bid pricing is estimating all the costs that will apply to each job. This may sound easy, but a complicated bid may involve thousands of cost components. Further, management must include an overhead charge and a charge for profit.

Demand must be considered, too

Competition must be considered when adding in overhead and profit. Usually, the customer will get several bids and accept the lowest one. So unthinking addition of "typical" overhead and profit rates should be avoided. Some bidders use the same overhead and profit rates on all jobs—regardless of competition—and then are surprised when they don't get some jobs.

Because bidding can be expensive, a marketing manager may want to be selective about which jobs to bid on and choose those where he feels he has the greatest chance of success. Firms can spend thousands—or even millions—of dollars just developing bids for large industrial or government orders.[13]

Sometimes bids are negotiated

Some buying situations (including much government buying) require the use of bids—and the purchasing agent must take the lowest bid. In other cases, however, the customer asks for bids and then singles out the company that submits the *most attractive* bid—not necessarily the lowest—for further bargaining.

Negotiated prices— what will a specific customer pay?

The list price or bidding price the seller would like to charge is sometimes only the *starting point* for discussions with individual customers. What a customer will buy—if the customer buys at all—depends on the **negotiated price**, a price set based on bargaining between the buyer and seller.

As with simple bid pricing, negotiated pricing is most common in situations where the marketing mix is adjusted for each customer—so bargaining may involve the whole marketing mix, not just the price level. For example, a firm that produces machine tools used by other manufacturers to make their products might use this approach. Each customer may need custom-designed machines and different types of installation service. Through the bargaining process, the seller tries to determine what aspects of the marketing mix are most important to the customer. For one customer, the selling price may be what is most important. There, the seller might try to find ways to reduce costs of other elements of the marketing mix—consistent with the customer's needs—so that a profit could be obtained. Another customer might want more of some other element of the marketing mix—like more technical help after the sale—and be less sensitive to the price level.

A seller must know his costs to negotiate price effectively. However, negotiated pricing *is* a demand-oriented approach. Here, the seller is very carefully analyzing a particular customer's position on a demand curve—or on different possible demand curves based on different offerings—rather than the overall demand curve for a group of customers. This is a challenging job and the details are beyond the scope of this book. You should see, however, that the techniques for analysis of supply and demand we have been discussing apply here as they do with other price setting approaches.

CONCLUSION

In this chapter, we discussed various approaches to price setting. Generally, retailers and wholesalers use traditional markups. Some use the same markups for all their items. Others find that varying the markups increases turnover and profit. In other words, they consider demand and competition!

Cost-oriented pricing seems to make sense for many middlemen because they handle small quantities of many items. Producers must take price setting more seriously. They are the ones that set the list price to which others apply markups. They should use demand-oriented pricing.

Producers commonly use average-cost curves to help set their prices. But this approach sometimes ignores demand completely. A more realistic approach to average-cost pricing requires a sales forecast— maybe just assuming that sales in the next period will be roughly the same as in the last period. This approach *does* enable the marketing manager to set a price—but the price may or may not cover all costs and earn the desired profit.

Break-even analysis is useful for evaluating possible prices. It provides a rough-and-ready tool for eliminating unworkable prices. But management must estimate demand to evaluate the chance of reaching these possible break-even points.

Traditional demand and supply analysis is a useful tool for finding the most profitable price—and the quantity to produce. The most profitable quantity is found at the intersection of the marginal revenue and marginal cost curves. To determine the most profitable price, a manager takes the most profitable quantity to the firm's demand curve to find the price target customers will be willing to pay for this quantity.

The major difficulty with demand-oriented pricing is estimating the demand curve. But experienced managers—aided perhaps by marketing research—can estimate the nature of demand for their products. Such estimates are useful—even if they aren't exact. They get you thinking in the right "ballpark." Sometimes, when all you need is a decision about raising or lowering price, even "rough" demand estimates can be very revealing.

Further, a firm's demand curve does not cease to exist simply because it is ignored. Some information is better than none at all. And it appears that some marketers do consider demand in their pricing. We see this with value in use pricing, leader pricing, bait pricing, odd-even pricing, psychological pricing, full-line pricing, and even bid pricing.

Throughout the book, we stress that firms must consider the customer before they do anything. This certainly applies to pricing. It means that when managers are setting a price, they have to consider what customers will be willing to pay. This isn't always easy. But it's nice to know that there is a profit range around the "best" price. Therefore, even "guesstimates" about what potential customers will buy at various prices will probably lead to a better price than mechanical use of traditional markups or cost-oriented formulas.[14]

Questions and Problems

1. Why do many department stores seek a markup of about 40 percent when some discount houses operate on a 20 percent markup?

2. A producer distributed its riding lawnmowers through wholesalers and retailers. The retail selling price was $800, and the manufacturing cost to the company was $312. The retail markup was 35 percent and the wholesale markup 20 percent. (a) What was the cost to the wholesaler? To the retailer? (b) What percentage markup did the producer take?

3. Relate the concept of stock turnover to the growth of mass-merchandising. Use a simple example in your answer.

4. If total fixed costs are $200,000 and total variable costs are $100,000 at the output of 20,000 units, what are the probable total fixed costs and total variable costs at an output of 10,000 units? What are the average fixed costs, average variable costs, and average costs at these two output levels? Explain what additional information you would want to determine what price should be charged.

5. Explain how experience curve pricing differs from average-cost pricing.

6. Construct an example showing that mechanical use of a very large or a very small markup might still lead to unprofitable operation while some intermediate price would be profitable. Draw a graph and show the break-even point(s).

7. The Davis Company's fixed costs for the year are estimated at $200,000. Its product sells for $250. The variable cost per unit is $200. Sales for the coming year are expected to reach $1,250,000. What is the break-even point? Expected profit? If sales are forecast at only $875,000, should the Davis Company shut down operations? Why?

8. Distinguish among marginal revenue, average revenue, and price.

9. Draw a graph showing a demand and supply situation where marginal analysis correctly indicates that the firm should continue producing even though the profit and loss statement shows a loss.

10. Discuss the idea of drawing separate demand curves for different market segments. It seems logical because each target market should have its own marketing mix. But won't this lead to many demand curves and possible prices? And what will this mean with respect to functional discounts and varying prices in the marketplace? Will it be legal? Will it be practical?

11. Nicor Company is having a profitable year. Its only product sells to wholesalers for 80 cents a can.

Its managers feel that a 60 percent gross margin should be maintained. Its manufacturing costs consist of: material, 50 percent of cost; labor, 40 percent of cost; and overhead, 10 percent of cost. Both material and labor costs increased 10 percent since last year. Determine the new price per can based on its present pricing method. Is it wise to stick with a 60 percent margin, if a price increase would mean lost customers? Answer, using graphs and MC–MR analysis. Show a situation where it would be most profitable to (*a*) raise price, (*b*) leave price alone, (*c*) reduce price.

12.   How does a prestige pricing policy fit into a marketing mix? Would exclusive distribution be necessary?

13.   Cite a local example of odd-even pricing and evaluate whether it makes sense.

14.   Cite a local example of psychological pricing and evaluate whether it makes sense.

15.   Distinguish between leader pricing and bait pricing. What do they have in common? How can their use affect a marketing mix?

16.   Is a full-line pricing policy available only to producers? Cite local examples of full-line pricing. Why is full-line pricing important?

Suggested Cases

26.   Wireco, Inc.

30.   Chemco, Inc.

34.   Kenny Chrysler, Inc.

Suggested Computer-Aided Problem

19.   Break-Even/Profit Analysis

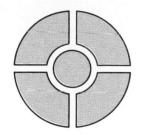

Chapter 20

Planning and Implementing Marketing Programs

When You Finish This Chapter, You Should

1. Know that strategy planning is much more than assembling the four Ps.

2. Understand the basic forecasting approaches and why they are used.

3. Know how response functions can help plan marketing strategies.

4. Understand why typical mixes are a good starting point for planning.

5. Know the content of and differences among strategies, marketing plans, and a marketing program.

6. Know about allocating budgets for marketing plans.

7. Know about some graphic aids for implementing a marketing program.

8. Understand the important new terms (shown in red).

More than strategies must be planned.

In NutraSweet's first five years on the market, its sales climbed to over $700 million—about 65 percent of the total market. But, in forecasting future sales and market share, NutraSweet's marketing managers knew that the earlier trend would not continue into the 1990s. Heavyweight competitors like Pfizer and Hoechst Celanese were already developing plans to enter the market—and NutraSweet's patent protection expires in December of 1992.

NutraSweet built its original success on an innovative product that met consumers' needs. But the strategy planned by NutraSweet's marketing managers involved more than a good product. The "typical" marketing strategy for suppliers of ingredients to food and soft-drink companies had emphasized personal selling to producers. In contrast, NutraSweet's marketing managers used mass selling to promote their brand name and red swirl logo directly to consumers. They also persuaded producers who used the ingredient to feature the NutraSweet brand name prominently on containers and in ads. In addition, because there was little direct competition, they used a profitable skimming approach to pricing—and charged different producer-customers different prices depending on the value NutraSweet added to their product.

Now, even as NutraSweet's patent expires, competitors will face a challenge entering the market because it will take a huge marketing effort—and a high promotion budget—to offset consumers' familiarity with the NutraSweet name. Moreover, Nutrasweet is targeting new markets to spark new growth in sales. For example, NutraSweet is planning and implementing new marketing mixes to appeal to consumers who now use sugar, rather than just focusing on people who are interested in artificial sweeteners. Further, it is also developing totally new products—

like its Simplesse fat substitute—and complete strategies to reach markets for its new products.[1]

This case—and this whole chapter—show why an individual firm should see each of its internal activities as part of a whole—and why a marketing manager must plan whole marketing mixes to satisfy target markets, rather than looking at only one of the four Ps.

MARKETING PLANNING IS MORE THAN ASSEMBLING THE FOUR Ps

They must be blended together

Marketing planning involves much more than assembling the four parts of a marketing mix. The four Ps must be creatively *blended* so the firm develops the "best" mix for its target market. This may mean that ideas of some specialists—the product manager, advertising manager, sales manager, and physical distribution manager—may have to be adjusted to improve the whole mix.

Throughout the text, we've given the job of integrating the four Ps to the marketing manager. Now you should see the need for this integrating role. It is easy for specialists to focus on their own areas and expect the rest of the company to work for or around them. This is especially true in larger firms—where specialists are needed—just because the size of the whole marketing job is too big for one person.

Need plans and program

Marketing managers must plan strategies, marketing plans, and finally, a whole marketing program. As we said earlier, a marketing *strategy* is a "big picture" of what a firm will do in some target market. A marketing *plan* includes the time-related details for that strategy. A marketing *program* is a combination of the firm's marketing plans.

Some time schedule is implicit in any strategy. A marketing plan simply spells out this time period—and the time-related details. Usually, we think in terms of some reasonable length of time—such as six months, a year, or a few years. But it might be only a month or two in some cases—especially when style and fashion are important. Or a strategy might be implemented over several years—perhaps the length of a product life cycle or at least the early stages of the life of the product.

You can see that marketing strategy planning is a creative process. But it is also a logical process. The marketing concept emphasizes that all of a firm's activities should focus on its target markets. Further, firms should try to meet the needs of some target market(s) that is (are) large enough to support its efforts—and yield a profit.

FORECASTING TARGET MARKET POTENTIAL AND SALES

Estimates of target **market potential**—what a whole market segment might buy—and a **sales forecast**—an estimate of how much an industry or firm hopes to sell to a market segment—are necessary for effective strategy planning. Without such information, it's hard to know if a strategy is potentially profitable.

We must first try to judge market potential before we can estimate what share a particular firm may be able to win with its particular marketing mix.

Without a sales forecast, it's hard to know if a strategy is potentially profitable.

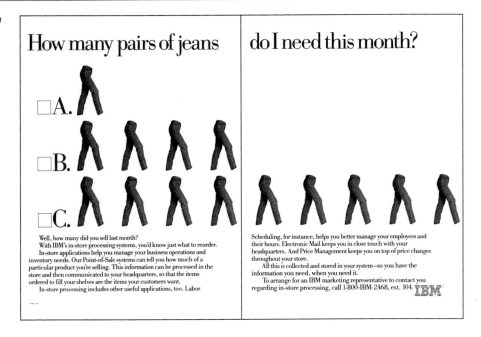

Two approaches to forecasting

Many methods are used to forecast market potential and sales, but they can all be grouped into two basic approaches: (1) extending past behavior and (2) predicting future behavior. The large number of methods may seem confusing at first, but this variety is an advantage. Forecasts are so important that management often prefers to develop forecasts in two or three different ways and then compare the differences before preparing a final forecast.

Extending past behavior can miss important turning points

When we forecast for existing products, we usually have some past data to go on. The basic approach—called **trend extension**—extends past experience into the future. With existing products, for example, the past trend of actual sales may be extended into the future. See Exhibit 20–1.

Ideally, when extending past sales behavior, we should decide why sales vary. This is the difficult and time-consuming part of sales forecasting. Usually we can gather a lot of data about the product or market—or about aspects of the uncontrollable environment. But unless we know the *reason* for past sales variations, it's hard to predict in what direction—and by how much—sales will move. Graphing the data and statistical techniques—including correlation and regression analysis—can be useful here. (These techniques, which are beyond our scope, are discussed in beginning statistics courses.)

Once we know why sales vary, we can usually develop a specific forecast. Sales may be moving directly up as population grows, for example. So we can just get an estimate of how population is expected to grow and project the impact on sales.

The weakness of the trend extension method is that it assumes past conditions will continue unchanged into the future. In fact, the future isn't always like the past. For example, for years the trend in sales of disposable diapers moved closely with the number of new births. However, as the number of women in the work force

Exhibit 20–1 Straight-Line Trend Projection—Extends Past Sales into the Future

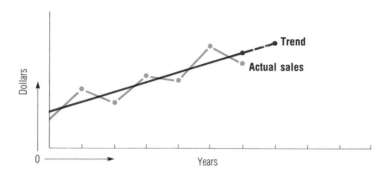

increased and as more women returned to jobs after babies were born, the use of disposable diapers increased and the trend changed. As in this example, trend extension estimates will be wrong whenever big changes occur. For this reason—although they may extend past behavior for one estimate—most managers look for another way to help them forecast sharp economic changes.

Predicting future behavior takes judgment

When we try to predict what will happen in the future—instead of just extending the past—we have to use other methods and add a bit more judgment. Some of these methods (to be discussed later) include juries of executive opinion, salespeople's estimates, surveys, panels, and market tests.

Knowing past trends helps in forecasting—but trend projecting can be dangerous.

THREE LEVELS OF FORECAST ARE USEFUL

We are interested in forecasting the potential in specific market segments. To do this, it helps to make three levels of forecasts.

Some economic conditions affect the entire economy. Others may influence only one industry. And some may affect only one company or one product's sales potential. For this reason, a common approach to forecasting is to:

1. Develop a *national income forecast* and use this to:
2. Develop an *industry sales forecast,* which then is used to:
3. Develop *specific company* and *product forecasts.*

Generally, a marketing manager doesn't have to make forecasts for the national economy or his industry. This kind of forecasting—basically trend projecting—is a specialty in itself. Such forecasts are available in business and government publications. Managers can use just one source's forecast or combine several together. Unfortunately, however, the more targeted the marketing manager's earlier segmenting efforts have been, the less likely that industry forecasts will match the firm's product-markets. So a manager has to move directly to estimating potential for his own company—and for specific products.

FORECASTING COMPANY AND PRODUCT SALES BY EXTENDING PAST BEHAVIOR

Past sales can be extended

At the very least, a marketing manager ought to know what the firm's present markets look like—and what it has sold to them in the past. A detailed sales analysis—for products and geographic areas—helps to project future results.

Just extending past sales into the future may not seem like much of a forecasting method. But it's better than just assuming that next year's total sales will be the same as this year's.

Factor method includes more than time

Simple extension of past sales gives one forecast. But it's usually desirable to tie future sales to something more than the passage of time. The factor method tries to do this.

The **factor method** tries to forecast sales by finding a relation between the company's sales and some other factor (or factors). The basic formula is: something (past sales, industry sales, etc.) *times* some factor *equals* sales forecast. A **factor** is a variable that shows the relation of some other variable to the item being forecast. For instance, in our example above, both the birth rate and the number of working mothers are factors that are related to sales of disposable diapers.

A bread producer example

The following example—about a bread producer—shows how firms can make forecasts for many geographic market segments—using the factor method and available data. This general approach can be useful for any firm—producer, wholesaler, or retailer.

Analysis of past sales relationships showed that the bread manufacturer regularly sold one half of 1 percent (0.005) of the total retail food sales in its various target markets. This is a single factor. By using this single factor, a manager could

estimate the producer's sales for the coming period by multiplying a forecast of expected retail food sales by 0.005.

Sales & Marketing Management magazine makes retail food sales estimates each year. Exhibit 20–2 shows the kind of geographically detailed data available.

Let's carry this bread example further—using the data in Exhibit 20–2 for Evanston, Illinois. Evanston's food sales were $84,575,000 for the last year. By simply accepting last year's food sales as an estimate of next year's sales—and multiplying the food sales estimate for Evanston by the 0.005 factor (the firm's usual share in such markets), the manager would have an estimate of his next year's bread sales in Evanston. That is, last year's food sales estimate ($84,575,000) times 0.005 equals this year's bread sales estimate of $422,875.

Factor method can use several factors

The factor method is not limited to using just one factor. Several factors can be used together. For example, *Sales & Marketing Management* regularly gives a "buying power index" (BPI) as a measure of the potential in different geographic areas. See Exhibit 20–2. This index considers (1) the population in a market, (2) the market's income, and (3) retail sales in that market. The BPI for Evanston, Illinois, for example, is 0.0375—that is, Evanston accounts for 0.0375 percent of the total U.S. buying power. This means that Evanston is a fairly attractive market because its BPI is much higher than would be expected based on population alone. Although Evanston accounts for 0.0291 percent of U.S. population, it has a much larger share of the buying power because its income and retail sales are above average.

Exhibit 20–2   Sample of Pages from *Sales and Marketing Management's* Survey of Buying Power

ILL. S&MM ESTIMATES	POPULATION—12/31/87									RETAIL SALES BY STORE GROUP 1987						
METRO AREA County City	Total Population (Thousands)	% Of U.S.	Median Age of Pop.	18–24 Years	25–34 Years	35–49 Years	50 & Over	House-holds (Thousands)	Total Retail Sales ($000)	Food ($000)	Eating & Drinking Places ($000)	General Mdse. ($000)	Furniture/ Furnish./ Appliance ($000)	Auto-motive ($000)	Drug ($000)
CHICAGO	6,177.3	2.5150	32.6	10.8	18.0	20.2	25.5	2,273.0	40,744,473	7,120,592	4,199,587	4,912,243	2,493,073	7,993,034	2,018,455
Cook	5,264.0	2.1432	32.8	10.9	17.6	19.7	26.5	1,945.7	33,252,656	5,997,815	3,644,658	4,024,336	2,151,580	6,251,599	1,724,715
Arlington Heights	69.6	.0283	34.6	8.8	15.9	26.1	23.3	24.1	616,856	103,026	53,255	30,338	44,138	221,404	26,639
Berwyn	45.1	.0184	43.2	8.9	14.5	17.5	42.7	19.3	242,132	29,012	31,841	21,488	15,759	55,638	20,919
● Chicago	3,021.7	1.2302	32.1	11.4	17.9	18.5	26.3	1,135.9	14,759,998	2,892,340	1,899,538	1,704,425	973,570	1,910,342	894,116
● Chicago Heights	35.4	.0144	30.4	11.6	16.2	17.7	24.8	11.8	341,504	42,794	26,762	18,177	6,814	170,828	8,427
Cicero	61.2	.0249	36.9	10.2	16.1	17.8	34.7	24.9	196,020	47,086	35,664	2,919	7,309	40,690	8,996
Des Plaines	56.5	.0230	35.7	9.9	16.3	22.6	28.4	20.5	457,412	62,569	67,646	18,319	8,847	167,106	21,135
● Evanston	71.4	.0291	33.1	15.5	20.5	18.4	27.8	27.9	564,442	84,575	47,499	26,694	43,212	204,722	18,823
Mount Prospect	54.0	.0220	34.0	10.9	16.8	24.3	24.0	19.9	575,349	109,736	34,646	114,853	35,762	59,737	24,223
Oak Lawn	57.9	.0236	38.6	10.2	12.6	20.1	34.6	20.6	686,009	111,152	45,567	65,199	34,721	262,514	30,728
Oak Park	54.4	.0221	33.3	9.5	22.4	19.2	27.0	23.2	336,263	71,107	23,736	22,242	22,149	98,381	19,263
Schaumburg	61.0	.0248	29.9	9.2	26.0	24.6	12.2	22.9	1,400,653	106,363	74,181	291,695	124,934	488,565	22,698
Skokie	59.3	.0241	41.8	8.5	13.4	20.7	38.8	22.7	764,534	70,620	55,604	133,739	68,851	178,013	27,036
DuPage	745.1	.3033	31.5	10.0	20.3	23.1	19.8	268.7	6,721,777	953,000	496,632	820,212	307,501	1,523,296	255,213
Downers Grove	44.0	.0179	33.6	8.7	19.5	23.3	23.9	17.0	479,014	93,049	25,816	186	24,323	166,613	22,879

ILL. S&MM ESTIMATES	EFFECTIVE BUYING INCOME 1987							ILL. S&MM ESTIMATES	EFFECTIVE BUYING INCOME 1987						
METRO AREA County City	Total EBI ($000)	Median Hsld. EBI	(A) $10,000–$19,999 A	(B) $20,000–$34,999 B	(C) $35,000–$49,999 C	(D) $50,000 & Over D	Buying Power Index	METRO AREA County City	Total EBI ($000)	Median Hsld. EBI	(A) $10,000–$19,999 A	(B) $20,000–$34,999 B	(C) $35,000–$49,999 C	(D) $50,000 & Over D	Buying Power Index
CHICAGO	93,727,146	31,491	16.5	23.5	19.5	25.0	2.7573	Peoria	3,002,587	31,079	16.9	25.5	19.6	23.8	.0874
Cook	76,746,999	29,583	17.7	23.6	18.6	23.0	2.2724	● Peoria	1,606,886	29,043	18.0	24.8	17.6	23.0	.0564
Arlington Heights	1,345,045	46,877	9.8	18.1	23.1	44.4	.0387	Tazewell	1,853,051	31,142	16.2	29.7	22.4	19.9	.0532
Berwyn	706,071	28,132	20.8	25.7	18.9	19.7	.0194	● Pekin	449,935	26,698	20.8	26.6	20.1	15.7	.0153
● Chicago	37,916,342	23,622	20.3	24.2	15.7	16.8	1.1246	Woodford	422,883	29,345	17.4	32.3	22.5	15.8	.0117
● Chicago Heights	424,116	28,237	18.0	24.8	19.8	19.2	.0161	SUBURBAN TOTAL	3,021,700	32,490	15.2	29.3	23.0	22.0	.0806
Cicero	839,728	25,928	22.4	26.9	18.6	16.0	.0219	ROCKFORD	3,890,816	29,642	18.0	28.9	22.2	16.9	.1197
Des Plaines	968,092	39,638	12.7	23.6	24.2	32.8	.0286	Boone	349,628	26,848	20.5	32.0	22.1	10.4	.0105
● Evanston	1,329,323	32,559	17.6	25.7	17.4	28.7	.0375	Winnebago	3,541,188	29,970	17.8	28.5	22.2	17.6	.1092
Mount Prospect	1,009,786	41,868	11.0	22.0	24.3	36.9	.0313	● Rockford	1,917,344	27,375	19.9	28.6	19.4	15.7	.0643
Oak Lawn	960,825	37,458	14.3	23.3	22.2	31.7	.0330	SUBURBAN TOTAL	1,973,472	31,859	16.2	29.1	25.1	18.1	.0554
Oak Park	969,528	31,387	18.6	26.1	18.7	25.5	.0261	SPRINGFIELD	2,497,911	24,135	23.2	28.7	18.4	12.0	.0798
Schaumburg	1,095,215	41,394	10.6	23.6	28.4	33.4	.0493	Menard	122,756	21,347	25.8	34.9	12.9	5.6	.0334
Skokie	1,212,339	42,021	13.3	20.9	20.9	38.7	.0386	Sangamon	2,375,155	24,358	23.1	28.2	18.8	12.4	.0764
Du Page	14,496,796	44,142	9.8	20.6	24.4	40.3	.4175	● Springfield	1,360,009	22,421	24.4	27.0	16.6	11.8	.0502
Downers Grove	909,636	44,892	11.6	18.6	22.7	41.9	.0271	SUBURBAN TOTAL	1,137,902	26,315	21.6	31.1	20.7	12.2	.0296

Using several factors rather than only one uses more information. And in the case of the BPI, it gives a single measure of a market's potential. Rather than falling back to using population only, or income only, or trying to develop a special index, the BPI can be used in the same way that we used the 0.005 factor in the bread example.

Manufacturers of industrial products can use several factors, too

Exhibit 20–3 shows how one manufacturer estimated the market for fiber boxes for a particular county. This approach could be used county by county to estimate the potential in many geographic target markets.

Note that the manufacturer used SIC code data. This is common in the industrial area because SIC code data is readily available and often very relevant. A trade association collected the data on the value of box shipments by SIC code. The rest of the data was available from government sources.

The basic approach is to calculate the typical consumption per employee—for each SIC industry group in the particular county—to get a market potential estimate for each group. Then, the sum of these estimates becomes the total market potential in that county. A firm thinking of going into that market would have to estimate the share it could get with its own marketing mix in order to get its sales forecast.

Note that this approach can also aid management's control job. If the firm is already in this industry, it can compare its actual sales (by SIC code) with the potential to see how it's doing. If its typical market share is 10 percent of the market—and it has only 2 to 5 percent of the market in various SIC submarkets—then it may need to change its marketing mix.

Times series and leading series may help estimate a fluctuating future

Not all past economic or sales behavior can be neatly extended with a straight line or some manipulation. Economic activity has ups and downs, and other uncontrollable factors change. To cope with such variation, statisticians have developed time series analysis techniques. **Time series** are historical records of the fluctuations in economic variables. We can't give a detailed discussion of these techniques here, but note that there *are* techniques to handle daily, weekly, monthly, seasonal, and annual variations.[2]

All forecasters dream of finding an accurate **leading series**—a time series that changes in the same direction *but ahead of* the series to be forecast. For example, car producers watch trends in the "Index of Consumer Sentiment" which is based on regular surveys of consumers' attitudes about their likely future financial security. People are less likely to buy a car or other "big ticket" item if they are worried about their future income. As this suggests, a drop in the index usually "leads" a drop in car sales. It is important that there be some logical relation between the leading series and what is being forecast.

No single series has yet been found that leads GNP—or other "national" figures. Lacking such a series, forecasters develop **indices**—statistical combinations of several time series—in an effort to find some time series that will lead the series they are trying to forecast. Some indices of this type are published by the U.S. Department of Commerce. And business magazines, like *Business Week,* publish their own time series—updating them weekly.

Exhibit 20–3   Estimated Market for Corrugated and Solid Fiber Boxes by Industry Groups, Phoenix, Arizona, Metropolitan Statistical Area

SIC major group code industry	(1) Value of box shipments by end use ($000)*	(2) Employment by industry groups†	(3) Consumption per employee by industry groups (1 ÷ 2) (dollars)	Maricopa County (4) Employment by industry groups†	(5) Estimated share of the market (3 × 4) ($000)
20 Food and kindred products	586,164	1,578,305	371	4,973	1,845
21 Tobacco	17,432	74,557	233	—	—
22 Textile mill products	91,520	874,677	104	—	—
23 Apparel	34,865	1,252,443	27	1,974	53
24 Lumber and products (except furniture)	19,611	526,622	37	690	26
25 Furniture and fixtures	89,341	364,166	245	616	151
26 Paper and allied products	211,368	587,882	359	190	68
27 Printing, publishing, and allied industries	32,686	904,208	36	2,876	104
28 Chemicals and allied products	128,564	772,169	166	488	81
29 Petroleum refining and related industries	28,328	161,367	175	—	—
30 Rubber and miscellaneous plastic products	67,551	387,997	174	190	33
31 Leather and leather products	8,716	352,919	24	—	—
32 Stone, clay, and glass products	226,621	548,058	413	1,612	666
33 Primary metal industries	19,611	1,168,110	16	2,889	46
34 Fabricated metal products	130,743	1,062,096	123	2,422	298
35 Machinery (except electrical)	58,834	1,445,558	40	5,568	223
36 Electrical machinery, equipment, and supplies	119,848	1,405,382	391	6,502	553
37 Transportation equipment	82,804	1,541,618	53	5,005	265
38 Professional, scientific instruments, etc.	13,074	341,796	38	—	—
39 Miscellaneous manufacturing industries	200,473	369,071	543	376	204
90 Government	10,895	—	—	—	—
Total	2,179,049	—	—	—	4,616

*Based on data reported in *Fibre Box Industry Statistics,* Fibre Box Association.

†U.S. Bureau of the Census, *County Business Patterns.*

PREDICTING FUTURE BEHAVIOR CALLS FOR MORE JUDGMENT AND SOME OPINIONS

These past-extending methods use quantitative data—projecting past experience into the future and assuming that the future will be like the past. But this is risky in competitive markets. Usually, it's desirable to add some judgment to other forecasts before making the final forecast yourself.

Jury of executive opinion adds judgment

One of the oldest and simplest methods of forecasting—the **jury of executive opinion**—combines the opinions of experienced executives—perhaps from marketing, production, finance, purchasing, and top management. Each executive estimates market potential and sales for the *coming years.* Then they try to work out a consensus.

The main advantage of the jury approach is that it can be done quickly and easily. On the other hand, the results may not be very good. There may be too much extending of the past. Some of the executives may have little contact with outside market influences. But their estimates could point to major shifts in customer demand or competition.

Estimates from salespeople can help, too

Using salespeople's estimates to forecast is like the jury approach. But salespeople are more likely than home office managers to be familiar with customer reactions—and what competitors are doing. Their estimates are especially useful in some industrial markets where the few customers may be well known to the salespeople. But this approach may be useful in any type of market. Good retail clerks have a "feel" for their markets—their opinions shouldn't be ignored.

However, managers who use estimates from salespeople should be aware of the limitations. For example, new salespeople may not know much about their mar-

When PepsiCo introduced Slice, forecasts based on surveys and market tests were shared with middlemen—to help them do better planning.

Please use this calendar to write in your schedule of Slice Programs

	1st Mo.	2nd Mo.	3rd Mo.	4th Mo.	5th Mo.	6th Mo.	7th Mo.
TV Radio Outdoor							
Wet Sampling Intercept Couponing							
Trial Bins and Motion Displays							
1000 Line BFD ROP Ads with Coupons and/or Mail-in Offer							
Continuity Programs							
Holiday Programs							

kets. Even experienced salespeople may not be aware of possible changes in the national economic climate or the firm's other uncontrollable environments. And if salespeople think that the manager is going to use the estimates to set sales quotas, the estimates may be low!

Surveys, panels, and market tests

Special surveys of final buyers, retailers, and/or wholesalers can show what's happening in different market segments. Some firms use panels of stores—or final consumers—to keep track of buying behavior and to decide when just extending past behavior isn't enough.

Surveys are sometimes combined with market tests when the company wants to estimate customers' reactions to possible changes in its marketing mix. A market test might show that a product increased its share of the market by 10 percent when its price was dropped one cent below competition. But this extra business might be quickly lost if the price were increased one cent above competition. Such market experiments help the marketing manager make good estimates of future sales when one or more of the four Ps is changed.

ACCURACY OF FORECASTS

The accuracy of forecasts varies a lot. The more general the number being forecast, the more accurate the forecast is likely to be. This is because small errors in various parts of the estimate tend to offset each other—and make the whole estimate more accurate. Annual forecasts of national totals—such as GNP—may be accurate within 5 percent. When style and innovation are important in an industry, forecast errors of 10 to 20 percent for *established products* are common. The accuracy of specific *new-product* forecasts is even lower.[3]

Accuracy depends on the marketing mix

Forecasting can help a marketing manager estimate the size of possible market opportunities. But the accuracy of any sales forecast depends on whether the firm selects and implements a marketing mix that turns these opportunities into sales and profits.

BLENDING THE FOUR Ps TAKES UNDERSTANDING OF A TARGET MARKET

Developing a good marketing mix requires blending many of the ideas discussed in this text. Exhibit 20–4 reviews the marketing strategy decision areas we've been talking about. Now we must integrate them into logical marketing mixes, marketing strategies, marketing plans—and a marketing program.

If we fully understand the needs and attitudes of a target market, then combining the four Ps should be "easy." There are three gaps in this line of reasoning, however. (1) We don't always know as much as we would like to about the needs and attitudes of our target markets. (2) Competitors are also trying to satisfy these or similar needs—and their efforts may force shifts of a firm's marketing mix. (3) The other uncontrollable variables may be changing—which may require more changes in marketing mixes.

Exhibit 20–4   Strategy Decision Areas Organized by the Four Ps

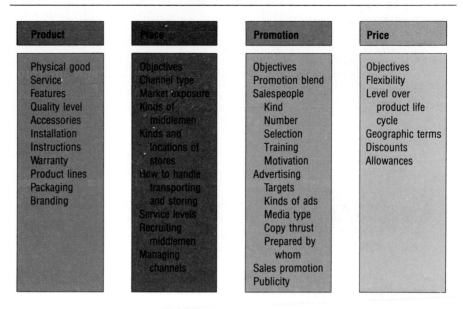

Product	Place	Promotion	Price
Physical good	Objectives	Objectives	Objectives
Service	Channel type	Promotion blend	Flexibility
Features	Market exposure	Salespeople	Level over
Quality level	Kinds of	Kind	product life
Accessories	middlemen	Number	cycle
Installation	Kinds and	Selection	Geographic terms
Instructions	locations of	Training	Discounts
Warranty	stores	Motivation	Allowances
Product lines	How to handle	Advertising	
Packaging	transporting	Targets	
Branding	and storing	Kinds of ads	
	Service levels	Media type	
	Recruiting	Copy thrust	
	middlemen	Prepared by	
	Managing	whom	
	channels	Sales promotion	
		Publicity	

Understanding leads to profitable mixes—maybe

An understanding of the needs and attitudes of the firm's target market can help a manager develop a more effective marketing mix—even in the face of competition.

Zenith Data Systems was one of the early firms to recognize the personal computer needs of business users. Zenith developed powerful personal computers to serve them. It sold the computers through established dealers already selling other office products to business firms. These middlemen delivered—and installed—complete computer systems for their business customers—and also provided support and training. Zenith also used personal selling and sales promotion to increase interest—and awareness—among business customers. The strategy worked very well.

But competitors—including IBM—soon targeted the profitable business market. And Zenith began to lose market share. Zenith marketing managers knew their firm lacked the financial resources and brand familiarity to compete head-to-head with IBM. So they looked for other markets—with unmet needs.

Zenith discovered that government computer users were very concerned about security. Most personal computers—including the popular IBM models—gave off radio waves that made it possible for an outsider to "hear" information entered on the computer. Zenith developed special computers to block these "eavesdroppers" —and targeted a marketing mix to military buyers. Personal selling informed everyone who might influence the purchase decision about the special features of the Zenith machines. Zenith offered quantity discounts. But, when Zenith won large contracts with the Air Force and other military agencies, the discounted prices still resulted in large total profits.

Zenith also realized that many businesspeople were not satisfied with the portable computers that could be used away from the office. So Zenith developed a line of powerful, lightweight laptop computers—including one that is about the size of a notebook. This strategy required more mass selling and closer work with middle-

Targeting specific markets has been successful for Zenith Data Systems.

men. However, because Zenith targeted its marketing mix on the needs of a specific target market, its strategy was very successful.[4]

Superior mixes may be breakthrough opportunities

When marketing managers fully understand their target markets, they may be able to develop marketing mixes that are superior to "competitive mixes." Such understanding may provide breakthrough opportunities—until competitors reach the same understanding of the market and decide to meet them "head-on." Taking advantage of these kinds of opportunities can lead to large sales—and profitable growth. This is why we stress the importance of looking for breakthrough opportunities rather than just trying to patch up or improve present mixes.

Inferior mixes are easy to reject

Just as some mixes are superior, some mixes are inferior—or unsuitable. For example, a national TV advertising campaign might make sense for a large company—but it might be completely out of the question for a small manufacturer offering a new product on the East Coast.

In-between mixes are harder to develop

Where competitors are hitting each other "head-on," it's even more important to understand the target market—and how it is likely to respond to alternative marketing mixes. Here, we have more need for estimating response functions.

RESPONSE FUNCTIONS MAY HELP PLAN BETTER STRATEGIES

A **response function** shows (mathematically and/or graphically) how the firm's target market is expected to react to changes in marketing variables. So, trying to estimate relevant response functions can be a real help in developing better marketing mixes.

Response functions are usually plotted as curves showing how sales and profit will vary at different levels of marketing expenditures. But other relationships may be helpful, too. Possibilities include how sales and profits will vary if a company (1) changes prices or (2) uses different promotion blends.

To increase your understanding of response functions, we'll first focus on response functions for each of the four Ps. See Exhibit 20–5, where possible response functions are graphed for each of the four Ps. We'll discuss the response function for the whole marketing mix a little later.

These are just examples of the general shape of curves you *might* find. A particular company aiming at a particular target market—and facing a particular group of competitors—might have very different response functions.

The shape of such response functions is critical to the selection of the "best" blend for each particular P—and for a whole marketing mix. Yet we don't know much about the precise shapes of the functions. Worse, there is no published source of response functions for different situations. The manager usually has to develop his own response functions—using past experience and judgment, perhaps aided by marketing research. Difficult as such estimating may be, it's still necessary in any careful evaluation of alternatives. Response functions do not "go away" if they are ignored—and decisions made without them may be just crude guesses.

Product quality response function

A response function for product quality may show that adding more quality (and features) will increase sales (perhaps even continuously up to a point). But adding

Exhibit 20–5   Four "Illustrative Only" Response Functions

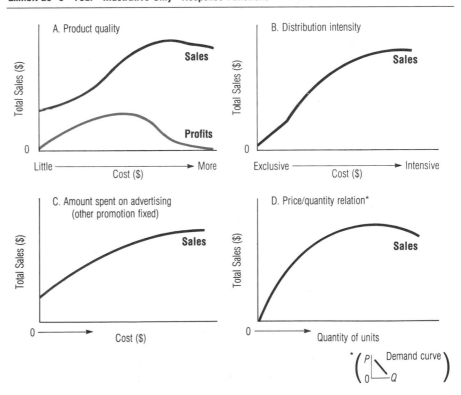

more quality may also increase costs and, at some point, customers may not be willing to pay more for more quality. This results in a profit response function that reaches a high point and then declines. This "maximum point" is the "best" level for product quality—depending on the firm's objectives, of course! See Exhibit 20–5A.

Place-distribution intensity response function

A Place-related response function that focuses on the degree of market exposure desired (ranging from exclusive to intensive) may look like the response function in Exhibit 20–5B. Sales level off near the extreme of intensive distribution because, when most outlets already carry the product, little increase in sales can be expected from the last few, perhaps marginal, outlets.

Promotion—advertising response function

Exhibit 20–5C shows a possible response function for advertising. This figure suggests that even with no advertising, personal selling (and other promotion efforts) will get some sales. But sales will be higher with some advertising. On the extreme right of the response function, the curve starts to level off—showing declining results from extra advertising. (Although picking the best level is beyond the scope of this text, it's important to note that the best point may not be at the highest sales level. Marginal analysis can be used here to show that, as the response function begins to flatten out, the marginal return of sales to advertising dollar begins to decline.)

Price-demand curve response function

The Price-oriented response function shown in Exhibit 20–5D shows the impact of price level variations on sales and quantity sold. This figure is simply another way of showing the down-sloping demand curve we discussed earlier. Note that a down-sloping demand curve means that total sales will start declining at some quantity. Recall that marginal revenue can go negative—which means that total revenue is declining. You can't increase total dollar sales indefinitely with price cuts!

A manager must estimate his own response functions

Estimating response functions isn't easy. They are probably changing all the time. Further, there are different response functions for each target market. Nevertheless, each marketing manager should make some estimate about how customers are likely to respond to the various ingredients he controls. This is where past experience is useful—and so is careful analysis of how the same or similar customers are responding to competitors' mixes. Suppose a competitor tries a 10 percent price cut to encourage retailers to sell more by cutting their own prices. If retailers simply absorb the extra margin, then the response function for this kind of price cutting is not attractive. But another competitor may have increased the number of calls made on each retailer—with great results. Some marketing research might help a manager decide whether he also has such a response function—and whether increasing sales effort would be equally successful for his firm.

Estimating general marketing effort response functions

Besides trying to estimate response functions for each of the four Ps, managers should estimate the general response function for all the marketing effort in one marketing mix. Then they can compare different response functions for alternative mixes when seeking the "best" mix for any particular target market. Such a response function is presented in Exhibit 20–6—showing the relation between marketing effort (in dollars) and sales (or profits) for one marketing mix.

Exhibit 20–6 A Marketing Effort Response Function for One Marketing Mix

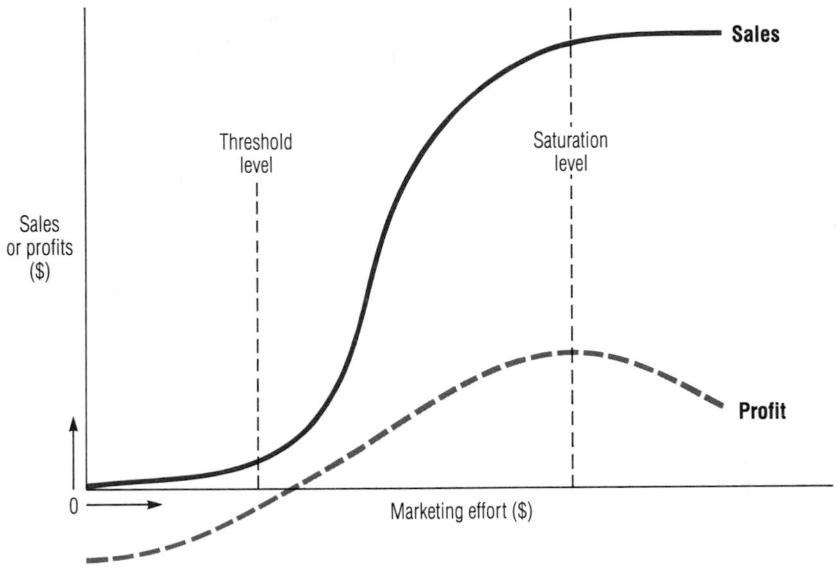

Threshold effort is needed to get any sales

The shape of this response function is typical of the alternatives marketing managers face. It shows that a higher level of marketing expenditures *may* yield a higher level of sales (or profits). But just spending more and more money for marketing won't guarantee better profits. Further, there is no straight-line relationship between marketing expenditures and sales (or profits). Instead, some expenditure may be necessary to get *any sales at all.* This is called the **threshold expenditure level**—the minimum expenditure level needed just to be in a market. After this level, small increases in expenditures may result in large increases in sales for a while (as the curve rises rapidly). But ultimately sales flatten out at the **saturation level**—the level where additional expenditures may lead to little or no increase in sales and a decline in profits.

The response function for a whole marketing mix is the result of the interaction of all the mix ingredients. There are techniques for estimating these functions—if we know the shape of all the mix ingredient functions. But this topic is beyond our scope.[5]

For our purposes, we'll have to be satisfied to know that it's possible to roughly estimate response functions for alternative mixes and that, therefore, it's possible to select the best one—given the firm's resources and objectives. Exhibit 20–7 shows three estimated response functions for three different mixes. If the marketing manager's budget were fixed at the level shown in Exhibit 20–7—and he wanted to maximize sales in the short run—then Mix A is clearly best.

ANALYSIS OF COSTS AND SALES CAN GUIDE PLANNING

If a manager doesn't want to estimate whole functions, he should estimate the sales and costs of "reasonable" alternative marketing mixes and compare them for

The threshold expenditure level for soft drinks is very high—so it is costly for new brands to enter the market.

profitability. Exhibit 20–8 shows such a comparison for a small appliance currently selling for $15—Mix A in the example. Here, the marketing manager simply estimated the costs and likely results of four "reasonable"" alternatives. And, assuming profit is the objective *and* there are adequate resources to consider each of the alternatives, marketing Mix C is obviously the best alternative.

Spreadsheet analysis speeds through calculations

Comparing the alternatives in Exhibit 20–8 is quite simple. But sometimes much more detail is needed to evaluate a plan. Hundreds of calculations may be required to see how specific marketing resources relate to expected outcomes—like total costs, expected sales, and profit. To make that part of the planning job simpler and faster, marketing managers often use spreadsheet analysis. With **spreadsheet analysis**, costs, sales, and other information related to a problem

Exhibit 20–7 Response Functions for Three Different Marketing Mixes for Next Year

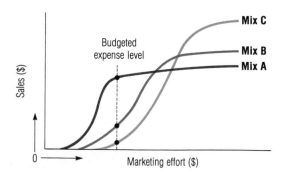

Exhibit 20–8   Comparing the Estimated Sales, Costs, and Profits of Four "Reasonable" Alternative Marketing Mixes*

Marketing mix	Price	Selling cost	Advertising cost	Total units	Sales	Total cost	Total profit
A	$15	$20,000	$ 5,000	5,000	$ 75,000	$ 70,000	$ 5,000
B	15	20,000	20,000	7,000	105,000	95,000	10,000
C	20	30,000	30,000	7,000	140,000	115,000	25,000
D	25	40,000	40,000	5,000	125,000	125,000	0

*For the same target market, assuming product costs per unit are $5 and fixed (overhead) costs are $20,000.

are organized into a data table—a spreadsheet—to show how changing the value of one or more of the numbers affects the other numbers. This is possible because the relationships among the variables are programmed in the computer software. Lotus 1-2-3, Excel, VisiCalc and Appleworks are examples of well-known spreadsheet programs.

A spreadsheet helps answer "What if" questions

Spreadsheet analysis also allows the marketing manager to evaluate "what if" type questions. For example, a marketing manager might be interested in the question "What if I charge a higher price and the number of units sold stays the same? What will happen to profit?" To look at how a spreadsheet program might be used to help answer this "what if" question, let's take a closer look at Exhibit 20–8.

The data in this table might be set up as a computer spreadsheet. The table involves a number of relationships. For example, price times total units is equal to sales; and total cost is equal to selling cost plus advertising cost plus overhead cost plus total product costs (7,000 units times $5 per unit). If these relationships have been programmed in the spreadsheet, a marketing manager can ask ques-

Many marketing managers use spreadsheet analysis to evaluate alternative marketing plans.

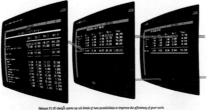

Exhibit 20–9   A Spreadsheet Analysis Showing How a Change in Price Affects Sales and Profit (based on Marketing Mix C from Exhibit 20–8).

Price	Selling cost	Advertising cost	Total units	Sales	Total cost	Total profit
$19.80	$30,000	$30,000	7,000	$138,600	$115,000	$23,600
19.90	30,000	30,000	7,000	139,300	115,000	24,300
20.00	30,000	30,000	7,000	140,000	115,000	25,000
20.10	30,000	30,000	7,000	140,700	115,000	25,700
20.20	30,000	30,000	7,000	141,400	115,000	26,400

tions like: "What if I raise the price to $20.20 and still sell 7,000 units? What will happen to profit?" To get the answer, all he needs to do is type the new price in the spreadsheet and the program will compute the new profit—$26,400.

In addition, he may also want to do many "what if" analyses—for example, to see how sales and profit change over a range of prices. Computerized spreadsheet analysis does this quickly and easily. For example, if the manager wants to see what happens to total revenue as the price varies between some minimum value (say, $19.80) and a maximum value (say, $20.20), the program can show the total revenue and profit for a number of price levels in the range from $19.80 to $20.20. See Exhibit 20–9.

In a problem like this, the marketing manager might be able to do the same calculations quickly by hand. But, with more complicated problems the spreadsheet program can be a big help—making it very convenient to more carefully analyze different alternatives or different possible response functions.[6]

FACTORS THAT AFFECT MARKETING MIX PLANNING

In this section, we will briefly review some of the factors that affect marketing mix planning. During this discussion, try to develop a feel for which mix ingredients seem "most important." These will probably be the ones with the most steeply rising response functions over reasonable cost levels. For example, if personal selling is very important in a particular mix, this probably means that the personal selling response function is more attractive than the other marketing mix ingredients. Even so, a marketing manager should evaluate how good personal selling is (over a range of expenditures) before naively spending all his promotion money on personal selling—or (maybe worse) all his marketing money on this one ingredient.

Typical mixes are a good starting point for marketing mix planning

Typical mixes are a good starting point for developing possible marketing mixes—and for estimating their profitability. What others have done in similar situations must have satisfied someone—and that can serve as a guide. And, if actual sales and cost data are available—or can be estimated—then you can estimate at least a few points on response functions. Beyond this, you need judgment or some marketing research. In this way, you can make use of past experience—while not relying on it blindly.

"Typical" marketing mixes related to product classes

Ideally, the ingredients of a good marketing mix flow logically from all the relevant dimensions of a target market. Exhibit 20–10 shows the kinds of market dimensions you might like to know—and their effect on the strategy decision

Special characteristics of the product or target market must be considered in planning and implementing the marketing mix.

areas. Usually, however, you don't or can't know all that you would like to about a potential target market. But you may know enough to decide whether the product is a consumer product or an industrial product—and which product class is most relevant.

A first step, then, is to decide the proper product class because that suggests how a "typical" product would be distributed and promoted. So, if you don't know as much as you would like about the potential customers' needs and attitudes, at

Exhibit 20–10   Relation of Potential Target Market Dimensions (including ones that are related to product classes) to Marketing Mix Decisions Areas

Potential target market dimensions	Effects on decision areas
1. Geographic location and other demographic characteristics of potential customers	Affects size of *Target Markets* (economic potential) and *Place* (where products should be made available) and *Promotion* (where and to whom to advertise)
2. Behavioral needs, attitudes, and how present and potential products or services fit into customers' consumption patterns	Affects *Product* (design, packaging, length or width of product line) and *Promotion* (what potential customers need and want to know about the product offering, and what appeals should be used)
3. Urgency to get need satisfied and desire and willingness to compare and shop	Affects *Place* (how directly products are distributed from producer to consumer, how extensively they are made available, and the level of service needed) and *Price* (how much potential customers are willing to pay)

Quick Metal Strategy Planning Fastens on Customer Needs—and Profits

Loctite Corporation, a producer of industrial supplies, used careful strategy planning to launch Quick Metal—a putty-like adhesive for repairing worn machine parts. Loctite chemists had developed similar products in the past. But managers had paid little attention to developing a *complete marketing strategy*—and sales had been poor.

Before creating Quick Metal, Loctite identified some attractive target customers. Research showed that production people were eager to try any product that helped get broken machines back into production. Quick Metal was developed to meet the needs of this target market. Ads appealed to such needs with copy promising that Quick Metal "keeps machinery running until the new parts arrive." Channel members also received attention. During the introduction stage, sales reps made frequent phone calls and sales visits to the nearly 700 wholesalers who handle Loctite products. Loctite awarded cash prices to those selling the most Quick Metal.

A tube of Quick Metal was priced at $17.75—about twice the price (and profit margin) of competing products. But Loctite's customers weren't concerned about price. They responded to a quality product that could keep their production lines operating.

Based on past experience, some estimated that a "typical" product for this market might reach sales of $300,000 a year. But Loctite didn't rely on a "typical" strategy. Instead the company offered a carefully targeted marketing mix to meet the needs of a *specific* target market. It sold 100,000 tubes the first week—and within seven months sales were over $2.2 million. Loctite's careful planning paid off in an immediate market success—and high profits.[7]

least knowing how they would classify the company's product can give you a head start on developing a marketing mix. Further, it's reassuring to see that product classes do summarize some of what you would like to know about target markets—as seen in Exhibit 20–10.

"Typical" is not necessarily "right"

The typical marketing mix for a given product class is not necessarily right for all situations. Some very profitable marketing mixes depart from the typical—to satisfy some target markets better.

A marketing manager may have to develop a mix that is *not* typical because of various market realities—including special characteristics of the product or target market, the competitive environment, and his own firm's capabilities and limitations. It is useful to see how some of these market realities may affect marketing mix decisions.

Not all targets look the same

Size and geographic concentration affect sales contacts needed

If the sales potential of the target market is large enough, it may be possible to go directly to retailers, consumers, or users. This is especially true if the target customers are highly concentrated—like the customers for many industrial products. Examples are auto manufacturers in Michigan and electronic manufacturers around Boston, New York, Minneapolis, Los Angeles, and the "Silicon Valley" near San Francisco. For final consumer products, however, customers are usually numerous and widely scattered—and they buy in small quantities. Although the total market may be relatively large, it's often split up into small geographic segments—with too little demand in each market to support a direct approach.

Value of item and frequency and regularity of purchase

Even low-priced items such as newspapers may be handled directly if they are purchased often and the total volume is large. But for products purchased infrequently—even though purchases are large—specialists such as commission merchants, agents, brokers, and other middlemen are useful. A critical factor is the cost—in relation to actual sales—of regularly providing the needed marketing functions.

Customer preferences for personal contact

Customer preferences vary even within the same product class. Some target customers—especially some industrial customers—don't like to buy from middlemen. Even though they may want only small quantities, they prefer to buy directly from manufacturers. The manufacturers may tolerate this occurrence because these customers sometimes buy larger quantities.

Other buyers, however, prefer the convenience of buying through a middleman—because they can telephone orders and get immediate action from a local source. Two very different marketing mixes may be needed to fully satisfy both types of customers.

Not all products are the same

Some products—because of their technical nature, perishability, or bulkiness—require *more direct* distribution than their product class implies.

Technical products

Complicated products—such as conveyor systems and electronic data processing equipment—call for much technical selling, expert installation, and servicing. Wholesalers often are not interested in or able to provide all these required services.

Perishability

Perishable items—cut flowers, milk, and fresh seafood—may have to be handled directly. If many small producers are clustered together, specialists may develop to handle transportation, refrigeration, and storage. Complicated terminal markets—such as those that handle fresh produce—may develop, along with many specialized commission merchants, brokers, merchant wholesalers, and truck wholesalers.

High-fashion items also are "perishable"—and they call for more direct distribution to speed the flow to retailers. Sometimes retailers and final consumers even go directly to the producers—to see the latest fashion showings in New York or Paris.

Services are also "perishable." If a service isn't sold, the opportunity may be lost. The service can't be produced and then stored to sell later. Services usually require direct distribution.

Bulkiness

Transporting, handling, and storing costs rise when bulky products are moved—making it hard for middlemen to operate. If a producer can't make enough sales contacts when selling bulky items direct, he may use brokers, manufacturers' agents, and especially drop-shippers. They make the sales contacts—and the producer ships the product directly to the customer.

Not all channel structures are the same

The marketing manager's "ideal" channel system may not be available or even possible—as we'll see next.

Availability of suitable and cooperative middlemen

The kinds of middlemen the marketing manager would like to use may not even be available—or willing to cooperate. This is more likely if the company enters a market late and competitors already have tied up the best middlemen—perhaps as part of a selective or exclusive distribution policy. Aggressive market-oriented middlemen usually aren't just waiting for someone to use them. They may be receptive to good proposals—but just another "me-too" mix won't interest them.

The customers already being reached by each middleman are very important. If these customers aren't part of the marketing manager's target markets, then that middleman doesn't have much to offer. A wholesaler specializing in groceries has a valuable customer list for the food business—but it isn't of much value in distributing electronic office equipment.

Uniformity of market coverage

The middlemen available in large urban areas may be very effective there—but they may not cover outlying areas. A producer may need two channels to reach both areas. But this may also lead to a dual distribution problem. Middlemen who are suitable for outlying areas may also cover urban areas—but not as well. Everyone likes to work where sales are plentiful and easy to make.

Even distribution through national or international companies doesn't guarantee uniform coverage. For example, A&P has a much larger share of the retail grocery market in the East than in the Midwest. And Sears is relatively stronger in the Midwest and West than in other regions. This simply means that, in practice, every channel must be custom-made for every target market.

Financing required in channel system

Adequate credit may be critical to smooth the flow through a channel system. Some middlemen enter a channel mainly because they can give financial help to the members. This is the role of factors. But some merchant wholesalers also hold a secure position in a channel because of their strong financial position—and their willingness to meet the financial needs of other channel members. This is especially true in international markets.

Nature of the company itself—is it big, rich, and unprejudiced?

In deciding what kind of mix to offer and how to work within a channel system, each marketing manager—at every level in the system—must evaluate his company's capabilities, needs, and potential contributions to the channel. It may be best to join a strong system—rather than try to be the channel captain.

Size of company and width of product line

A company's size affects its place in a channel system because size affects discrepancies of quantity and assortment. A large producer already making a wide line of food or soap products, for example, may be in a good position to take on an

additional product of the same type and handle it the same way—perhaps directly. In contrast, a smaller producer—or one with unrelated lines—may suffer from a discrepancy of quantity or discrepancy of assortment—or both—and would probably find middlemen more practical.

Financial strength

A company's financial strength is relevant if its customers need financial help. Firms unable to provide this financing may need specialized middlemen. Selling agents, factors, merchant wholesalers, or large retailers may be able to finance a producer or channel members—including users or final consumers. In fact, a channel captain's strength may depend heavily on financing ability.

PLANNING MUST USE THE PRODUCT LIFE CYCLE

So far we've emphasized developing the "best" marketing strategy for some target market. This can be risky, however, if you forget that markets are continually changing. This means that you must plan strategies that can adjust to changing conditions. The product life cycle can be a big help here because marketing variables, typically, should change throughout a product's life cycle.[8]

Exhibit 20–11 shows some changes in marketing variables that might be needed over the course of a product life cycle. This exhibit is a good review. Notice that as the product life cycle moves on, the marketing manager should expect to find more products entering "his" market—and pushing the market closer to pure competition or oligopoly. This means that as the cycle moves along, he may want to shift from a selective to an intensive distribution policy *and* move from a skimming to a penetration pricing policy. The original marketing plan may even include these likely adjustments and their probable timing.

It isn't necessary to make a plan for the full length of a product life cycle. A firm can drop out of a market. But you must be aware that the cycle will move on—and you should make your own plan accordingly.

COMPANIES PLAN AND IMPLEMENT MARKETING PROGRAMS

Several plans make a program

Most companies implement more than one marketing plan at the same time. A *marketing program* blends all of a firm's marketing plans into one "big" plan.

When the various plans in the company's program are different, managers may be less concerned with how well the plans fit together—except as they compete for the firm's usually limited financial resources.

When the plans are more similar, however, the same sales force may be expected to carry out several plans. Or the firm's advertising department may develop the publicity and advertising for several plans. In these cases, product managers try to get enough of the common resources, say, salespeople's time, for their own plans.

A company's resources are usually limited—so the marketing manager must make hard choices. You can't launch plans to pursue every promising opportunity. Instead, limited resources force you to choose among alternative plans—while you develop the program.

Exhibit 20–11   Typical Changes in Marketing Variables over the Product Life Cycle

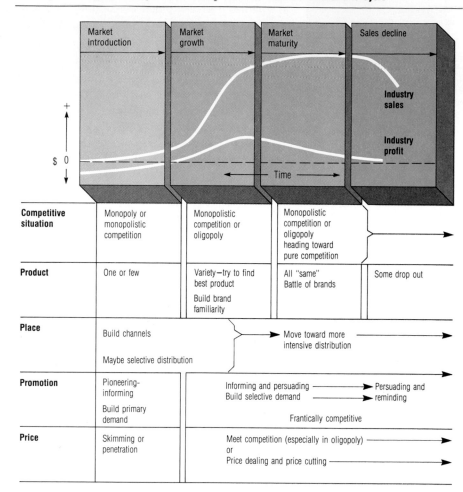

	Market introduction	Market growth	Market maturity	Sales decline
Competitive situation	Monopoly or monopolistic competition	Monopolistic competition or oligopoly	Monopolistic competition or oligopoly heading toward pure competition	→
Product	One or few	Variety—try to find best product Build brand familiarity	All "same" Battle of brands	Some drop out
Place	Build channels Maybe selective distribution		→ Move toward more intensive distribution	
Promotion	Pioneering-informing Build primary demand		Informing and persuading → Persuading and Build selective demand → reminding Frantically competitive	
Price	Skimming or penetration		Meet competition (especially in oligopoly) → or Price dealing and price cutting →	

Find the best program by trial and error

How do you find the "best" program? There is no one best way to compare various plans. Firms have to rely on management judgment and the evaluation tools discussed in Chapter 4. Some calculations are helpful, too. If a five-year planning horizon seems realistic for the firm's markets, then managers can compare expected profits over the five-year period for each plan.

Assuming the company has a profit-oriented objective, managers can evaluate the more profitable plans first—in terms of both potential profit and resources required. Also, they need to evaluate a plan's impact on the entire program. One profitable-looking alternative might be a poor first choice because it will eat up all the company's resources—and sidetrack several plans that together will be more profitable and will spread the risks.

Some juggling among the various plans—comparing profitability versus resources needed and available—moves the company toward the most profitable program. See Exhibit 20–12.

A computer program can help if managers have to evaluate a large number of alternatives. But the computer merely does the same function—trying to match potential revenues and profits against available resources.[9]

Big problems can develop if managers do not create good plans and implement them carefully.

ALLOCATING BUDGETS FOR A MARKETING PROGRAM

Once a company sets its overall marketing program and long-term plans, it also has to work out its shorter-term plans. Typically, companies use annual budgets—both to plan what they are going to do and to control various functions. Each department may be allowed to spend its budgeted amount—perhaps monthly. As long as departments stay within their budgets, they are allowed considerable (or complete) freedom.

Exhibit 20–12   A Marketing Manager May Evaluate Many Marketing Plans—Using ''Trial and Error'' to Find the Best Use of Available Resources—before Selecting the Plans to Be Implemented as ''The Marketing Program''

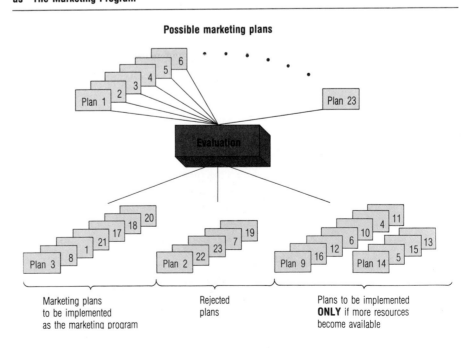

Budgeting for marketing—50 percent, 30 percent, or 10 percent is better than nothing

The most common method of budgeting for marketing expenditures is to compute a percentage of sales—either past or forecast sales. The virtue of this method is its simplicity. A similar percentage can be used automatically each year—eliminating the need to keep evaluating the kind and amount of marketing effort needed and its probable cost. It allows executives who aren't too tuned into the marketing concept to "write off" a certain percentage or number of dollars—while controlling the amount spent. When a company's top managers have this attitude, they often get what they deserve—something less than the best results.

Find the task, budget for it

Mechanically budgeting a certain percentage of past or forecast sales leads to expanding marketing expenditures when business is good and sales are rising, and cutting back when business is poor. It may be desirable to increase marketing expenditures when business is good. But when business is poor, the most sensible approach may be to be *more*, not less, aggressive!

Other methods of budgeting for marketing expenditures are:

1. Match expenditures with competitors.
2. Set the budget as a certain number of cents or dollars per sales unit (by case, by thousand, or by ton), using the past year or estimated year ahead as a base.
3. Set aside all uncommitted revenue—perhaps including budgeted profits. Companies willing to sacrifice some or all their current profits for future sales may use this approach—that is, they *invest* in marketing.
4. Base the budget on the job to be done—perhaps the number of new customers desired or the number required to reach some sales objective. This is called the **task method**—basing the budget on the job to be done.

Task method can lead to budgeting without agony

In the light of our continuing discussion about planning marketing strategies to reach objectives, the most sensible approach to budgeting marketing (and other functional) expenditures is the task method.

The amount budgeted using the task method can be stated as a percentage of sales. But calculating the right amount is much more involved than picking up a past percentage. It requires careful review of the firm's strategic (and marketing) plans and the specific tasks to be accomplished this year as part of each of these plans. The costs of these tasks are then totaled to determine how much should be budgeted for marketing and the other business functions provided for in the plans. In other words, the firm can assemble its budgets directly from detailed strategic plans—rather than from historical patterns or ratios.

After the marketing department receives its budget for the coming year, it can, presumably, spend its money any way it sees fit. But if the firm follows the previous planning-budgeting procedure, it makes sense to continue allocating expenditures within the marketing function according to the plans in the program.

Again, everyone in the marketing department—and in the business—should view the company as a total system and plan accordingly. This eliminates some of the traditional planning-budgeting "fights"—which are often so agonizing because managers and departments are pitted against each other.[10]

PROGRAM IMPLEMENTATION MUST BE PLANNED

Up to now, we've mainly been concerned with planning strategies—that is, the "big picture." Plans and a program bring this down to earth by adding the time-

Inexpensive computer programs for personal computers make it easier for marketing managers to plan and implement marketing programs.

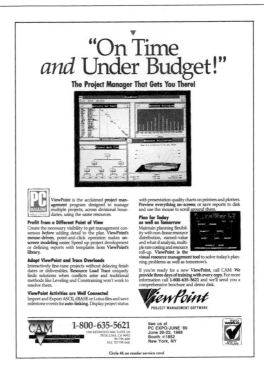

related details. Now we want to go a step further—illustrating graphic techniques that help marketing managers carry out their plans and program. First, we'll discuss techniques that are helpful for introducing new products or controlling special projects. Then we'll consider aids for an ongoing program.

New products or projects can use PERT flowcharts

Some marketing managers draw flowcharts or diagrams of all the tasks that must be accomplished on schedule. In recent years, many firms have successfully applied such flowcharting techniques as CPM (critical path method) or PERT (program evaluation and review technique). These methods were originally developed as part of the U.S. space program (NASA) to ensure that the various contractors and subcontractors stayed on schedule—and reached their goals as planned. PERT and CPM are now even more popular since inexpensive programs for personal computers make them easier and faster to use. Updating is easier, too.

The computer programs develop detailed flowcharts to show which marketing activities must be done in sequence and which can be done concurrently. These charts also show the time needed for various activities. Totaling the time allotments along the various chart paths shows the most critical (the longest) path—as well as the best starting and ending dates for the various activities.

Flowcharting is not really complicated. Basically, it requires that all the activities—which have to be performed anyway—be identified ahead of time and their probable duration and sequence shown on one diagram. (It uses nothing more than addition and subtraction.) Working with such information should be part of the planning function anyway. Then the chart can be used to guide implementation and control.

Regular plans call for monthly charts

Some marketing managers find that flowcharts are helpful for keeping track of all the tasks in their ongoing plans. Each week or month in an ongoing 12-month

plan, for example, can be graphed horizontally. Then managers can see how long each activity should take—and when it should be started and completed. If it is impossible to accomplish some of the jobs in the time allotted, the flowcharting process will make this clear—and managers will be able to make adjustments. Adjustments might be necessary, for example, when several product managers have planned more work than the salespeople can do during one month.

Basically, this kind of flowcharting is like the scheduling done by production planners—where wall-size graphic aids are used. Without such aids, it's easy to neglect some tasks—or just naively assume that enough time will be available to do all the necessary jobs. By planning ahead—aided by a visual approach—it's easier to avoid conflicts that can wreck implementation of the company's plans and program.[11]

CONCLUSION

In this chapter, we stressed the importance of developing whole marketing mixes—not just developing policies for the individual four Ps and hoping they will fit together into some logical whole. The marketing manager is responsible for developing a workable blend—integrating all of a firm's efforts into a coordinated whole that makes effective use of the firm's resources and guides it toward its objectives.

This usually requires that the manager use some approach to forecasting. We talked about two basic approaches to forecasting market potential and sales: (1) extending past behavior and (2) predicting future behavior. The most common approach is to extend past behavior into the future. This gives reasonably good results if market conditions are fairly stable. Methods here include extension of past sales data and the factor method. We saw that projecting the past into the future is risky when big market changes are likely. To make up for this possible weakness, marketers predict future behavior using their own experience and judgment. They also bring in the judgment of others—using the jury of executive opinion method and salespeople's estimates. And they may use surveys, panels, and market tests.

We saw that the accuracy of forecasts depends on how general a forecast is being made. The most error occurs with specific forecasts for products—especially new products.

Even though forecasts are subject to error, they are still necessary to help the firm choose among possible marketing plans. Sloppy forecasting can lead to poor strategies. No forecasting at all is stupid!

Of course, any sales forecast depends on the marketing mix that the firm actually selects. Developing the most effective marketing mix often requires thinking about response functions—how the four Ps affect sales and profit. Ultimately, however, managers must compare the market's responsiveness to possible marketing mixes. Ideally, they know the exact shape of the alternative response functions, but, in practice, they have to rely on past experience (to some extent), marketing research if they have the time, plus a lot of judgment. They also can study typical marketing mixes—and their apparent effectiveness in the marketplace—for clues about what works and how well.

As a starting place for developing new marketing mixes, a marketing manager can use the product classes that have served as a thread through this text. Even though he may not be able to fully describe the needs and attitudes of his target markets, he may be able to select the appropriate product class for a particular product. This, in turn, will help set Place and Promotion policies.

Throughout the text, we've emphasized the importance of marketing strategy planning. In this chapter, we went on to show that the marketing manager must develop a marketing plan for carrying out each strategy and then merge a set of plans into a marketing program. If this planning is effective, then budgeting should be relatively simple.

Finally, it's the marketing manager's job to coordinate implementation of the whole marketing program. We discussed two types of flowcharting techniques. Both may help in the difficult job of coordinating the firm's activities—to better satisfy its target customers.

Questions and Problems _____

1. Explain the difference between a forecast of market potential and a sales forecast.

2. Suggest a plausible explanation for sales fluctuations for (*a*) bicycles, (*b*) ice cream, (*c*) lawnmowers, (*d*) tennis rackets, (*e*) oats, (*f*) disposable diapers, and (*g*) latex for rubber-based paint.

3. Explain the factor method of forecasting. Illustrate your answer.

4. Based on data in Exhibit 20–2, discuss the relative market potential of Chicago Heights and Evanston, Illinois, for: (*a*) prepared cereals, (*b*) automobiles, and (*c*) furniture.

5. Distinguish between competitive marketing mixes and "superior" mixes that lead to breakthrough opportunities.

6. Explain how the use of response functions—even if they must be crudely estimated—can be helpful in developing a marketing strategy.

7. Explain why the threshold expenditure level might prevent a firm from entering a market. Use an example to illustrate your reasoning.

8. Why is spreadsheet analysis a popular tool for marketing strategy planning?

9. Distinguish clearly between marketing plans and marketing programs.

10. Consider how the job of the marketing manager becomes more complex as he must develop and plan *several* strategies as part of a marketing program. Be sure to discuss how he might have to handle different strategies at different stages in the product life cycle. To make your discussion more concrete, consider the job of a marketing manager for a sporting product manufacturer.

11. Briefly explain the task method of budgeting.

12. Discuss how a marketing manager could go about choosing among several possible marketing plans, given that choices must be made because of limited resources. Would the job be easier in the consumer product or in the industrial product area? Why?

13. Explain why the budgeting procedure is typically such an agonizing procedure, usually consisting of extending past budgets, perhaps with small modifications from current plans. How would the budgeting procedure be changed if the marketing program planning procedure discussed in the chapter were implemented?

Suggested Cases _____

18. Tandy versus IBM

30. Chemco, Inc.

34. Kenny Chrysler, Inc.

35. Visiting Nurses Services (VNS)

36. Lever, Ltd.

Suggested Computer-Aided Problem _____

20. Comparing Marketing Mixes

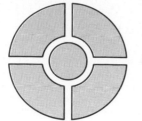

Chapter 21

Controlling Marketing Plans and Programs

When You Finish This Chapter, You Should

1. Understand how sales analysis can aid marketing strategy planning.

2. Understand the differences among sales analysis, performance analysis, and performance analysis using performance indexes.

3. Understand the difference between natural accounts and functional accounts—and their relevance for marketing cost analysis.

4. Know how to do a marketing cost analysis for customers or products.

5. Understand the difference between the full-cost approach and the contribution margin approach.

6. Understand how planning and control can be combined to improve the marketing management process.

7. Understand what a marketing audit is—and when and where it should be used.

8. Understand the important new terms (shown in red).

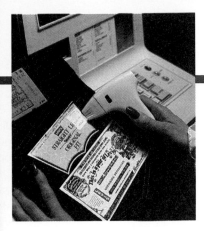

Planning, implementing, and control—that's the basic management process.

East Coast Packaging Corporation developed a new strategy to target producers of high-tech electronic equipment. This fast-growing market had a variety of packaging needs not being met by other suppliers. East Coast designed unique styrofoam "inserts" to protect electronic equipment during shipping. It assigned order getters to develop new accounts and recruited agent middlemen to develop distant markets. The whole marketing mix was well received—and the firm's "skimming" price led to good profits. But over time competition increased as other suppliers entered the market.

Marketing managers at East Coast routinely analyzed information stored in their marketing information system. To their surprise, this revealed that their once-successful strategy was slipping. Personal selling expense as a percent of sales had doubled because it took longer to find and sell new accounts. Moreover, it was costly to design special products for the many customers who purchased only small quantities. Profit margins were falling, too, because of increased price competition. In contrast, the analysis showed that sales of ordinary cardboard shipping boxes for agricultural products were very profitable.

East Coast stopped calling on *small* electronics firms and developed a new plan to build the firm's share of the less glamorous—but more profitable—cardbox box business.

Our primary emphasis so far has been on planning. Now we'll discuss **control**—the feedback process that helps the marketing manager learn (1) how ongoing plans are working and (2) how to plan for the future.

Keeping a firmer hand on the controls

A good manager wants to know: which products' sales are highest and why, which products are profitable, what is selling where, and how much the marketing process is costing. Managers need to know what's happening—in detail—to improve the "bottom line."

But traditional accounting reports are too general to be much help to the marketing manager. As East Coast Packaging discovered, a company may be showing a profit, while 80 percent of its business is coming from only 20 percent of its products—or customers. The other 80 percent may be unprofitable. But without special analyses, managers won't know it. This 80/20 relationship is fairly common—and it is often referred to as the *80/20 rule.*

It *is* possible for the marketing manager to get detailed information about how his plans are working. This chapter discusses the kind of information that can be available to the marketing manager—*but only if he asks for and helps develop the necessary data.*

This is an important chapter. And the techniques are not really complicated. They basically require only simple arithmetic—and perhaps a computer if a large volume of sorting, adding, and subtracting is required.[1]

SALES ANALYSIS SHOWS WHAT'S HAPPENING

Sales analysis—a detailed breakdown of a company's sales records—can be very informative—especially the first time it's done. Detailed data can keep marketing executives in touch with what's happening in the market. In addition, routine sales analyses prepared each week, month, or year may show trends—and enable managers to check their hypotheses and assumptions.[2]

Some managers resist sales analysis—or any analysis for that matter—because they don't appreciate how valuable it can be. One top executive in a large consumer products firm made no attempt to analyze his company's sales—even by geographic area. When asked why, he replied: "Why should we? We're making money!"

But today's profit is no guarantee that you'll make money tomorrow. In fact, ignoring sales analysis can lead not only to poor sales forecasting but to poor decisions in general. One manufacturer did much national advertising on the assumption that the firm was selling all over the country. But a simple sales analysis showed that most present customers were within a 250-mile radius of the factory! In other words, the firm didn't know who and where its customers were—and it was wasting most of the money it spent on national advertising.

But a marketing manager must ask for it

Detailed sales analysis is only a possibility until a manager asks for the data. Valuable sales information is often buried in sales invoices, which are filed away after the usual accounting functions are completed. Manual analysis of such records is so burdensome that it's seldom done.

Today, with computers and organized marketing information systems, effective sales analysis can be done easily and at relatively small cost—if marketing managers decide they want it done. In fact, the desired information can be obtained as a by-product of basic billing and accounts receivable procedures. The manager simply must see that identifying information—on important dimensions such as territory, sales reps, and so forth—is captured. Then, the computer can easily run sales analysis and simple trend projections.

What to ask for varies

There is no one "best" way to analyze sales data. Several breakdowns may be useful—depending on the nature of the company and product and what dimensions are relevant. Typical breakdowns include:

1. Geographic region—state, county, city, sales rep's territory.
2. Product, package size, grade, or color.
3. Customer size.
4. Customer type or class of trade.
5. Price or discount class.
6. Method of sale—mail, telephone, or direct sales.
7. Financial arrangement—cash or charge.
8. Size of order.
9. Commission class.

Too much data can drown a manager

While some sales analysis is better than none—or better than getting data too late for action—sales breakdowns that are too detailed can "drown" a manager in reports. Computers can print over 1,000 lines per minute—faster than any manager can read. So wise managers only ask for breakdowns that will help them make decisions. Further, they use computer programs that draw graphs and figures to make it easy to "see" patterns that otherwise might be hidden in a one-inch thick computer printout. But to avoid having to cope with mountains of data—much of which may be irrelevant—most managers move on to *performance analysis.*

Computer-produced graphs can make it easy to "see" patterns that might otherwise be hidden in a table of numbers.

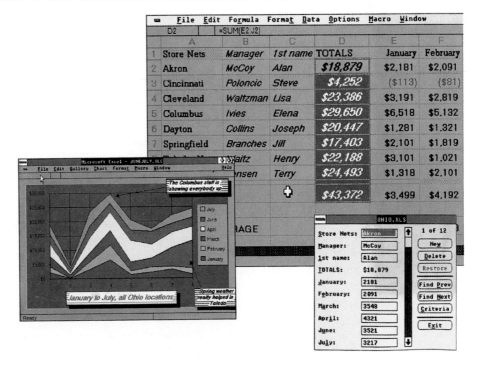

PERFORMANCE ANALYSIS LOOKS FOR DIFFERENCES

Numbers are compared

Performance analysis looks for exceptions or variations from planned performance. In simple sales analysis, the figures are merely listed or graphed—they aren't compared against standards. In performance analysis, managers make comparisons. They might compare one territory against another, against the same territory's performance last year, or against expected performance.

The purpose of performance analysis is to improve operations. The salesperson, territory, or other factors showing poor performance can be identified—and singled out for detailed analysis and corrective action. Or outstanding performances can be analyzed to see if the successes can be explained and made the general rule.

Performance analysis doesn't have to be limited to sales. Other data can be analyzed, too. This data may include miles traveled, number of calls made, number of orders, or the cost of various tasks.

A performance analysis can be quite revealing—as shown in the following example.

Straight performance analysis—an illustration

A manufacturer of industrial products sells to wholesalers through five sales reps—each serving a separate territory. Total net sales for the year amount to $2,386,000. Sales force compensation and expenses come to $198,000, yielding a direct-selling expense ratio of 8.3 percent—that is, $198,000 ÷ $2,386,000 × 100.

This information—taken from a profit and loss statement—is interesting, but it doesn't explain what's happening from one territory to another. To get a clearer picture, the manager has to compare the sales results with other data *from each territory.* See Exhibits 21–1 and 21–2. Keep in mind that exhibits like these and

Exhibit 21–1   Comparative Performance of Sales Reps

Sales area	Total calls	Total orders	Order-call ratio	Sales by sales rep	Average sales rep order	Total customers
A	1,900	1,140	60.0%	$ 912,000	$800	195
B	1,500	1,000	66.7	720,000	720	160
C	1,400	700	50.0	560,000	800	140
D	1,030	279	27.1	132,000	478	60
E	820	165	20.1	62,000	374	50
Total	6,650	3,284	49.3%	$2,386,000	$634	605

Exhjibit 21–2   Comparative Cost of Sales Reps

Sales area	Annual compensation	Expense payments	Total sales rep cost	Sales produced	Cost-sales ratio
A	$ 22,800	$11,200	$ 34,000	$ 912,000	3.7%
B	21,600	14,400	36,000	720,000	5.0
C	20,400	11,600	32,000	560,000	5.7
D	19,200	24,800	44,000	132,000	33.3
E	20,000	32,000	52,000	62,000	83.8
Total	$104,000	$94,000	$198,000	$2,386,000	8.3%

others that follow in this chapter are now very easy to generate. Popular computer programs like Lotus 1-2-3® and dBASE IV® make it easy to apply the ideas discussed here, even on inexpensive desktop computers.

The reps in sales areas D and E aren't doing well. Sales are low—and marketing costs are high. Perhaps sales reps with more "push" could do a better job, but the number of customers suggests that the potential might be low. Perhaps the whole plan needs revision.

The figures themselves, of course, don't provide the answers. But they do reveal the areas that need improvement. This is the main value of performance analysis. It's up to management to find the remedy—either by revising or changing the marketing plan.

PERFORMANCE INDEXES SIMPLIFY HUMAN ANALYSIS

Comparing against "what ought to have happened"

With a straight performance analysis, the marketing manager can evaluate the variations among sales reps to try to explain the "why." But this takes time. And "poor" performances are sometimes due to problems that bare sales figures don't reveal. Some uncontrollable factors in a particular territory—tougher competitors or ineffective middlemen— may lower the sales potential. Or a territory just may not have much potential.

To get a better check on performance effectiveness, the marketing manager compares what did happen with "what ought to have happened." This involves the use of performance indexes.

A performance index is like a batting average

When a manager sets standards—that is, quantitative measures of what "ought to happen"—it's relatively simple to compute a **performance index**—a number like a baseball batting average—that shows the relation of one value to another.

Baseball batting averages are computed by dividing the actual number of hits by the number of times at bat (the possible number of times the batter could have had a hit) and then multiplying the result by 100 to get rid of decimal points. A sales performance index is computed the same way—by dividing actual sales by expected sales for the area (or sales rep, product, etc.) and then multiplying this figure by 100. If a sales rep is "batting" 82 percent, the index is 82.

A simple example shows where the problem is

Computing a performance index is shown in the following example—which assumes that population is an effective measure of sales potential.

In Exhibit 21–3, the population of the United States is broken down by regional population—as a percent of the total population. The regions are Northeastern, Southern, Midwestern, and Western.

The firm already has $1 million in sales—and now it wants to evaluate performance in each region. Column 2 shows the actual sales of $1 million broken down in proportion to the population in the five regions. This is what sales *should* have been if population were a good measure of future performance. Column 3 in Exhibit 21–3 shows the actual sales for the year for each region. Column 4 shows measures of performance (performance indexes)—Column 3 ÷ Column 2 × 100.

The Western region isn't doing as well as expected. It has 20 percent of the total population—and expected sales (based on population) are $200,000. Actual sales, however, are only $120,000. This means that the Western region's perfor-

Exhibit 21–3   Development of a Measure of Sales Performances (by region)

Regions	(1) Population as percent of United States	(2) Expected distribution of sales based on population	(3) Actual sales	(4) Performance index
Northeastern	20	$ 200,000	$ 210,000	105
Southern	25	250,000	250,000	100
Midwestern	35	350,000	420,000	120
Western	20	200,000	120,000	60
Total	100	$1,000,000	$1,000,000	

mance index is only 60—(120,000 ÷ 200,000) × 100—because actual sales are much lower than expected on the basis of population. If population is a good basis for measuring expected sales (an important *if*), the poor sales performance should be analyzed further. Perhaps sales reps in the Western region aren't working as hard as they should. Perhaps promotion there isn't as effective as elsewhere. Or competitive products may have entered the market.

Whatever the cause, it's clear that performance analysis does not solve problems. It only points out potential problems—and it does this well.

A SERIES OF PERFORMANCE ANALYSES MAY FIND THE REAL PROBLEM

Performance analysis helps a marketing manager to see if the firm's marketing plans are working properly—and, if they are not, it can lead to solutions to the problems. But this may require a series of performance analyses, as shown in the following example.

To get a feel for how performance analysis can be part of a problem-solving process, follow this example carefully—one exhibit at a time. Try to anticipate the marketing manager's decision.

The case of Stereo, Inc.

Stereo's sales manager found that sales for the Pacific Coast region were $130,000 below the quota of $14,500,000 (that is, actual sales were $14,370,000) for the January through June period. The quota was based on forecast sales of the various types of stereo equipment the company sells. Specifically, the quota was based on forecasts for each product type in each store in each sales rep's territory.

John Dexter, the sales manager, felt this difference was not too large (1.52 percent) and was inclined to forget the matter—especially since forecasts are usually in error to some extent. But he thought about sending a letter to all sales reps and district supervisors in the region—a letter aimed at stimulating sales effort.

Exhibit 21–4 shows the overall story of what was happening to Stereo's sales on the Pacific Coast. What do you think the manager should do?

The Portland district had the poorest performance—but it wasn't too bad. Before writing a "let's get with it" letter to Portland and then relaxing, the sales manager decided to analyze the performance of the four sales reps in the Portland district. Exhibit 21–5 shows a breakdown of the Portland figures by sales rep. What conclusion or action do you suggest now?

Exhibit 21–4   Sales Performance—Pacific Coast Region, January–June ($000)

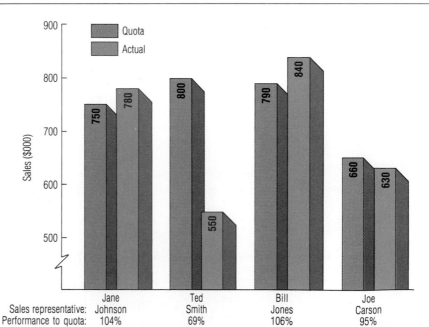

Since Ted Smith previously had been the top sales rep, the sales manager wondered if Smith was having trouble with some of his larger customers. Before making a drastic move, he obtained an analysis of Smith's sales to the five largest customers. See Exhibit 21–6. What action could the sales manager take now? Should Smith be fired?

Smith's sales in all the large stores were down significantly—although his sales in many small stores were holding up well. Smith's problem seemed to be general. Perhaps he just wasn't working. Before calling him, the sales manager decided to

Exhibit 21–5   Sales Performance—Portland District, January–June ($000)

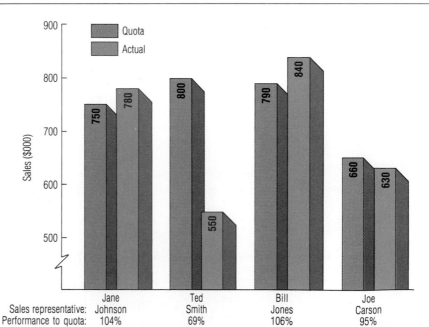

Exhibit 21–6   Sales Performance——Selected Stores of Ted Smith in Portland District, January–June ($000)

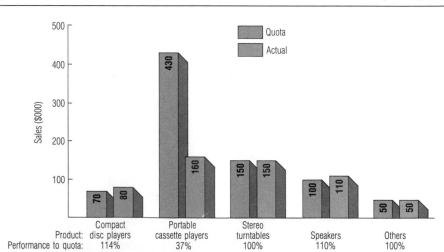

Store:	#1	#2	#3	#4	#5	Others
Performance to quota:	46%	69%	57%	50%	73%	127%

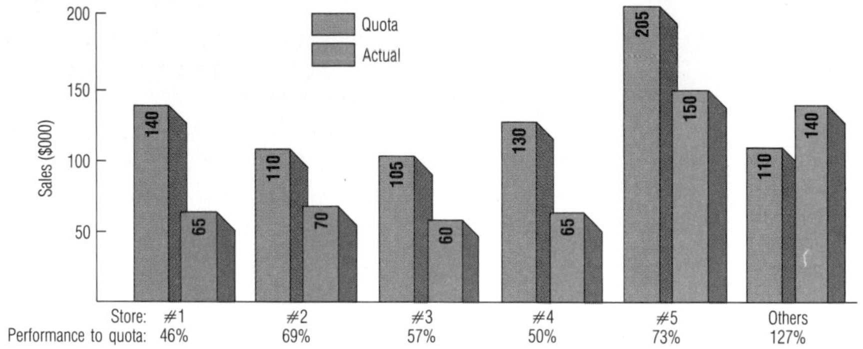

look at Smith's sales of the four major products. Exhibit 21–7 shows Smith's sales. What action is indicated now?

Smith was having real trouble with portable cassette players. Was the problem Smith or the players?

Further analysis by products for the whole region showed that everyone on the Pacific Coast was having trouble with portable players because a regional competitor was cutting prices. But higher sales on other products had hidden this fact. Since portable player sales had been doing all right nationally, the problem was only now showing up. You can see that this is the *major* problem.

Since overall company sales were going fairly well, many sales managers wouldn't have bothered with this analysis. They might have traced the problem to Smith. But, without detailed sales records and performance analysis, the natural human reaction for Smith would be to blame business conditions—or aggressive competition—or some other handy excuse.

Exhibit 21–7   Sales Performance by Product for Ted Smith in Portland District, January–June ($000)

Product:	Compact disc players	Portable cassette players	Stereo turntables	Speakers	Others
Performance to quota:	114%	37%	100%	110%	100%

Stay home and use the computer

This case shows that total figures can be deceiving. Marketing managers should not jump on the first plane—or reach for the phone—until they have all the facts. Even worse than rushing to the scene would be a rash judgment based on incomplete information. Some students want to fire Smith after they see the store-by-store data (Exhibit 21–6).

The home office should have the records and facilities to isolate problem areas—then rely on the field staff for explanations and help with locating the exact problem. Continuing detailed analysis usually gives better insights into problems, as this case shows. With computers, this can be done routinely and in great detail—*provided marketing managers ask for it.*

The "iceberg principle"—90 percent is below the surface

One of the most interesting conclusions from the Stereo illustration is the **iceberg principle**—much good information is hidden in summary data. Icebergs show only about 10 percent of their mass above water level. The other 90 percent is below water level—and not directly below, either. The submerged portion almost seems to be searching out ships that come too near.

The same is true of much business and marketing data. Since total sales may be large and company activities varied, problems in one area may be hidden below the surface. Everything looks calm and peaceful. But closer analysis may reveal jagged edges that can severely damage or even "sink" the business. The 90:10 ratio—or the 80/20 rule we mentioned earlier—must not be ignored. Averaging and summarizing data can be helpful, but you should be sure that summaries don't hide more than they reveal.

Sales analysis often reveals that much useful information is hidden in summary sales data.

K mart's Spring Sales Cool Off

In late 1988, marketing managers at K mart were implementing a long-range plan to change the company from a "no frills" discount store to a retailer of quality, brand-name products. For example, they had developed a new advertising campaign to promote their upgraded home furnishings line. They were also adding many new stores in areas where they were not reaching their target customers. The plan seemed to be working well—and the company was posting healthy gains in both sales and profits.

By the end of the first quarter of 1989, growth had slowed. Total sales were up 3.9 percent, but most of the increase was from new stores. In fact, analysis showed that sales at existing stores grew only .2 percent. Some K mart managers worried that new competition from Sears, Roebuck & Co. might be the problem. Sears had just switched to a new "everyday low-price" policy. However, further analysis showed that sales had fallen off even at K mart stores that were not near a Sears store.

To help isolate the problem, the K mart managers broke down total sales by product lines. Their analysis showed that the major problem area was poor performance on important seasonal items—such as patio furniture and gardening products. The analysis could not explain *why* sales for these products had been poor, but K mart's managers thought that a likely reason was that the spring weather had been much cooler than usual.[3]

MARKETING COST ANALYSIS—CONTROLLING COSTS, TOO

So far we've emphasized sales analysis. But sales come at a cost. And costs can and should be analyzed and controlled, too.

Detailed cost analysis has been very useful in the factory—but much less has been done with *marketing cost analysis*.[4] Accountants often show little interest in the marketing process. Many think of salespeople as swingers who wine and dine customers, play golf all afternoon, and occasionally pick up orders. Some accountants think it's impossible to tie the costs of selling to particular products or customers. And many think that advertising is a waste of money—that there's no way of relating it to particular sales. They wind up treating advertising as a general overhead cost—and then forget about it.

Marketing costs have a purpose

But careful analysis of most marketing costs shows that the money is spent for a specific purpose—either to develop or promote a particular product or to serve particular customers. So it makes sense to allocate costs to specific market segments—or customers—or to specific products. In some situations, it is practical to allocate costs directly to the various geographical market segments being served. This may let managers directly analyze the profitability of the firm's target markets. In other cases, it may be desirable to allocate costs to specific customers or specific products—and then add these costs for market segments depending on how much of which products each customer buys.

In either case, marketing cost analysis usually requires a new way of classifying accounting data. Instead of using the type of accounts typically used for financial analysis, we have to use functional accounts.

Natural versus functional accounts—what is the purpose?

Natural accounts are the categories to which various costs are charged in the normal financial accounting cycle. These accounts include salaries, wages, social security, taxes, supplies, raw materials, auto, gas and oil expenses, advertising,

Levi Straus's advertising costs can often be allocated to specific products, just as the cost of labor in the factory can be allocated to specific products.

REAL LIFE WEARS REAL JEANS.

REAL JEANS FOR WOMEN.

and others. These accounts are called "natural" because they have the names of their expense categories.

However, this is not the approach to cost analysis that factories use—and it's not the one we will use. In the factory, **functional accounts** show the *purpose* for which the expenditures are made. Factory functional accounts include shearing, milling, grinding, floor cleaning, maintenance, and so on. Factory cost accounting records are organized so that the cost and likely contribution to profit of particular products or jobs can be determined.

Marketing jobs are done for specific purposes, too. With some planning, the costs of marketing can also be assigned to specific categories—such as customers and products. Then their profitability can be calculated.

First, get costs into functional accounts

The first step in marketing cost analysis is to reclassify all the dollar cost entries in the natural accounts into functional cost accounts. For example, the many cost items in the natural *salary* account may be allocated to functional accounts with the following names: storing, inventory control, order assembly, packing and shipping, transporting, selling, advertising, order entry, billing, credit extension, and accounts receivable. The same is true for rent, depreciation, heat, light, power, and other natural accounts.

The way natural account amounts are shifted to functional accounts depends on the firm's method of operation. It may require time studies, space measurements, actual counts, and managers' estimates.

Then reallocate to evaluate profitability of profit centers

The next step is to reallocate the functional costs to those items—or customers or market segments—for which the costs were spent. The most common reallocation of functional costs is to products and to customers. After these costs are allocated, the detailed totals can be combined in any way desired—for example, by product or customer class, region, and so on.

The costs allocated to the functional accounts equal, in total, those in the natural accounts. They are just organized in a different way. But instead of being used only to show *total* company profits, the costs can now be used to calculate the profitability of territories, products, customers, salespeople, price classes, order sizes, distribution methods, sales methods, or any other breakdown desired. Each unit can be treated as a profit center.

Cost analysis finds "no-profit Jones"—tracking down the loser

These ideas can be seen more clearly in the following example. In this case, the usual financial accounting approach—with natural accounts—shows that the company made a profit of $938 last month (Exhibit 21–8). But such a profit and loss statement doesn't show the profitability of the company's three customers. So the managers decide to use marketing cost analysis because they want to know whether a change in the marketing mix will improve profit.

First, we distribute the costs in the five natural accounts to four functional accounts—sales, packaging, advertising, and billing and collection (see Exhibit 21–9)—according to the functional reason for the expenses. Specifically, $1,000 of the total salary cost was for sales reps who seldom even come into the office since their job is to call on customers; $900 of the salary cost was for packaging labor;

Exhibit 21–8   Profit and Loss Statement

Sales		$17,000
Cost of sales		11,900
Gross margin		5,100
Expenses:		
Salaries	$2,500	
Rent	500	
Wrapping supplies	1,012	
Stationary and stamps	50	
Office equipment	100	
		4,162
Net profit		$ 938

Exhibit 21–9   Spreading Natural Accounts to Functional Accounts

		Functional accounts			
Natural accounts		Sales	Packaging	Advertising	Billing and collection
Salaries	$2,500	$1,000	$ 900	$300	$300
Rent	500		400	50	50
Wrapping supplies	1,012		1,012		
Stationery and stamps	50			25	25
Office equipment	100			50	50
Total	$4,162	$1,000	$2,312	$425	$425

and $600 was for office help. Assume that the office force split its time about evenly between addressing advertising material and the billing and collection function. So we split the $600 evenly into these two functional accounts.

The $500 for rent was for the entire building. But the company used 80 percent of its floor space for packaging and 20 percent for the office. Thus $400 is allocated to the packaging account. We divide the remaining $100 evenly between the advertising and billing accounts because these functions used the office space about equally. Stationery, stamps, and office equipment charges are allocated equally to the latter two accounts for the same reason. Charges for wrapping supplies are allocated to the packaging account because these supplies were used in packaging. In another situation, different allocations and even different accounts may be sensible—but these are workable here.

Calculating profitability of three customers

Now we can calculate the profitability of the company's three customers. But we need more information before we can allocate these functional accounts to customers or products. It is presented in Exhibit 21–10.

Exhibit 21–10 shows that the company's three products vary in cost, selling price, and sales volume. The products also have different sizes, and the packaging costs aren't related to the selling price. So when packaging costs are allocated to products, size must be considered. We can do this by computing a new measure—a packaging unit—which is used to allocate the costs in the packaging account. Packaging units adjust for relative size and the number of each type of product sold. For example, Product C is six times larger than A. While the company sells only 10 units of Product C, it is bulky and requires 10 times 6, or 60 packaging units. So we must allocate more of the costs in the packaging account to each unit of Product C.

Exhibit 21–10 also shows that the three customers require different amounts of sales effort, place different numbers of orders, and buy different product combinations.

Exhibit 21–10 Basic Data for Cost and Profit Analysis Example

Products:

Products	Cost/unit	Selling price/unit	Number of units sold in period	Sales volume in period	Relative "bulk" per unit	Packaging "units"
A	$ 7	$ 10	1,000	$10,000	1	1,000
B	35	50	100	5,000	3	300
C	140	200	10	2,000	6	60
			1,110	$17,000		1,360

Customers:

Customers	Number of sales calls in period	Number of orders placed in period	Number of each product ordered in period		
			A	B	C
Smith	30	30	900	30	0
Jones	40	3	90	30	3
Brown	30	1	10	40	7
Total	100	34	1,000	100	10

Jones seems to require more sales calls. Smith places many orders that must be processed in the office—with increased billing expense. Brown seems to be a great customer. He placed only one order—and it was for 70 percent of the sales of high-valued Product C.

Exhibit 21–11 shows the computations for allocating the functional amounts to the three customers. There were 100 sales calls in the period. Assuming that all calls took the same amount of time, we can figure the average cost per call by dividing the $1,000 sales cost by 100 calls—giving an average cost of $10. Similar reasoning is used to break down the billing and packaging account totals. Advertising during this period was for the benefit of Product C only—so we split this cost among the units of C sold.

Calculating profit and loss for each customer

Now we can compute a profit and loss statement for each customer—combining his purchases and the cost of serving him. This is done in Exhibit 21–12. A statement is prepared for each customer. The sum of each of the four major components (sales, cost of sales, expenses, and profit) is the same as on the original statement (Exhibit 21–8)—all we've done is rearrange and rename the data.

For example, Smith bought 900 units of A at $10 each and 300 units of B at $50 each—for the respective sales totals ($9,000 and $1,500) shown in Exhibit 21–12. We compute cost of sales in the same way. Expenses require various calculations. Thirty sales calls cost $300—30 times $10 each. Smith placed 30 orders at an average cost of $12.50 each for a total ordering cost of $375. Total packaging costs amounted to $1,530 for A (900 units purchased times $1.70 per unit) and $153 for B (30 units purchased times $5.10 per unit). There were no packaging costs for C because Smith didn't buy any of Product C. Neither were any advertising costs charged to Smith—all advertising costs were spent promoting Product C, which he didn't buy.

Analyzing the results

We now see that Smith was the most profitable customer, yielding over 75 percent of the net profit.

This analysis shows that Brown was profitable, too—but not as profitable as Smith, because Smith bought three times as much. Jones was unprofitable. He didn't buy very much and received one-third more sales calls.

The iceberg principle is operating again here. Although the company as a whole is profitable, customer Jones is not. But before dropping Jones, the marketing manager should study the figures and the marketing plan very carefully. Perhaps Jones should be called on less frequently. Or maybe he will grow into a profitable account. Now he is at least covering some fixed costs. Dropping him may only

Exhibit 21–11   Functional Cost Account Allocations

Sales calls	$1,000/100 calls	=	$10/call
Billing	$425/34 orders	=	$12.50/order
Packaging units costs	$2.312/1,360 packaging units	=	$1.70/packaging unit or $1.70 for product A $5.10 for product B $10.20 for product C
Advertising	$425/10 units of C	=	$42.50/unit of C

Exhibit 21–12   Profit and Loss Statements for Customers

	Smith	Jones	Brown	Whole company
Sales				
A	$9,000	$ 900	$ 100	
B	1,500	1,500	2,000	
C		600	1,400	
Total sales	$10,500	$ 3,000	$ 3,500	$ 17,000
Cost of sales				
A	6,300	630	70	
B	1,050	1,050	1,400	
C		420	980	
Total cost of sales	7,350	2,100	2,450	11,900
Gross margin	3,150	900	1,050	5,100
Expenses				
Sales calls ($10 each)	300	400.00	300.00	
Order costs ($12.50 each)	375	37.50	12.50	
Packaging costs				
A	1,530	153.00	17.00	
B	153	153.00	204.00	
C		30.60	71.40	
Advertising		127.50	297.50	
	2,358	901.60	902.40	4,162
Net profit (or loss)	$ 792	$ (1.60)	$ 147.60	$ 938

shift those fixed costs to the other two customers—making them look less attractive. (See the discussion on contribution margin later in this chapter.)

The marketing manager may also want to analyze the advertising costs against results since a heavy advertising expense is charged against each unit of Product C. Perhaps the whole marketing plan should be revised.

Cost analysis is not performance analysis

Such a cost analysis is not a performance analysis, of course. If the marketing manager had budgeted costs to various jobs, it would be possible to extend this analysis to a performance analysis. This would be logical—and desirable—but many companies have not yet moved in this direction.

Now that more accounting and marketing information is routinely available on computers—and software to analyze it is easier to use—many managers are seizing the opportunity to do marketing cost and performance analysis—just like factory cost accounting systems develop detailed cost estimates for products. These changes also mean that more managers are able to compare marketing cost and performance figures with "expected" figures to evaluate and control their marketing plans.

SHOULD ALL COSTS BE ALLOCATED?

So far we've discussed general principles. But allocating costs is tricky. Some costs are likely to be fixed for the near future—regardless of what decision is

When a company sells many products, some costs may be difficult to allocate.

made. And some costs are likely to be *common* to several products or customers—making allocation difficult.

Two basic approaches to handling this allocating problem are possible—the full-cost approach and the contribution-margin approach.

Full-cost approach—everything costs something

In the **full-cost approach**, all functional costs are allocated to products, customers, or other categories. Even fixed costs and common costs are allocated in some way. Because all costs are allocated, we can subtract costs from sales and find the profitability of various customers, products, and so on. This *is* of interest to some managers.

The full-cost approach requires that difficult-to-allocate costs be split on some basis. Here the managers assume that the work done for those costs is equally beneficial to customers, to products, or to whatever group they are allocated. Sometimes this allocation is done mechanically. But often logic can support the allocation—if we accept the idea that marketing costs are incurred for a purpose. For example, advertising costs not directly related to specific customers or products might be allocated to *all* customers based on their purchases—on the theory that advertising has helped bring in the sales.

Contribution margin—ignores some costs to get results

When we use the **contribution-margin approach**, all functional costs are not allocated in *all* situations. Why?

When we compare various alternatives, it may be more meaningful to consider only the costs that are directly related to specific alternatives. Variable costs are relevant here.

The contribution-margin approach focuses attention on variable costs—rather than on total costs. Total costs may include some fixed costs that do not change in the short run and can safely be ignored or some common costs that are more difficult to allocate.[5]

The two approaches can lead to different decisions

The difference between the full-cost approach and the contribution-margin approach is important. The two approaches may suggest different decisions, as we'll see in the following example.

Full-cost example

Exhibit 21–13 shows a profit and loss statement—using the full-cost approach—for a department store with three operating departments. (These could be market segments or customers or products.)

The administrative expenses—which are the only fixed costs in this case—have been allocated to departments based on the sales volume of each department. This is a typical method of allocation. In this case, some managers argued that Department 1 was clearly unprofitable—and should be eliminated—because it showed a net loss of $500. Were they right?

To find out, see Exhibit 21–14, which shows what would happen if Department 1 were eliminated.

Several facts become clear right away. The overall profit of the store would be reduced if Department 1 were dropped. Fixed costs of $3,000—now being charged to Department 1—would have to be allocated to the other departments. This would reduce net profit by $2,500, since Department 1 previously covered $2,500 of the $3,000 of fixed costs. Such shifting of costs would then make Department 2 unprofitable!

Exhibit 21–13   Profit and Loss Statement by Department

	Totals	Dept. 1	Dept. 2	Dept. 3
Sales	$100,000	$50,000	$30,000	$20,000
Cost of sales	80,000	45,000	25,000	10,000
Gross margin	20,000	5,000	5,000	10,000
Other expenses				
Selling expenses	5,000	2,500	1,500	1,000
Administrative expenses	6,000	3,000	1,800	1,200
Total other expenses	11,000	5,500	3,300	2,200
Net profit or (loss)	9,000	(500)	1,700	7,800

Exhibit 21–14   Profit and Loss Statement by Department if Department 1 Were Eliminated

	Totals	Dept. 2	Dept. 3
Sales	$50,000	$30,000	$20,000
Cost of sales	35,000	25,000	10,000
Gross margin	15,000	5,000	10,000
Other expenses			
Selling expenses	2,500	1,500	1,000
Administrative expenses	6,000	3,600	2,400
Total other expenses	8,500	5,100	3,400
Net profit or (loss)	6,500	(100)	6,600

Contribution-margin example

Exhibit 21–15 shows a contribution-margin income statement for the same department store. Note that each department has a positive contribution-margin. Here the Department 1 contribution of $2,500 stands out better. This actually is the amount that would be lost if Department 1 were dropped. (Our example assumes that the fixed administrative expenses are *truly* fixed—that none of them would be eliminated if this department were dropped.)

A contribution-margin income statement shows the contribution of each department more clearly—including its contribution to both fixed costs and profit. As long as a department has some contribution-margin—and as long as there is no better use for the resources it uses—the department should be retained.

Contribution-margin versus full cost—choose your side

Using the full-cost approach often leads to arguments within a company. Any method of allocation can make some products or customers appear less profitable than if some other allocation method is used.

For example, it's logical to assign all common advertising costs to customers based on their purchases. But this approach can be criticized on the grounds that it may make large-volume customers appear less profitable than they really are—especially if the marketing mix aimed at the larger customers emphasizes price more than advertising.

Those in the company who want the smaller customers to look more profitable usually argue *for* this allocation method on the grounds that general advertising helps "build" good customers because it affects the overall image of the company and its products.

Arguments over allocation methods can be deadly serious. The method used may reflect on the performance of various managers—and it may affect their salaries and bonuses. Product managers, for example, are especially interested in how the various fixed and common costs are allocated to their products. Each, in turn, might like to have costs shifted to others' products.

Arbitrary allocation of costs also may have a direct impact on sales reps' morale. If they see their variable costs loaded with additional common or fixed costs over which they have no control, they may ask what's the use?

To avoid these problems, firms often use the contribution-margin approach. It's especially useful for evaluating alternatives—and for showing operating managers and salespeople how they're doing. The contribution-margin approach shows what they've actually contributed to covering general overhead and profit.

Exhibit 21–15 Contribution-Margin Statement by Departments

	Totals	Dept. 1	Dept. 2	Dept. 3
Sales	$100,000	$50,000	$30,000	$20,000
Variable costs				
Cost of sales	80,000	45,000	25,000	10,000
Selling expenses	5,000	2,500	1,500	1,000
Total variable costs	85,000	47,500	26,500	11,000
Contribution margin	15,000	2,500	3,500	9,000
Fixed costs				
Administrative expenses	6,000			
Net profit	9,000			

Top management, on the other hand, often finds full-cost analysis more useful. In the long run, some products, departments, or customers must pay for the fixed costs. Full-cost analysis has its place, too.

PLANNING AND CONTROL COMBINED

We've been treating sales and cost analyses separately up to this point. But management often combines them to keep a running check on its activities—to be sure the plans are working—and to see when and where new strategies are needed.

Sales + Costs + Everybody helps = $163,000

Let's see how this works at the XYZ Hardware Company, a typical hardware retailer.

This firm netted $155,000 last year. Jim Smith, the owner, expects no basic change in competition and slightly better local business conditions. So he sets this year's profit objective at $163,000—an increase of about 5 percent.

Next he develops tentative plans to show how he can make this higher profit. He estimates the sales volumes, gross margins, and expenses—broken down by months and by departments in his store—that he would need to net $163,000.

Exhibit 21–16 is a planning and control chart Smith developed to show the contribution each department should make each month. At the bottom of Exhibit 21–16, the plan for the year is summarized. Note that space is provided to insert the actual performance and a measure of variation. So this chart can be used to do both planning and control.

Exhibit 21–16 shows that Smith is focusing on the monthly contribution by each department. The purpose of monthly estimates is to get more frequent feedback and allow faster adjustment of plans. Generally, the shorter the planning and control period, the easier it is to correct problems before they become emergencies.

In this example, Smith is using a modified contribution-margin approach—some of the fixed costs can be allocated logically to particular departments. On this chart, the balance left after direct fixed and variable costs are charged to departments is called "Contribution to Store." The idea is that each department will contribute to covering *general* store expenses—such as top-management salaries and Christmas decorations—and to net profits.

In Exhibit 21–16, we see that the whole operation is brought together when Smith computes the monthly operating profit. He totals the contribution from each of the four departments and then subtracts general store expenses to obtain the operating profit for each month.

Each department must plan and control, too

Exhibit 21–17 shows a similar planning and control chart for a single XYZ department—Department B. In this exhibit, actual results have been entered for the month of January. The chart shows an unfavorable difference between planned and actual sales performance (−$14,000) and gross profit (−$1,700).

Now the marketing manager must decide why actual sales were less than projected and begin to make new plans. Possible hypotheses are: (1) prices were too high; (2) promotion was ineffective; (3) the product selection did not appeal to the target customers; and (4) errors might have been made in marking the prices or in totaling the sales figures.

Exhibit 21-16   XYZ Hardware Company Planning and Control Chart

| | Contribution to store | | | | | Store expense | Operating profit | Cumulative operating profit |
	Dept. A	Dept. B	Dept. C	Dept. D*	Total			
January								
Planned	27,000	9,000	4,000	−1,000	39,000	24,000	15,000	15,000
Actual								
Variation								
February								
Planned	20,000	6,500	2,500	−1,000	28,000	24,000	4,000	19,000
Actual								
Variation								
November								
Planned	32,000	7,500	2,500	0	42,000	24,000	18,000	106,500
Actual								
Variation								
December								
Planned	63,000	12,500	4,000	9,000	88,500	32,000	56,500	163,000
Actual								
Variation								
Total								
Planned	316,000	70,000	69,000	−4,000	453,000	288,000	163,000	163,000
Actual								
Variation								

*The objective of minus $4,000 for this department was established on the same basis as the objectives for the other departments, i.e., it represents the same percentage gain over last year, when Department D's loss was $4,200. Plans call for discontinuance of the department unless it shows marked improvement by the end of the year.

Corrective action could take either of two courses: improving implementation efforts or developing new, more realistic strategies.

SPEED UP THE INFORMATION FOR BETTER CONTROL

The marketing manager must take charge

Computers are now readily available to take the drudgery out of analyzing data. But this kind of analysis is not possible unless the data is in machine-processable form—so it can be sorted and analyzed quickly. Here, the creative marketing manager plays a crucial role by insisting that the necessary data be collected. If the data he wants to analyze is not captured as it comes in, information will be difficult—if not impossible—to get later.

Speed is a key factor

A marketing manager may need many different types of information to improve implementation efforts or develop new strategies. In the past, this has often caused delays—even if the information was in a machine-processable form. In a large company, for example, it could take days or even weeks for a marketing manager to find out how to get needed information from another department. Imagine how long it could take for a marketing manager to get needed sales data from sales offices in different countries all over the world.

Exhibit 21–17   XYZ Hardware Company Planning and Control Chart—Department B

| | Sales | Gross profit | Direct expense | | | Contribution to store | Cumulative contribution to store |
			Total	Fixed	Variable		
January							
Planned	60,000	18,000	9,000	6,000	3,000	9,000	9,000
Actual	46,000	16,300	8,300	6,000	1,150	8,000	8,000
Variation	−14,000	−1,700	700	0	700	−1,000	−1,000
February							
Planned	50,000	15,000	8,500	6,000	2,500	6,500	15,500
Actual							
Variation							
November							
Planned	70,000	21,000	13,500	10,000	3,500	7,500	57,500
Actual							
Variation							
December							
Planned	90,000	27,000	14,500	10,000	4,500	12,500	70,000
Actual							
Variation							
Total							
Planned	600,000	180,000	110,000	80,000	30,000	70,000	70,000
Actual							
Variation							

New approaches for electronic data interchange are helping some managers get information and adjust their strategies more quickly.

New approaches for electronic data interchange are helping to solve these problems. For example, many companies are using fiber optic telephone lines or satellite transmission systems to *immediately* transfer data from a computer at one location to another. A sales manager with a portable computer can use a regular telephone to pull data off his firm's mainframe computer. And marketing managers working at different locations on different aspects of a strategy can communicate through "networks" that link their computers together for easy data transfer.

This type of electronic "pipeline" means that needed data is often available instantly. A sales or performance analysis that in the past was done once a month now might be done weekly or even daily.

Of course, many firms have not considered or used these types of approaches. But in the future they will become much more common—especially if more marketing managers find that they are losing out to more nimble competitors who get information more quickly and adjust their strategies more often.[6]

THE MARKETING AUDIT

While crises pop, planning and control must go on

The analyses we've discussed so far are designed to help a firm plan and control its operations. They can help a marketing manager do a better job. Often, however, the control process tends to look at only a few critical elements—such as sales variations by product in different territories. It misses such things as the effectiveness of present and possible marketing strategies and mixes.

The marketing manager usually is responsible for day-to-day implementing as well as planning and control—and he may not have the time to evaluate the effectiveness of the firm's efforts. Sometimes, crises are popping in several places at the same time. Attention must focus on adjusting marketing mixes—or on shifting strategies in the short run.

To make sure that the whole marketing program is evaluated *regularly,* not just in times of crisis, marketing specialists have developed a new concept—the marketing audit. A marketing audit is similar to an accounting audit or a personnel audit, both of which have been accepted by business for some time.

The **marketing audit** is a systematic, critical, and unbiased review and appraisal of the basic objectives and policies of the marketing function—and of the organization, methods, procedures, and people employed to implement the policies.[7]

A marketing audit requires a detailed look at the company's current marketing plans to see if they are still the "best" plans the firm can offer. Customers' needs and attitudes change—and competitors are continually developing new and better plans. Plans that are more than a year or two old may be getting out of date—or may even be obsolete. Sometimes, marketing managers are "so close to the trees that they can't see the forest." An outsider can help the firm see whether it really has focused on some unsatisfied needs and is offering appropriate marketing mixes. Basically, the auditor uses our strategy planning framework. But instead of developing plans, he works backward—and evaluates the plans that are being implemented. He also evaluates the quality of the effort—looking at who is doing what and how well. This means interviewing customers, competitors, channel members, and employees. A marketing audit can be a big job. But if it helps ensure that the company's strategies are on the right track—and being implemented properly—it can be well worth the effort.

<table>
</table>

An audit shouldn't be
necessary—but usually it is

A marketing audit takes a big view of the business—and it evaluates the whole marketing program. It might be done by a separate department within the company—perhaps by a "marketing controller." Or, to avoid bias, it might be better to have it done by an outside organization such as a management consulting firm.

Ideally, a marketing audit should not be necessary. Good managers do their very best in planning, implementing, and control—and they should be continually evaluating the effectiveness of the operation.

In practice, however, managers often become identified with certain strategies—and pursue them blindly—when other strategies might be more effective. Since an outside view can give needed perspective, marketing audits may be more common in the future.

CONCLUSION

In this chapter, we saw that sales and cost analyses can help a marketing manager control a marketing program—and that control procedures can be useful in planning. Controls lead to feedback that aids future planning.

Simple sales analysis just gives a picture of what has happened. But when sales forecasts or other data showing expected results are brought into the analysis, we can evaluate performance using performance indexes.

Cost analysis also can be useful—if "natural" account costs are moved to functional cost accounts and then allocated to market segments, customers, products, or other categories. There are two basic approaches to cost analysis—full-cost and contribution-margin. Using the full-cost approach, all costs are allocated in some way. Using the contribution-margin approach, only the variable costs are allocated. Both methods have their advantages and special uses.

Ideally, the marketing manager should arrange for a constant flow of data that can be analyzed routinely—preferably by computer—to help control present plans and plan new strategies. A marketing audit can help this ongoing effort. Either a separate department within the company or an outside organization may conduct this audit.

A marketing program must be controlled. Good control helps the marketing manager locate and correct weak spots—and at the same time find strengths that may be applied throughout the marketing program. Control works hand in hand with planning.

Questions and Problems

1. Various breakdowns can be used for sales analysis, depending on the nature of the company and its products. Describe a situation (one for each) where each of the following breakdowns would yield useful information. Explain why.

  a. By geographic region.
  b. By product.
  c. By customer.
  d. By size of order.
  e. By size of sales rep commission on each product or product group.

2. Distinguish between a sales analysis and a performance analysis.

3. Carefully explain what the "iceberg principle" should mean to the marketing manager.

4. Explain the meaning of the comparative performance and comparative cost data in Exhibits 21–1 and 21–2. Why does it appear that eliminating sales areas D and E would be profitable?

5. Most sales forecasting is subject to some error (perhaps 5 to 10 percent). Should we then expect variations in sales performance of 5 to 10 percent above or below quota? If so, how should we treat such variations in evaluating performance?

6. Why is there controversy between the advocates of the full-cost and the contribution-margin approaches to cost analysis?

7. The June profit and loss statement for the Browning Company is shown. If competitive conditions make price increases impossible—and management has cut costs as much as possible—should the Browning Company stop selling to hospitals and schools? Why?

8. Explain why it's so important for the marketing manager to be directly involved in the planning of control procedures.

9. Explain why a marketing audit might be desirable—even in a well-run company. Who or what kind of an organization would be best to conduct a marketing audit? Would a marketing research firm be good? Would the present CPA firms be most suitable? Why?

Browning Company Statement

	Retailers	Hospitals and schools	Total
Sales			
80,000 units at $0.70 . . .	$56,000		$56,000
20,000 units at $0.60 . . .		$12,000	12,000
Total	56,000	12,000	68,000
Cost of sales	40,000	10,000	50,000
Gross margin	16,000	2,000	18,000
Sales and administrative expenses			
Variable	6,000	1,500	7,500
Fixed	5,600	900	6,500
Total	11,600	2,400	14,000
Net profit (loss)	$ 4,400	$ (400)	$ 4,000

Suggested Cases _____

37. Young & Whitney, CPAs

39. Speedy Pizza, Inc.

Suggested Computer-Aided Problem _____

21. Marketing Cost Analysis

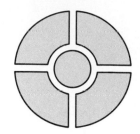

Chapter 22

Marketing Strategy Planning for International Markets

When You Finish This Chapter, You Should

1. Understand the various ways that businesses can get into international marketing.

2. Understand what multinational corporations are.

3. Understand the kinds of opportunities in international markets.

4. Understand the market dimensions that may be useful in segmenting international markets.

5. Understand the important new terms (shown in red).

International markets offer new opportunities.

Twenty years ago, when many small American companies were content to build their businesses in the huge U.S. market, marketing managers at H. B. Fuller Co. saw international markets as an opportunity—and also as a matter of survival. It was hard for their small firm, a producer of paints, adhesives, and industrial coatings, to compete against giant suppliers like Du Pont and Dow Chemical for a larger share of the U.S. market. Fuller's marketing managers didn't want to diversify into some other business, so they decided to go where the competition wasn't. They quickly found that developing a competitive advantage with overseas customers required constant sales and service contacts. So instead of exporting from the United States, Fuller now produces customized products in plants run by local people in 27 countries across Latin America, Europe, and Asia. That allows the company to be close to its customers and to deliver products quickly. The effort has not been without problems. For example, in 1979 a group of revolutionaries burned down the Fuller plant in Nicaragua. Even so, targeting international opportunities has been worth the effort. The company's sales have grown to over $500 million, and foreign business accounts for half of its profit.[1]

Procter & Gamble sells its products in 140 countries. Overseas markets account for more than a third of its sales. But success did not come easily. In fact, P&G initially piled up losses because marketing managers failed to see important cultural differences. For example, when they first tried to sell the U.S. version of Cheer to Japanese consumers they promoted it as an effective "all temperature" laundry detergent. The problem was that many Japanese wash clothes in cold tap water or leftover bath water—so they don't care about all temperature washing. In addition, Cheer didn't make suds when it was used with the fabric softeners that were popular with Japanese consumers. When P&G's marketing managers discovered these problems, they changed Cheer so it wouldn't be affected by the fabric softeners. They also changed Cheer ads to promise "superior" cleaning *in cold water*. Now Cheer has become one of P&G's best selling products in Japan.[2]

As these cases show, a marketing manager may find exciting opportunities in international markets. Moreover, the same ideas we have been discussing throughout this book apply to international markets. But planning strategies for international markets can be even harder than for domestic markets. Cultural differences are more important and the other uncontrollable variables may vary more. Each foreign market may need to be treated as a separate market—with its own submarkets. Simply lumping together all people outside the United States as "foreigners"—or assuming they are just like U.S. customers—almost guarantees failure.

Too much stereotyped thinking is applied to international marketing: "We wouldn't want to risk putting a plant over there and then having it nationalized," or "Fighting all that 'red tape' would be too much trouble," or "It sold here—it'll sell there" or "Just have the ad put into Spanish (or French, or German or—) and run it in all the papers."

In this chapter, we try to get rid of some of these misconceptions. And we discuss how firms have to adjust their marketing strategy planning when they go into international marketing. We'll see that a marketing manager must make several strategy decisions about international marketing: (1) whether the firm even wants to work in international markets at all and, if so, its degree of involvement, (2) in which markets, and (3) what organizational arrangements should be made to do so. See Exhibit 22–1.

Let's look first at how important international marketing is. Then we'll consider the strategy decisions a marketing manager must make when planning strategies for international markets.

THE IMPORTANCE OF INTERNATIONAL MARKETS

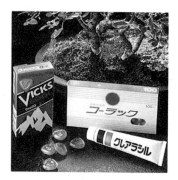

International markets are very important to the United States—and to many U.S. firms. There are many opportunities outside this country. In fact, many firms are finding that their *best opportunities* are in international markets that they were not even considering five years ago.

Many U.S. producers are already deeply involved in international marketing—nearly 5 million U.S. jobs are related to the export of manufactured products. Some U.S. companies earn more abroad than they do in the United States. For example Colgate-Palmolive Co. does 68 percent of its business overseas and Johnson & Johnson and Gillette earn more than 40 percent of their profits from international operations. Many service firms—such as banks and other financial institutions, travel businesses, and entertainment companies—are also building

Exhibit 22–1   Strategy Decisions about International Marketing

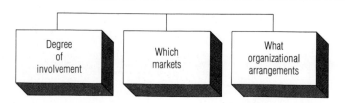

profits in overseas markets. Large corporations are not the only ones involved. There are now about 100,000 U.S. firms that are doing business overseas. And increased attention to international opportunities means that many more firms are likely to move in that direction soon.[3]

As a nation grows, its trade grows

All countries trade to some extent—we live in an interdependent world. In general, trade expands as a country develops and industrializes. The largest traders are highly developed nations. For example, the United States, Japan, and West Germany are the largest exporters. In combination, exports from these three countries account for about 40 percent of world trade in manufactured goods. The United States exports about 20 percent of all its manufactured goods and 40 percent of all agricultural output. In addition, the United States imports about 18 percent of the goods traded among countries.[4]

The largest changes in world trade are usually seen in rapidly developing economies. Over the last decade, for example, exports from Hong Kong, Taiwan, and Singapore have risen dramatically.

WHY BOTHER WITH INTERNATIONAL MARKETS?

It's easy for a marketing manager to fall into the trap of forgetting about international markets. After all, the United States is one of the most prosperous markets in the world. Why go to the trouble of looking elsewhere for opportunities?

The world is getting smaller

The answer to that question is important. The world is getting smaller. Advances in communications and transportation are making it easier to reach international customers. Product-market opportunities are often no more limited by national boundaries than they are by state lines within the United States. Around the

Pepsi sees new opportunities for growth—and a new life cycle in Thailand.

world there are potential customers with needs and money to spend. Ignoring those customers doesn't make any more sense than ignoring potential customers in the same town. The real question is whether the firm can effectively use its resources to meet customers' needs at a profit.

New markets may have new product life cycles

International expansion sometimes offers the firm a way to extend its product life cycle. You already know that profits from a product-market ultimately decline as growth slows. But the same product may be at different life cycle stages in different markets. That is good motivation to consider potential markets in other countries, especially if the product life cycle is not as far along and the marketing manager can "transfer" marketing know-how—or some other competitive advantage—it has already developed. The marketing manager who carefully looks for those opportunities overseas often finds them. Different countries are at different stages of economic and technological development, and their consumers have different needs at different times.

Develop an advantage at home and abroad

Regardless of the life cycle stage, if overseas customers are interested in the products a firm offers—or could offer—serving them may make it possible to lower costs by achieving better economies of scale. And that may give a firm a competitive advantage both in its home markets *and* abroad. This sort of competitive pressure may actually *force* a marketing manager to expand into international markets. A marketing manager who is only interested in the "convenient" customers in his own backyard may be rudely surprised to find that an aggressive, low-cost foreign producer is willing to pursue those customers—even if doing it is not convenient. Many companies that thought they could avoid the struggles of international competition have learned this lesson the hard way.

Find better trends in uncontrollable variables

Unfavorable trends in the uncontrollable variables at home—or favorable trends in other countries—may make international marketing particularly attractive. For example, population growth in the United States has slowed and income is also leveling off. In most other places in the world, population is increasing rapidly and income is increasing. Marketing managers will not be able to rely on the constant market growth that drove increased sales in the United States during the last 30 years. For many firms, growth—and perhaps even survival—will come only by taking aim at more distant customers.

Our point here is basic. In today's world, it doesn't make sense to ignore international markets and casually assume that all of the best opportunities are "at home." Careful analysis of all of the facts may lead to that conclusion. But not stopping to consider international opportunities can be a costly mistake.

DEGREES OF INVOLVEMENT IN INTERNATIONAL MARKETING

Attractive opportunities in foreign countries have led many firms into international marketing, and varying degrees of involvement are possible. We will discuss six basic kinds of involvement—as shown in Exhibit 22–2—exporting, licensing, contract manufacturing, management contracting, joint venturing, and wholly-owned subsidiaries. Let's look at these possibilities.

Exporting often comes first

Some companies get into international marketing just by **exporting**—selling some of what the firm is producing to foreign markets. Some firms start exporting

Exhibit 22–2   Kinds of Involvement in International Marketing that a Marketing Manager Can Choose

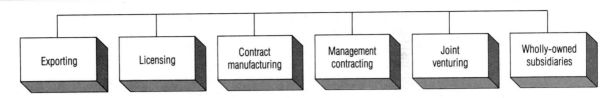

| Exporting | Licensing | Contract manufacturing | Management contracting | Joint venturing | Wholly-owned subsidiaries |

just to "get rid of" surplus output. For others, exporting comes from a real effort to look for new opportunities.

Some firms try exporting without changing the product—or even the service or instruction manuals! As a result, some early efforts are not very satisfying—to buyers or sellers. When Toyota first exported cars to the United States, the effort was a failure. Americans were not at all interested in the Toyota model that sold well in Japan. Toyota tried again three years later with a new design—and a new marketing mix. This second effort was a real success.[5]

Specialists can cut through red tape

Exporting does involve some government "red tape"—but firms can learn to handle it fairly quickly. Or that job can be turned over to middleman specialists. Export agents can handle the paperwork as the products are shipped outside the country. Then agents or merchant wholesalers can handle the importing details. Even large producers with many foreign operations use international middlemen for some products or markets. Such middlemen know how to handle the sometimes confusing formalities and specialized functions. Even a small mistake can tie products up at national borders for days—or months.[6]

Exporting doesn't have to involve permanent relationships. Of course, channel relationships take time to build and shouldn't be treated lightly—sales reps' con-

Exporting is often the first step into international marketing.

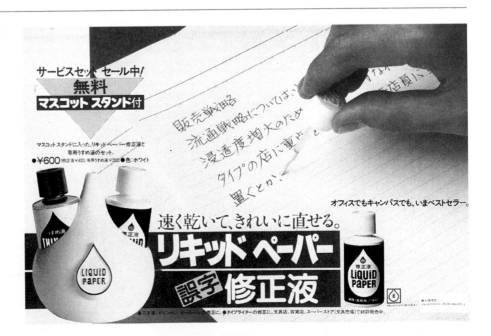

tacts in foreign countries are "investments." But it's relatively easy to cut back on these relationships—or even drop them.

Some firms, on the other hand, develop more formal and permanent relationships with nationals in foreign countries—including licensing, contract manufacturing, management contracting, and joint venturing.

Licensing is an easy way

Licensing is a relatively easy way to enter foreign markets. **Licensing** means selling the right to use some process, trademark, patent, or other right for a fee or royalty. The licensee takes most of the risk because it must invest some capital to use the right.

This can be an effective way of entering a market if good partners are available. Gerber entered the Japanese baby food market this way but still exports to other countries.[7]

Contract manufacturing takes care of the production problems

Contract manufacturing means turning over production to others while retaining the marketing process. Sears used this approach as it opened stores in Latin America and Spain.

This approach can be especially desirable where labor relations are difficult or where there are problems obtaining supplies and "buying" government cooperation. Growing nationalistic feelings may make this approach more attractive in the future.

Management contracting sells know-how

Management contracting means the seller provides only management skills—others own the production facilities. Some mines and oil refineries are operated this way—and Hilton operates hotels all over the world for local owners. This is a relatively low-risk approach to international marketing. The company makes no commitment to fixed facilities—which can be taken over or damaged in riots or wars. If conditions get too bad, key management people can fly off on the next plane—and leave the nationals to manage the operation.

Joint venturing is more involved

Joint venturing means a domestic firm entering into a partnership with a foreign firm. As with any partnership, there can be honest disagreements over objectives—for example, about how much profit is desired and how fast it should

Gillette recently established a joint venture near New Delhi, India.

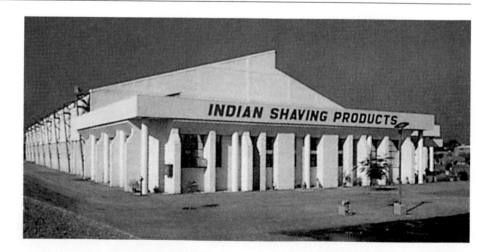

be paid out—as well as operating policies. Where a close working relationship can be developed—perhaps based on a U.S. firm's technical and marketing know-how and the foreign partner's knowledge of the market and political connections—this approach can be very attractive to both parties.

In some situations, a joint venture is the only type of involvement that is possible. For example, IBM wanted to increase its 2 percent share of the $1 billion a year that industrial customers in Brazil spend on data processing services. But a Brazilian law severely limited expansion by foreign computer companies. To be able to grow, IBM had to develop a joint venture with a Brazilian firm. Because of Brazilian laws, IBM could own only a 30 percent interest in the joint venture. But IBM decided it was better to have a 30 percent share of a business—and be able to pursue new market opportunities—than to stand by and watch competitors take the market.[8]

A joint venture usually requires a big commitment from both parties. When the relationship doesn't work out well it can be a nightmare that causes the U.S. firm to want to go into a wholly-owned operation. But the terms of the joint venture may block this for years.[9]

Wholly-owned subsidiaries give more control

When a firm feels that a foreign market looks really promising, it may want to take the final step. A **wholly-owned subsidiary** is a separate firm—owned by a parent company. This gives complete control and helps a foreign branch work more easily with the rest of the company.

Some multinational companies have gone this way. It gives them a great deal of freedom to move products from one country to another. If a firm has too much capacity in a country with low production costs, for example, it can move some production there from other plants and then export to countries with higher production costs. This is the same way that large firms in the United States ship products from one area to another—depending on costs and local needs.

MULTINATIONAL CORPORATIONS EVOLVE TO MEET INTERNATIONAL CHALLENGE

Multinational corporations have a direct investment in several countries and run their businesses depending on the choices available anywhere in the world. Well-known U.S.-based multinational firms include Coca-Cola, Eastman Kodak, Warner-Lambert, Pfizer, Anaconda, Goodyear, Ford, IBM, ITT, Corn Products, 3M, National Cash Register, and H. J. Heinz. They regularly earn over a third of their total sales or profits abroad.[10]

Many multinational companies are American. But there are also many well-known foreign-based companies—such as Nestle, Shell (Royal Dutch Shell), Lever Brothers (Unilever), Sony, and Honda. They have well-accepted "foreign" brands—not only in the United States, but around the world.

Multinational operations make sense to more firms

As firms become more involved in international marketing, some reach the point where the firm sees itself as a worldwide business. As a chief executive of Abbott Laboratories—a pharmaceutical company with plants all over the world—said, "We are no longer just a U.S. company with interests abroad. Abbott is a worldwide enterprise, and many major decisions must be made on a global basis."

Multinational corporations transcend national boundaries to seek market opportunities around the world.

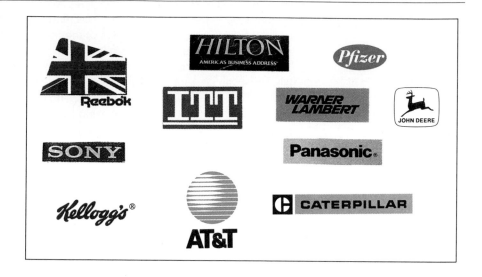

Much of the multinational activity in the 1960s and early 70s was U.S.-based firms expanding to other countries. As these opportunities became less attractive in the mid-1970s—due to the energy crisis, inflation, currency devaluations, labor unrest, and unstable governments—foreign multinational companies started to move into the United States. The United States is, after all, one of the richest markets in the world.

Foreign firms are beginning to see that it may be attractive to operate in this large—if competitive—market. The Japanese entry into the field of electronic products is well known. The Japanese are building plants here, too. Sony has had a TV plant in southern California since 1972. And Honda makes cars in Ohio. Kagome, the leading brand of ketchup in Japan, has even set up a factory in California to produce ketchup for export to consumers back in Japan.[11]

One reason for the movement of some multinational firms into the United States is that labor costs in their own countries (including Japan) are rising. Considering the total cost—including transportation costs—it may be more economical to produce products for the U.S. market here.

Multinational companies overcome national boundaries

From an international view, multinational firms do—as a GM manager said—"transcend national boundaries." They see world market opportunities and locate their production and distribution facilities for greatest effectiveness. This has upset some nationalistic business managers and politicians. But these multinational operations may be hard to stop. They are no longer just exporting or importing. They hire local workers—and build local plants. They have business relationships with local business managers and politicians. These are powerful organizations. And they have learned to deal with nationalistic feelings and typical border barriers— treating them simply as uncontrollable variables.

We don't have "one world" politically as yet—but business is moving in that direction. We may have to develop new kinds of corporations and laws to govern multinational operations. In the future, it will make less and less sense for business and politics to be limited by national boundaries.

Cybex Flexes Its Marketing Muscle

Many Americans are fanatics about staying in shape. The rapid growth of the "fitness" market in the United States created many opportunities—and attracted attention from companies as varied as Nike, Schwinn, Nautilus, and General Nutrition Corporation. Now that growth in the U.S. fitness market has slowed, many marketing managers who had been competing for consumers' fitness dollars are seeking new opportunities.

Many of those opportunities are in other countries—where interest in health and fitness started later. That's not news to Cybex, a company that sells Nautilus-like exercise equipment, including some high-tech units that hook up to computers to analyze lower back muscle injuries. Cybex has a head start in taking advantage of the growth in overseas markets. During the 1980s, Cybex exports grew an average of 40 percent a year. It now sells about $5 million worth of equipment in 30 foreign markets, and it hopes to increase its exports from 13 percent to 23 percent of sales in the next few years.

To get that increase, Cybex has a director of international marketing and its own international sales staff of 14 people who speak seven languages. With help from middlemen who specialize in international trade, they are selling Cybex's specialized $40,000 products in markets, like Japan, where customers have never before paid more than $3,000 for fitness equipment.

At a time when many major manufacturers of such goods as chemicals and paper appear to have reached an export plateau, Cybex is but one of about 10,000 smaller U.S. firms whose foreign sales are growing rapidly. Some experts think that this broad base of interest will help to keep growth in U.S. exports strong.[12]

IDENTIFYING DIFFERENT KINDS OF INTERNATIONAL OPPORTUNITIES

Firms usually start from where they are

A multinational firm that has accepted the marketing concept looks for opportunities in the same way we've been discussing throughout the text. That is, it looks for unsatisfied needs that it might be able to satisfy given its resources and objectives.

The typical approach is to start with the firm's current products and the needs it knows how to satisfy, and then try to find new markets—wherever they may be—for the same or similar unsatisfied needs. Next, the firm might adapt the Promotion, and then the Product. Later, the firm might think about developing new products and new promotion policies. Some of these possibilities are shown in Exhibit 22–3. Here, the emphasis is on Product and Promotion. But Place obviously has to be changed for new markets—and Price adjustments probably would be needed, too.

The "Same-Same" box in Exhibit 22–3 can be illustrated with McDonald's (the fast-food chain) entry into European markets. As McDonald's director of international marketing said, "Our target audience is the same worldwide—young families with children—and our advertising is designed to appeal to them." The basic promotion messages must be translated, of course. But the company applies the same strategy decisions that it made for the U.S. market. McDonald's has adapted its Product in Germany, however, by adding beer to appeal to adults who prefer beer to soft drinks. Its efforts have been extremely successful so far.[13]

Exhibit 22–3 International Marketing Opportunities as Seen by a U.S. Firm from the Viewpoint of Its Usual Product-Market in the United States

		Product		
		Same	**Adaptation**	**New**
Promotion	**Same**	Same needs and use conditions (McDonald's usual strategy)	Basically same needs and use conditions (McDonald's strategy with beer in Germany)	Basically same needs, but different incomes and/or applications (street vendor with low-cost hamburgers)
	Adaptation	Different needs but same use conditions (bicycles)	Different needs and use conditions (clothing)	Different needs and different incomes and/or applications (hand-powered washing machines)

McDonald's and other firms expanding into international markets usually move first into markets with good economic potential—such as Western Europe and Japan. But if McDonald's or some other fast-food company wanted to move into much lower-income areas, it might have to develop a whole new Product—perhaps a traveling street vendor with "hamburgers" made from soybean products. This kind of opportunity is in the upper right-hand corner of Exhibit 22–3.

The lower left-hand box in this exhibit is illustrated by the different kinds of Promotion needed for a simple bicycle. In some parts of the world, bicycles provide basic transportation, while in the United States people use them mainly for recreation. So a different Promotion emphasis is needed in these different target markets.

Both Product and Promotion changes are needed as we move to the right along the bottom row of Exhibit 22–3. Such moves increase the risk—and obviously require more market knowledge.

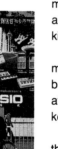

The risk of opportunities varies by environmental sensitivity

International marketing often means going into unfamiliar markets. This can increase risk. The farther you go from familiar territory, the greater the chance of making big mistakes. But not all products offer the same risk. Think of the risks running along a "continuum of environmental sensitivity." See Exhibit 22–4. Some products are relatively insensitive to the economic or cultural environment they're placed in. These products may be accepted as is—or they may require just a little adaptation to make them suitable for local use. Most industrial products are near the insensitive end of this continuum.

At the other end of the continuum, we find highly sensitive products that may be difficult or impossible to adapt to all international situations. At this end are "faddy" or high-style consumer products. It's sometimes difficult to understand why a par-

Exhibit 22–4   Continuum of Environmental Sensitivity

Insensitive		Sensitive
Industrial products	Basic commodity-type consumer products	Faddy or high-style consumer products

ticular product is well accepted in a home market. This, in turn, makes it even more difficult to predict how it might be received in a different environment.

This continuum helps explain why many of the early successes in international marketing were basic commodities such as gasoline, soap, transportation vehicles, mining equipment, and agricultural machinery. It also helps explain why some consumer products firms have been successful with the same promotion and products in different parts of the globe.

Yet some managers don't understand the reason for these successes. They think that a "global" marketing mix can be developed for just about *any* product. They fail to see that firms producing and/or selling products near the sensitive end of the continuum should carefully analyze how their products will be seen and used in new environments—and plan their strategies accordingly.[14] American-made blue jeans, for example, have been "status symbols" in Western Europe and Latin America—and producers have been able to sell them at premium prices through the "best" middlemen.

IBM products meet the same basic needs in different markets around the world.

**Evaluating opportunities
in possible international
markets**

Judging opportunities in international markets uses the same ideas we've been discussing throughout this text. Basically, each opportunity must be evaluated considering the uncontrollable variables. But in international markets there may be more of these—and they may be harder to evaluate. Estimating the risk involved in particular opportunities may be very difficult. Some countries are not as politically stable as the United States. Their governments and constitutions come and go. An investment that was safe under one government might become the target for a take-over under another. Further, the possibility of foreign exchange controls—and tax rate changes—can reduce the chance of getting profits and capital back to the home country.[15]

Because the risks are hard to judge, it may be wise to enter international marketing by exporting first—building know-how and confidence over time. Experience and judgment are even more important in unfamiliar areas. Allowing time to develop these skills among a firm's top management—as well as its international managers—makes sense. Then the firm will be in a better position to judge the prospects and risks of going further into international marketing.

INTERNATIONAL MARKETING REQUIRES EVEN MORE SEGMENTING

Success in international marketing requires even more attention to segmenting. There are over 140 nations with their own unique differences! There can be big differences in language, customs, beliefs, religions, race, and income distribution patterns from one country to another. This obviously complicates the segmenting process. But what makes it even worse is that there is less dependable data as firms move into international markets. While the number of variables increases, the quantity and quality of data go down. This is one reason why some multinational firms insist that local operations be handled by natives. They, at least, have a "feel" for their markets.

**There are more
dimensions—but there
is a way**

Segmenting international markets may require more dimensions. But a practical method adds just one step before the seven-step approach discussed in Chapter 3. See Exhibit 22–5. First, segment by country or region—looking at demographic, cultural, and other characteristics, including stage of economic development. This may help find reasonably similar submarkets. Then—depending on whether the firm is aiming at final consumers or intermediate customers—apply the seven-step approach discussed earlier.

In the rest of this chapter we'll emphasize final consumer differences, because they are likely to be greater than intermediate customer differences. Also, we'll consider regional groupings and stages of economic development—which can aid your segmenting.

REGIONAL GROUPINGS MAY MEAN MORE THAN NATIONAL BOUNDARIES

Consumers in the same country often share a common culture, and other uncontrollable variables may be homogeneous. For this reason it may be logical to treat consumers' countries as a dimension for segmenting markets. But sometimes it makes more sense to treat several nearby countries with similar cultures as one

Exhibit 22–5   Segementing in International Markets

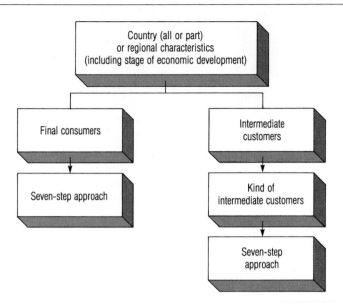

region—Central America or Latin America, for example. Or several nations that have banded together to have common economic boundaries can be treated as a unit. The outstanding example is the movement toward economic unification of the 12 European Community (EC) countries. See Exhibit 22–6.

Unification of Europe in 1992

The countries that form the European Community have dared to abandon old squabbles and nationalistic prejudices in favor of cooperative efforts to reduce taxes and other controls commonly applied at national boundaries.

Exhibit 22–6   Twelve Member Countries of the European Community

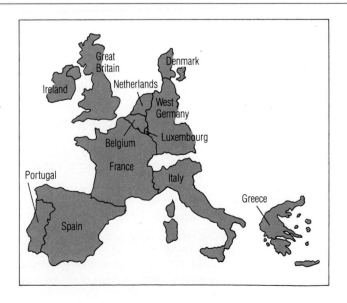

In the past, each country has had its own trade rules and regulations. These differences made it difficult to move products from one country to the other—or to develop economies of scale. Now, a commission with representatives from each nation has developed a plan to reshape the individual countries into a unified economic superpower—what some have called the "United States of Europe."

The plan, which will be nearly complete by the end of 1992, will eliminate nearly 300 separate barriers to inter-European trade. Trucks will be able to move from Denmark to Belgium and dentists from Belgium to Greece. Products will spill across the European continent and Britain. The increased efficiency that comes from eliminating these barriers is expected to cut consumer prices in Europe by 6 percent and create 5 million new jobs.

What's more, with 320 million prospering consumers, Europe will become the world's richest market. Of course, centuries of cultural differences will not instantly disappear at the end of 1992—and they may never disappear. So removal of economic barriers will not eliminate the need to adjust strategies to reach submarkets of European consumers. Yet, the cooperative arrangement will give firms that operate in Europe easier access to larger markets, and the European countries will have a more powerful voice in protecting their own interests.[16]

Tariffs and quotas may reduce marketing opportunities

These cooperative arrangements are very important. Taxes and restrictions at national or regional borders are not only annoying but also can greatly reduce marketing opportunities. **Tariffs**—taxes on imported products—vary, depending on whether the country is trying to raise revenue or limit trade. Restrictive tariffs often block all movement. But even revenue-producing tariffs cause red tape and discourage free movement of products.

Quotas act like restrictive tariffs. **Quotas** set the specific quantities of products that can move into or out of a country. Great market opportunities may exist in a unified Europe, for example, but import quotas (or export controls applied against a specific country) may discourage outsiders from entering.

The impact of such restrictions can be seen in South Korea. When Ford Motor Co. introduced the Mercury Sable, Korean trade restrictions blocked Ford from selling the Sable there. In late 1987, Korea lifted the restrictions. In their place, however, the Korean government imposed special taxes and tariffs. As a result, a 1988 Sable that sold for $14,800 in the United States cost $44,400 in Korea—and very few Korean consumers were willing or able to pay that much for a Sable.

Trade restrictions can be a potential source of conflict between nations. For example, in 1988 the U.S. government charged Japan, Brazil, and India with "unfair" trading practices that restricted opportunities for U.S. firms. Of course, the United States has also worked to control Japan's export of cars into the country. (Otherwise, we would have had even more Japanese cars entering the U.S. market!)[17]

STAGES OF ECONOMIC DEVELOPMENT HELP DEFINE MARKETS

International markets vary widely—within and between countries. Some markets are more advanced and/or growing more rapidly than others. And some countries—or parts of a country—are at different stages of economic development. This means their demands—and even their marketing systems—vary.

To get some idea of the many possible differences in potential markets—and how they affect strategy planning—we'll discuss six stages of economic develop-

Mexico hopes to attract investment from multinational companies to help speed economic development.

ment. These stages are helpful, but they greatly oversimplify the real world for two reasons. First, different parts of the same country may be at different stages of development—so it isn't possible to identify a single country or region with only one stage. Second, some countries skip one or two stages due to investment from multinational companies or from their own eager governments. For example, the building of uneconomical steel mills to boost national pride—or the arrival of multi-national car producers—might lead to a big jump in stages. This "stage-jumping" does not destroy the six-stage process—it just explains why more rapid movements take place in some situations.

Stage 1—Self-supporting agriculture

In this stage, most people are subsistence farmers. There may be a simple marketing system—perhaps weekly markets—but most of the people are not even in a money economy. Some parts of Africa and New Guinea are in this stage. In a practical marketing sense, these people are not a market because they have no money to buy products.

Stage 2—Preindustrial or commercial

Some countries in sub-Saharan Africa and the Middle East are in this second stage. During this stage, we see more market-oriented activity. Raw materials such as oil, tin, and copper are extracted and exported. Agricultural and forest crops such as sugar, rubber, and timber are grown and exported. Often this is done with the help of foreign technical skills and capital. A commercial economy may develop along with—but unrelated to—the subsistence economy. These activities may re-quire the beginnings of a transportation system to tie the extracting or growing areas to shipping points. A money economy operates in this stage.

Industrial machinery and equipment are imported. And huge construction projects may import component materials and supplies. Such countries also need imports—including luxury products—to meet the living standards of technical and supervisory people. These items may be handled by company stores rather than local retailers.

The few large landowners—and those who benefit by this new business activity—may develop expensive tastes. The few natives employed by these larger firms—and the small business managers who serve them—may form a small, middle-income class. But most of the population is still in the first stage—for practical purposes, they are not in the market. The total market in Stage 2 may be so small that local importers can easily handle the demand. There is little reason for local producers to try to supply it.

Stage 3—Primary manufacturing

In this third stage, there is some processing of the metal ores or agricultural products that once were shipped out of the country in raw form. Sugar and rubber, for example, are both produced and processed in Indonesia. The same is true for oil in the Persian Gulf. Multinational companies may set up factories to take advantage of low-cost labor. They may export most of the output, but they do stimulate local development. More local labor becomes involved in this stage. A domestic market develops. Small local businesses start to handle some of the raw material processing.

Even though the local market expands in this third stage, a large part of the population is still at the subsistence level—almost entirely outside the money economy. But a large foreign population of professionals and technicians may still be needed to run the developing agricultural-industrial complex. The demands of this group—and the growing number of wealthy natives—are still quite different from the needs of the lower class and the growing middle class. A domestic market among the local people begins to develop. But local producers still may have trouble finding enough demand to keep them in business.

Stage 4—Nondurable and semidurable consumer products manufacturing

At this stage, small local manufacturing begins—especially in those lines that need only a small investment to get started. Often, these industries grow out of small firms that developed to supply the processors dominating the last stage. For example, plants making sulfuric acid and explosives for extracting mineral resources might expand into soap manufacturing. And recently, multinational firms have speeded development of countries in this stage by investing in promising opportunities.

Paint, drug, food and beverage, and textile industries develop in this stage. Because clothing is a necessity, the textile industry is usually one of the first to develop. This early emphasis on the textile industry in developing nations is one reason the world textile market is so competitive.

Some of the small producers become members of the middle- or even upper-income class. They help to expand the demand for imported products. As this market grows, local businesses begin to see enough volume to operate profitably. So there is less need for imports to supply nondurable and semidurable products. But consumer durables and capital equipment are still imported.

Stage 5—Capital equipment and consumer durable products manufacturing

In this stage, the production of capital equipment and consumer durable products begins—including cars, refrigerators, and machinery for local industries. Such manufacturing creates other demands—raw materials for the local factories, and food and fibers for clothing for the rural population entering the industrial labor force.

Industrialization has begun. But the economy still depends on exports of raw materials—either wholly unprocessed or slightly processed.

Japan—like the United States—is at the stage of economic development where exporting manufactured products is important.

The country may still have to import special heavy machinery and equipment in this stage. Imports of consumer durables may still compete with local products. The foreign community and the status-conscious wealthy may prefer these imports.

Stage 6—Exporting manufactured products

Countries that have not gone beyond the fifth stage are mainly exporters of raw materials. They import manufactured products to build their industrial base. In the sixth stage, exporting manufactured products becomes most important. The country specializes in certain types of manufactured products—such as iron and steel, watches, cameras, electronic equipment, and processed food.

Many opportunities for importing and exporting exist at this stage. These countries have grown richer and have needs—and the purchasing power—for a wide variety of products. In fact, countries in this stage often carry on a great deal of trade with each other. Each trades those products in which it has production advantages. In this stage, almost all consumers are in the money economy. And there may be a large middle-income class. The United States, most of the Western European countries, and Japan are at this last stage.[18]

It is important to see that it is not necessary to label a whole country or geographic region as being in one stage. In fact, different parts of the United States have developed differently and are in different stages.

HOW THESE STAGES CAN BE USEFUL IN FINDING MARKET OPPORTUNITIES

A good starting point for estimating present and future market potentials in a country—or part of a country—is to estimate its present stage of economic development and how fast it's moving to another stage. The speed of movement, if any, and the possibility that stages may be skipped may suggest whether market opportunities exist—or are likely to open. But just naming the present stage can be very useful in deciding what to look at and whether there are prospects for the firm's products.

Fitting the firm to market needs

Producers of cars, expensive cameras, or other consumer durables, for example, should not plan to set up a mass distribution system in an area that is in Stage 2 (preindustrial) or even Stage 3 (primary manufacturing). Widespread selling of these consumer items requires a large base of cash or credit customers— and as yet too few people are part of the money economy.

On the other hand, a market in the nondurable products manufacturing stage (Stage 4) has more potential—especially for durable products producers. Incomes and the number of potential customers are growing. There is no local competition yet.

Opportunities might still be good for durable products imports in Stage 5—even though domestic producers are trying to get started. But more likely, the local government will raise some controls to aid local industry. Then the foreign producer has to license local producers—or build a local plant.

Pursuing that tempting mass market

Areas or countries in the final stage often are the biggest and most profitable markets. While there may be more competition, many more customers have higher incomes. We've already seen how income distribution shifted in the United States—leading to more families with middle and upper incomes. This should be expected during the latter stages—when a "mass market" develops.

OTHER MARKET DIMENSIONS MAY SUGGEST OPPORTUNITIES, TOO

Considering country or regional differences—including stages of economic development—can be useful as a first step in segmenting international markets. After finding some possible areas (and eliminating unattractive ones), we must look at more specific market characteristics.

We discussed potential dimensions in the U.S. market. It's impossible to cover all possible dimensions in all world markets. But many of the ideas discussed for the United States certainly apply in other countries, too. So here we'll outline some dimensions of international markets—and we'll show some examples to emphasize that depending on half-truths about "foreigners" won't work in increasingly competitive international markets.

Where the people are

Although our cities may seem crowded with people, the U.S. population is less than 5 percent of the world's population—which is over 5 billion. A map of the world redrawn to show land area in proportion to population makes the United States seem unimportant. See Exhibit 22–7. This is also true of Latin America and Africa. In contrast, Western Europe is much larger. India (with a population of over 800 million) and China (with a population over a billion) are even larger. You can see why many firms are interested in these markets.

People everywhere are moving off the farm and into industrial and urban areas. Shifts in population—combined with already dense populations—have led to extreme crowding in some parts of the world. And the crowding is likely to continue to get worse. By the year 2010, it is expected that more than 50 percent of the world's population will live in urban areas.

Exhibit 22–7   Map of the World Showing Area in Proportion to Population

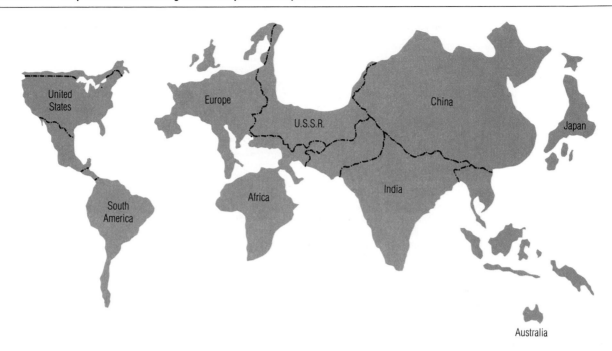

In addition, birth rates in most parts of the world are high—higher in Africa, Latin America, Asia, Australia, and New Zealand than in the United States. And death rates are declining as modern medicine is more widely accepted. Generally, population growth is expected in most countries. But the big questions are: How rapidly?—and—Will output increase faster than population? This is important to marketers. It affects how rapidly these countries move to higher stages of development and become new markets for different kinds of products.

You must sell where the income is

Profitable markets require income—as well as people. The best available measure of income in most countries is **gross national product (GNP)**—the total market value of goods and services produced in a year. Unfortunately, this may not give a true picture of consumer well-being in many countries because the method commonly used for figuring GNP may not be accurate for very different cultures and economies. For instance, do-it-yourself activities, household services, and the growing of produce or meat by family members for their own use are not usually figured as part of GNP. Since the activities of self-sufficient family units are not included, GNP can give a false picture of economic well-being in less-developed countries. At the other extreme, GNP may not do a good job measuring service-oriented output in highly developed economies.

But gross national product *is* useful—and sometimes it's the only available measure of market potential. The countries with the largest GNPs are shown in Exhibit 22–8. The Soviet Union and its allies are not listed because reliable data are not available. You can see that the more developed industrial nations have the biggest share of the world's GNP. This is why so much trade takes place between these countries—and why many companies see them as the more important markets.[19]

Income per person can be more helpful

GNP per person is a useful figure because it gives some idea of the income level of people in a country. See Exhibit 22–8. But GNP per person can be a mis-

Exhibit 22–8   Countries with the Largest GNP

Country	1988 GNP in billions of U.S. dollars	Population (in millions)	GNP per person
United States	$4,864.3	246.5	$19,733
Japan	2,858.9	122.6	23,318
West Germany	1,208.3	60.6	19,938
France*	945.9	55.9	16,921
Italy*	828.8	57.4	14,439
Britain*	812.1	56.9	14,272
Canada*	486.5	25.9	18,783
Brazil*	384.6	144.5	2,661
China*	370.6	1,085.3	341
Spain*	342.3	39.0	8,776
Iran*	338.4	52.9	6,396
India*	283.8	801.5	354
Australia*	246.0	16.6	14,819
Netherlands	230.2	14.7	15,659
Switzerland*	184.8	6.6	28,000
Mexico*	181.2	84.0	2,157
Sweden*	178.5	8.4	21,250
South Korea*	164.6	42.7	3,854
Belgium	152.0	9.9	16,888
Austria*	126.6	7.6	16,657
Taiwan*	116.2	19.9	5,839
Denmark*	107.8	5.1	21,137
Finland*	104.2	4.9	21,265
Norway*	88.1	4.2	20,976
Saudi Arabia*	74.5	12.9	5,775

*Note: Data for these countries excludes net income earned from abroad.

leading estimate of market potential. When GNP per person is used for comparison, we assume that the wealth of each country is distributed evenly among all consumers. This is seldom true. In a developing economy, 75 percent of the population may be on farms and receive 25 percent or less of the income. And there may be unequal distribution along class or racial lines.

A business, and a human opportunity

It is important to keep in mind that much of the world's population lives in extreme poverty. Even among the countries with the largest overall GNPs you see some sign of this. In India, for example, the GNP per person is only $354 a year. Many countries are in the early stages of economic development. Most of their people work on farms—and live barely within the money economy. At the extreme, in Ethiopia the GNP per person per year is only about $132 (in U.S. dollars).

These people, however, have needs. And many are eager to improve themselves. But they may not be able to raise their living standards without outside help. This presents a challenge and an opportunity to the developed nations—and to their business firms.

Some companies—including American firms—are trying to help the people of less-developed countries. Corporations such as Pillsbury, Corn Products, Monsanto, and Coca-Cola have developed nutritious foods that can be sold cheaply—but still profitably—in poorer countries. One firm sells a milk-based drink

(Samson)—with 10 grams of protein per serving—to the Middle East and the Caribbean areas. Such a drink can make an important addition to diets. Poor people in less-developed lands usually get only 8 to 12 grams of protein per day in their normal diet, while 60 to 75 grams per day are considered necessary for an adult.[20]

Reading, writing, and marketing problems

The ability of a country's people to read and write has a direct influence on the development of the economy—and on marketing strategy planning. The degree of literacy affects the way information is delivered—which in marketing means promotion. Unfortunately, only about two thirds of the world's population can read and write.

Low literacy sometimes causes difficulties with product labels and instructions—for which we normally use words. In highly illiterate countries, some producers found that placing a baby's picture on food packages is unwise. Natives believed that the product was just that—a ground-up baby! Singer Sewing Machine Company met this lack of literacy with an instruction book that used pictures instead of words.

Even in Latin America—which has generally higher literacy rates than Africa or Asia—a large number of people cannot read and write. Marketers have to use symbols, colors, and other nonverbal means of communication if they want to reach the masses.

ORGANIZING FOR INTERNATIONAL MARKETING

Until a firm develops a truly worldwide view of its operations, it should have someone in charge of international matters. The basic concern should be to see that the firm transfers its domestic know-how into international operations.

Organization should transfer know-how

As a firm moves beyond just a few international locations, its managers might want to develop regional groupings—clustering similar countries into groups. This smooths the transfer of know-how among operations in similar environments. Regional groupings may also reduce the cost of supervision.

But regional groups may be less useful than groups based on other relevant dimensions—such as the stage of economic development or language. The important thing is to develop an organization that enables the local managers to control matters that require "local feel" while, at the same time, to share their accumulating experience with colleagues who face similar problems.

Each national market should be thought of as a separate market. And if they are really different from each other, top management should delegate a great deal of responsibility for strategy planning to local managers. In extreme cases, local managers may not even be able to fully explain some parts of their plans because they are based on subtle cultural differences. Then plans must be judged only by their results. The organizational setup should be such that these managers are given a great deal of freedom in their planning—but are tightly controlled against their own plans. Top management can simply insist that managers stick to their budgets and meet the plans that they, themselves, create. When a firm reaches this stage, it is being managed like a well-organized domestic corporation—which insists that its managers (of divisions and territories) meet their own plans, so that the whole company's program works as intended.[21]

CONCLUSION

The international market is large—and it keeps growing in population and income. More American companies are becoming aware of the opportunities open to alert and aggressive businesses.

Involvement in international marketing usually begins with exporting. Then a firm may become involved in joint ventures or wholly-owned subsidiaries in several countries. Companies that become this involved are called multinational corporations. These corporations have a global outlook—and they are willing to move across national boundaries as easily as national firms move across state boundaries.

But markets in different countries vary greatly in stages of economic development, income, population, culture, and other factors. These differences must be studied and carefully considered in developing marketing strategies. Lumping foreign nations together under the common and vague heading of "foreigners"—or, at the other extreme, assuming that they are just like U.S. customers—almost guarantees failure. So does treating them like common Hollywood stereotypes.

Much of what we've said about marketing strategy planning throughout the text applies directly in international marketing. Sometimes Product changes are needed. Promotion messages must be translated into the local languages. And, of course, new Place arrangements and Prices are needed. But blending the four Ps still requires a knowledge of the all-important customer. The major "roadblock" to success in international marketing is an unwillingness to learn about and adjust to different peoples and cultures. To those who are willing to make these adjustments, the returns can be great.

Questions and Problems

1. Discuss the "typical" evolution of corporate involvement in international marketing. What impact would complete acceptance of the marketing concept have on the evolutionary process?

2. Distinguish between licensing and contract manufacturing in a foreign country.

3. Distinguish between joint ventures and wholly-owned subsidiaries.

4. Discuss the long-run prospects for (a) multinational marketing by U.S. firms producing in the United States only and (b) multinational firms willing to operate anywhere.

5. How can a producer interested in finding new international marketing opportunities organize its search process? What kinds of opportunities would it look for first, second, and so on?

6. Discuss how market segmenting (discussed in Chapter 3) might have to be modified when a firm moves into international markets.

7. Explain why tariffs and quotas affect international marketing opportunities.

8. Will the elimination of trade barriers between countries in Europe eliminate the need to consider submarkets of European consumers? Why or why not?

9. Discuss the prospects for a Latin American entrepreneur who is considering building a factory to produce machines that make cans for the food industry. His country is in Stage 4—the nondurable and semidurable consumer products manufacturing stage. The country's population is approximately 20 million, and there is some possibility of establishing sales contacts in a few nearby countries.

10. Discuss the value of gross national product per capita as a measure of market potential. Refer to specific data in your answer.

11. Discuss the possibility of a multinational marketer using the same promotion campaign in the United States and in many international markets.

12. Describe an effective organization for a multinational firm.

Suggested Cases

33. Multifoods, Ltd.

36. Lever, Ltd.

38. Alco Manufacturing Co.

Suggested Computer-Aided Problem

22. Export Opportunities

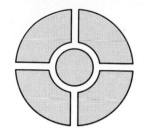

Chapter **23**

Marketing in a Consumer-Oriented Society: Appraisal and Challenges

When You Finish This Chapter, You Should

1. Understand why marketing must be evaluated differently at the micro and macro levels.

2. Understand why the text argues that micro-marketing costs too much.

3. Understand why the text argues that macro-marketing does not cost too much.

4. Know some of the challenges facing marketers in the future.

Does marketing cost too much?

Mikhail S. Gorbachev, the Soviet leader, is pushing for *perestroika*—reforms intended to lead to a more market-driven economy in Russia. There are good reasons for Gorbachev to worry about reforms. The Soviet Union is in serious trouble. Its centrally planned macro-marketing system is not working. There are shortages of basic foods like potatoes, meat, and sugar. Consumers must wait in lines for hours to get a pair of shoes, if shoes are available at all. And the shoes that are available are poor quality. Shortages are so common that about 84 percent of the Soviet population gets the goods they need on the illegal black market. For example, blue jeans are rarely found on the shelves of state stores. They are available on the black market—but the price of 150 rubles is about three weeks' pay for the average Russian worker.[1]

The challenges faced by consumers—and marketing managers—in the United States seem minor in contrast. When we worry about products being available, we are more likely to be worried about "instant gratification." We expect our Domino's Pizza to arrive in less than 30 minutes. We want McDonald's to have our Egg Mc-Muffin ready when we pull up at the "drive-thru" at 7:00 in the morning. We want supermarkets and drugstores handy. And we expect everything from fresh tropical fruits to camera batteries to brand name fashions to be available when—and where—we want them. There are few other places in the world where consumers expect so much—and get so much of what they expect. All of this has a price—and we, as consumers, pay the bill.[2]

When you think about these two cases, it's not hard to decide which set of consumers is better off. But is that just a "straw man" comparison? Is the Soviet situation one extreme, with our system just as extreme—only in a different way? Could we be better off if we were not putting quite so much emphasis on marketing? Do we need so many brands of products? Does money spent on advertising really help consumers? Do middlemen just add to the price consumers pay? In other words, does marketing cost too much? This is a fundamental question. Some people feel strongly that marketing does cost too much—that it's a waste of resources that would be better used elsewhere.

Now that you have a better understanding of what marketing is all about—and how the marketing manager contributes to the *macro*-marketing process—you should be able to consider whether marketing costs too much. That's what this chapter is about.

Your answer is very important. Your own business career and the economy in which you will live will be affected by your answer.

Do car producers, for example, produce lower quality cars than they could? Do producers of food and drug products spend too much money advertising "trivial differences" between their own brands? Should they stop trying to brand their products at all—and instead sell generics at lower prices? Does marketing encourage us to want "too much" of the wrong products? Are there too many retailers and wholesalers—all taking "too big" markups? Some critics of marketing would answer Yes! to *all* these important questions. Such critics believe we should change our political and legal environments—and the world in which you live and work. Do you agree with these critics? Or are you fairly satisfied with the way our system works? How will you "vote" on your consumer ballot?

HOW SHOULD MARKETING BE EVALUATED?

We must evaluate at two levels

As we saw in Chapter 1, it is useful to distinguish between two levels of marketing: the *micro* level (how individual firms run) and the *macro* level (how the whole system works). Some complaints against marketing are aimed at only one of these levels at a time. In other cases, the criticism *seems* to be directed to one level— but actually it is aimed at the other. Some critics of specific ads, for example, prob-

Many consumers in Russia buy shoes on the black market because the centrally planned Soviet economy does not satisfy their needs.

ably would not be satisfied with *any* advertising. When evaluating marketing, we must treat each of these levels separately.

Nation's objectives affect evaluation

Different nations have different social and economic objectives. Dictatorships, for example, may be concerned mainly with satisfying the needs of society as seen by the political elite. In a socialist state, the objective might be to satisfy society's needs—as defined by government planners.

While different nations may have different objectives, each nation needs some kind of macro-marketing system to accomplish those objectives. How a macro-marketing system operates should depend on the objectives of a particular nation. Therefore, the effectiveness of any nation's macro-marketing system can only be evaluated in terms of that nation's objectives.

Consumer satisfaction is the objective in the United States

In the United States, *the basic objective of our market-directed economic system has been to satisfy consumer needs as they—the consumers—see them.* This objective implies that political freedom and economic freedom go hand in hand— and that citizens in a free society have the right to live as they choose.

This is no place for a long discussion of whether this objective is right or wrong. Economists, philosophers, politicians, and business managers have long debated the trade-offs between consumer satisfaction and efficient use of resources. Perhaps the debate—along with changing social and economic conditions—will eventually lead to a change in our basic objective. However, this hasn't happened yet. And there is little reason to think that the majority of American consumers are willing to give up the freedom of choice they now enjoy.

Therefore, let's try to evaluate the operation of marketing in the American economy—where the present objective is to satisfy consumer needs *as consumers see them.* This is the essence of our system. The business firm that ignores this fact is asking for trouble.

CAN CONSUMER SATISFACTION BE MEASURED?

Since consumer satisfaction is our objective, marketing's effectiveness must be measured by *how well* it satisfies consumers. Unfortunately, consumer satisfaction is hard to define—and even harder to measure.

Measuring macro-marketing isn't easy

Economists believe that consumer satisfaction is derived from the amount of economic utility—form, time, place, and possession utility provided by goods and services. However, no satisfactory method of measuring economic utility has been developed. Further, some consumers may consider "psychic utility" more important than economic utility for some products.

Satisfaction depends on individual aspirations

Measuring consumer satisfaction is even more difficult because satisfaction depends on your level of aspiration or expectation. Less prosperous consumers begin to expect more out of an economy as they see the higher living standards of others. Also, aspiration levels tend to rise with repeated successes—and fall with failures. Products considered satisfactory one day may not be satisfactory the next day, or vice versa. A few years ago, most of us were more than satisfied with a 19-inch color TV that pulled in three or four channels. But once you've watched one of the newer large-screen models and enjoyed all of the options possible with

Car and truck producers use consumer surveys to track customer satisfaction.

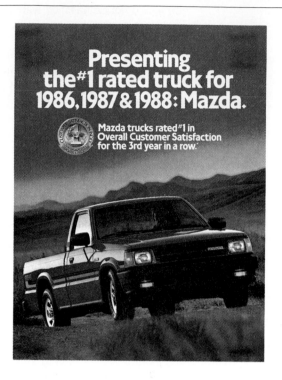

a cable hook-up or VCR, that old TV is never the same again. And when high-definition TVs become available, today's satisfying units won't seem quite so acceptable. Thus, consumer satisfaction is a highly personal concept that does not provide a reliable standard for evaluating macro-marketing effectiveness.[3]

Measuring macro-marketing must be subjective

Macro-marketing is concerned with *efficiency* (in terms of use of resources) and *fairness* (in terms of distribution of output to all parties involved)—while accomplishing the society's objectives.

If the objective is maximizing consumer satisfaction, then we must measure total satisfaction—of everyone. But there is no quantitative way to measure aggregate consumer satisfaction. So our evaluation of macro-marketing effectiveness has to be subjective.

The consumer-citizens' votes can be your guide

Probably the supreme test is whether the macro-marketing system satisfies enough individual consumer-citizens so that they vote—at the ballot box—to keep it running. So far, we've done so in the United States.

Measuring micro-marketing can be less subjective

Measuring micro-marketing effectiveness is also difficult. But it can be done. And individual business firms can and should try to measure how well their products satisfy their customers (or why their products fail). Some firms measure customer satisfaction with attitude research studies. For example, the J. D. Powers marketing research firm is well known for its studies of consumer satisfaction with different makes of automobiles. Other methods that have been used include unsolicited consumer responses (usually complaints), opinions of middlemen and salespeople, market test results, and profits.[4]

Satisfaction can be loosely measured by company profits

In our market-directed system, it's up to each customer to decide how effectively individual firms satisfy his or her needs. Usually, customers are willing to pay higher prices or buy more of the products that satisfy them. Thus, efficient marketing plans can increase profits—and profits can be used as a rough measure of a firm's efficiency in satisfying customers.

Evaluating marketing effectiveness is difficult—but not impossible

Because it's hard to measure consumer satisfaction—and, therefore, the effectiveness of micro- and macro-marketing—it's easy to see why there are different views on the subject. If the objective of the economy is clearly defined, however—and the argument is stripped of emotion—the big questions about marketing effectiveness probably *can* be answered.

In this chapter, we argue that micro-marketing (how individual firms and channels operate) frequently *does* cost too much but that macro-marketing (how the whole marketing system operates) *does not* cost too much, *given the present objective of the American economy—consumer satisfaction.* This position should not be accepted as "the" answer—but rather as a point of view. In the end, you'll have to make your own decision.[5]

MICRO–MARKETING OFTEN *DOES* COST TOO MUCH

Throughout the text, we've explored what marketing managers could or should do to help their firms do a better job of satisfying customers—while achieving company objectives. Many firms are implementing highly successful marketing programs. But, at the same time, many other firms are still too production oriented and inefficient. For customers of these latter firms, micro-marketing often does cost too much.

Many consumers are not satisfied

While American consumers are not in a revolutionary mood, many of them are unhappy with the marketing efforts of some firms. Many consumers are concerned about the high price and poor quality of many products—products whose performance doesn't live up to advertised claims—and poor after-sale service and repairs.[6]

Many consumers are complaining

Despite the usual claim, "Satisfaction Guaranteed," many consumers find reason to complain. The Better Business Bureau in a large city like Chicago may receive more than 1,200 complaints and inquiries *daily* from consumers and businesses. Multiply this figure by the number of Better Business Bureaus all across the United States. Add to this the complaints filed with federal, state, and local consumer protection agencies. Finally, add in the complaints made directly to businesses and nonprofit organizations. Obviously, many consumers are dissatisfied with many individual purchases.

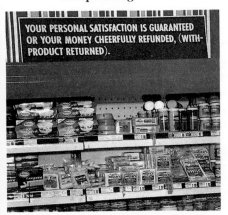

Consumers should be encouraged to complain

To further dramatize the problem, a study of consumer complaints suggested that as many as 50 percent of all serious consumer complaints are never reported. Further, many complaints that are reported never get fully resolved. The authors of the study concluded that "business should be alarmed at the amount of unresolved dissatisfaction that apparently exists in the marketplace." They advised firms to: (1)

encourage customers to speak out when things go wrong, (2) make it more convenient for them to do so, and (3) develop careful, speedy procedures to handle
complaints. Most important, companies must change their attitudes to ensure they
don't view complaining consumers as "the enemy."[7]

The failure rate is high

Further evidence that most firms are too production-oriented—and not nearly as
efficient as they could be—is the fact that so many new products fail. New and old
businesses fail regularly, too. The main reason for these failures is poor
management—or managerial incompetence. This leads to higher costs of
operation—and reduces the effectiveness of the entire business system.

Generally speaking, marketing inefficiencies are due to one or more of three
reasons:

1. Lack of interest in—or understanding of—the sometimes fickle customer.
2. Improper blending of the four Ps—caused in part by overemphasis on production and/or internal problems as contrasted with a customer orientation.
3. Lack of understanding of—or adjustment to—uncontrollable variables.

The high cost of poor marketing mixes

Perhaps lack of concern for the customer is most noticeable in the ways the
four Ps are sometimes combined—or forced—into a marketing mix. This can happen in many ways, as the following discussion shows.

Product—"Forget the customer, full speed ahead!"

Too many firms develop a new product to satisfy some manager's pet idea—not
to meet the needs of certain target customers. Or they see another company with
a successful product and try to jump into the market with another "me-too"
imitation—without even thinking about the competition they will encounter. Some
just want long production runs of easy-to-make standardized products to lower
costs. Often they aren't worried about quality control. In fact, until very recently,
most U.S. manufacturers lacked *any* quality control procedures. Then, to com-
pound these errors, the packaging people frequently put the ill-conceived product
in a container that is easy to make and fill—but that doesn't really protect the product or appeal to the customer. These poorly designed, poorly packaged products
are then turned over to the sales department to unload on the market!

Place—"The big retail chains will love this product"

Some marketing managers don't pay as much attention as they should to getting needed support from middlemen. A producer may just assume that the big
retail chains will be eager to carry a new product. They don't even stop to consider
the possibility that the retailer may see better profit potential in someone else's
product—or want to save scarce shelf space for its own brands.

Sales managers don't make adjustments in channels as often as they should.
Salespeople develop personal relationships with old customers and that makes
business more pleasant. But that doesn't necessarily contribute to efficiency and
profits. Such inflexibility can be costly—especially in view of the "scrambling" we
see in the channels of distribution.

Price—"Pick a price, any high price"

Firms often set prices on a cost-plus basis. This method of pricing may ignore
customer demand—and lead to unnecessarily high (*and* less profitable) prices.

Many business managers consider both margin and expected sales volume in pricing products. While margins are fairly definite, volume can only be predicted. So they choose high margins—which may lead to high prices and reduced volume.

Promotion—"Let our advertising geniuses and star sales reps do it"

If a product is poorly designed—or if a firm uses inadequate channels or pricing that isn't competitive—it's easy to see why promotion may be costly. Even the most aggressive selling isn't likely to overcome those earlier mistakes.

Even if a firm does a good job on the other three Ps, its Promotion is sometimes inefficient and costly. As we saw, sales managers and advertising managers may not cooperate. Each may think that his own techniques are the most effective and need no support from the other.

Some advertising executives still feel that all a promotion campaign needs is their creative genius. Or they may like the idea of glitzy TV advertising—regardless of how much it costs or what audience it reaches.

Sales managers also have their problems. There are many types of sales jobs. And careful analysis and management are needed to build a productive sales force at a reasonable cost. Unfortunately, many sales managers—although former "star" sales reps—are not up to this tough management job.

Company objectives may force higher-cost operation

Top-management decisions on company objectives may increase the cost of marketing unnecessarily. Seeking growth for growth's sake, for example, might lead to too much spending for promotion. Diversification for diversification's sake may take the firm into unfamiliar markets where marketing managers don't understand customers' needs, competitors' strengths, or what marketing mix is required to meet customers' expectations. In the last decade, many companies—including some very large ones—have learned this lesson the hard way.

For these reasons, marketing managers should be involved in shaping the firm's objectives. Progressive firms recognize the importance of marketing—and give marketing managers a greater voice in determining company objectives. Unfortunately, many more firms still look on marketing as the department that "gets rid of" the product.

Micro-marketing does cost too much—but things are changing

Marketing does cost too much in many firms. Despite much publicity, the marketing concept is not really applied in many places. Sales managers may be renamed "marketing managers" and vice presidents of sales called "vice presidents of marketing," but nothing else changes. Marketing mixes are still put together by production-oriented managers in the same old ways.

But not all firms and marketers should be criticized. More of them *are* becoming customer oriented. And many are paying more attention to market-oriented planning to carry out the marketing concept more effectively.

One encouraging sign is the end of the idea that anybody can run a business successfully. This never was true. Today, the growing complexity of business is drawing more and more professionals into the field. This includes not only professional business managers but computer specialists, psychologists, statisticians, and economists.

Another good sign is that some organizations have developed codes of ethics to guide members' behavior. For an example, see Exhibit 23–1. Some firms have adopted a code of ethics in response to criticisms of their marketing practices. But many other codes reflect long-established company policies of treating customers

Exhibit 23–1   Code of Ethics, American Marketing Association

CODE OF ETHICS

Members of the American Marketing Association (AMA) are committed to ethical professional conduct. They have joined together in subscribing to this Code of Ethics embracing the following topics:

Responsibilities of the Marketer

Marketers must accept responsibility for the consequences of their activities and make every effort to ensure that their decisions, recommendations, and actions function to identify, serve, and satisfy all relevant publics: customers, organizations and society.

Marketers' professional conduct must be guided by:

1. The basic rule of professional ethics: not knowingly to do harm;
2. The adherence to all applicable laws and regulations;
3. The accurate representation of their education, training and experience; and
4. The active support, practice and promotion of this Code of Ethics.

Honesty and Fairness

Marketers shall uphold and advance the integrity, honor, and dignity of the marketing profession by:

1. Being honest in serving consumers, clients, employees, suppliers, distributors and the public;
2. Not knowingly participating in conflict of interest without prior notice to all parties involved; and
3. Establishing equitable fee schedules including the payment or receipt of usual, customary and/or legal compensation for marketing exchanges.

Rights and Duties of Parties in the Marketing Exchange Process

Participants in the marketing exchange process should be able to expect that:

1. Products and services offered are safe and fit for their intended uses;
2. Communications about offered products and services are not deceptive;
3. All parties intend to discharge their obligations, financial and otherwise, in good faith; and
4. Appropriate internal methods exist for equitable adjustment and/or redress of grievances concerning purchases.

It is understood that the above would include, *but is not limited to,* the following responsibilities of the marketer:

In the area of product development and management,

- disclosure of all substantial risks associated with product or service usage;

- identification of any product component substitution that might materially change the product or impact on the buyer's purchase decision;
- identification of extra-cost added features.

In the area of promotions,

- avoidance of false and misleading advertising;
- rejection of high pressure manipulations, or misleading sales tactics;
- avoidance of sales promotions that use deception or manipulation.

In the area of distribution,

- not manipulating the availability of a product for purpose of exploitation;
- not using coercion in the marketing channel;
- not exerting undue influence over the reseller's choice to handle a product.

In the area of pricing,

- not engaging in price fixing;
- not practicing predatory pricing;
- disclosing the full price associated with any purchase.

In the area of marketing research,

- prohibiting selling or fund raising under the guise of conducting research;
- maintaining research integrity by avoiding misrepresentation and omission of pertinent research data;
- treating outside clients and suppliers fairly.

Organizational Relationships

Marketers should be aware of how their behavior may influence or impact on the behavior of others in organizational relationships. They should not demand, encourage or apply coercion to obtain unethical behavior in their relationships with others, such as employees, suppliers or customers.

1. Apply confidentiality and anonymity in professional relationships with regard to privileged information;
2. Meet their obligations and responsibilities in contracts and mutual agreements in a timely manner;
3. Avoid taking the work of others, in whole, or in part, and represent this work as their own or directly benefit from it without compensation or consent of the originator or owner;
4. Avoid manipulation to take advantage of situations to maximize personal welfare in a way that unfairly deprives or damages the organization or others.

Any AMA members found to be in violation of any provision of this Code of Ethics may have his or her Association membership suspended or revoked.

---

fairly and honestly. Even more industry groups might be willing to get together with the good intentions of discussing how to do a better job, but they are held back by fear of possible antitrust action.[8]

Managers who adopt the marketing concept as a way of business life do a better job. They look for target market opportunities and carefully blend the elements of the marketing mix to meet their customers' needs. As more of these managers rise in business, we can look forward to much lower micro-marketing costs.

MACRO—MARKETING DOES *NOT* COST TOO MUCH

Many critics of marketing take aim at the macro-marketing system. They think (1) that advertising and promotion in general are socially undesirable and (2) that the macro-marketing system causes improper allocation of resources, restricts income and employment, and leads to an unfair distribution of income. Most of these complaints imply that some micro-marketing activities should not be permitted—and, because they are, macro-marketing costs too much or yields poor results.

These critics have their own version of the ideal way to run an economy. Some of the most severe critics of our marketing system are theoretical economists who use the pure-competition model as their ideal. They want consumers and producers to have free choice in the market—but they are critical of the way the present market operates. Meanwhile, other critics would like to scrap our market-directed system and substitute the decisions of government planners—thus reducing freedom of choice in the marketplace. These different views should be kept in mind when evaluating criticisms of marketing.

In the following discussion, the word *business* probably could be substituted for *marketing* in most places. Marketing is the most exposed arm of business, but it is nearly impossible to separate this arm from the rest of the body. A criticism of marketing at the macro level usually (1) implies a criticism of our entire market-directed economic system as it now exists and (2) suggests that some modification—or an entirely different system—would be more effective. Let's look at some of these positions to help you form your own opinion.

Is pure competition the welfare ideal?

A major criticism of our macro-marketing system is that it permits—or even encourages—the allocation of too many resources for marketing activities, thus reducing consumer "welfare." This argument is concerned with how the economy's

---

People are different—and want different things.

resources (land, labor, and capital) are allocated for producing and distributing products. Such critics usually feel that scarce resources could be better spent on producing products than on marketing them. This argument assumes that marketing activities are unnecessary and do not create value. It also assumes that pure competition is the ideal for maximizing consumer welfare.

In pure competition, economists assume that consumers are "economic men"— that is, that they are well informed about all available offerings and will rationally choose among the alternatives to maximize their own welfare. Presumably, they will choose the "economical" alternatives—the "basic" or "stripped-down" versions of products. Therefore, these critics feel that emotional or persuasive advertising (1) discourages the economic comparisons needed for an ideal pure-competition economy and (2) is wasteful because society doesn't need it.

Theoretical economic analysis can show convincingly that pure competition will provide greater consumer welfare than monopolistic competition—*provided* all the conditions and assumptions of pure competition are met. But are they?

Different people want different things

Our present knowledge of consumer behavior and people's desire for different products pretty well demolishes the economists' "economic man" assumption—and therefore the pure-competition ideal. People, in fact, are different. And they want different products—even "fancy" versions of products, including more services. With this type of demand (down-sloping demand curves), monopoly elements naturally develop. A pioneer in monopolistic competition analysis concluded that "monopoly is necessarily a part of the welfare ideal. . . ."[9]

Once we admit that not all consumers know everything about the market—and that they have varied demands—we can see the need for a variety of micro-marketing activities.

Micro-efforts help the economy grow

Some critics feel that marketing helps create monopoly, or at least monopolistic competition. Further, they feel that this leads to higher prices, restricted output, and reduction in national income and employment.

It is true that firms in a market-directed economy try to carve out separate monopolistic markets for themselves with new products. But consumers don't *have* to buy the new product unless they feel it's a better value. The old products are still available. Ironically, the prices may go even lower on the old products—to meet the new competition.

Over several years, the profits of the innovator may rise—but rising profits also encourage further innovation by competitors. This leads to new investments—which contribute to economic growth and higher levels of national income and employment.

Increased profits also attract competition. Profits then begin to drop as new competitors enter the market and begin producing somewhat similar products. (Recall the rise and fall of industry profit during the product life cycle.)

The performance of micro-marketing activities in monopolistic competition *can* lead to a different allocation of resources than would be found in a pure-competition economy. But this allocation of resources probably results in greater consumer satisfaction. Let's look at advertising, for example.

Is advertising a waste of resources?

Advertising is the most criticized of all micro-marketing activities. Indeed, many ads *are* annoying, insulting, misleading, and downright ineffective. This is one reason why micro-marketing often does cost too much. However, advertising can also make both the micro- and macro-marketing processes work better.

Advertising can result in lower prices

Advertising is an economical way to inform large numbers of potential customers about a firm's products. Provided that a product satisfies customer needs, advertising can increase demand for the product—resulting in economies of scale in manufacturing, distribution, and sales. Because these economies may more than offset advertising costs, advertising can actually *lower* prices to the consumer.[10] In addition, advertising can reduce the time and effort consumers spend searching for products. It may also increase competition. In recent years, for example, advertising by doctors, lawyers, optometrists, and pharmacists has stimulated price competition.

Advertising stimulates economic growth

At the macro level, the increased demand brought about by advertising gives producers a faster return on their investment. This, in turn, stimulates further investment, encourages innovation, creates jobs, raises personal incomes, and generates economic growth.

Does marketing make people buy things they don't need?

From our discussion so far, it seems that the performance of micro-marketing activities aimed at satisfying consumer needs does *not* lead to an improper allocation of resources. Giving individuals what they want, after all, is the purpose of our market-directed economic system. However, some critics feel that most firms—especially large corporations—do not really cater to the needs and wants of the consumer. Rather, they use powerful persuasive techniques to manipulate consumers into buying whatever the firms want to sell.

Historian Arnold Toynbee, for example, felt that American consumers have been manipulated into buying products that are not necessary to satisfy "the minimum material requirements of life." Toynbee saw American firms as mainly trying to fulfill "unwanted demand"—demand created by advertising—rather than "genuine wants." He defined genuine wants as "wants that we become aware of spontaneously, without having to be told by Madison Avenue that we want something that we should never have thought of wanting if we had been left in peace to find out our wants for ourselves."[11]

What are the minimum requirements of life?

One problem with this line of reasoning is how to determine "the minimum material requirements of life." Does this mean that people should go back to living in caves or log cabins? Which products consumed today are unnecessary—and should not be produced?

Obviously, we have to make some value judgments to answer such questions—and few of us share the same values. One critic suggested that Americans could and should do without such items as pets, newspaper comic strips, second family cars, motorcycles, snowmobiles, campers, recreational boats and planes, cigarettes, aerosol products, pop and beer cans, and hats.[12] You may agree with some of those. But who should determine "minimum material requirements of life"—consumers or critics?

In the 1920s, few consumers saw the need for an electric "icebox." Now we all feel a refrigerator is a necessity—but some consumers don't see the need for special features. Who should decide what you need?

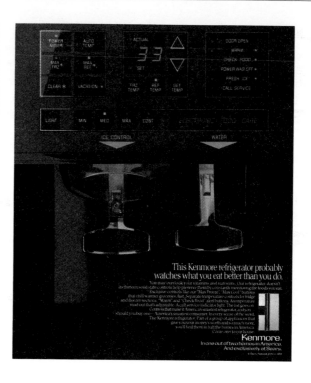

Which wants are really "genuine?"

Another problem with Toynbee's argument is the notion that people should be "left in peace" to discover their own wants. Actually, while our basic needs may be innate, almost all our wants for specific need-satisfying goods and services are learned. Moreover, these wants are learned not only through advertising, but also through other sources—including our family, friends, teachers, reference groups, and so on.

For example, American consumers did not stand up and demand refrigerators, cars, kidney dialysis machines, or microwave ovens before they were told that such products were available. Does this mean these products don't satisfy genuine needs and wants?

Consumers are not puppets

The idea that firms can manipulate consumers to buy anything they choose to produce simply isn't true. A consumer who buys a soft drink that tastes terrible won't buy another can of that brand—regardless of how much it's advertised. In fact, many new products fail the test of the market. Not even large corporations are assured of success every time they launch a new product. Consider, for example, the dismal fate of products such as Ford's Edsel, Du Pont's Corfam, Campbell's Red Kettle Soups, and RCA's computers.

Needs and wants change

Consumer needs and wants are constantly changing. Few of us would care to live the way our grandparents lived when they were our age—let alone like the pioneers who traveled west in covered wagons. The critics must realize that marketing's job is not just to satisfy consumer wants as they exist at any particular point in time. Rather, as Engledow stated:

One of marketing's most critical functions is the creative function—utilizing the capabilities of the firm to produce a better solution to a want than any that might be envisioned by the consumer *with his limited perception of technological and marketing possibilities.* [Emphasis added.][13]

Indeed, this continuous search for better solutions to consumer needs is what makes our competitive market-directed system work so effectively.

Does marketing make people materialistic?

There is no doubt that marketing relies heavily on materialistic values. However, people disagree as to whether marketing creates materialistic values—or simply appeals to already existing values.

Even in the most primitive societies, people want to accumulate possessions. In fact, in some tribal villages, a person's social status is measured by how many goats or sheep he owns. Further, the tendency for ancient pharaohs and kings to surround themselves with wealth and treasures can hardly be attributed to the persuasive powers of advertising agencies!

The idea that marketers create and serve "false tastes"—as defined by individual critics—was answered by a well-known economist who said:

The marketplace responds to the tastes of consumers with the goods and services that are salable, whether the tastes are elevated or depraved. It is unfair to criticize the marketplace for fulfilling these desires, when clearly the defects lie in the popular tastes themselves. I consider it a cowardly concession to a false extension of the idea of democracy to make sub rosa attacks on public tastes by denouncing the people who serve them. It is like blaming waiters in restaurants for obesity.[14]

Marketing reflects our own values

Scholars who study materialism seem to agree that—in the short run—marketing reflects social values, while—in the long run—it enhances and reinforces them. One expert pointed out that consumers vote for what they want in the marketplace and in the polling place. Saying that what they choose is wrong is "challenging the foundation of democracy and capitalism."[15]

Products do improve the quality of life

The issue is not really materialism versus some other option—really it's how much materialism is "necessary." More is not always better. The quality of life should not be measured strictly in terms of quantities of material goods. But when products are viewed as the means to an end—rather than the end itself—they *do* make it possible to satisfy higher-level needs. Microwave ovens, for example, greatly reduced the amount of time and effort people must spend preparing

meals—leaving them free to pursue other interests. And more dependable cars expanded people's geographic horizons—affecting where they can live and work and play. Not having "wheels" would drastically change many people's lifestyles—and even their self-images.

Consumers ask for it, consumers pay for it

The monopolistic competition typical of our economy is the result of customer preferences—*not* manipulation of markets by business. Monopolistic competition may seem costly at times when we look at micro-level situations. But it works fairly well at the macro level in serving the welfare of consumers who have many varied demands.

All these demands add to the cost of satisfying consumers. The total cost is larger than it would be if spartan, undifferentiated products were offered at the factory door on a take-it-or-leave-it basis to long lines of buyers.

But if the role of the marketing system is to serve consumers, then the cost of whatever services they demand cannot be considered excessive. It is just the cost of serving consumers the way they want to be served.

Does macro-marketing cost enough?

The role of marketing and business in our economy is to satisfy consumers. Neither production nor marketing can do this job alone. Mass production needs mass distribution—and our macro-marketing system helps make our entire market-directed economic system work.

In this sense, then, macro-marketing does *not* cost too much. Some of the activities of individual business firms may cost too much. And if these micro-level activities are improved, the performance of the macro system probably will improve. But regardless, our macro-marketing system performs a vital role in our economic system—and does not cost too much.

CHALLENGES FACING MARKETERS

We have said that our macro-marketing system does *not* cost too much—given the present objective of our economy. But we admit that the performance of many

Mass distribution makes mass production possible.

Marketing managers face the challenge of developing new strategies in ever-changing markets.

business firms leaves a lot to be desired. This presents a challenge to serious-minded students and marketers. What needs to be done—if anything?

We need better performance at the micro level

Some business executives seem to feel that they should be completely "free" in a market-directed economy. They don't understand that ours is a market-directed system—and that the needs of consumer-citizens must be served. Instead, they focus on their own internal problems—and don't satisfy consumers very well.

We need better market-oriented planning

Many firms are still production-oriented. Some hardly plan at all. Others simply extend this year's plans into next year. Progressive firms are beginning to realize that this doesn't work in our fast-changing markets. Market-oriented strategy planning is becoming more important in many companies. More attention is being paid to changes in the market—including trends in the uncontrollable environments—and how marketing strategies need to be adapted to consider these changes. Exhibit 23–2 lists some of the trends and changes we have been discussing throughout this text.

Good marketing strategy planning needs to focus on a specific target market and developing a marketing mix to meet its needs. And the basic frameworks and ideas about how to do that have not changed as much as the long list in Exhibit 23–2 might seem to suggest. At the same time, thinking about all these changes highlights the fact that marketing is dynamic. Marketing managers must constantly evaluate their strategies to be sure they are not being left "in the dust" by competitors who see new and better ways of doing things.

It's crazy for a marketing manager to constantly change a strategy that's working well. But too many fail to see or plan for needed changes. They are afraid to

Exhibit 23–2   Some Important Changes and Trends Affecting Marketing Strategy Planning

Communication Technologies
Computer-to-computer data exchange
Satellite communications
FAX machine transmissions
Cable television
Telemarketing
Cellular telephones

Role of Computerization
Personal computers and laptops
Spreadsheet analysis
Computer networks
Check-out scanners
"Bar codes" for tracking inventory
Computer-to-computer ordering

Marketing Research
Growth of marketing information systems
Decision support systems
Single source data
People meters
Use of scanner data
Easy-to-use statistical packages

Demographic Patterns
Aging of the baby boomers
Slow-down in overall population growth
Growth of Hispanic and black submarkets
Geographic shifts in population

Industrial and Intermediate Customers
Closer buyer/seller relationships
Just-in-time inventory systems
More single vendor sourcing

Product Area
More attention to innovation/new-product development
Faster new-product development
Market-driven focus on research and development
More attention to quality and quality control
More attention to services
Advances in packaging
Extending established family brand names to new products

Channels and Physical Distribution
More vertical market systems
Larger, more powerful retail chains
More conflict between producers/chains
More attention to physical distribution service
Automated warehouses
Integrated distribution centers
More competition among transportation companies

Channels and Physical Distribution (*continued*)
Growth of mass merchandising
Catalog, TV retailing
Growing role of air freight

Sales Promotion
Increased promotion to middlemen
Event sponsorships
Greater use of coupons
Stocking allowances

Personal Selling
Automated order taking
Use of portable computers
More specialization
   National accounts
   Telemarketing

Mass Selling
More targeted mass media
   Direct-mail advertising (computer mail lists)
   Specialty publications
   Cable TV
Shorter TV commercials
Larger advertising agencies
Changing agency compensation

Pricing
Less reliance on "traditional" markups by middlemen
Overuse of "sales" and trade "deals" for temporary price cuts
Bigger differences in functional discounts
Exchange rate impacts (in international markets)
Focus on higher stockturn at lower margins

International Marketing
Market development opportunities overseas
New and different competitors—at home and abroad
Need to adjust to unfamiliar markets, cultures
Widely spread markets
Trading restrictions (unification of Europe, tariffs, quotas, etc.)
More attention to exporting
Growth of multinational corporations

General
Less regulation of business
More attention to marketing ethics
Shift of emphasis away from diversification
Increasing concern about short-term profit
Greater attention to competitive advantage
More attention to profitability, not just sales

do anything different and adhere to the idea that "if it ain't broke, don't fix it." The problem is that a firm can't always wait until it is totally obvious that there is a problem to do anything about it. At the point when customers have moved on and profits have disappeared, it may be too late to "fix" the problem. Marketing managers who take the lead in finding innovative new markets and approaches get a competitive advantage.

The time horizon for planning is important. Some firms neglect a market orientation in pursuit of *short-run* profits. Some financial managers push their companies into unfamiliar markets, with little understanding of customer needs. Others milk profits in the short run and disregard long-term growth. Too often these firms make ineffective marketing decisions that add to the cost of our macro-marketing system.

May need more social responsiveness

A good business manager should put himself in the consumer's position. A useful rule to follow might be: Do unto others as you would have others do unto you. In practice, this means developing satisfying marketing mixes for specific target markets. It may mean building in more quality or more safety. The consumers' long-run satisfaction should be considered, too. How will the product hold up in use? What about service guarantees? What is the impact on the environment?

It seems doubtful that production-oriented approaches will work in the future. Tougher competition—from companies at home and abroad—may force the old-style production-oriented business managers to change their thinking—just to survive.

May need attention to consumer privacy

While focusing on consumers' needs, marketers also must be sensitive to other consumer concerns. Today, sophisticated marketing research methods and new technologies are making it easier to abuse consumers' rights to privacy. For example, credit card records—revealing much about consumers' purchases and private lives—are routinely computerized and sold to anybody who pays for the list.

Most consumers don't realize how much data about their personal lives—some of it incorrect but treated as factual—is collected and available. A simple computer billing error may land a consumer on a computer "bad credit" list—without his knowledge. Marketing managers should use technology responsibly to improve the quality of life, not disrupt it.

Socially responsible marketing managers are concerned with consumers' long-run satisfaction and safety.

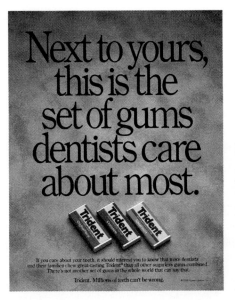

We may need new laws

One of the advantages of a market-directed economic system is that it operates automatically—but in our version of this system, consumer-citizens provide certain constraints (laws). And these constraints can be modified at any time. Managers who ignore consumer attitudes must realize that their actions may cause new restraints.

Need to rethink some present laws

Before piling on too many new rules, however, we should review the ones we have. Some of them may need to be changed—and others may need to be enforced more carefully. The antitrust laws, for example, are often applied to protect competitors from each other—when they were really intended to encourage competition.

On the other hand, the antitrust laws in the United States were originally developed with the idea that all firms competing in a market would be "playing by the same rules." That is no longer always the case. For example, in many markets individual U.S. firms compete with foreign firms whose governments have urged them to cooperate with each other. They don't see each other as competitors, but rather see U.S. firms—as a group—as the competitors.

Laws should affect top management

Strict enforcement of present laws could have far-reaching results if more price fixers, fraudulent or deceptive advertisers, and others who violate existing laws—thus affecting the performance of the macro-marketing system—were sent to jail or given heavy fines. A quick change in attitudes might occur if top managers—those who plan strategy—were prosecuted, instead of the salespeople or advertisers who are expected to "deliver" on weak or undifferentiated strategies.

In other words, if the government made it clear that it was serious about improving the performance of our economic system, much could be achieved within the present system—*without* adding new constraints or trying to "patch up" the present ones.

Need better-informed consumers

We also may need some changes to help potential customers choose among the confusing array of goods and services on the market. Legislation to ensure that consumers do have a basis for comparing products (for example, life expectancy of light bulbs and appliances) would be useful. Consumer education programs designed to teach people how to buy more effectively could also help.

But care must be used to preserve the consumers' free choice. If only quantitative measures are used, some qualitative criteria (for example, style, taste, or fun in use) might be overlooked. For many buyers these factors may be the most important.

Need socially responsible consumers

We've stressed that producers should act responsibly—but consumers have responsibilities, too. Consumer advocates usually ignore this point.[16] Some consumers abuse policies about returning goods, change price tags in self-service stores, and expect attractive surroundings and courteous, well-trained sales and service people—but want discount prices. Some are downright abusive to salespeople. Others think nothing of "ripping off" businesses because "they're rich." Shoplifting is a major problem for most retailers—and honest consumers pay for the cost of shoplifting in higher prices.

Wal-Mart Wants Consumers to Buy Products that Won't Last

Every day in the news we hear concerns about how we pollute our land, air, and water. As consumers, however, we enjoy the convenience of unbreakable plastic bottles, aerosol spray cans, disposable diapers, and styrofoam-wrapped fast food—all of which can have long-lasting effects on the environment.

Wal-Mart's marketing managers decided that consumers who really do want a cleaner environment should be able to vote for one—with their dollars. Wal-Mart told all of its suppliers that it would devote special in-store promotion and shelf space to improved products that "help prevent lasting environmental problems."

Wal-Mart also developed ads to inform consumers about the program and to ask them for ideas on how to expand it.

Wal-Mart's promise of promotion help should spur some of its suppliers to put more emphasis on this area. But some marketing managers are already working to satisfy consumers who are worried about the environment. For example, ads for Tender Care, a degradable disposable diaper, urge consumers to "change the world one diaper at a time." The Tender Care strategy shows that a marketing manager can do well by doing good. Tender Care sales doubled when the degradable diapers replaced the old ones—even though the price of the new diapers is 5 to 10 percent higher than before. Tender Care is not alone in making changes. Mobil Chemical Company has developed a degradable version of its popular Hefty trash bag. In California, Atlantic Richfield is offering a new fuel designed to reduce smog problems. Procter & Gamble uses recycled paper in 80 percent of its packaging, and 90 percent of its plastic packages can be recycled.[17]

Americans tend to perform their dual role of consumer-citizens with a split personality. We often behave one way as consumers—and then take the opposite position at the ballot box. For example, while our beaches and parks are covered with garbage and litter, we urge our legislators to take stiff action to curb pollution. We protest sex and violence in the media—and then flock to see the latest R- or X-rated movies. Parents complain about advertising aimed at children—then use TV as a "baby-sitter" on Saturday morning.

Consumers share in the responsibility for preserving an effective macro-marketing system. And they should take this responsibility seriously.

Let's face it. There's a wealth of information already available to aid consumer decision making. The consumerism movement has encouraged nutritional labeling, open dating, unit pricing, truth-in-lending, plain-language contracts and warranties, and so on. And government agencies publish many consumer buying guides, as do organizations such as Consumers Union. Yet the majority of consumers continue to ignore most of this information.

We may need to modify our macro-marketing system

Our macro-marketing system is built on the assumption that we are trying to satisfy consumers. But how far should the marketing concept be allowed to go?

Should marketing managers limit consumers' freedom of choice?

Achieving a "better" macro-marketing system is certainly a desirable objective. But what part should a marketer play in making decisions about what products to offer on the market? As a consumer-citizen, he has the right and obligation to contribute his view and vote to improve our system. But as a marketing manager, what should he do?

Leftover plastic packages last for centuries—unless they are recycled.

This is extremely important, because some marketing managers—especially those in large corporations—can have an impact far larger than in their role as a consumer-citizen. For example, should they deliberately refuse to produce hazardous products—like skis or motorcycles—even though such products are in strong demand? Should they be expected to install safety devices that increase costs—but that customers don't want?

These are difficult questions to answer. Some things marketing managers can do are clearly in both the firm's and consumers' interests because they lower costs and/or improve consumers' options. But other choices may actually reduce consumer choice and are at odds with a desire to improve the effectiveness of our macro-marketing system.

Consumer-citizens should vote on the changes

It seems fair to suggest, therefore, that marketing managers should be expected to improve and expand the range of goods and services they make available to consumers—always trying to better satisfy their needs and preferences. This is the job we've assigned to business.

If pursuing this objective makes "excessive" demands on scarce resources—or causes an "intolerable" level of ecological damage—then consumer-citizens have the right and the responsibility to vote for laws to restrict the individual firms that are trying to satisfy consumers' needs. This is the role that we, as consumers, have assigned to the government—to ensure that the macro-marketing system works effectively.

It is important to recognize that some *seemingly minor* modifications in our present system *might* result in very big, unintended problems. Allowing some government agency (for example, the FDA or Consumer Product Safety Commission) to prohibit the sale of products for seemingly good reasons may establish a precedent that would lead to major changes we never expected. (Bicycles, for example, are a very hazardous consumer product. Should they continue to be sold?) Clearly,

Maryland wants to attract businesses—because, in our society well-managed companies contribute to a higher quality of life.

THE BIGGEST
INCENTIVE
OF ALL: WE'RE
PRO-BUSINESS

In Maryland, we offer you
a solidly pro-business attitude
that's here today and
here tomorrow.
A commitment to help protect
the profits we know are the
lifeblood of Maryland.
And that's making Maryland
the best place in America
to do business. Isn't that
the biggest incentive of all?
Come for the carrot.
You'll stay for the greens.

MARYLAND

Write or call Michael Lofton,
Director, Business and Industrial
Development, Dept. 114, 45 Calvert
Street, Annapolis, Maryland 21401.
(301) 269-3514

such government actions could seriously reduce consumers' present "right" to freedom of choice—including "bad" choices.[18]

We, as consumer-citizens, should be careful to distinguish between proposed changes designed simply to modify our system and those designed to change it—perhaps drastically. In either case, we should have the opportunity to make the decision (through elected representatives). This decision should not be left in the hands of a few well-placed managers or government planners.

Marketing people may be even more necessary in the future

Regardless of the changes that might be voted by consumer-citizens, some kind of a marketing system will be needed in the future. Further, if satisfying more subtle needs—such as for the "good life"—becomes our objective, it could be even more important to have market-oriented firms. It may be necessary, for example, not only to define an individual's needs, but also society's needs—perhaps for a "better neighborhood" or "more enriching social experiences," and so on. As we go beyond tangible physical goods into more sophisticated need-satisfying blends of goods and services, the trial-and-error approach of the typical production-oriented manager will become even less acceptable.

CONCLUSION

Macro-marketing does *not* cost too much. Consumers have assigned business the role of satisfying their needs. Customers find it satisfactory—and even desirable—to permit businesses to cater to them and even to stimulate wants. As long as consumers are satisfied, macro-marketing will not cost too much—and business firms will be permitted to continue as profit-making entities.

But business exists at the consumers' discretion. It is mainly by satisfying the consumer that a particular firm—and our economic system—can justify its existence and hope to keep operating.

In carrying out this role—granted by consumers—business firms are not always as effective as they could be. Many business managers don't understand the marketing concept—or the role that marketing plays in our way of life. They seem to feel that business has a God-given right to operate as it chooses. And they proceed in their typical production-oriented ways. Further, many managers have had little or no training in business management—and are not as competent as they should be. Others fail to adjust to the changes that are taking place around them. As a result, micro-marketing often *does* cost too much. But the situation is improving. More business training is now available and more competent people are being attracted to marketing and business generally. Clearly, *you* have a role to play in improving marketing activities in the future.

Marketing has new challenges to face in the future. *Our* consumers may have to settle for a lower standard of living. Resource shortages, slower population growth, and a larger number of elderly—with a smaller proportion of the population in the work force—may all combine to reduce our income growth. This may force consumers to shift their consumption patterns—and politicians to change some of the rules governing business. Even our present market-directed system may be threatened.

To keep our system working effectively, individual firms should implement the marketing concept in a more efficient and socially responsible way. At the same time, we—as consumers—should consume goods and services in an intelligent and socially responsible way. Further, we have the responsibility to vote and ensure that we get the kind of macro-marketing system we want. What kind do you want? What should you do to ensure that fellow consumer-citizens will vote for your system? Is your system likely to satisfy you as well as another macro-marketing system? You don't have to answer these questions right now—but your answers will affect the future you'll live in and how satisfied you'll be.

Questions and Problems

1. Explain why marketing must be evaluated at two levels. What criteria should be used to evaluate each level of marketing? Defend your answer. Explain why your criteria are "better" than alternative criteria.

2. Discuss the merits of various economic system objectives. Is the objective of the American economic system sensible? Do you feel more consumer satisfaction might be achieved by permitting some sociologists—or some public officials—to determine how the needs of the lower-income or less-educated members of the society should be satisfied? If you approve of this latter suggestion, what education or income level should be required before an individual is granted free choice by the social planners?

3. Should the objective of our economy be maximum efficiency? If your answer is yes, efficiency in what? If not, what should the objective be?

4. Cite an example of a critic using his own value system when evaluating marketing.

5. Discuss the conflict of interests among production, finance, accounting, and marketing executives. How does this conflict affect the operation of an individual firm? Of the economic system? Why does this conflict exist?

6. Why does adoption of the marketing concept encourage a firm to operate more efficiently? Be specific about the impact of the marketing concept on the various departments of a firm.

7. In the short run, competition sometimes leads to inefficiency in the operation of the economic system. Many people argue for monopoly in order to eliminate this inefficiency. Discuss this solution to the problem of inefficiency.

8. How would officially granted monopolies affect the operation of our economic system? Consider the effect on allocation of resources, the level of income and employment, and the distribution of income. Is the effect any different if a firm obtains monopoly by winning out in a competitive market?

9. Could a pure-competition economy evolve naturally? Could legislation force a pure-competition economy?

10.   Comment on the following statement: "Ultimately, the high cost of marketing is due only to consumers."

11.   How far should the marketing concept go? How should we decide this issue?

12.   Should marketing managers, or business managers in general, refrain from producing profitable products that some target customers want but that may not be in their long-run interest? Should firms be expected to produce "good" products that offer a lower rate of profitability than usual? A break-even level? What if the products will be unprofitable, but the company makes other products that are profitable—so on balance the company will still make some profit? What criteria are you using for each of your answers?

13.   Should a marketing manager or a business refuse to produce an "energy-gobbling" appliance that some consumers are demanding? Should a firm install an expensive safety device that will increase costs but that customers don't want? Are the same principles involved in both these questions? Explain.

14.   Discuss how one or more of the trends or changes shown in Exhibit 23–2 is affecting marketing strategy planning for a specific firm that serves the market where you live.

15.   Discuss how slower economic growth or no economic growth would affect your college community—in particular, its marketing institutions.

Suggested Cases

29.   Fruitco, Inc.

30.   Chemco, Inc.

31.   American Tools, Inc.

32.   Castco, Inc.

33.   Multifoods, Ltd.

36.   Lever, Ltd.

Appendix C

Career Planning in Marketing

When You Finish This Appendix, You Should

1. Know that there is a job—or a career—for you in marketing.

2. Know that marketing jobs can pay well.

3. Understand the difference between "people-oriented" and "thing-oriented" jobs.

4. Know about the many marketing jobs you can choose from.

One of the hardest jobs facing most college students is the choice of a career. Of course, we can't make this decision for you. You must be the judge of your own objectives, interests, and abilities. Only you can decide what career *you* should pursue. However, you owe it to yourself to at least consider the possibility of a career in marketing.

THERE'S A PLACE IN MARKETING FOR YOU

We're happy to tell you that many opportunities are available in marketing. Regardless of your abilities or training, there's a place in marketing for everyone—from a supermarket bagger to a vice president of marketing in a large consumer products company such as Procter & Gamble or General Foods. The opportunities range widely—so it will help to be more specific. In the following pages, we'll discuss (1) the typical pay for different marketing jobs, (2) setting your own objectives and evaluating your interests and abilities, and (3) the kinds of jobs available in marketing.

MARKETING JOBS CAN PAY WELL

There are many challenging jobs for those with marketing training. Fortunately, marketing jobs open to college-level students do pay well! At the time this went to press, marketing undergraduates were being offered starting salaries ranging from $15,000 to $36,000 a year. Of course, these figures are extremes. Starting salaries can vary considerably—depending on your background, experience, and location.

As shown in Exhibit C–1, starting salaries in sales-marketing compare favorably with many other fields—although they are lower than those in such fields as computer science where college graduates are currently in very high demand. How far and fast your income rises above the starting level, however, depends on many factors—including your willingness to work, how well you get along with people, and your individual abilities. But most of all, it depends on *getting results*—individually and through other people. And this is where many marketing jobs offer the newcomer great opportunities. It is possible to show initiative, ability, and judgment in marketing jobs. And some young people move up very rapidly in marketing. Some even end up at the top in large companies—or as owners of their own businesses.

Marketing is often the route to the top

Marketing is where the action is! In the final analysis, a firm's success or failure depends on the effectiveness of its marketing program. This doesn't mean the other functional areas aren't important. It merely reflects the fact that a firm won't have much need for accountants, finance people, production managers, and so on if it can't successfully sell its products.

Because marketing is so vital to a firm's survival, many companies look for people with training and experience in marketing when filling key executive positions. A survey of the nation's largest corporations showed that the greatest proportion of chief executive officers had backgrounds in marketing and distribution (see Exhibit C–2).

DEVELOP YOUR OWN PERSONAL MARKETING STRATEGY

Now that you know there are many opportunities in marketing, your problem is matching the opportunities to your own personal objectives and strengths. Basi-

Exhibit C–1   Average Starting Salaries of 1988 College Graduates (with bachelor's degrees) in Selected Fields

Field	Average starting salary (per year)
Liberal arts	$22,596
Sales—marketing	22,848
Business administration	22,920
Accounting	24,324
Chemistry	25,692
Mathematics or statistics	26,112
Computer science	27,372
Engineering	29,820

Exhibit C–2   Main Career Emphasis of Corporate Chief Executive Officers*

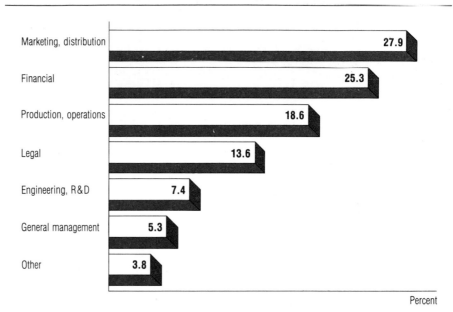

Percent

*Based on a survey of the chief executive officers of the nation's 500 largest industrial corporations and 300 non-industrial corporations (including commercial banks, life insurance firms, retailers, transportation companies, utilities, and diversified financial enterprises).

cally the problem is a marketing problem: developing a marketing strategy to "sell" a product—yourself—to potential employers. Just as in planning strategies for products, developing your own strategy takes careful thought. Exhibit C–3 shows how you can organize your own strategy planning. This exhibit shows that you should evaluate yourself first—a personal analysis—and then analyze the environment for opportunities. This will help you sharpen your own long- and short-run objectives—which will lead to developing a strategy. And, finally, you should start implementing your own personal marketing strategy. These ideas are explained more fully below.

CONDUCT YOUR OWN PERSONAL ANALYSIS

You are the "Product" you are going to include in your own marketing plan. So first you have to decide what your long-run objectives are—what you want to do, how hard you want to work, and how quickly you want to reach your objectives. Be honest with yourself—or you will eventually face frustration. Evaluate your own personal strengths and weaknesses—and decide what factors may become the key to your success. Finally, as part of your personal analysis, set some preliminary timetables to guide your strategy planning and implementation efforts. Let's spell this out in detail.

Set broad long-run objectives

Strategy planning requires much "trial-and-error" decision making. But at the very beginning, you should make some tentative decisions about your own objectives—what you want out of a job—and out of life. At the very least, you should decide whether you are just looking for a "job"—or whether you want to

Exhibit C–3   Organizing Your Own Personal Marketing Strategy Planning

```
   Personal analysis                    Environment analysis
┌─────────────────────────┐      ┌─────────────────────────┐
│ —Set broad long-run     │      │ —Identify current       │
│   objectives            │      │   opportunities         │
│ —Evaluate personal      │      │ —Examine trends which   │
│   strengths             │      │   may affect            │
│   and weaknesses        │      │   opportunities         │
│ —Set preliminary        │      │ —Evaluate business      │
│   timetables            │      │   practices             │
└─────────────────────────┘      └─────────────────────────┘
             │                                │
             └───────────────┬────────────────┘
                             ▼
                  ┌─────────────────────────┐
                  │ Develop objectives      │
                  │   —Long-run             │
                  │   —Short-run            │
                  └─────────────────────────┘
                             │
                             ▼
                  ┌─────────────────────────┐
                  │ Develop your marketing  │
                  │ plan                    │
                  │   —Identify likely      │
                  │     opportunities       │
                  │   —Plan your product    │
                  │   —Plan your promotion  │
                  └─────────────────────────┘
                             │
                             ▼
                  ┌─────────────────────────┐
                  │ Implement your          │
                  │   marketing plan        │
                  └─────────────────────────┘
```

build a "career." Beyond this, do you want the position to be personally satisfying—or is the financial return enough? And just how much financial return do you need—or are you willing to work for? Some people work only to support themselves and their leisure-time activities. Others work to support themselves and their families. These people seek only financial rewards from a job. They try to find job opportunities that provide adequate financial returns but aren't too demanding of their time or effort. Other people, however, look first for satisfaction in their job—and they seek opportunities for career advancement. Financial rewards may be important, too, but these are used only as measures of success. In the extreme, the career-oriented individual may be willing to sacrifice a lot—including leisure and social activities—to achieve success in a career.

Once you've tentatively decided these matters, then you can get more serious about whether you should seek a job—or a career—in marketing. If you decide to pursue a career, you should set your broad long-run objectives to achieve it. For example, one long-run objective might be to pursue a career in marketing management (or marketing research). This might require more academic training than you planned—as well as a different kind of training. If your objective is to get a "job" that pays well, on the other hand, then this calls for a different kind of training and different kinds of job experiences before completing your academic work.

Evaluate personal strengths and weaknesses

What kind of a job is right for you?

Because of the great variety of marketing jobs, it's hard to generalize about what aptitudes you should have to pursue a career in marketing. Different jobs attract people with various interests and abilities. We'll give you some guidelines about what kinds of interests and abilities marketers should have. Note: If you're completely "lost" about your own interests and abilities, see your campus career counselor and take some vocational aptitude and interest tests. These tests will help you to compare yourself with people who are now working in various career positions. They will *not* tell you what you should do, but they can help—especially in eliminating possibilities you are less interested in and/or less able to do well in.

Are you "people-oriented" or "thing-oriented?"

One of the first things you need to decide is whether you are basically "people-oriented" or "thing-oriented." This is a very important decision. A "people-oriented" person might be very unhappy in a bookkeeping job, for example, while a "thing-oriented" person might be miserable in a personal selling job that involves a lot of customer contact.

Marketing has both "people-oriented" and "thing-oriented" jobs. People-oriented jobs are primarily in the promotion area—where company representatives must make contact with potential customers. This may be direct personal selling or customer service activities—for example, in technical service or installation and repair. Thing-oriented jobs focus more on creative activities and analyzing data—as in advertising and marketing research—or on organizing and scheduling work—as in operating warehouses, transportation agencies, or the "back-end" of retailers.

People-oriented jobs tend to pay more, in part because such jobs are more likely to affect sales—the life blood of any business. Thing-oriented jobs, on the other hand, are often seen as "cost-generators" rather than "sales-generators." Taking a big view of the whole company's operations, the thing-oriented jobs are certainly necessary—but without sales no one is needed to do them.

Thing-oriented jobs are usually done at a company's facilities. Further, especially in lower-level jobs, the amount of work to be done—and even the nature of the work—may be spelled out quite clearly. The time it takes to design questionnaires and tabulate results, for example, can be estimated with reasonable accuracy. Similarly, running a warehouse, totaling inventories, scheduling outgoing shipments, and so on are more like production operations. It's fairly easy to measure an employee's effectiveness and productivity in a thing-oriented job. At the least, time spent can be used to measure an employee's contribution.

A sales rep, on the other hand, might spend all weekend thinking and planning how to make a half-hour sales presentation on Monday. For what should the sales rep be compensated—the half-hour presentation, all of the planning and thinking that went into it, or the results? Typically, sales reps are rewarded for their sales results—and this helps account for the sometimes extremely high salaries paid to effective order getters. At the same time, some people-oriented jobs can be routinized and are lower paid. For example, sales clerks in some retail stores are paid at or near the minimum wage.

Managers needed for both kinds of jobs

Here we have oversimplified deliberately to emphasize the differences among types of jobs. Actually, of course, there are many variations between the two extremes. Some sales reps must do a great deal of analytical work before they make a presentation. Similarly, some marketing researchers must be extremely people-sensitive to get potential customers to reveal their true feelings. But the division is still useful because it focuses on the primary emphasis in different kinds of jobs.

Managers are needed for the people in both kinds of jobs. Managing others requires a blend of both people and analytical skills—but people skills may be the more important of the two. Therefore, people-oriented persons are often promoted into managerial positions.

What will differentiate your "product"?

After deciding whether you're generally "people-oriented" or "thing-oriented," you're ready for the next step—trying to identify your specific strengths (to be built on) and weaknesses (to be avoided or remedied). It is important to be as specific as possible so you can develop a better marketing plan. For example, if you decide you are more people-oriented, are you more skilled in verbal *or* in written communication? Or if you are more thing-oriented, what specific analytical or technical skills do you have? Are you good at working with numbers, solving complex problems, or coming to the root of a problem? Other possible strengths include past experience (career-related or otherwise), academic performance, an outgoing personality, enthusiasm, drive, motivation, and so on.

It is important to see that your plan should build on your strengths. An employer will be hiring you to do something—so "promote" yourself as someone who is able to do something *well.* In other words, find your "competitive advantage" in your unique strengths—and then "promote" these unique things about *you* and what you can do.

While trying to identify strengths, you also must realize that you may have some important weaknesses—depending on your objectives. If you are seeking a career that requires technical skills, for example, then you need to get these skills. Or if you are seeking a career that requires a lot of self-motivation and drive, then you should try to develop these characteristics in yourself—or change your objectives.

Set some timetables

At this point in your strategy planning process, set some timetables to organize your thinking and the rest of your planning. You need to make some decisions at this point to be sure you see where you're going. You might simply focus on getting your "first job," or you might decide to work on two marketing plans: (1) a short-run plan to get your first job and (2) a longer-run plan—perhaps a five-year plan—to show how you're going to accomplish your long-run objectives. People who are basically job-oriented may "get away with" only a short-run plan—just drifting from one opportunity to another as their own objectives and opportunities change. But those interested in "careers" need a longer-run plan. Otherwise, they may find themselves pursuing attractive first job opportunities that satisfy short-run objectives—but quickly leave them frustrated when they realize that they can't achieve their long-run objectives without additional training or other experiences.

ENVIRONMENT ANALYSIS

Strategy planning is a matching process. For your own strategy planning, this means matching yourself to career opportunities. So let's look at opportunities available in the marketing environment. (The same approach applies, of course, in the whole business area.) Some of the possibilities and salary ranges are shown in Exhibit C–4.

Identifying current opportunities in marketing

Because of the wide range of opportunities in marketing, it's helpful to narrow your possibilities. After deciding on your own objectives, strengths, and weaknesses, think about where in the marketing system you might like to work. Would you like to work for manufacturers, or wholesalers, or retailers? Or doesn't it really matter? Do you want to be involved with consumer products or industrial products? By analyzing your feelings about these possibilities, you can

Exhibit C–4   Some Career Paths and Salary Ranges

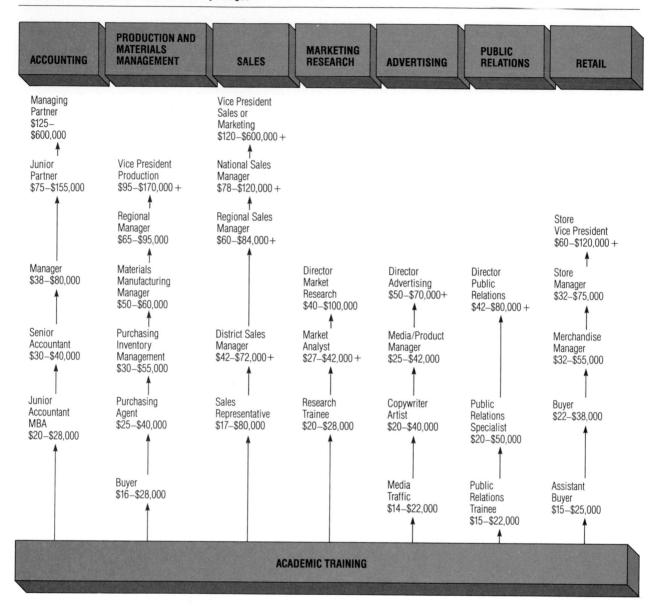

begin to zero in on the kind of job and the functional area that might interest you most.

One simple way to get a better idea of the kinds of jobs available in marketing is to review the chapters of this text—this time with an eye for job opportunities rather than new concepts. The following paragraphs contain brief descriptions of job areas that marketing graduates are often interested in with references to specific chapters in the text. Some, as noted below, offer good starting opportunities, while others do not. While reading these paragraphs, keep your own objectives, interests, and strengths in mind.

Marketing manager (Chapter 2)

This is usually not an entry-level job, although aggressive students may move quickly into this role in smaller companies.

Marketing research opportunities (Chapter 5)

There are entry-level opportunities at all levels in the channel (but especially in large firms where more formal marketing research is done) and in advertising agencies and marketing research firms. Quantitative and behavioral science skills are extremely important in marketing research, so many firms prefer to hire statistics or psychology graduates rather than business graduates. But there still are many opportunities in marketing research for marketing graduates. A recent graduate might begin in a training program—conducting interviews or summarizing open-ended answers from questionnaires—before being promoted to assistant project manager and subsequent management positions.

Customer or market analyst (Chapters 3 and 5)

Opportunities as consumer analysts and market analysts are commonly found in large companies, marketing research organizations, and advertising agencies. Beginners start in "thing-oriented" jobs until their judgment and people-oriented skills are tested. The job may involve collecting or analyzing secondary data or preparation of reports and plans. Because knowledge of statistics, computer software and/or behavioral sciences is very important, marketing graduates often find themselves competing with majors in fields such as psychology, sociology, statistics, and computer science. Graduates who have courses in marketing *and* one or more of these areas may have the best opportunities.

Purchasing agent/buyer (Chapter 7)

Opportunities are commonly found in large companies. Beginners start as trainees or assistant buyers under the supervision of experienced buyers.

Product planner (Chapter 10)

This is usually not an entry-level position. Instead, people with experience on the technical side of the business and/or in sales might be moved into new-product development as they demonstrate judgment and analytical skills.

Product/brand manager (Chapters 9 and 10)

Many multiproduct firms have brand or product managers handling individual products—in effect, managing each product as a separate business. Some firms hire marketing graduates as assistant brand or product managers, although typically only MBAs are considered. Most firms prefer that recent college graduates spend some time in the field doing sales work before moving into brand or product management positions.

Packaging specialists (Chapter 9)

Packaging manufacturers tend to hire and train interested people from various backgrounds—there is little formal academic training in packaging. There are many sales opportunities in this field—and with training, interested people can become specialists fairly quickly in this growing area.

Distribution channel management (Chapter 11)

This work is typically handled or directed by sales managers—and therefore it is not an entry-level position.

Retailing opportunities (Chapter 12)

Most entry-level marketing positions in retailing involve some kind of sales work. Retailing positions tend to offer lower than average starting salaries—but they often provide opportunities for very rapid advancement. Most retailers require new employees to have some selling experience before managing others—or buying. A typical marketing graduate can expect to do some sales work and manage one or several departments before advancing to a store management position—or to a staff position that might involve buying, advertising, marketing research, and so on.

Physical distribution opportunities (Chapter 14)

There are many sales opportunities with physical distribution specialists—but there are also many "thing-oriented" jobs involving traffic management, warehousing, and materials handling. Here, training in accounting, finance, and quantitative methods could be very useful. These kinds of jobs are available at all levels in the channels of distribution.

Sales promotion opportunities (Chapter 15)

There are not many entry-level positions in this area. Creativity and judgment are required, and it is difficult for an inexperienced person to demonstrate these skills. A beginner would probably move from sales or advertising jobs into sales promotion.

Personal sales opportunities (Chapter 16)

Most of the job opportunities—especially entry-level jobs—are in personal selling. This might be order getting, order taking, or missionary selling. Many students are reluctant to get into personal selling—but this field offers benefits that are hard to match in any other field. These include the opportunity to earn extremely high salaries and commissions—quickly—a chance to develop your self-confidence and resourcefulness, an opportunity to work with minimal supervision—almost to the point of being your own boss—and a chance to acquire product and customer knowledge that many firms consider necessary for a successful career in product/ brand management, sales management, and marketing management. Many salespeople spend their entire careers in selling—preferring the freedom and earning potential that go with a sales job over the headaches and sometimes lower salaries of sales management positions.

Advertising opportunities (Chapter 17)

Job opportunities are varied in this area—and highly competitive. And because the ability to communicate and knowledge of the behavioral sciences are important, marketing graduates often find themselves competing with majors from fields such as English, journalism, psychology, and sociology. There are "thing-oriented" jobs such as copywriting, media buying, art, and so on. And there are "people-oriented" positions involving sales—which are probably of more interest to marketing graduates. This is a glamorous, but small and extremely competitive industry where young people can rise very rapidly—but they can also be as easily displaced by new "bright young people." Entry-level salaries in advertising are typically low.

Pricing opportunities (Chapters 18 and 19)

Pricing is generally handled by experienced executives, so there are no entry-level opportunities here. In fact, in some companies pricing is not even handled by the sales or marketing people, as explained in the text.

Credit management opportunities

Specialists in credit have a continuing need for employees who are interested in evaluating customers' credit ratings and ensuring that money gets collected. Both people skills and "thing" skills can be useful here. Entry positions normally involve a training program—and then working under the supervision of others until your judgment and abilities are tested.

International marketing opportunities (Chapter 22)

Many marketing students are intrigued with the adventure and foreign travel promised by careers in international marketing. Some firms hire recent college graduates for positions in international marketing, but more often these positions go to MBA graduates from schools that specialize in international trade. It's an advantage in seeking an international marketing job to know a second language and to know about the culture of countries where you would like to work. Your college may have courses that would help in these areas. Graduates aiming for a career in international marketing usually must spend time mastering the firm's domestic marketing operations before being sent abroad.

Marketing cost and revenue analysis opportunities

Only progressive large firms use these kinds of techniques—usually as analytical tools in sales or marketing management. Some larger firms have staff departments to do these kinds of analyses. But in most companies, they are simply tools applied by the more analytical researchers and managers in their own jobs. An MBA degree probably would be needed to go directly into a staff position requiring this sort of work. But, graduates who know spreadsheet analysis and show that they have the ability to "work with numbers" often have good opportunities to move into these jobs.

Customer relations/consumer affairs opportunities (Chapters 16 and 23)

Some firms are becoming more concerned about their relations with customers and the general public. Employees in this kind of work, however, usually have held various positions with the firm before doing customer relations.

Study trends that may affect your opportunities

A strategy planner should always be evaluating the future because it's easier to go along with trends than to buck them. This means you should watch for political, technical, or economic changes that might open—or close—career opportunities.

If you can spot a trend early, you may be able to prepare yourself to take advantage of it as part of your long-run strategy planning. Other trends might mean you should avoid certain career options. For example, rapid technological changes in computers and communications are likely to lead to major changes in retailing and advertising—as well as in personal selling. Cable television, telephone selling, and direct-mail selling may reduce the need for routine order takers—while increasing the need for higher-level order getters. More targeted and imaginative sales presentations for delivery by mail and by phone or by TV screen may be needed. The retailers who survive may need a better understanding of their target markets. And they may need to be supported by wholesalers and manufacturers who can plan targeted promotions that make economic sense. This will require a better understanding of the production and physical distribution side of business—as well as the financial side. And this means better training in accounting, finance, inventory control, and so on. So plan your personal strategy with such trends in mind.

Evaluate business practices

Finally, you need to know how businesses really operate—and the kind of training required for various jobs. We've already seen that there are many opportunities in marketing—but not all jobs are open to everyone, and not all jobs are entry-level jobs. Positions such as marketing manager, brand manager, and sales manager are higher rungs on the marketing career ladder. They become available only when you have a few years of experience and have shown leadership and judgment. Some positions require more education than others. So take a hard look at your long-run objectives—and then see what you need for the kinds of opportunities you might like. Will a two-year degree get you where you want to go? Or will you need a four-year degree or even a graduate degree? Is a degree really necessary, or will it only be "helpful"—perhaps to make up for lack of experience or to speed your progress toward your objective?

DEVELOP OBJECTIVES

Once you've done a personal analysis and environment analysis—identifying your personal interests, your strengths and weaknesses, and the opportunities in the environment—you must define your objectives more specifically—both long-run and short-run.

Develop long-run objectives

Your long-run objectives should clearly state what you want to do—and what you will do for potential employers. You might be as specific as indicating the exact career area you want to pursue over the next 5 to 10 years. For example, your long-run objective might be to apply a set of marketing research and marketing management tools to the food manufacturing industry—with the objective of becoming director of marketing research in a small food manufacturing company.

Your long-run objectives should be realistic and attainable. They should be objectives you have thought about and for which you think you have the necessary skills (or the capabilities to develop those skills) as well as the motivation to reach the objectives.

Develop short-run objectives

To achieve your long-run objective(s), you should develop one or more short-run objective(s). These should spell out what is needed to reach your long-run objective(s). For example, you might need to develop a variety of marketing research skills *and* marketing management skills—because both are needed to reach the longer-run objective. Or you might need an entry-level position in marketing research for a large food manufacturer—to gain experience and background. An even shorter-run objective might be to take the academic courses that are necessary to get that desired entry-level job. In this example, you would probably need a minimum of an undergraduate degree in marketing—with an emphasis on marketing research. (Note that, given the longer-run objective of managerial responsibility, a business degree would probably be better than a degree in statistics or psychology.)

DEVELOPING YOUR MARKETING PLAN

Now that you've developed your objectives, move on to developing your own personal marketing plan. This means zeroing in on likely opportunities and developing a specific marketing strategy for these opportunities. Let's talk about that now.

Identify likely opportunities

An important step in strategy planning is identifying potentially attractive opportunities. Depending on where you are in your academic training, this can vary all the way from preliminary exploration to making detailed lists of companies that offer the kinds of jobs that interest you. If you're just getting started, talk to your school's career counselors and placement officers about the kinds of jobs being offered to your school's graduates. Your marketing instructors can help you be more realistic about ways you can match your training, abilities, and interests to job opportunities. Also, it helps to read business publications such as *Business Week, Fortune, The Wall Street Journal,* the *Journal of Marketing,* and *Advertising Age.* Don't overlook the business sections of your local newspapers to keep in touch with marketing developments in your area. And take advantage of any opportunity to talk with marketers directly. Ask them what they're doing—and what satisfactions they find in their jobs. Also, if your college has a marketing club, join it and participate actively in the club's programs. It will help you meet marketers and students with serious interest in the field. Some may have had interesting job experiences and can provide you with leads on part-time jobs or exciting career opportunities.

If you're far along in your present academic training, list companies that you know something about or are willing to investigate—trying to match your skills and interests with possible opportunities. Narrow your list to a few companies you might like to work for.

If you have trouble narrowing down to specific companies, make a list of your personal interest areas—sports, travel, reading, music, or whatever. Think about the companies that compete in markets related to these interests. Often your own knowledge about these areas—and interest in them—can give you a competitive advantage in getting a job. This helps you focus on companies that serve needs you think are important or interesting.

Then do some research on these companies. Find out how they are organized, their product lines, and their overall strategies. Try to get clear job descriptions for the kinds of positions you're seeking. Match the job descriptions against your understanding of these jobs and your objectives. Jobs with similar titles may offer very different opportunities. By researching job positions and companies in depth, you should begin to have a feel for where you would be comfortable as an employee. This will help you narrow your "target market" of possible employers to perhaps five firms. For example, you may decide that your "target market" for an entry position is large corporations with: (1) in-depth training programs, (2) a wide product line, and (3) a wide variety of marketing jobs that will enable you to get a range of experiences and responsibilities within the same company.

Planning your "Product"   Just like any strategy planner, you must decide what "Product" features are necessary to appeal to your target market. Identify which credentials are mandatory—and which are optional. For example, is your present academic program enough, or will you need more training? Also, identify what technical skills are needed—such as computer programming or accounting. Further, are there any business experiences or extracurricular activities that might help make your "Product" more attractive to employers? This might involve active participation in college organizations or work experience—either on the job or in internships.

Planning your promotion   Once you identify target companies and develop a Product you hope will be attractive to them, you have to tell these potential customers about your Product. You can write directly to prospective employers—sending a carefully developed résumé that reflects your strategy planning. Or you can visit them in person (with your résumé). Many colleges run well-organized interviewing services. Seek their advice early in your strategy planning effort.

IMPLEMENTING YOUR MARKETING PLAN

When you complete your personal marketing plan, you have to implement it—starting with working to accomplish your short-run objectives. If, as part of your plan, you decide that you need specific outside experience, then arrange to get it. This may mean taking a low-paying job—or even volunteering to work in political organizations or volunteer organizations where you can get that kind of experience. If you decide that you need skills you can learn in academic courses, plan to take these courses. Similarly, if you don't have a good understanding of your opportunities, then learn as much as you can about possible jobs by talking to professors, taking advanced courses, and talking to businesspeople. And, of course, trends and opportunities can change—so continue to read business publications, talk with professionals in your areas of interest, and be sure that the planning you've done still makes sense.

Strategy planning must adapt to the environment. If the environment changes or your personal objectives change, you have to develop a new plan. This is an ongoing process—and you may never be completely satisfied with your strategy planning. But even trying will make you look much more impressive when you begin your job interviews. Remember, while all employers would like to hire a Superman or a Wonder Woman, they are also impressed with candidates who know what they want to do and are looking for a place where they can fit in—and make a contribution. So planning a personal strategy and implementing it almost guarantee you'll do a better job of career planning, which will help ensure that you reach your own objectives—whatever they are.

Whether or not you decide to pursue a marketing career, the authors wish you the best of luck in your search for a challenging and rewarding career—wherever your interests and abilities may take you.

Cases

GUIDE TO THE USE OF THESE CASES

Cases can be used in many ways. And the same case can be analyzed several times for different purposes.

"Suggested cases" are listed at the end of most chapters, but these cases can also be used later in the text. The main criterion for the order of the cases is the amount of technical vocabulary—or text principles—which are needed to read the case meaningfully. The first cases are "easiest" in this regard. This is why an early case can easily be used two or three times—with different emphasis. Some early cases might require some consideration of Product and Price, for example, and might be used twice, perhaps in regard to place planning and later pricing. In contrast, later cases which focus more on Price might be treated more effectively *after* the Price chapters are covered.

1. McDonald's "Fast-Food" Restaurant

Mary Marino manages a McDonald's restaurant. She has noticed that some senior citizens have become not just regular patrons—but patrons who come for breakfast and stay on until about 3:00 P.M. Many of these older customers were attracted initially by a monthly breakfast special for people aged 55 and older. The meal costs $.99 and refills of coffee are free. Every fourth Monday, 100 to 150 seniors jam Mary's McDonald's for the special offer. But now almost as many of them are coming every day—turning the fast-food restaurant into a meeting place. They sit for hours with a cup of coffee, chatting with friends. On most days, as many as 100 will stay from one to five hours.

About a year ago, as a goodwill gesture, Mary brought in a team from the American Red Cross to check her regular customers' blood pressure—free of charge. Mary's employees have been very friendly to the seniors, calling them by their first names and visiting with them each day. In fact, Mary's McDonald's is a "happy place"—and her employees develop close relationships with the seniors. Some employees have even visited customers who have been hospitalized. "You know," Mary says, "I really get attached to the customers. They're like my family. I really care about these people." They are all "friends" and being friendly with the customers is a part of McDonald's corporate philosophy.

These older customers are an orderly group—and very friendly to anyone who comes in. Further, they are neater than most customers, and carefully clean up their tables before they leave. Nevertheless, Mary is beginning to wonder if anything should be done about her growing "non-fast-food" clientele. There's no crowding problem yet during the time when the seniors like to come. But if the size of the senior citizens group continues to grow, crowding could become a problem. Further, Mary is concerned that her restaurant might come to be known as an "old people's" restaurant—which might discourage some younger customers. And if customers felt the restaurant was crowded, some might feel that they wouldn't get fast service. On the other hand, a place that seems busy might be seen as "a good place to go" and a "friendly place."

Mary also worries about the image she is projecting. McDonald's is a "fast-food restaurant," and normally customers are expected to "eat and run." Will encouraging—or not discouraging—people to stay and visit change the whole concept? In the extreme, Mary's McDonald's might become more like a "European style" restaurant where the customers are never rushed, where they feel very comfortable about lingering over coffee for an hour or two! Mary Marino knows that the amount her senior customers spend is similar to the average customer's purchase—but the seniors do use the facilities for a much longer time. However, most of the older customers leave McDonald's by 3:00—before the "after school" crowd comes in.

Evaluate Mary Marino's current strategy regarding senior citizens. Does her current strategy improve McDonald's image? What should she do about the senior citizen market—should she encourage, ignore, or discourage her seniors? Explain.

2. Alta Foods, Inc.

It is now 1989, and Bob Bullard, newly elected president of Alta Foods, Inc., faces some serious problems. Alta Foods is a 120-year-old California-based food processor. Its multiproduct lines are widely accepted under the "Alta" brand. The company and its subsidiaries prepare, package, and sell canned and frozen foods—including fruits, vegetables, pickles, and condiments. Alta, which operates more than 27 processing plants in the United States, is one of the largest U.S. food processors, with annual sales (in 1988) of about $625 million.

Until 1986, Alta Foods was a subsidiary of a major midwestern food processor (Multi, Inc.), and many of the present managers came from the parent company. Alta's last president recently said: "Multi's influence is still with us. As long as new products show a potential for an increase in the company's sales volume, they are produced. Traditionally, there has been little, if any, attention paid to margins. We are well aware that profits will come through good products."

Dave Zappe, a 25-year employee and now production manager, is in full agreement with the multiproduct-line policy. Mr. Zappe says: "Volume comes from satisfying needs. We will can, pack, or freeze any vegetable or fruit we think the consumer might want." He also admits that much of the expansion in product lines was encouraged by economics. The typical plants in the industry are not fully used. By adding new products to use this excess capacity, costs are spread over greater volume. So the production department is always looking for new ways to make more effective use of its present facilities.

The wide expansion of product lines coupled with Alta's line-forcing policy has resulted in 85 percent of the firm's sales coming from supermarket chain stores—such as Safeway, Kroger, and A&P. Smaller stores are generally not willing to accept the Alta policy—which requires that any store wanting to carry its brand name must be willing to carry the whole line of 68 varieties of fruits and vegetables. Mr. Zappe explains, "We know that only large stores can afford to invest the amount of money in inventory that it would take to adequately stock our products. But, the large stores are the volume! We give consumers the choice of any Alta product they want, and the result is maximum sales." Many small retailers have complained about Alta's policy, but they have been considered too small in potential sales volume per store to be of any significance.

In 1989, a stockholders' revolt over low profits (only $100,000 in 1988) resulted in Alta's president and two of its five directors being removed. Bob Bullard, a lawyer who had been a staff assistant to the chairman of the board, was elected president. One of the first things he focused on was the variable and low levels of profits earned in the past several years. A comparison of Alta's results with comparable operations of some large competitors supported Mr. Bullard's concern. In the past 10 years, Alta's closest competitors have had an average profit return on shareholder's investment of 6 to 12 percent, while Alta averaged only 3.8 percent. Further, Alta's sales volume, $625 million in 1988, has not increased much from the 1956 level (after adjusting for inflation)—while operating costs have soared upward. Profits for the firm were about $8 million in 1956. The closest they have come since then is about $6 million—in 1964.

The outgoing president blamed his failure on an inefficient marketing department. He said, "Our marketing department has deteriorated. I can't exactly put my finger on it, but the overall quality of marketing people has dropped, and morale is bad. The team just didn't perform." When Mr. Bullard confronted Don Sharp, the vice president of marketing, with this charge, his reply was, "It's not our fault. I think the company made a key mistake after World War II. It expanded horizontally—by increasing its number of

product offerings—while major competitors were expanding vertically, growing their own raw materials and making all of their packing materials. They can control quality and make profits in manufacturing that can be used in marketing. I lost some of my best people from frustration. We just aren't competitive enough to reach the market the way we should with a comparable product and price."

In further conversation with Don Sharp, Mr. Bullard learned more about the nature of Alta's market. Although all the firms in the food-processing industry advertise heavily, the size of the market for most processed foods hasn't grown much. Further, most consumers aren't very selective. If they can't find the brand of food they are looking for, they'll pick up another brand rather than go without a basic part of their diet. No company in the industry has much effect on the price at which its products are sold. Chain store buyers are very knowledgeable about prices and special promotions available from all the competing suppliers, and they are quick to play one supplier off against another to keep the price low. Basically, they have a price they are willing to pay—and they won't exceed it. However, the chains will charge any price they wish on a given brand sold at retail. (That is, a 48-can case of sweet peas might be purchased from any supplier for $17.90, no matter whose product it is. Generally, the shelf price for each is no more than a few pennies different, but chain stores occasionally attract customers by placing a well-known brand on "sale.")

At this point, Mr. Bullard is wondering why Alta Foods isn't as profitable as it once was. Also, he is puzzled as to why the competition is putting products on the market with low potential sales volume. For example, one major competitor recently introduced a line of "gourmet" fruits.

Evaluate Alta Foods' situation. What should Mr. Bullard do to improve Alta's situation? Explain.

3. *Gerber Products Company*

Kathy Delaney, newly hired marketing manager for Gerber Products Company—a large baby foods producer—is trying to decide what product-market opportunities might make sense for Gerber. She is under serious pressure because the new CEO, David

Johnson, has just "cleaned out" some weak "diversification" efforts—including trucking, furniture, and toy ventures—which tended to take the company away from its core baby food business. Now he is looking for new opportunities close to the food business. But Mr. Johnson has made it clear that Gerber may want to move beyond baby foods because less than 5 percent of U.S. households have babies.

Mr. Johnson says that he would like Kathy and other Gerber managers to come up with new ideas for "premium-quality, value-added products in niche markets." It might be possible, for example, to extend the sales of its baby food products to adults (in general) and/or senior citizens. Some of its current "chunky" food items—no-salt, easy-to-chew foods—are intended for older tots and might be attractive to some adults. But care may be needed in expanding into these markets. Gerber had troubles in the 1970s with some products that were intended for adult tastes—one was beef stroganoff in a baby-food jar. Yet Mr. Johnson now wonders, "How come we can't develop food products that target everyone over the toddler age?"

Recent new product offerings include a line of applesauce-based fruit cups, bottled water, and shelf-stable homogenized milk. All three of these were seen to fit with Gerber's growth plans—offering more premium-quality, value-added products to niche markets. Growth efforts might also include selecting products that will enable the company to get enough experience to understand a market area and be able to pursue joint ventures or acquisitions.

Mr. Johnson's background includes not only domestic but international marketing with major companies that sell cleaning products, health and beauty aids, drug products, and baked goods. So it is likely that he will be willing to consider going quite far from baby foods. And given that Gerber is a major U.S. food processor—with sales of about $1 billion—it is clear the company has the production, distribution, and financial resources to consider a good-sized product-market opportunity. The problem is whether there are any attractive new opportunities—or whether Gerber must simply copy someone else's earlier developments.

Evaluate what Mr. Johnson wants to do. Suggest five product-market opportunities that might make sense for Gerber Products Company and explain why.

4. Bill's Cleaning, Inc.

Bill Brown is getting desperate about his new business. He's not sure he can make a go of it—and he really wants to stay in his hometown of Traverse City, Michigan. This is a beautiful summer resort area along the eastern shore of Lake Michigan. The area's permanent population of 25,000 more than triples in the summer months.

Bill spent seven years in the Navy after high school graduation, returning home in June 1988. He decided to go into business for himself because he couldn't find a good job in the Traverse City area. He set up Bill's Cleaning, Inc. He thought that his savings would allow him to start the business without borrowing any money. His estimates of required expenditures were: $6,000 for a used panel truck, $525 for a steam-cleaning machine adaptable to carpets and furniture, $375 for a heavy-duty commercial vacuum cleaner, $50 for special brushes and attachments, $75 for the initial supply of cleaning fluids and compounds, and $200 for insurance and other incidental expenses. This total of $7,225 still left Bill with about $2,800 in savings to cover living expenses while getting started.

One of the reasons Bill chose the cleaning business was his previous work experience. From the time he was 16, Bill had worked part-time for Joe Trust. Mr. Trust operates the only other successful carpet-cleaning company in Traverse City. There is one other cleaning company in Traverse City, but it is rumored to be near bankruptcy.

Mr. Trust prides himself on quality work and has a loyal clientele. Specializing in residential carpet cleaning, Trust has built a strong customer franchise. For 35 years, Trust's major source of new business—besides retailer recommendations—has been satisfied customers who tell friends about the quality service received from Mr. Trust. He is so highly thought of that the leading carpet and furniture stores in Traverse City always recommend Trust for preventive maintenance in quality carpet and furniture care. Often Trust is given the keys to Traverse City's finest homes for months at a time when owners are out of town and want his services. Trust's customers are so loyal, in fact, that Vita-Clean—a national household carpet-cleaning franchise—found it impossible to compete with him. Even price cutting was not an effective weapon against Mr. Trust.

Bill Brown thought that he knew the business as well as Mr. Trust—having worked for him many years.

Bill was anxious to reach his $50,000-per-year sales objective because he thought this would provide him with a comfortable living in Traverse City. While aware of opportunities for carpet cleaning in businesses such as office buildings and motels, Bill felt that the sales volume available there was only about $30,000 because most businesses had their own cleaning staffs. As Bill saw it, his only opportunity was direct competition with Mr. Trust.

To get started, Bill allocated $900 to advertise his business in the local newspaper. With this money he bought two large "announcement" ads and 52 weeks of daily three-line ads in the classified section listed under Miscellaneous Residential Services. All that was left was to paint a sign on his truck and wait for business to "take off."

Bill had a few customers and was able to gross about $120 a week. Of course, he had expected much more. These customers were usually Trust regulars who, for one reason or another (usually stains, spills, or house guests), weren't able to wait the two weeks until Trust could work them in. While these people agreed that Bill's work was of the same quality as Mr. Trust's, they preferred Trust's "quality-care" image. Sometimes Bill did get more work than he could handle. This happened during April and May—when resort owners were preparing for summer openings and owners of summer homes were ready to "open the cottage." The same rush occurred in September and October as resorts and homes were being closed for the winter. During these months, Bill was able to gross about $120 to $150 a day—working 10 hours.

Toward the end of his discouraging first year in business, Bill Brown is thinking about quitting. While he hates to think about leaving Traverse City, he can't see any way of making a living in the carpet- and furniture-cleaning business in Traverse City. Mr. Trust has the whole residential market sewed up—except in the rush seasons and for people who need emergency cleaning.

Why wasn't Bill Brown able to reach his objective of $50,000? What should Bill do?

5. Dow Chemical Company

Bruce Chin, a chemist in Dow Chemical Company's polymer resins laboratory, is trying to decide how hard to fight for the new product he has developed. Bruce's job is to find new, more profitable applications for the company's present resin products—and his current efforts are running into unexpected problems.

During the last five years, Bruce has been under heavy pressure from top management to come up with an idea that will open up new markets for the company's foamed polystyrene.

Two years ago, Bruce developed the "spiral-dome concept"—a method of using the foamed polystyrene to make dome-shaped roofs and other structures. He described the procedure for making domes as follows: The construction of a spiral dome involves the use of a specially designed machine that bends, places, and bonds pieces of plastic foam together into a predetermined dome shape. In forming a dome, the machine head is mounted on a boom, which swings around a pivot like the hands of a clock, laying and bonding layer upon layer of foam board in a rising spherical form.

According to Bruce, polystyrene foamed boards have several advantages:

1. Foam board is stiff—but it can be formed or bonded to itself by heat alone.
2. Foam board is extremely lightweight and easy to handle. It has good structural rigidity.
3. Foam board has excellent and permanent insulating characteristics. (In fact, the major use for foam board is as an insulator.)
4. Foam board provides an excellent base on which to apply a variety of surface finishes.

Using his good selling abilities, Bruce easily convinced top management that his idea had potential.

According to a preliminary study by the marketing research department, the following were areas of construction that could be served by the domes:

1. Bulk storage.
2. Cold storage.
3. Educational construction.
4. Covers for industrial tanks.
5. Light commercial construction.
6. Planetariums.
7. Recreational construction (such as a golf-course starter house).

The study focused on uses for existing dome structures. Most of the existing domes are made of cement-based materials. The study showed that large savings would result from using foam boards due to the reduction of construction time.

Because of the new technology involved, the company decided to do its own contracting (at least for the first four to five years after starting the sales program). Bruce thought this was necessary to make sure that no mistakes were made by inexperienced contractor crews. (For example, if not applied properly, the plastic may burn.)

After building a few domes to demonstrate the concept, Bruce contacted some leading architects across the country. Reactions were as follows:

"It's very interesting, but we're not sure the fire marshal of Chicago would ever give his OK."

"Your tests show that foamed domes can be protected against fires, but there are no *good* tests for unconventional building materials as far as I am concerned."

"I like the idea, but foam board does not have the impact resistance of cement."

"We design a lot of recreational facilities, and kids will find a way of poking holes in the foam."

"Building codes in our area are written for wood and cement structures. Maybe we'd be interested if the codes change."

After this unexpected reaction, management didn't know what to do. Bruce still thinks Dow should go ahead. He is convinced that a few reports of well-constructed domes in leading newspapers will go a long way toward selling the idea. But his managers aren't sure they want to OK spending more money on "his" product.

What should Bruce do? What should Dow Chemical do? Explain how Dow Chemical got into the present situation.

6. Inland Steel Company

Inland Steel Company is one of the two major producers of wide-flange beams in the Chicago area. The other major producer in the area is the U.S. Steel Corporation (now USX), which is several times larger than Inland in terms of production capacity on this particular product. Bethlehem Steel Company and U.S. Steel have eastern plants that produce this product, and some small firms compete. But generally U.S. Steel and Inland Steel are the major competitors in wide-flange beams in the Chicago area because typically the mill price charged by all producers is the

same and customers must pay freight from the mill. Therefore, the large eastern mills' delivered prices wouldn't be competitive in the Chicago area.

Wide-flange beams are one of the principal steel products used in construction. They are the modern version of what are commonly known as "I-beams." U.S. Steel rolls a full range of wide flanges from 6 to 36 inches. Inland entered the field about 25 years ago when it converted an existing mill to produce this product. Inland's mill is limited to flanges up to 24 inches, however. At the time of the conversion, Inland felt that customer usage of sizes over 24 inches was likely to be small. In the past few years, however, there has been a definite trend toward the larger and heavier sections.

The beams produced by the various competitors are almost identical since customers buy according to standard dimensional and physical-property specifications. In the smaller size range, there are a number of competitors. But above 14 inches only U.S. Steel and Inland compete in the Chicago area. Above 24 inches, U.S. Steel has no competition.

All the steel companies sell these beams through their own sales forces. The customer for these beams is called a "structural fabricator." This fabricator typically buys unshaped beams and other steel products from the mills and shapes them according to the specifications of each customer. The fabricator sells to the contractor or owner of the structure being built.

The structural fabricator usually must sell on a competitive-bid basis. The bidding is done on the plans and specifications prepared by an architectural or structural engineering firm and forwarded to him by the contractor who wants the bid. Although several hundred structural fabricators compete in the region, relatively few account for the majority of wide-flange tonnage. Since the price is the same from all producers, they typically buy beams on the basis of availability (i.e., availability to meet production schedules) and performance (i.e., reliability in meeting the promised delivery schedule).

Several years ago, Inland's production schedulers saw that they were going to have an excess of hot-rolled plate capacity in the near future. At the same time, a new production technique allowed a steel company to weld three plates together into a section with the same dimensional and physical properties and almost the same cross-section as a rolled wide-flange beam. This development appeared to offer two advantages to Inland: (1) it would enable

Inland to use some of the excess plate capacity, and (2) larger sizes of wide-flange beams could be offered. Cost analysts showed that by using a fully depreciated plate mill and the new welding process it would be possible to produce and sell larger wide-flange beams at competitive prices—the same price charged by U.S. Steel.

Inland's managers were excited about the possibilities because customers usually appreciate having a second source of supply. Also, the new approach would allow the production of up to a 60-inch flange. With a little imagination, these larger sizes might offer a significant breakthrough for the construction industry.

Inland decided to go ahead with the new project. As the production capacity was converted, the salespeople were kept well informed of the progress. They, in turn, promoted this new capability to their customers—emphasizing that soon they would be able to offer a full range of beam products. Several general information letters were sent to a broad mailing list, but no advertising was used. The market development section of the sales department was very busy explaining the new possibilities of the process—particularly to fabricators—at engineering trade associations and shows.

When the new production line was finally ready to go, the market reaction was disappointing and no orders had been obtained. In general, customers were wary of the new product. The structural fabricators felt they couldn't use it without the approval of their customers because it would involve deviating from the specified rolled sections. And, as long as they could still get the rolled section, why make the extra effort for something unfamiliar—especially with no price advantage? The salespeople were also bothered with a very common question: How can you take plate that you sell for about $450 per ton and make a product that you can sell for $460? This question came up frequently and tended to divert the whole discussion to the cost of production—rather than to the way the new product might be used.

Evaluate Inland's situation. What should Inland do?

7. Pillsbury's Häagen-Dazs

Assume you are the newly hired product-market manager for Häagen-Dazs—the market leader in the

U.S. "super premium ice cream market." The company has seen its sales continue to grow during the 1980s, but this market may be on the edge of significant change and very aggressive competition—and you are now responsible for Häagen-Dazs' strategy planning.

Super premium ice cream sales are slowing down, in part because of competition from other products, such as lower calorie yogurts and ice milk. Some producers' sales, including Häagen-Dazs', are continuing to grow at attractive rates—10 percent to 50 percent a year. But other super premium producers are reporting flat sales—and some are going out of business.

There is some evidence, also, that the urge to indulge in super desserts may be giving way to diet and health concerns. Some people are reducing or even eliminating "super" desserts. And some "dessert junkies" who want to indulge without too much guilt are turning to soft frozen yogurt and low calorie ice milk. This has encouraged some super premium ice cream competitors to offer these products too. Pillsbury's Häagen-Dazs, International Dairy Queen, Inc., and Baskin Robbins are selling frozen yogurt. And Kraft, Inc., which makes Frusen Glädjé, and Dreyer's Grand Ice Cream, Inc., are among many other ice cream makers who are promoting gourmet versions of ice milk. Some producers are even seeking government approval to call such ice milk "light ice cream."

Most ice cream products are considered economy and regular brands—priced at $2.00 to $3.00 a half gallon. But the higher priced—and higher profit—super premium products provided most of the growth in the ice cream market in the 1980s. The super premium ice cream category accounted for about 12 percent of total ice cream sales ($7 billion) in 1989 compared to almost 5 percent in 1980.

Super premium ice cream, with more than 14 percent butter fat (economy ice cream has a minimum of 10 percent) is the ultimate "yuppie" product—rich, indulgent, and fashionable. It retails for $2.00 to $2.50 a *pint*, or $8.00 to $10.00 a half gallon.

The rapid growth of the super premium market may be over, however. More and more consumers are becoming concerned about cholesterol—and ice cream is high in cholesterol.

Some of the super premium producers remain optimistic, however. Häagen-Dazs, for example, feels that because "people like to make every calorie count—they want wonderful food." But other competitors are more concerned because they see many close competitors going out of business. Frozen yogurt seems to be a big factor. Also the easy availability of super premium ice cream in supermarkets has hurt some competitors who sell through ice cream stores, which specialize in take-out cones, sundaes, and small containers of ice cream.

Many ice cream producers are turning to frozen yogurt for growth. A fad in the 1970s, frozen yogurt went into a long slump because many people didn't like the tart taste. But now the product has been reformulated and is winning customers. The difference is that today's frozen yogurt tastes more like ice cream.

The yogurt market leader, TCBY Enterprises, Inc., which had sales of only about $2 million in 1983, has risen to over $100 million in sales. Yogurt makers are using aggressive promotion against ice cream. TCBY ads preach: "Say goodbye to high calories—say goodbye to ice cream" and "All the pleasure, none of the guilt." And the ads for its nonfat frozen yogurt emphasize: "Say goodbye to fat and high calories with the great taste of TCBY Nonfat Frozen Yogurt."

Baskin Robbins has introduced yogurt in many of its stores and has even changed its name to Baskin Robbins Ice Cream and Yogurt. Häagen-Dazs also offers yogurt in most of its stores.

A new threat to super premium ice cream comes from ice milk. Traditionally, ice milk was an "economical" product for families on a budget. The butter fat content was at the low end of the 2 percent to 7 percent range. And, in part because of this, it was dense, gummy, stringy, and had a coarse texture. But the new "gourmet" ice milk products taste better due to 6 percent to 7 percent butter fat, less air content, and improved processing. And they still have only about half the calories of ice cream. Some producers of these products find their sales increasing nicely. Dreyer's, for example, is experiencing rapid growth of its Dreyer's Light, which retails for about $4.30 a half gallon.

Other ice cream producers, including Häagen-Dazs, say they are not planning to offer ice milk—under any name. These firms feel their brands stand for high quality and the best ingredients and they do not want to offer a "cheap product." As one marketing manager put it, "Ice milk is a failure, and that is why some producers are trying to reposition it as light ice cream."

Evaluate what is happening in the "ice cream market." What should you advise Häagen-Dazs about the apparent leveling off of the super premium ice cream market and the possible growth of the "ice milk market"? Should you plan to have Häagen-Dazs offer an ice milk product? Why?

8. *Mario's*

Mario Santini, the owner of Mario's, is reviewing the slow growth of his restaurant. He's also thinking about the future and wondering if he should change his strategy. Mario's is a fairly large restaurant—about 2,000 square feet—located in the center of a small shopping center that was completed early in 1987. In addition to Mario's restaurant, other businesses in the shopping center include a supermarket, a beauty shop, a liquor store, and a video rental store. Ample parking space is available.

The shopping center is located along a heavily traveled major traffic artery in a residential section of a growing suburb in the East. The nearby population is made up of middle-income families. Although the ethnic background of the residents is fairly heterogeneous, a large proportion are Italians.

Mario's sells mostly full-course dinners (no bar) and is owned and managed by Mario Santini. He graduated from a local high school and a nearby university and has lived in this town with his wife and two children for many years. He has been self-employed in the restaurant business since his graduation from college in 1959. His most recent venture—before opening Mario's—was a large restaurant that he operated successfully with his brother from 1977 to 1983. In 1983, Mario sold out his share because of illness. Following his recovery, Mario was anxious for something to do and opened the present restaurant in April 1987.

Mario feels his plans for the business and his opening were well thought out. When he was ready to start his new restaurant, he looked at several possible locations before finally deciding on the present one. Mario explained: "I looked everywhere, and this is one of the areas I inspected. I particularly noticed the heavy traffic when I first looked at it. This is the crossroads from north to south for practically every main artery statewide. So obviously the potential is here."

Having decided on the location, Mario eagerly attacked the problem of the new building. He tiled the floor, put in walls of surfwood, installed new plumbing and electrical fixtures and an extra washroom, and purchased the necessary restaurant equipment. All this cost $65,000—which came from his own cash savings. He then spent an additional $1,200 for glassware, $2,000 for his initial food stock, and $1,525 to advertise his opening in the local newspaper. The paper served the whole metro area, so the $1,525 bought only three quarter-page ads. These expenditures also came from his own personal savings. Next, he hired five waitresses at $140 a week and one chef at $250 a week. Then, with $15,000 cash reserve for the business, he was ready to open. (His wife—a high school teacher—was willing to support the family until the restaurant caught on.) Reflecting his "sound business sense," Mario knew he would need a substantial cash reserve to fall back on until the business got on its feet. He expected this to take about one year. He had no expectations of "getting rich overnight."

The restaurant opened in April and by August had a weekly gross revenue of only $1,500. Mario was a little discouraged with this, but he was still able to meet all his operating expenses without investing any "new money" in the business. By September business was still slow, and Mario had to invest an additional $2,000 in the business "for survival purposes."

Business had not improved in November, and Mario stepped up his advertising, hoping this would help. In December, he spent $500 of his cash reserve for radio advertising—10 late evening spots on a news program at a station that aims at "middle-income America." Mario also spent $1,000 more during the next several weeks for some metro newspaper ads.

By April 1988, the situation had begun to improve, and by June his weekly gross was up to between $2,000 and $2,100. By March of 1989, the weekly gross had risen to about $2,500. Mario increased the working hours of his staff six to seven hours a week and added another cook to handle the increasing number of customers. Mario was more optimistic for the future because he was finally doing a little better than "breaking even." His full-time involvement seemed to be paying off. He had not put any new money into the business since the summer of 1988 and expected business to continue to rise. He had not yet taken any salary for himself, even though he had built up a small "surplus" of about $7,000. Instead, he planned to put in a new air-conditioning system at a cost of $6,000. He was also planning to use what

salary he might have taken for himself to hire two new waitresses to handle the growing volume of business. And he saw that if business increased much more he would have to add another cook.

Evaluate Mario's past and present marketing strategy. What should he do now?

9. *Holiday Inn versus Days Inn*

Tom Spur is trying to decide whether he should make some minor changes in the way he operates his Sleepy Inn motel or if he should join either the Days Inn or Holiday Inn motel chains. Some decision must be made soon because his present operation is losing money. But joining either of the chains will require fairly substantial changes, including new capital investment if he goes with Holiday Inn.

Tom bought the recently completed 60-room motel two years ago, after leaving a successful career as a production manager for a producer of industrial machinery. He was looking for an interesting opportunity that would be less demanding than the production manager position. The Sleepy Inn is located about one-half mile off an interstate highway at the edge of a small town in a rapidly expanding resort area. It is 15 miles from a tourist area with several nationally franchised full-service resort motels suitable for "destination" vacations. There is a Best Western, a Ramada Inn, and a Hilton Inn, as well as many "mom and pop" motels in the tourist area. The interstate highway carries a great deal of traffic since the resort area is between several major metropolitan areas.

Initially, Tom was satisfied with his purchase. He had traveled a lot himself and stayed in many different hotels and motels—so he had some definite ideas about what travelers wanted. He felt that a relatively plain but modern room with a comfortable bed, standard bath facilities, and free cable TV would appeal to most customers. Further, Tom thought a swimming pool or any other nonrevenue producing additions were not necessary. And he felt a restaurant would be a greater management problem than any benefits it would offer could offset. However, after many customers commented, Tom arranged to serve a free Continental breakfast of coffee and rolls in a room next to the registration desk.

Day-to-day operations went fairly smoothly in the first two years, in part because Tom and his wife handled registration and office duties as well as general management. During the first year of operation, occupancy began to stabilize around 55 percent of capacity. But according to industry figures, this was far below the average of 68 percent for his classification—motels without restaurants.

After two years of operation, Tom was concerned because his occupancy rates continued to be below average. He decided to look for ways to increase both occupancy rate and profitability—and still maintain his independence.

Tom wanted to avoid direct competition with the resort areas offering much more complete services. He stressed a price appeal in his signs and brochures—and he was quite proud of the fact that he had been able to avoid all the "unnecessary expenses" of the resorts. As a result, Tom was able to offer lodging at a very modest price—about 30 percent below that of even the lowest-priced resort area motels. The customers who stayed at the Sleepy Inn said they found it quite acceptable. But he was troubled by what seemed to be a large number of people driving into his parking lot, looking around, and not coming in to register.

Tom was particularly interested in the results of a recent study by the regional tourist bureau. This study revealed the following information about area vacationers:

1. 68 percent of the visitors to the area are young couples and older couples without children.
2. 40 percent of the visitors plan their vacations and reserve rooms more than 60 days in advance.
3. 66 percent of the visitors stay more than three days in the area and at the same location.
4. 78 percent of the visitors indicated that recreational facilities were important in their choice of accommodations.
5. 13 percent of the visitors had family incomes of less than $20,000 per year.
6. 38 percent of the visitors indicated that it was their first visit to the area.

After much thought, Tom began to seriously consider affiliating with a national motel chain. After some investigating, he focused on two: Days Inn and Holiday Inn.

Days Inn of America, Inc., is an Atlanta-based chain of economy lodgings. It has been growing rapidly—and is willing to take on new franchisees. A major advantage of Days Inn is that it would not require a major capital investment by Tom. The firm is targeting people interested in lower-priced motels—in particular senior citizens, the military, school sports teams, educators, and business travelers. In contrast, Holiday Inn would probably require Tom to upgrade some of his Sleepy Inn facilities, including adding a swimming pool. The total new capital investment would be between $250,000 and $500,000 depending on how "fancy" he got. But then Tom would be able to charge higher prices—perhaps $60 per day on the average, rather than the $40 per day per room he's charging now.

The major advantages of going with either of these national chains would be their central reservations system—and their national names. Both companies offer toll-free reservation lines—nationwide—and these reservations produce about 40 percent of all bookings in affiliated motels.

A major difference between the two national chains is their method of promotion. Days Inn uses little TV advertising and less print advertising than Holiday Inn. Instead, Days Inn emphasizes sales promotions. In a recent campaign, for example, Blue Bonnet margarine users could exchange "proof-of-purchase seals" for a free night at a Days Inn. This tie-in led to the Days Inn system *selling* an additional 10,000 rooms. Further, Days Inn operates a "September Days Club" for over 300,000 senior citizens who receive such benefits as discount rates and a quarterly travel magazine. This club accounts for about 10 percent of the chain's room revenues.

Both firms charge 8 percent of gross room revenues for belonging to their chain to cover the costs of the reservation service and national promotion. This amount is payable monthly. In addition, franchise members must agree to maintain their facilities and make repairs and improvements as required. Failure to maintain facilities can result in losing the franchise. Periodic inspections are conducted as part of supervising the whole chain and helping the members operate more effectively.

Evaluate Tom Spur's present strategy. What should he do?

10.   Polar Ice Rink

Fred Miller, the manager of Polar Ice Rink, is trying to decide what strategies to use to do better than breaking even.

Polar is an ice-skating rink with a conventional hockey rink surface (85 feet × 200 feet). It is the only indoor ice rink in a northern city of about 300,000. Some outdoor rinks are operated by the city in the winter, but they don't offer regular ice skating programs because of weather variability.

Fred has a successful hockey program and is almost breaking even—which is about all he can expect if he emphasizes hockey. To try to improve his financial situation, Fred is trying to develop a public skating program. With such a program, he could have as many as 700 people in a public session at one time, instead of limiting the use of the ice to 12 to 24 people per hour. While the receipts from hockey can be as high as $130 an hour (plus concessions), the receipts from a two-hour public skating session—charging $3 per person—could yield up to $2,100 for a two-hour period (plus much higher concession revenue). The potential revenue from such large public skating sessions could add significantly to total receipts—and make Polar a profitable operation.

Fred has included several public skating sessions in his ice schedule, but so far they haven't attracted as many people as he hoped. In fact, on the average, they don't generate any more revenue than if the times were sold for hockey use. Even worse, more staff people are needed to handle a public skating session—guards, a ticket seller, skate rental, and more concession help.

The Sunday afternoon public skating sessions have been the most successful—with an average of 200 people attending during the winter season. Typically, this is a "kid-sitting" session. More than half of the patrons are young children who have been dropped off by their parents for several hours. There are some family groups.

In general, the kids and the families do have a good time—and a fairly loyal group comes every Sunday during the winter season. In the spring and fall, however, attendance drops about in half, depending on how nice the weather is. (Fred schedules no public sessions in the summer—focusing instead on hockey clinics and figure skating.)

It is the Friday and Saturday evening public sessions that are a big disappointment. The sessions run from 8 until 10—a time when he had hoped to attract couples. At $3 per person, plus 75 cents for skate rental, this would be a more economical date than going to the movies. In fact, Fred has seen quite a few young couples—and some keep coming back. But he also sees a surprising number of 8- to 12-year-olds who have been dropped off by their parents. The younger kids tend to race around the rink, playing tag. This affects the whole atmosphere—making it less appealing for dating couples.

Fred feels that it should be possible to develop a teenage and young-adult market by adapting the format used by roller-skating rinks. Their public skating sessions feature a variety of "couples-only" skates and "group games" as well as individual skating to dance music. Turning ice skating sessions into social activities is not common, however, although industry "rumors" suggest that a few operators have had success with the roller-skating format.

Fred installed some soft lights to try to change the evening atmosphere. The music was designed to encourage couples to skate together. For a few sessions, Fred even tried to have some "couples-only" skates, but this was strongly resisted by the young boys who felt that they had paid their money and there was no reason why they should be "kicked off the ice." Fred also tried to attract more young couples by bringing in a local disk jockey to broadcast from Polar—playing music and advertising the public sessions. But this had no effect on attendance—which varies from 50 to 100 per two-hour session.

Fred seriously considered the possibility of limiting the weekend evening sessions to people over 13 to try to change the environment. But when he counted the customers, he realized this would be risky. More than half of his customers on an average weekend night are 12 or under. This means that he would have to make a serious commitment to building the teenage and young-adult market. And, so far, his efforts haven't been successful. He has already invested over $2,000 in lighting changes and over $6,000 promoting the sessions over the rock music radio station—with disappointing results.

Some days, Fred feels it's hopeless. Maybe he should accept that a public ice skating session is a "mixed-bag." Or maybe he should just sell the time to hockey groups.

Evaluate Polar Ice Rink's situation. What should Fred do? Why?

11. Nike and Walking Shoes

Kathy Zang, owner of the Runners House, is trying to decide what she should do with her retail store and how committed she should be to Nike.

Kathy is a runner herself—and Runners House grew with the "jogging boom." The jogging boom helped make Runners House a profitable business. Throughout this period, Kathy emphasized Nike shoes, which were well accepted and seen as "top quality." This positive image made it possible to get $5 to $7 "above the market" for Nike shoes—and some of this was left with the retailers, which led to attractive profits for Kathy Zang.

Committing so heavily to Nike seemed like a good idea when its quality was up and the name was good. But around 1985, Nike quality began to slip. It hurt not only Nike but also retailers such as Kathy, who were heavily committed to them. Now, Nike has gotten its house in order again, but it is putting greater emphasis on other kinds of athletic equipment—and on walking shoes in particular. The jogging boom has flattened out and may actually be declining as many people find that jogging is hard work—and hard on the body, especially the knees. This is forcing Kathy to reconsider the emphasis in her store and to question whether she should continue committing so completely to Nike.

Nike's move into the walking shoe market is supported by U.S. Census Bureau estimates that between 50 and 80 million Americans walk for exercise—with between 15 and 20 million of these considering themselves serious "health" walkers. After several years of internal research, Nike is introducing shoes designed specifically for walkers. Nike found that walkers' feet are on the ground more often than a runner's feet—but receive about half the impact. So Nike reduced the size of its midsole and grooved it for flexibility. Nike also eliminated inside seams at the toe to avoid irritation and lowered the back tab of the shoe to avoid pressure on the Achilles tendon. The manager of the Nike walking shoe effort is optimistic about the potential for walking shoes. In fact, she's convinced it's a lot larger than the jogging market—especially since no experience or practice is necessary to be "good right away."

Many competitors are entering the walking shoe market, including the popular Avia, but the exact nature and size of the market isn't too clear. For one thing, it's likely that some ex-runners may just stop exercising—especially if they've damaged their knees. Further, the medical and biomechanical evidence about the need for specific walking shoes is not at all clear. One problem is that a shoe made for running can be used for walking, but not vice versa. Only very serious walkers may be interested in "only a walking shoe." Further, fashion has invaded the athletic wear markets, so it may be necessary to have many different colors and quality levels. But Nike has tended to emphasize function. This may be a problem because about 75 percent of current walkers are women, many of them older.

The main question that Kathy is debating is whether there really is a market for walking shoes. Further, is there a market for the Nike version of walking shoes, which will emphasize function more than fashion? What she must decide is whether she should shift her emphasis to walking shoes, while continuing to carry jogging shoes for her regular customers, and whether she should carry brands other than Nike. Should she put much greater emphasis on fashion rather than function? This would require, at the least, retraining current salespeople, and perhaps bringing in more fashion-oriented salespeople.

Just a small shift in emphasis probably won't make much of a difference. But a real shift to a heavy emphasis on walking shoes might require Kathy to change the name of her store—and perhaps even to hire salespeople who will be more sympathetic with nonjoggers and their needs.

One of the reasons she might want to broaden her line beyond Nike is that many other companies have entered the athletic shoe market, including Avia with its cantilevered-sole, Adidas, and many lesser-known and unknown brands. Many customers purchase "running shoes" with no intention of ever running in them. "Running shoes" are the new casual shoe, prices have dropped, and many producers are emphasizing fashion over function.

Still another problem that worries Kathy is whether she really wants to help pioneer a "specialty walking shoe" market. Those people who accept the need for "quality" walking shoes seem to be satisfied with running shoes or hiking boots. Selling a whole new walking shoe concept will require a lot of expensive introductory promotion. And, if it is successful, lower-priced versions will probably enter the market and be sold in most sporting goods stores and large shoe stores. So the larger margins that are available now will erode as the size of the "specialty walking shoe" market becomes clearer. The basic questions bothering Kathy are: Is there really a "specialty walking shoe" market and, if so, how big is it? To get a better idea of how people feel about "specialty walking shoes," she started asking some of her present customers how they felt about special shoes for walking. The following are representative responses:

"What? I can walk in my running shoes!"

"I might be interested if I could really notice the difference, but I think my running shoes will work fine."

"No, my running shoes walk good!"

To get a better feel for how noncustomers felt, she talked to some friends and neighbors and a few people in a nearby shopping mall. Typical responses were:

"My regular shoes are fine for walking."

"I really don't do much walking and don't see any need for such things!"

"I might be interested if you could explain to me why they were better than my present running shoes, which I got at K mart."

"My hiking boots work pretty well, but I'd be willing to hear how yours are better."

"I do a lot of walking and might be really interested if they were a lot better than the running shoes I'm using now."

"I'm always interested in looking at new products!"

Evaluate Kathy Zang's present strategy. Evaluate the alternative strategies she is considering. Which do you suggest? Why?

12. Union Carbide

Pat Cohen, a new product manager for Union Carbide, must decide what to do with a new antifreeze product that is not doing well compared to the company's other antifreeze products. Union Carbide is one of the large chemical companies in the United States—it makes a wide line of organic and inorganic chemicals, plastics, bio-products, and metals. Technical research has played a vital role in the company's growth.

Recently, one of Carbide's research laboratories developed a new antifreeze product—C-20. Much time and money was spent on the technical phase, involving various experiments concerned with the quality of the new product. Then Pat Cohen took over and has been trying to develop a strategy for the product.

The antifreeze commonly used now is ethylene glycol. If it leaks into the crankcase oil, it forms a thick, pasty sludge that can cause bearing damage, cylinder scoring, or a dozen other costly and time-consuming troubles for both the operator and the owner of heavy-duty equipment.

Carbide researchers believed that the new product—C-20—would be very valuable to the owners of heavy-duty diesel and gasoline trucks as well as to other heavy-equipment owners. Chemically, C-20 uses a propanol product instead of the conventional glycol and alcohol products. It cannot prevent leakage, but if it does get into the crankcase, it won't cause any problems.

The suggested price of C-20 is $20 per gallon—more than twice the price of regular antifreeze. The higher price was set because of higher production costs and to obtain a "premium" for making a better antifreeze.

At first, Pat thought she had two attractive markets for C-20: (1) the manufacturers of heavy-duty equipment and (2) the users of heavy-duty equipment. Carbide sales reps have made numerous calls. So far neither type of customer has shown much interest, and their sales manager is discouraging any more calls for C-20. The manufacturer prospects are reluctant to show interest in the product until it has been proven in actual use. The buyers for construction companies and other firms using heavy-duty equipment have also been hesitant. Some say the suggested price is far too high for the advantages offered. Others don't understand what is wrong with the present antifreeze and refuse to talk any more about paying extra for "just another" antifreeze.

Explain what has happened so far. What should Pat Cohen do?

13. Office Systems, Inc. (OSI)*

Max Lupe, marketing manager for Office Systems, Inc. (OSI) must decide whether he should permit his largest customer to buy some of OSI's best-selling file folders for resale under the customer's brand rather than OSI's brand. He is afraid that if he refuses, this customer—National Office Supplies, Inc.—will go to

---

*Adapted from a case written by Professor Hardy, University of Western Ontario, Canada.

another file folder producer and OSI will lose this business.

National Office Supplies (NOS) is a major distributor of office supplies and has already managed to put its own brand on more than 40 large selling office supply products. It distributes these products—as well as the branded products of many manufacturers—through its nationwide distribution network. Now, Rita Lopez, Vice President of Marketing for National Office Supplies, is seeking a line of file folders similar in quality to OSI's "Excel" brand, which now has over 50 percent of the market.

This is not the first time that NOS has asked OSI to produce a file folder line for NOS. On both previous occasions, Max Lupe has turned down the request and NOS continued to buy. In fact, NOS not only continued to buy the file folders but also the rest of OSI's lines. And total sales continued to grow. NOS accounts for almost 25 percent of Max's business. And Excel brand file folders account for about 40 percent of this volume.

OSI has consistently refused such "dealer branding" requests as a matter of corporate policy. This policy was set some years ago because of a desire (1) to avoid excessive dependence on any one customer and (2) to sell its own brands so that success depends on the quality of its products rather than just a low price. The policy developed from a concern that if it started making products under other customers' brands, then those customers could "shop around" for a low price and the business would be very fickle. At the time the policy was set, Max Lupe realized that it might cost them some business. But the policy was felt to be wise nevertheless because it allowed OSI to better control its future.

Office Systems, Inc. (OSI) has been in business 22 years and now has a sales volume of $30 million. Its primary products are file folders, file markers and labels, and a variety of indexing systems. OSI offers such a wide range of size, color, and type that no competition can match them in their part of the market. About 30 percent of OSI's file folder business is in specialized lines such as oversized blueprint and engineer drawings; "see through" files for medical markets; and greaseproof and waterproof files for marine, oil field, and other hazardous environmental markets. OSI's competitors are mostly small paper converters. But excess capacity in the industry is substantial and these converters are always hungry for orders and willing to cut price. Further, the raw materials for the Excel line of file folders are readily available.

OSI's distribution system consists of 10 regional stationery suppliers, NOS, and more than 35 local stationers who have wholesale and retail operations. The 10 regional stationers each have about six branches, while the local stationers each have one wholesale and three or four retail locations. The regional suppliers sell directly to large corporations and to some retailers. In contrast, NOS's main volume comes from retail sales to small businesses and walk-in customers.

Max Lupe has a real concern about the future of the local stationers' business. Some are seriously discussing the formation of buying groups to obtain volume discounts from vendors and thus compete more effectively with NOS's 60 retail stores and the large regionals. None of Max's other accounts is nearly as effective in retailing as NOS—which has developed a good reputation in every major city in the country. NOS's profits are the highest in the industry. Further, its brands are almost as well known as those of some key producers—and its expansion plans are aggressive.

Max is sure that OSI's brands are well entrenched in the market, despite the fact that most available money has been devoted to new product development rather than promotion of existing brands. But Max is concerned that if NOS brands its own file folders it will sell them at a discount and may even bring the whole market price level down. Across all the lines of file folders, Max is averaging a 35 percent gross margin, but the high-volume file folders sought by NOS are averaging only a 20 percent gross margin. And cutting this margin further does not look very attractive to Max.

Max is not sure whether NOS will continue to sell Office Systems' Excel brand of folders along with NOS's file folders if NOS is able to find a source of supply. NOS's history has been to sell its own brand and a major brand side by side, especially if the major brand offers high quality and has strong brand recognition.

Max is having a really hard time deciding what to do about the existing branding policy. OSI has excess capacity and could easily handle the NOS business. And he fears that if he turns down this business, NOS will just go elsewhere and its own brand will cut into OSI's existing sales at NOS. Further, what makes NOS's offer especially attractive is that OSI's variable manufacturing costs would be quite low in relation in any price charged to NOS—with substantial economies of scale, the "extra" business could be very profitable—if Max doesn't consider the possible impact on the Excel line. This NOS business would be easy to get, but it will require a major change in policy which Max will have to "sell" to Bob Murdock, OSI's president. This may not be easy, because Bob's primary interest is in developing new and better products so the company can avoid the "commodity end of the business."

Evaluate OSI's current strategy. What should Max Lupe do about Rita Lopez's offer? Explain.

14. Kodak's Ektar

Assume you were just appointed Product Manager for Kodak's new film products: Ektar 25, Ektar 125, and Ektar 1,000. You were not in on the initial strategy planning, but now you are responsible for the success of these products. From your previous experience at Kodak, you know that your success will be measured primarily on sales, although you will have to control your costs. And you also realize that you are mainly responsible for implementing the present strategy in the immediate future. You also know that you can make (1) small changes as the competitive situation demands and (2) recommendations for major long run changes. So now you are evaluating what you have "inherited" and deciding what you should do with your product.

Kodak already offers a wide range of color film, of various types and speeds. It offers film to make black and white or color prints or slides. Its film speeds range from ASA 25 through 64, 100, 160, 200, 400, and 1,000. So Ektar 25, Ektar 125 and Ektar 1,000 are additions to the existing line—which is well accepted as a market leader. Your job is to take care of Ektar 25, 125, and 1,000—not the whole line.

Eastman Kodak Company claims that Ektar film will produce the sharpest color prints in the world. Ektar's slogan is: "The genius is in the detail."

Ektar is said to be sharper, in part, because the grains on the film absorb light more efficiently. The 25 ASA speed film (which is very slow film) is especially good for enlargements—even as large as poster-size. Some users of the 25 speed film feel the quality of

these larger prints is "breathtaking." The 125 ASA and 1,000 ASA speed films also provide good detail. They produce a grainier print than the 25 speed film, but they are sharper than any similar-speed film on the market.

Ektar has its limitations. It can be used only by owners of single-lens reflex cameras (SLRs) which can adjust for the 25, 125 or 1,000 film speeds. In other words, it cannot be used in most of the increasingly popular point-and-shoot 35 mm cameras.

Kodak is targeting advanced amateur photographers with Ektar. Kodak feels that this advanced amateur photographer market is substantial and will appreciate a better film. Kodak research suggests that advanced amateurs consider themselves "artier" than occasional picture takers. This market uses an estimated 400 million rolls of film a year and makes up about 20 percent of the users of 35 mm cameras. Kodak is expecting the potential market for Ektar to be in the range of 1 to 1.5 billion U.S. dollars worldwide.

Ektar is priced about 15 percent to 20 percent higher than Kodak's existing films. The initial plan is to sell Ektar to specialty camera stores and photo minilabs so that knowledgeable salespeople can explain the advantages of the new film—and can keep "point-and-shoot customers" away from the film. Similarly, Kodak's advertising is in photography magazines and "upscale" consumer magazines such as *Travel and Leisure* and *Smithsonian*. The copy emphasizes high-quality pictures rather than "warm memories."

One of the factors that may slow acceptance of Ektar 25 is that it is so slow that a tripod or flash may be needed, except in bright sunlight. Early color films were similarly slow, and the desire for faster films led to the development of color films with speeds of ASA 64, 100, 160, 200, 400, and 1,000. Some cameras and lenses are designed to use the faster films. Some zoom lenses, for example, cannot be used easily with Ektar 25.

Some photography specialists have already raised questions about whether advanced amateurs will be willing to put up with the slower speed of Ektar 25 or appreciate the extra quality of Ektar 125 or 1,000—especially when the price is 15 percent to 20 percent more.

Evaluate Kodak's strategy planning for Ektar and your situation. What should you do? Why?

15. McMiller's Ski Shop

Joe and Janet McMiller are trying to decide what downhill skis to carry in their new store in Vail. They graduated from a state university in Colorado in 1987 and, with some family help, plan to open a small ski equipment shop in Vail, Colorado. The McMillers are sure that by offering friendly, personal service they will have something unique—and be able to compete with the many other ski shops in town. They are well aware that they will have many competitors because many "ski bums" choose the Vail area as a place to live—and then try to find a way to earn a living there. By keeping the shop small, however, the McMillers hope they'll be able to manage most of the activities themselves—keeping costs down and also being sure of good service for their customers.

Their current problem is deciding which line—or lines—of skis they should carry. Almost all the major manufacturers' skis are offered in the competing shops, so Joe and Janet are seriously considering specializing in the K-10 brand, which is not now carried by any local stores. In fact, the K-10 sales rep has assured them that if they are willing to carry the line exclusively, then K-10 will not sell its skis to any other retailers in Colorado. This appeals to Joe and Janet because it would give them something unique—a new kind of American-made ski that is just being introduced into the U.S. market with supporting full-page ads in skiing magazines. The skis have an injected foam core that is anchored to boron and composite layers above and below by a patented process that causes the composite to penetrate the foam. The process is the result of several years of experimenting by a retired space materials designer, Cal Kline, who applied space technology to building lighter and more responsive skis. Now his small firm—K-10 Manufacturing Company—is ready to sell the new design as recreational skis for the large beginner and intermediate skier markets. Eric Humes, the K-10 sales rep, is excited about the possibilities and compares the K-10 ski development to the Head ski (first metal ski) and Prince tennis racket (first "outsize" racket) developments, which were big winners. Both of these successes were built on the pioneering work of one man, Mr. Head, who Eric thinks is very much like Mr. Kline—a "hard-working genius."

The McMillers are interested because they would have a unique story to tell about skis that could satisfy almost every skier's needs. Further, the suggested retail prices and markups are similar to those of other manufacturers, so the McMiller Ski Shop could emphasize the unique features of the K-10 skis—and still keep their prices competitive.

The only thing that worries the McMillers about committing so completely to the K-10 line is that there are many other manufacturers—both domestic and foreign—that claim to offer unique features. In fact, most ski manufacturers regularly come out with new models and features, and the McMillers realize that most consumers are confused about the relative merits of all of the offerings. In the past, Joe himself has been reluctant to buy "off-brand" skis—preferring instead to stay with major names like Hart, Head, and Rossignol. So Joe wonders if a complete commitment to the K-10 line is wise. On the other hand, the McMillers want to offer something unique. They don't want to run just another ski shop carrying lines available "everywhere."

The K-10 line isn't their only possibility, of course. There are other "off-brands" that are not yet carried in Vail. But the McMillers like the idea that K-10 is planning to give national promotion support to the skis during the introductory campaign. They think that this might make a big difference in how rapidly the new skis are accepted. And if they provide friendly sales assistance and quick binding-mounting service, perhaps their chances for success will be even greater.

Another reason for committing to the K-10 line is that they like the sales rep, Eric Humes, and are sure he would be a big help in their initial stocking and set-up efforts. They talked briefly with some other firms' salespeople at the major trade shows, but had not gotten along nearly so well with any of them. In fact, most of the sales reps didn't seem too interested in helping a newcomer—preferring instead to talk with and entertain buyers from established stores. The major ski shows are over, so any more contacts with manufacturers will mean the McMillers must take the initiative. But based on their past experience, this doesn't sound too appealing. Therefore, they seem to be drifting fast toward specializing in the K-10 line.

Evaluate the McMillers' and Eric Humes's thinking. What should the McMillers do?

16. Visual Tools, Inc.

Paul Hunt, manager of Visual Tools, Inc., is looking for ways to increase profits. But he's turning cautious after seeing the poor results of his last effort during the previous Christmas season. Visual Tools, Inc., is located in a residential area, along a cross-town street, about two miles from the downtown of a metropolitan area of 450,000, and near a large university. It sells high-quality still and movie cameras, accessories, and projection equipment—including 8 mm and 16 mm movie projectors, 35 mm slide projectors, opaque and overhead projectors, and a large assortment of projection screens. Most of the sales of this specialized equipment are made to area school boards for classroom use, to industry for use in research and sales, and to the university for use in research and instruction.

Visual Tools (VT) also offers a wide selection of film and a specialized film-processing service. Instead of processing film on a mass production basis, VT gives each roll individual attention to bring out the particular features requested by a customer. This service is really appreciated by local firms that need high-quality pictures of lab or manufacturing processes for analytical and sales work.

To encourage the school and industrial trade, VT offers a graphics consultation service. If a customer wants to build a display—whether large or small—professional advice is readily available. Along with this free service, VT carries a full line of graphic arts supplies.

VT employs four full-time store clerks and two outside sales reps. These sales reps make calls on business firms, attend trade shows, make presentations for schools, and help both present and potential customers in their use and choice of visual aids.

The people who make most of the over-the-counter purchases are (1) serious amateur photographers and (2) some professional photographers who buy in small quantities. Price discounts of up to 25 percent of the suggested retail price are given to customers who buy more than $1,500 worth of goods per year. Most regular customers qualify for the discount.

In recent years, many more "amateurs" have been taking 35 mm pictures (slides) using compact automatic and semiautomatic full-frame cameras priced under $150. These cameras are easy to carry and use and have attracted many people who had never taken 35 mm pictures (slides)—or any pictures (slides)—before. Because of this, Paul Hunt felt that there ought to be a good opportunity to expand sales during the Christmas gift-giving season. Therefore, he planned a special pre-Christmas sale of two of the

most popular brands of these compact cameras and discounted the prices to competitive discount store levels. To promote the sale, he posted large signs in the store windows and ran ads in a Christmas gift-suggestion edition of the local newspaper. This edition appeared each Wednesday during the four weeks before Christmas. At these prices and with this promotion, Paul hoped to sell at least 600 cameras. However, when the Christmas returns were in, total sales were 67 cameras. Paul was extremely disappointed with these results—especially because trade "experts" suggested that sales of compact cameras in this price and quality range were up 300 percent over last year.

Evaluate what Visual Tools, Inc., is doing and what happened with the special promotion. What strategies should Paul Hunt implement to increase sales and profits?

17.   *National Sales Company*

Herb Miner, owner of National Sales Company, is deciding whether to take on a new line. He is very concerned, however, because although he wants to carry more lines he feels that something is "wrong" with his latest possibility.

Herb Miner graduated from a large midwestern university in 1985 with a B.S. in business. He worked as a car salesman for a year. Then Herb decided to go into business for himself and formed National Sales Company. Looking for opportunities, Herb placed several ads in his local newspaper in Cleveland, Ohio, announcing that he was interested in becoming a sales representative in the area. He was quite pleased to receive a number of responses. Eventually, he became the sales representative in the Cleveland area for three local manufacturers: Boxer Company, which manufactures portable drills; Silver Company, a manufacturer of portable sanding machines; and Tower Mfg. Company, a producer of small lathes. All of these companies were relatively small—and were represented in other areas by other sales representatives like Herb Miner.

Herb's main job was to call on possible producer customers. Once he made a sale, he would send the order to the respective manufacturer, who would ship the goods directly to the customer. The manufacturer would bill the customer, and Miner would receive a commission varying from 5 percent to 10 percent of the dollar value of the sale. Miner was expected to pay his own expenses.

Miner called on anyone in the Cleveland area who might use the products he sold. At first, his job was relatively easy, and sales came quickly because he had little competition. Many national companies make similar products, but at that time, they were not well represented in the Cleveland area.

In 1987, Miner sold $250,000 worth of drills, earning a 10 percent commission; $100,000 worth of sanding machines, also earning a 10 percent commission; and $200,000 worth of small lathes, earning a 5 percent commission. He was encouraged with his progress and looked forward to expanding sales in the future. He was especially optimistic because he had achieved these sales volumes without overtaxing himself. In fact, he felt he was operating at about 70 percent of his capacity.

Early in 1988, however, a local manufacturer with a very good reputation, the Tucker Mfg. Company, started making a line of portable drills. By April 1988, Tucker had captured approximately one half of Boxer's Cleveland drill market by charging a much lower price. Tucker used its own sales force locally and probably would continue to do so.

The Boxer Company assured Miner that Tucker couldn't afford to continue to sell at such a low price and that shortly Boxer's price would be competitive with Tucker's price. Herb Miner was not as optimistic about the short-run prospects, however. He began looking for other products he could sell in the Cleveland area. A manufacturer of hand trucks had recently approached him, but Herb wasn't too enthusiastic about this offer because the commission was only 2 percent on potential annual sales of $150,000.

Now Herb Miner is faced with another decision. The True Paint Company, also in Cleveland, has made what looks like an attractive offer. They heard what a fine job Herb was doing and felt that he could help them solve their present problem. True Paint is having trouble with its whole marketing effort and would like Herb Miner to take over.

The True Paint Company sells mainly to industrial customers in the Cleveland area and is faced with many competitors selling essentially the same products and charging the same low prices. True Paint is a small manufacturer. Last year's sales were $350,000. They could handle at least four times this sales volume with ease—and they are willing to

expand to increase sales, their main objective in the short run. They are offering Herb a 12 percent commission on all sales if he will take charge of their pricing, advertising, and sales efforts. Herb is flattered by their offer, but he is a little worried because the job might require a great deal more traveling than he is doing now. For one thing, he would have to call on new potential customers in Cleveland, and he might have to travel up to 200 miles around Cleveland to expand the paint business. Further, he realizes that he is being asked to do more than just sell. But he did have marketing courses in college, and he thinks the new opportunity might be challenging.

Evaluate Herb Miner's current strategy and how the proposed paint line fits in with what he is doing now. What should he do? Why?

18.   *Tandy versus IBM*

Assume that you are the newly hired marketing manager for The Tandy Corp. of Fort Worth, Texas—which is trying to become "America's Technology Company." This giant electronics concern, which produces a wide variety of consumer electronics products distributed through its Radio Shack stores, is seeking to challenge the "blue-chip" computer makers, including International Business Machines Corporation (IBM), Compaq Computer Corp., and Apple Computer, Inc. Already, Tandy has about 25 percent of the personal computer market (in unit sales).

Making Tandy into "America's Technology Company" won't happen immediately. Tandy's computers are sold through almost 5,000 Radio Shacks and similar retail outlets. But these retail stores generally do not use outside sales reps, relying instead on customers coming into the store to buy Tandy's "lower-priced" computers. So Radio Shacks have tended to cater to hobbyists and small business people who are willing to come into the stores. This is often necessary for small businesses because the major computer companies' sales reps do not find such companies good prospects. Radio Shacks are not seen as "high-tech" outlets. Instead they are seen as low-tech suppliers of wires and electronic parts. And in recent years they have offered toys, telephones, and other consumer-electronic products. This "low-tech" image makes it difficult for its outside computer sales reps when they call on major corporations.

In its move to become "America's Technology Company," Tandy has invested in new automated factories, which have earned it a reputation as an efficient maker of very reliable low-cost computers. Tandy is able to undercut IBM's PC prices by 20 percent to 30 percent. As a result, Tandy was the obvious choice when Matsushita decided to purchase computers in the United States for sale to U.S. customers. A company spokesman said that Tandy makes "quality computers at high volumes." Matsushita's decision to buy from Tandy was a major achievement because Matsushita—known in America for the brand names Panasonic, Quasar, and Technics—is known as a quality producer. And it's likely to make a major promotion effort to sell Tandy products, especially to office products retailers and major corporations—customers that Radio Shack sales reps have had trouble selling. Tandy is also going to make desktop computers for Digital Equipment Corporation—a respected producer of business computers. And Tandy bought Grid Systems Corporation, a successful maker of laptop computers. These developments advance Tandy's goal of becoming "America's Technology Company."

In another move to increase its personal computer sales, Tandy is testing selling personal computers through Wal-Mart Stores, Inc.—the United States's second largest discount retailer. These stores could obviously compete with Radio Shack stores, so Tandy is supplying Wal-Mart with a standard computer which has been replaced by an updated model in Radio Shack stores.

Another effort to sell more computers is using direct-mail—via American Express Company and J. C. Penney Company mailings—to attract buyers who probably wouldn't shop at a Radio Shack.

Part of the reason for these new moves is that Tandy recognizes that its products have not penetrated all of the available markets. Further, Tandy knows that the Radio Shack image is, in many cases, holding it back. Further, it seems that Tandy's less-expensive computers are not doing as well as its more expensive models. And more broadly, Tandy computer sales have not been growing as fast as the sales of other IBM compatibles that sell to larger companies.

Tandy executives were expecting that sales of its IBM-compatible computers outside of its Radio Shack stores could reach 100,000 computers in 1989–90,

compared to something over 400,000 computers sold through its Radio Shack stores. Note that these are the "higher-end" computers, which would compete with IBM and other major producers of business computers. In addition to these IBM-compatible computers, Tandy sells almost 150,000 "lower-end" computers.

Another reason for attempting to broaden the way it sells computers is that Tandy has concluded that it cannot continue to grow by simply opening new Radio Shack stores, which tended to generate profit margins almost double what most consumer-electronic retailers were able to earn (50 percent). A company executive says, "There is no place for new stores—we're pretty much saturated."

Thus, Tandy is trying to find new ways to continue to grow. It is building, or planning to build, additional automated factories and a research and development center. It is planning to add as many as 200 people to the research and development staff—a move which Tandy believes will further its efforts to become "America's Technology Company."

Evaluate Tandy's strategy planning for the computer market. Be sure to stress the advantages and risks of what it is doing. What should you do now? Why?

19. Nelson Company

Hank Nelson, owner of Nelson Company, feels his business is threatened by a tough new competitor. And now Hank must decide about an offer that may save his business.

Hank Nelson has been a salesman for over 30 years. He started selling in a clothing store, but gave it up after 10 years to work in a lumber yard because the future looked much better in the building materials industry. After drifting from one job to another, Hank finally settled down and worked his way up to manager of a large wholesale building materials distribution warehouse in Charlotte, North Carolina. In 1969, he formed Nelson Company and went into business for himself, selling carload lots of lumber to lumber yards in the western parts of North and South Carolina.

Hank works with five large lumber mills on the West Coast. They notify him when a carload of lumber is available to be shipped, specifying the grade, condition, and number of each size board in the shipment. Hank isn't the only person selling for these mills—but he is the only one in his area. He isn't required to take any particular number of carloads per month—but once he tells a mill he wants a particular shipment, title passes to him and he has to sell it to someone. Hank's main function is to buy the lumber from the mill as it's being shipped, find a buyer, and have the railroad divert the car to the buyer.

Hank has been in this business for 20 years, so he knows all of the lumber yard buyers in his area very well—and he is on good working terms with them. Most of his business is done over the telephone from his small office, but he tries to see each of the buyers about once a month. He has been marking up the lumber between 4 and 6 percent—the standard markup, depending on the grades and mix in each car—and has been able to make a good living for himself and his family. The "going prices" are widely publicized in trade publications, so the buyers can easily check to be sure Hank's prices are competitive.

In the last few years, the regional building boom slowed down. Hank's profits did too, but he decided to stick it out—figuring that people still needed housing and that business would pick up again.

Six months ago, an aggressive young salesman set up in the same business, covering about the same area but representing different lumber mills. This new salesman charges about the same prices as Hank, but undersells him once or twice a week in order to get the sale. Many lumber buyers—feeling that they are dealing with a homogeneous product—seem to be willing to buy from the lowest-cost source. This has hurt Hank financially and personally—even some of his "old friends" are willing to buy from the new competitor if the price is lower. The near-term outlook seems dark, since Hank doubts that there is enough business to support two firms like his, especially if the markup gets shaved any closer. Now, they seem to be splitting the business about equally as the newcomer keeps shaving his markup. The main reason Hank is getting some orders is because the lumber mills make up different kinds of carloads (varying the number of different sized products) and specific lumber yards happen to want his cars rather than his competitor's cars.

A week ago, Hank was called by Mr. Wilson, of Talbord Mfg. Co., a new particleboard manufacturing firm. Mr. Wilson knows Hank is well-acquainted with the local lumber yards and has asked Hank if he will

be the exclusive distributor for Talbord Mfg. Co. in his area—selling carload lots of particleboard, just as he does lumber. Mr. Wilson gave Hank a brochure on particleboard, a product introduced about 20 years ago by another company. The brochure explains how particleboard can be used as a cheaper and better subflooring than the standard lumber usually used. Particleboard is also made with a wood veneer so that it can be used as paneling in homes and offices. Mr. Wilson said that the lumber yards can specify the types and grades of particleboard they need—unlike lumber where they must choose from carloads that are already made up. Hank knows that a carload of particleboard costs about 30 percent more than a carload of lumber—and that sales will be less frequent. In fact, he knows that this kind of product is not as well accepted in his area as in many others because no one has done much promotion. But the 20 percent average markup is very tempting—and the particleboard market is expanding nationwide. Further, the other particleboard manufacturers don't have anyone calling on lumber yards in his area at this time.

Hank thinks he has three choices:

1. Take Mr. Wilson's offer and sell both products.
2. Take the offer and drop lumber sales.
3. Stay strictly with lumber and forget the offer.

Mr. Wilson is expecting an answer within one week, so Hank has to decide soon.

Evaluate Hank Nelson's current strategy and how the present offer fits in. What should he do now? Why?

20.   Hudson's, Inc.

Ann Korn, manager of Hudson's health and beauty aids (HBA) department, is considering an offer from the Block Drug Company. She thinks it might be attractive to senior citizens but has doubts about whether it really "fits" with the rest of Hudson's strategies.

Hudson's, Inc., is a full-line department store chain operating in and around Los Angeles, California. The company began in the 1920s in the downtown business district of Los Angeles and has now expanded until it operates not only the downtown store but also branches in eight major shopping centers around Los Angeles.

One of the more successful departments in the Hudson's stores is the HBA department. This department sells a wide variety of products—ranging from face powder to vitamins. But it has not been in the prescription business and does not have a registered pharmacist in the department. Its focus in the drug area has been on "proprietary" items—packaged and branded items that are sold without professional advice or supervision—rather than on the "ethical" drugs—which are normally sold only with a doctor's prescription that is filled by a registered pharmacist.

Ann now has a proposal from Block Drug Company to introduce a wholesale prescription service into Hudson's HBA department. Block is a well-established drug wholesaler that is trying to expand its business by serving retailers such as Hudson's.

Basically, the Block Drug Company's proposal is as follows:

1. Hudson's customers will leave their prescriptions in the HBA department one day and then pick up their medicines the following day.
2. A Block representative will pick up the prescriptions every evening at closing time and return the filled prescriptions before each store opens the following day. Hudson's stores will not have to hire any pharmacists or carry any drug inventories.
3. Hudson's could offer savings of from 30 to 50 percent to all customers—and an extra 10 percent discount for senior citizens. These savings will be due to the economies of the operation, including the absence of pharmacists and the elimination of inventories in each store.
4. Hudson's will earn a 40 percent commission on the retail selling price of each prescription sale.
5. Hudson's name will be identified with the service and be printed on all bags, bottles, and other materials. In other words, the Block Drug Company will serve as a wholesaler in the operation and will not be identified to Hudson's customers.

Block's sales rep, Barbara Salem, claims that retail drug sales are expanding and continued growth is expected as the average age of the population continues to rise—and especially as more people become "senior citizens" (a major market for medicines). Further, she says that prescription drug prices are rising, so Hudson's will participate in an expanding business. By offering cost savings to its customers, Hudson's will be providing another service—and also building return business and stimulating store traffic. Since Hudson's won't need to hire additional personnel or carry inventory, the 40 percent margin will be almost all net profit.

The Block Drug Company is anxious to begin offering this service to the Los Angeles area and has asked Ann to make a decision very soon. If Hudson's accepts Block's proposal, the Block executives have agreed not to offer their service to any other Los Angeles stores. Otherwise, Block plans to approach other Los Angeles retailers.

Evaluate Block's proposal. What should Ann Korn do? Why?

21. DeWitt State Bank

Andy Brog isn't having much luck convincing his father that their bank needs a "new look."

Andy Brog was recently appointed director of marketing by his father, Tom Brog, long-time president of the DeWitt State Bank. Andy is a recent marketing graduate of the nearby state college. He worked in the bank during summer vacations—but this is his first full-time job.

The DeWitt State Bank is a profitable, family-run business located in DeWitt—the county seat. The town itself has only about 20,000 population, but it serves farmers as far away as 20 miles. About 15 miles south is a metropolitan area of 350,000. Banking competition is quite strong there. But DeWitt has only one other bank—of about the same size. The DeWitt State Bank has been quite profitable, last year earning about $350,000—or 1 percent of assets—a profit margin that would look very attractive to big-city bankers.

DeWitt State Bank has prospered over the years by emphasizing its friendly, small-town atmosphere. The employees are all local residents and are trained to be friendly with all customers—greeting them on a first-name basis. Even Andy's father tries to know all the customers personally and often comes out of his office to talk with them. The bank has followed a conservative policy—for example, insisting on 25 percent down payments on homes and relatively short maturities on loans. The interest rates charged are competitive or slightly higher than in the nearby city, but they are similar to those charged by the other bank in town. In fact, the two local banks seem to be following more or less the same approach—friendly, small-town service. Since they both have fairly convenient downtown locations, Andy feels that the two banks will continue to share the business equally unless some change is made.

Andy has an idea that he thinks will attract a greater share of the local business. At a recent luncheon meeting with his father, he presented his plan and was disappointed when it wasn't enthusiastically received. Nevertheless, he has continued to push the idea.

Basically, Andy wants to differentiate the bank by promoting a new image. His proposal is to try to get all the people in town to think of the bank as "The Contemporary Bank." Andy wants to paint the inside and outside of the bank in current designers' colors (e.g., pastels) and have all the bank's advertising and printed materials refer to "The Contemporary Bank" campaign. The bank would give away pastel shopping bags, offer pastel deposit slips, mail out pastel interest checks, advertise on pastel billboards, and have pastel stationery for the bank's correspondence. Andy knows that his proposal is different for a conservative bank. But that's exactly why he thinks it will work. He wants people to notice his bank, instead of just assuming that both banks are alike. He is sure that after the initial surprise, the local people will think even more positively about DeWitt State. Its reputation is very good now, but he would like it to be recognized as "different." Andy feels that this will help attract a larger share of new residents and businesses. Further, he hopes that his "The Contemporary Bank" campaign will cause people to talk about DeWitt State Bank—and given that word-of-mouth comments are likely to be positive, the bank might win a bigger share of the present business.

Andy's father, Tom, is less excited about his son's proposal. He thinks the bank has done very well under his direction—and he is concerned about changing a "good thing." He worries that some of the older farmers who are loyal customers will question the integrity of the bank. His initial request to Andy was to come up with some other way of differentiating the bank without offending present customers. Further, Tom Brog thinks that Andy is talking about an important change that will be hard to undo once the decision is made. On the plus side, Tom agrees that the proposal will make the bank appear quite different from its competitor. Further, people are continuing to move into DeWitt, and he wants an increasing share of this business.

Evaluate DeWitt State Bank's situation and Andy's proposal. What should the bank do to differentiate itself?

22. *Outdoor Sports, Inc.*

Tim Boxer, owner of Outdoor Sports, is worried about his business' future. He has tried various strategies for two years now, and he's still barely breaking even.

Two years ago, Tim Boxer bought the inventory, supplies, equipment, and business of Seattle Sports Sales—located in a suburb of Seattle, Washington. The business is in an older building along a major highway leading out of town—several miles from any body of water. The previous owner had sales of about $350,000 a year—but was just breaking even. For this reason—plus the desire to retire to southern California—the owner sold to Tim for roughly the value of the inventory.

Seattle Sports Sales had been selling two well-known brands of small pleasure boats, a leading outboard motor, two brands of snowmobiles and jet-skis, and a line of trailer and pickup-truck campers. The total inventory was valued at $120,000. Tim used all of his own savings and borrowed some from two friends to buy it. At the same time, he took over the lease on the building so he was able to begin operations immediately.

Tim had never operated a business of his own before, but he was sure that he would be able to do well. He had worked in a variety of jobs—as an auto repair man, service man, and generally a jack-of-all-trades in the maintenance departments of several local businesses.

Soon after starting his business, Tim hired his friend, Bud, who had a similar background. Together, they handle all selling and set-up work on new sales and do maintenance work as needed. At the peaks of each sport season the two men are extremely busy. Then both sales and maintenance keep them going up to 16 hours a day. At these times it's difficult to have both new and repaired equipment available as soon as customers want it. At other times however, Tim and Bud have almost nothing to do.

Tim usually charges the prices suggested by the various manufacturers—except at the end of a weather season when he is willing to make deals to clear the inventory. He is annoyed that some of his competitors sell mainly on a price basis—offering 10 to 30 percent off a manufacturer's suggested list prices. Tim doesn't want to get into that kind of business, however. He hopes to build a loyal following based on friendship and personal service. Further, he doesn't think he really has to cut price because all of his lines are "exclusive" for his store. No stores within a 10-mile radius carry any of his brands, although many brands of similar products are offered by nearby retailers.

To try to build a favorable image for his company, Tim occasionally places ads in local papers and buys some radio spots. The basic theme of this advertising is that Outdoor Sports is a good place to buy the equipment needed for the current season. Sometimes he mentions the brand names he carries, but generally Tim tries to build an image for friendly service—both in new sales and repairs. He chose this approach because, although he has exclusives on the brands he carries, there generally are 10 to 15 different manufacturers' products being sold in each product category at any one time—and most of the products are quite similar. Tim feels that this similarity among competing products almost forces him to try to differentiate himself on the basis of his own store's services.

The first year's operation wasn't profitable. In fact, after paying minimal salaries to Bud and himself, the business just about broke even. And this was without making any provision for return on his investment.

In hopes of improving profitability, Tim jumped at a chance to add a line of lawn mowers, tractors, and trimmers as he was starting into his second year of business. This line was offered by a well-known equipment manufacturer who was expanding into Tim's market. The equipment is similar to that offered by other lawn equipment manufacturers. The manufacturer's willingness to do some local advertising and to provide some point-of-purchase displays appealed to Tim. And he also liked the idea that customers probably would want this equipment sometime earlier than boats and other summer items. So he could handle this business without interfering with his other peak selling seasons.

It's two years since Tim started Outdoor Sports, Inc.—and he's still only breaking even. Sales have increased a little, but costs have gone up too because he had to hire some part-time help. The lawn equipment helped to expand sales—as he had

expected—but unfortunately, it did not increase profits. The part-time helpers were needed to handle this business—in part because the manufacturer's advertising had generated a lot of sales inquiries. Relatively few of these resulted in sales, however, because many people seemed to be shopping for "deals." So Tim may have even lost money handling the new line. But he hesitates to give up on it because he has no other attractive choices right now—and he doesn't want to lose that sales volume. Further, the manufacturer's sales rep has been most encouraging—assuring Tim that things will get better and that his company will be glad to continue its promotion support during the coming year.

Evaluate Tim Boxer's overall strategy. What should he do now?

23.   Du Pont

Bob Medick is marketing manager of Du Pont's plastic business. Bob is reconsidering his promotion effort. He is evaluating what kind of promotion—and how much—should be directed to U.S. car producers. Currently, Bob has one salesperson who devotes most of his time to the car industry. This man is based in the Detroit area and focuses on the "Big Three"—GM, Ford, Chrysler—and the various molders who supply the car industry. This approach was adequate as long as relatively little plastic was used in each car *and* the auto producers did all of the designing themselves and then sent out specifications for very price-oriented bidding. But now the whole product planning and buying system is changing—and "foreign" producers in the United States are becoming more important.

The "new system" can be explained in terms of Ford's "program management" approach—developed in 1980 and used on the Taurus-Sable project. Instead of the normal five-year process of creating a new automobile in sequential steps, the new system is a "team approach." Under the old system, product planners would come up with a general concept and then expect the design team to give it "artistic" form. Next Engineering would develop the specifications and pass them on to Manufacturing and suppliers. There was little communication between the groups—and no overall project responsibility. Under the new "program management" approach, representatives from all the various functions—Planning, Design, Engineering,

Marketing, and Manufacturing—work together. The whole team takes final responsibility for a car. Because all of the departments are involved from the start, problems are resolved as the project moves on—before they cause a crisis. Manufacturing, for example, can suggest changes in design that will result in higher productivity—or better quality.

In the Taurus-Sable project, Ford engineers followed the Japanese lead and did some "reverse engineering" of their own. This helped them learn how the parts were assembled—and how they were designed. Ford actually bought several Japanese cars and dismantled them, piece by piece, looking for ideas they could copy or improve. Further, Ford engineers carefully analyzed over 50 similar cars to find the best parts of each. The Audi 5000 had the best accelerator-pedal feel. The Toyota Supra was best for fuel-gauge accuracy. The best tire and jack storage was in the BMW 228e. Eventually, Ford incorporated almost all of the "best" features into their Taurus-Sable.

In addition to "reverse engineering," Ford researchers conducted the largest series of market studies the company had ever done. This led to the inclusion of additional features, such as oil dipsticks painted a bright yellow for faster identification and a net in the trunk to hold grocery bags upright.

At the same time, a five-member ergonomics group studied ways to make cars more comfortable and easier to operate. They took seats from competing cars and tested them in Ford cars to learn what customers liked—and disliked. Similarly, dashboard instruments and controls were tested. Eventually the best elements in competing models were incorporated into the Taurus-Sable.

Ford also asked assembly-line workers for suggestions before the car was designed—and then incorporated their ideas into the new car. All bolts had the same size head, for example, so workers didn't have to switch from one wrench to another.

Finally, Ford consulted its suppliers as part of the program management effort. Instead of turning to a supplier after the car's design was completed, the Ford team signed long-term contracts with suppliers and invited them to participate in product planning. This project was so successful that it appears that most auto producers will follow a similar approach in the future.

The suppliers selected for the Taurus project were major suppliers who had already demonstrated a serious commitment to the car industry and who had not only the facilities, but also the technical and professional managerial staff who could understand—and become part of—the program management approach. Ford expected that these major suppliers would be able to provide the "just-in-time delivery system" pioneered by the Japanese and that the suppliers could apply statistical quality-control procedures in their manufacturing processes. These criteria led Ford to ignore suppliers whose primary sales technique is to entertain buyers and then submit bids on standard specifications.

Assuming that the program management approach will spread through the car industry and that plastics will be used more extensively in cars in the 1990s, Bob Medick is trying to determine if Du Pont's present effort is still appropriate. Bob's strategy has focused primarily on responding to inquiries and bringing in Du Pont technical people as the situation seems to require. Potential customers with technical questions are sometimes referred to other customers already using the materials or to a Du Pont plant. But basically, car producer customers are treated like any other customers. The sales rep makes calls and tries to find good business wherever it is.

Bob now sees that some of his major competitors—including General Electric and Dow Chemical—are becoming more aggressive in the car industry. They are seeking to affect specifications and product design from the start, rather than entering the picture after the car design is completed. This takes a lot more effort and resources, but Bob thinks that it may get better results. A major problem he sees, however, is that he may have to drastically change the nature of Du Pont's promotion. Instead of focusing primarily on buyers and responding to questions, it may be necessary to try to contact *all* the multiple buying influences, and not only answer their questions, but also help them understand what questions should be raised—and then help them answer them. Some competitors are already moving in this direction.

But it is too soon to be sure how effective their efforts are because the car industry is just beginning to think seriously about plastics as it moves further into "program management."

Contrast Ford Motor Company's previous approach to designing and producing cars to its program management approach. Assuming most U.S. car producers move in this direction, what strategy should Bob Medick develop for Du Pont? Explain.

24. *Republic Wire, Inc.*

John Watson, Vice President of Marketing for Republic Wire, Inc., is deciding how to organize and train his sales force—and what to do about Tony Conti.

Republic Wire, Inc., produces wire cable—ranging from one-half inch to four inches in diameter. The plant is in Chicago, Illinois. Republic sells across the United States. Principal users of its products are firms using cranes and various other overhead lifts in their own operations. Ski resorts and amusement parks, for example, are good customers because cables are used in the various lifts. The main customers, however, are cement plants, railroad and boat yards, heavy-equipment manufacturers, mining operations, construction companies, and steel manufacturers.

Republic employs its own "sales specialists" to call on the buyers of potential users. All of Republic's sales reps are engineers who go through an extensive training program covering the different applications, product strengths, and other technical details concerning wire rope and cable. Then they are assigned their own district—the size depending on the number of potential customers. They are paid a good salary plus generous travel expenses—with small bonuses and prizes to reward special efforts.

Tony Conti went to work for Republic in 1958, immediately after receiving a civil engineering degree from the University of Wisconsin. After going through the training program, he took over—as the only company rep—in the Ohio district. His job was to call on and give technical help to present customers of wire rope and cable. He was also expected to call on new customers, especially when inquiries came in. But his main activities were to: (1) call on present customers and supply the technical assistance needed to use cable in the most efficient and safe manner, (2) handle complaints, and (3) provide evaluation reports to customers' management regarding their use of cabling.

Tony Conti soon became Republic's outstanding representative. His exceptional ability to handle customer complaints and provide technical assistance was noted by many of the firm's customers. He also brought in a great deal of new business—mostly from heavy-equipment manufacturers in Ohio.

Tony's success established Ohio as Republic's largest-volume district. Although the company's sales in Ohio have not continued to grow in the past few years, the replacement market has been steady and profitable. This fact is mainly due to Tony Conti. As one of the purchasing agents for a large machinery manufacturer mentioned, "When Tony makes a recommendation regarding use of our equipment and cabling, even if it is a competitor's cable we are using, we are sure it's for the best of our company. Last week, for example, a cable of one of his competitors broke, and we were going to give him a contract. He told us it was not a defective cable that caused the break, but rather the way we were using it. He told us how it should be used and what we needed to do to correct our operation. We took his advice and gave him the contract as well!"

Four years ago, Republic introduced a unique and newly patented wire sling device for holding cable groupings together. The sling makes operations around the cable much safer—and its use could reduce hospital and lost-time costs due to accidents. The slings are expensive—and the profit margin is high. Republic urged all its representatives to push the sling, but the only sales rep to sell the sling with any success was Tony Conti. Eighty percent of his customers are currently using the wire sling. In other areas, sling sales are disappointing.

As a result of his success, John Watson is now considering forming a separate department for sling sales and putting Tony Conti in charge. His duties would include traveling to the various sales districts and training other representatives to sell the sling. The Ohio district would be handled by a new rep.

Evaluate John Watson's strategy(ies). What should he do about Tony Conti—and his sales force? Explain.

25. *Conn Furniture Company*

Carol Conn is discouraged with her salespeople and is even thinking about hiring some "new blood." Mrs. Conn has been running Conn Furniture Company for 10 years and has slowly built the sales to $1.5 million a year. Her store is located in the downtown shopping area of a growing city of 175,000 population. This is basically a factory city, and she has deliberately selected blue-collar workers as her target market. She carries some higher-priced furniture lines but emphasizes budget combinations and easy credit terms.

Table 1

In shopping for furniture I found (find) that	Demographic groups				Marital status	
	Group A	Group B	Group C	Group D	Newly-weds	Married 3–10 yrs.
I looked at furniture in many stores before I made a purchase	78%	57%	52%	50%	66%	71%
I went (am going) to only one store and bought (buy) what I found (find) there . . .	2	9	10	11	9	12
To make my purchase I went (am going) back to one of the stores I shopped in previously	48	45	39	34	51	49
I looked (am looking) at furniture in no more than three stores and made (will make) my purchase in one of these	20	25	24	45	37	30
No answer	10	18	27	27	6	4

Mrs. Conn is concerned that she may have reached the limit of her sales growth—her sales have not been increasing during the last two years even though total furniture sales have been increasing in the city as new people move in. Her newspaper advertising seems to attract her target customers, but many of these people come in, shop around, and leave. Some of them come back—but most do not. She thinks her product selections are very suitable for her target market and is concerned that her salespeople don't close more sales with potential customers. She has discussed this matter several times with her 10 salespeople. Her staff feels they should treat all customers alike—the way they personally want to be treated. They argue that their role is just to answer questions when asked—not to make suggestions or help customers make decisions. They think this would be too "hard sell."

Mrs. Conn says their behavior is interpreted as indifference by the customers attracted to the store by her advertising. She has tried to convince her salespeople that customers must be treated on an individual basis—and that some customers need more help in looking and deciding than others. Moreover, Mrs. Conn is convinced that some customers actually appreciate more help and suggestions than the salespeople themselves might. To support her views, she showed her staff the data from a study of furniture store customers (Tables 1 and 2). She tried to explain the differences in demographic groups and pointed out that her store was definitely trying to aim at specific

Table 2   The sample design

Demographic status

Upper class (group A); 13% of sample
  This group consisted of managers, proprietors, or executives of large businesses. Professionals, including doctors, lawyers, engineers, college professors and school administrators, research personnel. Sales personnel, including managers, executives, and upper-income salespeople above level of clerks.
  Family income over $40,000

Middle class (group B); 37% of sample
  Group B consists of white-collar workers including clerical, secretarial, salesclerks, bookkeepers, etc. It also includes school teachers, social workers, semiprofessionals, proprietors or managers of small businesses; industrial foremen and other supervisory personnel.
  Family income between $20,000 and $40,000.

Lower middle class (group C); 36% of sample
  Skilled workers and semiskilled technicians were in this category along with custodians, elevator operators, telephone linemen, factory operatives, construction workers, and some domestic and personal service employees.
  Family income between $10,000 and $40,000.
  No one in this group had above a high school education.

Lower class (group D); 14% of sample
  Nonskilled employees, day laborers. It also includes some factory operatives and domestic and service people.
  Family income under $15,000.
  None had completed high school; some had only grade school education.

people. She argued that they (the salespeople) should cater to the needs and attitudes of their customers—and think less about how they would like to be treated themselves. Further, Mrs. Conn announced that she is considering changing the sales compensation plan or hiring "new blood" if the present employees can't "do a better job." Currently, the sales reps are paid $25,000 per year plus a 1 percent commission on sales.

Evaluate Mrs. Conn's strategy and thinking about her salespeople. What should she do now? Explain.

26. Wireco, Inc.

Janet Eggers, marketing manager of consumer products for Wireco, Inc., is trying to set a price for her most promising new product—a kitchen flower pot holder.

Wireco, Inc.—located in Atlanta, Georgia—is a custom producer of industrial wire products. The company has a lot of experience bending wire into many shapes—and it can also chrome- or gold-plate finished products. The company was started 10 years ago and has slowly built its sales volume to $1.5 million a year. Just one year ago, Janet Eggers was appointed marketing manager of the consumer products division. It is her responsibility to develop this division as a producer and marketer of the company's own branded products—as distinguished from custom orders, which the industrial division produces for others.

Janet Eggers has been working on a number of different product ideas for almost a year now and has developed several designs for letter holders, message holders, towel holders, key and pencil holders, and other novelties. Her most promising product is a flower pot holder that can stand over kitchen sinks. It is very similar to one the industrial division produced for a number of years for another company. In fact, it was experience with the sales volume of that product that interested Wireco, Inc., in the market—and led to the development of the consumer products division.

Janet has sold hundreds of units of her products to various local food and general merchandise stores and wholesalers on a trial basis, but each time the price has been negotiated, and no firm policy has been set. Now she must determine what price to set on the flower pot holder—which she plans to push aggressively wherever she can. Actually, she hasn't decided on exactly which channels of distribution to use. But trials in the local area have been encouraging, and, as noted above, the experience in the industrial division suggests that there is a large market for this type of product.

The manufacturing cost on this product—when made in reasonable quantities—is approximately 35 cents if it is painted black and 45 cents if it is chromed or gold-plated. Similar products have been selling at retail in the $1.25 to $2.50 range. The sales and administrative overhead to be charged to the division will amount to $70,000 a year. This will include Janet's salary and some office expenses. It is expected that a number of other products will be developed in the near future. But for the coming year, it is hoped that this flower pot holder will account for about half the consumer products division's sales volume.

Evaluate Janet Eggers' strategy planning so far. What should she do now? What price should she set for the flower pot holder? Explain.

27. A-1 Photos, Inc.

Chris Conner, marketing manager of A-1 Photos, is faced with price cutting and wants to fight "fire with fire." But his boss feels that they should promote harder to retailers and/or final consumers.

A-1 Photos, Inc., is one of the four major Colorado-based photo-finishers—each with annual sales of about $7 million.

A-1 was started in 1950 by three people who had a lot of experience in the photo-finishing industry from working in Kodak's photo-finishing division in Rochester, New York. A-1 started in a small rented warehouse in Boulder, Colorado. Today the company has seven company-owned plants in five cities in Colorado and western Kansas. They are located in Boulder, Pueblo, Denver, and Colorado Springs, Colorado, and Hays, Kansas.

A-1 does all of its own black-and-white processing. While it has color-processing capability, A-1 finds it more economical to have most color film processed by the regional Kodak processing plant. The color film processed by A-1 is either "off-brand" film or special work done for professional photographers. A-1 has always given its customers fast, quality service. All pictures—including those processed by Kodak—can be returned within three days of receipt by A-1.

A-1 Photos started as a wholesale photo-finisher and later developed its own processing plants in a move for greater profit. A-1's major customers are drugstores, camera stores, department stores, photographic studios, and any other retail outlets where photo-finishing is offered to consumers. These retailers insert film rolls, cartridges, negatives, and so on into separate bags—marking on the outside the kind of work to be done. The customer is handed a receipt, but seldom sees the bag into which the film has been placed. The bag has the retailer's name on it—not A-1's.

Each processing plant has a small retail outlet for drop-in customers who live near the plant. This is a minor part of A-1's business.

The company also does direct-mail photo-finishing within the state of Colorado. Each processing plant in Colorado is capable of receiving direct-mail orders from consumers. All film received is handled in the same way as the other retail business.

A breakdown of the dollar volume by type of business is shown in Table I.

All retail prices are set by local competition—and all major competitors charge the same prices. A-1 sets a retail list price, and each retailer then is offered a trade discount based on the volume of business generated for A-1. The pricing schedule used by each of the major competitors in the Colorado-Kansas market is shown in Table 2.

All direct-mail processing for final consumers is priced at 33⅓ percent discount off the usual store price. But this is done under the Colorado Prints name—not the A-1 name—to avoid complaints from retailer customers. Retail walk-in accounts are charged the full list price for all services.

Retail stores offering photo-finishing are served by A-1's own sales force. Each processing plant has at

Table 1

Type of business	Percent of dollar volume
Sales to retail outlets	82%
Direct-mail sales.	15
Retail walk-in sales	3
	100%

Table 2

Monthly dollar volume (12-month average)	Discount (2/10, net 30)
$ 0–$100	33⅓%
$ 101–$500	40
$ 501–$1,000	45
$1,001–above	50

least three people servicing accounts. Their duties include daily visits to all present accounts to pick up and deliver all photo-finishing work. These sales reps also make daily trips to the nearby bus terminal to pick up and drop off color film to be processed by Kodak. The reps are not expected to call on possible new accounts.

Since the final consumer does not come in contact with A-1, the firm has not advertised its retail business to final consumers. Similarly, possible retailer accounts are not called on or advertised to—except that A-1 Photos is listed under "Photo-finishing: Wholesale" in the Yellow Pages of all telephone books in cities and towns served by its seven plants. Any phone inquiries are followed up by the nearest sales rep.

The direct-mail business—under the Colorado Prints name—is generated by regular ads in the Sunday pictorial sections of newspapers serving Pueblo, Denver, Colorado Springs, and Boulder. These ads usually stress low price, fast service, and fine quality. Mailers are provided for consumers to send to the plant. Some people in the company feel this part of the business might have great potential if pursued more aggressively.

A-1's president, Mr. Ken, is worried about the loss of several retail accounts in the $501 to $1,000 monthly sales volume range (See Table 2). He has been with the company since its beginning—and has always stressed quality and rapid delivery of the finished products. Demanding that all plants produce the finest quality, Mr. Ken personally conducts periodic quality tests of each plant through the direct-mail service. Plant managers are advised of any slips in quality.

To find out what is causing the loss in retail accounts, Mr. Ken is reviewing sales reps' reports and talking to employees. In their weekly reports, A-1's sales reps report a major threat to the company—price cutting. Fast Processing, Inc.—a competitor of equal size that offers the same services as A-1—is offering an additional 5 percent trade discount in each sales volume category. This really makes a difference at some stores because these retailers think that all the major processors do an equally good job. Further, they note, consumers apparently feel that the quality is acceptable because no complaints have been heard so far.

A-1 has faced price cutting before—but never by an equally well-established company. Mr. Ken can't understand why these retailer customers would leave A-1 because A-1 is offering higher quality and the price difference is not that large. Mr. Ken thinks the sales reps should sell "quality" a lot harder. He is also considering a radio or TV campaign to consumers to persuade them to demand A-1's quality service from their favorite retailer. Mr. Ken is convinced that consumers demanding quality will force retailers to stay with—or return to—A-1 Photos. He says: "If we can't get the business by convincing the retailer of our fine quality, we'll get it by convincing the consumer."

Chris Conner, the marketing manager, disagrees with Mr. Ken. Chris thinks that they ought to at least meet the price cut or cut prices another 5 percent wherever Fast Processing has taken an A-1 account. This would do two things: (1) get the business back and (2) signal that continued price cutting will be met by still deeper price cuts. Further, he says: "If Fast Processing doesn't get the message, we ought to go after a few of their big accounts with 10 percent discounts. That ought to shape them up."

Evaluate A-1's present and proposed strategies. What should they do now? Explain.

28. Western Mfg., Inc.

Tom Nason, the marketing manager of Western Mfg., Inc., wants to add sales reps rather than "play with price." That's how Tom describes what Jim Hicks, Western's president, is suggesting. Jim is not sure what to do. But he does want to increase sales, so something "new" is needed.

Western Mfg., Inc. of Los Angeles, California, is a leading producer in the wire machinery industry. It has patents covering over 200 machine variations, but Western's customers seldom buy more than 30 different types in a year. The machines are sold to wire and small-tubing manufacturers to increase production capacity or replace old equipment.

Established in 1895, the company has enjoyed steady growth to its present position with annual sales of $45 million.

Ten U.S. firms compete in the U.S. wire machinery market—no foreign firms have appeared yet. Each is about the same size and manufactures basically similar machinery. Each of the competitors has tended to specialize in its own geographic area. None has exported much because of high labor costs in the United States. Five of the competitors are in the East, three in the Midwest, and two—including Western—on the West Coast. The other West Coast firm is in Portland, Oregon. All of the competitors offer similar prices and sell F.O.B. their factories. Demand has been fairly strong in recent years. As a result, all of the competitors have been satisfied to sell in their geographic areas and avoid price cutting. In fact, price cutting is not a popular idea in this industry. About 20 years ago, one firm tried to win more business and found that others immediately met the price cut—but industry sales (in units) did not increase at all. Within a few years, prices returned to their earlier level, and since then competition has tended to focus on promotion and avoid price.

Western's promotion depends mainly on five company sales reps, who cover the West Coast. In total, these reps cost about $360,000 per year when all the costs of salary, bonuses, supervision, travel, and entertaining are added. When the sales reps are close to making a sale, they are supported by two sales engineers—at a cost of about $110,000 per year per engineer. Western does some advertising in trade journals—less than $25,000—and occasionally uses direct mailings. But the main promotion emphasis is on personal selling. Personal contact outside the West Coast market, however, is handled by manufacturers' agents who are paid 4 percent on sales.

Jim Hicks, Western's president, is not satisfied with the present situation. Industry sales have leveled off and so have Western's sales—although the firm continues to hold its share of the market. Jim would like to find a way to compete more effectively in the other regions because he sees great potential outside of the West Coast.

Competitors and buyers agree that Western is the top-quality producer in the industry. Its machines have generally been somewhat superior to others in terms of reliability, durability, and productive capacity. Since the others are able to do the necessary job, the difference usually has not been great enough to justify a higher price— unless a Western sales rep convinces the customer that the extra quality will improve the customer's product and lead to fewer production line breakdowns. The sales rep also tries to "sell" the company's better sales engineers and technical service people—and sometimes is successful. But if a buyer is only interested in comparing delivered prices for basic machines, Western's price must be competitive to get the business. In short, if such a buyer has a choice between Western's and another machine *at the same price,* Western will usually win the business in "its" part of the West Coast market. But it's clear that Western's price has to be at least competitive in such cases.

The average wire machine sells for about $180,000, F.O.B. shipping point. Shipping costs within any of the three major regions average about $3,000—but another $2,500 must be added on shipments between the West Coast and the Midwest (either way) and another $2,500 between the Midwest and the East.

Jim Hicks is thinking about expanding sales by absorbing the extra $2,500 to $5,000 in freight cost that occurs if a Midwestern or Eastern customer buys from his West Coast location. By doing this, he would not be cutting price in those markets but rather reducing his net return. He thinks that his competitors would not see this as price competition—and therefore would not resort to cutting prices themselves.

Tom Nason, the marketing manager, thinks that the proposed freight absorption plan might actually stimulate price competition in the Midwest and East—and perhaps on the West Coast. He proposes instead that Western hire some sales reps to work the Midwest and Eastern regions—selling "quality"—rather than relying on the manufacturers' agents. He argues that two additional sales reps in each of these regions would not increase costs too much—and might greatly increase the sales from these markets over that brought in by the agents. With this plan, there would be no need to absorb the freight and risk disrupting the status quo. This is especially important, he argues, because competition in the Midwest and East is somewhat "hotter" than on the West Coast due to the number of competitors in those regions. A lot of expensive entertaining, for example, seems to be required just to be considered as a potential supplier. In contrast, the situation has been rather quiet in the West because only two firms are sharing this market and working harder near their home offices. The

Eastern and Midwestern competitors don't send any sales reps to the West Coast—and if they have any manufacturers' agents, they haven't gotten any business in recent years.

Jim Hicks agrees that Tom Nason has a point, but industry sales are leveling off and Jim wants to increase sales. Further, he thinks the competitive situation may change drastically in the near future anyway, and he would rather be a leader in anything that is likely to happen than a follower. He is impressed with Tom Nason's comments about the greater competitiveness in the other markets, however, and therefore is unsure about what should be done.

Evaluate Western's current strategies. Given Jim Hicks' sales objective, what should Western do? Explain.

29. Fruitco, Inc.

Dave Corning, President of Fruitco, Inc., is not sure what he should propose to the board of directors. His recent strategy change isn't working. And Jerry Turner, Fruitco's only sales rep (and a board member), is so frustrated that he refuses to continue his discouraging sales efforts. Turner wants Dave Corning to hire a sales force or do something else instead.

Fruitco, Inc., is a long-time processor in the highly seasonal fruit canning industry. Fruitco packs and sells canned raspberries, boysenberries, plums, strawberries, apples, cherries, and "mixed fruit." Sales are made mainly through food brokers to merchant wholesalers, supermarket chains (such as Kroger, Safeway, A&P, and Jewel), cooperatives, and other outlets—mostly in the San Francisco Bay area. Of less importance, by volume, are sales to local institutions, grocery stores, and supermarkets and sales of dented canned goods at low prices to walk-in customers.

Fruitco is in Oregon's Willamette River Valley. The company has more than $25 million in sales annually (exact sales data is not published by the closely held corporation). Plants are located in strategic places along the valley and main offices are in Eugene. The Fruitco brand is used only on canned goods sold in the local market. Most of the goods are sold and shipped under a retailer's label or a broker's/wholesaler's label.

Fruitco is well-known for the consistent quality of its product offerings. And it's always willing to offer competitive prices. Strong channel relations were built by Fruitco's former chairman of the board and chief executive officer, F. Monroe. Mr. Monroe—who owns controlling interest in the firm—"worked" the Bay area as the company's salesman in its earlier years, before he took over from his father as president in 1940. Monroe was an ambitious and hard-working top manager—the firm prospered under his direction. He became well known within the canned food processing industry for technical/product innovations.

During the off-canning season, Mr. Monroe traveled widely. In the course of his travels, he arranged several important business deals. His 1968 and 1975 trips resulted in the following two events: (1) inexpensive pineapple was imported from Formosa and sold by Fruitco—primarily to expand the product line; and (2) a technically advanced continuous process cooker (65 feet high) was imported from England and installed at the Eugene plant in February–March 1980. It was the first of its kind in the United States and cut process time sharply.

Mr. Monroe retired in 1986 and named his son-in-law, 35-year-old Dave Corning, as his successor. Mr. Corning is intelligent and hard-working. He had been concerned primarily with the company's financial matters and only recently with marketing problems. During his seven-year tenure as financial director, the firm received its highest credit rating ever and was able to borrow working capital ($5 million to meet seasonal can and wage requirements) at the lowest rate ever received by the company.

The fact that the firm isn't unionized allows some competitive advantage. However, minimum wage law changes have increased costs. And these and other rising costs have squeezed profit margins. This led to the recent closing of two plants as they became less efficient to operate. The remaining two plants were expanded in capacity (especially warehouse facilities) so that they could operate more profitably due to maximum use of existing processing equipment.

Shortly after Mr. Monroe's retirement, Dave Corning reviewed the company's situation with his managers. He pointed to narrowing profit margins, debts contracted for new plant and equipment, and an increasingly competitive environment. Even considering the temporary labor-saving competitive advantage of the new cooker system, there seemed to be no way to improve the status quo unless the firm could sell direct, as it does in the local market—absorbing the food brokers' 5 percent commission on

sales. This was the plan decided on, and Jerry Turner was given the new sales job for six months.

Turner, who lives in Eugene, Oregon, is the only full-time salesman for the firm. Other top managers do some selling—but not much. Being a nephew of Mr. Monroe, Jerry Turner is also a member of the board of directors. He is well-qualified in technical matters and has a college degree in food chemistry. Although Mr. Turner formerly did call on some important customers with the brokers' sales reps, he is not well known in the industry or even by Fruitco's usual customers.

It is now five months later. Jerry Turner is not doing very well. He has made several selling trips and hundreds of telephone calls with discouraging results. He is unwilling to continue sales efforts on his own. There seem to be too many potential customers for one person to reach. And more "wining and dining" is needed. Turner insists that a sales staff be formed if the present way of operating is to continue. Sales are down in comparison both to expectations and to the previous year's results. Some regular supermarket chain customers have stopped buying—though basic consumer demand has not changed. Further, some potential new customers have demanded quantity guarantees much larger than the firm can supply. Expanding supply would be difficult in the short run because the firm typically must contract with growers to assure supplies of the type and quality they normally offer.

Evaluate Fruitco's strategy planning. What should Dave Corning do now?

30. Chemco, Inc.

Susan O'Keefe is trying to decide whether to leave her present job for what may be a great chance to buy into a business and be part of "top management."

Susan is now a sales rep for a plastics components manufacturer. She calls mostly on large industrial accounts—such as refrigerator manufacturers—who might need large quantities of custom-made products, like door liners. She is on a straight salary of $30,000 per year, plus expenses and a company car. She expects some salary increases but doesn't see much long-run opportunity with this company. As a result, she is seriously considering changing jobs and investing $35,000 in Chemco, Inc.—an established

Long Island (New York) thermoplastic molder (manufacturer). Mr. Larson, the present owner, is nearing retirement and has not trained anyone to take over the business. He has agreed to sell the business to Ted Swift, a lawyer, who has invited Susan O'Keefe to invest and become the sales manager. Ted Swift has agreed to match Susan's current salary plus expenses, plus a bonus of 2 percent of profits. However, Susan must invest to become part of the new company. She will get a 5 percent interest in the business for the necessary $35,000 investment.

Chemco, Inc., is well-established. Last year it had sales of $2 million, but zero profits (after paying Mr. Larson a salary of $35,000). In terms of sales, cost of materials was 46 percent; direct labor, 13 percent; indirect factory labor, 15 percent; factory overhead, 13 percent; and sales overhead and general expenses, 13 percent. The company has not been making any profit for several years, but it has been continually adding new machines to replace those made obsolete by technological developments. The machinery is well maintained and modern, but most of it is similar to that used by its many competitors. Most of the machines in the industry are standard. Special products are made by using specially made dies with these machines.

Sales have been split about two thirds custom-molded products (that is, made to the specification of other producers or merchandising concerns) and the balance proprietary items (such as housewares and game items, like poker chips and cribbage sets). The housewares are copies of articles developed by others—and indicate neither originality nor style. Mr. Larson is in charge of selling the proprietary items, which are distributed through any available wholesale channels. The custom-molded products are sold through three full-time sales engineers and three

manufacturers' reps who receive a 5 percent commission on individual orders up to $10,000 and then 3 percent above that level.

The company seems to be in fairly good financial condition—at least as far as book value is concerned. The $35,000 investment will buy almost $50,000 in assets—and ongoing operations should pay off the seven-year note. See Table 1.

Mr. Swift thinks that—with new management—the company has a good chance to make big profits. He expects to make some economies in the production process because he feels most production operations can be improved. He plans to keep custom-molding sales at approximately the present $1.3 million level. The new strategy will try to increase the proprietary sales volume from $700,000 to $2 million a year. Susan O'Keefe is expected to be a big help here because of her sales experience. This will bring the firm up to about capacity level—but it will mean adding additional employees and costs. The major advantage of expanding sales will be spreading overhead.

Some of the products proposed by Ted Swift for expanding proprietary sales are listed below.

New products for consideration:

Water bottles for cyclists.

Picnic lunch boxes.

Closet organizer/storage boxes for toys.

Short legs for furniture.

Step-on garbage can without liner.

Formed wall coverings.

Outside house shutters.

Bird houses.

Importing and distributing foreign housewares.

Table 1 Chemco Manufacturing Company, Statement of Financial Conditions, December 31, 199x

Assets			Liabilities and Net Worth		
Cash		$ 13,000	Liabilities:		
Accounts receivable		35,000	Accounts payable		$ 51,000
Building	$ 225,000		Notes payable—		
Less: depreciation	75,000		7 years (machinery)		194,000
		150,000			
Machinery	1,200,000		Net worth:		
Less: depreciation	450,000		Capital stock		700,000
		750,000	Retained earnings		4,000
Total assets		$948,000	Total liabilities and net worth		$948,000

Chemco faces heavy competition from many other similar companies. Further, most retailers expect a wide margin—sometimes 50 to 60 percent. Even so, manufacturing costs are low enough so Chemco can spend some money for promotion, while still keeping the price competitive. Apparently, many customers are willing to pay for novel new products—if they see them in stores. Susan isn't worried too much by tough competition. She sees plenty of that in her present job. And she does like the idea of being an "owner and sales manager."

Evaluate Chemco, Inc.'s situation and Ted Swift's strategy. What should Susan O'Keefe do? Why?

31. American Tools, Inc.

Bill Patch, president and marketing manager of American Tools, Inc., is deciding what strategy—or strategies—to pursue.

American Tools, Inc., is a manufacturer of industrial cutting tools. These tools include such items as lathe blades, drill press bits, and various other cutting edges used in the operation of large metal cutting, boring, or stamping machines. Bill Patch takes great pride in the fact that his company—whose $4.3 million sales in 1988 is small by industry standards—is recognized as a producer of the highest-quality line of cutting tools.

Competition in the cutting-tool industry is intense. American Tools competes not only with the original machine manufacturers, but also with many other larger manufacturers offering cutting tools as one of their many different product lines. This has had the effect, over the years, of standardizing the price, specifications, and, in turn, the quality of the competing products of all manufacturers.

About a year ago, Mr. Patch was tiring of the financial pressure of competing with larger companies enjoying economies of scale. At the same time, he noted that more and more potential cutting-tool customers were turning to small tool-and-die shops because of specialized needs that could not be met by the mass production firms. Mr. Patch thought perhaps he should consider some basic strategy changes. Although he was unwilling to become strictly a custom producer, Mr. Patch thought that the recent trend toward buying customized cutting edges suggested new markets might be developing—markets too small

for the large, multiproduct-line companies to serve profitably, but large enough to earn a good profit for a flexible company of American Tools' size.

A research company, Harrel Associates, was hired to study the feasibility of serving these markets. The initial results were encouraging. It was estimated that American Tools might increase sales by 60 percent and profits by 80 percent by serving the emerging markets.

Next, Mr. Patch had the sales manager hire two technical specialists (at a total cost of $60,000 each per year) to maintain continuous contact with potential cutting-tool customers. The specialists were supposed to identify any present—or future—needs that might exist in enough cases to make it possible to profitably produce a specialized product. The technical specialists were not to take orders or "sell" American Tools to the potential customers. Mr. Patch felt that only through this policy could these reps talk to the right people.

The initial feedback from the technical specialists was most encouraging. Many firms (large and small) had special needs—although it often was necessary to talk to the shop foreman or individual machine operators to find these needs. Most operators were "making do" with the tools available. Either they didn't know customizing was possible or doubted that their supervisors would do anything about it if they suggested that a more specialized tool would increase productivity. But these operators were encouraging because they said that it would be easier to persuade supervisors to order specialized tools if the tools were already produced and in stock than if they had to be custom-made. So Mr. Patch decided to continually add high-quality products to meet the ever-changing, specialized needs of users of cutting tools and edges.

American Tools' potential customers for specialized tools are located all over the country. The average sale per customer is likely to be less than $400, but the sale will be repeated several times within a year. Because of the widespread market and the small order size, Mr. Patch doesn't think that selling direct—as is done by small custom shops—is practical. At the present time, American Tools, Inc., sells 90 percent of its regular output through a large industrial wholesaler—Millco, Inc.—which serves the area east of the Mississippi River. This wholesaler, although very large and well known, is having trouble moving cutting tools. Millco is losing sales of cutting tools in some cities to newer wholesalers specializing in the cutting-tool industry. The new wholesalers are able to give more technical help to potential customers, and therefore better service. Millco's president is convinced that the newer, less-experienced concerns will either realize that a substantial profit margin can't be maintained along with their aggressive strategies, or they will eventually go broke trying to "overspecialize."

From Mr. Patch's standpoint, the present wholesaler has a good reputation and has served American Tools well in the past. Millco has been of great help in holding down Mr. Patch's inventory costs by increasing the inventory in its own 34 branch locations. Although Mr. Patch has received several complaints about the lack of technical assistance given by the wholesaler's sales reps—as well as their lack of knowledge about the new American Tools products—he feels that the present wholesaler is providing the best service it can. All its sales reps have been told about the new products at a special training session, and a new page has been added to the catalog they carry with them. So, regarding the complaints, Mr. Patch says: "The usual things you hear when you're in business."

Mr. Patch thinks there are more urgent problems than a few complaints. Profits are declining and sales of the new cutting tools are not nearly as high as forecast—even though all reports indicate the company's new products meet the intended markets' needs perfectly. The high costs involved in producing small quantities of special products and in adding the technical specialist team—together with lower-than-expected sales—have significantly reduced American Tools' profits. Mr. Patch is wondering whether it is wise to continue to try to cater to the needs of many specific target markets when the results are this discouraging. He also is considering increasing advertising expenditures in the hope that customers will "pull" the new products through the channel.

Evaluate American Tools' situation and Bill Patch's strategy. What should he do now?

32. Castco, Inc.

Milo West, marketing manager for Castco, Inc., is trying to figure out how to explain to his boss why a proposed new product line doesn't make sense for them. Milo is sure it's wrong—but he isn't able to explain why.

Castco, Inc., is a producer of malleable iron castings for automobile and aircraft manufacturers—and a variety of other users of castings. Last year's sales of castings amounted to over $65 million.

Castco also produces about 55 percent of all the original equipment bumper jacks installed in new automobiles each year. This is a very price-competitive business, but Castco has been able to obtain its large market share with frequent personal contact between the company's executives and its customers—supported by very close cooperation between the company's engineering department and its customers' buyers. This has been extremely important because the wide variety of models and model changes frequently requires alterations in the specifications of the bumper jacks. All of Castco's bumper jacks are sold directly to the automobile manufacturers. No attempt has been made to sell bumper jacks to final consumers through hardware and automotive channels—although they are available through the manufacturers' automobile dealers.

Mr. Bill Butler, Castco's production manager, now wants to begin producing hydraulic jacks for sale through automobile-parts wholesalers to retail auto parts stores. Mr. Butler saw a variety of hydraulic jacks at a recent automotive show and knew immediately that his plant could produce these products. This especially interested him because of the possibility of using excess capacity now that auto sales are down. Further, he thinks "jacks are jacks," and that the company would merely be broadening its product line by introducing hydraulic jacks.

As Butler became more enthusiastic about the idea, he found that Castco's engineering department already had a design that appeared to be at least comparable to the products now offered on the market. None of these products has any patent protection. Further, Mr. Butler says that the company would be able to produce a product that is better made than the competitive products (i.e., smoother castings, etc.)—although he agrees that most customers probably wouldn't notice the differences. The production department estimates that the cost of producing a hydraulic jack comparable to those currently offered by competitors would be about $38 per unit.

Milo West, the marketing manager, has just received a memo from Phil Armity, the company president, explaining the production department's enthusiasm for broadening Castco's jack line into hydraulic jacks. Armity seems enthusiastic about the idea, too, noting that it may be a way to make fuller use of the company's resources and increase its sales. Armity's memo asks for Milo's reaction, but Armity already seems sold on the idea.

Given Armity's enthusiasm, Milo West isn't sure how to respond. He's trying to develop a good explanation of why he isn't excited about the proposal. He knows he's already overworked and couldn't possibly promote this new line himself—and he's the only salesman the company has. So it would be necessary to hire someone to promote the line. And this "sales manager" would probably have to recruit manufacturers' agents (who probably would want a 10 to 12 percent commission on sales) to sell to automotive wholesalers who would stock the jack and sell to the auto parts retailers. These wholesalers would probably expect trade discounts of about 20 percent, trade show exhibits, some national advertising, and sales promotion help (catalog sheets, mailers, and point-of-purchase displays). Further, Milo West sees that the billing and collection system would have to be expanded because many more customers would be involved. It would also be necessary to keep track of agent commissions and accounts receivable.

Auto parts retailers are currently selling similar hydraulic jacks to "do-it-yourself" consumers for about $89.00. Milo has learned that retailers typically expect a trade discount of about 35 percent off of the suggested list price for their auto parts.

All things considered, Milo feels that the proposed hydraulic-jack line is not very closely related to the company's present emphasis. He has already indicated his lack of enthusiasm to Bill Butler, but this made little difference in Bill's thinking. Now it's clear that Milo will have to convince the president or he will soon be responsible for selling hydraulic jacks.

Evaluate Castco's current strategy and the proposed strategy. What should Milo West say to Phil Armity?

33.   *Multifoods, Ltd.**

Bruce Rains, marketing manager of Multifoods, Ltd., is being urged to approve the creation of a

separate marketing plan for Quebec—a major policy change.

Bruce Rains has been the marketing manager of Multifoods, Ltd., for the last four years—since he arrived from international headquarters in Minneapolis. Multifoods, Ltd.—headquartered in Toronto—is a subsidiary of a large U.S.-based consumer packaged-food company with worldwide sales of more than $2 billion in 1988. Its Canadian sales are just under $330 million—with the Quebec and Ontario markets accounting for 67 percent of the company's Canadian sales.

The company's product line includes such items as cake mixes, puddings, pie fillings, pancakes, and prepared foods. The company has successfully introduced at least six new products every year for the last five years. Its most recent new product was a line of frozen dinners successfully launched last year. Products from Multifoods are known for their high quality and enjoy much brand preference throughout Canada—including the Province of Quebec.

The company's sales have risen every year since Mr. Rains took over as marketing manager. In fact, the company's market share has increased steadily in each of the product categories in which it competes. The Quebec market has closely followed the national trend except that, in the past two years, total sales growth in that market began to lag.

According to Bruce Rains, a big advantage of Multifoods over its competitors is the ability to coordinate all phases of the food business from Toronto. For this reason, Mr. Rains meets at least once a month with his product managers to discuss developments in local markets that might affect marketing plans. While each manager is free to make suggestions—and even to suggest major departures from current marketing practices—Bruce Rains has the final say.

One of the product managers, Marie Rhone, expressed great concern at the last monthly meeting about the poor performance of some of the company's products in the Quebec market. While a broad range of possible reasons—ranging from inflation to politics—was reviewed to try to explain the situation, Marie insisted that it was due to a basic lack of understanding of that market because not enough managerial time and money had been spent on the Quebec market.

As a result, Marie Rhone felt the current marketing approach to the Quebec market should be reevaluated. An inappropriate marketing plan may be

*This case was adapted from one written by Professor Roberta Tamilia, University of Windsor, Canada.

responsible for the sales slowdown. After all, she said, "80 percent of the market is French-speaking. It's in the best interest of the company to treat that market as being separate and distinct from the rest of Canada."

Marie Rhone supported her position by showing that Quebec's per capita consumption of many product categories (in which the firm competes) is above the national average (Table 1). Research projects conducted by Multifoods also support the "separate and distinct" argument. Over the years, the firm has found many French-English differences in brand attitudes, lifestyles, usage rates, and so on.

Marie argued that the company should develop a unique Quebec marketing plan for some or all of its brands. She specifically suggested that the French-language advertising plan for a particular brand be developed independently of the plan for English Canada. Currently, the agency assigned to the brand just translates its English-language ads for the French market. Bruce Rains pointed out that the existing advertising approach assured Multifoods of a uniform brand image across Canada. However, the discussion that followed suggested that a different brand image might be needed in the French market if the company wanted to stop the brand's decline in sales.

The managers also discussed the food distribution system in Quebec. The major supermarket chains have their lowest market share in that province. Independents are strongest there—the "mom-and-pop" food stores fast disappearing outside Quebec remain alive and well in the province. Traditionally, these stores have stocked a higher proportion (than supermarkets) of their shelf space with national brands—an advantage for Multifoods.

Finally, various issues related to discount policies, pricing structure, sales promotion, and cooperative advertising were discussed. All of this suggested that things were different in Quebec—and that future marketing plans should reflect these differences to a greater extent than they do now.

After the meeting, Bruce Rains stayed in his office to think about the situation. Although he agreed with

the basic idea that the Quebec market was in many ways different, he wasn't sure how far his company should go in recognizing this fact. He knew that regional differences in food tastes and brand purchases existed not only in Quebec, but in other parts of Canada as well. People were people, after all, with far more similarities than differences.

Mr. Rains was afraid that giving special status to one region might conflict with top management's objective of achieving standardization whenever possible—one "global" strategy for Canada, on the way to one worldwide global strategy. He was also worried about the long-term effect of such a policy change on costs, organizational structure, and brand image. Still, enough product managers had expressed their concern over the years about the Quebec market to make him wonder if he shouldn't modify the current approach. Perhaps he could experiment with a few brands—and just in Quebec. He could cite the language difference as the reason for trying Quebec rather than any of the other provinces. But Bruce realizes that any change of policy could be seen as the beginning of more change, and what would Minneapolis think? Could he explain it successfully there?

Evaluate Multifoods, Ltd.'s present strategy. What should Bruce Rains do now? Explain.

34. Kenny Chrysler, Inc.

Tony Kenny owns Kenny Chrysler, Inc., a full-line Chrysler dealership in suburban St. Louis, Missouri. Tony is seriously considering moving into a proposed auto mall—a large display and selling area for 10 to 15 competing auto dealers. This mall will be a few miles away from his current location but easily available to his present customers and quite convenient to many more potential customers. He can consider moving now because the lease on his current location will be up in one year. He is sure he can renew the lease for another five years, but he feels the owner is likely to want to raise the lease terms so his total fixed costs will be about $100,000 more per year than his current fixed costs of $600,000 per year. Moving to the new mall will probably increase his total fixed costs to about $1 million per year. Further, it is likely that these fixed costs—wherever he is—will continue to rise with inflation. But this is not a major

Table 1   Per Capita Consumption Index, Province of Quebec (Canada = 100)

Cake mixes	105	Soft drinks	125
Pancakes	89	Pie fillings	117
Puddings	113	Frozen dinners	81
Salad dressings	88	Prepared packaged foods	87
Molasses	131	Cookies	121

problem in his mind. Car prices tend to rise at about the same rate as inflation, so these rising revenues and costs tend to offset each other.

Tony Kenny is considering moving to an auto mall because he feels this may be the future trend. Already, about 100 malls are operating in the United States and they do seem to lead to increases in sales per dealership. Some dealers in auto malls have reported increases in sales of as much as 30 percent over what they were doing in their former locations outside the mall.

Another reason Tony is considering moving to a mall is the growing number of competing brands and the desire of some consumers to shop more conveniently. Instead of the old competition of "the Big Three," there are now over 30 different brands of cars and 15 brands of trucks in the U.S. market—not including "specialty" cars such as Lambroghini and Rolls-Royce. This increasing competition is already taking its toll on some domestic and foreign car dealers, as they have to take less profit on each sale. For example, even owners of luxury car franchises such as Porsche, Audi, Sterling, and Acura are having troubles. Dealer ranks have thinned considerably too. Once there were 50,000 dealerships in the U.S. Now, there are less than half that number—and failures are reported all the time. Recently, some dealers tried to become "mega-dealers" operating in several markets, but this did not work too well because they could not achieve economies of scale. Now, owners of multiple dealerships seem to be going to malls to reduce their overhead and promotion costs. And if customers begin to go to these malls, then this may be *the* place to be—even for a dealer with only one auto franchise. That is the position that Tony Kenny is in. And he wonders if he should become well-positioned in a mall before it is too late.

Tony Kenny's dealership is now selling between 550 and 700 cars per year—at an average price of about $10,000. With careful management, he is grossing about 10 percent per car or $1,000 per car. This $1,000 is not all net profit, however. It must go towards covering his fixed costs of about $600,000 per year. So, if he sells more than 600 cars he will more than cover these fixed costs and make a profit. Obviously, the more cars he sells the more likely he is to make a profit—even a large profit—assuming he controls his costs. So he is thinking that moving to a mall might increase his sales and therefore lead to a larger profit. A major question in his mind is whether he is likely to sell enough extra cars in a mall to help pay for the increase in fixed costs. He is also

concerned about how his Chrysler products will stand up against all of the other cars when consumers can more easily shop around and compare. Right now, Tony has some loyal customers who regularly buy from him because of his seasoned, helpful sales force *and* his dependable repair shop. But he is worried that making it easy for these customers to compare other cars might lead to brand switching or put greater pressure on price to keep some of his "loyal" customers.

Another of Tony's concerns is whether the "Big Three" car manufacturers will discourage dealers from going into auto malls. Now, these auto manufacturers do not encourage dealers to go into a "supermarket setting." Instead, they prefer their dealers to devote their full energies to one brand in a free-standing location. But, as real estate prices rise, it becomes more and more difficult to insist upon free-standing dealerships in all markets—and still have profitable dealerships. The rising number of bankruptcies or dealerships in financial difficulties has caused the manufacturers to be more relaxed about insisting upon a free-standing location.

Adding to the competitiveness in the U.S. auto market is the increasing aggressiveness of auto importers as well as Japanese auto companies which are now producing in the United States. As they increase their penetration and capacity on the East and West Coasts, they are moving into the center of the United States. While imports represent more than half of car sales in some East and West Coast markets, they account for as little as 15 percent to 25 percent of the market in the Midwest. But now foreign producers are setting up more dealers in this area and competition is likely to become even more intense. In Tony Kenny's area—Missouri—imports account for approximately 25 percent of the market, but this share will probably rise in the future.

Evaluate Tony Kenny's present and possible new strategy. What would you recommend to Tony Kenny? Why?

35. Visiting Nurses Services (VNS)

Elsie Hollers, executive director of VNS, is trying to clarify her agency's strategies. She's sure some changes are needed, but she's less sure about how *much* change is needed and/or can be handled by her people.

The Visiting Nurses Services (VNS) is a nonprofit organization that has been operating—with varying degrees of success—for 25 years. Some of its funding comes from the local United Way to provide emergency nursing services for those who can't afford to pay. The balance of the revenues—about 90 percent of the $1.7 million annual budget—comes from charges made directly to the client or to third-party payers—including insurance companies and the federal government for Medicare or Medicaid services.

Elsie Hollers has been executive director of VNS for two years now. She has developed an organization that functions well and is able to meet most requests for service that come from some local doctors and from the discharge officers at local hospitals. Some business also comes by self-referral—the client finds the VNS name in the Yellow Pages of the local phone directory.

The last two years have been a rebuilding time because the previous director had personnel problems. This led to a weakening of the agency's image with the local referring agencies. Now the image is more positive. But Elsie is not completely satisfied with the situation. By definition, the Visiting Nurses Services is a nonprofit organization. But it still must cover all its costs to meet the payroll, rent payments, phone expenses, and so on—including Elsie's own salary. She can see that while VNS is growing slightly and is now breaking even, it doesn't have much of a cash "cushion" to fall back on if (1) the demand for VNS nursing services declines, (2) the government changes its rules about paying for the VNS's kind of nursing services—either cutting back on what it will pay for or reducing the amount it will pay for specific services—or (3) new competitors enter the market. In fact, the latter possibility is of great concern to Elsie. Some hospitals—squeezed for revenue—are expanding into home health care. And "for-profit" organizations (e.g., Kelly Home Care Services) are expanding around the country to provide home health care services—including nursing services of the kind offered by VNS. These for-profit organizations appear to be efficiently run—offering good service at competitive and sometimes even lower prices than some nonprofit organizations. And they seem to be doing this at a profit—which suggests that it would be possible for these for-profit companies to lower their prices if nonprofit organizations try to compete on price.

Elsie is considering whether she should ask her board of directors to let her move into the whole "home health care" market—to move beyond just nursing.

Currently, the VNS is primarily concerned with providing professional nursing care in the home. But VNS nurses are much too expensive for routine health-care activities—helping fix meals, bathing and dressing patients, and so on. The "full cost" of a nurse to VNS (including benefits and overhead) is about $55 per hour. Besides, a registered nurse is not needed for routine jobs. All that is required is someone who can get along with all kinds of people and is willing to do this kind of work. Generally, any mature person can be trained fairly quickly to do the job—following the instructions and under the general supervision of a physician, a nurse, or family members. The "full cost" of aides is $5 to $10 per hour for short visits—and as low as $50 per 24 hours for a live-in aide who has room and board supplied by the client.

The demand for home health care services seems to be growing as more women join the work force and can't take over home health care when the need arises due to emergencies or long-term disabilities. And with people living longer, there are more single-survivor family situations where there is no one nearby to take care of the needs of these older people. But often some family members—or third-party payers such as the government or insurers—are willing to pay home care services. Now, Elsie occasionally recommends other agencies, or suggests one or another of three women who have been doing this work on their own, part-time. But with growing demand, Elsie wonders if the VNS should get into this business—hiring aides as needed.

Elsie is concerned that a new, full-service home health care organization may come into "her" market and provide both nursing services *and* less-skilled home health care services. This has happened already in two nearby, but somewhat larger cities. Elsie fears that this might be more appealing than VNS to the local hospitals and other referrers. In other words, she can see the possibility of losing nursing service business if the VNS does not begin to offer a more complete service. This would cause real problems for VNS—because overhead costs are more or less fixed. A loss in revenue of as little as 10 percent would require some cutbacks—perhaps laying off some nurses or secretaries, giving up part of the office, and so on.

Another reason for expanding beyond nursing services—using paraprofessionals and relatively unskilled personnel—is to offer a better service to present customers *and* make more effective use of the organization structure that has been developed over the last two years. Elsie estimates that the administrative and office capabilities could handle 50 to 100 percent more clients without straining the system. It would be necessary to add some clerical help—if the expansion were quite large—as well as to expand the hours when the switchboard is open. But these increases in overhead would be minor compared to the present proportion of total revenue that goes to covering overhead. In other words, additional clients could increase revenue and assure the survival of the VNS, provide a cushion to cover the normal fluctuations in demand, and assure more job security for the administrative personnel.

Further, Elsie thinks that if the VNS were successful in expanding its services—and therefore could generate some surplus—it could extend services to those who aren't now able to pay. Elsie says one of the worst parts of her job is refusing service to clients whose third-party benefits have run out or who, for whatever reason, can no longer afford to pay. Elsie is uncomfortable about having to cut off service, but she must schedule her nurses to provide revenue-producing services if she's going to meet the payroll every two weeks. By expanding to provide more services, she might be able to keep serving more of these nonpaying clients. This possibility excites Elsie because her nurse's training has instilled a deep desire to serve people—whether they can pay or not. This continual need to cut off service because people can't pay has been at the root of many disagreements—and even arguments—between the nurses serving the clients and Elsie, as executive director and representative of the board of directors.

Elsie knows that expanding into home health care services won't be easy. The nurses' union must be convinced that the nurses should be available on a 24-hour schedule rather than the eight-to-five schedule six days a week that is typical now. Some decisions would be needed about relative pay levels for nurses, paraprofessionals, and home health care aides. VNS would also have to set prices for these different services and tell the present customers and referral agencies about the expanded services.

These problems aren't bothering Elsie too much, however—she thinks she can handle them. She is sure that home health care services are in demand and could be supplied at competitive prices.

Her primary concern is whether this is the right thing for a nurses' organization to do. The name of her group is the Visiting Nurses Services, and its whole history has been oriented to supplying *nurses' services.* Nurses are dedicated professionals who bring high standards to any job they undertake. The question is whether the VNS should offer "less professional" services. Inevitably, some of the home health care aides will not be as dedicated as the nurses might like them to be. And this could reflect unfavorably on the nurse image. At the same time, however, Elsie worries about the future of VNS—and her own future.

Evaluate VNS's present strategy. What should Elsie Hollers propose to the board of directors? Explain.

36.   Lever, Ltd.*

Al Feta is product manager for Protect Deodorant Soap. He was just transferred to Lever, Ltd., a Canadian subsidiary of Lever Group, Inc., from world headquarters in New York. Al is anxious to make a good impression and is working on developing and securing management approval of next year's marketing plan for Protect. His first step involves submitting a draft marketing plan to Mike Holden—his recently appointed group product manager.

Al's marketing plan is the single most important document he will produce on his brand assignment. This annual marketing plan does three main things:

1. It reviews the brand's performance in the past year, assesses the competitive situation, and highlights problems and opportunities for the brand.
2. It spells out marketing, advertising, and sales promotion strategies and plans for the coming year.
3. Finally, and most importantly, the marketing plan sets out the brand's sales objectives and advertising/promotion budget requirements.

In preparing this marketing plan, Al gathered the information in Table 1.

Al was aware of the regional differences in the bar soap market and recognized the significant regional skews:

a. The underdevelopment of the deodorant bar segment in Quebec with a corresponding overdevelopment of the beauty bar segment. Research showed

---

*Adapted from a case prepared by Mr. Daniel Aronchick, who at the time of its preparation was Marketing Manager at Thomas J. Lipton, Limited.

Table 1 Past 12-Month Share of Soap Market (percent)

	Maritimes	Quebec	Ontario	Manitoba/ Saskatchewan	Alberta	British Columbia
Deodorant segment						
Zest	21.3%	14.2%	24.5%	31.2%	30.4%	25.5%
Dial	10.4	5.1	12.8	16.1	17.2	14.3
Lifebuoy	4.2	3.1	1.2	6.4	5.8	4.2
Protect	2.1	5.6	1.0	4.2	4.2	2.1
Beauty bar segment						
Camay	6.2	12.3	7.0	4.1	4.0	5.1
Lux	6.1	11.2	7.7	5.0	6.9	5.0
Dove	5.5	8.0	6.6	6.3	6.2	4.2
Lower-priced bars						
Ivory	11.2	6.5	12.4	5.3	5.2	9.0
Sunlight	6.1	3.2	8.2	4.2	4.1	8.0
All others (including stores' own brands)	26.9	30.8	18.6	17.2	16.0	22.6
Total soap market	100.0	100.0	100.0	100.0	100.0	100.0

this was due to cultural factors. An identical pattern is evident in most European countries where the adoption of deodorant soaps has been slower than in North America. For similar reasons, the development of perfumed soaps is highest in Quebec.

b. The overdevelopment of synthetic bars in the Prairies. These bars, primarily in the deodorant segment, lather better in the hard water of the Prairies. Nonsynthetic bars lather very poorly in hard-water areas—and leave a soap film.

c. The overdevelopment of the "all-other" segment in Quebec. This segment, consisting of smaller brands, fares better in Quebec where 40 percent of the grocery trade is done by independent stores. Conversely, large chain grocery stores predominate in Ontario and the Prairies.

Al's brand, Protect, is a highly perfumed, deodorant bar. His business is relatively weak in the key Ontario market. To confirm this share data, Al calculated consumption of Protect per thousand people in each region (see Table 2).

These differences are especially interesting since per capita sales of total bar soap products are roughly equal in all provinces.

A consumer attitude and usage research study was conducted approximately a year ago. This study revealed that consumer top-of-mind awareness of the Protect brand differed greatly across Canada. This was true despite the even expenditure of advertising funds in past years. Also, trial of Protect was low in the Maritimes, Ontario, and British Columbia (Table 3).

The attitude portion of the research revealed that consumers who had heard of Protect were aware of its main attribute of deodorant protection via a high fragrance level. This was the main selling point in the copy strategy, and it was well communicated through Protect's advertising. The other important finding was that consumers who had tried Protect were satisfied with the product. Some 72 percent of those trying Protect had repurchased the product at least twice.

One last pressing issue for Protect was the pending delisting of the brand by two key Ontario chains. These chains, which controlled about half the grocery

Table 2 Standard Cases of Three-Ounce Bars Consumed per 1,000 People in 12 Months

	Maritimes	Quebec	Ontario	Manitoba/ Saskatchewan	Alberta	British Columbia
Protect	4.1	10.9	1.9	8.1	4.1	6.2
Sales index	66	175	31	131	131	100

Table 3 Usage Results (in percent)

	Maritimes	Quebec	Ontario	Manitoba/ Saskatchewan	Alberta	British Columbia
Respondents aware of Protect.........	20%	58%	28%	30%	32%	16%
Respondents ever trying Protect.......	3	18	2	8	6	4

Table 4 Allocation of Marketing Budget, by Population

	Maritimes	Quebec	Ontario	Manitoba/ Saskatchewan	Alberta	British Columbia	Canada
Percent of population...............	10%	27%	36%	8%	8%	11%	100%
Possible allocation of budget based on population...................	$76M	$205M	$273M	$61M	$61M	$84M	$760M
Percent of Protect business at present ..	7%	51%	12%	11%	11%	8%	100%

volume in Ontario, were dissatisfied with the level at which Protect was moving off the shelves.

With this information before him, Al now has to resolve the key aspect of the brand's marketing plan for the following year: how to allocate the advertising and sales promotion budget by region.

Protect's total advertising/sales promotion budget is 20 percent of sales. With forecast sales of $3.8 million, this budget amounts to a $760,000 marketing expenditure. Traditionally such funds have been allocated in proportion to population (Table 4).

Al feels he should spend more heavily in Ontario where the grocery chain delisting problem exists. In the previous year, 36 percent of Protect's budget was allocated to Ontario, which accounted for only 12 percent of Protect's sales. Al wants to increase Ontario spending to 47 percent of the total budget by taking funds evenly from all other areas. Al expects this will increase business in the key Ontario market, which has over a third of Canada's population.

Al presented this plan to Mike, his newly appointed group product manager. Mike strongly disagrees. He has also been reviewing Protect's business and feels that advertising and rally promotion funds have historically been misallocated. It is his strong belief that, to use his words: "A brand should spend where its business is." Mike believes that the first priority in allocating funds regionally is to support the areas of strength. He suggested to Al that there was more business to be had in the brand's strong areas, Quebec and the Prairies, than in chasing sales in Ontario. Therefore, Mike suggested that spending for Protect in the coming year be proportional to the brand's sales by region rather than to regional population.

Al is convinced this is wrong, particularly in light of the Ontario situation. He asked Mike how the Ontario market should be handled. Mike said that the conservative way to build business in Ontario is to invest incremental promotion funds. However, before these incremental funds are invested, a test of this Ontario investment proposition should be conducted. Mike recommended that an investment-spending test market be conducted in a small area or town in Ontario for 12 months. This will enable Al to see if the incremental spending results in higher sales and profits—profits large enough to justify the higher spending. In other words, an investment payout should be assured before spending any extra money in Ontario.

Al feels this approach would be a waste of time and unduly cautious, given the importance of the Ontario market.

Evaluate the present strategy for Protect and Al's proposed approach. How should the advertising and sales promotion money be allocated? Why?

37. Young & Whitney, CPAs

The partners of Young & Whitney are having much disagreement about what the firm should do in the near future.

Young & Whitney, CPAs (Y&W) is a large regional certified public accounting firm based in Grand Rapids, Michigan, with branch offices in Lansing and Detroit. Y&W has 10 partners and a professional staff of approximately 100 accountants. Gross service billings for the fiscal year ending June 30, 1989, were $6.8 million. Financial data for 1987, 1988, and 1989 are presented in Table 1.

Y&W's professional services include: auditing, tax preparation, and bookkeeping. A breakdown of gross service revenue by service area for 1987, 1988, and 1989 is presented in Table 1. Y&W's client base includes municipal governments (cities, villages, and townships), manufacturing companies, professional organizations (attorneys, doctors, and dentists), and various other small businesses.

The majority of revenue comes from the firm's municipal practice. A breakdown of Y&W's gross revenue by client industry for 1987, 1988, and 1989 is presented in Table 1.

At the monthly partners' meeting held in July 1989, Chuck Amboy, the firm's managing partner (CEO), expressed concern about the future of the firm's municipal practice. Mr. Amboy's presentation to his partners appears below:

Although our firm is considered to be a leader in municipal auditing in our geographic area, I am concerned that as municipals attempt to cut their operating costs, they will solicit competitive bids from other public accounting firms to perform their annual audits. Due to the fact that the local offices of most of the "Big 6" firms* in our area concentrate their practice in the manufacturing industry—which typically has December 31 fiscal year-ends—they have "available" staff during the summer months.†

Therefore, they can afford to "low-ball" competitive bids to keep their staff busy and benefit from on-the-job training provided by municipal clientele. I am concerned that we may begin to lose clients in our most established and profitable practice area.

Janet Lynch, a senior partner in the firm and the partner-in-charge of the firm's municipal practice, was the first to respond to Chuck Amboy's concern.

Chuck, we all recognize the potential threat of being underbid for our municipal work by our "Big 6" competitors. However, Y&W is a recognized leader in municipal auditing, and we have much more local experience than our competitors. Furthermore, it is a fact that we offer a superior level of service quality to our clients—which goes beyond the services normally expected during an audit to include consulting on financial and other operating issues. Many of our less sophisticated clients are dependent on our nonaudit consulting assistance. Therefore, I believe, we have been successful in differentiating our services from our competitors. In many recent situations, Y&W was selected over a field of as many as 10 competitors even though our proposed prices were much higher than those of our competitors.

The partners at the meeting agreed with Janet Lynch's comments. However, even though Y&W had many success stories regarding their ability to retain their municipal clients—despite being underbid—they had lost three large municipal clients during the past year. Janet Lynch was asked to comment on the loss of those clients. She explained that the lost clients are larger municipalities with a lot of "in-house" financial expertise—and therefore less dependence on Y&W's "consulting" assistance. As a result, Y&W's service differentiation went largely unnoticed. Janet explained that the larger, more sophisticated municipals regarded audits as a "necessary evil" and usually selected the low-cost reputable bidder.

Table 1

	Fiscal year ending June 30		
	1989	1988	1987
Gross billings	6,800,000	6,400,000	5,800,000
Gross billings by service area:			
Auditing	3,100,000	3,200,000	2,750,000
Tax preparation ...	1,990,000	1,830,000	1,780,000
Bookkeeping	1,090,000	745,000	660,000
Other	620,000	625,000	610,000
Gross billings by client industry:			
Municipal........	3,214,000	3,300,00	2,908,000
Manufacturing	2,089,000	1,880,000	1,706,000
Professional......	1,355,000	1,140,000	1,108,000
Other	142,000	80,000	78,000

*The "Big 6" firms are a group of the six largest public accounting firms in the United States. They maintain offices in almost every major U.S. city. Until recently, these firms were known as the "Big 8," but after several mergers they have come to be known as the "Big 6."

†Organizations with December fiscal year-ends require audit work to be performed during the fall and in January and February. Those with June 30 fiscal year-ends require auditing during the summer months.

Chuck Amboy then requested ideas and discussion from the other partners at the meeting. One partner suggested that Y&W should protect itself by diversifying. Specifically, he felt a substantial practice development effort should be directed toward manufacturing. He reasoned that since manufacturing work would occur during Y&W's "off-season," Y&W could afford to price very low to gain new manufacturing clients. This strategy would also help to counter (and possibly discourage) "Big 6" competitors' "low-ball" pricing for municipals.

Evaluate Young & Whitney, CPAs' situation. What strategy(ies) should they select? Why?

38. *Alco Manufacturing Co.**

Tom Malone, newly-hired VP of Marketing for Alco Mfg. Co., is reviewing the firm's international distribution arrangements because they don't seem to be very well thought out. He is not sure if anything is wrong, but he feels that perhaps the company should go to a "global strategy" rather than continuing to follow the current policies.

Alco, based in Miami, Florida, produces finished aluminum products, such as garden furniture, aluminum ladders, umbrella-type clothes lines, scaffolding, moldings, and cabinet edgings. Sales in 1988 reached $20 million—primarily to U.S. customers.

In 1985, Alco decided to try foreign markets. The sales manager, John Potvin, believed the growing affluence of European workers, their developing taste for leisure, and their lifestyle preferences would help the company's products gain market acceptance quickly.

John's first step in investigating foreign markets was to join a trade mission to Europe—a tour organized by the U.S. Department of Commerce. This trade mission visited Italy, Germany, Holland, France, and England. During this trip, John was officially introduced to leading buyers for department store chains, import houses, wholesalers, and buying groups. The two-week trip convinced John that there was ample buying power to make exporting a profitable opportunity.

*Adapted from a case written by Professor Peter Banting, McMaster University, Canada.

On his return to Miami, John's next step was to obtain credit references for the firms he considered potential distributors. To those who were judged creditworthy, he sent letters expressing interest and included samples, prices, and other relevant information.

The first orders were from a German wholesaler. Sales in this market totaled $60,000 in 1986. Similar success was achieved in France and England. Italy, on the other hand, did not produce any sales. John felt the semiluxury nature of the company's products and the lower incomes in Italy encouraged Italians to take a "make do" attitude rather than to look for goods and services that would make life easier.

In the United States, Alco distributes through merchant hardware distributors and buying groups, such as cooperative and voluntary hardware chains. In its foreign markets, however, there is no recognizable pattern. Channel systems vary from country to country. To avoid mixing channels of distribution, Alco has only one account in each country. The chosen distributor is the exclusive distributor.

In Germany, Alco distributes through a wholesaler based in Munich, in the south of Germany. This wholesaler has five salespeople covering the country. The firm specializes in small housewares and has contacts with leading buying groups, wholesalers, and department store chains. John is impressed with the firm's aggressiveness and knowledge of merchandising techniques.

In France, Alco sells to a Paris-based buying group for hardware wholesalers throughout the country. John felt this group would provide excellent coverage of the market because of its extensive distribution network.

In Denmark, Alco's line is sold to a buying group representing a chain of hardware retailers. This group recently expanded to include retailers in Sweden, Finland, and Norway. Together, this group purchases goods for about five hundred hardware retailers. The buying power of Scandinavians is quite high, and it is expected that Alco's products will prove very successful there.

In the United Kingdom, Alco uses an importer-distributor, who both buys on his own account and acts as a sales agent. This firm sells to department stores and hardware wholesalers. This firm has not done very well yet, but John is convinced that this market has the highest potential of all the foreign countries. So far, the do-it-yourself market has led to a lot of business in aluminum moldings.

Australia is handled by an importer who operates a chain of discount houses. After much correspondence, this firm discovered it could land aluminum furniture in Melbourne at prices competitive with Japanese imports. So it started ordering, because it wanted to cut prices in what is now a high-priced garden furniture market.

The Venezuelan market is handled by an American who came to the United States from Venezuela in search of new lines. Alco attributes success in Venezuela to the efforts of this aggressive and capable agent. He has built a sizable trade in aluminum ladders.

In Trinidad and Jamaica, Alco's products are handled by traders who carry such diversified lines as insurance, apples, plums, and fish. They have been successful in selling aluminum ladders.

John Potvin's export policies for Alco are as follows:

1. Product: No product modifications will be made in selling to foreign customers. This may be considered later after a substantial sales volume develops.
2. Price: The company will not publish suggested list prices. Distributors add their own markup to their landed costs. Supply prices will be kept as low as possible. This is accomplished by:
   a. Removing advertising expenses and other strictly domestic overhead charges from price calculations.
   b. Finding the most economic packages for shipping (smallest volume per unit).
   c. Bargaining with carriers to obtain the lowest shipping rates possible.
3. Promotion: The firm does no advertising in foreign markets. Brochures and sales literature already being used in the United States are supplied to foreign distributors. Alco will continue to promote its products by participating in overseas trade shows. These are handled by the sales manager. All inquiries are forwarded to the firm's distributor in that country.
4. Distribution: New distributors will be contacted through foreign trade shows. John Potvin considers large distributors desirable. He feels, however, that they are not as receptive as smaller distributors to a new, unestablished product line. Therefore, he prefers to appoint small distributors. Larger distribu-

tors may be appointed after the company has gained a strong consumer franchise in a country.
5. Financing: Alco sees no need to provide financial help to distributors. The company views its major contribution as providing good products at the lowest possible prices.
6. Marketing and Planning Assistance: John Potvin feels that foreign distributors know their own markets best. Therefore, they are best equipped to plan for themselves.
7. Selection of Foreign Markets: The evaluation of foreign market opportunities for the company's products is based primarily on disposable income and lifestyle patterns. For example, John fails to see any market in North Africa for his products, which he thinks are of a semiluxury nature. He thinks that cheaper products such as wood ladders (often homemade) are preferred to prefabricated aluminum ladders in regions such as North Africa and Southern Europe. He thinks Venezuela, on the other hand, is a more highly industrialized market with luxury tastes. Thus, John sees Alco's products as better suited for more highly industrialized and affluent societies.

Evaluate Alco's present "foreign markets" strategies. Should it develop a "global strategy?" What strategy or strategies should Tom Malone develop?

39. *Speedy Pizza, Inc.*

Trudy Hall, manager of Speedy Pizza, Inc.'s Pontiac, Michigan store, is trying to develop a plan for the "sick" store she just took over. She sees several alternatives, but none is "obviously right."

Speedy Pizza, Inc. (SP) is an owner-managed pizza take-out and delivery business with three stores located in Ann Arbor, Southfield, and Pontiac, Michigan. Speedy's business comes from telephone or walk-in orders. Each Speedy store prepares its own pizzas. In addition to pizzas, SP also sells and delivers a limited selection of soft drinks.

SP's Ann Arbor store has been very successful. Much of the store's success is attributed to being close to the University of Michigan's campus—with more than 35,000 students. Most of these students live within five miles of SP's Ann Arbor store.

The Southfield store has been moderately successful. It serves mostly residential customers in the Southfield area. Recently, the store advertised—using direct-mail flyers—to several office buildings within three miles of the store. The flyers described SP's willingness and ability to cater large orders for office parties, business luncheons, and so forth. This promotion was quite successful. With this new program and SP's solid residential base of customers in Southfield, improved profitability at the Southfield location seems assured.

SP's Pontiac location has had mixed results during the last three years. The Pontiac store receives only about half of its customer orders from residential delivery requests. The Pontiac store's new manager, Trudy Hall, believes the problem with residential pizza delivery in Pontiac is due to the location of residential neighborhoods in the area. Pontiac has several large industrial plants (mostly auto industry-related) located throughout the city. Small, mostly factory-worker neighborhoods are distributed in between the various plant sites. As a result, SP's store location can serve only two or three of these small neighborhoods on one delivery run.

Most of the Pontiac store's potential seems to be in serving the large industrial plants. Many of these plants work two or three work shifts—five days a week. During each work shift, workers are allowed one half-hour "lunch" break—which usually occurs at 11 A.M., 8 P.M., or 2:30 A.M. (depending on the shift).

Generally, a customer will call from a plant about 30 minutes before a scheduled lunch break and order several (5 to 10) pizzas for a work group. SP may receive many orders of this size from the same plant (i.e., from different groups of workers). The plant business is very profitable for several reasons. First, a large number of pizzas can be delivered at the same time to the same location, saving transportation costs. Second, plant orders usually involve many different toppings (double cheese, pepperoni, mushrooms, hamburger) on each pizza. This results in $11 to $14 revenue per pizza. The delivery drivers also like delivering plant orders because the tips are usually $1 or $2 per pizza.

Despite the profitability of the plant orders, several factors make it difficult to serve the plant market. SP's store is located 5 to 8 minutes from most of the plant sites, so SP must prepare the orders within 20 to 25 minutes after it receives the telephone order. Often, inadequate oven capacity means heating all the orders at the same time is impossible. Further, the current preparation crew often can't handle peak order loads in the time available.

Generally, plant workers will wait as long as 10 minutes past the start of their lunch break before ordering from various vending trucks that arrive at the plant sites during lunch breaks. (Currently, no other pizza delivery stores can service plant locations.) But there have been a few instances when workers refused to pay for pizzas that were only five minutes late! Worse yet, if the same work group gets a couple of late orders, they are lost as future customers. Trudy Hall believes that the inconsistent profitability of the Pontiac store is partly the result of such lost customers.

In an effort to rebuild the plant delivery business, Trudy is considering various methods to assure prompt customer delivery. She thinks that the potential demand during lunch breaks is significantly above SP's present capacity. Trudy also knows that if she tries to satisfy all phone orders on some peak days, she won't be able to provide prompt service—and may lose more plant customers.

Trudy has outlined three alternatives that may win back the plant business for the Pontiac store. She has developed these alternatives to discuss with SP's owner. Each alternative is briefly described below:

Alternative 1: Determine practical capacities during peak volume periods using existing equipment and personnel. Accept orders only up to that capacity and decline orders beyond. This approach will assure prompt customer service and high product quality. It will also minimize losses resulting from customers' rejection of late deliveries. Financial analysis of this alternative—shown in Table 1—indicates that a potential daily profit of $1,230 could result if this alternative is implemented successfully.

Alternative 2: Add additional equipment (one oven and one delivery car) and hire additional staff to handle peak loads. This approach would assure timely customer delivery and high product quality—as well as provide additional capacity to handle unmet demand. Table 2 is a conservative estimate of potential daily demand for plant orders compared to current capacity and proposed increased capacity. Table 3 gives the

Table 1   Practical Capacities and Sales Potential of Current Equipment and Personnel

	11 A.M. break	8 P.M. break	2:30 A.M. break	Daily totals
Current capacity (pizzas)............................	48	48	48	144
Average selling price per unit..........................	12.50	12.50	12.50	12.50
Sales potential................................	$600	$600	$600	$1,800
Variable cost (approximately 40 percent of selling price*	240	240	240	720
Contribution margin of pizzas...........................	360	360	360	1,080
Beverage sales (2 medium-sized beverages per pizza ordered at 75¢ a piece)†	72	72	72	216
Cost of beverages (30% per beverage)	22	22	22	66
Contribution margin of beverages	50	50	50	150
Total contribution margin of pizza and beverages	$410	$410	$410	$1,230

*The variable cost estimate of 40% of sales includes variable costs of delivery to plant locations.
†Amounts shown are not physical capacities (there is almost unlimited physical capacity), but potential sales volume is constrained by number of pizzas that can be sold.

Table 2   Capacity and Demand for Plant Customer Market

	Estimated daily demand	Current daily capacity	Proposed daily capacity
Pizza units (1 pizza)	320	144	300

Table 3   Cost of Required Additional Assets

	Cost	Estimated useful life	Salvage value	Annual depreciation*	Daily depreciation†
Delivery car (equiped with pizza warmer)	$ 8,000	5 years	$1,000	$1,400	$4.00
Pizza oven	$20,000	8 years	$2,000	$2,250	$6.43

*Annual depreciation is calculated on a straight-line basis.
†Daily depreciation assumes a 350-day (plant production) year. All variable expenses related to each piece of equipment (e.g., utilities, gas, oil) are included in the variable cost of a pizza.

cost of acquiring the additional equipment and relevant information related to depreciation and fixed costs.

Using this alternative, the following additional pizza preparation and delivery personnel costs would be required:

	Hours required	Cost per hour	Total additional required hour daily cost
Delivery personnel	6	5	$30.00
Preparation personnel	8	5	$40.00
			$70.00

The addition of even more equipment and personnel to handle all unmet demand was not considered in this alternative because the current store is not large enough.

Alternative 3: Add additional equipment and personnel as described in alternative 2, but move to a new location that would reduce delivery lead times to two to five minutes. This move would probably allow SP to handle all unmet demand because the reduction in delivery time will provide for additional "oven" time. In fact, SP might have excess capacity using this approach.

A suitable store is available near about the same number of residential customers (including many of the store's current residential customer neighborhoods). The available store is slightly larger than needed. And the rent is higher. Relevant cost information on the proposed store appears below:

Additional rental expense of proposed store over current store	$ 1,600 per year
Cost of moving to new store (one-time cost)	$16,000

Trudy Hall presented each of the three alternatives to SP's owner, Ted McClintock. Ted was pleased that Trudy had "done her homework." He decided that Trudy should make the final decision on what to do (being sure that profits increase) and offered the following comments and concerns:

1. Ted agreed that the plant market was extremely sensitive to delivery timing. Product quality and pricing, although important, were of secondary importance to delivery.
2. He agreed that plant demand estimates were conservative. "In fact they may be 10 to 20 percent low."
3. Ted expressed concern that under alternative 2, and especially under alternative 3, much of the store's capacity would go unused over 80 percent of the day.
4. He was also concerned that SP's store had a bad reputation with plant customers because the prior store manager was not sensitive to timely plant delivery.

At the end of the meeting, Ted also suggested that Trudy develop a promotion plan to improve SP's reputation in the plants.

Evaluate Trudy's possible strategies for the Pontiac store. What should Trudy do? Why? Suggest possible promotion plans for your preferred strategy.

Notes

Chapter 1

1. Christopher H. Lovelock and Charles B. Weinberg, *Marketing for Public and Nonprofit Managers* (New York: John Wiley & Sons, 1984); Ruby Roy Dholakia, "A Macromarketing Perspective on Social Marketing: The Case of Family Planning in India," *Journal of Macromarketing* 4, no. 1 (1984), pp. 53–61.

2. Gregory D. Upah and Richard E. Wokutch, "Assessing Social Impacts of New Products: An Attempt to Operationalize the Macromarketing Concept," *Journal of Public Policy and Marketing* 4 (1985), pp. 166–78.

3. Malcolm P. McNair, "Marketing and the Social Challenge of Our Times," in *A New Measure of Responsibility for Marketing*, ed. Keith Cox and Ben M. Enis (Chicago: American Marketing Association, 1968).

4. An American Marketing Association committee developed a similar—but more complicated—definition of marketing: "Marketing is the process of planning and executing conception, pricing, promotion, and distribution of ideas, goods, and services to create exchanges that satisfy individual and organizational objectives." See *Marketing News*, March 1, 1985, p. 1. See also Ernest F. Cooke, C. L. Abercrombie, and J. Michael Rayburn, "Problems With the AMA's New Definition of Marketing Offer Opportunity to Develop an Even Better Definition," *Marketing Educator*, Spring 1986, p. 1ff.; O. C. Ferrell and George H. Lucas, Jr., "An Evaluation of Progress in the Development of a Definition of Marketing," *Journal of the Academy of Marketing Science*, Fall 1987, pp. 12–23.

5. George Fisk, "Editor's Working Definition of Macromarketing," *Journal of Macromarketing* 2, no. 1 (1982), pp. 3–4; Shelby D. Hunt and John J. Burnett, "The Macromarketing/Micromarketing Dichotomy: A Taxonomical Model," *Journal of Marketing*, Summer 1982, pp. 11–26; J. F. Grashof and A. Kelman, *Introduction to Macro-Marketing* (Columbus, Ohio: Grid, 1973); John L. Crompton and Charles W. Lamb, Jr., "The Importance of the Equity Concept in the Allocation of Public Services," *Journal of Macromarketing* 3, no. 1 (1983), pp. 28–39.

6. For a more complete discussion of this topic see Y. H. Furuhashi and E. J. McCarthy, *Social Issues of Marketing in the American Economy* (Columbus, Ohio: Grid, 1971), pp. 4–6.

7. Patricia E. Goeke, "State Economic Development Programs: The Orientation Is Macro But the Strategy Is Micro," *Journal of Macromarketing*, Spring 1987, pp. 8–21; Jacob Naor, "Towards A Socialist Marketing Concept—The Case of Romania," *Journal of Marketing*, January 1986, pp. 28–39; *Advertising Age*, September 16, 1985, pp. 74–79; "Free Enterprise Helps to Keep Russians Fed but Creates Problems," *The Wall Street Journal*, May 2, 1983, p. 1ff.; Coskun Samli, *Marketing and Distribution Systems in Eastern Europe* (New York: Praeger Publishers, 1978); John F. Gaski, "Current Russian Marketing Practice: A Report of the 1982 AMA Study Tour of the Soviet Union," in *1983 American Marketing Association Educators' Proceedings*, ed. P. Murphy et al. (Chicago: American Marketing Association, 1983), pp. 74–77; Jerzy Dietl, "Industrial Product-Buyer Behavior in a Centrally Planned Economy," *Journal of Business Research*, August 1986, pp. 285–95; "Economic Problems Spur Soviets to Consider Changes in Industrial Organization—Even a 'Profit' Experiment,"

The Wall Street Journal, November 7, 1984, p. 36; William Lazer, "Soviet Marketing Issues: A Content Analysis of Pravda," *Journal of Business Research*, April 1986, pp. 117–32.

8. James M. Carman and Robert G. Harris, "Public Regulation of Marketing Activity, Part III: A Typology of Regulatory Failures and Implications for Marketing and Public Policy," *Journal of Macromarketing*, Spring 1986, pp. 51–64; John Kenneth Galbraith, *Economics and the Public Purpose* (Boston: Houghton-Mifflin, 1973); Bernard J. Cunningham, S. Prakash Sethi, and Thomas Turicchi, "Public Perception of Government Regulation," *Journal of Macromarketing* 2, no. 2 (1982), pp. 43–51; Venkatakrishna V. Bellur et al., "Strategic Adaptations to Price Controls: The Case of Indian Drug Industry," *Journal of the Academy of Marketing Science*, Winter/Spring 1985, pp. 143–59.

9. Arnold Reisman, Raj Aggarwal, and Duu-Cheng Fuh, "Seeking Out Profitable Countertrade Opportunities," *Industrial Marketing Management*, February 1989, pp. 65–72; "How to Sell to Cashless Buyers," *Fortune*, November 7, 1988, pp. 147–54; "Countertrading Grows as Cash-Short Nations Seek Marketing Help," *The Wall Street Journal*, March 13, 1985, p. 1ff.; Arnold Reisman, Duu-Cheng Fuh, and Gang Li, "Achieving an Advantage with Countertrade," *Industrial Marketing Management*, February 1988, pp. 55–64; David Shipley and Bill Neale, "Industrial Barter and Countertrade," *Industrial Marketing Management*, February 1987, pp. 1–8.

10. Van R. Wood and Scott J. Vitell, "Marketing and Economic Development: Review, Synthesis and Evaluation," *Journal of Macromarketing* 6, no. 1 (1986), pp. 28–48; Robert W. Nason and Phillip D. White, "The Visions of Charles C. Slater: Social Consequences of Marketing," *Journal of Macromarketing* 1, no. 2 (1981), pp. 4–18; Jean C. Darian, "Marketing and Economic Development: A Case Study from Classical India," *Journal of Macromarketing* 5, no. 2 (1985), pp. 14–26; Franklin S. Houston and Jule B. Gassenheimer, "Marketing and Exchange," *Journal of Marketing*, October 1987, pp. 3–18; Suzanne Hosley and Chow Hou Wee, "Marketing and Economic Development: Focusing on the Less Developed Countries," *Journal of Macromarketing*, Spring 1988, pp. 43–53.

11. William McInnes, "A Conceptual Approach to Marketing," in *Theory in Marketing*, second series, ed. Reavis Cox, Wroe Alderson, and Stanley J. Shapiro (Homewood, Ill.: Richard D. Irwin, 1964), pp. 51–67.

12. Reed Moyer, *Macro Marketing: A Social Perspective* (New York: John Wiley & Sons, 1972), pp. 3–5; see also Roger A. Layton, "Measures of Structural Change in Macromarketing Systems," *Journal of Macromarketing*, Spring 1989, pp. 5–15.

13. *Forging America's Future: Strategies for National Growth and Development*, Report of the Advisory Committee on National Growth Policy Processes, reprinted in *Challenge*, January/February 1977.

Chapter 2

1. "Foot's Paradise," *Time*, August 28, 1989, pp. 54–55; "Pricey Sneakers Worn in Inner City Help Set Nation's Fashion Trend," *The*

Wall Street Journal, December 1, 1988, p. A1ff.; "Nike Catches Up with the Trendy Frontrunner," *Business Week,* October 24, 1988, p. 88; "Sneaker Maker Uses James Dean Color to Revive Canvas Classics," *Marketing News,* October 24, 1988, p. 10ff.; "Reebok Trails Nike in Fight for Teens' Hearts and Feet," *The Wall Street Journal,* September 23, 1988, p. 21; "Foot Fashion Is Off and Running," *USA Today,* July 26, 1988, pp. B1–2; *1987 Annual Report,* Nike, Inc.

2. "Inside the Mind of Jack Welch," *Fortune,* March 27, 1989, pp. 38–50; "Marketing: The New Priority," *Business Week,* November 21, 1983, pp. 96–106; Neal Gilliatt and Pamela Cuming, "The Chief Marketing Officer: A Maverick Whose Time Has Come," *Business Horizons,* January/February 1986, pp. 41–48. For an early example of how the marketing revolution affected one firm, see Robert J. Keith, "The Marketing Revolution," *Journal of Marketing,* January 1960, pp. 35–38. For an overview of some of Procter & Gamble's recent marketing efforts, see "Stalking the New Consumer," *Business Week,* August 28, 1989, pp. 54–62; "P&G's Rusty Marketing Machine," *Business Week,* October 21, 1985, pp. 111–12. See also Thomas Masiello, "Developing Market Responsiveness Throughout Your Company," *Industrial Marketing Management,* May 1988, pp. 85–94; Robert F. Lusch and Gene R. Laczniak, "The Evolving Marketing Concept, Competitive Intensity and Organizational Performance," *Journal of the Academy of Marketing Science,* Fall 1987, pp. 1–11; Robert W. Ruekert and Orville C. Walker, Jr., "Marketing's Interaction with Other Functional Units: A Conceptual Framework and Empirical Evidence," *Journal of Marketing,* January 1987, pp. 1–19; Benson P. Shapiro, "What the Hell Is 'Market Oriented?' " *Harvard Business Review,* November–December 1988, pp. 119–25; Franklin S. Houston, "The Marketing Concept: What It Is and What It Is Not," *Journal of Marketing,* April 1986, pp. 81–87.

3. "Accountants Struggle as Marketers," *The Wall Street Journal,* July 10, 1989, p. B1; "Pediatric Centers Spring Up to Provide Off-Hour Care," *The Wall Street Journal,* February 13, 1989, p. B1; "Supreme Court Overturns Ban on Direct Mail Ads by Lawyers," *Marketing News,* July 4, 1988, p. 5; Valarie A. Zeithaml, A. Parasuraman, and Leonard L. Berry, "Problems and Strategies in Services Marketing," *Journal of Marketing,* Spring 1985, pp. 33–46; Paul N. Bloom, "Effective Marketing for Professional Services," *Harvard Business Review,* September–October 1984, pp. 102–10; "Hospitals Compete for Affluent Patients by Offering Luxury Suites and Hot Tubs," *The Wall Street Journal,* February 3, 1986, p. 19; "Lawyers Learn the Hard Sell—and Companies Shudder," *Business Week,* June 10, 1985, pp. 70–71; "Banks Get Aggressive," *Advertising Age,* March 10, 1986, p. S84; "A New Marketing Blitz in the War of Plastic Cards," *Business Week,* July 23, 1984, pp. 126–28; Betsy D. Gelb, Samuel V. Smith, and Gabriel M. Gelb, "Service Marketing Lessons from the Professionals," *Business Horizons,* September/October 1988, pp. 29–34; Robert W. Hite, Norman O. Schultz, and Judith A. Weaver, "A Content Analysis of CPA Advertising in National Print Media from 1979 to 1984," *Journal of the Academy of Marketing Science,* Fall 1988, pp. 1–15.

4. "Nonprofits Learn How-To's of Marketing," *Marketing News,* August 14, 1989, pp. 1–2; "Nonprofit Venture Learns About Cash," *The Wall Street Journal,* April 14, 1989, p. B15; "Nonprofits' Bottom-Line: They Mix Lofty Goals and Gutsy Survival Strategies," *Marketing News,* February 13, 1989, pp. 1–2; "There's Big Money in the 'Nonprofits,' " *Newsweek,* January 5, 1987, p. 38ff.; Alan R. Andreasen, "Nonprofits: Check Your Attention to Customers," *Harvard Business Review,* May–June 1982, pp. 105–10; Jeffrey A. Barach, "Applying Marketing Principles to Social Causes," *Business Horizons,* July/August 1984, pp. 65–69; J. N. Green, "Strategy, Structure, and Survival: The Application of Marketing Principles in Higher Education During the 1980s," *Journal of Business* 10 (1982), pp. 24–28; C. Scott Greene and Paul Miesing, "Public Policy, Technology, and Ethics: Marketing Decisions for NASA's Space Shuttle," *Journal of Marketing,* Summer 1984, pp. 56–67; Regina E. Herzlinger and William S. Krasker, "Who Profits from Nonprofits?" *Harvard Business Review,* January–February, 1987, p. 93ff.

5. "A Crackdown on 'Charity' Sweepstakes," *The Wall Street Journal,* March 6, 1989, p. B1; Roger C. Bennett and Robert G. Cooper, "The Misuses of Marketing: An American Tragedy," *Business Horizons,* November/December 1981, pp. 51–61; Alan R. Andreasen, "Judging Marketing in the 1980s," *Journal of Macromarketing* 2, no. 1 (1982), pp. 7–13; Leslie M. Dawson, "Marketing for Human Needs in a Humane Future," *Business Horizons,* June 1980, pp. 72–82; Peter C. Riesz, "Revenge of the Marketing Concept," *Business Horizons,* June 1980, pp. 49–53; G. R. Laczniak, R. F. Lusch, and P. E. Murphy, "Social Marketing: Its Ethical Dimensions," *Journal of Marketing,* Spring 1979, pp. 29–36.

6. David W. Cravens, "Strategic Forces Affecting Marketing Strategy," *Business Horizons,* September/October 1986, pp. 77–86; Joel E. Ross and Ronnie Silverblatt, "Developing the Strategic Plan," *Industrial Marketing Management,* May 1987, pp. 103–8; Barton A. Weitz and Robin Wensley, eds., *Strategic Marketing: Planning, Implementation and Control* (Boston: Kent, 1984); Robert H. Hayes, "Strategic Planning—Forward In Reverse?" *Harvard Business Review,* November–December 1985, pp. 111–19; William A. Cohen, "War in the Marketplace," *Business Horizons,* March/April 1986, pp. 10–20.

7. *1987 Annual Report,* Compaq Computer Corporation.

8. "At Toddler University, the Chairman Is Getting A's," *Business Week,* January 16, 1989, p. 61.

9. Orville C. Walker, Jr., and Robert W. Ruekert, "Marketing's Role in the Implementation of Business Strategies: A Critical Review and Conceptual Framework," *Journal of Marketing,* July 1987, pp. 15–33; Thomas V. Bonoma, "A Model of Marketing Implementation," *1984 AMA Educators' Proceedings* (Chicago: American Marketing Association, 1984), pp. 185–89; Robert E. Spekman and Kjell Gronhaug, "Insights on Implementation: A Conceptual Framework for Better Understanding the Strategic Marketing Planning Process," in *1983 American Marketing Association Educators' Proceedings,* ed. P. Murphy et al. (Chicago: American Marketing Association, 1983), pp. 311–14.

10. *1987 Annual Report,* Gillette Company.

11. "General Motors: What Went Wrong," *Business Week,* March 16, 1987, pp. 102–10; "Special Report: Automotive Marketing," *Advertising Age,* February 29, 1988, pp. S1–26; "Restyled Fords Take on GM's Coupes," *The Wall Street Journal,* December 7, 1988, p. B1; "Battle Lines Drawn in Minivan Market," *The Wall Street Journal,* January 5, 1989, p. B1; "Despite Record Profits, Big Three Auto Firms Seek More Protection," *The Wall Street Journal,* January 24, 1989, p. 1ff.; "GM's Bumpy Ride on the Long Road Back," *Business Week,* February 13, 1989, pp. 74–78; "Motor City Madness," *Business Week,* March 6, 1989, pp. 22–23; Alfred P. Sloan, Jr., *My Years with General Motors* (New York: MacFadden Books, 1965), Introduction, Chaps. 4 and 9; Jack Honomichl, "Consumer Signals: Why U.S. Auto Makers Ignored Them," *Advertising Age,* August 4, 1980, pp. 43–48; "Ford's Fragile Recovery," *Fortune,* April 2, 1984, pp. 42–48; "The American Small Car Keeps Getting More Japanese," *Business Week,* June 24, 1985, p. 50; "A Maxirush to Chrysler's Minivans," *Time,* February, 1984, p. 50.

12. "Timex, Swatch Push Fashion," *Advertising Age,* July 18, 1988, p. 4; "Swatch Catches Up with Itself," *The New York Times, Sunday,* August 16, 1987.

Chapter 3

1. "Regional Profiles, Motel 6," *Advertising Age,* November 9, 1988, p. 24; "No Frills Motels Upgrade to Grab Business Travelers," *The Wall Street Journal,* June 9, 1988, p. 33; "Cheap Dreams: The Budget Inn Boom," *Business Week,* July 14, 1986, pp. 76–77; "Motel 6 Adds Frills, Keeps Low-End Bills," *USA Today,* March 25, 1986, pp. B1–2.

2. "Marriott Sees Green in a Graying Nation," *The Wall Street Journal,* February 11, 1988, p. 11; "Hotels Offer More Amenities for Travel," *USA Today,* September 16, 1985; *1987 Annual Report,* Marriott Corporation; "That Thingamajig in the Bath Means You Have Arrived," *The Wall Street Journal,* April 4, 1989, p. A1ff.; "Hotels Dream Up New Ways to Dazzle Guests," *USA Today,* November 3, 1986, p. B5.

3. George S. Day and Robin Wensley, "Assessing Advantage: A Framework for Diagnosing Competitive Superiority," *Journal of Marketing,* April 1988, pp. 1–20; Kevin P. Coyne, "Sustainable Competitive Advantage—What It Is, What It Isn't," *Business Horizons,* January/February 1986, pp. 54–61; William A. Cohen, "War in the Marketplace," *Business Horizons,* March/April 1986, pp. 10–20; Peter Wright, "The Strategic Options of Least-Cost, Differentiation, and Niche," *Business Horizons,* March/April 1986, pp. 21–26; Michael E. Porter, *Competitive Strategy: Techniques for Analyzing Industries and Competitors* (New York: Free Press, 1980); Michael E. Porter, *Competitive Advantage—Creating and Sustaining Superior Performance* (New York: Free Press, MacMillan, 1986).

4. "The Cola Superpowers' Outrageous New Arsenals," *Business Week,* March 20, 1989, p. 162ff.; "Coke Mates Cola with Coffee Break," *USA Today,* September 28, 1988, p. B1; *1987 Annual Report,* AT&T; *1987 Annual Report,* McDonald's Corporation; *1987 Annual Report,* Microsoft Corporation; "A Changing Sony Aims to Own the 'Software' that Its Products Need," *The Wall Street Journal,* December 30, 1988, p. A1ff.; "Holiday Inn Scrambles for New Profits," *The New York Times,* April 22, 1984.

5. "Hallmark Now Marketing by Color," *Marketing News,* June 6, 1988, p. 18.

6. F. R. Bacon, Jr., T. W. Butler, Jr., and E. J. McCarthy, *Planned Innovation Procedures* (printed by authors, 1983). See also George S. Day, A. D. Shocker, and R. K. Srivastava, "Customer-Oriented Approaches to Identifying Product-Markets," *Journal of Marketing,* Fall 1979, pp. 8–19; Rajendra K. Srivastava, Mark I. Alpert, and Allan D. Shocker, "A Customer-Oriented Approach for Determining Market Structures," *Journal of Marketing,* Spring 1984, pp. 32–45.

7. Terry Elrod and Russell S. Winer, "An Empirical Evaluation of Aggregation Approaches for Developing Market Segments," *Journal of Marketing,* Fall 1982, pp. 32–34; Frederick W. Winter, "A Cost-Benefit Approach to Market Segmentation," *Journal of Marketing,* Fall 1979, pp. 103–11.

8. "The Riches in Market Niches," *Fortune,* April 27, 1987, pp. 227–30.

9. Peter R. Dickson and James L. Ginter, "Market Segmentation, Product Differentiation, and Marketing Strategy," *Journal of Marketing,* April 1987, pp. 1–10; Russell I. Haley, "Benefit Segmentation—20 Years Later," *Journal of Consumer Marketing* 1, no. 2 (1984), pp. 5–14. See also Roger J. Calantone and Alan G. Sawyer, "The Stability of Benefit Segments," *Journal of Marketing Research,* August 1978, pp. 395–404; Valarie A. Zeithaml, "The New Demographics and Market Fragmentation," *Journal of Marketing,* Summer 1985, pp. 64–75; "The Mass Market Is Splitting Apart," *Fortune,* November 28, 1983, pp. 76–82; Lynn R. Kahle, "The Nine Nations of North America and the Value Basis of Geographic Segmentation," *Journal of Marketing,* April 1986, pp. 37–47.

10. Cornelis A. de Kluyver and David B. Whitlark, "Benefit Segmentation for Industrial Products," *Industrial Marketing Management,* November 1986, pp. 273–86; Peter Doyle and John Saunders, "Market Segmentation and Positioning in Specialized Industrial Markets," *Journal of Marketing,* Spring 1985, pp. 24–32; Richard E. Plank, "A Critical Review of Industrial Market Segmentation," *Industrial Marketing Management,* May 1985, pp. 79–92; Herbert E. Brown, Ramesh Shivashankar, and Roger W. Brucker, "Requirements Driven Market Segmentation," *Industrial Marketing Management,* May 1989, pp. 105–12; Rowland T. Moriarty and David J. Reibstein, "Benefit Segmentation in Industrial Markets," *Journal of Business Research,* December 1986, pp. 463–86.

11. Girish Punj and David W. Stewart, "Cluster Analysis in Marketing Research: Review and Suggestions for Application," *Journal of Marketing Research,* May 1983, pp. 134–48; Fernando Robles and Ravi Sarathy, "Segmenting the Computer Aircraft Market with Cluster Analysis," *Industrial Marketing Management,* February 1986, pp. 1–12; Rajendra K. Srivastava, Robert P. Leone, and Allan D. Shocker, "Market Structure Analysis: Hierarchical Clustering of Products Based on Substitution-in-Use," *Journal of Marketing,* Summer 1981, pp. 38–48.

12. David A. Aaker and J. Gary Shansby, "Positioning Your Product," *Business Horizons,* May/June, 1982, pp. 56–62; Al Ries and Jack Trout, *Positioning: The Battle for Your Mind* (New York: McGraw-Hill, 1981), p. 53; D. W. Cravens, "Marketing Strategy Positioning," *Business Horizons,* December 1975, pp. 47–54; "Playing for Position," *Inc.,* April 1985, pp. 92–97.

Chapter 4

1. *1987 Annual Report,* Rubbermaid; "Rubbermaid's Acquisitions Take It Beyond the Kitchen," *The Wall Street Journal,* February 13, 1989, p. B2; "Tupperware: Sales Rebound Underway," *Advertising Age,* March 3, 1986, p. 32; "New Hustle for an Old Product," *Newsweek,* August 26, 1985, p. 48.

2. See Peter F. Drucker, *Management: Tasks, Responsibilities, Practices, and Plans* (New York: Harper and Row, 1973).

3. This point of view is discussed at much greater length in a classic article by T. Levitt, "Marketing Myopia," *Harvard Business Review,* September–October 1975, p. 1ff.

4. "Why Inflation Is Not Inevitable," *Fortune,* September 12, 1988, pp. 117–24.

5. "Reichhold Chemicals: Now the Emphasis is on Profits Rather than Volume," *Business Week,* June 20, 1983, pp. 178–79; Carolyn Y. Woo, "Market-Share Leadership—Not Always So Good," *Harvard Business Review,* January–February 1984, pp. 50–55; Robert Jacobson and David A. Aaker, "Is Market Share All That It's Cracked Up to Be?" *Journal of Marketing,* Fall 1985, pp. 11–22.

6. "Having a Hard Time with Just-in-Time," *Fortune,* June 9, 1986, pp. 64–66.

7. "Industrial Rebound: Factories Lead U.S. Economy Once Again," *The Wall Street Journal,* January 26, 1988, p. 1ff.

8. "Technology in the Year 2000," *Fortune,* July 18, 1988, pp. 92–98; "DNAP Seeks to Revolutionize Produce," *The Wall Street Journal,* November 28, 1988, p. B3; "The Portable Executive: From Faxes to Laptops, Technology Is Changing Our Work Lives," *Business Week,* October 10, 1988, pp. 102–12; John D. Ela and Manley R. Irwin, "Technology Changes Market Boundaries," *Industrial Marketing Management,* July 1983, pp. 153–56; Geoffrey Kiel, "Technology and Marketing: The Magic Mix?" *Business Horizons,* May/June 1984, pp. 7–14; "Information Power: How Companies Are Using New Technologies to Gain a Competitive Edge," *Business Week,* October 14, 1985, pp. 108–14; Noel Capon and Rashi Glazer, "Marketing and Technology: A Strategic Coalignment," *Journal of Marketing,* July 1987, pp. 1–14.

9. "Fighting Back: The Resurgence of Social Activism," *Business Week,* May 22, 1989, pp. 34–35; "Attorneys General Flex Their Muscles: State Officials Join Forces to Press Consumer and Antitrust Concerns," *The Wall Street Journal,* July 13, 1988, p. 25; "The Second Coming of Ralph Nader," *Business Week,* March 6, 1989, p. 28; "Winnebago's Breakdown-Prone Diesels Assailed by Owners and Consumer Groups," *The Wall Street Journal,* November 3, 1988, p. B1; "Consumers Union Tests Products In Ways Manufacturers Don't," *The Wall Street Journal,* January 14, 1985, p. 19; Paul N. Bloom and Stephen A. Greyser, "The Maturing of Consumerism," *Harvard Business Review,* November–December 1981, pp. 130–39;

"The Resurrection of Ralph Nader," *Fortune,* May 22, 1989, pp. 106–16.

10. "What Led Beech-Nut Down the Road to Disgrace," *Business Week,* February 22, 1988, pp. 124–28; "Beech-Nut Ready to Fight Back," *Advertising Age,* November 14, 1988, p. 6; Louis W. Stern and Thomas L. Eovaldi, *Legal Aspects of Marketing Strategy: Antitrust and Consumer Protection Issues* (Englewood Cliffs, N.J.: Prentice-Hall, 1984); "Packaging Firm Is Found Guilty of Price Conspiracy," *The Wall Street Journal,* January 21, 1977, p. 3. See also T. McAdams and R. C. Milgus, "Growing Criminal Liability of Executives," *Harvard Business Review,* March–April 1977, pp. 36–40.

11. Joseph C. Miller and Michael D. Hutt, "Assessing Societal Effects of Product Regulations: Toward An Analytic Framework," in *1983 American Marketing Association Educators' Proceedings,* ed. P. E. Murphy et al. (Chicago: American Marketing Association, 1983), pp. 364–68; Rachel Dardis and B. F. Smith, "Cost-Benefit Analysis of Consumer Product Safety Standards," *Journal of Consumer Affairs,* Summer 1977, pp. 34–46; Paul Busch, "A Review and Critical Evaluation of the Consumer Product Safety Commission: Marketing Management Implications," *Journal of Marketing,* October 1976, pp. 41–49.

12. Ray O. Werner, "Marketing and the Supreme Court in Transition, 1982–1984," *Journal of Marketing,* Summer 1985, pp. 97–105; Ray O. Werner, "Marketing and the United States Supreme Court, 1975–1981," *Journal of Marketing,* Spring 1982, pp. 73–81; Dorothy Cohen, "Trademark Strategy," *Journal of Marketing,* January 1986, pp. 61–74; A. R. Beckenstein, H. L. Gabel, and Karlene Roberts, "An Executive's Guide to Antitrust Compliance," *Harvard Business Review,* September–October 1983, pp. 94–102; Susan L. Holak and Srinivas K. Reddy, "Effects of a Television and Radio Advertising Ban: A Study of the Cigarette Industry," *Journal of Marketing,* October 1986, pp. 219–27.

13. "The U.S. Beef Industry Just Can't Seem to Get the Hang of Marketing," *The Wall Street Journal,* January 4, 1989, pp. A1–2; "Real Food Stages a Comeback," *Time,* October 12, 1987, p. 61; "By End of Year, Poultry Will Surpass Beef in the U.S. Diet," *The Wall Street Journal,* September 17, 1987, p. 1ff.

14. "Despite Skepticism, a Once-Lowly Bran Now Aspires to the Level of Oat Cuisine," *The Wall Street Journal,* March 28, 1989, p. B1; "Oscar Mayer Repositions Failing Line to Attract Health-Conscious Consumers," *Marketing News,* August 15, 1988, p. 6; "The Age of Cholesterol Dawns for Marketers at Food, Drug Makers," *The Wall Street Journal,* June 14, 1988, p. 1ff.; "Lance Cuts Fat from Junk Foods to Sell Snacks as Healthier Fare," *The Wall Street Journal,* March 28, 1988, p. 36; "Marketers Serve Up Low-Salt Products as Consumers Shed Their Sodium Habit," *Marketing News,* March 28, 1987, pp. 1–2; "Something to Cluck About," *Time,* November 21, 1988, p. 122; "Michael Foods Corners the Rights to Making Low-Cholesterol Eggs," *The Wall Street Journal,* June 9, 1988, p. 36; "A Bounty of Good Health," *Advertising Age,* May 30, 1988, p. 47.

15. Frank R. Bacon, Jr., and Thomas W. Butler, Jr., *Planned Innovation,* rev. ed. (Ann Arbor: Institute of Science and Technology, University of Michigan, 1980).

16. Paul F. Anderson, "Marketing, Strategic Planning and the Theory of the Firm," *Journal of Marketing,* Spring 1982, pp. 15–26; George S. Day, "Analytical Approaches to Strategic Market Planning," in *Review of Marketing 1981,* ed. Ben M. Enis and Kenneth J. Roering (Chicago: American Marketing Association, 1981), pp. 89–105; Ronnie Silverblatt and Pradeep Korgaonkar, "Strategic Market Planning in a Turbulent Business Environment," *Journal of Business Research,* August 1987, pp. 339–58.

17. Richard N. Cardozo and David K. Smith, Jr., "Applying Financial Portfolio Theory to Product Portfolio Decisions: An Empirical Study," *Journal of Marketing,* Spring 1983, pp. 110–19; Yoram Wind, Vijay Mahajan, and Donald J. Swire, "An Empirical Comparison of Standardized Portfolio Models," *Journal of Marketing,* Spring 1983, pp. 89–

99; Philippe Haspeslagh, "Portfolio Planning: Uses and Limits," *Harvard Business Review,* January–February 1982, pp. 58–73; H. Kurt Christensen, Arnold C. Cooper, and Cornelius A. de Kluyver, "The Dog Business: A Re-examination," *Business Horizons,* November/December 1982, pp. 12–18; Samuel Rabino and Arnold Wright, "Applying Financial Portfolio and Multiple Criteria Approaches to Product Line Decisions," *Industrial Marketing Management,* October 1984, pp. 233–40.

Chapter 5

1. "Modified Computer System Helps Kraft Make Plans," *Marketing News,* May 23, 1986, p. 31.

2. "Symphony Strikes a Note for Research as It Prepares to Launch a New Season," *Marketing News,* August 29, 1988, p. 12.

3. "Marketers Increase Their Use of Decision Support Systems," *Marketing News,* May 22, 1989, p. 29; Thomas H. Davenport, Michael Hammer, and Tauno J. Metsisto, "How Executives Can Shape Their Company's Information Systems," *Harvard Business Review,* March–April 1989, pp. 130–34; Bernard C. Reimann, "Decision Support Systems: Strategic Management Tools for the Eighties," *Business Horizons,* September/October 1985, pp. 71–77; Martin D. Goslar and Stephen W. Brown, "Decision Support Systems in Marketing Management Settings," in *1984 American Marketing Association Educators' Proceedings,* ed. R. W. Belk et al. (Chicago: American Marketing Association, 1984), pp. 217–21; L. M. Lodish and D. J. Reibstein, "Keeping Informed," *Harvard Business Review,* January–February 1986, p. 168ff.

4. M. E. Porter and V. E. Millar, "How Information Gives You Competitive Advantage," *Harvard Business Review,* July–August 1985, pp. 149–61; Martin D. J. Buss, "Managing International Information Systems," *Harvard Business Review,* September–October 1982, pp. 153–62; Lindsay Meredith, "Developing and Using a Customer Profile Data Bank," *Industrial Marketing Management,* November 1985, pp. 255–68; Johny K. Johansson and Ikujiro Nonaka, "Market Research the Japanese Way," *Harvard Business Review,* May–June 1987, pp. 16–23; Naresh K. Malhotra, Armen Tashchian, and Essam Mahmoud, "The Integration of Microcomputers in Marketing Research and Decision Making," *Journal of the Academy of Marketing Science,* Summer 1987, pp. 69–82.

5. Dik Warren Twedt, *1983 Survey of Marketing Research* (Chicago: American Marketing Association, 1983); see also Bruce Stern and Scott Dawson, "How to Select a Market Research Firm," *American Demographics,* March 1989, p. 44; Bodo B. Schlegelmilch, K. Boyle, and S. Therivel, "Marketing Research in Medium-Sized U.K. and U.S. Firms," *Industrial Marketing Management,* August 1986, pp. 177–86.

6. For more details on doing marketing research, see Harper W. Boyd, Jr., Ralph Westfall, and Stanley F. Stasch, *Marketing Research: Text and Cases* (Homewood, Ill.: Richard D. Irwin, 1988). See also Rohit Deshpande and Gerald Zaltman, "A Comparison of Factors Affecting Researcher and Manager Perceptions of Market Research Use," *Journal of Marketing Research,* February 1984, pp. 32–38; James R. Krum, Pradeep A. Rau, and Stephen K. Keiser, "The Marketing Research Process: Role Perceptions of Researchers and Users," *Journal of Advertising Research,* December 1987–January 1988, pp. 9–22.

7. "Dr Pepper Is Bubbling Again After Its 'Be a Pepper' Setback," *The Wall Street Journal,* September 25, 1985, p. B1.

8. An excellent review of commercially available secondary data may be found in Donald R. Lehmann, *Marketing Research and Analysis,* 3rd ed. (Homewood, Ill.: Richard D. Irwin, 1988), pp. 231–72. See also Ronald L. Vaughn, "Demographic Data Banks: A New Management Resource," *Business Horizons,* November/December 1984, pp. 38–56; "Information Brokers: New Breed with Access to Secondary Research," *Marketing News, Collegiate Edition,* April 1987, p. 14.

9. Jeffrey Durgee, "Richer Findings from Qualitative Research," *Journal of Advertising Research,* August–September 1986, pp. 36–44; Kathleen M. Wallace, "The Use and Value of Qualitative Research Studies," *Industrial Marketing Management,* August 1984, pp. 181–86. For more on focus groups see "Researcher: Focus Groups Are the Best Way to Spot Trends," *Marketing News,* March 28, 1988, p. 16; William Wells, "Group Interviewing," In *Handbook of Marketing Research,* ed. R. Ferber (New York: McGraw-Hill, 1975); Bobby J. Calder, "Focus Groups and the Nature of Qualitative Marketing Research," *Journal of Marketing Research,* August 1977, pp. 353–64; Joe L. Welch, "Researching Marketing Problems and Opportunities with Focus Groups," *Industrial Marketing Management,* November 1985, pp. 245–54.

10. Frederick Wiseman and Maryann Billington, "Comment on a Standard Definition of Response Rates, *Journal of Marketing Research,* August 1984, pp. 336–38; Jolene M. Struebbe, Jerome B. Kernan, and Thomas J. Grogan, "The Refusal Problem in Telephone Surveys," *Journal of Advertising Research,* June–July 1986, pp. 29–38.

11. Tyzoon T. Tyebjee, "Telephone Survey Methods: The State of the Art," *Journal of Marketing,* Summer 1979, pp. 68–77; Nicolaos E. Synodinos and Jerry M. Brennan, "Computer Interactive Interviewing in Survey Research," *Psychology and Marketing,* Summer 1988, pp. 117–38; A. Dianne Schmidley, "How to Overcome Bias in a Telephone Survey," *American Demographics,* November 1986, pp. 50–51.

12. "VideOcart Is Set to Roll into Supermarket Aisles," *Marketing News,* November 7, 1988, p. 32; "Coming to a Shopping Cart near You: TV Commercials," *Business Week,* May 30, 1988, pp. 61–62; "VideOcart Shopping Cart with Computer Screen Creates New Ad Medium that Also Gathers Data," *Marketing News,* May 9, 1988, pp. 1–2; "IRI Rolls into Future with Video Carts," *Advertising Age,* May 2, 1988, p. 6.

13. For more detail on observational approaches, see "Buy the Numbers," *Inc.,* March 1985; "Market Research by Scanner," *Business Week,* May 5, 1980, pp. 113–16; "License Plates Locate Customers," *The Wall Street Journal,* February 5, 1981, p. 23; "Taking Measure of the People Meter," *Marketing and Media Decisions,* August 1985, p. 62ff.; Eugene Webb et al., *Unobtrusive Measures: Nonreactive Research in the Social Sciences* (Chicago: Rand McNally, 1966); "Single-Source Ad Research Heralds Detailed Look at Household Habits," *The Wall Street Journal,* February 16, 1988, p. 39; "High-Tech Shocks in Ad Research," *Fortune,* July 7, 1986, pp. 58–62; "Collision Course: Stakes High in People-Meter War," *Advertising Age,* July 27, 1987, p. 1ff.

14. Alan G. Sawyer, Parker M. Worthing, and Paul E. Fendak, "The Role of Laboratory Experiments to Test Marketing Strategies," *Journal of Marketing,* Summer 1979, pp. 60–67; "Bar Wars: Hershey Bites Mars," *Fortune,* July 8, 1985, pp. 52–57.

15. A number of surveys have been done that reveal which marketing research areas and techniques are most common. See, for example, Barnett A. Greenberg, Jac L. Goldstucker, and Danny N. Bellenger, "What Techniques Are Used by Marketing Researchers in Business," *Journal of Marketing,* April 1977, pp. 62–68.

16. See John G. Keane, "Questionable Statistics," *American Demographics,* June 1985, pp. 18–21. Detailed treatment of confidence intervals is beyond the scope of this text, but it is covered in most marketing research texts, such as Donald R. Lehmann, *Marketing Research and Analysis,* 3rd ed. (Homewood, Ill.: Richard D. Irwin, 1988).

17. "GM Seeks Revival of Buick and Olds," *The Wall Street Journal,* April 12, 1988, p. 37.

18. Alan R. Andreasen, "Cost-Conscious Marketing Research," *Harvard Business Review,* July–August, 1983, pp. 74–81; A. Parasuraman, "Research's Place in the Marketing Budget," *Business Horizons,* March/April 1983, pp. 25–29; R. J. Small and L. J. Rosenberg, "The Marketing Researcher as a Decision Maker: Myth or Reality?" *Journal*

of Marketing, January 1975, pp. 2–7; Danny N. Bellenger, "The Marketing Manager's View of Marketing Research," *Business Horizons,* June 1979, pp. 59–65.

Chapter 6

1. "U.S. Companies Go for the Gray," *Business Week,* April 3, 1989, pp. 64–67; "Banks Woo Older Adults," *Advertising Age,* March 6, 1989, p. S54; Ellen Day et al., "Reaching the Senior Citizen Market(s)," *Journal of Advertising Research,* December 1987–January 1988, pp. 23–30.

2. Based on U.S. Census data and Judith Waldrop, "2010," *American Demographics,* February 1989, pp. 18–21ff.

3. Based on U.S. Census data and Cheryl Russell, *100 Predictions for the Baby Boom: The Next 50 Years* (Ithaca, NY: American Demographics Press, 1988).

4. Based on U.S. Census data and "Pregnant Pause May Be Over," *The Wall Street Journal,* March 20, 1989, p. B1; "Birth Rate Hits a Record Low," *The Wall Street Journal,* May 5, 1987, p. 39; "Boomlet Market," *American Demographics,* March 1989, pp. 14–16.

5. Based on U.S. Census data and Jeff Ostroff, "An Aging Market: How Businesses Can Prosper," *American Demographics,* May 1989, pp. 26–33ff.; "Special Report: Marketers Slow to Catch Age Wave," *Advertising Age,* May 22, 1989, pp. S1–6; "Marketers Err by Treating Elderly as Uniform Group," *The Wall Street Journal,* October 31, 1988, p. B1; "Designs for the Elderly but Not 'Geriatric,'" *The Wall Street Journal,* March 31, 1988, p. 25; William Lazer and Eric H. Shaw, "How Older Americans Spend Their Money," *American Demographics,* September 1987, pp. 36–41; "Marketers Mine for Gold in the Old," *Fortune,* March 31, 1986, pp. 70–78.

6. "Sony Line Tunes in Kids," *Advertising Age,* September 21, 1987, p. 12.

7. For more on the changing nature of families, see "America's Households," *American Demographics,* March 1989, pp. 20–27; "The Life of a Marriage," *American Demographics,* February 1989, p. 12; Kathryn A. London and Barbara Foley Wilson, "D-I-V-O-R-C-E," *American Demographics,* October 1988, pp. 23–26; Blayne Cutler, "Bachelor Party," *American Demographics,* February 1989, pp. 22–26ff.

8. Based on U.S. Census data and "Beliefs Bound to the Land Hold Firm as Times Change," *Insight,* December 7, 1987, pp. 10–11.

9. Based on U.S. Census data and G. Scott Thomas, "Micropolitan America," *American Demographics,* May 1989, pp. 20–24; "The New Boom Towns," *The Wall Street Journal,* March 27, 1989, p. B1; "Mad about Metros," *American Demographics,* March 1989, p. 17; "The MSA Mess," *American Demographics,* January 1989, pp. 53–56; "Metropolitan Growth," *American Demographics,* October 1988, p. 62.

10. William Dunn, "Americans on the Move," *American Demographics,* October 1986, pp. 48–51; John Gottko, "Marketing Strategy Implications of the Emerging Patterns of Consumer Geographic Mobility," in *1985 American Marketing Association Educators' Proceedings,* ed. R. F. Lusch et al. (Chicago: American Marketing Association, 1985), pp. 290–95; Michael R. Hyman, "Long-Distance Geographic Mobility and Retailing Attitudes and Behaviors: An Update," *Journal of Retailing,* Summer 1987, pp. 187–208; James R. Lumpkin and James B. Hunt, "Mobility as an Influence on Retail Patronage Behavior of the Elderly: Testing Conventional Wisdom," *Journal of the Academy of Marketing Science,* Winter 1989, pp. 1–12.

11. Based on U.S. Census data and Blayne Cutler, "Up the Down Staircase," *American Demographics,* April 1989, pp. 32–36ff.; "Many Americans Fear U.S. Living Standards Have Stopped Rising," *The Wall Street Journal,* May 1, 1989, p. A1ff.; "American's Income Gap: The Closer You Look, the Worse It Gets," *Business Week,* April 17, 1989, pp. 78–79; Thomas J. Stanley and George P. Moschis, "America's Affluent," *American Demographics,* March 1984, pp. 28–33; William Dunn, "In Pursuit of the Downscale," *American Demographics,* May 1986, pp. 26–33; Richard L. Pfister, "Are Incomes Really Declining?" *Business Horizons,* January/February 1989, pp. 54–58.

12. *Consumer Expenditure Survey: Interview Survey, 1986, News Bulletin,* U.S. Department of Labor, April 14, 1988; David E. Bloom and Sanders D. Korenman, "Spending Habits of American Consumers," *American Demographics,* March 1986, pp. 22–25.

13. Patrick E. Murphy and William A. Staples, "A Modernized Family Life Cycle," *Journal of Consumer Research,* June 1979, pp. 12–22; William D. Wells and George Gubar, "Life Cycle Concept in Marketing Research," *Journal of Marketing Research,* November 1966, pp. 355–63; Janet Wagner and Sherman Hanna, "The Effectiveness of Family Life Cycle Variables in Consumer Expenditure Research," *Journal of Consumer Research,* December 1983, pp. 281–91.

14. "Teen Spenders," *American Demographics,* June 1988, p. 21; "The ABC's of Marketing to Kids," *Fortune,* May 8, 1989, pp. 114–20; Horst H. Stipp, "Children as Consumers," *American Demographics,* February 1988, pp. 27–32; "As Kids Gain Power of Purse, Marketing Takes Aim at Them," *The Wall Street Journal,* January 19, 1988, p. 1ff.

15. "Between Two Worlds," *Time,* March 13, 1989, pp. 58–68; "The Black Middle Class," *Business Week,* March 14, 1988, pp. 62–70; "Segmenting the Black Market," *Marketing Communications,* July 1985, p. 17ff.

16. Joe Schwartz and Thomas Exter, "All Our Children," *American Demographics,* May 1989, pp. 34–37; "Hispanic Supermarkets Are Blossoming," *The Wall Street Journal,* January 23, 1989, p. B1; "If You Want a Big, New Market . . . ," *Fortune,* November 21, 1988, pp. 181–88; James P. Allen and Eugene J. Turner, "Where to Find the New Immigrants," *American Demographics,* September 1988, pp. 22–27ff; "Special Report: Marketing to Hispanics," *Advertising Age,* September 26, 1988, pp. S1–26; Humberto Valencia, "Hispanic Values and Subcultural Research," *Journal of the Academy of Marketing Science,* Winter 1989, pp. 23–28.

17. Horst H. Stipp, "What Is a Working Woman," *American Demographics,* July 1988, pp. 24–27ff; "People Patterns," *The Wall Street Journal,* October 20, 1988, p. B1; "Why Women Work," *USA Today,* June 10, 1988, p. B1; "The Lasting Changes Brought by Women Workers," *Business Week,* March 15, 1982, pp. 59–67; Michael D. Reilly, "Working Wives and Convenience Consumption," *Journal of Consumer Research,* March 1982, pp. 407–18; "Wives Are Bringing Home More of the Bacon," *Business Week,* June 23, 1986, pp. 33–34; W. Keith Bryant, "Durables and Wives' Employment Yet Again," *Journal of Consumer Research,* June 1988, pp. 37–47.

Chapter 7

1. "Luxury-Car Makers Scrambling to Stand Out in Crowded Market," *The Wall Street Journal,* February 17, 1988, p. 31; "Allante Goes High-Brow," *Advertising Age,* March 2, 1987, p. 24; "Cadillac Wants to Attract Younger Buyers but Its 'Old Man' Image Gets in the Way," *The Wall Street Journal,* November 18, 1985, p. 33; "Luxury Cars: New Leaders in an Upscale Upheaval," *Fortune,* April 10, 1989, pp. 66–74.

2. K. H. Chung, *Motivational Theories and Practices* (Columbus, Ohio: Grid, 1977), pp. 40–43; A. H. Maslow, *Motivation and Personality* (New York: Harper & Row, 1970). See also M. Joseph Sirgy, "A Social Cognition Model of Consumer Problem Recognition," *Journal of the Academy of Marketing Science,* Winter 1987, pp. 53–61.

3. Frances K. McSweeney and Calvin Bierley, "Recent Developments in Classical Conditioning," *Journal of Consumer Research,* September 1984, pp. 619–31; Walter R. Nord and J. Paul Peter, "A Behavior Modification Perspective on Marketing," *Journal of Marketing,* Spring 1980, pp. 36–47; James R. Bettman, "Memory Factors in Consumer

Choice: A Review," *Journal of Marketing,* Spring 1979, pp. 37–53; Richard Weijo and Leigh Lawton, "Message Repetition, Experience and Motivation," *Psychology and Marketing,* Fall 1986, pp. 165–80.

4. For just a few references, see Alvin A. Achenbaum, "Advertising Doesn't Manipulate Consumers," *Journal of Advertising Research,* April 1972, pp. 3–14; Joseph P. Manning and Susan P. Haynie, "How to Read Your Customers' Minds," *American Demographics,* July 1989, pp. 40–42; Sharon E. Beatty and Lynn R. Kahle, "Alternate Hierarchies of the Attitude-Behavior Relationship: The Impact of Brand Commitment and Habit," *Journal of the Academy of Marketing Science,* Summer 1988, pp. 1–10; Calvin P. Duncan and Richard W. Olshavsky, "External Search: The Role of Consumer Beliefs," *Journal of Marketing Research,* February 1982, pp. 32–43; M. Joseph Sirgy, "Self-Concept in Consumer Behavior: A Critical Review," *Journal of Consumer Research,* December 1982, pp. 287–300; Joel E. Urbany, Peter R. Dickson, and William L. Wilkie, "Buyer Uncertainty and Information Search," *Journal of Consumer Research,* September 1989, pp. 208–15.

5. Harold H. Kassarjian and Mary Jane Sheffet, "Personality and Consumer Behavior: An Update," in H. Kassarjian and T. Robertson, *Perspectives in Consumer Behavior* (Glenview, Ill.: Scott, Foresman, 1981), p. 160; H. H. Kassarjian, "Personality and Consumer Behavior: A Review," *Journal of Marketing Research,* November 1971, pp. 409–18; Raymond L. Horton, *Buyer Behavior: A Decision Making Approach* (Columbus, Ohio: Charles E. Merrill, 1984).

6. "Color Nuprin's Success Yellow," *Advertising Age,* October 31, 1988, p. 28.

7. Martha Farnsworth Riche, "Psychographics For the 1990s," *American Demographics,* July 1989, pp. 24–31; W. D. Wells, "Psychographics: A Critical Review," *Journal of Marketing Research,* May 1975, pp. 196–213; Alvin C. Burns and Mary C. Harrison, "A Test of the Reliability of Psychographics," *Journal of Marketing Research,* February 1979, pp. 32–38; Jack A. Lesser and Marie Adele Hughes, "The Generalizability of Psychographic Market Segments Across Geographic Locations," *Journal of Marketing,* January 1986, pp. 18–27; Lynn R. Kahle, Sharon E. Beatty, and Pamela Homer, "Alternative Measurement Approaches to Consumer Values: The List of Values (LOV) and Values and Life Styles (VALS)," *Journal of Consumer Research,* December 1986, pp. 405–10.

8. G. M. Munsinger, J. E. Weber, and R. W. Hansen, "Joint Home Purchasing Decisions by Husbands and Wives," *Journal of Consumer Research,* March 1975, pp. 60–66; George J. Szybillo et al., "Family Member Influence in Household Decision Making," *Journal of Consumer Research,* December 1979, pp. 312–16; Ellen R. Foxman, Patriya S. Tansuhaj, and Karin M. Ekstrom, "Adolescents' Influence in Family Purchase Decisions: A Socialization Perspective," *Journal of Business Research,* March 1989, pp. 159–72; Daniel T. Seymour, "Forced Compliance in Family Decision-Making," *Psychology and Marketing,* Fall 1986, pp. 223–40; Thomas C. O'Guinn, Ronald J. Faber, and Giovann Imperia, "Subcultural Influences on Family Decision Making," *Psychology and Marketing,* Winter 1986, pp. 305–18.

9. Richard P. Coleman, "The Continuing Significance of Social Class to Marketing," *Journal of Consumer Research,* December 1983, pp. 265–80; "What Is Happening to the Middle Class?" *American Demographics,* January 1985, pp. 18–25; Donald W. Hendon, Emelda L. Williams, and Douglas E. Huffman, "Social Class System Revisited," *Journal of Business Research,* November 1988, pp. 259–70.

10. George P. Moschis, "Social Comparison and Informal Group Influence," *Journal of Marketing Research,* August 1976, pp. 237–44; James H. Donnelly, Jr., "Social Character and Acceptance of New Products," *Journal of Marketing Research,* February 1970, pp. 111–16; Jeffrey D. Ford and Elwood A. Ellis, "A Reexamination of Group Influence on Member Brand Preference," *Journal of Marketing Research,* February 1980, pp. 125–32; Dennis L. Rosen and Richard W. Olshavsky, "The Dual Role of Informational Social Influence: Implications for Marketing Management," *Journal of Business Research,* April 1987, pp. 123–44.

11. James H. Myers and Thomas S. Robertson, "Dimensions of Opinion Leadership," *Journal of Marketing Research,* February 1972, pp. 41–46; Charles W. King and John O. Summers, "Overlap of Opinion Leadership Across Consumer Product Categories," *Journal of Marketing Research,* February 1970, pp. 43–50.

12. Grant McCracken, "Culture and Consumption: A Theoretical Account of the Structure and Movement of the Cultural Meaning of Consumer Goods," *Journal of Consumer Research,* June 1986, pp. 71–84; Walter A. Henry, "Cultural Values Do Correlate with Consumer Behavior," *Journal of Marketing Research,* May 1976, pp. 121–27. See also Lynn R. Kahle, "The Nine Nations of North America and the Value Basis of Geographic Segmentation," *Journal of Marketing,* April 1986, pp. 37–47.

13. Russell W. Belk, "Situational Variables and Consumer Behavior," *Journal of Consumer Research* 2 (1975), pp. 157–64; John F. Sherry, Jr., "Gift Giving in Anthropological Perspective," *Journal of Consumer Research,* September 1983, pp. 157–68; C. Whan Park, Easwar S. Iyer, and Daniel C. Smith, "The Effects of Situational Factors on In-Store Grocery Shopping Behavior: The Role of Store Environment and Time Available for Shopping," *Journal of Consumer Research,* March 1989, pp. 422–33.

14. Adapted and updated from James H. Myers and William H. Reynolds, *Consumer Behavior and Marketing Management* (Boston: Houghton Mifflin, 1967), p. 49.

15. Wayne D. Hoyer, "An Examination of Consumer Decision Making for a Common Repeat Purchase Product," *Journal of Consumer Research,* December 1984, pp. 822–29; James R. Bettman, *An Information Processing Theory of Consumer Choice* (Reading, Mass.: Addison-Wesley Publishing, 1979); Richard W. Olshavsky and Donald H. Granbois, "Consumer Decision Making—Fact or Fiction?" *Journal of Consumer Research,* September 1979, pp. 93–100; Lawrence X. Tarpey, Sr., and J. Paul Peter, "A Comparative Analysis of Three Consumer Decision Strategies," *Journal of Consumer Research,* June 1975, pp. 29–37.

16. Raj Arora, "Consumer Involvement—What It Offers to Advertising Strategy," *International Journal of Advertising* 4, no. 2 (1985), pp. 119–30; Don R. Rahtz and David L. Moore, "Product Class Involvement and Purchase Intent," *Psychology and Marketing,* Summer 1989, pp. 113–28; Banwari Mittal, "Measuring Purchase Decision Involvement," *Psychology and Marketing,* Summer 1989, pp. 147–62; James D. Gill, Sanford Grossbart, and Russell N. Laczniak, "Influence of Involvement, Commitment, and Familiarity on Brand Beliefs and Attitudes of Viewers Exposed to Alternative Ad Claims," *Journal of Advertising* 17, no. 2 (1988), pp. 33–43; Marsha L. Richins and Peter H. Bloch, "After the New Wears Off: The Temporal Context of Product Involvement," *Journal of Consumer Research,* September 1986, pp. 280–85.

17. Adapted from E. M. Rogers, *The Diffusion of Innovations* (New York: Free Press, 1962); E. M. Rogers with F. Shoemaker, *Communication of Innovation: A Cross Cultural Approach* (New York: Free Press, 1968).

18. "3M's Aggressive New Consumer Drive," *Business Week,* July 16, 1984, pp. 114–22.

19. William Cunnings and Mark Venkatesan, "Cognitive Dissonance and Consumer Behavior: A Review of the Evidence," *Journal of Marketing Research,* August 1976, pp. 303–8.

Chapter 8

1. "Polaroid Corp. Is Selling Its Technique for Limiting Supplier Price Increases," *The Wall Street Journal,* February 13, 1985, p. 36.

2. "Toshiba Official Finds Giving Work to Firms in U.S. Can Be Tricky," *The Wall Street Journal,* March 20, 1987, p. 1ff.

3. U.S. Bureau of the Census, *County Business Patterns 1986, United States* (Washington, D.C.: U.S. Government Printing Office, 1988); *Information Please Almanac 1989* (Boston, Mass.: Houghton-Mifflin, 1988); "Looking to Lure Suppliers, USX Plays Up a Town," *The Wall Street Journal,* August 17, 1989, p. B1; "Migratory Habits of the 500," *Fortune,* April 24, 1989, pp. 400–401.

4. For more detail, see "SIC: The System Explained," *Sales and Marketing Management,* April 22, 1985, pp. 52–113; "Enhancement of SIC System Being Developed," *Marketing News Collegiate Edition,* May 1988, p. 4.

5. Edward F. Fern and James R. Brown, "The Industrial/Consumer Marketing Dichotomy: A Case of Insufficient Justification," *Journal of Marketing,* Spring 1984, pp. 68–77; Peter Banting et al., "Similarities in Industrial Procurement Across Four Countries," *Industrial Marketing Management,* May 1985, pp. 133–44; John Seminerio, "What Buyers Like From Salesmen," *Industrial Marketing Management,* May 1985, pp. 75–78.

6. Joseph A. Bellizzi and Phillip McVey, "How Valid Is the Buy-Grid Model?" *Industrial Marketing Management,* February 1983, pp. 57–62; Erin Anderson, Wujin Chu, and Barton Weitz, "Industrial Purchasing: An Empirical Exploration of the Buyclass Framework," *Journal of Marketing,* July 1987, pp. 71–86; Rowland T. Moriarty, Jr., and Robert E. Spekman, "An Empirical Investigation of the Information Sources Used During the Industrial Buying Process," *Journal of Marketing Research,* May 1984, pp. 137–47; Barbara C. Perdue, "The Size and Composition of the Buying Firm's Negotiation Team in Rebuys of Component Parts," *Journal of the Academy of Marketing Science,* Spring 1989, pp. 121–28.

7. "Shaping Up Your Suppliers," *Fortune,* April 10, 1989, pp. 116–22; Vincent G. Reuter, "What Good Are Value Analysis Programs?" *Business Horizons,* March/April 1986, pp. 73–79.

8. W. E. Patton III, Christopher P. Puto, and Ronald H. King, "Which Buying Decisions Are Made by Individuals and Not by Groups?" *Industrial Marketing Management,* May 1986, pp. 129–38; Donald W. Jackson, Jr., Janet E. Keith, and Richard K. Burdick, "Purchasing Agents' Perceptions of Industrial Buying Center Influence: A Situational Approach," *Journal of Marketing,* Fall 1984, pp. 75–83; Wesley J. Johnston and Thomas V. Bonoma, "The Buying Center: Structure and Interaction Patterns," *Journal of Marketing,* Summer 1981, pp. 143–56; Lowell E. Crow and Jay D. Lindquist, "Impact of Organizational and Buyer Characteristics on the Buying Center," *Industrial Marketing Management,* February 1985, pp. 49–58; Michael H. Morris and Stanley M. Freedman, "Coalitions in Organizational Buying," *Industrial Marketing Management,* May 1984, pp. 123–32; Donald L. McCabe, "Buying Group Structure: Constriction at the Top," *Journal of Marketing,* October 1987, pp. 89–98; Melvin R. Mattson, "How to Determine the Composition and Influence of a Buying Center," *Industrial Marketing Management,* August 1988, pp. 205–14.

9. "Detroit Raises the Ante for Parts Suppliers," *Business Week,* October 14, 1985, pp. 94–97; Madhav N. Segal, "Implications of Single vs. Multiple Buying Sources," *Industrial Marketing Management,* August 1989, pp. 163–78.

10. Peter Kraljic, "Purchasing Must Become Supply Management," *Harvard Business Review,* September–October 1983, pp. 109–17; Christopher P. Puto, Wesley E. Patton III, and Ronald H. King, "Risk Handling Strategies in Industrial Vendor Selection Decisions," *Journal of Marketing,* Winter 1985, pp. 89–98; John L. Graham, "The Problem-Solving Approach to Negotiations in Industrial Marketing," *Journal of Business Research,* December 1986, pp. 549–66.

11. Ralph W. Jackson and William M. Pride, "The Use of Approved Vendor Lists," *Industrial Marketing Management,* August 1986, pp. 165–70.

12. "Machine-Tool Makers Lose Out to Imports Due to Price, Quality," *The Wall Street Journal,* August 17, 1987, p. 1ff.

13. "You Buy My Widgets, I'll Buy Your Debt," *Business Week,* August 1, 1988, p. 85. See also Robert E. Weigand, "The Problems of Managing Reciprocity," *California Management Review,* Fall 1973, pp. 40–48.

14. U.S. Bureau of the Census, *County Business Patterns 1986, United States* (Washington, D.C.: U.S. Government Printing Office, 1988); "Can Anyone Duplicate Canon's Personal Copiers' Success?" *Marketing and Media Decisions,* Special Issue, Spring 1985, pp. 97–101.

15. *1987 Annual Report,* Super Valu.

16. Dan Hicks, "MEGA Means Superior Service and Super Selection," *Boise Cascade Quarterly,* August 1985, p. 9.

17. Janet Wagner, Richard Ettenson, and Jean Parrish, "Vendor Selection Among Retail Buyers: An Analysis by Merchandise Division," *Journal of Retailing,* Spring 1989, pp. 58–79; *1987 Annual Report,* Food Lion; *1988 Annual Report,* Wal-Mart; "Supermarkets Demand Food Firms' Payments Just to Get on the Shelf," *The Wall Street Journal,* November 1, 1988, p. A1ff. For a historical perspective on supermarket chain buying, see J. F. Grashof, *Information Management for Supermarket Chain Product Mix Decisions,* Ph.D. thesis, Michigan State University, 1968.

18. "For Drug Distributors, Information Is the Rx for Survival," *Business Week,* October 14, 1985, p. 116; Robert E. Spekman and Wesley J. Johnston, "Relationship Management: Managing the Selling and the Buying Interface," *Journal of Business Research,* December 1986, pp. 519–32.

19. "Create Open-to-Buy Plans the Easy Way," *Retail Control,* December 1984, pp. 21–31.

20. Based on U.S. Census data and "How Do You Chase a $17 Billion Market? With Everything You've Got," *Business Week,* November 23, 1987, pp. 120–22; M. Edward Goretsky, "Market Planning for Government Procurement," *Industrial Marketing Management,* November 1986, pp. 287–92; Warren H. Suss, "How to Sell to Uncle Sam," *Harvard Business Review,* November–December 1984, pp. 136–44; M. Edward Goretsky, "When to Bid for Government Contracts," *Industrial Marketing Management,* February 1987, pp. 25–34.

Chapter 9

1. "Right Package Is Vital to Wrap Up More Sales," *USA Today,* April 2, 1986, p. B3; "Volvo Flags New Road Service," *Advertising Age,* May 5, 1986, p. 34.

2. Ross Johnson and William O. Winchell, *Marketing and Quality* (Milwaukee, Wisc.: American Society for Quality Control, 1989); Robert Jacobson and David A. Aaker, "The Strategic Role of Product Quality," *Journal of Marketing,* October 1987, pp. 31–44; "Victories in the Quality Crusade," *Fortune,* October 10, 1988, pp. 80–88; John R. Hauser and Don Clausing, "The House of Quality," *Harvard Business Review,* May–June 1988, pp. 63–73; Y. K. Shetty, "Product Quality and Competitive Strategy," *Business Horizons,* May/June 1987, pp. 46–52; V. K. Shetty, "Product Quality and Competitive Strategy," *Business Horizons,* May/June 1987, pp. 46–52; Jack Reddy and Abe Berger, "Three Essentials of Product Quality," *Harvard Business Review,* July–August 1983, pp. 153–59; Henry J. Kohoutek, "Coupling Quality Assurance Programs to Marketing," *Industrial Marketing Management,* August 1988, pp. 177–88.

3. Leonard L. Berry, "Services Marketing Is Different," in Christopher H. Lovelock, *Services Marketing* (Englewood Cliffs, N.J.: Prentice-Hall, 1984), pp. 29–37; G. Lynn Shostack, "Designing Services That Deliver," *Harvard Business Review,* January–February 1984, pp. 133–39; Sak Onkvisit and John J. Shaw, "Service Marketing: Image, Branding, and Competition," *Business Horizons,* January/February 1989, pp. 13–18; Dan R. E. Thomas, "Strategy Is Different in Service Industries,"

Harvard Business Review, July–August 1978, pp. 158–65; Leonard L. Berry, A. Parasuraman, and Valarie A. Zeithaml, "The Service-Quality Puzzle," *Business Horizons,* September/October 1988, pp. 35–43; "How to Handle Customers' Gripes," *Fortune,* October 24, 1988, pp. 88–100; "America Still Reigns in Services," *Fortune,* June 5, 1989, pp. 64–68; "Stars of the Service 500," *Fortune,* June 5, 1989, pp. 54–62; James R. Stock and Paul H. Zinszer, "The Industrial Purchase Decision for Professional Services," *Journal of Business Research,* February 1987, pp. 1–16.

4. J. B. Mason and M. L. Mayer, "Empirical Observations of Consumer Behavior as Related to Goods Classification and Retail Strategy," *Journal of Retailing,* Fall 1972, pp. 17–31; Edward M. Tauber, "Why Do People Shop?" *Journal of Marketing,* October 1972, pp. 46–49; Christopher H. Lovelock, "Classifying Services to Gain Strategic Marketing Insights," *Journal of Marketing,* Summer 1983, pp. 9–20.

5. Danny N. Bellenger, Dan H. Robertson, and Elizabeth C. Hirschman, "Impulse Buying Varies by Product," *Journal of Advertising Research,* December 1978, pp. 15–18; Dennis W. Rook, "The Buying Impulse," *Journal of Consumer Research,* September 1987, pp. 189–99; Cathy J. Cobb and Wayne D. Hoyer, "Planned versus Impulse Purchase Behavior," *Journal of Retailing,* Winter 1986, pp. 384–409.

6. William S. Bishop, John L. Graham, and Michael H. Jones, "Volatility of Derived Demand in Industrial Markets and Its Management Implications," *Journal of Marketing,* Fall 1984, pp. 95–103.

7. M. Manley, "To Buy or Not to Buy," *Inc.,* November 1987, pp. 189–90; Paul F. Anderson and William Lazer, "Industrial Lease Marketing," *Journal of Marketing,* January 1978, pp. 71–79.

8. P. Matthyssens and W. Faes, "OEM Buying Process for New Components: Purchasing and Marketing Implications," *Industrial Marketing Management,* August 1985, pp. 145–57; Ralph W. Jackson and Philip D. Cooper, "Unique Aspects of Marketing Industrial Services," *Industrial Marketing Management,* May 1988, pp. 111–18.

9. Ruth H. Krieger and Jack R. Meredith, "Emergency and Routine MRO Part Buying," *Industrial Marketing Management,* November 1985, pp. 277–82; Warren A. French et al., "MRO Parts Service in the Machine Tool Industry," *Industrial Marketing Management,* November 1985, pp. 283–88.

10. "Sunkist, a Pioneer in New Product Promotions," *Advertising Age,* November 9, 1988, p. 22ff.; "Special Report: Licensing," *Advertising Age,* June 1, 1987, pp. S1–12.

11. "New Trademark Law Aids U.S. in Foreign Markets," *Marketing News,* February 13, 1989, p. 7; "Name That Brand," *Fortune,* July 4, 1988, pp. 9–10; "The Big Brands Are Back in Style," *Business Week,* January 12, 1987, p. 74; "Firms Grapple to Find New Names as Images and Industries Change," *The Wall Street Journal,* November 17, 1986, p. 35; "Putting Muscle into Trademark Protection," *Advertising Age,* June 9, 1986, p. S13; "Judge Takes a 'Functional' Look at Trademarks," *Advertising Age,* April 21, 1986, p. 52; "Putting Teeth in the Trademark Laws," *Business Week,* November 8, 1984, pp. 75–79; Dorothy Cohen, "Trademark Strategy," *Journal of Marketing,* January 1986, pp. 61–74; George Miaoulis and Nancy D'Amato, "Consumer Confusion and Trademark Infringement," *Journal of Marketing,* April 1978, pp. 48–55; Sak Onkvisit and John J. Shaw, "Service Marketing: Image, Branding, and Competition," *Business Horizons,* January–February 1989, pp. 13–18; Ronald F. Bush, Peter H. Bloch, and Scott Dawson, "Remedies for Product Counterfeiting," *Business Horizons,* January–February 1989, pp. 59–65.

12. "Chrysler's Jeep Fuels New Licensing Efforts," *Advertising Age,* September 6, 1988, p. 53; "Special Report: Licensing," *Advertising Age,* June 6, 1988, pp. S1–6; "Hot Raisins: It's Licensed Products that Bring Big Bucks," *Advertising Age,* May 16, 1988, p. 30; "Special Report: Corporate Licensing," *Advertising Age,* June 9, 1986, pp. S1–16; "The Marketing of Licensed Characters for Kids, or How the Lovable Care Bears Were Conceived," *The Wall Street Journal,* September 24, 1982, p. 44; "What's in a Name? Millions, if It's Licensed," *Business Week,* April 8, 1985, pp. 97–98.

13. "Drugs: What's in a Name Brand? Less and Less," *Business Week,* December 5, 1988, pp. 172–76; "Ten Years May Be Generic Lifetime," *Advertising Age,* March 23, 1987, p. 76; Brian F. Harris and Roger A. Strang, "Marketing Strategies in the Age of Generics," *Journal of Marketing,* Fall 1985, pp. 70–81; "No-Frills Products: 'An Idea Whose Time Has Gone,' " *Business Week,* June 17, 1985, pp. 64–65; Martha R. McEnally and Jon M. Hawes, "The Market for Generic Brand Grocery Products: A Review and Extension," *Journal of Marketing,* Winter 1984, pp. 75–83.

14. "Supermarkets Push Private-Label Lines," *The Wall Street Journal,* November 15, 1988, p. B1; "Clothing Retailers Stress Private Labels," *The Wall Street Journal,* June 9, 1988, p. 33; "A&P to Sell a Private-Label Food Line to Compete against Top-Shelf Brand," *The Wall Street Journal,* June 2, 1988, p. 28; "Fighting the Goliaths," *Advertising Age,* August 3, 1987, p. 24ff.; J. A. Bellizzi et al., "Consumer Perceptions of National, Private, and Generic Brands," *Journal of Retailing* 57 (1981), pp. 56–70; Walter J. Salmon and Karen A. Cmar, "Private Labels Are Back in Fashion," *Harvard Business Review,* May–June 1987, pp. 99–106.

15. "Special Report: Packaging," *Advertising Age,* December 12, 1988, p. S1–4; "Why the Heat-and-Eat Market Is Really Cooking," *Business Week,* June 27, 1988, pp. 90–91; "Small-Size Foods Are a Big Deal," *Advertising Age,* May 16, 1988, p. 12; "Aluminum Maker's Big Coup: The Resealable Beverage Can," *The Wall Street Journal,* October 30, 1987, p. 25; "Package Redesign Helps Soft Cookie Contender Attract National Attention," *Food Processing,* March 1986, pp. 69–70; "Containers and Packaging," chap 7; *U.S. Industrial Outlook 1980,* p. 75; "Packaging for the Elderly," *Modern Packaging,* October 1979, pp. 38–39; "Consumers Examine Packages Very Closely Since Tylenol Tragedy," *The Wall Street Journal,* November 5, 1982, p. 1; "Paper Bottles Are Coming On Strong," *Business Week,* January 16, 1984, pp. 56–57; "Wrapping Up Sales," *Nation's Business,* October 1985, pp. 41–42; James H. Barnes, Jr., "Recycling: A Problem in Reverse Logistics," *Journal of Macromarketing* 2, no. 2 (1982), pp. 31–37.

16. "Warning Labels on Alcohol: Just What Is 'Prominent?' " *The Wall Street Journal,* May 4, 1989, p. B1; "Nestle to Drop Claim on Label of Its Formula," *The Wall Street Journal,* March 13, 1989, p. B5; Dennis L. McNeill and William L. Wilkie, "Public Policy and Consumer Information: Impact of the New Energy Labels," *Journal of Consumer Research,* June 1979, pp. 1–11.

17. J. E. Russo, "The Value of Unit Price Information," *Journal of Marketing Research,* May 1977, pp. 193–201; David A. Aaker and Gary T. Ford, "Unit Pricing Ten Years Later: A Replication," *Journal of Marketing,* Winter 1983, pp. 118–22.

18. "UPC Registers Retailing Impact," *Advertising Age,* April 7, 1986, p. 3ff; "Bar Codes: Beyond the Checkout Counter," *Business Week,* April 8, 1985, p. 90; "Bar Codes Are Black-and-White Stripes and Soon They Will Be Read All Over," *The Wall Street Journal,* January 8, 1985, p. 39; "Firms Line Up to Check Out Bar Codes," *USA Today,* December 4, 1985, pp. B1–2.

19. "Guarantees at Fever Pitch: From Appliances to Antifreeze," *Advertising Age,* October 26, 1987, p. 3; "What's in a Lifetime Guarantee? Often Value, Sometimes a Catch," *The Wall Street Journal,* April 29, 1987, p. 33; Joshua Lyle Wiener, "Are Warranties Accurate Signals of Product Reliability?" *Journal of Consumer Research,* September 1985, p. 245ff.; Laurence P. Feldman, "New Legislation and the Prospects for Real Warranty Reform," *Journal of Marketing,* July 1976, pp. 41–47; F. K. Shuptrine and Ellen Moore, "Even after the Magnuson-Moss Act of 1975, Warranties Are Not Easy to Understand," *Journal of Consumer Affairs,* Winter 1980, pp. 394–404; C. L. Kendall and Frederick A. Russ, "Warranty and Complaint Policies: An Opportunity for Marketing Management," *Journal of Marketing,* April 1975, pp. 36–43; Craig A. Kelley, "An Investigation of Consumer Product Warranties as Market Signals of Product Reliability," *Journal of the Academy of Marketing Science,* Summer 1988, p. 72ff.

Chapter 10

1. "Fax Fixation," *Advertising Age,* August 15, 1988, p. 3ff.; "Facsimile Machines: They're Everywhere," *USA Today,* June 6, 1988, p. E4; "Sony Isn't Mourning the 'Death' of Betamax," *Business Week,* January 25, 1988, p. 37; "Sony to Begin Selling VCRs in VHS Format," *The Wall Street Journal,* January 12, 1988, p. 39.

2. George Day, "The Product Life Cycle: Analysis and Applications Issues," *Journal of Marketing,* Fall 1981, pp. 60–67; John E. Swan and David R. Rink, "Fitting Marketing Strategy to Varying Product Life Cycles," *Business Horizons,* January/February 1982, pp. 72–76; Igal Ayal, "International Product Life Cycle: A Reassessment and Product Policy Implications," *Journal of Marketing,* Fall 1981, pp. 91–96; George W. Potts, "Exploit Your Product's Service Life Cycle," *Harvard Business Review,* September–October, 1988, pp. 32–39; Roger C. Bennett and Robert G. Cooper, "The Product Life Cycle Trap," *Business Horizons,* September/October 1984, pp. 7–16; Sak Onkvisit and John J. Shaw, "Competition and Product Management: Can the Product Life Cycle Help?" *Business Horizons,* July/August 1986, pp. 51–62; Mary Lambkin and George S. Day, "Evolutionary Processes in Competitive Markets: Beyond the Product Life Cycle," *Journal of Marketing,* July 1989, pp. 4–20.

3. "Is the Computer Business Maturing?" *Business Week,* March 6, 1989, pp. 68–78; "RCA to Cut Prices on Eight Color TVs in Promotion Effort," *The Wall Street Journal,* December 31, 1976, p. 16; "Sales of Major Appliances, TV Sets Gain but Profits Fail to Keep Up: Gap May Widen," *The Wall Street Journal,* August 21, 1972, p. 22; "What Do You Do When Snowmobiles Go on a Steep Slide?" *The Wall Street Journal,* March 8, 1978, p. 1ff; "After Their Slow Year, Fast-Food Chains Use Ploys to Speed Up Sales," *The Wall Street Journal,* April 4, 1980, p. 1ff.; "Home Smoke Detectors Fall on Hard Times as Sales Apparently Peaked," *The Wall Street Journal,* April 3, 1980, p. 1; "As Once Bright Market for CAT Scanners Dims, Smaller Makers of the X-Ray Devices Fade Out," *The Wall Street Journal,* May 6, 1980, p. 40.

4. "Searle Fights to Keep Red-Hot Aspartame Hot for a Long Time," *The Wall Street Journal,* September 18, 1984, p. 1ff.; "Calories and Cash: Sugar and Its Substitutes Fight for an $8 Billion Market," *Newsweek,* August 26, 1985, p. 54ff.

5. "High-Speed Management for the High-Tech Age," *Fortune,* March 5, 1984, pp. 62–68; "How Xerox Speeds Up the Birth of New Products," *Business Week,* March 19, 1984, pp. 58–59; "How Managers Can Succeed Through Speed," *Fortune,* February 13, 1989, pp. 54–59.

6. "Cookie Marketers Keep Mixing It Up," *Advertising Age,* February 24, 1986, p. 12; Steven P. Schnaars, "When Entering Growth Markets, Are Pioneers Better than Poachers?" *Business Horizons,* March/April 1986, pp. 27–36.

7. "The Winning Organization," *Fortune,* September 26, 1988, pp. 50–58.

8. "Riches from Rags: Sandra Garratt Designs a Fashion Sensation but Hits Many Snags," *The Wall Street Journal,* March 20, 1989, p. A1ff.; "Can Ms. Fashion Bounce Back?" *Business Week,* January 16, 1989, pp. 64–70; "This Season, Fashion Is Anything That Sells," *Business Week,* October 31, 1988, pp. 157–59; "Multiple Successes in Sportswear Field," *Advertising Age,* October 24, 1988, pp. 44–45; "Short Ties Make Comeback After 40 Years of Neglect," *The Wall Street Journal,* August 9, 1988, p. 29; George B. Sproles, "Analyzing Fashion Life Cycles—Principles and Perspectives," *Journal of Marketing,* Fall 1981, pp. 116–24; "Fad, Fashion, or Style?" *Saturday Review,* February 5, 1977, pp. 52–53; "Playtex: Buying Its Way from Function to Fashion," *Business Week,* July 7, 1980, pp. 40–41.

9. "Nabisco Ad Acknowledges AMA Award," *Marketing News,* March 27, 1989, p. 17; "AMA to Honor Top New-Product Marketers," *Marketing News,* January 30, 1989, p. 5.

10. " 'Good Products Don't Die,' P&G Chairman Declares," *Advertising Age,* November 1, 1976, p. 8; "Industry Is Shopping Abroad for

Good Ideas to Apply to Products," *The Wall Street Journal,* April 29, 1985, p. 1ff.; "P&G Takes Lead with High-Tech Detergent," *Advertising Age,* April 14, 1986, p. 3ff.; "P&G's High Tide Sinks Wisk to No. 2," *Advertising Age,* May 26, 1986, p. 88; "P&G Unleashes Flood of New Tide Products," *Advertising Age,* June 16, 1986, p. 3ff.

11. "Ten Ways to Restore Vitality to Old, Worn-Out Products," *The Wall Street Journal,* February 18, 1982, p. 25; William Lazer, Mushtaq Luqmani, and Zahir Quraeshi, "Product Rejuvenation Strategies," *Business Horizons,* November/December, 1984, pp. 21–28; Patrick M. Dunne, "What Really Are New Products," *Journal of Business,* December, 1974, pp. 20–25; "From Making Hearts to Winning Them," *Business Week,* November 16, 1987, pp. 153–56; "Alza Finally Finds a Cure for Losses," *Fortune,* April 28, 1986, p. 80; "3M's Aggressive New Consumer Drive," *Business Week,* July 16, 1984, pp. 114–22; "Teflon Is 50 Years Old, but Du Pont Is Still Finding New Uses for Invention," *The Wall Street Journal,* April 7, 1988, p. 34.

12. "A New Spin on Videodiscs," *Newsweek,* June 5, 1989, pp. 68–69; "Videodisks Make a Comeback as Instructors and Sales Tools," *The Wall Street Journal,* February 15, 1985, p. 25.

13. "Firms Grow More Cautious About New-Product Plans," *The Wall Street Journal,* March 9, 1989, p. B1; "Formal Process Can Improve Success of New Products," *Marketing News,* September 12, 1988, p. 22.

14. C. Merle Crawford, "Marketing Research and the New-Product Failure Rate," *Journal of Marketing,* April 1977, pp. 51–61.

15. "Manufacturers Strive and Slice Time Needed to Develop Products," *The Wall Street Journal,* February 23, 1988, p. 1ff.

16. Adapted from Frank R. Bacon, Jr., and Thomas W. Butler, Jr., *Planned Innovation,* rev. ed. (Ann Arbor: Institute of Science and Technology, University of Michigan, 1980). See also John R. Rockwell and Marc C. Particelli, "New Product Strategy: How the Pros Do It," *Industrial Marketing,* May 1982, p. 49ff.; G. Urban and J. Hauser, *Design and Marketing of New Products* (Englewood Cliffs, N.J.: Prentice Hall, 1985); David S. Hopkins, "New Emphasis in Product Planning and Strategy Development," *Industrial Marketing Management Journal* 6 (1977), pp. 410–19; Shelby H. McIntyre and Meir Statman, "Managing the Risk of New Product Development," *Business Horizons,* May/June 1982, pp. 51–55; "Listening to the Voice of the Marketplace," *Business Week,* February 21, 1983, p. 90ff.; F. Axel Johne and Patricia A. Snelson, "Product Development Approaches in Established Firms," *Industrial Marketing Management,* May 1989, pp. 113–24; Gordon R. Foxall, "User Initiated Product Innovations," *Industrial Marketing Management,* May 1989, pp. 95–104; David T. Wilson and Morry Ghingold, "Linking R&D to Market Needs," *Industrial Marketing Management,* August 1987, pp. 207–14.

17. Booz, Allen & Hamilton, *Management of New Products* (1968); "More New Products Die Abourning Than in 1968," *Marketing and Media Decisions,* May 1982, p. 48. See also Albert V. Bruno and Joel K. Leidecker, "Causes of New Venture Failure: 1960s vs. 1980s," *Business Horizons,* November/December 1988, pp. 51–56; Peter L. Link, "Keys to New Product Success and Failure," *Industrial Marketing Management,* May 1987, pp. 109–18.

18. "How Ford Hit the Bull's Eye with Taurus," *Business Week,* June 30, 1986, pp. 69–70; Shelby H. McIntyre, "Obstacles to Corporate Innovation," *Business Horizons,* January/February 1982, pp. 23–28; "Cutting Costs Without Killing the Business," *Fortune,* October 13, 1986, pp. 70–78.

19. Marisa Manley, "Product Liability: You're More Exposed Than You Think," *Harvard Business Review,* September–October, 1987, pp. 28–41; Phillip E. Downs and Douglas N. Behrman, "The Products Liability Coordinator: A Partial Solution," *Journal of the Academy of Marketing Science,* Fall 1986, p. 66ff.; "Gun Dealer Is Held Liable in Accident for Not Teaching Customer Safe Use," *The Wall Street Journal,* June 6, 1989, p. B8; "Liability Waivers Hold Up in More Sports-Injury Suits," *The Wall Street Journal,* November 11, 1988, p. B1; "Lawsuits Over Accutane Start to Mount," *The Wall Street Journal,* August 3, 1988, p.

21; "Why Throw Money at Asbestos?" *Fortune,* June 6, 1988, pp. 155–70; "Perils of the Tanning Parlor," *Time,* May 23, 1988, p. 76; T. M. Dworkin and M. J. Sheffet, "Product Liability in the 80s," *Journal of Public Policy and Marketing* 4 (1985), pp. 69–79; "When Products Turn Liabilities," *Fortune,* March 3, 1986, pp. 20–24; Fred W. Morgan, "Marketing and Product Liability: A Review and Update," *Journal of Marketing,* Summer 1982, pp. 69–78; "Marketers Feel Product Liability Pressure," *Advertising Age,* May 12, 1986, p. 3ff.; Ronald J. Adams and John M. Browning, "Product Liability in Industrial Markets," *Industrial Marketing Management,* November 1986, pp. 265–72.

20. "Grocer 'Fee' Hampers New-Product Launches," *Advertising Age,* August 3, 1987, p. 1ff.; "Want Shelf Space at the Supermarket? Ante Up," *Business Week,* August 7, 1989, pp. 60–61.

21. Adapted from Frank R. Bacon, Jr., and Thomas W. Butler, Jr., *Planned Innovation,* rev. ed. (Ann Arbor: Institute of Science and Technology, University of Michigan, 1980).

22. "Oops! Marketers Blunder Their Way Through the 'Herb Decade,' " *Advertising Age,* February 13, 1989, p. 3ff.

23. Ibid.

24. "Test Marketing—The Next Generation," *Nielsen Researcher,* no. 3 (1984), pp. 21–23; "Test Marketing Enters a New Era," *Dun's Business Month,* October 1985, p. 86ff.; Steven H. Star and Glen L. Urban, "The Case of the Test Market Toss-Up," *Harvard Business Review,* September–October 1988, pp. 10–27.

25. Phillip R. McDonald and Joseph O. Eastlack, Jr., "Top Management Involvement with New Products," *Business Horizons,* December 1971, pp. 23–31; Peter F. Drucker, "A Prescription for Entrepreneurial Management," *Industry Week,* April 29, 1985, p. 33ff.; E. F. McDonough III and F. C. Spital, "Quick-Response New Product Development," *Harvard Business Review,* September–October 1984, pp. 52–61.

26. "Masters of Innovation," *Business Week,* April 10, 1989, pp. 58–67.

27. "Brand Managers: '90s Dinosaurs?" *Advertising Age,* December 19, 1988, p. 19; "The Marketing Revolution at Procter & Gamble," *Business Week,* July 25, 1988, pp. 72–76; "P&G Widens Power Base—Adds Category Managers," *Advertising Age,* October 12, 1987, p. 1ff.; "P&G Creates New Posts in Latest Step to Alter How Firm Manages Its Brands," *The Wall Street Journal,* October 12, 1987, p. 6; "P&G Makes Changes in the Way It Develops and Sells Its Products," *The Wall Street Journal,* August 11, 1987, p. 1ff.; "Brand Managers Shelved?" *Advertising Age,* July 13, 1987, p. 81; Richard T. Hise and J. Patrick Kelly, "Product Management on Trial," *Journal of Marketing,* October 1978, pp. 28–33; Robert W. Eckles and Timothy J. Novotny, "Industrial Product Managers: Authority and Responsibility," *Industrial Marketing Management,* May 1984, pp. 71–76; William Theodore Cummings, Donald W. Jackson, Jr., and Lonnie L. Ostrom, "Differences between Industrial and Consumer Product Managers," *Industrial Marketing Management,* August 1984, pp. 171–80; Thomas J. Cosse and John E. Swan, "Strategic Marketing Planning by Product Managers—Room for Improvement?" *Journal of Marketing,* Summer 1983, pp. 92–102; P. L. Dawes and P. G. Patterson, "The Performance of Industrial and Consumer Product Managers," *Industrial Marketing Management,* February 1988, pp. 73–84.

Chapter 11

1. "An IBM Tagalong Sets Independent Course with Plenty of Risks," *The Wall Street Journal,* April 21, 1989, p. A1ff.; "Compaq vs. IBM: Peace Comes to Shove," *Business Week,* March 13, 1989, p. 132; "Compaq Computer Drops Businessland as Distributor," *The Wall Street Journal,* February 22, 1989, p. B1ff.

2. For a classic discussion of the discrepancy concepts, see Wroe Alderson, "Factors Governing the Development of Marketing Channels," in *Marketing Channels for Manufactured Goods,* ed. Richard M.

Clewett (Homewood, Ill.: Richard D. Irwin, 1954), pp. 7–9; Louis W. Stern and Adel I. El-Ansary, *Marketing Channels* (Englewood Cliffs, N.J.: Prentice-Hall, 1988). See also "Distributors: No Endangered Species," *Industry Week,* January 24, 1983, pp. 47–52; "Coke in the Cooler? Fountain Device Targets Small Offices," *Advertising Age,* November 28, 1988, p. B1; "Coke Unveils Compact Dispenser, Hoping to Sell More Soft Drinks in Small Offices," *The Wall Street Journal,* November 17, 1988, p. B1; Louis W. Stern and Frederick D. Sturdivant, "Customer-Driven Distribution Systems," *Harvard Business Review,* July–August 1987, pp. 34–41.

3. "Apple Promises Big Role for Retailers and Producers of Computer Accessories," *The Wall Street Journal,* June 27, 1985, p. 8; "High Cost of Direct Sales Spurs Strong Partnership," *Marketing News,* March 27, 1989, p. 10.

4. Robert D. Buzzell, "Is Vertical Integration Profitable?" *Harvard Business Review,* January–February 1983, pp. 92–102; Louis W. Stern and Torger Reve, "Distribution Channels as Political Economies: A Framework for Comparative Analysis," *Journal of Marketing,* Summer 1980, pp. 52–64; Michael Etgar and Aharon Valency, "Determinants of the Use of Contracts in Conventional Marketing Channels," *Journal of Retailing,* Winter 1983, pp. 81–92; "Why Manufacturers Are Doubling as Distributors," *Business Week,* January 17, 1983, p. 41; "Beer and Antitrust," *Fortune,* December 9, 1985, pp. 135–36; "Car Megadealers Loosen Detroit's Tight Rein," *The Wall Street Journal,* July 1, 1985, p. 6; Wilke D. English and Donald A. Michie, "The Impact of Electronic Technology upon the Marketing Channel," *Academy of Marketing Science,* Summer 1985, pp. 57–71.

5. "Esprit's Spirited Style Is Hot Seller," *USA Today,* March 25, 1986, p. B5; "Apparel Firm Makes Profits, Takes Risks by Flouting Tradition," *The Wall Street Journal,* June 11, 1985, p. 1ff.; "Is Häagen-Dazs Trying to Freeze Out Ben & Jerry's?" *Business Week,* December 7, 1987, p. 65; "Card Rivals Deal Ads: Convenience vs. New Lines," *Advertising Age,* July 27, 1987, p. 28; "Apparel Makers Seek Nontraditional Consumers with Own Outlets," *Marketing News,* May 22, 1987, p. 1ff; "Little Publisher Has Big Ideas on Where to Sell His Books," *The Wall Street Journal,* March 19, 1987, p. 1ff.; "Reebok: Keeping a Name Hot Requires More Than Aerobics," *The Wall Street Journal,* August 21, 1986, p. 21.

6. "This Isn't the Legend Acura Dealers Had in Mind," *Business Week,* November 28, 1988, pp. 106–10; "Car Dealers Mull Going Public at Cost of Independence," *The Wall Street Journal,* May 23, 1988, p. 6; "Retailers Take Tentative Steps as Auto Brokers," *The Wall Street Journal,* December 4, 1987, p. 41; "The New Super-Dealers," *Business Week,* June 2, 1986, pp. 60–66.

7. "Antitrust Issues and Marketing Channel Strategy" and "Case 1— Continental T.V., Inc., et al. v. GTE Sylvania, Inc.," in Louis W. Stern and Thomas L. Eovaldi, *Legal Aspects of Marketing Strategy* (Englewood Cliffs, N.J.: Prentice-Hall, 1984), pp. 300–361.

8. See also James R. Burley, "Territorial Restriction and Distribution Systems: Current Legal Developments," *Journal of Marketing,* October 1975, pp. 52–56; "Justice Takes Aim at Dual Distribution," *Business Week,* July 7, 1980, pp. 24–25; Saul Sands and Robert J. Posch, Jr., "A Checklist of Questions for Firms Considering a Vertical Territorial Distribution Plan," *Journal of Marketing,* Summer 1982, pp. 38–43; Debra L. Scammon and Mary Jane Sheffet, "Legal Issues in Channels Modification Decisions: The Question of Refusals to Deal," *Journal of Public Policy and Marketing* 5 (1986), pp. 82–96.

9. See, for example, Michael Levy, John Webster, and Roger Kerin, "Formulating Push Marketing Strategies: A Method and Application," *Journal of Marketing,* Winter 1983, pp. 25–34; Alvin A. Achenbaum and F. Kent Mitchel, "Pulling Away from Push Marketing," *Harvard Business Review,* May-June 1987, pp. 38–42.

10. Gul Butaney and Lawrence H. Wortzell, "Distributor Power versus Manufacturer Power: The Customer Role," *Journal of Marketing,* January 1988, pp. 52–63; Bruce J. Walker, Janet E. Keith, and Donald W. Jackson, Jr., "The Channels Manager: Now, Soon or Never?" *Acad-*

emy of Marketing Science, Summer 1985, pp. 82–96; Patrick L. Schul, William M. Pride, and Taylor L. Little, "The Impact of Channel Leadership Behavior on Intrachannel Conflict," *Journal of Marketing,* Summer 1983, pp. 21–34; Bert Rosenbloom and Rolph Anderson, "Channel Management and Sales Management: Some Key Interfaces," *Academy of Marketing Science,* Summer 1985, pp. 97–106; Roy D. Howell et al., "Unauthorized Channels of Distribution: Gray Markets," *Industrial Marketing Management,* November, 1986, pp. 257–64; *1988 Annual Report,* Wal-Mart.

11. "Channel Coalitions Benefit All Partners," *Marketing News,* March 13, 1989, p. 24; N. Mohan Reddy and Michael P. Marvin, "Developing a Manufacturer-Distributor Information Partnership," *Industrial Marketing Management,* May 1986, pp. 157–64.

12. Shelby D. Hunt, Nina M. Ray, and Van R. Wood, "Behavioral Dimensions of Channels of Distribution: Review and Synthesis," *Academy of Marketing Science,* Summer 1985, pp. 1–24; Peter R. Dickson, "Distributor Portfolio Analysis and the Channel Dependence Matrix: New Techniques for Understanding and Managing the Channel," *Journal of Marketing,* Summer 1983, pp. 35–44; Shelby D. Hunt and John R. Nevin, "Power in a Channel of Distribution: Sources and Consequences," *Journal of Marketing Research,* May 1974, pp. 186–93; Louis P. Bucklin, "A Theory of Channel Control," *Journal of Marketing,* January 1973, pp. 39–47; James R. Brown, "A Cross-Channel Comparison of Supplier-Retailer Relations," *Journal of Retailing,* Winter 1981, pp. 3–18; John E. Robbins, Thomas W. Speh, and Morris L. Mayer, "Retailers' Perceptions of Channel Conflict Issues," *Journal of Retailing,* Winter 1982, pp. 46–67; John F. Gaski, "The Theory of Power and Conflict in Channels of Distribution," *Journal of Marketing,* Summer 1984, pp. 9–29; Allan J. Magrath and Kenneth G. Hardy, "Avoiding the Pitfalls in Managing Distribution Channels," *Business Horizons,* September/October, 1987, pp. 29–33.

Chapter 12

1. "Woolworth to Rule the Malls," *Fortune,* June 5, 1989, pp. 145–56; "Specialty Stores Spruce Up Bottom Line," *USA Today,* February 26, 1988, pp. B1–2.

2. U.S. Bureau of the Census, *County Business Patterns 1986, United States* (Washington, D.C.: U.S. Government Printing Office, 1988), p. 49; U.S. Bureau of the Census, *Current Business Reports: Monthly Retail Trade, Sales and Inventories, February, 1989* (Washington, D.C.: U.S. Government Printing Office, 1989), p. 7.

3. For additional examples, see "Zayre's Major Task Is to Re-Store Itself," *The Wall Street Journal,* March 11, 1988, p. 6; "Zayre's Strategy of Ethnic Merchandising Proves to be Successful in Inner-City Stores," *The Wall Street Journal,* September 25, 1984, p. 31; "The Art of Selling to the Very Rich," *The New York Times,* Sunday, June 15, 1986, pp. F1–3; "Selling to the Poor: Retailers that Target Low-Income Shoppers Are Rapidly Growing," *The Wall Street Journal,* June 24, 1985, p. 1ff.; "The Green in Blue-Collar Retailing," *Fortune,* May 27, 1985, pp. 74–77.

4. "Upscale Look for Limited Puts Retailer Back on Track," *The Wall Street Journal,* February 24, 1989, p. B1; "Casual Corner Repositions Itself, Adopts Upscale Image for Stores," *Marketing News,* October 24, 1988, p. 8; "Specialty Retailing, a Hot Market, Attracts New Players," *The Wall Street Journal,* April 2, 1987, p. 1.

5. U.S. Bureau of the Census, *County Business Patterns 1986, United States,* p. 49; U.S. Bureau of the Census, *Current Business Reports,* p. 7.

6. "Why Big-Name Stores Are Losing Out," *Fortune,* January 16, 1989, pp. 31–32; "Stores Try On New Markets," *Advertising Age,* December 5, 1988, p. 48S; "Stores See Loyal Customers Slip Away," *Advertising Age,* July 11, 1988, p. 12; "How Three Master Merchants Fell from Grace," *Business Week,* March 16, 1987, pp. 38–40; "Department Stores Shape Up," *Fortune,* September 1, 1986, pp. 50–52;

"How Department Stores Plan to Get the Registers Ringing Again," *Business Week,* November 18, 1985, pp. 66–67.

7. David Appel, "The Supermarket: Early Development of an Institutional Innovation," *Journal of Retailing,* Spring 1972, pp. 39–53.

8. "Special Report: Grocery Marketing," *Advertising Age,* May 8, 1989, pp. S1–22; "New Grocery Store Design Gets Shoppers In and Out Quickly," *Marketing News,* June 6, 1988, p. 24; *Industry Surveys,* January 26, 1984, p. R1–7; "The Transformation of the Nation's Supermarkets," *New York Times,* September 2, 1984, p. 1ff.; Edward W. McLaughlin and Gene A. German, "Supermarketing Success," *American Demographics,* August 1985, pp. 34–37.

9. "At Today's Supermarket, the Computer Is Doing It All," *Business Week,* August 11, 1986, pp. 64–65; "Bigger, Shrewder, and Cheaper Cub Leads Food Stores into the Future," *The Wall Street Journal,* August 26, 1985, p. 19; " 'Super Warehouses' Chomp into the Food Business," *Business Week,* April 16, 1984.

10. "Catalog Showrooms Revamp to Keep Their Identity," *Business Week,* Industrial/Technology Edition, June 10, 1985, pp. 117–20; "Discount Catalogs: A New Way to Sell," *Business Week,* April 29, 1972, pp. 72–74; Pradeep K. Korgaonkar, "Consumer Preferences for Catalog Showrooms and Discount Stores," *Journal of Retailing,* Fall 1982, pp. 76–88; "Best Products: Too Much Too Soon at the No. 1 Catalog Showroom," *Business Week,* July 23, 1984, pp. 136–38.

11. *1987 Annual Report,* K mart Corporation.

12. "Wal-Mart, Will It Take Over the World?" *Fortune,* January 30, 1989, pp. 52–61; *1988 Annual Report,* Wal-Mart.

13. "Discounters Try 'Store-in-Store,' " *Advertising Age,* March 13, 1989, p. 66; "Bookshop 'Super-Store' Reflects the Latest Word in Retailing," *The Wall Street Journal,* February 23, 1987, p. 29; "Hechinger's: Nobody Does It Better in Do-It-Yourself," *Business Week,* May 5, 1986, p. 96; "Electronics Superstores Are Devouring Their Rivals," *Business Week,* June 24, 1985, pp. 84–85.

14. "Wal-Mart Hatches a 'Super' Winner," *Discount Store News,* December 19, 1988, pp. 93–94; "New Super K marts Test Grocery Sales," *Discount Store News,* December 19, 1988, p. 94; "Retailers Fly into Hyperspace," *Fortune,* October 24, 1988, pp. 48–52; "The Return of the Amazing Colossal Store," *Business Week,* August 22, 1988, pp. 59–61; "Special Report: Grocery Marketing," *Advertising Age,* April 28, 1986, p. S1ff.

15. "Special Report: Retail Marketing," *Advertising Age,* April 24, 1989, pp. S1–18; "The Final Word in No-Frills Shopping," *Fortune,* March 13, 1989, p. 30; "Club Format's Popularity, Sales Grow," *Discount Store News,* December 19, 1988, pp. 101–2; "The Mad Rush to Join the Warehouse Club," *Fortune,* January 6, 1986, pp. 59–61; Jack G. Kaikati, "The Boom in Warehouse Clubs," *Business Horizons,* March/April, 1987, pp. 68–73.

16. "Karl Eller's Big Thirst for Convenience Stores," *Business Week,* June 13, 1988, pp. 86–88; "Convenience Stores Try Cutting Prices and Adding Products to Attract Women," *The Wall Street Journal,* July 3, 1987, p. 15; "Convenience Chains Chase Buying Trends," *USA Today,* June 11, 1986, p. B3; "Convenience Stores Battle Lagging Sales by Adding Items and Cleaning Up Image," *The Wall Street Journal,* March 28, 1980, p. 16.

17. "The World's Most Valuable Company," *Fortune,* October 10, 1988, pp. 92–104; "Pay Now, Buy Later Starts to Take Off," *The Wall Street Journal,* August 26, 1988, p. 19; " 'Upscale' Vending Machine Designed for One-Stop Shopping," *Marketing News,* June 30, 1988, pp. 1–2; "How Sweet It Is for Granola Bars," *Business Week,* August 12, 1985, pp. 61–62.

18. "The Chic Is in the Mail," *Time,* July 17, 1989, pp. 74–75; "Retailing Clips Wings of High Flying Mail-Order Firms," *The Wall Street Journal,* January 6, 1989, p. B2; "Catalog Overload Turns Off Consumers," *The Wall Street Journal,* October 28, 1988, p. B1; "Special Report: "Spiegel Writes the Primer on Catalog Sales," *Advertising Age,* August 1, 1988, p. S1ff.; "Last Chapter for Big Catalog?" *Advertising Age,* July 18, 1988, p. 26; "Special Report: Cacophony of Catalogs Fill All Niches," *Advertising Age,* October 26, 1987, p. S1ff.; "Mail Order: Continuing Its Maturation, Competitiveness," *Direct Marketing,* July 1985, pp. 64–86; "Montgomery Ward Is Planning to Shut 300 Catalog Stores," *The Wall Street Journal,* January 14, 1985, p. 6; Roy A. Festervand, Don R. Snyder, and John D. Tsalikis, "Influence of Catalog vs. Store Shopping and Prior Satisfaction on Perceived Risk," *Journal of the Academy of Marketing Science,* Winter 1986, pp. 28–36.

19. "Electronic Retailing Filling Niche Needs," *Discount Store News,* December 19, 1988, p. 111; "Home Shopping Tries a Tonic for Its Sickly Stock," *Business Week,* April 25, 1988, p. 110; "Home Shopping," *Business Week,* December 15, 1986, pp. 62–69; "Direct Marketing on the Air: Hoopla, Growth, Video Sales," *Insight,* September 15, 1986, pp. 44–46; "Shoppers Tune in National Cable Network," *Advertising Age,* March 6, 1986, p. 35; "Home Shopping Gets Push from Cable Systems," *Advertising Age,* June 9, 1986, p. 64; Joel E. Urbany and W. Wayne Talarzyk, "Videotex: Implications for Retailing," *Journal of Retailing,* Fall 1983, pp. 76–92; George P. Moschis, Jac L. Goldstucker, and Thomas J. Stanley, "At-Home Shopping: Will Consumers Let Their Computers Do the Walking?" *Business Horizons,* March/April 1985, pp. 22–29.

20. Ruth Hamel, "Food Fight," *American Demographics,* March, 1989, pp. 36–39ff.; "No Holds Barred," *Time,* August 11, 1988, pp. 46–48; "Special Report: Stores Juggle Space, Specialties," *Advertising Age,* October 12, 1987, p. S1ff.; "There Are Two Kinds of Supermarkets: The Quick and the Dead," *Business Week,* August 11, 1986, pp. 62–63.

21. "K mart's Antonini Moves Far Beyond Retail 'Junk' Image," *Advertising Age,* July 25, 1988, p. 1ff.; "K mart Dangles Lure for Affluent Shoppers," *Advertising Age,* August 24, 1987, p. 12; "K mart Celebrates 25 Years with Revitalization of Marketing Strategy and Severing Its Kresge Roots," *Marketing News,* April 24, 1987, p. 1ff.; "K mart Spruces Up the Bargain Basement," *Business Week,* September 8, 1986, pp. 45–48; "Video Chain Aims to Star as Industry Leader," *USA Today,* July 22, 1988, pp. B1–2; Rom J. Markin and Calvin P. Duncan, "The Transformation of Retailing Institutions: Beyond the Wheel of Retailing and Life Cycle Theories," *Journal of Macromarketing* 1, no. 1 (1981), pp. 58–66; R. C. Curhan, W. J. Salmon, and R. D. Buzzell, "Sales and Profitability of Health and Beauty Aids and General Merchandise in Supermarkets," *Journal of Retailing,* Spring 1983, pp. 77–99; Ronald Savitt, "The 'Wheel of Retailing' and Retail Product Management," *European Journal of Marketing* 18, no. 6/7 (1984), pp. 43–54; "Safeway: Selling Nongrocery Items to Cure the Supermarket Blahs," *Business Week,* March 7, 1977, pp. 52–58.

22. "What Ails Retailing," *Fortune,* January 30, 1989, pp. 61–64; Jack G. Kaikati, "Don't Discount Off-Price Retailers," *Harvard Business Review,* May–June 1985, pp. 85–92.

23. "Retailers Grab Power, Control Marketplace," *Marketing News,* January 16, 1989, pp. 1–2; Dale D. Achabal, John M. Heineke, and Shelby H. McIntyre, "Issues and Perspectives on Retail Productivity," *Journal of Retailing,* Fall 1984, p. 107ff.; Charles A. Ingene, "Scale Economies in American Retailing: A Cross-Industry Comparison," *Journal of Macromarketing* 4, no. 2 (1984), pp. 49–63; "Mom-and-Pop Videotape Shops Are Fading Out," *Business Week,* September 2, 1985, pp. 34–35; Vijay Mahajan, Subhash Sharma, and Roger Kerin, "Assessing Market Penetration Opportunities and Saturation Potential for Multi-Store, Multi-Market Retailers," *Journal of Retailing,* Fall 1988, pp. 315–34.

24. "How Toys 'R' Us Controls the Game Board," *Business Week,* December 19, 1988, pp. 58–60; "Germans 'R' Us," *Advertising Age,* November 9, 1987, p. 56; "Toys 'R' Us Goes Overseas—And Finds that Toys 'R' Them, Too," *Business Week,* January 26, 1987, pp. 71–72; "Toys 'R' Us Uses Tax Savings to Cut Prices," *The Wall Street Journal,* January 16, 1987, p. 6.

25. "Going for the Golden Arches," *The Wall Street Journal,* May 1, 1989, p. B1; "Corporate Giants Drawn to Franchising," *The Wall Street Journal,* December 20, 1988, p. B1; "FTC Puts a Damper on Tupperware Party," *The Wall Street Journal,* November 14, 1988, p. B1; "Franchising Across the Nation," *USA Today,* October 3, 1988, pp. B5–8; "New Owners of Franchises Belie Mom-and-Pop Image," *The Wall Street Journal,* August 28, 1988, p. 15; "Kwik Kopy College," *The Wall Street Journal,* June 10, 1988, p. R25; "Want to Buy a Franchise? Look Before You Leap," *Business Week,* May 23, 1988, pp. 186–87; "Franchising Across the Nation," *USA Today,* March 2, 1988, pp. B5–8; "The Stunning Franchise Explosion," *New York Times,* January 20, 1985; "Franchisee Cuts Risk of Going into Business," *USA Today,* February 10, 1986, p. E6; Jeffrey S. Bracker and John N. Pearson, "The Impact of Franchising on the Financial Performance of Small Firms," *Journal of the Academy of Marketing Science,* Winter 1986, pp. 10–17.

26. "Say G'Day to the Megamall," *Business Week,* March 6, 1989, p. 29; Jennifer Stoffel, "What's New in Shopping Malls," *The New York Times,* Sunday, August 7, 1988; "Regional-Mall Developers Try New Tactics as Market Shrinks," *The Wall Street Journal,* September 21, 1987, p. 21; " 'Mini-Mall' Boom Fades as Developers Face Economic and Political Pressures," *The Wall Street Journal,* June 25, 1987, p. 27; "The Wholesale Success of Factory Outlet Malls," *Business Week,* February 3, 1986, pp. 92–94; "Now That Nation Is 'Malled,' Can 'Stripping' Be Far Off?" *The Wall Street Journal,* July 31, 1985, p. 21; Glen R. Jarboe and Carl D. McDaniel, "A Profile of Browsers in Regional Shopping Malls," *Journal of the Academy of Marketing Science,* Spring 1987, pp. 46–53.

27. "IBM, Sears—Their Gamble May Set Pace for Videotex," *USA Today,* September 20, 1988, p. B1; "Electronic Retailing Goes to the Supermarket," *Business Week,* March 25, 1985, pp. 78–79; "Computer Users Shop at Home over the Phone," *The Wall Street Journal,* February 20, 1985, p. 35.

28. "Lessons of '80s to Make Retailers Leaner in the '90s," *Marketing News,* May 22, 1989, p. 37; "Glitzy Video Booths Proposed to Replace Car Showrooms," *Marketing News,* February 27, 1989, p. 5; "Shopping Can Be Less Trying When It's All Done with Mirrors," *Advertising Age,* February 16, 1987, p. 47; Terry R. Hiller, "Going Shopping in the 1990s," *The Futurist,* December 1983, pp. 63–68; Leonard L. Berry and Larry G. Greshan, "Relationship Retailing: Transforming Customers into Clients," *Business Horizons,* November/December 1986, pp. 43–47; Larry J. Rosenberg and Elizabeth C. Hirschman, "Retailing without Stores," *Harvard Business Review,* July–August 1980, pp. 103–12; Patrick J. Kelly and William R. George, "Strategic Management Issues for the Retailing of Services," *Journal of Retailing,* Summer 1982, pp. 26–43; Jon M. Hawes and James R. Lumpkin, "Perceived Risk and the Selection of a Retail Patronage Mode," *Journal of the Academy of Marketing Science,* Winter 1986, pp. 37–42; Dale D. Achabal and Shelby H. McIntyre, "Guest Editorial: Information Technology Is Reshaping Retailing," *Journal of Retailing,* Winter 1987, pp. 321–25.

Chapter 13

1. "The Produce Marketer," *Savvy,* June 1988, pp. 26–28; "Quickie-Divorce Curbs Sought by Manufacturers' Distributors," *The Wall Street Journal,* July 13, 1987, p. 27; "Merger of Two Bakers Teaches Distributors a Costly Lesson" (3-parts), *The Wall Street Journal,* September 14, 1987, p. 29; October 19, 1987, p. 35; November 11, 1987, p. 33.

2. "American Hospital Supply: Snaring New Business with Freebies and Bonuses," *Business Week,* April 8, 1985, pp. 88–89; "Baxter Eases into Its Big Acquisition," *The Wall Street Journal,* July 19, 1985, p. 6.

3. Richard Greene, "Wholesaling," *Forbes,* January 2, 1984, pp. 226–28; Lyn S. Amine, S. Tamer Cavusgil, and Robert I. Weinstein, "Japanese Sogo Shosha and the U.S. Export Trading Companies," *Journal of the Academy of Marketing Science,* Fall 1986, pp. 21–32.

4. James D. Hlavacek and Tommy J. McCuistion, "Industrial Distributors—When, Who, and How?" *Harvard Business Review,* January–February 1983, pp. 96–101; Steven Flax, "Wholesalers," *Forbes,* January 4, 1982; N. Mohan Reddy and Michael P. Marvin, "Developing a Manufacturer-Distributor Information Partnership," *Industrial Marketing Management,* May 1986, pp. 157–64; Michael Levy and Michael Van Breda, "How to Determine Whether to Buy Direct or through a Wholesaler," *Retail Control,* June/July 1985, pp. 35–55; Donald M. Jackson and Michael F. d'Amico, "Products and Markets Served by Distributors and Agents," *Industrial Marketing Management,* February 1989, pp. 27–34; Thomas L. Powers, "Switching from Reps to Direct Salespeople," *Industrial Marketing Management,* August 1987, pp. 169–72.

5. "Sysco Corp.'s Bill of Fare Is Inviting," *USA Today,* August 11, 1989, p. B3; "Dean Foods Thrives among the Giants," *The Wall Street Journal,* September 17, 1987, p. 6; "Food Distribution: The Leaders Are Getting Hungry for More," *Business Week,* March 24, 1986, pp. 106–8.

6. "Special Report: Direct Marketing," *Advertising Age,* May 18, 1987, pp. S1–30; "Business-to-Business Mail Order Sales Reached $31B in '84," *Direct Marketing,* September 1985, pp. 72–82.

7. "Why Farm Cooperatives Need Extra Seed Money," *Business Week,* March 21, 1988, p. 96; "Independent Farmers Oppose Rules Letting Cartels Decide Output," *The Wall Street Journal,* June 17, 1987, p. 1ff.; "Farmers Try Processing to Reap Profit," *USA Today,* August 26, 1986, pp. B1–2; Kenneth G. Hardy and Allan J. Magrath, "Buying Groups: Clout for Small Businesses," *Harvard Business Review,* September–October, 1987, pp. 16–27.

8. "Independent TV Distributors Losing a Starring Role," *The Wall Street Journal,* April 14, 1989, p. B2.

9. "Brazil Captures a Big Share of the U.S. Shoe Market," *The Wall Street Journal,* August 27, 1985, p. 35; Jim Gibbons, "Selling Abroad with Manufacturers' Agents," *Sales & Marketing Management,* September 9, 1985, pp. 67–69; Evelyn A. Thomchick and Lisa Rosenbaum, "The Role of U.S. Export Trading Companies in International Logistics," *Journal of Business Logistics,* September 1984, pp. 85–105.

10. "Why Manufacturers Are Doubling as Distributors," *Business Week,* January 17, 1983, p. 41.

11. "Sanyo Sales Strategy Illustrates Problems of Little Distributors," *The Wall Street Journal,* September 10, 1984, p. 33; "Four Strategies Key to Success in Wholesale Distribution Industry," *Marketing News,* March 13, 1989, pp. 22–23.

12. "A Few Big Retailers Rebuff Middlemen," *The Wall Street Journal,* October 21, 1986, p. 6; J. A. Narus, N. M. Reddy, and G. L. Pinchak, "Key Problems Facing Industrial Distributors," *Industrial Marketing Management,* August 1984, pp. 139–48; J. A. Narus and J. C. Anderson, "Turn Your Industrial Distributors into Partners," *Harvard Business Review,* March–April 1986, pp. 66–71; J. J. Withey, "Realities of Channel Dynamics: A Wholesaling Example," *Academy of Marketing Science,* Summer 1985, pp. 72–81; "Napco: Seeking a National Network as a Nonfood Supermarket Supplier," *Business Week,* November 8, 1982, p. 70; James A. Narus and Tor Guimaraes, "Computer Usage in Distributor Marketing," *Industrial Marketing Management,* February 1987, pp. 43–54.

Chapter 14

1. "Making Them Rich Down Home," *Fortune,* August 15, 1988, pp. 51–55; "That Roar You Hear Is Food Lion," *Business Week,* August 24, 1987, pp. 65–66; *1987 Annual Report,* Food Lion; "TWST Names Ketner Best Chief Executive Retail/Food Chains," *The Wall Street Transcript,* April 7, 1986, pp. 81, 417.

2. Lloyd M. Rinehart, M. Bixby Cooper, and George D. Wagenheim, "Furthering the Integration of Marketing and Logistics Through Customer Service in the Channel," *Journal of the Academy of Marketing Science,* Winter 1989, pp. 63–72; Ernest B. Uhr, Ernest C. Houck, and John C. Rogers, "Physical Distribution Service," *Journal of Business Logistics* 2, no. 2 (1981), pp. 158–69; Martin Christopher, "Creating Effective Policies for Customer Service," *International Journal of Physical Distribution and Materials Management* 13, no. 2 (1983), pp. 3–24; William D. Perreault, Jr., and Frederick A. Russ, "Physical Distribution Service in Industrial Purchase Decisions," *Journal of Marketing,* April 1976, pp. 3–10; Gary L. Frazier, Robert E. Spekman, and Charles R. O'Neal, "Just-In-Time Exchange Relationships in Industrial Markets," *Journal of Marketing,* October 1988, pp. 52–67.

3. "Getting Ready: Businessmen Brace for a Trucking Strike, but There's a Limit to What They Can Do," *The Wall Street Journal,* March 29, 1979, p. 46.

4. Bernard J. LaLonde and P. H. Zinszer, *Customer Service: Meaning and Measurement* (Chicago: National Council of Distribution Management, 1976).

5. For more detail on deregulation of transportation, see J. J. Coyle, Edward J. Bardi, and Joseph L. Cavinato, *Transportation* (St. Paul, Minn.: West Publishing, 1986); "Deregulating America," *Business Week,* November 28, 1983; James C. Nelson, "Politics and Economics in Transport Regulation and Deregulation—A Century Perspective of the ICC's Role," *The Logistics and Transportation Review,* March, 1987, pp. 5–32; Karl M. Ruppentha, "U.S. Airline Deregulation—Winners and Losers," *The Logistics and Transportation Review,* March 1987, pp. 65–82.

6. For a more detailed comparison of mode characteristics, see Donald J. Bowersox, David L. Closs, and Omar K. Helferich, *Logistical Management* (New York: Macmillan, 1986); Edward R. Bruning and Peter M. Lynagh, "Carrier Evaluation in Physical Distribution Management," *Journal of Business Logistics,* September 1984, pp. 30–47; Ronald L. Coulter et al., "Freight Transportation Carrier Selection Criteria: Identification of Service Dimensions for Competitive Positioning," *Journal of Business Research,* August 1989, pp. 51–66; Prabir K. Bagchi, T. S. Raghumathan, and Edward J. Bardi, "The Implications of Just-In-Time Inventory Policies on Carrier Selection," *The Logistics and Transportation Review,* December 1987, pp. 373–84.

7. "Trains Double Up to Get Truck Business," *The Wall Street Journal,* July 28, 1989, p. B3; "Railroad Brings Far-Flung Dispatchers Together in Huge Computerized Bunker," *The Wall Street Journal,* May 9, 1989, p. B9; "New Train Control Systems Pass Big Tests," *The Wall Street Journal,* October 26, 1988, p. B6; "Why Santa Fe Wants the Southern Pacific," *Business Week,* June 2, 1980, p. 29; "N&W and Southern Railroads Propose $2 Billion Merger, Response to Big Consolidation Announced This Year," *The Wall Street Journal,* June 3, 1980, p. 3; "Back to Railroading for a New Era," *Business Week,* July 14, 1980, p. 64.

8. George L. Stern, "Surface Transportation: Middle-of-the-Road Solution," *Harvard Business Review,* December 1975, p. 82.

9. Gunna K. Sletmo and Jacques Picard, "International Distribution Policies and the Role of Air Freight," *Journal of Business Logistics* 6, no. 1 (1985), pp. 35–53; "Federal Express Rides the Small-Package Boom," *Business Week,* March 31, 1980, p. 108.

10. Judith A. Fuerst, "Sorting Out the Middlemen," *Handling and Shipping Management,* March 1985, pp. 46–50; Joseph T. Kane, "Future Shock Is Now for Freight Forwarders," *Handling and Shipping Management,* October 1983, pp. 65–68.

11. C. H. White and R. B. Felder, "Turn Your Truck Fleet into a Profit Center," *Harvard Business Review,* May–June 1983, pp. 14–17.

12. "Holly Farms' Marketing Error: The Chicken that Laid an Egg," *The Wall Street Journal,* February 9, 1988, p. 44.

13. Michael D. Hutt and Thomas W. Speh, "Realigning Industrial Marketing Channels," *Industrial Marketing Management,* July 1983, pp. 171–78; "How Just-in-Time Inventories Combat Foreign Competition," *Business Week,* May 14, 1984, pp. 176D–76G; David J. Armstrong, "Sharpening Inventory Management," *Harvard Business Review,* November–December 1985, pp. 42–59; Hal E. Mather, "The Case for Skimpy Inventories," *Harvard Business Review,* January–February 1984, pp. 40–49.

14. Wade Ferguson, "Buying an Industrial Service Warehouse Space," *Industrial Marketing Management,* February 1983, pp. 63–66; "Warehousing: Should You Go Public?" *Sales & Marketing Management,* June 14, 1976, p. 52; G. O. Pattino, "Public Warehousing: Supermarket for Distribution Services," *Handling and Shipping,* March 1977, p. 59; "Public Warehouses Perform Many Marketing Functions," *Marketing News,* February 8, 1980, p. 12.

15. Kenneth B. Ackerman and Bernard J. LaLonde, "Making Warehousing More Efficient," *Harvard Business Review,* April 1980, p. 94–102.

16. Roy D. Shapiro, "Get Leverage from Logistics," *Harvard Business Review,* May–June 1984, pp. 119–26; James E. Morehouse, "Operating in the New Logistics Era," *Harvard Business Review,* September–October 1983, pp. 18–19; Graham Sharman, "The Rediscovery of Logistics," *Harvard Business Review,* September–October 1984, pp. 71–79.

17. William D. Perreault, Jr., and Frederick R. Russ, "Physical Distribution Service: A Neglected Aspect of Marketing Management," *MSU Business Topics,* Summer 1974, pp. 37–46; Frances G. Tucker, "Creative Customer Service Management," *International Journal of Physical Distribution and Materials Management* 13, no. 3 (1983), pp. 34–50; John T. Mentzer, Roger Gomes, and Robert E. Krapfel, Jr., "Physical Distribution Service: A Fundamental Marketing Concept?" *Journal of the Academy of Marketing Science,* Winter 1989, pp. 53–62.

18. Arthur M. Geoffrion, "Better Distribution Planning with Computer Models," *Harvard Business Review,* July–August 1976, pp. 92–99; David P. Herron, "Managing Physical Distributor for Profit," *Harvard Business Review,* May–June 1979, pp. 121–32; " 'What If' Help for Management," *Business Week,* January 21, 1980, p. 73.

19. "Satellites Help Firms Keep on Trucking," *The Wall Street Journal,* April 5, 1989, p. B1; "A Scramble for Global Networks," *Business Week,* March 21, 1988, pp. 140–48; "A Smart Cookie at Pepperidge," *Fortune,* December 22, 1986, pp. 67–74.

20. "Push for Tighter U.S. Supervision of Railroads Is a Threat to Success of Reagan Deregulators," *The Wall Street Journal,* January 7, 1985, p. 50; "Living without Shackles," *Time,* December 12, 1983, p. 51; "Big Carriers Rely on Commuter Lines," *The Wall Street Journal,* September 13, 1985, p. 6; "Small Towns Would Miss Their Buses," *USA Today,* May 6, 1986, pp. B1–2.

21. R. F. Lusch, J. G. Udell, and G. R. Laczniak, "The Future of Marketing Strategy," *Business Horizons,* December 1976, pp. 65–74. See also "A Dark Tunnel Ahead for Mass Transit," *Business Week,* April 18, 1977, pp. 121–23; Walter F. Friedman, "Physical Distribution: The Concept of Shared Services," *Harvard Business Review,* March–April 1975, pp. 24–26; "Back to Railroading for a New Era," *Business Week,* July 14, 1980, pp. 64–69; "A Sickly Conrail Heads for Radical Surgery," *Business Week,* July 28, 1980, p. 78; John J. Burbridge, Jr., "Strategic Implications of Logistics Information Systems," *The Logistics and Transportation Review,* December 1988, pp. 368–83.

Chapter 15

1. "P&G Dives into New Media Strategies," *Advertising Age,* April 24, 1989, p. 3; "P&G Boosts Nontraditional Marketing," *The Wall Street Journal,* November 25, 1988, p. 13.

2. "Cabbage Patch Campaigner Tells Secret," *The Chapel Hill News-paper,* December 1, 1985, p. D1.

3. "Despite Ban, Liquor Marketers Finding New Ways to Get Products on Television," *The Wall Street Journal,* March 14, 1988, p. 31; "More Prime-Time TV Shows Plug Airlines, Hotels in Scripts," *The Wall Street Journal,* May 28, 1987, p. 33; "Small Firms Push Their Own Stock on Cable TV's New 'Infomercials,' " *The Wall Street Journal,* October 3, 1986, p. 31; "Public Relations Firms Offer 'News' to TV," *The Wall Street Journal,* April 2, 1985, p. 6.

4. "PR on the Offensive," *Advertising Age,* March 13, 1989, p. 20; E. Cameron Williams, "Product Publicity: Low Cost and High Credibility," *Industrial Marketing Management,* November 1988, pp. 355–60.

5. "More Firms Turn to Translation Experts to Avoid Costly Embarrassing Mistakes," *The Wall Street Journal,* January 13, 1977, p. 32; "How Does Slogan Translate?" *Advertising Age,* October 12, 1987, p. 84.

6. "High-Tech Hype Reaches New Heights," *The Wall Street Journal,* January 12, 1989, p. B1; "Listerine Goes on the Offensive," *Advertising Age,* May 9, 1988, p. 40; "Car Ads Turn to High-Tech Talk—But Does Anybody Understand It?" *The Wall Street Journal,* March 7, 1988, p. 23; Christy Marshall, "It Seemed Like a Good Idea at the Time," *Forbes,* December 28, 1987, pp. 98–99; "Prisoners of the Past: When It Comes to Understanding Women, Most Marketers Are Caught in a Time Warp," *The Wall Street Journal,* March 24, 1986, pp. D17–18. For interesting perspectives on this issue, see Jacob Jacoby and Wayne D. Hoyer, "The Comprehension/Miscomprehension of Print Communication: Selected Findings," *Journal of Consumer Research,* March 1989, pp. 434–43. See also Reed Sanderlin, "Information Is Not Communication," *Business Horizons,* March/April 1982, pp. 40–42.

7. Everett M. Rogers and F. Floyd Shoemaker, *Communication of Innovations: A Cross-Cultural Approach* (New York: Free Press, 1971), pp. 203–9; Kenneth Uhl, Roman Andrus, and Lance Poulsen, "How Are Laggards Different? An Empirical Inquiry," *Journal of Marketing Research,* February 1970, pp. 43–50; Thomas S. Robertson, "The Process of Innovation and the Diffusion of Innovation," *Journal of Marketing,* January 1967, pp. 14–19; Mary Dee Dickerson and James W. Gentry, "Characteristics of Adopters and Non-Adopters of Home Computers," *Journal of Consumer Research,* September 1983, pp. 225–35; Meera P. Venkatraman, "Opinion Leaders, Adopters, and Communicative Adopters: A Role Analysis," *Psychology and Marketing,* Spring 1989, pp. 51–68.

8. "Selling Software That's Hard to Describe," *The Wall Street Journal,* July 11, 1988, p. 23; Marsha L. Richins, "Negative Word-of-Mouth by Dissatisfied Consumers: A Pilot Study," *Journal of Marketing,* Winter 1983, pp. 68–78; Joseph R. Mancuso, "Why Not Create Opinion Leaders for New Product Introductions?" *Journal of Marketing,* July 1969, pp. 20–25; Leon G. Schiffman and Vincent Gaccione, "Opinion Leaders in Institutional Markets," *Journal of Marketing,* April 1974, pp. 49–53; Jacqueline Johnson Brown and Peter H. Reingen, "Social Ties and Word-of-Mouth Referral Behavior," *Journal of Consumer Research,* December, 1987, pp. 350–62; John A. Czepiel, "Word-of-Mouth Processes in the Diffusion of a Major Technological Innovation," *Journal of Marketing Research,* May 1974, pp. 172–80; Diane Lynn Kastiel, "Converse Takes a Test Run," *Advertising Age,* February 6, 1986, p. 34; John A. Martilla, "Word-of-Mouth Communication in the Industrial Adoption Process," *Journal of Marketing Research,* May 1971, pp. 173–78; Robin A. Higie, Lawrence F. Feick, and Linda L. Price, "Types and Amount of Word-of-Mouth Communications about Retailers," *Journal of Retailing,* Fall 1987, pp. 260–78.

9. "Personal Touch Costs More," *USA Today,* July 27, 1988, p. B1.

10. "Hershey's Sweet Tooth Starts Aching," *Business Week,* February 7, 1970, pp. 98–104; "Big Chocolate Maker, Beset by Profit Slide, Gets More Aggressive," *The Wall Street Journal,* February 18, 1970, p. 1ff.

11. "What's New in Joint Promotions," *New York Times,* March 10, 1985; Henry H. Beam, "Preparing for Promotion Pays Off," *Business*

Horizons, January/February 1984, pp. 6–13; P. Rajan Varadarajan, "Horizontal Cooperative Sales Promotion: A Framework for Classification and Additional Perspectives," *Journal of Marketing,* April 1986, pp. 61–73.

12. J. F. Engel, M. R. Warshaw, and T. C. Kinnear, *Promotional Strategy* (Homewood, Ill.: Richard D. Irwin, 1988).

13. "Special Report: Marketing's Rising Star, Sales Promotion 1989," *Advertising Age,* May 1, 1989, pp. S1–20; "Special Report: Premiums, Incentives," *Advertising Age,* May 2, 1988, pp. S1–12; "Burgeoning Sales Promotion Spending to Top $100 Billion," *Marketing News,* May 22, 1987, p. 9ff.; "Special Report: No End in Sight to Promotion's Upward Spiral," *Advertising Age,* March 12, 1987, p. S1ff.

14. "The Party's Over: Food Giants Pull Back on Marketing, but Boost Promotion," *Advertising Age,* February 27, 1989, p. 1ff.; "Sales-Promo Surge Has Shops Scrambling," *Advertising Age,* April 14, 1986, p. 114.

15. "Laundry Soap and Pantyhose Hitch a Ride on Racing Cars," *The Wall Street Journal,* August 13, 1987, p. 23; "Nothing Sells like Sports," *Business Week,* August 31, 1987, pp. 48–53; "Sports Score Big for Sponsors," *Advertising Age,* September 7, 1987, p. 45; "Game Plan: Firms Race to be Sponsors," *USA Today,* October 1, 1987, pp. B1–2; "Special Report: Sports Marketing," *Advertising Age,* November 9, 1987, pp. S1–12; "Sponsors Flock to Local Fetes," *Advertising Age,* January 25, 1988, p. S48.

16. "Red Letter Cut from Coupon War," *Advertising Age,* April 3, 1989, p. 38; "Prom Night: Free Samples with Tux," *Advertising Age,* March 13, 1989, p. 53; "Coupon Growth Is Attributed to FSI Rate War," *Advertising Age,* March 13, 1989, p. 70; Joe Schwartz, "Frito-Lay Makes Friends by Building Playgrounds," *American Demographics,* February 1989, p. 44; "Coupons Gain Favor with U.S. Shoppers," *Advertising Age,* November 14, 1988, p. 64; "Coupon Clippers of America," *American Demographics,* May 1988, p. 60; "Big Investments in Small Packages," *Savvy,* February 1986, p. 14.

17. "Trade Shows Can Pay Off for New Firms," *The Wall Street Journal,* January 1, 1989, pp. B1–2; Christopher H. Lovelock and John A. Quelch, "Consumer Promotions in Service Marketing," *Business Horizons,* May/June 1983, pp. 66–75; Thomas V. Bonoma, "Get More out of Your Trade Shows," *Harvard Business Review,* January-February 1983, pp. 75–83; Daniel C. Bello and Hiram C. Barksdale, Jr., "Exporting at Industrial Trade Shows," *Industrial Marketing Management,* August 1986, pp. 197–206; Kenneth G. Hardy, "Key Success Factors for Manufacturers' Sales Promotions in Package Goods," *Journal of Marketing,* July 1986, pp. 13–23; "Airlines Try New Efforts to Lure Overseas Fliers," *Advertising Age,* May 26, 1986, p. 89; "How Coors Picks Its Winners in Sports," *Business Week,* August 26, 1985, pp. 56–61; "Product Sampling Getting off the Ground," *Advertising Age,* May 5, 1986, p. S30; "Retailers Turn to Glitzy 'Special Events' to Create Excitement and Lure Shoppers," *The Wall Street Journal,* September 10, 1985, p. 33; Donald W. Jackson, Janet E. Keith, and Richard K. Burdick, "The Relative Importance of Various Promotional Elements in Different Industrial Purchase Situations," *Journal of Advertising* 16, no. 4 (1987), pp. 25–33; Rockney G. Walters, "An Empirical Investigation into Retailer Response to Manufacturer Trade Promotions," *Journal of Retailing,* Summer 1989, pp. 253–72; Ronald C. Curhan and Robert J. Kopp, "Obtaining Retailer Support for Trade Deals: Key Success Factors," *Journal of Advertising Research,* December 1987-January 1988, pp. 51–60.

18. John A. Quelch, "It's Time to Make Trade Promotion More Productive," *Harvard Business Review,* May–June 1983, pp. 130–36; "Retailing May Have Overdosed on Coupons," *Business Week,* June 13, 1983, p. 147; Sunil Gupta, "Impact of Sales Promotions on When, What, and How Much to Buy," *Journal of Marketing Research,* November 1988, pp. 342–55.

19. "Oh, the Romance of Travel: Nothing Motivates the Sales Staff Like an Exotic Trip," *Marketing News,* March 13, 1989, pp. 1–2; "Rewards for Good Work," *USA Today,* April 8, 1988, p. B1; "GM's New Compensation Plan Reflects General Trend Tying Pay to Performance," *The Wall Street Journal,* January 26, 1988, p. 39; Joanne Y. Cleaver, "Employee Incentives Rising to Top of Industry," *Advertising Age,* May 5, 1986, p. S1ff.; Curt Schleier, "Travel Business Gets Mileage out of Incentives," *Advertising Age,* May 5, 1986, p. S14.

20. "Promotion 'Carnival' Gets Serious," *Advertising Age,* May 2, 1988, p. S1ff.

Chapter 16

1. "How IBM Teaches Techies to Sell," *Fortune,* June 6, 1988, pp. 141–46; "Big Changes at Big Blue," *Business Week,* February 15, 1988, pp. 92–98; "IBM's Big Blues: A Legend Tries to Remake Itself," *Fortune,* January 19, 1987, pp. 34–54.

2. Tom Richman, "Seducing the Customer: Dale Ballard's Perfect Selling Machine," *Inc.,* April, 1988, pp. 96–104; *1987 Annual Report,* Ballard Medical Products.

3. Kenneth R. Evans and John L. Schlacter, "The Role of Sales Managers and Salespeople in a Marketing Information System," *Journal of Personal Selling and Sales Management,* November 1985, pp. 49–58; P. Ronald Stephenson, William L. Cron, and Gary L. Frazier, "Delegating Pricing Authority to the Sales Force: The Effects on Sales and Profit Performance," *Journal of Marketing,* Spring 1979, pp. 21–24; "Reach Out and Sell Something," *Fortune,* November 26, 1984, p. 127ff.; James H. Fouss and Elaine Solomon, "Salespeople as Researchers: Help or Hazard?" *Journal of Marketing,* Summer 1980, pp. 36–39; George J. Avlonitis, Kevin A. Boyle, and Athanasios G. Kouremenos, "Matching the Salesmen to the Selling Job," *Industrial Marketing Management,* February 1986, pp. 45–54.

4. "Pushing Doctors to Buy High Tech for the Office," *Business Week,* September 2, 1985, pp. 84–85.

5. "Truck-Driving 'Sales Force' Hauls in Extra Customers," *Marketing News,* May 8, 1989, p. 2; "Telemarketing Foes: Don't Reach Out to Us," *Marketing News,* July 3, 1989, p. 1ff.; "New Era of Telemarketing to Rely on High Tech and Integration of Services," *Marketing News,* July 3, 1989, p. 14; "Telemarketers Take Root in the Country," *The Wall Street Journal,* February 2, 1989, p. B1; "What Flexible Workers Can Do," *Fortune,* February 13, 1989, pp. 62–64; "Apparel Makers Play Bigger Part on Sales Floor," *The Wall Street Journal,* March 2, 1988, p. 31; David W. Cravens and Raymond W. LaForge, "Salesforce Deployment Analysis," *Industrial Marketing Management,* July 1983, pp. 179–92; Michael S. Herschel, "Effective Sales Territory Development," *Journal of Marketing,* April 1977, pp. 39–43; John Barrett, "Why Major Account Selling Works," *Industrial Marketing Management,* February 1986, pp. 63–74; Jerome A. Colletti and Gary S. Tubridy, "Effective Major Account Sales Management," *Journal of Personal Selling and Sales Management,* August 1987, pp. 1–10; Frank C. Cespedes, Stephen X. Doyle, and Robert J. Freedman, "Teamwork for Today's Selling," *Harvard Business Review,* March–April, 1989, pp. 44–59.

6. "If Only Willy Loman Had Used a Laptop," *Business Week,* October 12, 1987, p. 137.

7. "Retailers Discover an Old Tool: Sales Training," *Business Week,* December 22, 1980; Wesley J. Johnston and Martha Cooper, "Analyzing the Industrial Salesforce Selection Process," *Industrial Marketing Management,* April 1981, pp. 139–47; Richard Nelson, "Maybe It's Time to Take Another Look at Tests as a Sales Selection Tool?" *Journal of Personal Selling and Sales Management,* August 1987, pp. 33–38; Thomas W. Leigh, "Cognitive Selling Scripts and Sales Training," *Journal of Personal Selling and Sales Management,* August 1987, pp. 49–56; A. J. Dubinsky, "Recruiting College Students for the Salesforce," *Industrial Marketing Management,* February 1980, pp. 37–46; Ronald H. King and Martha B. Booze, "Sales Training and Impression Management," *Journal of Personal Selling and Sales Management,* August 1986, pp. 51–60; Robert H. Collins, "Sales Training: A Microcomputer-Based Approach," *Journal of Personal Selling and Sales Management,* May 1986, p. 71; Barry J. B. Robinson, "Role Playing as a Sales Training Tool," *Harvard Business Review,* May–

June, 1987, pp. 34–37; Earl D. Honeycutt and Thomas H. Stevenson, "Evaluating Sales Training Programs," *Industrial Marketing Management,* August 1989, pp. 215–22.

8. Stephen X. Doyle and Benson P. Shapiro, "What Counts Most in Motivating Your Sales Force," *Harvard Business Review,* May–June 1980, pp. 133–40; O. C. Walker, Jr., G. A. Churchill, and N. M. Ford, "Motivation and Performance in Industrial Selling: Present Knowledge and Needed Research," *Journal of Marketing Research,* May 1977, pp. 156–68; Thomas N. Ingram and Danny N. Bellenger, "Motivational Segments in the Sales Force," *California Management Review,* Spring 1982, pp. 81–88; "Motivating Willy Loman," *Forbes,* January 30, 1984, p. 91; Z. S. Demirdjian, "A Multidimensional Approach to Motivating Salespeople," *Industrial Marketing Management,* February 1984, pp. 25–32; William L. Cron, Alan J. Dubinsky, and Ronald E. Michaels, "The Influence of Career Stages on Components of Salesperson Motivation," *Journal of Marketing,* January 1988, pp. 78–92; Richard F. Beltrami and Kenneth R. Evans, "Salesperson Motivation to Perform and Job Satisfaction: A Sales Contest Participant Perspective," *Journal of Personal Selling and Sales Management,* August 1988, pp. 35–42.

9. "Now Salespeople Really Must Sell for Their Supper," *Business Week,* July 31, 1989, pp. 50–52; John P. Steinbrink, "How to Pay Your Sales Force," *Harvard Business Review,* July–August 1978, pp. 111–22; Leon Winer, "A Sales Compensation Plan for Maximum Motivation," *Industrial Marketing Management* 5 (1976), pp. 29–36; Pradeep K. Tyagi and Carl E. Block, "Monetary Incentives and Salesmen Performance," *Industrial Marketing Management,* October 1983, pp. 263–70; William Strahle and Rosann L. Spiro, "Linking Market Share Strategies to Salesforce Objectives, Activities, and Compensation Policies," *Journal of Personal Selling and Sales Management,* August 1986, pp. 11–18; Russell Abratt and Michael R. Smythe, "A Survey of Sales Incentive Programs," *Industrial Marketing Management,* August 1989, pp. 209–14.

10. Jan P. Muczyk and Myron Gable, "Managing Sales Performance Through a Comprehensive Performance Appraisal System," *Journal of Personal Selling and Sales Management,* May 1987, pp. 41–52; Douglas N. Behrman and William D. Perreault, Jr., "Measuring the Performance of Industrial Salespersons," *Journal of Business Research,* September 1982, pp. 350–70; "High-Tech Sales: Now You See Them, Now You Don't?" *Business Week,* November 18, 1985, pp. 106–7; J. S. Schiff, "Evaluate the Sales Force as a Business," *Industrial Marketing Management,* April 1983, pp. 131–38; Douglas N. Behrman and William D. Perreault, Jr., "A Role Stress Model of the Performance and Satisfaction of Industrial Salespersons," *Journal of Marketing,* Fall 1984, pp. 9–21; Lawrence B. Chonko, Roy D. Howell, and Danny N. Bellenger, "Congruence in Sales Force Evaluations: Relation to Sales Force Perceptions of Conflict and Ambiguity," *Journal of Personal Selling and Sales Management,* May 1986, pp. 35–48.

11. Paul Busch and David T. Wilson, "An Experimental Analysis of a Salesman's Expert and Referent Bases of Social Power in the Buyer-Seller Dyad," *Journal of Marketing Research,* February 1976, pp. 3–11; Rosann L. Spiro, William D. Perreault, Jr., and Fred D. Reynolds, "The Personal Selling Process: A Critical Review and Model," *Industrial Marketing Management,* December 1977, pp. 351–64; Rosann L. Spiro and William D. Perreault, Jr., "Influence Use by Industrial Salesmen: Influence Strategy Mixes and Situational Determinants," *Journal of Business,* July 1979, pp. 435–55.

12. John I. Coppett and Roy Dale Voorhees, "Telemarketing: Supplement to Field Sales," *Industrial Marketing Management,* August 1985, pp. 213–16; Roy Voorhees and John Coppett, "Telemarketing in Distribution Channels," *Industrial Marketing Management,* April 1983, pp. 105–12; "Better Than a Smile: Salespeople Begin to Use Computers on the Job," *The Wall Street Journal,* September 13, 1985, p. 29; Eugene M. Johnson and William J. Meiners, "Selling and Sales Management in Action: Telemarketing—Trends, Issues, and Opportunities," *Journal of Personal Selling and Sales Management,* November 1987, pp. 65–68; Judith J. Marshall and Harrie Vredenburg, "Successfully Using Telemarketing in Industrial Sales," *Industrial Marketing Management,* February 1988, pp. 15–22; Herbert E. Brown and Roger W. Brucker, "Telephone Qualifications of Sales Leads," *Industrial Marketing Management,* August 1987, pp. 185–90; J. David Lichtenthal, Saameer Sikri, and Karl Folk, "Teleprospecting: An Approach for Qualifying Accounts," *Industrial Marketing Management,* February 1989, pp. 11–18; William C. Moncrief, Charles W. Lamb, Jr., and Terry Dielman, "Developing Telemarketing Support Systems," *Journal of Personal Selling and Sales Management,* August 1986, pp. 43–50.

13. Robert H. Collins, "Microcomputer Applications in Selling and Sales Management: Portable Computers—Applications to Increase Salesforce Productivity," *Journal of Personal Selling and Sales Management,* November 1984, p. 75ff.; "Rebirth of a Salesman: Willy Loman Goes Electronic," *Business Week,* February 27, 1984, pp. 103–4; Margery Steinberg and Richard E. Plank, "Expert Systems: The Integrative Sales Management Tool of the Future," *Journal of the Academy of Marketing Science,* Summer 1987, pp. 55–62; Al Wedell and Dale Hempeck, "Sales Force Automation: Here and Now," *Journal of Personal Selling and Sales Management,* August 1987, pp. 11–16; Michael H. Morris, Alvin C. Burns, and Ramon A. Avila, "Computer Awareness and Usage by Industrial Marketers," *Industrial Marketing Management,* August 1989, pp. 223–32.

14. For more on sales presentation approaches, see C. A. Pederson, M. D. Wright, and B. A. Weitz, *Selling: Principles and Methods,* (Homewood, Ill.: Richard D. Irwin, 1986), pp. 224–356. See also Marvin A. Jolson, "Canned Adaptiveness: A New Direction for Modern Salesmanship," *Business Horizons,* January/February, 1989, pp. 7–12; Don Meisel, "Add Sales Power! Ask Questions," *Industrial Distribution,* December 1976, p. 64.

Chapter 17

1. "Campbell Ups Budget 15%," *Advertising Age,* July 24, 1989, p. 1ff.; "Campbell Soup Agrees to Ad Guidelines in 9 States to Settle Dispute over Claims," *The Wall Street Journal,* May 11, 1989, p. B8; "Campbell Rated Nation's Most Innovative Company. . .But It's Accused of False Advertising," *Marketing News,* February 27, 1989, p. 6; "FTC Attacks Campbell Ad Health Claim," *Advertising Age,* January 30, 1989, p. 2ff.; "FTC Alleges Campbell Ad Is Deceptive," *The Wall Street Journal,* January 27, 1989, p. B1.

2. "Ad Spending to Rise 6.9% in '89, Coen Says in a Warmer Forecast," *The Wall Street Journal,* June 15, 1989, p. B4.

3. "Ad Spending Outlook Brightens," *Advertising Age,* May 15, 1989, p. 24.

4. Exact data on this industry are elusive, but see U.S. Bureau of the Census, *Statistical Abstract of the United States 1988* (Washington, D.C.: U.S. Government Printing Office, 1987), p. 376.

5. "Special Issue: 100 Leading National Advertisers," *Advertising Age,* September 24, 1987, pp. S1–166; "Chemical Firms Press Campaigns to Dispel Their 'Bad Guy' Image," *The Wall Street Journal,* September 20, 1988, p. 1ff.; "Spiffing up the Corporate Image," *Fortune,* July 21, 1986, pp. 68–72; "Cars Go from Ragtops to Riches," *Advertising Age,* May 29, 1989, p. 44; "Ford Decides to Fight Back in Truck Ads," *The Wall Street Journal,* February 28, 1989, p. B1; "A Pained Bayer Cries 'Foul,'" *Business Week,* July 25, 1977, p. 142; Lewis C. Winters, "The Effect of Brand Advertising on Company Image: Implications for Corporate Advertising," *Journal of Advertising Research,* April–May, 1986, p. 54ff.

6. "New Law Adds Risk to Comparative Ads," *The Wall Street Journal,* June 1, 1989, p. B6; William L. Wilkie and Paul W. Farris, "Comparison Advertising: Problems and Potential," *Journal of Marketing,* October 1975, pp. 7–15; Linda L. Golden, "Consumer Reactions to Explicit Brand Comparisons in Advertisements," *Journal of Marketing Research,* November 1979, pp. 517–32; "Should an Ad Identify Brand X?" *Business Week,* September 24, 1979, pp. 156–61; Kenneth L. Bernhardt, Thomas C. Kinnear, and Michael B. Mazis, "A Field Study of Corrective Advertising Effectiveness," *Journal of Public Policy and Marketing* 5 (1986), pp. 146–62; Steven A. Meyerowitz, "The Developing Law of Comparative Advertising," *Business Marketing,* August 1985, pp. 81–86.

7. "Co-op Ads Attempt to Look More Like Brand-Name Commercials," *The Wall Street Journal,* July 21, 1989, p. B7; "Out-of-Home Drives Home," *Advertising Age,* October 19, 1987, p. S10ff.; "Sears Pulls in Its Advertising Umbrella," *Advertising Age,* May 5, 1986, p. 32; "Co-op: A Coup for Greater Profits," *Marketing Communications,* September 1985, pp. 66–73; "Ad Agencies Press Franchisees to Join National Campaigns," *The Wall Street Journal,* January 17, 1985, p. 29; "Block, Block, Fizz, Fizz—Alka-Seltzer and H&R Block Join Forces Against Tax Headaches," *Business Week,* March 30, 1987, p. 36.

8. "Special Report: Media Outlook," *Advertising Age,* November 28, 1988, p. S1ff.; "Special Report: Media Outlook," *Advertising Age,* November 30, 1987, pp. S1–32; Richard W. Pollay, "The Subsiding Sizzle: A Descriptive History of Print Advertising, 1900–1980," *Journal of Marketing,* Summer 1985, pp. 24–37; Murphy A. Sewall and Dan Sarel, "Characteristics of Radio Commercials and Their Recall Effectiveness," *Journal of Marketing,* January 1986, pp. 52–60; Michael Heges, "Radio's Lifestyles," *American Demographics,* February 1986, pp. 32–35; "Special Report: Outdoor Marketing," *Advertising Age,* October 9, 1989, p. 1ff.; "Signs Point to Great Reach via Outdoors," *Advertising Age,* March 7, 1988, p. S2ff.; "Breakout in Billboards," *Dun's Business Month,* May 1985, pp. 40–44; "Confused Advertisers Bemoan Proliferation of Yellow Pages," *The Wall Street Journal,* February 27, 1986, p. 23; "Cost of TV Spot Pegged at $145,600," *Advertising Age,* March 6, 1989, p. 68; "Advertisers Bristle as Charges Balloon for Splashy TV Spots," *The Wall Street Journal,* June 20, 1985, p. 31; Carol Sonenklar, "Women and Their Magazines," *American Demographics,* June 1986, p. 44.

9. "Why Jockey Switched Its Ads from TV to Print," *Business Week,* July 26, 1976, pp. 140–42; "Bike Racks, Phone Booths Are New 7–11 Ad Vehicles," *Marketing News,* February 27, 1989, p. 5; " '900' Numbers, Ad Tie-ins Connect," *Advertising Age,* June 5, 1989, p. 12; "Ad Attack: No Place to Escape," *USA Today,* March 22, 1988, pp. B1–2; "Bags to Take Ads Again," *Advertising Age,* May 30, 1988, p. 30; "Attention, Shoppers," *Fortune,* November 23, 1987, p. 12; "More Ads Bombard Airplane Passengers," *The Wall Street Journal,* February 14, 1989, p. B1; "Ads Spread to Video Covers," *Advertising Age,* September 14, 1987, p. 82; "Video Renters Watch the Ads, Zapping Conventional Wisdom," *The Wall Street Journal,* April 28, 1989, p. B1; "Advertising on Blimps Grows in Popularity," *The Wall Street Journal,* November 9, 1988, p. B1; "In-Store Video Ads Can Reinforce Media Campaigns," *Marketing News,* May 22, 1989, pp. 5–7; "What's Free, Full of Ads, and Read All Over," *Business Week,* November 2, 1987, p. 122ff.; Donald R. Glover, Steven W. Hartley, and Charles H. Patti, "How Advertising Message Strategies Are Set," *Industrial Marketing Management,* February 1989, pp. 19–26.

10. "Study of Olympics Ads Casts Doubts on Value of Campaigns," *The Wall Street Journal,* December 6, 1984, p. 33; "Cost of TV Sports Commercials Prompts Cutbacks by Advertisers," *The Wall Street Journal,* January 15, 1985, p. 37; "Cheers for Real Winners of Super Bowl XXIII: Bud and Coke," *Advertising Age,* January 23, 1989, p. 1ff.

11. "Special Report: Newspapers," *Advertising Age,* March 6, 1989, pp. S1–14; "Newspapers: Stretching to Deliver Readers' Needs," *Advertising Age,* July 20, 1987, pp. S1–8; "More Newspapers Plan Sunday Editions," *The Wall Street Journal,* January 19, 1989, p. B1; "Newspapers Target 'Techies' with Media Buying Diskette," *Marketing News,* January 30, 1989, p. 16; "Special Issue: Magazines, Facing the Challenges of the '90s," *Advertising Age,* May 24, 1989, pp. S1–84; "Magazines Offer 'Extras' in Battle for Ads," *The Wall Street Journal,* January 4, 1989, p. B1; "Special Report: Cable TV," *Advertising Age,* March 30, 1987, pp. S1–12; "Advertisers Are Flocking to Fledgling Fox," *The Wall Street Journal,* February 28, 1989, p. B6; *Lists of 14 Million Businesses* (American Business Lists, Inc.: Omaha, Nebraska), July 1989; "Direct Marketing for Packaged Goods," *The Wall Street Journal,* May 26, 1988, p. 29; "Why Melinda S. Gets Ads for Panty Hose, Melinda F., Porsches," *The Wall Street Journal,* May 6, 1988, p. 1ff.; "Special Report: Direct Marketing," *Advertising Age,* January 18, 1988, pp. S1–20; "Carmakers Take Spin with Computer Discs," *Advertising Age,* February 8, 1988, p. 30; "Advertisers Provide Tapes Free with Videos," *Advertising Age,* February 16, 1987, p. 22; Helen

E. Katz and Kent M. Lancaster, "How Leading Advertisers and Agencies Use Cable Television," *Journal of Advertising Research,* February–March 1989, pp. 30–38.

12. "Satellite Programs Enter In-Store Act," *Advertising Age,* March 20, 1989, p. 54; "An Upstart Is Upsetting Actmedia's Shopping Carts," *Business Week,* September 7, 1987, pp. 28–29.

13. "A New Role for Ads in the Yellow Pages," *The Wall Street Journal,* June 26, 1989, p. B1; "Invasion of the Yellow Pages," *Time,* October 5, 1987, p. 52; "Price Hikes Loom for TV's Hot :15s," *Advertising Age,* August 29, 1988, p. 1ff.; "And Now, A Wittier Word from Our Sponsors," *Business Week,* March 24, 1986, pp. 90–94; "Don't Gimme Gimmicks: Novelty Ads Flood Media," *Advertising Age,* November 9, 1987, p. 12; "New Olds Ad Campaign Updates the Old," *The Wall Street Journal,* August 23, 1989, p. B3; "New Ads Give a Boost to the Olds Image but Don't Help the Old Sales Woes Much," *The Wall Street Journal,* June 19, 1989, p. B1; "Advertisers See Big Gains in Odd Layouts: Page Position Can Make Ads More Prominent," *The Wall Street Journal,* June 29, 1988, p. 25; "You Can't (Hum) Ignore (Hum) That Ad: Novel Sound Effects Are Making the Video-Blitzed Listen Up," *Business Week,* September 21, 1987, p. 56; "Ads in Magazines Get Personalized Touch as *Time,* Others Test High-Tech Process," *The Wall Street Journal,* October 27, 1988, p. B1; Joel Saegert, "Why Marketing Should Quit Giving Subliminal Advertising the Benefit of the Doubt," *Psychology and Marketing,* Summer 1987, pp. 107–20; "Marketers Resurrect Ads from the Past: Golden Oldies Offer Awareness That's Built-In," *The Wall Street Journal,* July 18, 1988, p. 25; Michael L. Ray and Peter H. Webb, "Three Prescriptions for Clutter," *Journal of Advertising Research,* February–March 1986, pp. 69–78.

14. Daniel B. Wackman, Charles T. Salmon, and Caryn C. Salmon, "Developing an Advertising Agency-Client Relationship," *Journal of Advertising Research,* December 1986–January 1987, pp. 21–28; "Gambling on a Client's Success: Agencies Debate Equity Payment," *The Wall Street Journal,* August 22, 1989, p. B4; "Demand for Hispanic Ads Outstrips Specialists in Field," *The Wall Street Journal,* June 29, 1989, p. B1; "Confessions of an Advertising Man," *Fortune,* June 5, 1989, pp. 131–32; "As Ad Research Gains Followers, Agencies Point Out Its Failures," *The Wall Street Journal,* April 5, 1989, p. B11; "Carnation Links Pay, Research," *Advertising Age,* March 6, 1989, p. 1ff.; "Big Agencies Call for End to Free Pitches," *The Wall Street Journal,* February 22, 1989, p. B7; "P&G Seeks New Creative Thrust: Boosts Compensation to Ad Agencies," *Advertising Age,* February 20, 1989, p. 3ff.; "Power Charts, Media Charts, Agency Power," *Advertising Age,* December 26, 1988, pp. 11–13; "More Companies Offer Their Ad Agencies Bonus Plans that Reward Superior Work," *The Wall Street Journal,* July 26, 1988, p. 37; "Wanted: Media Muscle—Ad Agencies Race to Form Buying Linkups," *Advertising Age,* July 11, 1988, p. 1ff.; "A Word from the Sponsor: Get Results—or Else," *Business Week,* July 4, 1988, p. 66; "General Foods to Cut Commission to Ad Firms, Award Some Bonuses," *The Wall Street Journal,* May 19, 1988, p. 40; "Can Young & Rubicam Keep the Crown?" *Business Week,* April 4, 1988, pp. 74–80; "Haggling Grows over Ad Agency Fees," *The Wall Street Journal,* March 3, 1988, p. 22; "How Three Small Agencies Thrive in the Megamerger Era," *Business Week,* November 2, 1986, pp. 74–76; "Do Media Buying Services Sell Their Clients Short?" *Marketing and Media Decisions,* August 1985, p. 49ff.; Michael G. Harvey and J. Paul Rupert, "Selecting an Industrial Advertising Agency," *Industrial Marketing Management,* May 1988, pp. 119–28.

15. "Behind the Scenes at an American Express Commercial," *Business Week,* May 20, 1985, pp. 84–88.

16. "Television Ads Ring Up No Sale in Study," *The Wall Street Journal,* February 15, 1989, p. B6; "TvB Rebuts Prof: Adds Its Voice to Defense of Ads," *Advertising Age,* May 1, 1989, p. 26; "Prof: TV Ads Not as Effective as Price and Promotions," *Marketing News,* March 27, 1989, p. 7; "IRI Research Bolsters Value of Advertising," *Advertising Age,* March 6, 1989, p. 71; George M. Zinkhan, "Rating Industrial Advertisements," *Industrial Marketing Management,* February 1984,

pp. 43–48; Pradeep K. Korgaonkar, Danny N. Bellenger, and Allen E. Smith, "Successful Industrial Advertising Campaigns," *Industrial Marketing Management,* May 1986, pp. 123–28; Lawrence C. Soley, "Copy Length and Industrial Advertising Readership," *Industrial Marketing Management,* August 1986, pp. 245–52; David W. Stewart, "Measures, Methods, and Models in Advertising Research," *Journal of Advertising Research,* June–July 1989, p. 54ff.

17. "FTC under Industry Pressure, Shows New Life in Backing Deceptive Ad Laws," *The Wall Street Journal,* April 17, 1989, p. B4; "Lowest-Price Claims in Ads Stir Dispute," *The Wall Street Journal,* August 12, 1988, p. 17; William L. Wilkie, Dennis L. McNeil, and Michael B. Mazis, "Marketing's Scarlet Letter: The Theory and Practice of Corrective Advertising," *Journal of Marketing,* Spring 1984, pp. 11–31; Jacob Jacoby, Margaret C. Nelson, and Wayne D. Hoyer, "Corrective Advertising and Affirmative Disclosure Statements: Their Potential for Confusing and Misleading the Consumer," *Journal of Marketing,* Winter 1982, pp. 61–72.

18. Gary T. Ford and John E. Calfee, "Recent Developments in FTC Policy on Deception," *Journal of Marketing,* July 1986, pp. 82–103; Dorothy Cohen, "Unfairness in Advertising Revisited," *Journal of Marketing,* Winter 1982, pp. 73–80; "Lysol's Maker Keeps Fighting FTC over Advertising Claims," *The Wall Street Journal,* February 24, 1983, p. 29; J. J. Boddewyn, "Advertising Regulation in the 1980s: The Underlying Global Forces," *Journal of Marketing,* Winter 1982, pp. 27–35; John S. Healey and Harold H. Kassarjian, "Advertising Substantiation and Advertiser Response: A Content Analysis of Magazine Advertisements," *Journal of Marketing,* Winter 1983, pp. 107–17; Michael A. Kamins and Lawrence J. Marks, "Advertising Puffery: The Impact of Using Two-Sided Claims on Product Attitude and Purchase," *Journal of Advertising* 16, no. 4 (1987), pp. 6–15.

19. "Do Toll Phone Services Play Fair by Advertising Directly to Kids?" *The Wall Street Journal,* July 7, 1989, p. B1; "Advertisers Draw up TV Boycott Lists," *The Wall Street Journal,* June 21, 1989, p. B4; "NAD Tackles Kids' 900-Number Ads," *Advertising Age,* February 20, 1989, p. 64; "Watchdog Group Lashes out at Ads that Demean Men," *Marketing News,* March 27, 1989, p. 2; "Double Standard for Kids' TV Ads," *The Wall Street Journal,* June 10, 1988, p. 25; "Watchdogs Zealously Censor Advertising Targeted to Kids," *The Wall Street Journal,* September 5, 1985, p. 35; Priscilla A. LaBarbera, "The Diffusion of Trade Association Advertising Self-Regulation," *Journal of Marketing,* Winter 1983, pp. 58–67.

Chapter 18

1. "Sears Breaks Biggest Blitz," *Advertising Age,* February 27, 1989, p. 2ff.; "Sears Will Close Stores 42 Hours to Cut Prices," *The Wall Street Journal,* February 24, 1989, p. B1ff.; "Sears Delays 'Neighborhood Store' Plan," *Advertising Age,* August 8, 1988, p. 45; "Sears Expands Staff as Part of Revision of Electronic Lines," *The Wall Street Journal,* August 2, 1988, p. 27; "Sears Plans to Test More Name Brands in Both Electronic and Appliance Lines," *The Wall Street Journal,* July 29, 1988, p. 22; "Sears Has Everything, Including Messy Fight over Ads in New York," *The Wall Street Journal,* June 28, 1988, p. 1ff.

2. "Car Makers Seek to Mask Price Increases," *The Wall Street Journal,* August 16, 1989, p. B1.

3. Alfred Rappaport, "Executive Incentives versus Corporate Growth," *Harvard Business Review,* July–August 1978, pp. 81–88.

4. Pricing "in the public interest" is often an issue in pricing government services; for an interesting example, see "Price Policy on Space Shuttle's Commercial Use Could Launch—or Ground—NASA's Rockets," *The Wall Street Journal,* March 21, 1985, p. 64.

5. "Computer Price Cuts Seem Likely Despite Efforts to Hold the Line," *The Wall Street Journal,* September 5, 1985, p. 25.

6. "Harvester Sells Many Trucks below Cost, Citing Need to Maintain Dealer Network," *The Wall Street Journal,* April 19, 1983, p. 8.

7. "Leave the Herd and Leap off the Old Price Treadmill," *Chicago Tribune,* November 11, 1985, Sec. 4, p. 21ff.

8. "Aluminum Firms Offer Wider Discounts but Price Cuts Stop at Some Distributors," *The Wall Street Journal,* November 16, 1984, p. 50.

9. Elliot B. Ross, "Making Money with Proactive Pricing," *Harvard Business Review,* November–December 1984, pp. 145–55; Thomas Nagle, "Pricing as Creative Marketing," *Business Horizons,* July/August 1983, pp. 14–19. See also Subhash C. Jain and Michael B. Laric, "A Framework for Strategic Industrial Pricing," *Industrial Marketing Management* 8 (1979), pp. 75–80; Mary Karr, "The Case of the Pricing Predicament," *Harvard Business Review,* March–April, 1988, pp. 10–23; Saeed Samiee, "Pricing in Marketing Strategies of U.S. and Foreign-Based Companies," *Journal of Business Research,* February 1987, pp. 17–30; Gerard J. Tellis, "Beyond the Many Faces of Price: An Integration of Pricing Strategies," *Journal of Marketing,* October 1986, pp. 146–60.

10. For an interesting discussion of the many variations from a one-price system in retailing, see Stanley C. Hollander, "The 'One-Price' System—Fact or Fiction?" *Journal of Marketing Research,* February 1972, pp. 35–40. See also Michael J. Houston, "Minimum Markup Laws: An Empirical Assessment," *Journal of Retailing,* Winter 1981, pp. 98–113; "Flexible Pricing," *Business Week,* December 12, 1977, pp. 78–88; Michael H. Morris, "Separate Prices as a Marketing Tool," *Industrial Marketing Management,* May 1987, pp. 79–86.

11. "Squeezin' the Charmin," *Fortune,* January 16, 1989, pp. 11–12; "Grocers Join Winn-Dixie," *Advertising Age,* November 7, 1988, p. 3; "Grocery Chains Pressure Suppliers for Uniform Prices," *The Wall Street Journal,* October 21, 1988, p. B1; "Grocery Chain Dumps Major Package Goods," *Advertising Age,* October 10, 1988, p. 1ff.

12. Alan Reynolds, "A Kind Word for 'Cream Skimming,' " *Harvard Business Review,* November–December 1974, pp. 113–20.

13. Stuart U. Rich, "Price Leadership in the Paper Industry," *Industrial Marketing Management,* April 1983, pp. 101–4; "OPEC Member Offers Discounts to Some Amid Downward Pressure on Oil Prices," *The Wall Street Journal,* November 16, 1984, p. 4.

14. "Campbell's Taste of the Japanese Market is Mm-Mm Good," *Business Week,* March 28, 1988, p. 42; "Most U.S. Firms Seek Extra Profits in Japan, at the Expense of Sales," *The Wall Street Journal,* May 15, 1987, p. 1ff.

15. "Cash Discounts," *Electrical Wholesaling,* May 1989, pp. 90–96; "Retailers Buy Far in Advance to Exploit Trade Promotions," *The Wall Street Journal,* October 9, 1986, p. 37; "Feeding the Card Habit," *Newsweek,* July 8, 1985, pp. 52–53; Michael Levy and C. A. Ingene, "Retailers: Head Off Credit Cards with Cash Discounts?" *Harvard Business Review,* May–June 1983, pp. 18–25; George S. Day and Adrian B. Ryans, "Using Price Discounts for a Competitive Advantage," *Industrial Marketing Management,* February 1988, pp. 1–14; James B. Wilcox et al., "Price Quantity Discounts: Some Implications for Buyers and Sellers," *Journal of Marketing,* July 1987, pp. 60–70.

16. "What Looks Like a Sale, but Isn't a Sale?" *The Wall Street Journal,* April 27, 1989, p. B1; "Who Wins with Price Matching Plans," *The Wall Street Journal,* March 16, 1989, p. B1; "The 'Sale' Is Fading as a Retailing Tactic," *The Wall Street Journal,* March 1, 1989, p. B1ff.

17. "Want Shelf Space at the Supermarket? Ante Up," *Business Week,* August 7, 1989, pp. 60–61; "Product Glut Sparks Struggle for Shelf Space," *Marketing News,* January 16, 1989, p. 2; "Supermarkets Demand Food Firms' Payments Just to Get on the Shelf," *The Wall Street Journal,* November 1, 1988, p. A1ff.

18. "Camera Owners Find a Market in Used Models," *The Wall Street Journal,* September 3, 1987, p. 21; "Postal Probe Clips $1M-a-Week Coupon Scam," *Advertising Age,* March 31, 1986, p. 10; P. Rajan Varadarajan, "Coupon Fraud: A $500 Million Dilemma," *Business,* July/August/September 1985, pp. 23–29; "Grocery Coupons Are Seen Threatened by Growth of Fraudulent Redemptions," *The Wall Street Journal,* April 12, 1976, p. 26; "Marketers Tighten Rules on Rebate Offers in Effort to Reduce Large Fraud Losses," *The Wall Street Journal,* March 18, 1987, p. 33.

19. For an excellent discussion of laws related to pricing, see Louis W. Stern and Thomas L. Eovaldi, *Legal Aspects of Marketing Strategy: Antitrust and Consumer Protection Issues* (Englewood Cliffs, N. J.: Prentice-Hall, 1984).

20. Donald R. Lichtenstein and William O. Bearden, "Contextual Influences on Perceptions of Merchant-Supplied Reference Prices," *Journal of Consumer Research,* June 1989, pp. 55–66; John Liefeld and Louise A. Heslop, "Reference Prices and Deception in Newspaper Advertising," *Journal of Consumer Research,* March 1985, pp. 868–76. Individual states often have their own laws; see, for example, "States Crack Down on Phony Price-Cutting 'Sales,' " *The Wall Street Journal,* January 30, 1986, p. 1; Willard F. Mueller and Thomas W. Paterson, "Effectiveness of State Sales-Below-Cost Laws: Evidence from the Grocery Trade," *Journal of Retailing,* Summer 1986, pp. 166–85.

21. "Firms Face Bigger Exposure to Liability for Price Fixing because of Court Ruling," *The Wall Street Journal,* April 20, 1989, p. B6; "Court Says Indirect Buyers Can Sue Violators of State Antitrust Laws," *The Wall Street Journal,* April 19, 1989, p. B7; "Panasonic to Pay Rebates to Avoid Antitrust Charges," *The Wall Street Journal,* January 19, 1989, p. B1ff.; "Cola Seilers May Have Bottled Up Their Competitors," *The Wall Street Journal,* December 9, 1987, p. 6; "Price-Fix Case Naming Bottlers Is Stepped Up," *The Wall Street Journal,* October 15, 1987, p. 3; "The FTC Redefines Price Fixing," *Business Week,* April 18, 1983, p. 37. See also Mary Jane Sheffet and Debra L. Scammon, "Resale Price Maintenance: Is It Safe to Suggest Retail Prices?" *Journal of Marketing,* Fall 1985, pp. 82–91.

22. Morris L. Mayer, Joseph B. Mason, and E. A. Orbeck, "The Borden Case—A Legal Basis for Private Brand Price Discrimination," *MSU Business Topics,* Winter 1970, pp. 56–63; T. F. Schutte, V. J. Cook, Jr., and R. Hemsley, "What Management Can Learn from the Borden Case," *Business Horizons,* Winter 1966, pp. 23–30.

23. "Is the Cost Defense Workable?" *Journal of Marketing,* January 1965, pp. 37–42; B. J. Linder and Allan H. Savage, "Price Discrimination and Cost Defense—Change Ahead?" *MSU Business Topics,* Summer 1971, pp. 21–26; "Firms Must Prove Injury from Price Bias to Qualify for Damages, High Court Says," *The Wall Street Journal,* May 19, 1981, p. 8.

24. "FTC Accuses Six Large Book Publishers of Price Bias Against Independent Stores," *The Wall Street Journal,* December 23, 1988, p. B4; Lawrence X. Tarpey, Sr., "Who Is a Competing Customer?" *Journal of Retailing,* Spring 1969, pp. 46–58; John R. Davidson, "FTC, Robinson-Patman and Cooperative Promotion Activities," *Journal of Marketing,* January 1968, pp. 14–18; L. X. Tarpey, Sr., "Buyer Liability under the Robinson-Patman Act: A Current Appraisal," *Journal of Marketing,* January 1972, pp. 38–42.

Chapter 19

1. "Seeking Big Money in Paper and Pens," *Fortune,* July 31, 1989, pp. 173–74.

2. Marvin A. Jolson, "A Diagrammatic Model for Merchandising Calculations," *Journal of Retailing,* Summer 1975, pp. 3–9.

3. Mary L. Hatten, "Don't Get Caught with Your Prices Down: Pricing in Inflationary Times," *Business Horizons,* March 1982, pp. 23–28; "Why Detroit Can't Cut Prices," *Business Week,* March 1, 1982, p. 110; Douglas G. Brooks, "Cost Oriented Pricing: A Realistic Solution to a Complicated Problem," *Journal of Marketing,* April 1975, pp. 72–74.

4. George S. Day and David B. Montgomery, "Diagnosing the Experience Curve," *Journal of Marketing,* Spring 1983, pp. 44–58; Alan R. Beckenstein and H. Landis Gabel, "Experience Curve Pricing Strategy: The Next Target of Antitrust?" *Business Horizons,* September/October 1982, pp. 71–77; William W. Alberts, "The Experience Curve Doctrine Reconsidered," *Journal of Marketing,* July, 1989, pp. 36–49.

5. G. Dean Kortge, "Inverted Breakeven Analysis for Profitable Marketing Decisions," *Industrial Marketing Management,* October 1984, pp. 219–24; Thomas L. Powers, "Breakeven Analysis with Semifixed Costs," *Industrial Marketing Management,* February 1987, pp. 35–42.

6. Approaches for estimating price-quantity relationships are reviewed in Kent B. Monroe, *Pricing: Making Profitable Decisions* (New York: McGraw-Hill, 1979). For a specific example see Frank D. Jones, "A Survey Technique to Measure Demand under Various Pricing Strategies," *Journal of Marketing,* July 1975, pp. 75–77; or Gordon A. Wyner, Lois H. Benedetti, and Bart M. Trapp, "Measuring the Quantity and Mix of Product Demand," *Journal of Marketing,* Winter 1984, pp. 101–9. See also Michael H. Morris and Mary L. Joyce, "How Marketers Evaluate Price Sensitivity," *Industrial Marketing Management,* May 1988, pp. 169–76.

7. "Miatific Bliss in Five Gears," *Time,* October 2, 1989, p. 91; "Sexy Ragtop Puts Buyers in Scramble," *USA Today,* August 11–13, 1989, pp. A1–2; "Miata Success Story Has Curious Twists," *The Wall Street Journal,* August 3, 1989, p. B1; "Romancing the Roadster," *Time,* July 24, 1989, p. 39; "Mazda Rolls Out a Poor Man's Maserati," *Business Week,* June 26, 1989, p. 66.

8. Benson P. Shapiro and Barbara P. Jackson, "Industrial Pricing to Meet Customer Needs," *Harvard Business Review,* November–December 1978, pp. 119–27; "The Race to the $10 Light Bulb," *Business Week,* May 19, 1980, p. 124; see also Michael H. Morris and Donald A. Fuller, "Pricing an Industrial Service," *Industrial Marketing Management,* May 1989, pp. 139–46.

9. For an example applied to a high-price item, see "Sale of Mink Coats Strays a Fur Piece from the Expected," *The Wall Street Journal,* March 21, 1980, p. 30.

10. B. P. Shapiro, "The Psychology of Pricing," *Harvard Business Review,* July–August 1968, pp. 14–24; C. Davis Fogg and Kent H. Kohnken, "Price-Cost Planning," *Journal of Marketing,* April 1978, pp. 97–106.

11. "Strategic Mix of Odd, Even Prices Can Lead to Increased Retail Profits," *Marketing News,* March 7, 1980, p. 24.

12. "Special Report: Marketing to the Affluent," *Advertising Age,* October 19, 1987, pp. S1–32; Peter C. Riesz, "Price versus Quality in the Marketplace," *Journal of Retailing,* Winter 1978, pp. 15–28; John J. Wheatly and John S. Y. Chiu, "The Effects of Price, Store Image, and Product and Respondent Characteristics on Perceptions of Quality," *Journal of Marketing Research,* May 1977, pp. 181–86; N. D. French, J. J. Williams, and W. A. Chance, "A Shopping Experiment on Price-Quality Relationships," *Journal of Retailing,* Fall 1972, pp. 3–16; J. Douglas McConnell, "Comment on 'A Major Price-Perceived Quality Study Reexamined,'" *Journal of Marketing Research,* May 1980, pp. 263–64; K. M. Monroe and S. Petroshius, "Buyers' Subjective Perceptions of Price: An Update of the Evidence," in *Perspectives in Consumer Behavior,* ed. T. Robertson and H. Kassarjian (Glenview, Ill.: Scott Foresman 1981), pp. 43–55; Valarie A. Zeithaml, "Consumer Perceptions of Price, Quality, and Value: A Means-End Model and Synthesis of Evidence," *Journal of Marketing,* July 1988, pp. 2–22.

13. Stephen Paranka, "Competitive Bidding Strategy," *Business Horizons,* June 1971, pp. 39–43; Wayne J. Morse, "Probabilistic Bidding Models: A Synthesis," *Business Horizons,* April 1975, pp. 67–74; Kenneth Simmonds and Stuart Slatter, "The Number of Estimators: A Critical Decision for Marketing under Competitive Bidding," *Journal of Marketing Research,* May 1978, pp. 203–13.

14. For references to additional readings in the pricing area, see Kent B. Monroe, D. Lund, and P. Choudhury, *Pricing Policies and Strate-* gies: An Annotated Bibliography* (Chicago: American Marketing Association, 1983). See also "Pricing of Products Is Still an Art, Often Having Little Link to Costs," *The Wall Street Journal,* November 25, 1981, p. 29ff.

Chapter 20

1. "NutraSweet Rivals Stirring," *Advertising Age,* June 26, 1989, p. 3ff.; "New Sweeteners Head for the Sugar Bowl," *The Wall Street Journal,* February 6, 1989, p. B1; "NutraSweet Sets Out for Fat-Substitute City," *Business Week,* February 15, 1988, pp. 100–103; "NutraSweet May Develop Its Own Simplesse Brands," *Advertising Age,* February 8, 1988, p. 4ff.; "Marketing NutraSweet in Leaner Times," *The Wall Street Journal,* May 7, 1987, p. 36.

2. See most basic statistics textbooks under time series analysis.

3. Checking the accuracy of forecasts is a difficult subject. See D. M. Georgoff and R. G. Murdick, "Manager's Guide to Forecasting," *Harvard Business Review,* January–February 1986, pp. 110–20; P. L. Bernstein and T. H. Silbert, "Are Economic Forecasters Worth Listening to?" *Harvard Business Review,* September-October 1984, pp. 32–41; E. Jerome Scott and Stephen K. Keiser, "Forecasting Acceptance of New Industrial Products with Judgment Modeling," *Journal of Marketing,* Spring 1984, pp. 54–67; "And Now, the Home-Brewed Forecast," *Fortune,* January 20, 1986, p. 53ff.; Arthur J. Adams, "Procedures for Revising Management Judgments Forecasts," *Journal of the Academy of Marketing Science,* Fall 1986, pp. 52–57; Robert H. Collins and Rebecca J. Mauritson, "Microcomputer Applications: Artificial Intelligence in Sales Forecasting Applications," *Journal of Personal Selling and Sales Management,* May 1987, pp. 77–80; F. William Barnett, "Four Steps to Forecast Total Market Demand," *Harvard Business Review,* July-August 1988, pp. 28–40; Anthony D. Cox and John D. Summers, "Heuristics and Biases in the Intuitive Projection of Retail Sales," *Journal of Marketing Research,* August 1987, pp. 290–97; D. M. Georgoff and R. G. Murdick, "Manager's Guide to Forecasting," *Harvard Business Review,* January–February 1986, pp. 110–20.

4. "Zenith Likely to Introduce 'Notebook'-Size Computer," *The Wall Street Journal,* July 11, 1989, p. B1; *1987 Annual Report,* Zenith Electronics Corporation; "Changing Channels at Zenith," *Time,* March 10, 1986, p. 66; *1985 Annual Report,* Zenith Electronics Corporation.

5. Gordon A. Wyner, Lois H. Benedetti, and Bart M. Trapp, "Measuring the Quality and Mix of Product Demand," *Journal of Marketing,* Winter 1984, pp. 101–9; J. B. Wilkinson, J. Barry Mason, and Christie H. Paksoy, "Assessing the Impact of Short-Term Variables," *Journal of Marketing Research,* February 1982, pp. 72–86; Paul W. Farris and Mark S. Albion, "The Impact of Advertising on the Price of Consumer Products," *Journal of Marketing,* Summer 1980, pp. 17–35; Leonard M. Lodish, "A User-Oriented Model for Sales Force Size, Product, and Market Allocations Decisions," *Journal of Marketing,* Summer 1980, pp. 70–78; Scott A. Neslin and Robert W. Shoemaker, "Using a Natural Experiment to Estimate Price Elasticity: The 1974 Sugar Shortage and the Ready-to-Eat Cereal Market," *Journal of Marketing,* Winter 1983, pp. 44–57; "Using Scanning Data to Analyze the Effects of Manufacturers' Coupons," *Nielsen Researcher,* no. 1 (1985), pp. 6–11; Stephen J. Arnold et al., "Advertising Quality in Sales Response Models," *Journal of Marketing Research,* February 1987, pp. 106–13; Ruth N. Bolton, "Sales Response Modeling: Gains in Efficiency from System Estimation," *Journal of Business Research,* March 1989, pp. 107–26.

6. For a "hands on" introduction to the use of spreadsheet analysis for marketing strategy planning, see E. J. McCarthy and William D. Perreault, Jr., *Computer-Aided Problems for Use with Basic Marketing* (Homewood, Ill.: Irwin, 1990); see also Gary L. Lilien, *Marketing Mix Analysis with Lotus 1–2–3* (Palo Alto, Calif.: Scientific Press, 1986).

7. "Companies to Watch: Loctite Corporation," *Fortune,* June 19, 1989, p. 148; "Loctite: Home Is Where the Customers Are," *Business Week,* April 13, 1987, p. 63; *1987 Annual Report,* Loctite Corporation; "Loctite 'Listens' to the Marketplace," in Ronald Alsop and Bill

Abrams, *The Wall Street Journal on Marketing* (New York: Dow Jones & Co., 1986), pp. 281–83.

8. John E. Smallwood, "The Product Life Cycle: A Key to Strategic Marketing Planning," *MSU Business Topics,* Winter 1973, pp. 29–35; Richard F. Savach and Laurence A. Thompson, "Resource Allocation within the Product Life Cycle," *MSU Business Topics,* Autumn 1978, pp. 35–44; Peter F. Kaminski and David R. Rink, "PLC: The Missing Link between Physical Distribution and Marketing Planning," *International Journal of Physical Distribution and Materials Management* 14, no. 6 (1984), pp. 77–92.

9. For further discussion on evaluating and selecting alternative plans, see Francis Buttle, "The Marketing Strategy Worksheet—A Practical Planning Tool," *Long Range Planning,* August 1985, pp. 80–88; Douglas A. Schellinck, "Effect of Time on a Marketing Strategy," *Industrial Marketing Management,* April 1983, pp. 83–88; George S. Day and Liam Fahey, "Valuing Market Strategies," *Journal of Marketing,* July 1988, pp. 45–57.

10. Jerry A. Viscione, "Small Company Budgets: Targets Are Key," *Harvard Business Review,* May–June 1984, pp. 42–53; Neil C. Churchill, "Budget Choice: Planning vs. Control," *Harvard Business Review,* July–August 1984, pp. 150–65; Vincent J. Blasko and Charles H. Patti, "The Advertising Budgeting Practices of Industrial Marketers," *Journal of Marketing,* Fall 1984, pp. 104–10; Douglas J. Dalrymple and Hans B. Thorelli, "Sales Force Budgeting," *Business Horizons,* July/August 1984, pp. 31–36.

11. Gordon J. Badovick and Sharon E. Beatty, "Shared Organizational Values: Measurement and Impact Upon Strategic Marketing Implementation," *Journal of the Academy of Marketing Science,* Spring 1987, pp. 19–26; Thomas V. Bonoma, "Making Your Marketing Strategy Work," *Harvard Business Review,* March–April 1984, pp. 68–76; Barbara J. Coe, "Key Differentiating Factors and Problems Associated with Implementation of Strategic Market Planning," in *1985 American Marketing Association Educators' Proceedings,* ed. R. F. Lusch et al. (Chicago: American Marketing Association, 1985), pp. 275–81; Robert E. Spekman and Kjell Gronhaug, "Insights on Implementation: A Conceptual Framework for Better Understanding the Strategic Marketing Planning Process," in *1983 American Marketing Association Educators' Proceedings,* ed. P. Murphy et al. (Chicago: American Marketing Association, 1983), pp. 311–14; Thomas V. Bonoma, "Enough About Strategy! Let's See Some Clever Executions," *Marketing News,* February 13, 1989, p. 10ff.

Chapter 21

1. Bernard J. Jaworski, "Toward a Theory of Marketing Control: Environmental Context, Control Types, and Consequences," *Journal of Marketing,* July 1988, pp. 23–39; Subhash Sharma and Dale D. Achabal, "STEMCOM: An Analytical Model for Marketing Control," *Journal of Marketing,* Spring 1982, pp. 104–13; James M. Hulbert and Norman E. Toy, "A Strategic Framework for Marketing Control," *Journal of Marketing,* April 1977, pp. 12–21; Sam R. Goodman, *Techniques of Profitability Analysis* (New York: John Wiley & Sons, 1970), especially chap. 1; Kenneth A. Merchant, "Progressing Toward a Theory of Marketing Control: A Comment," *Journal of Marketing,* July 1988, pp. 40–44.

2. Ed Weymes, "A Different Approach to Retail Sales Analysis," *Business Horizons,* March/April 1982, pp. 66–74; R. I. Haley and R. Gatty, "Monitor Your Markets Continuously," *Harvard Business Review,* May–June 1968, pp. 65–69; D. H. Robertson, "Sales Force Feedback on Competitors' Activities," *Journal of Marketing,* April 1974, pp. 69–71. See also Robert H. Collins, Regan F. Carey, and Rebecca F. Mauritson, "Microcomputer Applications: Maps on a Micro—Applications in Sales and Marketing Management," *Journal of Personal Selling and Sales Management,* November 1987, p. 83ff.

3. "K mart Corp. Stands Pat Despite Sears' Offensive," *Advertising Age,* June 5, 1989, p. 55; "K mart's Hyperactive," *Advertising Age,* January 23, 1989, p. 1ff.; "Attention K mart Shoppers: Style Coming to This Aisle," *The Wall Street Journal,* August 9, 1988, p. 6; "CEO's Plan Adds Glitter to K mart," *USA Today,* July 16, 1986, pp. B1–2.

4. Patrick M. Dunne and Harry I. Wolk, "Marketing Cost Analysis: A Modularized Contribution Approach," *Journal of Marketing,* July 1977, pp. 83–94; Nigel F. Piercy, "The Marketing Budgeting Process: Marketing Management Implications," *Journal of Marketing,* October 1987, pp. 45–59; Leland L. Beik and Stephen L. Buzby, "Profitability Analysis by Market Segments," *Journal of Marketing,* July 1973, pp. 48–53; Frank H. Mossman, Paul M. Fischer, and W. J. E. Crissy, "New Approaches to Analyzing Marketing Profitability," *Journal of Marketing,* April 1974, pp. 43–48; V. H. Kirpalani and Stanley J. Shapiro, "Financial Dimensions of Marketing Management," *Journal of Marketing,* July 1973, pp. 40–47; Michael J. Sandretto, "What Kind of Cost System Do You Need?" *Harvard Business Review,* January–February 1985, pp. 110–18; Douglas M. Lambert and Jay U. Sterling, "What Types of Profitability Reports Do Marketing Managers Receive?" *Industrial Marketing Management,* November 1987, pp. 295–304.

5. Technically, a distinction should be made between variable and direct costs, but we will use these terms interchangeably. Similarly, not all common costs are fixed costs, and vice versa. But the important point here is to recognize that some costs are fairly easy to allocate, and other costs are not. See Stewart A. Washburn, "Establishing Strategy and Determining Costs in the Pricing Decision," *Business Marketing,* July 1985, pp. 64–78.

6. "The Personal Computer Finds Its Missing Link," *Business Week,* June 5, 1989, pp. 120–29; "An Electronic Pipeline That's Changing the Way America Does Business," *Business Week,* August 3, 1987, pp. 80–82; "Computer Finds a Role in Buying and Selling, Reshaping Businesses," *The Wall Street Journal,* March 18, 1987, p. 1ff.; "Computers Bringing Changes to Basic Business Documents," *The Wall Street Journal,* March 6, 1987, p. 33; "Networking: Japan's Latest Computer Craze," *Fortune,* July 7, 1986, pp. 94–96; William J. Bruns, Jr., and W. Warren McFarlan, "Information Technology Puts Power in Control Systems," *Harvard Business Review,* September-October 1987, pp. 89–94.

7. John F. Grashof, "Conducting and Using a Marketing Audit," in *Readings in Basic Marketing,* ed. E. J. McCarthy, J. J. Grashof, and A. A. Brogowicz (Homewood, Ill.: Richard D. Irwin, 1984); Edward M. Mazze and John T. Thompson, Jr., "Organization Renewal: Case Study of a Marketing Department," *MSU Business Topics,* Summer 1973, pp. 39–44; Alice M. Tybout and John R. Hauser, "A Marketing Audit Using a Conceptual Model of Consumer Behavior: Application and Evaluation," *Journal of Marketing,* Summer 1981, pp. 82–101.

Chapter 22

1. "Most U.S. Companies Are Innocents Abroad," *Business Week,* November 16, 1987, pp. 168–69.

2. "After Early Stumbles, P&G Is Making Inroads Overseas," *The Wall Street Journal,* February 6, 1989, p. B1.

3. "Colgate Misfires in U.S.," *Advertising Age,* June 5, 1989, p. 3ff.; *1987 Annual Report,* Colgate-Palmolive Co.; "U.S. Firms Adapt to Japan's Market," *USA Today,* February 10, 1989, p. B5; *1987 Annual Report,* Johnson & Johnson; *1987 Annual Report,* the Gillette Company; "How to Sell to Cashless Buyers," *Fortune,* November 7, 1988, pp. 147–54; "The New Export Entrepreneurs," *Fortune,* June 6, 1988, pp. 87–102.

4. M. Frank Bradley, "Nature and Significance of International Marketing: A Review," *Journal of Business Research,* June 1987, pp. 205–20; "For All Its Difficulties, U.S. Stands to Retain Its Global Leadership," *The Wall Street Journal,* January 23, 1989, p. A1ff.; "Will Japan Gain Too Much Power?" *Fortune,* September 12, 1988, pp. 150–53; "Currency Shifts Muddle the Export Picture," *Business Week,* February 16, 1987, p. 22.

5. "America's 50 Biggest Exporters," *Fortune,* July 17, 1989, pp. 50–51; "A Top Japanese Firm in Electronics Finds U.S. Market Difficult," *The Wall Street Journal,* March 25, 1985, p. 1ff. See also "Forest-Products Concerns Urge Using Wood for Latin Houses," *The Wall Street Journal,* September 19, 1984, p. 35; S. Tamer Cavusgil and Jacob Naor, "Firm and Management Characteristics as Discriminators of Export Marketing," *Journal of Business Research,* June 1987, pp. 221–36; Camille P. Schuster and Charles D. Bodkin, "Market Segmentation Practices of Exporting Companies," *Industrial Marketing Management,* May 1987, pp. 95–102; Refik Culpan, "Export Behavior of Firms: Relevance of Firm Size," *Journal of Business Research,* May, 1989, pp. 207–18; Anthony C. Koh and Robert A. Robicheaux, "Variations in Export Performance Due to Differences in Export Marketing Strategy: Implications for Industrial Marketers," *Journal of Business Research,* November 1988, pp. 249–58.

6. "'Papa-Mama" Stores in Japan Wield Power to Hold Back Imports," *The Wall Street Journal,* November 14, 1988, p. A1ff.; "U.S. Concerns Trying to Do Business in Japan Face Government, Market, Cultural Barriers," *The Wall Street Journal,* July 8, 1985, p. 16; F. H. Rolf Seringhaus, "Using Trade Missions for Export Market Entry," *Industrial Marketing Management,* November, 1987, pp. 249–56.

7. John A. Quelch, "How to Build a Product Licensing Program," *Harvard Business Review,* May–June 1985, p. 186ff.

8. "The Steel Deal That Could Boost Big Blue in Brazil," *Business Week,* May 19, 1986, p. 66.

9. "Top U.S. Companies Move into Russia," *Fortune,* July 31, 1989, pp. 165–71; "When U.S. Joint Ventures with Japan Go Sour," *Business Week,* July 24, 1989, pp. 30–31; "More Competitors Turn to Cooperation: Joint Ventures Are Encouraged by Government," *The Wall Street Journal,* June 23, 1989, p. B1; "Your Rivals Can Be Your Allies," *Fortune,* March 27, 1989, pp. 66–76; "How a German Firm Joined with Soviets to Make Good Shoes," *The Wall Street Journal,* February 14, 1989, p. A1ff.; "PepsiCo Accepts Tough Conditions for the Right to Sell Cola in India," *The Wall Street Journal,* September 20, 1988, p. 44; "Why Mitsubishi Is Right at Home in Illinois," *Business Week,* May 30, 1988, p. 45; F. Kingston Berlew, "The Joint Venture—A Way into Foreign Markets," *Harvard Business Review,* July–August 1984, pp. 48–55; Robert B. Reich and Eric D. Mankin, "Joint Ventures with Japan Give Away Our Future," *Harvard Business Review,* March–April 1986, pp. 78–86; D. Robert Webster, "International Joint Ventures with Pacific Rim Partners," *Business Horizons,* March/April 1989, pp. 65–71.

10. "Why There's Still Promise in China," *Fortune,* February 27, 1989, pp. 95–101; "U.S. Companies Going It Alone in China Find Road Bumpy But Have Few Regrets," *The Wall Street Journal,* October 24, 1988, p. A12; Theodore Levitt, "The Globalization of Markets," *Harvard Business Review,* May–June 1983, pp. 92–102; Gary Hamel and C. K. Prahalad, "Do You Really Have a Global Strategy," *Harvard Business Review,* July–August 1985, pp. 139–48.

11. "American Food Companies Look Yummy to Japan," *Business Week,* February 27, 1989, pp. 94–96; "Battling a High Yen, Many Japanese Firms Shift Work Overseas," *The Wall Street Journal,* February 27, 1989, p. 1ff.; "What Foreigners Will Buy Next," *Fortune,* February 13, 1989, pp. 94–98; "Japanese Firms Set Up More Factories in U.S., Alarm Some Americans," *The Wall Street Journal,* March 29, 1985, p. 1ff.; Thomas Hout, Michael E. Porter, and Eileen Rudden, "How Global Companies Win Out," *Harvard Business Review,* September-October 1982, pp. 98–108; "Japanese Multinationals Covering the World with Investment," *Business Week,* June 16, 1980, pp. 92–99.

12. "The Little Guys Are Making It Big Overseas," *Business Week,* February 27, 1989, pp. 94–96.

13. "McWorld? McDonald's Can Make a Big Mac Anywhere, But Duplicating Its Culture Abroad Won't Be So Easy," *Business Week,* October 13, 1986, pp. 78–86; "McDonald's Brings Hamburger (with Beer) to Hamburg," *Advertising Age,* May 30, 1977, p. 61.

14. Kamran Kashani, "Beware the Pitfalls of Global Marketing," *Harvard Business Review,* September-October 1989, pp. 91–98; "How to Go Global—and Why," *Fortune,* August 28, 1989, pp. 70–76; "Coke to Use 'Can't Beat the Feeling' as World-Wide Marketing Theme," *The Wall Street Journal,* December 12, 1988, p. 35; "Japanese Firm That Specializes in Cute Stumbles with Black Sambo Caricatures," *The Wall Street Journal,* August 31, 1988, p. 20; "Marketers Turn Sour on Global Sales Pitch Harvard Guru Makes," *The Wall Street Journal,* May 12, 1988, p. 1ff.; "Marketing Can Be Global, But Ads Must Remain Cultural," *Marketing News, Collegiate Ed.,* September, 1987, p. 12; John A. Quelch and E. J. Hoff, "Customizing Global Marketing," *Harvard Business Review,* May–June 1986, pp. 59–68; "Playtex Kicks Off a One-Ad-Fits-All Campaign," *Business Week,* December 16, 1985, pp. 48–49; Barbara Mueller, "Reflections of Culture: An Analysis of Japanese and American Advertising Appeals," *Journal of Advertising Research,* June–July 1987, p. 51ff.; Subhash C. Jain, "Standardization of International Marketing Strategy: Some Research Hypotheses," *Journal of Marketing,* January 1989, pp. 70–79.

15. "What's Next for Business in China," *Fortune,* July 17, 1989, pp. 110–12; "U.S. Importers Aren't Jumping Ship—Yet," *Business Week,* June 26, 1989, p. 78; "Has Beijing Burned Its Bridges with Business?" *Business Week,* June 19, 1989, pp. 32–33; "U.S. Companies Vow to Stay in China," *Fortune,* June 19, 1989, p. 8; "Business Copes with Terrorism," *Fortune,* January 6, 1986, pp. 47–55; "Dole and Del Monte Are Staying Put—No Matter What," *Business Week,* November 18, 1985, pp. 58–59; Thomas W. Shreeve, "Be Prepared for Political Changes Abroad," *Harvard Business Review,* July–August 1984, pp. 111–18; "Ford's Mexico Plant to Heed Export Call," *Chicago Tribune,* April 7, 1985, Sec. 7, p. F9; Victor H. Frank, Jr., "Living with Price Control Abroad," *Harvard Business Review,* March–April 1984, pp. 137–42; Michael G. Harvey and James T. Rothe, "The Foreign Corrupt Practices Act: The Good, the Bad and the Future," in *1983 American Marketing Association Educators' Proceedings,* ed. P. E. Murphy et al. (Chicago: American Marketing Association, 1983), pp. 374–79.

16. "Juggling the Scepter in a Unified Europe," *Insight,* June 19, 1989, pp. 8–10; "The Coming Boom in Europe," *Fortune,* April 10, 1989, pp. 108–14; "Europe Will Become Economic Superpower as Barriers Crumble," *The Wall Street Journal,* December 28, 1988, p. A1ff.; "Reshaping Europe: 1992 and Beyond," *Business Week,* December 12, 1988, pp. 48–73; "Multinationals Eye Spain," *Advertising Age,* October 17, 1988, p. 38; "U.S. to Boost Tariffs on European Pasta in Response to EC Citrus Discrimination," *The Wall Street Journal,* June 21, 1985, p. 31; "Philips Finds Obstacles to Intra-Europe Trade Are Costly, Inefficient," *The Wall Street Journal,* August 7, 1985, p. 1ff. See also John R. Darling and Danny R. Arnold, "Foreign Consumers' Perspective of the Products and Marketing Practices of the United States versus Selected European Countries," *Journal of Business Research,* November 1988, pp. 237–48; Sandra Vandermerwe and Marc-Andre L'Huillier, "Euro-Consumers in 1992," *Business Horizons,* January/February, 1989, pp. 34–40; James M. Higgins and Timo Santalainen, "Strategies for Europe 1992," *Business Horizons,* July/August, 1989, pp. 54–58.

17. "Perils of Getting Tough on Korea," *Fortune,* June 5, 1989, pp. 263–68; "An $85,000 Lincoln Will Become Reality Soon in South Korea," *The Wall Street Journal,* March 22, 1988, p. 53; "As EC Markets Unite, U.S. Exporters Face New Trade Barriers," *The Wall Street Journal,* January 19, 1989, p. A1ff.; "Europe Gives Break to Franchisers," *The Wall Street Journal,* January 5, 1989, p. B1; "EC's Auto Plan Would Keep Japan at Bay," *The Wall Street Journal,* October 27, 1988, p. A1ff.; "Rethinking Japan: The New, Harder Line Toward Tokyo," *Business Week,* August 7, 1989, pp. 44–52; "Where Global Growth Is Going," *Fortune,* July 31, 1989, pp. 71–92; "Getting Tough with Tokyo," *Time,* June 5, 1989, pp. 50–52; "Export Barriers the U.S. Hates Most," *Fortune,* February 27, 1989, pp. 88–93; "The Rage for U.S. Goods That's Rocking Taiwan," *Business Week,* March 21, 1988, pp. 63–64; "We're All in This Together," *Fortune,* February 2, 1987, pp. 26–29.

18. John S. McClenahen, "The Third World Challenge," *Industry Week,* May 28, 1984, pp. 90–95.

19. "Where Global Growth Is Going," *Fortune,* July 31, 1989, pp. 71–92; "Keeping Up," *American Demographics,* January 1989, p. 8; U.S. Bureau of the Census, *Statistical Abstract of the United States 1988* (Washington, D.C.: U.S. Government Printing Office, 1987), pp. 798–99; U.S. Bureau of the Census, *Statistical Abstract of the United States 1986* (Washington, D.C.: U.S. Government Printing Office, 1985), p. 838; J. S. Hill and R. R. Still, "Adapting Products to LDC Tastes," *Harvard Business Review,* March/April 1984, pp. 92–101; *Yearbook of National Account Statistics, 1981, Vol. II* (New York: United Nations, 1983), pp. 5–10; "Country Shares of World Population, 1986," *Business Horizons,* March/April 1989, p. 17; "Economic and Social Indicators on the Pacific Rim," *Business Horizons,* March/April 1989, pp. 3–13.

20. "The Chief Executives in Year 2000 Will Be Experienced Abroad," *The Wall Street Journal,* February 27, 1989, p. A1ff.; Christopher A. Bartlett, "MNCs: Get off the Reorganization Merry-Go-Round," *Harvard Business Review,* March–April 1983, pp. 138–46; James M. Hulbert, William K. Brant, and Raimar Richers, "Marketing Planning in the Multinational Subsidiary: Practices and Problems," *Journal of Marketing,* Summer 1980, pp. 7–16; Raj Aggarwal, "The Strategic Challenge of the Evolving Global Economy," *Business Horizons,* July/August 1987, pp. 38–44.

Chapter 23

1. "Gorbachev's Reforms: Will They Work?" *Business Week,* June 5, 1989, pp. 52–89.

2. "After the Beep: The Message Is Convenience Matters Most," *The Wall Street Journal,* September 19, 1989, pp. B1–2; "Design Is Hot in the Cold Business," *Insight,* September 18, 1989, pp. 44–45; "Will U.S. Warm to Refrigerated Dishes?" *The Wall Street Journal,* August 18, 1989, p. B1; "As 'Fresh Refrigerated' Foods Gain Favor, Concerns about Safety Rise," *The Wall Street Journal,* March 11, 1988, p. 27; "Life in the Express Lane," *Time,* June 16, 1986, p. 64.

3. "Smart Cards: Pocket Power," *Newsweek,* July 31, 1989, pp. 54–55; "How America Has Run Out of Time," *Time,* April 24, 1989, pp. 58–67; Cheryl Russell, "What's Your Hurry," *American Demographics,* April 1989, p. 2; Ruth Hamel, "Living in Traffic," *American Demographics,* March 1989, pp. 49–51.

4. Jagdip Singh, "Consumer Complaint Intentions and Behavior: Definitional and Taxonomical Issues," *Journal of Marketing,* January 1988, pp. 93–107; "Most Consumers Shun Luxuries, Seek Few Frills But Better Service," *The Wall Street Journal,* September 19, 1989, pp. B1–2; "Don't Just Meet Customer Expectations—Exceed Them," *Marketing News,* March 13, 1989, p. 5ff.; "Business Marketers Make Customer Service Job for All," *Marketing News,* January 30, 1989, pp. 1–2; "Keep 'em Satisfied: Competitive Heat Is on to Learn What the Customer Really Wants," *Marketing News,* January 2, 1989, p. 1ff.; "Banks Stress Resolving Complaints to Win Small Customers' Favor," *The Wall Street Journal,* December 8, 1986, p. 31; Robert B. Woodruff, Ernest R. Cadotte, and Roger L. Jenkins, "Modeling Consumer Satisfaction Processes Using Experience-Based Norms," *Journal of Marketing Research,* August 1983, pp. 296–304; James U. McNeal, "Consumer Satisfaction: The Measure of Marketing Effectiveness," *MSU Business Topics,* Summer 1969, p. 33; John F. Gaski and Michael J. Etzel, "The Index of Consumer Sentiment Toward Marketing," *Journal of Marketing,* July 1986, pp. 71–81; A. Parasuraman, Valarie A. Zeithaml, and Leonard L. Berry, "SERVQUAL: A Multiple-Item Scale for Measuring Consumer Perceptions of Service Quality," *Journal of Retailing,* Spring 1988, pp. 12–40; Teresa A. Swartz and Stephen W. Brown, "Consumer and Provider Expectations and Experiences in Evaluating Professional Service Quality," *Journal of the Academy of Marketing Science,* Spring 1989, p. 189ff.

5. Cheryl Russell, "People Who Lust after Big Numbers," *American Demographics,* May 1989, p. 2; "TvB Rebuts Prof: Adds Its Voice to Defense of Ads," *Advertising Age,* May 1, 1989, p. 26; "Prof: TV Ads Not as Effective as Price and Promotions," *Marketing News,* March

27, 1989, p. 7; "IRI Research Bolsters Value of Advertising," *Advertising Age,* March 6, 1989, p. 71; "Don't Blame Television, Irate Readers Say," *The Wall Street Journal,* March 1, 1989, p. B6; "Television Ads Ring Up No Sale in Study," *The Wall Street Journal,* February 15, 1989, p. B6. For classic discussions of the problem and mechanics of measuring the efficiency of marketing, see Stanley C. Hollander, "Measuring the Cost and Value of Marketing," *Business Topics,* Summer 1961, pp. 17–26; Reavis Cox, *Distribution in a High-Level Economy* (Englewood Cliffs, N.J.: Prentice-Hall, 1965).

6. Hiram C. Barksdale and William D. Perreault, Jr., "Can Consumers Be Satisfied?" *MSU Business Topics,* Spring 1980, pp. 19–30.

7. "If You Can't Trust the BBB, to Whom Do You Turn Then?" *The Wall Street Journal,* January 15, 1988, p. 1ff.; Jon Han, "How the BBB Works on the Consumer's Behalf," *Chicago Daily News,* May 8, 1976, p. 26; Claes Fornell and Robert A. Westbrook, "The Vicious Circle of Consumer Complaints," *Journal of Marketing,* Summer 1984, pp. 68–78; Hiram C. Barksdale, Jr., Terry E. Powell, and Earnestine Hargrove, "Complaint Voicing by Industrial Buyers," *Industrial Marketing Management,* May 1984, pp. 93–100; Theodore Levitt, "After the Sale Is Over . . . ," *Harvard Business Review,* September–October 1983, pp. 87–93; Alan R. Andreasen and Arthur Best, "Consumers Complain—Does Business Respond?" *Harvard Business Review,* July–August 1977, pp. 100–101; Claes Fornell and Birger Wernerfelt, "Defensive Marketing Strategy by Customer Complaint Management: A Theoretical Analysis," *Journal of Marketing Research,* November 1987, pp. 337–46.

8. "Ethics Codes Spread Despite Skepticism," *The Wall Street Journal,* July 15, 1988, p. 19; "What Bosses Think About Corporate Ethics," *The Wall Street Journal,* April 6, 1988, p. 27; "For These M.B.A.s, Class Became Exercise in Corporate Espionage," *The Wall Street Journal,* March 22, 1988, p. 37; "Businesses Are Signing Up for Ethics 101," *Business Week,* February 15, 1988, pp. 56–57; "Unfuzzing Ethics for Managers," *Fortune,* November 23, 1987, pp. 229–34; "Nature or Nurture? Study Blames Ethical Lapses on Corporate Goals," *The Wall Street Journal,* October 9, 1987, p. 31; Robert Bartels, "Is Marketing Defaulting Its Responsibilities?" *Journal of Marketing,* Fall 1983, pp. 32–35; Gene Laczniak, "Frameworks for Analyzing Marketing Ethics," *Journal of Macromarketing* 3, no. 1 (1983), pp. 7–8; Alan R. Andreasen, "Judging Marketing in the 1980s," *Journal of Macromarketing* 2, no. 1 (1982), pp. 7–13; Shelby D. Hunt, Van R. Wood, and Lawrence B. Chonko, "Corporate Ethical Values and Organizational Commitment in Marketing," *Journal of Marketing,* July 1989, pp. 79–90; Clarke Caywood and Gene R. Laczniak, "Ethics and Personal Selling: Death of a Salesman as an Ethical Primer," *Journal of Personal Selling and Sales Management,* August 1986, p. 81; Jerry W. Anderson, Jr., "Social Responsibility and the Corporation," *Business Horizons,* July/August 1986, pp. 22–27.

9. E. H. Chamberlin, "Product Heterogeneity and Public Policy," *American Economic Review,* May 1950, p. 86.

10. For more on this point, see Robert L. Steiner, "Does Advertising Lower Consumer Prices?" *Journal of Marketing,* October 1973, pp. 19–26; Robert L. Steiner, "Marketing Productivity in Consumer Goods Industries—A Vertical Perspective," *Journal of Marketing,* January 1978, pp. 60–70; see also Robert B. Archibald, Clyde A. Haulman, and Carlisle E. Moody, Jr., "Quality, Price, Advertising, and Published Quality Ratings," *Journal of Consumer Research,* March 1983, pp. 347–56.

11. Arnold J. Toynbee, *America and World Revolution* (New York: Oxford University Press, 1966), pp. 144–45; see also John Kenneth Galbraith, *Economics and the Public Purpose* (Boston: Houghton Mifflin, 1973), pp. 144–45.

12. Russell J. Tomsen, "Take It Away," *Newsweek,* October 7, 1974, p. 21.

13. J. L. Engledow, "Was Consumer Satisfaction a Pig in a Poke?" *MSU Business Topics,* April 1977, p. 92.

14. "Deregulating America," *Business Week,* November 28, 1983, pp. 80–82; E. T. Grether, "Marketing and Public Policy: A Contemporary View," *Journal of Marketing,* July 1974, pp. 2–7; "Intellectuals Should Re-Examine the Marketplace: It Supports Them, Helps Keep Them Free," *Advertising Age,* January 28, 1963; David A. Heenan, "Congress Rethinks America's Competitiveness," *Business Horizons,* May/June 1989, pp. 11–16; Irvin Grossack and David A. Heenan, "Cooperation, Competition, and Antitrust: Two Views," *Business Horizons,* September/October 1986, pp. 24–28; Donald P. Robin and R. Eric Reidenbach, "Identifying Critical Problems for Mutual Cooperation Between the Public and Private Sectors: A Marketing Perspective," *Journal of the Academy of Marketing Science,* Fall 1986, pp. 1–12.

15. Frederick Webster, *Social Aspects of Marketing* (Englewood Cliffs, N.J.: Prentice-Hall, 1974), p. 32.

16. "The Community's Persuasive Power," *Insight,* December 12, 1988, pp. 58–59; "It's All Relative: Mutual Funds Discover 'Socially Responsible' Is in Eye of Beholder," *The Wall Street Journal,* May 20, 1987, p. 37; "Companies as Citizens: Should They Have a Conscience?" *The Wall Street Journal,* February 19, 1987, p. 29; "New Book Rates Consumer Firms on Social Issues," *The Wall Street Journal,* January 16, 1987, p. 25; John H. Antil, "Socially Responsible Consumers: Profile and Implications for Public Policy," *Journal of Macromarketing* 4, no. 2 (1984), pp. 18–39; James T. Roth and Lissa Benson, "Intelligent Consumption: An Attractive Alternative to the Marketing Concept," *MSU Business Topics,* Winter 1974, pp. 30–34; "As Firms' Personnel Files Grow, Worker Privacy Falls," *The Wall Street Journal,* April 19, 1989, p. B1; "The $3 Billion Question: Whose Info Is It, Anyway?" *Business Week,* July 4, 1988, pp. 106–7; "Privacy: Companies Are Delving Further into Employees' Personal Lives . . . ," *Business Week,* March 28, 1988, pp. 61–68; "Federal Agencies Press Data-Base Firms to Curb Access to 'Sensitive' Information," *The Wall Street Journal,* February 5, 1987, p. 23; Warren A. French, Melvin R. Crask, and Fred H. Mader, "Retailers' Assessment of the Shoplifting Problem," *Journal of Retailing,* Winter 1984, pp. 108–15; "How Shoplifting Is Draining the Economy," *Business Week,* October 15, 1979,

pp. 119–23; Robert E. Wilkes, "Fraudulent Behavior by Consumers," *Journal of Marketing,* October 1978, pp. 67–75; Donald P. Robin and R. Eric Reidenbach, "Social Responsibility, Ethics, and Marketing Strategy: Closing the Gap between Concept and Application," *Journal of Marketing,* January 1987, pp. 44–58.

17. "Trashing a $150 Billion Business," *Fortune,* August 28, 1989, pp. 90–98; "For Consumers, Ecology Comes Second," *The Wall Street Journal,* August 23, 1989, p. B1; "Wal-Mart Throws 'Green' Gauntlet," *Advertising Age,* August 21, 1989, p. 1ff.; "A New Sales Pitch: The Environment," *Business Week,* July 24, 1989, p. 50; "Waste Not, Want Not? Not Necessarily," *Business Week,* July 17, 1989, pp. 116–17; "Cash from Trash," *Fortune,* June 19, 1989, p. 16; Cheryl Russell, "Guilty, as Charged," *American Demographics,* February 1989, p. 2; "Here Comes the Big New Cleanup," *Fortune,* November 21, 1988, pp. 102–18; "Florida Readies Broad Assault on Garbage," *The Wall Street Journal,* July 20, 1988, p. 25; "Garbage, Garbage, Everywhere," *Time,* September 5, 1988, pp. 81–82.

18. "Exxon's Army Scrubs Beaches, but Many Don't Stay Cleaned," *The Wall Street Journal,* July 27, 1989, p. 1ff.; "An Oil Slick Trips Up Exxon," *Time,* April 24, 1989, p. 46; "The Two Alaskas," *Time,* April 17, 1989, pp. 56–67; "CFC Curb to Save Ozone Will Be Costly," *The Wall Street Journal,* March 28, 1988, p. 6; "Du Pont Plans to Phase Out CFC Output," *The Wall Street Journal,* March 25, 1988, p. 2; "Big Electric Utilities and Consumers Push Conservation Strategy," *The Wall Street Journal,* December 8, 1987, p. 1ff.; Dan R. Dalton and Richard A. Cosier, "The Four Faces of Social Responsibility," *Business Horizons,* May/June 1982, pp. 19–27; Y. Hugh Furuhashi and E. Jerome McCarthy, *Social Issues of Marketing in the American Economy* (Columbus, Ohio: Grid, 1971); James Owens, "Business Ethics: Age-Old Ideal, Now Real," *Business Horizons,* February 1978, pp. 26–30; Steven F. Goodman, "Quality of Life: The Role of Business," *Business Horizons,* June 1978, pp. 36–37; Stanley J. Shapiro, "Marketing in a Conserver Society," *Business Horizons,* April 1978, pp. 3–13; Johan Arndt, "How Broad Should the Marketing Concept Be?" *Journal of Marketing,* January 1978, pp. 101–3.

Illustration Credits

Chapter 1   3 (left) Boy drinking orange juice, *Minute Maid Country Style Juice is a registered trademark of The Coca-Cola Company and is used with permission;* (center) Fast-food checkout, *courtesy Marriott Corporation;* (right) Jeans, *courtesy Lands' End, Inc.;* 4 (left) Prince ad, *courtesy Prince Manufacturing, Inc.;* (right) Spaulding ad, *courtesy Spaulding;* 6 New York City neon, *Roy Morsch/The Stock Market,* 7 (left) Fantastic, *courtesy Dow Brands;* (right) Sony ad, *courtesy Sony Corporation of America;* 8 Supermarket, *Joseph Sterling/Tony Stone Worldwide;* 9 (left) Family in bank, *courtesy Household International;* (right) Banana shopping, *© Tom Tracy/ After Image, 1987;* 11 Chinese students, *Peter Turnley/ Black Star;* 12 Sale sign, *© Brent Jones;* Gun control ad, *courtesy, Handgun Control, Inc., Washington, D.C.;* 14 Central market, *Luis Villotai/The Stock Market;* Exhibit 1–2, *adapted from Wroe Alderson, "Factors Governing the Development of Marketing Channels,"* in Marketing Channels for Manufactured Products, *ed. Richard M. Clewett (Homewood, Ill.: Richard D. Irwin, 1954), p. 7;* 16 Women weaving, *Cameramann International;* 17 Broccoli farmer, *Sergio Dorantes;* Cars, *Robert Essel/The Stock Market;* 18 Exhibit 1–3, *adapted from William McInnes, "A Conceptual Approach to Marketing,"* in Theory in Marketing, *2nd ser., ed. Reavie Cox, Wroe Alderson, and Stanley J. Shapiro (Homewood, Ill.: Richard D. Irwin, 1964), pp. 51–67;* 19 Fruit packing, *Jay Freis/The Image Bank;* (left) Billboards, *courtesy Gannett Company, Inc.;* (right) UPS ad, *courtesy United Parcel Service of America, Inc.;* 20 Exhibit 1–4, *model suggested by Professor A. A. Brogowicz, Western Michigan University;* 21 Airplane assembly, *Martin Rogers/Stock Boston*

Chapter 2   25 (left) Nike Air Max, *courtesy of NIKE, Inc.;* (center) Pizza take-out, *reproduced with permission, © PepsiCo, Inc. 1988;* (right) Woman with Borden products, *courtesy Borden, Inc.;* 28 Product development team, *Ron Seymour/Tony Stone Worldwide;* 29 (left) National Guard ad, *courtesy Army National Guard;* (right) Drug abuse ad, *courtesy of Partnership for a Drug-Free America;* 31 Exhibit 2–3, *adapted from R. F. Vizza, T. E. Chambers, and E. J. Cook,* Adoption of the Marketing Concept—Fact or Fiction *(New York: Sales Executive Club, Inc., 1967), pp. 13–15;* ATM, *© 1985 Joe Bator/The Stock Market;* 32 Smyrna Hospital ad, *courtesy Smyrna Hospital;* Neighborhood Watch sign, *Scott Wanner/Journalism Services;* Alcoholic beverage control ad, *courtesy Virginia Department of Alcoholic Beverage Control;* 33 Slice, *Michael J. Hruby;* 35 Compaq logo, *reprinted with permission of Compaq Computer Corporation; all rights reserved;* 36 People, *Tom Biethaume/Parallel Productions;* Stereo shopping, *Gabe Palmer/The Stock Market;* 38 Minute Maid ads, *Minute Maid is a registered trademark of The Coca-Cola Company and is used with permission;* 40 (left) Chevy Astro ad, *courtesy General Motors Corporation;* (right) GM ad, *reproduced with permission from General Motors Corporation;* 45 Van at beach, *Roy Morsch/The Stock Market;* 47 Watch ads, *reprint permission granted by Timex Corporation*

Chapter 3   63 (left) Toothpaste, *Jim Whitmer Photography;* (center) Magazine covers, *Phillip Saltonstall/Onyx/*Sports Illustrated for Kids; *Heinz Kluetmeier/*Sports Illustrated; (right) Motel sign, *courtesy of Marriott Corporation;* 65 L'Oréal ad, *courtesy of Cosmair, Inc.;* 66 Exhibit 3–2, *Igor Ansoff,* Corporate Strategy *(New York: McGraw-Hill, 1965);* 68 Hallmark shop, *Kirk Schlea/Berg & Associates;* 69 (left) Check-Up gum, *courtesy Minnetonka, Inc.;* (right) Crest toothpaste, *© The Procter & Gamble Company; used with permission;* 71 Map presentation, *Don Albrecht/ Camera Graphics;* 75 Nissan ads, *courtesy Nissan Motor Corporation in the U.S.A.;* 76 Ketchup ads, *courtesy Heinz U.S.A.;* 78 (left) Pentax camera ad, *courtesy Pentax Corporation;* (right) Sony camera ad, *courtesy Sony Corporation of America;* 82 Rental sign, *Glennon Donahue/Tony Stone Worldwide;* 83 Young couple, *David Stoecklein/The Stock Market;* 86 People at pool, *Rich Meyer/The Stock Market;* Computer training, *Chris Jones/The Stock Market;* 87 (left) Colgate toothpaste, *courtesy Colgate-Palmolive Company;* (right) EpiSmile toothpaste, *© 1989 EPI Products USA, Inc.;* 89 Exhibit 3–16, *Russell I. Haley, "Benefit Segmentation: A Decision-Oriented Research Tool,"* Journal of Marketing, *July 1968, p. 33*

Chapter 4   93 (left) UPS plane, *courtesy United Parcel Service of America, Inc.;* (center) Computer training, *reproduced with permission of AT&T;* (right) Refrigerator, *courtesy Motorola;* 94 Little Tikes ad, *courtesy The Little Tikes Company;* 96 Close-out sign, *Joan Sloane/Berg & Associates;* 98 Nike ads, *courtesy of NIKE, Inc.;* 100 Potato farmer, *Martin Rogers/Tony Stone Worldwide;* 102 Ginger-

bread ad, *courtesy Hammermill Papers;* 103 Clorox, *Michael J. Hruby;* 105 Exhibit 4–5, Statistical Abstract of the United States, 1988, *p. 450;* 106 Communication chain, *courtesy NEC America, Inc.;* 107 Consumer magazines, *Scott Wanner/Journalism Services;* 108 Wal-Mart shopper, *courtesy Wal-Mart, Inc.;* 111 (left) Wastewater ad, *courtesy Matlack, Inc.;* (right) Birth control ad, *courtesy Lexis Pharmaceuticals, Inc.;* 113 Bicycle ads, *courtesy Schwinn Bicycle Company;* 117 Exhibit 4–11, *adapted from M. G. Allen, "Strategic Problems Facing Today's Corporate Planner," speech given at the Academy of Management, 36th Annual Meeting, Kansas City, Missouri, 1976*

Chapter 5   123 (left) Computer graphics, *courtesy Information Resources, Inc.;* (center) Consumer survey, *courtesy Campbell Soup Company;* (right) Reading data output, *courtesy General Cinema;* 124 Compass ad, *courtesy Claritas;* 126 IRI Prompt TV screen, *courtesy Information Resources, Inc.;* 127 Marketing managers, *Comstock, Inc.;* 128 Aldus Pagemaker, *portions reprinted with the permission of and copyright Aldus Corporation®, all rights reserved;* 132 Statistical Abstract cover, *courtesy U.S. Department of Commerce, Bureau of the Census;* 133 Information Services catalog, *courtesy National Decision Systems, a target marketing and marketing information company, San Diego, California;* 134 Focus group, *© Stock Imagery/Richard Gross, 1987;* 135 Questionnaire, *courtesy Mid-America Research, Inc.;* 136 Telephone survey, *courtesy U.S. Testing Company, Market Research, Inc.;* 137 Census ad, *courtesy U.S. Census Bureau;* Market researcher, *Ellis Herwig/The Picture Cube;* 139 Bar codes and printout, *Cameramann International;* Store, *courtesy Dominick's Finer Foods, Inc.;* Taste test, *Don Albrecht/Camera Graphics;* 140 SPSS ad, *courtesy of SPSS, Inc.*

Chapter 6   147 (left) Older couple playing croquet; (center) Walking on beach, *reproduced with permission, © PepsiCo, Inc. 1988;* (right) People with fast food, *courtesy of Marriott Corporation;* 149 Exhibit 6–1, *map developed by the authors based on data from* Statistical Abstract of the United States, 1988, *p. 23;* 150 Exhibit 6–2, *map developed by the authors based on data from* Statistical Abstract of the United States, 1988, *p. 23;* 151 Cuban grocery, *Jacques Charlas/Stock Boston;* Fixing bike, *Comstock, Inc.;* 152 (left) Learning Window ad, *courtesy Video Technology Industries, Inc.;* (right) Baby Monitor ad, *courtesy of Hasbro, Inc.;* Exhibit 6–3, Statistical Abstract of the United States, 1988, *p. 59;* 153 Exhibit 6–4, Statistical Abstract of the United States, 1988, *pp. 13, 15, 25;* 154 Clothes shopping, *Victoria Beller-Smith/The Stock Market;* 156 U-Haul truck, *courtesy U-Haul®/Navistar International;* 157 Exhibit 6 5, Statistical Abstract of the United States, 1988, *p. 427;* 158 Exhibit 6–6, Statistical Abstract of the United States, 1988, *p. 428;* 159 Exhibit 6–7, *map developed by the authors based on data from* Statistical Abstract of the United States, 1988, *p. 417;* 160 (left) Jewelry ad, *courtesy Erwin Pearle, Inc.;* (right) Flatware ad, *courtesy Oneida, Inc.;* 161 Exhibit 6–8, *adapted by the authors from* Consumer Expenditure Survey, Interview Survey, 1987, *News Bulletin, U.S. Department of Labor, April 14, 1988;* 163 Exhibit 6–9, *adapted from William D. Wells and George Gubar, "Life Cycle Concept in Marketing Research,"* Journal of Marketing Research, *August 1968, p. 267; see also Patrick E. Murphy and William A. Staples, "A Modernized Family Life Cycle,"* Journal of Consumer Research, *June 1979, pp. 12–22;* 164 Reading The Wall Street Journal, *reproduced with permission, © PepsiCo, Inc. 1988;* (left) Bran Flakes ad, *courtesy of General Foods;* (right) AT&T ad, *courtesy AT&T;* 165 Boy on bike, *George Fry/Genentech, Inc.*

Chapter 7   169 (left) Buying car, *Jeffry Myers/Stock Boston;* (center) Buying stereo, *Chuck Keeler, Jr./Tony Stone Worldwide;* (right) Family shopping, *© Walter Bibikow/The Image Bank;* 172 Exhibit 7–3, *adapted from C. Glenn Walters,* Consumer Behavior, *3rd ed. (Homewood, Ill.: Richard D. Irwin, 1979);* 174 (left) Dog Chow ad, *© 1988 Ralston Purina Company;* (right) Benedryl ad, *courtesy Warner-Lambert Co.;* 176 Lemon Clorox, *courtesy The Clorox Company;* 177 (left) Jewelry ad, *courtesy Mayor's;* (right) Deodorant ad, *courtesy The Gillette Company;* 178 Exhibit 7–6, *Joseph T. Plummer, "The Concept and Application of Life-Style Segmentation,"* Journal of Marketing, *January 1974, pp. 33–37;* 179 Betty Crocker, *used with the permission of General Mills, Inc.;* Buying furniture, *Bohdan Hrynew/Stock Boston;* 180 Buying TV, *courtesy of Sears, Roebuck & Co., 1987 Annual Report;* 181 Exhibit 7–7, *adapted from Steven L. Diamond, Thomas S.*

Robertson, and F. Kent Mitchel, "Consumer Motivation and Behavior," in Marketing Manager's Handbook, ed. S. H. Britt and N. F. Guess (Chicago: Dartnell, 1983), p. 239; 182 Little Tikes products, courtesy of Rubbermaid, Inc.; 184 Buying iron, Frank Cezus/Tony Stone Worldwide; 187 Muesli coupon, courtesy Ralston Purina Company

Chapter 8 193 (left) Aluminum wheels, courtesy Alcoa; (center) Textile vendors, courtesy of Wal-Mart, Inc.; (right) Forest products, courtesy of Canadian Pacific Limited; 194 Exhibit 8–1, County Business Patterns—United States, 1986; Statistical Abstract of the United States, 1988; Information Please Almanac, 1989 (Boston: Houghton Mifflin, 1988); 196 Exhibit 8–2, data adapted from County Business Patterns—United States, 1986, p. 6; 197 Exhibit 8–3, adapted from Standard Industrial Classification Manual, 1987; 199 Exhibit 8–5, Patrick J. Robertson and Charles W. Faris, Industrial Buying and Creative Marketing (Boston: Allyn & Bacon, 1967), p. 33, reprinted by permission of the publisher; Exhibit 8–6, Rowland T. Moriarty, Jr., and Robert E. Spekman, "An Empirical Investigation of the Information Sources Used during the Industrial Buying Process," Journal of Marketing Research, May 1984, pp. 137–47; 200 (left) R.O.I. ad, courtesy Cushman, a Division of Outland Marine Corporation; (right) Welder ad, courtesy GMF Robotics Corporation; 201 Buying group, courtesy Textron/Mason Morfit Photo; 202 GE ad, courtesy GE Lighting; 204 (left) Grain inspection, Cameramann International; (right) Steel inspection, © 1989, Paul Fusco/Magnum Photos; 205 Guaranteed availability ad, courtesy Copeland Corporation; 206 Buying by computer, courtesy The Southland Corporation; 209 Canon copier ad, courtesy Canon USA, Inc.; 210 Supermarket, Ted Horowitz/The Stock Market; Druggist, Charles Gupton/Stock Boston; 211 Retail buying, courtesy of Toys "R" Us, Inc.; 212 (left) BigToys ad, courtesy of BigToys; (right) Edmont ad, courtesy of Edmont

Chapter 9 217 (left) Inspecting refrigerator, Gabe Palmer/General Electric Company; (center) Product development, courtesy The Clorox Company; (right) Pizza delivery reproduced with permission, © PepsiCo, Inc. 1989; 219 (left) Stanley tape rule, courtesy of Stanley Tools; (right) Toyota Quality ad, courtesy of Toyota Motor Sales, U.S.A., Inc.; 221 (left) Construction pipe, courtesy United Brands; (right) Registration desk, courtesy of Marriott Corporation; 222 Procter & Gamble products, Jim Whitmer Photography; 223 (left) Man drinking Gatorade, courtesy Quaker Oats/Bayer, Bess, Vanderwarker; (right) Gatorade Fluid Performance ad, courtesy The Quaker Oats Company; 224 Ice cream truck, William D. Perreault, Jr.; 225 Buying stove, Jim Pickerell/Tony Stone Worldwide; 226 Dannon yogurt, Michael J. Hruby; Holiday Inn sign, Don Smetzer/Tony Stone Worldwide; 228 Earthmover, courtesy Caterpillar Inc.; 230 Lumber and diapers, courtesy of The Procter & Gamble Company; 232 (left) Checking wheels, courtesy of Ford Motor Co.; (right) Supply room, courtesy Boise Cascade Corporation; 234 Window washers, Dario Perla/After Image; 237 HERSHEY'S syrup ad, courtesy of Hershey Foods Corporation. HERSHEY'S is a registered trademark of Hershey Foods Corporation and is used with permission; 239 Fun Fruit ad, courtesy Sunkist Growers, Inc.; 242 (left) Delivery package, courtesy Boise Cascade Corporation; (right) Pop Quartet, reproduced with the permission of Del Monte Corporation; 244 (left) Service guarantee ad, courtesy AT&T, © 1989; (right) Roadside assistance ad, courtesy Volvo North America Corporation

Chapter 10 249 (left) Design engineers, courtesy Alcoa; (center) Fax machine, Stacy Pick/Stock Boston; (right) Pull-top cans, courtesy Anheuser-Busch Companies, Inc.; 251 Syringe ad, photo courtesy of Amoco Chemical Company; 252 Executive on cellular phone, Frank White, © 1987; 253 Extra gum, Michael J. Hruby; Almost Home cookies, Scott Wanner/Journalism Services; 254 (left) Hanes Activewear, © 1988 Gable Estates & Co., represented by the Roger Richman Agency, Inc., Beverly Hills, CA; (right) American Lifestyle rugs, courtesy Burlington Industries, Inc.; 256 Saran Wrap, Scott Wanner/Journalism Services; 257 Teddy Grahams, Michael J. Hruby; 258 Liquid Tide, Michael J. Hruby; 260 Plenum Cable ad, courtesy Du Pont Company; advertising for Du Pont by Ketchum Advertising, Philadelphia, PA; 261 Exhibit 10–5, adapted from Frank R. Bacon, Jr., and Thomas W. Butler, Planned Innovation (Ann Arbor: University of Michigan Institute of Science and Technology, 1980); 262 Exhibit 10–6, adapted from Management Research Department, Booz, Allen, and Hamilton, Inc.; 263 Bomb ad, courtesy M/A/R/C; 264 Exhibit 10–7, adapted from Philip Kotler, "What Consumerism Means for Marketers," Harvard Business Review, May-June 1972, pp. 55–56; Jet ski, Focus on Sports, Inc.; 265 Lee Iacocca ad, courtesy Chrysler Corporation; 267 CADAM ad, photo courtesy of CADAM, Inc.; Pringles lab, courtesy The Procter & Gamble Company; 268 Taste test, courtesy of The Clorox Company

Chapter 11 273 (left) Bread delivery, courtesy Anheuser-Busch Companies, Inc.; (center) Outdoor market, Arthur Meyerson/The Coca-Cola Company; (right) Stocking toothpaste, courtesy Wetterau, International; 276 (left) Golf ball imprinting, Richard Pasley/Stock Boston; (center) Packing golf balls, Richard Pasley/Stock Boston; (right) Golf shop, Richard Pasley/Stock Boston; (bottom) Sporting

goods store, courtesy of Outdoor Sports Headquarters, Inc.; 277 Bulk breaking, courtesy The Southland Corporation; 278 Video store, David Strick; 279 (left) Carousel ad, courtesy The Franklin Mint; (right) Egg ad, courtesy The Travelers Insurance Company; 280 Fuller Brush catalog, courtesy The Fuller Brush Company; 281 7-Eleven store, courtesy The Southland Corporation; 283 (left) Doublemint gum, Wm. Wrigley Jr. Company; (right) Godiva chocolates, courtesy Godiva Chocolatier, Inc.; 284 Espirit logo, courtesy Espirit De Corp; 285 Televisions, Rob Nelson/Stock Boston; 288 (left) Toshiba fax machine, courtesy Toshiba America Information Systems Inc.; (right) Canon faxphone, courtesy Canon USA, Inc.; 289 Map ad, courtesy Sherwood; 290 Ace Hardware logo, courtesy Ace Hardware Corporation; 291 Exhibit 11–4, adapted from D. J. Bowersox and E. J. McCarthy, "Strategic Development of Planned Vertical Marketing Systems," in Vertical Marketing Systems, ed. Louis Bucklin (Glenview, Ill.: Scott, Foresman, 1970)

Chapter 12 295 (left) Eddie Bauer store, copyright Steve Niedorf, 1989; (center) Checkout lines, courtesy of Toys "R" Us, Inc.; (right) Shopping for children's clothes, Chuck Keeler/Tony Stone Worldwide; 298 Exhibit 12–2, adapted from Louis Bucklin, "Retail Strategy and the Classification of Consumer Goods," Journal of Marketing, January 1963, pp. 50–55; 299 Talbots' store, General Mills, Inc., copyright Steve Niedorf, 1989; 301 Oscar de la Renta counter, courtesy of Avon Products; 302 Grocery cart, reprinted from Marketing News, published by the American Marketing Association, January 2, 1989, p. 51; 303 Service Merchandise store, courtesy of Service Merchandise; 304 Wal-Mart interior, courtesy of Wal-Mart, Inc.; Bigg's superstore, Henry Groskinsky © 1989; 305 Man eating soup, courtesy of Campbell Soup Company; 306 Mail-order catalogs, Scott Wanner/Journalism Services, courtesy L. L. Bean, Inc., courtesy Lands' End, Inc., courtesy Marshall Field's, copyright © The Sharper Image; 307 Home Shopping Club, courtesy of Home Shopping Network; 309 (left) No Nonsense ad, courtesy Kayser-Roth Hosiery, Inc.; (right) Microwave popcorn, courtesy Golden Valley Microwave Foods, Inc.; 312 Exhibit 12–7, based on data from 1982 Census of Retail Trade; 313 J. C. Penney store, Joseph H. Jacobson/Journalism Services; 316 Shopping center, Craig Hammell; 317 Greetings Express, courtesy Electronic Greetings

Chapter 13 323 (left) Wholesale Only sign, Cameramann International; (center) Oranges, Glenn Steiner/Joan Kramer & Associates; (right) Delivery truck, Joe Jacobson/Journalism Services; 325 Warehouse storage, Chuck Keeler/Tony Stone Worldwide; Southland ad, courtesy Southland Distribution Center; 326 Exhibit 13–1, based on data from 1982 Census of Wholesale Trade; 328 Restaurant supply truck, courtesy IU International; 329 Specialty wholesaler, courtesy Phoenix Distributors; 331 Mail-order catalog, courtesy Rand Material Handling Equipment; Blue Diamond almonds, Michael J. Hruby; Rack jobbers, Mary Ellen Zang; 335 Oriental shipment, David Barnes/The Stock Market; 337 (left) Teklogix ad, courtesy Teklogix; (right) Buschman ad, courtesy The Buschman Company; 338 Computer inventory, Charles Gupton/Stock Boston; 339 Bar codes ad, courtesy of Dennison Industrial Systems; 340 Federal Express plane, Brian Seed/Tony Stone Worldwide

Chapter 14 343 (left) Banana cartons, Will McIntyre; (center) Distribution person, courtesy of The Clorox Company; (right) Coke trucks, Coca-Cola is a registered trademark of The Coca-Cola Company and is used with permission; 344 UPS ad, courtesy of United Parcel Service; 345 Compact disks, photo: courtesy Best Buy Co., Inc.; 346 Satellite dish, Cameramann International; 347 Budweiser truck, courtesy Anheuser-Busch Companies, Inc.; 348 Exhibit 14–2, adapted from B. J. LaLonde and P. H. Zinzer, Customer Service: Meaning and Measurement (Chicago: National Council of Physical Distribution Management, 1976); and D. Phillip Locklin, Transportation for Management (Homewood, Ill.: Richard D. Irwin, 1972); 349 Exhibit 14–3, Statistical Abstract of the United States, 1988, p. 570; Box cars, Brownie Harris/The Stock Market; 351 Pressureaide railroad car, courtesy ACF Shippers Car Line Division; 352 Sony video ad, courtesy Sony Corporation of America; 353 CSX ad, courtesy of CSX Corporation; APC truck trailer, Ovak Arslanian; 354 Grain storage facility, Wayne Bladholm; 355 Pepsi, Scott Wanner/Journalism Services; 356 Public warehouse, Joe Jacobson/Journalism Services; Exhibit 14–5, adapted from Louis W. Stern and Adel I. El-Ansary, Marketing Channels (Englewood Cliffs, N.J.: Prentice-Hall, 1977), p. 150; 357 Distribution center, photo: courtesy Best Buy Co., Inc.; 361 (left) Subaru car lot, A. & M. Pechter/The Stock Market; (right) Computer system, photo courtesy of Unisys Corporation; Pepperidge Farm cookies, Michael J. Hruby

Chapter 15 365 (left) Pepsi logo on sail, reproduced with permission, © PepsiCo, Inc., 1988; (center) Checking magazine layout, reprinted courtesy of Eastman Kodak Company; (right) Hot-air balloons, Vince Streano/Tony Stone Worldwide; 367 (left) Polaroid videocassette ad, courtesy of Polaroid Corporation; (right) Eveready ad, courtesy of Eveready Battery Company; 370 Sassy ad, courtesy of Sassy Magazine; 372 Good Housekeeping seal, courtesy of Good Housekeeping;

3-D pop-up ads, *Ted Morrison;* 373 Spiegel ad, *courtesy of Spiegel, Inc., photographer: Dennis Manarchy;* 376 McGraw-Hill ad, *courtesy of McGraw-Hill, Inc.;* 377 Yellow Pages directories, *courtesy of Bell Atlantic Corporation;* 378 *Target Marketing* magazine, *courtesy of North American Publishing Company;* 379 Crayola crayons, *Michael J. Hruby;* 380 (left) Froot Loops ad, *® Kellogg Company © 1988 Kellogg Company;* (right) Ruffles ad, *courtesy of Frito-Lay, Inc.;* 381 Wholesaling sales reps, *courtesy of Dean Foods;* 383 Billboard, *Scott Wanner/Journalism Services;* Yellow Pages ad, *Scott Wanner/Journalism Services;* Frequent Flier card, *courtesy of United Airlines;* 384 Bicycle race, *Tim Welsh/Stock Imagery;* 385 Pepsi display, *courtesy PepsiCo, Inc.;* 386 Promotion managers, *Gabe Palmer/After Image;* 387 Trade show, *J. Maenza/The Image Bank*

Chapter 16   393 (left) Asking for order, *Jim Pickerell/Tony Stone Worldwide;* (center) Salesmen with map, *Jon Feingersh Photography;* (right) Missionary salesman, *Greg Mancuso/Uniphoto;* 395 Two men with computer and parts, *Steve Dunwell;* 398 Order getter in meeting, *photo: courtesy Best Buy Co., Inc.;* 399 Sales rep with retailer, *photo courtesy of Hewlett-Packard Company;* 400 Konica fax machine ad, *courtesy Konica Business Machines U.S.A., Inc.;* 402 Retail order taker, *courtesy of Batus, Inc.;* 403 Bartles & Jaymes display, *© Bartles & Jaymes Co. 1986, photograph by John Harding;* Missionary salesperson, *Mary Ellen Zang;* Gore-Tex fabric, *courtesy Du Pont;* 406 IBM training class, *© Bill Ballenberg Photography;* 407 Sales training center, *courtesy The Goodyear Tire & Rubber Company;* 409 Sales by region, *produced with Harvard Graphics from Software Publishing Corporation;* 411 Exhibit 16–2, *suggested by Professor A. A. Brogowicz, Western Michigan University;* 412 Sales rep on phone, *courtesy of Nekoosa Packaging;* 413 Toshiba ad, *courtesy of Toshiba America Information Systems, Inc., Computer Systems Division;* 415 Sales presentation, *Comstock, Inc.*

Chapter 17   419 (left) California Raisin, *courtesy California Raisin Advisory Board;* (center) Supermarket shopper, *Dick Loria/After Image;* (right) Planning advertising program, *courtesy of The Gillette Company;* 421 Exhibit 17–2, *Advertising Age, September 27, 1989, p. 1;* 422 (left) Log Cabin ad, *LOG CABIN is a registered trademark of General Foods Corporation;* (right) Certs ad, *courtesy Warner-Lambert Co.;* 423 Exhibit 17–3, *adapted from R. J. Lavidge and G. A. Steiner, "A Model for Predictive Measurements of Advertising Effectiveness,"* Journal of Marketing, *October 1961, p. 61;* 424 (left) Webster's dictionary ad, *by permission, Merriam-Webster, Inc., publisher of the Merriam-Webster ® dictionaries. © 1988;* (right) Dow college student ad, *photo courtesy The Dow Chemical Company;* 425 (left) California Raisins, *courtesy California Raisin Advisory Board;* (right) Sun Maid raisin ad, *courtesy Sun Maid Growers of California;* 426 Tyco versus Lego ad, *courtesy Tyco Toys, Inc.;* 427 Billboard, *courtesy BMW of North America, Inc.;* 429 Exhibit 17–4, *data from Standard Rate and Data Service and estimates from* Advertising Age, *May 15, 1989, p. 24;* 430 MTV ad, *courtesy of MTV Networks, Inc.;* 431 Consumer magazines, *Don Smetzer/Tony Stone Worldwide;* 432 Yellow Pages ad, *courtesy Yellow Pages Publishers Association;* 433 Billboard, *courtesy The Des Moines Register/Muller + Co.;* 435 Cheerios ad, *courtesy General Mills, Inc.;* 436 Exhibit 17–6, Advertising Age, *March 20, 1989, p. 3;* 437 Ad campaign, *Richard Gross/The Stock Market;* 439 Kodak film ad, *reprinted courtesy of Eastman Kodak Company*

Chapter 18   445 (left) Fruit stand, *J. Myers/H. Armstrong Roberts;* (center) Price changes, *Frank Williams/Bookworks, Inc.;* (right) Advertising department, *photo: courtesy Best Buy Co., Inc.;* 450 Sears store, *© Marc Pokempner;* 453 UPS ad, *courtesy United Parcel Service of America, Inc.;* 454 Hewlett-Packard logo, *courtesy of Hewlett-Packard Company;* 455 (left) Dinner Supreme ad, *courtesy of Stouffer Foods Corporation;* (right) Budget Gourmet ad, *courtesy of The All American Gourmet Company/Dilorio Wergeles;* 457 Crown Books, *Sue Markson;* 458 Invoice, *courtesy Servco, Inc.;* 459 American Express sign, *Larry Mulvehill/Photo Researchers;* 460 Sale in store, *Andy Freeberg Photography;* 461 Nut & Honey Crunch coupon, *® Kellogg Company © 1989 Kellogg Company;* 462 Pearle Vision promotion, *courtesy Pearle, Inc.;* 463 Truck hauling products, *courtesy of IU International;* 465 Borden's condensed milk, *Michael J. Hruby*

Chapter 19   483 (left) Calculator, *© Stock Imagery/Richard Gross, 1990;* (center) Sign, *courtesy of Wal-Mart, Inc.;* (right) Furniture sale, *John Coletti/The Picture Cube;* 485 Electric drill, *Don Smetzer/Tony Stone Worldwide;* 487 Milk on shelves, *Peter Menzel/Stock Boston;* 489 Orange juice assembly line, *Minute Maid is a registered trademark of The Coca-Cola Company and is used with permission;* 493 Owens/Corning Fiberglas logo, *courtesy of Owens-Corning Fiberglas Corporation;* 495 Dodge Daytona ad, *courtesy of Dodge Division, Chrysler Motors;* 505 Osram ad, *courtesy of OSRAM Corporation;* Coffee on store shelf, *Scott Wanner/Journalism Services;* 506 Prices in window, *Cameramann International;* 507 Rolex ad, *courtesy of Rolex Watch USA, Inc.;* 508 Affordable Furniture ad, *courtesy of Affordable Furniture®*

Chapter 20   515 (left) Computer bar graph, *Gabe Palmer/The Stock Market;*

(center) Marketing meeting, *courtesy of The Clorox Company;* (right) Perishable product, *Robert Frerck/Odyssey Productions;* 517 IBM ad, *courtesy of International Business Machines Corporation;* 518 Discussing computer sales graph, *Camera Graphics;* 520 Bread on shelves, *Gabe Palmer/The Stock Market;* Exhibit 20–2, Sales and Marketing Management, *December 1988;* 521 *Paperboard Packaging* magazine, *courtesy of Paperboard Packaging;* 523 Manager at table, *Jon Feingersh Photography;* Slice ad and survey, *© PepsiCo, Inc., 1985;* 526 Zenith Data Systems ads, *courtesy of Zenith Data Systems Corporation;* 527 Estimated response graph, *William D. Perreault, Jr.;* 530 Jolt ad, *courtesy The Jolt Company, Inc.;* 531 Lotus 1–2–3 ad, *courtesy Lotus Development Corporation;* 533 Parade Publications ad, *courtesy of Parade Publications, Inc., and Warwick Baker & Fiore, Inc.;* 535 Technical rep and manager, *Cameramann International/Courtesy Best Kosher Sausage Co.;* Seafood on ice, *courtesy of Sara Lee Corporation;* 537 Orange juice assembly line, *Ron Sherman/Uniphoto;* 539 Emergency sale sign, *Ken Sexton/Nawrocki Stock Photo;* 541 Viewpoint ad, *courtesy of Full Spectrum Graphic Design, Santa Rosa;* 542 Managers and scheduling board, *courtesy of Sears, Roebuck & Co.*

Chapter 21   545 (left) Budgeter, *courtesy Raytheon/Brownie Harris photo;* (center) Manager with printout, *Jon Feingersh Photography;* (right) Hand-held scanner, *Cameramann International;* 546 Managers with map, *Mary Ellen Zang;* 547 Computer graphics, *reprinted from* PC Magazine, *December 22, 1987, copyright © 1987 Ziff Communications Company;* 553 Sales analysis, *Gabe Palmer/The Stock Market;* 555 (left) Worker cutting denim, *© Philip Saltonstall/Onyx;* (right) Levi ad, *courtesy Levi Strauss Associates, Inc.;* 560 Homelite ad, *courtesy of Homelite Division of Textron Inc.;* 563 Hardware store, *Gabe Palmer/After Image;* 565 Hewlett-Packard ad, *courtesy of Hewlett-Packard Company*

Chapter 22   571 (left) London street, *William D. Perreault, Jr.;* (center) Kentucky Fried Chicken in China, *reproduced with permission, © PepsiCo, Inc. 1988;* (right) Marketing meeting, *Alvis Upitis/The Image Bank;* 572 Vicks products in Japan, *courtesy The Procter & Gamble Company;* 573 Pepsi in Thailand, *courtesy Compaq Computer Corporation;* 575 Japanese Liquid Paper ad, *courtesy of The Gillette Company;* 576 Gillette joint venture in India, *courtesy of The Gillette Company;* 578 Multinational corporations, *courtesy of Reebok International Ltd., courtesy of ITT, courtesy of Pfizer, Inc., courtesy of Hilton Hotels Corporation, courtesy of Warner-Lambert Company, courtesy of Deere & Company, courtesy of Sony Corporation of America, courtesy of Panasonic, courtesy Kellogg Company, courtesy AT&T, courtesy Caterpillar Inc.;* Japanese plant in United States, *Billy Barnes/Tony Stone Worldwide;* 579 Tokyo McDonald's *Greg Davis/The Stock Market;* 580 Exhibit 22–3, *adapted from Warren Keegan, "Multinational Product Planning: Strategic Alternatives,"* Journal of Marketing, *January 1969, p. 59;* Chinese bicyclists and billboards, *Catherine Leroy/Time magazine;* 581 Thai IBM Personal System/2 keyboard, *courtesy International Business Machines Corporation;* 583 Exhibit 22–6, *European Community Directorate-General for Information;* 584 Bumper sticker, *© 1989 John Vink/Contact Press Images;* 585 Banca Serfin ad, *Banca Serfin/Albert Frank-Guenther Law Advertising Agency;* 586 Chinese toy company workers, *© 1989 Mary Beth Camp/Matrix;* 587 Canon ad, *courtesy of Canon USA, Inc.;* 588 British Lean Cuisine transit ad, *Mary Ellen Zang;* 590 Exhibit 22–8, Edward C. Baig, *"Where Global Growth Is Going,"* Fortune, *July 31, 1989, pp. 71–92;* 591 Foreign soda signs, *William S. Nawrocki/Nawrocki Stock Photo;* International flags, *courtesy of Dow Chemical*

Chapter 23 and Appendix C   595 (left) Furniture display, *Robert Frerck/Tony Stone Worldwide;* (center) Midas Brochure, *Mary Ellen Zang;* (right) Quality control, *W. Strode/Four by Five;* 596 Soviet black market line, *Marc Garanger;* 598 Mazda truck ad, *Courtesy Mazda Motors of America (Central), Inc.;* 599 Customer satisfaction sign, *Cameramann International;* 603 Phylrich International ad, *courtesy of Phylrich International;* 606 (left) 1920s GE refrigerator ad; (right) Kenmore refrigerator ad, *courtesy of Sears, Roebuck & Co.;* 607 Using microwave, *Mary Ellen Zang;* 608 Men's clothing store, *Craig Hammell;* 609 House & Garden ad, *courtesy HG. Copyright © 1989 by The Condé Nast Publications Inc.;* 610 Exhibit 23–2, *adapted from discussions of an American Marketing Association Strategic Planning Committee;* 611 (left) Trident gum ad, *courtesy of Warner-Lambert Company;* (right) Du Pont ad, *courtesy of Du Pont;* 612 Shoplifter sign, *Mary Ellen Zang;* 614 Recycling plastic bottles, *Terry Parke/Time magazine;* 615 Maryland business ad, *courtesy The State of Maryland;* 619 Exhibit C–1, Northwestern Lindquist-Endicott Report, 1988 *(Evanston, Ill.: Northwestern University, The Placement Center);* 620 Exhibit C–2, *adapted and updated from Charles G. Burck, "A Group Profile of the Fortune 500 Chief Executive,"* Fortune, *May 1976, p. 172;* 624 Exhibit C–4, *adapted and updated from Lila B. Stair,* Careers in Business: Selecting and Planning Your Career Path *(Homewood, Ill.: Richard D. Irwin, 1980); and Northwestern Lindquist-Endicott Report, 1988 (Evanston, Ill.: Northwestern University, The Placement Center)*

Author Index

Subject Index

Glossary

Accessories short-lived capital items—tools and equipment used in production or office activities.

Accumulating collecting products from many small producers.

Administered channel systems various channel members informally agree to cooperate with each other.

Administered prices consciously set prices aimed at reaching the firm's objectives.

Adoption curve shows when different groups accept ideas.

Adoption process the steps individuals go through on the way to accepting or rejecting a new idea.

Advertising any *paid* form of nonpersonal presentation of ideas, goods, or services by an identified sponsor.

Advertising agencies specialists in planning and handling mass selling details for advertisers.

Advertising allowances price reductions to firms further along in the channel to encourage them to advertise or otherwise promote the firm's products locally.

Advertising managers managers of their company's mass selling effort in television, newspapers, magazines, and other media.

Agent middlemen wholesalers who do not own (take title to) the products they sell.

AIDA model consists of four promotion jobs—(1) to get *Attention*, (2) to hold *Interest*, (3) to arouse *Desire*, and (4) to obtain *Action*.

Allowance (accounting term) occurs when a customer is not satisfied with a purchase for some reason and the seller gives a price reduction on the original invoice (bill), but the customer keeps the goods or services.

Allowances reductions in price given to final consumers, customers, or channel members for doing "something" or accepting less of "something."

Assorting putting together a variety of products to give a target market what it wants.

Attitude a person's point of view toward something.

Auction companies agent middlemen who provide a place where buyers and sellers can come together and complete a transaction.

Automatic vending selling and delivering products through vending machines.

Average cost (per unit) the total cost divided by the related quantity.

Average-cost pricing adding a "reasonable" markup to the average cost of a product.

Average fixed cost (per unit) the total fixed cost divided by the related quantity.

Average variable cost (per unit) the total variable cost divided by the related quantity.

Bait pricing setting some very low prices to attract customers but trying to sell more expensive models or brands once the customer is in the store.

Balance sheet an accounting statement that shows the assets, liabilities, and net worth of a company.

Basic list prices the prices that final customers or users are normally asked to pay for products.

Basic sales tasks *order getting, order taking,* and *supporting.*

Battle of the brands the competition between dealer brands and manufacturer brands.

Belief a person's opinion about something.

Bid pricing offering a specific price for each possible job rather than setting a price that applies for all customers.

Birthrate the number of babies per 1,000 people.

Brand familiarity how well customers recognize and accept a company's brand.

Brand insistence customers insist on a firm's branded product and are willing to search for it.

Brand managers manage specific products, often taking over the jobs formerly handled by an advertising manager—sometimes called product managers.

Brand name a word, letter, or a group of words or letters.

Brand nonrecognition a brand is not recognized by final customers at all—even though middlemen may use the brand name for identification and inventory control.

Brand preference target customers will usually choose the brand over other brands, perhaps because of habit or past experience.

Brand recognition customers remember the brand.

Brand rejection the potential customers won't buy a brand—unless its image is changed.

Branding the use of a name, term, symbol, or design—or a combination of these—to identify a product.

Break-even analysis an approach to determine whether the firm will be able to break even—that is, cover all its costs—with a particular price.

Break-even point (BEP) the sales quantity where the firm's total cost will just equal its total revenue.

Breakthrough opportunities opportunities that help innovators develop hard-to-copy marketing strategies that will be very profitable for a long time.

Brokers agent middlemen who specialize in bringing buyers and sellers together.

Bulk-breaking dividing larger quantities into smaller quantities as products get closer to the final market.

Buying center all the people who participate in or influence a purchase.

Buying function looking for and evaluating goods and services.

Capital item a long-lasting product that can be used and depreciated for many years.

Cash-and-carry wholesalers like service wholesalers, except that the customer must pay cash.

Cash discounts reductions in the price to encourage buyers to pay their bills quickly.

Catalog showroom retailers stores that sell several lines out of a catalog and display showroom with backup inventories.

Central markets convenient place where buyers and sellers can meet face-to-face to exchange goods and services.

Chain store one of several stores owned and managed by the same firm.

Channel captain a manager who helps direct the activities of a whole channel and tries to avoid—or solve—channel conflicts.

Channel of distribution any series of firms or individuals who participate in the flow of goods and services from producer to final user or consumer.

Clustering techniques approaches used to try to find similar patterns within sets of data.

Combination export manager a blend of manufacturers' agent and selling agent—handling the entire export function for several producers of similar but noncompeting lines.

Combined target market approach combining two or more submarkets into one larger target market as a basis for one strategy.

Combiners firms that try to increase the size of their target markets by combining two or more segments.

Commission merchants agent middlemen who handle products shipped to them by sellers, complete the sale, and send the money (minus their commission) to each seller.

Communication process a source trying to reach a receiver with a message.

Community shopping centers planned shopping centers that offer some shopping stores as well as convenience stores.

Comparative advertising advertising that makes specific brand comparisons using actual product names.

Competitive advantage means that a firm has a marketing mix that the target market sees as better than a competitor's mix.

Competitive advertising advertising that tries to develop demand for a specific brand rather than a product category.

Competitive bids the terms of sale offered by different suppliers in response to the buyer's purchase specifications.

Competitive environment the number and types of competitors the marketing manager must face, and how they may behave.

Complementary product pricing setting prices on several related products as a group.

Components processed expense items that become part of a finished product.

Concept testing getting reactions from customers about how well a new product idea fits their needs.

Confidence intervals the range on either side of an estimate from a sample that is likely to contain the "true" value for the whole population.

Consumer panel a group of consumers who provide information on a continuing basis.

Consumer Product Safety Act a 1972 law that set up the Consumer Product Safety Commission to encourage more awareness of safety in product design—and better quality control.

Consumer products products meant for the final consumer.

Consumer surplus the difference to consumers between the value of a purchase and the price they pay.

Consumerism a social movement that seeks to increase the rights and powers of consumers.

Containerization grouping individual items into an economical shipping quantity and sealing them in protective containers for transit to the final destination.

Contract manufacturing turning over production to others while retaining the marketing process.

Contractual channel systems channel members agree by contract to cooperate with each other.

Contribution-margin approach a cost analysis approach in which all functional costs are not allocated in *all* situations.

Control the feedback process that helps the marketing manager learn (1) how ongoing plans are working and (2) how to plan for the future.

Convenience (food) stores a convenience-oriented variation of the conventional limited-line food stores.

Convenience products products a consumer needs but isn't willing to spend much time or effort shopping for.

Convenience store a convenient place to shop—either centrally located near other shopping or "in the neighborhood."

Cooperative advertising middlemen and producers sharing in the cost of ads.

Cooperative chains retailer-sponsored groups, formed by independent retailers, to run their own buying organizations and conduct joint promotion efforts.

Copy thrust what the words and illustrations of an ad should communicate.

Corporate chain store one of several stores owned and managed by the same firm.

Corporate channel systems corporate ownership all along the channel.

Corrective advertising   ads to correct deceptive advertising.

Cost of sales   total value (at cost) of the sales during the period.

Cues   products, signs, ads, and other stimuli in the environment.

Cultural and social environment   affects how and why people live and behave as they do.

Culture   the whole set of beliefs, attitudes, and ways of doing things of a reasonably homogeneous set of people.

Cumulative quantity discounts   reductions in price for larger purchases over a given period, such as a year.

Customer service level   how rapidly and dependably a firm can deliver what customers want.

Dealer brands   brands created by middlemen.

Decision support system (DSS)   a computer program that makes it easy for a marketing manager to get and use information *as he is making decisions*.

Decoding   the receiver in the communication process translating the message.

Demand-backward pricing   setting an acceptable final consumer price and working backward to what a producer can charge.

Demand curve   a graph of the relationship between price and quantity demanded in a market—assuming that all other things stay the same.

Department stores   larger stores that are organized into many separate departments and offer many product lines.

Derived demand   demand for industrial products is derived from the demand for final consumer products.

Description (specification) buying   buying from a written (or verbal) description of the product.

Determining dimensions   the dimensions that actually affect the customer's purchase of a *specific* product or brand in a *product-market*.

Direct-mail advertising   selling directly to customers via their mailboxes.

Direct type advertising   competitive advertising that aims for immediate buying action.

Discount houses   stores that sell "hard goods" (cameras, TVs, appliances) at substantial price cuts.

Discounts   reductions from list price that are given by a seller to a buyer who either gives up some marketing function or provides the function himself.

Discrepancy of assortment   the difference between the lines a typical producer makes and the assortment wanted by final consumers or users.

Discrepancy of quantity   the difference between the quantity of products it is economical for a producer to make and the quantity normally wanted by final users or consumers.

Discretionary income   what is left of disposable income after paying for necessities.

Disposable income   income that is left after taxes.

Dissonance   tension caused by uncertainty about the rightness of a decision.

Distribution center   a special kind of warehouse designed to speed the flow of goods and avoid unnecessary storing costs.

Diversification   moving into totally different lines of business—which may include entirely unfamiliar products, markets, or even levels in the production-marketing system.

Diversion in transit   redirection of railroad carloads already in transit.

Door-to-door selling   going directly to the consumer's home.

Drive   a strong stimulus that encourages action to reduce a need.

Drop-shippers   wholesalers who take title to the products they sell—but do not actually handle, stock, or deliver them.

Dual distribution   when a producer uses several competing channels to reach the same target market.

Early adopters   the second group in the adoption curve to adopt a new product, these people are usually well-respected by their peers and often are opinion leaders.

Early majority   a group in the adoption curve that avoids risk and waits to consider a new idea after many early adopters have tried it—and liked it.

Economic and technological environment   affects the way firms and the whole economy use resources.

Economic men   people who know the facts and logically compare choices in terms of cost and value received to get the greatest satisfaction from spending their time and money.

Economic needs   needs concerned with making the best use of a consumer's time and money—as the consumer judges it.

Economic system   the way an economy organizes to use scarce resources to produce goods and services and distribute them for consumption by various people and groups in the society.

Economies of scale   as a company produces larger numbers of a particular product, the cost for each of these products goes down.

Elastic demand   if prices are dropped, the quantity demanded will stretch enough to increase total revenue.

Elastic supply   the quantity supplied does stretch more if the price is raised.

Emergency products   products that are purchased immediately when the need is great.

Empty nesters   people whose children are grown and who are now able to spend their money in other ways.

Encoding   the source in the communication process deciding what it wants to say and translating it into words or symbols that will have the same meaning to the receiver.

Equilibrium point   the quantity and the price sellers are willing to offer are equal to the quantity and price that buyers are willing to accept.

Equilibrium price   the going market price.

Exclusive distribution   selling through only one middleman in a particular geographic area.

Expense item   a product whose total cost is treated as a business expense in the period when it is purchased.

Expenses   all the remaining costs that are subtracted from the gross margin to get the net profit.

Experience curve pricing   average-cost pricing using an estimate of *future* average costs.

Experimental method   a research approach in which researchers compare the responses of groups that are similar, except on the characteristic being tested.

Export agents   manufacturers' agents who specialize in export trade.

Export brokers   brokers in international marketing.

Export commission houses   brokers in international trade.

Exporting   selling some of what the firm is producing to foreign markets.

Extensive problem solving   the type of problem solving involved when a need is completely new or important to a consumer and much effort is taken to decide how to satisfy the need.

Facilitators   firms that provide one or more of the marketing functions other than buying or selling.

Factor   a variable that shows the relation of some other variable to the item being forecast.

Factor method   an approach to forecast sales by finding a relation between the company's sales and some other factor (or factors).

Factors   wholesalers of credit.

Fad   an idea that is fashionable only to certain groups who are enthusiastic about it—but so fickle that it is even more short-lived than a regular fashion.

Family brand   a brand name that is used for several products.

Farm products   products grown by farmers, such as oranges, wheat, sugar cane, cattle, poultry, eggs, and milk.

Fashion   currently accepted or popular style.

Federal Fair Packaging and Labeling Act   a 1966 law requiring that consumer goods be clearly labeled in easy-to-understand terms.

Federal Trade Commission (FTC)   federal government agency that polices antimonopoly laws.

Field warehouser   a firm that segregates some of a company's finished products on the company's own property and issues warehouse receipts that can be used to borrow money.

Financing   provides the necessary cash and credit to produce, transport, store, promote, sell, and buy products.

Fixed-cost (FC) contribution per unit   the selling price per unit minus the variable cost per unit.

Flexible-price policy   offering the same product and quantities to different customers at different prices.

Floor planning   the financing of display stocks for auto, appliance, and electronics dealers.

F.O.B.   a transportation term that means "free on board" some vehicle at some point.

Focus group interview   an interview of 6 to 10 people in an informal group setting.

Form utility   provided when someone produces something tangible.

Franchise operation   a franchiser develops a good marketing strategy, and the retail franchise holders carry out the strategy in their own units.

Freight absorption pricing   absorbing freight cost so that a firm's delivered price meets the price of the nearest competitor's.

Freight forwarders   transportation "wholesalers" who combine the small shipments of many shippers into more economical shipping quantities.

Full-cost approach   all functional costs are allocated to products, customers, or other categories.

Full-line pricing   setting prices for a whole line of products.

Functional accounts   categories of costs that show the *purpose* for which the expenditures are made.

General merchandise wholesalers   service wholesalers who carry a wide variety of nonperishable items such as hardware, electrical supplies, plumbing supplies, furniture, drugs, cosmetics, and automobile equipment.

General stores   early retailers who carried anything they could sell in reasonable volume.

Generic market   a market with *broadly* similar needs—and sellers offering various and *often diverse* ways of satisfying those needs.

Generic products   have no brand at all other than identification of their contents and the manufacturer or middleman.

Gross margin (gross profit)   the money left to cover the expenses of selling and operating the business.

Gross national product (GNP)   the total market value of goods and services produced in a year.

Gross sales   the total amount charged to all customers during some time period.

Heterogeneous shopping products   shopping products that the customer sees as different—and wants to inspect for quality and suitability.

Homogeneous shopping products   shopping products that the customer sees as basically the same—and wants at the lowest price.

Hypotheses   educated guesses about the relationships between things or what will happen in the future.

Iceberg principle   much good information is hidden in summary data.

Ideal market exposure   when a product is widely enough available to satisfy target customers' needs—but not to exceed them.

Implementation   putting marketing plans into operation.

Import agents   manufacturers' agents who specialize in import trade.

Import brokers   brokers in international marketing.

Import commission houses   brokers in international trade.

Impulse products   products that are bought quickly as *unplanned* purchases because of a strongly felt need.

Indexes   statistical combinations of several time series used to find some time series that will lead the series to be forecast.

Indirect type advertising   competitive advertising that points out product advantages—to affect future buying decisions.

Individual brands   separate brand names used for each product.

Individual product   a particular product within a product line.

Industrial products   products meant for use in producing other products.

Inelastic demand   the quantity demanded would increase if the price were decreased, but the quantity demanded would not "stretch" enough to avoid a decrease in total revenue.

Inelastic supply   the quantity supplied does not stretch much (if at all) if the price is raised.

Innovation   the development and spread of new ideas and products.

Innovators   the first group to adopt new products.

Inspection buying   looking at every item.

Installations   industrial products that are important capital items such as buildings, land rights, and major equipment.

Institutional advertising   advertising that tries to develop goodwill for a company or even an industry instead of a specific product.

Intensive distribution   selling a product through all responsible and suitable wholesalers or retailers who will stock and/or sell the product.

Intermediate customers   any buyers who buy for resale or to produce other goods and services.

Introductory price dealing   temporary price cuts to speed new products into a market.

Inventory   the amount of goods being stored.

Job description   a written statement of what an employee (for example, a salesperson) is expected to do.

Joint venturing   in international marketing, a domestic firm entering into a partnership with a foreign firm.

Jury of executive opinion   forecasting by combining the opinions of experienced executives—perhaps from marketing, production, finance, purchasing, and top management.

Just-in-time delivery   reliably getting products to the customer *just* before the customer needs them.

Laggards   prefer to do things the way they have been done in the past and are very suspicious of new ideas—sometimes called nonadopters—see *adoption curve*.

Late majority   a group of adopters who are cautious about new ideas—see *adoption curve*.

Law of diminishing demand   if the price of a product is raised, a smaller quantity will be demanded—and if the

price of a product is lowered, a greater quantity will be demanded.

Leader pricing   setting very low prices on some products to get customers into retail stores.

Leading series   a time series that changes in the same direction *but ahead of* the series to be forecast.

Learning   a change in a person's thought processes caused by prior experience.

Licensed brand   well-known brand that sellers pay a fee to use.

Licensing   selling the right to use some process, trademark, patent, or other right for a fee or royalty.

Life-style analysis   the analysis of a person's day-to-day pattern of living as expressed in his *A*ctivities, *I*nterests, and *O*pinions—sometimes referred to as AIOs or psychographics.

Limited-function wholesalers   merchant wholesalers who provide only *some* wholesaling functions.

Limited-line stores   stores that specialize in certain lines of related products rather than a wide assortment—sometimes called single-line stores.

Limited problem solving   when a consumer is willing to put *some* effort into deciding the best way to satisfy a need.

Long-run target return pricing   pricing to cover all costs and over the "long-run" achieve an average target return.

Low-involvement purchases   purchases that do not have high personal importance or relevance for the customer.

Lower-lower class   (13 percent of the population) consists of unskilled laborers and people in very low-status occupations.

Lower-middle class   (36 percent of the population) consists of small business people, office workers, teachers, and technicians—the "white-collar" workers.

Macro-marketing   a social process that directs an economy's flow of goods and services from producers to consumers in a way that effectively matches supply and demand and accomplishes the objectives of society.

Magnuson-Moss Act   a 1975 law requiring that producers provide a clearly written warranty if they choose to offer any warranty.

Mail-order wholesalers   sell out of catalogs that may be distributed widely to smaller industrial customers or retailers.

Management contracting   the seller provides only management skills—the production facilities are owned by others.

Manufacturer brands   brands created by manufacturers.

Manufacturers' agents   agent middlemen who sell similar products for several noncompeting producers for a commission on what is actually sold.

Manufacturers' sales branches   separate businesses that producers set up away from their factories.

Marginal analysis   evaluating the change in total revenue and total cost from selling one more unit to find the most profitable price and quantity.

Marginal cost   the change in total cost that results from producing one more unit.

Marginal profit   profit on the last unit sold.

Marginal revenue   the change in total revenue that results from the sale of one more unit of a product.

Markdown   a retail price reduction that is required because customers won't buy some item at the originally marked-up price.

Markdown ratio   a tool used by many retailers to measure the efficiency of various departments and their whole business.

Market   a group of potential customers with similar needs and sellers offering various products—that is, ways of satisfying those needs *or* a group of sellers and buyers who are willing to exchange goods and/or services for something of value.

Market development   trying to increase sales by selling present products in new markets.

Market-directed economic system   the individual decisions of the many producers and consumers make the macro-level decisions for the whole economy.

Market growth   a stage of the product life cycle when industry sales are growing fast—but industry profits rise and then start falling.

Market information function   the collection, analysis, and distribution of all the information needed to plan, carry out, and control marketing activities.

Market introduction   a stage of the product life cycle when sales are low as a new idea is first introduced to a market.

Market maturity   a stage of the product life cycle when industry sales level off—and competition gets tougher.

Market penetration   trying to increase sales of a firm's present products in its present markets—usually through a more aggressive marketing mix.

Market potential   what a whole market segment might buy.

Market segment   a relatively homogeneous group of customers who will respond to a marketing mix in a similar way.

Market segmentation   a two-step process of: (1) *naming* broad product-markets and (2) *segmenting* these broad product-markets in order to select target markets and develop suitable marketing mixes.

Marketing audit   a systematic, critical, and unbiased review and appraisal of the basic objectives and policies of the marketing function and of the organization, methods, procedures, and people employed to implement the policies.

Marketing company era   a time when, in addition to short-run marketing planning, marketing people develop long-range plans—sometimes 10 or more years ahead—and the whole company effort is guided by the marketing concept.

Marketing concept   the idea that an organization should aim *all* its efforts at satisfying its *customers*—at a *profit*.

Marketing department era   a time when all marketing activities are brought under the control of one department to improve short-run policy planning and to try to integrate the firm's activities.

Marketing information system (MIS)   an organized way of continually gathering and analyzing data to provide marketing managers with information they need to make decisions.

Marketing management process   the process of (1) *planning* marketing activities, (2) directing the *implementation* of the plans, and (3) *controlling* these plans.

Marketing mix   the controllable variables that the company puts together to satisfy a target group.

Marketing model   a statement of relationships among marketing variables.

Marketing orientation   trying to carry out the marketing concept.

Marketing plan   a written statement of a marketing strategy *and* the time-related details for carrying out the strategy.

Marketing program   blends all of the firm's marketing plans into one "big" plan.

Marketing research   procedures to develop and analyze new information to help marketing managers make decisions.

Marketing research process   a five-step application of the scientific method that includes (1) defining the problem, (2) analyzing the situation, (3) getting problem-specific information, (4) interpreting the data, and (5) solving the problem.

Marketing strategy   specifies a target market and a related marketing mix.

Markup   a dollar amount added to the cost of products to get the selling price.

Markup chain   the sequence of markups used by firms at different levels in a channel—determining the price structure in the whole channel.

Markup (percent)   the percentage of selling price that is added to the cost to get the selling price.

Mass marketing   the typical production-oriented approach that vaguely aims at "everyone" with the same marketing mix.

Mass-merchandisers   large, self-service stores with many departments that emphasize "soft goods" (housewares, clothing, and fabrics) and selling on lower margins to get faster turnover.

Mass-merchandising concept   the idea that retailers can get faster turnover and greater sales volume by charging lower prices that will appeal to larger markets.

Mass selling   communicating with large numbers of potential customers at the same time.

Merchant wholesalers   wholesalers who own (take title to) the products they sell.

Message channel   the carrier of the message.

Metropolitan Statistical Area (MSA)   an integrated economic and social unit with a large population nucleus.

Micro-macro dilemma   what is "good" for some producers and consumers may not be good for society as a whole.

Micro-marketing   the performance of activities that seek to accomplish an organization's objectives by anticipating customer or client needs and directing a flow of need-satisfying goods and services from producer to customer or client.

Middleman someone who specializes in trade rather than production.

Missionary salespeople supporting salespeople who work for producers by calling on their middlemen and their customers.

Modified rebuy the in-between process where some review of the buying situation is done—though not as much as in new-task buying or as little as in straight rebuys.

Monopolistic competition a market situation that develops when a market has (1) different products and (2) sellers who feel they do have some competition in this market.

Multinational corporations firms that make a direct investment in several countries and run their businesses depending on the choices available anywhere in the world.

Multiple buying influence the buyer shares the purchasing decision with several people—perhaps even top management.

Multiple target market approach segmenting the market and choosing two or more segments, each of which will be treated as a separate target market needing a different marketing mix.

National accounts sales force salespeople who sell directly to large accounts such as major retail chain stores.

Nationalism an emphasis on a country's interests before everything else.

Natural accounts the categories to which various costs are charged in the normal financial accounting cycle.

Natural products products that occur in nature—such as fish and game, timber and maple syrup, and copper, zinc, iron ore, oil, and coal.

Need-satisfaction approach a type of sales presentation in which the salesperson develops a good understanding of the individual customer's needs before trying to close the sale.

Needs the basic forces that motivate a person to do something.

Negotiated contract buying agreeing to a contract that allows for changing the purchase arrangements.

Negotiated price a price set based on bargaining between the buyer and seller.

Neighborhood shopping centers planned shopping centers that consist of several convenience stores.

Net an invoice term that means that payment for the face value of the invoice is due immediately—also see *cash discounts*.

Net profit what the company has earned from its operations during a particular period.

Net sales sales dollars the company will receive.

New product a product that is new *in any way* for the company concerned.

New-task buying when a firm has a new need and the buyer wants a great deal of information.

New unsought products products offering really new ideas that potential customers don't know about yet.

Noise any distraction that reduces the effectiveness of the communication process.

Nonadopters prefer to do things the way they have been done in the past and are very suspicious of new ideas—sometimes called laggards—see *adoption curve*.

Noncumulative quantity discounts reductions in price when a customer purchases a larger quantity on an *individual order*.

Nonprice competition aggressive action on one or more of the Ps other than Price.

Odd-even pricing setting prices that end in certain numbers.

Oligopoly a special market situation that develops when a market has (1) essentially homogeneous products, (2) relatively few sellers, and (3) fairly inelastic industry demand curves.

One-price policy offering the same price to all customers who purchase products under essentially the same conditions and in the same quantities.

Open to buy a buyer has budgeted funds that he can spend during the current time period.

Operating ratios ratios of items on the operating statement to net sales.

Operating statement a simple summary of the financial results of the operations of a company over a specified period of time.

Operational decisions short-run decisions to help implement strategies may be needed.

Opinion leader a person who influences others.

Order getters salespeople concerned with getting new business.

Order getting seeking possible buyers with a well-organized sales presentation designed to sell a product, service, or idea.

Order takers salespeople who sell the regular or typical customers.

Order taking the routine completion of sales made regularly to the target customers.

Packaging promoting and protecting the product.

Penetration pricing policy trying to sell the whole market at one low price.

Perception how we gather and interpret information from the world around us.

Performance analysis analysis that looks for exceptions or variations from planned performance.

Performance index a number that shows the relation of one value to another.

Personal needs an individual's need for personal satisfaction unrelated to what others think or do.

Personal selling direct face-to-face communication between a seller and a potential customer.

Phony list prices misleading prices that customers are shown to suggest that the price they are to pay has been discounted from "list."

Physical distribution (PD)   the transporting and storing of goods so as to match target customers' needs with a firm's marketing mix—within individual firms and along a channel of distribution.

Physical distribution (PD) concept   all transporting and storing activities of a business and a channel system should be coordinated as one system—which should seek to minimize the cost of distribution for a given customer service level.

Physiological needs   biological needs such as the need for food, drink, rest, and sex.

Piggyback service   transporting truck trailers or flat-bed trailers carrying containers on rail cars to provide both speed and flexibility.

Pioneering advertising   advertising that tries to develop demand for a product category rather than a specific brand.

Place   making products available in the right quantities and locations—when customers want them.

Place utility   having the product available *where* the customer wants it.

Planned economic system   government planners decide what and how much is to be produced and distributed by whom, when, and to whom.

Planned shopping center   a set of stores planned as a unit to satisfy some market needs.

Pool car service   allows groups of shippers to pool their shipments of like goods into a full rail car.

Population   in marketing research, the total group you are interested in.

Portfolio management   treats alternative products, divisions, or strategic business units (SBUs) as though they are stock investments to be bought and sold using financial criteria.

Positioning   shows where customers locate proposed and/or present brands in a market.

Possession utility   obtaining a product and having the right to use or consume it.

Prepared sales presentation   a memorized presentation that is not adapted to each individual customer.

Prestige pricing   setting a rather high price to suggest high quality or high status.

Price   what is charged for "something."

Price discrimination   injuring competition by selling the same products to different buyers at different prices.

Price fixing   sellers illegally getting together to raise, lower, or stabilize prices.

Price leader   a seller who sets a price that all others in the industry follow.

Price lining   setting a few price levels for a product line and then marking all items at these prices.

Primary data   information specifically collected to solve a current problem.

Primary demand   demand for the general product idea, not just the company's own brand.

Private warehouses   storing facilities owned or leased by companies for their own use.

Producers' cooperatives   operate almost as full-service wholesalers—with the "profits" going to the cooperative's customer-members.

Product   the need-satisfying offering of a firm.

Product advertising   advertising that tries to sell a specific product.

Product assortment   the set of all product lines and individual products that a firm sells.

Product development   offering new or improved products for present markets.

Product liability   the legal obligation of sellers to pay damages to individuals who are injured by defective or unsafe products.

Product life cycle   the stages a new product idea goes through from beginning to end.

Product line   a set of individual products that are closely related.

Product managers   manage specific products, often taking over the jobs formerly handled by an advertising manager—sometimes called brand managers.

Product-market   a market with *very* similar needs—and sellers offering various *close substitute* ways of satisfying those needs.

Production   actually *making* goods or *performing* services.

Production era   a time when a company focuses on production of a few specific products—perhaps because few of these products are available in the market.

Production orientation   making whatever products are easy to produce and *then* trying to sell them.

Professional services   specialized services that support the operations of a firm.

Profit maximization objective   an objective to get as much profit as possible.

Promotion   communicating information between seller and potential buyer to influence attitudes and behavior.

Prospecting   following down all the "leads" in the target market to identify potential customers.

Psychographics   the analysis of a person's day-to-day pattern of living as expressed in his *A*ctivities, *I*nterests, and *O*pinions—sometimes referred to as AIOs or life-style analysis.

Psychological pricing   setting prices that have special appeal to target customers.

Public relations   communication with noncustomers—including labor, public interest groups, stockholders, and the government.

Public warehouses   independent storing facilities.

Publicity   any *unpaid* form of nonpersonal presentation of ideas, goods, or services.

Pulling   getting consumers to ask middlemen for the product.

Purchase discount   a reduction of the original invoice amount for some business reason.

Purchasing agents   buying specialists for their employers.

Pure competition   a market situation that develops when a market has (1) homogeneous products, (2) many buyers and sellers who have full knowledge of the market, and (3) ease of entry for buyers and sellers.

Pure subsistence economy   each family unit produces everything it consumes.

Push money (or prize money) allowances   allowances (sometimes called "PMs" or "spiffs") given to retailers by manufacturers or wholesalers to pass on to the retailers' salesclerks for aggressively selling certain items.

Pushing   using normal promotion effort—personal selling, advertising, and sales promotion—to help sell the whole marketing mix to possible channel members.

Qualifying dimensions   the dimensions that are relevant to including a customer-type in a product-market.

Qualitative research   seeks in-depth, open-ended responses.

Quality   the ability of a product to satisfy a customer's needs or requirements.

Quantitative research   seeks structured responses that can be summarized in numbers—like percentages, averages, or other statistics.

Quantity discounts   discounts offered to encourage customers to buy in larger amounts.

Quotas   the specific quantities of products that can move in or out of a country.

Rack jobbers   merchant wholesalers who specialize in nonfood products that are sold through grocery stores and supermarkets—and they often display them on their own wire racks.

Random sampling   each member of the research population has the same chance of being included in the sample.

Raw materials   unprocessed expense items—such as logs, iron ore, wheat, and cotton—that are handled as little as needed to move them to the next production process.

Rebates   refunds to consumers after a purchase has been made.

Receiver   the target of a message in the communication process, usually a customer.

Reciprocity   trading sales for sales—that is, "if you buy from me, I'll buy from you."

Reference group   the people to whom an individual looks when forming attitudes about a particular topic.

Regional shopping centers   large planned shopping centers that emphasize shopping stores and shopping products.

Regrouping activities   adjusting the quantities and/or assortments of products handled at each level in a channel of distribution.

Regularly unsought products   products that stay unsought but not unbought forever.

Reinforcement   occurs in the learning process when the consumer's response is followed by satisfaction—that is, reducing the drive.

Reminder advertising   advertising to keep the product's name before the public.

Requisition   a request to buy something.

Research proposal   a plan that specifies what marketing research information will be obtained and how.

Resident buyers   independent buying agents who work in central markets for several retailer or wholesaler customers from outlying areas.

Response   an effort to satisfy a drive.

Response function   a mathematical and/or graphic relationship that shows how the firm's target market is expected to react to changes in marketing variables.

Response rate   the percent of people contacted in a research sample who complete the questionnaire.

Retailing   all of the activities involved in the sale of products to final consumers.

Return   when a customer sends back purchased products.

Return on assets (ROA)   the ratio of net profit (after taxes) to the assets used to make the net profit—multiplied by 100 to get rid of decimals.

Return on investment (ROI)   ratio of net profit (after taxes) to the investment used to make the net profit—multiplied by 100 to get rid of decimals.

Risk taking   bearing the uncertainties that are part of the marketing process.

Robinson-Patman Act   a 1936 law that makes illegal any price discrimination—i.e., selling the same products to different buyers at different prices—if it injures competition.

Routinized response behavior   regularly selecting a particular way of satisfying a need when it occurs.

Rule for maximizing profit   the firm should produce that output where marginal cost is just less than or equal to marginal revenue.

Safety needs   needs concerned with protection and physical well-being.

Sale price   a temporary discount from the list price.

Sales analysis   a detailed breakdown of a company's sales records.

Sales decline   a stage of the product life cycle when new products replace the old.

Sales era   a time when a company emphasizes selling because of increased competition.

Sales finance companies   firms that finance inventories.

Sales forecast   an estimate of how much an industry or firm hopes to sell to a market segment.

Sales managers   managers concerned with managing personal selling.

Sales-oriented objective   an objective to get some level of unit sales, dollar sales, or share of market—without referring to profit.

Sales presentation   a salesperson's effort to make a sale.

Sales promotion   promotion activities—other than advertising, publicity, and personal selling—that stimulate interest, trial, or purchase by final customers or others in the channel.

Sales promotion managers   managers of their company's sales promotion effort.

Sales territory   a geographic area that is the responsibility of one salesperson or several working together.

Sample   a part of the relevant population.

Sampling buying   looking at only part of a potential purchase.

Saturation level   the level where additional expenditures may lead to little or no increase in sales—and to a decline in profits.

Scientific method   a decision-making approach that focuses on being objective and orderly in *testing* ideas before accepting them.

Scrambled merchandising   retailers carrying any product lines that they think they can sell profitably.

Seasonal discounts   discounts offered to encourage buyers to stock earlier than present demand requires.

Secondary data   information that has been collected or published already.

Segmenters   aim at one or more homogeneous segments and try to develop a different marketing mix for each segment.

Segmenting   an aggregating process that clusters together people with similar needs into a market segment.

Selective demand   demand for a specific brand rather than a product category.

Selective distribution   selling through only those middlemen who will give the product special attention.

Selective exposure   our eyes and minds seek out and notice only information that interests us.

Selective perception   people screen out or modify ideas, messages, and information that conflict with previously learned attitudes and beliefs.

Selective retention   people remember only what they want to remember.

Selling agents   agent middlemen who take over the whole marketing job of producers—not just the selling function.

Selling formula approach   a sales presentation that starts with a prepared presentation outline, gets customers to discuss needs, and then leads the customer through some logical steps to a final close.

Selling function   promoting the product.

Senior citizens   people over 65.

Service   a deed performed by one party for another.

Service wholesalers   merchant wholesalers who provide all the wholesaling functions.

Shopping products   products that a customer feels are worth the time and effort to compare with competing products.

Shopping stores   stores that attract customers from greater distances because of the width and depth of their assortments.

Simple trade era   a time when families traded or sold their surplus output to local middlemen, who sold these goods to other consumers or distant middlemen.

Single-line (or general-line) wholesalers   service wholesalers who carry a narrower line of merchandise than general merchandise wholesalers.

Single-line stores   stores that specialize in certain lines of related products rather than a wide assortment—sometimes called limited-line stores.

Single target market approach   segmenting the market and picking one of the homogeneous segments as the firm's target market.

Situation analysis   an informal study of what information is already available in the problem area.

Skimming price policy   trying to sell the top of the demand curve at a high price before aiming at more price-sensitive customers.

Social class   a group of people who have approximately equal social position as viewed by others in the society.

Social needs   needs concerned with love, friendship, status, and esteem—things that involve a person's interaction with others.

Sorting   separating products into grades and qualities desired by different target markets.

Source   the sender of a message.

Specialty products   consumer products that the customer really wants and is willing to make a special effort to find.

Specialty shop   a type of limited-line store—usually small and with a distinct "personality."

Specialty stores   stores for which customers have developed a strong attraction.

Specialty wholesalers   service wholesalers who carry a very narrow range of products and offer more information and service than other service wholesalers.

Spreadsheet analysis   organizing costs, sales, and other information into a data table to show how changing the value of one or more numbers affects the other numbers.

Standard Industrial Classification (SIC) codes   codes used to identify groups of firms in similar lines of business.

Standardization and grading   sorting products according to size and quality.

Staples   products that are bought often and routinely—without much thought.

Statistical packages   easy-to-use computer programs that analyze data.

Status quo objectives   "don't rock the boat" pricing objectives.

Stimulus-response model   the idea that people respond in some predictable way to a stimulus.

Stocking allowances   allowances given to middlemen to get shelf space for a product—sometimes called slotting allowances.

Stockturn rate   the number of times the average inventory is sold in a year.

Storing   the marketing function of holding goods.

Storing function   holding goods until customers need them.

Straight rebuy   a routine repurchase that may have been made many times before.

Strategic business unit (SBU)   an organizational unit (within a larger company) that focuses its efforts on some product-markets and is treated as a separate profit center.

Strategic (management) planning   the managerial process of developing and maintaining a match between the resources of an organization and its market opportunities.

Substitutes   products that offer the buyer a choice.

Supermarket   a large store specializing in groceries—with self-service and wide assortments.

Super-stores   very large stores that try to carry not only foods, but all goods and services the consumer purchases *routinely.*

Supplies   expense items that do not become a part of a finished product.

Supply curve   the quantity of products that will be supplied at various possible prices.

Supporting salespeople   salespeople who support the order-oriented salespeople—but don't try to get orders themselves.

Target market   a fairly homogeneous (similar) group of customers to whom a company wishes to appeal.

Target marketing   a marketing mix is tailored to fit some specific target customers.

Target return objective   a specific level of profit as an objective.

Target return pricing   pricing to cover all costs and achieve a target return.

Tariffs   taxes on imported products.

Task method   an approach to developing a budget—basing the budget on the job to be done.

Team selling   different sales reps working together on a specific account.

Technical specialists   supporting salespeople who provide technical assistance to order-oriented salespeople.

Technological base   the technical skills and equipment that affect the way the resources of an economy are converted to output.

Telemarketing   using the telephone to "call" on customers or prospects.

Telephone and direct-mail retailing   allows consumers to shop at home—usually placing orders by mail or a toll-free long-distance telephone calls and charging the purchase to a credit card.

Threshold expenditure level   the minimum expenditure level needed just to be in a market.

Time series   historical records of the fluctuations in economic variables.

Time utility   having the product available *when* the customer wants it.

Ton-mile   the movement of 2,000 pounds (one ton) of goods one mile.

Total cost   the sum of total fixed and total variable costs.

Total cost approach   evaluating each possible PD system and identifying *all* of the costs of each alternative.

Total fixed cost   the sum of those costs that are fixed in total—no matter how much is produced.

Total variable cost   the sum of those changing expenses that are closely related to output—such as expenses for parts, wages, packaging materials, outgoing freight, and sales commissions.

Trade (functional) discount   a list price reduction given to channel members for the job they're going to do.

Trade-in allowance   a price reduction given for used products when similar new products are bought.

Trademark   those words, symbols, or marks that are legally registered for use by a single company.

Traditional channel systems   a channel in which the various channel members make little or no effort to cooperate with each other.

Transporting   the marketing function of moving goods.

Transporting function   the movement of goods from one place to another.

Trend extension   extends past experience to predict the future.

Truck wholesalers   wholesalers who specialize in delivering products that they stock in their own trucks.

2/10, net 30   means that a 2 percent discount off the face value of the invoice is allowed if the invoice is paid within 10 days.

Unfair trade practice acts   set a lower limit on prices, especially at the wholesale and retail levels.

Uniform delivered pricing   making an average freight charge to all buyers.

Unit-pricing   placing the price per ounce (or some other standard measure) on or near the product.

Universal functions of marketing   buying, selling, transporting, storing, standardizing and grading, financing, risk taking, and providing market information.

Universal product code (UPC)   special identifying marks for each product that can be "read" by electronic scanners.

Unsought products   products that potential customers don't yet want or know they can buy.

Upper class   (2 percent of the population) consists of people from old, wealthy families (upper-upper class)—as well as the socially prominent new rich (lower-upper class).

Upper-lower class   (38 percent of the population) consists of factory production line workers, skilled workers, and service people—the blue-collar workers.

Upper-middle class   (11 percent of the population) consists of successful professionals, owners of small businesses, or managers of large corporations.

Utility   the power to satisfy human needs.

Validity   the extent to which data measures what it is intended to measure.

Value in use pricing   setting prices that will capture some of what customers will save by substituting the firm's product for the one currently being used.

Vendor analysis   formal rating of suppliers on all relevant areas of performance.

Vertical integration acquiring firms at different levels of channel activity.

Vertical marketing systems a whole channel focuses on the same target market at the end of the channel.

Voluntary chains wholesaler-sponsored groups that work with "independent" retailers.

Wants "needs" that are learned during a person's life.

Warranty what the seller promises about its product.

Wheeler Lea Amendment a law that bans unfair or deceptive acts in commerce.

Wheel of retailing theory new types of retailers enter the market as low-status, low-margin, low-price operators and then—if they are successful—evolve into more conventional retailers offering more services—with higher operating costs and higher prices.

Wholesalers firms whose main function is providing *wholesaling activities*.

Wholesaling the *activities* of those persons or establishments that sell to retailers and other merchants, and/or to industrial, institutional, and commercial users, but who do not sell in large amounts to final consumers.

Wholly-owned subsidiary a separate firm owned by a parent company.

Zone pricing making an average freight charge to all buyers within specific geographic areas.